Development in an Inflationary World

This is a volume in
ECONOMIC THEORY, ECONOMETRICS, AND MATHEMATICAL ECONOMICS

A Series of Monographs and Textbooks

Consulting Editor: KARL SHELL

A complete list of titles in this series appears at the end of this volume.

Development in an Inflationary World

Edited by *M June Flanders*

Assaf Razin

THE PINHAS SAPIR CENTER FOR DEVELOPMENT
TEL AVIV UNIVERSITY
RAMAT AVIV, TEL AVIV
ISRAEL

Proceedings of the 1979 Pinhas Sapir Conference, The Pinhas Sapir Center for Development, Tel Aviv University, 17–19 June 1979

1981

ACADEMIC PRESS
A Subsidiary of Harcourt Brace Jovanovich, Publishers
New York London Toronto Sydney San Francisco

ACADEMIC PRESS, INC.
111 Fifth Avenue, New York, New York 10003

United Kingdom Edition published by
ACADEMIC PRESS, INC. (LONDON) LTD.
24/28 Oval Road, London NW1 7DX

Library of Congress Cataloging in Publication Data
Main entry under title:

Development in an inflationary world.

(Economic theory, econometrics, and mathematical economics)
"Proceedings of the 1979 Pinhas Sapir conference, the Pinhas Sapir Center for Development, Tel Aviv University, 17-19 June 1979."
Includes bibliographies and index.
1. Inflation (Finance)--Congresses. 2. Inflation (Finance)--Israel--Congresses. 3. Economic development--Congresses. I. Flanders, M June, Date. II. Razin, Assaf. III. Merkaz le-fituah al-shem P. Sapir.
HG229.D48 332.4'1 80-28548
ISBN 0-12-259750-8

PRINTED IN THE UNITED STATES OF AMERICA

81 82 83 84 9 8 7 6 5 4 3 2 1

To the memory of Elisha Pazner

Photograph by M June Flanders

Contents

PART 3 INDEXATION AND PRICING

PART 4 FINANCIAL ASSETS, FOREIGN EXCHANGE, AND CAPITAL MARKETS

The Permanent Effects of Inflation on Development and Choice of Production Technique

Allan Drazen

Equilibrium Business Cycle Theory with Centralized Trading in Some Assets

Edi Karni

Inflation and Balance of Payments Adjustments with Maximizing Consumers

Elhanan Helpman

Exchange Rates and Price Movements in a World of Capital Mobility

Assaf Razin

PART 6 MACRO PUBLIC FINANCE

Public Debt and Taxes

Robert J. Barro

Fiscal Policies, Inflation, and Capital Formation

Martin Feldstein

On the Almost Neutrality of Inflation

Notes on Taxation and the Welfare Costs of Inflation

Joseph E. Stiglitz

PART 7 REVIEW AND CRITIQUE

List of Contributors

Numbers in parentheses indicate the pages on which the authors' contributions begin.

Robert J. Barro (377), Department of Economics, University of Rochester, Rochester, New York 14627

Brian Bentley (131), Department of Economics, University of Western Ontario, London, Canada N6A 5C2

Mario I. Blejer (343), Hebrew University of Jerusalem, Jerusalem, Israel and Center for Latin American Development Studies, Boston University, Boston, Massachusetts

Alan S. Blinder (61), Department of Economics, Princeton University, Princeton, New Jersey 08540

Domingo F. Cavallo (103), Institute of Economic Studies, Cordoba, Argentina

Kenneth W. Clements* (283), Graduate School of Business, University of Chicago, Chicago, Illinois 60637

Rudiger Dornbusch (319, 461), Department of Economics, Massachusetts Institute of Technology, Cambridge, Massachusetts 02139

Allan Drazen (211), University of Chicago, Chicago, Illinois 60637

Christina Fader (131), Department of Economics, University of Western Ontario, London, Canada N6A 5C2

Martin Feldstein (395), Department of Economics, Harvard University, Cambridge, Massachusetts 02138 and National Bureau of Economic Research, Cambridge, Massachusetts 02138

Stanley Fischer (319), Department of Economics, Massachusetts Institute of Technology, Cambridge, Massachusetts 02139

M June Flanders (1), The Pinhas Sapir Center for Development, Tel Aviv University, Ramat Aviv, Tel Aviv, Israel

Jacob A. Frenkel (283), Department of Economics, University of Chicago, Chicago, Illinois 60637

Arnold C. Harberger (35), Department of Economics, University of Chicago, Chicago, Illinois 60637

*Present Address: Macquarie University and Reserve Bank of Australia, Sydney, N.S.W. 2001, Australia.

Elhanan Helpman (243), Department of Economics, Tel Aviv University, Ramat Aviv, Tel Aviv, Israel

Edi Karni (233), Department of Economics, Tel Aviv University, Ramat Aviv, Tel Aviv, Israel

Abraham Knobel (173), Department of Economics, Tel Aviv University, Ramat Aviv, Tel Aviv, Israel

Leonardo Leiderman (343), Department of Economics, Tel Aviv University, Ramat Aviv, Tel Aviv, Israel

Abba P. Lerner (47), Department of Economics, Florida State University, Tallahassee, Florida 32306

Yair Mundlak (359), Department of Agricultural Economics, Hebrew University of Jerusalem, Faculty of Agriculture, Rehovot, Israel

Michael Parkin (131), Department of Economics, University of Western Ontario, London, Canada N6A 5C2

Don Patinkin (31), Department of Economics, Hebrew University of Jerusalem, Jerusalem, Israel

Elisha A. Pazner* (155), Department of Economics, Tel Aviv University, Ramat Aviv, Tel Aviv, Israel

Douglas D. Purvis (469), Department of Economics, Queen's University, Kingston, Canada K7L 3N6

Assaf Razin (1, 259), The Pinhas Sapir Center for Development, Tel Aviv University, Ramat Aviv, Tel Aviv, Israel

E. Sheshinski (195), Department of Economics, Hebrew University of Jerusalem, Jerusalem, Israel

Joseph E. Stiglitz (419), Department of Economics, Princeton University, Princeton, New Jersey 08540

A. Tishler (195), Department of Economics, Tel Aviv University, Ramat Aviv, Tel Aviv, Israel

James Tobin (19), Department of Economics, Yale University, New Haven, Connecticut 06520

Y. Weiss (195), Department of Economics, Tel Aviv University, Ramat Aviv, Tel Aviv, Israel

Ben-Zion Zilberfarb (163), Department of Economics, Bar-Ilan University, Ramat-Gan, Israel

Preface

In choosing a topic for the first annual conference sponsored by the Pinhas Sapir Center for Development, it seemed apt to focus on the concepts of development and inflation (and their juxtaposition). The center is concerned with all aspects of development—and at that time (fall, 1978), inflation was ubiquitous. Pinhas Sapir, Israel's seventh minister of trade and industry (1955–1963) and third minister of finance (1963–1974), had been deeply concerned about development in Israel. He undoubtedly contributed greatly to it, as even his most severe critics admit. And though his own tenure as minister was not marked by rapid inflation, some would argue that many of his policies helped make the Israeli economy particularly fertile ground for the subsequent growth of inflation. His approach to development, while often brilliant, one might say inspired, was a highly pragmatic one in which every problem was to be "solved" or at least "settled" as it arose. To maximize the short-run employment effects of development, he chose to encourage industry, *inter alia*, on the basis of its labor intensivity. But his encouragement took the form of heavy subsidy to capital, tending to make capital–labor ratios high, often in a way that was distorting. The combination of personalism, particularism, and the aforementioned pragmatism was antithetical to long-range, consistent, indicative planning. As the economy was gradually opened up to international trade, it became apparent that Sapir's approach had reinforced other factors in the economy in creating a highly distorted productive structure, rigidity and inflexibility with regard to mobility of labor and other factors, and a large and growing public sector.

In any event, when we planned the conference, the rate of inflation in Israel was about 40% per annum. When the conference took place, in June 1979, it was about 80% per annum. As this is being written, in early 1980, it is about 140% per annum.

For a variety of reasons, perhaps regrettable, there is more in this volume about inflation than about development. In part this is due to accident, in that several invitees were unable to prepare papers or, at the last minute, were unable to attend the conference.

In part, however, it is probably due to the more basic cause that inflation, today, by virtue (?) of its immediacy, demands and gets more attention from the profession than the longer-run and inherently more vital problem of development. Some lessons about inflation and development can be gleaned from the papers in Part II on stagflation. But basically we are forced to admit that the economics profession at this juncture does not have a great deal to say about the precise relationship(s) between development and inflation—not because it is not interested, but because the problem is so difficult.

When the conference was announced in the local press, we were besieged by reporters and commentators eagerly inquiring whether or not we hoped to hear "solutions" and "remedies" for Israel's inflation. We replied that this was not a how-to-do-it session and we were not expecting nostrums to be dispensed. The profession, indeed, does not have any quick and ready answers. Only Abba Lerner, of those who attended the conference and, perhaps, Milton Friedman, who did not, are willing to say, "Take my advice and you will stop inflation." Why neither has found a readier market for his cure-all is a question that deserves attention, but not here.

Rudiger Dornbusch and Douglas Purvis graciously agreed to write "critical surveys" of the papers given at the conference. They have done a magnificent job, and the editors wish, at this juncture, to thank them. We wish to thank, as well, the Editorial Selection Committee: Eitan Berglas, Martin Feldstein, Edi Karni, and James Tobin. Their help in making some difficult choices was invaluable.

Relieved of the task of surveying the proceedings of the conference, we have decided to use the editorial prerogative to describe, ever so briefly, the Israeli experience with respect to both development and inflation. It can be argued that the causes and effects of 140% inflation in Israel and 14% in the United States are not radically different: Israeli wags are fond of noting that the rates are much the same—only we in Israel achieve in less than a month what takes a year in the United States. In the ensuing we present, then, a thumbnail sketch of the Israeli economy.

We conclude here with the pleasant task of thanking the many people whose assistance has made the conference and the book possible. Professor Haim Ben-Shahar, M. Bernard Gitter, Israel Pollack, and the late Yehoshua Rabinowitz, all members of the Executive Committee of the Sapir Center, were particularly strong in their support and helpful in the arrangement of the conference. Mali Nudel and Deborah Kestenbaum ran the office and coordinated the conference activities cheerfully and efficiently, Barbara Karni prepared the subject and country indexes, and Connie Wilsack performed editorial services above and beyond the call of either duty or reasonable expectation.

We decided, after some consideration, not to include transcripts of the discussions at the conference. Nevertheless, the contribution of the discussants was invaluable. Their work improved the quality of the final papers submitted, helped the selection committee in its difficult decisions, and was a basic input in the summaries which Dornbusch and Purvis provided. We thank them heartily. They are

Chaim Barkai	Benjamin Eden	Efraim Kleiman
Simon Beninga	Stanley Fischer	Leonardo Leiderman
Mario I. Blejer	Jacob A. Frenkel	Nissan Liviatan
Alan S. Blinder	Giora Hanoch	Yoram Mayshar
Hollis B. Chenery	Arnold Harberger	Douglas D. Purvis
Alex Cukierman	Milton Harris	Eytan Sheshinski
Leif Danziger	Elhanan Helpman	Yoram Weiss
Allan Drazen	Edi Karni	

Elisha A. Pazner: 1941–1979

The death of Elisha A. Pazner in Jerusalem on 28 March 1979 was indeed untimely. He was thirty-eight years old. The profession has lost a promising young scholar; the Department of Economics at Tel Aviv University has been deprived of one of its senior and most active members, a dear friend, and a valued colleague; and his family has been bereft of a loved son, husband, and father.

Elisha, the son of an Israeli diplomat, was born in Switzerland and grew up there, in Argentina, and in Israel. From this polyglot environment he acquired facility in five languages, wide-ranging intellectual curiosity, and artistic and aesthetic sophistication, as well as what can only be described as "continental charm."

He began his university studies at the Hebrew University of Jerusalem, where he received both the B.A. and the M.A. degrees. At that stage he began to specialize and to develop his interest in public economics, while continuing to be concerned with macroeconomics, industrial organization —and economics.

He completed his graduate studies at Harvard in 1971, and immediately thereafter joined the then-young Economics Department at Tel Aviv University. He remained an active member of the department until his death, but managed frequent visits abroad, including a visiting appointment at Northwestern University.

At a time at which the major emphasis in public economics was being placed on issues of efficiency, Elisha was among the few scholars who were beginning to be concerned, formally and analytically, with questions of economic justice. Of particular interest to him was the issue of the trade-off between justice in distribution on the one hand and economic efficiency on the other, taking into account differences in individual preferences and individual abilities.

Important contributions in this area were his papers with David Schmeidler, "A difficulty in the concept of fairness" (*Review of Economic Studies*, 1975) and "Egalitarian equivalent allocations, a new concept of economic equity" (*Quarterly Journal of Economics*, 1979), as well as his own "Pitfalls in the theory of fairness" (*Journal of Economic Theory*, 1977).

Elisha was keenly interested in other branches of economics, including macroeconomic theory and the macroeconomic problems of the Israeli economy. A draft of a paper on wage indexation and macroeconomic stability has been included in this volume. Decision making under uncertainty was another of his interests, and he was actively involved in current analysis of Israel's tax and fiscal policies.

Characteristic of his approach to economics was his penchant for thinking in the simplest possible terms about deep issues. He was a theorist truly concerned with the problems of the society in which he lived; a true scholar; a very special person. We miss him.

Introduction

Development in an Inflationary World: Israel

M JUNE FLANDERS AND ASSAF RAZIN

Though only a small country with a very brief history, Israel is rich in examples of economic experiences, good and bad, "right" and "wrong": mass immigration, rapid development, industrialization, periods of price stability and of three-digit inflation, a full spectrum of foreign trade and exchange control regimes, financial inventiveness (such as indexation of various kinds), the coexistence of a relatively lively private sector and a public and quasi-governmental sector almost unparalleled in the western world, huge defense expenditures, massive inflows from abroad, disruptive wars—and underlying all, political stability and a vigorous democracy. For this reason, we choose to open this volume with a capsule history of the Israeli economy.

Population growth in the early years of statehood occurred at rates perhaps unprecedented in modern history (Fig. 1, Chart A). The population doubled from 758,000 in 1948 to 1.7 million in 1953. The immediate impact was a much larger increase in demand than in output. Since most of the immigrants in these years came from the countries of the Middle East and North Africa, they lacked the skills prevalent in developed economies. (Families were large, furthermore, so that a high proportion of the immigrants were children.) And since, in addition to skilled labor, there was very little by way either of productive plant and equipment or economic infrastucture, the problems facing the early planners were formidable indeed.

The initial surge in population was difficult to absorb, but in the "ingathering of the exiles," a major goal of the Jewish State, if not its primary raison d'être, the absorption of immigrants was never perceived as a burden to the economy.

ISBN 0-12-259750-8

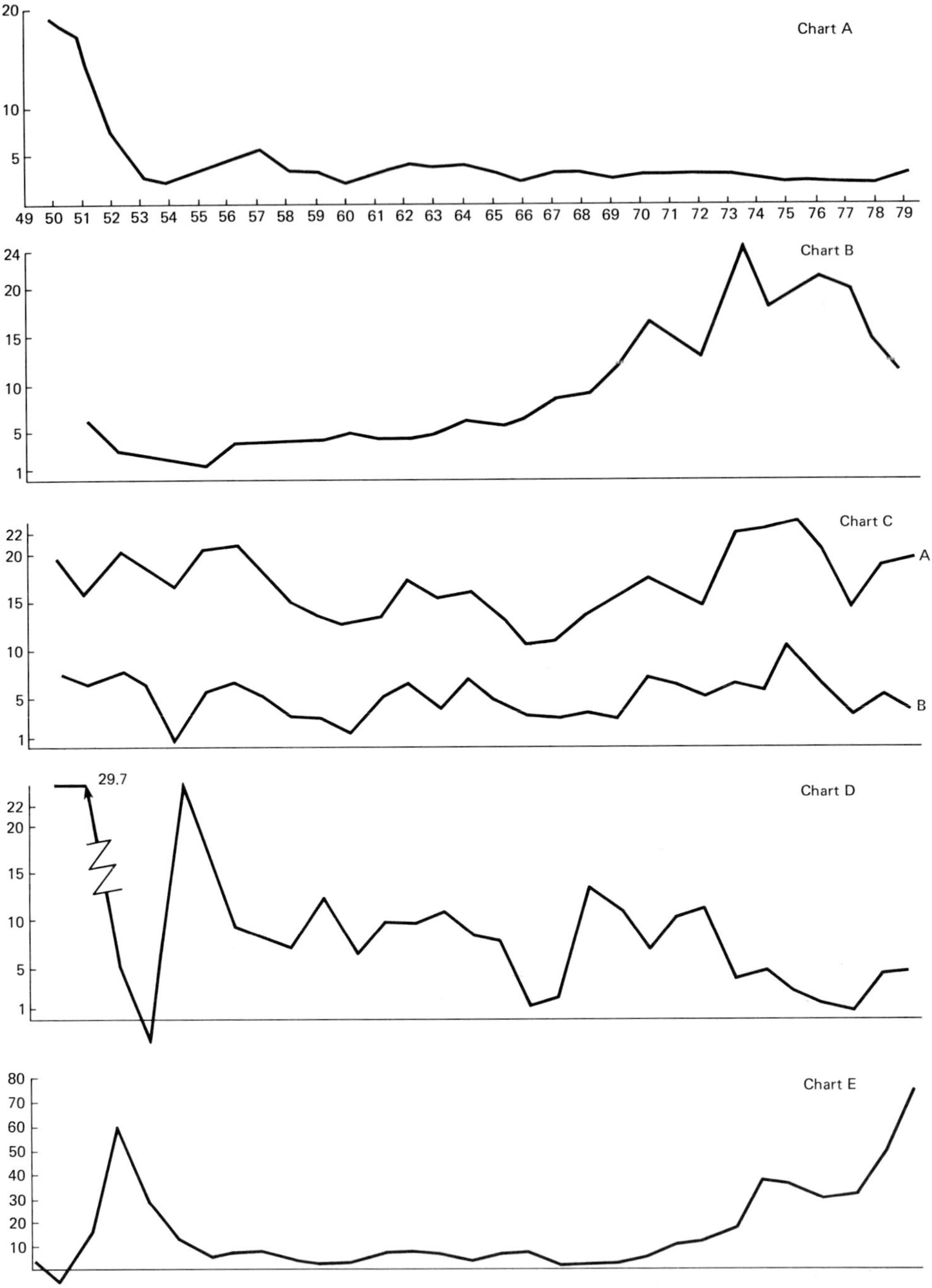

Fig. 1. Long-term trends in the Israeli economy. Chart A: population: annual rate of change; Chart B: defense expenditure: percentage of total resources; Chart C: current account deficit: percentage of total resources; Chart D: gross national product: annual rate of change; Chart E: inflation. Note: Total resources are defined as GNP plus imports. Chart C, line A represents balance on goods and services account. Line B represents current account balance: goods and services plus unilateral transfers. [Source: Central Bureau of Statistics, *Statistical Abstract of Israel* (annual).]

There is, however, no argument as to the burden imposed by *defense expenditures*, which have taken a large, and growing, bite out of total available resources over the years.[1] Chart B in Fig. 1 shows this clearly. After the War of Independence, the defense budget declined as a percentage of total resources until the Sinai Campaign of 1956. At that time it rose and held at the higher level until the Six Day War in 1967. It then spurted up again and continued to rise through the War of Attrition, falling back in the early 1970s only to shoot up once more with the Yom Kippur War in 1973, since when it has continued to rise. It is currently about 12–14% of resources, or 26% of GNP. (Part of the rise in the ratio of the defense budget to resources in the late 1970s is due to the stability in the denominator of that ratio, since resources actually declined in real terms in 1976 and held constant or fell slightly in 1977.)

The large and chronic *current account deficit* has been a striking feature of the Israeli economy, whether regarded as a problem or a blessing—or both. As a percentage of resources it is, and always has been, high. It began to fall in the early 1970s, but rose and remained high during and after the Yom Kippur War. That it is not an unmitigated "bad" stems in part from the nature of the financing available for it. This can be seen in Chart C in Fig. 1. The two lines represent, respectively, the deficit on account of trade in goods and services and the deficit on current account including unilateral transfers, both as percentages of total resources. The gap between them (large and variable, but with no clearly discernible trend) represents receipts of several kinds: contributions from Jewish communities around the world, especially in the United States; immigrant transfers (highly variable, depending on both the level and source of immigration); government-to-government reparations payments from Germany; government-to-individual compensation payments from Germany; and aid from the United States, to the extent that this takes the form of grants rather than loans. These transfers, *in toto*, have financed on the average 60–70% of the current account deficit. That they were enormously helpful in financing the construction of apartments to house and factories to employ the immigrants and the investment in capital equipment for industry and agriculture and, in general, were one of the stimuli to the rapid growth of the Israeli economy is not disputed. However, none of this contradicts the fact that many people today are worried about how the economy—and the society—are preparing to shift gears and adjust to the eventual reductions of such inflows. This, in the face of an existing

[1] Inflow of capital and unilateral transfers have loomed so large in the Israeli economy that GNP is a totally inadequate approximation of available resources, or total absorption. "Resources for domestic use" (which are definitionally equal to "total uses") are defined in the national accounts as GNP plus the import surplus (the current account deficit).

external debt of impressive proportions, can indeed be viewed as one of the serious future problems facing the country. At present the debt, equal to about $14 billion at the end of 1979, amounts to roughly $4000 per capita—that is, the current annual average wage!

Now for *growth and inflation* (Fig. 1, Charts D and E, respectively). Israel has indeed experienced both, and in good measure, as we can see in the charts, though rather more growth and on the whole rather less inflation in the earlier years than in the later period, especially since 1973. The earliest inflation figures are highly erratic (and probably not very reliable), primarily because a period of tight controls and repressed inflation was followed by a devaluation and liberalization which lifted the lid.

Throughout the 1950s and 1960s prices rose and inflation was a constant feature of the economy, but at rates which by today's standards appear moderate. The upswing in 1962 followed a devaluation, and the downturn in the rate of inflation in 1966 and 1967 was the result of a government engineered recession. We shall return to the post-1973 period below, but the oil price shock, worldwide inflation, the Yom Kippur War, and the large and growing level of government expenditures since, have all worked in the same direction (they are, of course, themselves interrelated), while counteracting forces are difficult to discern.

The rate of growth has been high, on the average, over the 30 year period, but rates have varied considerably, and there have been three major lows. In the early years of statehood, growth rates were phenomenal, though the precise numbers on the graph ought not to be taken too seriously, particularly since the base line was, in every respect, very low indeed. After the War of Independence, output increased rapidly until the trough of 1952. This trough was the result of a stringent anti-inflationary policy. The mass immigration of 1950 and 1951 had put tremendous pressure on aggregate demand. The inflation was first suppressed, then released, then attacked by a reduction in investment spending which slowed the growth rate.

The next trough, in 1966–1967 (which is still referred to as the recession) seems to have been to a large extent a "mistake." Prices had not been particularly volatile, but a deteriorating balance of payments worried the government. A slowing in immigration provided the excuse to cut a major form of government and government influenced spending, namely, residential construction. Construction, which constituted roughly a third of total gross domestic investment, rose in real terms by 7.1% in 1965, and fell by 22 and 33.3% in 1966 and 1967. The resulting recession was much deeper than anybody in government had intended. The crunch was so severe that real estate prices actually fell, despite the reduction in housing starts. This decline and the widespread unemployment (10% of the labor force) were unique in the history of the State. The overall price index continued, indeed, to rise but at a very slow rate—less than 2%. The war of June 1967 ended the recession, but the slack in the economy was a major reason why the 1967 war did not have the kind of aftereffects that the 1973 war was to have.

The average growth rate in the 1960s and early 1970s was 10%. Since 1973 it has been much lower. The shocks to output and prices caused by both the Yom Kippur War and the import price increases of 1973, and the subsequent worsening in the current account, led the government to adopt a restrictive policy in 1975. Gross national product in real terms increased by 11.6% per annum in 1971 and 1972 (on average), 4.5% in 1973 and 1974 (average for the two years), 2% in 1975, 1.6% in 1976, and at most 1% in 1977 (there are those who argue that it decreased). Since then total output has increased, but a large part of this increase is accounted for by government spending, much of it on defense and on services. Consumers have been expecting, and achieving, rising standards of living; per capita consumption continues to increase, albeit more slowly than in the early 1970s. In addition, net capital inflow has been declining; that is, more resources are devoted to servicing and repaying the foreign debt (as Israel becomes a "mature" economy in this sense). As more and more of the total resources are devoted to uses other than investment, the future growth prospects of the economy are to that extent impaired. It is thus doubtful whether the growth rates of the 1960s can be matched in the near future.

The decade of the 1970s is worth somewhat closer scrutiny—both because it is nearer in time and because it witnessed several major changes in policy as well as in the behavior of a number of important macrovariables.

Figure 2 shows the time pattern of three variables: the real exchange rate (to be defined), the current account deficit, and the level of net autonomous domestic expenditures (approximately $G + I - T$).

Before we discuss these time series, a note about Israeli exchange rate policy during the period. From the establishment of the State until June 1975, there was a system of pegged exchange rates which were changed relatively infrequently. Between the major official devaluations (1952, 1962, 1967, 1971, and 1974) changes in what was called the "effective exchange rate" were made frequently through changes in subsidies to exports and import surcharges. The effective exchange rate (which has been used in the computation of the series in the figure) thus moved much more smoothly than the "official rate" would indicate.

In June 1975 a crawling peg was adopted, with small changes in the official rate about once a month, and with export subsidies being held roughly constant (as a percentage of the official rate).

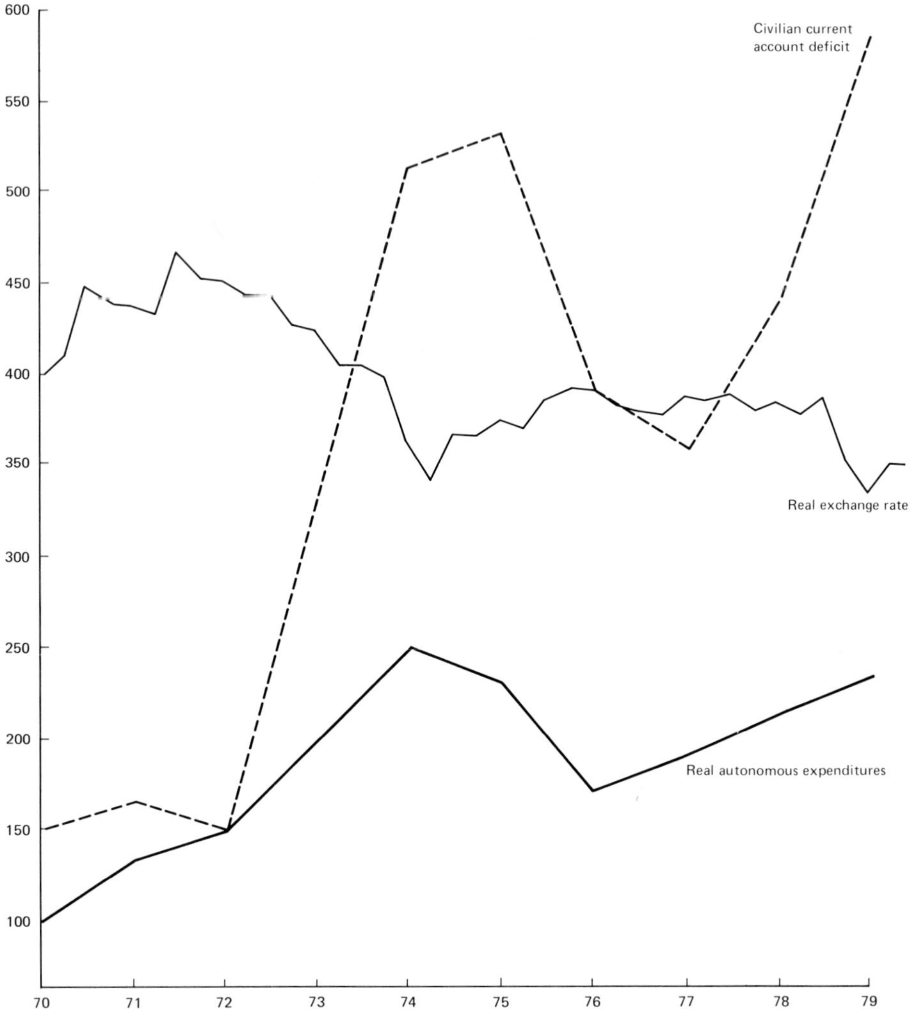

Fig. 2. Real autonomous expenditures, real exchange rate, and civilian current account deficit, annual percentage rate of change. Note: D/p = real autonomous expenditures: [$(G - T + I)$ divided by the consumer price index], $M - X$ = imports minus exports, $\bar{e}$ = ep^*/p = (price of U.S. dollars)(U.S. consumer price index)/(Israeli consumer price index). [Source: Central Bureau of Statistics, *Statistical Abstract of Israel* (annual), Bank of Israel, *Annual Report*.]

From November 1977 Israel has had a floating exchange rate regime, and export subsidies (and the import surcharge, though not tariffs) were abolished.

One of the interesting features of the story, as we see in Fig. 2, is that the proverbial man from Mars would be unable, by looking at the real exchange rate, to discern the dates (or even the existence) of these changes in regime. This is due to two factors. In the first place, the real exchange rate is, of course, the result of market forces as well as policy regarding nominal exchange rates; to the extent that the former were important, the formal exchange rate regime was clearly irrelevant. The nominal exchange rate was, and continues to be, a policy variable of the government and the central bank, not systematically linked to the choice of formal exchange rate regime. (Note that the system of exchange controls, coupled with export subsidies and import surcharges, meant that there was a dual exchange rate system up to the time of the liberalization of 1977. Thus when we speak of effective and nominal exchange rates here we are referring only to the rates applicable to current account transactions.) The "reform" of October 1977 was more important in its impact in that it liberalized foreign exchange holdings and international capital flows than in its shift from a "fixed" to a putatively "floating" rate.

The real exchange rate is here defined as the ratio of the domestic price of tradable goods to that of nontradable goods. If the law of one price holds at all times, then multiplying the world price index by the nominal effective exchange rate and dividing by the domestic price index should yield a precise proxy for (changes in) this variable. We have taken the United States consumer price index as a representation of world price and have multiplied it by the effective exchange rate (defined above) in terms of the U.S. dollar. This represents the domestic price of tradables. We have divided by the Israeli consumer price index, a weighted average of tradable and nontradable prices. The resulting ratio represents the real exchange rate. An increase in this value is equivalent to a depreciation of the Israeli pound. The figures in the graph are quarterly averages.

The second line in Fig. 2 represents the civilian (nondefense) current account balance (on goods and services) in constant dollars. Not surprisingly, it is related inversely to changes in the real exchange rate. As relative appreciations occurred, the current account worsened.

The third line represents real autonomous net domestic expenditures (hereafter autonomous expenditure). This is private gross investment (minus direct import of investment goods) plus government domestic expenditures (net of imports of defense goods) minus taxes (net of subsidies). These expenditures can plausibly be assumed to have a high component of expenditure on nontradables, so that changes in these expenditures can be interpreted as involving an increase in demand for nontraded goods. Unless the nominal effective exchange rate is adjusted (by policy or in the market) immediately, this should, by putting upward pressure on the relative prices of nontradables, lead to a fall in the real exchange rate. On the whole, this is what we in fact observe in Fig. 2.

The general picture is that increasing autonomous expenditure is associated with increasing current account deficits and appreciation (decline) of the real exchange rate. That the deficit on current account "fits" the movement of autonomous expenditure better than the real exchange rate does is not surprising. A change in autonomous expenditures can be expected to spill over quickly into current account changes. The effect on the real exchange rate, on the other hand, must work through a change in the prices of nontradables, and can be dampended in the short run by simultaneous changes in the nominal exchange rate and in world prices. Government exchange rate policy is clearly an important determinant of the real exchange rate in the short run. (Note that the figures for the real exchange rate are quarterly; the other two series are annual.)

Two sharp declines in the real exchange rate are unaccounted for by comparable changes in autonomous expenditures. One occurred in 1973–1974 and the other in 1978.

In 1973 and 1974 autonomous expenditures rose about 33 and 28%, respectively; both the decline in the real exchange rate and the increase in the current account deficit were considerably greater than this.

As far as the deficit is concerned, this is reasonably easy to explain. In the face of expenditure increases, all output, including the output of tradables, was affected by supply constraints as manpower and equipment (most notably, but not exclusively, transport equipment) were diverted to military use.

Though all output was affected, however, nontradables appear to have been affected more. If we assume that the government and nonprofit institutions are heavily weighted by nontradables, then the ratio of GNP to real private sector output can be used as a crude proxy of the relative share of nontraded goods. Real private sector output[2] rose by 8% in 1971, 12% in 1972, 1% in 1973, and 7% in 1974. Real GNP rose by 4% in 1973 and 4.9% in 1974. The ratio of GNP to private sector output, therefore, fell in 1974, indicating a relative decline in the output of nontraded goods.

The fall in the real exchange rate in 1973 and 1974 can be broken into components, as seen in Table 1.

Though the price of the U.S. dollar increased substantially over the period (there was a large devaluation), the cost of living index increased very much more, as we can see. This can be attributed both to the output changes discussed above and to policy developments during the period. There was a drastic reduction in the subsidies on basic foodstuffs and on energy and transport. This caused a large increase in the cost of living, though the breakdown of this increase between traded and nontraded goods is difficult to assess. The nominal exchange rate applicable to

[2] This is GNP minus imputed rents and output of government and nonprofit institutions, deflated by the GNP deflator (see Cukierman *et al.*, 1976).

TABLE 1

COMPONENTS OF CHANGES IN THE REAL EXCHANGE RATE[a]

	Change in U.S. CPI	Change in Israeli CPI	Change in price of U.S. dollar	Change in real exchange rate
1972	3.3	12.9	8	– 1.6
1973	6.0	20.0	4	– 10.0
1974	11.0	40.0	11	– 18.0

[a]Source: Bank of Israel (1972–1974), *Annual Report*; IMF (1972–1974), *International Financial Statistics*.

current transactions increased much less, particularly since the official devaluation was accompanied by a reduction in the direct export subsidy.

In sum, the relative decline in the output of nontraded goods put upward pressure on the relative price of these goods. This, plus the policy actions, caused a deterioration in the real exchange rate. This in turn, combined wlth a decline in the rate of growth of output of traded goods, while total demand continued to expand, resulted in the sharp increase in the balance of trade deficit.

The 1978–1979 story is somewhat different. In stylized version it is approximately as follows: A sizeable increase in real autonomous spending in a period of accelerating inflation exacerbated the inflation (which hit 8.4% *per month* in July 1978). Meanwhile the exchange rate situation was that following the "liberalization" of November 1977—there was (officially) a floating rate. The rate was heavily managed, however, and the Bank of Israel's intervention policy appeared to be to induce devaluations approximately parallel to Israeli inflation (minus "world" inflation) but with a lag, so that the price of foreign exchange rose more slowly than the overall price level. As the market became aware of this, expectations formed that this would continue. At the same time, due mainly to fiscal expansion, domestic interest rates went up. Borrowing abroad, which became possible with the aforementioned liberalization, was expected to be profitable, since nominal interest rates in Israel were greater than foreign interest rates plus the expected depreciation (see Table 2). As expectations of this nature become crystallized, and as the market learned what was possible under the new regulations, borrowing from abroad accelerated.

In the fall of 1978 the Bank of Israel attempted a tight money policy, including strict enforcement of reserve requirements (deficits in required reserves having been subject to fines which were low enough to make such deficits profitable for the banks). As a result, the capital inflow increased further. There was strong downward pressure on the exchange rate, despite

TABLE 2

REPRESENTATIVE INTEREST RATES (DOMESTIC AND FOREIGN) AND RATES OF EXCHANGE RATE DEPRECIATION[a,b]

	Domestic interest rates	Rates of exchange rate depreciation	Foreign interest rates
1978 : 1	50.3	30.0	6.41
1978 : 2	49.4	39.0	6.48
1978 : 3	49.4	12.0	7.32
1978 : 4	52.0	15.0	8.68
1979 : 1	62.5	61.0	9.36
1979 : 2	69.0	93.0	9.38
1979 : 3	91.8	73.0	9.63
1979 : 4	121.0	122.0	11.87

[a]Source: Bank of Israel (1978–1979) and IMF (1978–1979), *International Financial Statistics*.

[b]Note: Exchange rates are expressed in Israeli pounds per U.S. dollar. Domestic interest rates were computed from a sample of overdraft rates. Foreign interest rates are U.S. Treasury bill rates.

the fact that by the end of the year the Bank of Israel finally began to buy, briefly, rather than sell foreign exchange. The pressure was so strong that during the month of December, the price of the U.S. dollar, the nominal exchange rate, actually fell; this was true also of the nominal exchange rate expressed in terms of a trade-weighted basket of currencies. All this, while the price level continued to rise by 5–6% per month.

The increase in autonomous spending in 1978 and 1979 was considerable. It and the relative appreciation of the currency, together, account for the sharp rise in the current account deficit.

Finally, a few comments on the salient features of the Israeli inflation. Inflation has been a characteristic of the Israeli economy from the inception of the State, but during the 1970s and particularly in the post-1973 period, it reached unprecedented proportions. We are now easily what Harberger has characterized in this volume as an "acute" inflation country. While virtually all Israeli economists (and outside observers) are agreed on at least some of the causes of the Israeli inflation, nobody has yet offered a satisfactory explanation of why the current rate of inflation is 140%—rather than 200 or 80%.

A large and growing government deficit, constituting a high percentage of the autonomous expenditures we discussed previously, is clearly one of the causes (there are those who argue *the* cause) of the present inflation. The oil price and other foreign shocks particularly in 1974 and 1976 also played a role, though in a stable world with no other inflationary pressures they should have resulted in a once-for-all price increase rather than in continuing inflation. Thus, they may explain the beginning of the spiral, but not its continuation and, by themselves, surely not the acceleration that has characterized the last two years. The role of strong and persistent wage demands is here, as elsewhere, more controversial as a factor in inflation. Without entering into that particular debate, we may note, however, that the government employs roughly one-third of the labor force and that government wage negotiations not only influence private sector wages but also enter directly into autonomous expenditures, since wages constitute a high percentage of government expenditures. (In this sense "autonomous expenditures" are not strictly autonomous.)

The relationship between money supply and prices is shown in Fig. 3. For the 1970s the relationship between the money supply narrowly defined (M_1) and the price level is not very close; that between M_4 (a broad definition, to be described below) and prices is much closer, almost surprisingly so, considering the openness of the economy.

A characteristic of the Israeli economy is the existence of two highly liquid financial assets, which are in fact not near-moneys but hypermoneys, since they are very nearly inflation proof. These are linked government securities and foreign exchange accounts, to be described in turn.

Linked government securities have existed in Israel for some time. They have been variously linked to the consumer price index, the exchange rate, or both, with linkage ranging from 80 to 100%. Currently the majority are 80% linked to the price index. Initially they were regarded as a low-risk asset which provided a comfortable and yet liquid hedge against inflation. They are, incidentally, one of the reasons that inflation has for years constituted, in Israel, a subsidy from the government to the public rather than a tax. The other major reason is that the government, through borrowing by issuing assets linked to the cost of living, has traditionally made low-interest unlinked loans, primarily for housing and for industry. Since the government is a very large lender, and borrower, the amount of inflation subsidy can be very large indeed. Furthermore, the amount of the subsidy has varied very dramatically with the rate of inflation; in recent years the government's debtors have gained mightily.

The acceleration of inflation brought with it, of course, an increase in the subsidy. This interrelationship constituted a built-in destabilizer; the increased capital values of existing assets provided a stimulus to further spending. More important perhaps, the government budget for "intermediation" in the capital market developed ever growing deficits as inflation progressed. Since late 1979 an additional stimulus to inflation has been the lending to export industries on the part of the Bank of Israel. This form of export subsidy constitutes an automatic system of monetary injections following cost increases.

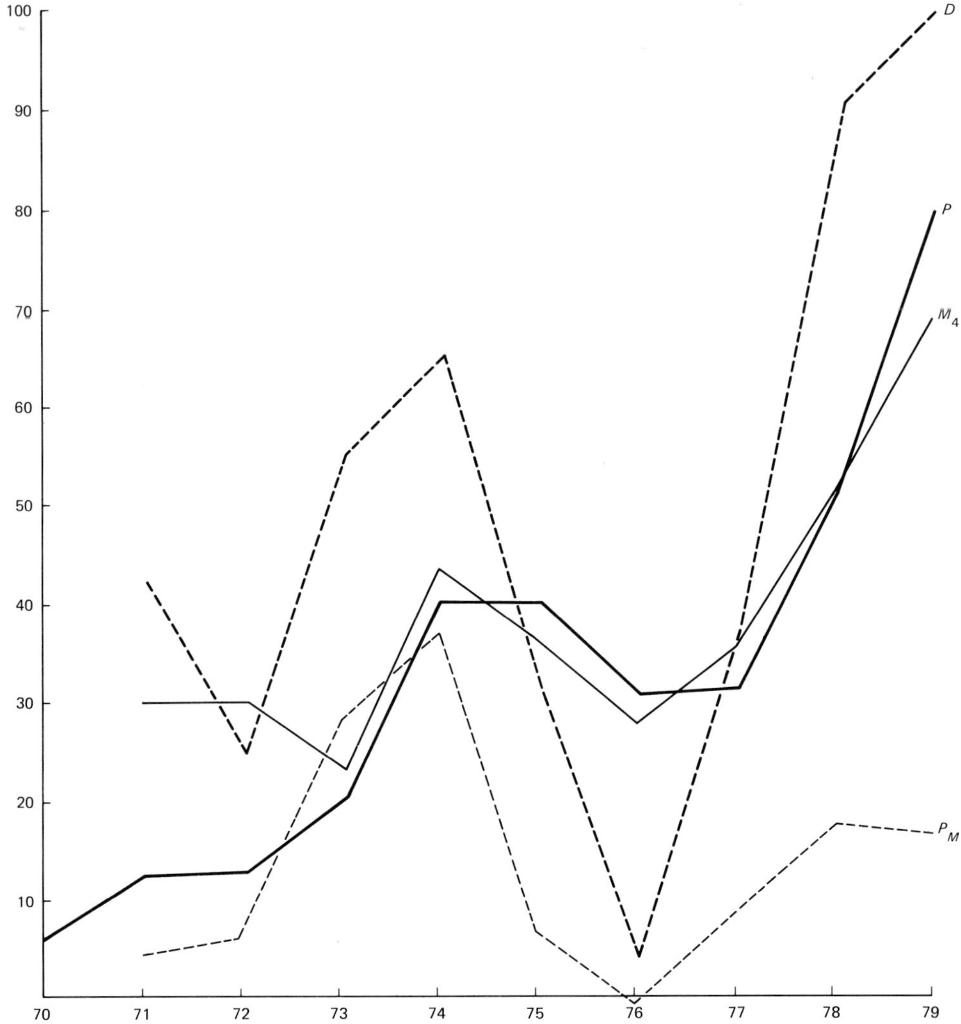

Fig. 3. Prices, money, and autonomous expenditures annual percentage rates of change. Note: P is consumer price index, M is currency, demand deposits, time deposits, foreign-denominated demand and time deposits, government bonds held by the public, P_M is index of U.S. dollar price of imports, D is nominal autonomous domestic expenditures: $G - T + I$. [Source: Central Bureau of Statistics, *Statistical Abstract of Israel* (annual), Bank of Israel, *Annual Report.*]

As inflation accelerated and holding cash and demand deposits became more costly, the linked government securities became an ever more liquid asset and began to be held, apparently, instead of cash and demand deposits. Transaction costs in their purchase and sales are relatively low; and though figures are not available there is evidence that in recent years they have been used as actual means of payments in relatively large transactions.

The second type of hyper-money, foreign exchange deposits, is of more recent origin. Prior to the liberalization of 1977 only nonresidents and recipients of German compensation payments could hold convertible foreign-currency denominated deposits. Now any Israeli resident may have demand or time deposits, in any amount, denominated in foreign currency. These are convertible freely into domestic currency or demand deposits. They may be used to purchase foreign exchange, but for the same purposes and with the same limitations that domestic currency can be used to acquire foreign exchange. So these foreign exchange deposits are virturally dollar-linked (or other currency-linked) Israeli pounds and are widely used in direct transfer between Israel residents.[3] These accounts are different from eurodollar and other offshore currencies in that the banks, as aforesaid, are not obligated—in fact, are not allowed—to deliver foreign exchange to their depositors on demand, above the limits established by the foreign exchange regulations. The banks in turn are required to hold very high reserves (between 80 and 100%) at the Bank of Israel. As long as the Bank of Israel's foreign exchange reserves do not increase pari passu with the increase in foreign-currency-denominated deposits this means that the Bank of Israel is, in effect, supplying the market with the dollars demanded for these accounts. As a matter of fact, these accounts have increased in the past year and a half much more rapidly than the foreign exchange reserves of the central bank, which implies, or is consistent with, the hypothesis that the Bank has, indeed, been "supplying" the dollars being held by the public.

The large and growing share of these hyper-moneys in the total supply of highly liquid assets M_4, and the velocity of circulation of the various measures of M are shown in Tables 3 and 4.

An outstanding feature of Table 4 is the enormous increase in the velocity of M_1 over time, as inflation accelerated and the hyper-moneys became more widely used. This is particularly striking in the last two years, since the liberalization and the use of foreign-currency-denominated deposits. It is interesting, though not surprising, that M_4 is much more stable.

The decline in the share of currency and demand deposits, M_1, in the total means of payment, or liquid assets, weakens the effectiveness of

[3] On February 22, 1980, as this book was being compiled, the Israeli currency was changed from the pound, or lira, to the shekel, in a 10:1 ratio. Since this is a technical currency reform with no apparent monetary repercussions, we have continued using the older nomenclature. A more substantive change occurred on February 26, when the Bank of Israel and the Treasury decreed that henceforth these foreign-currency-denominated accounts could no longer be transferred from one holder to another. The effect of this will presumably be to lower the liquidity of this asset; what impact that will have on its "moneyness" is too early to tell.

TABLE 3

SHARE OF HYPER-MONEYS IN M_4[a]

		Negotiable government securities held by public	Foreign currency denominated deposits
1977:	12	0.29	0.48
1978:	1	0.28	0.50
	2	0.27	0.52
	3	0.27	0.51
	4	0.27	0.51
	5	0.26	0.52
	6	0.25	0.52
	7	0.25	0.53
	8	0.24	0.54
	9	0.25	0.54
	10	0.26	0.55
	11	0.27	0.53
	12	0.25	0.55
1979:	1	0.26	0.54
	2	0.27	0.54
	3	0.28	0.54
	4	0.28	0.54
	5	0.27	0.55
	6	0.27	0.56
	7	0.29	0.55
	8	0.29	0.55
	9	0.27	0.57
	10	0.27	0.58
	11	0.27	0.59
	12	0.27	0.60

[a] Source: Bank of Israel (1977–1979).

traditional monetary policy. For example, exchanging money for linked government securities in such a world will have little if any effect—given the hyper-money nature of linked bonds, it may even have a perverse effect. Similarly, government intervention in the foreign exchange market as a monetary tool will, in such a situation, have little or no effect on the level of total spending.

Although these relatively "pure" monetary tools, involving money-market interventions, may have become ineffective, the same is not at all true of the fiscal-monetary mix implied by changing government deficits. In a sense, it strengthens the effectiveness of this tool, since it no longer depends as heavily as heretofore on the method of financing a deficit. In the current Israeli institutional framework, financing a government deficit

TABLE 4

VELOCITIES OF MONEY AGGREGATES[a,b]

	Velocity of M_1	Velocity of M_4
1970	5.85	1.44
1971	5.97	1.40
1972	5.91	1.39
1973	5.93	1.42
1974	7.00	1.41
1975	7.60	1.47
1976	8.30	1.48
1977	8.51	1.58
1978	9.96	1.69
1979	13.91	1.84

[a]Source: Bank of Israel (1970–1979), and Central Bureau of Statistics (1970–1979), *Statistical Abstract*.

[b]Note: Velocity = Y/M, where Y = GNP, M_1 = currency, demand deposits (average over year); M_4 = currency, demand and time deposits; foreign-denominated demand and time deposits, and tradable government bonds held by the public (average over year).

involves an increase in one or some components of M_4, and total spending power is increased to almost the same extent whether the increase is in M_1 or in another magnitude. In Fig. 3 we see that the rate of inflation is closely connected with nominal autonomous expenditures and with changes in M_4. The relationship between price level changes and variations in M_1 is weak, particularly in recent years.

Once more, we see that the 1973–1974 period is atypical. The supply constraints imposed by the Yom Kippur War, the oil price increase, and more generally the sharp increase in import prices, and the decline in subsidies to basic commodities combined to produce inflation above what could have been predicted on the basis of either autonomous expenditure increases or changes in M_4, or both. In general, M_4 and autonomous expenditures both include components which are linked to the price index, so that they are a cause as well as an effect of inflation. It is noteworthy that the 1978–1979 rise in autonomous expenditures reversed the downward trend in these expenditures in 1975–1977 and was thus very likely unanticipated. The sharp acceleration in inflation is partly due to this fact.

In conclusion, our purpose in presenting this brief survey has been to offer a set of "stylized facts." We make no pretense at completeness; our interest was to highlight the unusual, if not unique, aspects of that history. We make no claim to either comprehensiveness or balance. Excellent detailed histories are available to the interested reader in Patinkin (1960), Halevi and Klinov-Malul (1968), and Michaely (1975).

REFERENCES

Cukierman, Alex, Pazner, Elisha, and Razin, Assaf (1976). A Macroeconomic Model of the Israeli Economy: 1956–1974. *Bank of Israel Economic Review* **44**, 23–51.

Halevi, Nadav, and Klinov-Malul, Ruth (1968). *The Economic Development of Israel*. Praeger, New York.

Kleiman, Efraim (1975). Inflation and the Redistribution of Public Capital. *Economic Quarterly* **83**, 238–257. (In Hebrew.)

Michaely, Michael (1975). *Foreign Trade Regimes and Economic Development: Israel*. National Bureau of Economic Research, New York.

Patinkin, Don (1960). *The Israeli Economy: The First Decade*. Falk Project for Economic Research, Jerusalem.

THE PINHAS SAPIR CENTER FOR DEVELOPMENT
TEL AVIV UNIVERSITY
RAMAT AVIV, TEL AVIV, ISRAEL

PART 1

Inflation: Causes, Characteristics, Cure(s)

Diagnosing Inflation: A Taxonomy

JAMES TOBIN

1. Introduction

For nearly a decade the advanced democratic societies of Western Europe, North America, and Japan have been struggling with inflation and losing. Their problem, still as far from resolution as ever, has been to keep price inflation under control at low rates while sustaining economic growth and high employment. While the countries of the Organization of Economic Development (OECD), individually and collectively, have failed to reconcile these goals, the aspirations of their peoples have not shrunk nearly enough to fit actual performance.

The resulting economic, political, and social frustrations are very serious. They are fueling, at least in some countries, cynical distrust of existing political and economic institutions. They are eroding national consensus and weakening the social inhibitions on self-interest and group interest in economic and political behavior. They are stimulating autarkic and protectionist threats to the international financial and commercial cooperation that helped so much to support the remarkable growth of trade after World War II. They are sharpening conflicts with the less developed countries, both those whose progress makes them formidable competitors in the world markets and those whose continued stagnation exasperates both sides of the dialogue of haves and have-nots.

The macroeconomic impasse of the West must certainly gratify communist governments and ideological opponents of democratic capitalism and socialism everywhere. Inflation, stagflation, and unemployment are rarely overt problems in centrally directed economies. The Marxists badly needed some such consolation. The flaws they had detected in capitalism

ISBN 0-12-259750-8

proved to be far from fatal; the organism whose collapse they had so long awaited so expectantly seemed to be stubbornly robust. Capitalism seemed immune to the grand dialectics of accumulation, technological change, and class conflict. Ironically, its unforeseen weakness appears to be an ancient, technical, and relatively trivial malady, instability of prices (Gordon, 1975). If this truly is our Achilles' heel, our world ends not with a bang but with a whimper.

In diagnosing the malady and prescribing remedies, the economic physicians of the West have exhibited as much disarray as their sick patients. One important reason, I shall agree, is that there are several kinds of inflation and several diseases of which inflation is a highly visible symptom. Some of our countries suffer from one of these maladies, some from another, some from more than one simultaneously or sequentially. Some cure themselves, some are easy to remedy, some are intractable. There is no single sovereign remedy.

2. A Monetary Phenomenon?

What I have just said may sound like heresy to those who recall Milton Friedman's famous aphorism "Inflation is at all times and everywhere a monetary phenomenon." It certainly is, if only by definition. Since inflation means that *money* prices of commodities generally increase—in other words that the commodity value of the monetary unit generally declines—it is necessarily a monetary phenomenon. The author of the quotation and other monetarists mean much more than that. They mean to attribute all inflation to excessive rates of expansion of monetary aggregates, excessive relative to the sustainable growth of real output. For example, if the growth of labor supply and other productive resources, augmented by the normal technological trend of productivity, is 3% per year, then monetary expansion that brings about a growth of more than 3% per year in nominal spending for goods and services is excessive. Insert the word *continuous* in the last sentence, and it too is almost tautological. The difficult question remains: Why does the monetary authority acquiesce in "excessive" growth of monetary aggregates and nominal spending? What would happen if it did not?

A purely *monetary inflation* is one variety of the disease. It is far more than a logical possibility, as the historical inflations resulting from surges of gold production attest. But modern central bankers do not capriciously or gratuitously expand money supplies, and they are not friends of inflation. There are several explanations why they have nonetheless been engines or accomplices of inflation.

One explanation, offered by Friedman himself, is simply intellectual error. Central banks did not know what they were doing. They misunderstood the monetary and financial system and the economy and inadvertently overexpanded money supplies. They paid too much attention to nominal interest rates or to credit market conditions. Underestimating the lags in transmission of their monetary impulses, they destabilized the economy like an idiot trying to regulate the temperature of a shower or the thermostat of a home furnace. Whatever the merit of these allegations, they do not imply an inflationary bias. Moreover, they do not apply to the inflation of the 1970s. This inflation has coincided with the conversion of central bankers to a belief in monetarist theories, statistics, and targets.

3. Excess Demand and Trade-Off Inflations

It is more credible that central banks have assisted their governments in pursuing fiscal and macroeconomic policies with inflationary consequences. Classic *excess demand* inflation occurs when new government demands for resources are piled on to labor and product markets lacking slack capacity. The government does not have the courage to tax its citizens enough to obtain the needed resources in an orderly way, and the central bank lacks the will or the power to raise interest rates enough to release the resources from private use. Pressure to keep the treasury's borrowing rates low when the government is selling securites has often constrained the central bank.

In the United States our most recent example of excess demand inflation was quantitatively modest in historical perspective, but turned out to be important beyond all expectation and proportion in the genesis of the inflation that still plagues us. It was the financing of the Vietnam war in 1966–1969, which raised the inflation rate in the United States by three points, from 2% in 1965 to 5% in 1969 and 1970.

A variant of excess demand inflation, somewhat different both in theory and in motivation, could be called *trade-off inflation*. The Phillips curve blurred the line defining excess demand into a continuum of trade-offs, with increasing marginal cost in inflation for additional employment and production. In its primitive form, the theory certainly understated the long-run inflation cost of low rates of unemployment and excess capacity.

Today a widespread version of recent history is that governments deliberately sought higher inflation in order to reduce unemployment and underestimated the severity of the trade-off. Such a policy was clearly and explicitly followed by the first Roosevelt administration in 1933 to 1936. As an explanation of recent inflation in the United States, I believe this account is enormously exaggerated. In 1961–1965 the Kennedy–Johnson administration sought successfully to reduce unemployment from 7% to 4%, which was its estimate of full employment or of what would later be called the "natural rate of unemployment." Far from welcoming inflation, the administration adopted "wage–price guideposts" to hold it down during the hoped-for recovery. In the event, the 4% unemployment goal was reached in 1965 with inflation still no higher than 2%. The 1966–1969 ride up the Phillips curve was not a conscious choice of novel macroeconomic strategy but a time-worn political decision about wartime finance. Against the advice of his Keynesian advisors, President Johnson chose for his own reasons of domestic and international politics not to ask Congress for increased taxes to finance his ill-starred escalation of the conflict in Indochina.

In 1971 President Nixon and Treasury Secretary Connally, frustrated by the failure of the 1970–1971 recession to cure inflation (it actually reached new heights while unemployment was rising by $2\frac{1}{2}$ points), slapped on wage and price controls and shifted into stimulative monetary and fiscal gear. The recovery of 1971–1974 ended with double-digit inflation and 5% unemployment. The abrupt counterinflationary response brought the worst recession and highest unemployment of postwar history. The subsequent recovery of 1975–1979 is ending with double-digit inflation and 6% unemployment. Whatever the reasons for these misfortunes, it is clear that none of these episodes can be fairly described as an attempt to make full employment fuller by inviting higher inflation.

4. The Political Business Cycle

Observers within and outside the economics profession claim to discern a political rhythm in the stop–go alternation of expansionary and restrictive macroeconomic policies. (It is widely believed, for example, that the Federal Reserve's 1972 monetary expansion was a deliberate assist to Nixon's campaign for reelection. I do not know the inside facts, but I observe that the policy was understandable in the economic circumstances and was within the normal range of "leaning against the wind" characteristic of recovery periods.) The incumbent administration, it is alleged, times prosperity for election months, calculating that the inflation pain will come later. Cooling off the economy comes after the election, long enough before the next one to be forgotten and to set the stage for the next well-timed "go" policy. These commentators have an extravagant view of the precision of fine tuning, as well as a contemptuous view of voters and politicians. The more cynical among them regard expansionary policies as purely political, never seeing intrinsic economic benefit in reducing unemployment and raising production. In any event, the theory of the political stop–go business cycle, resting as it does on the premise that votes depend not on levels of economic activity but on the rate of increase of real incomes in the year prior to election, implies an inflationary trend only because the structure of the economy is so asymmetrical that symmetrical cycles in real economic activity generate irreversible accelerations of inflation.

5. Accommodation

Whether or not they engage in stop–go electoral calculations and manipulations, the makers of macroeconomic policy are always seeking politically acceptable compromises. There is really no great mystery why governments and central banks have in the 1970s allowed monetary expansions "excessive" in relation to actual and sustainable real growth rates. They have usually accommodated ongoing inflation because they regard the consequences of nonaccommodation as unacceptable economically and politically. Those consequences are exemplified by the severe worldwide recession of 1974–1975, which may be attributed to nonaccommodative policies, deliberate or accidental.

6. Inertial Inflation

The inflations of the 1970s confronted monetary and other macroeconomic policy makers with cruelly difficult choices. To describe these inflations, I must add two more types to the taxonomy I have gradually been introducing. I will call them *inertial inflation* and *specific-price inflation*. By "inertial inflation" I mean the self-replicating pattern of wage and price inflation with which we all have become familiar. Whatever the historical origins of the inflation, once it is built into the system in a consistent manner it continues very much on its own. The nonagricultural private sector of the U.S. economy is a natural habitat of such a closed system. Unions and employers relate their wage increases to recent settlements in other markets and to recent price trends. Employers mark up the increases in labor costs, with allowance for normal productivity gains. These markups determine price trends, which in turn feed into the wage increases.

The behavior that sustains these patterns may be interpreted as backward looking—emulating the behavior of other unions and other industries, catching up with reference groups, passing through historical costs, fulfilling explicit or implicit contractual agreements and mutual understandings. Or it may be interpreted as forward looking—estimating from past experience and other information the likely course of other prices and of market conditions during the periods of decision. It is doubtless both, and the two are tied together. In any case, what matters is the stubborn persistence of the built-in pattern, in particular its resistance to slowdown in monetary demand. Refusal to accommodate inertial inflation will not cause the pattern to collapse. Rather it will bring severe contraction in employment and production for several years, while the built-in wage/price pattern subsides very slowly. This is the fear that motivates accommodative policies.

7. Specific Price Inflation

Similar dilemmas of accommodation arise when nonmonetary events raise prices in specific markets, and as a result raise economy-wide price indexes. A few years ago, admitting the possibility of "specific price inflation" would have invited excommunication from the guild of monetary economists. The important distinction between absolute and relative prices is still fundamental. It is still vulgar fallacy to refer to the declining prices of computers and digital watches as "deflation" and to rising oil prices as "inflation." These are not monetary but real phenomena!

Nevertheless, the same wage and price setting institutions that sustain inertial inflation make it impossible to keep dramatic increases in specific prices out of the average price level. Given the stubbornness of built-in patterns of wage and price inflation, it was inevitable that absorption of quadrupled oil prices would create a bulge of general inflation. Indeed, OPEC's blow was a prototypical stagflationary shock, transferring money and real income and wealth to nonspenders and at the same time raising prices. Fully accommodative macropolicies not only would have covered the rise in prices but would have compensated for the contractionary diversion of purchasing power. A nonaccommodative policy was bound to lead to recession unless wages and prices in sectors and markets other than oil were very quickly flexible downward. They were not.

Specific price shocks are not always inflationary, though since 1973 we in the United States can be excused for thinking they are. In addition to oil and energy, we have suffered from increases in food prices, from the dollar-price consequences of exchange depreciation, and from various "self-inflicted wounds." The latter included farm price supports and crop restrictions that deprived us of the full counterinflationary advantages of favorable agricultural developments, import restrictions, increases in payroll taxes and other indirect taxes, increases in minimum wages and unemployment insurance benefits, and environmental and safety regulations.

8. Disinflation by Nonaccommodation

In general, I submit, it is fatuous and disingenuous to argue that inertial inflation can be painlessly expunged from the economic scene by disinflationary macroeconomic policy, monetary and fiscal, as if all that is required is for government to exercise self-control in the amount and financing of its expenditures and so forth. If this orthodox prescription will work at all, it will take years of high unemployment and subnormal growth of real income, with lasting damage to the stock of physical and human capital and to the social contract. The econometric consensus for the United States suggests that the real costs would be large and protracted: an extra point of unemployment diminishes inflation by only a quarter or half point per year. Maybe disinflation is worth that cost. Maybe this policy is the least of all evils. Those are arguable propositions, and some monetarists have argued them. But other monetarists, including the new classical macroeconomists, have contributed to the increasingly frequent and vocal claim that prudent government policy can conquer inflation without real pain.

Confronting the problem squarely, Professor William Fellner has argued that pessimistic econometric estimates of the short-run Phillips tradeoff are misleading. These estimates, he argues, are generated by the statistics of an era of accommodative policies. The disinflationary response would be much faster and much less costly, he asserts, if economic agents believed that the government and central bank had resolutely shifted to nonaccommodation (Fellner, 1976).

Fellner dates the advent of accommodative policy in the early 1960s. Prior to the "new economics," he observes, the inflation rate fell fairly sharply in postwar cyclical recessions; afterwards, it did not. He concludes that the government must visibly and ostentatiously lock up the money supply and destroy the key. Once it is clear to workers, unions, and employers that there is going to be only so much monetary demand, they will see that the more they take in inflation the less they will have in employment and output. Then they will very quickly opt for the natural rate of unemployment. Rational expectations theorists will put it the other way round—whatever they opt for is the natural rate. I do not understand Fellner to say that but to make an assertion that is at least in principle empirically testable.

One practical problem in a democracy is to make credible the threat that the government will do nothing about recession, unemployment, stagnation—nothing either macroeconomic or microeconomic for the relief of particular industries, regions, or groups. This congress or this parliament, this president or this prime minister, may stand tough, but may not survive. During the Vietnam war, our presidents and secretaries of state used to complain that we would win the war if only domestic opposition to it, causing the enemy to suspect irresolution, would cease.

Even if the Fellner threat could be made credible, there remains the question: What behavior would it induce in a decentralized but not perfectly competitive economy? There would be no problem at all if all prices and wages were made, and frequently remade, in impersonal competitive auction markets. The problem arises because in a modern economy most wages and prices are administered, decided, or negotiated periodically by identifiable individuals. At the same time, in the United States at any rate, there is no concerted economy-wide bargain or price decision. Fellner models the situation as a 2-person game, the unruly inflation-prone economy versus a disciplinarian government. More accurately, it is an $n + 1$-person game, with the n private groups playing mainly against each other. Each is interested in its volume of employment or sales, to be sure, but also in its real wage or price relative to those of other groups. Your line of least resistance, of apparently least risk, is to follow the inertial pattern, expecting everyone else to do likewise. The result—assuming the government means business—is generally low volume but no loss of relative status. And if others do disinflate, you will gain in real income and relative position and lose less in volume. On the other hand, if you disinflate without assurance that others will do likewise, you risk great loss of real income and status for what will likely be a small gain of volume.

To succeed, I think, the threat must be a promise, the mutual promise of all major interested groups to de-escalate together, forswearing the temptation to gain relative position from the restraint of other groups. In this respect income policies or social compacts go hand-in-hand with announcement of plans to diminish the rate of growth of aggregate nominal spending. Countries with traditions and institutions of economy-wide wage bargaining, with government participation, may be better positioned to conjoin monetary disinflation and incomes policies than those like the United States with decentralized collective bargaining and price setting.

9. Equilibrium Paths

The discussion so far has taken for granted the existence of a viable economic and political equilibrium of real outcomes, a path along which expectations of relative prices and real incomes are mutually consistent and are by and large fulfilled. Such an economy can have any rate of inflation—or even any other path of nominal prices—to which it has adapted its conventions, institutions, and expectations and to which it accommodates its monetary and fiscal policies.

That is surely the view of monetarists, old-fashioned and new. It is also the view of those who diagnose current inflation as basically inertial. They would say there is no intrinsic difference between the U.S. economy of 1965 and that of 1978 to explain the difference between their wage–price patterns: increases of 4% in wages and 2% in prices in 1965, as against the 9% in wages and 7% in prices in 1978. The inflation difference is purely historical in origin. If the slate could be wiped clean of the patterns of behavior and expectation that keep the inflation going, the economy could go on its merry way with lower inflation or even with stable prices. Unlike the monetarists, the diagnosticians of intertial inflation do not think it is easy to wipe the slate clean. That is why they favor incomes policies rather than restrictive macropolicies unassisted.

These diagnoses are consistent with the possibility that the amount of structural, frictional, and voluntary unemployment has risen since the 1960s and 1950s. A number of reasons, varying in plausibility, have been advanced and need not be reviewed here. Some of them say merely that, for various demographic and statistical reasons, the official overall unemployment rate is higher for the same essential tightness of labor and product markets. It is more disturbing if at the same degree of resource utilization we now experience greater acceleration of prices. Moreover, deterioration of both kinds may be an unintended and unwelcome by-product of the counterinflationary macroeconomic measures of the 1970s. I have in mind that slowdown in capital investment can turn Keynesian unemployment into classical structural unemployment, that lack of jobs for cohorts of teenagers and young adults can make them unemployable, and that extensions and improvements of unemployment insurance and other measures to relieve economic distress can convert some involuntary unemployment into voluntary. Maybe there are several equilibrium paths, and we have shifted to a less desirable one.

10. Conflict Inflation

Quite a different diagnosis is that inflation is the symptom of deep-rooted social and economic contradiction and conflict. There is no real equilibrium path. The major economic groups are claiming pieces of pie that together exceed the whole pie. Inflation is the way that their claims, so far as they are expressed in nominal terms, are temporarily reconciled. But it will continue and indeed accelerate so long as the basic conflicts of real claims and real power continue (Holzman, 1950).

Will restrictive macroeconomic policies resolve *conflict inflation*? If the players cannot agree how to divide a larger pie, will they agree how to divide a smaller one? The hope is that the exclusion of more and more people from the game weakens the more assertive groups. The fear is that the shrinking of the pie just makes the insiders more intransigent and protectionist. Reasoning by competitive logic does not help us in this syndicalist world.

There are a number of possible scenarios of conflict inflation in the 1970s. A common story is that a combination of misfortunes—OPEC, long-run energy shortage, environmental dangers and costs—has sharply lowered the paths of potential output, real wages, and real returns on capital investment. But it has not lowered the standards of real income progress to which employed workers are accustomed or the profit rates that managers and shareowners expect.

Workers expect their employers and unions to continue to deliver the usual gains, and they are willing to exert their organized power to that end. Presumably in the long run workers and unions adapt to whatever rate of productivity growth the economy can provide. But in a painfully long meanwhile, insiders may in effect find in restriction of members a substitute source of increasing real wages. Similarly, unrealistic profit goals result in excessive markups and exaggerated hurdles for new investment.

In this scenario the relative price shocks of the mid-1970s are the source of serious and lasting conflict, not simply of a temporary bulge of inflation statistics. If hamburger and gasoline become more expensive, will urban workers accelerate wage inflation for decades in hopeless quest for compensation from employers who profit from neither beef nor petroleum? Will they do the same when sales or payroll or income taxes are raised? One theory of British inflation goes along the following lines: Although they voted for MPs who gave them the welfare state, British workers did not really regard the benefits for which they were taxed as the equivalent of take-home pay. Consequently, they sought to get them back at the bargaining table (Bacon and Eltis: 1976).

Among OECD countries there were large differences in the paths of real wages following the adverse shift of terms of trade with OPEC and with producers of food and materials. In the United States money wages stayed pretty close to their inertial trend, and labor, organized as well as unorganized, absorbed absolute reductions in real wages, as well as declines in the growth of real disposable incomes. In Britain, thanks partly to untimely indexation and partly to political power, major unions were able to maintain real wages and shunt the national losses to other social groups via accelerated inflation. One lesson we should all learn, incidentally, is the danger of casual indexing by cost-of-living measures inclusive of prices that represent unavoidable costs to the whole society. Somebody has to pay OPEC for oil, and not everyone can have incomes, wages, or social benefits insured against such risks.

The distinction I have tried to make between inertial inflation and conflict inflation invites a metaphor. Consider a stadium where everyone stands up to see the spectacle. They can all see equally well if everyone sits down. The problem is to get people to sit down; but that is the only problem. A more serious situation occurs when there are not enough places in the stadium, and no way to agree on taking turns.

I am not sure how to classify the inflations of our countries in this decade. I have been pretty sure that United States inflation was of the inertial species, but I would not exclude the possibility that more fundamental social conflict is arising from the frustrations of continued economic reverses. In either event we face problems much more serious than their inflationary symptoms, problems that we cannot expect a central bank to solve.

REFERENCES

Bacon, Robert, and Eltis, Walter (1976). *Britain's Economic Problem: Too Few Producers*. St. Martin's, New York.

Fellner, William (1976). *Towards a Reconstruction of Macroeconomics: Problems of Theory and Policy*. American Enterprise Institute for Public Policy Research, Washington, D.C.

Gordon, David, M. (1975). Recession is Capitalism as Usual. *New York Times Magazine* April 27, 1975.

Holzman, Franklyn D. (1950). Income Determination in Open Inflation. *Review of Economics and Statistics* **32**, 150–158.

DEPARTMENT OF ECONOMICS
YALE UNIVERSITY
NEW HAVEN, CONNECTICUT

Some Observations on the Inflationary Process

DON PATINKIN

I would like to take advantage of this opportunity to make some general observations on the inflationary process.

Let me begin by saying—as several others at this conference have also said—that I have never found the familiar statement that inflation is everywhere and at all times a monetary phenomenon to be a very edifying one: for the price level is the inverse of the purchasing power of money, so that by the same token one can say that the price of potatoes is everywhere and at all times a potato phenomenon. The real question is whether the quantity of money is an exogenous variable or an endogenous one. Does the monetary increase come from outside the system, or is it generated by the dynamics of the system itself? Is it the cause of the increase in the price level, or is it the result? We all know that statistical correlations do not determine causal relationships, so on the basis of a high correlation alone, we cannot say which variable is affecting which. Moreover, there is always a possibility that some third variable is affecting both of them simultaneously.

Let me put this question of causal relationships in another way. Political leaders and ministers of finance have from time immemorial known how to print money. Why do they sometimes suddenly decide to print more? The statistical correlation between inflation and money-supply growth does not answer that basic question.

Some have attempted to provide an answer by saying that the government generates inflation as a means of levying a tax on cash balances. This approach to inflation is not a new one. A vivid and eloquent analysis of it can be found in Keynes's *Tract on Monetary Reform*, which was written

ISBN 0-12-259750-8

immediately after World War I. In the *Tract* Keynes described inflation as a tax, and he even had the notion (which only in recent years has been developed rigorously) of the optimum rate of this inflation tax.

There are, however, several reasons why I do not feel that this can be a complete answer to the question. First, the inflation tax is levied not on the total money supply, but on the monetary base—and in an economy like that of the United States, the real proceeds of such a tax would seem to be too small to provide an explanation of the continuation and even exacerbation of an inflationary process that has clear political disadvantages for the government.

In any event, the case of Israel provides a vivid counterexample to this explanation, for in Israel every time the price level goes up, the government suffers a real loss! This results from the situation during the past decade and more in which the Israel government has borrowed by means of indexed loans and has lent from its development budget without indexing. Thus every increase in the price level increases the government's debt to the public without affecting the public's debt to the government, and this loss more than offsets the government's real gain on the nominal debt that it owes the public on account of the monetary base. Thus every time inflation occurs, the government loses in real terms. This situation could, of course, be rationalized by saying that the government decides to use its "receipts" from the inflation tax to "finance" subsidies to people to whom it is lending, but such an explanation turns the statement that inflation is a tax on cash balances into a vacuous one that can never be falsified.

There is a further, and far more general, reservation that I have about explaining inflation in terms of a tax on cash balances. In order that this be a full explanation, one must also explain why the fiscal structure of so many Western countries during the past decade has shifted in the direction of increased dependence on this tax. And one should also explain why there seems to have been less of such a shift in the case of Eastern European countries, where (even after due account is taken of price controls and of deficiencies in the price-index statistics) the rate of inflation seems to have been lower than in the West.

At the risk of expressing views on questions on which I have no expertise, let me be more concrete. There was a major shift in the U.S. federal fiscal structure from dependence on import duties and excise taxes before World War I to dependence on a progressive income tax afterwards. Any student of fiscal history in the United States is accordingly faced with the challenge of explaining this shift, an explanation which may proceed in terms of (a) the increase in government expenditures, which required it to find new sources of tax revenues; and (b) the increased concern to reduce inequality in the distribution of income. I would like to have a similar explanation for the increased use of inflation as a tax by Western counties. Perhaps it too is related to the increased level of government expenditures in the period after World War II—to the emergence of the welfare state and the consequent need to find new sources of finance. But this hardly serves as an explanation for the highly varying rates of inflation that have prevailed in certain economies (for example, Israel during the past 5 years) despite a fairly stable structure of welfare services. Similarly, the administrative ease of the inflation tax—the possibility of levying it without the assistance of tax collectors—cannot serve as an explanation of *changes* in the rate of inflation. Indeed, except for countries in a state of serious wartime disruption, I do not feel that this administrative ease has been an important cause of inflation.

I do, however, feel that we will get a better insight into the origins of inflation if we abandon the view (which is implicit in the notion of inflation as a tax) of government as a single, monolithic decision-making unit. A democratic government—and maybe even a nondemocratic one—is a coalition. Sometimes it is a formal coalition, as in Israel and many European countries; and sometimes it is an informal one, as in the United States. Inflation might then be viewed (and I must admit that these views have been much influenced by my observations of the Israeli scene during the past three decades) as the imposition of a tax by the finance minister on all the other ministries. That is, in a situation where the finance minister—because of coalition considerations—does not have the power to force individual ministries to make adequate reductions in their respective budgets and is thus confronted with an overall budget whose planned expenditures far exceed its expected revenues, he may simply finance the deficit by printing money and letting the resulting inflation enforce the necessary real reduction in expenditure. Indeed, since this amounts to an across-the-board reduction, it may be the path of least resistance for him.

A direct implication of this "coalition theory of inflation" is that the weaker the coalition, the higher the rate of inflation. And I think this is one of the major reasons for the much higher rate of inflation in Israel's present coalition government as compared with that of the preceding coalition.

Let me draw on Israel's experience to make another comment (that has also been made by others at this conference) on a completely different topic—cost inflation. It has long been recognized that such an inflationary process can be generated by the government levying indirect taxes. But in an economy in which the government is a major employer (and that is certainly the case in Israel), it may also generate cost inflation by the wage contracts it makes with its own employees. In such situations the government provides both the "supply shock" of a wage increase that initiates or reinforces the inflation and the accommodating increase in the quantity of money that permits it to continue.

I would like to conclude by expressing my general impression that during the past decade the formal theory of inflation has drawn much closer to the folk wisdom of inflation—and in large part that means that in the eternal banking-school/currency-school controversy it has drawn closer to the position of the banking school. I see four main manifestations of this. The first is the increasing respectability of talking about "supply shocks" and, more generally, cost inflation. A prime example of this is the frequent analysis of the impact of the increase in OPEC oil prices on the inflationary process. The man in the street (together with Thomas Tooke!) was always ready to describe inflation as the consequence of increases in specific prices, but there was a time when an economist was in danger of being read out of the profession for doing so. The second, and related, manifestation is the increased tendency to regard the money supply as an endogenous variable. Once again, for the man in the street, this was the natural view: The real-bills doctrine of the banking school was for him not a fallacy, but a true description of the world. The third manifestation is the increased emphasis being placed in the theory of inflation on the role of expectations. The folk wisdom of inflation frequently described it as a psychological phenomenon; on the other hand, the economists of the 1950s and 1960s just as frequently cited Cagan's classic study of hyperinflation as proof that even in such extreme situations, the process was stable and would not have continued on the basis of expectations alone. Contrast this with the spirit of (say) the expectations-augmented Phillips curve of today, based on the assumption that the actual rate of inflation is the expected one, adjusted at most for the state of excess demand in the market.

The fourth manifestation has to do with rational expectations. The Israeli public (and I am sure that this was true of the public in other countries as well) always knew better than to take at face value the finance minister's annual declarations that he was going to reduce budget expenditures, or the central bank's repeated declarations that it was going to limit the growth in the money supply. And I am glad to see that folk wisdom of this kind has finally found a place in our formal economic analysis.

DEPARTMENT OF ECONOMICS
HEBREW UNIVERSITY OF JERUSALEM
JERUSALEM, ISRAEL

In Step and Out of Step with the World Inflation

A Summary History of Countries, 1952–1976

ARNOLD C. HARBERGER

1. Introduction

This paper can be looked upon as a progress report on a broad and general study of inflation throughout the world in the period since World War II. The study has several facets to which successive sections of the paper will be devoted. In Section 2 I present evidence on the world inflation. In Sections 3 and 4, two types of deviation from the world inflation are identified, and in Section 5 the phenomenon of devaluation crisis is explored. Finally, in Section 6 certain aspects of the Israeli inflation are highlighted.

2. The World Inflation, 1952–1976

Table 1 presents data on the average rates of inflation for the major industrial countries for three subperiods. The most notable attribute of this table is the tendency for inflation rates to be similar across the countries within each of the different periods. Indeed, as is shown at the bottom of the table, ranges can be chosen so as to include, in each subperiod, 80% of the observations in such a way as to leave the ranges for the different subperiods completely disjoint (that is, without any overlap). The picture is one of a common inflationary process, accelerating as one moves from one subperiod to the next.

Table 2 shows that this same attribute applies to a wide range of less-developed countries (LDCs). The ranges for the LDCs span those for

ISBN 0-12-259750-8

TABLE 1

INDUSTRIAL COUNTRIES AVERAGE ANNUAL INFLATION RATES[a]

	1952–1967	1967–1972	1972–1976
United States	1.5	4.6	9.5
Canada	1.7	3.9	9.2
Japan	4.3	5.9	13.9
Australia	2.5	4.3	13.2
New Zealand	3.2	6.6	12.7
Austria	3.1	4.3	8.2
Belgium	1.9	4.0	10.3
Denmark	3.9	6.1	11.0
France	3.7	4.7	10.5
Germany	1.9	3.5	6.1
Italy	3.1	3.9	15.9
Netherlands	3.0	6.0	9.2
Norway	3.3	6.1	9.4
Sweden	3.5	5.1	9.2
Switzerland	2.1	4.3	6.7
United Kingdom	2.8	6.6	16.4
Median	3.0	4.6	9.9
Range encompassing 80% of observations	1.7–3.7	3.9–6.1	8.2–13.9

[a] Percent per annum.

the industrial countries, but there seems to be no systematic tendency for the LDCs to have higher average rates of inflation than the countries in Table 1.

What is left to be pondered here is the relevance of thinking about these inflations as being in any sense "national" phenomena. Are these 44 inflations the creatures of 44 different central banks and/or ministries of finance? Or are they rather separate reflections of a single process of world inflation? Personally, I strongly incline to the latter interpretation. As evidence, consider the following: All 44 of the countries in the two tables shared in the progression from medium inflation to high inflation as one moves from 1967–1972 to 1972–1976. That is to say, all 44 inflation rates increased. Now if these were independent phenomena, with a 50% probability that the inflation rate would increase or decrease from one period to the next, the probability of this result occurring would be equal to that of getting 44 heads in 44 consecutive tosses of a coin. That probability is less than one in eighteen quadrillion!!

The progression from low to medium inflation (that is, from 1952–1967 to 1967–1972) was shared by only 38 of the 44 countries. But the probabil-

TABLE 2

SELECTED LESS-DEVELOPED COUNTRIES AVERAGE ANNUAL INFLATION RATES[a]

	1952–1967	1967–1972	1972–1976
Costa Rica	1.8	3.8	16.2
Dominican Republic	0.8	3.4	12.6
Ecuador	2.2	6.4	15.5
Egypt	1.4	3.3	8.8
El Salvador	1.4	1.5	12.2
Guatemala	0.6	1.3	13.6
Haiti	1.8	3.3	15.7
Honduras	1.3	2.9	7.3
India	4.8	3.7	9.9
Iran	4.7	4.3	12.0
Iraq	0.5	4.2	8.2
Jamaica	2.8	6.9	18.3
Malaysia	− 0.2	3.2	8.6
Mexico	4.3	4.4	16.6
Morocco	2.7	2.5	9.5
Nigeria	3.4	8.3	18.1
Pakistan	3.8	4.0	19.2
Panama	0.3	2.7	7.7
Philippines	2.7	8.5	14.2
Portugal	2.4	8.8	18.5
Spain	6.3	5.9	15.4
Sri Lanka	0.9	5.6	7.4
Sudan	2.7	3.9	16.4
Syria	0.9	2.7	16.5
Taiwan	6.7	4.4	14.5
Thailand	2.7	2.2	10.7
Trinidad/Tobago	2.4	5.2	16.0
Venezuela	0.9	2.5	7.5
Median	2.3	3.8	13.9
Range encompassing 80% of observations	0.8–4.8	2.2–6.9	7.4–16.5

[a]Percent per annum.

ity of its happening by chance under 44 separate causal mechanisms is still astounding—the probability of 38 or more heads in 44 tosses of a coin is less than one in a million.

Without stopping to analyze these results, let me simply point out that we as a profession have not devoted enough attention to world inflation as a single interconnected process. We have too much taken the country as our sole object of analysis. We badly need more work trying to identify the underlying, common causes of the 44 inflations recorded in the tables, plus those of many other countries not listed that shared the same experience. The world money supply is a meaningful concept here, and its movements broadly "explain" the world inflation. But then we must still ask what lies behind the speeding up of the rate of expansion of the world money supply, from the first subperiod to the second and from the second to the third.

3. Chronic and Acute Inflations

Tables 3 and 4 present evidence on two important types of behavior that deviate from the world pattern. In defining the category of chronic inflation, I imposed the criterion of an inflation rate of 20% or more for at least five consecutive years. For acute inflation the criterion was a rate of 80% or more for at least two years. It is worth noting (a) how few such deviations there are and (b) how concentrated they are in the southern cone of South America. Additional points of interest are (c) that in chronic inflation the money supply tends to rise faster than prices—as the demand function for real cash balances shifts outward with income and population growth, while the cost of holding money, though high, does not rise dramatically and (d) that in acute inflation, prices rise faster than money since the movement along the demand curve for real balances, reflecting a sharp rise in the cost of holding money, is sufficient to dominate whatever rightward shift of the function might be taking place over the relatively short acute phase of the inflation disease.

TABLE 3

EXAMPLES OF CHRONIC INFLATION[a]

		Average annual percentage increase	
Country	Period	Consumer prices[b]	Money supply[c]
Argentina	1949–1974	27	29
Brazil	1957–1976	35	42
Chile	1952–1970	32	38
Uruguay	1958–1965	26	34

[a] Source: International Monetary Fund, *International Financial Statistics*, 1977 *Supplement*.

[b] Basic data were yearly averages of monthly price levels.

[c] Basic data were end-of-year money supply figures.

TABLE 4

EXAMPLES OF ACUTE INFLATION[a]

Country	Period	Average annual percentage increase	
		Prices[b]	Money supply[c]
Argentina	1974–1976	293	262
Bolivia	1952–1959	117	100
Chile	1971–1976	273	231
Indonesia	1965–1968	306	223
Paraguay	1951–1953	81	54
South Korea	1950–1955	102	101
Uruguay	1965–1968	95	66
Uruguay	1971–1974	83	63

[a]Source: See Table 3.
[b]See note *b* to Table 3.
[c]See note *c* to Table 3.

4. Looking beyond the Money Supply

In this section we take for granted that expansions in the money supply were the proximate causes of the chronic and acute inflations reported above. But what lay behind those monetary expansions? They surely were not the result of pure whim of central bankers. In a very exploratory effort, we defined three variables that in one sense or other may help explain movements in money and hence in prices. These variables are

β the net increase during the year of banking system credit to the public sector, expressed as a percentage of the year's gross domestic product (GDP). Thus, if the public sector's borrowings from the banking system stood at 200 at the beginning of the year and went to 300 by year's end, the net increase would be 100. If GDP of the year were 800, then β would be 12.5% (100/800).

γ the fraction of total banking system credit going to the public sector. Thus, if at the beginning of the year total bank credit were 400 and if at the end it were 500, then (using public sector credit figures from above) γ would be 0.50 (200/400) at the beginning of the year and 0.60 (300/500) at the end. In the tables presented in this paper γ is always measured from end-of-year data. Whenever the public sector is a net lender to the banking system, γ is simply recorded as less than zero.

TABLE 5

MEDIAN OBSERVATIONS OF INDICATED VARIABLE DURING PERIOD SPECIFIED

		β (%)	γ	λ (%)	π (%)
		Cases of Acute Inflation			
Indonesia	(1966–1968)	2.0	0.542	145	128
Bolivia	(1954–1957)	4.4	0.800	81	120
Chile	(1973–1976)	33.0	0.850	433	365
Uruguay	(1966–1968)	1.7	0.215	40	89
Uruguay	(1972–1975)	3.0	0.234	95	80
Argentina	(1975–1976)	13.3	0.394	220	310
Median		3.7	0.467	120	124
		Cases of Chronic Inflation			
Argentina	(1954–1974)	2.6	0.333	27	26
Uruguay	(1954–1965, 1969–1971)	1.2	0.120	26	21
Chile	(1959–1972)	2.9	0.477	41	28
Brazil	(1954–1976)	2.0	0.300	43	29
Median		2.3	0.316	34	27

TABLE 6

CONTROL GROUP—STABLE EXCHANGE RATE COUNTRIES[a]

		β (%)	γ	λ (%)	π (%)
Taiwan	(1960–1972)	0.5	0.267	18.6	3.0
Honduras	(1954–1970)	0.2	0.288	12.1	1.2
Haiti	(1954–1970)	0.5	0.680	07.7	1.4
Jamaica	(1954–1965)	0.3	<0	21.8	2.1
Iran	(1960–1970)	1.8	0.345	20.2	1.6
Thailand	(1954–1970)	0.1	0.251	11.9	2.1
Portugal	(1954–1970)	0.2	0.164	11.0	3.0
Guatemala	(1954–1970)	0.3	0.174	11.4	0.6
El Salvador	(1954–1970)	0.5	0.093	10.3	1.5
Dominican Republic	(1954–1970)	0.6	0.379	15.7	0.3
Morocco	(1960–1970)	0.3	0.439	10.2	3.0
Iraq	(1954–1970)	1.4	0.246	26.6	8.2
Nigeria	(1960–1970)	1.8	0.248	41.7	5.2
Malaysia	(1954–1970)	0.8	0.017	19.0	−0.1
Sudan	(1954–1970)	2.6	<0	25.4	2.4
Trinidad/Tobago	(1954–1965)	0.4	0.070	14.3	2.1
Median		0.5	0.247	13.0	2.1
First quartile		0.3	0.082	11.0	1.3
Third quartile		1.1	0.317	21.0	3.0

[a] Data are median observations of indicated variables during period specified.

λ the percentage increase during the year in total domestic credit of the banking system. This, with the figures just presented, would be 25% [(500/400) − 1].

These three variables have the great virtue of being strictly policy variables, regardless of whether the country in question is on a fixed or fluctuating exchange rate system. By contrast, the money supply itself and its rate of increase are endogenous variables under a fixed exchange rate system. These variables have the added advantage of being readily calculated from the data regularly presented for nearly all International Monetary Fund (IMF) member countries in *International Financial Statistics* (*IFS*). We also define

π rate of inflation (usually of consumer prices) during the year, also taken from *IFS*.

Tables 5 and 6 give median values of β, γ, λ, and π for the acute inflation countries, the chronic inflation countries, and for a control group of countries which successfully maintained stable exchange rates during the period of observation. The comparison across groups is made in Table 7, in which it is seen that the acute inflation cases exhibit a higher frequency distribution for each of the four variables than the chronic

TABLE 7

COMPARISON OF INFLATIONARY COUNTRIES WITH CONTROL GROUP

	Acute inflation countries		Chronic inflation countries		Control group of stable LDCs
β (Net increase in banking system credit to the public sector, expressed as a percentage of GDP)					
First quartile	2.0	>	1.6	>	0.3
Median	3.7	>	2.3	>	0.5
Third quartile	13.3	>	2.8	>	1.1
γ (Public sector bank credit/Total bank credit)					
First quartile	0.234	>	0.210	>	0.082
Median	0.467	>	0.316	>	0.247
Third quartile	0.800	>	0.405	>	0.317
λ (Percent increase in total bank credit)					
First quartile	81		26		11
Median	120	→	34	→	13
Third quartile	220	→	42	→	21
π (Percent increase in price level)					
First quartile	89		23		1.3
Median	124	→	27	→	2.1
Third quartile	310	→	28	→	3.0

inflation countries, and these latter in turn have higher frequency distributions than the control group of stable exchange rate countries.

5. The Devaluation Crisis Countries

The results just reported suggest that the variables β, γ, and λ may indeed have some value in indicating the underlying conditions that produce inflationary pressures out of line with the general "world infla-

TABLE 8

DEVALUATION COUNTRIES: KEY VARIABLES IN YEAR OF DEVALUATION

Country	Year	β (Δ pub. sect. credit as % of GDP)	γ (Pub. sect. credit/ Total credit)	λ (% increase total credit)
Bolivia	1972	2.1	0.58	28.2
Burma	1975	3.0	0.87	14.2
Colombia	1957	1.8	0.24	21.8
Costa Rica	1974	1.6	0.16	50.6
Ecuador	1970	3.0	0.32	22.4
Egypt	1962	3.6	0.50	17.0
Finland	1957	< 0	0.06	3.0
Finland	1967	0	0.03	14.2
Ghana	1967	5.9	0.76	18.5
Greece	1975	3.3	0.24	25.0
Iceland	1960	< 0	0.01	7.1
Iceland	1967	2.0	0.09	15.2
India	1966	1.5	0.59	8.7
Indonesia	1968	2.1	0.47	145.0
Israel	1962	< 0	0.03	< 0
Israel	1971	5.6	0.43	27.9
Italy	1976	7.2	0.36	22.1
Korea	1960	< 0	0.35	< 0
Mexico	1976	1.7	0.63	21.3
New Zealand	1967	1.2	0.29	7.0
Pakistan	1972	2.9	0.48	17.4
Peru	1958	1.5	0.28	9.7
Peru	1967	1.6	0.38	13.0
Philippines	1962	< 0	0.23	12.1
Philippines	1970	0.3	0.32	12.4
Rwanda	1966	2.2	0.83	50.2
Spain	1958	2.4	0.42	15.0
Sri Lanka	1967	3.6	0.68	17.9
Venezuela	1964	< 0	< 0	4.2
First quartile		0.15	0.200	9.2
Median		1.80	0.350	15.0
Third quartile		3.00	0.490	22.25

tion." We turn now to an attempt to test this hypothesis by applying it to yet another group of countries that might be said also to suffer from a form of the inflation disease that differs from the "general" inflation. The obvious group is the set of countries which, while attempting to maintain fixed exchange rates, find themselves ultimately forced to devalue their currencies. The thought is that the pressures that ultimately force a devaluation are likely to be similar to those that cause chronic and acute inflations in other countries. Moreover, one can extend the hypothesis a bit further to speculate that the pressures that ultimately force a devaluation do not just arise from nowhere to topple the currency, but rather build up over some significant period of time. The particular hypothesis that we will examine is that the key symptoms of inflationary pressure are present in the year prior to the devaluation, as well as in the year of the devaluation itself.

Table 8 lists 29 cases of devaluation during the period 1952–1976. The criterion for inclusion was that the devaluation had to be of at least 20% and that it had to be preceded by at least four years of exchange stability. As can be seen, several countries managed to qualify twice under this criterion.

Table 9 compares the chronic inflation countries with the devaluation countries and with the control group of stable exchange rate LDCs. The case is quite clear. With respect to β and γ, the devaluation countries are quite like the chronic inflation countries. Only with respect to λ are they more like the control group. This, in turn, is to be expected since λ, a credit expansion variable, is almost certain to be higher in a chronic inflation

TABLE 9

COMPARISON OF DEVALUATION COUNTRIES (IN YEAR OF DEVALUATION) WITH CHRONIC INFLATION COUNTRIES AND CONTROL GROUP

first quartile	Chronic inflation countries		Devaluation countries (year of devaluation)		Control group of stable LDCs
β (Net increase in banking system credit to the public sector, expressed as percentage of GDP)					
First quartile	1.6	>	0.2	~	0.3
Median	2.3	>	1.8	>	0.5
Third quartile	2.8	<	3.0	>	1.1
γ (Public sector bank credit/Total bank credit)					
First quartile	0.210	~	0.200	>	0.082
Median	0.316	<	0.350	>	0.247
Third quartile	0.405	<	0.490	>	0.317
λ (Percent increase in total bank credit)					
First quartile	26	>	9.2	~	11
Median	34	>	15.0	~	13
Third quartile	42	>	22.3	~	21

setting than in countries that have for some time been maintaining (however precariously) a fixed exchange rate.

Table 10 reports the status of the devaluation countries, one year prior to their devaluation crisis, and Table 11 compares them (a) to themselves in the year of the crisis and (b) to the control group of stable LDCs. Here there is no perceptible difference between the devaluation countries in the year before as compared with the year of the crisis.

TABLE 10

KEY VARIABLES IN YEAR PRIOR TO DEVALUATION

Country	Year	β (Δ pub. sect. credit as % of GDP)	γ (Pub. Sect. credit/ Total credit)	λ (% increase total credit)
Bolivia	1971	1.8	0.61	21.2
Burma	1974	7.0	0.90	17.8
Colombia	1956	1.9	0.20	32.7
Costa Rica	1973	0	0.16	10.5
Ecuador	1969	2.2	0.26	19.4
Egypt	1961	2.7	0.50	10.9
Finland	1956	0.2	0.07	5.9
Finland	1966	0.8	0.03	14.7
Ghana	1966	3.6	0.68	16.9
Greece	1974	3.0	0.23	23.0
Iceland	1959	<0	0.01	17.8
Iceland	1966	<0	<0	13.2
India	1965	1.6	0.60	12.1
Indonesia	1967	1.0	0.54	91.0
Israel	1961	<0	0.28	13.3
Israel	1970	5.4	0.41	28.1
Italy	1975	11.3	0.36	23.5
Korea	1959	0.6	0.54	7.7
Mexico	1975	3.0	0.66	27.1
New Zealand	1966	0.1	0.24	5.3
Pakistan	1971	5.9	0.51	14.7
Peru	1957	1.2	0.23	17.7
Peru	1966	1.9	0.35	13.8
Philippines	1961	1.9	0.28	34.5
Philippines	1969	3.3	0.35	16.6
Rwanda	1965	4.2	0.87	108.0
Spain	1957	3.0	0.43	15.8
Sri Lanka	1966	0.5	0.67	4.7
Venezuela	1963	<0	0.02	3.6
First quartile		0.35	0.215	11.50
Median		1.90	0.350	16.75
Third quartile		3.15	0.570	23.25

TABLE 11

COMPARISON OF YEAR PRIOR TO DEVALUATION CRISIS WITH YEAR OF CRISIS, AS WELL AS WITH CONTROL GROUP

	Devaluation countries year of devaluation		Devaluation countries one year earlier		Control group of stable LDCs
	β (Net increase in banking system credit to public sector, expressed as percentage of GDP)				
First quartile	0.2	~	0.4	~	0.3
Median	1.8	~	1.9	>	0.5
Third quartile	3.0	~	3.2	>	1.1
	γ (Public sector bank credit/Total bank credit)				
First quartile	0.200	~	0.215	>	0.082
Median	0.350	=	0.350	>	0.247
Third quartile	0.490	<	0.570	>	0.317
	λ (Percent increase in total bank credit)				
First quartile	9.2	~	11.5	~	11
Median	15.0	~	16.8	>	13
Third quartile	22.3	~	23.3	~	21

6. A Brief Note on Israel's Inflation

Israel has recently come close to meeting our criterion for chronic inflation and may now also be on the brink of meeting that for acute inflation as well. It seems worthwhile, therefore, to explore its own behavior with respect to our criterion variables β, γ, and λ. Here we have, for 1974–1977, β equal to 6.0—above the third quartile for the chronic inflation countries, below the third quartile but above the median for acute inflation countries. For γ we have 0.284, below the median for both classes of countries. And for λ we have 58%, above the third quartile for chronic inflation countries but below the median for acute inflation countries. The impression is clear that Israel has recently been fluttering on the borderline between our two categories of chronic and acute inflation.

Israel stands out in another sense as well. Most inflationary countries have relatively high values of β, indicating substantial amounts of bank credit expansion for the purpose of financing the government. There are only a few cases (of which Uruguay has historically been the most notable, but Brazil from 1964 to 1974 has also been a significant example) of what I call private sector credit inflations—in which the government has not shared significantly as a beneficiary of credit expansion.

Israel is to my knowledge the only case that fits in both categories. It has a very high β, indicating substantial borrowing by the government from the banking system. At the same time the government does not use the proceeds of its borrowing to spend in the usual ways, but rather to relend to the private sector. So the government is a substantial net debtor vis-a-vis the banking system, but much less so vis-a-vis the private sector as a whole. It seems that the government borrows largely on an indexed basis and lends largely on a nonindexed basis and that much of its overall deficit can be accounted for by the difference in interest rates on these two classes of loans!

DEPARTMENT OF ECONOMICS
UNIVERSITY OF CHICAGO
CHICAGO, ILLINOIS

A Mutation in the Aggregate Price and Employment Equilibrating Mechanism of a Market Economy

ABBA P. LERNER

Classical economic theory and many neoclassical monetarists claim that we can and should rely on an automatic equilibrating mechanism in our economic system through which a stable money supply restores, if slowly, a stable price level and a satisfactory level of employment whenever these are disturbed. A very simple form of the theory runs in terms of the law of supply and demand: Whenever the demand for any good is greater than the supply, its price rises; when the supply is greater than the demand, the price falls. The price moves, up or down, until it brings demand and supply into equality.

For this form of the theory unemployment is simply an excess of the supply of labor over the demand. A fall in its price (that is, in the wage) would accordingly reduce the supply and increase the demand, thus automatically curing the unemployment. The unemployment is naturally not cured if the automatic process is blocked because the price (the wage) refuses to fall.

Similarly with the simple explanation of inflation. It assumes that rising prices must be due to excess demand (that is, to demand being greater than supply). Since inflation is usually found together with increasing total spending, the increasing spending is taken to be the excess demand that causes the inflation; so that stabilizing the money supply would limit the increase in total spending, eliminate the excess demand, and cure thc inflation. The inflation is naturally not cured if the government, instead of stabilizing the money supply, keeps on increasing it.

These very simple formulations have gained wide acceptance, but only at very great theoretical and practical cost. The theoretical cost is the

ISBN 0-12-259750-8

omission of an essential (but very unattractive) element in the full theory. The practical cost is the failure to note that a mutation has made this essential element unavailable.

The simple law of supply and demand is a microeconomic device that is not applicable to macroeconomic problems like the demand and supply for labor as a whole or the level of overall economic activity. The microeconomic response to a fall in price comes from buyers switching to the cheapened good from uncheapened alternatives and from producers shifting away from the cheapened product to relatively more profitable lines. For labor as a whole, and for overall economic activity, this makes no sense because there is no alternative from or to which to shift.

The microeconomic device is represented by Fig. 1a which shows the operation of the market for a single commodity. It assumes (quite reasonably) that although changes here will have effects on other part of the economy, the repercussions back on this market (the feedback) from these changes in other parts are small enough to be neglected. Figure 1a shows (horizontally) how the quantity of the commodity (Q_i) that the sellers want to sell (supply S_i), and that the buyers want to buy (demand D_i) responds to various prices of the commodity (P_i), given the general price level. The S_i curve slopes northeastward, showing that at a lower price suppliers will shift *from* producing Q_i to producing other items. The D_i curve slopes southeastward, showing that at a lower price buyers will shift from buying other goods *towards* Q_i. The arrows show that P_i falls when S_i is greater than D_i, and rises when D_i is greater than S_i, bringing P_i and Q_i to the stable equilibrium position represented by the intersection of the two curves at E.

Figure 1b shows the attempt to apply this microeconomic device to the macroeconomic problem with W (the wage rate) taking the place of P_i, and N (overall employment) taking the place of Q_i. This does not work because (a) there are no substitutes for overall employment (which changes together with overall output), either by the demanders or by the suppliers;

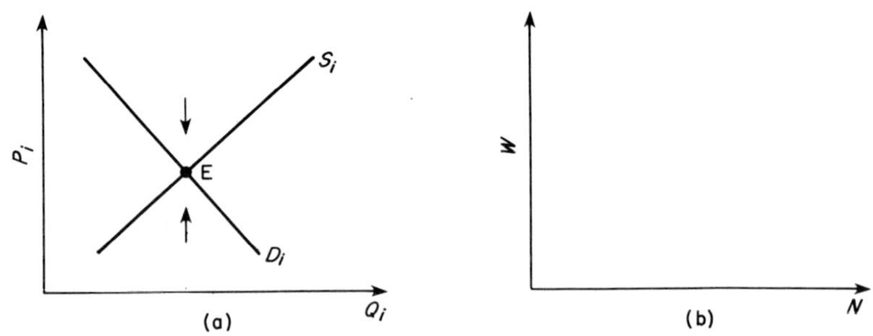

Fig. 1. (a) Microeconomic market equilibrium; (b) Macroeconomic market equilibrium.

and (b) when W (the general wage level) changes, P (the general price level) changes together with it (whichever is considered as adjusting to the other) so that we cannot draw the S and D curves with the northeastward and southeastward slopes or the vertical arrows as in Fig. 1a. (Figure 1b can be given a meaning by measuring W/P, the *real wage*, on the vertical axis instead of W, but the present argument is concerned with changes in the *money wage*.)

The not-quite-so-simple full theory recognizes that there is indeed no solution by "shifting," and it dispenses with the microeconomic argument. It says instead that in a depression ($S > D$), a smaller number of dollars is needed as wages, prices, and incomes fall. (The original number of dollars comes to constitute more "real" dollars—more purchasing power.) The public try to lend the spare money to each other, and this makes it cheaper and easier for business to borrow money at lower interest i for investment I. When they invest more, economic activity, income (Y), and consumption (C), are increased and increase each other further, and the unemployment is cured. Diagramatically:

$$(S > D) \rightarrow P\downarrow = (M/P)\uparrow \rightarrow i\downarrow \rightarrow (Y \rightleftarrows C)\uparrow \rightarrow \text{full employment.} \quad (1)$$

This still glides over the very unattractive essential ingredient in the recipe. What makes the prices and incomes fall is not any shifting between goods demanded or between products supplied, but a fall in money wages (70% of the total cost); and what makes the wages fall is the *unemployment* (U) inserted in the diagram:

$$(S > D) \underline{\rightarrow U\uparrow \rightarrow W\downarrow} \rightarrow P\downarrow$$
$$= (M/P)\uparrow \rightarrow i\downarrow \rightarrow I\uparrow \rightarrow (Y \rightleftarrows C)\uparrow \rightarrow \text{full employment.} \quad (2)$$

The crucial issue is how much unemployment must be created, and how long must it last, to reduce the wages enough to reduce prices enough to reduce incomes enough to reduce the need for money enough to make borrowing easy enough to get investors to borrow and invest enough to increase income and consumption enough to cure the unemployment.

The answer to "how much unemployment" is fundamentally "how hungry must the unemployed become?" They must become hungry enough to overcome their reluctance to start a wage-cutting race with fellow workers and earn the stigma (or more concrete penalties) of being a "scab."

$$(S > D) \rightarrow \underline{U\uparrow \rightarrow H\uparrow} \rightarrow W\downarrow \rightarrow P\downarrow$$
$$= (M/P)\uparrow \rightarrow i\downarrow \rightarrow I\uparrow \rightarrow (Y \rightleftarrows C)\uparrow \rightarrow \text{full employment.} \quad (3)$$

This brings us to the mutation. In the last few decades, with the increasing per capita income, savings, and sources of credit, with the greater possibilities for women to earn money and help out the family, with unemployment pay, social welfare, medical benefits, food stamps, and the like, it takes much more unemployment to bring about the required degree of hunger—so much more that governments always give up waiting for the unemployment to cure itself automatically by hunger, and they take positive Keynesian monetary and fiscal steps to increase employment. This means increasing the money supply and the spending on goods that the unemployed can produce.

$$\begin{array}{l}
(S > D) \rightarrow U\uparrow \nrightarrow H\bar{\uparrow},\ W\underline{\downarrow},\ P\underline{\downarrow},\ (M/P)\bar{\uparrow}. \\
\downarrow \qquad (M/P)\uparrow \rightarrow i\downarrow \rightarrow I\uparrow \rightarrow (Y \leftrightarrows C)\uparrow \rightarrow \text{full employment} \\
\left(\begin{array}{l}\text{Keynesian}\\ \text{bypasses}\end{array}\right) \begin{array}{l}\text{—monetary} \rightarrow (M/P)\uparrow \\ \text{—fiscal} \rightarrow I\uparrow,\ (Y \leftrightarrows C)\uparrow\end{array}
\end{array} \tag{4}$$

The symbols $\bar{\uparrow}$ and $\underline{\downarrow}$ indicate movements blocked; $\nrightarrow$, the mutation, not enough hunger.

The story is essentially the same for inflation. If we had a *demand inflation* (which is due to a continuing excess of total spending in the economy—due to "too much money chasing too few goods") the cure, naturally enough, would be to stop the excess spending. But what we have is an *expectational inflation*, due not to too much spending, but to an established expectation of continuing inflation. Labor has to raise wages to keep up with the cost of living; business has to raise prices to keep up with the wages and costs; and the government, to avoid catastrophic depression, has to keep expanding the money supply and total spending to keep up with the rising prices.

$$M\uparrow \rightleftarrows (P \rightleftarrows W)\uparrow \quad \text{or} \quad \begin{array}{ccc} & M\uparrow & \\ \nearrow & & \searrow \\ P\uparrow & \leftarrow & W\uparrow \end{array}. \tag{5}$$

The observation that an increasing rate of total spending regularly *accompanies* the inflation has suggested to many people, including the government, that that must be the *cause* of the inflation—so that stabilizing the spending would cure the inflation. But this also works only by creating enough hunger to get workers to give up trying to maintain their level of living; and the social mutation has rendered hunger unavailable as an instrument of economic policy.

Mistakenly applying the cure for *demand* inflation, the government *restrains* the expansion, and simple macro becomes *monetarism*.

$$M\bar{\uparrow} \rightarrow U\uparrow \rightarrow W\bar{\uparrow} \rightarrow P\bar{\uparrow} \quad \text{(disinflation).} \tag{6}$$

But this is not what happens. Monetary restraint does not cure the inflation. It only makes spending fall behind prices and wages so that we get increasing unemployment. Because of the mutation

$$U\uparrow \nrightarrow W\bar{\uparrow} \text{ (wages refuse to \textit{fall behind}), and}$$
$$(W \rightleftarrows P)\uparrow \to (M/P)\downarrow \to i\uparrow \to I\downarrow \to (Y \rightleftarrows C)\downarrow. \tag{7}$$

What we get is

$$M\bar{\uparrow} \to U\uparrow \quad \text{together with} \quad (W \rightleftarrows P)\uparrow, \tag{8}$$

that is, deepening depression with continuing inflation. If we have "too few goods" it is only because there is "not enough money chasing them" so that it does not pay to produce more.

The only difference between this and the case of unemployment without inflation is that workers, instead of trying to maintain their level of living by refusing to let their money wage *fall*, now try to maintain their level of living by refusing to let their wages *fall behind* the rising prices in the inflationary race, so wages, prices, and unemployment all keep on increasing.

Monetarism is then abandoned. As a catastrophic money crunch and deepending depression threaten, M is allowed to increase again. We then have

$$M\overset{\uparrow}{\underset{\uparrow}{-}} \to U\bar{\uparrow} \quad \text{and} \quad M\overset{\uparrow}{\underset{\uparrow}{-}} \to (W \rightleftarrows P)\uparrow. \tag{9}$$

Otherwise stated, unemployment stops increasing and inflation continues, so we have stagflation, and we are back to the vicious cycle with wages, prices, and spending chasing each other, each of the three actors continuing the dance because he has to keep up with the others in a continuing *expectational inflation*.

$$\begin{array}{ccc} & M\uparrow & \\ \nearrow & & \nwarrow \\ P\uparrow & \leftarrow & W\uparrow \end{array}.$$

It might seem that if any one of the three participants in the dance stopped running, the inflation would have to stop, but this turns out not to be so. *Spending* is the item that has the most consistently been chosen as the one to be stopped. The weapon used for this is "sound finance," which we have already analyzed.

A few plans have been devised to work on *price increases.* However, these plans do not overcome the administrative problems stemming from the ease with which quality changes can be used to obscure, or to be disguised as, price changes.

It is also possible to work on *wage increases*. Limiting the average increase in wages to the average increase in output per man would stabilize average cost and average price. A number of plans on these lines are currently receiving wide attention. (They mostly propose only to *reduce* wage increases slightly so as to moderate the inflation slightly.) But all such plans give the impression of discriminating against labor by holding down wage increases while leaving profits unchecked. This is bound to make the plans unacceptable to labor and thus impossible to implement in a democratic society.

What we learn from this is that it is not enough to stop only one of the three inflationary elements in the tripartite expectational inflation. It turns out to be necessary to deal with wages and profits together. Once this is done the government will no longer have to keep expanding total spending to keep up with any rising prices. Since it will not have to prove it is not responsible for an ongoing inflation, the government will also feel free to give up the monetarist "anti-inflationary" monetary and fiscal restraint that is responsible for the *stag* in the stagflation.

To be able to cure both inflation and unemployment, the economy needs a replacement for the instrument it has lost. Such a device is MAP—the market anti-inflation plan—a painless substitute for hunger. It could quickly cure inflation and remove the occasion for the "dis-inflationary" restraint in spending that results in stagflation.

The futile inflationary race of wages, prices, and total spending all increasing so as to keep up with each other can also be considered as the result of a *social* flaw in the *private* accounting of firms. The inflationary impacts of wage and price decisions are not taken into account, just as environmental impacts, health impacts, and other socially important consequences are often not taken fully into account in the decisions of individuals or firms. (It is, of course, the absence of "hunger" as an effective reducer or restrainer of wages that makes the private accounting socially inadequate.)

Individuals and firms can be made, and are being made, to take these environmental impacts into account through the imposition of incentives (usually taxes or subsidies) to correct the accounting, to make the private decisions responsible from a social point of view. The inflation cure must apply similar incentives to stop the excessive (that is, inflationary) wage and price increases.

Total spending in the economy must still increase enough to be able to buy the output of full employment, though not more than enough as this would bring excess-demand inflation. Functional finance is still essential. But the cure for inflation is now faced with an additional *twofold task*:

1. It must stabilize the *average* price (the price level).
2. At the same time, it must leave *actual* prices and wages free to be

adjusted individually, by the market and by free bargaining, to the continuing changes in tastes, techniques, and availabilities.

MAP achieves this twofold task by providing a disincentive that makes inflationary "price increasing" decisions *more costly* to the firm. It works like a tax on a pollutant poured into a river, except that instead of merely *reducing* the pollution (inflation) it would *completely stop* it.

Attempts to cure the inflation have failed so far, because they have not satisfied all the necessary conditions. The same seems also to be true of the anti-inflation proposals now being considered.

Wage and price controls, when applied in the crudest possible way (sometimes as a preparatory step only) as a freeze of all wages and prices, immediately achieve objective 1, but they do nothing at all for objective 2. As the controls develop, they attempt to adjust the wages and prices to the changing tastes, techniques, and availabilities, but they do this not by using market and bargaining methods but by centralized administration. The task is too much for this method and the attempt regularly breaks down in an "administrative nightmare." Wage and price guidelines and guideposts have been greatly discredited, but are proposed again from time to time only because nothing better has come up.

Similarly desperate (which means without hope) are attempts to stop the inflation by "jawboning"—attempts to persuade the public, even while they are experiencing the inflation going on, that the inflation is ending—so that they will stop raising wages and prices. This attacks the problem precisely the wrong way around. We must first stop the inflation. Only when the public sees that the inflation has stopped will they stop expecting it to continue.

Prices in general rise, which is what we mean by inflation, when total national dollar net sales is increasing faster than total national (net) real output. This also means that national net sales per unit of input is increasing faster than national average output per unit of input—"productivity." A device that prevents every firm from increasing its net sales per unit of input by more than the national (average) increase in productivity would stop the inflation. But this would achieve only objective 1. It would *freeze* the economy, preventing the adjustments of *relative* net sales (the relative wages and profits) that are essential for the efficient working of a free and unregimented economy.

To achieve objective 2, MAP must eliminate the nonfunctional, inflationary part of the increase which is *proportional* without interfering with the functional *relative* changes.

The excess of a firm's increase in *net sales* per unit of input over the national average increase in *output* per unit of input may be called its "*inflationary impact*." It constitutes the firm's contribution to the inflation —in the sense that the sum of these excesses and deficits constitutes the overall excess of the increase in national net sales over the increase in national net output, which is the inflation. If general inflation is to be prevented, this sum must be made to add up to zero.

To achieve this, MAP (1) grants each firm a basic amount of "MAP credit;" (2) requires each firm to buy or rent additional MAP credit to cover any excess of its net sales over its total MAP credit, or to sell or rent out any MAP credit and remove any *excess* of its total MAP credit over its net sales (= *deficit* of net sales below its MAP credit); and (3) lets a free market set the price of MAP credit at the equilibrium level, which makes the demand (by "excess net sales" firms) equal to the supply (from "deficit net sales" firms).

The price of MAP credit, as set by the free market, is the MAP incentive, which induces each firm, in setting its prices and in negotiating its wages, to take into account the inflationary impacts on the economy. In setting the price of MAP credit where the supply equals the demand, the market makes it strong enough an incentive to offset the inflationary expectations and eliminate the inflationary impacts. It induces all firms to restrain price increases or reduce prices so as to hold down their net sales to just the right degree—some to avoid having to buy so much MAP credit and some to set free more MAP credit to sell.

All firms remain free to set their individual net sales as high or as low as they wish, after taking into account what they will have to pay, or receive, for the MAP credit they buy or sell. This is how the social flaw in the private accounting is corrected. The firms are induced by the price of the MAP credit freely to set their net sales, and thereby also the wages and prices, at the levels required for an inflation-free economy.

When the supply of MAP credit equals the demand, the excess and the deficit net sales just cancel each other. Total net sales (which is what the net output is sold for) grows in the same proportion as total net output, so that the *average* price (the price level) is stable. The inflation has been conquered. There is then no pressure on the government to increase the money supply to keep up with rising prices and no occasion for any "disinflationary" monetary or fiscal restraint, which would induce stagflation.

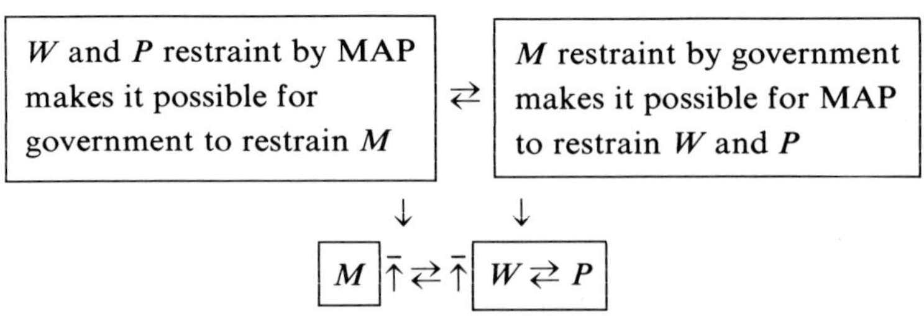

(10)

The actual rules for MAP are the following:

1. The Federal Reserve carries responsibility for maintaining a sound money supply, which means one that is *compatibe* with prosperity and with price stability. For this to be possible, price stability and prosperity must be made compatible with each other. The Federal Reserve's responsibility is therefore extended by Congress to include responsibility for the *maintenance* of price stability through MAP.

2. A Federal Reserve MAP credit office credits each firm with basic MAP credit equal to 102% of its previous year's net sales, (2% being the estimated national increase in producivity). Net sales is gross sales minus purchases from other *firms*, which makes it equal to profit *plus* wages paid to *individuals.*

3. When a firm hires a new employee, it gets additional free MAP credit equal to his wage (including fringe benefits) in his previous employment. (It has to be his wage in his previous employment to avoid the device of employers firing people and then rehiring them at a higher pay to get extra free MAP credits.) Conversely, on the separation of an employee from a firm its MAP credit is reduced by the amount of wage. New capital investment similarly entitles a firm to additional free MAP credit equal to the interest on the new investment at the prime rate of interest. This represents a payment for the services of the new capital. And conversely, when invested capital is retired, this reduces the firm's MAP credit correspondingly.

4. Net sales in excess of a firm's MAP credit requires the firm to buy or rent that additional amount of MAP credit. A deficit in a firm's net sales below its MAP credit calls for the sale or renting out of its unused MAP credit.

5. The MAP credit office starts up a free market in MAP credit: buying, selling, borrowing, and lending it freely to all comers at the market price or rental.

6. In the case of government enterprises or nonprofit institutions, the same rules hold except that instead of net sales (which is inapplicable) the rules apply to "individual incomes generated" (which is what net sales comes to if profit is taken out).

7. The MAP credit office keeps a continuous record of each firm's total MAP credit, adjusted by hirings and separation of employees, by increases and reductions in capital invested, and by its purchases and sales of MAP credit. With this updated record it is able to check whether the firm's net sales corresponds to its total MAP credit.

Let me go through a drastically simplified example of how MAP would work. If MAP is imposed when prices have been rising at 6% (annually), with productivity increasing at 2%, and the inputs of labor and capital services increasing at 2%, total net sales will have been increasing at 10%. Suddenly, the increase in net sales is reduced to 4% (2% for "productivity" plus an additional 2% for the annual increase in inputs of labor and capital services), this being the total increase in MAP credit to which the net sales has to conform. This is just enough to buy the increased output *at last year's prices*. There will be demand for additional MAP credit to legitimize any expected increase in net sales from an expected continuation in the increase in prices. The price of MAP credit will be correspondingly high. But as it becomes apparent that the *actual* increase in net sales is only 4%, the expectation of price increases will diminish, and with it both the demand for extra MAP credit and its price.

MAP deflates the inflation, it also deflates itself. When the inflation and the expectation of inflation cease, the price of MAP credit falls to zero (or to whatever counterinflationary pressure is still needed to offset any remaining inflationary pressures other than inflationary expectations).

As with all anti-inflation plans, there is a temptation for firms and unions to beat the gun and establish higher basic MAP credit claims by raising net sales *before* the plan starts. But once MAP is installed, average price stabilization would still be reached as soon as the rules are understood and obeyed.

If, as seems pretty certain, there is a lively prior discussion, the price stabilization would take very little time, or no time at all, or even *less than no time*!

MAP could never be adopted without a general expectation having been established that MAP would at least reduce the inflation. Such an anticipation of smaller future price increases would make sellers ready to accept lower price increases now rather than wait, and make buyers willing to wait rather than buy now. This could stop the inflation even *before* MAP came into effect.

Other incentive-based anti-inflation plans also avoid the administrative nightmare of government officials having to authorize all wage and price changes, but MAP differs from them in two ways:

1. The MAP disincentive is set not by government taxes or subsidies, but by the market. This insulates it from politics, automatically sets it at the appropriate strength, and adjusts it to changing conditions.
2. The MAP disincentive, being based on *net sales* (which is wages *plus* profits) instead of focusing entirely on wages, is not disqualified as "unfair" by labor, and it is automatically adjusted for changes in the labor–capital ratio.

MAP will indeed seem to many people a wild-eyed revolutionary dream too good to be true. But it is, on the contrary, a well-established device that is operating under our eyes all the time. It is so familiar that it has become invisible—like G. K. Chestertons' invisible postman. This device regularly achieves the same twofold task of keeping the *average* of a large number of quantities of some item fixed, while the *actual* quantity bought by any consumer remains unregulated, for free determination by himself. *MAP is no new invention*. MAP is just a plagiarism, a copy of this ancient device. What makes MAP seem strange is only that until now the item to which MAP is applied has not been treated in this normal way.

One example of the only too familar miracle will suffice. The price of oranges is adjusted by the market to make the demand equal to the supply. It achieves objective 1 by making the *average* number demanded per consumer equal to the average number available per consumer, even while achieving objective 2 by permitting the *actual* number of oranges demanded by each consumer to be freely chosen by him when he takes the price into consideration.

For this miracle to work, society at one time had to decide to make the ownership of oranges a legal property-right of individuals. This undoubtedly was a shocking, impious, revolutionary, and antisocial idea when first suggested to the head of an individualized tribe. We expect some of the same resistance to MAP even if it is accompanied by the claim that it could cure the inflation so quickly.

This sketch of MAP is no finished blueprint, but it does, I hope, give a good idea of the general way MAP works. But many, if not most, of the actual numbers or time periods baldly pronounced here may well be changed and improved.

One possible variation of MAP is the extension of "the previous year" (for the determination of the grants of free MAP credit) to an average of several years, so as to diminish distortion from specially favorable or unfavorable years. Another is the restriction of MAP to firms above a certain size. This would be very important if some bureaucratic administration of wages or prices were involved, but it does not seem necessary since MAP calls only for the *monitoring* of the truthfulness of the reports. This task is not different in kind from the monitoring and auditing of income tax and social security taxes. There will, of course, be some cheating, but the incentives for cheating will be very much less than with income tax. The actual accounting task is comparable to what is being done by organizations like Master Charge.

There are many secondary problems—like the determination of the amount of free MAP credit for new entrants to the labor force with no previous wage. There might be some minimum wage before an employee is included in MAP. There is the possible hiring of retirees only for the sake of large free MAP credit based on their last wage. Some adjustment may have to be made to prevent shrinkage of a firm's total MAP credit from the retirement of high-wage senior employees and the recruitment of low-wage beginners, though this could be provided for in the automatic annual increase in MAP credit.

Among the possible variations in the application of MAP is the possible *slowing* of the disinflation. Many people would be hurt by a sudden end to the inflation. Assets such as houses bought at superinflated prices based on the anticipation of further inflation will fall in value if the further inflation does not come about. There will also be other serious inequities. Workers with contracts for wage increases for several years at the high rates appropriate in continuing inflation will benefit from being able to spend their inflated future incomes on goods with stable prices, while everybody else will have to get *less* than the 2% average rate of increase to balance these gains. A quick MAP would be very hard on those with contractual future monetary obligations undertaken in the expectation that they would be paid in more easily earned depreciated dollars. To soften such inequities, a *gradual* disinflation has been suggested. There are many considerations for and against such gradualism, but even if a careful weighting of the pros and cons should come out definitely in favor of a quick MAP, a gradual disinflation may be dictated by the political need to reduce resistance to MAP from those who would lose, or who think they might lose, as well as from those to whom all quick measures seem dangerous.

The details of MAP and some of the possible variations will be spelled out in a book, *MAP, A Market Anti-inflation Plan* by Lerner and Colander, to be published by Harcourt Brace Javanovich.

DEPARTMENT OF ECONOMICS
FLORIDA STATE UNIVERSITY
TALLAHASSEE, FLORIDA

PART 2

Stagflation

Supply-Shock Inflation

Money, Expectations, and Accommodation

*ALAN S. BLINDER**

1. Introduction

This paper will focus on a very particular, and particularly onerous, variety of inflation—stagflation. More specifically, I will concentrate on stagflation caused by adverse developments on the supply side of the economy—so called "supply shocks." Where factual, historical, or empirical evidence is brought to bear, the setting will be the United States; but the principles are applicable to almost any industrialized economy.

A few facts will help put the tasks of the paper into perspective. Table 1 shows the rates of inflation and unemployment in the United States between 1971 and 1976. While rather puny by Israeli standards, the inflation rates recorded in 1973 and 1974 were stunningly large by U.S. standards. Economists need to explain why the inflation rate *rose* from only 3.4% in 1971 and 1972 (a low rate achieved partly with the aid of wage–price controls) to 8.8% in 1973 and 12.2% in 1974, and then *fell* to 7% in 1975 and 4.8% in 1976. We also need to explain why the worst of the inflation nearly coincided with the worst unemployment performance since the 1930s.

*The author wishes to thank Jeffrey Sachs and Leif Danziger, his discussants at the conference, for a number of valuable suggestions; and also Gregory Chow, Jonathan Eaton, Stephen Goldfeld, Robert Gordon, Burton Malkiel, Robert Solow, and John Taylor for helpful comments on portions of the draft manuscript. It seems important, however, not to implicate any of them in the opinions expressed herein. Research support from the National Science Foundation is gratefully acknowledged.

ISBN 0-12-259750-8

TABLE 1

INFLATION AND UNEMPLOYMENT IN THE UNITED STATES, 1971–1976[a]

Year	Inflation rate (%)[b]	Unemployment rate (%)[c]
1971	3.4	5.9
1972	3.4	5.6
1973	8.8	4.9
1974	12.2	5.6
1975	7.0	8.5
1976	4.8	7.7

[a] Source: U.S. President, *Economic Report of the President, 1979.* U.S. Government Printing Office, Washington, D.C.

[b] Percentage change in consumer price index from December of previous year to December of stated year.

[c] Yearly average; unemployed as a percentage of civilian labor force.

While tied very closely to real-world events, this paper has its eye on current debates in economic theory and, in particular, on the competing macroeconomic models offered by the Keynesian, monetarist, and rational expectations schools. I shall argue that, contrary to what seems to have become the conventional nonwisdom, there is indeed a perfectly coherent Keynesian explanation of what happened in the mid-1970s—an explanation that captures not only the broad qualitative outlines of these events, but many of their quantitative features as well. I shall argue further that there is no comparably coherent monetarist or rational expectations explanation of these events.

As this is a long paper, a reader's guide may be useful before the journey begins. Section 2, one of the two long sections of the paper, offers a description and analysis of the major economic events in the United States between 1971 and 1976. It summarizes several chapters in my book on the U.S. stagflationary experience (Blinder, 1979) and provides an entirely Keynesian interpretation of these events. In this section I raise the central policy issue of the paper: Should the authorities "accommodate" supply shocks? Tentatively, I give an affirmative answer. Some estimates of how much *more* inflation and how much *less* unemployment the United States would have experienced under an accommodative policy are offered.

Section 3, a very short section, takes up one possible objection to the scenario outlined in Section 2—a scenario of inflation without money, which therefore seems to fly in the face of monetarist doctrine.

Section 4, by far the longest section of the paper, takes up a second objection. Adverse effects on inflationary expectations have been raised as an objection to (a) the policy recommendation that supply shocks ought to be accommodated (a matter of normative economics) and (b) the quantitative estimates of the higher inflation and lower unemployment that an accommodative policy might have achieved (a matter of positive economics). Both empirical and theoretical evidence (of both the formal and informal varieties) are brought to bear on this issue, with the focus mainly on positive issues.

Finally, Section 5 wraps up the paper by drawing out its implications for economic theory and policy.

2. The Great Stagflation: A Keynesian Interpretation

A. A Conceptual Framework for Supply-Shock Stagflation

I think it is by now widely agreed that, for better or for worse, the hallmark of Keynesian economics is the assumption—which is well-grounded empirically, but not so well-grounded theoretically—that money wages move rather sluggishly. With nominal wages relatively fixed in the short run, it is a simple matter to show that an exogenous increase in the supply price of output—caused, for example, by higher oil prices—will lead to both higher prices and lower output, that is, to stagflation (Phelps 1978). Alternatively, the same conclusion can be reached by ignoring wages and considering instead two types of output: one whose price adjusts instantly to clear the market, and hence is very sensitive to a restriction of supply ("farm prices"), and the other whose price is quite sticky ("industrial prices"). In this case, stagflation will result, *ceteris paribus*, if the supply of farm output is reduced (Gordon, 1975). In either case, the basic idea is that downward rigidities of prices or wages mean that *inflation* is the way the economy adjusts to what are essentially shocks to *relative* prices.

In Keynesian analysis these ideas are usually couched in terms of aggregate demand and supply curves.[1] The fixity of the nominal wage, for example, is sufficient to rationalize the upward slope of the aggregate supply curves depicted in Fig. 1. Supply shocks such as those of the mid-1970s shift the aggregate supply curve upward to the left, leading to both higher prices and lower output. If we interpret these diagrams as applying to deviations of P and y from their normal trends, then the implications are that a supply shock causes (a) a recession and (b) a

[1] Though I have some misgivings about this paradigm, it seems serviceable enough in the present context.

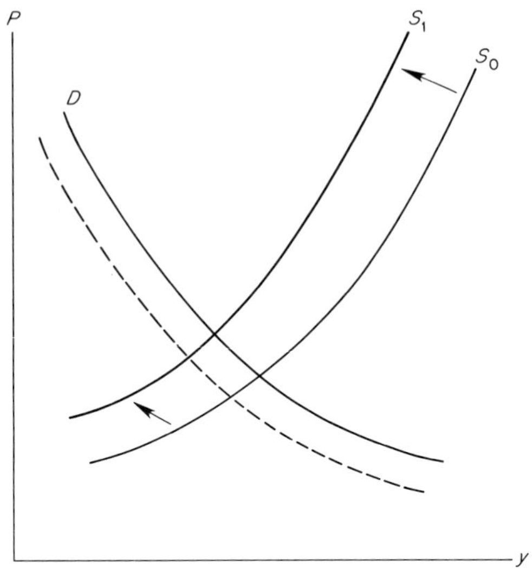

Fig. 1. Keynesian analysis of a supply shock.

temporary acceleration of inflation, leading to a *permanently* higher price level.[2]

Two distinct sets of effects that supply shocks have on aggregate demand are worth spelling out explicitly. First, adverse supply shifts move the economy upward to the left along any given demand curve by (a) shrinking the supply of real balances, (b) raising real tax burdens if the income tax code is not indexed, (c) destroying real consumer wealth, and (d) potentially having adverse effects on the balance of trade. But, second, the particular supply shocks experienced in the 1970s also shifted the aggregate demand curve to the left because they were typically accompanied by large-scale redistributions of income in favor of people with unusually low short-run marginal propensities to spend. (See the dotted line in Fig. 1.)

Finally, an obvious point follows from Fig. 1: In a world of perfectly flexible prices and wages it is far from clear that such shocks to *relative* prices should raise the *general* price level. Nonoil prices, for example, could fall as oil prices rise.

[2]The long run effect on the natural rate of output depends on the nature of the shock. Higher oil prices, for example, probably lead to a permanent drop in the natural rate of output, but no change in the natural rate of unemployment. A crop failure, by contrast is probably transitory, leaving the natural rate unaffected. It is characteristic of Keynesian analysis to let long-run effects play second fiddle.

B. The "Shocks" of the 1970s

This simple story of stagflation caused by supply shocks provides an excellent explanation of what actually happened during the sorry seventies, though not all the shocks were of the stagflationary variety. I proceed now to a brief description of the major shocks that buffeted the U.S. economy between 1971 and 1974. As will be clear, some of these shocks (such as food and oil prices) affected the entire world at more or less the same time, while others (such as price controls) were specifically American maladies.

(1) Devaluation of the Dollar

De facto floating of the U.S. dollar began in August 1971, when President Nixon suspended convertibility into gold and, in effect, ended the Bretton Woods system. During the few months before rates were repegged by the Smithsonian agreements, the dollar dropped about 6% relative to a multilateral trade weighted average of other currencies. Then, when the new parities were abandoned in December 1972, the dollar lost another 13% during the first 6 months of 1973, for a cumulative decline of about 19% over 2 years. Experts on such matters use an empirically based multiplier of about 0.15 to convert changes in the exchange value of the dollar into changes in the consumer price index (CPI). Based on this rule of thumb, the devaluation probably raised the U.S. price level by about 2.8%.[3] This constituted a sizeable inflationary shock which accounts for part of the increase of the inflation rate from 1972 to 1973.

(2) Monetary and Fiscal Policy

Monetary and fiscal policy in the United States were extremely expansionary during 1971 and 1972. Among the possible explanations for this policy stance are

1. We were coming out of the 1970 recession and needed stimulus.
2. Potential GNP was overestimated.
3. Policymakers mistakenly thought wage–price controls had "taken care of" inflation, so that they could concentrate on reducing unemployment.
4. Floating exchange rates eased the balance of payments constraint on domestic policy.

[3] A more careful estimate made with Peter Kenen and associates (1978) model of the balance of payments implies that the devaluation (which was 16.6% in the index Kenen used) added 2.4% to the implicit deflator for personal consumption expenditures by 1973 : 2, and the adjustment was not yet complete.

5. President Nixon was eager to be reelected, and Federal Reserve Board Chairman Arthur Burns was not averse to this outcome.

For present purposes it is not important to know the reason, because the facts are incontrovertible. Using a variant of some measures of fiscal and monetary policy that Stephen Goldfeld and I (Blinder and Goldfeld, 1976) developed on another occasion, I have estimated that fiscal and monetary policy actions *each* raised the annual growth rate of GNP between 1971 : 1 and 1973 : 1 by about $3\frac{1}{2}$–4 percentage points—for a combined effect of around $7\frac{1}{2}$ percentage points (more than the total growth).[4] This is a stunning degree of stimulus, which both undermined the wage–price controls program and left the United States with a legacy of inflationary pressures going into 1973. More significant, however, for the maladies of the mid-1970s was the abrupt turn taken by both monetary and fiscal policy shortly after the November 1972 election. According to the measures just cited, the swing toward restrictive fiscal policy chopped about 3 percentage points off the growth rate of real GNP between 1973 : 1 and 1974 : 1. The swing in monetary policy was just as sudden, but owing to longer lags, had less effect on the economy in 1973. It did, however, probably preordain a recession in 1974 even if nothing else had happened.

Plainly, however, lots of other things did happen—most of them bad. I turn next, and in somewhat more detail, to the three major stagflationary shocks of 1973–1974: food, oil, and the demise of price controls.

(3) The Food Shock

The problems in the world food market, which began with a series of bad harvests in 1972, are probably too well-known to require recounting here. Rapidly rising food prices began to plague American consumers at the retail level in early 1973. The consumer price index (CPI) for food, which rose less than 5% during 1972, increased 20% during 1973 and 12% during 1974. This constituted a major inflationary shock whose importance, I think, has still not been adequately appreciated. For example, from December 1972 to September 1973, the CPI rose at an 8.7% annual rate, but the CPI excluding food rose at only a 4.4% annual rate—not much above its rate in 1972. The acceleration of inflation in early 1973 was, in a word, mostly a food inflation. After early 1973 food prices ceased being an engine of accelerating inflation, though they kept contributing to the *high* inflation rate. I have made some estimates of the contribution of food prices to overall inflation (as measured by the deflator for personal

[4] This sentence hardly does justice to the calculations. Details can be found in Blinder (1979, Chaps. 7 and 8).

consumption expenditures), including both the *direct* effects (food is a component of the index) and the *indirect* effects operating through the wage–price spiral. These calculations suggest that, from mid-1973 to mid-1975, about 5 percentage points of the annual inflation rate were attributable to food—and that this contribution was relatively steady during those 2 years (Blinder, 1979, Chap. 5).

The food price increases also cut into aggregate demand. While the deleterious effects of OPEC on aggregate demand have been much discussed, far less attention has been given to the corresponding effects of higher food prices. Considered as an external price shock, the food price increases of 1972–1974 were substantially greater than the energy price increases of 1973–1974. However, the food price increases were more spread out in time, which allowed for a smoother adjustment, and they primarily represented a redistribution of income *within* U.S. borders.[5] Nonetheless, it has been well known for some time that farmers have unusually high marginal propensities to save, so the redistribution of income no doubt shifted the aggregate demand curve to the left.

(4) The Energy Shock

As just noted, the inflationary consequences of the OPEC shock in 1973–1974 were smaller than those of the food shock. But the consequences for aggregate demand were probably more severe nonetheless, owing to the massive redistribution of income from the United States (and, indeed, the entire Western world) to OPEC. In addition, the OPEC shock temporarily disrupted industrial activity in a way that the food shock never did. Finally, whereas agricultural harvests returned to normal after 1974, leaving the natural rate of output unperturbed, the OPEC cartel did not oblige the world by vanishing. In these respects, then, the OPEC shock can be considered the more severe of the two.

A first step toward appraising the severity of the oil shock is to estimate its direct effect on consumer prices. I have estimated that the increase in prices of *directly consumed* energy accounted for a 2.4% increase in the level of the CPI between 1973 : 3 and 1974 : 3. To this must be added an (admittedly crude) estimate of the energy costs embodied on other consumer goods. George Perry's (1975a) work suggests that this amounted to another 1% or so, for a total of about $3\frac{1}{2}\%$. But this is only a measure of the *initial* upward push on the price level. When we consider the general equilibrium reactions of the whole macroeconomic system, at least two further effects are potentially quite important. On the one hand, higher consumer prices lead to higher wage settlements, which lead in turn to still

[5] This, of course, was not true for nations that were major food importers.

higher prices, in a typical wage–price spiral that magnifies the initial shock.[6] On the other hand, however, the deleterious effects of the OPEC shock on aggregate demand served to mitigate its inflationary consequences. Simulations by Perry (1975a) and by Pierce and Enzler (1974) with the MIT-Penn-SSRC (MPS) model suggest that these two effects roughly canceled each other in the short run, so that on balance the oil shock raised the *level* of consumer prices by about 3%, $3\frac{1}{2}\%$, and $4\frac{1}{2}\%$ as of the third quarters of 1974, 1975, and 1976, respectively.

(5) The End of Wage–Price Controls

Mandatory controls over wages and prices in time of peace came to the United States for the first time in August 1971, as the cornerstone of President Nixon's "new economy policy" (NEP). But Nixon's NEP was less successful than Lenin's.

The controls apparatus, which began with a 90-day freeze covering all wages and about 90% of prices, evolved through several phases (including a brief second "freeze" in the summer of 1973) before it lapsed in April 1974. The American public believed that the acceleration of inflation from 3.4% in 1972 to 8.8% in 1973 proved that controls had failed—a view which, of course, was wrong since the bulk of the acceleration of inflation in 1973 can be traced directly to food. It seems that if we want to appraise the effects of price controls on inflation, we must concentrate on nonfood (and also nonenergy, due to OPEC) prices.

William Newton and I (Blinder and Newton, 1979) have recently carried out a detailed study of the Nixon controls, using a specially constructed measure of the fraction of the (nonfood and nonenergy) CPI that was subject to controls each month. Our findings to date can be summarized briefly as follows. While price controls were in effect, they slowed inflation modestly. The maximum cumulative downward deflection of the price *level*, according to our estimates, was about 2–3%; and it occurred in February 1974. Thereafter, and especially after controls lapsed in April, extra post-controls "catchup" inflation in the decontrolled sector began to overwhelm any dampening effect of controls in the controlled sector. By November 1974 the price level was somewhere between 0 and 1.5% below where it would have been had there never been a controls program.

On balance, the controls program gave us almost the same *mean*

[6] Rational expectation raises the possibility that, owing to their explicitly one-shot nature, price increases attributable to the oil and food shocks had less than one-for-one effects on wage increases. My examination of the data seems to support this idea, and to suggest that in fact only about half of these price increases got into wages (Blinder, 1979, Chap. 5).

inflation rate over the 4-year period from mid-1971 to mid-1975 that we would have had without controls, but added greatly to the *variance* of inflation. According to virtually any reasonable view of the social costs of inflation, this was a very bad bargain.

The post-controls catchup inflation also explains why the inflation rate in the United States—which had been pushed into the double-digit range by energy prices—stayed there through the end of 1974, even though energy prices ceased escalating. According to our estimates, the controls program *reduced* the annual inflation rate (as measured by the CPI) by between 0.9 and 1.3 percentage points during the 8-month period ending in February 1974, and *raised* the inflation rate by between 1.5 and 3.6 percentage points during the 8-month period beginning in February 1974 —a net acceleration of between 2.8 and 4.5 points. This represents a good deal of the observed acceleration and prevented what would otherwise have been a rather quick end to double-digit inflation.

C. The Case for Accommodation

What could conventional stabilization policy have done in the face of these massive exogenous price shocks? I include myself among the large number of economists who thought then, and still think, that a more enlightened policy would have accommodated these shocks—probably in two ways. First, a cut in personal income taxes could have offset (at least some of) the decline in aggregate demand caused by the distribution effects mentioned earlier, as well as by the damaging effects of higher prices on consumer purchasing power (via Pigou effects and the unindexed income tax). Second, an increase in the nominal money supply could have limited the decline in real balances—which fell 7% from cyclical peak to cyclical trough.[7]

In terms of the framework of Fig. 1, such a policy response would be designed to (a) offset the downward shift in the aggregate demand curve (the dotted line in the graph) caused by the redistribution of income, and to (b) push the aggregate demand curve upward to offset some of the deleterious effects of the supply shift on real output. As the graph makes clear, one cost of such an accommodative policy would have been even more inflation than we actually had in 1974. How much more?

There obviously is no answer to this question that will command universal assent. For one thing, there are probably as many different

[7] Real balances are defined here as M_1 deflated by the GNP deflator. As Phelps (1978) points out, if real output declines, the increase in money can be less than the increase in the price level. So accommodation would have implied an increase of somewhat less than 7%.

TABLE 2

EFFECTS OF HIGHER ENERGY PRICES ON CONSUMER PRICES[a]

	Price level in		
	1974 : 3	1975 : 3	1976 : 3
1. No accommodation[b]	+ 2.9%	+ 3.6%	+ 4.4%
2. No recession[c]	+ 3.9%	+ 5.5%	+ 7.4%
3. Difference (effect of lower aggregate demand)	− 1.0%	− 1.9%	− 3.0%
	Inflation rate during		
	1973 : 3–1974 : 3	1974 : 3–1975 : 3	1975 : 3–1976 : 3
4. No accommodation[b]	+ 2.9%	+ 0.6%	+ 0.8%
5. No recession[c]	+ 3.9%	+ 1.5%	+ 1.8%
6. Difference (effect of lower aggregate demand)	− 1.0%	− 0.9%	− 1.0%

[a] Source: Blinder (1979, Table 5-4).
[b] From Perry (1975a) and Pierce and Enzler (1974).
[c] Author's calculations.

versions of accommodative policy as there are accommodationists. For another, there is a wide range of estimates of the effect of changes in aggregate demand on the price level. Let me offer a couple of indicative calculations.

Start with the OPEC shock. The simulations of Perry and Pierce–Enzler that I cited earlier suggest that the OPEC shock decreased real GNP by about 3% and raised prices by the amounts shown in Table 2, lines 1 and 4. Suppose instead that policy was adjusted so that OPEC caused no recession. I have estimated that, in this case, the effect of the oil shock on the price level and inflation would have been as shown in lines 2 and 5 of Table 2. The differences, shown in lines 3 and 6, are what allowing the recession to proceed bought for us in terms of reduced inflation—approximately a one percentage point reduction in the inflation rate for three years.

Or we can pose a different question. Define an accommodating monetary policy as something like an additional 6–7% monetary growth in 1974, and ask how much more inflation and how much less unemployment such a policy would have given us. Policies like this, sometimes with a fiscal component as well, have been simulated by Perry (1975b), Ando and Palash (1976), and Eckstein (1978). They show that the recession could have been considerably muted at little short-run inflationary costs.[8] For example, Perry's policy of holding the commercial paper rate at 7% after 1974 : 1 (which requires a money stock 7.3% higher than actual history by 1974 : 3) and cutting personal income taxes by $20 billion (about half the increase in fuel bills), reduces the unemployment rate of 1975 : 1 by 1.1 percentage points while increasing the inflation rate over this year by only half a percentage point.

It is clear, of course, that no amount of *positive* economic analysis will ever answer the question: *Should* we have accommodated the supply shocks? Value judgments are needed to weigh the relative social costs of unemployment versus inflation. And here it may well be that Keynesians, monetarists, and rational expectationists will never agree.

D. A Summary and Some Objections

A very brief summary of the paper so far might run as follows.

1. Because prices and wages are unresponsive to changes in demand in the short run, the massive realignments of *relative* prices required by poor agricultural harvests, OPEC, and the end of wage–price controls caused most of the great inflation of 1973–1974 and most of the great recession of 1973–1975. (A positive statement.)
2. By some sort of accommodative monetary and fiscal policy, the authorities could have prevented, or at least cushioned, the recessionary blow at the cost of slightly more inflation. (Another positive statement.)
3. The authorities should have behaved in this way. (A normative statement.)

It seems fruitless to go over the arguments defending or attacking the normative statement 3. Instead, I want to spend the bulk of this paper considering some possible objections to the Keynesian analysis of the great stagflation that I have sketched so far—sticking strictly to positive economics. In particular, monetarists have been offended by the distinctly nonmonetary explanation of the inflationary burst of the mid-1970s (statement 1). Did money play no role in this inflation? Second, a number of economists have objected to statement 2 on the grounds that an accommodative policy stance would have had damaging effects on inflationary expectations. Have accommodationists been naively sanguine about the

[8] Of course, in the long run we suspect that the price level will rise in proportion to the additional money that is created. But if this is a long drawn out process, the additional inflation in any one year may be slight.

short-run trade-off between inflation and unemployment? The next two sections take up these arguments in turn.

3. Is Inflation Always and Everywhere a Monetary Phenomenon?

Monetarism is an elusive doctrine. Were it not, economists would not have spilled so much ink in arguing what it is and what it is not. But surely one of the hallmarks of positive monetarism (as opposed to normative monetarism) is the claim that money is the root of all inflation. The Friedmanian dictum alluded to in the title of this part is well-known and widely quoted. Yet I have sketched in Section 2 an explanation of the acceleration of inflation in the mid-1970s that allows no role whatsoever for money. How can there be inflation without money? It is time to confront this question directly.

A. Steady versus One-Shot Inflation

Let me start by posing the question differently: What can possibly be meant by saying that money is the only cause of inflation? Surely inflation will accelerate if *either* the growth of aggregate demand accelerates *or* the growth of aggregate supply decelerates. A surge in aggregate demand could be fueled by expansionary fiscal policy, or by an increase in the propensity to consume, or, I hasten to add, by an increase in the money supply. Aggregate supply growth could be slowed by shocks of the kind considered already, by a slowdown in the rate of growth of productivity, and so on. Monetarists, presumably, would not deny that any of these developments can speed the rise of the price level.

In what sense, then, is inflation "always and everywhere a monetary phenomenon"? In the very limited sense that money is normally the only one of these factors that *permanently* changes the *inflation rate*. An upward shift of the consumption or investment function, an increase in government expenditures, or an increase in the *level* of the money stock will all give rise to a *temporary* upward "blip" in the inflation rate as the *price level* adjusts to its new equilibrium path. Only if these fillips to demand are repeated period after period will there be any *permanent* effect on the inflation rate. But clearly the consumption and investment functions cannot continue to shift up period after period, government spending does not steadily rise faster than potential GNP, and so on. Hence the non-monetary influences on aggregate demand normally will not affect the baseline inflation rate. Money is different, however. A policy of permanently increasing the money *growth rate*—which we can think of as a succession of one-shot increases in the *level* of the money *stock*—will have a permanent effect on the inflation rate.

Turn now to supply-side factors. The supply shocks I discussed in Section 2 were all of the one-shot variety, not events that are repeated year after year. A permanent inflationary change emanating from the supply side *is* conceivable—just think of a permanent reduction in the growth rate of productivity that is not accompanied by a slowdown in aggregate demand growth. The fact of the matter, however, is that such things normally do not occur. This leaves money as the only factor likely to account for long-run swings in the inflation rate.

The conclusion, then, is that we must distinguish between two very different phenomena that nonetheless look very similar to the proverbial man in the street (and also to the folks who compile the price indexes!): steady continual inflation and one-shot bursts of inflation. The former, in practice if not in theory, probably is strictly a "monetary phenomenon." But the latter type of inflation can be kicked off by a bewildering variety of nonmonetary factors, and often is. The supply shocks considered here are precisely of this character.

B. How Can We Tell Which We Have?

A good question follows from this analysis. When we see an acceleration of inflation, how do we know if we have witnessed a steady monetary sort of inflation or a one-time special factors inflation? A number of tests suggest themselves, all of which really amount to little more than opening our eyes.

The crudest sort of evidence is often the most convincing. Look at Fig. 2, which is taken from (of all places!) the *Federal Reserve Bank of St. Louis Review*. This diagram charts the time series behavior of inflation (as measured by the GNP deflator) and growth of the money stock (M_1) from 1954 to 1977.[9] Comment is hardly necessary. Can anyone looking at this chart seriously maintain that the acceleration of inflation in 1973 and 1974 and the deceleration in 1975 were attributable to changes in the growth rate of the money stock?

A more sophisticated way to make the same point is to estimate a regression model explaining inflation by its own past values and by current and past monetary growth rates. I have done this using the deflator for personal consumption expenditures to measure inflation and this time

[9] A twenty-quarter annual growth rate is used to smooth M_1; a four-quarter annual growth rate is used to smooth the GNP deflator.

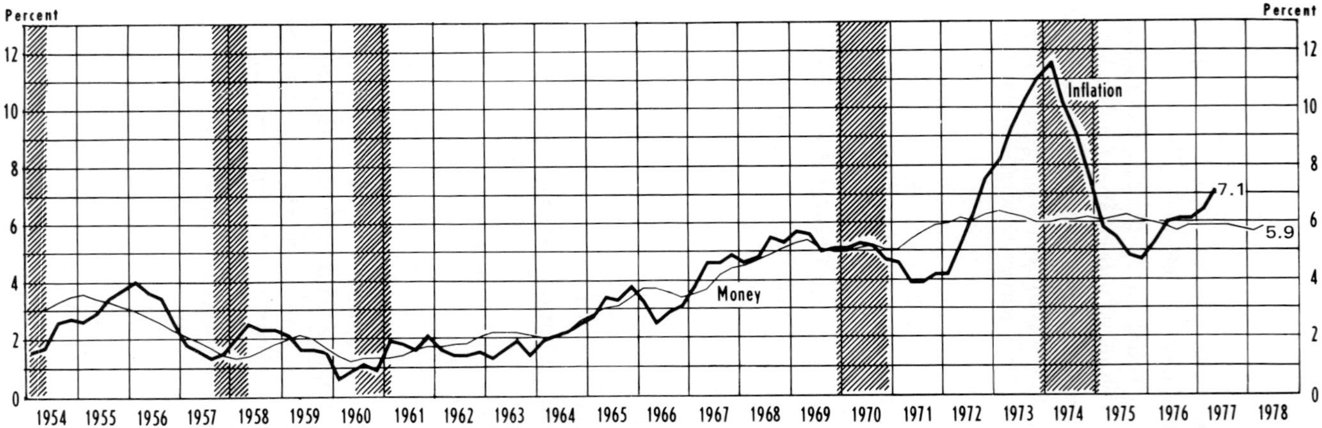

Fig. 2. Money growth and inflation. Bold line is inflation; light line is money. Shaded areas represent periods of business recessions. A twenty-quarter annual growth rate is used to smooth M_1; a four-quarter annual growth rate is used to smooth the GNP deflator. Latest data plotted: Inflation, second quarter, 1977; Money, second quarter, 1978. (From Tatom, 1978.)

TABLE 3

INFLATION PREDICTIONS FROM A MONETARIST EQUATION

Year and quarter	Actual Inflation[a]	Predicted Inflation[b]	Error[c]
1973 : 1	5.4	4.2	+ 1.2
1973 : 2	7.7	5.8	+ 1.9
1973 : 3	6.8	7.6	− 0.7
1973 : 4	10.0	8.2	+ 1.8
1974 : 1	12.9	9.4	+ 3.5
1974 : 2	12.3	10.9	+ 1.4
1974 : 3	11.4	10.8	+ 0.6
1974 : 4	10.9	9.9	+ 1.0
1975 : 1	6.3	9.3	− 3.0
1975 : 2	5.6	6.9	− 1.3
1975 : 3	7.2	5.7	+ 1.5
1975 : 4	5.3	6.1	− 0.8

[a] Quarterly change in deflator for personal consumption expenditures at annual rates, in percentage points.

[b] Predictions from a regression of inflation on money growth rates and lagged inflation.

[c] Actual minus predicted.

using M_2 to measure money.[10] The results for an estimation period covering 1951 : 3 through 1977 : 4 were

$$\dot{P}_t = \underset{(0.38)}{-0.60} + \sum_{j=1}^{11} a_j \dot{P}_{t-j} + \sum_{j=0}^{17} b_j \dot{M}_{t-j},$$

$$R^2 = 0.73, \quad DW = 1.98, \quad \text{s.e.} = 1.42, \quad \sum a_j = 0.67, \quad \sum b_j = 0.27.$$

Table 3 shows the (within sample) predictions of the inflation rate made by this equation for 1973–1975. They are not impressive.

The equation starts off precisely on track in 1972 : 4, but misses the (food-induced) acceleration of inflation in early 1973. It gets back on track by 1973 : 3 owing to the large coefficients on lagged inflation,[11] but misses the effects of the oil shock in 1973 : 4 and 1974 : 1. Though the positive residuals for the remaining three quarters of 1974 are not large, they may

[10] This choice was motivated by the well-known problems with the conventional demand function for M_1, which misbehaved badly in 1974–1976. By contrast, velocity of M_2 remained quite constant.

[11] The coefficient of lagged inflation is 0.43 and the coefficient of inflation lagged two quarters is 0.22. Without this built-in error-correction mechanism the equation would perform much worse.

be due to the equation's inability to cope with the post-controls bout of catchup inflation. For the 1973–1974 period as a whole, the inflation forecasts are too low in seven out of eight quarters, and cumulate to an underprediction of the 1974 : 4 price level of almost 3%. The equation also badly misses the sharp deceleration of inflation in early 1975.

Both of the abovementioned pieces of evidence deny the cogency of the monetary explanation of the acceleration and deceleration of inflation in 1973–1975. What of the special factors explanation? I have already offered some supporting evidence on food and energy. Let me now turn to nonfood nonenergy prices, where the principal factor was wage–price controls.[12]

The version of the "special factors" model of inflation in which downward price rigidities translate *relative* price adjustments into bursts of *inflation* suggests that when wage–price controls end, there should be a temporary blip in the inflation rate. That is, we should find an acceleration of inflation followed by a deceleration of roughly equal magnitude because decontrol does not affect the basic underlying inflation rate.

What do we actually find? Table 4 shows the annual rate of inflation of a specially constructed price index for nonfood nonenergy personal consumption expenditures (roughly 70% of total expenditures) during 1973–1975. The bulge is clear, and the degree of symmetry is remarkable. If we call the three-quarter period of double-digit inflation the peak period and mark off prepeak and postpeak periods of equal length, we find that the annual rate of inflation rose from 5.9% in the pre-peak period to 11% in the peak period, and then fell back precisely to 5.9% in the post-peak period. Monthly data from the CPI confirm this general pattern, though not with quite so much symmetry (see Blinder, 1979, Table 5-10). A coincidence? I doubt it. And in any case it seems inconceivable that money could have

TABLE 4

INFLATION RATE OF NONFOOD NONENERGY CONSUMER PRICES[a,b]

	1973	1974	1975
1st quarter	3.7	7.7	7.2
2nd quarter	4.7	10.2	5.2
3rd quarter	4.3	12.3	5.2
4th quarter	5.5	10.6	5.9

[a]Source: Constructed by author from data in *Survey of Current Business*, various issues.

[b]Quarter-to-quarter percentage change in price index, at seasonally adjusted annual rates.

[12]Blinder (1979) offers more evidence on all these matters.

had anything to do with this roller coaster pattern. The great inflation of the mid-1970s simply was not a monetary phenomenon.

4. Monetary Accommodation and Expectations

A. The Arguments

Since the debate over accommodation started in 1974, a number of economists have pointed out that econometric model simulations suggesting that accommodation would have caused rather little extra inflation fail to come to grips properly with inflationary expectations. (A proposition with which even the model builders would probably agree!) Often appealing to some sort of rational expectations argument, these economists oppose accommodation because of its alleged adverse effects on inflationary expectations.

In dealing with the expectationists' objections, I would like to divide them into two distinct families. In the first group, which I will call "present disaster" arguments, are variants of the following story. A policy of monetary accommodation (or even the announcement of such a policy) would increase inflationary expectations, shifting the short-run Phillips curve upward and defeating the purpose of the expansionary policy. Instead of getting a big improvement in production with only a little deterioration on the inflation front (as the models suggest), we would get a big burst of (runaway?) inflation with little improvement in real economic activity.

Arguments in the second group, which I will call future disaster arguments, are more subtle, but also more elusive. The idea is that by informing private agents of the intention to accommodate supply shocks in the future, the monetary authorities would exacerbate the rigidity of wages and prices, thus making it more difficult to deal with future supply shocks.

Both of these sets of arguments have a ring of plausibility. The problem is that it is hard to know how to evaluate them, based as they are on a priori assertions without empirical support. But to say something is an a priori assertion is not to say that it is *wrong*, and it would be nice to have a way of conducting this debate at a scientific level higher than that of a shouting match.

The rest of this section tries to do just that by dealing with the expectationist arguments at three different levels. First, and very briefly, come the shouting-match aspects—some reasons why I am not persuaded by the a priori assertions used to oppose accommodation. Next, I take an empirical approach, using the recent estimates of Barro and Rush (1980) to appraise the inflation–unemployment trade-offs that might have resulted from two accommodative monetary policies. Finally, I try to analyze the argument at a purely theoretical level, using two popular rational expectations macromodels.

B. A Priori Counterassertions

First, it is worth pointing out that the MPS model, upon which I have relied heavily in making numerical estimates of inflation–unemployment trade-offs, *does* incorporate inflationary expectations. It models the expected rate of inflation as a (geometric) distributed lag on past actual rates of inflation—a procedure I do not necessarily wish to defend against the rational expectations alternative. However, for the present disaster argument to have any force, it must be the case that the (rational) inflationary expectations that would arise from a policy of accommodation are systematically and substantially *higher* than the inflationary expectations derived from the mechanical distributed lag formulation. But why should this be so? Especially if the announced policy was a step increase in the money *stock* with no change thereafter in its *growth rate*.[13]

The second problem I find in the expectationist argument is its assumption of a direct and rapid link between government policy actions (or even announcements) and private pricing decisions. It is as if the gigantic, decentralized U.S. economy could be modeled as a two-person game. My guess is that in setting the price of a Chevrolet, the management of General Motors must weigh and evaluate scores (hundreds? thousands?) of factors, among which next quarter's money supply is not terribly important. For the many businesses whose prospects are less well correlated with the state of aggregate demand than is GM's, the link from monetary policy announcements to their own pricing policy must be more tenuous still. In this respect industrial prices differ greatly from the prices of financial instruments, where the money supply may be of paramount importance.

I hasten to add that I do not mean to imply by this that money is unimportant for the price level. Like any respectable economist, I pledge allegiance to the long-run neutrality of money. My point is simply that money may work on prices primarily through markets, rather than directly through expectations. If this is the case, then accommodative monetary policy will raise prices only gradually and therefore will stimulate real economic activity in the interim.

Third, the behavior of workers and firms that is implied by the

[13] See, for example, note 6.

expectationist argument strikes me as somewhat implausible. For an antiaccommodative policy to work, firms must voluntarily reduce their margins of selling prices over costs because they fear that otherwise monetary stringency will damage sales. The important aspect of this argument is that firms must *not* wait for the damage to occur, but must act *now* in anticipation of it. Alternatively, it could be workers who take the lead—willingly settling for slower wage growth out of fear that if they refuse, widespread unemployment might result. Again, what distinguishes this argument from the Keynesian analysis is that the lower wages *come in anticipation of future unemployment*, whereas Keynesians see the lower wages coming (grudgingly) only *as a result of actual unemployment*. The difference in views is fundamental, and while the expectationist case certainly is not outlandish, I would like to see some evidence in support of it.

Finally, we should not lose sight of the fact that the U.S. monetary authorities did in fact follow nonaccommodative policies in 1974. Are prices and wages in the industrial sector now more flexible as a result? Again, I would like to see the evidence.

C. Empirical Evidence Based on Rational Expectations

A critical plank in the present disaster argument is the notion that empirical macromodels grossly overstate the benefits (less unemployment) and understate the costs (more inflation) of monetary accommodation. Where can we look for evidence on this matter? Clearly, standard econometric models will not do, since their validity is precisely what is being questioned.

At the level of a priori assertion, some simple rational expectations models imply that any *fully anticipated* increase in the money supply will reap no real gains, but will instead cause a jump in the price level. And Barro (1977, 1978) has even purported to demonstrate the empirical validity of this extreme point of view. So perhaps it is best to consider *unanticipated* monetary accommodation.

Recent quarterly estimates by Barro and Rush (1980) make it possible to estimate output–inflation trade-offs for an unanticipated (and who could have anticipated it?) policy of monetary accommodation in 1974—estimates which presumably are fully consistent with rational expectations. Does this trade-off look worse than what the MPS model suggests?

Since it is less than perfectly clear how to capture accommodation in the Barro–Rush equations, I have conducted two different experiments. Before describing them, a brief review of the Barro model is appropriate.

The model consists of three equations:

$$DM_t = \sum_{i=1}^{n} \hat{\alpha}_i DM_{t-i} + X_t\hat{\beta} + DMR_t, \tag{1}$$

$$\log y_t = \sum_{i=0}^{m} \hat{a}_i DMR_{t-i} + Z_t\hat{b} + \hat{e}_t, \tag{2}$$

$$\log P_t = \log M_t - \sum_{i=0}^{k} \hat{\gamma}_i DMR_{t-i} + Y_t\hat{\delta} + \hat{u}_t, \tag{3}$$

where M_t is the money supply, DM_t is the first difference of $\log M_t$ (quarterly growth rate of M), y_t is real output, P_t is the price level, X_t, Z_t, Y_t are other variables entering each equation, which are of no concern here, DMR_t, $\hat{e}_t$, $\hat{u}_t$ are estimated residuals in each equation, and $\hat{\alpha}$, $\hat{\beta}$, $\hat{a}$, $\hat{b}$, $\hat{\gamma}$, $\hat{\delta}$ are estimated coefficients. Equation (1) is the money reaction function. Its purpose is to divide each quarter's monetary growth into an anticipated part ($\widehat{DM} \equiv DM - DMR$), which depends on past monetary growth and some other variables (X), and on an unanticipated part (DMR). Equation (2) estimates the distributed lag effect of unanticipated money growth on real output, and Eq. (3) estimates the effects of actual and unanticipated money on the price level.

For the first experiment I define accommodative policy to be a 6% *unanticipated* increase in the money supply in 1974 : 1. Thereafter, DM_t returns to its historical path, leaving the level of the money supply 6% higher. To model this policy, I suspend Eq. (1) and simply raise DMR by 0.06 in 1974 : 1, leaving it at its historical value in all other quarters. From the distributed lag coefficients in Eqs. (2) and (3)[14] it is easy to generate the predicted effects (expressed as deviations from actual history) on log y and log P. These are shown in Table 5.

The results, are indeed, quite different from what the MPS model would predict. However, instead of undermining the accommodationist argument, they are actually much more favorable to it! According to Table 5, output responds immediately and very strongly to the monetary stimulus. By 1975 : 1 (the recession trough) real GNP is increased by almost 10%. Since the actual decline in real GNP from 1973 : 4 to 1975 : 1 was 5.7% and normal trend growth over this period would have been another 4.6%, the implication is that the recession would have been almost entirely avoided. What of the inflationary price tag? According to the Barro–Rush equations, there would have been a brief and short acceleration of inflation (about a $7\frac{1}{2}$% annual rate) in the initial quarter followed by an even sharper deceleration of inflation (about an 11% annual rate) in the next

[14]Equation (2) is Eq. (4) in Table 1 of Barro and Rush (1980); Eq. (3) is their Eq. (5) in Table 2.

TABLE 5

EFFECTS OF AN UNANTICIPATED 6% INCREASE OF THE MONEY SUPPLY IN 1974 : 1[a]

Quarter	Effect on log y_t	Effect on log P_t
1974 : 1	+ 0.031	+ 0.018
1974 : 2	+ 0.068	− 0.008
1974 : 3	+ 0.075	− 0.011
1974 : 4	+ 0.092	− 0.003
1975 : 1	+ 0.096	− 0.001
1975 : 2	+ 0.068	+ 0.002
1975 : 3	+ 0.045	− 0.010
1975 : 4	+ 0.017	− 0.006
1976 : 1	0	− 0.004
⋮	⋮	⋮
1977 : 4	0	+ 0.060

[a] Source: Author's computations, based on equations in Barro and Rush (1980).

quarter, leaving the 1974 : 2 price level about 1% *lower* as a result of accommodation.[15] After this, nothing much happens to the inflation rate until all real effects have vanished. Thereafter, however, a significant inflation develops, carrying the price level up to 6% by 1977 : 4. Frankly, I find the predictions in Table 5 rather difficult to believe.

As an alternative representation of accommodative policy, I considered raising *actual* DM_t by 0.015 in each of the four quarters from 1973 : 4 through 1974 : 3. In the first quarter this implies a *DMR* of 0.015, but in subsequent quarters—according to the autoregressive aspects of Eq. (1)—agents begin to catch on. Column (1) of Table 6 lists the quarterly values of *DMR* implied by Eq. (1), and columns (2) and (3) record the implications for log y and log P.

The results of this policy seem much more in line with the predictions of Keynesian macromodels. Output responds more slowly and less vigorously than in the previous case. Since the peak effect on real GNP is about 5%, about half the recession is avoided. Prices also exhibit a more "reasonable" pattern of response. The gradual 6% increase in money leads to very little additional inflation in the first two quarters, about 2.2% more inflation during the first year and about 1.6% more during the next year. Eventually, of course, prices will rise by 6%. In sum, for this policy the Barro–Rush model seems slightly more optimistic than the standard

[15] Unanticipated money *lowers* the price level because in Barro and Rush's Eq. (3) the coefficients of *DMR* generally exceed unity at lags 1–9.

TABLE 6

EFFECTS OF INCREASING THE ANNUAL GROWTH RATE OF MONEY BY 6% FOR FOUR QUARTERS (1973 : 4–1974 : 3)[a]

Quarter	(1) DMR_t	(2) $\log y_t$	(3) $\log P_t$
1973 : 4	+ 0.015	+ 0.008	+ 0.005
1974 : 1	+ 0.007	+ 0.021	+ 0.008
1974 : 2	+ 0.008	+ 0.031	+ 0.014
1974 : 3	+ 0.007	+ 0.044	+ 0.022
1974 : 4	− 0.009	+ 0.048	+ 0.027
1975 : 1	− 0.001	+ 0.038	+ 0.033
1975 : 2	− 0.004	+ 0.028	+ 0.035
1975 : 3	− 0.003	+ 0.009	+ 0.38
1975 : 4	− 0.002	− 0.009	+ 0.040
1976 : 1	− 0.002	− 0.017	+ 0.041
⋮	⋮	⋮	⋮
1977 : 4	0	− 0.001	+ 0.073

[a] Source: Author's computations, based on equations in Barro and Rush (1980).

macromodels about the potential output gains, but slightly more pessimistic about the short-run inflationary costs. The differences, however, are not great.

D. ACCOMMODATION UNDER RATIONAL EXPECTATIONS: THEORY

One nagging problem with Barro's empirical work is that, since he estimates only reduced-form equations, we are left unenlightened about the structure from which these reduced forms may have come. In addition, the Barro–Rush empirical model is no more able to come to grips with the future disaster argument than is the MPS model (or any empirical model?). For both of these reasons, I turn next to a theoretical examination of the extent to which rational expectations might undermine the case for accommodating supply shocks.

The basic ideas are simple enough to explain but somewhat tedious to work out precisely. At least where *anticipated* monetary policy is concerned, the simplest rational expectations models imply that the aggregate supply curve is vertical, even in the short run. Hence, if there is a supply shock, the supply curve moves inward as shown in Fig. 3. Apparently, the case for accommodation has now evaporated because the only thing an upward shift in the aggregate demand curve could accomplish would be to

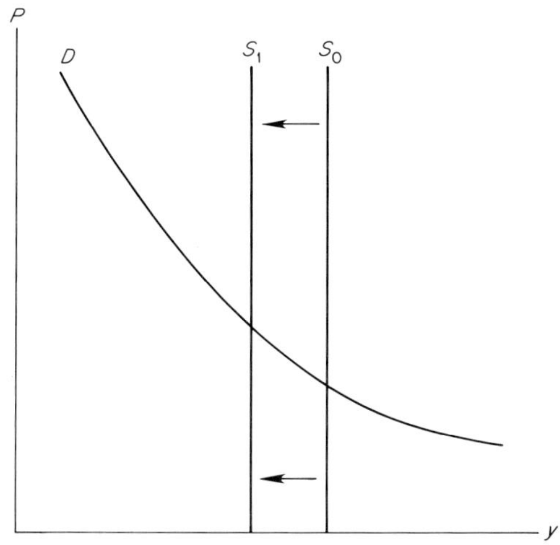

Fig. 3. Rational expectations analysis of a supply shock.

raise the price level—not raise real output. In fact, the optimal policy seems to be to reduce aggregate demand enough to prevent the price level from rising (see Section 4.D.2).

I will argue here, however, that this simple story leaves out at least three pertinent aspects of the OPEC shock. The first simply applies a point made already by Fischer (1977), Phelps and Taylor (1977), and others: If wages (or prices) are sticky for some reason, then the short-run aggregate supply curve retains some upward slope despite rational expectations. In such a case, Fig. 1 again becomes relevant, and a potential case for accommodation arises. The second point is that the OPEC shock shifted the aggregate demand curve to the left, through the previously mentioned distribution effects. There is a potential role for stabilization policy in offsetting this shift. Finally, I suggest that since OPEC posts a *nominal* price of oil, the short-run aggregate supply curve acquires a positive slope despite rational expectations even without wage or price stickiness. The remainder of this section is devoted to spelling out these arguments in somewhat greater detail.

The rational expectations models represented schematically by Fig. 3 are elaborations of the following simple model developed by Lucas (1973):

$$y_t = k_t + \alpha(P_t - {}_{t-1}P_t) + e_t, \qquad \alpha > 0, \tag{4}$$

$$m_t + v_t = y_t + P_t, \tag{5}$$

where y_t is the log of output, P_t is the log of the price level, m_t is the log of the money supply, e_t and v_t are random output and velocity shocks (assumed to be white noise), k_t and α are constants, and the notation ${}_{t-s}X_t$ is used throughout the paper for the (rational) expectation of X_t formulated in period $t - s$. Equation (4) is the Lucas specification of aggregate supply, and Eq. (5) is the simple quantity-theory specification of aggregate demand. Since the same symbol is used for both demand and supply, the model implies that prices are perfectly flexible and move to clear the market each period.

Two very different rationales for (4) can be provided. The first, which is prominent in the work of Lucas and his followers, is based on agents (there is no important distinction between workers and firms) who, lacking knowledge of the current price level, mistakenly view any unanticipated inflation as being, in part, an increase in their own *relative* price.

The second rationale simply appeals to standard production theory to derive output supply as a decreasing function of the real wage, $y_t = k_t - \alpha(W_t - P_t) + e_t$, and then assumes that wages for period t are proportional to the expected price level of period t, $W_t = {}_{t-1}P_t$. There is no question here about whether P_t is known in period t; full current knowledge is assumed.

In what follows, both of these rationales for (4) will be exploited. I begin with a model based on the work of Fischer (1977) in which the real wage rationale is used, and wage stickiness gives monetary policy stabilizing powers.

(1) A Model with Sticky Wages

In the Fischer (1977) model, half the firms pay wages that were set last period, and half pay wages that were set two periods ago. If we extend that model to allow for a second factor of production (energy), the supply function for firms that set their wages in period $t - 1$ would be

$$y_{1t} = k_{1t} - \alpha({}_{t-1}W_t - P_t) - \delta(R_t - P_t) + e_{1t},$$

where ${}_{t-i}W_t$ is the (log of the) contract wage for period t set in period $t - i$ and R_t is the (log of the) *nominal* price of oil. Production theory implies that α and δ are positive.

Assume that nominal input prices are given by:

$${}_{t-i}W_t = {}_{t-i}P_t, \tag{6}$$

$$R_t = {}_{t-1}\hat{P}_t + r_t. \tag{7}$$

Equation (6) is carried over from Fischer (1977). Equation (7) states that OPEC sets its nominal price one period ahead in order to achieve a target real price r_t, according to its own price expectations ${}_{t-1}\hat{P}_t$. Since the real price that it actually achieves is $r_t - (P_t - {}_{t-1}\hat{P}_t)$, the supply function follows:

$$y_{1t} = k_{1t} + \alpha(P_t - {}_{t-1}P_t) + \delta(P_t - {}_{t-1}\hat{P}_t) - \delta r_t + e_{1t}.$$

A similar supply function holds for the firms that set their wages in period $t-2$:

$$y_{2t} = k_{2t} + \alpha(P_t - {}_{t-2}P_t) + \delta(P_t - {}_{t-1}\hat{P}_t) - \delta r_t + e_{2t}.$$

Since half the firms fall in each category, the aggregate supply function follows directly (with obvious notation):

$$y_t = k_t + \tfrac{1}{2}\alpha(P_t - {}_{t-1}P_t) + \tfrac{1}{2}\alpha(P_t - {}_{t-2}P_t) + \delta(P_t - {}_{t-1}\hat{P}_t) - \delta r_t + e_t.$$

For convenience, I write this as:

$$y_t = k_t + \alpha_1(P_t - {}_{t-1}P_t) + \alpha_2(P_t - {}_{t-2}P_t) + \delta(P_t - {}_{t-1}\hat{P}_t) - \delta r_t + e_t, \tag{8}$$

where $\alpha_1 = \alpha_2 = \frac{1}{2}\alpha$. This form has the advantage that we can see what happens in the absence of wage stickiness by setting $\alpha_2 = 0$, $\alpha_1 = \alpha$.

For aggregate demand, Fischer (1977) used (5), and I modify this only slightly to allow for the aforementioned distribution effects on demand. Thus let the aggregate demand curve remain a rectangular hyperbola, but let its position depend on the real price of oil (which can be thought of as the terms of trade):

$$y_t + P_t = m_t + v_t - c(R_t - P_t). \tag{9}$$

To solve the model, substitute (7) into (9), and equate the result to (8). After taking all the appropriate expectations, the following expressions can be derived:

$$P_t = \frac{\delta - c}{1+\alpha}(r_t - {}_{t-1}r_t) + \frac{1}{1+\alpha+\delta-c}(m_t - {}_{t-1}m_t) - k_t + \frac{(\delta - c)({}_{t-1}\hat{m}_t - {}_{t-1}m_t)}{(1+\alpha)(1+\alpha+\delta-c)} + \frac{1}{1+\alpha_2}({}_{t-1}m_t + \alpha_2\, {}_{t-2}m_t) + \frac{\delta - c}{1+\alpha_2}({}_{t-1}r_t + \alpha_2\, {}_{t-2}r_t) + \eta_t, \tag{10}$$

$$P_t - {}_{t-1}P_t = \frac{\delta - c}{1+\alpha}(r_t - {}_{t-1}r_t) + \frac{1}{1+\alpha+\delta-c}(m_t - {}_{t-1}m_t) + \frac{(\delta - c)({}_{t-1}\hat{m}_t - {}_{t-1}m_t)}{(1+\alpha)(1+\alpha+\delta-c)} + \eta_t, \tag{11}$$

$$P_t - {}_{t-2}P_t = (P_t - {}_{t-1}P_t) + \frac{1}{1+\alpha_2}({}_{t-1}m_t - {}_{t-2}m_t) + \frac{\delta - c}{1+\alpha_2}({}_{t-1}r_t - {}_{t-2}r_t), \tag{12}$$

$$P_t - {}_{t-1}\hat{P}_t = \frac{m_t - {}_{t-1}\hat{m}_t}{1+\alpha+\delta-c} + \eta_t, \tag{13}$$

where $\eta_t \equiv (v_t - e_t)/(1 + \alpha + \delta - c)$ is a white-noise error term, and where ${}_{t-1}\hat{m}_t$ denotes OPEC's expectation of the money stock.

One obvious feature of the model can be seen in (10). The "OPEC shock" is basically a shock to a *relative* price. In this model, it will be *inflationary* only if $\delta > c$, that is, only if a rise in the real price of energy reduces supply by more than it reduces demand. In reality, it is far from clear that this condition is met, yet OPEC shocks are pretty clearly inflationary; this, I believe, is a weakness of any model that assumes downward flexibility of prices. To maintain some semblance of realism, I shall assume $\delta > c$, so that increases in r_t are indeed inflationary.

Equations (11)–(13) reflect the standard implication of rational expectations: "Unexpected" inflation can only be attributable to events that have taken place since the expectations were formed.

To take up the issue of accommodation, I now introduce the following class of monetary rules:

$$m_t = k_t + \beta(R_t - {}_{t-1}R_t) + b_{t-1}R_t. \tag{14}$$

If $b = \beta = 0$, this is the Friedman rule of letting money grow at the growth rate of potential GNP. The parameters b and β indicate the elasticity of the money stock with respect to anticipated and unanticipated OPEC price increases, respectively. Any rule with b and/or β positive will be considered accommodating. Since the rule has no "noise," m_t and ${}_{t-1}\hat{m}_t$ will always be identical.

Use of (14) in (11) and (12) leads to

$$P_t - {}_{t-1}P_t = \frac{\beta + \delta - c}{1 + \alpha - \beta}(r_t - {}_{t-1}r_t) + \eta_t, \tag{15}$$

$$P_t - {}_{t-2}P_t = (P_t - {}_{t-1}P_t) + \frac{b + \delta - c}{1 + \alpha_2 - b}({}_{t-1}r_t - {}_{t-2}r_t). \tag{16}$$

Substitution of these expressions into the supply function leads to the following expression for output:

$$y_t = k_t + \left[\frac{\alpha(\beta + \delta - c)}{1 + \alpha - \beta} - \delta\right](r_t - {}_{t-1}r_t)$$
$$+ \left[\frac{\alpha_2(b + \delta - c)}{1 + \alpha_2 - b} - \delta\right]({}_{t-1}r_t - {}_{t-2}r_t) - \delta_{t-2}r_t + u_t, \tag{17}$$

where $u_t \equiv (\delta + \alpha)\eta_t + e_t$. The nature of the accommodation issue is pretty clear from these equations.

Consider first accommodation of an *unanticipated* OPEC shock. This is possible, it will be recalled, since *both* the monetary authority *and* all private agents are assumed to know R_t at the beginning of period t. From (15), the price level can be insulated from unanticipated OPEC shocks by setting $\beta = c - \delta$, which I have assumed to be negative. This is an antiaccommodating stance of the sort that is associated with rational expectations models in which the short-run supply curve is vertical (see Fig. 3). However, as (17) makes clear, such a policy would allow the full negative effect of any unanticipated OPEC shock on production to take place. Instead, a policy of insulating output from the unanticipated portion of any OPEC price increase would set $\beta = (\delta + \alpha c)/(\delta + \alpha) > 0$. The trade-off is pretty clear, and value judgments are necessary to decide on the appropriate β.

The issue of accommodation of "anticipated" shocks is more subtle since, owing to the assumed structure of contracts, it matters whether the shock was anticipated at time $t-1$ or at time $t-2$. Equation (17) makes it clear that there are no output gains to be reaped by trying to offset ${}_{t-2}r_t$, and Eq. (10) shows that any monetary reaction whereby ${}_{t-2}m_t$ was raised in response to ${}_{t-2}r_t$ would simply cause inflation. Thus there is no case for accommodating such shocks. In the real world, this translates to the statement that there is no case for accommodating (and perhaps a case for antiaccommodating) any OPEC shock that has been anticipated since before the longest existing contractual arrangement was made. I leave it to the reader to appraise the practical significance of this result.

Of greater interest are shocks that become anticipated in $t-1$ but were not anticipated in $t-2$, for here a trade-off does appear. Equation (17) shows that a positive value of b will help offset the output reducing effects of such a shock, while equation (16) shows that a negative value of b will help offset its inflationary consequences. Specifically, $b = c - \delta < 0$ will make it impossible for OPEC shocks to cause unanticipated inflation while $b = (\delta + \alpha_2 c)/(\alpha_2 + \delta) > 0$ will insulate real output from such shocks.

Optimal policy rules in this model are not straightforward unless OPEC obliges by following a stationary policy, for Eqs. (15)–(17) show that OPEC's decisions drive the whole model. One simple policy rule for OPEC that *is* stationary is

$$r_t = \bar{r} + \epsilon_t,$$

where ϵ_t is a white-noise error term. This states that, except for random noise, OPEC always shoots for a constant real price. Under such a policy, the natural rate of output will be $k_t - \delta\bar{r} \equiv \bar{k}_t$, and the variance of output around this mean will be

$$\operatorname{Var}(y_t - \bar{k}_t) = \sigma_u^2 + \left[\frac{\alpha(\beta + \delta - c)}{1 + \alpha - \beta} - \delta\right]^2 \sigma_\epsilon^2,$$

and the variances of both types of domestic unanticipated inflation and actual inflation all turn out to be:

$$\operatorname{Var}(P_t - {}_{t-1}P_t) = \operatorname{Var}(P_t - {}_{t-2}P_t),$$

$$\operatorname{Var}({}_{t-1}P_t - P_{t-1}) = \sigma_\eta^2 + \left(\frac{\beta + \delta - c}{1 + \alpha - \beta}\right)^2 \sigma_\epsilon^2 .$$

Under steady state conditions a reasonable goal for policy is to minimize a weighted average of these variances, where the weights reflect both welfare costs and value judgments:

$$W = \lambda_1 \operatorname{Var}(y_t - \bar{k}_t) + \lambda_2 \operatorname{Var}(P_t - {}_{t-1}P_t) + \lambda_3 \operatorname{Var}(P_t - {}_{t-2}P_t) + \lambda_4 \operatorname{Var}({}_{t-1}P_t - P_{t-1}),$$

where $\lambda_1, \ldots, \lambda_4 \geqslant 0$, $\lambda_1 + \cdots + \lambda_4 = 1$, and $\lambda_3 < \lambda_2$.

Minimizing this with respect to β (b is irrelevant since OPEC's assumed behavior now eliminates any difference between ${}_{t-1}r_t$ and ${}_{t-2}r_t$) yields the following optimal policy rule:

$$\beta = \frac{\alpha\lambda_1(\alpha c + \delta) - (1 - \lambda_1)(\delta - c)}{\alpha\lambda_1(\alpha + \delta) + (1 - \lambda_1)},$$

which calls for a positive β if and only if

$$\lambda_1 > \frac{\delta - c}{\alpha(\alpha c + \delta) + (\delta - c)} .$$

Clearly, an accommodating policy ($\beta > 0$) is more likely: (a) the higher the relative welfare weight attached to output deviations λ_1; and (b) the greater the demand-reducing aspects of the OPEC shock c.

To summarize the results from this model: In a rational expectations model with sticky wages there is a case for providing some degree of monetary accommodation to *both* anticipated and unanticipated OPEC shocks. This holds even if OPEC knows that a policy of accommodation will be followed, and uses this knowledge in setting its price. The strength of the case for accommodation, of course, depends on value judgments because any such accommodation, while partially insulating real output from OPEC shocks, exacerbates the inflationary consequences of such shocks.

In the long run, which in this context is a period longer than that of the longest contract, there is no output-inflation trade-off, and hence no reason to accommodate an OPEC shock. Indeed, since real output is permanently lower on account of higher oil prices, it makes sense to reduce the money supply.

(2) A Model with a Nominal OPEC Pricing Rule

I turn now to the other entering wedge for monetary accommodation—the possibility that OPEC will set a price in *nominal* terms and not react fully to an increase in the U.S. price level. To focus squarely on this aspect of the problem, I abandon the Fischer (1977) framework of sticky prices and use instead a variant of the Lucas (1973) model in which all prices are perfectly flexible.

It is worth reiterating that the rationale for the basic Lucas supply function differs substantially between the two models. In the model to be considered now, agents do not know the current price level and instead must infer it from the information available to them. In Lucas' (1973) analysis, this information set consisted of the agent's own price and his knowledge of the distribution of P_t as of time $t-1$. As he shows, optimal use of this information leads to a supply function like (4). In the model of this section I add one further piece of data to the agent's information set: the current price of oil R_t. As will be shown in the Appendix, this leads to the following amendment to the Lucas supply function:

$$y_t = k_t + \alpha(P_t - {}_{t-1}P_t) - \delta(R_t - {}_{t-1}P_t) + e_t. \tag{18}$$

Aggregate demand is modeled in the same way as before:

$$y_t + P_t = m_t + v_t - c(R_t - P_t), \tag{19}$$

and the following pricing rule for OPEC is introduced:

$$R_t = r_t + \omega_{t-1}\hat{P}_t + (1-\omega)Z_t, \tag{20}$$

where Z_t is an exogenous variable.

This rule merits some discussion. First, if $\omega = 1$, it is the same rule as before: OPEC sets a target real price r_t for each period. At the other extreme, if $\omega = 0$, then OPEC's *nominal* price R_t becomes exogenous, and monetary policy can—in principle—push the real price as low as it wants. Intermediate cases with $0 < \omega < 1$ imply partial adjustment of the nominal OPEC price to anticipated inflation. Let us provide a rationale for such partial adjustment.

It is critical to note that the country being modeled here is the United States and that OPEC fixes the price of oil in U.S. dollars. OPEC presumably cares about the *purchasing power* of the nominal price it sets, but not in terms of U.S. prices only. If OPEC directs a fraction ω of its purchases to U.S. goods and a fraction $(1-\omega)$ to other countries, then (20) implies no irrationality if Z_t is the expected price level of the rest of the world (converted to U.S. dollars), for then $\omega_{t-1}\hat{P}_t + (1-\omega)Z_t$ is the price index OPEC expects to pay. The question then becomes: Under that condition can Z_t be independent of the U.S. price level?

In the first place, it matters very much whether we are talking about the policy response of the United States *acting alone* or of the whole non-OPEC world *acting in unison*. If all countries follow a cooperative policy of accommodating OPEC and raise their money supplies together, Z_t will probably rise proportionately with P_t, and we are back to the case $\omega = 1$. So long as OPEC anticipates this policy response, the policy will be self-defeating. Personally, however, I find this scenario of coordinated monetary expansion somewhat fanciful. Can anyone imagine the Germans going along?

So consider next the case where *only* the United States raises its money supply in response to a higher nominal price of oil. The price levels in foreign countries (measured in their own currencies) ought then to be mostly unaffected by the U.S. money supply, but the exchange value of the dollar should depreciate. In fact, if purchasing power parity held in the short run, then the exchange rate would move point for point with the inflation differential between the United States and the rest of the world, so that Z_t would again become proportional to P_t. However, I think we may safely assume that purchasing power parity does *not* hold in the very short run. In this case, the fraction ω in (20) can reasonably be expected to be less than unity.

To summarize this discussion, the parameter ω in (20) reflects two factors: the extent to which other countries follow suit in pursuing an accommodating monetary policy, and the extent to which purchasing power parity holds. For short-run analysis it seems likely that both of these will be quite incomplete, so ω will be substantially below unity.

To develop a better understanding of the workings of the model, I will deal separately with two extreme cases: $\omega = 1$ and $\omega = 0$. The analysis with (20) clearly is a blend of these two extremes.

The case $\omega = 1$ lies behind rational expectations analyses of the OPEC shock which tacitly assume that OPEC in effect changes the *real* price of oil. In this case the solutions for the anticipated price level, unanticipated inflation, and output under the same monetary rule as before [Eq. (14)] are:

$$ {}_{t-1}P_t = \frac{b+\delta-c}{1-b}\, {}_{t-1}r_t, \tag{21} $$

$$ P_t - {}_{t-1}P_t = \left(\frac{\beta+\delta-c}{1+\alpha-c-\beta} \right)(r_t - {}_{t-1}r_t) + \eta_t, \tag{22} $$

where $\eta_t = (v_t - e_t)/(1 + \alpha - c)$.

$$ y_t = (k_t - \delta_{t-1}r_t) + \left[\frac{(\alpha-\delta)(\beta+\delta-c)}{1+\alpha-c-\beta} - \delta \right](r_t - {}_{t-1}r_t) + u_t, \tag{23} $$

where u_t is a composite error term.

These equations make several points quite obvious. First, a policy of trying to offset anticipated OPEC price hikes completely through money creation ($b = 1$) is not viable. It leads to an indeterminate price level because OPEC fully anticipates the policy. Second, and more importantly, there is no reason in this model to accommodate such a shock at all. In fact, since positive values of b yield no output gains [see (23)], but cause anticipated inflation [see (21)], b should be *negative* if there is any cost at all of anticipated inflation. More specifically, setting $b = c - \delta$ (which I have assumed to be negative) would appear optimal in this model, just as the expectationists have claimed.

Interestingly, however, the case for accommodating an *unanticipated* OPEC shock remains much the same as it was in the sticky-wage model. A positive value of β will exacerbate the inflationary consequences of an unanticipated OPEC price hike [see (22)], but will mitigate the output reducing effects [see (23)]. The optimal policy depends, as always, on the relative social costs of output losses versus unanticipated inflation.

Why does a case for activist monetary policy appear in this model, whereas none exists in the standard Lucas model (the case $\delta = c = 0$)? The reason is pretty clear. *By hypothesis*, OPEC introduces a disturbance which is recognized *contemporaneously* by the monetary authority.[16] Since R_t pushes P_t up, this additional information gives the authority some ability to react to the contemporaneous price-level disturbance—the right-hand side of (22). This is an ability the central bank would use even in the Lucas model without OPEC—if only it could.

I now turn to the opposite extreme case, where R_t is an exogenous variable. I should emphasize that this does not mean that R_t is fixed for long periods of time in nominal terms, but only that R_t does not react *contemporaneously* to either P_t or its expectation. Under the same monetary rule as before, the model (18)–(20) with $\omega = 0$ produces the following solutions:

$$_{t-1}P_t = \frac{b + \delta - c}{1 + \delta - c}\, {}_{t-1}R_t, \tag{24}$$

$$P_t - {}_{t-1}P_t = \left(\frac{\beta + \delta - c}{1 + \alpha - c} \right)(R_t - {}_{t-1}R_t) + \eta_t, \tag{25}$$

$$y_t = k_t - \frac{\delta(1 - b)}{1 + \delta - c}\, {}_{t-1}R_t + \left[\frac{\alpha(\beta + \delta - c)}{1 + \alpha - c} - \delta \right](R_t - {}_{t-1}R_t) + u_t. \tag{26}$$

The dimensions of the policy problem with respect to *unanticipated* OPEC

[16] And also by everyone else. There is no issue of informational asymmetry here.

shocks are exactly as they were in the previous case (with $\omega = 1$), except that OPEC is now characterized by its nominal price, rather than its real price. Nothing further need be said about this.

The situation with respect to *anticipated* OPEC shocks is, however, quite different. Clearly, (24) says once again that any monetary accommodation of an OPEC hike will be inflationary. However, (26) now says that such a policy will, in effect, raise the natural rate of output,

$$k_t - \delta\left(\frac{1-b}{1+\delta-c}\right)_{t-1}R_t.$$

There is, then, an output–inflation trade-off for accommodating an anticipated OPEC shock when $\omega = 0$.

This trade-off, of course, is only a short-run phenomenon. OPEC's price cannot be independent of the U.S. price level in the long run because (24) implies that the real price OPEC expects to receive from its sales to the United States is

$${}_{t-1}R_t - {}_{t-1}P_t = \frac{1-b}{1+\delta-c}\,{}_{t-1}R_t,$$

which is lower the higher is b. Furthermore, the factors I used to rationalize $\omega < 1$ cannot be expected to persist in the long run. Nonetheless, macroeconomists should not have to be reminded that the short run also matters.

(3) Dimensions of the Future Disaster Argument

Let me review briefly what has been done in this section so far. I have considered three rational expectations models of an OPEC shock, and in each of them considered the advisability of an accommodating monetary rule of the form (14). The three models all used the same simple specification of aggregate demand, but differed in their specification of aggregate supply. The models were as follows.

Model 1 (sticky wages):

$$y_t = k_t + \alpha_1(P_t - {}_{t-1}P_t) + \alpha_2(P_t - {}_{t-2}P_t) - \delta(R_t - P_t) + e_t, \quad (8)$$

$$R_t = {}_{t-1}\hat{P}_t + r_t \quad (r_t \text{ exogenous}). \quad (7)$$

Model 2 (extended Lucas model):

$$y_t = k_t + \alpha(P_t - {}_{t-1}P_t) - \delta(R_t - {}_{t-1}P_t) + e_t, \quad (18)$$

$$R_t = {}_{t-1}\hat{P}_t + r_t \quad (r_t \text{ exogenous}). \quad (7)$$

Model 3 (nominal OPEC price):

$$y_t = k_t + \alpha(P_t - {}_{t-1}P_t) - \delta(R_t - {}_{t-1}P_t) + e_t \quad (R_t \text{ exogenous}). \quad (18)$$

In each case, an output–inflation trade-off appeared when responses to *unanticipated* OPEC price hikes were considered. In models 1 and 3, there was also such a trade-off with respect to *anticipated* OPEC price increases.

In the inelegant terminology introduced at the start of Section 4, this analysis pertains only to the present disaster argument—that the short-run output–inflation trade-off is really much worse than standard Keynesian models suggest. Nothing has been said so far about the more elusive future disaster arguments. Let me close this part with some brief remarks on this subject.

In the context of model 1 (the sticky-wage model), the natural way for the future disaster argument to enter the picture would be to drop the assumption that each time the market for labor contracts opens, the result of the bargaining is a fixed real wage. We might assume instead that the real wage expected in period $t-i$ for period t would be a decreasing function of ${}_{t-i}r_t$. It seems clear that such a feature of the labor contract would lessen the severity of OPEC shocks, since part of the adjustment problem is getting real wages down. The issue then would be: Would an accommodating monetary policy reduce the sensitivity of expected real wages to OPEC's expected real price? I hope to explore this possibility further in future work.

In the context of models 2 and 3, two aspects of the future disaster argument seem to arise. Most obviously, the behavior of the central bank may help determine whether OPEC acts as assumed in model 2 or as assumed in model 3. Specifically, once it becomes known (or suspected) that the Federal Reserve will aggressively accommodate any nominal OPEC shock (that is, b will be high), OPEC may decide to abandon its nominal pricing policy and try to establish a real price instead. In this case, a policy of accommodating an anticipated OPEC price increase might reap some gains at first (under model 3) but leave us with the more vexing model 2 in the long run. This would undercut, but not necessarily eliminate, the case for accommodation.

Second, it was noted in Section 4.D.2 that an activist monetary response to unanticipated OPEC price changes is advisable because of the informational content of R_t as a predictor of the price level. This informational content, however, depends critically on the correlation between R_t and P_t, and this correlation, in turn, depends in a fundamental way on the policy rule being followed. This, of course, is just another instance of Lucas' (1976) econometric policy critique: it suggests that the parameters of the aggregate supply function (18) might not be invariant to the policy rule.

This possibility is explored in the Appendix, where the following is established. Under the class of monetary rules considered here [Eq. (14)], α

in Eq. (18) *is* structural; that is, it does not depend on the policy rule. But the parameter δ *is not* structural, and we would expect it to rise as policy becomes more accommodating toward unanticipated shocks (that is, as β rises). Since the inherent difficulties caused by OPEC shocks depend directly on the size of the parameter δ, the future disaster argument again undercuts the case for accommodation. How important this problem is quantitatively is, of course, another question entirely. It is also worth noting that δ does not depend on the choice of b—the way policy responds to an *anticipated* OPEC shock—because this response does not affect the correlation between unanticipated R_t and unanticipated P_t. So the parameter-change problem is less devastating under model 3 than under model 2.

5. Implications for Macroeconomic Theory and Policy

It has often been said that the events of the 1970s discredited both Keynesian theory and the practical manifestation of that theory in econometric models, and that, consequently, the policy advice given by Keynesian economists is no longer to be trusted. This section might aptly be subtitled "Keynes lives!" for I want to argue instead that the Keynesian paradigm held up very well during the 1970s, while it was monetarism and the rational expectations approach to macroeconomics that were dealt heavy blows by the force of real events.

A. Keynesian Theory

There seem to be two main reasons why the 1970s are thought to have been destructive of Keynesian doctrine. First, it has been said that Keynesian theory cannot explain the coexistence of high (or rising) inflation and low (or declining) levels of economic activity. But I began this essay by outlining a perfectly coherent (if oversimplified) theory of stagflation along Keynesian lines, and then showed that—at least in its broad outlines—the data conform to the picture suggested by the theory. So we can dismiss this charge out of hand.

Second, it has been pointed out that Keynesians in the early 1970s held an overly optimistic view of the Phillips curve trade-off—a view that was questioned on theoretical grounds by Friedman (1968) and Phelps (1968) and subsequently proven wrong by events. This charge is certainly correct.

The prevailing view among Keynesians as of, say, 1970, was that, despite the very cogent theoretical arguments of Friedman and Phelps, the long-run Phillips curve was indeed negatively sloped—a view that now seems hopelessly naive. It is, however, worth recalling how things appeared then. Empirically estimated Phillips curves did indeed display long-run negative slopes, so economists had to choose between a neat theoretical argument that the long-run Phillips curve *had to be* vertical and seemingly strong empirical evidence that it *was in fact* negatively sloped. Keynesians tended to be more impressed by the empirical evidence which, in this case, put them on the wrong side of the issue.[17]

A more fundamental point is this. Only extreme mental gymnastics can equate Keynesian theory with a negatively sloped long-run Phillips curve. Mainstream Keynesianism today incorporates a Phillips curve which, while negatively sloped in the short run, is approximately vertical in the long run. Just as the postwar disaster in forecasting consumption led Keynesians to abandon the *simpliste* consumption function in favor of newer models invented by Friedman (1957) and Modigliani and Brumberg (1954), so the 1970s disaster in forecasting inflation led to an improved Phillips curve, without in any way overthrowing basic Keynesian ideas.[18]

B. Monetarism

The verdict on monetarism seems less auspicious. Let me distinguish between *positive* monetarism and *normative* monetarism.

At least where inflation is concerned, the cutting edge of positive monetarism must be the assertion that "inflation is (almost?) always and (almost?) everywhere a monetary phenomenon." From this perspective, the events of the 1970s were mostly bad news for monetarists. The big burst of inflation in 1973 and 1974, I have argued, cannot in any way be explained by money.[19]

[17] A clear statement of the uneasy state of affairs as then perceived can be found in Solow (1970). Subsequent work by Gordon (1972) and Eckstein and Brinner (1972) reconciled the natural rate theory with the empirical evidence.

[18] Lest I sound too much like a Pollyanna, I should state that there are plenty of empirical problems for which Keynesian economists lack good answers at present. Macroeconometrics has not yet succeeded in recovering God's model. My point is simply that none of these puzzles seems to call for jettisoning the basic theoretical structure—at least not yet.

[19] Nor, by the way, can the terrible recession be explained by money—unless you adopt the accommodationist attitude and blame the recession on the Federal Reserve's refusal to accommodate the supply shocks.

Normative monetarism—with its stress on constant monetary growth—did not fare much better. It is striking that the growth rate of money from 1973 : 1 to 1974 : 4—precisely the period in which everything was deteriorating—was as constant as it has ever been for an extended period (see Table 7). While no doubt more variable than Friedman would have liked, these growth rates are far less variable than those that prevailed during the preceding seven quarters (while the economy boomed) or the following seven quarters (while the economy recovered).

On balance, it seems to me that the great stagflation did about as much good for monetarism as the great depression did for Say's law.

TABLE 7

MONEY GROWTH RATES AND THEIR VARIABILITY

Period	Average quarterly growth rate[a]	Highest	Lowest	Standard deviation
1971 : 2 to 1973 : 1	7.4	9.4	2.8	2.1
1973 : 1 to 1974 : 4	5.2	7.6	4.0	1.1
1974 : 4 to 1976 : 3	4.8	7.5	2.0	1.8

[a] Seasonally adjusted annual rates in percentage points.

C. RATIONAL EXPECTATIONS

Lately, the main battle among macroeconomic theorists has shifted away from traditional monetarist–Keynesian lines. Lines are currently drawn between those who argue from rational expectations to the impotence of systematic monetary policy and those who oppose this view. How have events treated the adherents to the rational expectations approach to macrotheory?[20]

First, the essence of this theory is that departures of actual from potential output are primarily due to misperceptions caused by unanticipated inflation—an idea neatly captured by the Lucas supply function. While persistent deviations of output from potential are possible within this framework,[21] the fact that it took the U.S. economy two or three years

[20] I stress that what is at issue here is not whether expectations are formed rationally but whether this expectations-formation mechanism robs systematic monetary policy of its real effects.

[21] See, for example, Lucas (1975), Taylor (1980), and Blinder and Fischer (1979).

to get back to something approximating full employment seems anomalous from this point of view.

Second, it is hard to see when and how we experienced enough unanticipated *deflation* to cause such a deep recession. The inflation rate did, of course, drop sharply in the winter of 1974–1975, but by then the recession had been in progress for some time. More importantly, it seems that agents with rational expectations should have perceived the one-shot nature of the inflationary surge of 1974 and hence should have expected inflation to decline. Could unanticipated money have been the culprit? The Barro–Rush quarterly estimates show small negative values of DMR in 1974 : 3, 1974 : 4, and 1975 : 1 (respectively, -0.005, -0.002, and -0.010), but these can hardly account for such a severe recession. In fact, Barro and Rush's output equation predicts virtually no change in $\log y$ for 1974 : 4 (in fact, it fell by 0.014) and a very small decline (-0.002) in 1975 : 1 (in fact, the change was -0.023).

Third, since it is not the rationality of expectations that gives the new classical models their anti-Keynesian implications, but rather the instant flexibility of prices, it seems fair to ask how the relative price shocks of 1973–1974 could have led to so much inflation and to such a deep recession if the world behaved like these models.

Finally, as I argue at length in my book (Blinder, 1979, Chaps. 7 and 8), both monetary and fiscal policy in 1974 approximately followed the nonaccommodative policies that are suggested by rational expectations models. Yet the results seem quite different from what these models led us to expect.

In sum, events of the 1970s seem to have dealt devastating blows to any model in which expectational errors are the chief cause of economic fluctuations and prices are perfectly flexible. The manner in which expectations are modeled is mostly beside the point.

Appendix: Microeconomics of the Augmented Lucas Model

Assume that all oil is imported, and follow Lucas (1973) in assuming that there are a large number of domestic competitive firms, indexed by a continuous variable z, producing in isolated markets and selling their outputs at prices $P_t(z)$. The absolute price of each product differs from the absolute price level P_t according to some relative price shock Z_t. Letting lower case symbols denote natural logs of upper case symbols, Lucas writes $p_t(z) = p_t + z_t$, where z_t is assumed to have mean 0 and variance σ_z^2.

The firm at location z makes an estimate of the (unknown) price level $E_z(p_t)$, given the information available to it, and produces output as an increasing function of its own estimate of its own relative price, viz.,

$$x_t(z) = a[p_t(z) - E_z(p_t)], \qquad a > 0, \tag{A1}$$

where x is the deviation of output from trend. To allow OPEC into the picture, I add the notion that output is a decreasing function of the perceived relative price of oil:

$$x_t(z) = a[p_t(z) - E_z(p_t)] - d[R_t - E_z(p_t)], \qquad d > 0, \tag{A2}$$

where R_t is the log of the *nominal* price of energy—a random variable with known probability distribution. I assume that firms observe the absolute price of energy *before* they make production decisions.

The inference problem considered by Lucas is dealt with slightly differently here, but with very similar results. Firm z has *three* pieces of data to use in forming its (rational) expectation of the current price level: $p_t(z)$ (its own price), R_t (the price of oil), and ${}_{t-1}p_t$ (the mean of the distribution of p_t before $p_t(z)$ is known). It seeks an unbiased and efficient estimator of the form

$$E_z(p_t) = \theta_1 p_t(z) + \theta_2 R_t + \theta_3\, {}_{t-1}p_t, \qquad \theta_1 + \theta_2 + \theta_3 = 1. \tag{A3}$$

As we know from Lucas, the parameters θ_1, θ_2, and θ_3 depend on the variances of the relative price shock z, the absolute price level p, the OPEC price R. The major new wrinkle here, as noted in the text, is that the covariance between p and R becomes relevant to the θs, which thus *do* depend on the policy rule.

To see this, consider the problem of selecting the weights θ_1, θ_2, θ_3 to minimize the mean-squared prediction error $M \equiv E[p_t - E_z(p_t)]^2$. If any deterministic trend in R_t relative to p_t is removed, then all unbiased estimators will have $\theta_1 + \theta_2 + \theta_3 = 1$ since the expectation of the right-hand side of (A3), given the information available at time $t-1$, is

$$\begin{aligned}
&\theta_1({}_{t-1}p_t + {}_{t-1}z_t) + \theta_2\, {}_{t-1}R_t + \theta_3\, {}_{t-1}p_t \\
&\quad = (\theta_1 + \theta_2 + \theta_3)\, {}_{t-1}p_t \qquad \text{if} \quad {}_{t-1}R_t = {}_{t-1}p_t.
\end{aligned}$$

Restricting ourselves to unbiased estimators, then, the prediction error is

$$\begin{aligned}
p_t - E_z(p_t) &= p_t - \theta_1 p_t(z) - \theta_2 R_t - \theta_3\, {}_{t-1}p_t \\
&= (1 - \theta_1) p_t - \theta_1 z_t - \theta_2 R_t - \theta_3\, {}_{t-1}p_t \\
&= -\theta_1 z_t - \theta_2(R_t - p_t) - \theta_3\, {}_{t-1}p_t + \theta_3 p_t \\
&= -\theta_1 z_t + \theta_3(p_t - {}_{t-1}p_t) - \theta_2[(R_t - {}_{t-1}R_t) - (p_t - {}_{t-1}p_t)],
\end{aligned}$$

since $\theta_1 + \theta_2 + \theta_3 = 1$ and ${}_{t-1}R_t = {}_{t-1}p_t$. Thus

$$M = \theta_1^2\sigma_z^2 + \theta_2^2(\sigma_R^2 + \sigma_P^2 - 2\sigma_{RP}) + \theta_3^2\sigma_P^2 - 2\theta_3\theta_2\sigma_{RP} + 2\theta_3\theta_2\sigma_P^2,$$

where $\sigma_p^2 = E(p_t - {}_{t-1}p_t)^2$ and $\sigma_{RP} = E(R_t - {}_{t-1}R_t)(p_t - {}_{t-1}p_t)$. Minimizing this with respect to θ_1 and θ_3 (noting that $\theta_2 = 1 - \theta_1 - \theta_3$) gives

$$\partial M/\partial\theta_1 = 2\theta_1\sigma_z^2 - 2\theta_2(\sigma_R^2 + \sigma_P^2 - 2\sigma_{RP}) + 2\theta_3\sigma_{RP} - 2\theta_3\sigma_P^2 = 0,$$

$$\partial M/\partial\theta_3 = 2\theta_3\sigma_P^2 - 2\theta_2(\sigma_R^2 + \sigma_P^2 - 2\sigma_{RP}) + 2(\sigma_P^2 - \sigma_{RP})(\theta_2 - \theta_3) = 0.$$

Eliminating θ_2 gives

$$\theta_1(\sigma_z^2 + \sigma_R^2 + \sigma_P^2 - 2\sigma_{RP}) + \theta_3(\sigma_R^2 - \sigma_{RP}) = \sigma_R^2 + \sigma_P^2 - 2\sigma_{RP},$$

$$\theta_1(\sigma_R^2 - \sigma_{RP}) + \theta_3\sigma_R^2 = \sigma_R^2 - \sigma_{RP}.$$

Solving for θ_1 and θ_3 leads to

$$\theta_1 = (\sigma_R^2\sigma_P^2 - \sigma_{RP}^2)/\Delta, \tag{A4}$$

$$\theta_3 = \sigma_z^2(\sigma_R^2 - \sigma_{RP})/\Delta, \tag{A5}$$

so that

$$\theta_2 = 1 - \theta_1 - \theta_3 = \sigma_z^2\sigma_{RP}/\Delta, \tag{A6}$$

where $\Delta \equiv \sigma_R^2\sigma_z^2 + \sigma_R^2\sigma_P^2 - \sigma_{RP}^2$. By substituting (A4)–(A6) into (A3) and (A3) into (A2) and simplifying, we obtain the supply function for firm z:

$$x_t(z) = [a + (d - a)\theta_1][p_t(z) - {}_{t-1}p_t] - [d + (a - d)\theta_2](R_t - {}_{t-1}p_t),$$

which, following Lucas, aggregates to

$$X_t = \alpha(p_t - {}_{t-1}p_t) - \delta(R_t - {}_{t-1}p_t), \tag{A7}$$

where

$$\alpha \equiv a + (d - a)\theta_1, \tag{A8}$$

$$\delta \equiv d + (a - d)\theta_2. \tag{A9}$$

This is Eq. (18). [If R is irrelevant to predicting the price level ($\sigma_{RP} = 0$), these formulas reduce to Lucas' results.]

It follows from (22) that

$$\sigma_P^2 = \left(\frac{\beta + \delta - c}{1 + \alpha - c - \beta}\right)^2 \sigma_R^2 + \sigma_\eta^2, \qquad \sigma_{RP} = \left(\frac{\beta + \delta - c}{1 + \alpha - c - \beta}\right)\sigma_R^2.$$

Thus, using (A4) and (A6), (A8) and (A9) can be written

$$\alpha = \left[\frac{\sigma_\eta^2}{\sigma_z^2 + \sigma_\eta^2}\right] d + \left[\frac{\sigma_z^2}{\sigma_z^2 + \sigma_\eta^2}\right] a, \tag{A10}$$

$$\delta = d + (a - d)\frac{\delta + \beta - c}{1 + \alpha - c}\,\frac{\sigma_z^2}{\sigma_z^2 + \sigma_\eta^2}. \tag{A11}$$

From (A10) it follows that α *is* structural: It does *not* depend on the policy rule. From (A11) it follows that δ *does* depend on the policy rule. In particular, δ is an increasing function of β, so that more accommodation of unanticipated OPEC shocks increases the economy's sensitivity to these shocks.

REFERENCES

Ando, Albert, and Palash, Carl (1976). Some Stabilization Problems of 1971–75, with an Application of Optimal Control Algorithms. In *Frontiers of Quantitative Economics* (M. Intriligator, ed.), Vol. 3, pp. 385–421. North-Holland Publ., Amsterdam.

Barro, Robert J. (1977). Unanticipated Money Growth and Unemployment in the United States. *American Economic Review* **67**(2), 101–115.

Barro, Robert J. (1978). Unanticipated Money, Output, and the Price Level in the United States. *Journal of Political Economy* **86** (4), 549–580.

Barro, Robert J., and Rush, Mark (1980). Unanticipated Money and Economic Activity. In *Rational Expectations and Economic Policy* (Stanley Fischer, ed.). pp. 23–48. University of Chicago Press, Chicago, Illinois.

Blinder, Alan S. (1979). *Economic Policy and the Great Stagflation.* Academic Press, New York.

Blinder, Alan S., and Fischer, Stanley (1979). Inventories, Rational Expectations, and the Business Cycle. NBER Working Paper No. 381, August.

Blinder, Alan S., and Goldfeld, Stephen M. (1976). New Measures of Fiscal and Monetary Policy, 1958–73. *American Economic Review* **66**, 780–796.

Blinder, Alan S., and Newton, William J. (1979). The 1971–1974 Controls Program and the Price Level: An Econometric Post-Mortem. NBER Working Paper No. 279, September.

Eckstein, Otto (1978). *The Great Recession*. North-Holland Publ., Amsterdam.

Eckstein, Otto, and Brinner, Roger (1972). *The Inflation Process in the United States* (Study for the Joint Economic Committee, 92nd Congress, 2nd Session). U.S. Government Printing Office, Washington, D.C.

Fischer, Stanley (1977). Long-Term Contracts, Rational Expectations, and the Optimal Money Supply Rule. *Journal of Political Economy* **85** (1), 191–205.

Friedman, Milton (1968). The Role of Monetary Policy. *American Economic Review* **58** (Mar.), 1–17.

Friedman, Milton (1957). *A Theory of the Consumption Function*. Princeton University Press, Princeton, New Jersey.

Gordon, Robert J. (1972). Wage–Price Controls and the Shifting Phillips Curve. *Brookings Papers on Economic Activity* **1972** (2), 385–421.

Gordon, Robert J. (1975). Alternative Responses of Policy to External Supply Shocks. *Brookings Papers on Economic Activity* **1975** (1), 183–204.

Kenen, Peter B., and associates (1978). *A Model of the U.S. Balance of Payments*. Heath, Lexington, Massachusetts.

Lucas, Robert E., Jr. (1973). Some International Evidence on Output-Inflation Trade-Offs. *American Economic Review* **63** (3), 326–334.

Lucas, Robert E., Jr. (1975). An Equilibrium Model of the Business Cycle. *Journal of Political Economy* **83** (6), 1113–1144.

Lucas, Robert E., Jr. (1976). Economic Policy Evaluation: A Critique. In *The Phillips Curve and Labor Markets* (K. Brunner and A. H. Meltzer, eds.), pp. 19–46. Carnegie–Rochester Conference Series, North-Holland Publ., Amsterdam.

Modigliani, Franco, and Brumberg, Richard (1954). Utility Analysis and the Consumption Function: An Interpretation of Cross-Section Data. In *Post-Keynesian Economics* (K. K. Kurihara, ed.), pp. 71–104. Rutgers University Press, New Brunswick, New Jersey.

Perry, George L. (1975a). The United States. In *Higher Oil Prices and the World Economy* (E. R. Fried and C. L. Schultze, eds.), pp. 71–104. Brookings Institution, Washington, D.C.

Perry, George L. (1975b). Policy Alternatives for 1974. *Brookings Papers on Economic Activity* **1975** (1), 222–235.

Phelps, Edmund S. (1968). Money-Wage Dynamics and Labor-Market Equilibrium. *Journal of Political Economy* **76**, 678–711.

Phelps, Edmund S. (1978). Commodity-Supply Shock and Full-Employment Monetary Policy. *Journal of Money, Credit and Banking* **10** (2), 206–221.

Phelps, Edmund S., and Taylor, John B. (1977). Stabilizing Powers of Monetary Policy Under Rational Expectations. *Journal of Political Economy* **85** (1), 163–190.

Pierce, James L., and Enzler, Jared J. (1974). The Effects of External Inflationary Shocks. *Brookings Papers on Economic Activity* **1974** (1), 13–54.

Solow, Robert M. (1970). *Price Expectations and the Behaviour of the Price Level.* Manchester University Press, Manchester, England.

Tatom, John A. (1978). Does the Stage of the Business Cycle Affect the Inflation Rate? *Federal Reserve Bank of St. Louis Review* **60** (9), 7–15.

Taylor, John B. (1980). Aggregate Dynamics and Staggered Contracts. *Journal of Political Economy* **88** (1), 1–23.

DEPARTMENT OF ECONOMICS
PRINCETON UNIVERSITY
PRINCETON, NEW JERSEY

Stagflationary Effects of Monetarist Stabilization Policies in Economies with Persistent Inflation

DOMINGO F. CAVALLO

1. Introduction

It is generally accepted that the credit conditions of an economy affect the process of capital accumulation and therefore the long-run aggregate supply of commodities. Monetarists would agree with the statement insofar as it refers to credit conditions which reflect the saving behavior and the productivity characteristics of the economy. They would probably dismiss the possibility that credit affects the long-run aggregate supply of commodities through transitory changes in the credit conditions caused by discretionary monetary and fiscal policy (Friedman, 1968). Keynesians would accept even this possibility (Tobin, 1972). But in discussing the short-run effect of changes in credit conditions, both would surely concentrate on the links between aggregate demand commodities and the interest rate and/or the quantity of money.[1]

Recent literature on the natural rate of unemployment has considered short-run aggregate supply effects.[2] It is argued that in the short run, aggregate supply may respond to changes in the general price level (or its

[1] For a very good synthesis of what could be considered one of the most accepted views about the linkages between real and monetary phenomena in the developed western economies see Modigliani (1963) and Ando (1974). For a similar synthesis referred to Latin American economies see Arnaudo (1972, Chap. 9).

[2] See Lucas (1972, 1973). For a very careful econometric application see also Fernandez (1977).

ISBN 0-12-259750-8

rate of change) as suppliers are unable to distinguish between changes in the relative price of their goods and changes in the general level of prices. In any case, if real income and price level change, it will be because aggregate demand has shifted, whether because of changes in credit conditions or for any other reason. There are also frequent references to aggregate supply changes due to "shocks," such as sudden increases in import prices or wages, or crop failures [see, for example, Gordon, (1973) and Solow (1975)]. Theoretical references to aggregate supply changes due to changes in credit conditions are rather more rare.[3]

This paper analyzes how credit conditions affect the short-run aggregate supply of commodities. It is argued that this may explain why the application of monetarist stabilization policies to economies with persistent inflation often produces "stagflationary" initial results.

In the past three decades this phenomenon has been observed in several Latin American countries. Characteristically, economic agents in these countries have deeply rooted expectations of high and volatile rates of price changes. At any time there are some nominal prices (typically factor prices) that are being revised upward, generally by some sort of institutional mechanism, to restore their relative position. These adjustments, together with the previous history of inflation, feed inflationary expectations for subsequent periods. These phenomena do not seem to be deterred significantly by such forces as the behavior of other variables, and the pattern seems extremely persistent. We refer to this kind of chronic economic problem as *persistent inflation.*

While wages and price controls may reduce inflation in the short run, the positive effects do not endure. However, monetary restrictions, generally considered capable of lowering inflation in the long run, have strong perverse effects in the short run, especially in the absence of fiscal restrictions, wage controls, or price controls. These perverse effects consist of a fall in real output and sometimes an acceleration of inflation.

This initial stagflation greatly reduces the social acceptability of stabilization plans based on monetary restrictions. During the period in which real growth declines while inflation continues at its previous rate or even accelerates, the government faces strong opposition to its restrictive policy and may be forced to abandon it before the (presumably positive) "second-run" effects can begin. This study is devoted to identifying the economic mechanism behind the effects of monetary restriction in the hope that this will permit the design of better stabilization plans. The Argentine economy will be our case study.

[3] Some exceptions are Maynard and Van Rijckeghem (1968), Morley (1971), Baez (1975), Reca (1969), and Almonacid and Pastore (1975). All use the quantity of credit in real terms as an argument of the short-run supply of commodities.

While one of the aims of this paper is to analyze a phenomenon that was particularly important for the Argentine economy in recent decades, the main objective is more ambitious: to show that the kind of financial influence on the nonfinancial economy discussed in this paper is not the result of institutional arrangements specific to the Argentine economy, but has a rather general theoretical basis that may make it relevant for other economies plagued by inflation.

Section 2 presents the theoretical underpinning. The characteristics of the Argentine economy relevant to the level of aggregation and the variables chosen are presented in Section 3. Next we consider the basic structure of the econometric model and discuss the main assumptions, especially those related to how economic agents form their expectations on the future course of inflation (Section 4). Finally, we apply the model and interpret the results.

The main hypothesis should ideally be tested using a macro econometric model of greater complexity, but limited resources prevent this. The present approach considers the market for manufactured commodities only and does not analyze how future factor prices respond to current and past monetary and fiscal policies. Nevertheless, it strongly suggests that the perverse effects of monetarist stabilization may be explained by the way in which commodity supply responds to credit conditions in the short run.

2. Theoretical Discussion

The model is based on an aggregate supply equation that captures the effects of changes in credit conditions. It assumes an imaginary economy resembling in almost all respects that of microeconomics textbooks, the only difference being the introduction of working capital by assuming a time lag between paying for inputs and receiving payment for outputs.

There are two factors of production: fixed capital, assumed given in the short run; and labor, which is assumed variable. The technology is described by a constant-returns-to-scale Cobb–Douglas function. The firm is a price taker in every market, and its objective is to maximize the expected utility of profits. Wages are paid a fraction u of a period before payment for output is received. When the firm chooses its level of production, it knows with certainty the wage rate, the nominal rate of interest, and the spot price of output. The rate of sale price inflation is a normally distributed random variable. The firm's utility function displays constant relative risk aversion. Under these assumptions the firm's short-run output can be derived as follows:

$$V = P_{t-u}\exp(u\pi_t)Q_t - W_{t-u}\exp(ur_t)L_t, \tag{1}$$

$$U[V(\pi_t)] = \frac{1}{n!}\sum_{n=0}^{\infty} U^n[uP_{t-u}\exp(u\pi_t^e)Q_t]^n(\pi_t - \pi_t^e)^n, \tag{2}$$

where $U^n = (d^nU/dV^n)\,|\,\pi_t = \pi_t^e$.

$$E(U(V)) = \sum_{n=0}^{\infty} \frac{1}{2^n n!} U^{2n}\left[uP_{t-u}\exp(u\pi_t^e)Q_t^{2n}\right]\sigma_{\pi_t}^{2n}, \tag{3}$$

$$U(V) = \frac{V^{1-\gamma}}{1-\gamma} \tag{4}$$

$$Q_t = (1-a)^{(1-a)/a}K_t \frac{W_{t-u}}{P_{t-u}} \exp[u(r_t - \pi_t^e)]^{(1-a)/a} \times \left(1 - \frac{u\gamma\sigma_{\pi_t}^2}{a}\right)^{(1-a)/a}, \tag{5}$$

where V is excess of sales proceeds over variable cost production, P is price of output, W is wage rate, Q is level of output, L is level of labor input, u is fraction of a period by which payment for inputs precede the sale of output, r is nominal rate of interest, U is utility function, π is rate of inflation of output price, π^e is expected rate of inflation, σ^2 is variance of unexpected inflation, and a is elasticity of output with respect to K, γ is the parameter of utility function.

Equation (1) defines the relevant profits. Looking at utility of profits as a function of the rate of inflation and computing the Taylor expansion around expected inflation, we get (2). Taking expected value on both sides and applying the formulas for the moments of a normal variable, we get (3). Finally, using specification (4) for the utility function, rearranging terms, and using

$$1 - a = \frac{W_{t-u}L_t}{P_{t-u}Q_t} \exp u(r_t - \pi_t^e)$$

as a first approximation, we arrive at the supply equation (5). Inspection of (5) provides the first of our conclusions on the effect of introducing working capital into the model:

1. *Short-run aggregate supply of commodities depends on the real interest rate (defined as the difference between the nominal interest rate and the expected rate of inflation) and on the variance of the unexpected rate of inflation. (Of course, it also depends on the stock of fixed capital and the real costs of the variable factors of production.)*

Next we move to an aggregate model of output and price level determination that includes the previously derived supply equation but in all other aspects involves very conventional assumptions:

$$\log E = \log P^{e} + \log Q^{e} + e_{\rho}(\rho - \bar{\rho}) + e_{m}(\log MS - \log MD'),$$
$$e_{\rho} < 0, \quad e_{m} > 0, \quad (6)$$

$$\log Q = \log K - \frac{1-a}{a}(\log W - \log P) - u\frac{1-a}{a}\rho - \frac{u\gamma(1-a)}{a^{2}}\sigma^{2}_{\pi_{t}}, \quad (7)$$

$$\rho = \bar{\rho} + \theta(\log MD' - \log MS) \qquad \theta > 0, \quad (8)$$

$$\log E = \log P^{e} + \log Q^{e} + (e_{m} - e_{\rho}\theta)(\log MS - \log MD'), \quad (6a)$$

$$\log Q = \log K - \frac{1-a}{a}(\log W_{-u} - \log P_{-u}) + u\frac{1-a}{a}\theta$$
$$\times(\log MS - \log MD') - \frac{u\gamma(1-a)}{a^{2}}\sigma^{2}_{\pi t}, \quad (7a)$$

$$\log W - \log P = \bar{w} + \epsilon(\log Q - \log Q^{e}), \quad (9)$$

where E is total expenditures, ρ is real rate of interest, w is real wage rate, MS is money supply, MD' is money demand evaluated at the long-run equilibrium real interest rate and at a level of expenditures equal to $P^{e}Q^{e}$, and e_{ρ}, e_{m}, θ, and ϵ are parameters. The superscript e means expected; a bar above the letters indicates a long-run equilibrium level. Other symbols have the same meaning as in Eq. 1–5. Equation (7) is the aggregate supply equation that results from taking logs in (5) and disregarding intercepts and terms above the first order. Equation (6) is a nominal expenditure equation that assumes unitary price elasticity of aggregate demand. We assume that expenditure will equal expected nominal income when the real rate of interest is equal to a long-run equilibrium level $\bar{\rho}$ and the money market is in equilibrium. A real rate of interest higher than that long-run level will depress expenditures. A lower real rate of interest will cause expenditures to rise. Further, a positive excess supply of money will increase expenditures while a negative excess supply of money will depress them. The demand for money used to compute monetary disequilibrium is evaluated at the long-run equilibrium level ρ, assuming expected nominal income. We further assume in (8) that the real rate of interest will move away from the long-run level as a consequence of monetary disequilibrium.

Using (8) in substituting for $\rho - \bar{\rho}$ in (6) and (7), we get (6a) and (7a). Equation (6a) tells us that given expectations and a real wage rate, the elasticity of expenditures with respect to the supply of money is $e_{m} - e_{\rho}\theta$, which is greater than zero because e_{ρ} is negative and the other two parameters involved are positive. Equation (7a) says that the elasticity of real output with respect to money supply is $u[(1-a)/a]\theta$, which is also positive. If we further assume that the commodity market clears within the period of the analysis, we can derive two additional conclusions:

2. *If the real wage rate is fixed, and working capital exists* ($u > 0$) *and the real interest rate is affected by monetary policy* ($\theta > 0$), *the rate of growth of output will necessarily decline as a consequence of a restrictive monetary policy. The condition for this is* $u = [(1-a)/a]\theta > 0$, *which is always satisfied under the above conditions.*

3. *With the real wage rate fixed if* $u[(1-a)/a]\theta > e_m - e\theta$, *the restrictive monetary policy will accelerate inflation.*

We next relax the assumption of unchanged real wages and allow the real wage rate to be sensitive to changes in real output according to an elasticity ϵ in Eq. (9). The condition for output to fall as a consequence of a restrictive monetary policy is then $u\{(1-a)/[a+(1-a)\epsilon]\}\theta > 0$; and the conditions for inflation to accelerate is $u\{(1-a)/[a+(1-a)\epsilon]\}\theta > e_m - e_\rho\theta$. The higher the response of real wages to current output (or unemployment), the less likely both conditions become.

3. Adaptation of the Model to the Argentine Economy

In a previous paper (Cavallo, 1977) I discussed some special features of the financial and real sectors of the Argentine economy that can be considered the result of persistent inflation or of institutional arrangements historically associated with it. The general conclusion was that these special features (lack of an active capital market, high debt equity ratios, imperfect credit markets, less competitive commodity markets) cause the aggregate supply of commodities to respond more strongly to changes in credit conditions. More specifically, it was argued that with imperfect credit markets and with the government controlling interest rates on bank loans, the interest rate relevant to production and investment decisions would be the one charged in the free markets where the firms procure their marginal funds, that is, the interest rate that firms take as the marginal cost of credit.

The recorded nominal interest rate charged on bank acceptances turned out to be a poor proxy for the marginal cost of credit. Ther is much evidence that even in the bank acceptance market (supposedly a free market for loans) banks have changed the effective rate charged to borrowers by indirect methods such as compensatory balances, administrative charges, and making the supplementary guarantee of shorter term than the loan, rather than by adjusting nominal rates. There also seems to have been some credit rationing. Unfortunately, records of the *effective* rates charged to borrowers in the bank acceptance markets or of the rates charged in other free markets (such as acceptances by *financieras*, where credit rationing was probably less frequent) are incomplete.

For these reasons the main hypothesis must be tested using aggregate demand and supply equations in which the real rate of interest is replaced by a function of its main argument: the measure of ex ante disequilibrium in the money market. In other words, instead of using adapted versions of (6) and (7), we use adapted versions of (6a) and (7a).

The sectoral structure and institutional arrangements of the Argentine economy imply that the anti-inflationary effects of government macropolicies must first become apparent in the market for manufactured goods and services with freely determined prices. The government's ability to reduce the rate of inflation of labor costs or the prices of agricultural and imported goods, energy, transportation, and gas will show up in the administrative determination of the exchange rate, taxes on exports and imports, prices of public utilities and public enterprise, or on the level of nominal wages. However, the ability to exercise control through pricing policies in specific markets is virtually unrelated to the ability to change fiscal and monetary macropolicies. Prices in the construction sector are not directly set by the government, but because of long-term contracts they tend to follow the price of manufactured goods and nominal wages.

We are especially interested in how monetary policy affects output and prices through commodity supply. Agriculture and manufacturing are the two sectors where one would expect this kind of effect to be relevant. As services usually have a very short production period, working capital is generally unimportant. In the construction industry working capital *is* important, but given the kind of contracts under which construction projects are carried out, output is basically demand determined, and prices move in strict response to some long-run cost formula.

As the development of a complete structural macromodel of the Argentine economy is beyond our present possibilities, the empirical testing of the main hypothesis focuses on what we consider to be the market that plays the most important role as receiver and transmitter of the short-run effects of anti-inflationary monetary policy: the market for manufactured commodities.

For specification and estimation purposes nominal wages, the prices of agricultural and imported goods, and the prices of services, such as energy, transportation, and gas, are assumed to be either predetermined or exogenous policy variables. The same assumption is made regarding the real output of agriculture and construction, and the changes in money supply originating in domestic credit expansion or in government induced inflows or foreign capital. Real output of the service sectors is considered a function of the output of the three commodity sectors. Hence, once the real output of manufacturing is determined, total output follows. These assumptions mean that there are only two endogenous variables to be explained: real output and prices in the manufacturing industry.

4. The Basic Structure of the Econometric Model

Basically, we work with an adapted version of the model presented in (6)–(9) which includes the aggregate demand for and aggregate supply of manufactured goods. Supply and demand for other goods, services, and factors of production are excluded because their prices are considered exogenous. Each commodity is purchased and sold several times before it reaches the final consumer. We have to decide at which stage of the commercialization process to draw the line separating demand from supply. It has often been observed that retail prices follow, with some lag, the behavior of wholesale prices. Moreover, if the wholesale stage is chosen as the object of our analysis, supply can be identified with output, and any change in inventories not strictly proportional to changes in output can be transferred to the demand side. This permits simple statistical differentiation between working capital and surplus or speculative inventories. (A manufacturing firm that chooses to keep some portion of its current production in the form of surplus inventories instead of selling all its production at the market wholesale price will be considered, to the extent of that inventory decision, to be a consumer rather than a supplier in the market for manufactured goods.) The quantity transacted will thus be taken to be equal to current-quarter production of manufactured goods. Therefore, the two endogenous variables we try to explain are current-quarter production of manufactured goods and wholesale prices.

A. Aggregate Demand for Manufactured Goods

The basic econometric model discussed in this section is as follows:

$$\log Q_{\mathrm{ma}}^{\mathrm{d}} = cPDL(\log Y) + c_m PDL(\log MS' - \log MD'), \qquad (10)$$

$$\log p_{\mathrm{ma}} - \log p_{\mathrm{ma}}^{\mathrm{e}} = f(\log Q_{\mathrm{ma}}^{\mathrm{d}} - \log Q_{\mathrm{ma}}), \qquad (11)$$

$$\log p_{\mathrm{ma}} = \log p_{\mathrm{ma}}^{\mathrm{e}} + fc_y PDL(\log Y) + fc_m \times PDL(\log MS' - \log MD') - f \log Q_{\mathrm{ma}} \qquad (12)$$

$$\begin{aligned}\log Q_{\mathrm{ma}} = {} & b_k PDL(\log K) + b_{\mathrm{vf}} PDL\left\{\log\left[\left(W^{0.35} p_{\mathrm{a}}^{0.20} p_{\mathrm{im}}^{0.16} p_{\mathrm{es}}^{0.29}\right)/p_{\mathrm{ma}}\right]\right\} \\ & + b_m PDL(\log MS' - \log MD') + b_\sigma PDL\left(\sigma_\pi^2\right) + b_{\mathrm{bc}} \\ & \times PDL\left\{\log\left[BC/\left(W^{0.35} p_{\mathrm{a}}^{0.20} p_{\mathrm{im}}^{0.16} p_{\mathrm{es}}^{0.29}\right)\right]\right\}, \qquad (13)\end{aligned}$$

$$p_{\mathrm{ma}} = a_\pi \pi^{\mathrm{e}} + a_y PDL(y) + a_m PDL(ms' - md') + a_q q_{\mathrm{ma}}, \qquad (14)$$

$$\begin{aligned} q_{\mathrm{ma}} = {} & b_k PDL(k) + b_{\mathrm{vf}} PDL(p_{\mathrm{vf}} - p_{\mathrm{ma}}) + b_m PDL(ms' - md') \\ & + b_\sigma \cdot PDL\left(D\sigma_\pi^2\right) + b_{\mathrm{bc}} PDL(bc - p_{\mathrm{vf}}), \qquad (15)\end{aligned}$$

where a, b, c, and f are parameters to be estimated; lower-case letters are continuously compounded rates of growth of the variables denominated by the respective capital letters, for example, $q_{\mathrm{ma}} = \log Q_{\mathrm{ma}} - \log Q_{\mathrm{ma}_{-1}}$; *PDL* means polynomial distributed lags. $Q_{\mathrm{ma}}^{\mathrm{d}}$ is the quantity of manufacturing commodities demand. Y is real income in terms of manufacturing prices, computed as

$$Q_{\mathrm{a}} \frac{P_{\mathrm{a}}}{P_{\mathrm{ma}}} + Q_{\mathrm{ma}} + Q_{\mathrm{c}} \frac{P_{\mathrm{c}}}{P_{\mathrm{ma}}} + (Q_{\mathrm{a}} + Q_{\mathrm{ma}} + Q_{\mathrm{c}})0.70 \frac{P_{\mathrm{s}}}{P_{\mathrm{ma}}},$$

where Q_{a}, Q_{ma}, and Q_{c} are agricultural, manufacturing, and construction GDP, respectively, and GDP in the service sectors is estimated as 0.70 times the GDP in the sectors that produce goods. P_{ma}, P_{a}, P_{c}, and P_{s} are price indices for manufacturing, agriculture, construction, and services, respectively. Other terms used are as follows: MS' is money supply in an ex ante sense discussed later, MD' is money demand, discussed in the next section, Q_{ma} is quantity produced by manufacturing industry, K is stock of capital at the beginning of the quarter, obtained by accumulation of investments using a rate of depreciation of 1% per quarter and a benchmark of capital stock for the end of 1960, W is index of nominal wages, P_{im} is index of domestic prices of imported goods, P_{es} is price index for economic services (energy, transportation, and gas), σ_π^2 is variance of predicted inflation, BC is bank credit to manufacturing firms, π^{e} is expected inflation, $P_{\mathrm{ma}}^{\mathrm{e}}$ is index of the expected price of manufactured goods computed as $P_{\mathrm{ma}_{-1}} \exp(\pi^{\mathrm{e}})$, and p_{vf} is rate of change of variable cost of production, computed as $0.35w + 0.20p_{\mathrm{a}} + 0.16P_{\mathrm{im}} + 0.29p_{\mathrm{es}}$.

Aggregate demand for manufactured goods in real terms is assumed to be dependent upon present and past levels of real income and upon the measure of disequilibrium in the money market (10). The distinction between demand for consumption and for investment is dropped for lack of information on the proportions of expenditure on manufactured goods in each category. However, the distributed lag on real income should capture both the dependence of consumption demand upon permanent income and the dependence of investment demand upon current and past levels of output. Monetary disequilibrium is also entered as a distributed lag in order to capture the usually lagged response of investment expenditures (both fixed and in the form of surplus inventories) to credit conditions. Initially, an attempt was made to introduce relative prices for other sectors because of the possibility of substitution effects, but as preliminary regressions showed these effects to be insignificant, relative prices are omitted from (10).

The theory discussed in Section 2 assumed that the commodity market reached equilibrium within each individual period and that the demand for commodities had unitary price elasticity. While these two assumptions greatly simplified the exposition, it seems inconvenient to impose them as a priori restrictions in a quarterly model for an actual economy. We assume instead the price adjustment mechanism of (11) according to which the actual price level differs from the expected price level as a function of the difference between the quantity demanded and the quantity supplied at the expected level of prices. The value of the coefficient is not specified a priori but is subject to estimation.[4]

Combining the demand equation with the price adjustment mechanism we obtain (12), in which the unobservable quantity demanded at the expected price level is replaced by a function of its arguments. Equation (12) is therefore the specification suited for estimation.

Note that the measure of monetary disequilibrium enters into (10) for two reasons. First, monetary disequilibrium can have direct spillover effects on the commodity market. Second, the relevant real rate of interest (which should be an argument of the demand equation) is not observable but is assumed to be a function of current and past monetary disequilibrium.

Equation (14) results from taking first differences in (12). For reasons explained below, this is the version finally used in the estimation.

B. Aggregate Supply of Manufactured Goods

Aggregate supply of manufactured goods is specified as a function of the stock of fixed capital, the cost of the variable factors of production relative to the prices of manufactures, the measure of monetary disequilibrium, the variance of expected inflation, and the total bank credit in terms of variable factor costs as shown in (13). This aggregate supply equation differs from (7) in three main respects. First, the variable factor of production is a composite that includes labor, agricultural and imported goods, and economic services. Second, the real rate of interest is replaced

[4] The assumptions used in Section 2 are equivalent to making f equal to unity.

by a measure of monetary disequilibrium. Third, following other economists (see note 3) real bank credit is introduced as an additional argument. In addition, all arguments are entered as polynomial distributed lags to capture partial adjustments and differences in the length of the production processes of the variety of goods aggregated.

Equation (15) results from taking first differences in (13). Again, this is the version used in the estimation.

C. The Demand for Money and the Measure of Monetary Disequilibrium

Defining money as an aggregate including not only currency and demand deposits but also interest-bearing financial assets is very inappropriate in economies with persistent inflation. In these economies the difference between a demand deposit and a savings or time deposit (or any other interest-bearing financial asset) is measured by nominal interest rates on the order of several times 10%. Furthermore, once interest-bearing financial assets are included in the money aggregate, it becomes very difficult to decide where to stop.

Moreover, as interest rates in Argentina are set by the central government, savings and time deposits have gradually become less important. Thus the balances that have remained since the mid-1950s reflect the behavior of some groups of the population that behave more traditionally than rationally; one should therefore not expect, for our sample period, strong substitution effects between this kind of financial asset and others available in the portions of the financial market where free interest rates prevail. The demand for the more liquid assets, such as currency and demand deposits, is motivated by transactions purposes and undoubtedly has closer connections with the demand for commodities and the supply of and demand for short-term loans in free financial markets. Firms and households whose liquidity levels fall short of the desired level according to the planned level of transactions and the opportunity cost of money will tend to decrease transactions or to demand more loans (if they are net demanders in the loan market) or supply less loans (if they are net suppliers) in order to rebuild their liquidity levels. If situations of liquidity deficit predominate, transactions will be adjusted downward, and the net demand for loans will be increased. The opposite will happen if excess liquidity predominates.[5]

[5] We prefer to describe the relationship between money and the loan and commodity markets in this fashion rather than as a problem of allocation of wealth among alternative assets because in economies with persistent inflation the "speculative" or "asset" motive for holding money tends to disappear.

For these reasons we define money in the most conventional and restrictive sense, that is, including only currency outside the banking system and demand deposits in the commercial banks.

The conventional determinants of the transactions demand for money are expenditures in nominal terms and some measure of the opportunity cost of holding money. For this reason, the real rate of interest and the expected rate of inflation should both enter as arguments. We also want to test the frequently proposed hypothesis that the demand for money depends on the variance of predicted inflation. The main reason for introducing the variance of predicted inflation is that uncertainty about the level of prices may induce higher precautionary balances. Therefore, we should expect this variable to have a positive coefficient. As in the case of the commodity market, we do not want to impose an a priori restriction that monetary equilibrium has to be achieved within the quarter.

D. Expected Inflation

The model formed by (12) and (13), or for that matter (14) and (15), involves three nonobservable variables. One is money demand before the working of the commodity market MD', as discussed in the previous section. The others are expected inflation π^e and the variance of expected inflation σ_π^e. As these enter into the model's three basic equations and into the estimation of money demand, we have to make some assumptions about how economic agents form their expectations.

Before going into details about specification, we must consider a practical issue: What precise price index should expected inflation refer to? In the aggregate demand and supply equations for manufactured goods there is no doubt that it should refer to the wholesale price index for domestic manufactured goods. In the demand for money equations other price aggregates may be relevant. For simplicity the basic expected inflation variable is the same as that used in the aggregate supply and demand equations, but we shall check how using other versions of the rate of inflation affects the estimation of the relevant parameters.

Having chosen the aggregate price index, we next have to make an assumption about the information and procedures that economic agents use to make their predictions.

Previous formulations of the demand for money equations for the Argentinian economy have used Cagan's adaptive expectations model and Muth–Sargent–Lucas's rational expectations model. Adaptive expectations have given rather suspicious results (Diz, 1970; Mallon and Sourrouille, 1975), and while Fernandez (1977) found evidence favorable to the rational expectations approach, his results were not very conclusive either. Independently of empirical evidence we do not consider either of these methods appropriate to the Argentine economy. On the one hand, with inflation of several tens of percents a year and subject to strong fluctuation prediction errors are very costly; it is therefore difficult to accept that people will not try to use whatever information can be obtained at a cost, as long as the cost is less than the gains to be had from predictive accuracy. On the other hand, the Muth–Sargent–Lucas-type of rational expectations specified by Fernandez (estimated by using information for the *whole* sample period) involves the use of information that the economic agent could not have used simply because it belonged to the future.

Another specification of "rational expectations," which will be referred to as Muth–Friedman "best one can do" expectations, is much more appealing. Economic agents are assumed to use all relevant information *available at the moment of making the prediction.* They are supposed not to know the true value of the parameters in the relevant relationships of the economy, but rather to estimate them using the least-squares method. They then use the estimated equation to predict the future value of the desired variable. Under certain assumptions, this is known to be optimal in the minimum quadratic error sense. B. Friedman (1979) has recently shown that this kind of expectation is also adaptive in form, but with the coefficient of adaptation not necessarily constant [as in the Cagan (1963) scheme] but dependent on the past values of the exogenous variables. This is very interesting because it implies that economic agents are neither irrational nor seers. In addition, it allows for the computation not only of a predicted (or expected) value for each period but also of the variance of the prediction error, precisely what is needed to replace the two remaining unobservable variables.

It is well known that, except for short-run misperceptions of facts by economic agents in Muth–Sargent–Lucas's rational expectations framework, every kind of real effects of monetary policy will vanish and (except for random shocks) the economy will always be in long-run equilibrium. This is not obvious with the "best one can do" expectations. Therefore, under this assumption, it is still meaningful to try to test the empirical relevance of the supply-side effects in which we are interested.

For these reasons this paper is based on "best one can do" expectations. In order to implement it, we must identify (within the limits of our structural model) the variables people use in predicting inflation. The first step will be to estimate a reduced-form equation for the quarterly rate of inflation, in terms of the current and lagged values of the observable exogenous variables and the lagged values of the endogenous variables.

We began by running a regression with the current and first lagged value of all the exogenous variables and the first lagged value of the endogenous variables. We then eliminated those variables having a t statistic smaller than one. For the two remaining variables in lagged form (rate of increase in wages, and rate of growth of money supply) additional lags were introduced. The wage rate lagged more than one quarter failed to satisfy the above signficance requirement. Therefore, values lagged two or more quarters were retained only for the rate of growth of money supply. To reduce the number of parameters we adopted a second-degree polynomial distributed lag assumption. The appropriate formulation for the period 1963 : 1–1976 : 2 is given by

$$\begin{aligned}\pi = {} & \underset{(1.820)}{0.126}\, w + \underset{(1.112)}{0.064}\, w_{-1} + \underset{(5.346)}{0.436}\, p_{\mathrm{a}} + \underset{(3.246)}{0.282}\, p_{m} + \underset{(3.421)}{0.154}\, p_{\mathrm{es}} \\ & - \underset{(-1.794)}{0.154}\, ms - \underset{(-1.763)}{0.071}\, ms_{-1} - \underset{(-0.507)}{0.009}\, ms_{-2} + \underset{(1.156)}{0.033}\, ms_{-3} \\ & + \underset{(1.444)}{0.055}\, ms_{-4} + \underset{(1.535)}{0.057}\, ms_{-5} + \underset{(1.577)}{0.039}\, ms_{-6}, \end{aligned} \tag{16}$$

$$R^2 = 0.045, \qquad DW = 2.059, \qquad SE = 0.037.$$

The following characteristics of this equation are worth noting:

1. The sum of the coefficients of w, w_{-1}, p_{a}, p_{m}, and p_{es} is 1.071. The standard error is 0.064. This means that the sum is not significantly different from unity.

2. The sum of the coefficients of the current and lagged rates of growth of money supply is 0.050 with a standard error of 0.099, that is, not significantly different from zero.

3. Current and previous-quarter rates of growth of money supply have negative coefficients. The two-quarters lag has a coefficient still negative, but very close to zero, while the lags for three or more quarters have positive coefficients.

Since w, p_{a}, p_{im}, and p_{es} are precisely the prices of the main manufacturing inputs, it is tempting to interpret their coefficients as the share of each input in total production costs. But this is not strictly so. The effects of changes in these input prices on manufacturing prices come from the supply *and* demand sides. The comparison of the estimated coefficients with the input shares as obtained from the input–output data available suggests that agricultural prices may have stronger demand effect for manufactured goods than wages and the prices of services (energy, transportation, and gas).

In the same way, monetary expansion comes to the reduced-form equation for the rate of inflation from both the demand and supply equations. The signs of the coefficients seem to suggest that supply-side effects predominate during two quarters, but only structural equations can really illustrate the economic mechanism that brings about the observed relationship between the variables.

Equation (16), which can be taken to be a simplified reduced-form equation for the rate of inflation, could be reestimated with all the information available in every quarter and then used to predict inflation one quarter ahead. But for this to hold, economic agents should have not only the historical information needed to estimate the parameters of (16) but also the value of input prices and monetary expansion one period ahead. However, as Argentina's monetary policy has never been announced in advance it is unrealistic to assume prior knowledge of the rate of growth of money supply.

The exchange rate and export and import taxes (the main determinants of agricultural and import prices) have usually been kept constant for rather long periods, and devaluations and drastic changes in taxes have always been preceded by balance of payments crises and strong speculation in the black market for foreign exchange. In the same way prices for services like electricity, transportation, and gas have not been modified continually, but kept constant for a while and then adjusted upward according to actual cost increases since the last adjustment. Nominal wages have been modified either at preestablished dates and by proportions decided in long-run negotiations or by government decisions following periods of social unrest due to deterioration of real wages. In both circumstances, the final outcome could usually be guessed reasonably well even several months before the adjustment. All this means that at any moment economic agents surely know more than what one can mechanically ascribe to them from some average of past values.

As a compromise assumption, we postulate that economic agents correctly predict the future price of inputs one quarter ahead and use this information together with the past values of all relevant economic variables to predict the quarterly rate of inflation that will prevail on average over the next *two* quarters. There are several reasons why this assumption is appropriate. On the one hand, the 180-day loan is the typical operation in free credit markets; in the aggregate supply equation, where the variance of expected inflation enters via the uncertain real cost of credit, the variance of expected inflation should refer to the same 180-day period. On the other hand, even when the relevant expected inflation refers to only one quarter ahead (as in the aggregate demand equation), it seems likely that economic agents will assign to the next quarter the average inflation they expect over the longer time span which is relevant to them in making their financial decisions.[6] Finally, selecting two quarters as the time span

[6] In the preliminary regression we found that the quarterly average expected inflation over the next two quarters performed as well in the demand equation as the one-quarter future expected inflation and was more adequate in the supply equation. We therefore decided to use the quarterly average expected inflation over the next *two* quarters in both contexts.

of the prediction and assuming that input prices are known with certainty only for one quarter ahead sets a framework of imperfect information that is probably closer to reality than are the alternative assumptions of absolute lack of information or perfect certainty about future input prices.

Summing up, we assume that economic agents predict inflation using all relevant past information, as well as the price of inputs that will prevail in the following quarter. They then do the best they can to predict the average quarterly rate of inflation during the next half year.

With only this information available (16) is not directly applicable. Instead, we must try to estimate how average inflation two quarters ahead relates to the rates of change of input prices one quarter ahead and to past values of whatever variable may prove to be relevant. Our model does not explain how the wage rate and prices of agricultural goods, services, and imports behave over time, nor does it say anything about the determinants of changes in money supply through time. It thus cannot provide precise indications of what variables should replace the unknown future values of input prices and monetary expansion in (16). We have tried to obtain this from a statistical analysis of the historical data.

Equation (17) began from a regression like (16), with the following differences: The dependent variable is the arithmetic average of the rates of inflation in quarters 5 and 5 + 1; the explanatory variables are the rates of input price inflation in quarter t, the rate of wage inflation in quarter t, and six lagged values of the rate of growth on money supply ($t-1$ to $5-6$). We then tried adding additional lags for the rate of inflation of input prices and all other exogenous and endogenous variables in (14) and (15). Variables that did not have a t statistic higher than unity were discarded. When several lags appeared to be significant, we tried polynomial distributed lags of different degrees and lengths. The regression finally chosen for the period 1963 : 1–1976 : 1 was

$$(\pi_{t+1}+\pi_t)/2 = \underset{(2.930)}{0.233}\,w - \underset{(-3.082)}{0.207}\,w_{-1} + \underset{(4.260)}{0.346}\,p_{\mathrm{a}} - \underset{(-3.396)}{0.432}\,p_{\mathrm{a}_{-1}}$$

$$+ \underset{(4.000)}{0.396}\,p_{\mathrm{im}} + \underset{(4.391)}{0.643}\,\pi_{-1} + \textstyle\sum_{i=1}^{20}\gamma_{-i}ms_{-i}, \qquad (17)$$

$\gamma_1 = -0.008\ (-0.125)$, $\gamma_8 = 0.059\ (2.111)$, $\gamma_{15} = -0.037\ (-1.738)$,
$\gamma_2 = 0.024\ (0.590)$, $\gamma_9 = 0.048\ (1.795)$, $\gamma_{16} = -0.045\ (-1.956)$,
$\gamma_3 = 0.047\ (1.812)$, $\gamma_{10} = 0.034\ (1.407)$, $\gamma_{17} = -0.049\ (-2.065)$,
$\gamma_4 = 0.062\ (2.997)$, $\gamma_{11} = 0.019\ (0.877)$, $\gamma_{18} = -0.047\ (-2.118)$,
$\gamma_5 = 0.070\ (3.084)$, $\gamma_{12} = 0.003\ (0.159)$, $\gamma_{19} = -0.039\ (-2.141)$,
$\gamma_6 = 0.071\ (2.746)$, $\gamma_{13} = -0.012\ (-0.653)$, $\gamma_{20} = -0.024\ (-2.149)$,
$\gamma_7 = 0.068\ (2.414)$, $\gamma_{14} = -0.026\ (-1.323)$,

$R^2 = 0.932$, $DW = 2.065$, $SE = 0.036$.

The main differences between (16) and (17) are as follows:

1. Inflation in the prices of agricultural and manufactured goods, lagged one period, enters as explanatory variables in (17) but not in (16). Service price inflation, which appears in (16), is not significant in (17).
2. In (17), 20 lagged rates of growth of money supply enter as explanatory variables instead of the 7 that appear in (16).

These differences are not surprising: Inflation in the prices of agricultural and manufactured goods in the immediate past is probably the main determinant of future nominal wage increases and adjustments in the exchange rate. The adjustment in the price of services (energy, transportation, and gas) within a two-quarter span must be closely related to past changes in other prices entering into the costs of services. For this reason the rate of increase in the price of services one quarter ahead becomes uninformative once current and past increases on other prices are introduced. Finally, in the absence of information about the rate of growth of money supply in the next two quarters, central bank behavior patterns are inferred from past changes in money supply.

We next generate the values of expected inflation and the variance of unexpected inflation for our basic sample period 1963 : 1–1976 : 1:

1. The parameters of (17) are estimated using information for the preceding 48 quarters (12 years).[7] The length of the sample period is kept constant. Therefore, every time a new observation becomes available, the oldest observation is dropped. The 48-quarter "moving" sample period is the longest that published information permits. The size of the sample used in estimating (17) for more recent quarters is not increased because there is no reason to assume that economic agents in recent quarters were actually exposed to a longer learning period than were their counterparts in previous quarters.
2. Having estimated (17) on the basis of information from quarters $t-1$ to $t-48$, we predict $(\pi_{t+1}+\pi_t)/2$ using the actual values of the explanatory variables (w_t, w_{t-1}, p_{a_t}, $p_{a_{t-1}}$, p_{im_t}, π_{t-1}, ms_{t-i}, $i = 1, \ldots, 20$). This predicted value is taken to be expected inflation in period t (π_t^e).
3. The variance of unexpected inflation is computed as $\sigma_\pi^2 = s^2[1 + \mathbf{x}_p'(X'X)\mathbf{x}_p]$, where $\mathbf{x}_p$ is the vector of actual values of the explanatory variables used to compute expected inflation in step 2, X is a matrix with the historic information on the explanatory variables used to estimate (17) in step 1, and s^2 is the standard error of the estimated equation.

[7] Note that we are still giving people too much information in letting them know in advance the right specification.

E. Estimation of the Demand for Money

Having estimated expected inflation and the variance of unexpected inflation, we proceed to estimate the equation for the demand for money:

$$\log(M/E) = \underset{(13.67)}{0.62} \log(M/E)_{-1} - \underset{(-12.53)}{0.80} \pi^e + \underset{(5.04)}{92.57} \sigma_\pi^2$$

$$+ \underset{(2.33)}{0.03} DPC - \underset{(-8.72)}{0.78}, \tag{18}$$

$$R^2 = 0.95, \qquad SE = 0.041, \qquad DW = 1.624, \qquad h = 1.460.$$

$$\log(M/E) = \underset{(34.55)}{0.74} \log(M_{-1}/E) + \underset{(3.70)}{59.65} \sigma_\pi^2 + \underset{(2.05)}{0.04} DPC - \underset{(10.95)}{0.52}, \tag{19}$$

$$R^2 = 0.963, \qquad SE = 0.038, \qquad DW = 1.662, \qquad h = 1.152,$$

where *DPC* is a dummy variable that assumes value 1 from 1967 : 2–1970 : 4 and then declines by 0.25 each quarter beginning at 0 again in 1971 : 4. It is also 1 from 1973 : 3–1974 : 2 and then declines by 0.25 each quarter until it reaches zero in 1975 : 3. Note that in both regressions, a dummy was introduced to represent periods during which price controls were effective.[8] Expected inflation does not appear in (19) because it was excluded from the regression.

The main difference between (18) and (19) is, precisely, the role of expected inflation. In (18), which corresponds to the partial adjustment in terms of *real* money, expected inflation is a crucial explanatory variable ($t = -12.53$), but in (19), which corresponds to the partial adjustment assumption in terms of *nominal* money, $t = 0$.

From the point of view of the statistical results Eq. (19), that is, the regression that implies a partial adjustment assumption in terms of *nominal* money, has a smaller standard error and a Durbin–Watson statistic closer to 2. In spite of these statistical results, the choice between (18) and (19) is still difficult because it implies deciding between two very different values of the elasticity of demand for money with respect to expected inflation.

Almost all estimation of the demand for money made by other researchers have shown the significance of expected inflation, whatever the form in which this expectation was specified [see, for example, Diz (1970), and Mallon and Sourrouille (1975)]. Why do our results in (19) differ from

[8] The dummy assumes value 1 from 1967 : 2 to 1970 : 4 when wage controls and price agreements were applied. Since 1971 : 1, the value of the dummy is decreased by 0.25 each quarter and becomes zero in 1971 : 4. This way we try to capture the gradual elimination of the wage and price control system during 1971. In 1973: 3 wages and price controls were again imposed. The dummy is set equal to 1 from 1973 : 3 to 1974 : 2. Since 1971 : 3 the system began to be relaxed; by 1975 : 3 it was practically inoperative. The dummy is again decreased by 0.25 each quarter beginning in 1974 : 3.

theirs? Simply because many of the previous estimations used a partial adjustment assumption in terms of real money. If the true adjustment takes place in nominal terms but with $\log(M/E)_{-1}$ as the explanatory variable as in (18) instead of $\log(M_{-1}/E)$ as in (19), $\log(E_{-1}/E)$ is left out of the regression and, as a consequence, expected inflation which is highly correlated with $\log(E/E_{-1})$, acquires statistical significance. Once $\log(M_{-1}/E)$ is substituted for $\log(M/E_{-1})$, expected inflation is no longer significant.[9]

Only after preliminary regressions indicated that the choice did not significantly affect the estimation of the parameters of the aggregate demand and supply equations was (19) selected as the demand for money equation. Note that (19) implies that, except for the influence of the variance of expected inflation and the effect of price controls, "desired" velocity is a constant. The variance of expected inflation, which turns out to be highly significant, has a positive effect on the demand for money; that is, desired velocity of money decreases when people's prediction of future inflation becomes more uncertain. Price controls also increase the demand for money.

5. Estimation of Aggregate Demand for and Supply of Commodities

Having estimated the coefficients of the demand for money, we can undertake the estimation of the aggregate demand and supply equations.

A. Preliminary Regression

The results of preliminary regression by ordinary least-squares (OLS) analysis showed that residuals in (12) and (13) were highly autocorrelated, with an estimated autocorrelation coefficient very close to unity. We therefore, decided to work with first differences in (12) and (13), that is, with specifications (14) and (15), after which autocorrelation disappeared.

The results of these preliminary regressions were also used to choose the lag structure for the different explanatory variables. The following were the main findings:

1. The capital stock variable in the aggregate supply equation showed completely insignificant coefficients up to the third lag and after the ninth lag. A polynomial lag structure of the second degree was chosen and the estimated temporal weights for the capital stock variable were 0.11, 0.18, 0.21, 0.21, 0.18, and 0.11 for lags 4–9, respectively.

[9] Modigliani *et al.* (1970) obtained the same results for the United States.

2. The real wage rate in the current quarter was completely insignificant and had the wrong sign in the aggregate supply equation. But from lags 1 to 6 it was significant and had the right sign. A second degree polynomial lag structure was used and the estimated weights turned out to be 0.32, 0.25, 0.18, 0.13, 0.08, and 0.04 for lags 1–6, respectively.

3. Real bank credit to manufacturing and variance of expected inflation proved significant *only* for the current quarter, so for these two variables no lagged values were included in the aggregate supply equation.

4. In the aggregate demand equation, real income in the current quarter appeared to be insignificant, but the values for lags 1–6 proved to have significant coefficients. The estimated "weights" were, in order, 0.42, 0.28, 0.17, 0.09, 0.03, and 0.01.

5. The monetary disequilibrium variable appeared to be significantly positive in the aggregate supply equation for the current quarter and lags 1 and 2. In the aggregate demand the coefficients of the monetary disequilibrium variable were in general insignificant and had alternate signs.

If the real wage rate of the current quarter in the aggregate supply equation and the real income of the current quarter in the aggregate demand equation (both of which turned out to be insignificant in the preliminary regressions) were eliminated, (14) and (15) would become a recursive system, and the use of OLS estimates would be justified. But the lack of significance could be due to a simultaneity problem that biases the OLS estimates. For this reason the whole model was estimated using the full information maximum likelihood (FIML) procedure.

For simplicity in estimation we decided to retain the previously estimated weights for the lagged capital stock, real wage rate, and real income variables. But the real wage rate and the real income of the current quarter were kept in the supply and demand equations, respectively. For the monetary disequilibrium variables no results from the previous regression were used, so that for these variables not only the sum but also each of the coefficients was computed by the FIML run.

B. Main Results

The FIML estimation of the structural model of the commodity market produced the following results:

$$
\begin{aligned}
q_{\mathrm{ma}} = {} & \underset{(6.86)}{1.07}\,(k)_{-4\text{ to }-10} + \underset{(0.46)}{0.04}\,(p_{\mathrm{vf}} - p_{\mathrm{ma}}) - \underset{(-2.41)}{0.54}\,(p_{\mathrm{vf}} - p_{\mathrm{ma}})_{-1\text{ to }-6} \\
& + \underset{(2.92)}{0.01}\,(bc - p_{\mathrm{vf}}) - \underset{(-1.44)}{0.99}\,D\sigma_{\pi}^{2} + \underset{(3.45)}{0.13}\,(ms - md) \\
& + \underset{(2.37)}{0.07}\,(ms - md)_{-1} + \underset{(1.10)}{0.02}\,(ms - md)_{-2},
\end{aligned}
\tag{20}
$$

$$\begin{aligned}
p_{\text{ma}} = {} & \underset{(24.32)}{1.03}\,\pi^{\text{e}} - \underset{(-3.41)}{0.20}\,q_{\text{ma}} + \underset{(1.45)}{0.12}\,y + \underset{(1.87)}{0.28}\,(y)_{-1\text{ to }-6} \\
& - \underset{(-1.02)}{0.01}\,(ms - md) + \underset{(1.98)}{0.03}\,(ms - md)_{-1} \\
& + \underset{(1.46)}{0.02}\,(ms - md)_{-2} - \underset{(-1.62)}{0.04}\,\Delta DPC, \qquad (21)
\end{aligned}$$

$$\begin{aligned}
q_{\text{ma}} = {} & \underset{(6.77)}{1.06}\,(k)_{-4\text{ to }-9} - \underset{(-2.57)}{0.57}\,(p_{\text{vf}} - p_{\text{ma}})_{-1\text{ to }-6} \\
& + \underset{(2.90)}{0.01}\,(bc - p_{\text{vf}}) - \underset{(-1.36)}{0.93}\,D\sigma_{\pi}^{2} + \underset{(3.40)}{0.12}\,(ms - md) \\
& + \underset{(2.40)}{0.07}\,(ms - md)_{-1} + \underset{(1.38)}{0.02}\,(ms - md)_{-2}, \qquad (22)
\end{aligned}$$

$$R^2 = 0.931, \qquad SE = 0.025, \qquad DW = 2.17,$$

$$\begin{aligned}
p_{\text{ma}} = {} & \underset{(26.07)}{1.05}\,\pi^{\text{e}} - \underset{(-3.33)}{0.15}\,q_{\text{ma}} + \underset{(1.79)}{0.25}\,(y)_{-1\text{ to }-6} - \underset{(-1.07)}{0.02}\,(ms - md) \\
& + \underset{(2.02)}{0.04}\,(ms - md)_{-1} + \underset{(1.98)}{0.04}\,(ms - md)_{-1} - \underset{(-1.07)}{0.04}\,\Delta DPC, \qquad (23)
\end{aligned}$$

$$R^2 = 0.944, \qquad SE = 0.031, \qquad DW = 2.14.$$

Numbers in parentheses are observed *t*s. The weights for k are 0.11, 0.18, 0.12, 0.21, 0.18, 0.11. The weights for p_{vf} are 0.32, 0.25, 0.18, 0.13, 0.08, 0.04. The weights for y are 0.42, 0.28, 0.17, 0.09, 0.03. 0.01.

Equations (20) and (21) are the estimated equations. Both current real income in the demand equation and current real wage in the supply equation are still insignificant, so the model was finally reestimated without these variables. The final results are given by (22) and (23).

Beginning with the aggregate supply (22), the following aspects of the estimation results are worth noting:

1. The coefficient of the capital stock variable (weighted average of lags 4–9) is 1.06, with $t = 6.77$. According to the theory in Section 2, under constant returns to scale that coefficient should be unity; our results do not differ significantly from that a priori value.

2. The coefficient of the variable factors (weighted average of lags 1–6) is -0.57, with $t = -2.57$. This implies an elasticity of manufacturing output with respect to the variable factors of production of 0.35. Although a bit low, this does not seem completely implausible, especially if one takes into account that in Argentina the possibility of firing workers is rather limited.

3. The coefficient of real bank credit to manufacturing firms is very small (0.01), but still significant ($t = 2.90$).

4. The variance of unexpected inflation has the expected sign, but has a relatively low t value (-1.36). We nevertheless decided to retain this

variable in the estimated equation because in all preliminary regressions its coefficient was not responsive to the inclusion or removal of other variables and on several occasions we did indeed get a higher t statistic.

5. The sum of the coefficients for the monetary disequilibrium variable was estimated at 0.21, with $t = 3.13$. The estimated coefficient for monetary disequilibrium in the current quarter is 0.12 ($t = 3.40$). For the first lag the coefficient is 0.07 ($t = 2.40$). For the second lag the coefficient is 0.02 ($t = 1.38$).

For the aggregate demand equation (23) the main results are the following:

6. The estimated coefficient for expected inflation is 1.05 ($t = 26.07$). It is not possible to reject the hypothesis of its being equal to unity that is implied in the price-adjustment scheme specified in (11).

7. The coefficient of current-quarter production is -0.15 ($t = 3.33$). The coefficient of permanent income is 0.25 ($t = 1.79$). This implies a long-run elasticity of 1.67 for the demand for manufactured goods with respect to permanent income.

8. The sum of the coefficients for the monetary disequilibrium variable is 0.06 ($t = 1.45$). Therefore, it is not significantly different from zero at the 5% level. Individually considered, the coefficient of the monetary disequilibrium in the same quarter is completely insignificant (and negative), but the coefficients become positive and more significant for the first and second lags. Further lags proved totally insignificant.

The overall performance of the model is fairly satisfactory. The R^2 of the aggregate supply function is 0.931 with a standard error of 0.025 and a Durbin–Watson statistic of 2.17. For the aggregate demand function the R^2 is 0.944 with a standard error of 0.031 and a Durbin–Watson statistic of 2.14. Note that while the reduced-form equation (16) predicted inflation with a standard error of 0.037, the structural system permits a reduction of the standard error for the same variable to 0.031.

C. Implications for Our Theory

Our main thesis regarding the monetary influence of aggregate supply is confirmed by the statistical results. Not only are the coefficients of the monetary disequilibrium variable in the supply equation statistically significant, but if this variable is omitted, the sign of the real wage rate variable reverses, and its coefficient becomes insignificant. In other words, it is only after introducing the monetary disequilibrium variable that the supply equation comes close to resembling the conventional short-run supply of the theory of the firm.

Monetary influences on the demand equation are weaker, but it should be remembered that the expected inflation already accounts for the effects of monetary expansion, especially of that which took place one or more quarters earlier.

The demand-side effect of monetary disequilibrium is insignificant in the first quarter; the supply-side effect is strong. This means that the *first* effect of monetary *contraction* is to depress manufacturing output, which in turn increases the rate of inflation within the same quarter. In other words, "stagflation" is the initial effect of monetary restriction on the market for manufactured commodities. Setting aside the effects of this initial acceleration of inflation on factor-price inflation over the next quarters, the direct supply-side effect will still be strong one quarter ahead, but will then tend to peter out. The deflationary demand-side effects begin to operate with a lag of one quarter, and considering the role that such effects play in the regression used for generating expected inflation, they increase in importance from there on.

D. Implications in Relation to Other Economists' Work

In Section 2 we saw that most other researchers have regarded bank credit as an argument of the production function. This is true in particular of Almonacid and Pastore (1975) and McKinnon (1973). In terms of the specification of aggregate supply, that means that the log of real bank credit should be the relevant financial variable used as the explanatory variable. Such a variable was used in (13) and (15) together with the monetary disequilibrium variable; our results therefore enable us to comment on their views. Note that the real bank credit variable for the current quarter had a statistically significant coefficient in (20) and (22), but that its lagged values were insignificant. This means that we may not reject the hypothesis that real bank credit helps to explain aggregate supply. But note that the coefficient of real bank credit is less than one tenth that of the measure of monetary disequilibrium, even when the order of magnitude of both variables is approximately the same.[10] Thus monetary disequilibrium is a much more important determinant of supply than the specific amount of bank credit received by manufacturing industry.

Other economists, particularly those in the United States, have argued that real cash balances are an argument of the production function

[10] Note that the real bank credit variable that enters in (20) and (22) is the percentage change in nominal bank credit to manufacturing industry, minus the percentage change in the price of the variable factors of production. The monetary disequilibrium variable is, practically speaking, the percentage change in the nominal money supply minus the percentage change in expected expenditure.

because they render "commercial services." They have not suggested that this fact could play a relevant role in the course of stabilization plans, but the point has been made mainly in the context of the "optimum quantity of money" discussion. The money disequilibrium variable used here is for all practical purposes almost collinear with the amount of real cash balances. Therefore, without having observations on the relevant real interest rate, there is no way to discriminate between the specification of those economists and that presented in Section 2. Evaluating the relative merits of either can be answered only by comparing the quality of the respective theoretical underpinnings rather than by looking at the statistical results.

E. Sensitivity to the Exogeneity Assumptions

The estimates reported in (20) and (21) may be affected by a simultaneity bias if some of the variables assumed to be exogenous are actually correlated with the stochastic error of the aggregate demand and supply equations. This may be the case both for factor prices and for the money supply.

Factor prices in the current quarter enter the aggregate demand equation via expected inflation. They do not enter as an argument in the aggregate supply function because in going from (20) to (22) the real wage rate variable for the current quarter was dropped; but one could argue that the lack of significance of the latter in (20) is in fact due to a simultaneity bias. Therefore, it is convenient to analyze the possible effects of eliminating the assumption of exogenous factor prices on the estimate for both the aggregate demand and the aggregate supply equations. Even if factor prices responded within the current quarter to the actual rate of inflation or to the rate of real growth, instrumental variable estimators are still consistent if the instruments used are uncorrelated with the random errors of the equations.

In Table 1 we compare the FIML estimates with instrumental variables estimates (IV). We used as instruments: four-lagged values of the rate of inflation and of the rate of growth of nominal wages, two-lagged values of the rates of growth of the other three factor prices (prices of agricultural goods, imports, and services), and four-lagged rates of growth of the real output of manufacturing industry. All of these may be thought of as arguments of reduced-form equations for each of the factor prices. Being lagged values, they must be uncorrelated with the random shocks of the current quarter. Note that the FIML and instrumental variables estimates reported in Table 1 are very close. This must mean that the estimates appearing in (20)–(23) are free of any significant simultaneity problem originating in the behavior of factor prices.

TABLE 1

INSTRUMENTAL VARIABLE ESTIMATES OF AGGREGATE DEMAND AND SUPPLY

Aggregate supply	(k) -4 to -10	$P_{vf} - P_{ma}$	$(P_{vf} - P_{ma})$ -1 to -7	$(b_c - p_{vf})$	$D\sigma_{\pi}^2$	$ms - md$	$ms - md_{-1}$	$(ms - md)_{-2}$	R^2	
FIML	1.07 (6.86)	0.04 (0.46)	−0.54 (−2.41)	0.01 (2.91)	−0.99 (−1.44)	0.13 (3.45)	0.07 (2.37)	0.02 (1.10)	0.931	0.025
IV	1.10 (6.46)	0.12 (1.38)	−0.50 (−2.02)	0.01 (2.52)	−1.16 (−1.55)	0.12 (3.30)	0.06 (2.30)	0.02 (0.89)	0.933	0.025
Aggregate demand	π^e	q_{ma}	y	y -1 to -6	$ms - md$	$(ms - md)_{-1}$	$(ms - md)_{-2}$	DPC	R^2	
FIML	1.03 (24.32)	−0.20 (−3.21)	0.12 (0.15)	0.28 (1.87)	−0.01 (−1.02)	0.03 (1.98)	0.02 (1.46)	−0.04 (−1.62)	0.944	0.031
IV	1.04 (24.47)	−0.18 (−3.05)	0.07 (0.73)	0.27 (1.75)	−0.01 (−0.04)	0.02 (1.67)	0.02 (1.91)	−0.04 (−1.40)	0.944	0.031

It is also possible to get some insight into the possible simultaneity bias that results from assuming the money supply is endogenous. Suppose that a random shock occurred that increased the rate of inflation during the current quarter and that the monetary authority responded in an accommodating fashion. This is probably a realistic assumption for Argentina at several points throughout our sample period. That kind of central bank behavior would create a *positive* covariance between the random error in the aggregate demand equation on the one hand, and the money supply on the other. This would create an upward bias in our estimates of the coefficient of the monetary disequilibrium variable in the aggregate demand equation. In this case the actual effect of monetary disequilibrium on the demand side would be weaker than that estimated in (23). Suppose further that the monetary authority reacted to random shock that tended to diminish real output by trying to shorten the fall through a compensatory expansion of money supply (more often than not, this is the realistic possibility for Argentina). Such behavior would register in the form of a negative covariance between the random shock of aggregate supply and the money supply. That in turn would have a downward bias on the estimates of the monetary disequilibrium variable in (22). In other words, the supply-side effects of monetary disequilibrium would be underestimated by the results reported in (22)–(23).

Summing up, the kind of simultaneity bias that might arise from money supply being endogenous would reinforce, rather than weaken, our substantive findings. For this reason we conclude that our main results are acceptably robust with respect to the possibility that the main arguments of the structural equations may be endogenous.

REFERENCES

Almonacid, R., and Pastore, A. (1975). Gradualismo ou Tratamento de Choque. *Pesquisa e Planyamento Economico* **5**, 331–384.

Ando, A. (1974). Some Aspects of Stabilization Policies, the Monetarist Controversy, and the MPS Model. *International Economic Review* **15**, 541–572.

Arnaudo, A. (1972). *Economia Monetaria*. Centro de Estudios Latinoamericanos, Mexico City.

Baez, G. C. (1975). Producto Agropecuario, Crédito y Precios. Serie Estudios Tecnicos, No. 4, Centro de Estudios Monetarios y Bancarios, Banco Central de la República Argentina. Mimeo.

Cagan, P. (1963). The Monetary Dynamics of Hyperinflation. In *Studies in the Quantity Theory of Money* (M. Friedman, ed.), pp. 25–117. University of Chicago Press, Chicago, Illinois.

Cavallo, D. (1977). Stagflationary Effects of Monetarist Stabilization Policies in Economies with Persistent Inflation. Ph.D. Thesis, Harvard University.

Diz, A. (1970). Money and Prices in Argentina, 1935–62. In *Varieties of Monetary Experience* (D. Meiselman, ed.), pp. 69–162. University of Chicago Press, Chicago, Illinois.

Fernandez, R. (1977). An Empirical Inquiry on the Short-run Dynamics of Output and Prices. *American Economic Review* **67**, 595–609.

Friedman, B. (1979). Optimal Expectations and the Extreme Information Assumptions of "Rational Expectations" Macromodels. *Journal of Monetary Economics* **5**, 23–43.

Friedman, M. (1968). The Role of Monetary Policy. *American Economic Review* **58** (Mar), 1–17.

Gordon, R. (1973). Alternative Responses of Policy to External Supply Shocks. *Brooking Papers on Economic Activity* **4**, 133–195.

Lucas, R. E. (1972). Expectations and the Neutrality of Money. *Journal of Economic Theory* **4** (Apr.), 103–124.

Lucas, R. E. (1973). Some International Evidence on Output Inflation Tradeoff. *American Economic Review* **63**, 326–334.

Mallon, R. D., and Sourrouille, I. V. (1975). *Economic Policy-Making in a Conflict Society: The Argentine Case*. Harvard University Press, Cambridge, Massachusetts.

Maynard, G., and Van Rijckeghem, W. (1968). Stabilization Policy in an Inflationary Economy: Argentina. In *Development Policy—Theory and Practice* (Gustav Papanek, ed.), pp. 207–235. Harvard University Press, Cambridge, Massachusetts.

McKinnon, R. (1973). *Money and Capital in Economic Development*. Brookings Institution, Washington, D.C.

Modigliani, F. (1963). The Monetary Mechanism and its Interaction with Real Phenomena. *Review of Economics and Statistics* Suppl. (Feb.), 79–107

Modigliani, F., Rasche, R., and Cooper, J. P. (1970). Central Bank Policy, the Money Supply, and the Short Term Rate of Interest. *Journal of Money, Credit and Banking* **2**(2), 166–218.

Morley, S. (1971). Inflation and Stagnation in Brazil. *Economic Development and Cultural Change* **19**, 203.

Reca, L. (1969). Determinantes de la Oferta Agropecuaria in la Argentina 1934/35–1966/67. *Estudios sobre la Economia Argentina* No. 5 (Aug.).

Solow, R. (1975). The intelligent citizen's guide to inflation. *Public Interest* Winter, pp. 30–66.

Tobin, J. (1972). Inflation and Unemployment. *American Economic Review* **62** (Mar.).

INSTITUTE OF ECONOMIC STUDIES
CORDOBA, ARGENTINA

Some International Evidence on Output–Inflation Trade-Offs: A Reappraisal

*MICHAEL PARKIN, BRIAN BENTLEY, AND CHRISTINA FADER**

This paper reappraises Lucas's (1973) seminal empirical study of real output–inflation trade-offs based on annual time-series from 18 countries over the years 1951–1967. While Lucas's results were broadly favorable to the natural-rate and rational expectations hypotheses, the specific model developed "account[ed] for output and inflation rate movements only moderately well" (p. 334) and "the goodness of fit statistics [were] generally considerably poorer than we have come to expect from annual time-series models" (pp. 331–332). It is perhaps not surprising that a model as general and abstract as that developed by Lucas fails to perform well when confronted with time-series data. The model contained only one good, which Barro (1976) subsequently called "back-scratching services"; postulated rational agents whose supply decisions depended only on one relative price (the price observed in some local market relative to the price level expected to prevail in the economy as a whole); and postulated an exogenous level of nominal aggregate demand to be divided between real output and the price level in a manner dependent upon the slope of the aggregate supply function. What is surprising about the model is not that it performed relatively poorly on annual time-series data within each of the

*We are grateful to many people for their helpful discussions and suggestions, especially to Alex Cukierman and Jacob Frenkel; to Monica Malkus for excellent secretarial assistance; and to the Social Science and Humanities Research Council of Canada for funding the research.

ISBN 0-12-259750-8

18 countries, but that it yielded predictions about the cross-country variability of real output and inflation that the data broadly confirmed. The key prediction, of course, was that the greater the variance of nominal aggregate demand, the steeper (with inflation on the vertical axis and output deviations on the horizontal axis) would be the aggregate supply function.

The chief aim of the work reported in this paper is to see whether we can develop a model of the output–inflation trade-off that retains the natural rate and rational expectations hypotheses and that possesses a degree of simplicity similar to Lucas's but performs better in explaining the annual time-series data. The model developed is estimated and tested using the now-extended sample available from the 18 countries featured in Lucas's study, together with 3 additional countries (France, Japan, and Switzerland).

It turns out that we have not been entirely successful in achieving our aim. Our major conclusion is that the short-run trade-off between inflation and output is not a simple and easily observed relationship. Second, the cross-country variability in the division of nominal demand shocks between output and price responses is not simply explained by the variance of those nominal demand shocks.

Many modifications to Lucas's basic hypothesis could yield improved explanatory power if pursued; the one used here is that of explicitly modeling economic openness—that is, the trading relations between an individual economy and the rest of the world. The line of inquiry is prompted by the simple and somewhat primitive observation that inflation is a monetary phenomenon, namely the rate of change in the value of money. This being the case, intercountry inflation differences should be heavily influenced by the exchange rate regime linking the value of one country's currency to that of another's. It would be a curious study that examined the interstate evidence on output–inflation trade-offs and drew conclusions from the cross-section data generated by Alabama/Wymoing. The reason why this would be a curious study is that the states of the Union are, from a monetary point of view, linked together by an exchange rate for all practical purposes irrevocably fixed at unity. Thus movements in prices in one state different from those in another do not reflect differences in inflation rates, but rather reflect changing *relative* prices. It is therefore perhaps equally curious to attempt to investigate output–inflation trade-offs using a cross-country sample of 18 countries, 16 of which had, throughout the selected sample period, fixed exchange rates between each other. Only one country had a flexible exchange rate throughout the entire period—Argentina—and one other country, Canada, had a flexible rate for much of the period. (A third country, Paraguay, had a flexible rate from 1957 to 1960.)

The key difference between the model developed in this paper and that of Lucas is that here we pay explicit attention to the openness of the national economies whose inflation–output trade-offs are being studied. We cannot, of course, say a priori that taking account of this additional detail will resolve the puzzles and remedy the deficiencies of Lucas's simpler and more abstract formulation. Whether or not it does is an empirical matter. It does, however, seem to be an avenue worthy of investigation regardless of the nature of the empirical findings. It will be interesting, perhaps even more interesting, to discover that economic openness is irrelevant and that one can proceed as if the economy were closed when investigating its inflation–output trade-off.

To keeps things as simple as possible and also to keep the results as comparable as possible with Lucas's, his theoretical framework will only be minimally modified. Specifically, the theoretical model developed will display the natural rate hypothesis and assume expectations to be formed rationally. Following Lucas, a major simplification will be achieved by treating nominal aggregate demand as exogenous, rather than providing a detailed modeling of the aggregate demand side of the economy. Lucas's model will be a special case of that developed here, namely, the special case in which the economy is closed. Two alternative economies are modeled, one in which the exchange rate is flexible and the other in which it is fixed. Predictions concerning the nature of the trade-offs between output and inflation in the two cases are derived, the resulting reduced-form relationships estimated, and the hypotheses embodied in them tested.

The paper is divided into two major sections. Section 1 develops the model and Section 2 presents the empirical results.

1. An Aggregate Model of an Open Economy

The economy to be modeled is open to trade with the rest of the world. Some of the output produced in the domestic economy is sold in the rest of the world, and agents in the domestic economy consume good produced in the rest of the world. Supply decisions are made in response to expected relative prices where the denominator of the relative price is a weighted average of the average price of domestic output and the average price of "foreign output." This, together with necessary augmentation of the stochastic specification, is the only change introduced to what is otherwise the same model as that employed in Lucas (1973).

We follow Lucas in imposing equilibrium on the aggregate economy (equality of aggregate supply and aggregate demand), rather than Barro (1976) and Cukierman and Wachtel (1979), who impose equilibrium in each and every market. We have two reasons for doing so, but neither is strongly convincing. First, we wanted to keep our analysis as simple and close to Lucas's as possible. Second, some initial attempts to pursue the alternative route suggested it would be necessary to model the whole world as a simultaneous general equilibrium system, thereby losing the simplicity of the small open economy approach adopted here.

The domestic economy and the rest of the world are to be regarded as having identical structures, though only the domestic economy is explicity modeled. What distinguishes the domestic economy from the rest of the world is the speed with which information flows between individual markets.

A. Aggregate Supply

As in the Lucas model, economic agents are located in a large number of scattered competitive markets, and because demand for goods in each period is distributed unevenly over markets, there are relative as well as general price movements. Individual agents in the domestic economy are viewed as producing a single homogeneous commodity, some of which is traded domestically and some of which is traded in the rest of the world. Some "island markets" will be located entirely within the domestic economy, and others will span the domestic economy and the rest of the world economy. The agents in the domestic economy consume two goods, one produced domestically and a different homogeneous commodity produced in the rest of the world.

The output supplied by domestic producers in some individual market z is

$$y_t(z) = y_{nt} + y_{ct}(z), \tag{1}$$

where y equals the log of output, subscript n denotes normal, subscript c denotes cyclical, z indexes the market, and t is a time subscript. The normal component of output is assumed to follow a linear logarithmic trend. That is,

$$y_{nt} = \alpha + \beta t, \tag{2}$$

where t denotes time. The cyclical component of output varies with the price observed in market z relative to the relevant price index for the basket of goods consumed by the typical agent. That is,

$$y_{ct}(z) = \gamma\{ p_t(z) - E[p_{It} \mid I_t(z)]\} + \lambda y_{c,t-1}(z), \tag{3}$$

where $p_t(z)$ is the price in market z, p_{It} denotes the price index relevant to the consumption decisions of individual agents, and I_t denotes the stock of information available to agents in market z at time t. E is the mathematical expectations operator. The lagged cyclical output variable captures inerita in the adjustment of cyclical supply to the perceived relative price movements. The price index relevant to individual supply decisions is hypothesized to be

$$p_{It} = \mu p_t + (1 - \mu)(p_t^* + \epsilon_t), \tag{4}$$

where p_t^* is the log of the price (in foreign currency) of the foreign good, ϵ_t is the log of the exchange rate (units of domestic currency per unit of foreign currency), and μ is the share of domestic output in the domestic consumption bundle.

The price observed in an individual market z is assumed to deviate from the average price in the domestic economy p_t in accordance with

$$p_t(z) = p_t + z \tag{5}$$

and the domestic price level (average) is assumed to be related to the world price level in accordance with

$$p_t = p_t^* + \epsilon_t + \omega_t. \tag{6}$$

The deviation, z, of the price in market z from the economy average price is assumed to be a zero-mean normally distributed random variable with a constant variance τ^2, namely,

$$z \sim N(0, \tau^2). \tag{7}$$

This assumption reflects the notion that there is incomplete information and a lack of instantaneous arbitrage between individual island markets. However, over time there is full arbitrage in the sense that the expectation of $p_{t+i}(z) = p_{t+i}$. This captures the notion that although information is costly and arbitrage opportunities are costly to exploit, they will, over time, be fully exploited. Price deviations within the domestic economy cannot persist.

Equation (6) can be thought of as a statement about international purchasing power parity. The term ω_t represents the real terms of trade between domestic and foreign output. It seems reasonable to assume that while in the long run purchasing power parity will prevail, costs of information and transportation will permit some persistence in deviations from purchasing power parity. Specifically, it is hypothesized that $\Delta\omega_t$ follows a first-order autoregressive process. That is,

$$w_t = \Delta\omega_t - \rho\,\Delta\omega_{t-1} \sim N(0, \psi^2). \tag{8}$$

Foreign inflation is also assumed to follow a first-order autoregressive process. That is,

$$v_t = \Delta p_t^* - \kappa\,\Delta p_{t-1}^* \sim N(0, \phi^2). \tag{9}$$

The previous equations describe completely the aggregate supply side of the economy. The difference between the specification contained here and that of Lucas is that in (3) an expected price index (rather than the expectation of the average of prices over all domestic markets) is the relevant denominator for the relative price term and that (6), (8), and (9) specify a source of potential confusion between permanent and transitory shocks to the economy which augment the absolute-relative shocks incorporated in (5).

To derive the aggregate supply function, first write the expected price index as

$$E[p_{It} \mid I_t(z)] = \mu E(p_t \mid I_{t-1}, p_t(z), \epsilon_t) + (1-\mu)E(p_t^* \mid I_{t-1}, p_t(z), \epsilon_t) + (1-\mu)\epsilon_t. \tag{10}$$

Using the method of recursive projection [see Sargent (1979, p. 327)], this becomes (after straightforward but tedious manipulation)

$$\begin{aligned} E[p_{It} \mid I_t(z)] = {} & \mu[\bar{p}_t + \beta_1(p_t(z) - \bar{p}_t) + \beta_2(p_t - \bar{p}_t - v_t - w_t)] \\ & + (1-\mu)[p_{t-1}^* + \kappa\,\Delta p_{t-1}^* + \epsilon_t + \beta_3(p_t(z) - \bar{p}_t) \\ & + \beta_4(p_t - \bar{p}_t - v_t - w)], \end{aligned} \tag{11}$$

where

$$\bar{p}_t = E(p_t \mid I_{t-1}), \tag{12}$$

$$\left.\begin{aligned} \beta_1 &= \frac{1}{D}\left\{\sigma^2(\phi^2+\psi^2) - \pi^2(\phi^2+\psi^2)^2\right\}, \\ \beta_2 &= \frac{1}{D}\left\{\tau^2[\sigma^2 - \pi(\sigma^2+\psi^2)]\right\}, \\ \beta_3 &= \frac{1}{D}\left\{\sigma^2 - \pi^2(\phi^2+\psi^2)\right\}\phi^2, \\ \beta_4 &= \frac{1}{D}\left\{\tau^2(\pi-1) - [\sigma^2 - \pi^2(\phi^2+\psi^2)]\right\}\phi^2 \\ D &= \sigma^2(\phi^2+\psi^2+\tau^2) + \tau^2(1-2\pi)(\phi^2+\psi^2) - \pi^2(\phi^2+\psi^2)^2, \end{aligned}\right\} \tag{13}$$

$$\sigma^2 = E[p_t - E(p_t \mid I_{t-1})]^2 \tag{14}$$

and π is the coefficient on $v_t + w_t$ in the reduced-form domestic price level (p_t) equation.

Inserting (11) in (3), aggregating over all markets (z), and noting that $p_t - p_t^* - \kappa\,\Delta p_{t-1}^* - \epsilon_t = v_t + w_t + \omega_{t-1} + \Delta\omega_{t-1}$ gives

$$y_{ct} = \gamma\theta_1(p_t - \bar{p}_t) + \gamma\theta_2(v_t + w_t) + \gamma(1-\mu)(\omega_{t-1} + \rho\,\Delta\omega_{t-1}) + \lambda y_{c,t-1}, \tag{15}$$

where

$$\theta_1 = \mu(1 - \beta_1 - \beta_2) - (1-\mu)(\beta_3 + \beta_4)$$

and

$$\theta_2 = \mu\beta_2 + (1-\mu)(1+\beta_4).$$

This is directly analogous to Lucas's equation [1973, Eq. (7), p. 328]. The equation embodies the natural rate hypothesis in the sense that if $p_t = \bar{p}_t$ (that is, if there are no domestic price surprises) and if $v_t + w_t = 0$ (that is, if there are no foreign price level or international relative price surprises), then deviations of output from normal, y_{ct}, will depend only on real variables, namely, the real terms of trade expected conditional on information available prior to the current period and on the lagged level of deviations of output from normal. For output to converge to its normal rate, the model predicts that it is essential not only that there be no domestic or foreign price surprises but also that the real terms of trade return to their (normalized) level of unity (so that their logarithm is zero). The way in which domestic price and foreign price surprises affect cyclical output is quite complicated and does not appear to lend itself to the simple qualitative cross-country predictions in the simpler Lucas formulation. This matter will be returned to, however, after the model has been completely solved.

B. Aggregate Demand

The aggregate demand for goods will be postulated to depend in exactly the same way as Lucas supposed on the level of nominal demand x_t and the price level p_t. That is, in logarithms,

$$y_t = x_t - p_t, \tag{16}$$

where x_t equals the log of nominal aggregate demand. It will be assumed that in the case of an economy with a flexible exchange rate, x_t is an exogenous random variable generated by the process

$$\{\Delta x_t\} \sim N(\delta, \sigma_x^2). \tag{17}$$

However, if the economy has a fixed exchange rate, the exchange rate will be treated as exogenous. Nominal aggregate demand will be an endogenous variable generated as a consequence of supply decisions, the value of the exchange rate, and the movements of foreign prices together with the random drawing of ω_t.

C. Model Summary and Solution

The model may be summarized as follows: The aggregate supply function is

$$y_t = y_{nt} + \gamma\theta_1(p_t - \bar{p}_t) + \gamma\theta_2(v_t + w_t) + \gamma(1-\mu)(\omega_{t-1} + \rho\,\Delta\omega_{t-1}) + \lambda y_{c,t-1}; \tag{18}$$

aggregate demand is given by

$$y_t = x_t - p_t; \tag{19}$$

and international relative prices are given by

$$p_t = p_t^* + \epsilon_t + \omega_t. \tag{20}$$

In the flexible exchange rate version, these three equations determine the endogenous variables p_t, y_t, and ϵ_t, given y_{nt}, x_t, p_t^*, ω_t, and the values of the predetermined variables appearing in (18). The expectation of p_t, $\bar{p}_t$, which is the expectation of p_t independent of information available in market z at t, is the prediction of p_t given by these three equations.

In a fixed exchange rate regime the exchange rate is an exogenous random variable, and the three equations serve to determine the endogenous variables y_t, p_t, and x_t. In that case the system becomes recursive in the sense that (20) determines the price level, (18) determines output [given the price level from (20)], and finally (19) simply determines nominal output. In fact, given that the focus of attention is the output–inflation trade-off, nominal output is not a very interesting variable in the fixed exchange rate variant of the model. Imposing rational expectations and solving the above model for the flexible exchange rate case yields:

$$y_{ct} = \pi_1(\Delta x_t - \delta) + \pi_2(v_t + w_t) + \gamma(1-\mu)(\omega_{t-1} + \rho\,\Delta\omega_{t-1}) + \lambda y_{c,t-1}, \tag{21}$$

where

$$\pi_1 = \gamma\theta_1/(1+\gamma\theta_1) \qquad \text{and} \qquad \pi_2 = \gamma\theta_2/(1+\gamma\theta_1).$$

As was pointed out by Lucas (1976), given the structure of this model, there is only one linearly independent equation, so that, although we may obtain the reduced-form expressions for p_t and ϵ_t, they do not contain any additional information not already incorporated in (21).

Under fixed exchange rates, (18) and (20) give the output solution as

$$y_{ct} = \pi_3(v_t + w_t) + \gamma(1-\mu)(\omega_{t-1} + \rho\,\Delta\omega_{t-1}) + \lambda y_{c,t-1}, \tag{22}$$

where

$$\pi_3 = \gamma(\theta_1^* + \theta_2^*)$$

and the asterisks on θ_i signify that the values of these composite parameters are different under a fixed exchange rate regime than under flexible rates since the values of σ^2 and π will differ between the regimes.

Although (21) and (22) look somewhat different from Lucas's equation [1973, Eq. (11)], their interpretations are analogous. $\Delta x_t - \delta$, which appears in (21), is identical to the term that appears in Lucas's equation and is the surprise in domestic nominal demand. The term $v_t + w_t$ is the total foreign surprise. It appears in both the flexible exchange rate and fixed exchange rater reduced-form output equations. Its effect, however, is different in the two cases, as will be discussed more fully below. Movements in the expected real terms of trade and in the lagged value of real output affect current cyclical output under both regimes in an identical manner. This is not surprising since these variables, being entirely predictable on the basis of information available prior to the current period, should in no way depend upon the way in which different exchange rate regimes generate different information. Under fixed exchange rates, since from the structure of the model, domestic nominal demand is determined recursively with respect to output and prices, deviations of its value from its expected value clearly have no effect upon output. The only "surprise" influencing output under fixed exchange rates therefore is the foreign surprise. In contrast, under flexible exchange rates, both the domestic and foreign surprises have an influence on output.

In Lucas's (closed economy) setting, it was possible to be very definite about the relationship between the variances of the exogenous variables and the slope of the output–inflation trade-off. In this open economy model, even though it represents an apparently only slight extension of the Lucas framework, simple predictions are available only in the fixed exchange rate case. Under flexible exchange rates, there are no straightforward qualitative predictions concerning the cross-country pattern of output–inflation trade-off slopes. This arises for two reasons. First, there are two sources of shock to cyclical output and the domestic price level. There are, therefore, two partial trade-offs depending on the source of the shock. Worse than this, however, the values of the parameters π_1 and π_2 (depending as they do on θ_1 and θ_2) depend in such a complex, nonlinear manner on the variances of the stochastic variables that no strong cross-country predictions concerning even the values of those parameters are available. This is apparent if the expressions for those parameters under flexible exchange rates are considered. They are

$$\theta_1 = \frac{[1 + \gamma(\theta_1 + \theta_2)](1 - \gamma\theta_1)(\phi^2 + \mu\psi^2)\tau^2}{(\phi^2 + \psi^2 + \tau^2)\sigma_x^2 + [1 + \gamma(\theta_1 + \theta_2)]^2(\phi^2 + \psi^2)\tau^2} \tag{23}$$

$$\theta_2 = \frac{\begin{aligned}[\mu\tau^2 - (1 - \mu)]\sigma_x^2 + \mu\gamma\theta_2[1 + \gamma(\theta_1 + \theta_2)](\phi^2 + \psi^2)\\ - (1 - \mu)(1 + \gamma\theta_1)[1 + \gamma(\theta_1 + \theta_2)]\tau^2\end{aligned}}{(\phi^2 + \psi^2 + \tau^2)\sigma_x^2 + [1 + \gamma(\theta_1 + \theta_2)]^2(\phi^2 + \psi^2)\tau^2}. \tag{24}$$

It is immediately apparent that the simplicity available in Lucas's closed economy model is now lost for the case of flexible exchange rates. It is not possible to say how the values of θ_1 and θ_2 will vary (in qualitative terms) as the underlying variances (σ_s^2, ϕ^2, ψ^2, and τ^2) vary.

Under the fixed exchange rates, matters are much more straightforward. There is a well-defined short-run trade-off in that case, the slope of which is given by $\gamma(\theta_1^* + \theta_2^*)$. Straightforward manipulation of the model enables the value of this slope to be derived as

$$\gamma(\theta_1^* + \theta_2^*) = \gamma\left[\tau^2 + (1 - \mu)(\phi^2 + \psi^2)\right] \Big/ (\phi^2 + \psi^2 + \tau^2). \tag{25}$$

Evidently, the slope of the trade-off in a fixed exchange rate world will depend on the aggregate foreign surprise variance, that is, the variance of unexpected foreign inflation and the variance of unexpected changes in the real terms of trade. If, following Lucas, we imagine that γ and τ^2 are the same for all economies, then our prediction would be that the slope of the short-run trade-off would vary inversely with $\phi^2 + \psi^2$. This follows directly from considering the derivative of π_3 with respect to $\phi^2 + \psi^2$, which is

$$\frac{\partial \pi_3}{\partial(\phi^2 + \psi^2)} = \frac{-\gamma\mu\tau^2}{\phi^2 + \psi^2 + \tau^2} < 0. \tag{26}$$

Evidently, if there is no variance to the foreign surprises, then the slope of the trade-off will equal γ. At the other extreme, as that foreign variance becomes infinitely large, the slope of the short-run trade-off will become $(1 - \mu)\gamma$.

To summarize, in the case of flexible exchange rates, we have a strong within-country time series prediction that cyclical output will respond positively to domestic nominal demand surprises and to foreign price surprises as well as to expected changes in the real terms of trade and lagged real output. In the flexible exchange rate case, there are no strong predictions concerning the cross-country relationship among the coefficients of output response or, equivalently, the slope of the output–inflation trade-off. Under fixed exchange rates, it is predicted that the cyclical output of an economy will be unresponsive to domestic nominal demand surprises, but will respond otherwise to the same things as in the flexible exchange rate case. The coefficients will be the same on the known real variables, but the coefficient on the foreign price surprise will differ between the two exchange rate regimes. Under flexible exchange rates, it is predicted that the smaller the variance of foreign price surprises is, the larger the response of real output to those foreign shocks will be.

2. Tests and Results

Again following Lucas, testing the hypotheses developed above is a two-stage process. First, within each country, the time series-model should perform well in the sense that it explains a high proportion of the variance of cyclical output. The second stage in the test procedure is to see whether the cross-country predictions of the model are supported by the data. For the flexible exchange rate periods, there are no such predictions. However, for the fixed exchange rate periods (the bulk of the period covered by the data used in this study), the model yields the prediction that the larger the variances of foreign inflation and the real terms of trade are, the steeper the short-run output–inflation trade-off will be (inflation measured on the vertical axis). Since what is foreign and what is domestic depends on the country we are dealing with, this does provide a basis for testing. If all countries but one had very stable price behavior, then from the point of view of the one country with unstable price behavior foreign inflation would have a low variance. However, from the point of view of all the stable-price countries foreign inflation would have a higher variance because the variance of the high-variance country would be included (weighted) in the appropriate definition of the foreign inflation rate for all the other countries.

Let us now proceed to the first stage of the test procedure, namely, the estimation of the models developed above on time-series data from each of the 21 countries. For most of the sample period that we are able to deal with here, 19 of the 21 countries were on fixed exchange rates. Only Argentina was on a flexible rate throughout the period from 1953. Canada had a flexible rate from 1953 to 1961. All the other economies were on fixed rates from 1953 to 1970 and, after that date most economies, though not quite all, began to float. A full catalog of the exchange rate regimes is set out in Table 1.

Inspection of (21) and (22) reveals that there are some coefficients in common between the fixed and flexible exchange rate periods. In view of the acute shortage of degrees of freedom it seems useful to try to exploit that fact in setting up the estimation of the equations. Evidently, the coefficients on $\omega_{t-1} + \rho\,\Delta\omega_{t-1}$ and $y_{c,t-1}$ are the same in both fixed and flexible regimes. The remaining variables have different coefficients between the two regimes. In order to minimize the degrees of freedom used up in the estimation, we define a dummy variable D_t that takes the value unity for the flexible exchange rate period and zero for the fixed exchange rate period. We can then form the following estimating equation for the entire period:

$$y_{ct} = \pi_1(\Delta x_t - \delta)D_t + \pi_2(v_t + w_t)D_t + \pi_3(v_t + w_t)(1 - D_t) + \gamma(1-\mu)(\omega_{t-1} + \rho\,\Delta\omega_{t-1}) + \lambda y_{c,t-1}. \tag{27}$$

Before we can estimate (27), we need to be more explicit about the definition and calculation of some of the variables. First, y_{ct} is simply the deviation of the log of the real gross national product (GNP) from an

TABLE 1

EXCHANGE RATE REGIMES[a]

Country	Fixed	Flexible
Argentina	—	1953–1978
Austria	1953–1970	1971–1978
Belgium	1953–1970	1971–1978
Canada	1962–1969	1953–1961
		1970–1978
Denmark	1953–1970	1971–1978
Germany (West)	1953–1969	1971–1978
Guatemala	1953–1978	—
Honduras	1953–1978	—
Ireland	1953–1970	1971–1978
Italy	1953–1970	1971–1978
Netherlands	1953–1970	1971–1978
Norway	1953–1970	1971–1978
Paraguay	1961–1978	1957–1961
Puerto Rico	1953–1978	—
Sweden	1953–1970	1971–1978
United Kingdom	1953–1970	1971–1978
United States	1953–1970	1971–1978
Venezuela	1953–1978	—
France	1953–1970	1971–1978
Japan	1953–1970	1971–1978
Switzerland	1953–1970	1971–1978

[a] *International Monetary Fund* (1975, pp. 2, 3, 119); International Monetary Fund, Annual Report on *Exchange Restrictions*, Washington, 1976, 1977, and 1978.

estimated linear trend. Δx_t is the change in the log of nominal GNP. δ is the mean of that variable for each country, estimated for the flexible exchange rate subperiod only. ϵ_t is defined to be the log of the exchange rate, expressed in units of domestic currency per U.S. dollar, (except for the United States, in which case it is expressed as an average exchange rate in terms of U.S. dollars per "basket" of relevant foreign currencies), as detailed below. ω_t is the log of the domestic GNP implicit deflator minus the log of the rest of the world implicit deflator (see below) minus the log of the exchange rate.

The foreign price and inflation variables need lengthier discussion. These were calculated in the following way. First, for each country except the United States, nominal GNP was converted into current U.S. dollars and real GNP was converted into U.S. dollars at the exchange rate for the base year of the series. Indexing countries by a presubscript i or j, the relevant foreign price level (in logs) for country j is given by

$$_jp_t^* \equiv \log\left[\frac{\sum_{i=1, i\neq j}^{21} {}_iY_{n\$t}}{\sum_{i=1, i\neq j}^{21} {}_iY_{r\$t}}\right], \tag{28}$$

where ${}_iY_{n\$t} = {}_iY_{nt}E_t$, ${}_iY_{r\$t} = {}_iY_{rt}E_0$, and Y is GNP, the subscripts n and r are nominal and real, respectively, and E is the exchange rate. The relevant foreign rate of inflation is simply the first difference of the variable defined in (28). For the United States, a weighted average of the other 20 countries' implicit GNP deflators was used as the relevant foreign price where the weights were countries' shares in the rest of world real GNP. That is,

$$_{\mathrm{USA}}p_t^* \equiv \log\left\{\sum_{\substack{i=1\\ i\neq \mathrm{USA}}}^{21} \frac{{}_iY_{r\$t}}{\sum_{i=1, i\neq \mathrm{USA}}^{21} {}_iY_{r\$t}}\, {}_iP_t\right\}. \tag{29}$$

Also, the relevant U.S. exchange rate was defined as the negative of the log of a weighted average of the remaining 20 countries' exchange rates vis-á-vis the U.S. dollar. That is,

$$_{\mathrm{USA}}\epsilon_t \equiv \log\left\{\sum_{\substack{i=1\\ i\neq \mathrm{USA}}}^{21} \frac{{}_iY_{r\$t}}{\sum_{i=1, i\neq \mathrm{USA}}^{21} {}_iY_{r\$t}}\, {}_iE_t\right\}. \tag{30}$$

For estimating the model set out in (27), two further preliminary matters were dealt with. First, (8) was estimated for each country, to yield estimates of the parameter $\rho\,(\hat{\rho})$—the coefficient of autocorrelation in the real terms of trade. In addition, the equation

$$_j\Delta p_t^* = \kappa_j\, \Delta p_{t-1}^* + \psi_t \tag{31}$$

was also estimated to yield estimates of the parameter κ ($\hat{\kappa}$). These parameter estimates, together with the prior estimates of δ, were imposed in the estimation of (27).

The results of the preliminary estimations of $\hat{\rho}$, $\hat{\kappa}$, ϕ^2, and ψ^2 are set out in Table 2. The estimates of δ and σ_x are given in Table 3. As a check on the specification of the stochastic process generating Δx we estimate

$$\Delta x_t = \phi_0 + \phi_1\, \Delta x_{t-1} + \eta_t \tag{32}$$

with the expectation that $\phi_0 = \delta$ and $\phi_1 = 0$. The results of this are also shown in Table 3. It is evident that we cannot reject our specification of the

TABLE 2

PRELIMINARY ESTIMATIONS[a]

Country	$\hat{\kappa}$	$\hat{\rho}$	ϕ^2	ψ^2
Argentina	1.045	− 0.032	0.00028	0.0044
	(14.36)	(0.14)		
Austria	0.899	0.620	0.00050	0.0007
	(10.02)	(3.69)		
Belgium	0.925	0.462	0.00058	0.0006
	(9.63)	(2.28)		
Canada	0.984	0.145	0.00088	0.0027
	(9.02)	(0.75)		
Denmark	0.900	0.315	0.00048	0.0011
	(10.23)	(1.68)		
Germany	0.971	0.563	0.00065	0.0013
	(10.13)	(3.38)		
Guatemala	0.901	0.619	0.00062	0.0014
	(9.38)	(3.54)		
Honduras	0.979	0.435	0.00078	0.0011
	(9.55)	(2.24)		
Ireland	0.901	0.108	0.00062	0.0036
	(9.39)	(.060)		
Italy	0.987	0.103	0.00074	0.0012
	(9.89)	(0.57)		
Netherlands	0.927	0.743	0.00079	0.0008
	(8.06)	(4.16)		
Norway	0.927	0.422	0.00059	0.0007
	(9.59)	(2.41)		
Paraguay	0.937	0.078	0.00069	0.0017
	(8.74)	(0.47)		
Puerto Rico	0.901	− 0.070	0.00062	0.0243
	(9.38)	(0.36)		
Sweden	0.972	0.199	0.00081	0.0008
	(9.22)	(0.99)		
United Kingdom	0.902	− 0.117	0.00060	0.0021
	(9.47)	(0.61)		
United States	0.906	0.373	0.00074	0.0161
	(9.07)	(1.83)		
Venezuela	0.893	− 0.191	0.00063	0.0120
	(9.11)	(0.96)		
France	1.001	− 0.194	0.00069	0.0026
	(10.12)	(0.94)		
Japan	0.904	0.620	0.00059	0.0020
	(10.01)	(3.32)		
Switzerland	0.970	0.425	0.00077	0.0026
	(9.53)	(2.09)		

[a]Figures in parentheses are t ratios; ϕ^2 and ψ^2 are the variances of the residuals in the regressions from which $\hat{\kappa}$ and $\hat{\rho}$, respectively, were estimated.

TABLE 3

PRELIMINARY ESTIMATIONS AND TESTS[a]

Country	δ	$\hat{\sigma}_x$	$\hat{\phi}_0$	$\hat{\phi}_1$	DW	n
Argentina	0.309	0.196	0.179	0.492	1.52	22
			(1.85)	(1.57)		
Austria	0.112	0.025	0.129	− 0.147	2.00	6
			(2.24)	(0.30)		
Belgium	0.114	0.026	0.142	− 0.233	1.64	7
			(2.26)	(0.45)		
Canada	0.086	0.046	0.036	0.545	1.61	18
			(1.66)	(2.52)		
Denmark	0.115	0.014	0.117	− 0.021	1.88	6
			(1.81)	(0.04)		
Germany	0.080	0.020	0.045	0.400	2.53	8
			(1.78)	(1.43)		
Ireland	0.171	0.042	0.185	− 0.090	2.34	7
			(2.84)	(0.23)		
Italy	0.167	0.050	0.057	0.680	1.11	8
			(1.23)	(2.53)		
Netherlands	0.118	0.018	0.152	− 0.288	1.72	7
			(2.44)	(0.56)		
Norway	0.124	0.016	0.089	0.270	1.12	7
			(1.59)	(0.62)		
Paraguay	0.137	0.022	—	—	—	2
Sweden	0.105	0.024	0.065	0.380	1.19	8
			(1.60)	(0.99)		
United Kingdom	0.145	0.039	0.145	0.105	2.17	7
			(0.039)	(1.87)		
United States	0.095	0.013	0.095	0.070	1.93	8
			(0.013)	(2.96)		
France	0.125	0.010	0.093	0.272	2.96	8
			(3.74)	(1.32)		
Japan	0.134	0.036	0.085	0.341	1.50	8
			(1.49)	(0.87)		
Switzerland	0.065	0.050	0.013	0.705	1.82	8
			(0.52)	(2.55)		

[a] All statistics are calculated for flexible exchange rate periods only. Figures in parentheses are t ratios. Column 2 ($\hat{\sigma}_x$) reports standard deviations. DW is the Durbin–Watson statistic. n is the sample size for estimation of Eq. (32).

Δx process for 17 of the countries. The values of $\hat{\delta}$, $\hat{\beta}$, and $\hat{\sigma}_x$ are very comparable to those in Lucas's original study of the 18 countries. Argentina has the largest amount of nominal demand variance; Italy and Switzerland come second, while many of the rest are much lower than these three.

Table 4 sets out estimates of the parameters in (27). From the specifica-

TABLE 4

ESTIMATES OF OUTPUT EQUATIONS[a]

Country	π_1	π_2	π_3	$\gamma(1-\mu)$	λ	h	R^2
Argentina	− 0.082	0.001	—	0.0007	− 0.009	—	0.254
	(2.20)	(0.03)		(0.31)	(0.04)		
Austria	0.990	0.125	0.057	− 0.0003	0.366	1.277	0.640
	(3.99)	(1.39)	(0.25)	(0.23)	(1.98)		
Belgium	0.836	0.092	0.963	0.0019	0.624	2.018	0.765
	(2.77)	(0.90)	(2.80)	(1.94)	(5.03)		
Canada	0.415	0.162	0.549	0.049	0.326	2.813	0.634
	(3.84)	(1.29)	(1.51)	(0.89)	(2.00)		
Denmark	0.650	− 0.074	0.113	0.002	0.834	—	0.546
	(0.79)	(0.53)	(0.44)	(0.63)	(3.93)		
Germany	1.033	− 0.102	0.598	− 0.001	0.710	0.267	0.841
	(3.17)	(1.12)	(2.86)	(0.16)	(7.17)		
Guatemala	—	—	0.157	− 0.021	0.568	0.433	0.565
			(1.45)	(1.54)	(3.47)		
Honduras	—	—	− 0.195	0.002	0.585	2.030	0.335
			(0.74)	(0.16)	(3.29)		
Ireland	− 0.023	0.095	− 0.056	− 0.003	0.891	1.208	0.817
	(0.09)	(0.70)	(0.55)	(0.03)	(9.45)		
Italy	0.106	− 0.083	0.054	0.0002	0.869	2.707	0.666
	(0.79)	(1.14)	(0.36)	(0.33)	(5.84)		
Netherlands	1.441	0.064	0.663	0.005	0.727	0.474	0.815
	(3.83)	(0.74)	(1.84)	(1.23)	(4.35)		
Norway	0.012	− 0.032	− 0.018	0.0009	0.691	0.986	0.603
	(0.04)	(0.49)	(0.19)	(0.71)	(5.14)		
Paraguay	9.985	− 3.252	0.183	− 0.002	1.323	—	0.812
	(4.01)	(4.21)	(1.66)	(1.94)	(7.27)		
Puerto Rico	—	—	− 0.589	0.100	0.736	0.874	0.651
			(3.26)	(1.76)	(4.84)		
Sweden	0.813	− 0.162	0.237	0.003	1.049	1.807	0.801
	(0.62)	(1.41)	(0.94)	(0.90)	(8.81)		
United Kingdom	− 0.288	− 0.123	− 0.045	0.0008	0.580	− 0.507	0.423
	(1.56)	(1.40)	(0.39)	(0.15)	(2.86)		
United States	1.658	0.063	− 0.070	− 0.004	0.750	0.552	0.659
	(2.89)	(1.25)	(1.65)	(0.50)	(5.75)		
Venezuela	—	—	− 0.072	− 0.001	0.686	− 0.337	0.702
			(1.60)	(0.41)	(5.82)		
France	− 0.701	− 0.096	0.115	0.0003	0.956	− 0.357	0.768
	(1.14)	(1.30)	(1.10)	(0.14)	(7.55)		
Japan	0.412	0.096	0.551	0.002	0.907	2.142	0.791
	(0.99)	(0.65)	(1.61)	(1.43)	(6.52)		
Switzerland	0.870	− 0.148	0.225	0.0003	0.738	1.454	0.880
	(4.40)	(2.08)	(0.65)	(0.06)	(7.57)		

[a] Figures in parenthesis are t ratios; h is Durbin's h; see the Appendix for notes on data and estimation.

tion of the model all the parameters should be positive, and π_1 and λ should lie between zero and one, but there is no upper restriction on π_2 and π_3. First consider the estimates of π_1. Four of the countries were on fixed exchange rates throughout the sample and so do not have an estimate of this parameter. Of the remaining 17 countries, 9 have estimates of π_1 that fall inside the predicted interval. Of the other 8 countries, 4 (Argentina, Ireland, United Kingdom, and France) have π_1 estimates that are less than zero. None of them, however, are significantly below zero, and we shall take it that these 4 countries have π_1s equal to zero. The other 4 countries (Germany, Netherlands, Paraguay, and United States) have π_1 estimates that exceed unity. Only in the case of Paraguay, however, does the coefficient significantly exceed unity, and we suspect that this arises from the fact that Paraguay had a flexible exchange rate for a very short period so that the true significance of that result is not properly reflected in the estimated coefficient and standard error. We take it, however, that our model does not fit Paraguay and is on this ground alone decisively rejected for that country. In the case of the other 3 countries, however, the estimated value if π_1 is not significantly greater than unity, and we take unity to be those countries' value of that parameter.

In summary, 16 of the 17 countries that have had a flexible exchange rate experience have estimated values of π_1 that, although in some cases lying outside the predicted interval, are consistent with (cannot lead to a rejection of) the maintained hypothesis. Viewed against a higher standard, however, the π_1 parameter estimates are not all that impressive. Only 4 of the estimated values of π_1 (Austria, Belgium, Canada, and Switzerland) are significantly nonzero and in the required interval.

Turning next to the estimates of π_2, recall that this parameter should be positive but, unlike π_1, has no predicted upper bound. In fact, 8 of the 17 flexible exchange rate experience countries have values of π_2 that estimate as positive, although none of them is significantly greater than zero. The remaining nine estimate as negative, although only one of them (Paraguay) is significantly less than one. The remarks made above concerning the estimated value of Paraguay's π_1 apply with equal force to the estimated value of π_2. It is evident that, under flexible exchange rates, foreign price surprises play an insignificant role in influencing domestic output fluctuations. This in no way constitutes a rejection of the model formulated since zero is a theoretical lower bound for the effects of that variable under a flexible exchange rate regime.

There are 20 countries that have experienced fixed exchange rates for some period during our sample. The model predicts that π_3, the coefficient on foreign price surprises during a fixed exchange rate regime, will be positive (with a theoretical upper limit of γ). Of the 20 estimated values of

π_3, 13 are positive, although only two of them are significantly greater than zero. Nevertheless, several of the estimated values of π_3, although not significantly greater than zero, do have a fairly high point estimate. Six of the coefficients estimate as negative, although not significantly so. Just one country has a value of π_3 that definitely rejects the model, namely, Puerto Rico.

Looking at the parameters that are common to both exchange rate regimes, it is evident that the expected international relative price variable, the coefficient on which is $\gamma(1 - \mu)$, performs very poorly. The variable always estimates with a very small coefficient, and it never does achieve statistical significance. The lagged value of cyclical output, in contrast, performs strongly in most cases (which is comparable to Lucas's finding). In this case, all the values of γ are as predicted by the model with the exception of Argentina, which is just below zero (although not significantly so), and may be assumed to be zero; Sweden, which is just above unity (though not significantly so); and Paraguay, which is above unity and this time significantly above.

The Durbin *h*-statistic indicates that the hypothesis that the residuals display first-order autocorrelation may not be rejected in the cases of Canada, Honduras, Italy, and Japan, although in all other cases that hypothesis may be rejected. The overall goodness of fit of the equation as indicated by R^2 is quite variable although in most cases better than that found by Lucas.

In overall terms, it is clear that the model does not explain the time-series evolution of the variables in an adequate manner. In this respect, it is no worse than Lucas's model, but the way in which we have modeled economic openness does not seem to have produced a dramatic improvement over Lucas's simpler formulation.

It is, however, interesting to examine whether the countries whose time-series behavior is reasonably well explained by this model display the cross-country relationships predicted by the fixed exchange rate variant of the above model.

Our model predicts that π_3 will be inversely correlated with $\phi^2 + \psi^2$. The relevant data for performing this test are contained in Table 5. While we have not computed the rank correlation coefficient between the two series, it is evident that there is a hint that the π_3 predictions of our model are not wildly at variance with the facts. There is, however, too much looseness in the relationship to be able to say that the data in Table 5 constitutes evidence in favor of our formulation.

It is of some interest to observe that the estimated values of the coefficients on foreign surprises are more often than not larger under fixed exchange rates than under flexible rates. While little statistical significance

TABLE 5

RELEVANT KEY SUMMARY STATISTICS[a]

Country	π_3		$(\phi^2 + \psi^2)10^4$	
Austria	0.057	(8)	12	(17)
Belgium	0.963	(18)	12	(17)
Canada	0.549	(14)	36	(4)
Denmark	0.113	(9)	16	(13)
Germany	0.598	(16)	20	(9)
Guatemala	0.157	(11)	20	(9)
Honduras	0	(1)	19	(11)
Ireland	0	(1)	42	(3)
Italy	0.054	(7)	19	(11)
Netherlands	0.663	(17)	16	(13)
Norway	0	(1)	13	(16)
Sweden	0.237	(13)	16	(13)
United Kingdom	0	(1)	27	(7)
United States	0	(1)	168	(1)
Venezuela	0	(1)	126	(2)
France	0.115	(10)	33	(6)
Japan	0.551	(15)	26	(8)
Sweden	0.225	(12)	34	(5)

[a]Figures in parentheses give the rank of each country.

can be attached to these observations, it is nevertheless noteworthy that in the 15 cases where a comparison of the coefficients π_2 and π_3 is possible, in 10 of those cases π_3 exceeds π_2. This conforms with a fairly commonly held belief concerning the efficacy of flexible exchange rates as a means of insulating domestic economic activity from shocks in the rest of the world and the tendency of fixed exchange rates to enhance the effects of those shocks on domestic output.

What are the implications of these empirical findings? First it will be recognized that we have in no way rejected the natural rate and rational expectations hypotheses. In order to formulate our model for empirical implementation we had to make a series of judgments en route, any one of which could be at the source of the overall failure of the model. For example, modeling the growth of nominal demand as an exogenous variable is an economical procedure, but may be the source of specification bias. Further, even allowing nominal demand growth to be exogenous, the assumption that it is a serially uncorrelated normally distributed random variable may require modification. The same remark would apply to the processes assumed to generate foreign inflation and the deviation from purchasing power parity. Both of these processes were modeled as simple first-order schemes. A more general characterization of all three of these stochastic processes could and perhaps should be pursued. However while we would not want to interpret the results presented here as a rejection of the natural rate-rational expectations-open economy model, we do interpret them as indicating that there is no simple trade-off, even in the short run, between inflation and output in most of the countries studied. If these countries do indeed have a short-run trade-off, it is very difficult to observe; more sophisticated modeling of the exogenous variables (and possibly of the aggregate demand side of the economy) is needed in order that the parameters of that short-run trade-off may be recovered.

A further possible interpretation of these results, and one to which we incline, is that the sample used is too heavily dominated by fixed exchange rate experience. In a fixed exchange rate world, differences in measured inflation rates across national economies reflect changing relative prices rather than different underlying monetary growth rates. The relevant aggregate entity at which to perform monetary analyses in such a world is the aggregate of countries whose exchange rates are pegged against each other. It may well be that at that level of "world" aggregation, there does indeed exist a trade-off between output and inflation, but that the distribution of output across individual economies is either in no way or only loosely related to the rate of inflation. A further useful line of inquiry would be to examine the performance of the closed economy model (as developed by Lucas) on world aggregate data through the fixed exchange rate period up to 1971–1972.

To conclude, we have specified a weaker version of the natural rate-rational expectations model developed by Lucas to allow for economic openness. We have had to make additional assumptions concerning the determination of the additional exogenous variables, but have otherwise retained Lucas's assumptions. We have estimated the model and found it to be rejected on a variety of sign and parameter-value criteria for only 2 of the 21 countries in the sample. For the 19 countries whose data do not reject the model, the cross-country relationship between the slope of the short-run trade-off and the variance of nominal demand, predicted by Lucas (but not by our model), is not found in the data. Further, the cross-country relationship between the slope of the trade-off and the variance of foreign shocks, predicted by our analysis, is not found in the data. Several further lines of inquiry seem to be suggested by these results, notably elaborating the modeling of aggregate demand, using more general assumptions about the stochastic processes generating the exogenous variables, and possibly examining the performance of the model on a more global aggregate economy through the fixed exchange rate years of the 1950s and 1960s.

Appendix

1. Estimation

Data manipulation and estimation were carried out using TSP CDC Cyber 73/16 of the Social Science Computing Laboratory at the University of Western Ontario.

2. Data Sources

Data for all countries, except Puerto Rico, are taken from IMP *International Financial Statistics* publications. The May 1978 issue provides the major protion of the data base, while the other issues cited are used to extend the series back to 1951 and forward to 1978 wherever possible. The output data (nominal and in 1975 prices) are either GDP (lines 99b and 99b, p) or GNP (lines 99a and 99a, p or 99a, r), whichever is published consistently. The exchange rate series (mainly lines rf or rh) are period average values. Some errors were corrected in the real output data for Canada (1951) and Norway (1967 to 1969).

The data for Puerto Rico were pieced together from the various United Nations bulletins noted below.

3. References

International Monetary Fund, *International Financial Statistics*, **29** (5) (May 1976); **30** (5) (May 1977); **31** (5) (May 1978); **32** (6) (June 1979).

United Nations, *Monthly Bulletin of Statistics*, **33** (6) (June 1979).

United Nations, *Yearbook of National Accounts Statistics*, 1961; 1966; 1970 (vols. 1 and 2); 1975 (vol. 1).

REFERENCES

Barro, R. J. (1976). Rational Expectations and the Role of Monetary Policy, *Journal of Monetary Economics* **2**, 1–32.

Cukierman, A., and Wachtel, P. (1979). Differential Inflationary Expectations and the Variability of the Rate of Inflation, *American Economic Review* **69**, 595–609.

Lucas, R. E. (1973). Some International Evidence on Output-Inflation Tradeoffs, *American Economic Review* **33**, 326–334.

Lucas, R. E. (1976). Some International Evidence on Output–Inflation Tradeoffs: Errata, *American Economic Review* **66**, 985.
Sargent, T. J. (1979). *Macroeconomic Theory*. Academic Press, New York.

DEPARTMENT OF ECONOMICS
UNIVERSITY OF WESTERN ONTARIO
LONDON, CANADA

PART 3

Indexation and Pricing

On Indexation and Macroeconomic Stability

ELISHA A. PAZNER[*†]

1. Introduction

As conjectured by Fischer (1976) and proved by Gray (1976), while indexing wages to the price level insulates the real sector of the economy from monetary disturbances, it exacerbates the real effects of real disturbances. In this paper I show, within Gray's model, that indexing nominal wages to aggregate nominal income rather than to the price level provides the same insulation from monetary shocks and eliminates the exacerbation of real shocks. In this sense, full indexation to nominal income is superior to full indexation to the price level.

I also show that an even better method of indexation involves differential indexation to the price level and to real income. This is better in the general setting considered here, where labor market contracts involve wage rigidity and employment flexibility during the contract period. It is only in such a context, in fact, that indexation is defensible on efficiency grounds. What kind of formal economic model one would require in order to explain the existence of this kind of institutional setting is an important question which is, however, beyond the scope of the present paper.

*This is an extensively edited version of a draft that Professor Pazner was apparently reworking, at the time of his death, for presentation at the conference.

†Helpful conversations with Robert J. Gordon on the general subject of indexation are gratefully acknowledged. I also wish to thank Assaf Razin for helpful comments on a previous draft.

ISBN 0-12-259750-8

2. Gray's Macroeconomic Model

Following Gray, the model of the economy is given by

$$Y = \alpha G(L), \qquad \alpha = 1 + \mu, \tag{1}$$

$$M^{S} = \beta\text{-}\overline{M}, \qquad \beta = 1 + \Sigma, \tag{2}$$

$$M^{D} = KPY, \tag{3}$$

$$M^{S} = M^{D}, \tag{4}$$

$$L^{D} = f(w/\alpha), \qquad w = W/P, \qquad f_{w/\alpha} < 0, \tag{5}$$

$$L^{S} = g(w), \qquad g_2 > 0, \tag{6}$$

where Y is aggregate output, L is aggregate labor input, $G(L)$ is aggregate production function (assumed to be homogeneous of degree less than one), μ is symmetrically distributed stochastic term with zero mean, M^S is nominal money supply, $\overline{M}$ is constant, Σ is symmetrically distributed stochastic term with zero mean (assumed to be uncorrelated with μ), M^D is demand for nominal balances, K is the Cambridge desired ratio of money to nominal income (assumed to be constant), L^D is demand for labor, L^S is supply of labor, W is nominal wage rate, P is price level, and w is real wage rate, $w = W/P$.

Again, following Gray, the base nominal wage rate is assumed to be set so as to satisfy $L^S = L^D$ when $\mu = \Sigma = 0$. Once this contract has been negotiated, the values of μ and Σ become known and production decisions are made. At this point the level of employment becomes completely demand determined.[1]

Indexation of nominal wages to nominal income means that during the contract period

$$d \log W = d \log PY = d \log P + d \log Y \tag{7}$$

so that the *real* wage w is allowed to change in proportion to the change in real income ($d \log w = d \log Y$). This new form of indexing thus differs fundamentally from indexation to the price level, where the real wage rate is not allowed to change during the contract period (as $d \log W = d \log P$ implies that $dw = 0$).

The following analysis assumes, like Gray's, that prices adjust instantaneously to ensure equilibrium in the money market as described by (4). I now proceed to show that indexing the wage rate to nominal income

[1] These assumptions are somewhat arbitrary (see Gray, 1976, pp. 223–224, especially notes 6 and 9).

prevents the transmission of monetary disturbances to the real sector *without* exacerbating the real effects of real disturbances.

3. Monetary Shocks

Real disturbances are assumed away in this section by postulating that $\mu = 0$, leaving aggregate output exclusively a function of total labor input:

$$Y = G(L). \tag{1'}$$

Likewise, the demand for labor in this case depends solely on the real wage rate:

$$L^{\mathrm{D}} = f(w). \tag{5'}$$

Equilibrium in the money market requires

$$\overline{M} = KPY, \qquad \beta = 1 + \textstyle\sum, \tag{8}$$

which can be rewritten as

$$(1 = \Sigma)\overline{M} = K \cdot (W/w) \cdot G[f(w)], \tag{9}$$

Assume that $\Sigma > 0$. The immediate impact of the increase in $M^{\mathrm{S}}(= M^{\mathrm{D}})$ by the factor $\beta > 1$ is to raise $P = W/w$ by the same factor. If the nominal wage rate is indexed to PY then, at the unchanged Y, W goes up by the factor β as well, leaving w unchanged. From (5′) it is then seen that L^{D} is unchanged, implying (in this demand-determined model) from (1′) that Y is unchanged as well. Hence, under indexation of wages to nominal income, the real sector is fully insulated from monetary disturbances. Note that the assumption about the clearing of (4) by means of instantaneous adjustments in P implies that prices may fall as well as rise. Therefore, a negative monetary shock ($\Sigma < 0$) has exactly the same result. Without indexation of wages, monetary disturbances would be transmitted to the real sector precisely as described in Gray (1976, pp. 226–227).

4. Real Shocks

Monetary disturbances are assumed away in this section by postulating $\Sigma = 0$, which implies

$$M^{\mathrm{S}} = \overline{M}. \tag{2'}$$

The equilibrium condition for the money market then becomes

$$\overline{M} = K \cdot (W/w) \cdot (1+\mu) \cdot G\{f[w/(1+\mu)]\}, \qquad G_{w/1} + \mu < 0. \quad (10)$$

where (1) has been used in its stochastic form.

In the nonindexed case, W is fixed. This implies that any increase (decrease) in μ will be offset by a proportionate increase (decrease) in w. It further implies that employment L stays constant while real income (output) Y changes by the factor $1 + \mu$ so that Y and w change by the same proportion up or down according to whether the real shock is positive or negative ($\mu \gtrless 0$). The price level P falls when $\mu > 0$ and rises when $\mu < 0$.

In the case of an indexed economy, it is easy to see that if wages are indexed to nominal income, precisely the same results obtain. At the level of employment prevailing prior to the real shock—that is, at that level of L which solves (5) and (6), real income Y changes by the factor $(1 + \mu)$. By the indexation rule, this implies a proportionate change in the nominal wage rate W as well. At this point the real wage rate has changed to $(1 + \mu)w$. At a fixed price level (that prevailing prior to the real shock), W/w is unchanged, implying that $M^D \neq M^S$. Therefore P must change, implying (because of the indexation method) a proportionate change in W, leaving the real wage rate at its new value $(1 + \mu)w$. Once the price level has changed by the factor $(1 - \mu)$, equilibrium is restored in the money (and commodity) market. The real wage rate is now $(1 + \mu)$ times what it would be under $\mu = 0$, employment is unchanged, and output is changed by the factor $(1 + \mu)$—precisely the same results as those obtained in a nonindexed system.[2] In both cases aggregate nominal income is unchanged, reflecting the fact that both M and K are assumed to be fixed.

Thus, indexation of nominal wages to nominal income, unlike indexation to the price level along, does *not* exacerbate the effects of real disturbances.

[2] Note that $d \log W = d \log P + d \log Y = -\mu + \mu = 0$, so that, in the final analysis, the *nominal* wage rate stays fixed at its contractual level.

This might also be the appropriate place to note that we could think of an indexation scheme under which nominal labor *income* (rather than the wage rate) is indexed to nominal income. This might seem more natural since the index base PY and the indexed variable WL would then have the same dimensions, in the sense that W and P are both price variables, making indexation to the price level a seemingly more "natural" procedure. It is easy to see, however, that the conclusions of this and the preceding sections would remain unaffected since in the expression $d \log W + d \log L = d \log P + d \log Y$, which would reflect the indexing formula in this case, we would again obtain $d \log L = 0$ under both monetary and real shocks.

5. On the Optimal Degree of Indexation

Gray has also considered the interesting problem of the optimal degree of indexation in the present kind of setting where noncontingent wages are contractually agreed upon at the beginning of the contract period, and the level of employment can adjust during the contract period so that employers are always on their demand curve. Within the context of indexation to the price level, Gray showed that the optimal degree of indexation is generally less than unity, under an objective function that makes some adjustments in employment desirable in the event of real shocks [see Gray (1976, p. 230, Eq. (10))].

It is easy to see that under Gray's objective function, if wages are indexed to nominal income instead of to the price level, the optimal degree of indexation will still generally differ from unity. However, a somewhat different and rather interesting result is obtained if the degree of indexation of wages to the price P and real output Y components of nominal income PY is *not* constrained to be the same.

The optimization problem regarding the degree and form of indexation can be looked upon in the following way. A *precise* simulation of labor–market equilibria in a perfectly frictionless version of the economy such as Gray assumes (which is the "first-best" state of affairs under Gray's objective function) is generally unattainable by indexation alone as the degree of indexation is not allowed to be state contingent. Allowing differential degrees of wage indexation to the P and Y components of PY permits greater flexibility. Irrespective of the optimal degrees of indexation to P and Y obtaining in this case, it is always possible to devise an equivalent indexation scheme that indexes W fully to P but only partially to Y. In other words, the optimal degree of indexation is always amenable to a scheme that specifies full indexation of wages to the price level but only partial indexation of wages to real income.

The moral of this section is the usual one regarding targets and instruments in the theory of economic policy. In the present model, given Gray's objective function, two separate pragmatic policy targets appear.

In the presence of monetary disturbances, the target is to reproduce *fully* the working of a frictionless competitive economy, which implies insulating the real sector from monetary shocks. This can be achieved by indexation only if wages are fully indexed to the price level. In the presence of real shocks, on the other hand, the aim is to approach *as closely as possible* the workings of a frictionless economy. (Complete success is unachievable in the absence of contingent contracts.) This generally requires partial indexation of wages to nominal income, which can be achieved in conjunction with full indexation to the price level by partial indexation to real income. Gray assumed that only one indexing instrument was available; her analysis is therefore "second-best" relative to the results attainable here. As noted, the present analysis is also "second best" relative to the solution attainable with a set of full-fledged contingent (indexation) contracts. As always, terms such as "optimal" are precise only when used in conjunction with well-defined objectives and instruments.

6. Concluding Remarks

A. Full Indexation to Nominal Income

1. The economics behind the nominal corrections proposed here in lieu of the standard monetary corrections are straightforward. Real shocks have only recently been subjected to close academic scrutiny. The classical case of inflation at full employment due to monetary excesses ("monetary disturbances") focused on inflation at a given level of aggregate output. With nominal wages lagging behind prices because of institutional rigidities, the idea of indexing wages to prices only was natural since the "classical" model of the macroeconomy admitted only one level of real wages compatible with full-employment equilibrium; indexation was thought to be a costless way of hastening convergence to equilibrium.

However, in view of real shocks, equilibrium considerations generally dictate a change in real wages at full employment equilibrium. Whereas indexation to the price level is problematic because the real wage is totally inflexible during the contract period, the method discussed here ensures that adjustments in full employment real wages will actually take place even under full indexation. Note also that its practical implementation is certainly no more of a problem than that of indexation to the price level (it is much easier to construct a reliable index of nominal income than a satisfactory price index).

2. By fixing the relative share of labor in national income as well as the distribution within the sector, the proposed method is also likely to minimize labor disputes and industrial unrest in the event of unforeseen shocks during the contract period. Casual empirical evidence over the long haul suggests that labor's relative share is approximately constant. This implies that the proposed method of indexation would operate as a smoothing device, maintaining the long-run distributional patterns of an unindexed economy. I consider these distributional effects of indexation important even if their ultimate effect is only the peaceful attainment of the "efficiency" objective assumed here and by Gray.

3. While the problem of full indexation, including the indexation of financial assets, has not been discussed, the principles applied here carry over. For instance, if part of the real capital stock in the economy is destroyed by shocks such as a war or an earthquake, indexation of financial assets to the price level only (which ensures a fixed real rate of return) is clearly inappropriate. Indexation to the nominal (present) value of assets (or partial indexation to real capital, on top of full indexation to prices) will, on the other hand, permit at least some of the necessary adjustments in the real rates of return to real shocks, while at the same time ensuring that price changes due purely to monetary disturbances are not allowed to affect (temporarily) the real rate of interest.

B. Partial Indexation

1. The optimal degree of partial indexation is less straightforward as it is sensitive both to objectives and to the additional instruments assumed to be available. However, it would seem reasonable that the optimal indexation policy should always specify *full indexation to the price level and partial indexation to real income* and possibly to some other key economic variables as well. Only this will provide full insulation from monetary shocks while also keeping the costs of real shocks to a minimum.

2. Finally, some implications for tax policy: Insofar as proportional taxes are concerned, indexation is obviously superfluous. As to progressive taxes, such as personal income tax, where the *real* average rate of taxation is to be an increasing function of *real* income, tax brackets ought to be fully escalated to the price level, which from the viewpoint of the present paper is a partial indexation scheme.

REFERENCES

Barro, R. J. (1979). Indexation in a Rational Expectations Model. *Journal of Economic Theory* **13**, 229–244.

Fischer, S. (1976). On Some Theoretical Considerations. In *The Role of Indexation* (A. Swoboda, ed.). International Center for Monetary and Banking Studies, Geneva.

Gray, J. A. (1976). Wage-Indexation: A Macroeconomic Approach. *Journal of Monetary Economics* **2**, 221–235.

DEPARTMENT OF ECONOMICS
TEL AVIV UNIVERSITY
RAMAT AVIV, TEL AVIV, ISRAEL

Partial Tax Indexation and Economic Stability

*BEN-ZION ZILBERFARB**

The high rates of inflation experienced by most economies in recent years have brought great pressure on governments to index their income tax systems. [A survey of the various tax adjustment schemes is provided in OECD (1976).] The most common argument for tax indexation is tax equity, mainly to protect the taxpayer from the effects of inflation in relation to his income tax liability. Friedman (1974) and others advance another argument: Tax indexation acts as a brake on the growth of government expenditures by removing the additional tax revenues caused by inflation. Opponents of the indexed tax system disagree. They claim that government expenditures are determined by public needs, independent of the way in which they are financed. The main argument against an indexed tax system, as stated, for example, in Canada's (1967) Carter Report, is that it causes irreparable damage to the built-in stability of the system. In an unindexed regime with a progressive tax system, tax revenues rise faster than nominal income when there is inflation. Thus, disposable income and subsequently consumption vary less than nominal income, and the economy is more stable.[1]

The purpose of this study is to measure the effect of partial tax indexing on economic stability. This is done by simulating an annual

* I would like to thank F. G. Adams, M. Feldstein, S. Fischer, E. Katz, L. R. Klein, L. Seidman, and R. Shiller for helpful comments on earlier versions of this paper.

[1] Recent experience has shown that this traditional argument is incomplete. In a period of stagflation the reduction in aggregate demand, caused by the inflation generated increase in taxes, will tend to stabilize the price level but aggravate unemployment.

ISBN 0-12-259750-8

model of the United States economy close in nature to the Wharton model. [A detailed description of the model is provided in Zilberfarb (1976); a summary is provided in the Appendix.] The results are reported and analyzed in Section 2. Conclusions are presented in Section 3.

1. The Income Tax Equation in Indexed and Unindexed Regimes

The income tax equation of the unindexed model relates income tax revenues (*PIT*) to national income (*NI*) minus the level of total personal exemptions (*EXMP*). Three dummy variables are included in the equation to account for the tax law revisions in 1964, 1968, and 1970. The estimated equation for the period 1947–1972 is

$$PIT = -3.21 + 0.175(NI - EXMP) + \text{dummies}, \tag{1}$$

where $EXMP = N$ (population) $\cdot$ XMP (the level of personal exemption). The progressive tax structure is not reflected in the model since indexation in this paper is limited to the level of personal exemptions.[2] However, it is expected that indexation of the progressive tax structure as well as personal exemptions would simply strengthen the results.

In the indexed model, the tax equation is adjusted by making exemptions proportionate to the GNP deflator P. The base year for indexing is 1950 and the indexed *PIT* equation is

$$PIT = -3.21 + 0.175(NI - EXMP \cdot P/P_{50}) + \text{dummies}. \tag{2}$$

The constant term in Eq. (1), which is carried over to Eq. (2), is negative, presumably reflecting other tax deductions not implicitly included in the equation. In an alternative version of the indexed model the constant term is also indexed and the tax equation is

$$PIT = -3.21 \cdot P/P_{50} + 0.175(NI - EXMP \cdot P/P_{50}) + \text{dummies}. \tag{3}$$

The simulation results obtained for the two versions are virtually the same because of the magnitude of the constant term compared with total personal exemptions (1950—$83 billion; 1972—$145 billion). The results reported later are those of the first version [Eq. (2)].[3]

[2] Personal exemptions were $83 billion in 1950 and $145 billion in 1972, or 34% and 15% of national income, respectively. When personal exemptions are indexed, the 1972 figure is $287 billion, or 28% of national income. The partial indexation discussed here therefore accounts for roughly one-quarter of national income.

[3] The results for the second version [Eq. (3)] are available from the author on request.

2. The Effect of Tax Indexation on Economic Stability: Simulation Results

To test the effect of tax indexation on economic stability, three types of external shocks are analyzed: shocks to aggregate demand (a stochastic shift of the *IS* curve), shocks to money supply (a stochastic shift of the *LM* curve), and shocks to prices. Their effect is calculated in the following way. First, a control solution is computed by ex post simulation of the model (for both the indexed and unindexed cases). Another solution is then computed for the same time period, with a change in one of the exogenous variables. This is the deviant solution. A comparison of the deviant solution with the control solution enables measurement of the response of economic variables to the exogenous shock as[4]

$$k_{it} = Y_{it}^{\mathrm{d}} - Y_{it}^{\mathrm{c}},$$

where k_{it} is the effect of an exogenous shock on an endogenous variable i at time t, and Y_{it}^{d}, Y_{it}^{c} are the values of an endogenous variable i at time t. The d, c superscripts denote the deviant and control solution, respectively. Indexing would reduce economic stability if the exogenous shocks induced greater movements in real output (or prices) in the indexed system than in an unindexed regime.

A. External Shocks to Aggregate Demand and to the Money Supply

The shock to aggregate demand (hereafter referred to as a real shock) is created by a sustained increase of \$1 billion in real government expenditures. The monetary shock is created by a sustained increase of \$1 billion in the money supply. The effect of these shocks on real GNP and the GNP deflator P is summarized in Table 1 and Fig. 1.

The results show that an exogenous shock induces greater fluctuations in real GNP and the price level when the economy is indexed than when it is not. It implies that indexing reduces the built-in stability of the economic system. The reason is that the fiscal and monetary shocks cause price increases which lead to higher real tax revenues in an unindexed economy, thereby reducing the effective marginal propensity to consume (MPC). In the indexed regime the level of personal exemptions is adjusted for infla-

[4] For a detailed analysis of simulation techniques, see Klein (1971).

TABLE 1

The Effects of Real and Monetary Shocks

	Real shock				Monetary shock			
	ΔGNP		ΔP		ΔGNP		ΔP	
Year	Indexed	Unindexed	Indexed	Unindexed	Indexed	Unindexed	Indexed	Unindexed
1	1.93	1.91	0.00	0.00	0.53	0.54	0.00	0.00
2	2.04	1.78	0.13	0.13	0.80	0.72	0.03	0.03
3	2.77	2.12	0.36	0.32	0.97	0.77	0.10	0.09
4	2.40	1.45	0.68	0.55	0.88	0.58	0.20	0.17
5	2.40	1.05	1.02	0.75	0.86	0.41	0.30	0.22
6	2.20	0.04	1.36	0.90	0.77	0.20	0.40	0.26
7	1.78	− 0.18	1.65	0.98	0.60	− 0.23	0.47	0.26
8	1.51	− 0.57	1.88	0.97	0.47	− 0.39	0.52	0.21

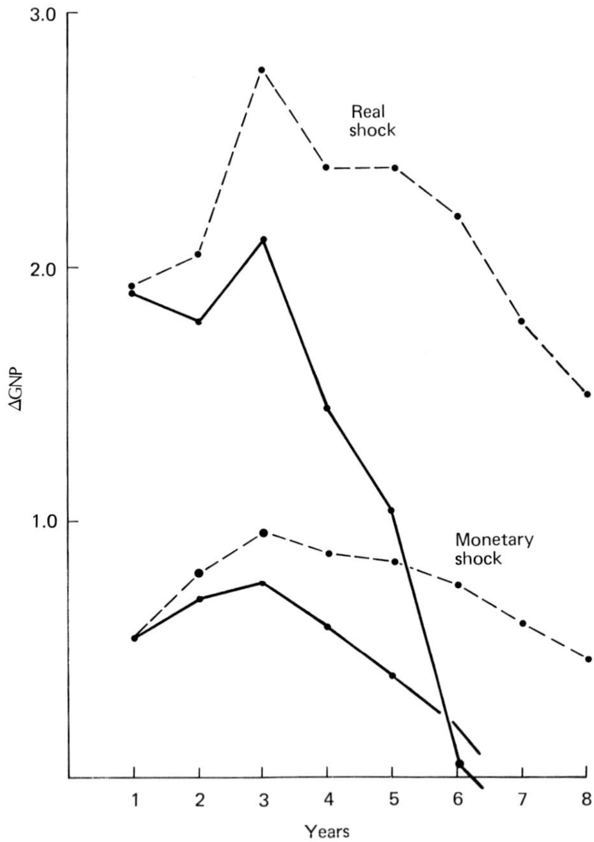

Fig. 1. The effects of real and monetary shocks. Solid line is unindexed regime; dashed line is indexed regime.

tion, and therefore the reduction in MPC is less than that of the unindexed economy. It is clear that the difference between the effect of these exogenous shocks on real GNP in the indexed and unindexed regimes widens as the price level rises. Since the simulation results show that the impact of these shocks on the price level increases with time, so also does the reduction in the built-in stability. The average effect of the real (monetary) shock on real GNP is higher in the indexed regime by 7.6% (5.6%) for the two-year average, and it increases to 16.0% (12.7%) and 39.2% (34.7%) for the three- and five-year averages. These results contradict Pierce and Enzler (1976), who found that complete tax indexation has a small effect on the built-in stability of the system. In their study a real shock causes an increase in GNP only 1.9% higher in the indexed regime than in the unindexed system six quarters after the shock. In the case of a monetary shock there is no difference at all between the two regimes in the short run. They do not report long-run effects.

One obvious explanation for these differences is the different models employed in these simulation studies. A more probable cause are the economic conditions for the period over which the simulation experiments were conducted. Pierce and Enzler (1976, p. 178) decided "to choose a 'typical' historical period during which the economy . . . was not subject to unusual influences." As most of the effects of the Vietnam war were therefore not included in their data, it is likely that the inflation rate in their simulation period was low. However, in this study, the inflation rate in the simulation period is quite high (between 2.1 and 4.8% per annum). Since the case for indexation grows stronger as inflation increases, it is more likely that such a system will be implemented in a period of high inflation; therefore the simulation period should be characterized by high inflation rates.

When interpreting the results of this study, one should remember that they are "upward biased." The personal income tax system is indexed by the *current* price level, assuming an immediate adjustment of the exemption level to price changes. In practice the adjustment mechanism must involve a lag, thereby reducing the destabilizing effects of indexation.[5]

[5] By ignoring the government budget constraint and assuming that government expenditures are independent of tax revenues, it is implicitly assumed that tax revenues lost due to indexation are financed by government bonds, and that these bonds are not part of private wealth (see Barro, 1974). However, if government bonds are part of private wealth, or if lost tax revenues are financed by fiat money, then the expansionary effect of tax indexing would be more pronounced, leading to a reduction in the built-in stability. In such a case our results are "downward biased."

B. Price Shocks

Recent experience has shown that the economy may be exposed to large external price shocks, such as a rise in oil prices. An argument against indexing is that it exacerbates the effect of these price shocks, making the indexed system less stable with respect to prices. An exogenous price shock increases domestic prices, thereby increasing real tax revenues and reducing consumption. The reduction in consumption, and therefore in aggregate demand, puts a downward pressure on prices. This restraining effect is weakened in an indexed regime, since real tax revenues increase less than in an unindexed regime.[6]

To examine this issue the model was simulated with a sustained exogenous shock of ten percentage points to import prices. The effect of this change on the GNP deflator is reported in Table 2 and Fig. 2. As expected, the change in *P* is higher in the indexed regime. The difference between the indexed and unindexed regimes increases from zero in the first year to 1.96 points, ten years after the shock. In both regimes the change in *P* reaches a peak seven years after the initial shock and declines thereafter. Thus, the results show that both regimes are stable when an exogenous shock to the price level occurs. However, indexing exacerbates the effect of this shock. Once again, the results contradict these reported by Pierce and Enzler (1976).

TABLE 2

The Effect of a Price Shock on the GNP Deflator (*P*)

	Change in *P*			Change in *P*	
Year	Indexed	Unindexed	Year	Indexed	Unindexed
1	1.31	1.31	6	8.85	7.55
2	3.28	3.18	7	9.25	7.66
3	5.16	4.85	8	9.24	7.43
4	6.78	6.16	9	8.85	6.90
5	7.99	7.02	10	8.01	6.05

3. Conclusions

This study explores how indexation of the level of personal exemptions affects economic stability. The simulation results suggest the following conclusions:

[6] This argument also implies that the change in real GNP caused by the price shock is more moderate in the indexed regime. The simulation results confirm this argument.

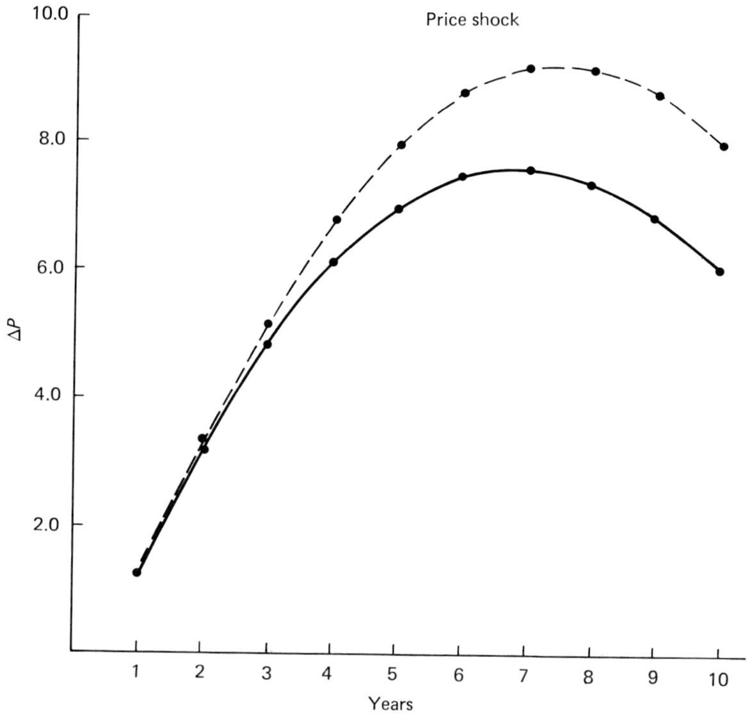

Fig. 2. The effects of a price shock. Solid line is unindexed regime; dashed line is indexed regime.

1. Tax indexing reduces the built-in stability of the economic system. This reduction increases with time. In the short run (one or two years) an exogenous shock to the *IS* (*LM*) curve causes changes in real GNP which are greater on the average by 7.6% (5.6%) in an indexed system than in an unindexed regime. These differences increase to 16.0% (12.7%) after three years and to 39.3% (34.7%) after 5 years.

2. Tax indexing exacerbates the effect of an exogenous price shock on the price level.

The results and conclusions should not be interpreted as opposition to tax indexation. The implementation of an indexed tax system is a social issue as well as an economic one. This paper tries to show some of the economic implications of such a system. It is clear that a decrease in the built-in stability of the economic system can be offset by discretionary government policy. However, in many real-world situations, government is politically unable to implement discretionary policies quickly. Hence the loss of automatic stability may be of some importance.

Appendix

(1) $C_d = -21.2 + 0.066 DPI/PC + 0.163(M + TD)/PC + 0.196\, C_{d-1}$

(2) $C_{nd} = 14.3 + 0.134 DPI/PC + 0.608\, C_{nd-1},$

(3) $C_s = -1.4 + 0.096 DPI/PC + 0.038 H + 0.696\, C_{s-1},$

(4) $IHN/N = -0.104 + 0.017\, \Delta(DPI/N) + 0.006(R - RCP) + 0.013(R - RCP)_{-1} + 0.225 PH/P - 0.088(N16 - N65)/N - 0.032(H/N)_{-1},$

(5) $INR/KNR_{-1} = 0.017 + 0.149 X/KNR_{-1} - 0.007(R + DEP - \hat{P}) + 0.0151 \Delta X/KNR_{-1} + 0.013 D62,$

(6) $EX = -22.6 + 0.266 XWT + 19.1 PX/P + DCA,$

(7) $IM = -1.18 + 0.041 X - 4.22 PM/P + 0.359 IM_{-1} + DCA,$

(8) $\Delta \ln L = 0.442 + 0.457 \ln X - 0.340(\ln L_{-1} + 0.410 \ln k) - 0.003 T,$

(9) $UNR = 0.393 - 0.670\, \Delta CL - 0.195 UNR_{-1} + 0.374(W/P)_{-1},$

(10) $\widehat{WR} = 5.35 - 0.761 UNR + 0.851 \hat{P} + 0.626(\widehat{X/L}),$

(11) $P = 3.85 + 0.856 W/X + 0.082 PM + 0.395 P_{-1},$

(12) $\Delta PC = -0.106 + 0.867\, \Delta P + 0.016\, \Delta PF,$

(13) $\Delta PH = 0.244 + 1.14\, \Delta P + 0.150\, \Delta(IH + INR),$

(14) $IBT = -2.91 + 0.096 P \cdot X,$

(15) $PIT = -3.21 + 0.175(NI - XMP \cdot N) + \text{dummies},$

(16) $SSC = -14.3 + 0.217 WC + BASE \cdot RATE \cdot (L - LG),$

(17) $CPIV = 1.76 + 0.399 NW,$

(18) $DIV = -0.652 + 0.069 CPIV + 0.830 DIV_{-1},$

(19) $IPGC = 15.1 + 1.14 R + 0.120 P,$

(20) $TP/(P \cdot N16) = -0.985 + 0.018 UNR + 2.73 N65/N16,$

(21) $RCP = 4.87 - 4.98 M/P + 0.011 X + 2.55 D69,$

(22) $R = 0.159 + 0.311 RCP + 0.045 \hat{P} + 0.726 R_{-1},$

(23) $TD = -60.4 + 0.383 NI - 5.54 RCP - 0.869 \hat{P} + LCD.$

IDENTITIES

(24) $X = C_{nd} + C_d + C_s + INR + IH + G + EX - IM,$

(25) $KNR = INR + KNR_{-1} - DEP \cdot KNR_{-1},$

(26) $H = IH + 0.95 H_{-1},$

(27) $NW = P \cdot W - WR \cdot L - IBT - P \cdot KNR \cdot DEP - P \cdot H \cdot 0.05,$

(28) $DPI = WR \cdot L + NW - CPIV + DIV - SSC + TP + IPGC - PIT,$

where Δ denotes changes (e.g., $\Delta X = X_t - X_{t-1}$), and the overhead caret denotes rates of change (e.g., $\hat{P} = \Delta P/P_{t-1}$)

LIST OF SYMBOLS

- **BASE* maximum wage for social security contributions
- C_d consumption of durable goods (in constant dollars),
- C_{nd} consumption of nondurable goods (in constant dollars)
- C_s consumption of services (in constant dollars)
- *CL* civilian employment
- *CPIV* corporate profits and inventory valuation adjustment
- **DCA* dummy variable for the U.S.–Canadian Auto Agreement
- **DEP* depreciation rate
- *DIV* dividends
- *DPI* disposable personal income

**D*62	dummy variable for investment credit
**D*69	dummy variable for the commercial paper market
EX	real exports
H	real stock of housing
IBT	indirect business tax
IH	real residential investment
IHN	net residential investment (in constant dollars)
IM	real imports
INR	real nonresidential investment
IPGC	interest paid by government and consumers
K	capital stock (in constant dollars)
KNR	nonresidential capital stock (in constant dollars)
L	unemployment
**LCD*	large certificate of deposits
**LG*	government employees
**M*	money supply (currency + demand deposits)
**N*	population
NI	national income
NW	nonwage income
*N*16	population aged 16 and above
**N*65	population aged 65 and above
P	GNP deflator
PC	personal consumption deflator
**PF*	price index of the farm sector
PH	price of housing
PIT	personal income tax
**PM*	imports price index
**PX*	exports price index
R	long-term interest rate
**RATE*	rate of social security contributions
RCP	short-term interest rate
SSC	social security contributions
**T*	time
TD	time deposits
TP	transfer payments
UNR	unemployment rate
X	real GNP
**XMP*	level of personal exemption
**XWT*	index of real-world trade
W	total wage bill
**WC*	wages covered by the social security program as percentage of total wages
WR	nominal wage rate

An asterisk indicates an exogenous variable.

REFERENCES

Barro, R. J. (1974). Are Government Bonds Net Wealth? *Journal of Political Economy* **82**, 1095–1117.

Canada (1967). *Report of the Royal Commission on Taxation*. Ottawa.

Friedman, M. (1974). Monetary Corrections. In *Essays on Inflation and Indexation*, pp. 25–62. American Enterprise Institute, Washington, D.C.

Klein, L. R. (1971). *An Essay on the Theory of Economic Prediction*. Markham, Chicago, Illinois.

OECD (1976). *The Adjustment of Personal Income Tax Systems for Inflation*. Paris.

Pierce, J. L., and Enzler, J. J. (1976). The Implication for Economic Stability of Indexing the Individual Income Tax. In *Inflation and the Income Tax*, H. J. Aaron, ed., pp. 173–195. Brookings Institute, Washington, D.C.

Zilberfarb, B. (1976). An Annual Model of the U.S. Economy 1947–1972. Mimeo, University of Pennsylvania.

DEPARTMENT OF ECONOMICS
BAR-ILAN UNIVERSITY
RAMAT-GAN, ISRAEL

Wage Indexation in an Open Economy

*ABRAHAM KNOBEL**

1. Introduction

Gray (1976) and Fischer (1977) have shown that while wage indexation has a stabilizing effect on an economy subject to monetary shocks, it has a destabilizing effect on an economy in which real shocks prevail.

The purpose of the present study is to extend the analysis of wage indexation to an open economy with pegged exchange rates. The complication added by permitting international trade is that now the economy is subject not only to domestic disturbances but also to shocks originating abroad. Furthermore, the policy goal of macroeconomic stability must be reinterpreted.

In a static closed economy a possible rationale for considering stability of output desirable is that it guarantees consumers a smooth consumption stream, which is preferable to a consumption path subject to random fluctuations. In an open economy a trade balance deficit or surplus may destroy the equality of output and consumption that necessarily prevails in a static closed economy. Consequently, stability of output alone does not entail stability of consumption; an appropriate policy goal would be stability of the sum of domestic output and excess of imports over exports.

*This paper evolved from my work on a Ph.D. thesis to be submitted to Tel Aviv University. I wish to thank Assaf Razin for his guidance and most valuable comments. Thanks are also due to Alex Cukierman, Rudiger Dornbusch, Douglas Purvis, and Zvi Sussman, who commented on a previous version of the paper. Partial financial support by the Foerder Institute for Economic Research is gratefully acknowledged.

ISBN 0-12-259750-8

Once a distinction is made between tradable goods and nontradables so that relative price changes become possible, a smooth aggregate consumption stream does not necessarily imply the absence of random fluctuations in the consumption of each of the goods. Insofar as these fluctuations are undesirable, the relevant policy goal in an open economy with two commodities should be redefined to include stability of output in the nontradable good industry, as well as stability of the sum of domestic output of the tradable good and the trade balance deficit.

As the main concern of this paper is to examine whether or not the results obtained by Gray and Fischer regarding the effect of wage indexation on economic stability carry over to open economies, an effort has been made to conduct the analysis in a framework that includes key features of their papers. In particular, it should be noted that following Gray's paper it is assumed that in the absence of real wage rigidity caused by indexation, real wages are flexible while nominal wages are not. While one might argue that real wages are not constant unless they are fixed by indexation, the flexibility of real wages in the absence of wage indexation does not necessarily imply nominal wage rigidity.

However, it should be realized that the very issue of wage indexation can emerge only in a world where market forces are not strong enough always to clear the labor market, as they would otherwise probably also overcome artificially imposed real wage rigidities. In other words, the standard of comparison for analyzing the effects of wage indexation should be an economy in which impediments may keep the labor market from clearing in the short run even though real wages are flexible. Assuming nominal wage rigidity is a convenient way to achieve this effect, although it might be more realistic to assume that nominal wages do adjust in situations of disequilibrium in the labor market, but not fast enough to clear the market at each and every instant.

The plan of the paper is as follows: Sections 2 and 3 consider, respectively, the effects of wage indexation on macroeconomic stability in a one-commodity two-country model and in a two-commodity model for a small open economy. Section 4 is concerned with the effectiveness of devaluation under wage indexation. The major conclusions are presented in Section 5.

2. A One-Commodity Two-Country Model

This model is a straightforward extension of Gray's article to an open economy. The aggregate output of each country is produced by means of capital and labor. The amount of capital in each firm is fixed. The nominal wages and the indexation formula are agreed upon at the beginning of the period during which the wage contract is valid. The wage agreement takes into account an anticipated rate of inflation equal to the anticipated rate of world money creation. Furthermore, the wage agreement in the home country takes into account an anticipated rate of devaluation of the home currency equal to the difference between the home country's rate of money creation and that abroad. Expectations on which the wage agreement is based are rational in the sense that they are correct on the average. In addition, wage contracts take into account a degree of labor productivity also correctly anticipated on the average. The wage rate agreed upon is the competitive wage rate that clears the labor market if all anticipated values are realized.[1] However, the realized real wage rate may deviate from the competitive one as a result of stochastic disturbances in money supply or in the production function. In this case, the way in which the amount of labor forthcoming is determined must be specified. Following a common assumption in the indexation literature, we assume that by adjusting the amount of leisure they consume, workers agree to supply any amount of labor demanded by employers once product prices have become known.[2] This amounts to postulating that any quantity of labor employed according to the demand for labor function is (ex post) an equilibrium quantity.

Consider now the market for final goods. The excess demand function Z_i is defined for each country. The demand for the final good in each country is a function of real balances and the expected value of lifetime income, which is constant throughout the analysis and can therefore be neglected. The supply of final goods in each country is a decreasing function of real wages. For simplicity assume that the rate of exchange of currencies is one. Equilibrium in the product market obtains when the world excess demand is zero:

$$Z_1(M, P, W_1, \pi_1) + Z_2(\overline{M} - M, P, W_2, \pi_2) = 0, \tag{1}$$

where W_i is the nominal wage rate in country i, M the supply of money in country 1, $\overline{M}$ the world money supply, P the price of the commodity, and π_i a productivity factor. Since money is the only other good in the model, fulfillment of equilibrium condition (1) entails equilibrium in the world money market as well.

[1] This assumption is not compatible with the existence of risk aversion. Nevertheless it is used to facilitate the comparison of macroeconomic stability under different degrees of wage indexation. In this context the important difference between indexed and nonindexed wages is their reaction to unanticipated price fluctuations, rather than the different levels of nominal wages agreed upon in each case.

[2] The results of this paper are extremely sensitive to this assumption. In a large number of cases the results would be reversed if the input of labor were allowed to be determined by the supply of labor that is a function of the real wage.

External balance in the home country requires that excess demand for the commodity in that country be zero:

$$Z_1(M, P, W_1, \pi_1) = 0. \tag{2}$$

If (2) holds, the excess demand for money in country 1 is zero, which can be seen by recalling that the labor market is by definition in equilibrium and then invoking Walras's law. But if both the home country money market and the world money market are in equilibrium, as implied by (1), then the money market in country 2 must also clear. From here it can be inferred that the product market in country 2 clears as well. It can therefore be concluded that whenever (1) and (2) hold simultaneously, all markets clear.

Figure 1 is a diagrammatic representation of equilibrium conditions (1) and (2). The home country's money supply is measured on the vertical axis, and product prices are measured on the horizontal axis. Along the vertical line XX the world product market is in equilibrium. To keep the world money supply constant, a decrease in M must be accompanied by an equal increase in the amount of money in country 2. If the world demand for commodities is affected only by the world money supply and not by its distribution between countries, the equilibrium price of commodities is not affected by a transfer of monetary reserves from one country to another. Therefore, for a given world money supply there is only one price that clears the world commodity market.[3]

Consider now the line BB^{NI} which is the locus of values of M and P that maintain external balance in country 1 when wages are not indexed.

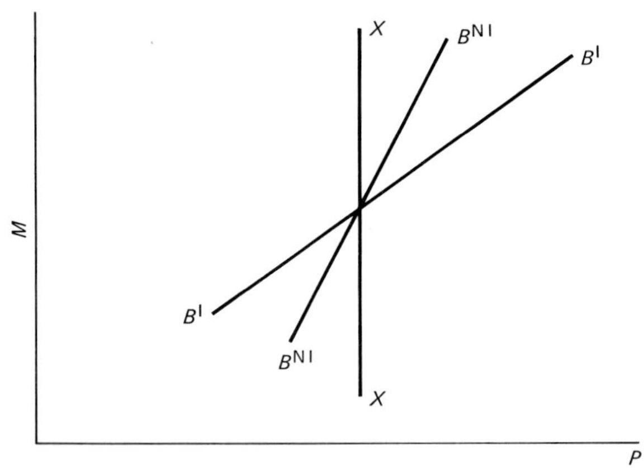

Fig. 1. Equilibrium in the world commodity market and the domestic commodity market.

[3] Differences between countries in the propensity to consume out of real balances could be permitted without affecting the conclusions.

Starting from a point of equilibrium, an increase in the money supply in country 1 will cause excess demand for commodities. In order for equilibrium to be reattained, the price of the commodity must increase. An increase of P has a twofold effect: On one hand it reduces real balances, thus reducing the demand for commodities. On the other hand, an increase of P with W_1 constant causes an increase in the amount of labor employed, and thereby in the amount of commodities supplied. From this argument, it is clear that the slope of the line BB^{NI} is positive.

The line BB^{I} is the counterpart of BB^{NI} when wages are indexed. The slope of BB^{I} is positive too (in fact, BB^{I} lies on a ray from the origin) but smaller than that of BB^{NI}. This is because the excess demand for commodities caused by an increase in M is reduced by an increase in P through the real balance effect, as in the nonindexed case. However, as the nominal wage increases proportionately to the price level, employment does not increase as it did in the previous case. Therefore, a larger increase in the price level is required to reestablish external balance.

As this section analyzes the stabilization effects of wage indexation when the sum of domestic output and the excess of imports over exports is the macroeconomic variable to be stabilized, we do not elaborate on the impact of wage indexation on the output of the commodity and on the trade balance deficit. Furthermore, macroeconomic stability as defined here amounts to stability of the demand for commodities, which in turn is directly related to the stability of the level of real balances. The following analysis therefore focuses on this variable.

A. Monetary Disturbances

Starting from a situation where all anticipated values are realized, so that the equilibrium values of M and P are the same for the indexed and the nonindexed economy, assume that the world supply of money exceeds its anticipated level, thereby causing world excess demand for commodities. To restore equilibrium in the world commodity market the price level must now increase, causing a rightward shift of the locus XX in Fig. 2. Given the indexation arrangement in country 2, an increase in P reduces the demand for commodities in country 1 through the real balance effect. If wages in country 1 are not indexed, the supply of commodities in that country will increase. The latter effect is absent if wages in country 1 are indexed. As a consequence, the increase in prices required to restore equilibrium will be larger if wages in country 1 are indexed.

It is assumed that commodity prices adjust instantaneously so as to clear the world commodity market. Therefore, if the monetary shock

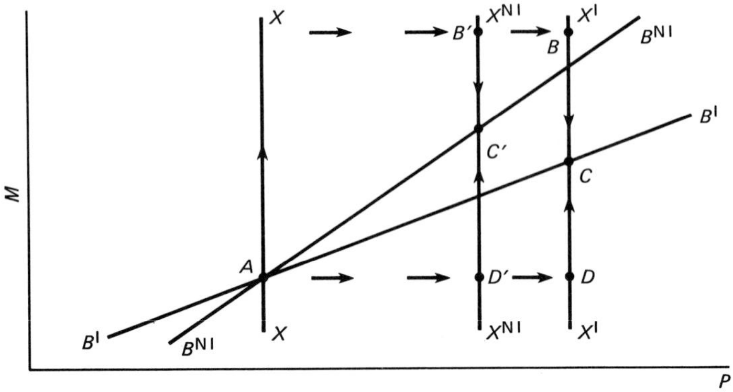

Fig. 2. Monetary disturbance.

occurred in country 1, the impact effect moves the economy from the initial point A to point B or B', depending on whether wages are linked to the price level.

As points B and B' in Fig. 2 are located to the left of the line BB^{I} along which the real balances are constant, it is easily seen that the impact effect of the monetary shock causes real balances to increase whether or not wages are indexed. However, while not completely insulating the economy from the destabilizing effects of domestic monetary disturbances, indexation is still desirable since it diminishes the deviation of the level of real balances from its target value.

In the long run,[4] as monetary reserves dwindle due to the home country's trade deficit, the economy gradually moves to points C' and C, respectively.[5] Hence, if indexation prevails the target value of real balances will be restored in the long run, but not if wages are not indexed. If the monetary expansion occurs in country 2, points C' and C in the diagram will be reached via D' and D, respectively, so that the long-run effect of wage indexation on macroeconomic stability will be the same whether the monetary disturbance occurs abroad or at home. In the short run however, indexation exacerbates instability, as can be observed by comparing the deviation of the level of real balances at points D' and D from the target level.

[4] The long run is defined in this paper as being the time span necessary for all monetary adjustments to take place. The analysis is conducted under the assumption that this occurs before the validity of wage agreements expires. The purpose of this assumption, which does not purport to be a close description of reality, is to allow an insight into the way in which different indexation arrangements affect macroeconomic stability beyond the impact effect. The long run as defined here should therefore be thought of as representing the point of time at which new wage agreements are negotiated, even if this occurs before all monetary adjustments have taken place.

[5] Point C must lie to the southeast of point C', as can easily be shown.

B. Real Disturbances

A decrease in productivity in country 2 causes a decrease in employment and hence in output in country 2 as long as commodity prices remain constant, thus creating world excess demand for the commodity. The rise in prices due to this excess demand for commodities decreases demand through the real balance effect. Given the indexation arrangement in country 2, the increase in prices causes an increase in output in country 1 unless wages in that country are indexed. Therefore the new equilibrium value of prices will be larger if wages in country 1 are indexed. Figure 3 shows this graphically by the larger rightward shift of the line XX^{I} than that of the line XX^{NI}. As there is no change in productivity in country 1, the lines BB^{I} and BB^{NI} do not shift.

The impact of a decrease in productivity abroad carries the home country's economy to point B' or B in the diagram. It is obvious that the decrease of real balances as compared to their target level is smaller at B', that is, in the nonindexed economy. In the long run, real balances return to their original level if wages are indexed; otherwise they overshoot it.[6]

Consider now a decrease of productivity at home. The decrease in country 1's output causes excess world demand for commodities, which in turn initiates an increase in prices. This decreases the world demand for commodities and simultaneously causes an increase in output in country 1 unless wages there are indexed. Therefore equilibrium in the world commodity market will be restored at a lower price level if wages in country 1 are not indexed. Furthermore, for any given price level, external balance in country 1 will continue to obtain only if nominal balances are reduced. This causes lines BB^{I} and BB^{NI} in Fig. 4 to shift downward.

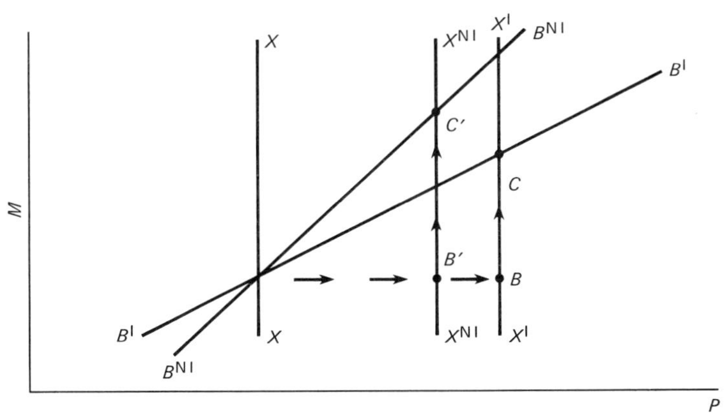

Fig. 3. Foreign real disturbance.

[6] Point C' in Fig. 3 must lie to the northwest of point C, as can easily be shown.

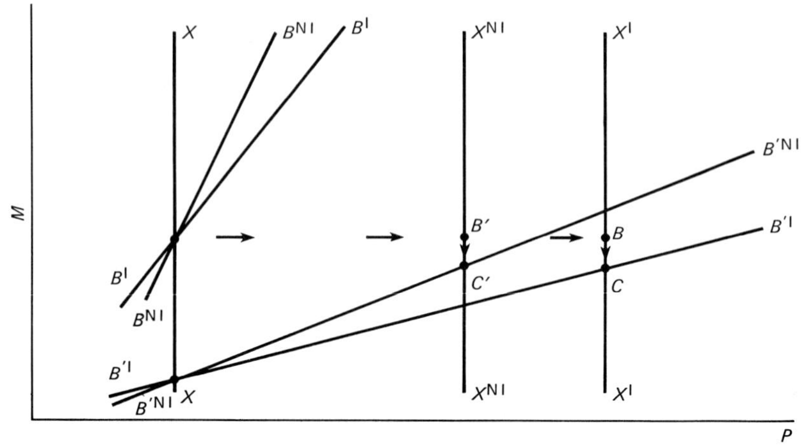

Fig. 4. Domestic real disturbance.

In the short run, the economy moves to points B' and B, respectively, and real balances fall short of their target level at each of these points. However, if wages are indexed, the deviation will be larger than otherwise. Moreover, wage indexation exacerbates the destabilizing effect of domestic real disturbances in the long run too. This can be seen by comparing the level of real balances at points C' and C in Fig. 4. Point C must lie to the southeast of C' as can be proved, so that the above-mentioned result obtains.

C. The Optimal Degree of Indexation

As suggested above, the optimal degree of wage indexation in an open economy depends on the contribution of indexation to the stability of domestic consumption, which equals the sum of domestic output and the excess of imports over exports. We have seen that in the short run, indexation contributes to macroeconomic stability in the above sense only in view of domestic nominal disturbances, but even then wage indexation does not insulate the economy completely from random disturbances; and in the presence of domestic real disturbances and foreign disturbances of either kind, lack of indexation has been shown to be preferable.

In the long run, the results are slightly modified. Here wage indexation insulates the economy completely from both foreign and domestic monetary disturbances and from foreign real disturbances, and is preferable when these are the predominant shocks. As far as domestic real disturbances are concerned, lack of indexation is preferable both in the short and long run.

The optimal degree of wage indexation is therefore a function of the importance policy makers attach to macroeconomic stability, in the short run and in the long run, and of the probability of real and monetary disturbances at home and abroad.

Generally, therefore, the optimal degree of wage indexation will lie between zero and one. However, if the country considered is sufficiently small that disturbances at home do not affect the world price level, domestic disturbances have the same effect on real balances (and therefore on macroeconomic stability) whether wages are indexed or not. Consequently, the decision on indexation must take into account the influence of indexation on macroeconomic stability in the presence of foreign disturbances. If attention is restricted to the short run, the conclusion is that the optimal degree of wage indexation in a small open economy is zero. However, if longer-run considerations are taken into account, partial indexation will be preferable to no wage indexation at all.

3. A Two-Commodity Model for a Small Open Economy

The drawback of the one-commodity model presented in Section 2 is that it does not take into account the relative price changes between traded and nontraded goods that are characteristic of an open economy with pegged exchange rates.

The model discussed in this section refers to a small economy with money as its only financial asset and two produced commodities. Each firm in the economy produces either traded or nontraded goods by means of labor and a fixed amount of capital. Labor is completely mobile between firms and industries at the time wage contracts are drawn up, but becomes completely immobile during the period for which these contracts are valid.[7] Wage contracts are based on rational expectations. If the real wage rate deviates from that anticipated, it is assumed that the amount of labor workers agree to supply is the amount demanded by employers according to the value of the marginal product of labor. Workers do so by adjusting accordingly the amount of leisure consumed.

In this model, deviations of the real wage rate from its expected value may be caused by domestic disturbances in the money supply or in

[7] Wage rigidities in models with traded and nontraded goods have been discussed previously by Helpman (1976, 1977) and Brecher (1978). The difference between their models and that presented here is the degree of factor mobility assumed. Helpman and Brecher assume that labor is completely mobile, thus treating wage rigidities as a long-run phenomenon. The model presented here treats wage rigidities as a short-run phenomenon that goes along with total immobility of factors of production.

production functions and by disturbances abroad that affect the price of the traded good.

The demand for domestic products is a function of their own price P, the price of traded goods e, the supply of money M, and expected real lifetime income, which is constant throughout the analysis and can therefore be neglected. The supply of domestic goods is a function of their price, nominal wages, and the productivity factor. The excess demand for domestic goods Z_d, is therefore

$$Z_d = \tilde{D}_d(P, e, M) - \tilde{S}_d(P, W, \pi), \tag{3}$$

where $\tilde{D}_d$ and $\tilde{S}_d$ are the demand and supply functions of domestic goods. Each of these functions is homogeneous of degree zero in all its arguments except π, so (3) can be rewritten:

$$Z_d = D_d(P/e, M/e) - S_d(P/e, W/e, \pi) = Z_d(P/e, M/e, W/e, \pi). \tag{4}$$

Similarly the excess demand function for tradables can be defined:

$$\begin{aligned} Z_I &= \tilde{D}_I(P, e, M) - \tilde{S}_I(e, W, \pi) \\ &= D_I(P/e, M/e) - S_I(W/e, \pi) = Z_I(P/e, M/e, W/e, \pi), \end{aligned} \tag{5}$$

where the subscript I indicates tradable goods.

According to our assumption, current income does not influence the demand for commodities. Any increase (decrease) of current real income Y over (below) its long-run average level will thus cause the demand for money to increase (decrease) by the same amount. Real income in terms of the traded goods is in turn a function of commodity prices, the nominal wage rate, and the productivity factor:

$$Y = (P/e)\tilde{S}_d(P, W, \pi) + \tilde{S}_I(e, W, \pi). \tag{6}$$

An increase in P, *ceteris paribus*, causes an increase in the value of the marginal product of labor in the domestic good industry, so that output in that industry expands. As long as only P changes, the tradable good industry is not affected at all. An increase in e, on the other hand, leaves the output of domestic goods unchanged but causes the output of tradable goods to expand through an increase in the demand for labor. An increase in W with both commodity prices constant decreases the demand for labor in both industries, so that output decreases too. A proportionate change in P, e, and W will not affect output in any industry, so that (6) can be rewritten:

$$Y = (P/e)S_d(P/e, W/e, \pi) + S_I(W/e, \pi). \tag{7}$$

Using (7), we get for the excess demand function for money:

$$Z_M = \tilde{D}_M(P, e, M, Y) - M = \hat{D}_M(P, e, M, P/e, W/e, \pi) - M. \tag{8}$$

As the demand function for money is homogeneous of degree one in P, e, and M, we get from (8):

$$Z_{\mathrm{M}} = eD_{\mathrm{M}}(P/e, M/e, W/e, \pi) - M = eZ_{\mathrm{M}}(P/e, M/e, W/e, \pi). \quad (9)$$

Consider now the nonindexed economy NI. Long-run equilibrium in this economy obtains if excess demand in each market is zero. The equilibrium conditions are therefore:

$$Z_{\mathrm{d}}^{\mathrm{NI}}(P/e, M/e, W/e, \pi) = 0, \quad (10)$$

$$Z_{\mathrm{I}}^{\mathrm{NI}}(P/e, M/e, W/e, \pi) = 0, \quad (11)$$

$$Z_{\mathrm{M}}^{\mathrm{NI}}(P/e, M/e, W/e, \pi) = 0. \quad (12)$$

In addition the labor market must be in equilibrium.

Yet, according to our assumptions this condition is always met with ex post, so that Walras's law can be invoked to drop one of the conditions (10)–(12). In the following, attention will be focused on (10) and (11).

Figure 5 is a diagrammatic representation of these equilibrium conditions, derived from Mundell (1968) and Berglas (1974). On the vertical axis the relative price of nontradables is measured in terms of tradables. On the horizontal axis real balances are measured in terms of tradables. The line XX^{NI} is the locus of values of P/e and M/e for which, given a specific value of W/e and π, the market for nontradables is in equilibrium. Starting from a point on that line, an increase in M/e causes an excess demand for

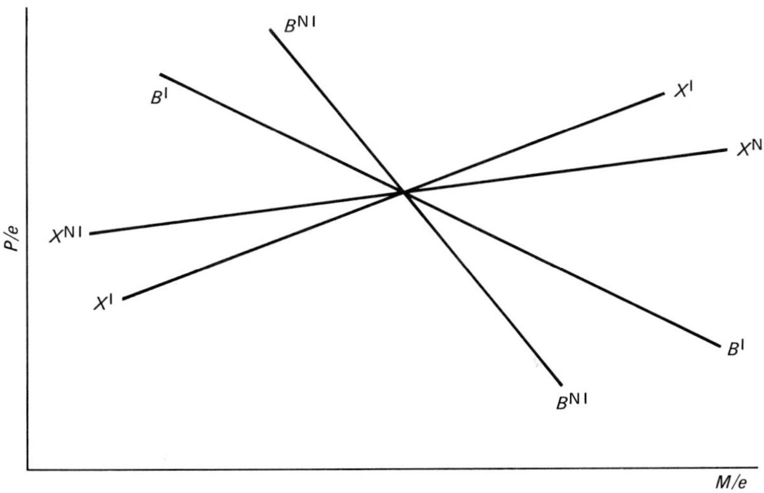

Fig. 5. Equilibrium in the tradable goods and nontradable goods markets.

nontradables: To return to equilibrium, domestic prices must rise. As nominal wages are kept constant, this rise in domestic prices decreases the demand for tradables and increases their supply so that eventually equilibrium is reattained. The slope of line XX^{NI} in Fig. 5 is therefore positive. The line BB^{NI} is the locus of those values of P/e and M/e that create equilibrium in the tradable good market. Starting from a point on that line, an increase in M/e causes an excess demand for tradables. To reestablish equilibrium, P/e must decrease, that is, the relative price of tradables must rise. Assuming that all goods in this model are gross substitutes, a decrease of P/e diminishes the demand for tradables so that equilibrium is reattained. The slope of BB^{NI} in Fig. 5 is therefore negative.

Consider now the indexed economy. For simplicity of exposition it will be assumed here that the wage in both industries is linked to the price of domestic goods so that we have

$$W = wP, \tag{13}$$

where w is a constant.

With (13) substituted into (4) and (5), the equilibrium conditions in the tradables and nontradables markets can be written:

$$Z_{\mathrm{d}}^{\mathrm{I}}(P/e, M/e, \pi) = 0, \tag{10'}$$

$$Z_{\mathrm{I}}^{\mathrm{I}}(P/e, M/e, \pi) = 0. \tag{11'}$$

Consider now the line XX^{I}, the locus of values of P/e and M/e that maintain equilibrium in the domestic goods market in the indexed economy. The slope of this line in Fig. 5 is positive since excess demand for domestic goods caused by an increase in the amount of money supplied can only be canceled by an increase in domestic prices. A rise in prices decreases the amount of domestic goods demanded, but as the nominal wage increases proportionately it does not cause any increases in the output of nontradables. Thus to restore equilibrium in the indexed economy, domestic prices must rise more than in the nonindexed economy. Consequently, the slope of XX^{I} in Fig. 5 is steeper than that of XX^{NI}. Note that the slope of any ray from the origin that cuts XX^{I} is steeper than the slope of that line, and therefore also steeper than the slope of XX^{NI}. To see this, consider an increase of e from any point on XX^{I}, so that we move toward the origin on the ray emanating from the origin through the initial point on XX^{I}. Due to assumed gross substitution between the goods, an increase in the price of tradables causes an excess demand for domestic goods, which can be canceled only by an increase in their price. The point on the ray from the origin through the initial point of equilibrium must therefore be to the right of the new point of equilibrium, yet this can only happen if any ray from the origin that cuts XX^{I} does so from below.

The line BB^{I} is the locus of values of P/e and M/e that maintain equilibrium in the tradable goods market in the indexed economy. The slope of this line in Fig. 5 must be negative since the excess demand for tradables caused by an increase in M can be canceled only by a decrease in P, which diminishes the demand for tradables. However, in contrast to the nonindexed economy, a decrease in P in the indexed economy causes a decrease in the nominal wage and therefore an expansion of output in the tradable good industry. Therefore the decrease of P required to reestablish equilibrium is smaller in the indexed than in the nonindexed economy. Consequently, the slope of BB^{I} in Fig. 5 is flatter than that of BB^{NI}.

As pointed out above, the assumed stabilization objectives in the two-sector economy amount to stability of output of the nontradable good and stability of demand for the tradable good. Therefore we now concentrate on these variables.

A. An Unanticipated Increase in the Supply of Money

Starting from the point of long-run equilibrium A in Fig. 6, an increase in the amount of money carries the indexed economy to point B in Fig. 6, while the nonindexed economy is carried to point B'. It is assumed that domestic prices adjust instantaneously to clear the nontradable good market. Let us now compare points B and B' with respect to the level of output in the nontradable good industry and the demand for tradables. At

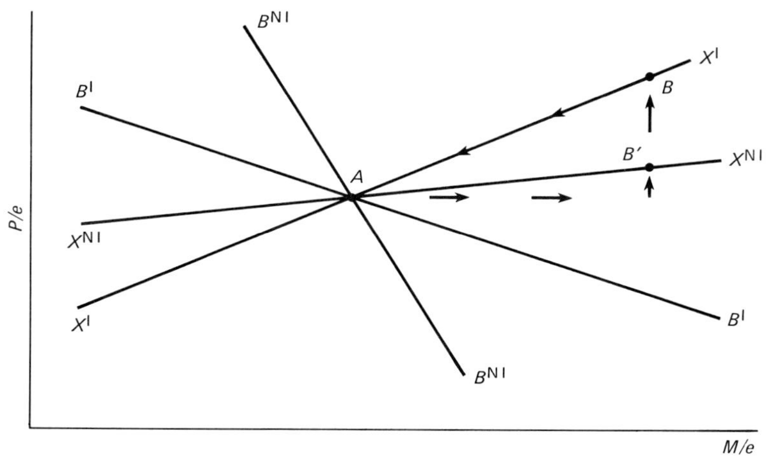

Fig. 6. Monetary disturbance.

point B'—that is, in the nonindexed economy—the rise in domestic prices has caused the output of nontraded goods to expand. In the indexed economy, located at point B, the rise in domestic prices has been accompanied by a proportionate increase in nominal wages, leaving output in the nontradable good industry unchanged. As far as the demand for tradables is concerned, it is easily seen that it exceeds the target level at both B and B'. The increase in demand is smaller if wages are not indexed, as domestic prices then increase to a smaller extent.

Due to the excess demand for traded goods at points B and B' and the resulting trade balance deficit, the domestic money supply gradually increases so that the economy moves toward the long-run equilibrium at point A on lines XX^{I} in the indexed case and on line XX^{NI} otherwise. At point A output of nontradable goods and demand for tradables have returned to their original levels.

B. An Unanticipated Decrease of Productivity

A decrease of labor productivity in both industries at the same time causes employment to decrease at given wages and prices. This decrease in labor input together with the negative effect that the real disturbance has on output engenders an excess demand for both goods. At given wages and prices this can be canceled only by a decrease in money supply. Graphically, this is demonstrated by a leftward shift of all equilibrium loci in Fig. 7. For simplicity, we assume that all loci shift by the same horizontal distance.

The impact of an adverse real disturbance moves the indexed economy to point B in Fig. 7. Note that the only factor influencing the demand for labor in the indexed economy is the decrease of productivity per se since real wages remain constant. The result is a fall of output of nontradables in the indexed economy greater than that in the nonindexed economy, located at point B', where the adverse effect of the disturbance is counteracted by the expansionary effect of the increase in domestic prices.[8]

The demand for tradables at each of the points B and B' is below target, but the decrease is smaller at point B (the indexed economy) due to the higher level of domestic prices at that point.

At the long-run equilibrium point A', representative of both the in-

[8] The net outcome of the counteracting forces in the nonindexed economy must be a decrease of production. This fact can be recognized by noting that the relative price of domestic good has risen, so the quantity demanded of that good must have declined. As the domestic good market is in equilibrium at point B, the quantity demanded equals the quantity supplied, so the above result holds.

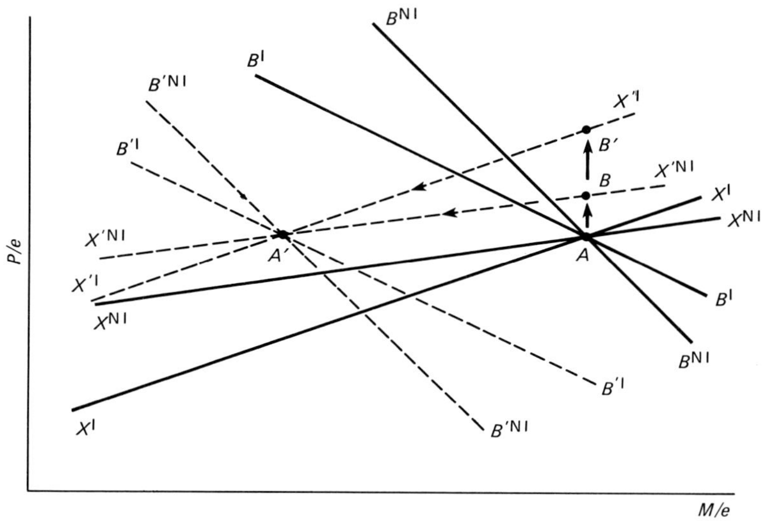

Fig. 7. Real disturbance.

dexed and the nonindexed economy, prices have returned to their original level. Any effects on output are due only to the real shock, and are the same in both economies.

The demand for tradables at that point is smaller than the target level and is the same in both economies.

C. An Unanticipated Increase in the Price of Tradables

Recall that in the nonindexed economy the loci XX^{NI} and BB^{NI} are defined for a given value of W/e. As the price of tradables increases, lines XX^{NI} and BB^{NI} both shift. To determine the direction of the shift, consider Fig. 8. For any given value of P/e there will be an excess supply of domestic goods at the level of M/e that maintained equilibrium in the nontraded good market before the disturbance. Since wages are constant, the increase in P necessary to keep relative prices constant causes an expansion of output in the domestic good industry. On the demand side, no change takes place if M, e, and P increase proportionately. The conclusion is that for any given value of P/e, to restore equilibrium in the domestic good market the value of M/e must rise. This is reflected in the rightward shift of the XX^{NI} locus in Fig. 8. Similarly, for any combination of values of P/e and M/e that maintained equilibrium in the traded good market before the disturbance occurred, there will not be an excess supply of traded goods as output has increased with no change in demand. Therefore for any given value of P/e, the new equilibrium value of M/e

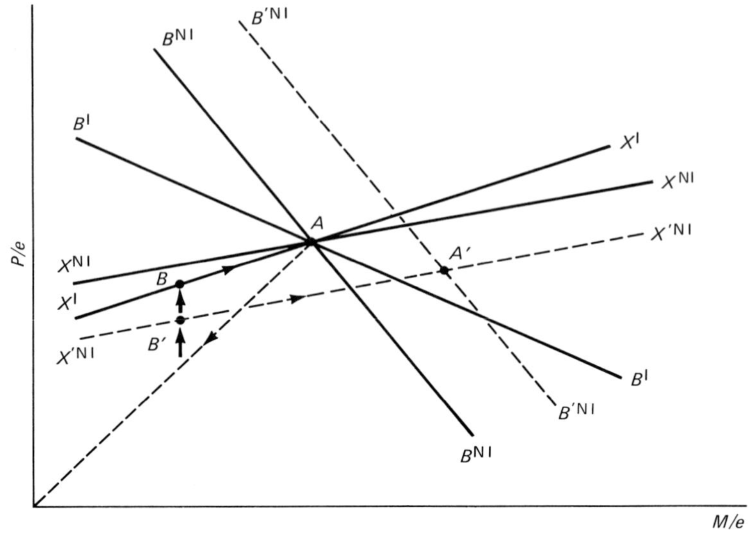

Fig. 8. Foreign disturbance.

will be larger than the previous one. This causes the rightward shift of BB^{NI} depicted in Fig. 8.

Starting from the initial point of long-run equilibrium A, the impact effect of a rise in e carries the indexed and nonindexed economies to points B and B', respectively.[9] In the indexed economy wages will rise proportionately to domestic prices leaving output of nontradables unchanged, while output increases if wages are not indexed. The demand for tradables at both B and B' falls short of the target level. However, in the indexed economy (point B) demand will fall less as domestic prices are higher than in the nonindexed economy.

In the long run the indexed economy returns to the initial equilibrium point A, where the target values of output of nontradables and demand for tradables are reattained. The nonindexed economy, on the other hand, settles at point A' where both the output of nontradables and the demand for tradables exceed the desired level. (The domestic price level at A' may be the same, higher, or lower than at A.)

D. The Optimal Degree of Wage Indexation

It has been argued above that output of nontradables as well as the aggregate of domestic output of tradables and the excess of imports over

[9] It can be shown easily that B' must be below B, given the assumption of gross substitution between the commodities.

TABLE 1

THE EFFECT OF WAGE INDEXATION ON MACROECONOMIC STABILITY[a]

Sector	Disturbance		
	Monetary	Real	Foreign
Short-run			
nontradables	+	–	+
tradables	–	+	+
Long-run			
nontradables	+ –	+ –	+
tradables	–	+ –	+

[a]The + indicates that indexation is preferable; – indicates that lack of indexation is preferable; and + – indicates that indexation has the same effect as lack of indexation.

exports should be the stabilization objectives of economic policy.[10] Table 1 summarizes the results obtained above concerning the contribution of wage indexation to macroeconomic stability in the sense defined here.

Table 1 shows clearly that indexation has an unambiguously stabilizing effect on the economy only in the presence of foreign disturbances. In other cases, desirability of wage indexation, particularly in the short run, depends critically on the importance attributed to stability in each sector as defined here. Therefore, the optimal degree of wage indexation will generally lie between zero and one in this model too.

4. Devaluation

Given a slightly different interpretation, the discussion of unanticipated changes in international prices in Section 3 may cast some light on an issue that has frequently been the subject of public debate in Israel: Does indexation hamper the effectiveness of devaluation?

The analytical framework of Section 3 can be conveniently applied to this issue. To begin with, note that a rise in the price of international goods may be caused not only by disturbances abroad but also by an unanticipated devaluation. Consequently, we will now return to Fig. 8 and use it to compare the effectiveness of devaluation in an indexed and a nonindexed economy.

At point B' in Fig. 8 output in the tradable good industry has increased due to the rise of the price of international goods with nominal wages

[10]An alternative view would be to consider aggregate consumption (rather than consumption of each good) as the stabilization objective. Under this criterion most of the results would be inconclusive as to the effect of wage indexation on stability.

constant. In the indexed economy, which is represented by point *B*, output in the traded good industry has also risen, but to a smaller extent than in the indexed economy. This is due to the fact that in the indexed economy the rise in domestic prices entails a proportionate increase in nominal wages, which counteracts the expansionary effect of the rise of international prices.

The demand for tradables is larger in the nonindexed economy where domestic prices rise to a smaller extent.

Combining the effects on demand and supply in the traded good sector, we find that the excess supply of traded goods, which equals the trade balance surplus, is larger if wages are not indexed.

A comparison of the cumulative trade balance surplus caused by a devaluation in either economy yields a similar result. The inflow of monetary balances following a devaluation is larger if wages are not indexed (point *A′* in Fig. 8 is located to the right of point *A*).

The analysis therefore substantiates the commonly held opinion that wage indexation hampers the effectiveness of devaluations.

Another issue connected to devaluations in an indexed economy is the question of whether the direct impact of devaluations on the price level should be taken into account when the cost of living allowance included in wage contracts is computed. In Israel this has been the subject of substantial public debate following devaluations. Those favoring payment of a cost of living allowance not including the direct impact of the devaluation on the price level usually argue that their suggested procedure would enhance the effectiveness of the devaluation. To examine this argument, let us interpret the suggested omission of the direct impact of the devaluation as calling for linkage of wages to domestic prices only. As this is exactly the case we analyzed above, lines XX^{I} and BB^{I} of Fig. 8 are representative for this proposal and are redrawn in Fig. 9.

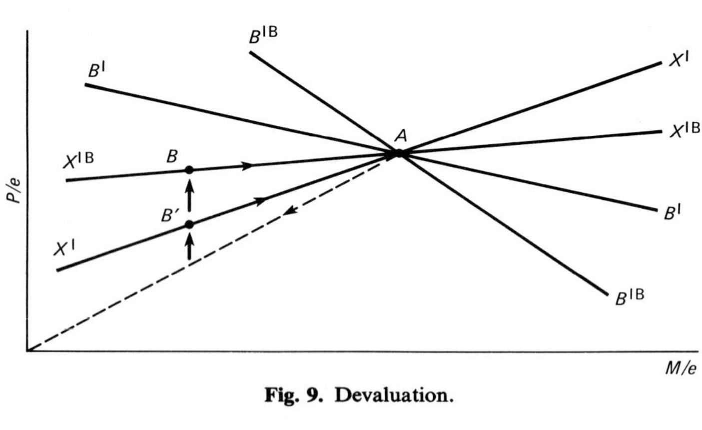

Fig. 9. Devaluation.

The other alternative is linkage to a consumption bundle that includes both domestic and international goods. In this case the excess demand functions will be of the form

$$Z_{\mathrm{d}}^{\mathrm{I}B} = \tilde{Z}_{\mathrm{d}}^{\mathrm{I}B}[P/e, M/e, \alpha wP/e + (1-\alpha)we/e] = Z_{\mathrm{d}}^{\mathrm{I}B}(P/e, M/e, \pi), \tag{4'}$$

$$Z_{\mathrm{I}}^{\mathrm{I}B} = Z_{\mathrm{I}}^{\mathrm{I}B}(P/e, M/e, \pi). \tag{5'}$$

In this formulation α is the share of domestic products in the historical consumption bundle used in computing the cost of living index.

From (4′) and (5′) it can be seen immediately that, following a devaluation, long-run equilibrium is restored only after domestic prices and money supply have increased by the same proportion as e. Point A in Fig. 8 is therefore the long-run equilibrium point for both economies considered here. An immediate consequence is that in the long run the amount of reserves accumulated by a devaluation does not depend on the way the cost of living allowance is computed.

Consider now the slopes of lines $XX^{\mathrm{I}B}$ and $BB^{\mathrm{I}B}$ in Fig. 9, as compared to those of XX^{I} and BB^{I}. Starting from a point of equilibrium in the domestic good market, an increased money supply causes excess demand for domestic goods that can be canceled only by an increase in domestic prices. With the price of the traded good constant, the rise in domestic prices causes a smaller increase in wages if linkage is to a consumption bundle rather than to domestic prices only. In the latter economy, therefore, output in the domestic good industry is not affected by a price increase, while in the former economy it expands. Consequently, the increase in domestic prices required to cancel the initial excess demand is smaller in the economy where wages are linked to a consumption bundle. This result is represented graphically by the smaller slope of $XX^{\mathrm{I}B}$ in Fig. 9, as compared to that of XX^{I}.

The excess demand in the traded goods market caused by an increase in M and the decrease in local prices (required to restore equilibrium in that market) expand output in the foreign sector of both economies as wages decrease. As the expansion of output is larger where wages are linked only to prices of domestic goods, a smaller decrease in domestic prices is sufficient to restore equilibrium in the traded good sector. Therefore BB^{I} has been drawn with a slope that is flatter than that of $BB^{\mathrm{I}B}$.

Consider now the impact effect of a devaluation of the currency. While the IB economy moves to point B in Fig. 9, the I economy moves to B'. At point B' the demand for traded goods is smaller than at point B since relative prices of domestic goods are lower at B'. Wages at point B have risen by a weighted average of the increase in domestic and international prices. This weighted average is necessarily larger than the increase in wages at point B', which equals the rise in domestic prices at that point. It is therefore clear that the excess supply of traded goods is larger at point B', where wages are linked to prices of domestic goods only.

In sum, the omission of the direct impact of a devaluation from the cost of living allowance will cause a faster improvement in the balance of payments, but will not affect the cumulative surplus created.

5. Conclusions

Various models of closed economies used by Gray and Fischer to examine the effect of wage indexation on macroeconomic stability showed that wage indexation is desirable in the case of monetary disturbances but not with respect to real disturbances. The major conclusion of the present paper is that policy recommendations as to the optimal degree of indexation that are based on findings from closed economy models cannot be carried over to open economies.

There are two major reasons for this: First, the stabilization goal, which in the closed economy model was taken to be output of the aggregate commodity, has to be redefined once an open economy is considered. Second, random shocks that occur abroad need not be taken into account in closed economies, while their existence in open economies affects the optimal degree of wage indexation.

Furthermore, not only has it been shown that the effects of wage indexation in an open economy differ from those in a closed economy, but also the results are much less clear cut than those reported by Gray and Fischer. We therefore remain with the general conclusion that neither full wage indexation nor absence of wage indexation are optimal with regard to macroeconomic stability. At least in this respect, the results presented here are in line with those for closed economies.

A particularly bothersome feature of the models presented here is the sensitivity of the results to the assumed behavior of labor input in disequilibrium situations. The assumption that labor input is determined by the demand for labor was used here to allow comparison with closed economy results. However, a more general treatment of the issue of wage indexation should replace ad hoc assumptions concerning the determination of the amount of labor forthcoming by using results from the theory of labor contracts as input for the analysis.

A similar caveat concerning the generality of the results applies to the influence of wage indexation on the effectiveness of devaluation. While the above analysis justifies commonly held opinions on this issue, opposite results would be obtained if the amount of labor forthcoming were allowed to be determined according to the supply function of labor.

Finally, it should be noted that an immediate extension of the analysis presented here would be to examine the effect of wage indexation on macroeconomic stability under flexible exchange rates.

REFERENCES

Berglas, Eitan (1974). Devaluation, Monetary Theory and Border Tax Adjustments. *Canadian Journal of Economics* **7**(Feb.), 1–11.

Brecher, Richard A. (1978). Money, Employment, and Trade-Balance Adjustment with Rigid Wages. *Oxford Economic Papers* **30**(Mar.), 1–15.

Fischer, Stanley (1977). Wage Indexation and Macro-Economic Stability. *Journal of Monetary Economics, Supplement (Carnegie–Rochester Conference Series)* **5**, 107–147.

Gray, Jo Anna (1976). Wage Indexation: A Macroeconomic Approach. *Journal of Monetary Economics* **2**, 221–235.

Helpman, Elhanan (1976). Macroeconomic Policy in a Model of International Trade with a Wage Restriction. *International Economic Review* **17**(June), 262–277.

Helpman, Elhanan (1977). Nontraded Goods and Macroeconomic Policy under a Fixed Exchange Rate. *Quarterly Journal of Economics* **91**(Aug.), 469–480.

Mundell, Robert A. (1968). *International Economics*. Macmillan, New York.

DEPARTMENT OF ECONOMICS
TEL AVIV UNIVERSITY
RAMAT AVIV, TEL AVIV, ISRAEL

Inflation, Costs of Adjustment, and the Amplitude of Real Price Changes

An Empirical Analysis

*E. SHESHINSKI, A. TISHLER, AND Y. WEISS**

1. Introduction

It is well-known that one of the damaging consequences of rapid inflation is frequent nonsynchronized nominal price changes, leading to increased variation in relative prices and to higher price uncertainty (Parks, 1978; Jaffee and Kleiman, 1978; Vining and Elwertowsky, 1976; Cagan, 1975; Cukierman and Wachtel, 1980). A less-known aspect of the same phenomenon is the increase in the amplitude of changes in the *real* price of each product over time. The typical firm is therefore further away from its regular profit-maximizing position and suffers a real loss. Investigating some theoretical aspects of this problem, Sheshinski and Weiss (1977, 1979) argued that the fluctuations in real prices constitute the major welfare loss associated with inflationary processes. These losses exist even if inflation is fully predicted in the aggregate as long as relative prices are allowed to vary randomly. Under such circumstances firms will find it profitable to inform customers of their specific prices; however, they will find it costly to change prices continually [see also Fischer and Modigliani (1978)].

We adopt a micro, partial equilibrium approach and consider a firm

*We wish to thank Dr. M. Shefer from the Bureau of Commerce for supplying data and providing helpful comments and Anat Babitz for her excellent research assistance. The financial assistance of the Foerder Institute for Economic Research is also gratefully acknowledged.

ISBN 0-12-259750-8

that operates under inflationary expectations. Following Arrow (1962), we assume that the firm possesses a monopoly power that allows it to set the nominal price of its output or, alternatively, the price of one of its inputs. The firm produces a nonstorable product whose demand depends on its price relative to the price of rival commodities considered as an aggregate. The firm expects the aggregate price level and its costs of production to increase at a certain given rate. In the absence of adjustment costs the optimal policy would be to increase its own price continually at the same rate. We assume, however, that a fixed real cost is associated with each price change (Barro, 1972). Consequently, the optimal policy is characterized by a sequence of finite intervals during which the *nominal* price is held constant, followed by discrete price adjustments (Scarf, 1959). The analysis focuses on the effect of the expected rate of inflation on the frequency and the magnitude of these price changes.

Sheshinski and Weiss (1977) showed that an increase in the rate of inflation leads to an increase in the initial real price and to a decrease in the terminal real price in each period, thereby increasing the magnitude of each price change and the amplitude of fluctuations in real prices. However, the effect on the frequency of price changes was shown to be ambiguous.

The objective of this paper is to test these implications of their model empirically. We examine the effects of the accelerating rate of inflation in Israel on the nominal and real price/time patterns of two branded commodities, instant coffee and noodles, both produced by local monopolies. Our preliminary findings suggest that *ceteris paribus*, an increase in the expected rate of inflation implies a higher frequency of nominal price changes. The nominal price is set at a level that implies a higher *initial* real price, but the nominal price is not held fixed until the *final* real price is reduced. The latter aspect of the firm's price adjustment strategy appears to be inconsistent with the simple model that we propose. In part, this may be due to the omission of the real interest rate from the empirical analysis. In future work we plan to examine additional products and to suggest some theoretical modifications of our simple price adjustment model in an attempt to resolve this discrepancy.

2. A Model of Price Adjustment

We consider a price-setting firm that operates under inflationary expectations, where costs and demand are subject to exogenous unexpected shocks. As there are real costs of adjustment associated with varying nominal prices, the firm does not change its prices immediately whenever conditions change, even if these changes are presumed to be permanent.

Instead, it will allow its real price to fluctuate between some predetermined bounds and will change the nominal price by a discrete jump only if the lower or upper bounds are met. Sheshinski and Weiss (1977) describe the determination of these bounds. They show that for each permanently fixed rate of inflation, real costs, and demand, there is an optimal price program in which, starting at the first price change, nominal prices are held constant over successive time intervals of *equal* duration. That is, at calendar time μ the firm plans to change its nominal price at times $t = \mu + \xi + \tau\epsilon$, $\tau = 0, 1, 2, \ldots,$ where $\xi \geqslant 0$ is the time that elapses until the first price change and ϵ is the time that elapses between all subsequent price changes. Furthermore, if g_μ is the rate of inflation expected to hold permanently from μ onward, then $p_\tau = p_{\tau-1}e^{g_\mu \epsilon}$, $\tau = 1, 2, \ldots$. The value of the optimal program [see Eq. (2) in Sheshinski and Weiss (1977)] can be written as follows:

$$v_\mu = \int_0^\xi F_\mu\left(\frac{p_\mu}{\bar{p}_\mu} e^{-g_\mu t}\right) e^{-rt}\,dt - \beta e^{-r\xi}$$
$$+ \frac{e^{-r\xi}}{1 - e^{-r\epsilon}}\left[\int_0^\epsilon F_\mu(Se^{-g_\mu t})e^{-rt}\,dt - \beta e^{-r\epsilon}\right], \tag{1}$$

where p_μ is the nominal *predetermined* price at time μ; $\bar{p}_\mu$, the general price level at time μ; S, the real price chosen at time μ for $t = \mu + \xi + \tau\epsilon$, $\tau = 0, 1, 2, \ldots$; F_μ, real profits as a function of real price at time $t \geqslant \mu$; β, real costs of a nominal price adjustment; and r, real rate of interest. It is assumed that r and β are positive constants independent of calendar time. On the other hand, the expected rate of inflation g_μ and the profit function may change over time. All such changes are unexpected; however, at each μ it is assumed that the inflation rate and the profit function will remain the same for $t \geqslant \mu$.

The optimal values of the choice variables ξ, S, and ϵ are obtained by maximizing (1). The first-order conditions are

$$F_\mu\left(\frac{p_\mu}{\bar{p}_\mu} e^{-g_\mu \xi}\right) + r\beta - \frac{r}{1 - e^{-r\epsilon}}\left[\int_0^\epsilon F_\mu(Se^{-g_\mu t})e^{-rt}\,dt - \beta e^{-r\epsilon}\right] \leqslant 0, \tag{2}$$

$$\int_0^\epsilon F'_\mu(Se^{-g_\mu t})e^{-(r+g_\mu)t}\,dt = 0, \tag{3}$$

$$F_\mu(Se^{-g_\mu \epsilon}) + r\beta - \frac{r}{1 - e^{-r\epsilon}}\left[\int_0^\epsilon F_\mu(Se^{-g_\mu t})e^{-rt}\,dt - \beta e^{-r\epsilon}\right] = 0. \tag{4}$$

We note that the optimal solution of S and ϵ is determined from (3) and (4) alone. Whenever there is a price change it will always be chosen so as to set the real price at S. The nominal price will then be held fixed until the real price drops to $s = Se^{-g_\mu \epsilon}$. Therefore, if the basic conditions remain unchanged, the real price will repeatedly fluctuate between S and s. If $\xi > 0$, that is, if the firm does not change its price immediately, then (2) and (4) imply that $F_\mu[(p_\mu/\bar{p}_\mu)e^{-g_\mu}] = F_\mu(s)$. A corner solution with an immediate price change, that is, with $\xi = 0$, will occur if $F_\mu(p_\mu/\bar{p}_\mu) < F_\mu(s)$. While the optimal values of s, S, and ξ depend on the expectations held at μ concerning the rate of inflation and the shape of the real profit function (Fig. 1), the actual nominal price at time μ is predetermined by previous conditions. If the firm finds itself with a real price $(p_\mu/\bar{p}_\mu) < s$ then it will increase its real price immediately to S. If $(p_\mu/\bar{p}_\mu) > \hat{S}$, where by definition $F_\mu(\hat{S}) = F_\mu(s)$, then the firm will reduce its real price immediately to S. If, however, $\hat{S} > (p_\mu/\bar{p}_\mu) > s$, the firm will *not* change its nominal price at time μ. Sheshinski and Weiss (1977) proved that an increase in the expected rate of inflation will lead to an increase in S and to a reduction in s, which implies that $\hat{S}$ must increase. One purpose of our work is to test this implication empirically.

The model outlined above, which is based on Sheshinski and Weiss (1977), is built upon a number of assumptions that may limit its empirical applicability. Consumers are assumed to act exclusively on the basis of current data, and substitution over time and the possibility of carrying inventories are ignored. Such assumptions may be justified in the case of some perishable commodities like newspapers and consumer services, whose consumption cannot be postponed, but when the typical period between price adjustments is relatively short, these assumptions may not be appropriate. A second limiting aspect is that the firm's optimal plans are chosen under the assumption of a *fixed* aggregate rate of inflation. Finally, we do not analyze the potential effects of price controls. In future work we intend to extend the model to incorporate the above elements.

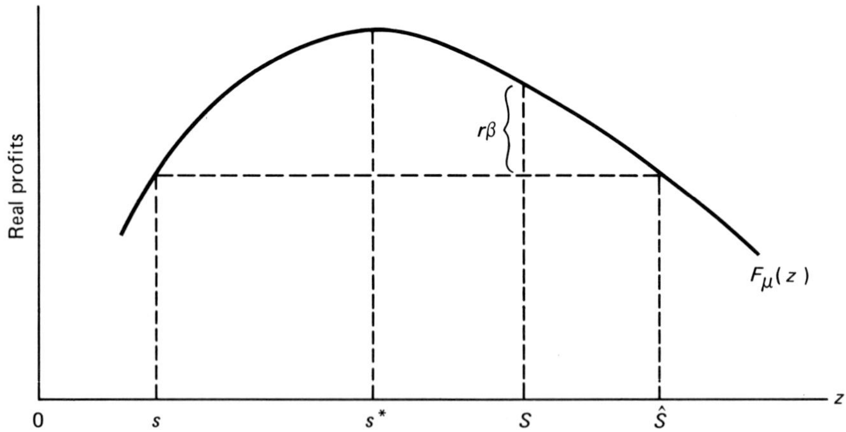

Fig. 1. The profit function of the firm.

3. Statistical Formulation

A. Methodology

Assume that the firm contemplates the possibility of a price change only at some discrete equally spaced points in time, say, every month. At such points the firm gathers information on the (continuously changing) aggregate price level, costs, and demand conditions. It forms expectations and determines the optimal values of s, S, and $\hat{S}$. Let p_t be the nominal price chosen by the firm at time t, and let $\bar{p}_t$ be the aggregate price level at time t, $t = 1, 2, 3, \ldots$. The firm's decision can be formulated as follows: If $p_{t-1}/\bar{p}_t < s_t$ the firm will increase its nominal price so as to raise the real price to S_t. Similarly, if $p_{t-1}/\bar{p}_t > \hat{S}_t$, the firm will reduce its nominal price and again set the real price at S_t. Finally if $s_t \leqslant p_{t-1}/\bar{p}_t \leqslant \hat{S}_t$, the firm will not change its nominal price and will set $p_t = p_{t-1}$.

The optimal levels of s, S: and $\hat{S}$ are determined by the first-order conditions (2)–(4) as functions of the exogenous variables. The linear approximations of these functions are

$$S_t = b_1' x_t + v_t, \qquad s_t = b_2' x_t + \gamma_2 v_t, \qquad \hat{S}_t = b_3' x_t + \gamma_3 v_t, \tag{5}$$

where the vector x_t includes the measured effects of inflationary expectations and costs of production, and b_1, b_2, and b_3 are vectors of parameters. The random variable v_t represents shifts in the profit function due to changes in the costs of unobserved inputs and changes in demand conditions. It is assumed that

$$v_t \sim h(0, \sigma^2). \tag{6}$$

The values of S, s, and $\hat{S}$ are potentially observable only when a price change occurs. For observations in which the nominal price is held constant we can only estimate the probability that the observed real price falls between the bounds $\hat{S}$ and s. Furthermore when a price change occurs we directly observe S, but not s and $\hat{S}$. We only know that the real price exceeds $\hat{S}$ when a price reduction occurs and is below s when the price is increased. This is due to the discrete nature of our observations on the price process.

The probabilities of prices increasing, remaining constant, and decreasing, are, respectively,

$$\begin{aligned}
\mathrm{pr}(p_t > p_{t-1}) &= \mathrm{pr}(p_{t-1}/\bar{p}_t \leqslant s_t) = \mathrm{pr}\left[(p_{t-1}/\bar{p}_t - b_2' x_t)\gamma_2^{-1} \leqslant v_t\right], \\
\mathrm{pr}(p_t = p_{t-1}) &= \mathrm{pr}(s_t < p_{t-1}/\bar{p}_t < \hat{S}_t) \\
&= \mathrm{pr}\left[(p_{t-1}/\bar{p}_t - b_3' x_t)\gamma_3^{-1} < v_t < (p_{t-1}/\bar{p}_t - b_2' x_t)\gamma_2^{-1}\right], \\
\mathrm{pr}(p_t < p_{t-1}) &= \mathrm{pr}(p_{t-1}/\bar{p} \geqslant \hat{S}_t) = \mathrm{pr}\left[(p_{t-1}/\bar{p}_t - b_3' x_t)\gamma_3^{-1} \geqslant v_t\right].
\end{aligned} \tag{7}$$

Estimates of the coefficient vectors b_2' and b_3', and of $\gamma_2\sigma$ and $\gamma_3\sigma$ can be obtained by maximizing the likelihood function

$$L = \prod_{t\in I_1} \Phi\left[\left(-\frac{p_{t-1}}{\bar{p}_t} + b_2' x_t\right)\frac{1}{\gamma_2\sigma}\right] \prod_{t\in I_2} \left\{\Phi\left[\left(\frac{p_{t-1}}{\bar{p}_t} - b_2' x_t\right)\frac{1}{\gamma_2\sigma}\right] - \Phi\left[\left(\frac{p_{t-1}}{\bar{p}_t} - b_3' x_t\right)\frac{1}{\gamma_3\sigma}\right]\right\} \prod_{t\in I_3} \Phi\left[\left(\frac{p_{t-1}}{\bar{p}_t} - b_3' x_t\right)\frac{1}{\gamma_3\sigma}\right], \tag{8}$$

where Φ is the standard normal distribution function and I_1, I_2, I_3 denote the set of indices for which p_t has increased, is unchanged, or has decreased, respectively.

Recalling that $S_t = p_t/\bar{p}_t$ whenever a price change occurs, we can obtain consistent estimates of the coefficients of b_1' from the regression

$$p_t/\bar{p}_t = b_1' x_t + \sigma\lambda_t + w_t, \qquad t \in I_1 \cup I_3. \tag{9}$$

The variable λ_t is added to eliminate the sample selection bias (Heckman, 1979) and is defined by:

$$\lambda_t = \begin{cases} \dfrac{1}{\sigma} E\left[v_t \mid v_t \geqslant \left(\dfrac{p_{t-1}}{\bar{p}_t} - b_2' x_t\right)\dfrac{1}{\gamma_2}\right] \\ \qquad = \dfrac{\phi\left[(p_{t-1}/\bar{p}_t - b_2' x_t)(\gamma_2\sigma)^{-1}\right]}{\Phi\left[(-p_{t-1}/\bar{p}_t + b_2' x_t)(\gamma_2\sigma)^{-1}\right]}, & t \in I_1, \\ \dfrac{1}{\sigma} E\left[v_t \mid v_t \leqslant \left(\dfrac{p_{t-1}}{\bar{p}_t} - b_3' x_t\right)\dfrac{1}{\gamma_3}\right] \\ \qquad = \dfrac{-\phi\left[(p_{t-1}/\bar{p}_t - b_3' x_t)(\gamma_3\sigma)^{-1}\right]}{\Phi\left[(p_{t-1}/\bar{p}_t - b_3' x_t)(\gamma_3\sigma)^{-1}\right]}, & t \in I_3, \end{cases} \tag{10}$$

where ϕ and Φ are the standard normal density and distribution functions, respectively. With this definition the residual w_t has an expectation equal to zero.

B. The Data

The products chosen for analysis were instant coffee and noodles, both of which are produced by local monopolies. Monthly data on the price of these commodities is available for the period 1965–1978. Monthly data on wages in the food-processing industry and on raw materials were used to construct an index of the variable costs of production; weightings of wages and raw materials were derived from data on the costs structure of the respective firms.[1]

The expected monthly rate of inflation was assumed to depend on past trends and on relevant macroeconomic variables. After some experimentation, a forecasting equation was chosen in which price changes in the previous 12 months and the rate of change in the foreign exchange rate were used as explanatory variables.[2] (Other macroeconomic variables such as money supply and wage rates were found to have negligible additional explanatory power.) This equation was used to produce estimates of the expected aggregate rate of inflation in each month.

Data on the nominal price profiles of the two commodities are to be found in the appendices, together with the values of the real price, real costs, and expected rate of inflation at the points at which price changes occurred. (To save space, we do not report the values of real variables at other dates. These data can be obtained from the authors upon request.)

In describing the data we may divide the sample into three distinct periods. Between August 1965 and August 1970 the average rate of inflation was only 0.25% per month. Despite some significant changes in the price of coffee beans, the nominal price of instant coffee was changed only twice, and at moderate rates. The price of noodles was changed more frequently but again at moderate rates. Between August 1970 and October 1973, the average rate of inflation accelerated to 1.1% per month. We do not find a marked increase in the frequency of nominal price changes, but rather an increase in the size of the jumps. Between October 1973 and December 1978 the rate of inflation accelerated further to an average of 2.9% per month. We now observe a higher frequency of nominal price changes as well as larger jumps in the prices of both products. The relative gap between real prices just before and just after the nominal price change is increased. There is thus an increase in real price variation. The overall variation in the real price of coffee is much larger than that of noodles, reflecting the sharp swings in the international price of raw coffee beans; in fact, for coffee we observe six cases of price *reduction*. In the case of noodles, prices only increase.

The two firms under discussion are subject to price control, meaning that they must submit applications for price changes to a supervising agency. If approved, the new price becomes the official price and cannot be

[1] Wages and raw materials account for 55% of the total production costs for noodles and 80% for instant coffee. For noodles the relative share of wages is 38% and of flour 62%. For instant coffee the relative share of wages is 25% and of coffee beans 75%.

[2] It may be argued that exchange rate changes are not exogenous variables; in alternative specifications we introduced dummy variables for the two major devaluations (instead of exchange rate changes) and a time trend, but obtained similar results.

changed without permission. While the presence of such controls entails certain costs, their effectiveness during the sample period was probably quite low.[3] There are nevertheless some indications that price controls had some effect on the timing of price increases, in that the periods after the Six Day War and the Yom Kippur War were both characterized by long periods of nominal price stability. It is difficult to obtain data on Israeli branded commodities that are *not* subject to formal price controls. In future work special effort will be made to obtain such data, possibly from other countries.

4. Some Preliminary Findings

The estimates of the effects of inflation and real costs on the price policies of the two firms are obtained in two stages. In the first stage we estimate these effects on the lower bound s, and when price reduction occurs, on $\hat{S}$ [see Eq. (8)]. These estimates also yield the inverse Mill's ratio (10), which is used in the second stage in (9) to estimate the upper bound S. The probit estimates for the first stage are presented in Table 1. The main finding is that an increase in the expected rate of inflation leads to a higher value of the lower bound on real price variation s. That is, the firm increases the nominal price whenever the real price falls below a critical value; the higher the expected rates of inflation, the higher the critical value. This result is obtained for both instant coffee and noodles whether price reductions are included or not. We find that the effect on $\hat{S}$ (the critical bound for price reductions) is not significant. This is not surprising as there are few price reductions in our sample. As expected, an increase in the real cost of production leads to an increase in the lower bound on real price variation. The larger coefficient of real costs in the case of instant coffee reflects the fact that the production cost index represents a larger part of total costs (88%, versus 55% for noodles).

The second-stage estimates are presented in Table 2. For purposes of comparison we also present the (inconsistent) ordinary least squares (OLS) estimates. As one would expect, sample selection is important. This is reflected by the significant effect of the inverse Mill's ratio λ and its marked effect on the size of the coefficient of the expected rate of inflation. For both products we find that, correcting for sample selection, an increase

[3] All price-increase requests appear to have been approved; moreover in several cases actual price increases were below the maximum approved by the authorities. In late 1977, a further restriction was introduced whereby changes were approved at most once every three months; however, this latter restriction appears to have been effective only during the second half of 1978.

TABLE 1

PROBIT ESTIMATES OF THE EFFECT OF EXPECTED INFLATION AND REAL COSTS ON s AND $\hat{S}$[a]

Sample and dependent variable	Constant	Expected inflation	Real cost	Standard deviation σ_i
		Instant Coffee		
All price changes				
s	−0.49	7.48	0.62	0.42
	(−3.26)	(3.68)	(7.04)	
$\hat{S}$	4.00	−19.61	−0.75	1.1
	(4.67)	(−1.14)	(−1.13)	
Price increases				
s	−0.51	7.33	0.66	0.40
	(−5.93)	(5.55)	(8.99)	
		Noodles		
s	0.29	3.26	0.33	0.25
	(5.39)	(5.19)	(6.55)	

[a] Asymptotic t values in parentheses.

in the expected rate of inflation leads to an *increase* in the upper bound on real price variation. That is, when the nominal price is increased, it is set at a level that implies a higher *initial* real price.

The findings that the effects of inflation on S and s are both positive and of similar magnitude imply that the relative gap between S and s tends to decrease as the rate of inflation increases.

Recalling the definition of s, we have the relation $\epsilon = (\ln S - \ln s)/g$. The results suggest that ϵ is reduced as the expected rate of inflation g is increased; in other words, the frequency of price changes increases.

Our finding that expected inflation has a positive effect on s may be due to missing explanatory variables, in particular, the real interest rate. Sheshinski and Weiss (1977, p. 296) show that an increase in the real interest rate should have a negative effect on both S and s. Since we do not have consistent unified data on the nominal interest rate we are unable to incorporate it in the estimation. However, from the partial data in our possession it appears that the real interest rate is negatively correlated with expected inflation, which brings about a positive bias in the parameter of the expected inflation in both s and S. We conjecture that this effect may be stronger in the case of s, since s is estimated for the entire sample period and not just for points at which price changes occurred.

TABLE 2

THE EFFECT OF EXPECTED INFLATION AND REAL COSTS ON INITIAL REAL PRICE[a]

Sample and estimation method	Constant	Expected inflation	Real cost	λ	Sample size	DW	R^2
			Instant coffee				
All price changes							
OLS	0.11	1.21	0.55	—	27	0.41	0.55
	(0.85)	(0.86)	(5.26)				
Two-stage	−0.02	1.76	0.60	0.03	27	0.43	0.61
	(−0.14)	(1.28)	(5.81)	(1.85)			
Price increases							
OLS	0.17	1.17	0.50	—	21	0.28	0.48
	(1.08)	(0.76)	(3.93)				
Two-stage	−0.97	7.21	0.82	0.19	21	1.30	0.96
	(−11.07)	(12.52)	(20.25)	(15.14)			
			Noodles				
OLS	0.57	−0.56	0.39	—	31	0.57	0.48
	(6.49)	(−0.99)	(5.00)				
Two-stage	0.21	1.96	0.42	0.05	31	1.51	0.84
	(3.07)	(4.22)	(9.28)	(7.64)			

[a] Asymptotic *t* values in parentheses.

For several reasons we view the above results as very preliminary: the results for the two specific commodities that we analyzed may not be applicable to other products. Differences may arise because of different storage possibilities, substitution over time, costs of price adjustment, degree of competition, and price controls. Other factors affecting the firm's price policy were only partially controlled; not all cost variables were available, and demand factors were ignored. Our statistical method did not incorporate all the restrictions of the theoretical model (for example, $S > s$) and is not the most efficient method. A separate test (outside the model) is necessary to determine whether or not our forecasting equation adequately represents the inflationary expectations.

In future work we plan to overcome some of these difficulties and to obtain a more precise estimate of the effects of inflation in price adjustment strategies.

Appendix 1

NOMINAL PRICE CHANGES AND THE REAL COST OF NOODLES

Date of price change	No. of months since last change	Rate of nominal price change (%)	Real unit cost	Expected monthly rate of inflation (%)	Real price after price change	Real price prior to price change
8.65	—	4.6	1.02	0.71	1.04	1.00
2.66	6	2.2	1.00	0.91	1.01	0.99
4.66	2	2.2	0.98	1.04	1.00	0.98
7.66	3	6.4	0.95	0.59	1.06	0.99
10.66	3	2.0	0.95	0.82	1.07	1.05
4.67	6	2.0	0.97	0.60	1.08	1.06
7.71	51	3.8	0.89	0.77	0.93	0.89
10.71	3	7.4	0.98	0.14	0.94	0.88
1.72	3	1.7	0.93	0.74	0.92	0.90
5.72	4	1.7	0.96	0.74	0.90	0.88
2.73	9	10.1	0.92	1.04	0.90	0.82
4.73	2	7.6	0.97	1.26	0.91	0.85
11.73	7	1.4	0.94	1.15	0.82	0.81
2.74	3	27.8	1.04	2.16	0.91	0.71
6.74	4	12.0	1.19	1.55	0.94	0.84
9.74	3	14.6	1.22	1.78	1.04	0.91
11.74	3	31.4	1.34	8.67	1.19	0.91
3.75	4	15.5	1.46	1.89	1.20	1.04
10.75	7	4.5	1.41	5.05	1.12	1.07
2.76	4	4.8	1.30	1.58	1.11	1.05
4.76	2	10.2	1.38	2.28	1.11	1.01
6.76	2	10.7	1.44	1.24	1.20	1.09
8.76	2	1.7	1.44	2.88	1.15	1.13
10.76	2	6.2	1.41	3.11	1.15	1.09
5.77	7	5.0	1.34	2.14	1.05	1.00
8.77	3	5.9	1.30	2.58	1.03	0.97
11.77	3	16.4	1.24	13.73	1.00	0.86
2.78	3	3.9	1.25	3.07	0.98	0.94
5.78	3	9.5	1.22	3.50	0.96	0.88
8.78	3	3.7	1.26	3.14	0.93	0.90
11.78	3	12.4	1.24	4.51	0.91	0.81

Appendix 2

NOMINAL PRICE CHANGES AND REAL COSTS OF INSTANT COFFEE

Date of price change	No. of months since last change	Rate of nominal price change (%)	Real unit cost	Expected monthly rate of inflation (%)	Real price after price change	Real price prior to price change
1.66	—	2.2	1.00	0.44	1.00	0.98
7.67	18	0.5	0.92	0.28	0.95	0.95
8.70	37	14.5	1.13	0.45	0.99	0.86
10.71	14	9.8	1.07	1.39	0.93	0.84
1.72	3	1.8	1.01	0.74	0.90	0.88
8.74	31	13.8	0.83	1.83	0.59	0.52
11.74	3	15.5	0.79	8.67	0.58	0.50
2.75	3	8.2	0.76	2.88	0.57	0.52
6.75[a]	4	− 1.4	0.77	1.85	0.53	0.54
7.75	1	1.4	0.77	1.52	0.54	0.53
10.75	3	13.9	0.96	5.05	0.56	0.49
1.76[a]	3	− 4.4	0.98	1.77	0.51	0.53
3.76	2	8.2	1.05	1.91	0.53	0.49
5.76	2	8.7	1.14	2.71	0.53	0.49
7.76	2	8.3	1.27	2.18	0.55	0.50
8.76	1	4.4	1.27	2.88	0.57	0.54
11.76	3	28.7	1.30	2.44	0.65	0.51
1.77	2	35.9	1.46	2.08	0.87	0.64
2.77[a]	1	− 1.3	1.58	2.04	0.85	0.86
4.77	2	40.5	2.05	2.50	1.16	0.81
6.77	2	23.4	2.07	2.04	1.36	1.11
9.77[a]	3	− 6.5	1.56	3.06	1.17	1.25
11.77	2	34.7	1.47	13.73	1.36	1.01
1.78[a]	2	− 10.8	1.57	1.79	1.17	1.31
3.78[a]	2	− 2.4	1.58	2.18	1.09	1.12
5.78	2	0.5	1.45	3.50	1.02	1.02
8.78	3	4.9	1.37	3.14	1.00	0.96

[a] Price decrease.

REFERENCES

Arrow, K. J. (1962). Toward a Theory of Price Adjustment. In *The Allocation of Economic Resources* (M. Abramovitz *et al.*, eds.), pp. 41–51. Stanford University Press, Stanford, California.

Barro, R. J. (1972). A Theory of Monopolistic Price Adjustment. *Review of Economic Studies* **39**, 17–26.

Cagan, P. (1975). Changes in the Recession Behavior of Wholesale Prices in the 1920s and Post World War II. *Explorations in Economic Research*, *NBER* **2**, 54–104.

Cukierman, A., and Wachtel, P. (1980). Differential Inflationary Expectations and the Variability of the Rate of Inflation. *American Economic Review* (to be published).

Fischer, S., and Modigliani, F. (1978). Towards Understanding of the Real Effects and Costs of Inflation. NBER Working Paper No. 303, November.

Heckman, J. (1979). Sample Selection Bias as a Specification Error. *Econometrica* **47**, 153–161.

Jaffee, D., and Kleiman, E. (1978). The Welfare Implications of Uneven Inflation. In *Inflation Among Countries* (E. Lundberg, ed.). Macmillan, London.

Parks, R. W. (1978). Inflation and Relative Price Variability. *Journal of Political Economy* **86**, 79–96.

Scarf, H. (1959). The Optimality of (s, S) Policies in the Dynamic Inventory Problem. In *Mathematical Methods in the Social Sciences* (K. Arrow, S. Karlin, and P. Suppes, eds.), pp. 196–204. Stanford University Press, Stanford, California.

Sheshinski, E., and Weiss, Y. (1977). Inflation and Costs of Price Adjustment. *Review of Economic Studies* **44**, 287–309.

Sheshinski, E., and Weiss, Y. (1979). Demand for Fixed Factors, Inflation and Adjustment Costs. *Review of Economic Studies* **49**, 31–45.

Vining, D. R., and Elwertowsky, T. C. (1976). The Relationship Between Relative Prices and the General Price Level. *American Economic Review* **66**, 699–708.

E. SHESHINSKI
DEPARTMENT OF ECONOMICS
HEBREW UNIVERSITY OF JERUSALEM
JERUSALEM, ISRAEL

A. TISHLER and Y. WEISS
DEPARTMENT OF ECONOMICS
TEL AVIV UNIVERSITY
RAMAT AVIV, TEL AVIV, ISRAEL

PART 4

Financial Assets, Foreign Exchange, and Capital Markets

The Permanent Effects of Inflation on Development and Choice of Production Technique

*ALLAN DRAZEN**

1. Introduction

The effect of inflation on capital accumulation is a central question in the theory of growth and development. In the basic two-asset growth model [as in Tobin (1965)] where money and capital are alternative assets, an increase in the inflation rate will, in general, increase demand for capital by reducing the return to holding money. This in turn will lead to an increase in the steady-state capital–labor ratio. (This result will not hold in models where saving behavior is derived from utility maximization over an infinite horizon, though this is a somewhat specialized result.) In seemingly sharp contrast to the Tobin result is the view, put forward by Edward Shaw (1973) and Ronald McKinnon (1976), among others, that inflation will hinder capital accumulation and growth. Their argument, based on the view that because of the process of financial intermediation money is often a claim to capital, implies that inflation will ultimately reduce capital accumulation. My general purpose in this paper is twofold. First, I want to examine the Shaw–McKinnon view carefully in order to derive conditions

*I wish to thank Milton Harris, Yoram Mayshar, Eytan Sheshinski, Yoram Weiss, and participants at the Faculty Seminar at the Hebrew University of Jerusalem and at this conference for helpful comments. Financial support from the Foerder Institute for Economic Research, Tel Aviv University, and from the University of Chicago Graduate School of Business is gratefully acknowledged.

ISBN 0-12-259750-8

for deciding when it is or is not a better description of an economy than the Tobin view. I shall argue that the two views are really not contradictory.

Having derived simple conditions for inflation to depress capital accumulation, I then want to address a second, more difficult question. The applicability of Shaw's debt intermediation view (as it has come to be called) rests on there being certain constraints on financial markets. From the basic theory of growth one would expect that if these constraints are temporary, the steady state that will be approached will be the same as if these constraints had not existed. That is, though constraints in the short run may affect the speed of approach to steady state, basic theory leads one to believe they will not affect the properties of the steady state itself, those being determined by certain underlying properties of the system. In the second part of the paper I want to examine circumstances under which the invariance of the steady state to the approach path does *not* hold, so that temporary constraints will have permanent effects. After examining certain general mechanisms, I shall argue that under rather plausible conditions, "dislocations" in financial markets caused by inflation will have permanent effects on the development path of an economy. I present a model of one such mechanism.

2. Alternative Views on Inflation and Capital Accumulation

The basic two-asset growth model is due to Tobin (1965) and extended by Sidrauski (1967a, 1967b). In models with a fixed saving rule (for example, a constant average propensity to save) a higher inflation rate, by reducing the return to holding money, will induce a substitution out of money and into capital, the alternative asset. A policy of secular inflation would therefore enhance capital accumulation.

Several economists have taken sharp exception to this view when applied to less-developed countries, arguing that secular inflation will, in fact, depress capital accumulation. The alternative view [see, e.g., Shaw (1973) or McKinnon (1976)] begins with the central role of financial intermediaries and the banking system in the money supply process. Money in the form of bank deposits (inside money, to use Shaw's term) is a bank liability, which must correspond to some asset in the bank's balance sheet. If the intermediary function of the banking system is to channel funds to investment, one may argue that inside money ultimately corresponds to capital. In countries where alternative methods of finance are not well developed, banks as providers of inside money will be crucial in the investment process, and inflation, by reducing demand for bank money, will reduce investment.

The apparent difference between the more common view on the effects of inflation and the Shaw–McKinnon view is easily explained. Clearly, Shaw considers money and capital to be the same asset (inside money ultimately being a claim to capital), whereas the opposing view considers money and capital to be alternative, competing assets. Differences on the effects of inflation and implied optimal policy flow directly from this underlying difference. The relevant question in assessing the applicability of the debt intermediation view then becomes one of the conditions that would make the treatment of money and capital as (ultimately) the same asset a better description of economic reality than the Tobin view of asset substitutability.

A reading of the work of Shaw and McKinnon suggests consideration of three types of conditions for accepting the framework and conclusions of the debt intermediatiation view. On a practical level there is the question of exactly how important banks are in the process of channeling funds to investors. How developed are private capital markets or other alternatives? Implicit in the Tobin view is the notion that capital markets are sufficiently well developed to make it sensible to consider money and capital as different assets. If capital markets are not well developed, such that an overwhelming fraction of new investment flows corresponds to increases in inside money, a second condition suggests itself. It begins with a distinction between those assets whose return is fixed in nominal terms and those with nominal returns which adjust to inflation. The relevant question becomes whether intermediary money falls in the first or the second category. If in the first, then Shaw is correct in arguing that if the financial sector is "repressed" (that is, characterized by poorly functioning capital markets), inflation will be inimical to growth. If, however, inside money falls in the latter category, inflation should have no effect on the real return to money (or, more precisely, the same effect on the return to capital). The implication is that secular inflation will not discourage investment, even though the debt intermediation view is the realistic description of the financial sector. Since money and capital are the same asset (but for costs of the intermediation process) in the Shaw–McKinnon world, the latter case is certainly plausible. Of course, the view that nominal interest rates are either absolutely fixed or adjust fully is unrealistic. The question is How much will nominal rates change in response to inflation? Put in practical terms, how effective are interest rate ceilings on bank deposits in economies with a repressed financial sector? In discussions of the debt intermediation view nominal deposit rates and interest rate ceilings loom exceedingly large, and they will play a central role in the discussion of the permanent effects of constraints presented below.

The comparison of money and capital brings up a third issue relevant to the debt intermediation view. To the extent that there is basically only one financial asset available to savers in an underdeveloped economy, the important question is not one of asset substitution but of total asset accumulation, that is, the total flow of saving. Government policies must be concerned not with substitution effects but with coaxing out saving to allow for higher investment. Here we return to the question of the efficiency of the banking sector. If no domestic capital markets exist, it is crucial that the banking sector offer savers instruments that are attractive in terms of liquidity and yield. One should then ask how elastic the total supply of savings is to nominal interest rates, and whether this elasticity varies with the degree of financial repression. Many macroeconomists would argue, on both theoretical and empirical grounds, that the interest elasticity of saving would be extremely small. I believe that the response of proponents of the debt intermediation view would run as follows. Whereas in a financially well-developed economy this might be true, the same would not hold when financial assets available to individuals are fairly limited. Funds that would flow to banks (and ultimately to investors) when yields are attractive may well end up going to consumer durables or even nondurables. That is, if the real return on bank liabilities is low or negative and if no alternatives exist to allocate saving efficiently, one would not be surprised to find low measured saving rates, reflecting a high propensity for consumer expenditures. In theory, the move away from financial repression should lead both to a better allocation of the existing flow of saving and to a significant increase in the fraction of income devoted to saving. For matters of policy one would like to know how large an effect could be expected.

To summarize, a comparison of the applicability of the debt intermediation view on the relation of money and growth with the more standard view will turn to a large extent on the answers to the three questions outlined above. How important empirically are banks as intermediaries in the flow of national product to investment? If they are of central importance, how important are interest rate ceilings in inducing nonadaptation of interest rates to inflation? Finally, how responsive is total saving to what may very loosely be called the financial environment, meaning, among other things, the efficiency of the banking system and the controls under which it operates? [A more detailed discussion of the conditions outlined here may be found in Drazen (1979).] The applicability of the policy prescriptions advanced by Shaw and McKinnon will depend on the answers to these questions.

Let us now suppose we are considering an economy in which banks do in fact play a central role in channeling funds to real investment. The real return on bank deposits will then be important in determining the supply of funds for investment. This in turn implies the importance of both the nominal interest rate and the expected rate of inflation. Policies that impose artificially low interest rate ceilings or increase the average rate of inflation for a given fixed level of nominal interest rates will tend to constrain the supply of capital. Artificially low interest rate ceilings will lead to an excess demand for capital and some form of capital rationing relative to what would happen if the deposit interest rate were allowed to find its market clearing level. All of this is fairly obvious. The economist who considers financial reform packages will be justified in saying that if low real deposit interest rates induce excess demand for capital and capital rationing and hence hamper development, a first step in a development plan must be either the freeing of bank deposit rates or a substantial increase in the deposit rate ceiling coupled with a commitment to maintain a low secular rate of inflation.

A discussion of the freeing of deposit interest rates to remove disequilibrium in the capital market raises the following question. It should be clear by now that in the sort of economy we are considering, investment will be hampered during the period in which deposit rate ceilings are effective. What will happen after they are lifted? More specifically, can such constraints, though temporary, have permanent effects on the pattern of capital accumulation and development? I address this question in Section 3.

3. Permanent Effects of Capital Rationing: General Mechanisms

The notion that in an economy whose financial sector is described by the Shaw–McKinnon model capital accumulation may be depressed during a period of binding interest rate ceilings is not surprising. Nor would it be surprising if one found that for a period of time after ceilings were lifted, the capital intensity of the economy is less than it would have been in the absence of such constraints. To argue, however, that a period of temporary rationing could have permanent effects in the sense of altering the steady state toward which the economy tends is considerably more controversial. Growth theory tells us that two economies with similar saving rules, similar possible choice of production techniques, and similar long-run resource utilization rates should display similar steady states. Why then, for a given economy, should a temporary period of rationing which leaves the basic characteristics of the economy unchanged alter its steady-state configuration? I argue here that the process of capital accumulation, especially in a developing economy is dependent not only on bank financing but also on a process of learning by doing which changes the set of available production techniques itself. The process is such that a temporary decrease in investment may permanently shift the economy to more labor intensive techniques, even after investment returns to its previous level. In Section 4 I present a model of the interaction of short-run capital rationing and learning by doing to show how an economy can get "stuck" at a relatively labor intensive technique. Before doing so I want to discuss the phenomenon of dependence of steady states on short-run disequilibrium more generally and consider what sort of mechanisms would give rise to it.

Most models of growth and capital accumulation are characterized by continual market clearing for factors in the short run. This approach is justified partially by the objective of much of growth theory, namely, the explanation of trends of output and productivity rather than fluctuation about trend, but also by the view that failure of markets to clear in the short run will affect the speed of approach to steady state and the likelihood of convergence, but should not affect the properties of the steady state itself [see, e.g., Fischer (1972) or Ito (1978)]. It seems more logical, however, when considering the possible invariance of steady states to factor availability in the short run, to ask what conditions might cause this to hold or not to hold, and then ask whether or not such conditions are likely to be satisfied. This is especially important given the phenomena of excess supply of or demand for factors associated with price rigidity in the short run. [For a survey of models in which markets do not clear in the short run, see Drazen (1980).]

When one considers a firm facing a decision on investment in one of several techniques or types of capital, the decision will often depend on, among other things, the amount invested in the given technique in the past. This is not necessarily because of myopia in the sense of weighing fixed costs too heavily. Rather, the cost of investing in a given technique may be an inverse function of the amount invested so far. This general observation forms the basis of the phenomenon considered in this paper. The specific mechanism giving rise to the inverse relation between cost of future investment and aggregate investment to date that I shall consider here is learning by doing, though other mechanisms are possible. The obvious implication is that a firm which has invested heavily in a technique in the past will continue to do so. This, in turn, raises the possibility that the path of capital accumulation will be strongly dependent on "initial conditions." How this dependence relates to the discussion of supply of investment in Section 2 should be clear. Constriction of the supply of total investment funds through government policies in financial markets may set the representative firm on a path of investment in labor intensive techniques. The nature of the capital accumulation process may be such that having invested in such techniques for a sufficiently long time, the firm continues to do so when total supply of investment funds returns to its previous level.

This is the "message" of this paper, which will be examined in detail in Section 4.

One final comment is appropriate. It may appear that what is being discussed is a case of multiple equilibria. This interpretation is not really correct. Possible steady states of the system are determined by the dynamics of capital accumulation and are not inherent in the underlying structure. As will become clear, an infinity of steady states is possible in this model. Which of them actually appears depends on the extent and duration of capital rationing.

4. The Interaction of Capital Constraints and Learning by Doing

The concept of learning at production processes is a well-known one (Arrow, 1962), applicable to both developed and developing economies. Unlike generalized technical progress, which is usually a shift in the entire production function or set of techniques over time, learning by doing is often seen as increasing output per unit input only in those techniques that are actually employed. For an economy that faces rationing in the short run this distinction is crucial. The decision to use one technique instead of another will change the relative profitability of the two techniques over time. When one technique is employed for a period of time, a second technique may no longer be profitable (relative to the first) at the wage–rental ratio at which it was previously profitable. Hence the "abandonment" of a technique during rationing may mean that when the economy returns to the original wage–rental ratio, the original technique is no longer profitable and will not be chosen. Hence the effect of rationing of a factor is to deprive firms of learning at techniques intensive in that factor. The development of the economy is characterized by specialization in techniques intensive in the factor that, at least temporarily, was more abundant. I believe that such a mechanism may help explain why different economies continue using dissimilar techniques for the production of similar commodities.

The basic model is of the "putty-clay" type used by Solow (1962), where capital and labor are freely substitutable ex ante but must be used in fixed proportions ex post. I shall first give a detailed outline of the model in the case where technical progress shifts the entire ex ante production function, concentrating on the behavior of the firm. The flow of output going to investment is exogenous to the representative firm, but will change when the changes in the nominal deposit rate change the real return to saving. The interest rate that firms face will *not* in general be equal to this rate. I shall first consider how a temporary period of low saving and investment will affect steady-state capital intensity in the usual technological progress case. In this case a temporary period of low investment will have no effect on the steady state of the economy. Two economies with the same average saving rate and other underlying parameters will tend toward the same steady state, even though one may have had a temporarily lower saving ratio at some earlier point. I shall then consider the same question for an economy where technological progress affects only techniques actually used. By looking at the firm's decision problem it will be shown that techniques initially profitable at a given wage–rental ratio that came to be dominated by another technique will never be chosen again, after a certain period of time, no matter what wage–rental ratio prevails.

A. The Firm's Behavior in the General Case

Firms in the basic model produce output by means of machinery and labor. Though it is common to think of the model as a two-sector one, where machines are produced by means of labor and consumption goods by use of machines and labor, I ignore the machine-producing sector by assuming no scarce inputs are used in producing machines.[1] Machines produced in period t, however, do not produce output till the following period. For simplicity machines are infinitely durable although they may fall out of use because of economic obsolescence. Physical depreciation will not change the basic results.

At each point in time the firm must choose which type of machine to produce. We summarize this by considering the machine's capacity y, which tells the maximum output the machine can produce, and the labor input n needed to produce capacity output. We assume capacity is a continuous, increasing, concave function of n, $y(n)$ (that is, $y' > 0$, $y'' < 0$), and we index machines by their labor input n. We could also assume that only a discrete set of techniques is available, but then could not use calculus to solve the problem. This will be important in the case considered below. Machines that use more labor at capacity produce more output, but obviously have a higher wage bill. We assume the capacity of a machine does not depreciate over its life.

Once a machine is built, its labor requirements and output capacity remain fixed. Hence if machines of type n are built, the fixed capital and labor coefficients per unit of output are $1/y(n)$ and $n/y(n)$, respectively.

[1] Of course, the number of machines is determined by the flow of investment funds. Hence there is no option of building two small machines (each half the size) rather than one large machine.

The firm continues to operate the machine as long as the revenues from the machine are at least as great as the wage cost of running the machine, that is, as long as quasi-rents are positive. Because of technological progress the producer predicts a constant rate of increase of wages. Therefore, he will anticipate operating the machine until a given date when quasi-rents fall to zero and then retire the machine permanently. Suppose the producer anticipates a constant rate of wage increase at time t, $\omega(t)$, so that if today's wage is $w(t)$, the wage expected at t to hold at time t', denoted $\hat{w}(t,t')$, is

$$\hat{w}(t,t') = w(t)e^{\omega(t)(t'-t)}. \tag{1}$$

Therefore, a machine of type (y,n) is expected to last T years, where T is determined by

$$\hat{w}(t,t+T)n = y \quad \text{or} \quad nw(t)e^{\omega(t)T} = y. \tag{2}$$

The total flow of investment at time t, $I(t)$, is exogenous to the firm. It is determined by the saving behavior of individuals, which (given the structure of financial markets outlined above) is dependent on government policies that fix nominal interest rates and change the rate of inflation. The important point is that in times of low investment, when firms calculate a high (shadow) interest rate, the high return to investment does not get communicated to savers and hence savings do not increase.

As total investment $I(t)$ in new machinery is exogenous, the firm's problem is one of choosing the optimal capacity or labor intensity of new machines. The firm also treats the wage $w(t)$ and the interest rate $r(t)$ as exogenous. (These will later be determined by the interactions of firm demand and supply of factors.) Given the expected rate of growth of wages at time t, $\omega(t)$, the expected time path of wages will be determined as in (1). It will be assumed firms anticipate that the rate of interest in the future $\hat{r}(t,t')$ will remain at its current level, that is, that

$$\hat{r}(t,t') = r(t), \qquad t' \geqslant t.$$

Of course, $r(t)$ may change through time, but this assumption is convenient for illustrating the basic structure of the model. When considering rationing, I shall discuss the effect of some modifications of this assumption.

Since coefficients are fixed ex post, a labor-intensive machine that yields high quasi-rents in the near future will not be the optimal machine in terms of highest quasi-rents in the distant future when wage rates have risen. Therefore, one may argue that a firm chooses the optimal labor intensity for a machine by maximizing the expected discounted value of quasi-rents, denoted V, over the expected life of the machine,

$$V = \int_t^{t+T} R(t,\chi)\exp[-r(t)(\chi - t)]\,d\chi, \tag{3}$$

where $R(t,\chi)$ is the quasi-rent expected as of t to accrue at time χ. From the assumptions made above, if technique $y(n)$ is chosen at time t, quasi-rents expected at χ are

$$R(t,\chi) = y - nw(t)\exp[\omega(t)(\chi - t)]. \tag{4}$$

Therefore,

$$V = y\int_t^{t+T} \exp[-r(t)(\chi - t)]\,d\chi - nw(t)\int_t^{t+T} \exp\{(\omega(t) - r(t))(\chi - t)\}\,d\chi, \tag{5}$$

which the firm maximizes with respect to n, subject to $y = y(n)$, and (2) determining T. Therefore, to find the optimal n we differentiate (5), letting both T and y vary with n, and set $\partial V/\partial n$ equal to zero. We obtain

$$\frac{\partial y}{\partial n}\int_t^{t+T} \exp\{-r(t)(\chi - t)\}\,d\chi - w(t)\int_t^{t+T} \exp\{(\omega(t) - r(t))(\chi - t)\}\,d\chi + \frac{\partial T}{\partial n}[y - nw(t)\exp\{\omega(t)T\}]\exp\{-r(t)T\} = 0. \tag{6}$$

We evaluate (6) at the optimal T. Therefore, the term in brackets equals zero and the third term on the left-hand side vanishes. Since the integrands in the first two terms are exponential functions, this expression can be simplified further, and we obtain

$$\partial y/\partial n = c(T)w(t), \tag{7}$$

where

$$c(T) \equiv \frac{r(t)}{r(t) - \omega(t)}\,\frac{1 - \exp\{-[r(t) - \omega(t)]T\}}{1 - \exp\{-r(t)T\}}.$$

At the optimum the marginal product of labor is set equal to the wage multiplied by a constant that is a function of expectations. If, for example, wages were expected to remain constant so that $\omega(t) = 0$, then $c(T) = 1$, and the marginal product of labor would be set equal to the wage. If interest rate expectations were not static, but followed a more complicated pattern, we could replace $r(t)$ by $\hat{r}(t,\chi)$ in (5) and (6). Equation (7) would still hold with the marginal product of labor proportional to the wage, but the function for the factor of proportion $c(T)$ would be more complicated.

The firm's problem is now completely characterized by (2) and (7), which determine the labor intensity and life of machines for given values of $r(t)$, $w(t)$, and $\omega(t)$. Demand for labor to man the new machines and output from these machines is determined by $I(t)$, the scale of investment.

To find total demand for labor and supply of output by the representative firm, we consider the set of machines of all vintages whose labor requirements are such that at the current wage they still yield positive quasi-rents. I assume that technological progress in the general model is labor augmenting, so that older machines have "on average" a higher labor intensity and hence eventually become unprofitable as wages rise. The set of all machines profitable to operate (except those just constructed, which by assumption cannot be operated until next period) then tells us total labor needed to operate them at capacity, that is, the firm's total labor demand. We find total output in a similar manner.

B. Determination of Wage, Interest, and Growth Rates

To close the model we would like to know how wage and interest rates are determined. The wage rate equates labor demand and supply. On the demand side assume every firm is like the representative firm. On the supply side assume supply of labor at time t, $L(t)$, is supplied inelastically. Heuristically, labor is "assigned first" to machines with the highest productivity per worker, then machines next highest, and so on, until all labor has been assigned. The level of the wage is such that on the marginal machine, quasi-rents are zero; wage thus equals the average product of labor on this machine. When a new machine comes on line, its owner, to attract labor, bids up the wage sufficiently to man the machine. Labor is released from the marginal machine, which with the higher wage is no longer profitable. The wage is bid up just enough to make it equal to the average product of a slightly more efficient machine.

The determination of the interest rate is a bit trickier. The real interest rate that savers receive is the difference between the fixed nominal deposit rate and the rate of inflation $(d - \pi)$ and hence is controlled by the government. We could set the interest rate which firms face as equal to this difference, but this exogenous interest rate raises the possibility of pure profit or pure loss in the machine-building industry. For example, if $d - \pi$ is "low," then $I(t)$ will be low. Setting $r(t)$ equal to $d - \pi$ means that firms' demand for capital will exceed supply at $r(t)$, and the allocation of investment funds to firms will take place via some rationing mechanism. Machine-producing firms lucky enough to get funds will make pure profits. At this artificially low interest rate, choice of technique is still determined by (7).

Alternatively, we could sever the connection between $r(t)$ and $d - \pi$. In that case $r(t)$ would be determined by the interaction of the given $I(t)$ and demand by firms and would adjust to eliminate any pure profit or loss in the machine-building sector. The rate of interest would then equal the marginal rate of return to investment. If $d - \pi$ and $I(t)$ were low, rationing of investment funds would be achieved via price rather than via quantity constraints. Demand equals supply $I(t)$, but it is not a full equilibrium in the sense that $r(t)$ will be greater than $d - \pi$. Profit which in the previous case accrued to machine builders now accrues to the banking sector. [Of course, in the alternative case where an exogenously high level of $r(t)$ would cause pure loss in the machine sector the argument will not carry over. If $I(t)$ is high, so that market clearing $r(t)$ is low, banks will not absorb a loss, but will lower deposit rates below their ceilings.]

The actual rate of wage growth ω will depend on the rate of labor-augmenting technical progress. Suppose technical progress takes place at an exponential rate γ, so that the entire "production function" shifts over time. If a technique requires n units of labor per machine at time t, it will require at time $t + t'$ only $ne^{-\gamma t'}$ units of labor to produce the same y units of output. As new machines are more productive than old machines, wages will have to rise from period to period to clear the labor market. The rate of wage increase ω will be exactly equal to γ only in steady state of course. As technical progress shifts the entire production relation, variation of technique due to variation of $w(t)$ according to (7) is as before.

The assumption that gross investment $I(t)$ is exogenous could be replaced by a saving rule, such as $I(t)$ being a constant fraction s of total output in the economy $y(t)$. Either implictly or explicitly there would thus be a direct relation between either s or $I(t)$ and the real return to saving $d - \pi$. The saving rule would allow us to cast this in terms of a standard growth model.

C. Steady States and the Effect of Capital Shortfalls

We can now consider how a temporary period of low saving would affect the long-run capital accumulation path in the case of general technical progress. One can show that if technical progress is of the general Harrod-neutral type, a model such as this with a constant saving rate is capable of steady-state growth (Sheshinski, 1967) and that the growth path is stable. In a steady state the choice of technique will be constant, dependent on the nature of the $y(n)$ function, the rate of growth of the labor force, and the saving ratio s. If these are given, the steady state is fully determined. A fall in s will lead to a lower wage and an increase in the labor intensity of machines in steady state. Suppose $I(t)$ falls because of the fall in s; $w(t)$ then determines the labor intensity of new machines. In period $t + 1$, however, the stock of machines in existence is lower than it would have been had investment remained at its old level. To maintain full employment of labor, machines that would otherwise have been retired must be kept running, meaning that the wage will be lower than at the old rate of investment. This in turn leads to a choice of higher labor intensity for new machines, and so on, until a steady state is achieved.

What happens when s returns to its previous higher level, say at time t'? Because technical progress shifts the entire $y(n)$ relation simply as a function of time (that is, independent of the techniques actually used), the production relation at time t' is the same as if the temporary fall in s had not occurred. Therefore, as the period of low investment recedes farther into the past, the economy comes closer to the path of capital accumulation that would have obtained had s always remained at its higher level. In other words, the temporary imposition of low interest rate ceilings (or, equivalently, a temporary high inflation period relative to the level of interest rate ceilings) will have no permanent effect on the path of capital accumulation. Let us now consider the same question in what appears to me the more realistic case where progress in a certain technique depends on that technique actually being employed.

D. Production Decisions with Learning at Techniques

The argument that technical progress will take the form of learning at techniques actually employed implies that the change in production relations over time [the $y(n)$ function] will be different than in the case of general labor-augmenting technical progress. As the firm's decision problem was described in detail in Section A, I shall now concentrate on the nature of the production relation itself.

Suppose initially that the production relation is represented by the continuous function $y(n)$. At the initial wage and interest rate technique n_i is chosen. Technical progress is labor augmenting, but is assumed to affect only technique n_i.[2] For simplicity let us assume for now that progress at technique i is a function only of the length of time it is used, not [as in the classic Arrow (1962) paper] the amount of output, or the investment undertaken in the technique. A modification will later be considered. At time $t + 1$ the labor requirement to produce y_i is $n_i e^{-\gamma}$, where γ is the rate of progress. Since technical progress affects no other technique, the production relation is clearly no longer everywhere continuous. More importantly, because the labor requirement to produce y_i has fallen, some techniques close to $y_i(n_i)$ will no longer be profitable relative to y_i. There are two such possibilities. If we consider a technique initially slightly less labor intensive

[2] It would be more realistic to assume that learning also affects techniques in the neighborhood of n_i. The polar assumption used here highlights the mechanism being considered. Moreover, as long as learning has a greater effect on n_i than on adjacent techniques, the basic results presented here still hold.

than i (which therefore produces less output per machine), labor-augmenting technical progress at i means that a type i machine will eventually produce more output with less labor input and hence will strictly dominate the alternative technique. Now consider a technique slightly more labor intensive than i (call it j), which is initially chosen at a lower wage rate. Technical progress at i means there will be a wage rate that makes the firm indifferent between the two techniques i and j, and as technical progress at i continues, the wage rate that makes i and j equally profitable falls. However, at this lower wage rate techniques more labor intensive than j are more profitable than either i or j. Therefore, if more labor intensive techniques exist, technique j will "disappear" as a profit-maximizing choice because of technical progress of i.

The notion of "disappearance" of adjacent techniques due to learning at a given technique is formalized in the following propositions.

Proposition 1. If there has been labor-augmenting technical progress in technique i, there exists a set of less labor intensive techniques which are strictly dominated by i in the sense that a machine of type i produces more output with less labor input.

Clearly, there is no wage at which these dominated techniques will be chosen, independent of the existence of other techniques. (If technical progress is capital or machine augmenting, some techniques that are more labor intensive will disappear.)

Proposition 2. If there has been labor-augmenting technical progress in technique i, there exists a set of more labor intensive techniques which are dominated by i or (at a sufficiently low wage) by an even more labor intensive technique.

That is, as long as even more labor intensive techniques are available, there is a set of techniques labor intensive relative to i which will appear at no wage. Similarly, we may write

Proposition 3. If there has been labor-augmenting technical progress in technique i, there exists a set of less labor intensive techniques which are dominated either by i or (at a sufficiently high wage) by an even less labor intensive technique.

(For machine-augmenting technical progress the relevant analogs of Propositions 2 and 3 hold.) The meaning and intuition of these propositions is straightforward and may be illustrated by Fig. 1. With technical progress in technique i there is no wage at which adjacent techniques are chosen.

The proofs of these propositions are fairly obvious and proceed as follows:

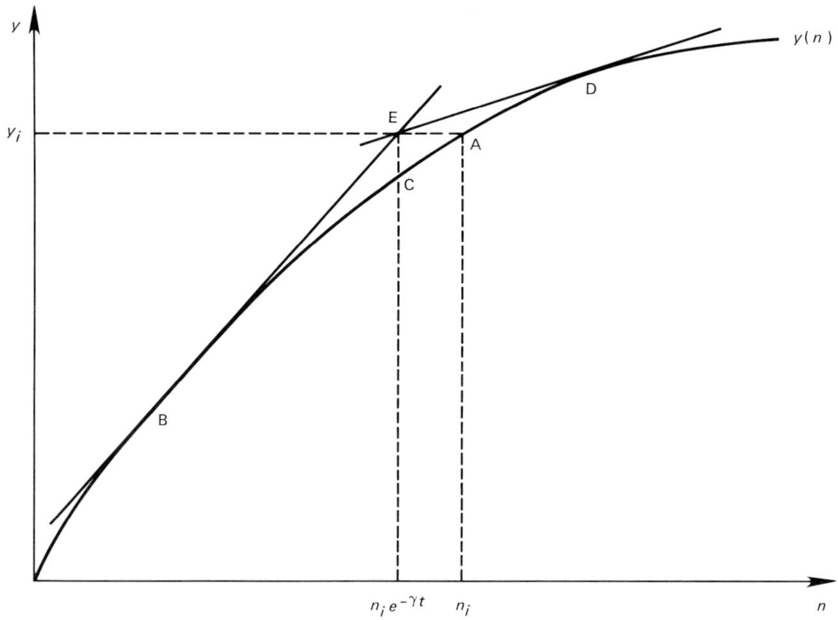

Fig. 1. The effect of learning. Learning reduces physical labor units needed to produce y_i from n_i to $n_i e^{-\gamma t}$. Points between C and A are strictly dominated (Proposition 1). Points between A and D are dominated either by technique i or by a technique to the right of D (Proposition 2). Points between B and C are dominated either by technique i or by a technique to the left of B (Proposition 3). Hence all techniques between B and D (with the exception of i) never reappear.

PROOF OF PROPOSITION 1. If at t_0, a machine of type i uses n_i workers to produce y_i, it will use $n_i e^{-\gamma t}$ workers at time $t_0 + t$ to produce y_i if it has been in use from t_0 to $t_0 + t$. Consider a machine of type j where $n_i e^{-\gamma t} < n_j < n_i$. The second inequality implies $y_j < y_i$. Therefore, from the first inequality we may write, for any w,

$$y_j - wn_j < y_i - wn_i e^{-\gamma t}.$$

Therefore, at any wage rate the quasi-rents obtainable from machine j must be less than those from machine i for all $t' > t$. Therefore, technique j will never be chosen.

PROOF OF PROPOSITION 2. We first show that for any technique for which $n_j > n_i$ (that is, for *all* techniques which are more labor intensive) there is some wage $\tilde{w}$ that implies higher quasi-rents for technique j. We then show that if the marginal product of labor with technique j, $\partial y/\partial n_j$, is greater than $\tilde{w}$, technique j is dominated at $\tilde{w}$ by some technique which is more labor intensive. Therefore, j must be dominated at any w either by i or by a more labor intensive technique.

Consider a technique $y_j(n_j)$, where $n_j > n_i > n_i e^{-\gamma t}$ and $y_j > y_i$. We ask if there exists a $\tilde{w}$ such that

$$y_j - \tilde{w} n_j > y_i - \tilde{w} n_i e^{-\gamma t}. \tag{8}$$

Rearranging, $\tilde{w}$ must satisfy

$$\tilde{w} < (y_j - y_i)/(n_j - n_i e^{-\gamma t}). \tag{9}$$

By the inequalities above $\tilde{w}$ exists. Equation (9) defines the set of wages at which j is preferred to i in terms of maximum quasi-rents. It is clear, however, from (9) that for n_j close to n_i, $\partial y_j/\partial n_j > \tilde{w}$ for any $\tilde{w}$ that satisfies (9). From the concavity of y a slightly more labor intensive technique $y(n_k)$ has a derivative $\partial y_k/\partial n_k$ such that

$$\partial y_j/\partial n_j > \partial y_k/\partial n_k > \tilde{w}. \tag{10}$$

k can be written $n_k = n_j + \epsilon$, $y_k = y_j + \delta\epsilon$ where $\delta \approx \partial y_k/\partial n_k$. Therefore, quasi-rents at $\tilde{w}$ from k are

$$y_k - \tilde{w} n_k = y_j + \delta\epsilon - (n_j + \epsilon)\tilde{w} = y_j - n_j\tilde{w} + (\delta - \tilde{w})\epsilon > y_j - n_j\tilde{w}.$$

Therefore, for any $\tilde{w}$ that satisfies (9) technique j will be dominated by any technique that satisfies (10). If there is no $\tilde{w}$ that satisfies (9), technique i dominates technique j. Therefore, subject to the existence condition (10), technique j will never be used.

Two comments on Proposition 2 might be useful. First, techniques that are highly labor intensive relative to i will not be dominated since the wage which satisfies (9) will be larger than the marginal product of labor in this technique. Hence there exists a k such that $\partial y_k/\partial n_k = (y_k - y_i)/(n_k - n_i e^{-\gamma t})$, and all techniques j with $n_k > n_j > n_i$ are dominated, while all techniques for which $n_j > n_k$ are not. Second, the existence condition (10) should be noted. If the choice of techniques is not continuous, there may exist a technique with $\partial y_j/\partial n_j > \tilde{w}$, but which may appear at a sufficiently low wage rate, because there may be no technique k that satisfies (10).

Proof of Proposition 3. This proof is analogous to the proof of Proposition 2. Consider $y_j(n_j)$ where $n_j < n_i e^{-\gamma t} < n_i$ and $y_j < y_i$. There exists $\tilde{w}$, such that

$$y_j - \tilde{w} n_j \geqslant y_i - \tilde{w} n_i e^{-\gamma t}, \tag{11}$$

$$\tilde{w} \geqslant \frac{y_i - y_j}{n_i e^{-\gamma t} - n_j}. \tag{12}$$

For n_j close to n_i, $\partial y_i/\partial n_j$ is less than the minimum $\tilde{w}$ satisfying (12). Therefore, consider a slightly less labor intensive technique $y(n_k)$, such that

$\partial y_j/\partial n_j < \partial y_k/\partial n_k < \tilde{w}$. y_k will dominate y_j at $\tilde{w}$ and as before, technique j will never be used.

The implication of these propositions for the problem we are considering is clear. If firms are temporarily pushed towards relatively labor intensive techniques because of low wage rates, they may acquire sufficient learning at these techniques that they do not return to less labor intensive techniques when wage rates rise. An individual firm that faces capital rationing in the short run acquires expertise at a labor intensive method of production and finds it optimal to remain with the labor intensive technique when the flow of investment funds increases.

Whether or not after a period of low investment the original technique in fact reappears clearly depends on two things: the length of time spent at the labor intensive technique and the difference in (trend adjusted) wage rates between the high and low investment periods, which comes down to the level of investment. The longer the labor intensive technique has been used, the larger the increase in the wage must be for the old technique to reappear. More specifically, suppose technique j was in use at time t_0 when interest rate ceilings cause investment to fall. Suppose the fall in wages causes a shift to technique i, which is used from t_0 to $t_0 + t'$. Under what conditions will j reappear at $t_0 + t'$? Given Proposition 3, we obtain first

$$\frac{\partial y_j}{\partial n_j} \geqslant \frac{y_i - y_j}{n_i e^{-\gamma t'} - n_j} > 0 \tag{13}$$

for j to reappear at all. Moreover, for j, rather than an even less labor intensive technique, to appear $w(t_0 + t')$ must obviously equal $\partial y_j/\partial n_j$ [divided by $c(T)$]. Therefore, for j to be just at the margin we have

$$w(t')c(T) = \frac{y_i - y_j}{n_i e^{-\gamma t'} - n_j}\,. \tag{14}$$

Conversely, we could ask how large the rise in wages must be for a technique other than i to be used. Since $(y_i - y_j)/(n_i e^{-\gamma t} - n_j)$ (when n_j is the marginal technique) is increasing in t, the larger is t, the greater is the marginal product of the most labor intensive technique less than i which will appear. This value $\partial y_j/\partial n_j$ tells us what wage is necessary to cause a shift out of i. Or, the longer the period for which interest rate ceilings are imposed, the more likely it is for a firm with static expectations of wage–rental rates (defined to include wage growth at rate ω) to continue using the labor intensive technique when ceilings or other such constraints are lifted.

Finally, to complete the model of the firm's behavior, we should consider the case where firms, instead of having static expectations, anticipate an increased flow in investment and a higher effective wage at some future date $t + t'$. This should clearly affect the decision about the type of machine to build at time t. Two aspects of this more realistic notion of expectations are important. The first concerns simply the effect of different wage expectations on today's choice of technique, ignoring the effect of today's choice on the production relation $y(n)$ at $t + t'$. Second, we must consider how the realization that future production possibilities depend on today's actions will affect today's choice of technique.

On the first aspect, suppose firms anticipate an increase in I at $t + t'$ and therefore a rise in w relative to trend. This should decrease the optimal labor intensity of those machines which the firm still expects to be in use at $t + t'$. To solve the problem precisely, we consider (5) with a more complicated structure of wage and interest rate expectations (still retaining the assumption of point expectations) and differentiate (5) with respect to n. The optimal solution for $n(t + k)$, $(k < t')$, will be more complicated than in (7) and could conceivably have multiple solutions. However, our assumptions about $y(n)$ ensure the existence of an optimal n, and the differentiation of (5) indicates how to find an optimum.

The second aspect is considerably more complicated. When firms realize that techniques become more efficient only when used and when they anticipate a change in the wage–rental ratio, they may choose a technique which is not profit maximizing today in order to accumulate learning at that technique in anticipation of an increase in the effective wage in the future. To solve this problem, we must introduce the dependence of the production constraint itself on the past history of the economy. Since $y(n)$ at $t + t'$ depends on the history of the economy, so does the optimal n at $t + t'$. Firms choosing techniques at t must take this dependence into account. The dependence of $n^*_{t+t'}$ on n_t gives rise to a dynamic programming problem where the transition law is the change in the production relation due to learning and where, to repeat, $y(n)$ at $t + t'$ depends on the state of the system at all previous dates. These characteristics make the problem extremely difficult; I have so far been unable to fully formulate and solve it rigorously, but hope to be able to report on this in the near future. I believe, however, that the basic question about permanence of labor intensive techniques can be answered in this framework.

The assumption that progress at a technique depends only on the length of time it is employed, independently of level, now becomes untenable. For if firms anticipated a change in wage ratio at $t + t'$, they would devote $I(t) - \epsilon$ to the technique that is currently profitable and ϵ to the technique that will be profitable beginning at $t + t'$, thereby gaining learning "costlessly" at the technique they anticipate using in the future. One must therefore assume, consistent with the Arrow model, that the amount of learning at a technique is proportional to the intensity at which it is used.

The results for the static expectations case will be unchanged by this assumption. We therefore ask Is it more or less likely that firms will permanently remain with the technique chosen in the short run when they explicitly take account of the dependence of the production relation on their actions? One's intuition is that if firms fully realize that an investment shortfall will be temporary, it is more likely that the long-run steady state will be unaffected by short-run constraints. My preliminary results for this case indicate the opposite. First, it is clear from the above that the anticipation of a rise in wage rates (above current trend) at some future date will cause firms to choose less labor intensive techniques. Recognition of the learning process will reinforce this. Let us consider two cases: first, where firms permanently remain with the short-run technique chosen (technique i) under static expectations and second, where the rise in wages is sufficiently great that they switch to a less labor intensive technique in the long run. Given nonstatic expectations, firms must weigh higher short-run profits from choosing a relatively labor intensive technique against the loss from the absence of learning at less labor intensive techniques that will be optimal in the long run.

In the first case, where with static expectations there was sufficient learning at the technique chosen in the short run to make it optimal to continue using it when wages rise, firms will still choose the same technique after $t + t'$ as before, when expectations were not static. In the case of nonstatic expectations they choose a less labor intensive technique than in the static expectations case. Therefore, if the wage rise is sufficiently small that quasi-rents from remaining with technique i are larger than those from changing techniques in the static expectations case, this will surely be true for the technique chosen under nonstatic expectations. In other words, for every case in which the short-run choice was permanent in the case of static expectations, the same will hold true in the case of nonstatic expectations.

I argue that there are cases where the short-run technique will not be permanent in the case of static expectations, but will be permanent with nonstatic expectations. Consider for example the case where, under static expectations, the rise in wages is sufficiently large that at $t + t'$ the firm switches to a less labor intensive technique and "loses" all learning accumulated in technique i. Suppose the wage change is such that the firm is just at the margin. Now consider a firm that anticipates the same wage change. By altering the technique chosen at t slightly and using instead a less labor intensive machine, they can remain with the same technique at $t + t'$ and reap the benefit of learning with higher profits in the future at a cost of only slightly lower profits in the short run. The firm uses its knowledge of the discontinuity in the ex post production relation to raise profits over what they would be with static expectations. In short, there is no case where the choice is permanent with static expectations but not with nonstatic expectations, but there are cases where, for a given wage path, nonstatic expectations implies permanence whereas static expectations leads to switching. Hence if firms are aware of the effects of their actions on future production constraints, permanence is more rather than less likely. I hope to have more to report on this in the near future.

E. Steady States in the Learning Model

In Section 4.C it was shown that if technical progress shifts the entire production relation, a temporary fall in the rate of investment or the saving ratio will have no permanent effect. The economy will return to the technique which would have been chosen if the saving rate had been at its long-run level. As shown in Section 4.D, the results on the behavior of the firm make it clear that this will not be the case here. If the economy has used a labor intensive technique when the saving rate was low for a sufficiently long period of time, it will continue to use this labor intensive technique when the saving rate rises. What remains is to demonstrate the existence of and convergence to a steady state if the firm behaves as in Section 4.D. On the first, after a period of time, a finite number of techniques will have been used and will dominate all techniques that have never been used. We can then consider the production function as a finite number of fixed coefficient techniques. One must then show that, eventually, only one technique is chosen for a reasonable variation in wage rates, which seems plausible. If this is so, we have, in essence, a clay–clay technology, and the existence and stability of steady state has been demonstrated by Solow *et al.* (1966).

5. Summary and Conclusions

The results of this paper can be summarized by pointing out three conclusions: First, on a theoretical level, I have presented a general mechanism which implies that the properties of the steady state in a growth model are not invariant to the path of approach to steady state, in sharp contrast to the standard model. It is worthwhile, in fact, to investigate conditions for hysteresis to be present or absent in growth models in order to answer the question of whether or not we are justified in constructing models where path invariance of the steady state is assumed to hold.

Therefore, a model without invariance is important in its own right, and my feeling is that we should devote more resources to constructing and studying such models.

Second, the model in Section 4 shows that how technical progress in using production techniques actually takes place is crucially important for a firm's behavior. The notion that firms learn only at techniques actually employed is certainly plausible.[3] Therefore, on an applied level, one hopes that this model may provide insight into the question of why two firms that produce the same product may use significantly different techniques even though they face the same economic environment. Having faced different circumstances at some point in the past, each firm has acquired sufficient learning at its technique to make it nonoptimal to switch to the other firm's technique. This point may have strong relevance to some of the differences in production technique between countries.

Finally, and most importantly for this conference, this paper has strong policy implications. It is well known that constraints on financial markets may hinder development in the short run. The results presented here make an even stronger case against policies such as putting ceilings on interest rates. For such policies may in fact imply a permanently lower capital intensity in the economy than if such constraints had been absent, even though the constraints themselves may be temporary. Once an economy has resorted to policies that depress real rates of interest received by savers, removing such constraints may not totally undo the damage. Therefore, the argument that such policies are temporarily imposed to attain short-run goals becomes somewhat suspect.

REFERENCES

Arrow, K. (1962). The Economic Implications of Learning by Doing. *Review of Economic Studies* **29**, 155–173.

Atkinson, A., and Stiglitz, J. (1969). A New View of Technological Change. *Economic Journal* **79**, 573–578.

Drazen, A. (1980). Recent Developments in Macroeconomic Disequilibrium Theory. *Econometrica* **48**, 283–306.

Drazen, A. (1979). Review of McKinnon, *Money and Finance in Economic Growth and Development. Journal of Political Economy* **87**, 901–909.

Fischer, S. (1972). Keynes–Wicksell and Neoclassical Models of Money and Growth. *American Economic Review* **62**, 880–890.

Ito, T. (1978). Disequilibrium Growth Theory: The Kaldor Model. NBER Working Paper No. 281, September.

[3] After completing this paper I became aware of a note by Atkinson and Stiglitz (1969) that presents a similar notion of localized technical progress, but does not study disappearance of techniques in the manner presented here.

McKinnon, R., ed. (1976). *Money and Finance in Economic Growth and Development.* Dekker, New York.

Shaw, E. (1973). *Financial Deepening in Economic Development.* Oxford University Press, London and New York.

Sheshinski, E. (1967). Balanced Growth and Stability in the Johansen Vintage Model. *Review of Economic Studies* **34**, 239–248.

Sidrauski, M. (1967a). Rational Choice and Patterns of Growth in a Monetary Economy. *American Economic Review* **57**, 534–544.

Sidrauski, M. (1967b). Inflation and Economic Growth. *Journal of Political Economy* **75**, 796–810.

Solow, R. M. (1962). Substitution and Fixed Proportions in the Theory of Capital. *Review of Economic Studies* **29**, 207–218.

Solow, R. M., Tobin, J., Yaari, M., and von Weizsäcker, C. (1966). Neoclassical Growth with Fixed Factor Proportions. *Review of Economic Studies* **33**, 79–116.

Tobin, J. (1965). Money and Economic Growth. *Econometrica* **33**, 671–684.

UNIVERSITY OF CHICAGO
CHICAGO, ILLINOIS

Equilibrium Business Cycle Theory with Centralized Trading in Some Assets

*EDI KARNI**

1. Introduction

In two recent articles Lucas (1975, 1977) proposes that the business cycle should be analyzed as an equilibrium phenomenon—that is, using a theoretical framework based on the premises that markets clear at all times and that agents act in their own self-interest. The novelty of Lucas's idea lies in his attempt to explain the mechanism that triggers cyclical fluctuations in output and employment as the result of incomplete information. According to this approach, decision makers receive information about some prices more often than about other prices and infer from the price information the extent to which the observed price changes represent absolute rather than relative price movements. Thus, if all prices change equiproportionally, all agents will observe increases in their own prices. Unaware of the situation, agents attribute part of the observed change to relative factors and respond by varying output; had they possessed full information, they would have preferred to leave output unchanged.

The importance of this observation is that expansions or contractions are triggered simultaneously across a wide range of seemingly unrelated markets. Furthermore, cyclical fluctuations may be triggered by a relatively simple one-shock process with relative and absolute components. In

*This paper was written while visiting the University of Chicago. I would like to thank Robert Kohn, Gary R. Skoog, and Robert E. Lucas Jr. for very helpful discussions.

ISBN 0-12-259750-8

Lucas's work this shock emanates from unanticipated variations in the quantity of money.

Once the system is set in motion, the theory postulates propagation mechanisms, which have the nature of stock adjustment, to convert the initial "pulse" into prolonged, serially correlated movements in output and employment.

In formal applications of these ideas the information that agents are assumed to possess includes the current equilibrium prices in the markets where they happen to be located, but excludes current prices in other markets. All prices become known with a lag of one period. The main purpose of this paper is to study the consequences for the equilibrium theory of the business cycle of variations in the information structure resulting from the incorporation of an additional asset traded in an economy-wide market. The significance of this issue is twofold: Its empirical importance stems from the fact that centralized trading in standardized stocks and bonds is a common feature of modern economies. The theoretical significance stems from the notion that the prices of these assets convey information about the aggregate state of the economy more accurately than local prices do and that this information is currently available to agents. Lucas addressed this issue as follows:

> The interesting issue, however, is to examine the consequences of a single *economy-wide* market for some standardized kind of bond which would clear in an integral sense, but not for each fixed market z. This modification would involve a major change in the information structure of the economy, since the equilibrium interest rate (or bond price) would depend only on *aggregate* state variables, and hence its value would convey to agents some aggregate information uncontaminated by local disturbances (Lucas, 1975, p. 1137).*

Lucas did not attempt to analyze these consequences in detail although he did conjecture that this information would dampen cyclical movements but not eliminate them or alter their qualitative character. Elsewhere (Karni, 1980), I have shown this conjecture to be incorrect. In the context of "one-shock" equilibrium models of the business cycle, the existence of economy-wide trading in one asset amounts to complete information regarding the current aggregate state of the economy, and the trigger mechanism is consequently rendered inoperative. If agents are to remain less than fully informed about the aggregate state of the economy, additional aggregate disturbances must be assumed. Moreover, to the extent that economy-

*Reprinted from: An Equilibrium Model of the Business Cycle by R. E. Lucas in *Journal of Political Economy* **83** (1975) by permission of The University of Chicago Press.

wide markets for assets give rise to independent equilibrium price equations, a meaningful framework for the study of the implications of incomplete information requires that the number of aggregate disturbances exceeds the number of such markets by at least one.

Barro (1980) has recently addressed the same problem within the context of a specific macroeconomic model with two aggregate disturbances, concentrating specifically on the implications for the behavior of the interest rate. The present paper attempts to provide a more general treatment of the issue. The broad features of the theory are maintained, but the specific behavioral relationships, namely the specific functions, are largely omitted. The conclusions therefore transcend specific details of macroeconomic behavior, while preserving the more essential ingredients of the equilibrium theory of the business cycle.

We shall start by considering the general structure of the class of models with incomplete information. In Section 3 we consider a "two-shock" setup and analyze the cyclical effects of unanticipated monetary disturbances. Section 4 summarizes the main findings and points to some additional implications.

2. Preliminaries and Notation

Consider an economy with two types of capital goods, K and H, and money M. Trading in this economy takes place in a continuum of distinct markets denoted by an index z, $0 < z \leqslant 1$. The market-specific, or local, characteristics of the first type of capital K (for example, housing) make its trade across markets at a given time prohibitively costly. Capital of the second type H, despite its fixed geographic location, has no market-specific features and thus may be traded in an economy-wide market. Let $z = 1$ be the index of this particular market, which will henceforth be deleted when the market is unambiguous. Finally, suppose that at the start of each period agents are distributed randomly but uniformly across markets $0 < z < 1$ and that they all have free access to $z = 1$.

Changes in the money supply are introduced by government spending and vary randomly across time and across markets at a given time. Let x_t denote the aggregate rate of change of the money supply at time t, and assume that $x_t \sim N(0, \sigma^2)$.

The random allocation of agents to markets assures that the distribution of agents by their money holdings is the same in all markets. The only changing moment of the distribution is its logarithmic mean m_t which follows the stochastic process:

$$m_{t+1} = m_t + x_t.$$

In addition to x_t, there is another aggregate disturbance y_t (for example, fiscal policy) which is a normally distributed random variable with mean zero and variance σ_y^2. Further "noise" is introduced through a market-specific disturbance $\epsilon_t(z)$, $0 < z < 1$, also a normally distributed random variable with mean zero and variance σ_2^2. We shall assume that x_t, y_t and $\epsilon_t(z)$, $0 < z < 1$, are stochastically independent.

Denote by $p_t^k(z)$ and p_t^h the equilibrium (log of) prices that prevail in market z and the economy-wide market of H at time t. We assume that these prices are linear functions of the aggregate and relative disturbances. We further assume that traders in the economy-wide market for H are independently drawn from the local markets $0 < z < 1$ and that their number is large. Thus, invoking the central limit theorem, the market specific disturbance $\epsilon_t(1) = \lim_{s \to 1} \int_0^s \epsilon_t(z) n_t(z)\, dz$ [where $n_t(z)$ is the proportion of traders in $z = 1$ that come from z in period t] has zero mean, and a variance that tends to zero as the number of agents tends to infinity.[1] Thus, for all practical purposes, agents behave as if $\epsilon_t(1) = 0$.[2] Finally, let $\hat{p}_t^k$ and $\hat{p}_t^h$ denote the prices of K and H that were expected, prior to trading, to prevail in period t.

Prior to trading, agents observe the equilibrium price of K in their local market as well as the equilibrium price of H. These prices are functions of unobserved variables including the aggregate and market specific disturbances. As such, they convey additional information which is used by agents to form a posterior distribution on the disturbances to be used in their output decisions. This problem of inference is considered next.

3. Two-Shock Systems and Equilibrium Business Cycles

Abstracting inessential details, consider the following signal-extraction problem. Let the deviations of the current prices of K and H from the values which prior to trading were expected to prevail be linear functions of the relevant aggregate and relative stochastic disturbances. Formally,

$$p_t^k(z) - \hat{p}_t^k = \pi_0 x_t + \pi_1 y_t + \pi_2 \epsilon_t(z), \tag{1}$$

and

$$W_t \equiv p_t^h - \hat{p}_t^h = \lambda_0 x_t + \lambda_1 y_t, \tag{2}$$

where π_i and λ_i are known parameters.

[1] The variance σ_ϵ^2 is assumed finite, so the central limit theorem applies.

[2] Note that if there is a disturbance specific to $z = 1$, it can be regarded as part of y_t, and thus this possibility does not represent a theoretical problem.

With no loss of generality, let money be neutral in the sense that variations in the quantity of money do not affect relative prices. In other words, $\pi_0 = \lambda_0$. Then subtracting (2) from (1), we get

$$q_t(z) = \{[p_t^k(z) - \hat{p}_t^k] - (p_t^h - \hat{p}_t^h)\} = a_1 y_t + \pi_2 \epsilon_t(z), \qquad 0 < z < 1, \tag{3}$$

where $a_1 = \pi_1 - \lambda_1$.

The basic problem now facing agents is to infer the actual magnitudes of x_t, y_t, and $\epsilon_t(z)$ from the pair of observations $[W_t, q_t(z)]$. Using a statistical procedure described by Anderson (1958, pp. 33–34), the conditional means are given by

$$E\{l_t \mid I_t(z)\} = \hat{l}_t + A^l W_t + B^l q_t(z), \tag{4}$$

where $I_t(z)$ is the set of current information available to agents in z, $0 < z < 1$,

$$A^l = (\sigma_{lW}/\sigma_W^2) - B^l(\sigma_{qW}/\sigma_W^2),$$

$$B^l = [\sigma_{lq} - (\sigma_{lW}\sigma_{qW}/\sigma_W^2)][\sigma_q^2 - (\sigma_{qW}^2/\sigma_W^2)]^{-1},$$

and $l = y, x, \epsilon(z)$.

To analyze the consequences of unanticipated aggregative monetary disturbances (that is, of a realization of x_t) for the business cycle, we begin by comparing the effects of two realizations of x_t on the conditional means. Let x_t^0 and x_t^1 be two realizations of x_t, and suppose that $x_t^1 > x_t^0$. Then, from (4), and since $q_t(z)$ is independent of x_t, we have

$$E\{l_t \mid I_t(z)\}|_{x_t = x_t^1} - E\{l_t \mid I_t(z)\}|_{x_t = x_t^0} = \lambda_0 A^l(x_t^1 - x_t^0), \tag{5}$$

where $l = x, y, \epsilon(z)$.

Since $q_t(z)$ is independent of x_t for all $0 < z < 1$, from (3) we have

$$0 = (a_1 A^y + \pi_2 A^\epsilon)\lambda_0(x_t^1 - x_t^0).$$

But $\lambda_0(x_t^1 - x_t^0) > 0$; hence

$$A^\epsilon = -(a_1/\pi_2)A^y. \tag{6}$$

Assuming $\pi_2 > 0$, A^ϵ and A^y will have the same or opposite signs when $a_1 < 0$ and $a_1 > 0$, respectively. Furthermore, from (2)

$$W_t|_{x_t = x_t^1} - W_t|_{x_t = x_t^0} = \lambda_0(x_t^1 - x_t^0). \tag{7}$$

Thus

$$W_t|_{x_t = x_t^1} - W_t|_{x_t = x_t^0} = (\lambda_0 A^x + \lambda_1 A^y)\lambda_0(x_t^1 - x_t^0). \tag{8}$$

Hence,

$$\lambda_0 A^x + \lambda_1 A^y = 1. \tag{9}$$

From (4), and since $\sigma_{qx} = 0$,

$$\lambda_0 A^x = \lambda_0 \frac{\sigma_{xW}}{\sigma_W^2}\left[1 + \frac{\sigma_{qW}^2}{\sigma_W^2 \sigma_q^2 (1+\rho^2)}\right] = \frac{\lambda_0^2 \sigma_x^2}{\sigma_W^2}\left(1 + \frac{\rho^2}{1-\rho^2}\right),$$

where ρ is the correlation coefficient of q_t, W_t. Thus

$$\lambda_0 A^x = \frac{\lambda_0^2 \sigma_x^2}{\sigma_W^2} \times \frac{\sigma_q^2 \sigma_W^2}{\sigma_q^2 \sigma_W^2 - \sigma_{Wq}^2}$$

$$= \frac{\lambda_0^2 \sigma_x^2 \left(a_1^2 \sigma_y^2 + \pi_2^2 \sigma_\epsilon^2\right)}{\left(a_1^2 \sigma_y^2 + \pi_2^2 \sigma_\epsilon^2\right)\left(\lambda_0^2 \sigma_x^2 + \lambda_1^2 \sigma_y^2\right) - (a_1 \lambda_1)^2 \sigma_y^4}$$

$$= \frac{\lambda_0^2 \sigma_x^2 \left(a_1^2 \sigma_y^2 + \pi_2^2 \sigma_\epsilon^2\right)}{\lambda_0^2 \sigma_x^2 \left(a_1^2 \sigma_y^2 + \pi_2^2 \sigma_\epsilon^2\right) + \lambda_1^2 \pi_2^2 \sigma_\epsilon^2 \sigma_y^2}.$$

Hence

$$0 < \lambda_0 A^x < 1, \tag{10}$$

and from (9)

$$0 < \lambda_1 A^y < 1, \tag{11}$$

and $\lambda_1 \gtrless 0 \Leftrightarrow A^y \gtrless 0$.

The interpretation of (5)–(11) is that agents are unable to trace observed price movements to their true source. If observed price changes are not attributed to their actual source, they must be attributed to other aggregate and market specific variables. In particular, an unanticipated monetary disturbance that increases all prices equiproportionally will be perceived in part as a change in y_t and $\epsilon_t(z)$. Therefore, the issues with which we are concerned are: Under what circumstances will the misperception of the underlying cause of the observed price movement trigger a systematic output response across markets, and what is the nature of this output response?

The answer depends, of course, on the modeling of agents' behavior in response to a given configuration $[W_t, q_t(z)]$. Lucas's analysis of the business cycle is based on a response pattern derived from Friedman (1969) and Phelps (1968). According to this scenario, there would be no real response to an unanticipated increase in prices if agents perceive the increase as a reflection of the general price movement; but if it is perceived as a deviation from the general price movement, a real response would ensue. Thus, to trigger a simultaneous expansion or contraction across markets, agents must be led either to underestimate or to overestimate the general price movement. Hence, in Lucas's words, "It is *essential* to this argument that general price movements not be perceived as such as they are occurring" (Lucas, 1977, p. 2).

Within the present context, there is no misperception regarding the price of H, since this price changes uniformly across all markets. Hence, the crucial issue is whether the change in p_t^k, which is not directly observed at time t, is underestimated or overestimated by all agents. As it turns out, the answer depends upon the nature of the aggregate disturbance y_t. To see this, consider two general cases: (a) a stochastic aggregate disturbance y_t that causes an *increase* in the average price of K relative to that of H, and (b) a stochastic aggregate disturbance y_t that causes a *decrease* in the average price of K relative to that of H.

Case 1. Suppose, without essential loss of generality, that $\lambda_0 > 0$ and $\lambda_1 > 0$. Let $\pi_1 > \lambda_1$; in other words, let an increase in y_t increase both p_t^k and p_t^h and also the relative price q_t.

Consider an unanticipated increase of the nominal money supply x_t. By the neutrality assumption this will cause an equiproportional increase of p_t^k and p_t^h. Let the realizations y_t, $\epsilon_t(z)$, $0 < z < 1$, be zero. If the source of the increase in prices is perceived correctly, the monetary disturbance will have no effect on output. However, in the absence of complete information, agents follow the statistical procedure described above and attribute the observed price increase in part to y_t.[3] Thus, from (11),

$$E\{y_t \mid I_t(z)\} > y_t = 0. \tag{12}$$

But $\pi_1 > \lambda_1$ implies $a_1 > 0$; hence, from (5) and (6),

$$E\{\epsilon_t(z) \mid I_t(z)\} < \epsilon_t(z) = 0 \qquad \forall z. \tag{13}$$

Across markets agents systematically overestimate the aggregate disturbance y_t and underestimate the market specific disturbance $\epsilon_t(z)$. Consequently, observing $p_t^k(z)$, they systematically overestimate the magnitude of p_t^k. This overestimate is positively related to x_t. Averaging across markets, the monetary shock has the effect of *reducing* the aggregate output of K

[3]This is since y_t is positively correlated with both p_t^h and $p_t^k(z)$ and the two prices are also positively correlated. Note also that no essential loss of generality results from the assumption that $y_t = \epsilon_t(z) = 0$, $0 < z < 1$. If $y_t \neq 0$ and/or $\epsilon_t(z) \neq 0$ for some z, we have

$$E\{y_t \mid I_t(z)\}|_{x_t = x_t^1} > E\{y_t \mid I_t(z)\}|_{x_t = x_t^0} \qquad \text{for} \quad x_t^1 > x_t^0.$$

In this case, the larger the unanticipated monetary disturbance is, the larger the conditional expectation of y_t. The relative magnitude of $E\{y_t \mid I_t(z)\}$ and the realization y_t is ambiguous. Similarly,

$$E\{\epsilon_t(z) \mid I_t(z)\}|_{x_t = x_t^1} < E\{\epsilon_t(z) \mid I_t(z)\}|_{x_t = x_t^0} \qquad \forall z.$$

relative to what it would have been in the absence of the shock. Furthermore, the perceived unanticipated increase in the price of K exceeds the observed but unanticipated increase in the price of H. Formally, averaging $q_t(z)$ across markets,

$$E\{p_t^k | I_t(z)\} - p_t^h - (\hat{p}_t^k - \hat{p}_t^h) = a_1 E\{y_t | I_t(z)\} > 0 \qquad \forall z. \quad (14)$$

Averaging across locations, the output of H will therefore *decline*. Otherwise stated, since the actual value of $p_t^k(z)$ and p_t^h increase equiproportionally (by the neutrality assumption), an overestimation of the increase of p_t^k causes $p_t^k(z)$ and p_t^h to deviate in the same direction from the general price movement.

Hence, under the assumed configuration of parameters, *an unanticipated increase in the nominal money supply produces a simultaneous contraction of the aggregate output of both H and K and triggers a cyclical downswing.*

Case 2. Maintaining the assumptions regarding λ_i, $i = 1, 2$, let $\lambda_1 > \pi_1 > 0$. Thus an increase in y_t increases both p_t^k and p_t^h and reduces the relative price q_t. Repeating the experiment described in Case 1, we find that (12) still holds. However, $a_1 < 0$; hence from (5) and (6),

$$E\{\epsilon_t(z) | I_t(z)\} > \epsilon_t(z) = 0 \qquad \forall z. \quad (15)$$

Across markets, agents now systematically overestimate the market specific shock facing them. Consequently, by the logic employed in the discussion of the preceding case, the aggregate output of K exceeds what it would have been in the absence of the monetary shock. Furthermore, the change in the sign of a_1 reverses the inequality (14). In other words, the price p_t^h exceeds the perceived average price of K. Hence the price of H is believed to have increased relative to the general price level, and agents respond by increasing the average (across locations) output of H.

We have therefore established that, in the present context, *an unanticipated monetary disturbance induces a simultaneous expansion of aggregate output of both H and K, thus producing the initial upswing of the business cycle.*

Finally we note that if the aggregative disturbance y_t is neutral in the sense that $a_1 = 0$, then we are back in the complete current information setup. Equation (3) permits an accurate assessment of $\epsilon_t(z)$. Although agents may still confuse changes in x_t with changes in y_t, this confusion will have no implications for output. In this case, changes in p_t^k are equiproportional to changes in p_t^h, and the latter is observed. Thus general price movements are perceived as such when they occur, and the trigger mechanism is defused.

4. Concluding Remarks

Building upon Lucas's equilibrium model of the business cycle, this paper studies the consequences of variations in the information structure associated with the incorporation into the model of economy-wide trading in one asset. The two main conclusions of the discussion are:

(a) In a "one-shock" economic system the existence of centralized trading in one asset amounts to possession of complete current information by all agents.

(b) In a "two-shock" economic system the consequences of incomplete information for aggregate economic activity depend upon the nature of the nonmonetary disturbances. In particular, an unanticipated monetary shock may trigger an expansion or recession according to the effect of the other disturbance upon the relative prices.

Some additional implications are discussed below.

Implications for the allocation of resources. It is worth noting that the agents' misperception of the price ratio (which is an essential part of the model) has no effect on the allocation of productive resources between the two sectors of the economy. This is because production takes place in the *local* markets, and the local price ratios are unaffected by variations in the quantity of money.

Implications for the Phillips curve analysis. Recent treatment of the Phillips curve by Lucas (1972) is based on the same notion as that which underlies the "trigger mechanism" of the business cycle. The analysis presented here therefore applies to the Phillips curve as well. In particular, the discussion suggests that in a "one-shock" system with economy-wide trading the Phillips curve is vertical, while in a "two-shock" system with economy-wide trading the slope of the Phillips curve may be negative or positive, depending on the character of the nonmonetary aggregate disturbance.

A remark on generality. The analysis of the "trigger mechanism" hinges on the confusion between aggregate and relative price movements. To preserve this feature of the decision making process in the presence of information emanating from economy-wide asset markets, it is necessary that the number of aggregate shocks exceed the number of markets. The present analysis is confined to the case of a "two-shock one-market" system, yet it seems that, except for minor details, this case is general in terms of its insights and implications. I suspect that adding shocks and markets will alter neither the basic analysis nor the main conclusions.

REFERENCES

Anderson, T. W. (1958). *An Introduction to Multivariate Statistical Analysis.* Wiley, New York.

Barro, R. J. (1980). A Capital Market in an Equilibrium Business Cycle Model. *Econometrica* (to be published).

Friedman, M. (1969). The Role of Monetary Policy. *American Economic Review* **58**, 1–17.

Karni, E. (1980). A Note on Lucas's Equilibrium Model of the Business Cycle. *Journal of Political Economy* (to be published).

Lucas, R. E. (1972). Expectations and the Neutrality of Money. *Journal of Economic Theory* **4**, 103–123.

Lucas, R. E. (1975). An Equilibrium Model of the Business Cycle. *Journal of Political Economy* **83**, 1113–1144.

Lucas, R. E. (1977). Understanding Business Cycles. *Journal of Monetary Economics* (*Supplement on Stabilization of the Domestic and International Economy*) pp. 7–21.

Phelps, E. S. (1968). Money Wage Dynamics and Labor Market Equilibrium. *Journal of Political Economy* **76**, 687–711.

DEPARTMENT OF ECONOMICS
TEL AVIV UNIVERSITY
RAMAT AVIV, TEL AVIV, ISRAEL

Inflation and Balance of Payments Adjustments with Maximizing Consumers

*ELHANAN HELPMAN**

1. Introduction

The hypothesis of maximizing behavior has a long tradition in economics. It has yielded powerful results in such diverse areas as general equilibrium theory, the theory of optimal economic growth, public finance, urban economics, international trade, and many more. Nevertheless, an explicit use of the maximizing hypothesis is virtually absent in the literature on international monetary problems. [For exceptions, see Helpman and Razin (1979), Kareken and Wallace (1978), Stockman (1978), and Helpman (1979a).] True, specifiers of portfolio balance equations and expenditure functions have in mind functions that represent maximizing behavior. But are the assumptions made about these functions consistent with maximizing behavior? And even if they are, is it not possible that maximizing behavior imposes *more* restrictions, thus adding more structure than admitted by these writers?

Since the expenditure function and the demand for money function are central to my analysis, the paper starts with a derivation of an expenditure function and a money demand function from intertemporal optimization,

*I would like to thank Larry Benveniste, Ron Jones, Edi Karni, Lionel McKenzie, Itzhak Venezia, and Ed Zabel for helpful discussions. The present version is based on Working Paper No. 17-79 of the Foerder Institute for Economic Research, Tel Aviv University, and was prepared while I was at the Institute for International Economic Studies at the University of Stockholm.

ISBN 0-12-259750-8

using an explicit microeconomic theory of money (Sections 2 and 3). The details of this derivation are not presented, since this part of the paper is based on Helpman (1979b). Here, money is used for transaction purposes and as a store of value, but it does not provide direct utility [see Dornbusch and Mussa, (1975)]. A well-defined money demand function arises nevertheless.

Following the characterization of the expenditure function and the money demand function that arise from intertemporal maximization of utility, these functions are applied to the problem of international adjustment under fixed exchange rates (Section 4). Contrary to the existing view, it is shown that for stationary economies without capital markets, the behavior of the price level during the process of balance of payments adjustments is predictable: Either it will be constant, or it will rise for a finite number of periods at the beginning of the adjustment process and remain constant thereafter. This is a general result; it is not based on any specific functional forms. It is proved first for countries populated by identical individuals and then extended to economies populated by many different individuals. The concluding remarks explain why in the presence of capital markets, and independently of whether or not international capital flows are permitted, the price level remains constant during the process of adjustment.

The results derived in this paper are encouraging. They suggest that the hypothesis of maximizing behavior coupled with a microeconomic foundation for the role of money can be used instead of the current ad hoc models to explain the course of economic variables, although, of course, much more work is needed.

2. The Basic Framework

The world consists of two countries: the home country, country H, and the foreign country, country F. Each country produces a single perishable good whose output level y_{it}, $i = \text{H}, \text{F}$, is given in every period: $y_{\text{H}t}$ (> 0) in the home country, and $y_{\text{F}t}$ (> 0) in the foreign country, $t = 1, 2, \ldots$. Outputs are perfect substitutes in consumption.

Every country has its own money. Purchases in the home country must be made with home money, while foreign goods must be purchased with foreign money. Monies are the only assets, so that apart from transaction purposes they also serve as the only stores of value.

At the beginning of period t a representative consumer has certain quantities of home and foreign money. He can—subject to his assets budget constraint—reallocate his asset holdings via trading with the Exchange Rate Stabilizing Authority (ERSA) to desired holding levels of each currency. During period t the consumer can spend part or all of his home currency holdings on home goods and part or all of his foreign currency holdings on foreign goods. Money not spent may be carried over to the next period, $t+1$. At the end of period t the consumer also receives dividends from firms, which are added to his initial money holdings at the beginning of period $t+1$; he cannot use the dividends distributed at the end of period t to buy goods in period t. The amounts of money that have not been spent during period t plus dividend payments at the end of period t determine the individual's money holdings at the beginning of period $t+1$. The process then repeats itself. It is assumed that home firms are owned by home residents, and foreign firms are owned by foreign residents.

Firms sell output and pay out dividends; otherwise they play a passive role in these economies. Monies accumulated from the sale of output are redistributed to stockholders at the end of each period.

The ERSA exchanges one currency for the other at a fixed rate of exchange that equals unity. If it is short on, say, home currency, the home government supplies it with the required quantity of home money. Similarly, if it is short on foreign currency, the foreign government supplies it with the required quantity of foreign money. This the cooperative peg regime described in Helpman (1979a), and it conforms to common modelings of a fixed exchange rate regime. Thus ERSA operations do not change the aggregate quantity of money in circulation in the world economy, only its composition. In what follows, it is assumed that individuals do not expect to pay taxes or receive transfers from their government, so that the aggregate quantity of money in the world economy is not expected to change.

Now we are prepared to state the decision problem of a representative individual of country i, $i = \mathrm{H}, \mathrm{F}$. The following decision problem is for period t. Prices for periods $t+\tau$, $\tau = 1, 2, \ldots,$ should be interpreted as expected prices (all expectations are point expectations). In order to avoid excessive notation, I do not introduce notations for country specific expectations. The decision problem of a representative individual of country i is

$$\text{Choose } \left(c^i_{\mathrm{H}t+\tau}, c^i_{\mathrm{F}t+\tau}, M^i_{\mathrm{H}t+\tau}, M^i_{\mathrm{F}t+\tau}\right) \geqslant 0,\ \tau = 0, 1, \ldots, \text{ to maximize} \tag{1}$$

$$\sum_{\tau=0}^{\infty} \left(\delta^i\right)^{\tau} u^i\left(c^i_{\mathrm{H}t+\tau} + c^i_{\mathrm{F}t+\tau}\right)$$

subject to

$$M^i_{Ht} + M^i_{Ft} \leqslant \overline{M}^i_{Ht} + \overline{M}^i_{Ft}, \tag{a}$$

$$\begin{aligned} M^i_{Ht+\tau} + M^i_{Ft+\tau} \leqslant & \left(M^i_{Ht+\tau-1} - p_{Ht+\tau-1}c^i_{Ht+\tau-1}\right) \\ & + \left(M^i_{Ft+\tau-1} - p_{Ft+\tau-1}c^i_{Ft+\tau-1}\right) \\ & + p_{it+\tau-1}y_{it+\tau-1}, \quad \tau = 1, 2, \ldots, \end{aligned} \tag{b}$$

$$p_{Ht+\tau}c^i_{Ht+\tau} \leqslant M^i_{Ht+\tau}, \quad \tau = 0, 1, \ldots, \tag{c1}$$

$$p_{Ft+\tau}c^i_{Ft+\tau} \leqslant M^i_{Ft+\tau}, \quad \tau = 0, 1, \ldots, \tag{c2}$$

where superscript i stands for the country, $i = \mathrm{H}, \mathrm{F}$; δ^i is the discount factor, equal to one over one plus the rate of time preference, $0 < \delta^i < 1$; u^i is a strictly increasing, strictly concave, twice continuously differentiable utility function, defined on $[0, +\infty)$; $c^i_{Ht+\tau}$ is consumption of home goods in period $t + \tau$; $c^i_{Ft+\tau}$ is consumption of foreign goods in period $t + \tau$; $M^i_{Ht+\tau}$ is holdings of home money in the beginning of period $t + \tau$; $M^i_{Ft+\tau}$ is holdings of foreign money in the beginning of period $t + \tau$; $\overline{M}^i_{Ht}$ is initial holdings of home money in period t; $\overline{M}^i_{Ft}$ is initial holdings of foreign money in period t; and $p_{it+\tau}$ is the price of country i's goods in terms of i's money in period $t + \tau$.

Since in an equilibrium the demand for each output should equal its supply, it implies that in an equilibrium $p_{Ht+\tau} = p_{Ft+\tau}$. For if $p_{Ht+\tau} > p_{ft+\tau}$, the demand for the home country's output in period $t + \tau$ is zero, and if $p_{Ht+\tau} < p_{Ft+\tau}$ the demand for the foreign country's output in period $t + \tau$ is zero. [This is an implication of (1).] With equal prices in both countries a consumer is indifferent to whether he buys home or foreign goods, as well as to whether he stores home or foreign money. Hence, letting $p_{t+\tau} = p_{Ht+\tau} = p_{Ft+\tau}$, $M^i_{t+\tau} = M^i_{Ht+\tau} + M^i_{Ft+\tau}$, $c^i_{t+\tau} = c^i_{Ht+\tau} + c^i_{Ft+\tau}$, $\overline{M}^i_t = \overline{M}^i_{Ht+\tau} + \overline{M}^i_{Ft+\tau}$, problem (1) can be rewritten as

$$\text{Choose } \left(c^i_{t+\tau}, M^i_{t+\tau}\right) \geqslant 0, \quad \tau = 0, 1, \ldots, \text{ to maximize}$$

$$\sum_{\tau=0}^{\infty} (\delta^i)^{\tau} u^i(c^i_{t+\tau}) \tag{2}$$

subject to

$$M^i_t \leqslant \overline{M}^i_t, \tag{a}$$

$$M^i_{t+\tau} \leqslant M^i_{t+\tau-1} - p_{t+\tau-1}c^i_{t+\tau-1} + p_{t+\tau-1}y_{it+\tau-1}, \qquad \tau = 1, 2, \ldots, \tag{b}$$

$$p_{t+\tau}c^i_{t+\tau} \leqslant M^i_{t+\tau}, \qquad \tau = 0, 1, \ldots. \tag{c}$$

In a temporary equilibrium in period t the demand for each output equals its supply and the quantity of each currency demanded for the beginning of period $t+1$ equals its supply, where demands are derived from the consumers' decision problems. Since the ERSA can provide any desired composition of currencies, and since country specific outputs are perfect substitutes in consumption the equilibrium conditions in period t are

$$c_t^{\mathrm{H}}(\cdot)+c_t^{\mathrm{F}}(\cdot)=y_{\mathrm{H}t}+y_{\mathrm{F}t},\qquad M_{t+1}^{\mathrm{H}}(\cdot)+M_{t+1}^{\mathrm{F}}(\cdot)=\overline{M}_t^{\mathrm{H}}+\overline{M}_t^{F},$$

where variables followed by parentheses indicate demand functions derived from (2). We shall be investigating the infinite sequence of temporary equilibria, which will be proved to exist for the specification adopted below.

As a temporary equilibrium depends on price expectations, these expectations must be defined prior to any analysis of the adjustment process. The decision problem presented above is rich enough to encompass a wide variety of expectational hypotheses. However, I have not been able to solve the problem for all interesting expectational hypothesis (like perfect foresight). As a result of this constraint, and for the sake of comparison with existing specifications of the adjustment process under fixed exchange rates in which current spending is written as a function of current variables only [see, e.g., Dornbusch (1973)], I concentrate on the case of static expectations, that is, the case in which the expected price of goods in all future periods is the present price. Under these circumstances $p_{t+\tau}=p_t$ for $\tau=1, 2, \ldots$ in (2). It is also assumed that each country's output level is constant over time, so $y_{\mathrm{H}t+\tau}=y_{\mathrm{H}}$, and $y_{\mathrm{F}t+\tau}=y_{\mathrm{F}}$, $\tau=0,1,\ldots$. Under these assumptions, and taking into account the fact that it is never optimal to have strict inequalities in constraints (a) and (b) in (2), problem (2) can be rewritten as follows:

$$\text{Choose } \left(c_{t+\tau}^i, m_{t+\tau}^i\right) \geqslant 0,\ \tau=0,1,\ldots, \text{ to maximize}$$

$$\sum_{\tau=0}^{\infty}\left(\delta^i\right)^{\tau} u^i\left(c_{t+\tau}^i\right) \tag{3}$$

subject to

$$m_t^i=\overline{m}_t^i, \tag{a}$$

$$m_{t+\tau}^i=m_{t+\tau-1}^i-c_{t+\tau-1}^i+y_i,\qquad \tau=1,2,\ldots, \tag{b}$$

$$c_{t+\tau}^i \leqslant m_{t+\tau}^i,\qquad \tau=0,1,\ldots, \tag{c}$$

where $m_{t+\tau}^i$ equals real balance holdings in period $t+\tau$ $(M_{t+\tau}^i/p_t)$ and $\overline{m}_t^i$ equals initial real balance holdings $(\overline{M}_t^i/p_t)$.

From (3) it is clear that, given δ^i and $u^i(\cdot)$, real spending in period t c_t^i depends only on initial real balance holdings $\overline{m}_t^i$ and permanent real income y_i. Moreover, the functional relationship between current real spending and the level of real balance holdings and permanent real income is invariant to the time period t. Hence, we can write

$$c_t^i = z^i(\overline{m}_t^i, y_i), \qquad i = \mathrm{H,F}, \tag{4}$$

where $z^i(\cdot)$ is the real spending function of country i. Also, using (a) and (b) from problem (3) and Eq. (4), we can define a demand function for real balances for the beginning of next period:

$$m_{t+1}^i = l^i(\overline{m}_t^i, y_i) \overset{\text{def}}{=} \overline{m}_t^i - z^i(\overline{m}_t^i, y_i) + y_i, \qquad i = \mathrm{H,F}. \tag{5}$$

Using (4) and (5), the temporary equilibrium conditions can be written as

$$z^{\mathrm{H}}(\overline{M}_t^{\mathrm{H}}/p_t, y_{\mathrm{H}}) + z^{\mathrm{F}}(\overline{M}_t^{\mathrm{F}}/p_t, y_{\mathrm{F}}) = y_{\mathrm{H}} + y_{\mathrm{F}}, \tag{6a}$$

$$l^{\mathrm{H}}(\overline{M}_t^{\mathrm{H}}/p_t, y_{\mathrm{H}}) + l^{\mathrm{F}}(\overline{M}_t^{\mathrm{F}}/p_t, y_{\mathrm{F}}) = (\overline{M}_t^{\mathrm{H}} + \overline{M}_t^{\mathrm{F}})/p_t. \tag{6b}$$

Observe that (6a) and (6b) are not independent since, via (5), (6a) implies (6b), and (6b) implies (6a).

Given the distribution of money in the beginning of period t, $\overline{M}_t^{\mathrm{H}}$ and $\overline{M}_t^{\mathrm{F}}$, temporary equilibrium is attained at a price level p_t that satisfies (6). This determines the distribution of money holdings in the beginning of period $t + 1$,

$$\overline{M}_{t+1}^i = \overline{M}_t^i - p_t z^i(\overline{M}_t^i/p_t, y_i) + p_t y_i, \qquad i = \mathrm{H,F}, \tag{7}$$

which determines, via (6), the price level in period $t + 1$, and so on. This is essentially the monetary mechanism of international adjustment. The deficit in country i's balance of payments is given by

$$\overline{M}_t^i - \overline{M}_{t+1}^i = p_t\left[z^i(\overline{M}_t^i/p_t, y_i) - y_i\right].$$

3. Properties of the Demand Functions

This section provides a characterization of the spending and demand for money functions. It is based on Helpman (1979b). Using the equilibrium conditions (6) and (7), I then derive the properties of the adjustment process. Since this section deals with a single country, the country-identifying index i is dropped for notational convenience.

In order to characterize the solution to (3), we need to define a sequence of auxiliary numbers $\mu_0, \mu_1, \ldots$. These numbers have the following meaning: If the country under consideration has real balances in the interval $(\mu_{T-1}, \mu_T]$, then it plans to arrive at its steady-state consumption level and real balance holdings in T periods. (The sequence $\{\mu_t\}$ is, of course, country specific.) This interpretation will become clear after the statement of the main theorem. At this stage, I define the sequence $\{\mu_t\}$ implicitly in the following way:

$$\mu_0 = 0, \tag{8a}$$

$$u'(\mu_1) = \delta u'(y), \tag{8b}$$

$$u'(\mu_T - \mu_{T-1} + y) = \delta^T u'(y), \qquad T = 2, 3, \ldots, \tag{8c}$$

where a prime indicates a derivative.

Due to the strict concavity of $u(\cdot)$, (8) implies

$$y < \mu_1 < \mu_2 < \cdots < \mu_T < \cdots, \tag{9}$$

$$\mu_2 - \mu_1 < \mu_3 - \mu_2 < \cdots < \mu_T - \mu_{T-1} < \cdots. \tag{10}$$

Hence the intervals $[\mu_{T-1}, \mu_T]$ are of increasing length. The solution to (3), choosing for simplicity $t = 1$, is completely characterized by the following theorem, whose proof is provided in Helpman (1979b).

Theorem. Let $u(\cdot)$ be strictly increasing, strictly concave, twice continuously differentiable, defined on $[0, +\infty)$, and let $0 < \delta < 1$, $y > 0$; then for every $0 < \bar{m} < +\infty$ there exists a unique solution to (3). The solution c_τ^*, $\tau = 1, 2, \ldots,$ is as follows:

(a) If $0 < \bar{m} \leqslant \mu_1$, then $c_1^* = \bar{m}$, and $c_\tau^* = y$, $\tau = 2, 3, \ldots$;
(b) if $\mu_{T-1} < \bar{m} \leqslant \mu_T$, $T \in \{2, 3, \ldots\}$, then $c_{T+\tau}^* = y$, $\tau = 1, 2, \ldots,$

and $c_1^* > c_2^* > \cdots > c_T^* > y$ are implicitly defined by the following system of $T + 1$ equations with λ being part of the solution:

(i) $u'(c_\tau^*) = \delta^{T-t}\lambda$, $\tau = 1, 2, \ldots, T$,
(ii) $\sum_{\tau=1}^{T} c_\tau^* = \bar{m} + (T-1)y$.

From this theorem it is clear that $c_1^* = z(\bar{m}, y)$. Hence the properties of the real spending function can be derived from the dependence of c_1^* on $\bar{m}$ and y. It is clear that $z(\cdot)$ is a continuous function. Also, for $\mu_{T-1} < \bar{m} < \mu_T$ it is differentiable in both arguments. For $\mu_{T-1} < \bar{m} < \mu_T$ we can calculate the partial derivatives $z_m(\cdot)$ and $z_y(\cdot)$ directly from conditions (i) and (ii) of the theorem, using the implicit function theorem.

It can be shown that the marginal propensity to spend out of real balance holdings is strictly between zero and one except for $0 < \bar{m} < \mu_1$ for which it equals one.[1] The marginal propensity to spend out of real (permanent) income is $T-1$ times larger than the marginal propensity to spend out of real balances; it is positive for $\overline{m} > \mu_1$, zero for $0 < \overline{m} < \mu_1$, but it need not be smaller than one [see Helpman (1979b)].

Usually, nominal spending is assumed to be a linear homogeneous function of two variables, nominal income and nominal money balances. This, however, is a misspecification; nominal spending should be specified as a linear homogeneous function of nominal income, nominal money balances, *and* the price level. The relevance of the price level as an independent variable is explained in Helpman (1979b).

4. Inflation and the Adjustment Process

In this section I investigate the behavior of the price level during the process of balance of payments adjustments. By the process of balance of payments adjustments I mean the process in which the temporary equilibria described in Section 2 shift as a result of the existence of deficits and surpluses in countries' balance of payments, but in the absence of other economic forces which may cause the temporary equilibria to shift (for example, monetary injections). The main argument that follows is that the price level never falls during the process of balance of payments adjustments; either it is constant, or it rises for several periods and from then on remains constant. This is in contrast to common arguments that the price level may either rise or fall, and that there is not presumption as to which will occur.

First, let me observe that with constant prices a single country's adjustment path can be described by means of a diagram, as shown in Fig. 1. Superscript i is reintroduced to identify countries.

In Fig. 1 I have drawn the real balance demand function $l^i(\overline{m}^i, y_i) \equiv \overline{m}^i - z^i(\overline{m}^i, y_i) + y_i$ based on the properties described in the previous section. In addition I have added a straight line C parallel to the 45° line that goes through the origin, but higher by y_i. For every real balance holding, the vertical difference between line C and $l^i(\cdot)$ represents real spending.

Now suppose $\overline{m}_1^i$ is between μ_2^i and μ_3^i, as in Fig. 1. Then real spending in period 1 is z_1^{*i} and second-period real balance holdings will be m_2^i, as

[1] It can also be shown that

$$\lim_{\substack{\epsilon>0,\\ \epsilon\to 0}} z_m(\mu_T - \epsilon, y) > \lim_{\substack{\epsilon>0\\ \epsilon\to 0}} z_m(\mu_T + \epsilon, y)$$

for all $T = 1, 2, \ldots$.

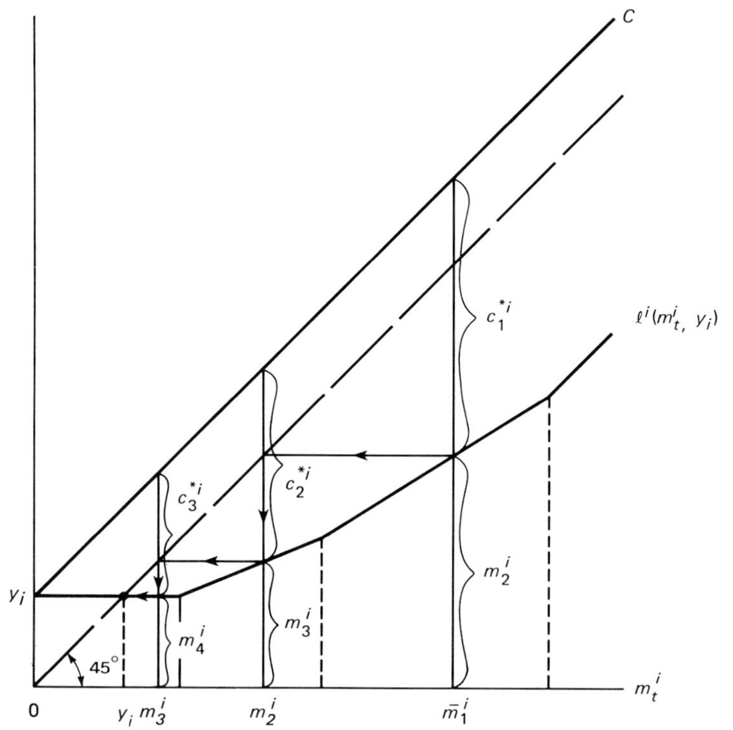

Fig. 1. The adjustment of a single country. $y_i = m_t^i = z^i(m_t^i, y_i)$, $t = 4, 5, \ldots$.

indicated in the figure. Given real balances in period 2 we can read off real spending in period 2 and real balance holdings in period 3. In the fourth period the economy reaches its steady state, with real spending equal to real income equal to real balance holdings. Thus the economy converges to its steady state in three steps. It is also clear that an economy with initial real balance holdings smaller than μ_1^i converges to its steady state in only one step.

The preceding discussion identifies a fundamental asymmetry between deficit and surplus countries. It is apparent from Fig. 1 that a country runs a surplus in its balance of payments if real balance holdings fall short of real income, while if real balance holdings exceed real income, it runs a deficit. Hence a surplus country attempts to work out its adjustment process in one period, while a deficit country may attempt to work out its adjustment process in more than one period, depending on the extent to which its real balances exceed its real income. The two types of country generate asymmetric pressures on the price level, and this will be shown to produce inflation during the international process of adjustment.

Suppose that the distribution of money holdings in period 1 is given by $(\overline{M}_1^{\text{H}}, \overline{M}_1^{\text{F}})$. Then the first-period equilibrium price level is implicitly defined by the following equilibrium condition:

$$\sum_i z^i(\overline{M}_1^i/p_1, y_i) = \sum_i y_i. \tag{11}$$

The equilibrium price level exists, and it is unique.[2] This price level also satisfies

$$\sum_i l^i(\overline{M}_1^i/p_1, y_i) = \sum_i \overline{M}_1^i/p_1. \tag{12}$$

Now either $\overline{M}_1^i/p_1 = y_i$, $i = \text{H}, \text{F}$, or it does not. Equilibrium real balances will equal real incomes only when initial money stocks are distributed proportionately to real income (when $\overline{M}_1^{\text{H}}/y_{\text{H}} = \overline{M}_1^{\text{F}}/y_{\text{F}}$). If this is not the case, there exists an i for which $l^i(\overline{M}_1^i/p_1, y_i) > \overline{M}_1^i/p_1$, with the opposite inequality holding for the other country. Suppose, for concreteness, that the home country satisfies $l^{\text{H}}(\overline{M}_1^{\text{H}}/p_1, y_{\text{H}}) > \overline{M}_1^{\text{H}}/\text{p}_1$. It therefore also satisfies $z^{\text{H}}(\overline{M}_1^{\text{H}}/p_1, y_{\text{H}}) < y_{\text{H}}$. The home country then spends all its money balances and runs a surplus in its balance of payments while the foreign country runs a deficit.

The second-period distribution of monies is given by

$$M_2^{\text{H}} = p_1 y_{\text{H}}, \tag{13}$$

$$M_2^{\text{F}} = \sum_i \overline{M}_1^i - p_1 y_{\text{H}} = \overline{M}_1^{\text{F}} - p_1 z^{\text{F}}(\overline{M}_1^{\text{F}}/p_1, y_{\text{F}}) + p_1 y_{\text{F}}. \tag{14}$$

Now there are two possibilities: Either $\overline{M}_1^{\text{F}}/p_1 \leqslant \mu_1^{\text{F}}$, or $\overline{M}_1^{\text{F}}/p_1 > \mu_1^{\text{F}}$. In the first case the foreign country also spends all its money balances in the first period, which implies

$$p_1 = \sum_i \overline{M}_1^i \Big/ \sum_i y_i. \tag{15}$$

From (13) through (15) it is clear that $(M_2^{\text{H}}, M_2^{\text{F}})$ is the steady-state distribution of money and that p_1 is the steady-state equilibrium price level. Hence in this case the world economy adjusts to its steady state in one period and without inflation.

In the second case (when $\overline{M}_1^{\text{F}}/p_1 > \mu_1^{\text{F}}$), using the price level p_1 in the second period, we find that there is excess demand for goods. This can be

[2]To see this, remember that $z^i(\cdot)$ is strictly increasing in its first argument. Now for p_1 sufficiently high so that $\overline{M}_1^i/p_1 < y_i$, $i = \text{H}, \text{F}$, $\sum_i z^i(\overline{M}_1^i/p_1, y_i) = \sum_i \overline{M}_1^i/p_1 < \sum_i y_i$, while for p_1 sufficiently low so that $\overline{M}_1^i/p_1 > y_i$, $i = \text{H}, \text{F}$, $\sum z^i(\overline{M}_1^i/p_1, y_i) > \sum_i y_i$. Hence there is a unique p_1 which satisfies (11).

shown as follows. Using (13) and (14), we have

$$\sum_i z^i(M_2^i/p_1, y_i) = z^{\mathrm{H}}(y_{\mathrm{H}}, y_{\mathrm{H}}) + z^{\mathrm{F}}\left[\overline{M}_1^{\mathrm{F}}/p_1 - z^{\mathrm{F}}(\overline{M}_1^{\mathrm{F}}/p_1, y_{\mathrm{F}}) + y_{\mathrm{F}}, y_{\mathrm{F}}\right]$$

$$= y_{\mathrm{H}} + \tilde{c}_2^{\mathrm{F}}(\overline{M}_1^{\mathrm{F}}/p_1, y_{\mathrm{F}}),$$

where $\tilde{c}_2^{\mathrm{F}}(\cdot)$ is the solution of c_2^* in the theorem as a function of real balances and permanent income. Since $\overline{M}_1^{\mathrm{F}}/p_1 > \mu_1^{\mathrm{F}}$, $\tilde{c}_2^{\mathrm{F}}(\overline{M}_1^{\mathrm{F}}/p_1, y_{\mathrm{F}}) > y_{\mathrm{F}}$. Hence $\sum_i z^i(M_2^i/p_1, y_i) > \sum_i y_i$, which means that with the price level p_1 in the second period, there is an excess demand for goods. The second-period equilibrium price level satisfies

$$\sum_i z^i(M_2^i/p_2, y_i) = \sum_i y_i, \tag{16}$$

and from the preceding argument we have $p_2 > p_1$. As a result, using (13), $M_2^{\mathrm{H}}/p_2 < y_{\mathrm{H}}$, so that the home country keeps running a surplus in its balance of payments, while the foreign country keeps running a deficit. The argument that was advanced for the second-period equilibrium can also be advanced for the third-period equilibrium. Therefore, by induction, we arrive at the following conclusions:

A country that starts with a deficit in its balance of payments will run deficits during the entire adjustment process, while a country which starts with a surplus in its balance of payments will run a surplus during the entire adjustment process. The adjustment process will work out in a finite number of periods, with the number of periods in which the deficit country works out its deficit at *constant* prices serving as an upper bound on the number of periods required for the international process of adjustment to work itself out. If the process of adjustment works itself out in $T > 1$ periods, the price level will rise during the first $T - 1$ periods.[3]

Some of these conclusions depend on the assumption that each country is composed of identical individuals, but the main conclusion does not: The process of international adjustment reaches a steady state in a finite number of periods, say T; and for $T > 1$ the price level during the first $T - 1$ period rises. For $T = 1$ the price level is constant.

[3]The fact that the number of periods in which the deficit country works out its deficit at constant prices serves as an upper bound on the number of periods in which the international process of adjustment works itself out can be shown as follows. Suppose $\mu_{T-1} < \overline{M}_1^{\mathrm{F}}/p_1 \leqslant \mu_T$, for $T > 1$. Then one can see from Fig. 1 that with rising prices the real balances in each period will be lower than with constant prices. Thus, since prices can never rise so as to make the deficit country a surplus country, rising prices reduce the number of periods required for convergence to a steady state.

This can be seen from the following. Suppose that there are a finite number of individuals of the type described above in the world economy. Every individual has his own utility function, rate of time preference, share of ownership in his country's output, and initial money holdings. Let $z^j(m^j, y^j)$ be individual j's real spending function, derivable from an optimization problem like (3). Let I^i be the set of individuals who reside in country i, $i = \mathrm{H, F}$. Then $\sum_{j\in I^i} y^j = y_i$, $i = \mathrm{H, F}$.

Let $\{\overline{M}_1^j\}$ be the initial distribution of money; $\sum_{j\in I^i} \overline{M}_1^j = \overline{M}_1^i$, $i = \mathrm{H, F}$. Then the first-period equilibrium price level is implicitly defined by

$$\sum_j z^j(\overline{M}_1^j/p_1, y^j) = \sum_j y^j = y_\mathrm{H} + y_\mathrm{F}. \tag{17}$$

The equilibrium price level p_1 exists, and it is unique (see footnote 3).

Now, for each τ, partition the set of individuals into two subsets: $A_\tau = \{j \mid M^j/p_\tau \leqslant \mu_1^j\}$ and $B_\tau = \{j \mid M^j/p_\tau > \mu_1^j\}$. The set A_1 is not empty, while B_1 may be empty. Then we have

$$M_2^j = p_1 y^j \qquad \text{for} \quad j \in A_1, \tag{18a}$$

$$M_2^j > p_1 y^j \qquad \text{for} \quad j \in B_1, \tag{18b}$$

which implies

$$\begin{aligned}\sum_j z^j(M_2^j/p_1, y^i) &= \sum_{j\in A_1} z^j(y^j, y^j) + \sum_{j\in B_1} z^j(M_2^j/p_1, y^j)\\ &= \sum_{j\in A_1} y^j + \sum_{j\in B_1} z^j(M_2^j/p_1, y^j).\end{aligned}$$

However, $M_2^j/p_1 > y^i$ implies $z^j(M_2^j/p_1, y^j) > y^i$, which together with (18) yields:

$$\sum_j z^j(M_2^j/p_1, y^j) = \sum_j y^j \qquad \text{if} \quad B_1 \text{ is empty}; \tag{19a}$$

$$\sum_j z^j(M_2^j/p_1, y^j) > \sum_j y^j \qquad \text{if} \quad B_1 \text{ is not empty}. \tag{19b}$$

Hence, if B_1 is empty, the second-period equilibrium price level is equal to p_1, and a steady state is reached in one period. If B_1 is not empty, the second-period price level is larger than p_1, and the adjustment process takes more than one period.

By induction we see that the price level cannot fall and that as long as the set B_τ is not empty, it has to rise. Once B_τ becomes empty, there are no further adjustments in the price level.

In order to see that the steady state is reached in a finite number of periods, observe that once an individual is in set A he will remain in set A in all future periods, because the price level cannot decline. Let $T(j)$ be implicitly defined by $\mu^j_{T(j)-1} < \overline{M}^j/p_1 \leqslant \mu^j_{T(j)}$. Then individual j can be in set B for at most $T(j)$ periods. Hence the process of adjustment can last at most $\max_j T(j)$ periods.

The preceding argument deals with individuals and is independent of the distribution of individuals between countries. It shows clearly that the inflationary bias of the adjustment process is independent of the characteristic of the countries. The number of countries is also irrelevant for this result.

The common argument about the behavior of the price level during the adjustment process is based on the following reasoning [see Dornbusch (1973)]. If, say, at time t, the home country runs a surplus in its balance of payments and the foreign country runs a deficit, the home country's money stock is increasing, and the foreign country's money stock is on the decline. The money transferred from the foreign country to the home country increases spending at home and reduces spending abroad. Hence, if the home country's marginal propensity to spend out of money balances exceeds the foreign country's marginal propensity to spend out of money balances, there would be an excess of spending over income in the world economy if the price level did not change. Thus the price level must increase. However, if the surplus country has the smaller marginal propensity to spend out of money balances, the price level will decline. Since there is no presumption as to which country has the larger marginal propensity to spend, and generally these marginal propensities will change during the adjustment process, the course of the price level during the adjustment process is unpredictable.

One way in which one may reconcile this with my analysis is to say that in the model adopted in this paper, the surplus country's marginal propensity to spend out of money balances must equal one, while that of the deficit country's is less than or equal to one. However, we have seen that the inflationary bias also exists in a world with many different consumers, which shows that the analogy is not as simple as it might appear on first sight.

With nonidentical consumers a *country's* marginal propensity to spend out of money balances may not be well defined, for the effect of a marginal increase in the stock of money on aggregate spending generally depends on the way in which the additional money is distributed among consumers. In any case, during the process of adjustment, some consumers of a deficit country may be accumulating money balances while others may be decumulating them; the terms deficit country and surplus country refer only to the *aggregate* result. Therefore, at constant prices the surplus country need *not* increase spending by the amount of money accumulated, so that its effective marginal propensity to spend out of money balances may be smaller than one. However, what I have shown is that at constant prices, aggregate spending in the world economy has to increase (or remain the same) during the process of adjustment, thus forcing prices to rise (or remain constant).

5. Closing Remarks

The hypothesis of maximizing behavior in conjunction with an explicit microeconomic theory of money has been shown to shed light on the behavior of the price level during the process of balance of payments adjustments in a fixed exchange rate regime. In particular, it has been shown that in the absence of financial assets other than money, a fixed exchange rate regime has an inherent inflationary bias, but that without autonomous monetary injections the process of inflation can only last for a finite time span.

The framework of this paper can readily be modified to take account of bonds. The interesting result that emerges in this case is that the price level remains constant during the adjusment process, independently of whether bonds are traded only within national borders or whether they are also internationally traded. This result contrasts sharply with the frequently expressed view that economies with nontraded bonds behave similarly to economies without bonds. I do not provide a formal derivation of this result because the reasoning is quite simple. In the presence of bonds the equilibrium interest rate must be positive. For if the interest rate is zero, it can be shown that consumer spending will go to infinity as long as there is a positive rate of time preference However, with a positive interest rate bonds dominate money for store of value purposes. Therefore, consumers will not use money to store wealth, implying that all money balances will be spent during every period. As a result, the equilibrium price level will equal the ratio of aggregate world money balances to aggregate world output, and it will be the same in each period.

Coming back to the framework without bonds, it is illuminating to describe the adjustment of the world economy to an unexpected monetary shock. Suppose the world economy is in long-run equilibrium and that at time t_0 the home country's government unexpectedly increases the domestic money supply. If the monetary injection amounts to, say, x percent of the world's initial stock of money, we know that in the new long-run equilibrium the price level will increase by x percent. We also know that the impact effect of the monetary expansion is to raise the price level, since at the *initial* price level the increase in the money supply generates an excess demand for goods. Now there are two possibilities: Either the price level

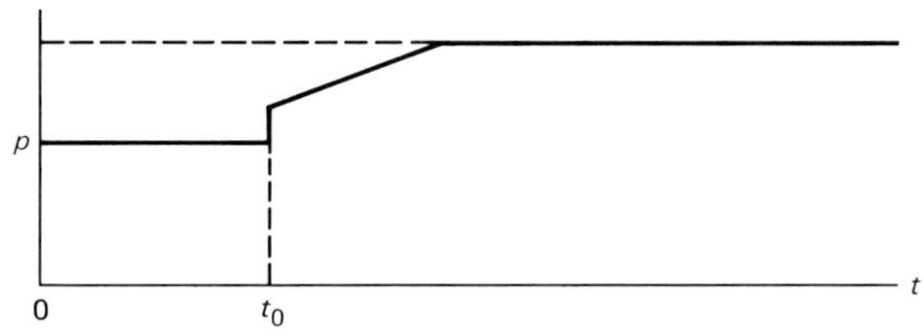

Fig. 2. The effect of a monetary expansion on the price level.

rises immediately by x percent, or it does not. Suppose it does not, which will be the case for sufficiently large x. Then during the process of balance of payments adjustments the price level has to increase over time. As a result, the impact effect will result in an increase in the price level of *less* than x percent, and this will be followed by a gradual upward adjustment of the price level to the x percent limit. The course of the price level is depicted in Fig. 2.

Now consider a monetary contraction that reduces the world's stock of money by x percent. Again, assume that x is sufficiently large so that the new long-run equilibrium is not reached in one period. We know that in the new long-run equilibrium the price level will be lower by x percent and that the impact effect of the monetary contraction is to reduce the price level. However, since during the process of balance of payments adjustments the price level has to rise, the impact effect of the monetary contraction reduces the price level by *more* than x percent. The course of the price level is described in Fig. 3.

This analysis again brings out the inherent asymmetry in the fixed exchange rate regime. Monetary contractions do not trigger an adjustment process that is the mirror image of the adjustment process that results from a monetary expansion. Similar asymmetries exist in response to other types of shocks, and they all stem from the fact that at the margin, deficit countries are fundamentally different from surplus countries.

Fig. 3. The effect of a monetary contraction on the price level.

REFERENCES

Dornbusch, R. (1973). Money, Devaluation and Nontraded Goods. *American Economic Review* **63**, 871–880.

Dornbusch, R., and Mussa; M. (1975). Consumption, Real Balances and the Hoarding Function. *International Economic Review* **16**, 415–421.

Helpman, E. (1979a). An Exploration in the Theory of Exchange Rate Regimes. *Journal of Political Economy* (to be published).

Helpman, E. (1979b). Optimal Spending and Money Holdings in the Presence of Liquidity Constraints. *Econometrica* (to be published).

Helpman, E., and Razin, A. (1979). Towards a Consistent Comparison of Alternative Exchange Rate Systems. *Canadian Journal of Economics* **12**, 394–409.

Kareken, J. H., and Wallace, N. (1978). Samuelson's Consumption-Loan Model with Country Specific Fiat Monies. Staff Report No. 24, Federal Reserve Bank of Minneapolis.

Stockman, A. C. (1978). A Theory of Exchange Rate Determination. Ph.D. Thesis, Department of Economics, University of Chicago.

DEPARTMENT OF ECONOMICS
TEL AVIV UNIVERSITY
RAMAT AVIV, TEL AVIV, ISRAEL

Exchange Rates and Price Movements in a World of Capital Mobility

ASSAF RAZIN

1. Introduction

This paper develops a simple framework for the study of exchange rates movements, trade balance changes, and capital movements under flexible exchange rates. Its basic features are that consumer behavior is derived from intertemporal utility maximization; there is allowance for foreign capital movements; expectations concerning future prices, particularly exchange rates, are self-fulfilling; and (in an extension in the latter part of the paper) traded and nontraded goods are treated separately.

Recent exchange rate models have one or more of those properties, but not all four. For example, Dornbusch (1976a, 1976b) and Calvo and Rodriguez (1977) deal with flexible exchange rates with capital movements, but they do not derive demand functions from utility maximization, and international transactions are not restricted by the country's intertemporal budget constraint. On the other hand, Kemp's (1969) model of flexible exchange rates, while consistent with utility maximization, does not permit capital movements. Mundell's (1968) classic paper on flexible exchange rates in the presence of capital movements assumes static exchange rate expectations and ad hoc demand functions.

The contribution of the paper is to show that when all four properties are combined in a single consistent model, the results are significantly different from those obtained from the models mentioned above.

The paper confirms the view that in the presence of capital movements,

ISBN 0-12-259750-8

flexible exchange rates fail to insulate a country from external disturbances, while in the absence of capital movements they completely insulate it from such disturbances. In the presence of capital movements a monetary expansion abroad raises foreign expenditure and that leads to a rise in foreign prices and in the real interest rate, reducing domestic money demand and causing domestic prices to rise as well. A fiscal expansion abroad has similar effects on domestic prices. The essential difference between fiscal expansion and monetary expansion is that with the former, public expenditure increases at the expense of private expenditure.

Thus, the present paper does not confirm Fleming's (1962) and Mundell's (1968) findings of sharp dichotomy between the two policies. Fleming and Mundell found that fiscal expansion abroad has expansionary effects at home while a monetary expansion abroad has contractionary effects at home. They, however, assumed that output is demand determined; their results are thus not strictly comparable to those of the present paper, which assumes completely flexible prices and hence full employment.

The so-called (extreme) asset market approach to exchange rate determination, which claims that the current exchange rate is determined by nominal asset supplies and is independent of the current account, is also not in accord with our results. We show that autonomous domestic increases in the current account deficit, of which fiscal expansion financed by lump-sum taxes is an example, have a direct influence on the current exchange rate and cause the domestic currency to depreciate. It is precisely the deficit in the current account that, in the presence of capital movements, serves as the channel for the transmission of disturbances in one country to the rest of the world. In the absence of this channel external disturbances will be fully offset by exchange rate movements, leaving domestic magnitudes intact.

An extension of the basic framework in Section 8 develops a model of the determination of exchange rates and the allocation of production and consumption for a small country when traded and nontraded goods are treated separately. Movements in exchange rates and in the relative prices of traded goods in terms of nontraded goods—known as real exchange rates—are explored in detail.

The analysis of fiscal expansion emphasizes the distinction between government spending on traded and nontraded goods. It modifies the Fleming–Mundell result that fiscal expansion must appreciate the currency (by inducing an incipient capital inflow resulting from the upward pressure on interest rates exerted by the rise in income and the demand for money). It is shown that the effect of government spending on traded goods induces a trade balance deficit and a depreciation of the currency, while spending on nontraded goods increases their production at the expense of traded goods and deteriorates the trade balance. The resulting effect on real income, and thereby on the demand for money and the exchange rate, is ambiguous.

2. The Framework

Assume a two-period one-good monetary model of trade between two countries. Let the home country's utility be a function of consumption, nominal balances, and prices. This is, of course, only a rough approximation for liquidity services provided by money. The utility function is homogeneous of degree zero in nominal balances and prices and assumed to be intertemporally separable. We can write

$$U(c_1, M_1, e_1, p_1^*, c_2, M_2, e_2, p_2^*) = u(c_1, M_1/e_1 p_1^*) + \beta u(c_2, M_2/e_2 p_2^*), \tag{1}$$

where c_i is consumption in period i, $i = 1, 2$; M_i is domestic money holdings in period i, $i = 1, 2$; e_i is exchange rate (units of domestic currency per unit of foreign currency) in period i, $i = 1, 2$; p_i^* is foreign price level in period i, $i = 1, 2$; $u(\cdot)$ is utility and has the properties: $u_c(\cdot) > 0$, $u_M(\cdot) > 0$, $u_{cc}(\cdot) < 0$, $u_{MM}(\cdot) < 0$, $u_{cM}(\cdot) \geqslant 0$; and β is a discount factor.

The country is assumed to maximize (1) subject to the budget constraints:

$$e_1 p_1^* c_1 + M_1 + e_1 A = e_1 p_1^* Y_1 + \overline{M}_1, \tag{2}$$

$$e_2 p_2^* c_2 + M_2 = e_2 p_2^* Y_2 + e_2 RA + \overline{M}_2, \tag{3}$$

where A is interest bearing tradable asset holdings (denominated in foreign currency) with a return given by R, Y_i is output in period $i, i = 1, 2$, and $\overline{M}_i$ is money supply in period $i, i = 1, 2$ ($\overline{M}_2 = M_1 + \Delta M$, where ΔM is a policy variable).

Prices are perfectly flexible; hence output is at full employment level. The first-order conditons yield the following equations:

$$\frac{u_c(c_1, M_1/e_1 p_1^*)}{\beta u_c(c_2, M_2/e_2 p_2^*)} = R \frac{p_1^*}{p_2^*} \equiv \rho, \tag{4}$$

$$\frac{u_M(c_1, M_1/e_1 p_1^*)}{u_c(c_1, M_1/e_1 p_1^*)} = 1 - \frac{e_1}{e_2} \frac{1}{R} \equiv 1 - \frac{e_1 p_1^*}{e_2 p_2^*} \frac{1}{\rho}, \tag{5}$$

$$\frac{u_M(c_2, M_2/e_2 p_2^*)}{u_c(c_2, M_2/e_2 p_2^*)} = 1, \tag{6}$$

where $\rho = p_1^*/Rp_2^*$ is the *real* return on tradable asset holdings.

Equation (4), well known from the theory of savings, is interpreted as an equality between the real interest factor and the marginal rate of substitution between present and future consumption. The left-hand side of (5) represents the marginal rate of substitution between real balances and consumption in the first period. The right-hand side is related to the nominal interest rate. To see this, let $\pi = (e_2 p_2^* / e_1 p_1^*) - 1$ be the rate of domestic price increase from the first to the second period, and let $s = \rho - 1$ be the real rate of interest. The term on the right-hand side of Eq. (5) is then equal to $(s + \pi + \pi s)/(1 + s)(1 + \pi)$, where $s + \pi$ is the nominal interest rate. Real money cannot be a store of value in the second period (being the last period), and one unit of real balances in the second period is worth one unit of consumption. Thus (6) is an equality between the marginal rate of substitution between real balances and consumption in the second period and the relative price and is equal to one.[1]

Since there are no sign restrictions on asset holdings, constraints (2) and (3) can be reduced to a single budget constraint

$$Rp_1^*(c_1 - Y_1) + p_2^*(c_2 - Y_2) = Re_1^{-1}(\overline{M}_1 - M_1) + e_2^{-1}(\overline{M}_2 - M_2). \quad (7)$$

Assume that domestic money balances are held by domestic residents only. This is not a restriction since domestic residents are permitted to hold the tradable interest bearing asset.

Money market clearing conditions are

$$M_1 = \overline{M}_1, \quad (8)$$

$$M_2 = \overline{M}_2, \quad (9)$$

Equations (7)–(9) can be seen to imply

$$Rp_1^*(c_1 - Y_1) + p_2^*(c_2 - Y_2) = 0. \quad (7a)$$

That is, the future value of the excess of consumption over income must total zero.

Similarly, using an asterisk to denote foreign magnitudes, the foreign country's choice problem is

$$\text{Choose } c_1^*, M_1^*, c_2^*, M_2^*, \text{ and } A^* \text{ to maximize}$$
$$u^*(c_1^*, M_1^*/p_1^*) + \beta^* u^*(c_2^*, M_2^*/p_2^*) \quad (10)$$

[1] Equation (6), which can be viewed as a terminal condition for the determination of equilibrium exchange rates, is different from that given in Helpman and Razin (1979). There, it was postulated that the economy starts off with a given quantity of domestic money in the first period and ends up with the same quantity of domestic money in the last period.

subject to

$$p_1^* c_1 + M_1^* + A^* = p_1^* Y_1^* + \overline{M}_1^*, \tag{11}$$

$$p_2^* c_2 + M_2^* = p_2^* Y_2^* + \overline{M}_2^* + RA^*. \tag{12}$$

The first-order conditions yield

$$\frac{u^*(c_1^*, M_1^*/p_1^*)}{\beta^* u_c^*(c_2^*, M_2^*/p_2^*)} = R\frac{p_1^*}{p_2^*} \equiv \rho, \tag{13}$$

$$\frac{u_M(c_1^*, M_1^*/p_1^*)}{u_c(c_1^*, M_1^*/p_1^*)} = 1 - \frac{1}{R} \equiv 1 - \frac{p_1^*}{p_2^*}\frac{1}{\rho}, \tag{14}$$

$$\frac{u_M(c_2^*, M_2^*/p_2^*)}{u_c(c_2^*, M_2^*/p_2^*)} = 1. \tag{15}$$

In equilibrium, foreign money balances are willingly held:

$$M_1^* = \overline{M}^*, \qquad M_2^* = \overline{M}_2. \tag{16}$$

This implies

$$\overline{R}p_1^*(c_1^* - Y_1^*) + p_2^*(c_2^* - Y_2^*) = 0. \tag{17}$$

The market clearing condition for consumption goods in the first period is

$$c_1 - Y_1 + c_1^* - Y_1^* = 0. \tag{18}$$

By Walras's law the second-period consumption goods market clears as well.

The set of Eqs. (4), (6), (7a), (8), (9), and (13)–(18) determines equilibrium quantities $c_1, c_2, M_1, M_2, A, c_2^*, c_2^*, M_2^*, M_2^*$, and A^*; and equilibrium prices e_1, e_2, p_1^*, p_2^*, and ρ.

3. Diagrammatic Exposition

It is convenient to analyze the real and the monetary sectors separately before analyzing the interactions between them.

A. The Real Sector

Real equilibrium can be represented by means of offer curves showing various combinations of first-period capital exports and second-period capital imports for different values of the real interest ρ. The home

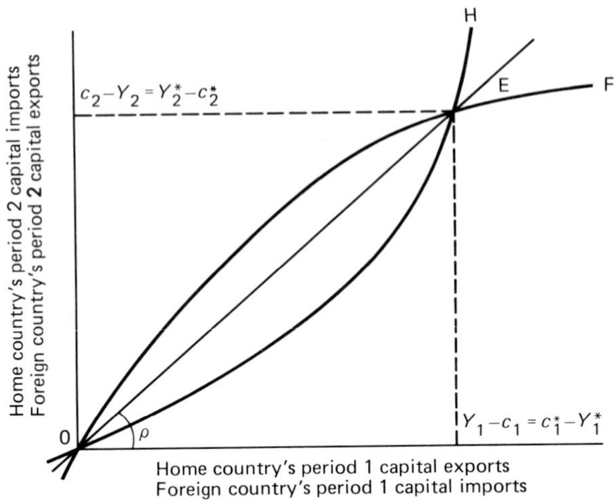

Fig. 1. Two-country real equilibrium.

country's first-period capital exports are $Y_1 - c_1$, and its second-period capital imports are $c_2 - Y_2$. The foreign country's capital exports in period i are given by $Y_i^* - c_i^*$, $i = 1, 2$.

Figure 1 shows how the real equilibrium interest is determined. $0H$ is the home country's offer curve and $0F$ is the foreign offer curve. The home country's offer curve is implicitly defined (with ρ to be solved out of the equations) by

$$u_c(x_1 + Y_1, M_1/e_1p_1^*) - \beta\rho u_c(x_2 + Y_2, M_2/e_2p_2^*) = 0 \tag{19}$$

and

$$\rho x_1 + x_2 = 0, \tag{20}$$

where $x_i = c_i - Y_i$ represents capital imports in period i, $i = 1, 2$ [see Eqs. (14) and (7a)]. Similarly, the foreign offer curve is implicitly defined by

$$u_c^*(x_1^* + Y_1^*, M_1^*/p_1^*) - \beta\rho u_i^*(x_2^* + Y_2^*, M_2^*/p_2^*) = 0 \tag{21}$$

and

$$\rho x_1^* + x_2^* = 0. \tag{22}$$

Observe that along an offer curve real balances and output levels are held constant and that changes in either real balances or outputs will shift the curve. For example, an increase in the home country's real balances in the first period would switch $0H$ to the left around the origin and an increase in the foreign country's real balances would switch $0F$ to the right. This is because higher first-period real balances would raise the marginal utility of first-period consumption and thereby induce an increase in first-period consumption at the expense of second-period consumption. An increase in first-period output in the home country switches $0H$ to the right, and an increase in first-period output in the foreign country switches $0F$ to the left. Increases in real balances and the output levels in the second period result in shifts in the opposite direction.

At point E an equilibrium real interest ρ obtains. First-period capital exports by the home country are equal to first-period capital imports by the foreign country, and the second-period capital imports by the home country are equal to the second-period capital exports by the foreign country.

B. The Monetary Sector

By assumption, only domestic residents hold domestic currency, and only foreign residents hold foreign currency. We thus have two sets of money market clearing conditions, one for the domestic and the other for the foreign country. These are shown in Figs. 2a and 2b, respectively.

In Fig. 2a M_1M_1 shows various combinations of domestic prices in the first and second period that satisfy

$$u_M(c_1, \overline{M}_1/e_1p_1^*) - (1 - (e_1p_1^*/e_2p_2^*)\rho^{-1})u_c(c_1, \overline{M}_1/e_1p_1^*) = 0 \quad (23)$$

[from (5) and (8)]. That is, the first-period domestic money market is in equilibrium along M_1M_1. Note that the curve is upward sloping and steeper than a ray through the origin and a point on the curve. Along the curve c_1, ρ and $\overline{M}_1$ are held constant. If c_1 goes up, $u_M(\cdot)$ increases, and $u_c(\cdot)$ declines. Thus, for a given level of $e_1p_1^*$, $e_2p_2^*$ must increase to restore equilibrium, and M_1M_1 shifts up and to the left.

In Fig. 2a M_2M_2 shows various combinations of domestic prices in the first and the second period that satisfy

$$u_M(c_2, \overline{M}_2/e_2p_2^*) - u_c(c_2, \overline{M}_2/e_2p_2^*) = 0 \quad (24)$$

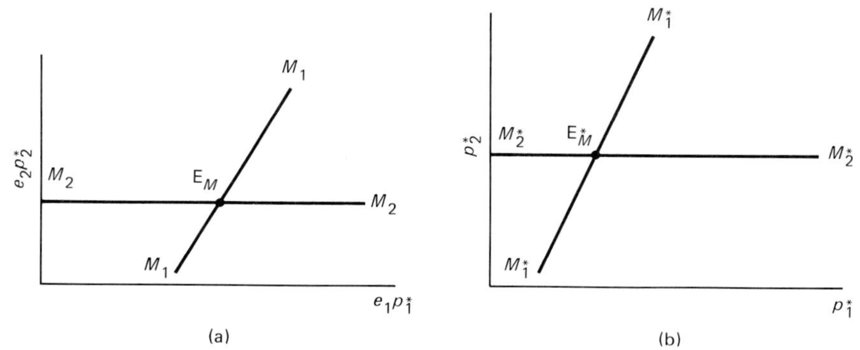

Fig. 2. (a) Domestic monetary equilibrium, (b) foreign monetary equilibrium.

[from (6) and (9)]; that is, an equilibrium condition for the second-period domestic money market. Note that the M_2M_2 curve is independent of first-period domestic prices, and that second-period consumption c_2 and $\overline{M}_2$ are held constant along the curve. An increase in c_2 increases $u_M(\cdot)$ and reduces $u_c(\cdot)$ and thus necessitates a decrease in $e_2p_2^*$, given the level of $e_1p_1^*$, to restore the initial balance. Hence M_2M_2 shifts downward. Full money market clearing obtains at point E_M.

The curves $M_1^*M_1^*$ and $M_2^*M_2^*$ in Fig. 2b are defined by

$$u_M^*\left(c_1^*, \overline{M}_1^*/p_1^*\right) - (1 - p_1^*/p_2^*\rho)u_c^*\left(c_1^*, \overline{M}_1^*/p_1^*\right) = 0 \tag{25}$$

and

$$u_M^*\left(c_2^*, \overline{M}_2^*/p_2^*\right) - u_c^*\left(c_2^*, \overline{M}_2^*/p_2^*\right) = 0, \tag{26}$$

respectively. Their properties can be explained as in the home country's case above. Foreign money market clearing obtains at point E_M^*.

A remark on the case of no mobility of capital is now in order. If capital is immobile, $A = A^* = 0$. The home country's budget constraints are

$$e_1p_1^*M_1 + A^{\mathrm{d}} = e_1p_1^*Y_1 + \overline{M}_1,$$

$$e_2p_2^*C_2 + M_2 = e_2p_2^*Y_2 + R^{\mathrm{d}}A^{\mathrm{d}} + \overline{M}_2,$$

where A^{d} are domestic bonds and R^{d} is the domestic interest factor. In equilibrium

$$A^{\mathrm{d}} = 0, \qquad M_1 = \overline{M}_1, \qquad M_2 = \overline{M}_2.$$

This implies that $C_1 = Y_1$ and $C_2 = Y_2$. Similarly, in conjunction with the foreign country we have $C_1^* = Y_1^*$ and $C_2^* = Y_2^*$. That is, the trade balance deficit is zero in every period.

Equations (4)–(6) now give the first-order conditions for the home country, provided that R^{d} substitutes for R_1. Substituting Y_1 for C_1 in (5) and (6), it can be seen that, given money supplies, any change in foreign prices or income is completely offset by exchange rate movements, so that domestic prices are left unchanged. Thus flexible exchange rates completely insulate countries from disturbances abroad in the absence of capital mobility. Complete insulation would not hold, however, in the presence of capital mobility. This is discussed in the next section.

4. Monetary Policies

A domestic monetary expansion in the first period (which can be regarded as a *transitory* monetary expansion since second-period money supply is held constant) shifts M_1M_1 down in Fig. 2a and thus raises domestic prices $e_1 p_1^*$ and real balances $M_1/e_1 p_1^*$ in the home country. From (23), domestic prices *undershoot* and rise proportionally less than $\overline{M}_1$. The offer curve $0H$ in Fig. 1 shifts up and to the left, reflecting a first-period increase in expenditure. Consequently the real interest rate ρ increases. The resulting decrease in foreign consumption in the first period shifts $M_1^* M_1^*$ in Fig. 2b down and to the right [see Eq. (25)], thereby raising foreign prices in the first period. These changes feed back into the monetary and real sectors in a way that would mitigate the immediate impact on first-period prices. They also spill over to the second period in the form of increased prices. By Hicksian stability, the ultimate changes in the variables are in the same direction as the changes indicated above. Note that it is precisely the current account deficit that is the vehicle for transmitting the inflation in the home country to the foreign country.

This discussion illustrates one important property of the model: Monetary expansion at home is transmitted to the rest of the world in the form of inflation there. Flexible exchange rates do not insulate the rest of the world from domestic monetary expansion, and vice versa. Other kinds of monetary changes at home and abroad, in the present or in the future, can also be analyzed in a straightforward fashion using the analytical framework developed here.

In contrast with transitory monetary changes, an equiproportional change in the home country's money supply in every period (which can be regarded as a steady-state change) has no effect except that the exchange rate in every period rises in a proportion equal to that by which the money supply increases.

The fact that equiproportional changes in the money supply in every period do not affect the equilibrium (except in nominal exchange rates), while a monetary expansion that increases the supply of money by different proportions in different periods *does* have real effects, is of course not surprising. We remember that in order for monetary policies to be effective at least one nominal variable should be held constant; in the case of steady-state change all nominal variables, including prices and exchange rates, vary by an equal proportion.

5. Fiscal Policies

The conditions underlying the home country's offer curve in the presence of first-period government spending, (19) and (20), can be rewritten as follows:

$$u_c(x_1 + Y_1 - G, M_1/e_1 p_1^*) - \beta\rho u_c(x_1 + Y_2, M_2/e_2 p_2^*) = 0, \qquad (11a)$$

$$\rho x_1 + x_2 = 0, \qquad (20a)$$

where $x_1 = c_1 + G - Y_1$, and G is government spending financed by first-period lump-sum taxes.[2]

The government can, alternatively, finance its spending by the issuance of bonds paying interest at the rate $\rho - 1$. To cover the costs of interest and debt repayment in a nondistorting fashion, second-period lump-sum taxes have to be imposed. The present value of the tax is equal to G. It is obvious that this budgetary financing scheme is precisely equivalent to the tax financing scheme that we employ here. This is simply a reiteration of the Ricardian proposition that under perfect foresight and in the presence of a perfect capital market, which provides no advantages to government over individual household's in borrowing and lending, debt financing and tax financing of government spendings are equivalent.

An increase in government spending in the first period causes a switch to the left around the origin in the home country's offer curve (curve $0H$ in Fig. 1). Thus first-period capital exports decline, and the real interest rate ρ rises. At the same time private consumption c_1 declines. From (23), the M_1M_1 curve in Fig. 2a shifts to the right and domestic prices increase.

From (25), the reduction in foreign consumption and the increase in the interest rate shift $M_1^*M_1^*$ in Fig. 2b down and to the right. Assuming that the foreign offer curve is elastic, the reduction in second-period domestic consumption shifts M_2M_2 up, thereby causing a rise in second-period domestic prices. Further changes, including feedbacks from the monetary sectors to the real sectors, would mitigate the above-mentioned immediate effects, but would not alter the direction of these changes.

Again we see how domestic fiscal expansion is transmitted to the rest of the world through changes in current account deficits or surpluses, while flexible exchange rates fail to insulate one economy from disturbances in another. In contrast to the so-called (extreme) asset market approach to exchange rate determination [see Discussion Section in Whitman (1975)], which states that the current exchange rate is determined by nominal asset supplies and is independent of the current account, we find here that current account changes caused by fiscal expansion or by other autonomous changes have a *direct* influence on exchange rates.

6. Output Changes

An exogenous increase in domestic output in the first period switches the home country's offer curve $0H$ down and to the right around the origin. As a result, the world real interest rate declines. First-period domestic

[2]It is assumed that government expenditure takes place in the first period only. A generalization that included government spending in the second period as well is straightforward and thus need not be pursued here.

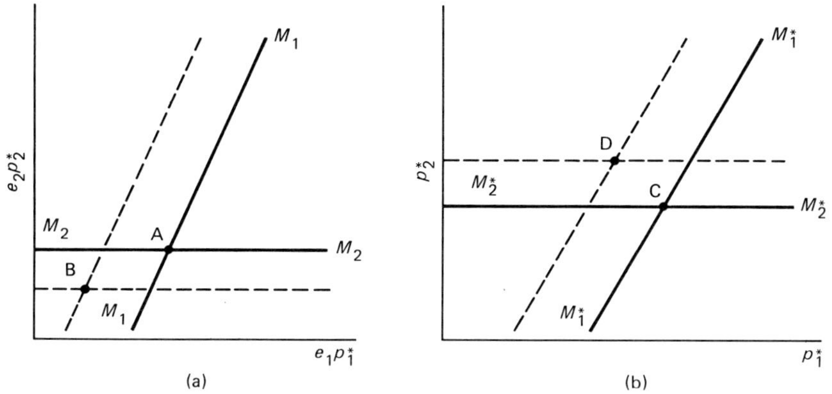

Fig. 3. Effects of an increase in domestic output on monetary equilibrium: (a) domestic, (b) foreign.

consumption rises (the income and substitution effects are working in the same direction) but less than the rise in output, so that domestic capital exports increase. Since foreign output is unchanged, this means that first-period foreign consumption rises. If the foreign offer curve is elastic, second-period consumption in the home country rises, and second-period consumption in the foreign country falls.

The consequent changes in money markets are shown by the dotted lines in Fig. 3. They follow from a straightforward analysis of Eqs. (23)–(26).

Equilibrium points change from *A* to *B* in Figure 3a and from *C* to *D* in Figure 3b. Domestic prices fall, while the change in foreign prices in the first period is ambiguous. The exchange rate movements are also indeterminate. Thus exchange rates and output levels do not seem to be linked in a predictable a priori way.

7. Optimal Policies

Optimal policies for an individual country involve two kinds of instruments—one directed at the timing (present or future) of capital exports, and the other directed at satisfying the optimal money rule. A special blend of present and future monetary expansion or contraction could be used to create a zero nominal interest rate, hence bringing real balances to a saturation level. But if this policy is used alone, the level of the country's capital exports or imports may not be adequate and the real interest rate may be either too high or too low. On the other hand a tax (or a subsidy) on capital exports, along the lines of the optimum tariff, could determine an adequate level for the real interest rate (assuming no retaliation by the rest of the world), but does not necessarily lead to an efficient level of money balances. Thus a policy mix that uses *both* instruments is necessary in order to achieve the full optimum. Fiscal policy is then an appropriate tool to achieve other goals such as the optimal provision of public goods.

8. Traded and Nontraded Goods: The Small Country Case

We now extend the model to treat traded and nontraded goods separately. To keep matters simple we confine the analysis to the small country case.

The utility level is assumed, again, to be a function of consumption and of real money balances. In order to avoid index number problems, we write utility as a function of nominal money balances, prices, and consumption. This function is homogeneous of degree zero in money holdings and prices in every period. To simplify the exposition, we assume that money balances may be separated from consumption in the utility function. This permits a simple analysis in terms of expenditures on consumption and money balances [see Berglas and Razin (1972)]. As an initial simplification we start by assuming that money balances and consumption are additively separable in the utility function. We proceed later to a more general formulation.

Assuming that the foreign price of traded goods is equal to one, the consumer's problem is

$$\begin{gathered}\text{Choose } c_1^{\mathrm{N}}, c_1^{\mathrm{T}}, M_1, X_1^{\mathrm{T}}, A, c_2^{\mathrm{N}}, c_2^{\mathrm{T}}, M_2, \text{ and } X_2^{\mathrm{T}} \text{ to maximize} \\ u(c_1^{\mathrm{N}}, c_1^{\mathrm{T}}) + v(M_1/e_1, p_1) + \beta u(c_2^{\mathrm{N}}, c_2^{\mathrm{T}}) + \beta v(M_2/e_2, p_2)\end{gathered} \tag{27}$$

subject to

$$e_1 G^{\mathrm{T}} + e_1 c_1^{\mathrm{T}} + M_1 + e_1 A = e_1 X_1^{\mathrm{T}} + \overline{M}_1, \tag{28}$$

$$e_2 c_2^{\mathrm{T}} + M_2 = e_2 X_2^{\mathrm{T}} + e_2 R A + \overline{M}_2 \tag{29}$$

and

$$c_1^{\mathrm{N}} = F(X_1^{\mathrm{T}}) - G^{\mathrm{N}}, \tag{30}$$

$$c_2^{\mathrm{N}} = F(X_2^{\mathrm{T}}), \tag{31}$$

where c_i^{N} is consumption of nontraded goods in period i, $i = 1,2$; c_i^{T}, consumption of traded goods in period i, $i = 1,2$; M_i, domestic money holdings in period i, $i = 1,2$; A, foreign asset holdings bearing interest r, and $R = 1 + r$ is the interest factor; X_i^{T}, production of traded goods in period i, $i = 1,2$; e_i, exchange rate in period i, $i = 1,2$; p_i, relative price of nontraded goods in terms of traded goods in period i; G^{T}, government spending on traded goods; G^{N}, government spending on nontraded goods; $\overline{M}_1$, first-period money supply; $\overline{M}_2$, second-period money supply; $F(\ )$, transformation function from traded to nontraded goods, with $p_i = [F'(X_i^T)]^{-1}$. Thus, in equilibrium, the marginal rate of transformation between traded and nontraded goods is equal to the relative price of nontraded goods in terms of traded goods.

For simplicity we assume that government spending takes place in the first period, financed by nondistorting taxes. Since there is perfect borrowing and lending, the period in which government spending on traded goods takes place is of no consequence for the private sector as long as the present value of spending is constant. The timing of government spending on nontraded goods *is* important, but as a straightforward analysis may be derived from the present model no further treatment is provided here.

Since there is no sign restriction on foreign asset holdings, constraints (28) and (29) can be reduced into a single intertemporal budget constraint:

$$R\left(G^{\mathrm{T}} + c_1^{\mathrm{T}} - X_1^{\mathrm{T}}\right) + \left(c_2^{\mathrm{T}} - X_2^{\mathrm{T}}\right) = Re_1^{-1}\left(\overline{M}_1 - M_1\right) + e_2^{-1}\left(\overline{M}_2 - M_2\right). \tag{32}$$

The left-hand side of (32) represents the future value of the excess of traded goods consumption and government spending over traded goods output. At equilibrium, money balances are willingly held:

$$M_1 = \overline{M}_1, \qquad M_2 = \overline{M}_2. \tag{33}$$

Substituting (33) into (32), the future value of traded goods consumption plus government spending on traded goods is equal, at an equilibrium, to the future value of tradable output.

The first-order conditions of the representative consumer's problem (27)–(31), yield the following equations:

$$\frac{u_{\mathrm{N}}\left(c_1^{\mathrm{N}}, c_1^{\mathrm{T}}\right)}{u_{\mathrm{T}}\left(c_1^{\mathrm{N}}, c_1^{\mathrm{T}}\right)} = \frac{-1}{F'\left(X_1^{\mathrm{T}}\right)} = p_1, \tag{34}$$

$$\frac{u_{\mathrm{N}}\left(c_2^{\mathrm{N}}, c_2^{\mathrm{T}}\right)}{u_{\mathrm{T}}\left(c_2^{\mathrm{N}}, c_2^{\mathrm{T}}\right)} = \frac{-1}{F'\left(X_2^{\mathrm{T}}\right)} = p_2, \tag{35}$$

$$\frac{u_{\mathrm{T}}\left(c_1^{\mathrm{N}}, c_1^{\mathrm{T}}\right)}{\beta u_{\mathrm{T}}\left(c_2^{\mathrm{N}}, c_2^{\mathrm{T}}\right)} = R, \tag{36}$$

$$\frac{v_M(M_1/e_1, p_1)}{u_{\mathrm{T}}\left(c_1^{\mathrm{N}}, c_1^{\mathrm{T}}\right)} = 1 - \frac{e_1}{e_2}\frac{1}{R}, \tag{37}$$

$$\frac{v_M(M_2/e_2, p_2)}{u_{\mathrm{T}}\left(c_2^{\mathrm{N}}, c_2^{\mathrm{T}}\right)} = 1, \tag{38}$$

where subscripts attached to u and v denote partial derivatives, and p_i is the relative price of nontraded in terms of traded goods in period i, $i = 1,2$.

We assume that u_N diminishes in c^N and increases in c^T, u_T diminishes in c^T and increases in c^N, and $v_M(M/e_i, p_i)$ diminishes in M/e_i and increases in p_i. (The last condition is plausible since an increase in the relative price of nontraded goods, holding e constant, amounts to an increase in the nominal price of nontraded goods and this would reduce the marginal utility of money balances.)

As explained before, equilibrium implies

$$R\left(c_1^T + G^T - X_1^T\right) + c_2^T - X_2^T = 0. \tag{39}$$

Equation (34) represents the equality between the first-period marginal rate of substitution and the first-period marginal rate of transformation between traded and nontraded goods. Equation (35) describes a similar condition for the second period.

Equation (36), well known from the theory of savings, is interpreted as an equality between the interest factor and the marginal rate of substitution between first-period and second-period consumption of traded goods. Marginal rates of substitution between first-period real balances and first-period consumption of traded goods, and similarly for the second period, are on the left-hand sides of (37) and (38), respectively. First- and second-period relative prices of real balances are shown on the right-hand sides of (37) and (38).

It is convenient now to analyze the real and the monetary sectors separately before analyzing the interactions between them.

A. The Real Sector

Equations (30), (31), (34), (36), and (39) characterize the real sector—they determine the trade balance, capital movements, and the relative prices of nontraded goods in terms of traded goods.

Figure 4 describes equilibrium for the case in which the subjective rate of discount is larger than the real interest rate, that is, $\beta R < 1$; a trade balance surplus can be similarly analyzed. In Fig. 4, TT describes the transformation curve between traded and nontraded goods. First-period equilibrium is given by the consumption point A_1^C and the production point A_1^P. The relative price of nontraded goods in terms of traded goods is p_1, and the income–consumption curve corresponding to that relative price is $0I_1$. The nontraded goods market clears, and there is a commodity trade deficit and a capital trade surplus whose magnitudes are represented by the distance between A_1^C and A_1^P. The second-period relative price of nontraded goods in terms of traded goods is p_2, which corresponds to an income–

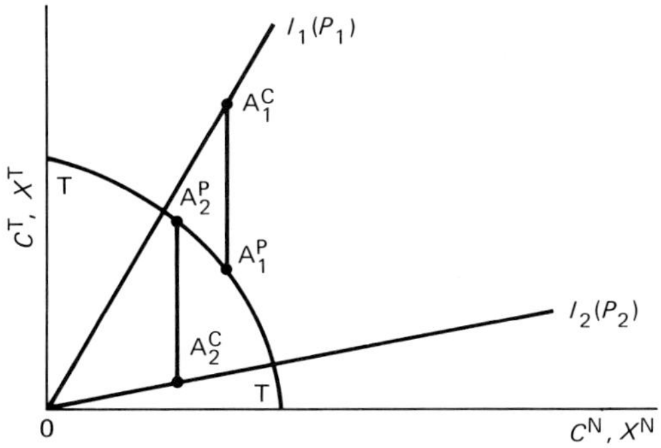

Fig. 4. Real equilibrium with nontraded goods.

consumption curve $0I_2$, consumption point A_2^C, and production point A_2^P. The nontraded goods market clears and there is a commodity trade surplus and a capital trade deficit measured by the distance between A_2^P and A_2^C, which is R times the distance between A_1^P and A_1^C (the first-period trade deficit). Observe that p_1 must be larger than p_2; that is, the relative price of traded goods must increase over time if there is an initial trade deficit. Note that the income consumption lines (indicating the allocation of consumption from a given expenditure) and the equilibrium levels of expenditure are not a function of monetary variables such as exchange rates.[3]

B. The Monetary Sector

Figure 5 shows how equilibrium exchange rates are determined, given consumption levels and relative prices of nontraded goods in terms of traded goods. It is derived from equations (37) and (38). The various combinations of e_1 and e_2 that, from (38), make the second-period marginal rate of substitution between real balances and traded goods consumption equal to one are depicted by the horizontal line M_2M_2. Note that this defines a unique level for every level of e_1. Along M_2M_2, second-period money supply, second-period consumption of traded goods, and the second-period relative price of nontraded goods are held constant. The various combinations of e_1 and e_2 that make the first-period marginal rate of substitution between real balances and traded goods consumption $MRS_{m_1c_1}$ equal to $1 - e_1/e_2R(\equiv \rho)$, the relative price of real balances in terms of traded goods, are represented by the curve M_1M_1. This curve is

[3] If the consumption and real balances are separable (but not additively separable) in the utility function, the allocation of consumption from a given expenditure is not affected by monetary variables. These do, however, affect the equilibrium *level* of expenditure, as discussed in Section 10.

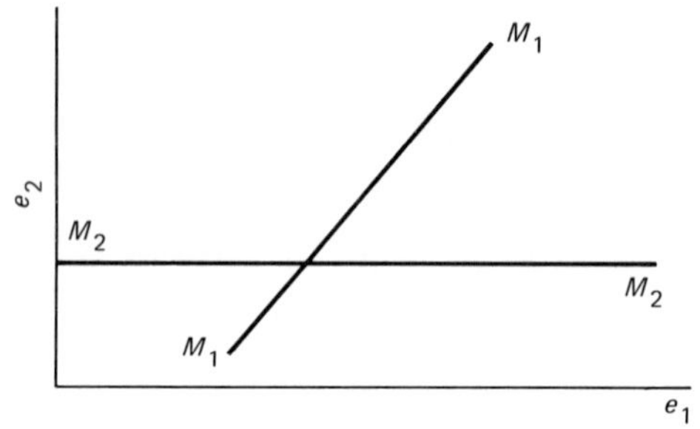

Fig. 5. Monetary equilibrium.

upward sloping and steeper than a ray through the origin for the following reason. Starting off from equality between $MRS_{m_1c_1}$ and ρ, suppose that e_1 and e_2 go up by an equal proportion. Then ρ remains unchanged while $MRS_{m_1c_1}$ increases since the level of real balances declines. To restore the initial equality by raising ρ, e_2 must increase further. Along M_1M_1, first-period money supply, first-period consumption of traded goods, first-period relative price of traded goods in terms of nontraded goods, and the interest rate are all held constant.

9. Fiscal Policies with Nontraded Goods

Fiscal policies have different effects on exchange rates, trade balances, and related magnitudes according to whether the government spends on traded goods or on nontraded goods.

A. Government Spending on Traded Goods

The present analysis of fiscal policies is similar to that in Razin (1978). There, I showed that an increase in G^{T} will reduce the level of traded goods consumption c_1^{T} and c_2^{T} and will increase the total trade deficit in the first period while reducing the private sector trade deficit. This can be explained as follows. Let $c_1^{\mathrm{N}} = c_1^{\mathrm{N}}(p_1; E_1)$ be first-period consumption of nontraded goods as a function of the relative price of nontraded goods and expenditure. Expenditure is, in turn, a function of the value of output minus government spending, and prices. The nontraded goods market in period i clears when $c_i^{\mathrm{N}}(p_i; E_i) = X^{\mathrm{N}}(p_i)$ where X^{N} is the production of nontradable goods. If G^{T} increases, at the initial prices E_i goes down and so does

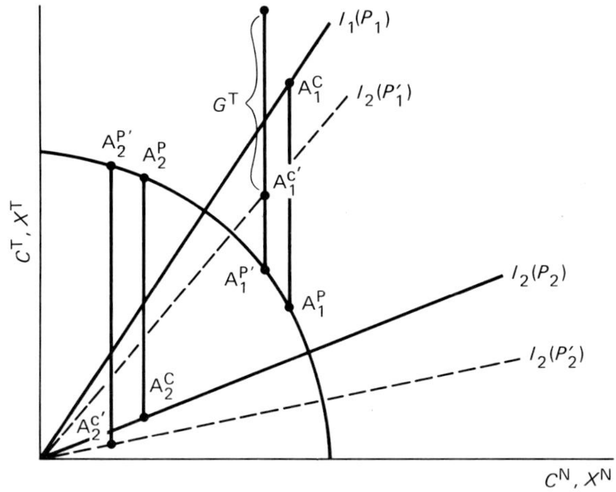

Fig. 6. Government spending on traded goods: Real equilibrium.

c_i^N. In order to restore equilibrium, the relative price of nontradables p_i must decrease. Because of the change in prices, as well as a marginal propensity to spend that is smaller than one, first-period decline in private sector demand for tradables is less than the increase in government demand. Thus the total first-period trade deficit increases while the private sector trade deficit improves.

Figure 6 reproduces the equilibrium shown in Fig. 4, which is now used to analyze the effect of this policy. The reduction in expenditure following fiscal expansion reduces the relative price of nontraded goods in terms of traded goods in both periods. As a result, the income–consumption lines move to the right—from $I_1(P_1)$ to $I_1(P_1')$ and from $I_2(P_2)$ to $I_2(P_2')$. First-period production and consumption points move to $A_1^{P'}$ and $A_1^{c'}$. Second-period production and consumption points move to $A_2^{P'}$ and $A_2^{c'}$, respectively. Thus the second-period trade surplus increases, implying an increase in the total first-period trade deficit (private as well as government). First-period production and consumption points move to $A_1^{P'}$ and $A_1^{c'}$. Government spending is shown by the distance G^T. The total trade deficit in the first period is the distance $A_1^{P'}A_1^{c'}$ plus G^T.

Monetary equilibrium is affected as follows. The reduction in c_1^T and p_1 reduce the first-period marginal rate of substitution between real balances and traded goods. Thus M_1M_1 in Fig. 7 shifts down and to the right. For a similar reason the reduction in c_2^T and p_2 shift M_2M_2 up. Thus equilibrium exchange rates must increase.

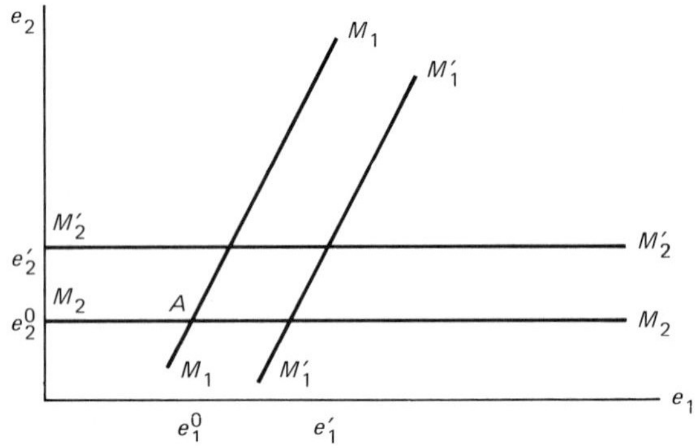

Fig. 7. Government spending on traded goods: Monetary equilibrium.

B. Government Spending on Nontraded Goods

Abstracting from monetary considerations, first-period government spending on nontraded goods was shown in Razin (1978) to result in a decrease in consumption on traded goods in every period, and a first-period increase in the trade deficit.

This is explained as follows. The nontraded goods market in the first period clears when $c_1^N(P_1; E_1) + G^N = X^N(p_1)$ and in the second period clears when $c_2^N(p_1; E_2) = X^N(p_2)$. Holding prices constant, the increase in G^N will reduce private demand for nontradables, through decreased expenditure, by less than the increase in government demand. To eliminate the excess demand, p_1 must rise, and the demand for nontradables must fall. Since E_2 declines at the initial level of p_2, an excess supply for nontradables emerges, and p_2 must fall.

Figure 8 describes the effect of the fiscal expansion. The income consumption lines pivot out from $I_1(P_1)$ to $I_1(P_1')$ and from $I_2(P_2)$ to $I_2(P_2')$. The second-period equilibrium changes from (A_2^P, A_2^c) to $(A_2^{P'}, A_2^{c'})$ indicating an increase in the second-period trade surplus. This implies that the first-period trade deficit has increased. The new first-period equilibrium is given by private consumption point $A_1^{c'}$, government spending G^N and production point $A_1^{P'}$, where total production of nontraded goods equals private consumption of nontradables plus government spending.

The effects on the monetary equilibrium are somewhat ambiguous. The decrease in traded goods consumption and the reduction in the relative price of nontraded goods in terms of traded goods reduce the marginal rate of substitution between real balances and traded goods in the second period. Therefore, in Fig. 9, M_2M_2 shifts upward to $M_2'M_2'$.

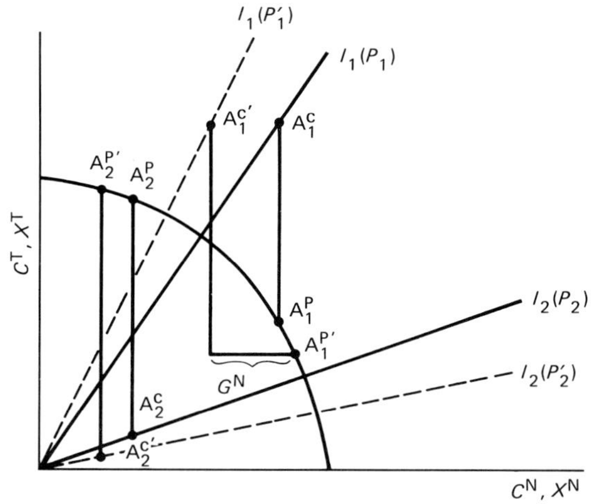

Fig. 8. Government spending on nontraded goods: Real equilibrium.

The increase in the consumption of traded goods and the increase in the relative price of nontraded goods raise the marginal rate of substitution between real balances and traded goods in the first period. Thus M_1M_1 in Fig. 9 shifts up and to the left. Whether or not the first-period exchange rate increases would depend on the magnitudes of the shifts in M_1M_1 and M_2M_2. the second-period exchange rate will, however, definitely increase. The nominal interest rate must increase since even if M_1M_1 had not moved, e_2 would have risen proportionally more than e_1; a fortiori, e_2/e_1 must rise in the present case since M_1M_1 actually moves to the left.

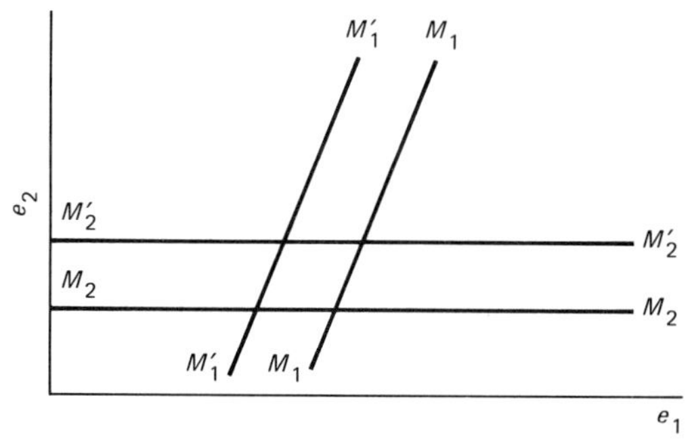

Fig. 9. Government spending on nontraded goods: Monetary equilibrium.

10. Feedbacks from the Monetary Sector to the Real Sector

Assume now a utility function of a more general form, which permits the marginal rate of substitution between commodities (tradable or nontradable) in every period to depend on monetary magnitudes, while retaining the simplicity of the previous formulation. Hence the utility function is

$$u\left[\phi(c^{\mathrm{N}},c^{\mathrm{T}}),M_1/e_1,p_1\right]+\beta u\left[\phi(c^{\mathrm{N}},c^{\mathrm{T}}),M_2/e_2,p_2\right], \tag{40}$$

where $u_{\phi M}>0$; that is, the marginal utility of consumption increases with money balances. This assumption can be shown to be sufficient for the stability of equilibrium.

To illustrate the role of feedbacks from the monetary to the real sector, we again consider monetary policy. A first-period monetary expansion causes a depreciation in domestic currency in the first period coupled with an increase in first-period real balances, while second-period real balances are left unchanged. Consider the consequent change in the marginal rate of substitution between first- and second-period traded goods:

$$MRS_{c_1^{\mathrm{T}}c_2^{\mathrm{T}}}=\frac{u_{\mathrm{T}}\left[\phi(c^{\mathrm{N}},c^{\mathrm{T}}),M_1/e_1,p_1\right]}{\beta u_{\mathrm{T}}\left[\phi(c_2^{\mathrm{N}},c_2^{\mathrm{T}}),M_2/e_2,p_2\right]}. \tag{41}$$

Given the level of consumption and relative prices of nontraded goods, the numerator on the right-hand side of (41) increases, while the denominator remains constant. Hence monetary expansion raises the marginal rate of substitution. To restore equality between the marginal rate of substitution and the interest factor [see (36)], first-period expenditure rises and second-period expenditure falls, thereby satisfying the intertemporal budget constraint. Figure 10 describes real sector equilibrium. The increase in first-

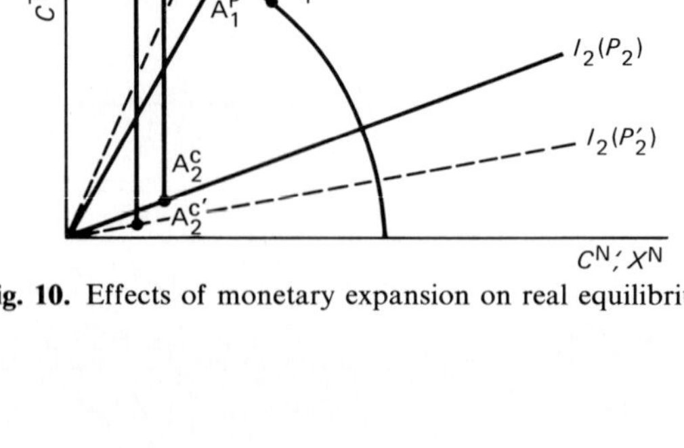

Fig. 10. Effects of monetary expansion on real equilibrium.

period expenditure must increase the relative price of nontraded goods in that period to clear the nontraded goods market. The decreased second-period expenditure lowers the relative price of nontraded goods. The income–consumption curves shift from $I_1(P_1)$ to $I_1(P_1')$, and from $I_2(P_2)$ to $I_2(P_2')$. The first-period equilibrium trade deficit, measured by the distance from $A_1^{c'}$ to $A_1^{P'}$ is therefore larger than that prior to the monetary expansion, which is measured by the distance from A_1^c to A_1^P. These real sector changes could be shown to mitigate the impact of monetary expansion on exchange rates, in that the first-period exchange rate would rise less in the presence of feedbacks from the monetary sector to the real sector.

REFERENCES

Berglas, E., and Razin, A. (1972). A Note on the Balance of Payments, and the Terms of Trade in Relation to Financial Controls. *Review of Economic Studies* **39**, 511–513.

Calvo, G. A., and Rodriguez, C. A. (1977). A Model of Exchange Rate Determination Under Currency Substitution and Rational Expectations. *Journal of Political Economy* **85**, 617–626.

Dornbusch, R. (1976a). The Theory of Flexible Exchange Rate Regimes and Macroeconomic Policy. *Scandinavian Journal of Economics* **2**, 225–275.

Dornbusch, R. (1976b). Expectations and Exchange Rate Dynamics. *Journal of Political Economy* **84**, 1161–1177.

Fleming, M. (1962). Domestic Financial Policies under Fixed and Floating Exchange Rates. *I.M.F. Staff Papers* **9**, 369–379.

Helpman, E., and Razin, A. (1979). Towards a Consistent Comparison of Alternative Exchange Rate Systems. *Canadian Journal of Economics*, **3**, 394–409.

Kemp, M. C. (1969). *The Pure Theory of International Trade and Investment.* Prentice-Hall, Englewood Cliffs, New Jersey.

Mundell, R. A. (1968). *International Economics*. Macmillan, New York.

Razin, A. (1978). Capital Movements, Nontraded Goods, and the Trade Balance. Working Paper No. 29-78, Foerder Institute for Economic Research, Tel Aviv University, September.

Whitman, M. V. N. (1975). Global Monetarism and the Monetary Approach to the Balance of Payments; also Discussion. *Brookings Papers on Economic Activity*, **2**, 491–555.

THE PINHAS SAPIR CENTER FOR DEVELOPMENT
TEL AVIV UNIVERSITY
RAMAT AVIV, TEL AVIV, ISRAEL

PART 5

Expectations and Macroeconometrics

Exchange Rates in the 1920s*

A Monetary Approach

JACOB A. FRENKEL AND KENNETH W. CLEMENTS[†]

1. Introduction

Current views about flexible exchange rate systems are based, to a large extent, on the lessons from the period of the 1920s, during which many exchange rates were flexible. The experience of that period has proven to be extremely important in shaping current thinking about, and understanding of, the operation of flexible exchange rates. It led to an examination of various issues associated with a regime of flexible exchange rates, such as speculation, the efficiency of the foreign exchange markets, the purchasing power parity doctrine, and the factors that determine equilibrium exchange rates.[1] This paper reexamines some of these issues from the perspective of the recently revived monetary approach (or more generally, asset market

*We are indebted to Izan Haji Yaakob for efficient research assistance and to John F. O. Bilson, Rudiger Dornbusch, Michael Mussa, and Arnold Zellner for helpful comments and suggestions. We have benefited from numerous comments during presentations of earlier versions of this paper at various seminars. In particular, we would like to acknowledge the useful comments we received during seminars at the University of Rochester, the University of Wisconsin, MIT, the Tenth Konstanz Seminar, and Tel Aviv University. J. A. Frenkel acknowledges financial support from a National Science Foundation grant, SOC 78-14480. The research reported here is part of the NBER's research program in International Studies. Any opinions expressed are those of the authors and not those of the NBER.

[†]Present address: MacQuarie University and Reserve Bank of Australia, Sydney, New South Wales 2001, Australia.

[1]See, for example, Aliber (1962), Dulles (1929), Farag and Ott (1964), Frenkel (1978), Hodgson (1972), Stolper (1948), and Tsiang (1959–1960).

ISBN 0-12-259750-8

approach) to the exchange rate. This reexamination could provide the necessary ingredient for a broader study of the lessons that could be learned from the important formative experience of the 1920s for the understanding of the economics of exchange rates during the 1970s.

Section 2 presents a simple monetary model of exchange rate determination. The key characteristic of the model lies in the notion that, being a relative price of two monies, the equilibrium exchange rate is attained when the existing stocks of the two monies are willingly held. The equilibrium exchange rate is shown to depend on both real and monetary factors which operate through their influence on the relative demands and supplies of monies. In Section 3 we examine some of the efficiency properties of the foreign exchange market and analyze the relationship between spot and forward rates for the franc/pound, dollar/pound, and franc/dollar exchange rates. Section 4 contains the results of the empirical test of the monetary model of exchange rate determination. Using monthly data we estimate various versions of the model and allow for interrelationships between the various exchange rates. We then use the estimated parameters for dynamic simulations. Section 5 contains some concluding remarks.

2. A Model of Exchange Rate Determination

In this section we outline a simple model of exchange rate determination that reflects the recent revival of the monetary approach (or more generally, the asset market approach) to the analysis of exchange rates.[2] The monetary view of exchange rate determination emphasizes that the exchange rate, being the relative price of two national monies, is determined primarily by factors that affect the relative supplies and demands for these monies. Since the demands for the various national monies depend on expectations, incomes, rates of return and other considerations relevant for portfolio choice, the approach is referred to as an asset market approach to the determination of exchange rates. The major building blocks of the theory are hypotheses concerning (a) the properties of the demand for money, (b) the purchasing power parity condition, and (c) the interest parity theory.

Consider first the equilibrium in the money markets. The supplies of domestic and foreign real balances are M/P and M^*/P^*, where M and P denote the nominal money supply and the price level, respectively, and

[2]For theoretical developments and applications of the approach see, for example, Dornbusch (1976a, 1976b), Kouri (1976), Mussa (1976), Frenkel (1976), Frenkel and Johnson (1978), Bilson (1978), and Hodrick (1978).

where variables pertaining to the foreign country are indicated by an asterisk. Denoting the demands for real balances by L and L^* (both of which functions will be specified below) equilibrium in the money markets is attained when

$$L = M/P \tag{1}$$

and

$$L^* = M^*/P^*. \tag{2}$$

From Eqs. (1) and (2), equilibrium in the money markets implies that the ratio of the two price levels is

$$P/P^* = (M/M^*)(L^*/L) \tag{3}$$

The second building block links domestic and foreign prices through the purchasing power parity condition according to which

$$P = SP^*, \tag{4}$$

where S denotes the spot exchange rate—the price of foreign exchange in terms of domestic currency.[3] Using (4) in (3) yields

$$S = (M/M^*)(L^*/L), \tag{5}$$

which expresses the exchange rate in terms of domestic and foreign supplies and demands for money. To gain further insight into the determinants of the exchange rate and to set the stage for the empirical estimation, assume that the demand for money depends on real income y and the rate of interest i according to

$$L = ay^{\eta}e^{-\alpha i}, \tag{6}$$

$$L^* = b^*y^{*\eta^*}e^{-\alpha^* i^*}. \tag{7}$$

Using Eqs. (6) and (7) in (5) and assuming for simplicity of exposition that foreign and domestic parameters of the demand for money are the same, that is, that $\alpha = \alpha^*$ and that $\eta = \eta^*$, we obtain

$$\ln S = C + \ln(M/M^*) + \eta \ln(y^*/y) + \alpha(i - i^*), \tag{8}$$

where $C \equiv \ln(b^*/a)$.

[3] For a discussion of the choice of the relevant price index to be used in (4) see Frenkel (1978). To the extent that *purchasing power parity* pertains to traded goods only, the exchange rate equation would also contain terms that relate to the relative prices of traded to nontraded goods; for a formulation along these lines see Dornbusch (1976b), and for an empirical application see Clements and Frenkel (1980). A more refined specification would allow for the effects of tariffs on the relationship between domestic and foreign prices as well as for short-run effects of unanticipated money on output rather than only on prices and the exchange rate.

Denoting a percentage change in a variable by a circumflex (for example $\hat{x} = \Delta x/x$), the percentage change in the exchange rate is

$$\hat{S} = (\hat{M} - \hat{M}^*) + \eta(\hat{y}^* - \hat{y}) + \alpha\,\Delta(i - i^*). \tag{9}$$

Equation (9) relates the percentage change in the exchange rate to the differences between domestic and foreign (a) rates of monetary expansion, (b) rates of growth of real incomes, and (c) changes in rates of interest.[4]

The third building block is the interest parity theory according to which, in equilibrium, the premium on a forward contract for foreign exchange for a given maturity is (approximately) equal to the interest rate differential

$$i - i^* = \pi, \qquad \pi \equiv \ln(F/S), \tag{10}$$

where π denotes the forward premium on foreign exchange and F denotes the forward exchange rate. Substituting (10) into (8) and (9) yields

$$\ln S = C + \ln(M/M^*) + \eta \ln(y^*/y) + \alpha\pi, \tag{11}$$

$$\hat{S} = (\hat{M} - \hat{M}^*) + \eta(\hat{y}^* - \hat{y}) + \alpha\,\Delta\pi. \tag{12}$$

One of the central implications of the monetary (or the asset market) approach is the key role assigned to expectations concerning future events. The role of expectations in the determination of exchange rates is summarized by the forward premium or discount on foreign exchange. The monetary approach summarized in (11) and (12) differs from the elasticities approach to exchange rate determination in that concepts such as exports and imports do not appear explicitly as being fundamentally relevant for the understanding of the evolution of the exchange rate. Rather, the relevant concepts relate to two groups of variables: those determined by the monetary authorities and those that affect the demands for domestic and foreign monies.[5]

The implications of the model are that, *ceteris paribus*, (a) a rise in the supply of domestic money will depreciate the home currency (that is, raise S), while a rise in the supply of foreign money will appreciate the home

[4]To the extent that purchasing power parity pertains only to traded goods, (9) will include another term describing the ratio of domestic to foreign relative prices of traded to nontraded goods (that is, the relative real exchange rates).

[5]It should be noted that when *properly specified*, other approaches to exchange rate determination would also yield reduced-form equations like (8) or (9), with money supplies, incomes, and interest rates appearing on the right-hand side. The virtue of the monetary approach in comparison with the elasticities approach is in bringing these variables to the foreground.

currency; (b) a rise in domestic income due, for example, to a rise in productivity will appreciate the currency (lower S), while a rise in foreign income will depreciate the currency; and (c) a rise in the forward premium on foreign exchange will depreciate the currency (raise S). This dependence of the current exchange rate on expectations concerning the future rate (as summarized by the forward premium) is a typical key characteristic of price determination in asset markets (and in markets for durable goods). Thus an expected future depreciation of the currency is reflected immediately in the current value of the currency. The model yields the following predictions concerning the values of the various elasticities: (a) The elasticity of the exchange rate with respect to the domestic money supply is unity, and the elasticity with respect to the foreign money supply is minus unity; (b) the elasticity with respect to domestic and foreign real incomes should approximate the income elasticities of the demand for money η (positive for foreign income and negative for domestic income), and (c) the (semi-) elasticity with respect to the forward premium should approximate (in absolute value) the interest (semi-) elasticity of the demand for money. These predictions are examined in Section 4.

The above model makes no distinction between "the demand for domestic money" and "the domestic demand for money." Implicitly, it has been assumed that domestic money is demanded only by domestic residents, while foreign money is demanded only by foreign residents. Furthermore, the formulation of the demands for real cash balances in (6) and (7) includes the domestic interest rate in the domestic demand and the foreign interest rate in the foreign demand; implicitly, it is assumed that the only relevant alternative for holding domestic money is domestic securities, while the only relevant alternative for holding foreign money is foreign securities. In principle, however, the alternatives to holding domestic money include domestic securities and foreign securities, as well as foreign exchange. It follows that a richer formulation of the demand for money would recognize that, as an analytical matter, the spectrum of alternative assets and rates of return relevant for the specification of the demand for money is rather broad, including both rates of interest, i and i^*, as well as the forward premium on foreign exchange π. Furthermore, to the extent that under a flexible exchange rate system, individuals might wish to diversify their currency holdings, the demand for domestic money would include a foreign component, which depends on foreign income, while the demand for foreign money would include a domestic component, which depends on domestic income.[6] These characteristics reflect the phenome-

[6] For a discussion of the specification of the demand for money under a flexible exchange rate regime see Frenkel (1977, 1979) and Abel *et al.* (1979).

non of currency substitution, which is likely to arise when the exchange rate is not pegged.[7]

The above discussion suggests the need for a more detailed specification of the demand for money. Let domestic demand for domestic money depend on domestic income and on the three alternative rates of return, according to

$$L_1 = ay^{\eta_1}\exp(-\alpha_1 i - \beta_1 i^* - \gamma_1 \pi), \tag{13}$$

and let the foreign demand for domestic money be

$$L_1^* = a^* y^{*\eta_1^*}\exp(-\alpha_1^* i - \beta_1^* i^* - \gamma_1^* \pi), \tag{14}$$

where the total demand for domestic money is $L_1 + L_1^* = L$. Analogously, the demand for foreign money is also composed of domestic and foreign components: domestic demand for foreign money L_2 and foreign demand for foreign money L_2^* according to

$$L_2 = by^{\eta_2}\exp(-\alpha_2 i - \beta_2 i^* + \gamma_2 \pi), \tag{15}$$

$$L_2^* = b^* y^{*\eta_2^*}\exp(-\alpha_2^* i - \beta_2^* i^* + \gamma_2^* \pi), \tag{16}$$

where the total demand for foreign money is $L_2 + L_2^* = L^*$.

Using the above relationships, the domestic and foreign demands for money are $L_1 + L_2$ and $L_1^* + L_2^*$, respectively. Substituting (13)–(16) into (5) yields the more general relationship between the exchange rate and the various components of the supplies and demands for the two monies. For expositional simplicity assume that all the various income elasticities of money demands are equal to η, that is, $\eta_1 = \eta_1^* = \eta_2 = \eta_2^* = \eta$; that the semi-elasticities of the demands for money with respect to both interest rates are equal, that is, $\alpha_i = \beta_i = \alpha_i^* = \beta_i^*$ $(i = 1, 2)$; and that the semi-elasticities of the demands for money with respect to the forward premium on foreign exchange are equal to γ, that is, $\gamma_1 = \gamma_1^* = \gamma_2 = \gamma_2^* = \gamma$. Under these assumptions the exchange rate can be written as

$$S = \frac{M}{M^*}\,\frac{by^{\eta} + b^* y^{*\eta}}{ay^{\eta} + a^* y^{*\eta}}\,e^{\beta\pi}, \tag{17}$$

where $\beta \equiv 2\gamma$.

From (17), the percentage change in the exchange rate is

$$\hat{S} = (\hat{M} - \hat{M}^*) + \eta(\lambda^* + \lambda - 1)(\hat{y}^* - \hat{y}) + \beta\,\Delta\pi, \tag{18}$$

where $\lambda^* \equiv L_2^*/L^*$ and $\lambda \equiv L_1/L$.

The implications of (18) are similar to those of (12), except for the inference concerning the elasticity of the exchange rate with respect to real

[7] For an analysis of the phenomenon of currency substitution see Boyer (1973), Chen (1973), Chrystal (1977), Girton and Roper (1976), Stockman (1976), Calvo and Rodriguez (1977), and Miles (1978). On the extent of currency substitution during the German hyperinflation, see Frenkel (1977).

incomes. When individuals hold diversified portfolios of currencies, the effects of income growth on the exchange rate depend on the income elasticity of the demand for money as well as on the parameters λ and λ^* indicating the currency mix of money holdings. If domestic and foreign residents hold portfolios with identical currency mixes, changes in incomes will not affect the exchange rate. In general, it is expected that the typical portfolio of currencies will be intensive in the local currency; thus both λ and λ^* are each larger than one-half, and therefore $\lambda + \lambda^* > 1$. Under these circumstances it is expected that the elasticity of the exchange rate with respect to domestic income would be negative. The elasticity with respect to foreign income would be positive, but somewhat less than the corresponding income elasticities of the demands for money since $(\lambda + \lambda^* - 1)$ is less than unity. In the special case where money holdings are not diversified, individuals hold only local currency, $\lambda = \lambda^* = 1$, and (18) reduces to (12).

Prior to concluding this section it should be emphasized that the monetary (or asset market) approach to the exchange rate *does not* claim that the exchange rate is "determined" only in the money or in the asset markets and that only stock rather than flow considerations are relevant for determining the equilibrium exchange rate. Obviously, general equilibrium relationships relevant for the determination of exchange rates include both stock and flow variables. In this respect, the asset market equilibrium relationship that has been used may be viewed as a reduced-form relationship. Furthermore, the fact that the analysis of the exchange rate has been carried out in terms of the supplies and the demands for monies *does not* imply that "only money matters" or that the exchange rate is determined only by the supply of domestic and foreign monies. On the contrary, the demand for money plays a critical role, and it depends on real variables like real income as well as on other real variables that underlie expectations. The rationale for concentrating on the relative supplies and demands for money is that they provide a convenient and a natural framework for organizing thoughts concerning the determinants of the relative price of monies. The same principle has been used by proponents of the monetary approach to the balance of payments in justifying the use of the money-demand money-supply framework for the analysis of the money account of the balance of payments under a pegged exchange rate system.[8]

[8] See, for example, Mussa (1974) and Frenkel and Johnson (1976). In the context of flexible exchange rates the same argument is made by Dornbusch (1976b) and Mussa (1976). It should be noted that the money-demand money-supply framework is not employed only for convenience; it reflects the hypotheses that money markets clear faster than goods markets, that the demands for real balances are relatively stable, and that the supply of nominal balances is a policy instrument controlled by the monetary authorities. The emphasis on the role of the money supply places a unique responsibility on the monetary authorities in affecting the rate of exchange.

3. Efficiency of Foreign Exchange Markets

In the previous section we outlined the basic building blocks of an asset market approach to the determination of exchange rates. We argued that since the exchange rate is the relative price of two assets, it depends (like other asset prices) on expectations concerning the future course of events. We suggested that these expectations be measured by using data from the forward market for foreign exchange.

The assumption underlying the use of data from the forward market for foreign exchange is that this market is indeed useful in conveying information concerning expectations held by market participants. Therefore, prior to incorporating such data in the empirical analysis of exchange rate determination, it is important to study some of the characteristics of the market. In this section we examine some of the efficiency properties of the market for foreign exchange.[9]

If the foreign exchange market is efficient and if the exchange rate is determined in a fashion similar to other asset prices, we should expect that current prices reflect all available information. Expectations concerning future exchange rates should be incorporated and reflected in forward exchange rates. To examine the efficiency of the market, we first regress the log of the current spot exchange rate $\ln S_t$ on the log of the one-month-forward exchange rate prevailing at the previous month $\ln F_{t-1}$, as in (19). Similar regressions are also computed using the levels of the exchange rates rather than their logs as in (19′).

$$\ln S_t = a + b \ln F_{t-1} + u_t, \tag{19}$$

$$S_t = a' + b' F_{t-1} + v_t. \tag{19'}$$

If the market for foreign exchange is efficient and if the forward exchange rate is an unbiased forecast of the future spot exchange rate, then we expect the following three properties: (a) The constant terms in (19) and (19′) should not differ significantly from zero;[10] (b) the slope coefficients should not differ significantly from unity, and (c) the residuals should be serially uncorrelated. We examine three exchange rates: the franc/pound, the dollar/pound and the franc/dollar. Obviously, only two of the three rates are independent, due to triangular arbitrage. Equations (19) and (19′)

[9] For an application of the same methodology in analyzing the efficiency properties of the foreign exchange market during the German hyperinflation between 1921 and 1923 see Frenkel (1976, 1977, 1979). For an application to the 1920s and the 1970s see Krugman (1977), and for a survey see Levich (1979).

[10] More precisely, if (assuming risk neutrality) the forward rate measures the expected value of the future spot rate, then the constant term in (19′) should be zero, and the constant term in the logarithmic equation (19) should be $-0.5\sigma_u^2$; see Frenkel (1979).

were estimated using monthly data for the 52 months between February 1921 and May 1925. Details of data and data sources are given in Appendix B. The resulting ordinary-least-squares estimates are reported in Tables 1 and 2. These tables also include regression results, with F_{t-2} as an additional explanatory variable.

As can be seen, the results are consistent with the three hypotheses outlined above. In all cases, the constant terms do not differ significantly from zero at the 95% confidence level. Furthermore, the Durbin–Watson statistics are consistent with the hypothesis of the absence of first-order autocorrelated residuals.[11] In all cases at the 95% confidence level we cannot reject the joint hypothesis that the constant terms are zero *and* that the slope coefficients are unity.

TABLE 1

EFFICIENCY OF FOREIGN EXCHANGE MARKETS (LOGARITHMIC EQUATION); MONTHLY DATA: FEBRUARY 1921–MAY 1925[a]

Dependent variable	Constant	$\ln F_{t-1}$	$\ln F_{t-2}$	R^2	s.e.	DW
$\ln S_t$(franc/pound)	0.169 (0.179)	0.962 (0.042)	—	0.91	0.07	1.92
$\ln S_t$(franc/pound)	0.177 (0.187)	0.992 (0.144)	− 0.032 (0.147)	0.91	0.07	1.97
$\ln S_t$(dollar/pound)	0.057 (0.056)	0.964 (0.038)	—	0.93	0.02	1.54
$\ln S_t$(dollar/pound)	0.073 (0.057)	1.181 (0.143)	− 0.229 (0.142)	0.93	0.02	2.11
$\ln S_t$(franc/dollar)	0.203 (0.149)	0.928 (0.054)	—	0.85	0.08	1.95
$\ln S_t$(franc/dollar)	0.206 (0.156)	0.945 (0.145)	− 0.018 (0.146)	0.85	0.08	1.98

[a]Standard errors are in parentheses below each coefficient; s.e. is the standard error of the equation; DW is the Durbin–Watson statistic.

[11]With $n = 50$ and with one explanatory variable and a constant, the lower and upper bounds of the 5% confidence level of the Durbin–Watson test statistic are $d_L = 1.50$ and $d_u = 1.59$. The corresponding bounds of the 1% confidence level are $d_L = 1.32$ and $d_u = 1.40$. Thus in all cases at the 1% confidence level we cannot reject the hypothesis that successive residuals are not correlated. At the 5% confidence level we reach the same conclusion in all cases except for the dollar/pound exchange rate for which the value of the Durbin–Watson statistic falls in the inconclusive range. We have also examined higher order correlation up to 12 lags; no correlation of any order was significant.

TABLE 2

EFFICIENCY OF FOREIGN EXCHANGE MARKETS; MONTHLY DATA: FEBRUARY 1921–MAY 1925[a]

Dependent variable	Constant	F_{t-1}	F_{t-2}	R^2	s.e.	DW
S_t(franc/pound)	3.801 (3.335)	0.955 (0.047)	—	0.89	5.43	1.95
S_t(franc/pound)	3.898 (3.500)	0.966 (0.145)	− 0.012 (0.148)	0.89	5.54	1.96
S_t(dollar/pound)	0.159 (0.163)	0.967 (0.037)	—	0.93	0.08	1.56
S_t(dollar/pound)	0.205 (0.167)	1.173 (0.143)	− 0.217 (0.143)	0.93	0.08	2.11
S_t(franc/dollar)	1.470 (0.942)	0.913 (0.059)	—	0.83	1.32	1.91
S_t(franc/dollar)	1.520 (0.990)	0.943 (0.145)	− 0.034 (0.147)	0.83	1.34	1.96

[a]See footnote *a* to Table 1.

We have argued above that in an efficient market, expectations concerning future exchange rates are reflected in forward rates and that spot exchange rates reflect all available information. If forward exchange rates prevailing at period $t-1$ summarize all relevant information available at that period, they should also contain the information summarized in data corresponding to period $t-2$. It thus follows that including additional lagged values of the forward rates in (19) and (19′) should not greatly affect the coefficients of determination and should not yield coefficients significantly different from zero. The results reported in Tables 1 and 2 are consistent with this hypothesis; in all cases the coefficients of F_{t-2} do not differ significantly from zero, and the inclusion of the additional lagged variables has not improved the fit.[12]

[12]To test whether F_{t-1} contains all available information, we have also followed the procedure used by Fama (1975) and included the lagged dependent variable S_{t-1} instead of the additional lagged independent variable F_{t-2}. Since, however, S_{t-1} and F_{t-1} are highly correlated, the resulting point estimates are imprecise. However, as expected, the sums of the coefficients of F_{t-1} and S_{t-1} do not differ significantly from unity. Since movements in both spot and forward rates are dominated by the response to new information, it is clear that S_{t-1} and F_{t-1} would be highly correlated since they summarize information concerning the same period and since they respond at the same time to the same flow of new information. In this sense the use of the pair F_{t-1} and F_{t-2} seems preferable. It is also noteworthy that while the forward rate seems to be an unbiased forecast of the future spot rate, the standard errors of

These results are consistent with our hypotheses about the period under consideration: The markets for foreign exchange seem to have been efficient, and the various forward exchange rates seem to have been unbiased forecasts of the future spot exchange rates. These results support the notion that data from the forward market for foreign exchange provide useful information on the expectations held by market participants. In the following section we use these data as measures of expectations in the analysis of the determinants of exchange rates.

4. Empirical Tests of the Monetary Approach to the Exchange Rate

In this section we incorporate the information about expectations into the estimation of the monetary model of exchange rate determination. We start by analyzing the sample information.

A. Estimates of the Model: Sample Information

The analysis in Section 2 implies that the exchange rate between two currencies can be expressed in terms of domestic and foreign monies, incomes, and the forward premium on foreign exchange, which reflects expectations. Thus, for estimation purposes, the exchange rate between currencies i and j at time t can be written as

$$\ln S_{ijt} = \alpha_{ij}^{0} + \alpha_{ij}^{1} \ln M_{it} + \alpha_{ij}^{2} \ln M_{jt} + \alpha_{ij}^{3} \ln y_{it} + \alpha_{ij}^{4} \ln y_{jt} + \alpha_{ij}^{5} \pi_{ijt} + u_{ijt}, \tag{20}$$

where u_{ijt} is a stochastic disturbance term. In terms of our previous notations, if i denotes the home country and j the foreign country, then $\ln M_i$ refers to $\ln M$, and $\ln M_j$ refers to $\ln M^*$. Analogous notations pertain to real incomes. As indicated above, the prior expectations are that the elasticity of the exchange rate with respect to domestic money supply is unity, while the corresponding elasticity with respect to foreign money supply is minus unity. The discussion concerning currency substitution suggests that we do not have clear prior expectations concerning the

the forecast are nonnegligible. As a matter of fact, only a small fraction of the percentage change in the spot rate is predicted by the lagged forward premium. This phenomenon is typical of the foreign exchange market, as well as of other stock markets where current variation in price reflects primarily the market response to new information [see Mussa (1979) and Frenkel and Mussa (1980)]. On the relationship between forward and spot rates see Fama (1976).

magnitude of the income elasticities, although we expect elasticity with respect to domestic income to be negative and elasticity with respect to foreign income to be positive. Finally, we expect the elasticity of the exchange rate with respect to the forward premium to be positive and to be related to the magnitude of the interest semi-elasticity of the demand for money.[13]

We have examined three pairs of currencies: the franc/pound, the franc/dollar, and the dollar/pound exchange rates. Since, however, only two of these rates are independent due to triangular arbitrage, we analyze in detail only the franc/pound and the franc/dollar exchange rates.[14] Using monthly data on exchange rates, monies, incomes and the forward premiums on foreign exchange, we have estimated (20) in first differences for the two rates.[15] These results are reported in Table 3. As is apparent, the individual parameter estimates are extremely imprecise; we describe our attempt to obtain more precise estimates in Section B. It should be noted, however, that in terms of overall fit, the regression equations as a whole are

TABLE 3

SINGLE-EQUATION LEAST-SQUARES ESTIMATES; MONTHLY DATA: FEBRUARY 1921–MAY 1925[a]

Equation	Constant	$\ln M$	$\ln M^*$	$\ln y$	$\ln y^*$	π	DW	RMSE	Quasi-R^2
Franc/pound	0.004	0.952	− 0.011	0.100	0.974	3.194	2.03	0.067	0.923
	(0.011)	(0.809)	(0.587)	(0.287)	(0.521)	(4.038)			
Franc/dollar	0.004	0.448	0.021	0.235	− 0.456	4.647	1.83	0.074	0.865
	(0.013)	(0.928)	(1.429)	(0.328)	(0.384)	(4.491)			

[a]For the exchange rate between the currencies of countries i and j the estimating equation is

$$\ln S_{ijt} = \alpha_{ij}^0 + \alpha_{ij}^1 \ln M_{it} + \alpha_{ij}^2 \ln M_{jt} + \alpha_{ij}^3 \ln y_{it} + \alpha_{ij}^4 \ln y_{jt} + \alpha_{ij}^5 \pi_{ijt} + u_{ijt},$$

where u_{ijt} is a stochastic disturbance term. In the table $\ln M$ and $\ln M^*$ refer to $\ln M_i$ and $\ln M_j$, respectively; similarly, $\ln y$ and $\ln y^*$ denote $\ln y_i$ and $\ln y_j$, respectively.

To eliminate residual autocorrelation, we have transformed the data by taking first differences. For equation i, root mean square error (RMSE) $= \sqrt{\text{var}(\hat{u}_i)}$, where $\hat{u}_i$ is the residual of that equation, quasi-$R^2 = 1 - \text{var}(\hat{u}_i)/\text{var}(z_i)$, where z_i is the untransformed dependent variable and DW is the Durbin–Watson statistic. Standard errors are given in parentheses below each estimated parameter.

[13]Equation (20) does not distinguish between short-run and long-run equilibrium. To the extent that such a distinction is relevant, the equation would include some lagged values of the variables; and depending on the nature of the dynamics, the error structure would be more complicated.

[14]It should be noted that some of the results obtained for the dollar/pound exchange rate are not in full agreement with the implications of the other two rates. We elaborate on the analysis in Clements and Frenkel (1980).

[15]Details on the data are provided in Appendix B.

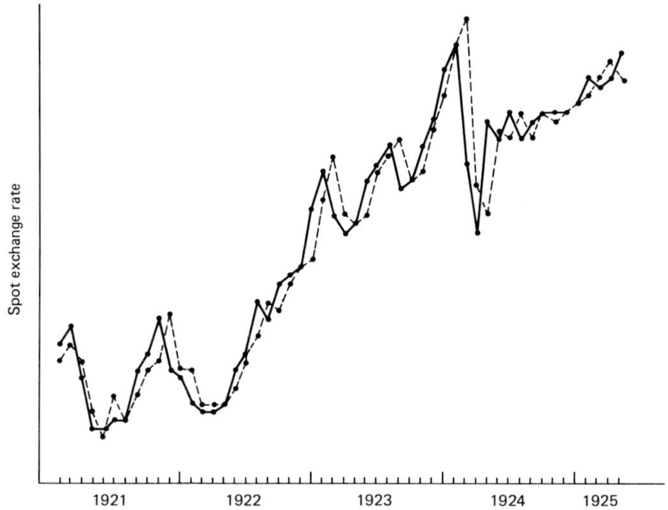

Fig. 1. Franc/pound spot exchange rate: Actual and fitted (single-equation least-squares estimates). Montly data: February 1921–May 1925. Solid line is actual spot exchange rates; broken line is fitted spot exchange rate.

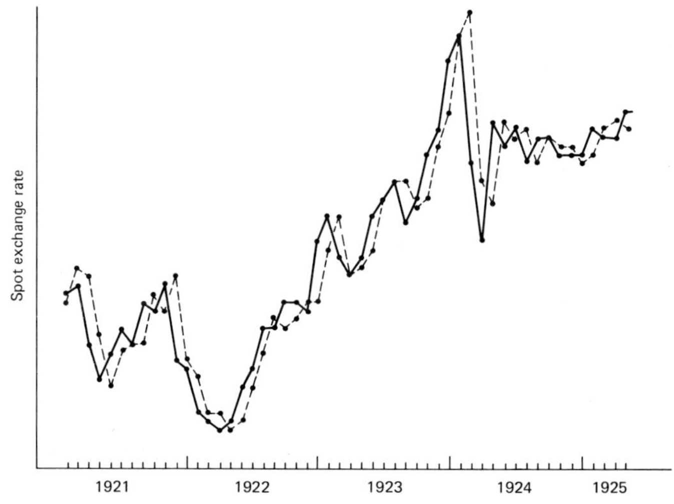

Fig. 2. Franc/dollar spot exchange rates: Actual and fitted (single-equation least-squares estimates). Monthly data: February 1921–May 1925. Solid line is actual spot exchange rate; broken line is fitted spot exchange rate.

somewhat more satisfactory, particularly in view of the fact that the model is estimated using monthly data. Figures 1 and 2 illustrate the overall fit by plotting actual and fitted values of the two exchange rates.[16]

In the foregoing analysis, the equation determining the franc/pound exchange rate was viewed as completely separate from the corresponding equation determining the franc/dollar exchange rate. Implicitly, we assumed that the right-hand side of (20) represents all that there is to know about the specific regression equation. In practice, however, various exchange rates may be subject to common shocks, reflecting the fact that markets are interrelated and that in a fundamental sense, the various exchange rates belong to a global system. To allow for the correlation among disturbances, we viewed the two exchange rates as forming a system of equations and have reestimated the system using Zellner's (1962) method for estimating seemingly unrelated regressions.[17] The estimates are listed in Table 4. As may be seen, the qualitative results are similar to those of the single-equation estimates: The individual parameter estimates are extremely imprecise (even though each parameter estimate has the predicted sign), and the overall fit is reasonably satisfactory. In what follows we attempt to improve the precision of the individual parameter estimates.

TABLE 4

SEEMINGLY UNRELATED ESTIMATES; MONTHLY DATA: FEBRUARY 1921–MAY 1925[a]

Equation	Constant	$\ln M$	$\ln M^*$	$\ln y$	$\ln y^*$	π	DW	RMSE	Quasi-R^2	ω
Franc/pound	0.006	1.021	−0.121	0.202	−0.024	1.163	1.93	0.072	0.910	0.973
	(0.011)	(0.808)	(0.239)	(0.280)	(0.216)	(3.639)				
Franc/dollar	0.005	0.634	−0.321	0.166	−0.197	2.575	1.91	0.074	0.863	
	(0.012)	(0.903)	(0.594)	(0.311)	(0.157)	(4.005)				

[a]The model is given in footnote *a* to Table 3. ω is the estimated correlation coefficient between the residuals of the two equations. For the meaning of the other notation, see the footnote to Table 3. To eliminate residual autocorrelation, we have transformed the data by taking first differences. Standard errors are given in parentheses below each estimated parameter.

[16]In computing the fitted values of the exchange rate we have added the fitted change in the exchange rate (from Table 3) to the actual level of the exchange rate in the previous period; thus, in effect, we have computed the one-period forecast. The dynamic simulations reported in Table 7 deal with the multiperiod forecast.

[17]This procedure allows for both heteroscedasticity and correlation across equations by applying the Aitken estimator to the model when it is stacked equation by equation.

B. Combining Sample and Prior Information

Due to the relatively small sample, the limited degree of variation in the series, and the high degree of colinearity the information in the sample is not sufficient to provide precise estimates of the various parameters; it can at best only provide estimates of the overall fit of the various regression equations. A proper procedure for obtaining more precise estimates would be to supplement the sample information with some prior information. In incorporating the prior information one may follow Bayesian procedures or, alternatively, apply the mixed estimation procedure.[18] In what follows we implement the mixed estimation procedure, which, as is shown in Appendix A, may be given a Bayesian interpretation.

We turn now to the specification of the prior information. The homogeneity postulate (together with other studies of the relationship among money, prices, and the exchange rate) yields prior information on the elasticity of the exchange rate with repect to domestic and foreign monies. Evidence on the demand for money provides prior information on the elasticity of the exchange rate with respect to the forward premium. The prior knowledge is formulated in terms of stochastic restrictions on these elasticities whereby it is assumed that

$$\begin{aligned}
r_{ij}^1 &= \alpha_{ij}^1 + v_{ij}, \qquad E(v_{ij}) = 0, \qquad E\left(v_{ij}^2\right) = 0.01 \qquad \text{for all} \quad i \text{ and } j, \\
&\qquad E(v_{ij}v_{i'j'}) = 0 \qquad \text{for all} \quad i \neq i', \quad j \neq j', \\
r_{ij}^2 &= \alpha_{ij}^2 + w_{ij}, \qquad E(w_{ij}) = 0, \qquad E\left(w_{ij}^2\right) = 0.01 \qquad \text{for all} \quad i \text{ and } j, \\
&\qquad E(w_{ij}w_{i'j'}) = 0 \qquad \text{for all} \quad i \neq i', \quad j \neq j', \\
&\qquad E(v_{ij}w_{i'j'}) = 0 \qquad \text{for all} \quad i, i', j, j',
\end{aligned} \tag{21}$$

where r_{ij} is the random prior estimate of the corresponding elasticity. It is further assumed that the homogeneity postulate generally holds and thus, consistent with other studies on the relationship between money prices and the exchange rate, our prior estimates of the elasticities of the exchange rate with respect to domestic and foreign money supplies are unity and minus unity, respectively. However, we allow for some uncertainty about these parameter values by including the random terms v and w, which are assumed to be distributed normally with a zero mean and a variance of

[18] For details on the mixed estimation procedure see Theil and Goldberger (1961), Theil (1963), and Theil (1971, Chap. 7); see also Appendix A. For an application of the mixed estimation procedure to the analysis of the DM/pound exchange rate between 1972 and 1976, see Bilson (1978).

0.01. Thus, using the 2-sigma range, the approximate 95% confidence intervals for r_{ij}^1 and r_{ij}^2 are (0.8, 1.2) and (−0.8, −1.2), respectively.

The prior knowledge about the elasticity of the exchange rate with respect to the forward premium stems from estimates of the demand for money and is formulated in a similar fashion. It is assumed that

$$\begin{aligned} r_{ij}^5 = \alpha_{ij}^5 + s_{ij}, \quad E(s_{ij}) = 0, \quad E(s_{ij}^2) = 1.00 \quad &\text{for all} \quad i \text{ and } j, \\ E(s_{ij}s_{i'j'}) = 0 \quad &\text{for all} \quad i \neq i', \ j \neq j', \\ E(v_{ij}s_{i'j'}) = E(w_{ij}s_{s'j'}) = 0 \quad &\text{for all} \quad i, i', j, j'. \end{aligned} \tag{22}$$

Our prior estimate of the coefficient on the forward premium is 4. In terms of (9), with a monthly interest rate of 1%, this amounts to an interest elasticity of the demand for money of −0.04. This is consistent with Goldfeld's (1973) estimates for the United States. The variance of the disturbance terms s implies that the 95% confidence interval for the prior estimate of the interest elasticity of the demand for money is approximately (−0.02, −0.06).[19]

The basic idea underlying the mixed estimation method is to combine the prior information about some of the parameters with the information contained in the sample. The prior information has been summarized in (21) and (22), and the sample information has been summarized in Tables 3 and 4. The mixed estimation procedure combines these two sources of information. Since neither of these two sources provides complete information about the coefficients, the estimates implied by the two sources may differ. Therefore, prior to implementing the mixed-estimation procedure, it is important to verify that the sample and the prior information are compatible. Under the null hypothesis that the sample and the prior information are compatible, the relevant test is a χ^2 test with degrees of freedom corresponding to the number of restrictions. We obtained χ^2 values of 2.88 and 0.74 for the franc/pound and the franc/dollar exchange rates, while the critical value for $\chi^2(3)$ at the 0.05 level is 7.82. Thus, since we cannot reject the compatibility hypothesis, we proceed with combining the two sources of information by implementing the mixed estimation procedure to the first differences of the data. Details on the estimation procedure are provided in Appendix A.

The resulting mixed estimates for the two exchange rates are reported in Table 5. As may be seen, the results are consistent with the predictions of the monetary model. For both exchange rates the constant terms do not differ significantly from zero. This indicates that when the economic variables are accounted for there is no autonomous trend in the exchange

[19] In terms of the currency substitution model presented in (18) this amounts to an interest elasticity of −0.02 with a 95% confidence interval of (−0.01, −0.03).

TABLE 5

SINGLE-EQUATION MIXED ESTIMATES; MONTHLY DATA: FEBRUARY 1921–MAY 1925[a]

Equation	Constant	ln M	ln M^*	ln y	ln y^*	π	DW	RMSE	Quasi-R^2	χ^{2b}
Franc/pound	0.001	0.999	− 0.972	0.188	0.926	3.914	1.86	0.069	0.917	2.88
	(0.010)	(0.099)	(0.099)	(0.281)	(0.520)	(0.970)				(7.82)
Franc/dollar	0.006	0.995	− 0.995	0.255	− 0.369	3.971	1.81	0.074	0.860	0.74
	(0.011)	(0.099)	(0.100)	(0.327)	(0.370)	(0.974)				(7.82)

[a] The model is given in footnote a to Table 3. The following stochastic prior information is used in estimation: $r_{ij}^1 = \alpha_{ij}^1 + v_{ij}$, $E(v_{ij}) = 0$, $E(v_{ij}^2) = 0.01 \ \forall \ i, j$; $E(v_{ij}v_{i'j'}) = 0 \ \forall \ i \neq i', j \neq j'$; $r_{ij}^2 = \alpha_{ij}^2 + w_{ij}$, $E(w_{ij}) = 0$, $E(w_{ij}^2) = 0.01 \ \forall \ i, j$; $E(w_{ij}w_{i'j'}) = 0 \ \forall \ i \neq i', j \neq j'$; $E(w_{ij}v_{i'j'}) = 0 \ \forall \ i, i', j, j'$; $r_{ij}^5 = \alpha_{ij}^5 + s_{ij}$, $E(s_{ij}) = 0$, $E(s_{ij}^2) = 1.00 \ \forall \ i, j$; $E(s_{ij}s_{i'j'}) = 0 \ \forall \ i \neq i', j \neq j'$; $E(s_{ij}w_{i'j'}) = E(s_{ij}v_{i'j'}) = 0 \ \forall \ i, i', j, j'$. The r_{ij}^k are random prior estimates of the α_{ij}^k and the v_{ij}, w_{ij}, and s_{ij} are stochastic disturbances. Our prior point estimate of $[\alpha_{ij}^1\alpha_{ij}^2\alpha_{ij}^5]$ is $[1, -1, 4]$. For further details, see text.

To eliminate residual autocorrelation, we have transformed the data by taking first differences. For the meaning of the notation see the footnote to Table 3. Standard errors are given in parentheses below each estimated parameter.

[b] The χ^2 statistic gives the result of testing the null hypothesis that the sample information as summarized by the single-equation least-squares estimates given in Table 3 and the stochastic prior information given in the previous footnote are compatible. Under the null hypothesis, the test statistic is distributed as $\chi^2(q)$, where q is the number of stochastic restrictions. Critical values of the χ^2 distribution at the 0.05 level are given in parentheses. The null hypothesis is rejected when the value of the test statistic exceeds the critical value. Details of the test are given in Theil (1971, pp. 350–351).

TABLE 6

SYSTEMS MIXED ESTIMATES; MONTHLY DATA: FEBRUARY 1921–MAY 1925[a]

Equation	Constant	ln M	ln M^*	ln y	ln y^*	π	DW	RMSE	Quasi-R^2	ω	χ^{2} [b]
Franc/pound	0.003	1.021	−0.866	0.271	−0.080	3.587	1.81	0.071	0.913		
	(0.010)	(0.096)	(0.092)	(0.277)	(0.213)	(0.876)					
										0.954	14.72
											(12.59)
Franc/dollar	0.006	0.979	−0.982	0.179	−0.129	4.190	1.87	0.075	0.862		
	(0.011)	(0.097)	(0.099)	(0.309)	(0.152)	(0.891)					

[a]The model and the stochastic prior information used in estimation are given in the footnotes to Tables 3 and 5. The systems estimator allows for cross-equation correlation of the disturbances. To eliminate residual autocorrelation, we have transformed the data by taking first differences. For the meaning of the notation see the footnotes to Tables 3 and 4. Standard errors are given in parentheses below each estimated parameter.

[b]The χ^2 statistic gives the results of testing the null hypothesis that the sample information as summarized by the seemingly unrelated estimates given in Table 4 and the stochastic prior information given in footnote *a* to Table 5 are compatible. The critical value of the χ^2 distribution at the 0.01 level is 16.81. For further details of the test see footnote *b* to Table 5.

rates. Also, for both exchange rates the elasticities with respect to domestic and foreign money supplies are unity and minus unity, respectively. These estimates are about ten times the size of the corresponding standard errors. The semi-elasticities of the exchange rates with respect to the forward premiums are about 4. This is about four times the size of the corresponding standard errors. The high level of significance of the parameter estimates reflects the fact that the sample provides very little information concerning the magnitude of the individual parameters. In consequence, a high weight is given to prior information in computing parameter estimates.[20] The income elasticities in Table 5 are not significant at the 95% confidence level. In the only case in which the income elasticity comes close to being significant (foreign income in the franc/pound exchange rate), it has the correct positive sign. The low values of the income elasticities may reflect a poor measure of income,[21] as well as some of the implications of diversified currency portfolios outlined in Section 2.

In an analogous manner to the procedure of the single-equation analysis we have also applied the mixed estimation procedure to the system of equations, using the method for estimating seemingly unrelated regressions. The results, which are reported in Table 6, are similar to those of the single-equation estimates: The estimates are consistent with the predictions of the monetary model of exchange rate determination. The constant terms do not differ significantly from zero; both the forward premiums and the elasticities of the exchange rates with respect to domestic and foreign money supplies are significant and have the expected size, and all income elasticities have the expected sign even though, as before, they are not significant. Table 6 also shows the correlation coefficient between the residuals of the two exchange rate equations. The high correlation (0.954) indicates the potential gain from the application of the estimation method of seemingly unrelated equations.[22]

[20] The fact that the sample provides very little information suggests that the data would also be compatible with different values of the prior information. It seems therefore that even though the sample from the 1920s is consistent with the predictions of the monetary approach, the test is not sufficiently powerful since the sample does not contain sufficient information for discriminating among alternative approaches.

[21] We have also estimated these equations using some measure of permanent income (a distributed lag of the measure of current income) instead of the income variable used here. The resulting income elasticities did not differ significantly from zero.

[22] It might be noted that in this case the χ^2 statistic testing for compatibility of the sample and prior information is 14.72 which exceeds 12.59—the critical value of $\chi^2(6)$ at the 0.05 level; it is, however, smaller than 16.81—the corresponding critical value at the 0.01 level. Note that the quasi-R^2 for each equation is only suggestive since, strictly speaking, the goodness of fit should be analyzed for the system as a whole.

TABLE 7

IN-SAMPLE DYNAMIC SIMULATION OF EXCHANGE RATE LEVELS; MONTHLY DATA: FEBRUARY 1921–MAY 1925[a]

Estimated parameters used in simulation and exchange rate	Squared correlation coefficient between actual and simulated	Mean error	Root mean square error	Mean absolute error	Theil's inequality coefficient
Single-equation least-squares estimates (Table 3)					
Franc/pound	0.887	0.018	0.082	0.063	0.010
Franc/dollar	0.634	−0.047	0.136	0.099	0.025
Seemingly unrelated estimates (Table 4)					
Franc/pound	0.854	−0.023	0.099	0.079	0.012
Franc/dollar	0.683	−0.059	0.139	0.100	0.025
Single-equation mixed estimates (Table 5)					
Franc/pound	0.893	0.007	0.079	0.058	0.009
Franc/dollar	0.558	−0.069	0.155	0.114	0.028
Systems mixed estimates (Table 6)					
Franc/pound	0.862	−0.034	0.102	0.078	0.012
Franc/dollar	0.616	−0.080	0.159	0.116	0.029

[a]The model is simulated dynamically by computing the predicted value of the exchange rate level as the simulated value of the previous period's level plus the predicted change for the current period. Recall that the model is estimated in first differences. Since the simulations refer to the logarithm of the exchange rate levels, the error statistics are percentages when multiplied by 100.

C. Dynamic Simulations of the Model

We now investigate how well the estimated models track the (log of the) levels of the exchange rates over the sample period. We simulate the model dynamically by taking only the initial value of the exchange rate as given and taking the simulated value to be the predicted rate of change plus the lagged (log of the) exchange rate as *predicted* by the model for the previous month. It should be emphasized that this dynamic simulation is a severe test of the predictive ability of the model since simulation errors may accumulate over time.

Table 7 contains the results of these dynamic simulations for the various models, using parameter estimates derived from the single-equation and the system-estimation methods.[23] As may be seen, the various models perform reasonably well. The mean error for the franc/pound exchange rate ranges from 0.7 to −3.4%, while the mean error for the franc/dollar exchange rate ranges from −4.7 to −8.0%. In general, the simulations of the franc/pound rate perform better than those of the franc/dollar rate. On the whole there is no marked difference between the performance of simulations based on the sample estimates and those based on the mixed estimates. This result is noteworthy since it highlights the fact that the sample does provide satisfactory information on the overall relationship and that the application of the mixed estimation procedure is aimed at improving the precision of the individual parameter estimates. Comparison of the performance of the single-equation estimates with those of the system estimates shows that the simulations based on the single equations perform somewhat better.

Table 7 also gives Theil's inequality coefficient. Its extremely low value indicates the reasonable quality of the predictive ability of the model.[24]

5. Concluding Remarks

The evolution of the international monetary system into a regime of floating exchange rates has led to a renewed interest in the economics of exchange rates, which has resulted in new developments in the theory of

[23]The simulation program we use is PREDIC, written by Clifford R. Wymer.

[24]Theil's inequality coefficient measures the quality of forecasts. Consider a series of prediction $P_1, \ldots, P_n$ and a series of outcomes $A_1, \ldots, A_n$. The inequality coefficient, which is bounded between zero and one, is

$$U = \sqrt{\frac{1}{n}\sum(P_i - A_i)^2} \Big/ \left(\sqrt{\frac{1}{n}\sum P_i^2} + \sqrt{\frac{1}{n}\sum A_i^2}\right).$$

Thus, in the case of perfect forecast, $P_i = A_i$ and $U = 0$, while at the other extreme $U = 1$.

exchange rate determination. The central insight of the monetary approach to the exchange rate is that the exchange rate is a financial variable determined in a macroeconomic setting. Thus, being a relative price of two monies, it is determined in a manner similar to that by which other asset prices are determined. Equilibrium is attained when the existing stocks are willingly held, and one of the important determinants of current prices is expectations concerning the future course of events. From the policy perspective the monetary approach to the exchange rate serves as a reminder that the exchange rate and the conduct of monetary policy are intimately linked to each other and that, as a first approximation, policies that affect the trend of domestic (relative to foreign) monetary growth affect the exchange rate in the same manner.

Since current views concerning the operation of flexible exchange rate systems are based, to a large extent, on the experience of the 1920s, we have chosen to reexamine the determinants of exchange rates during the 1920s from the analytical perspective of the monetary approach. Having developed a simple model of exchange rate determination, we examined the efficiency of the foreign exchange markets and estimated the model using monthly data. We found that the foreign exchange markets were efficient and that the forward exchange rate was an unbiased forecast of the future spot rate. We then used the forward premium on foreign exchange as a measure of expectations in estimating the monetary model of the exchange rate. The various results were consistent with the theoretical predictions, but the sample did not seem to contain sufficient information to make it possible to reject the predictions of alternative models.

Rather than summarizing the results we wish to highlight some of the methodological issues raised by the empirical work. The first involves the use of monthly data for the analysis of a macroeconomic phenomenon. Since it is believed that asset markets clear relatively fast, it is desirable to use frequent observations. We used monthly data since this is the shortest maturity for which data on forward contracts are available. Second, following Frenkel (1976, 1977), we used data from the forward market for foreign exchange as direct market measures of expectations. Third, since the various exchange rates may be subject to common shocks, it might be desirable to supplement single-equation estimates with system estimates. Fourth, since the various determinants of the exchange rate may not display sufficient variation and/or are likely to be highly colinear (like the time series of two national money supplies and incomes), estimates of individual parameters might be imprecise. In such cases it is desirable to apply techniques such as the mixed estimation procedure or Bayesian approaches, which complement the sample information with prior information. Using the monetary model, the prior information derives from the homogeneity postulate and from known properties of the demand for money.

One of the characteristics of the estimated model has been the assumption that purchasing power parities and money market equilibrium were maintained throughout the sample period. A useful extension would allow for a distinction between short-run and long-run equilibria and would examine the dynamics of adjustment. Another useful extension would examine the experience from the 1970s in the light of the lessons from the 1920s. The study of the recent evolution of exchange rates in the light of the lessons from the 1920s is of special interest since world capital markets have become much more integrated, the role of "real" shocks has become much more important (particularly in the 1970s), the roles of both tariff and nontariff barriers to trade and the degree of exchange rate management have changed, and the International Monetary Fund has been created.

Appendix A. Estimation Procedures

In this appendix we outline some of the details of the estimation procedures for incorporating prior knowledge with the sample information. We start with the mixed estimation procedure and then provide a Bayesian interpretation of the estimator.

Let the T vector of observations on the dependent variable y be generated according to

$$y = X\beta + u; \qquad u \sim N(0, \sigma^2 I_T), \tag{A1}$$

where X is a matrix of observations on the k independent variables, β is a parameter vector, and u is a disturbance vector. The stochastic prior information on the parameter values can be written as

$$r = R\beta + v; \qquad E(v) = 0, \qquad E(vv') = V, \qquad E(uv') = 0, \tag{A2}$$

where r is a vector of random prior estimates of $R\beta$, R is a known matrix, and v is an error vector. Combining (A1) and (A2) yields

$$\tilde{y} = \tilde{X}\beta + \tilde{u}; \qquad E(\tilde{u}) = 0, \qquad E(\tilde{u}\tilde{u}') = \Omega, \tag{A3}$$

in which

$$\tilde{y} = [y' \mid r']', \quad \tilde{X} = [X' \mid R']', \quad \tilde{u} = [u' \mid v']', \quad \text{and} \quad \Omega = \left[\begin{array}{c|c} \sigma^2 I_T & 0 \\ \hline 0' & V \end{array}\right].$$

Applying the Aitken principle to (A3) gives the mixed estimator of β:

$$\tilde{\beta} = (\tilde{X}'\Omega^{-1}\tilde{X})^{-1}\tilde{X}'\Omega^{-1}\tilde{y} = (R'V^{-1}R + X'X/\sigma^2)^{-1}(R'V^{-1}r + X'y/\sigma^2). \tag{A4}$$

The covariance matrix of $\tilde{\beta}$ is

$$V(\tilde{\beta}) = (R'V^{-1}R + X'X/\sigma^2)^{-1}.$$

To make these expressions operational, the unknown parameter σ^2 is replaced by an estimate. [For further details, see, e.g., Theil (1971, pp. 346–352).]

The mixed estimator can also be viewed in a Bayesian framework. The expression given in (A4) is the mean of the conditional (in the sense indicated below) posterior density of the parameter vector when the prior distribution is normal. To show this, let $\bar{\beta}$ and A^{-1} be the prior mean and covariance matrix of β, and let the prior density be multivariate normal:

$$\begin{aligned} p(\beta) &= (2\pi)^{-k/2}|A|^{1/2}\exp\left[-\tfrac{1}{2}(\beta-\bar{\beta})'A(\beta-\bar{\beta})\right] \\ &\propto \exp\left[-\tfrac{1}{2}(\beta-\bar{\beta})'A(\beta-\bar{\beta})\right], \end{aligned} \tag{A5}$$

where $\propto$ denotes proportionality. Assuming that the disturbance variance in (A1) σ^2 is known and denoting its known value by σ_0^2, the likelihood function associated with (A1) is

$$\begin{aligned} p(y\,|\,\beta,\sigma_0^2,X) &\propto \exp\left[-(2\sigma_0^2)^{-1}(y-X\beta)'(y-X\beta)\right] \\ &\propto \exp\left[-(2\sigma_0^2)^{-1}(\beta-\hat{\beta})'X'X(\beta-\hat{\beta})\right], \end{aligned} \tag{A6}$$

where

$$\hat{\beta} = (X'X)^{-1}X'y. \tag{A7}$$

Using Bayes's theorem to combine the prior density (A5) and the likelihood function (A6), we obtain the following conditional posterior density:

$$\begin{aligned} p(\beta\,|\,\sigma_0^2,y,X) &\propto p(\beta)p(y\,|\,\beta,\sigma_0^2,X) \\ &\propto \exp\left\{-\tfrac{1}{2}\left[(\beta-\hat{\beta})'X'X(\beta-\hat{\beta})/\sigma_0^2 \right.\right. \\ &\qquad \left.\left. +(\beta-\bar{\beta})'A(\beta-\bar{\beta})\right]\right\} \\ &\propto \exp\left[-\tfrac{1}{2}\left(\beta-\bar{\bar{\beta}}\right)'(A+X'X/\sigma_0^2)\left(\beta-\bar{\bar{\beta}}\right)\right], \end{aligned} \tag{A8}$$

where

$$\bar{\bar{\beta}} = (A+X'X/\sigma_0^2)^{-1}(A\bar{\beta}+X'X\hat{\beta}/\sigma_0^2). \tag{A.9}$$

Thus from (A8), the conditional posterior distribution of β is normal with the following mean and covariance matrix:

$$E(\beta) = \bar{\bar{\beta}}, \qquad V(\beta) = (A+X'X/\sigma_0^2)^{-1}.$$

The conditional posterior mean given in (A9) is a matrix weighted average of the prior mean $\bar{\beta}$ and the least squares estimator $\hat{\beta}$ defined in (A7). The weight matrices are the relative precisions of $\bar{\beta}$ and $\hat{\beta}$: the information contained in the data is given a larger weight the greater is its relative precision. The weight matrices are both positive definite, and they sum to the identity matrix.

The expression given in (A9) corresponds to the mixed estimator (A4) with $R = I_k$, $V = A^{-1}$, $\sigma^2 = \sigma_0^2$, and $r = \bar{\beta}$, hence the Bayesian interpretation. This analysis of the single-equation case generalizes to multiple-equation systems (such as in our application).

The Bayesian interpretation can also be extended to the situation in which σ^2 is an unknown parameter. Assuming that $\ln \sigma$ has a uniform prior distribution together with the normal prior for β, it can be shown that the quantity given in (A9) is the mean of the leading normal term in an asymptotic expansion approximating the posterior distribution of β. [For details, see Zellner (1971b, Chap. 4).] Thus in this case the previous interpretation of the mixed estimator applies approximately.

For an analysis of Bayesian and alternative approaches see Zellner (1971a).

Appendix B. The Data Base

In this appendix we give the detailed definitions of all the variables in the data base, the primary data sources, and a listing of the entire data base. The data base is made up of 53 monthly observations on each variable for the period January 1921–May 1925.

We use the following country subscripting convention: France, the United States, and the United Kingdom are denoted by the subscripts 1, 2, and 3, respectively.

1. Exchange Rates and Forward Premiums

The franc/pound and dollar/pound spot rates are taken from the weekly rates given in Einzig (1937, Appendix 1, pp. 450–458). We take the rate quoted nearest the end of the month as the monthly rate.

The spot franc/dollar rate is computed as the ratio of the spot franc/pound rate to the spot dollar/pound rate. That is, we use the triangular arbitrage condition.

The three spot exchange rates are given in Table B1. Here, we use S_{ij} to denote the spot rate between the currency of country i and that of country j. The term S_{ij} is the cost of a unit of the currency of country j in terms of the currency of country i. Country i can be thought of as the home country

TABLE B1

SPOT EXCHANGE RATES[a]

Year and month		S_{13}	S_{23}	S_{12}
1921	1	54.3700	3.8600	14.0855
	2	54.9800	3.8700	14.2067
	3	56.5800	3.9200	14.4337
	4	51.1900	3.9600	12.9268
	5	46.7000	3.8950	11.9897
	6	46.7400	3.7300	12.5308
	7	46.9200	3.5625	13.1705
	8	47.6500	3.6875	12.9220
	9	52.3500	3.7350	14.0161
	10	54.0000	3.9250	13.7580
	11	57.8000	3.9850	14.5044
	12	51.8800	4.2150	12.3084
1922	1	51.8000	4.2500	12.1882
	2	49.3000	4.3975	11.2109
	3	48.5000	4.3850	11.0604
	4	48.2700	4.4225	10.9146
	5	48.8700	4.4500	10.9820
	6	52.1600	4.4025	11.8478
	7	54.1700	4.4475	12.1799
	8	59.4000	4.4725	13.2812
	9	57.7700	4.3700	13.2197
	10	62.1500	4.4625	13.9272
	11	62.9700	4.5000	13.9933
	12	63.5700	4.6350	13.7152
1923	1	72.2500	4.6400	15.5711
	2	77.6000	4.7150	16.4581
	3	70.4000	4.6750	15.0588
	4	68.2200	4.6350	14.7185
	5	69.8700	4.6250	15.1070
	6	75.6200	4.5725	16.5380
	7	77.9000	4.5850	16.9902
	8	80.3500	4.5550	17.6400
	9	74.1700	4.5525	16.2922
	10	75.9200	4.5000	16.8711
	11	80.8700	4.3650	18.5269
	12	84.8200	4.3375	19.5551
1924	1	94.2500	4.2275	22.2945
	2	99.7500	4.3125	23.1304
	3	78.4500	4.3000	18.2442
	4	68.7500	4.3825	15.6874
	5	84.4000	4.3050	19.6051
	6	81.8000	4.3200	18.9352
	7	86.1200	4.4000	19.5727
	8	82.1200	4.5025	18.2388
	9	84.8000	4.4725	18.9603
	10	86.2000	4.4900	19.1982
	11	85.8200	4.6225	18.5657

(*continues*)

TABLE B1 (*continued*)

Year and month		S_{13}	S_{23}	S_{12}
	12	87.2700	4.7125	18.5188
1925	1	88.4000	4.7950	18.4359
	2	92.5700	4.7600	19.4475
	3	90.6000	4.7775	18.9639
	4	92.6000	4.8125	19.2416
	5	96.9200	4.8600	19.9424
Sample mean		69.2245	4.3651	15.7676
Standard deviation		16.2619	0.3202	3.1220

[a] See text for meaning of notation and data sources.

and j as the foreign country. For example, using our subscripting convention, S_{13} is the spot franc/pound rate. A rise in S_{13} means that the franc has depreciated relative to the pound.

The one month forward exchange rate for both the franc/pound and dollar/pound are also from Einzig (1937, Appendix 1, pp. 450–458). We again use the forward rate quoted for the last week in a month as that month's forward rate. The one month forward franc/dollar rate is computed from the triangular arbitrage relationship, as before.

The three one month forward rates are given in Table B2. Here F_{ij} is

TABLE B2

ONE MONTH FORWARD EXCHANGE RATES[a]

Year and month		F_{13}	F_{23}	F_{12}
1921	1	54.0700	3.87750	13.9446
	2	54.6800	3.88250	14.0837
	3	56.3100	3.92500	14.3465
	4	51.0400	3.96188	12.8828
	5	46.6200	3.90375	11.9424
	6	46.6600	3.73625	12.4885
	7	46.9600	3.56750	13.1633
	8	47.6800	3.69125	12.9170
	9	52.3600	3.73625	14.0141
	10	54.0300	3.93000	13.7481
	11	57.8200	3.99000	14.4912
	12	51.8900	4.21687	12.3053
1922	1	51.7900	4.25062	12.1841
	2	49.2950	4.39812	11.2082
	3	48.5000	4.38500	11.0604
	4	48.2775	4.42281	10.9156
	5	48.8800	4.45125	10.9812
	6	52.1800	4.40344	11.8498
	7	54.2500	4.45062	12.1893

(*continues*)

TABLE B2 (*continued*)

Year and month	F_{13}	F_{23}	F_{12}
8	59.5100	4.47500	13.2983
9	57.8000	4.37375	13.2152
10	62.2500	4.46875	13.9301
11	63.0700	4.51000	13.9845
12	63.6000	4.64625	13.6885
1923 1	72.3200	4.65000	15.5527
2	77.7000	4.72500	16.4444
3	70.4900	4.68500	15.0459
4	68.2500	4.64375	14.6972
5	69.9050	4.63375	15.0861
6	75.6800	4.57875	16.5285
7	77.9400	4.58875	16.9850
8	80.3950	4.55718	17.6414
9	74.2000	4.55625	16.2853
10	75.9650	4.50437	16.8647
11	80.9700	4.37187	18.5207
12	84.8650	4.34250	19.5429
1924 1	94.5200	4.23375	22.3254
2	100.3300	4.31625	23.2447
3	79.5700	4.30062	18.5020
4	68.9500	4.38437	15.7263
5	85.1000	4.30625	19.7620
6	82.1000	4.31937	19.0074
7	86.1900	4.39375	19.6165
8	82.1900	4.49687	18.2772
9	84.8900	4.46687	19.0044
10	86.3300	4.48687	19.2406
11	86.0700	4.62219	18.6211
12	87.7400	4.71281	18.6173
1925 1	88.6800	4.79562	18.4919
2	93.0500	4.76062	19.5458
3	90.9000	4.77687	19.0292
4	93.1300	4.80937	19.3643
5	97.4700	4.85625	20.0710
Sample mean	69.3474	4.3685	15.7825
Standard deviation	16.4215	0.3190	3.1607

[a] See text for meaning of notation and data sources.

used to denote the one month forward rate between the currency of country i and that of country j. The interpretation of F_{ij} is exactly analogous to that for S_{ij} given previously.

The one month forward premium π_{ij} is computed as

$$\pi_{ij} = \ln(F_{ij}/S_{ij}), \qquad j > i; \qquad i, j = 1, 2, 3.$$

Hence π_{ij} is the proportion by which the one month forward rate exceeds the current spot rate. A positive value of π_{ij} means that the currency of country j for delivery in one month's time is selling at a premium relative to the currency of country i—that is, the home country's currency is expected to depreciate relative to that of country j.

The forward premiums are given in Table B3. Notice that for each month, apart from rounding errors, the franc/dollar forward premium π_{12} is exactly the difference between the franc/pound and the dollar/pound premiums π_{13} and π_{23}. This is because the triangular arbitrage relation is used to construct both the spot and forward rates for the franc/dollar.

TABLE B3

ONE MONTH FORWARD PREMIUMS[a]

Year and month		π_{13}	π_{23}	π_{12}
1921	1	−0.553319	0.452420	−1.005740
	2	−0.547120	0.322437	−0.869557
	3	−0.478362	0.127506	−0.605867
	4	−0.293446	0.047302	−0.340748
	5	−0.171471	0.224400	−0.395870
	6	−0.171280	0.167465	−0.338744
	7	0.085258	0.140190	−0.054932
	8	0.062942	0.101662	−0.038720
	9	0.019074	0.033379	−0.014305
	10	0.055504	0.127220	−0.071716
	11	0.034523	0.125313	−0.090790
	12	0.019264	0.044441	−0.025177
1922	1	−0.019264	0.014687	−0.033951
	2	−0.010109	0.014210	−0.024319
	3	0.000000	0.000000	0.000000
	4	0.015545	0.007057	0.008488
	5	0.020504	0.028038	−0.007534
	6	0.038338	0.021267	0.017071
	7	0.147629	0.070190	0.077438
	8	0.184917	0.055885	0.129032
	9	0.051975	0.085735	−0.033760
	10	0.160789	0.139999	0.020790
	11	0.158691	0.221920	−0.063229
	12	0.047111	0.242424	−0.195312
1923	1	0.096798	0.215244	−0.118446
	2	0.128746	0.211906	−0.083160
	3	0.127697	0.213623	−0.085926
	4	0.043964	0.188637	−0.144672
	5	0.050068	0.188923	−0.138855
	6	0.079250	0.136566	−0.057316

(*continues*)

TABLE B3 (*continued*)

Year and month		π_{13}	π_{23}	π_{12}
	7	0.051308	0.081825	– 0.030517
	8	0.055981	0.047970	0.008011
	9	0.040436	0.082397	– 0.041962
	10	0.059318	0.097179	– 0.037861
	11	0.123596	0.157356	– 0.033760
	12	0.053024	0.115204	– 0.062180
1924	1	0.286007	0.147724	0.138283
	2	0.579736	0.086879	0.492857
	3	1.417540	0.014496	1.403040
	4	0.290489	0.042725	0.247764
	5	0.825974	0.028992	0.796983
	6	0.366116	– 0.014496	0.380611
	7	0.081253	– 0.142193	0.223446
	8	0.085163	– 0.125027	0.210190
	9	0.106049	– 0.125885	0.231934
	10	0.150681	– 0.069618	0.220299
	11	0.290871	– 0.006771	0.297642
	12	0.537108	0.006676	0.530432
1925	1	0.316238	0.013065	0.303172
	2	0.517178	0.013065	0.504112
	3	0.330544	– 0.013161	0.343704
	4	0.570773	– 0.064945	0.635717
	5	0.565812	– 0.077152	0.642965
Sample mean		0.133687	0.080497	0.053190
Standard deviation		0.313671	0.112800	0.378781

[a]See text for meaning of notation and data sources. All entries are to be divided by 100.

2. Money Supplies

For the French money supply, we use the Bank of France note circulation as quoted by Tinbergen (1934, pp. 66–67, column 17). The units of the French money supply are milliards of francs.

The U.S. money supply variable is currency held by the public, plus demand and time deposits at commercial banks ("M_2"), taken from Friedman and Schwartz (1970, pp. 19–23, column 9). The units of this variable are thousands of millions of dollars.

Our U.K. money supply variable is the total deposits of the London Clearing Banks. The available monthly series does not include total deposits of all banks. The London Clearing Banks accounted, on average, for

78% of total deposits in the U.K. during the interwar years [see Howson (1975, p. 146)]. The source for this is the Committee on Finance and Industry (1931, pp. 285–287). Here the units are tens of millions of pounds.

The three money supplies are given in Table B4. Here M_i denotes the money supply of country i.

TABLE B4

MONEY SUPPLIES[a]

Year and month		M_1	M_2	M_3
1921	1	37.90	34.21	179.40
	2	37.80	33.93	174.10
	3	38.40	33.37	169.40
	4	38.20	33.01	169.70
	5	38.20	32.92	171.50
	6	37.40	32.46	176.40
	7	36.90	32.15	176.80
	8	36.80	32.24	174.30
	9	37.10	31.98	175.40
	10	37.20	32.19	179.30
	11	36.30	32.24	176.50
	12	36.50	32.16	180.80
1922	1	36.40	31.93	180.10
	2	36.20	32.30	177.80
	3	35.50	32.44	171.60
	4	35.80	33.13	172.10
	5	35.70	33.40	172.30
	6	36.00	33.91	174.30
	7	36.00	34.28	171.00
	8	36.40	34.47	166.60
	9	36.60	34.76	163.80
	10	36.70	35.00	166.60
	11	36.10	35.00	165.10
	12	36.40	35.97	167.10
1923	1	36.80	35.87	167.00
	2	37.10	36.11	162.20
	3	37.20	36.08	157.90
	4	36.50	36.47	159.40
	5	36.70	36.73	158.90
	6	36.70	36.69	162.80
	7	36.90	36.66	161.80
	8	37.40	36.71	158.90
	9	37.60	36.90	159.10
	10	37.70	37.08	161.00
	11	37.30	37.21	160.80
	12	37.90	37.38	166.40

(continues)

TABLE B4 (*continued*)

Year and month	M_1	M_2	M_3
1924 1	38.80	37.22	165.20
2	39.80	37.36	160.70
3	39.90	37.52	158.90
4	39.80	37.75	160.00
5	39.60	37.97	160.20
6	39.70	38.33	164.70
7	40.30	38.78	162.10
8	40.00	39.21	159.30
9	40.30	39.66	160.40
10	40.50	39.93	160.90
11	40.40	40.42	160.60
12	40.60	40.30	165.40
1925 1	40.80	40.77	162.40
2	40.80	41.09	161.20
3	40.90	41.11	158.40
4	43.00	41.30	158.80
5	42.70	41.65	157.20
Sample mean	38.04	36.03	166.50
Standard deviation	1.88	2.94	7.07

[a]See text for meaning of notation and data sources.

3. Real Incomes

For real income in France, we use the General Index of Production from Tinbergen (1934, pp. 75–76, column 52).

The U.S. real income variable is the Index of Volume of Manufactured Output, also from Tinbergen (1934, pp. 213–214, column 42).

Real income data for the United Kingdom are readily available only on an annual basis. We use the monthly unemployment series to interpolate the annual industrial production index as follows. First, we regress annual industrial production on a time trend and on the annual unemployment rate. This yields (standard errors are given in parentheses below each estimated parameter)

$$\underset{}{y} = \underset{(3.59)}{98.46} + \underset{(0.1035)}{0.4277}\, t - \underset{(0.0007591)}{0.0007674}\, t^2 - \underset{(0.2023)}{1.2799}\, u$$

in which $R^2 = 0.9651$; y is the annual U.K. total industrial production index; $t = 6, 18, 30, \ldots, 126$, an annual time trend; and u is the U.K. unemployment rate in June expressed as a percentage (for example, $u = 3.0$ if the unemployment rate is 3%). This equation is estimated with data from 1920 to 1930. The source for the total industrial production index for the United Kingdom is Feinstein (1976, p. 1112, column 1).

Our measure of u is the Trade Union and National Unemployment Insurance "unemployed" percentages, given in International Industrial Relations Institute (1932, pp. 259–260). We then compute a monthly real income series by using a monthly time trend and the monthly unemployment rate in the estimated relationship. Hence we use the interpolated monthly industrial production index for real income in the United Kingdom.

The three income series are given in Table B5. Here y_i is the real income for country i.

TABLE B5

REAL INCOMES[a]

Year and month		y_1	y_2	y_3
1921	1	63.00	81.00	89.80
	2	60.00	81.00	88.18
	3	57.00	76.00	86.68
	4	54.00	75.00	80.83
	5	52.00	72.00	75.11
	6	53.00	74.00	74.63
	7	50.00	73.00	79.79
	8	51.00	78.00	80.59
	9	50.00	79.00	83.05
	10	52.00	80.00	82.57
	11	56.00	81.00	82.47
	12	62.00	84.00	82.75
1922	1	65.00	84.00	82.77
	2	68.00	89.00	83.56
	3	74.00	92.00	83.97
	4	73.00	91.00	83.60
	5	77.00	95.00	84.77
	6	78.00	98.00	86.07
	7	78.00	100.00	87.75
	8	81.00	97.00	88.66
	9	82.00	96.00	88.67
	10	86.00	99.00	89.58
	11	88.00	106.00	89.72
	12	88.00	108.00	90.62
1923	1	88.00	106.00	91.27
	2	82.00	108.00	92.55
	3	83.00	110.00	93.83
	4	82.00	113.00	95.50
	5	82.00	111.00	95.88
	6	87.00	111.00	96.52
	7	87.00	108.00	97.03
	8	89.00	104.00	97.15
	9	90.00	106.00	97.79
	10	93.00	104.00	98.68

(*continues*)

TABLE B5 (*continued*)

Year and month		y_1	y_2	y_3
	11	95.00	103.00	99.43
	12	98.00	105.00	100.96
1924	1	104.00	106.00	102.35
	2	105.00	108.00	103.11
	3	106.00	106.00	103.99
	4	104.00	100.00	104.74
	5	105.00	92.00	105.75
	6	106.00	89.00	105.85
	7	108.00	88.00	105.96
	8	111.00	92.00	105.68
	9	114.00	96.00	105.15
	10	116.00	97.00	105.37
	11	112.00	100.00	105.86
	12	113.00	103.00	105.45
1925	1	111.00	105.00	106.05
	2	109.00	105.00	105.90
	3	108.00	104.00	106.76
	4	107.00	104.00	106.59
	5	106.00	102.00	106.04
Sample mean		84.89	95.75	93.84
Standard deviation		20.68	11.77	9.80

[a]See text for meaning of notation and data sources.

REFERENCES

Abel, Andrew, Dornbusch, Rudiger, Huizinga, John, and Marcus, Alan (1979). Money Demand During Hyperinflation. *Journal of Monetary Economics* **5**(1), 97–104.

Aliber, Robert Z. (1962). Speculation in the Foreign Exchanges: The European Experience, 1919–1926. *Yale Economic Papers* Spring, pp. 171–245.

Bilson, John F. O. (1978). Rational Expectations and the Exchange Rate. In *The Economics of Exchange Rates: Selected Studies* (J. A. Frenkel and H. G. Johnson, eds.), pp. 75–96. Addison-Wesley, Reading, Massachusetts.

Boyer, Russel (1973). Substitutability between Currencies and between Bonds: A Theoretical Analysis of Gresham's Law. Unpublished manuscript, University of Western Ontario.

Calvo, Guillermo A., and Rodriguez, Carlos A. (1977). A Model of Exchange Rate Determination under Currency Substitution and Rational Expectations. *Journal of Political Economy* **85**(3), 617–626.

Chen, Chow-Nan (1973). Diversified Currency Holdings and Flexible Exchange Rates. *Quarterly Journal of Economics* **87**(1), 96–111.

Chrystal, K. Alec (1977). Demand for International Media of Exchange. *American Economic Review* **67**(5), 840–850.

Clements, Kenneth W., and Frenkel, Jacob A. (1980). Exchange Rates, Money and Relative Prices: The Dollar–Pound in the 1920's. *Journal of International Economy* **10**(2), 249–262.

Committee on Finance and Industry (1931). *Report*. Stationery Office, London.

Dornbusch, Rudiger (1976a). Capital Mobility, Flexible Exchange Rates and Macroeconomic Equilibrium. In *Recent Issues in International Monetary Economics* (E. Claassen and P. Salin, eds.), Pp. 29–48. North-Holland Publ., Amsterdam.

Dornbusch, Rudiger (1976b). The Theory of Flexible Exchange Rate Regimes and Macroeconomic Policy. *Scandinavian Journal of Economics* **78**(2), 255–275. (Reprinted in Frenkel, J. A., and Johnson, H. G., eds., *The Economics of Exchange Rates: Selected Studies*. Addison-Wesley, Reading, Massachusetts, 1978).

Dulles, Eleanor L. (1929). *The French Franc, 1914–1928*. Macmillan, New York.

Einzig, Paul (1937). *The Theory of Forward Exchange*. Macmillan, London.

Fama, Eugene F. (1975). Short-Term Interest Rates as Predictors of Inflation. *American Economic Review* **65**(3), 269–282.

Fama, Eugene F. (1976). Forward Rates as Predictors of Future Spot Rates. *Journal of Financial Economics* **3**(4), 361–377.

Farag, Attiat A., and Ott, David J. (1964). Exchange Rate Determination under Fluctuating Exchange Rates: Some Empirical Evidence. In *Money in the International Order* (Carter, Murphy, ed.), Southern Methodist University Press, Dallas, Texas.

Feinstein, Charles H. (1976). *Statistical Tables of National Income Expenditure and Output of the U.K. 1855–1965*. Cambridge University Press, London and New York.

Frenkel, Jacob A. (1976). A Monetary Approach to the Exchange Rate: Doctrinal Aspects and Empirical Evidence. *Scandinavian Journal of Economics* **78**(2), 200–224. (Reprinted in *The Economics of Exchange Rates: Selected Studies*. J. A. Frenkel, and H. G. Johnson, eds., Addison-Wesley, Reading, Massachusetts, 1978.)

Frenkel, Jacob A. (1977). The Forward Exchange Rate, Expectations and the Demand for Money: The German Hyperinflation. *American Economic Review* **64**(4), 653–670.

Frenkel, Jacob A. (1978). Purchasing Power Parity: Doctrinal Perspective and Evidence from the 1920's. *Journal of International Economics* **8**(2), 169–191.

Frenkel, Jacob A. (1979). Further Evidence on Expectations and the Demand for Money During the German Hyperinflation. *Journal of Monetary Economics* **5**(1), 81–96.

Frenkel, Jacob A., and Johnson, Harry G. (1976). The Monetary Approach to the Balance of Payments: Essential Concepts and Historical Origins. In *The Monetary Approach to the Balance of Payments* (J. A. Frenkel and H. G. Johnson, eds.), pp. 21–45. Allen & Unwin, London and University of Toronto Press, Toronto.

Frenkel, Jacob A., and Johnson, Harry G., eds. (1978). *The Economics of Exchange Rates: Selected Studies*. Addison-Wesley, Reading, Massachusetts.

Frenkel, Jacob A., and Mussa, Michael L. (1980). The Efficiency of Foreign Exchange Markets and Measures of Turbulence. *American Economic Review* **70**(2), 374–381.

Friedman, Milton, and Schwartz, Anna J. (1970). *Monetary Statistics of the United States: Estimates, Sources and Methods*. National Bureau of Economic Research, New York.

Girton, Lance, and Roper, Don (1976). Theory and Implications of Currency Substitution. International Finance Discussion Papers, No. 86, International Finance Section, Board of Governors of the Federal Reserve System.

Goldfeld, Steve M. (1973). The Demand for Money Revisited. *Brookings Papers on Economic Activity* **3**, 577–639.

Hodgson, John S. (1972). An Analysis of Floating Rates: The Dollar Sterling Rate, 1919–1925. *Southern Economic Journal* **34**(2), 249–257.

Hodrick, Robert J. (1978). An Empirical Analysis of the Monetary Approach to the Determination of the Exchange Rate. In *The Economics of Exchange Rates: Selected Studies* (J. A. Frenkel and H. G. Johnson, eds.), pp. 97–116. Addison-Wesley, Reading, Massachusetts.

Howson, Susan (1975). *Domestic Monetary Management in Britain 1919–39*. Cambridge University Press, London and New York.

International Industrial Relations Institute (1932). *International Unemployment* (N. L. Fledderus, ed.). The Hague.

Kouri, Pentti J. K. (1976). The Exchange Rate and the Balance of Payments in the Short Run and in the Long Run: A Monetary Approach. *Scandinavian Journal of Economics* **78**(2), 280–304.

Krugman, Paul (1977). The Efficiency of the Forward Exchange Market: Evidence from the Twenties and the Seventies. Unpublished manuscript, Yale University.

Levich, Richard M. (1979). The Efficiency of Markets for Foreign Exchange. In *International Economic Policy: Theory and Evidence* (Rudiger Dornbusch and Jacob A. Frenkel, eds.), pp. 246–267. Johns Hopkins Press, Baltimore, Maryland.

Miles, Marc A. (1978). Currency Substitution, Flexible Exchange Rates and Monetary Independence. *American Economic Review* **68**(3), 428–436.

Mussa, Michael (1974). A Monetary Approach to the Balance of Payments Analysis. *Journal of Money, Credit and Banking* **6**, 333–351.

Mussa, Michael (1976). The Exchange Rate, the Balance of Payments and Monetary and Fiscal Policy under a Regime of Controlled Floating. *Scandinavian Journal of Economics* **78**(2), 229–248. (Reprinted in J. A. Frenkel, and H. G. Johnson, eds., *The Economics of Exchange Rates: Selected Studies*. Addison-Wesley, Reading, Massachusetts, 1978.)

Mussa, Michael (1979). Empirical Regularities in the Behavior of Exchange Rates and Theories of the Foreign Exchange Market. *Journal of Monetary Economics, Supplement* (*Carnegie–Rochester Conference Series on Public Policy*) **22**, 19–57.

Stockman, Alan C. (1976). Monetary Cross-Substitution and the International Transmission of Monetary Shocks under Floating Exchange Rates. Unpublished manuscript, University of Chicago.

Stolper, Wolfgang F. (1948). Purchasing Power Parity and the Pound Sterling from 1919–25. *Kyklos* **2**, Fasc. 3 (1948): 240–269.

Theil, Henri (1963). On the Use of Incomplete Prior Information in Regression Analysis. *Journal of the American Statistical Association* **58**, 401–414.

Theil, Henri (1971). *Principles of Econometrics*. Wiley, New York.

Theil, Henri, and Goldberger, Arthur S. (1961). On Pure and Mixed Statistical Estimation in Economics. *International Economic Review* **2**(Mar.), 65–78.

Tinbergen, Jan, ed. (1934). *International Abstracts of Economic Statistics, 1919–1930.* International Conference of Economic Services, London.

Tsiang, S. C. (1959–1960). Fluctuating Exchange Rates in Countries with Relatively Stable Economies. *IMF Staff Papers* **7**, 244–273.

Zellner, Arnold (1962). An Efficient Method of Estimating Seemingly Unrelated Regressions and Tests for Aggregation Bias. *Journal of the American Statistical Association* **57**, 348–368.

Zellner, Arnold (1971a). The Bayesian Approach and Alternatives in Econometrics—I. In *Frontiers in Quantitative Economics* (M. D. Intriligator, ed.), pp. 178–193. North-Holland Publ., Amsterdam.

Zellner, Arnold (1971b). *Bayesian Inference in Econometrics*. Wiley, New York.

JACOB A. FRENKEL
DEPARTMENT OF ECONOMICS
UNIVERSITY OF CHICAGO
CHICAGO, ILLINOIS

KENNETH W. CLEMENTS
GRADUATE SCHOOL OF BUSINESS
UNIVERSITY OF CHICAGO
CHICAGO, ILLINOIS

Budget Deficits and Inflation

*RUDIGER DORNBUSCH AND STANLEY FISCHER**

The view that inflation is always and everywhere a monetary phenomenon is widely accepted as an explanation of at least long-run inflation. It then becomes necessary to explain monetary growth. The argument that monetary growth in fiat money systems is typically a result of government budget deficits has also been widely accepted. The two hypotheses together imply that inflation is in modern times (almost) always and everywhere a fiscal phenomenon.

The preceding paragraph, written before the empirical work to be discussed below was carried out, represents our prior beliefs about the relationship between money growth and budget deficits. However, it turns out that the link between monetary growth and budget deficits is not particularly strong, at least for the sample of seven countries with which we work. There is instead a stronger link between money growth and the rate of increase of wages, indicating typically accommodative monetary policies.

The aims of this paper are twofold. First, we examine the links between budget deficits and monetary growth, and also other determinants of money growth; and second, we consider the links between money growth and inflation. We work with a sample of seven countries, specified below, and chosen largely on grounds of data availability.

Aghevli and Khan (1978), Gordon (1977), Harberger (1978), and Willett and Laney (1978) have recently examined some of the same issues. Aghevli

*We are indebted to David Germany for valuable research assistance, going well beyond the call of duty. Financial support was provided by the National Science Foundation.

ISBN 0-12-259750-8

and Khan examine experience in Brazil, Colombia, the Dominican Republic, and Thailand, a group of countries chosen to provide a range of inflation rates. They construct and fit with some success a small dynamic model in which the price level is fundamentally determined by the stock of money, with appropriate lags, and the stock of money is determined by the government budget deficit, the latter in turn being affected by income and inflationary experience. The model includes a potentially destabilizing element in that inflation causes an increase in the government budget deficit as real tax collections lag. Gordon examines eight major OECD economies, comparing wage-push theories of monetary growth with those based on the view that monetary growth is determined by international factors. He finds some support for the wage-push view but more for the view that monetary growth reflects countercyclical policy responses.

Harberger paints with a broad brush, showing the correlation between the budget deficit and the inflation rate for 44 countries. He argues that the relationship between government budget deficits and the rate of inflation is not necessarily linear but that such a relationship does exist when the budget deficit is large. Willett and Laney examine the hypothesis that wages push money growth in the context of the United Kingdom and Italy and find evidence for such a relationship for both countries. In each of these cases there is also a link between the budget deficit and money growth.

Section 1 presents a simple supply and demand framework for the analysis of inflation, which is sufficiently general to encompass a broad variety of modern theories of inflation. Section 2 discusses factors that potentially affect the rate of growth of the money stock. Section 3 presents estimates of the money growth equations implied by the discussion in Section 2, showing in particular the apparent responsiveness of money growth to the behavior of wages. Sections 4 and 5 discuss price and wage behavior, respectively. Concluding comments on anti-inflationary policy are contained in Section 6. The Appendix describes the data.

1. Theories of the Inflation Process

Inflation appears to come in many types and from many causes. In one country the government has lost control of the ability to finance its spending and resorts in extremis to the printing press. In another an authoritarian government uses inflation as a relatively acceptable way of redistributing income away from labor towards industrialists; in other countries inflation is a means of saving wage earners from the consequences of their avarice. Somewhere else, inflation is the rational response to an external shock that would otherwise generate unemployment. At the level of political economy it is undoubtedly necessary to analyze factors such as these to understand the inflationary process in each country.

It is therefore particularly to be hoped that there is some simple and convenient analytical apparatus that subsumes a broad range of hypotheses about inflation. In this section we focus on the aggregate supply and demand framework of standard macroeconomic analysis. The framework is useful in understanding the process of inflation given the behavior of policy variables: differing theories of inflation are largely, but not entirely, theories about the determinants of policy. As currently presented, our framework does not encompass theories of inflation that emphasize issues of the income distribution, but it is probably sufficiently general that it could be extended to examine these issues.

Section A develops the basic framework. Rational expectations are discussed in Section B. Section C shifts the emphasis to wage setting as a determinant of inflation and discusses long-term contracts and the implications of autonomous wage behavior. The analysis is extended in Section D to import prices and supply shocks as determinants of inflation.

A. The Basic Model

The current inflation rate is determined by the interaction of aggregate demand and supply. On the aggregate supply side inflation is affected in part by cyclical factors, here measured by the GNP gap or the deviation of output from full employment. On the aggregate demand side inflation exerts an effect on aggregate spending through its effect on the real value of money. The interaction of aggregate demand and supply thus determines current inflation and current output, given various predetermined variables.

We start with the aggregate supply side of the economy. Inflation is determined by the GNP gap or the deviation of output from the full employment level λ and by a factor θ that will be given content below[1]:

$$\dot{p} = \theta + a\lambda, \tag{1}$$

where $\dot{p}$ is the rate of inflation, $\lambda = (y - \bar{y})$ is the GNP gap, and where time subscripts have been omitted. We show the aggregate supply side of the economy in Fig. 1 as the positively sloped schedule AS, drawn for a given level of θ. Equation (1) is sufficiently general that it can be interpreted as a conventional or expectations-augmented Phillips curve, or a Lucas aggregate supply function, or a function relating output supplied to the real wage —and no doubt as much else.

[1]We omit here growth considerations and thus discuss deviations of output from a constant full employment level rather than deviations from a full employment path.

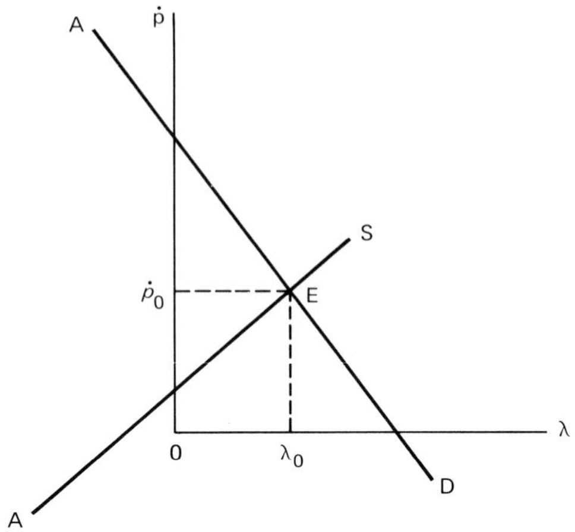

Fig. 1. The aggregate demand/supply framework.

On the aggregate demand side we draw on the standard IS–LM model to derive an aggregate demand function with real balances and fiscal policy as determinants of the equilibrium level of spending. Over time the change in real demand is determined by changes in real balances and changes in fiscal policy. Hence we can write

$$y = y_{-1} + b(\dot{m} - \dot{p}) + cf, \tag{2}$$

where $\dot{m} = (m - m_{-1})/m_{-1}$, the growth rate of nominal money, and f is a measure of the change in fiscal policy. Subtracting full employment output $\bar{y}$ from both sides we have

$$\lambda = \lambda_{-1} + b(\dot{m} - \dot{p}) + cf. \tag{2$'$}$$

Equation (2′) is shown in Fig. 1 as the downward sloping schedule *AD*, drawn for a given growth rate of nominal money, the past gap, and no change in fiscal policy.

The short-run equilibrium obtains at point *E* where inflation and the current gap are simultaneously determined.[2] The dynamics of the model are determined by the evolution of $\dot{m}$, f, and θ that appear as exogenous for the present.

The model of Eqs. (1) and (2′) or Fig. 1 sets out a general frame of reference. Particular theories of the inflation process can be identified with

[2] In deriving the aggregate demand side of the economy we have omitted the Mundell effect, namely, the effect of changes in expected inflation on aggregate demand. The complete model would be described by

$$\lambda = \lambda_{-1} + b(\dot{m} - \dot{p}) + cf + d\phi,$$

where ϕ denotes the change in expected inflation.

factors that randomly or systematically impinge on the aggregate demand or supply side of the economy. We have in mind, in particular, theories that draw on wage behavior or expectations or both as a theory of inflation on the supply side, and theories of the determinants of money growth and fiscal policy as supporting inflation on the demand side.

B. Rational Expectations and the Lucas Supply Function

The first view of (1) we examine is the Lucas rational expectations equilibrium approach. Lucas views the equation as reflecting the supply behavior of workers whose perception of the reward for working is positively related to the price level in the current period. In the simplest version of the hypothesis (Lucas, 1973), formulation (1) starts out essentially as a supply function of labor. Output is at the full employment level as long as there is full information about prices and other disturbances; hypothesized information lags make it necessary to estimate the current aggregate price level on the basis of limited information about current nominal variables. This estimation involves combining prior expectations with current information.

The Lucas approach leads to a relationship between inflation and the output gap (properly measured) that results entirely from expectational errors. The derivation of this result is straightforward once it is recognized that in this framework we want to interpret θ as the expected rate of inflation, contingent on information available at the end of the previous period.

Combining (1) and (2′) we obtain

$$\dot{p} = \theta + a(\lambda_{-1} + b(\dot{m} - \dot{p}) + cf). \tag{3}$$

Now interpreting θ as the rational expectation of $\dot{p}$, defined as $\dot{p}'$ we obtain

$$\dot{p}' = \dot{m}' + (1/b)(\lambda_{-1} + cf'), \tag{3′}$$

where a prime denotes the expectation of the relevant variable based on information available at the beginning of the current period.

Expected inflation thus depends on the expected growth rate of nominal money, with the conventional unit coefficient, but also on real variables. In particular, an anticipated fiscal expansion will be inflationary as will be the anticipated recovery from a position of overemployment. Substituting then for $\dot{p}' = \theta$ in (3) yields the equilibrium current rate of inflation:

$$\dot{p} = \dot{m} + v(\dot{m}' - \dot{m}) + (1/b)\lambda_{-1} + (c/b)f + (c/b)v(f' - f), \tag{4}$$

where $v \equiv 1/(1 + ab)$.

Equation (4) shows that under rational expectations, inflation is determined by nominal money growth, a cyclical variable λ_{-1}, and anticipated fiscal policy changes. Expectational errors appear as determinants of inflation in that unanticipated money growth and unanticipated fiscal expansions exert an effect on inflation. As is well known, unanticipated money growth is *not* fully reflected in inflation—the coefficient is $1/(1+ab)$ and depends on the slope of the aggregate supply schedule a and the effect of real balances on aggregate demand b.

The inflation equation has a counterpart in the equation for the GNP gap. The current GNP gap is *entirely* due to expectational errors $(\dot{p} - \dot{p}')$.[3] Using (1) and substituting for $\dot{p}'$ and $\dot{p}$ from (3) and (4) we have

$$\lambda = bv(\dot{m} - \dot{m}') + cv(f - f'). \tag{5}$$

The equation for the deviation of output from normal confirms the view that monetary or fiscal "surprises" are expansionary in real terms. The implication of the present model is that deviations of output from normal are serially uncorrelated. However, it is well known that subsidiary hypotheses can be introduced to generate serial correlation of output deviations.

In terms of Fig. 1 the model can be interpreted as follows: The position of the aggregate supply schedule AS is set by expectations of the rate of inflation $\dot{p}_0'$. The aggregate demand schedule depends on realizations of the monetary and fiscal variables. The case we show in Fig. 2, for example,

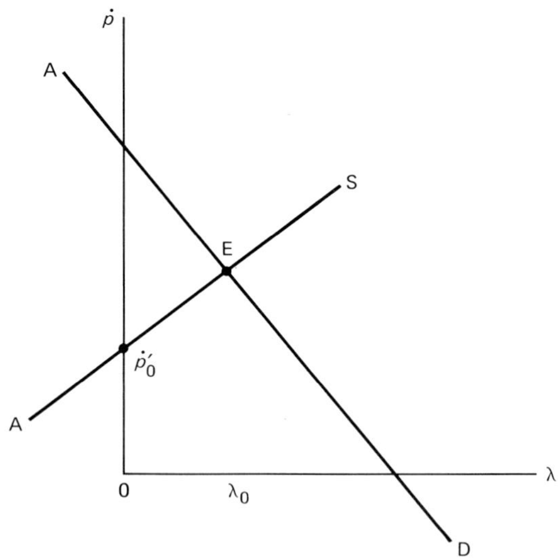

Fig. 2. The effects of unanticipated fiscal expansion.

[3]This particularly strong statement is a result of the absence of disturbances on the supply side in this model.

corresponds to unanticipated fiscal expansion leading to unanticipated inflation and output expansion. With no further changes in fiscal policy the economy would return subsequently to $\dot{p}_0$, implying a higher price level and real interest rate.[4]

The theory is easily extended to cope with supply disturbances. Unanticipated supply shocks shift the *AS* schedule, thus causing inflation and output to deviate from their anticipated levels.

C. Wage Setting and Aggregate Supply.

The rational expectations equilibrium model, as developed above, presents the strongest abstraction from institutional aspects of wage–price setting. A seemingly more realistic description of the institutional setting would view prices as determined by a markup over cost, where costs are for the present taken to be wages. With a constant markup the term θ in (1) could then be interpreted as the rate of wage inflation $\dot{w}$.[5]

Wage inflation in turn can be modeled in a number of ways. One view applies the conceptual framework of the rational expectations approach, but places it in a multiperiod context through the realistic feature of long-term labor contracts. Money wages are set over the life of the contract to produce full employment equilibrium given the expectation of monetary and fiscal policy. In such a model the current rate of wage inflation will be a weighted average of the predetermined rates of inflation in existing contracts of various maturities and of the rate of wage inflation of contracts currently entered into.

With *all* contracts predetermined relative to the current realizations of monetary and fiscal variables it will remain true that surprises in monetary or fiscal policy will cause output to deviate from its normal level. Further, with labor elastically supplied at the predetermined wage, deviations in output from normal will now be serially correlated since innovations in monetary or fiscal variables create real wage surprises and therefore unanticipated changes in employment and output. The duration of these surprises is determined by the length of labor contracts.

An important contribution by John Taylor (1979) has shown that relative wage considerations reinforce the potential for expectational errors in wage setting to give rise to persistent real effects. If short-term contracts currently entered into reflect not only the expectations of money wages

[4]However, the present framework does not model the real interest rate explicitly.

[5]We abstract from productivity growth. We should also note that the markup equation can be interpreted as being consistent with the theory of supply in competitive industries, where supply is a function of the real wage. Inverting the supply function, the price of output can be expressed as a function of the wage and output.

consistent with planned employment levels but also wage targets relative to contracts currently in force and continuing, then unanticipated monetary or fiscal policy actions have long-term real effects. Consider a world of zero expected inflation and long-term contracts in force reflecting that expectation. Suppose next that nominal money were reduced. Contracts that currently come due for renewal would, from a full-employment perspective, call for reduced money wages. Over time, as all contracts become flexible, this would lead to a reduction of money wages. If relative wages matter, though, we would have less of a reduction in current money wages since otherwise contracts currently being renewed would be too far out of line with existing contracts. In this case wage adjustment would become slower or wages stickier.

The wage contracting viewpoint lends plausibility to the inertia of wage behavior and makes that inertia consistent with rational expectations. Of course, such contracts are not invariant to the economic environment, but their current form is such, and adjusts sufficiently slowly, as to give considerable justification for an approach that assumes the existence of nominal long-term wage contracts in which output levels are determined by the firm. These assumptions imply the serial correlation of deviations of output from normal and focus attention on institutional features of the labor market.

What does this framework of analysis suggest about the impact of wage disturbances on inflation and real activity? Looking at Fig. 3, suppose we

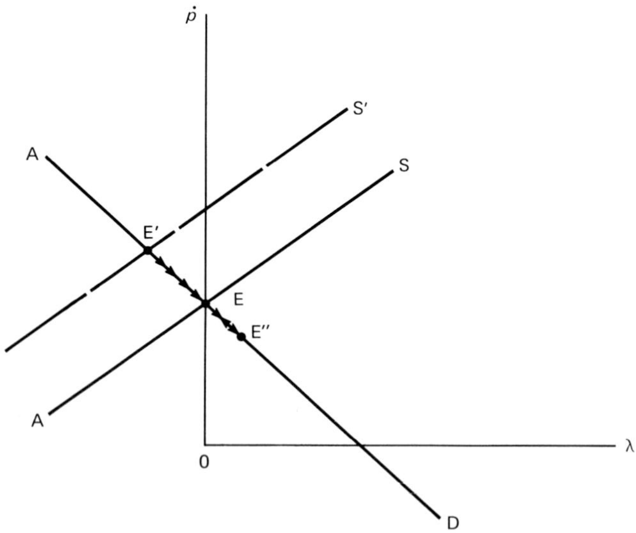

Fig. 3. The response to a supply shock that is not accommodated.

are initially in full equilibrium at point E and that there is a random increase in money wages on currently negotiated contracts. Suppose that policy does not respond to the disturbance, so that the aggregate demand schedule does not shift. The wage disturbance appears in the first place as an upward shift of the AS schedule since θ—the economy-wide average wage inflation—increases. As a result inflation increases, and output declines below normal because of the squeeze in real balances. Next we have adjustment of new contracts in part raising wage inflation because of the relative wage effect, in part reducing wage inflation because of under employment. For a while the former effect may dominate, shifting up the AS schedule further and raising inflation and unemployment. Ultimately unemployment comes to dominate, wage inflation falls, the AS schedule shifts downward, and inflation subsides. There has to be a period of below average inflation (moving to E'') to restore real balances to a level commensurate with full employment. The long-run effect of the wage disturbances is zero. In the transition, though, the random money-wage increase affects the path of inflation and output.

What scope is there for monetary or fiscal policy in stabilizing inflation and unemployment? The extreme rational expectations model of the previous section appears to suggest that the mere announcement of reduced monetary growth will cause expectations to fall in line with this pronouncement, and the economy will wind down its rate of inflation without tears.[6] The present formulation suggests that disinflation is a considerably more tricky issue. It is more tricky because the relative wage effect and long-term contracts make the rate of wage inflation, and hence price inflation, *largely* exogenous. Monetary policy in the short run primarily affects output and only over time acts on the rate of inflation. [In terms of Fig. 3 a strong relative wage effect and a low sensitivity of current contracts to unemployment imply a relatively flat (in the limit, horizontal) AS schedule.]

Can monetary or fiscal policy stabilize output in the face of autonomous wage disturbances, and at what price in terms of inflation? We noted above that for a given monetary and fiscal policy, as shown in Fig. 3, random wage disturbances have transitory real effects. If monetary policy sought to accommodate wage increases by an expansion in nominal money, then inflation in the short run might not be appreciably raised over and above the increase due to wage inflation, since the AS schedule is relatively flat. In the short run monetary accommodation thus appears as a full-employment policy. In the longer term, of course, expectations adjust to the increased nominal money growth; the accommodation policy implies in-

[6] Of course, the announcement has to be believed. We find it difficult to persuade ourselves, however, that inflation could be quickly reduced at essentially zero cost if only the policymakers could persuade economic agents of the strength of their resolution.

creased inflation or validation of the random behavior of wages. It is important to recognize, though, that a policy of monetary accommodation would imply inflation behavior and money supply behavior substantially governed by wages, not by deviations of output from trend.

D. Import Price Disturbances

An important extension of the model for practical purposes is to recognize the role of import prices as a separate source of inflation. The extension, still in the framework of a markup pricing model, is straightforward (Bruno, 1978). Our price equation now becomes

$$\dot{p} = x\theta + (1 - x)\dot{p}_m + a\lambda = \dot{p}_m + x(\theta - \dot{p}_m) + a\lambda, \tag{1'}$$

where $\dot{p}_m$ is the rate of import price inflation and x denotes the share of wages in costs.

In terms of our earlier model it is apparent that variations in the rate of import price inflation appear now as a separate shift term on the aggregate supply side of the economy. Thus in Eq. (1′) we represent import prices in their influence through intermediate imported goods.

A separate role for import prices appears of course on the aggregate demand side. Departing from the closed economy formulation here implies that changes in relative prices create changes in demand for domestic output. The equation for the GNP gap then becomes

$$\lambda = \lambda_{-1} + b(\dot{m} - \dot{p}) + cf + d(\dot{p}_m - \dot{p}). \tag{2''}$$

From (2″), we observe that an increase in import price inflation relative to domestic inflation lowers the relative price of domestic goods and thus shifts demand toward our output. For a given rate of import price inflation $\dot{p}_m$ the aggregate demand schedule now becomes steeper: Increased inflation exerts a deflationary effect both by squeezing real balances and by inducing a loss in competitiveness.[7]

What is the short-run response to an increase in the rate of import price inflation? Increased import price inflation will shift the aggregate supply schedule up and to the left, thereby exerting pressure toward increased inflation and reduced output. On the aggregate demand side the increase in import price inflation shifts the aggregate demand schedule up and to the right, exerting a tendency toward expansion and increased inflation. The impact is thus clearly inflationary. Whether output expands or contracts

[7] The formulation of the aggregate demand side assumes that there are no lags in the adjustment of demand to changes in relative prices. The assumption is convenient but implausible. Here is another place where expectations might play an important role.

will depend on the share of imports in costs and the response of aggregate demand to real balances and relative prices.

The effect of increased import price inflation on domestic inflation and output are, respectively,

$$d\lambda / d\dot{p}_m = d - (b + d)\, d\dot{p} / d\dot{p}_m \tag{6}$$

and

$$\frac{d\dot{p}}{d\dot{p}_m} = \frac{1 - x + ad + x\, d\theta / d\dot{p}_m}{1 + ab + ad} \equiv k. \tag{7}$$

With domestic wage inflation initially unresponsive to increased import price inflation ($d\theta / d\dot{p}_m = 0$) the term k is less than unity. Increased import price inflation is less than fully passed through. The impact on output is $d\lambda / d\dot{p}_m = d(1 - k) - kb$ and is positive if the relative price effect is large relative to the effect of real balances on aggregate demand and if the inflation pass-through k is small.

The extended model that recognizes the role of import price inflation can be used to make two important points. The first concerns a regime where a once and for all change in import price inflation (exchange depreciation) and money growth is undertaken. What is the adjustment path? Here the inertia of wage movements discussed above comes into play. With long-term contracts and relative wage considerations there will be a protracted adjustment, with inflation initially responding less than fully to increased money growth and depreciation. In the transition period real output will initially expand as competitiveness is gained through changes in relative prices sustained by slow wage inflation. The adjustment process will be more rapid the faster wage inflation reacts to the overemployment, money creation, and depreciation and the less it is guided by relative wage concerns.

The second point concerns changes in the real price of imported intermediate goods such as the oil price increase. In that event we have a discrepancy in the rates of inflation of import prices relevent to aggregate demand and supply. The oil price increase, for example, would appear as an upward shift of the aggregate supply schedule with a resulting increase in inflation and a reduction in output.[8]

In summary, import price inflation appears as one of the determinants, along with wages, of domestic inflation. Expectations about import price inflation, as much as expectations about monetary and fiscal policy, will determine wage inflation and will therefore feed back into price inflation.

The theory of the inflation process laid out here is appropriate to

[8] We abstract here from further effects, first, on aggregate demand through the international redistribution of income and, second, on potential output.

industrialized countries under circumstances where income distribution questions are not particularly relevant to the level of aggregate demand or to the inflation process. We should also draw attention to an entire strand of inflation theory built around the idea that the inflation process is designed to reconcile conflicting demands for income shares and that the process itself affects aggregate demand, growth, and productivity.[9] While the relative wage hypothesis goes some way in the direction of such theories —and perhaps as far as one might wish to go—these theories are quite different in orientation and are left out of consideration here.

2. Money Supply Behavior

Our review of the inflation process has focused on aggregate demand and supply. Wage and import price inflation were singled out as the proximate determinants of inflation on the aggregate supply side. Changes in monetary and fiscal policy and changes in relative prices appear as sources of inflationary disturbances on the aggregate demand side. We concentrate now on the money supply and ask what determines its evolution.

There are two broad hypotheses about the behavior of nominal money. One views the monetary authorities as using money creation to finance the public sector deficit. Such a view is developed formally in the discussion of hyperinflation, but it is also implicit in IMF policies that seek control of the public sector deficit as an essential element of monetary and balance of payments stabilization. A more appropriate view in many instances of inflation is that the authorities have imperfect control of the fiscal apparatus and that, under these conditions, money creation is the only source of finance. There is no need to distinguish these views closely. Either amounts to money creation determined by the budget deficit.

A second view of money creation, and one certainly important in industrialized countries, regards monetary policy as accommodating. The growth rate of money is used to stabilize economic activity through discretionary policy moves or explicit feedback rules. In such a view, as sketched in Section 1, the stability of output in the face of variations in aggregate demand or in aggregate supply requires offsetting variations in monetary growth. In particular, increased wage inflation requires an accommodating monetary expansion. There is a question whether monetary accommodation is full or only partial. In the former case increased wage inflation leads to higher inflation and no decrease in output, while in the

[9] See, for example, L. Taylor (1979).

latter case the output effect is negative. This case is less likely in that the central bank will typically have both inflation and employment targets.

An important question in determining the extent of accommodation, given inflation and employment targets, is the impact of accommodation on the wage inflation process. If wage disturbances are largely transitory, accommodation becomes plausible. If inertia and relative wages are important, then accommodation will certainly lengthen the adjustment process and may aggravate the cumulative inflationary impact of the wage disturbances. This is, of course, a fundamental problem facing the monetary authority.

A third view of the money supply process emphasizes the openness of the economy and the fact that, under fixed exchange rates, the money stock is directly affected by the balance of payments. The monetary base is equal to the sum of domestic credit and net foreign assets of the central bank. Changes in net foreign assets, as they arise in the process of pegging the exchange rate, directly affect the base and therefore the money stock. This view, accordingly, would explain money supply behavior in part by movements in net external assets. The view needs qualification, though, in two respects. First, net foreign assets are themselves endogenous and are determined by monetary policy. Second, a change in net foreign assets can be offset by changes in domestic credit that sterilize it. The extent, therefore, to which changes in net foreign assets affect the money stock depends on the central bank's willingness and ability to sterilize.

The model of the money supply that emerges from these considerations is one that emphasizes three sets of variables which reflect the need for accommodating and offsetting policy action (the budget deficit, inflation, and unemployment) as well as changes in net foreign assets:

$$\dot{m} = \dot{m}(\text{budget deficit}, \dot{w}, \lambda, \Delta \text{ net foreign assets}). \tag{8}$$

Before we turn to some empirical evidence on the determinants of the money supply process, we should point out that the perspective on monetary growth (and indeed on any other macroeconomic policy) of this paper is one that has become increasingly common and that serves to reconcile a variety of views on the causes of inflation. There is no doubt that inflation is a monetary phenomenon, in the sense that a determined monetary policy could eventually reduce the inflation rate provided the monetary authority or the government were willing to pay the price. It is precisely in considering the price of monetary tightness, and therefore adjusting the growth rate of money, that narrowly economic theories of inflation link up with other plausible theories that to some appear to emphasize the wrong variables.

In concluding this section we present a brief overview of selected indicators for the cross section of countries that we report on. Table 1

TABLE 1

SELECTED INDICATORS[a]

	Finland	Guatemala	Ireland	Israel	South Africa	Sri Lanka	Norway
Budget deficit/GNP							
Mean	0.4	0.9	6.0	13.2	3.2	5.7	2.1
Maximum	3.3	2.2	13.7	24.8	7.1	11.2	5.9
Minimum	– 1.8	– 0.1	2.5	2.4	8.3	– 0.2	0.4
Money growth (M_1)							
Mean	10.8	10.0	9.5	19.3	7.3	8.5	8.2
Maximum	34.5	40.9	11.4	38.8	20.4	34.9	16.6
Minimum	– 1.7	– 8.1	– 0.0	2.5	– 2.3	– 7.2	– 0.4
Money growth (M_2)							
Mean	12.6	12.5	10.9	28.5	10.5	10.1	9.1
Maximum	22.3	30.9	23.9	85.1	24.6	38.2	15.4
Minimum	3.6	– 4.3	– 0.2	12.1	– 2.3	– 4.4	3.3
Inflation							
Mean	7.0	3.5	6.8	13.6	4.9	3.3	5.3
Maximum	17.8	16.6	20.9	50.6	13.5	12.4	11.7
Minimum	0.0	– 1.1	0.0	1.2	– 2.3	– 1.7	2.3

[a]Data are generally for the period 1960–1977.

shows the budget deficit as a ratio of GNP, the growth rate of nominal money, and the rate of inflation for these countries. The high inflation country in this sample is Israel although every other country within the sample experienced double-digit inflation at some time. With respect to the budget deficit Israel again leads by a considerable margin. In this regard, though, Ireland and Sri Lanka also have high average deficit ratios. Finally money growth has been near the teens for every country in the sample. Casual inspection reveals the absence of a close relation between the budget deficit and the rate of inflation in this cross section of countries.

3. Money Growth Equations

In this section we present and discuss estimates of money supply equations for seven countries, using annual data. The seven countries were chosen, essentially on the basis of data availability, from the countries for which data are included in *International Financial Statistics*, but excluding the major industrialized economies.[10]

[10]Countries for which we had less than 15 annual observations and/or unemployment rates were excluded. The data sources are described in more detail in the appendix.

The time-series equations for the individual countries are based on the discussion of the previous section and include as right-hand side variables lagged growth rates of money, the growth rate of nominal wages, the unemployment rate, the budget deficit (as a ratio to high-powered money), and the change in net foreign assets (also as a ratio to high-powered money). Obviously most of the right-hand side variables are not exogenous. Since there is clearly serial correlation of the errors in almost all the equations, we have used Fair's method to estimate the equations presented in Table 2.[11]

Equations are presented for each country. We started with a general form of the equation, parameter estimates for which are given in the top line for each of the countries. For some countries there is a second line containing parameter estimates for forms of the more general equation in which some parameters in the first equation have been constrained to zero. There is obviously no reason the money supply process should be the same in each country, and the estimates indicate some diversity in the functions.

Before we discuss the economic content of the estimates, we should comment on some general features. First, the equations do not fit very well, even given the small number of observations for most of the countries. The standard error of the regression is typically of the order of 3% per annum, while the average growth rate of money over the entire sample for the (different) sample periods is about 12%. Second, there is generally substantial serial correlation of residuals from the regressions; surprisingly, a number of the coefficients of the estimated first order autoregressive process are negative.

We turn now to examine the coefficients on the last four variables listed among the regressors in Table 2. First, it is quite striking that the rate of change of wages enters significantly and positively in the regressions for five of the seven countries. This is evidence of monetary policy that accommodates wage pressures. The coefficient on the rate of change of wages is less than one in each case, so that the monetary authority is bending with the wind but still leaning into it. The coefficient on wages is not significant in the case of Guatemala, and has a negative sign in the case of Norway. The Norwegian coefficient could be interpreted as a sign of strong counterinflationary policy. Other coefficients in that equation, however, suggest caution in the interpretation.

Similarly, in five of the seven countries the growth rate of money is significantly affected by the rate of acquisition of foreign assets by the central bank. There is offsetting of the effects of capital inflows on money growth, but it is clear that it is not complete.

[11] See Fair (1970).

TABLE 2

MONEY GROWTH EQUATIONS[a]

Country (Money supply concept)	Const	$g_{m_{-1}}$	$g_{m_{-2}}$	g_w	u	BD/H_{-1}	$\Delta NFA/H_{-1}$	R^2	s.e.	ρ	DW
Finland ($M2$)	0.124* (2.1)	0.241 (0.6)	−0.235 (0.7)	0.634 (1.7)	−3.24 (1.5)	0.015 (0.5)	0.029 (0.7)	0.26	0.0404	0.232	2.08
	0.081* (3.2)	0.623* (2.8)	−0.484* (2.6)	0.240* (2.2)		−0.022 (1.3)	−0.081 (0.5)	0.50	0.0318	−0.854	2.54
Guatemala ($M2$)	0.066* (3.3)	−0.298 (0.1)	0.428 (1.7)	0.223 (0.44)	−0.713* (3.2)	0.403* (2.8)	0.366* (3.8)	0.864	0.0299	−0.566	2.02
Ireland ($M2$)	0.076* (2.9)	0.789* (2.9)	−1.023* (3.6)	0.904* (3.7)	−1.110* (3.0)	0.057 (0.7)	−0.051 (0.8)	0.864	0.0306	−0.618	2.40
Israel ($M1$)	−0.039 (0.8)	0.351* (4.4)	−0.162 (1.0)	0.295* (3.6)	0.287 (0.8)	0.078* (4.8)	0.191* (7.91)	0.942	0.0318	−0.833	2.1
	−0.032 (1.4)	0.284* (3.0)		0.182* (2.2)		0.082* (5.7)	0.199* (9.7)	0.896	0.0375	−0.517	2.95

Norway	0.076*	0.356*	0.057	− 0.307*	− 2.678*	0.164*	0.123*	0.945	0.0134	− 0.215	2.1
($M2$)	(4.0)	(1.96)	(0.4)	(2.2)	(3.3)	(4.2)	(3.9)				
South Africa	0.77	0.375	− 0.035	0.579	− 0.350	− 0.050	0.162*	0.737	0.0466	− 0.367	1.8
($M1$)	(1.1)	(1.6)	(0.1)	(1.1)	(0.8)	(0.9)	(3.5)				
	0.024	0.469*	− 0.086	0.827*		− 0.041	0.152*	0.715	0.0460	− 0.411	1.7
	(1.2)	(2.2)	(0.3)	(2.1)		(0.8)	(3.5)				
Sri Lanka	0.138*	− 0.413	− 0.281	0.555*	− 2.345	0.058	0.231*	0.646	0.0311	0.180	2.2
($M2$)	(2.7)	(2.0)	(1.3)	(3.5)	(1.4)	(0.65)	(3.18)				
	0.153*	− 0.408	− 0.438*	0.470*		− 0.037	0.204*	0.612	0.0310	0.050	2.3
	(3.1)	(1.9)	(2.3)	(3.0)		(0.6)	(3.0)				

[a] Asterisk denotes coefficient is significant at the 5% level. Sample period is generally 1960–1977.

There is little evidence from the regressions of systematic countercyclical policy that increases the growth rate of money when the unemployment rate rises. The coefficient on unemployment is typically negative and sometimes significant, suggesting that the reduction in demand for money that accompanies a reduction in the level of activity is typically not totally offset by the monetary authority.

One focus of this paper is, of course, on the relationship between the budget deficit and the growth rate of money. It turns out that this is not one of the stronger relationships observed in the table. Typically, an increase in the budget deficit does increase the growth rate of money, but in the sample of countries with which we are working, the coefficient is significant only in the case of Guatemala, Israel, and Norway.[12]

The conclusion that budget deficits do not appear as a dominant determinant of money growth does stand in contrast with a loose oral tradition. It does not, however, necessarily conflict with the evidence presented by Harberger (1978). Harberger noted that countries with acute inflation problems tended to have relatively large budget deficits by comparison with low inflation countries, but did not examine the direct relationship between money growth and deficit, which our evidence, by contrast, does.

There are, of course, reasons why the relation between deficits and money growth may not be very strong. The first is that the money supply is not invariant to the manner in which the deficit is financed. At one extreme we can think of a budget deficit financed entirely by debt sold in the open market; at the other we have a deficit fully financed by the central bank. Intermediate cases might involve requirements for the banking system to hold a share of their reserves in the form of government debt. Clearly, the range of possibilities will, in principle, have a range of implications for the money supply.[13] In the former case we need have no expansion in money, while in the latter case there is full monetization of the deficit. The intermediate case may or may not involve money creation depending on the extent to which credit to the government displaces credit to the private sector. The second reason for the weakness of the link between the budget deficit and money growth is that the method of financing could well be external.

[12]We have also worked with variants of the equations shown in Table 2, with similar results. The variants are (a) running a similar equation with high-powered money as the dependent variable, and (b) excluding the unemployment rate from the equation in case the collinearity of the budget deficit and the unemployment rate were responsible for the nonsignificance of the coefficient on the deficit.

[13]We should in this connection note that estimation of equations similar to those of Table 2 for high-powered money growth did not produce promising results; in particular, the link between deficits and high-powered money growth was weaker than that shown in Table 2.

4. The Price Equation

Markup pricing is consistent with the framework of Section 1. In the case of markup pricing the variable θ is interpreted as a cost variable that would include wages and import prices. In addition, the rate of change of the money stock and fiscal policy affect the behavior of prices through aggregate demand. Accordingly the implied price equation is, using (1′) and (2″)

$$\dot{p} = (1 + ab + ad)^{-1}\left[x\dot{w} + (1 - x + ad)\dot{p}_m + a\lambda_{-1} + ab\dot{m} + acf\right]. \quad (9)$$

Since some of the right-hand side variables are endogenous we have estimated the reduced-form equation in (9) using Fair's method. Furthermore, since the lagged gap (proxied by lagged unemployment) proved invariably insignificant and because of the serious lack of degrees of freedom, we excluded that variable from the regressions reported in Table 3.

TABLE 3

PRICE EQUATIONS[a]

Country	Const	$\dot{m}$	$\dot{w}$	$\dot{p}_m$	f	Rho	R^2	s.e.	DW
Finland	− 0.40 (3.77)*	0.22 (1.00)	1.64 (5.73)*	− 0.02 (0.20)	0.27 (3.49)*	− 0.17 (0.62)	0.89	0.02	2.19
Guatemala	− 0.04 (0.42)	0.07 (0.25)	1.09 (1.88)	0.61 (3.70)*	− 0.002 (0.03)	− 0.65 (2.94)*	0.83	0.03	1.89
Ireland	− 0.18 (2.56)*	− 0.28 (1.63)	0.81 (8.29)*	0.14 (1.57)	0.23 (2.66)*	− 0.60 (3.00)*	0.95	0.02	2.14
Israel	− 0.09 (3.51)*	− 0.03 (0.61)	0.76 (11.78)*	0.24 (3.55)*	0.01 (2.47)*	− 0.73 (3.89)*	0.99	0.01	2.57
Norway	0.08 (0.28)	− 0.25 (0.73)	0.08 (0.31)	0.31 (1.97)	− 0.01 (0.07)	− 0.27 (1.03)	0.66	0.02	1.58
South Africa	− 0.06 (1.13)	− 0.07 (1.61)	− 0.21 (0.71)	0.44 (6.94)*	0.03 (1.45)	− 0.36 (1.53)	0.94	0.01	2.10
Sri Lanka	− 0.03 (0.31)	− 0.06 (0.50)	0.08 (0.99)	0.03 (1.68)	0.04 (0.79)	0.76 (5.10)*	0.71	0.02	1.73

[a]Note: Estimated using Fair's method. Instruments included once and twice lagged values of the left- and right-hand side variables. Asterisk denotes coefficient is significant at the 5% level.

The most striking aspect of the results is the weak role of aggregate demand influences—monetary or fiscal policy—on the rate of inflation. Current monetary growth is not significant in any of the regressions and indeed has the wrong sign—though imprecisely estimated—in a good number of cases.[14] Fiscal policy is only significant in three cases (Finland, Ireland, and Israel) and, indeed, in these instances has the desired positive coefficient. In all cases, though, the numerical size of the effect of fiscal policy is quite small.

The role of costs, wages and import prices is supported in several of the regressions. Finland, Ireland, and Israel appear to have wage inflation as a significant determinant of price inflation. The size of coefficients for Ireland and Israel is smaller than unity, as expected from (9). In the case of Finland the coefficient of wages is inexplicably high.

Import price inflation appears as a significant determinant of price inflation in only three countries. The coefficients are below unity as expected. The interesting case is Israel since here the wages and import price coefficients add to unity; that number, unfortunately, is too high if (9) is taken as the theoretical specification.

5. The Wage Equation

The theoretical framework and the price equations reported above place strong emphasis on wage behavior as a determinant of price inflation. In this section we therefore investigate the determinants of wage behavior. Particularly, we investigate whether or not wage behavior can be satisfactorily explained in terms of expected inflation, expected growth of money, and unemployment. This hypothesis is shown in (10):

$$\dot{w} = \text{const} + a\dot{m}' + b\dot{p}' + c\lambda. \tag{10}$$

We do not have direct measures of the expectations of money growth and price inflation. However, under the hypothesis of rational expectations we can use the fact that

$$\dot{m} = \dot{m}' + \epsilon, \qquad \dot{p} = \dot{p}' + \eta, \tag{11}$$

where ϵ and η are white noise errors, and thus use realized inflation and money growth as right-hand side variables. Since the right-hand side variables in this estimation procedure are correlated with the error, we have to use instrumental variables estimation.

[14] In regressions not reported here we have considered inflation as a function of current and lagged rates of nominal money growth. This specification, which singles out money—including lagged money—as the sole determinant of inflation, proved altogether unsuccessful.

TABLE 4

WAGE EQUATIONS[a]

Country	Const	$\dot{p}'$	$\dot{m}'$	u	R^2	s.e.	DW
Ireland	− 0.008	0.55	0.6	0.33	0.86	0.028	2.48
	(0.18)	(1.36)	(2.12)*	(0.46)			
	0.04	0.66	0.89	− 0.68	0.64	0.046	2.49
	(0.77)	(1.31)	(1.63)	(0.72)			
Finland	0.07	0.67	0.31	− 2.17	0.64	0.03	1.80
	(1.88)	(2.19)*	(1.51)	(− 1.09)			
	−0.06	0.67	0.95	− 0.2	0.67	0.03	1.49
	(0.8)	(2.49)*	(1.87)	(0.13)			
Israel	0.03	0.95	− 0.07	0.36	0.96	0.026	1.97
	(0.19)	(6.49)*	(0.11)	(0.91)			
South Africa	0.09	0.64	− 0.1	− 0.68	0.75	0.028	0.96
	(2.1)	(2.36)	(0.7)	(2.35)			
	0.09	0.75	− 0.11	− 0.62	0.78	0.026	0.99
	(2.5)	(2.9)	(0.9)	(2.7)			
Norway	− 0.0	1.56	− 0.05	1.61	0.37	0.038	2.31
	(0.03)	(2.58)*	(0.12)	(0.46)			

[a]Note: Estimated using instrumental variables. Asterisk denotes coefficient is significant at the 5% level.

Table 4 reports the results for the wage equation for five countries only, as the first-stage equations for the remainder yielded negative R^2 for the final equation and were thus unsatisfactory. We also note that in interpreting the standard errors it is essential that there not be serial correlation in the error since otherwise the standard error estimates are inconsistent. Thus the results for South Africa should be interpreted with caution.

The role of expected price inflation as a determinant of wage behavior stands out strongly in the case of Israel, Finland, and Norway. In each case expected inflation has a significant positive coefficient. In the case of Israel the coefficient is quite close to unity, suggesting that a word of caution is in order: It is quite possible that with the annual data we might partly be capturing the impact of formal indexing mechanisms.

Anticipated monetary growth appears as a significant determinant of wage inflation only in the case of Ireland. For the remaining cases the coefficients of money growth are very imprecisely estimated and in some cases are of the wrong sign.

Unemployment does not appear to be important in explaining wage inflation. In none of the cases without significant serial correlation is unemployment significant and in some cases, including Israel, we get the wrong sign.

What conclusions about wage behavior are appropriate? It appears that with inflation as the only systematic determinant and with traditional explanations along aggregate demand or Phillips curve lines not showing up, we have to recognize that there is considerable autonomy in wage behavior.

6. Concluding Remarks

This paper has reviewed a theory of the inflation process, hypotheses about the proximate determinants of inflation, and some empirical evidence on these questions. We started out with the presumption that budget deficits could readily explain the inflationary experience in many small countries. The evidence that we present here, although it must, of course, be viewed with very considerable caution because of the small sample and the small number of observations, does not support such a view. The evidence rather suggests that wage inflation is an important determinant of money growth. Such a finding is consistent with a policy of accommodation in which the authorities validate money wage growth through a monetary expansion.

The finding on money growth led us to consider price and wage inflation. Wage and import price inflation appear as the significant determinants of price inflation. Wage inflation, in turn, is significantly affected by the expected rate of inflation.

The evidence discussed is, in our view, largely relevant to the short run of several years. We continue to believe that in the long run inflation control requires control over monetary growth. But the short run of several years is the context of much, if not most, policy discussion.

From a policy perspective we note the importance of the finding that neither unemployment nor money growth has an important effect on wage inflation. This finding, of course, suggests that the aggregate supply schedule, in terms of Fig. 1, would be quite flat. It suggests that aggregate demand governs the level of output, but that it does not exert an important effect on inflation. Certainly there is no direct channel through which monetary growth acts on wage settlements. What policy should the authorities follow in such a setting? If wage behavior is taken as largely autonomous then failure to accommodate wage disturbances would produce variability in aggregate demand and output. Accommodation is in the short run very effective with respect to output and largely inconsequential for inflation. On the other hand it is, of course, clear that such an accommodation policy cannot but validate the inflationary expectations that *are* a determinant of wage inflation. Thus from a longer run perspective accommodation policy is an inflation policy.

We have reached a very conventional lesson: Stabilization policy is effective in the short run, inflation is largely predetermined relative to aggregate demand and current policies, and accommodation policy in the long run validates the autonomy of wage behavior. In these respects our results confirm accepted wisdom, but they do not confirm the accepted wisdom that budget deficits are the dominant source of money growth.

Appendix. The Data

The *International Financial Statistics* (*IFS*) served as the major source for data in this study. The following series was adapted from the *IFS* for all seven countries.

Data concept	*IFS* line number
High-powered money	14
$M1$	34
Quasi-M ($M2$–$M1$)	35
Consumer price index	64
GNP (current prices)	99a
GDP (constant prices)	99b.p
Government Data	
Budget deficit	80
Revenues	81
Net foreign aid receipts[a]	81g
Expenditures	82
Net lending minus repayments[a]	83

[a] Where applicable.

Wage data for Guatemala and South Africa were taken from Table 19 of the *Yearbook of Labor Statistics* (*YLS*) published by the International Labor Organization. Wage data for the other countries were reported on line 65 of the *IFS*. The *IFS* also reported import prices for Ireland and South Africa on line 76.x. Import price data for the other countries were found in Table 8a of the United Nations *Yearbook of National Accounts Statistics* (*YNAS*). All unemployment data were adapted from Table 10 of the *YLS*. In the cases of Guatemala, South Africa, and Sri Lanka, however, a measure of total unemployment replaced the unemployment rate. These data were converted into a proxy for the unemployment rate by dividing the total figure by the country's population, found on line 99z of the *IFS*.

Data for the world level of import unit values and for the rate of change in the world CPI were adapted from the *IFS*. Finally, a data series for real GDP in the industrialized countries was developed by splicing together data series found in the *YNAS*, the OECD *Historical Statistics*, and the OECD *Main Economic Indicators.*

REFERENCES

Aghevli, B. B., and Khan, M. S. (1978). Government Deficits and the Inflationary Process in Developing Countries. *IMF Staff Papers* **25**, 383–415.

Bruno, M. (1978). An Analysis of Stagflation in the Industrial Countries: Some Preliminary Results. Discussion Paper No. 788, Falk Institute for Economic Research in Israel.

Fair, Ray (1970). The Estimation of Simultaneous Equation Models with Lagged Endogenous Variables and First Order Serially Correlated Errors. *Econometrica* **38** (3), 507–516.

Gordon, R. J. (1977). World Wide Inflation and Monetary Accommodation. *Brookings Papers on Economic Activity* **2**, 409–478.

Harberger, A. C. (1978). A Primer on Inflation. *Journal of Money Credit and Banking* **10**, 505–521.

Lucas, R. E. (1973). Some International Evidence on Output Inflation Tradeoffs, *American Economic Review* **63**, 326–334.

Taylor, J. B. (1979). Staggered Wage Setting in a Macro Model. *American Economic Review Papers and Proceedings* **69**, 108–113.

Taylor, L. B. (1979). *Macro Models for Developing Countries*. McGraw-Hill, New York.

Willett, T. D., and Laney, L. O. (1978). Monetarism, Budget Deficits, and Wage Push Inflation: The Cases of Italy and the U.K. *Banca Nationale del Lavoro Quarterly Review* **31**, 315–331.

DEPARTMENT OF ECONOMICS
MASSACHUSETTS INSTITUTE OF TECHNOLOGY
CAMBRIDGE, MASSACHUSETTS

Inflation and the Balance of Payments under a Crawling Peg Regime

*MARIO I. BLEJER AND LEONARDO LEIDERMAN**

1. Introduction

This paper develops and estimates a monetary framework for the analysis of the simultaneous determination of the rate of inflation, the exchange rate, and the balance of payments under a crawling peg regime. The model is estimated on the basis of quarterly data from Brazil covering the crawling peg period: 1968–1977.

The model presented can be considered as a variant of the monetary approach to the balance of payments and to the exchange rate. As is well known, modern versions of this approach have been pioneered by Mundell (1968, 1971), Johnson (1972), and Dornbusch (1973), and these contributions have been followed by a large number of studies which have adopted the framework of the monetary approach. According to this approach money and asset markets play a crucial role in the determination of the balance of payments and the exchange rate.[1]

*The authors would like to thank the Center for Latin American Development Studies of Boston University for valuable support.

[1] A number of important contributions on the topic are collected in Frenkel and Johnson (1976, 1978) and in the IMF (1977) volume. A review of the empirical evidence on the monetary approach to the balance of payments and exchange rates is presented in Magee (1976). Johnson (1977) and Whitman (1975) present comprehensive reviews of the recent contributions to the monetary approach literature, while a critique of some of the central aspects of that approach is elaborated by Hahn (1977). All these deal with fixed exchange rate regimes. Among those dealing with floating rates are Dornbusch (1976), Frenkel (1976), Frenkel and Clements (1981), Kouri (1975), and Mussa (1976).

ISBN 0-12-259750-8

Most of the previous literature on the monetary approach can be characterized by a dichotomy in the choice of the exchange rate regime analyzed: Either a fixed exchange rate *or* a freely floating system is assumed.[2] However, recent years have shown that many countries meet neither of these assumptions. These countries operate either under a "managed float" system, characterized by substantial government intervention in the foreign exchange market, *or* under a crawling peg system in which the authorities completely determine the path followed by the exchange rate.[3] In order to analyze the experience of countries with these characteristics within a monetary framework, previous formulations of the monetary approach must be extended. This paper represents one such extension, dealing with the case of the crawling peg.

The paper is organized as follows: Section 2 presents the basic model; Section 3 deals with the empirical implementation of the model; and Section 4 contains concluding remarks.

2. The Model

The model here developed extends the framework of the monetary approach to the balance of payments to consider different degrees of exchange rate flexibility, from a freely floating parity to a totally fixed exchange rate. We take the case of a small open economy for which the international price of its traded goods is exogenously determined, and we consider also nontraded goods. The latter are defined as goods whose price responds, at least in the short run, to domestic monetary variables. We also assume that the rate of growth of real income is not affected by monetary variables.

The basic relationships of the monetary sector are

$$M_{\mathrm{s}} \equiv a(R + D), \tag{1}$$

$$M_{\mathrm{d}} = Pm_{\mathrm{d}}, \tag{2}$$

$$m_{\mathrm{d}} = f(y, \pi^{\mathrm{e}}), \tag{3}$$

[2] An exception is the study by Girton and Roper (1977). They develop and test a monetary model of exchange market pressure, defined as a composite variable that includes changes in both the exchange rate and international reserves. As will be seen below, our model deals with the simultaneous determination of each of the components of exchange market pressure.

[3] A theoretical analysis which concludes that the optimal exchange rate regime will correspond to neither of the extremes of a completely fixed or a completely flexible rate is presented by Frenkel (1978, Appendix C). Frenkel concludes that "... for the purpose of empirical work it is useful to design a framework of the adjustment mechanism that can accommodate simultaneously changes in international reserves and changes in the exchange rate" (Frenkel, 1978, p. 39, footnote 1).

where M_s is the nominal supply of domestic money, a is the money multiplier, R is the foreign exchange reserves held by the central bank, D is the domestic credit component of the monetary base, M_d is the demand for nominal cash balances, P stands for a price index that includes traded and nontraded goods, and m_d is the real demand for money, assumed to be a function of real income y and of the alternative cost of holding money, proxied by π^e (the expected rate of inflation).[4]

Although it is possible to postulate a mechanism of lagged adjustments,[5] for simplicity we assume stock equilibrium. That is, the money market clears in each period so that the nominal stock of money is equalized, ex post, with the demand for nominal balances. The assumption requires the existence of the flow equlibrium

$$M_s^* = M_d^*, \tag{4}$$

where the asterisk indicates the percentage rate of change of the variable. Differentiating (1) and (2) logarithmically, the flow equilibrium condition can be rewritten as

$$a^* + (1 - \gamma)R^* + \gamma D^* = P^* + m_d^*, \tag{4'}$$

where γ is a factor of proportionality equal to $D/(R + D)$ and P^* is the domestic rate of inflation. The latter is a weighted average of the rate of change of the price of both traded and nontraded goods,

$$P^* = \lambda P_T^* + (1 - \lambda)P_{NT}^*, \tag{5}$$

where P_T is the price of traded goods in domestic currency, P_{NT} is the price of nontraded goods, and λ is the share of traded goods in total expenditure. Since we consider a small economy, P_T^* is determined by the world rate of inflation P_w^* and by the variations in the effective exchange rate ρ^*:

$$P_T^* = P_w^* + \rho^*. \tag{6}$$

The price of nontraded goods, on the other hand, may be affected by domestic factors. Since an ex ante excess supply of money implies excess demand in the goods market and if excess demand for nontraded goods varies monotonically with excess demand throughout the economy, we can expect the price of nontraded goods relative to that of traded goods to be a function of imbalance in the money market,

$$P_{NT}^* = P_T^* + \theta\Omega, \tag{7}$$

[4]As it happens, the following results are valid under a large variety of assumptions about the mechanism for the formation of π^e, provided that the latter depends on lagged variables. In the empirical application, we assume that π^e is formed by a version of rational expectations; see Section 3.

[5]Indeed, in Section 3 we postulate for the empirical analysis a mechanism of lagged adjustments in the money market.

where Ω is a measure of monetary imbalance and θ is the elasticity of the relative price with respect to the monetary variable.[6]

Regarding Ω, it is important to remember that a central conclusion of the monetary approach to the balance of payments is that in a small open economy the nominal supply of money may be beyond the control of the monetary authority. Under fixed exchange rates the monetary authority can determine the ex ante quantity of money only by changing the domestic credit component of the base or by affecting the money multiplier through the manipulation of variables under its control (such as legal reserve requirements). Such actions, in conjunction with the flow demand for real balances generated by adjustments in the desired stock, create an ex ante excess flow supply of money to which the public reacts by changing the level of the international reserve component of the base through the balance of payments and by affecting the rate of domestic inflation. The ex post nominal quantity of money in an open economy is then influenced by the behavior of the public in response to ex ante conditions in the money market.[7]

There is a presumption therefore that the relevant measure to account for the monetary effects on the goods market in an open economy should be an ex ante measure that does not include the endogenous reaction of the foreign component of the base. For that reason we define Ω in (7) as the gap (in percentage terms) between the ex ante change in the money supply (that is, a change in the domestic credit component of the base and in the money multiplier) and changes in demand. Equation (7) can therefore be rewritten as

$$P^*_{\mathrm{NT}} = P^*_{\mathrm{T}} + \theta(\gamma D^* + a^* - M^*_{\mathrm{d}}). \tag{7'}$$

Substituting (6) into (7′) and then (6) and (7′) into (5), we obtain, after some manipulation, the following expression for the rate of domestic inflation[8]:

$$P^* = \epsilon(P^*_{\mathrm{w}} + \rho^*) + (1 - \epsilon)(\gamma D^* - m^*_{\mathrm{d}}), \tag{8}$$

where $\epsilon = 1/[1 + \theta(1 - \lambda)]$.

In addition to changes in the price level, monetary equilibrium is restored also by changes in international reserves. Therefore, an expression

[6] θ is a function of the elasticity of substitution between traded and nontraded goods in consumption and production, as well as the income elasticity of the nontraded goods. For a detailed description of the dynamics of domestic price determination in a monetary model with traded and nontraded goods see, for example, Blejer (1977) and Parkin (1974).

[7] For time-series analysis and econometric tests of the interaction between changes in domestic credit and in international reserves implied by the monetary approach using European data, see Blejer (1980) and Leiderman (1980).

[8] Assuming, for simplicity, a constant money multiplier, that is $a^* = 0$. In the empirical section, however, changes in the money multiplier are explicitly considered.

for the money account of the balance of payments, which is equal to the change in the international reserves held by the central bank, may be obtained by substituting P^* in (4′)—the flow equlibrium condition for the money market—for its value in (8) and by rearranging the terms:

$$(1-\gamma)R^* = \epsilon(P_w^* + \rho^* + m_d^* - \gamma D^*). \qquad (9)$$

Equations (8) and (9) present the domestic rate of inflation and the balance of payments as functions of world inflation, exchange rate policy, and the rate of ex ante excess flow supply of money. When nontraded goods are absent ($\lambda = 1$) or when their price is not sensitive to monetary imbalance ($\theta = 0$), then $\epsilon = 1$ and the model is similar to the classical long-run formulation of the monetary approach [see Johnson (1972)]. In such cases domestic monetary variables do not affect the domestic rate of inflation, which if the exchange rate is not altered, is fully determined by the world rate, and every ex ante monetary shock will lead to reserve depletion due to a balance of payments deficit.

To complete the model, we must specify the exchange rate behavior. Except in a fully flexible exchange rate system fluctuations are generally influenced by policy decisions. Under a crawling peg system the exchange rate is changed frequently according to some set of rules designed to attain the government's objectives.[9] The variations of the exchange rate can therefore be considered as following a sort of reaction function which reflects policy goals as well as the parameters of the model adopted and the values of the exogenous and endogenous variables considered relevant for the desired goals. These goals, and therefore the crawling rules, may vary from country to country.[10]

With a view toward empirical implementation of the model for the case of Brazil we postulate here that the policy objective of the monetary authority is to avoid long-run changes in the real exchange rate and that the nominal rate ρ is therefore altered to maintain purchasing power parity.[11] We assume, in addition, that the full adjustment of the exchange rate may take more than one period. The reaction function implied by the

[9] A number of proposals for the operation of the crawling peg and analyses of the stability of the system have recently been presented; see, e.g., Cooper (1970), Kenen (1975), Levin (1975, 1977), Mathieson (1976), Williamson (1965).

[10] Kenen (1975) analyzes in detail the relative efficiency of a number of alternative sliding parity rules. Mathieson (1976) studies the consequences of using a welfare—instead of a balance of payments—objective as the guideline for the crawl.

[11] A discussion of the appropriateness of this assumption for the case of Brazil is presented in Section 3. In a previous version of this paper a number of alternative rules were incorporated into the model, among them maintaining a given level of nominal reserves ($R^* = 0$) and maintaining a given level of real reserves ($R^* - P_w^* = 0$). Although the dynamics of the system change with the policy rule, its basic structure is not affected. For presentational convenience the model is here confined to a single rule.

policy rule is

$$\rho_t^* = \beta \sum_{i=0}^{n} (1-\beta)^i L^i (P^* - P_w^*)_t, \tag{10}$$

where t is a time subscript, β indicates the portion of the current differential rate of inflation transmitted to the exchange rate in the current period, and L is the lag operator (such that $L^i x_t = x_{t-i}$).[12]

This formulation specifically assumes that (in addition to the current-period adjustment) the exchange rate will continue to be changed in each subsequent period by a portion β of the still unadjusted differential until the whole differential has been transmitted to the exchange rate. Obviously, the greater β is, the faster the adjustment of the rate will be. If $\beta = 1$, our model does not differ conceptually from the monetary approach model of free floating exchange rates since the rate of depreciation is then fully determined by the domestic–foreign inflation differential [see Frenkel (1976)].

The model can now be solved for the rate of inflation, the rate of change of foreign exchange reserves, and the rate of change of the exchange rate. Combining (8) and (10) to solve for ρ_t^*, we obtain

$$\rho_t^* = \frac{\beta(1-\epsilon)}{1-\beta\epsilon-(1-\beta)L}(\gamma D^* - m_d^* - P_w^*)_t. \tag{11}$$

Substituting this in (8) and (9), we obtain

$$P_t^* = \frac{\epsilon[(1-\beta)(1-L)]}{1-\beta\epsilon-(1-\beta)L}(P_w^*)_t + \frac{(1-\epsilon)[1-(1-\beta)L]}{1-\beta\epsilon-(1-\beta)L}(\gamma D^* - m_d^*)_t \tag{12}$$

and

$$(1-\gamma)R_t^* = \frac{\epsilon[(1-\beta)(1-L)]}{1-\beta\epsilon-(1-\beta)L}(P_w^* + m_d^* - \gamma D^*)_t. \tag{13}$$

It can be seen that the three endogenous variables are functions of current and lagged values of foreign inflation and of domestic monetary

[12] A reaction function of this type follows Dean's (1974) approach in the sense that endogenous target variables are functions of the current values of other endogenous variables on the grounds that they are a plausible representation of the structure of the model, allowing for the possibility of prior knowledge of the structural-form coefficients. This differs from the approach of earlier works such as Friedlaender (1973) where endogenous variables depend only on exogenous or lagged endogenous variables.

variables. Because the coefficients of P_w^* and $(\gamma D^* - m_d^*)$ in (12) add to unity, domestic and foreign inflation will be equalized ($P^* = P_w^*$) when the exogenous component of the supply of money (domestic credit) is expanded at a rate that exceeds the growth in the demand for real balances by the world rate of inflation, that is, when the ex ante excess flow supply of money $(\gamma D^* - m_d^*)$ is equal to the world inflation rate. When that takes place, the balance of payments will be in equilibrium and the exchange rate will not change ($R^* = \rho^* = 0$).[13]

From Eqs. (11)–(13) it is possible to infer that under a crawling peg system a small open economy can choose its long-run rate of domestic inflation independently from that of the rest of the world. Balance of payments deficits and surpluses are, however, experienced in the process of adjustment to a new rate of price increases due to the less than immediate full adjustment of the exchange rate.

3. Empirical Investigation

A. Methodology

In this section the model developed above is restated in econometric form. For estimation purposes, we work with the following system:

$$P_t^* = \epsilon(P_w^* + \rho^*)_t + (1 - \epsilon)(a^* + \gamma D^* - m_d^*)_t + \mu_{1t}, \tag{8'}$$

$$(1 - \gamma)R_t^* = \epsilon(P_w^* + \rho^* + m_d^* - \gamma D^* - a^*)_t + \mu_{2t}, \tag{9'}$$

$$\rho_t^* = \beta(P^* - P_w^*)_t + \beta(1 - \beta)(P^* - P_w^*)_{t-1} + \beta(1 - \beta)^2(P^* - P_w^*)_{t-2} + \mu_{3t}. \tag{10'}$$

Equations (8′), (9′), and (10′) could be referred to as the model's semistructural equations.[14] These equations correspond, with only slight modifications,[15] to (8), (9), and (10), respectively.

[13] For a detailed discussion of the functioning of a similar model, see Blejer and Leiderman (1981).

[14] This is because (8′) and (9′) do not represent "truly" structural equations in the sense of autonomous behavioral equations. Equation (10′), however, is one of the model's structural equations.

[15] Specifically, random disturbances have been added, and we are now taking into account changes in the money multiplier. Also, we consider only three terms in the exchange rate equation (see discussion that follows).

The following stochastic specification is adopted: It is assumed that the μs possess a first-order autoregressive representation

$$\mu_{it} = \phi_i \mu_{it-1} + v_{it}, \qquad i = 1, 2, 3,$$

where ϕ_i are the autoregressive parameters and v_{it} are error terms. Furthermore, we assume that the error vectors (v_{1t}, v_{2t}, v_{3t}), $t = 1, \ldots, T$, have zero mean and a constant variance–covariance matrix Γ; also, they are serially uncorrelated and drawn from a multivariate normal distribution.

Equations (8′), (9′), and (10′) constitute a simultaneous system, which is linear in the variables but nonlinear in (some of) the parameters. Given these characteristics, consistent estimation requires the use of some simultaneous-equation method. We have used a full information maximum likelihood (FIML) estimator. The FIML utilizes all the a priori restrictions on the system to estimate the coefficients of interest (ϵ, $\beta, \phi_1, \phi_2, \phi_3$), in our case by maximizing the model's likelihood function.[16]

To make the estimation operational, time series are required for m^*_{dt}, the rate of change of real money demand. Here we have assumed a semilogarithmic money demand equation, whereby the log of demand for real money balances depends, as in (3), on the log of real income and expected inflation. As the model is applied to quarterly data, we postulate a process of gradual adjustment of real money balances to their optimal value.[17] With these specifications it is appropriate to take the first-differences of the fitted values of the estimated money demand equation as corresponding to the variable m^*_{dt}.[18] Finally, the estimation of money demand requires a proxy for π^e. This proxy was constructed by assuming a version of Sargent's (1973) "partly rational" expectations. Specifically, it is postulated that agents form their inflation expectations on the basis of least-squares predictions of inflation which are conditional on lagged rates of inflation.[19]

[16] See Hendry (1971). The parameter estimates reported below were obtained by using Wymer's (1978) computer program, Resimul. The program uses a Newton–Raphson iterative procedure, beginning with arbitrary initial parameter values.

[17] Formally, the demand for money is given by $\log m_{dt} = \delta_0 + \delta_1 \log y_t - \delta_2 \pi^e_t$. Money demand equations of this form have been previously estimated for Brazil by Silveira (1973) and Khan (1977). We assume an adjustment mechanism of the form $(\log m_t - \log m_{t-1}) = h(\log m_{dt} - \log m_{t-1})$, $0 < h < 1$. Griliches (1967) gives a discussion of the conditions under which adjustment mechanisms of this class are likely to be optimal.

[18] Although it is possible to think of the complete system as being composed of (8′), (9′), (10′), and in addition (3), it will be noted that such a system is block recursive, with (3) forming the lowest-order block. Therefore, this equation can be consistently estimated at a first stage, even if its disturbance is contemporaneously correlated with those of (8′), (9′), and (10′). This is the strategy adopted here.

[19] That is, $\pi^e = \sum_{i=1}^{n} \hat{\psi}_i P^*_{t-i}$, where the $\hat{\psi}_i$s are the estimated parameters of this least-squares regression equation. In the empirical application we set $n = 6$.

B. Results

In this section we report estimates of the parameters of (8′), (9′), and (10′), as well as of the derived reduced-form equations. All estimates are based on quarterly data for Brazil. The sample period, 1968 : 3–1977 : 4, contains 38 observations.

As already mentioned, our empirical work is based on data for Brazil. Brazil adopted a crawling peg regime in August 1968. The adoption of such an exchange rate regime can be considered as an extension of indexation to the external sector.[20] Although there are no explicitly announced rules for the crawl, it is evident that the mechanism used is an application of a purchasing power parity clause to the domestic price of foreign exchange. The evolution of both domestic and foreign price levels is taken into account in making the adjustments of the exchange rate. In this way, and as emphasized by the Brazilian authorities, it is possible to neutralize the harmful effects of domestic inflation on the competitiveness of Brazilian products in international markets and hence on Brazil's balance of payments.[21] The specification of (10), the exchange rate reaction function, intends to capture these considerations. Most of the variables used in our empirical analysis are represented by readily available series.[22]

As indicated previously, the estimation of the model's semistructural equations (8′), (9′), and (10′) requires the construction of the m^*_{dt} variable. Therefore, at a first stage we estimated a semilogarithmic demand for money. The estimated equation is

$$\log m_t = \underset{(0.195)}{-\ 0.462} + \underset{(0.064)}{0.188}\log y_t - \underset{(0.283)}{1.665}\,\pi^e_t + \underset{(0.058)}{0.828}\log m_{t-1},$$

$$R^2 = 0.984, \qquad h = 1.12, \qquad \text{rho} = -0.627, \qquad \text{s.e.} = 0.042.$$

Figures in parentheses are standard errors. To account for serial correlation in the residuals, the equation was estimated using the Cochrane–Orcutt technique. Rho is the estimated autocorrelation coefficient, h is Durbin's

[20] On the various aspects of indexation in Brazil see the NBER volume edited by Nadiri and Pastore (1977). A comprehensive study of the recent Brazilian economic experience is presented by Lemgruber (1977). On the functioning of the crawling peg and its effects on the economy see Moura Da Silva (1977); see also Lara-Resende (1978).

[21] This appears to be the main rationale provided by the authorities for the adoption of the crawling peg (see Lemgruber (1977) and Moura Da Silva (1977)).

[22] For P, R, and M the following series were utilized: consumer price index, international reserves of the central bank, and the money supply. D was generated by subtracting R from the monetary base, and ρ is the exchange rate (average over the quarter). All of the preceding were taken from *International Financial Statistics*, various issues. y is represented by the quarterly real-income series constructed by Wachter (1976). (The series was extended through 1977 using exactly Wachter's method.)

serial-correlation statistic for autoregressive models, s.e. is the standard error of the regression, and π_t^e is our proxy for expectations of inflation, formed with the fitted values of a sixth-order inflation autoregressive process.[23]

All the coefficients in the estimated money demand equation have the expected signs and are significantly different from zero. The estimated coefficients are fairly similar to those reported by Khan (1977) and Silveira (1973) for the case of Brazil. Our parameter estimates imply a long-run income elasticity of real money demand equal to 1.093 and a long-run elasticity or real money demand with respect to expected inflation of -0.57. Given these results, we constructed m_{dt}^* by taking the first difference of the fitted values of the estimated money demand equation.

Results of estimating (8′), (9′), and (10′) are presented in Table 1. All the parameter estimates are of the proper sign and are reasonably well determined: In most cases asymptotic t ratios are well above two.[24] The reported $\tilde{R}^2$ are quite satisfactory for (9′) and (10′), considering that the model is estimated in first differences; the $\tilde{R}^2$ for Eq. (8′), however, is low.[25]

The results indicate that both foreign inflation and excess supply in the money market significantly affect the determination of the domestic rate of inflation. These two factors (world inflation and monetary imbalance) also affect significantly the balance of payments as shown by (9′). Specifically, an acceleration in the rate of domestic credit creation over and above the rate of growth in money demand will increase domestic inflation and reduce international reserves. The overall effect of such an increase, however, cannot be established solely from (8′) and (9′). This is because the departure of domestic from world inflation will induce, as indicated by (10′), a depreciation of the exchange rate which in turn, in this simultaneous model, further raises the rate of inflation and reduces the rate at which foreign exchange reserves are depleted. In order to analyze the full

[23] As noted previously, this methodology can be interpreted as a version of Sargent's (1973) "partly rational" expectations. The estimated equation is

$$\pi_t^e = \underset{(0.164)}{[0.876} - \underset{(0.218)}{0.471L} + \underset{(0.225)}{0.488L^2} - \underset{(0.220)}{0.041L^3} + \underset{(0.204)}{0.039L^4} - \underset{(0.150)}{0.125L^5}]P_{t-1}^*$$

$$+ \underset{(0.009)}{0.012} + \underset{(0.008)}{0.011S_1} - \underset{(0.007)}{0.005S_2} - \underset{(0.008)}{0.001S_3},$$

$$R^2 = 0.652, \qquad DW = 1.79, \qquad s.e. = 0.015.$$

Standard errors appear in parentheses; L is the lag operator, defined in the text; S_i represent seasonal dummies ($i = 1, 2, 3$).

[24] Asymptotic t ratios are defined as coefficient values divided by asymptotic standard errors.

[25] $\tilde{R}^2$ is defined as one minus the ratio of variance of structural residual to variance of endogenous variable. The meaning of these $\tilde{R}^2$ in simultaneous models is ambiguous at best.

TABLE 1

FIML ESTIMATES OF THE MODEL[a]

$$P_t^* = \underset{(0.019)}{0.955}\,(P_w^* + \rho^*)_t + \underset{(0.019)}{0.045}\,(a^* + \gamma D^* - m_d^*)_t,$$

$$\tilde{R}^2 = 0.054, \quad \phi_1 = -\underset{(0.083)}{0.015}, \quad C_1 = \underset{(0.002)}{0.002}. \qquad (8')$$

$$(1-\gamma)R_t^* = \underset{(0.019)}{0.955}\,(P_w^* + \rho^* + m_d^* - \gamma D^* - a^*)_t,$$

$$\tilde{R}^2 = 0.295, \quad \phi_2 = -\underset{(0.139)}{0.365}, \quad C_2 = \underset{(0.002)}{0.017}. \qquad (9')$$

$$\rho_t^* = \underset{(0.117)}{0.537}\,(P^* - P_w^*)_t + \underset{(0.009)}{0.245}\,(P^* - P_w^*)_{t-1} + \underset{(0.074)}{0.098}\,(P^* - P_w^*)_{t-2},$$

$$\tilde{R}^2 = 0.375, \quad \phi_3 = \underset{(0.060)}{0.017}, \quad C_3 = \underset{(0.003)}{0.007}, \qquad (10')$$

$$\hat{\Gamma} = \begin{pmatrix} 0.00053 & & \\ 0.00047 & 0.00480 & \\ -0.00047 & -0.00059 & 0.00048 \end{pmatrix}.$$

[a]Note: See text for notation. Numerals in parenthesis are asymptotic standard errors of regression coefficients. $\hat{\Gamma}$ is the estimated residuals' variance–covariance matrix. C_i, $i = 1, 2, 3$, is the estimated constant term.

effect of changes in the rate of growth of domestic credit (as well as in the other exogenous variables) reduced-form coefficients should be considered. These coefficients are reported below.

With respect to the exchange rate reaction function (10′) the parameter estimates indicate that more than 50% of the foreign–domestic inflation differential is transmitted to the exchange rate within the current quarter and an additional 25% in the following quarter. After only three quarters the full differential is completely reflected by the exchange rate adjustment. In this context it is important to note that (10′) embodies a specific restriction regarding the effects of current and lagged values of the domestic–foreign inflation differential on the exchange rate. Specifically, a pattern of geometrically decaying weights was postulated. Indeed, the results reported in Table 1 are derived under the imposition of this restriction. To test the empirical validity of the restriction, we estimated the system unrestricted and constructed a chi-square likelihood ratio test. In our case the likelihood ratio obtains a value of 2.255 with two degrees of freedom. This value is smaller than the 95% chi-square critical value; that is, the sample information does not reject the restrictions embodied in (10′) at the usual 5% significance level.

With the information contained in Table 1 it is possible to calculate the derived reduced-form estimates and their asymptotic standard errors. The

TABLE 2

DERIVED REDUCED-FORM ESTIMATES[a]

$$\rho_t^* = [\underset{(0.018)}{0.050} + \underset{(0.013)}{0.026}L + \underset{(0.012)}{0.024}L^2 + \underset{(0.011)}{0.023}L^3 + \underset{(0.010)}{0.022}L^4](\gamma D^* + a^* - m_d^* - P_w^*)_t. \quad (11')$$

$$P_t^* = [\underset{(0.029)}{0.907} - \underset{(0.014)}{0.045}L - \underset{(0.014)}{0.043}L^2 - \underset{(0.012)}{0.041}L^3 - \underset{(0.011)}{0.039}L^4](P_w^*)_t$$
$$+ [\underset{(0.029)}{0.093} + \underset{(0.015)}{0.045}L + \underset{(0.014)}{0.043}L^2 + \underset{(0.012)}{0.041}L^3 + \underset{(0.011)}{0.039}L^4](\gamma D^* + a^* - m_d^*)_t. \quad (12')$$

$$(1-\gamma)R_t^* = [-\underset{(0.029)}{0.907} + \underset{(0.015)}{0.045}L + \underset{(0.014)}{0.043}L^2 + \underset{(0.012)}{0.041}L^3 + \underset{(0.011)}{0.039}L^4](\gamma D^* + a^* - m_d^* - P_w^*)_t. \quad (13')$$

[a]Note: For notation and explanations see text.

reduced forms are given by (11)–(13). The estimates of these equations, with the corresponding standard errors as implied by the structural estimates reported in Table 1, are presented in Table 2.[26]

The overall effects of current and lagged rates of excess money supply and of foreign inflation on the exchange rate, the domestic rate of inflation, and the balance of payments can be assessed from the coefficients of (11′), (12′), and (13′).[27] The latter indicate that about 30% of the excess flow supply of money (the difference between the rates of growth of domestic credit and money demand) is transmitted to the inflation rate within five quarters. To the extent that the rate at which the excess supply of money is created exceeds the foreign rate of inflation, the exchange rate will depreciate (by about 15% of the difference during the first five quarters), and international reserves will fall. Monetary equilibrium is therefore maintained by a combination of reductions in the real value of the nominal stock due to the acceleration in the inflation rate and reductions in the monetary base through the loss of reserves.

The effects of foreign inflation on the three endogenous variables can also be analyzed from the estimates in Table 2. A higher rate of world inflation will reduce the rate of depreciation of the exchange rate and will have a positive effect on the rate of accumulation of foreign reserves. It will, however, significantly raise the domestic rate of inflation during the current quarter. Notice that lagged rates of foreign inflation appear with a

[26]Since in the empirical section we take into account changes in the money multiplier, Table 2 refers to Eqs. (11′), (12′), and (13′) which include such changes.

[27]Although only current and four-lagged coefficients are reported for purposes of illustration, coefficients for additional lags can be calculated from Table 1.

negative sign, which is indeed consistent with our version of the crawling peg regime. An acceleration of world inflation will tend, *ceteris paribus*, to induce subsequent appreciations of the exchange rate, thus attenuating the initial increase in both the domestic price of traded goods and the domestic rate of inflation.

4. Concluding Remarks

In this paper we have developed and tested a monetary model of the joint determination of inflation, the exchange rate, and the balance of payments under a crawling peg system. The framework presented represents an extension of the previous literature on the monetary approach.

Our analysis implies that a country that indexes its exchange rate can, by adopting a purchasing power parity clause, choose its rate of inflation independently from the rest of the world. To the extent that the exchange rate does not fully adjust to domestic–foreign inflation differentials, equilibrating flows of international reserves will emerge. As also implied by our analysis, an increase in the rate of growth of domestic credit tends to increase domestic inflation and the exchange rate (that is, a depreciation of the currency) and to reduce domestic holdings of international reserves. Overall, the model is capable of generating simultaneous deviations from purchasing power parity and from fluctuations in both the exchange rate and international reserves.

The empirical investigation consisted of FIML estimation of the model's basic equations for Brazilian quarterly time series for the crawling peg period from 1968 to 1977. The main hypotheses delivered by the model regarding signs and magnitudes of several parameters receive some support from the sample information.

REFERENCES

Blejer, Mario I. (1977). Short-Run Dynamics of Prices and the Balance of Payments. *American Economic Review* **68**, 419–428.

Blejer, Mario I. (1980). On Causality and the Monetary Approach to the Balance of Payments: The European Experience. *European Economic Review* (to be published).

Blejer, Mario I., and Leiderman, Leonardo, (1981). A Monetary Approach to the Crawling Peg System: Theory and Evidence. *Journal of Political Economy* (to be published).

Cooper, Richard N. (1970). Sliding Parities: A Proposal for Presumptive Rules. In *Approaches to Greater Flexibility of Exchange Rates: The Burgensto Papers* (George N. Halm, ed.), pp. 251–259. Princeton University Press, Princeton, New Jersey.

Dean, James W. (1974). Problems in the Specification and Interpretation of Central Bank Reaction Functions. *Economic and Social Review* **5**, 431–443.

Dornbusch, Rudiger (1973). Devaluation, Money, and Nontraded Goods. *American Economic Review* **63**, 871–880.

Dornbusch, Rudiger (1976). The Theory of Flexible Exchange Regimes and Macroeconomic Policy. *Scandinavian Journal of Economics* **78**, 255–275.

Frenkel, Jacob A. (1976). A Monetary Approach to the Exchange Rate: Doctrinal Aspects and Empirical Evidence. *Scandinavian Journal of Economics* **78**, 200–224.

Frenkel, Jacob A. (1978). International Reserves: Pegged Exchange Rates and Managed Float. University of Chicago, February.

Frenkel, Jacob A., and Clements, Kenneth W. (1981). Exchange Rates in the 1920's: A Monetary Approach. This volume.

Frenkel, Jacob A., and Johnson, Harry G., eds. (1976). *The Monetary Approach to the Balance of Payments.* Allen & Unwin, London and University of Toronto Press, Toronto.

Frenkel, Jacob A., and Johnson, Harry G., eds. (1978). *The Economics of Exchange Rates: Selected Studies*. Addison-Wesley, Reading, Massachusetts.

Friedlaender, Ann F. (1973). Macro Policy Goals in the Postwar Period: A Study in Revealed Preferences. *Quarterly Journal of Economics* **88**(Feb.), 25–43.

Girton, Lance, and Roper, Don (1977). A Monetary Model of Exchange Market Pressure Applied to Postwar Canadian Experience. *American Economic Review* **67**, 537–548.

Griliches, Zvi (1967). Distributed Lags: A Survey. *Econometrica* **35**(Jan.), 16–49.

Hahn, Frank H. (1977). The Monetary Approach to the Balance of Payments. *Journal of International Economics* **7**, 231–249.

Hendry, David F. (1971). Maximum Likelihood Estimation of Systems of Simultaneous Regression Equation with Errors Generated by a Vector Autoregressive Process. *International Economic Review* **22**, 257–272.

IMF (1977). *The Monetary Approach to the Balance of Payments*. Washington, D.C.

Johnson, Harry, G. (1972). The Monetary Approach to the Balance of Payments. In *Further Essays in Monetary Theory*, pp. 229–249. Allen & Unwin, London.

Johnson, Harry G. (1977). The Monetary Approach to the Balance of Payments: A Non-Technical Guide. *Journal of International Economics* **7**, 251–262.

Kenen, Peter B. (1975). Floats, Glides and Indicators: A Comparison of Methods for Changing Exchange Rates. *Journal of International Economics* **5**, 107–152.

Khan, Mohsin S. (1977). Variable Expectations and the Demand for Money in High-Inflation Countries. *Manchester School* Sept., pp. 270–293.

Kouri, Pentti J. K. (1975). Exchange Rate Expectations, and the Short-Run and the Long-Run Effects of Fiscal and Monetary Policies under Flexible Exchange Rates. Paper presented at the conference on Monetary Mechanisms in Open Economies, Helsinki, August.

Lara-Resende, Andre (1978). Interest Parity and the Brazilian Crawling Peg: The Official and the Parallel Markets. Unpublished manuscript, Massachusetts Institute of Technology, April.

Leiderman, Leonardo (1980). Relationships Between Macroeconomic Time-Series in a Fixed-Exchange-Rate Economy. *European Economic Review* (to be published).

Lemgruber, Antonio C. (1977). Inflation in Brazil. In *Worldwide Inflation* (Lawrence B. Krause and Walter S. Salant, eds.), pp. 395–442. Brookings, Washington, D.C.

Levin, Jay, II (1975). Monetary Policy and the Crawling Peg. *Economic Journal* **85**(Mar.), 20–32.

Levin, Jay, II (1977). Reserve Stocks as External Targets and the Stability of Alternative Exchange Rate Systems. *Review of Economic Studies* **44**(Feb.), 49–70.

Magee, Stephen P. (1976). The Empirical Evidence on the Monetary Approach to the Balance of Payments and Exchange Rates. *American Economic Review* **66**, 163–170.

Mathieson, D. J. (1976). Is There an Optimal Crawl? *Journal of International Economics* **6**, 183–202.

Moura Da Silva, Antonio (1977). The Basis of the Mini-devaluation Policy. *Explorations in Economic Research* **4**, 101–116.
Mundell, Robert A. (1968). *International Economics*. Macmillan, New York.
Mundell, Robert A. (1971). *Monetary Theory*. Goodyear, Pacific Palisades, California.
Mussa, Michael (1976). The Exchange Rate, the Balance of Payments, and Monetary and Fiscal Policy under a Regime of Controlled Floating. *Scandinavian Journal of Economics* **77**, 229–248.
Nadiri, Ishaq M., and Pastore, Alfonso C., eds. (1977). Indexation, the Brazilian Experience. *Explorations in Economic Research* **4**(Winter).
Parkin, Michael (1974). Inflation, the Balance of Payments, Domestic Credit Expansion, and Exchange Rate Adjustments. In *National Monetary Policies and the International Financial System* (R. Z. Aliber, ed.), pp. 49–63. University of Chicago Press, Chicago, Illinois.
Sargent, Thomas J. (1973). Rational Expectations, the Real Rate of Interest, and the Natural Rate of Unemployment. *Brookings Papers* **2**, 429–480.
Silveira, Antonio M. (1973). The Demand for Money: The Evidence from the Brazilian Economy. *Journal of Money, Credit and Banking* **5**(Feb.), 113–140.
Wachter, Susan M. (1976). *Latin American Inflation.* Lexington Books, Lexington, Massachusetts.
Whitman, Marina V. N. (1975). Global Monetarism and the Monetary Approach to the Balance of Payments. *Brookings Papers* **3**, 491–536.
Williamson, John H. (1965). *The Crawling Peg* (Princeton Essays in International Finance, No. 50). Princeton University Press, Princeton, New Jersey.
Wymer, Cliford (1978). *Computer Programs: Resimul Manual*. IMF, Washington, D.C.

MARIO I. BLEJER
HEBREW UNIVERSITY OF JERUSALEM
JERUSALEM, ISRAEL

and

CENTER FOR LATIN AMERICAN DEVELOPMENT STUDIES
BOSTON UNIVERSITY
BOSTON, MASSACHUSETTS

LEONARDO LEIDERMAN
DEPARTMENT OF ECONOMICS
TEL AVIV UNIVERSITY
RAMAT AVIV, TEL AVIV, ISRAEL

Elements of a Pure Theory of Forecasting and the After-Keynesian Macroeconometrics

*YAIR MUNDLAK**

1. Introduction

The development of the new macroeconomics is very much empirically oriented and influenced by the data. This can be clearly seen in a recent interesting testimony of two major participants, Lucas and Sargent (1978), who take inventory of the state of the art. They claim that basic issues which have been viewed as closed will have to be reopened in order to achieve a theory of business cycles. Their discussion is based on a fruitful interplay between economic and econometric analysis. It can therefore serve well in formulating some of the issues that have to do with the empirical content and usefulness of macro models and deserve some more attention.

The general framework suggested by Lucas and Sargent for evaluating macro models can be used here in bringing up the main issues to be discussed. A general macroeconometric system relates linearly vectors $\mathbf{y_t}$, $\mathbf{x_t}$, and $\boldsymbol{\epsilon}_\mathbf{t}$ of (respectively) endogenous variables, exogenous variables, and disturbances. Each of those vectors includes current and lagged values, a fact denoted here by the boldface subscript **t**. The reduced form expresses each element $\mathbf{y}_t$ as a linear function of $\mathbf{y}_{t-1}$, $\mathbf{x}_t$, and $\boldsymbol{\epsilon}_t$. As forecasting constitutes an important factor in empirical analysis, Lucas and Sargent remind the reader that (unrestricted) reduced-form forecasting takes no

*I should like to thank George M. Kuznets and Yakir Plessner for helpful discussions.

ISBN 0-12-259750-8

account of structural changes, and they therefore state that it has no value.[1] The recognition that parameters change over time (or over policies) has very important repercussions.[2] It limits the size of the sample that can be used for estimating any particular model. Thus it is intrinsic to this approach, from a statistical point of view, that one is working within a small sample framework. The essence of this framework is that the sampling error may have a relatively large variance.[3] This point is not recognized by the authors, and if anything, they follow procedures which do not coexist well with such a framework. This statement is explained below.

In line with the conventional wisdom, Lucas and Sargent insist that models should be identified.[4] However they criticize the Keynesian econometric models for achieving identification by imposing too many zero restrictions on the parameters. This simply amounts to ignoring or omitting too many variables. Their alternative calls for models with a larger number of variables. But in considering this alternative, an essential point is completely ignored: the number of variables that can be sustained by the data of a given sample size.

Another aspect of indentification criticized by Lucas and Sargent is the classification of variables as exogenous or endogenous. It is claimed that such a classification should be empirically based and determined from the sample, using the Sims test. It turns out that the actual performance of this test also involves the problem of statistical inference with many variables and finite (and relatively small) samples.

The criticism of the omission of variables is not an abstract one. To a large extent it is directed at improper handling of expectations with respect to variables which influence decisions and whose values are unknown. Their approach to a proper way of dealing with expectations is stated as follows:

> However the macro models . . . generally imply that a wise agent would use the current and many lagged values of many and usually

[1] Ex ante forecasting from the reduced form is "an exercise in sophisticated kind of extrapolation requiring no understanding of . . . the economic model." Alternatively, " . . . one needs to know the structural parameters. This is so because a change in policy *necessarily* alters some of the structural parameters . . . and therefore affects the reduced form parameters in a highly complex fashion" (Lucas and Sargent, 1979, p. 3).

[2] In criticizing Keynesian econometrics, Lucas and Sargent (1979) state that " . . . the track record of the major econometric models is, on any dimension other than very short-term unconditional forecasting, very poor. Formal statistical test for parameters instability . . . invariably reveals major shift" (p. 6).

[3] Sampling variance means a variance that declines monotonically with sample size.

[4] "The problem of identifying a structural model from a collection of economic time series is one that must be solved by anyone who claims the ability to give quantitative economic advice" (Lucas and Sargent, 1979, p. 3).

> most endogenous and exogenous variables in the model in order to form expectations about any one variable. Thus virtually any version of the hypothesis that agents behave in their own interest will contradict the identification restrictions imposed on expectations formation . . . the role of expectations is pervasive in the models and exerts a massive influence on their dynamic properties (a point Keynes himself insisted on). (Lucas and Sargent, 1979, p. 5).

Consequently, in the new econometric models, "[t]he hypothesis of rational expectation is being imposed . . . because agents are supposed to make the best possible use of limited information they have and are assumed to know the pertinent objective probability distributions" (Lucas and Sargent, 1979, p. 8).

If assumptions have to be explained or rationalized, it seems that it would be desirable to clarify how agents acquire the pertinent objective probability distributions in a world undergoing structural changes. Various authors use somewhat different definitions of rational expectations, and we return to this point below. However, the approach taken by Lucas and Sargent is of immediate interest to our discussion. Its essence is that all information is utilized by agents and in an optimal way. The criterion for optimality does not seem to play an important role at the theoretical level. At the practical level it leads to the utilization of many lagged values.

Other writers emphasize other aspects of rational expectations. For instance Cyert and DeGroot (1974, p. 521) state that "Muth's hypothesis was that the mean expectation of firms with respect to some phenomenon . . . was equal to the prediction that would be made by the relevant economic theory." The difficulty with such a statement is that it assumes that the "relevant economic theory" is a well-defined homogeneous product. As this is far from being the case, it does not provide a basis for deriving rational expectations. It seems that the notion of rational expectations should be defined differently. It should be viewed as a joint restriction on both model and expectations, rather than on the expectations alone. It thus converts the problem to that of model construction. It is under such an interpretation that the hypothesis can be considered as a " . . . scientific truth rather than a religious belief" (p. 522).

From a statistical point of view, the computation of rational expectations involves the formation of predictions on the basis of past data and estimated relationships. This problem is related to but is not the same as that of estimating the model and also involves a choice as to whether and how to utilize all the available information.

The foregoing remarks are all related to the confrontation of theory and data, a link that deserves some further analysis. The framework of such an analysis is largely statistical in nature, and that is also the framework adopted here. In order to make the analysis concrete, we begin by examining results obtained in a recently published empirical study which illustrates the difficulty in the empirical implementation of the concept of rational expectations. That discussion deals with a two-stage procedure where the first stage produces estimates for the unobserved expectation variables and the second stage utilizes the results of the first stage for estimating the structural parameters.

The problem of too many exogenous variables occurs in the first stage. This is discussed in Section 3 within the framework of the linear statistical model. The purpose of the discussion is to formulate the problem and to provide results; the details of the analysis are omitted. The question is Can the formation of expectations be obtained from a regression on a subset of regressors, or should a larger set of regressors be used? Section 3 deals with this by viewing expectations as the estimation of an unobserved variable. This framework is related to the discussion in Section 2 and also provides the basis for extending the analysis to simultaneous equations, a subject not pursued here. Section 4 extends the analysis to the case where the expectation is considered to be a prediction of a random variable. The choice criterion used in this discussion is the conditional variance of the estimator or of the prediction error. Such a criterion is different from statistical testing of the null hypothesis with respect to the marginal variables. Yet the various procedures have something in common: The verdict is always either to include a variable or to omit it. Such a discrete decision may not utilize the information in the sample in the best way; this problem is explained briefly in Section 5, in which reference is also made to an alternative approach. The discussion is concluded in Section 6.

2. Expectations as Unobservables

It emerges from the discussion in Section 1 that when the sample size is not very large, the addition of variables to an empirical equation may increase the sampling error significantly. I now illustrate this by referring to McCallum's (1976) attempt at testing the natural rate hypothesis using a model that views the expectation variable as an unobservable. As such it represents an important set of studies. His model is

$$y = y^*\gamma + X\boldsymbol{\beta} + \epsilon, \tag{1}$$

where y^* is the anticipated value at t of y_{t+1}. In order to examine the statistical aspects of this procedure, it is sufficient to deal with a simpler version

$$y_t = \gamma y_t^* + \epsilon_t, \tag{2}$$

where y_t^* is the expectation variable at time t with respect to future outcome affecting the decision variable y_t. The variable y_t^* is not observed and has to be estimated. An estimate of y_t^*, to be denoted by $\hat{y}_t^*$, can be obtained by relating y_t^* to observed variables. Thus let

$$y_t^* = \mathbf{x}_t\boldsymbol{\beta} + w_t. \tag{3}$$

Assume that

$$y_{t+1} = y_t^* + \eta_t, \qquad E(y_t^*\eta_t) = 0, \tag{4}$$

then $\hat{y}_t^*$ is obtained as an estimate of a point on the line

$$y_{t+1} = \mathbf{x}_t\boldsymbol{\beta} + u_t, \tag{5}$$

where $u_t = \eta_t + w_t$.

This is the first stage of a two-stage procedure. In the second stage $\hat{y}_t^*$ is used for estimating γ under the assumption that $\hat{y}_t^* = y_t^* + e_t$ and $E(y_t^* e_t) = 0$. If we also assume that $E(e_t\epsilon_t) = 0$, we have a model of errors in the variables. It is well known that

$$\hat{\gamma} = \sum \hat{y}_t^* y_t \Big/ \sum \hat{y}_t^{*2} \sim \gamma P^2, \tag{6}$$

where $P^2 = \sum y_t^{*2} / \sum \hat{y}_t^{*2}$, the proportion of the variance of $\hat{y}_t^*$ accounted for by the expectation variable. Thus the larger the sampling error of $\hat{y}_t^*$ is, the smaller P^2 is, and the larger the bias of $\hat{\gamma}$ is.

To summarize the procedure, in the first stage (5) is used to generate an estimator of the expection variable y^*. This in turn is used in the second stage to estimate γ from (2). The more variables included in the first stage, the better the fit of this equation. However, note that the dependent variable in this case is y_{t+1}, the same variable as in (2) but with a one-year lag. Adding more variables to (5) is thus also expected to improve the fit of (2). At the same time, as we show in Section 3, increasing the number of variables increases the variance of $\hat{y}^*$.

McCallum tried several options, with the number of explanatory variables in the first stage ranging from 9 to 17. He actually estimated an equation similar to (2), except that his formulation included two additional exogenous variables measuring the excess demand in the labor market. His y_t is the rate of change of wages, while y_t^* is the expected rate of change of prices. The purpose of his analysis was to test the natural rate hypothesis, $\gamma = 1$. His estimates of γ under the various options with respect to the number of regressors in stage 1 are given in Table 1, along with related measures.

The options differ in the number of variables but not in a monotonic way, which facilitates a simple comparison. The results are reported in declining order of $\hat{\gamma}$, which is also a rising order of R^2. The rank correlation

TABLE 1

SELECTED RESULTS FROM MCMALLUM (1976, TABLES I AND II)

Variables	VI	VII	II	I	III	IV	V
$\hat{\gamma}$	0.809	0.759	0.710	0.700	0.681	0.631	0.384
s.e. of $\hat{\gamma}$	0.183	0.172	0.154	0.156	0.151	0.144	0.100
R^2	0.391	0.419	0.443	0.447	0.456	0.475	0.518
t ratios	4.42	4.41	4.61	4.49	4.51	4.38	3.84
No. regressors	9	11	11	9	11	17	Perfect fit

between R^2 and $\hat{\gamma}$ is minus one, which is in line with our hypothesis. The order of the standard error of $\hat{\gamma}$ is basically the same as that of $\hat{\gamma}$, leading to t ratios that do not vary much across the options (except perhaps the last one, which will be explained below). Since for any given number of degrees of freedom the t ratios are monotonically correlated with the partial correlation coefficients, the lack of pronounced variations in the t ratios indicate a lack of such variations in the partial correlation. Thus the contribution of the additional variables was primarily to the error.

McCallum realized that if enough variables are added in the first stage, the estimator approaches the value of the dependent variable. He therefore considered using y_{t+1} instead of $\hat{y}_t^*$. This is option V which has the largest R^2 and the smallest $\hat{\gamma}$. He sensed that this may be due to errors in the variables and consequently tried another set of regressions with fewer variables. As he also made other changes, the results are not exactly comparable but nevertheless indicative. The value of $\hat{\gamma}$ in the four additional options varied between 0.861 and 0.968 with corresponding R^2 values of 0.339 and 0.259 and t ratios of 4.6 and 5.8.

All this is in line with the foregoing discussion, which has far-reaching implications for estimation methods in simultaneous equations models. The message is that it is not necessarily a blessing to have a large number of exogenous variables.[5] But this goes against common sense: How can additional information do harm? The key to this question is in differentiating between adding *variables* and adding *information*; the two are not necessarily identical. This is discussed more fully in Section 5.

Finally, the discussion has treated the expectation variable as if it were a deterministic variable. It is, however, a random variable, and the statisti-

[5] A similar phenomenon was observed by Sawa (1969) in his derivation of the exact sampling distribution of two-stage estimators. "It can be seen that with a decrease in the number of exogenous variables for fixed sample size, the bias and dispersion of the TSLS estimator became smaller" p. 936. I am indebted to James Heckman for calling my attention to this reference.

cal problem is therefore that of forecasting its value rather than of estimating it as a linear function of the parameters in stage 1. This modification is important, but does not change the basic conclusion. To show this, we must first examine the statistical framework underlying the foregoing discussion.

The model used by Blejer and Leiderman in the preceding chapter for their empirical analysis has a somewhat similar structure, as the expected rate of inflation π^e appears in the demand for money. They state that the expected inflation is formed with the fitted values of a sixth-order inflation autoregression process. The regression equation from which π^e is formed has ten coefficients of which only three coefficients are larger than two times their standard errors. Even though testing the null hypotheses individually with respect to each coefficient is not an appropriate criterion for selecting variables for prediction, low values for the ratio quoted above are indicative that there is a problem here with the precision of the constructed variable and, consequently, with the estimates in the regression of the demand for money.

3. The Sampling Variance

The linear statistical model deals with the question of inclusion or omission of variables in an equation by testing the null hypothesis with respect to the "marginal" variables. Such a procedure requires a prior decision as to what variables are the marginal ones. This decision is frequently made during the analysis itself, but even if the marginal variables are identified beforehand, such a procedure does not necessarily yield the most accurate estimates or forecasts (see Section 5). As such, it cannot be used as a criterion for the empirical construction of expectations. The remainder of this section is devoted to this point.

Suppose that y is generated by the process described by (7) and (8):

$$\mathbf{y} = X_1\boldsymbol{\beta}_1 + X_2\boldsymbol{\beta}_2 + \mathbf{u} \equiv X\boldsymbol{\beta} + \mathbf{u}, \tag{7}$$

$$\mathbf{u} \sim N(\mathbf{0}, \sigma^2 I_n), \qquad \text{rank } X = k = r + q, \tag{8}$$

where $\mathbf{y}$ and $\mathbf{u}$ are vectors of n random variables. X_1 and X_2 are $n \times r$ and $n \times q$ matrices of explanatory variables; $\boldsymbol{\beta}_1$ and $\boldsymbol{\beta}_2$ are the corresponding vectors of coefficients. The distribution of $\mathbf{u}$ is given by (8). Note that X, or some columns of it, can be random variables. In this case we add the assumption that $\mathbf{u}$ is distributed conditionally on X, or that (7) is rewritten as

$$E(\mathbf{y} \mid X) = X\boldsymbol{\beta}. \tag{9}$$

This result is obtained immediately when X is uncorrelated with $\mathbf{u}$.

At this stage, the decomposition of X into X_1 and X_2 is arbitrary. It is introduced in order to facilitate an evaluation of the effect of adding additional variables to the regression. The effect of additional variables depends on their relationships to the regressors already included. This statement can be formalized by the following equation:

$$X_1 = E(X_2 | X_1) + U_2 \equiv X_1 \Pi + U_2. \tag{10}$$

The term $E(X_2|X_1)$ may reflect the design of the experiment when X_2 is nonstochastic, or the population relationship if the Xs are random variables. The two possibilities may have different implications for the distribution of the rows of U_2. Basically, it is the second possibility that is interesting for economic analysis. Accordingly, it is assumed that the rows of U_2 have an independent q-variate normal distribution[6]:

$$\mathbf{u}_2 \sim N_q(\mathbf{0}, \Sigma_2) \tag{11}$$

Combining (7) and (10), yields

$$\mathbf{y} = X_1 \boldsymbol{\alpha} + \mathbf{u}_1, \tag{12}$$

where

$$\boldsymbol{\alpha} = \boldsymbol{\beta}_1 + \Pi \boldsymbol{\beta}_2, \qquad \mathbf{u}_1 = \mathbf{u} + U_2 \boldsymbol{\beta}_2,$$

and

$$\mathbf{u}_1 = \sim N(\mathbf{0}, \sigma_1^2 I_n), \qquad \sigma_1^2 = \sigma^2 + \boldsymbol{\beta}_2' \Sigma_2 \boldsymbol{\beta}_2. \tag{13}$$

σ_1^2 is the conditional variance of y given $\mathbf{x}_1$, a row vector having the same distribtion as the rows of X_1. The question to be decided on the basis of the data is whether to use (12) or (7). Let $\mathbf{b}$ be the ordinary least-squares (OLS) estimate of $\boldsymbol{\beta}$, so that $\operatorname{Var} \mathbf{b} = \sigma^2 (X'X)^{-1}$. Let $\hat{\Pi}$ be the OLS estimate of Π, so that $\hat{\Pi} = (X_1'X_1)^{-1} X_1' X_2$, and let V_2 be the residuals of X_2 from the computed regressions $X_1 \hat{\Pi} : V_2 = M_1 X_2$, where $M_1 = I_n - K_1$, $K_1 = X_1 (X_1'X_1)^{-1} X_1'$. Similarly, $\mathbf{a}$ is the OLS estimate of $\boldsymbol{\alpha}$ with $\operatorname{Var} \mathbf{a} = \sigma_1^2 (X_1'X_1)^{-1}$.

It simplifies the discussion if we begin with the choice of an estimator before taking up the prediction problem. Thus assume that we are interested in estimating $\psi = \mathbf{x}'\boldsymbol{\beta}$ where $\mathbf{x}'$ is a row vector subject to the restrictions imposed on the Xs in the model. It can be decomposed to $\mathbf{x}' = (\mathbf{x}_1', \mathbf{x}_2')$ and $\mathbf{x}_2'$ is in part accounted for by $\mathbf{x}_1$ as given by $\hat{\mathbf{x}}_2 = \hat{\Pi} \mathbf{x}_1$. The two alternative estimators are

$$\hat{y} = \mathbf{x}'\mathbf{b}, \tag{14}$$

$$\hat{y}_1 = \mathbf{x}_1'\mathbf{a}. \tag{15}$$

[6]Part of the discussion can be conducted without the normality assumption. For the present discussion it is not particularly important to separate the results according to their dependence on the normality assumption.

As is well known, the variance of $\hat{y}$ (conditional on X and $\mathbf{x}'$) as an estimator of ψ is given by

$$\sigma_{\hat{y}}^2 = \sigma^2 \mathbf{x}'(X'X)^{-1}\mathbf{x} \equiv \sigma^2 h. \tag{16}$$

Similarly, the variance of $\hat{y}_1$ (conditional on X_1 and $\mathbf{x}_1$) is

$$\sigma_{\hat{y}_1}^2 = \sigma_1^2 \mathbf{x}_1'(X_1'X_1)^{-1}\mathbf{x}_1 \equiv \sigma_1^2 h_1. \tag{17}$$

It can be shown that

$$h_2 \equiv h - h_1 = \mathbf{v}_2'(V_2'V_2)^{-1}\mathbf{v}_2, \tag{18}$$

where $\mathbf{v}_2 = \mathbf{x}_2 - \hat{\Pi}\mathbf{x}_1$. Note that

$$\hat{\Sigma}_2 = V_2'V_2/(n - r) \tag{19}$$

consititutes an unbiased estimator of Σ_2. Then

$$h_2 = \mathbf{v}_2'\hat{\Sigma}_2^{-1}\mathbf{v}_2/(n - r). \tag{20}$$

It thus appears that

$$\sigma_{\hat{y}}^2 - \sigma_{\hat{y}_1}^2 = \sigma^2 h_2 - (\sigma_1^2 - \sigma^2)h_1. \tag{21}$$

Consequently,

$$\sigma_{\hat{y}}^2 - \sigma_{\hat{y}_1}^2 \gtreqless 0 \Leftrightarrow h_2/h_1 \gtreqless \Delta, \tag{22}$$

where $\Delta = \boldsymbol{\beta}_2'\Sigma_2\boldsymbol{\beta}_2/\sigma^2$. As more variables are added to the regression, Δ tends to decline. On the other hand, h_2 tends to increase. Consequently, there *may* be an $r < k$ for which the conditional variance is minimized. This implies that adding more variables will result in an increase in the variance of $\hat{y}$.

The discussion to this point establishes the existence of a limit to the number of variables to be included in the regression. The limit itself cannot be computed in a deterministic way as the variances σ^2 and σ_1^2 are unknown. They can be estimated so as to yield a specific result for the estimates under consideration:

$$\hat{\sigma}_{\hat{y}}^2 - \hat{\sigma}_{\hat{y}_1}^2 \gtreqless 0 \Leftrightarrow h_2/h_1 \gtreqless \hat{\sigma}_1^2/\hat{\sigma}^2 - 1. \tag{23}$$

As is well known, unbiased estimators are obtained from $\hat{\sigma}^2 = \mathbf{y}'M\mathbf{y}/(n - k)$ and $\hat{\sigma}_1^2 = \mathbf{y}_1'M_1\mathbf{y}_1/(n - r)$.
Let F be the statistic used for testing the null hypothesis $\boldsymbol{\beta}_2 = 0$. By a simple transformation, it can be shown that $\hat{\sigma}_1^2/\hat{\sigma}_1^2 - 1 = (F - 1)q/(n - r)$. Consequently, rewrite (23) as

$$\hat{\sigma}_{\hat{y}}^2 - \hat{\sigma}_{\hat{y}_1}^2 \gtreqless 0 \Leftrightarrow h_2/h_1 \gtreqless q(F - 1)/(n - r). \tag{24}$$

It is then clear that when $F < 1$ the restricted regression is preferable. Furthermore, let F_α be the critical value for testing the null hypothesis, then the inequality $F \lesseqgtr F_\alpha$ is not directly related to that in (24) in the sense that the verdict on the null hypothesis is neither necessary nor sufficient for determining which estimator is more accurate. F can be larger than the critical value but yield a smaller right-hand side for (24), in which case the restricted forecast should be preferred. The converse is also possible.

This last conclusion is not in line with some current practices. For instance, in carrying out the Sims–Granger causality test Sargent (1976, Section III) tests the null hypothesis in order to determine whether or not a group of variables should be retained in a regression that generates estimates for unobservables.

4. Expectation as a Prediction

By its very nature expectation is a prediction of a random event. As such it is subject to error. The variance of the error consists of two components: the variance of the event itself and the variance of the predictor.[7] The formation of a "good" expectation is therefore a question of selecting an accurate predictor. This property should be demanded also of predictors based on sound economic theory and on assumptions with respect to the behavior of the economic agents.

The problem is formulated within the framework given by (7)–(13). The two alternative predictors are $\hat{y}$ and $\hat{y}_1$, as defined in (14) and (15), with prediction errors f and f_1, respectively. The errors are evaluated conditional on the xs used for the regression and the prediction in each case, $(X, \mathbf{x})$ for f and $(X_1, \mathbf{x}_1)$ for f_1. While the expected value of the errors are zero, their conditional variance depends on the explanatory variables:

$$\sigma_f^2 = \sigma^2(1 + h), \tag{25}$$

$$\sigma_{f_1}^2 = \sigma_1^2(1 + h_1), \tag{26}$$

where h and h_1 are defined as in Section 3. The two predictors have in common the reliance on $(X_1, \mathbf{x}_1)$. They differ in terms of whether or not they utilize $(X_2, \mathbf{x}_2)$. When $\mathbf{x}_2$ is a random vector, $\mathbf{v}_2$ can be considered as a computed residual given by

$$\mathbf{v}_2 = (\Pi - \hat{\Pi})'\mathbf{x}_1 + \mathbf{u}_2 \tag{27}$$

with a variance matrix

$$\Sigma_{\mathbf{v}_2} = \Sigma_2 + h_1\Sigma_2 = (1 + h_1)\Sigma_2. \tag{28}$$

[7] Assuming that y and its predictor are uncorrelated.

It can be shown that

$$\mathbf{v}_2' \hat{\Sigma}_{\mathbf{v}_2}^{-1} \mathbf{v}_2 n/(n-r) \sim T^2, \tag{29}$$

where T^2 is Hotelling's generalized T^2 statistic. Utilizing the relationships between T^2 and F we can write the following probability statement:

$$P\left\{ \left(\sigma_{f_1}^2 / \sigma_f^2 \right) \Big|_{X_1, \mathbf{x}_1} > 1 \right\} = P\{ F(\cdot) < \tau \} = \int_0^\tau F(\cdot)\, dF, \tag{30}$$

where $F(\cdot)$ has an F distribution with $(\cdot) \equiv (q, n-r+1)$ degrees of freedom and $\tau = [(n-r+1)/q]\Delta$, where Δ is as defined in Section 3. As $n \to \infty$, $P(\tau) \to 1$ so that the unrestricted model dominates $(\sigma_f^2 < \sigma_{f_1}^2)$ with probability 1. For a finite n (not "excessively large"), the model may be improved by eliminating variables that contain no net information. The net information is directly related to the size of the variance of these variables or more accurately to the quadratic form of the variance matrix, denoted by Δ. Thus it is desirable to eliminate variables that vary little and have low values for their coefficients.

The condition in (30) depends implicitly on the number of variables already included in the restricted model r. Other things being equal, the larger r is, the smaller the diagonal terms in Σ_2 (the variance of the unaccounted part of X_2) will be. Furthermore, Δ will decline with an increase in r. At the same time $\mathbf{v}_2' \Sigma_{\mathbf{b}_2} \mathbf{v}_2$ will increase, and consequently the "cost" of increasing r will rise.[8]

5. On the Information Contained in the Sample and Its Utilization

In some sense the foregoing discussion dealt with how to optimize the use of the information available in a given sample in terms of the number and choice of variables to be included in a regression, whether for estimation or prediction. As indicated, selecting variables by testing null hypotheses does not necessarily produce the most accurate prediction. This method also has other limitations:

(a) Eliminating variables amounts to imposing discrete, zero–one restrictions; either the variable is included or excluded. It would be preferable to have greater freedom in choosing the weights to be imposed.

(b) It does not necessarily produce a convergence in the sense of obtaining a regression with all coefficients being significantly different from zero.

[8] We use here another interpretation for $(V_2' V_2)^{-1}$: $\mathrm{Var}(\mathbf{b}_2) \equiv \Sigma_{b_2} = \sigma^2 (V_2' V_2)^{-1}$ and consequently, $h_2 = \mathbf{v}_2' \Sigma_{b_2} \mathbf{v}_2 / \sigma^2$.

There are some other objections, at least implicitly stated. For instance Sims (1972, p. 545) states:

> In applying the F tests for causal direction suggested in the previous section, one should bear in mind that the absolute size of the coefficients is important regardless of the F value. It is a truism too often ignored that coefficients which are "large" from the economic point of view should not be casually set to zero no matter how statistically "insignificant" they are.

This is a strong statement of position, axiomatic in nature, which one can accept or reject but may find it difficult to argue with. It can be interpreted as a suggestion to impose a prior restriction on the model. The consequences of this will depend on the "realism" of the prior, and no more can be stated at this level of generality. From the above discussion it is clear that this procedure has a cost; it may even be self-defeating, as the discussion of the McCallum results indicated. It is therefore desirable to approach the problem in a way which allows the distillation of the information contained in the sample without imposing any prior restriction.

The limitations to the sequential decision or testing process discussed above can be overcome in the following way. The question of convergence can be solved by dealing with orthogonal variables. Thus the variables must first be transformed. This brings us to the use of principal components, which also overcomes the first objection in that it assigns continuous weights to the various variables. The general limitation of principal components was lack of an optimality criterion for selecting variables (principal components). A solution for this is suggested in a recent paper (Mundlak, 1979), which serves as a basis for the following comments.

The question posed is How many homogeneous restrictions that are not significantly different from zero can be imposed on the columns of X? Assume that there are q such restrictions, $0 \leqslant q < k$. We then say that the statistical rank of the matrix X is $r = k - q$. Accordingly, if a variable is added to the regression so as to change the rank of X from k to $k + 1$, and also q changes to $q + 1$, we say that this variable does not change the statistical rank. It can also be said that it does not contribute (net) information over and above the information already contained in X. It should be noted that as we are operating within a statistical framework, the outcome depends on the critical level of the test statistic and the sampling distribution of the random vector $\mathbf{y}$.

The theory can be outlined as follows. A set of q linearly independent estimable functions generates a q-dimensional space of estimable functions, to be denoted by L. That is, let $\boldsymbol{\psi}' = (\psi_1, \ldots, \psi_q)' = C\boldsymbol{\beta}$; then $L = [\mathbf{h}'\boldsymbol{\psi} \mid C$ is $q \times k$ of rank $q \leqslant k$, and $\mathbf{h} \in R^q]$. The basic theorem (Scheffé, 1959, p. 69) is

Theorem. Under the model as specified by (7) and (8), the probability is $1 - \alpha$ that simultaneously for all $\psi \in L$

$$\hat{\psi} - S\hat{\sigma}_{\hat{\psi}} \leqq \psi \leqq \hat{\psi} + S\hat{\sigma}_{\hat{\psi}}, \tag{31}$$

where $\hat{\psi} = \mathbf{c}'\mathbf{b}$, and $S = (qF_{\alpha,q,n-k})^{1/2}$.

Let us apply this to our question What is the dimensionality of L, such that for all $\psi \in L$, the interval in (31) covers the origin? The answer is given by the relation that exists between the S method of multiple comparisons and the F test. The hypothesis $H: \psi_1 = \cdots = \psi_q = 0$ is rejected by the F test if and only if there exists ψ in L such that its OLS estimate ψ is significantly different from zero, that is, if used in (31), the interval does not cover the origin.

This rule facilitates the selection of q variables to be excluded from a regression of y on the principal components of X. This procedure gives a unique solution for any sample and level of significance. It thus eliminates that part of the sample the contribution of which to the estimation of the coefficients $\boldsymbol{\beta}$ (or linear coefficients thereof) is not significantly different from zero. This procedure overcomes the two objections to the use of statistical testing raised at the beginning of the section.

In operational terms the procedure yields regression coefficients on a subset of principal components of the matrix X. It is a simple matter to transform the coefficients to estimates of the coefficients of the original variables (**x**s) rather than of their principal components. This procedure still does not determine the optimal number of regressors from the point of view of forming the minimum variance predictors as discussed in Section 4. However, the procedure is very useful in that endeavor since it can be shown that for any prediction based on a subset of, say, r explanatory variables, the prediction obtained from the principal component regression has the lowest conditional variance. Once the prediction is optimized for any given r, the selection of the number of variables to be included in the regression follows the rule developed in Section 4.

In practice, the hypothesis of rational expectations is interpreted as suggesting the utilization of all available information, present and past, in the formation of expectations. Its empirical implementation takes the form of regressions with numerous regressors. It is shown that if the criterion for a construction of an expectation is precision then there exists a limit to the number of regressors to be used in any particular regression. This is so either when the expectation is considered to be a point on a regression line or a forecast of a random variable. The reason is that the sampling variance increases with the number of variables. This problem always exists in time-series analysis as the length of the time series is limited by the desire not to include in one sample periods with different structures.

Basically, the argument is that the amount of information that a sample contains is not proportional to the number of variables that can serve as regressors in any particular regression. The problem in empirical analysis is to find ways to represent the available information with the smallest number of variables, thereby reducing the sampling variance. A method that achieves this objective, based on a particular handling of principal components analysis, determines the statistical rank of the design or information matrix. The method is also applicable to the construction of forecasts that are both relatively precise and based on a relatively smaller number of variables as compared with the conventional techniques. The suggested techniques have repercussions in other areas of econometric work.

6. Concluding Remarks

Present work in macroeconomics is based on the confrontration of theory and data. As this is carried out within a statistical framework, it is relevant and pertinent to evaluate this work in a like manner. Current macro models are based to varying extents on modified classical models, with emphasis on the role of imperfect information. This approach has produced interesting and important results. The discussion in this paper is concerned not with the results but rather with the method of analysis. It is difficult at this point to gauge its ultimate substantive importance.

The concept of rational expectations plays an important role in current economic analysis. It is understood here to represent a constraint imposed jointly on the expectation and the model, and the framework used here accommodates such a constraint. It is believed that such an interpretation avoids various difficulties. It is, however, appropriate to indicate that it is not quite clear that the concept of rational expectations is fully adequate, nor is it clear how it should be defined in order to be so. The point particularly pertinent to our discussion is that the basic premise that markets clear is not immediately operational. The question is not whether markets clear eventually but rather *when* do they clear. The speed of convergence is an extremely important factor that must be taken explicitly into account: It should be treated as an endogenous variable in the economic system; as such, it is affected by economic variables. Since the economic system is in a continuous process of adjustment, it is not clear just what is the process responsible for the property that on the average the expectations of the agents are equal to the equilibrium value determined by the model. Which equilibrium? Of what run and in which market?

Finally, suppose that the statistical analysis is carried out as suggested here and the variances in question are minimized; how infallibly can one expect the econometric models to perform? Is the failure of the 1970s to be considered as a failure of methods or as an outcome which has a reasonable probability? This question is posed here not to provide an answer but rather to point out that to answer it properly one has to evaluate it within a framework that allows the exogenous variables to be stochastic and to evaluate the unconditional (on the regressors') variance of the forecasts in question. I shall address this problem elsewhere.

To conclude, the new macroeconometrics opens up some interesting areas of econometric research. Such research may indicate that it is not at all necessary that the new equations have a large number of variables.

REFERENCES

Cyert, Richard M., and DeGroot, Morris H. (1974). Rational Expectations and Bayesian Analysis. *Journal of Political Economy* **82**, 521–536.

Lucas, Robert E., and Sargent, Thomas J. (1979). After Keynesian Macroeconomics. *Quarterly Review, Federal Reserve Bank of Minneapolis* **Spring**, 1–16.

McCallum, B. T. (1976). Rational Expectations and the Natural Rate Hypothesis: Some Consistent Estimates. *Econometrica* **44**, 43–52.

Mundlak, Y. (1979). *On the Concept of Non Significant Functions and Its Implications for Regression Analysis*. Report No. 7914, Center for Mathematical Studies in Business and Economics, University of Chicago.

Muth, J. F. (1961). Rational Expectations and the Theory of Price Movements. *Econometrica* **24**, 315–335.

Rao, C. R. (1973). *Linear Statistical Inference and Its Applications*, 2nd ed. Wiley, New York.

Sargent, Thomas J. (1976). A Classical Macroeconometric Model for the United States. *Journal of Political Economy* **84**, 207–238.

Sawa, Takamitsu (1969). The Exact Sampling Distribution of Ordinary Least Squares and Two-Stage Least Squares Estimators. *Journal of the American Statistical Association* **64**, 923–937.

Scheffé, H. (1959). *Analysis of Variance*. Wiley, New York.

Sims, C. A. (1972). Money, Income, and Causality. *The American Economic Review* **62**, 540–552.

DEPARTMENT OF AGRICULTURAL ECONOMICS
HEBREW UNIVERSITY OF JERUSALEM
REHOVOT, ISRAEL

PART 6

Macro Public Finance

Public Debt and Taxes

*ROBERT J. BARRO**

The national debt, representing the accumulation of past choices to borrow rather than levy taxes, is frequently thought to constitute a burden on future generations. This burden is sometimes viewed as operating through direct income transfers from younger to older generations and sometimes described through the crowding out of private capital formation. Alternatively, it has been argued that (domestically held) government bonds represent internally canceling debts and credits and are therefore of negligible economic significance. The present paper is devoted to an economic analysis of these and related issues. The first section provides a brief examination of the historical development of national debt in the United States and the United Kingdom. The next section discusses how shifts between taxes and debt issue affect perceived private wealth. The final section relates this wealth effect to the central economic issues, which include the burden of the debt on future generations, the crowding out of private investment, and fiscal policy.

1. Some Data on Public Debt

Table 1 provides an overview of the behavior of the national debt in the United States since 1860. Column 1 shows the (par) value of nominal, interest-bearing federal debt net of holdings by U.S. government agencies

*This paper was published in M. J. Boskin, ed., *Federal Tax Reform*, San Francisco, Institute for Contemporary Studies, 1978. The work was carried out while I was a national fellow at the Hoover Institution, Stanford University. I have benefited from research support on related work by the National Science Foundation.

ISBN 0-12-259750-8

TABLE 1

VALUES OF GOVERNMENT DEBT AND EXPENDITURE IN THE UNITED STATES FOR SELECTED YEARS[a]

	Federal government				State and local government			
	(1) B_f	(2) B_f/P	(3) B_f/Py	(4) G_f/Py	(5) B_{s1}	(6) B_{s1}/P	(7) B_{s1}/Py	(8) G_{s1}/Py
1860	0.06	0.4	0.01[b]	0.01[b]	—	—	—	—
1865	2.22	8.7	0.24[b]	0.10[b]	—	—	—	—
1867	2.24	8.8	0.23[b]	0.04[b]	—	—	—	—
1880	1.71	9.1	0.13	0.02	—	—	—	—
1902	0.93	5.6	0.041	0.02	2.1	12.7	0.09	0.05
1916	0.91	3.8	0.018	0.02	4.5	19.0	0.09	0.06[c]
1918	20.5	59.9	0.26	0.23	5.1	14.9	0.06	—
1922	21.6	67.1	0.29	0.04	7.9	24.5	0.11	0.08
1929	14.9	45.3	0.14	0.03	13.6	41.3	0.13	0.07
1940	41.5	142.6	0.42	0.10	16.4	56.4	0.16	0.08
1945	228.2	600.5	1.07	0.40	13.4	35.3	0.06	0.04
1948	193.6	364.6	0.75	0.13	17.0	32.0	0.07	0.06
1956	198.1	314.9	0.47	0.17	44.5	70.7	0.11	0.08
1964	218.1	300.0	0.34	0.19	90.4	124.3	0.14	0.09
1974	269.9	231.9	0.19	0.21	211.2	181.4	0.15	0.11
1976	408.5	305.3	0.24	0.23	236.3	176.6	0.14	0.11

[a]Notes to data [for details see Barro (1978b)]: B_f is nominal, par value, interest-bearing federal debt in billions of dollars, net of holdings by federal agencies and trust funds and the Federal Reserve. Values since 1916 are at the end of the calendar year; earlier values are at midyear. P is the GNP deflator (1972 = 1.0); y is real GNP (1972 dollars). G_f is total nominal federal expenditure; B_{s1} is the end-of-year value in billions of dollars of net nominal state and local government debt; and G_{s1} is total nominal state and local government expenditure less transfers from the federal government to the state and local sector.

[b]Based on a trend value of real GNP.

[c]Value is for 1913.

and trust funds and the Federal Reserve. Column 2 expresses the quantity of debt in real terms after division by a general price index (the GNP deflator), and column 3 indicates the ratio of nominal debt to nominal GNP. The quantity of public debt outstanding in 1860 amounted to only 1% of GNP.[1] The extensive deficit finance during the Civil War raised the debt–GNP ratio to a value of about $\frac{1}{4}$ in 1865. The long, essentially

[1]An interesting note about the pre-1860 period is the experience in 1835 when the national debt was entirely paid off and the government sought desperately for outlets for its surplus. Apparently, this problem was solved by the motivation for deficit finance during the sharp economic contraction that began in 1837 (Dewey, 1931, p. 221).

peacetime period following the Civil War was accompanied by a steady decline of the national debt to about 2% of GNP in 1916. Outstanding debt rose sharply during World War I to a peak value of just under 30% of GNP and then fell during the postwar period to a value of about 14% of GNP in 1929. The large federal deficits and the decline in nominal income during the Great Depression produced a debt–GNP ratio of over 40% in 1940. The ratio then increased sharply to just over 100% as a consequence of the vast debt issues of World War II. The post-World War II period is similar to the principally peacetime period following the Civil War and World War I in exhibiting a steady decline of the debt–GNP ratio (although, because of the chronic inflation associated with the "new monetary standard" (Klein, 1975), the nominal debt figures do not show the steady decline that characterized the earlier postwar periods). The debt–GNP ratio fell below 20% in 1974, before rising as a consequence of the strong economic contraction to 24% in 1976 (a value that was maintained for 1977). An important observation is that the current debt–GNP ratio is not high by historical standards and is well below the values that prevailed during the 1950s.

Table 1, column 4, indicates the ratio of total federal spending to GNP. One observation is that the rise in this ratio from 3% in 1929 to 10% in 1940 to 13% in 1948 and to 23% in 1976 has not been associated with a systematic supporting movement of the debt–GNP ratio. Notably, the rise in the share of GNP flowing through the federal government during the post-World War II period has been accompanied by a steady decline in the debt–GNP ratio.

Columns 5–7 provide data on net debt and expenditures of the state and local government sector. The debt–GNP ratio (column 7) exhibits a pattern of secular increase from 1902 (9%) to 1940 (16%), except for the reduction in the ratio along with the rise in nominal GNP during World War I. After a sharp decline during World War II, the ratio of state and local government debt to GNP rose gradually to its pre-World War II level, which was attained by the mid-1960s. The ratio has remained steady at that value until the present.

An interesting comparison with the U.S. experience is provided by the British case. Figure 1, which is taken from ongoing research by Dan Benjamin and Levis Kochin, contains a plot of the ratio of British national debt to national income since 1801. As in the U.S. experience, major wars appear to have had a strong positive effect on the debt–income ratio. The extensive deficit financing of the Napoleonic Wars produced a debt–income ratio of almost 3.0 in 1821. This value was almost three times the peak ratio reached in the United States in 1945. The British experience shows a long period of declining debt–income ratios from 1821 until the

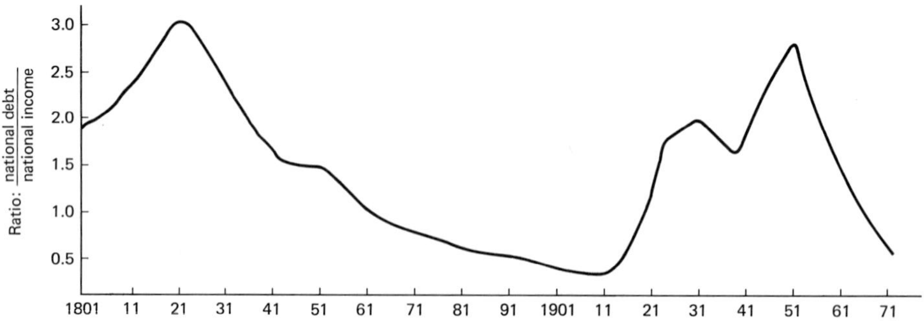

Fig. 1. The behavior of the British national debt.

start of World War I. A strong increase in the ratio during the war is extended to the depressed economic period of the 1920s and early 1930s. There is a further sharp expansion of national debt during World War II, although the peak debt–income ratio remains somewhat below that attained in 1821. Finally, as in the U.S. experience, the post-World War II period in Britain exhibits a steady decline in the debt–income ratio. Again, the current ratio of public debt to national income is not high by historical standards.

2. Economic Effects of the Debt/Tax Choice

What difference does it make for the economy if the national government finances its expenditures by public debt issue rather than by taxation? The argument that there is no first first-order difference, which dates back to Ricardo (1951, Vol. 1, pp. 244–248, Vol. 4, pp. 184–189), begins with the observation that public debt issue implies a stream of future interest payments and possible repayments of principal. These future payments must be financed either by future taxes (including future money creation, which is a form of taxation that works through its effect on the price level) or by additional deficits, which would raise further the required future time path of interest and principal payments. The option of financing interest payments solely through new debt issue raises the possibility that taxes could be escaped through perpetual deficit finance. However, this possibility depends on a chain-letter mechanism in which individuals would be willing to hold ever expanding amounts of public debt without regard to the government's limited capacity to raise revenue for debt repayment.[2] Generally, it seems safe to ignore this "free lunch" possibility and to assume that debt issue implies a corresponding increase in the present value of future taxes. As a simplification I also assume that the future interest payments implied by current debt issue are exactly matched in magnitude and timing by additions to future taxes. This case, in which future interest payments are not financed by additional debt issue and in which future taxes are not high enough to retire outstanding debt, turns out to be adequate for examining the major economic effects of the debt/tax choice.

Suppose that an additional $1 million of current government expenditure is financed either by current taxes or debt issue. In the former case individuals experience an additional one-time tax liability of $1 million. In the latter case, assuming the interest rate on government bonds to be 5% per year, government interest payments and, by assumption, tax collections are raised "forever" by $50,000 per year. I neglect any direct administrative costs associated with public debt issue, and I assume that, aside from the difference in timing, the incidence of the $50,000 annual tax is identical to that of the lump-sum $1 million collection. (Otherwise, an additional pure income redistribution effect would be added to the analysis.) Basically, the representative taxpayer would view the choice between debt issue and taxation as equivalent to the choice between a share of the $1 million current tax and a like share of the $50,000 annual tax in perpetuity. The two options would be viewed as equivalent—producing the so-called Ricardian equivalence theorem on the public debt[3]—under the following set of conditions: (a) there is no possibility of escaping part of the perpetual tax liability, either by dying (which introduces an effect of finite lives) or by leaving the jurisdiction of the government; (b) everyone can borrow and lend funds at the same interest rate as the government; (c) there is no uncertainty about future tax shares (which might be induced by uncertainty about individual income or other characteristics on which the tax shares are

[2] In the case where the interest rate (net of expected inflation) on the public debt exceeds the long-run real growth rate of the economy (which turns out to be a necessary condition for the efficient operation of the private sector), perpetual deficit finance would require a continually rising ratio of public debt to national income (Barro, 1976). The chain-letter aspect of perpetual deficit finance has been referred to as a Ponzi scheme by Miller and Upton (1974, p. 181) in honor of the "Boston money-manager" of the 1920s who paid people 50 per cent interest on funds deposited with him. He did so by using the proceeds of new deposits to pay off old depositors. While it worked, it was a good deal. Those who got in (and out) early made money, but the bubble eventually burst and those who still had deposits with Ponzi lost everything."

[3] See Ricardo (1951). A discussion of the Ricardian theorem is contained in Buchanan (1958, pp. 43–46, 114–122). See also de Marco (1936, pp. 377–398) and Bailey (1971, pp. 156–158).

contingent); (d) the future tax liabilities implied by public debt issue are accurately perceived; (e) the volume of government expenditures is independent of the method of finance; and (f) there are no other channels for effects of the choice of finance method on the prices, rates of return, and so on, faced by individuals. Considering the length of this list, it is apparent that not all of these conditions could be exactly satisfied. In evaluating these factors it is therefore useful to distinguish between first- and second-order effects and to weigh the likely balance of forces for assessing the net economic impact of the debt/tax choice. I discuss, first, the various issues from the viewpoint of the effect of debt issue on perceived private wealth, and second, the connection of these wealth perceptions to the burden of the public debt argument, to crowding out of private investment, and to fiscal policy.

A. Finite Lives and Related Matters

Suppose that the interest payments and associated tax liabilities extend beyond the expected lifetime of the representative current taxpayer (as is clearly the case when the debt principal is "never" paid off). In this situation an individual who is unconcerned with the welfare of his descendants and who can borrow and lend at the same interest rate as the government would be better off with a share of the \$50,000 per year liability than with the like share of the single payment of \$1 million. Consider an individual who expects to live 20 years and who meets the one-time tax cost of his share of \$1 million by effecting a like reduction in his interest-bearing assets. By assumption, these assets have a 5% yield, so that the reduction in annual income is by the share of \$50,000—the same annual cost that arises under the debt-finance option and which could just have been met from the interest on the taxpayer's assets, which could then have been maintained intact. Although the two finance options balance in this respect, there is a difference in the taxpayer's estate after 20 years. Under the tax option the estate is reduced by the share of \$1 million. Under the debt option, with no further tax payments required after 20 years (that is, after death), this reduction does not apply. A taxpayer wishing to leave a zero (or fixed size) estate would anticipate this outcome and would therefore engage in a higher level of lifetime expenditure under the debt option (financed by the eating up of the capital that would otherwise be left in the estate) than under the tax option.[4] In this respect

[4]The same conclusion applies if the taxpayer borrows to finance his share of the \$1 million tax cost, assuming that such loans at 5% interest must be secured by life insurance.

finite lives imply that the representative current taxpayer would perceive himself wealthier when debt issue is substituted for taxation.

The wealth effect associated with finite lives arises because a portion of the future tax liabilities corresponding to future interest payments are shifted to members of later generations. If the added liabilities on descendants were fully counted in wealth calculations by current taxpayers, then the present distinction between the debt and tax options would not arise. Essentially, public debt issue enables members of current generations to die in a state of insolvency by leaving a debt for their descendants. Current taxpayers are "wealthier" if they view the implied governmental shifting of income across generations as desirable. In fact, most individuals already have private opportunities for shifting income across generations that they have chosen not to exercise. Parents make voluntary contributions to children in the form of educational investments, other expenses in the home, and bequests. Children—especially before the expansion of social security—provide support for aged parents. To the extent that private, voluntary intergenerational transfers of this sort are operative—and casual observation suggests that such transfers in the appropriate broadly defined sense are pervasive—the shift from tax to debt finance (or, analogously, the introduction of a pay-as-you-go social security scheme) would not present the representative individual with a new opportunity for extracting funds from members of other generations. Rather, the private response to debt issue (or to more social security) would be a shifting of private, voluntary transfers by an amount sufficient to restore the balance of income across generations that was previously deemed optimal. In this case a shift from tax to debt finance would not affect the perceived wealth position of a finite-lived taxpayer.[5]

A taxpayer can also escape some part of the future taxes associated with debt issue by leaving the jurisdiction of the government. Presumably, this option is more pertinent for state and local governments than for the national government and is generally more important in cases where out-migration costs are low. However, the incentive for individuals to leave an area with a large accumulated debt would arise only to the extent that

[5] Barro (1974) gives a rigorous treatment of this private offset effect. A complication to the analysis arises when some taxpayers have more or less than the average number of descendants. For example, individuals without children may have no ties to future generations (and are therefore made better off by debt issue), although such individuals must be matched by other persons with an above-average number of children (who are likely to be made worse off by debt issue). A second-order wealth effect from debt issue would arise if these individual effects do not cancel out through aggregation. Another second-order effect is the stimulus of debt issue toward reduced family size, which would be motivated by the corresponding reduction in family liability for the stream of future taxes.

this debt was not matched by the quantity of government-owned real capital, which would generate a public income stream that offsets the debt-finance costs. Accordingly, at a local level, debt issue would tend to be associated more with large capital projects than with financing of current expenditures. A further consideration involves the capitalization of taxes—especially property taxes—into property values. To the extent that a higher flow of anticipated future taxes is already reflected in a drop in property values (and, correspondingly, in a reduced annual cost of housing, and so forth), individuals would not be motivated to move out of the jurisdiction with these higher future taxes.

B. Imperfect Private Capital Markets

The argument for equivalence between debt and tax finance depends also on the correspondence between private and governmental interest rates. Suppose, instead, that some individuals have poor collateral on private loan markets and therefore face borrowing rates that are much higher than the government's rate, which I still assume to be 5%. The high private borrowing rates would reflect both default risk and administrative costs associated with the operation of loan markets. Suppose that the government reduces current taxes by $1000 on an individual with a high (or infinite) borrowing rate—labeled person A—and substitutes the issue of a $1000 bond, which would be held by a different individual (or firm), person B, who regards 5% per year from the government as a satisfactory rate of return. I assume that the $50 per year flow of taxes to finance the interest payments on the bond are levied on person A, so that the operation involves no direct redistribution of income across different types of individuals. The net outcome of this debt-creation process is that individual A borrows $1000 at a 5% interest rate from individual B. Individual A is likely to be better off after this transaction because, with his high private borrowing rate, he may be willing to pay much more than 5% annual interest (even for a loan on which default is "impossible") in order to shift expenditures from the future to the present. Individual B is satisfied with the operation because the 5% yield is guaranteed by the government, although he would be unwilling to accept such a return on a direct loan to individual A. Apparently, the shift to debt finance would therefore raise the average perceived wealth of current taxpayers.

The government's debt issue functions as a successful intermediation in the credit market because it avoids the high transaction costs of private loan market operations that are implicit in the initially high borrowing rate of person A. There is a hidden assumption that the government is more efficient than the private market in carrying out credit market operations.

The omitted costs are those entailed by the collection of the flow of future taxes (rather than the single current tax) from individual A. If this individual is a poor credit risk who requires large "supervision" costs on the private market, he is likely, despite the government's coercive taxing powers, to be a similar risk on public loans. The argument that debt issue raises perceived wealth because of imperfect private capital markets depends on the assumption that the government is more efficient, at the margin, in carrying out the loan process than the private market is.[6]

A related argument is that the superior liquidity characteristics of public debt securities enable the government to market its debts at lower interest rates than those applicable to private obligations. This point seems to apply with most force to "high-powered" money (which consists in the United States of currency and reserves of commercial banks that are members of the Federal Reserve system), where the government has some clear monopoly power. In the United States this monopoly position does not seem to extend significantly to interest-bearing debt since the private market seems able to generate, at similar underlying administrative costs, close substitutes for both short- and long-term government securities. Therefore, from the liquidity standpoint, it seems unlikely that shifts between taxes and interest-bearing debt would, at the margin, significantly alter perceived private sector wealth in a developed country like the United States.

C. Uncertainty about Future Taxes

It has often been argued that the future individual tax liabilities implicit in public debt issue are uncertain and would therefore be heavily discounted in calculations of effective wealth positions.[7] In fact, risk-averse individuals would tend to give higher, rather than lower, weight to a given expected amount of future taxes when the variance attached to these liabilities increases.[8] On this count, the substitution of debt issue—and hence uncertain future individual tax liabilities—for current taxation would tend to diminish perceived effective wealth. The principal offset to this conclusion arises to the extent that variations in future individual tax liabilities reflect movements in (uncertain) future individual incomes, rather

[6] Private bail bondsmen are perhaps a response to a differential collection efficiency that favors the private sector. Casual observation of the federal government's student loan program suggests that relative governmental efficiency in the credit markets is actually an amusing idea.

[7] See, for example, Bailey (1971, pp. 157–158) and Buchanan and Wagner (1977, pp. 17, 101, 130). The contrary view is taken in Buchanan (1967, pp. 258–260) and in Barro (1974, pp. 1113–1115).

[8] I am assuming that private insurance markets and other institutions are not sufficient to provide full diversification of relative tax risks.

than changes in other individual characteristics that affect tax liability, shifts in tax procedures, and so on. A positive association between individual taxes and incomes would buffer changes in individual disposable incomes and would therefore offset the other effects of uncertainty on effective wealth calculations. The overall effect of uncertainty on the perceived wealth effect of debt issue is generally ambiguous.

D. Misperception of Future Taxes

It is also sometimes argued that the future taxes implicit in the public debt would be largely ignored because of the complexity involved with estimating these individual liabilities (Feldstein, 1976; Buchanan and Wagner, 1977, p. 130). Difficulties in making accurate computations seem similar to uncertainty about future tax procedures, as discussed above, which would tend to magnify, rather than diminish, the average effective weight assigned to future taxes. In any event it is unclear why misperceptions or "irrationality" would call particularly for underestimation of future taxes. At this level of analysis one could just as well argue that government deficits (which seem to be well publicized) make people sufficiently nervous to reduce their perceived wealth when taxes are replaced by debt issue.

A more plausible argument is that unusual movements (either up or down) in the public debt—that is, government deficits that do not arise from the usual pattern of association with the business cycle, government expenditure changes, etc.—would be temporarily misperceived. The adjustment of the measured government surplus to obtain a "full employment surplus" that takes account of the automatic stabilizer role of the tax system seems to be consistent with this viewpoint.[9] However, in a preliminary empirical investigation, I have been unable to isolate important effects of unusual (or usual) public debt movements on economic activity.

E. The Volume of Government Expenditure

The above analysis has treated the amount and composition of government spending as fixed while considering some consequences of different methods of finance. Therefore, it has been possible to abstract the analysis from evaluations of government expenditure programs. It has, however, sometimes been argued that the existence of the debt-finance option effectively "cheapens" government expenditure because deficits are politi-

[9] The full employment surplus is discussed in Council of Economic Advisers (1962, pp. 78–81).

cally more popular than taxes.[10] The argument for an important effect of this type seems equivalent to the proposition that a shift, at the margin, from taxes to debt issue would substantially raise perceived private sector wealth. It is only in this circumstance that a move toward deficit finance would actually be politically popular. Therefore, the very same analysis that questions the wealth effect of debt issue, at the margin, also raises doubts about the effect of the public debt option in stimulating governmental activity.

3. Public Debt and the Timing of Taxation

The set of arguments that includes finite lives, imperfect private capital markets, uncertainty about future taxes, and misperceptions of tax liabilities does not make an impressive a priori case for public debt issue to alter perceived private wealth in one direction or the other. A reasonable expectation for a country like the United States, in which technical advantages of the government, at the margin, in the loan process or in creating liquidity are likely to be minimal, is that substitution of debt issue for taxes would have a wealth effect of second-order magnitude (and of indeterminate sign).

One difficulty with this sort of negative conclusion is that it does not provide a basis for a positive theory of public debt issue. Elsewhere (Barro, 1978a), I have attempted to construct such a theory by accepting the idea that direct wealth effects are negligible and by focusing on the role of public debt issue as a mechanism for smoothing the time path of tax collections. Suppose that taxes entail collection costs or impose distortions on the private economy and that these costs are an increasing function of the fraction of current national income that the government is collecting in taxes. Although public debt issue does not permit a permanent escape from taxation, it does allow rearrangement of the timing of collections. With "collection costs" an increasing function of the ratio of taxes to national

[10] Buchanan and Wagner (1977) present this hypothesis as the major theme of their book. They attempt to explain much of the rise in the U.S. federal spending–GNP ratio since World War II as a response to a structural change to a "Keynesian debt policy" that made deficits politically more popular than before. However, this hypothesis seems to conflict with the observation that the federal debt–GNP ratio (Table 1) has actually fallen in the post-World War II period in a manner similar to that after World War I and the Civil War. Detailed empirical analysis of annual public debt movements that I have carried out, as discussed in Section 3, indicates that the economic structure that determines the amount of deficit finance has been reasonably stable since at least the 1920s.

income, the optimal method of public finance turns out to involve a pattern of debt issue that rules out any predictable changes in this ratio. This behavior raises a given total (present value) of tax revenues in a manner that minimizes the expected overall costs of collection. Some empirically important implications of this model are that temporary government expenditures, especially the large outlays during wartime, would be financed primarily by debt issue (in order to avoid large temporary movements in the tax–income ratio) and that debt issue would be large during recessions and small or negative during booms (so as to preserve stability of the tax–income ratio over the business cycle in the face of little cyclical fluctuation in government spending). Some other conclusions are that the debt–income ratio would tend to decline, rather than remain constant, during peacetime periods (in order to average out, ex ante, the large positive effects on debt issue of wars and severe contractions) and that nominal debt would grow, other things equal, one to one with the anticipated rate of growth of nominal national income. The last effect is especially important during the inflation of the past decade in the United States—in fact, much of the federal deficit for these years (although only about 30% of the total for 1975–1976) is associated merely with maintaining the anticipated real value of the outstanding interest-bearing public debt. Finally, the model also implies that certain variables—in particular, the size of the accumulated past debt and the level of government expenditure—would not be important determinants of current debt issue.

My empirical analysis suggests that the principal movements in publicly held, interest-bearing federal debt in the United States since World War I can, in fact, be explained by three variables: (a) the movement in federal expenditures relative to "normal," which captures, in particular, the strong response of debt issue to (temporary) wartime spending; (b) the movement in real GNP relative to trend, which captures the countercyclical response of debt issue; and (c) a one-to-one effect of the anticipated inflation rate on the growth rate of nominal debt. The debt creation process appears to be reasonably stable—in the sense of constant coefficients for expressing the effects on debt issue of the above three variables—over the post-World War I period. For example, the sharp expansion of federal debt for 1975–1976 emerges as a response of somewhat more than the usual size to the sharp contraction of output and to the high value of the anticipated rate of inflation. The overall extent of countercyclical debt movement does turn out to be stronger than that called for by the model. However, this phenomenon does not seem to be of recent origin, since results for the 1920s and 1930s appear similar in this respect to those for the post-World War II period. The propositions that the size of the outstanding debt (relative to GNP) and the level of government expenditure (expressed as a fraction of GNP) are irrelevant to current debt issue are supported by the data. Overall, there is a satisfactory empirical performance from the theory of public debt determination that neglects direct wealth effects and focuses on the tax-smoothing role of deficits.

4. The Burden of the Public Debt

The sense in which the (domestically owned) national debt constitutes a burden on future generations has substantially occupied economists' attention [see, e.g., Ferguson (1964) and Tobin (1965)]. This topic is intertwined with the wealth effect of debt issue, as can be illustrated for the case of finite-lived taxpayers discussed in Section 2.A. Suppose that the representative current taxpayer is unconcerned with his descendants and therefore experiences an increase in wealth when taxes are replaced by debt issue. As Buchanan (1958) has argued, the burden on future generations is direct and involves, in particular, the liability for taxes that greets members of future generations as they are born. This first-order argument for debt burden is independent of complications that involve the crowding out of private investment, the direct role of government expenditure programs, the observation that the resources utilized by government for its current expenditures must come out of current output, and so on. The debt burden on future generations is analogous to that which might arise under a pay-as-you-go social security scheme with no government purchases of goods and services. Currently old individuals receiving retirement payments would benefit initially at the expense of the currently young taxpayers. These currently young individuals would be able to recoup a portion of their losses because members of later generations will be born with the liability to pay taxes to finance social security benefits to retirees. Overall, there will be a transfer of wealth from younger generations (including the currently unborn) to older generations.

While the above type of analysis seems to capture the essence of the public debt-burden argument, it is incomplete because it does not discuss the restoration of economic equilibrium after the initial boost to wealth perceptions. Basically, because the rise in perceived wealth increases consumer demand, any increase in the supply of private loanable funds in response to the cut in current taxes (rise in current disposable income) must fall short of the rise in the government's demand for borrowings. Therefore, the rate of return must increase to restore equilibrium in the loanable funds market. The depressing effect of this higher required rate of return on private investment constitutes a crowding-out effect of public borrowing.

Modigliani (1961) has labeled the associated long-run decline in the economy's capital–labor ratio as the burden of the public debt on future generations (in the sense that each generation, in aggregate, bequeathes a smaller capital stock to its descendants). Although a capital stock reduction would, in fact, be predicted under the above assumption about wealth perceptions, it seems that this effect is not the essence of the debt burden argument, which has been captured above by the direct intergenerational income transfers that are implied by debt issue or social security.

The arguments for debt burden and for crowding out of private investment hinge on the assumption that debt issue raises perceived wealth. Neither a burden on future generations nor crowding out would occur in the case discussed above where the public intergenerational transfers implied by debt issue or social security are fully offset by compensating adjustments in voluntary private transfers. For example, there may be no net change in income distribution across generations if parents react to debt issue by increasing transfers to their children or if children react by reducing transfers to their aged parents. With the corresponding absence of a shift in perceived wealth consumer demand would not be stimulated by the movement from taxes to debt issue. It follows that the supply of private loanable funds would rise one to one with the cut in current taxes (increase in current disposable income), so that the extra governmental demand for funds implied by its debt issue would be fully absorbed by the private sector without an increase in the rate of return. Therefore, the crowding out of private investment would not arise when public debt issue leaves unchanged the value of perceived wealth.

Imperfect private capital markets (or the superior liquidity characteristics of government debt), which may be especially important for underdeveloped countries, also imply that public debt issue may raise perceived wealth. However, the analysis of debt burden and crowding out for this case is quite different from that just described. Substitution of debt issue for taxation can work, in part, as an effective governmental intermediation in the credit markets. By cutting current taxes the government can place some funds in the hands of individuals with high (or infinite) borrowing rates who have correspondingly high opportunity rates of return for investment or consumption purposes. These individuals would respond to the tax cut by raising their demands for commodities and—as they exhaust the opportunities with the highest imputed rates of return—by correspondingly reducing the interest rate they would be willing to pay on borrowed funds. On the other hand—with the government's collection costs for future taxes neglected—individuals or firms with interest rates equal to the government's rate would be initially unaffected by the tax cut. Because of the net increase in private commodity demand, it again follows that the government's increased demand for loanable funds would exceed the directly generated increase in private supply. Therefore, the interest rate on risk- and transaction-cost-free loans again rises with debt issue. However, for individuals with high borrowing rates, the net effect must be to lower the imputed rate of return. That is, the government's credit market intermediation implied by its debt issue leads to a convergence of rates of return across the economy. The net effect on investment versus consumption is ambiguous, but the diversion of funds from low opportunity rates of return to high rates is clear. If the government actually has a technical advantage in capital market operations, the perceived wealth increase associated with debt issue is neither an illusion nor an expropriation of future generations, but is rather a movement toward a more efficient allocation of resources. Although it is appropriate in this case to view debt issue as raising perceived private wealth, it would be inappropriate to speak of a public debt burden or of a crowding out of private investment.

5. Fiscal Policy

The perceived wealth effect of public debt issue (produced in this case by a finite life effect, by imperfect private capital markets, or by other reasons for heavy discounting of future tax liabilities) is also a necessary condition for the efficacy of fiscal policy.[11] Substitution of debt issue for taxation is assumed to raise perceived wealth and thereby to generate an expansion of aggregate demand. If the positive link between debt issue and perceived wealth is broken, the possibility of this sort of fiscal policy disappears. Therefore, the argument against a significant wealth effect of public debt issue is also an argument against the efficacy of fiscal policy.[12]

The weight of empirical evidence on the connection between public debt (or, analogously, the expected benefits less taxes implied by social security) and aggregate consumer demand suggests a minor impact of uncertain sign.[13] However, the evidence is surely not unanimous, and there are many estimation problems associated with this type of empirical analysis. Despite these results that raise doubts about the possibility of important

[11] I am abstracting here from the impact of changes in the level of government expenditures. That analysis would involve as a central element the economic function of these expenditures, as discussed in Bailey (1971, Chap. 9).

[12] It should not be inferred that the positive wealth effect of debt issue is sufficient to build a normative case for fiscal activism. Other considerations involve the adjustment of prices and rates of return, the timing of government policy, and the role of private expectations about government policy formation.

[13] The empirical literature includes Kochin (1974), Tanner (1970), David and Scadding (1974), Kormendi (1978), Feldstein (1974, 1977), Barro (1978c, with a reply by Feldstein), Barro and MacDonald (1977), and Darby (1978).

fiscal policy effects, it is not surprising that some large macroeconometric models imply that "expansionary" fiscal policy would have a substantial positive impact on economic activity. These models essentially constrain a shift from taxes to debt issue to have a positive effect on consumer demand —usually by writing consumption as a positive function of current disposable income, without attempting to hold constant the value of anticipated future taxes.[14] This restricted structural specification unreasonably requires the response of consumer demand to a tax cut to be the same as that induced by an exogenous rise in real net national product, independently of whether the tax cut is associated with a deficit that would raise future taxes or is instead accompanied by a decline in the anticipated long-run value of government expenditures. Reduced-form analyses of income determination, which do not impose these sorts of structural restrictions, do not seem to show significant fiscal policy effects.[15]

It seems fair to say that neither economic theories nor empirical analyses provide convincing supporting evidence for the effectiveness of fiscal policy. The area of fiscal policy exhibits a wide gap between, on the one hand, the weight of theory and evidence and, on the other hand, the general opinion of professional economists and policymakers.

REFERENCES

Andersen, L. C., and Jordon, J. L. (1968). Monetary and Fiscal Actions: A Test of their Relative Importance in Economic Stabilization. *Federal Reserve Bank of St. Louis Review* **50** (November), 11–24.

Bailey, M. J. (1971). *National Income and the Price Level*, 2nd ed. McGraw-Hill, New York.

Barro, R. J. (1974). Are Government Bonds Net Wealth? *Journal of Political Economy* **82**, 1095–1117.

Barro, R. J. (1976). Reply to Feldstein and Buchanan. *Journal of Political Economy* **84**, 343–349.

Barro, R. J. (1977). Unanticipated Money Growth and Unemployment in the United States. *American Economic Review* **67**, 101–115.

Barro, R. J. (1978a). On the Determination of the Public Debt. Working paper, University of Rochester.

Barro, R. J. (1978b). Comment from an Unreconstructed Ricardian. *Journal of Monetary Economics* **4**, 569–581.

Barro, R. J. (1978c). *The Impact of Social Security on Private Savings—Evidence from the U.S. Time Series*. American Enterprise Institute, Washington, D.C.

[14] For example, in the Federal Reserve–M.I.T.–Penn model, the key explanatory variable for consumption corresponds approximately to current personal disposable income (Modigliani, 1971). A similar current personal disposable income variable is used in the Brookings model, as reported by Suits and Sparks (1965).

[15] The "St. Louis model" reduced-form equations, which use high-employment government expenditures rather than a deficit variable as a fiscal measure, are reported in Andersen and Jordon (1968). An updated view of this model is contained in K. M. Carlson (1978). Some reduced-form effects on unemployment and output of debt issue and of the "unanticipated" part of this issue are reported in Barro (1977) and Barro (1978a, Section III).

Barro, R. J., and MacDonald, G. (1977). Social Security and Consumer Spending in an International Cross Section. Working paper, University of Rochester.

Buchanan, J. M. (1958). *Public Principles of Public Debt*. Irwin, Homewood, Illinois.

Buchanan, J. M. (1967). *Public Finance in Democratic Process*. University of North Carolina Press, Chapel Hill.

Buchanan, J. M., and Wagner, R. E. (1977). *Democracy in Deficit*. Academic Press, New York.

Carlson, K. M. (1978). Does the St. Louis Equation Now Believe in Fiscal Policy? *Federal Reserve Bank of St. Louis Review* **60** (February), 13–19.

Council of Economic Advisors (1962). *Economic Report of the President*. Washington, D.C.

Darby, M. R. (1978). The Effects of Social Security on Income and the Capital Stock. Working paper 95, University of California, Los Angeles.

David, P. A., and Scadding, J. (1974). Private Savings: Ultrarationality, Aggregation, and "Dennison's Law." *Journal of Political Economy* **82**, 225–249.

de Marco, A. de Viti (1936). *First Principles of Public Finance* (E. Marget, transl.). Jonathan Cape, London.

Dewey, D. R. (1931). *Financial History of the United States*, 11th ed. Longmans, Green, New York.

Feldstein, M. S. (1974). Social Security, Induced Retirement, and Aggregate Capital Accumulation. *Journal of Political Economy* **82**, 905–926.

Feldstein, M. S. (1976). Perceived Wealth in Bonds and Social Security: A Comment. *Journal of Political Economy* **84**, 331–336.

Feldstein, M. S. (1977). Social Security and Private Savings. In *The Economics of Public Services* (M. Feldstein and R. Inman, eds.), pp. 174–205.

Ferguson, J. M. (1964). *Public Debt and Future Generations*. University of North Carolina Press, Chapel Hill.

Klein, B. (1975). Our New Monetary Standard: The Measurement and Effects of Price Uncertainty 1800–1973. *Economic Inquiry* **13**, 461–484.

Kochin, L. (1974). Are Future Taxes Anticipated by Consumers? *Journal of Money, Credit, and Banking* **6**, 385–394.

Kormendi, R. C. (1978). Are Government Bonds Net Wealth? An Empirical Investigation. Working paper, Graduate School of Business, University of Chicago.

Miller, M., and Upton, C. (1974). *Macroeconomics: A Neoclassical Introduction*. Irwin, Homewood, Illinois.

Modigliani, F. (1961). Long-run Implications of Alternative Fiscal Policies and the Burden of the National Debt. *Economic Journal* **71**, 730–755.

Modigliani, F. (1971). Monetary Policy and Consumption: Linkages via Interest Rates and Wealth Effects in the FMP Model. In *Consumer Spending and Monetary Policy: The Linkages*. Federal Reserve Bank of Boston Conference Series 5:14.

Ricardo, D. (1951). *The Works and Correspondence of David Ricardo*. (P. Straffa, ed.). Cambridge University Press, London.

Suits, D. B., and Sparks, G. R. (1965). Consumption Regressions with Quarterly Data. In *The Brookings Quarterly Econometric Model of the U.S.* (J. S. Dusenberry, G. Fromm, L. R. Klein, and E. Kuh, eds.) pp. 203–223. Rand McNally, Chicago, Illinois.

Tanner, J. E. (1970). Empirical Evidence on the Short-Run Real Balance Effect in Canada. *Journal of Money, Credit and Banking* **2**, 473–485.

Tobin, J. (1965). The Burden of the Public Debt. *Journal of Finance* **20**, 679–682.

DEPARTMENT OF ECONOMICS
UNIVERSITY OF ROCHESTER
ROCHESTER, NEW YORK

Fiscal Policies, Inflation, and Capital Formation

*MARTIN FELDSTEIN**

1. Introduction

The unprecedented large government deficits in recent years have stimulated speculation about the adverse effects of such deficits on inflation and on private capital formation. While it is clear that deficits may have no adverse effect in an economy with sufficient unemployed resources, the effects of a deficit when there is full employment are less clear. Is a persistent increase in the government deficit necessarily inflationary? Does it necessarily reduce private capital formation? Is it possible to avoid both adverse effects? A primary purpose of this paper is to answer these questions in the context of a fully employed and growing economy.

A closely related issue is the relation between private saving and capital formation when money and other government liabilities are alternatives to real capital in individual portfolios. Keynes (1936), Harrod (1948), and Tobin (1965) have all emphasized the possibility of excess saving when individuals will not hold capital unless its yield exceeds some minimum required return. When the return on capital is too low, an increase in saving only reduces aggregate demand. If prices are flexible downward, this causes deflation until the increased value of real balances causes a sufficient

*This paper is part of the National Bureau of Economic Research (NBER) Program of Research on Capital Formation; a previous version was circulated as NBER Working Paper No. 275 (August 1978), and published in the *American Economic Review* (September 1980). I am grateful for financial support from the National Science Foundation and the NBER. The paper presents the view of the author and not necessarily of the NBER.

ISBN 0-12-259750-8

reduction in saving; if prices cannot fall, the excess saving results in unemployment.

Three ways of averting such "excess saving" have been emphasized in both theory and practice. The thrust of the Keynesian prescription was to increase the government deficit to provide demand for the resources that would not otherwise be used for either consumption or investment. In this way, aggregate demand would be maintained by substituting public consumption for private consumption A second alternative prescription was to reduce the private saving rate. Early Keynesians like Harris (1941) saw the new social security program as an effective way to reduce aggregate saving. The third type of policy, developed by Tobin (1965), relies on increasing the rate of inflation and making money less attractive relative to real capital. In Tobin's analysis the resulting increase in capital intensity offsets the higher saving rate and therefore maintains aggregate demand.

The current paper will examine ways of increasing capital intensity in this context without raising the rate of inflation. The analysis will also show why, contrary to Tobin's conclusion, a higher rate of inflation may not succeed in increasing investors' willingness to hold real capital.

An important feature of the analysis in this paper is a monetary growth model that distinguishes between money and interest-bearing government bonds. With this distinction we can compare government deficits financed by borrowing with deficits financed by creating money. It is possible also to examine the effect of changes in the interest rate on government debt while maintaining the fact that money is not interest bearing. The two types of government liabilities also permit analyzing the distinction between the traditional liquidity preference and a demand for government bonds that I shall call safety preference. In practice, this safety preference may be much more important than the traditional liquidity preference.

Section 2 of the paper develops the three-asset monetary growth model that will be used in the remaining analysis. Section 3 then considers the effects of changes in the government deficit. The effects of increased saving on aggregate demand and capital intensity are developed in Section 4. There is a brief concluding section.

2. A Three-Asset Model of Monetary Growth

The model developed here differs from traditional monetary growth models [such as Tobin (1965) and Levhari and Patinkin (1968)] in two important ways. First, instead of the usual assumption that all taxes are lump-sum levies, the current analysis recognizes taxes on capital income that lower the net rate of return.[1] Second, the government deficit is financed not only by increasing the money supply but also by issuing interest-bearing government debt.[2] Throughout the analysis we maintain the simplifying assumption that the savings rate out of real disposable income is fixed; the tax on capital income affects the allocation of saving but not the saving rate itself. Because the analysis in the sections that follow will focus on comparative steady-state dynamics, only these steady-state properties will be discussed here.[3] Note that this assumption of steady-state dynamics implies that all growth rates are constant and therefore that all quantities are correctly anticipated.

The economy is characterized by an exogenously growing population

$$N = N_0 e^{nt}. \tag{1}$$

The labor force is a constant fraction of the population, and technical progress is subsumed into population growth. Production can be described by an aggregate production function with constant returns to scale. The relation between per capita output y and per capita capital stock k is

$$y = f(k) \tag{2}$$

with $f' > 0$ and $f'' < 0$. For simplicity output is measured net of depreciation, and depreciation is not explicitly included in the analysis.

A. The Government Budget Constraint

Government spending G plus the payment of interest on the government debt must be financed by either tax receipts, money creation, or borrowing. Total real tax receipts T are the sum of a lump-sum tax T_0 and

[1] Feldstein (1976) and Feldstein *et al.* (1978) show the importance of recognizing capital income taxes in analyzing the effects of inflation in a monetary growth model. Corporate and personal taxes were distinguished there, but will not be in the current paper.

[2] Green and Sheshinski (1977) examine an economy with both bonds and money, but assume that such bonds are perfect substitutes for private capital in investors' portfolios. Their analysis generally focuses on quite different issues. Tobin and Buiter (1978) recently developed a three-asset model in which government bonds and money are imperfect substitutes for each other as well as for real capital. I received a copy of their unpublished paper only after the current paper was completed. Because the tax structure that they assume is very different from the taxes described in the current paper, their conclusions are frequently different from my own. Friedman (1979) also recently developed a three-asset model but used it to analyze quite different questions (the short-run effects of monetary and fiscal policies in an economy with unemployment and fixed prices) from those that are the focus of my own research.

[3] Section 4 will, however, consider the possibility of disequilibrium behavior associated with excess saving.

the revenue that results from taxing the income from real capital at rate τ.[4] The money created by the government M is the only money in the economy and does not bear interest. The time rate of change of the stock of nominal money is DM; the real value of the extra money created in this way is DM/p. Government bonds bear interest at rate i; the nominal market value of these bonds is B, and the real value of new borrowing is DB/p.[5]

The government's budget constraint may be written

$$G + iB/p = T + DM/p + DB/p. \tag{3}$$

Alternatively, it will be convenient to denote the real government deficit by Δ and write

$$\Delta = DM/p + DB/p. \tag{4}$$

In steady state the ratio of real money per unit of real capital M/pK must remain constant. This implies that the rate of growth of M is equal to the rate of growth of pK, or with $Dp/p = \pi$,[6]

$$DM/M = \pi + n. \tag{5}$$

Similarly, the steady-state rate of growth of nominal government bonds equals the inflation rate plus the real growth rate of the economy:

$$DB/B = \pi + n. \tag{6}$$

Substituting these expressions into (4) and dividing by the population gives the steady-state per capita deficit:

$$\Delta/N = (\pi + n)(M/pN) + (\pi + n)(B/pN). \tag{7}$$

With lower case letters representing real per capita values (7) can be rewritten

$$\delta = (\pi + n)(m + b). \tag{8}$$

The real per capita deficit equals the product of the economy's nominal growth rate and the real per capita government liabilities.

[4]The tax rate τ is best thought of as a corporate tax rate. The personal tax on real capital income and on the interest on government debt is not specially recognized.

[5]These bonds may be thought of as treasury bills although their maturity is irrelevant for steady-state analysis as long as that maturity is finite. We ignore changes in the market value that would temporarily result from changes in the interest rate if the maturity were not very short.

[6]This uses the fact that in steady state $k = K/N$ is constant, implying $DK/K = n$.

B. Portfolio Behavior[7]

The real value of household assets is the sum of the real values of government liabilities and the capital stock[8]:

$$a = b + m + k. \tag{9}$$

I shall simplify the description of the households' portfolio behavior by assuming that the equilibrium ratio of real bonds to capital depends on the difference between the net real yield on capital r and the real yield on government bonds $i - \pi$[9]:

$$b/k = \beta(r + \pi - i), \qquad \beta' < 0. \tag{10}$$

Because the depreciation method used in the United States and in most other countries is based on the original costs of plant and equipment, the tax liability per unit of capital increases with the rate of inflation.[10] I shall therefore write the net rate of return as

$$r = f' - \tau(f' + \lambda\pi), \tag{11}$$

where the parameter λ indicates the extent to which a higher inflation rate increases the tax liability.[11] Substituting (11) into (10) yields the equilibrium bond portfolio condition:

$$b/k = \beta\left[(1 - \tau)f'(k) + (1 - \tau\lambda)\pi - i\right], \qquad \beta' < 0. \tag{12}$$

With safe short-term interest-bearing government debt available, individuals should hold money only for transaction purposes. As Baumol (1952) and others have shown, this demand for money varies positively

[7] The description of portfolio behavior and saving in this model assumes that households as a whole regard government bonds as net wealth, implicitly ignoring the corresponding tax liabilities that they and future generations must bear in order to pay the interest and principle on these bonds. The alternative view, based on the so-called "Ricardian equivalence theorem," depends on extremely strong and improbable assumptions. To the extent that households do partially reduce their perceived value of government bonds because of future tax liabilities, the variable B (or b) in household portfolios might be scaled down to some fraction of B. This need not change any of the qualitative conclusions of the current analysis.

[8] The private bonds and equities that represent the ownership claims to the capital stock are not explicitly recognized. The tax rate τ can be regarded as the effective tax rate corresponding to the steady-state mix of debt and equity finance. See Feldstein *et al.* (1979).

[9] Recall that we are ignoring the *personal* tax on investment income.

[10] See Feldstein *et al.* (1978, especially the appendix by Auerbach) and Feldstein and Summers (1977).

[11] Accelerated depreciation affects τ and λ, but λ exceeds zero even if, at the equilibrium value of π, tax depreciation exceeds economic depreciation.

with the level of income and inversely with the rate of interest[12]:

$$m/y = L(i), \qquad L' < 0. \tag{13}$$

An important feature of an economy with money or other government liabilities is the possibility that individuals will be unwilling to hold capital unless its yield is above some minimum level. In the traditional two-asset Keynesian model this is represented as a liquidity trap, that is, as an infinitely elastic demand for money at some low rate of interest. A more realistic description is possible with the current three-asset model. When the real net yield on capital becomes very low relative to the real yield on government bonds, investors will want to hold government bonds instead of capital; in the notation of (12) the absolute value of β' becomes infinite when the real differential becomes very small.[13] The reason that investors prefer government bonds in this situation is that the pretax profitability of private capital is uncertain. The bond demand behavior will therefore be referred to as a "safety preference" relation to distinguish it from the liquidity preference relation that governs the demand for money.[14]

C. The Supply and Demand for Savings

The supply of savings S is proportional to the households' real disposable income H:

$$S = \sigma H. \tag{14}$$

The saving propensity will be assumed to be constant. Disposable income is equal to national income Y minus both the government's tax receipts T and the fall in the real value of the population's money and government bonds $\pi M/p$ and $\pi B/p$, respectively.[15]

Saving is therefore:

$$S = \sigma(Y - T - \pi M/p - \pi B/p + iB/p) \tag{15}$$

[12]This can be simplified by assuming that individuals regard the interest-bearing government debt rather than real capital as an alternative to transaction balances. Transaction balances are also assumed to depend on income rather than wealth when in reality both are important.

[13]This unwillingness to own real capital may also increase the demand for money, but that effect is likely to be small relative to the increased demand for bonds.

[14]The private securities are generally as marketable as government bonds, and to the extent that they have the same maturity structure, their price will be as sensitive to interest rate fluctuations. Their liquidity is therefore similar even though the safety and predictability of the yields differ substantially.

[15]Recall that this analysis assumes that households as a whole regard government bonds as net wealth.

or, using (13),

$$S = \sigma(Y - G + DM/p + DB/p - \pi M/p - \pi B/p). \tag{16}$$

Since $DM/p - \pi M/p = nM/p$ (with a similar equivalence for bonds),

$$S = \sigma(Y - G + nM/p + nB/p). \tag{17}$$

In a steady-state government spending must bear a stable relation to national income. The analysis that follows assumes that a fraction γ of national income is devoted to government spending exclusive of interest on the government debt. This implies that any increase in interest on the government debt causes a corresponding increase in the government deficit or in lump-sum taxes.

All saving must be absorbed in either real capital accumulation or additional real money and bonds:

$$S = DK + D(M/p) + D(B/p). \tag{18}$$

The constant ratio of capital to labor in steady-state growth implies $DK = nK$. Similarly, the constancy of $m = M/pN$ and $b = B/pN$ implies that $D(M/p) = nM/p$ and $D(B/p) = nB/p$. Thus

$$S = nK + nM/p + nB/p. \tag{19}$$

Combining (17) and (19), writing γY for G, and dividing by N yields the per capita growth equilibrium condition

$$\sigma[y(1 - \gamma) + nm + nb] = nk + nm + nb. \tag{20}$$

This completes the presentation of the model that will be analyzed in the remainder of this paper. Although the model contains important features that were lacking in earlier monetary growth models, it is still very simple. It would be desirable to investigate a richer class of models that includes personal taxes on portfolio income, that distinguishes households from institutional investors, that recognizes substitututes for business capital other than bonds and money, and that separates corporate bonds and equity. The reader should bear in mind the strong simplifying assumptions that have been made, and the fact that the subsequent analysis will compare steady-state growth patterns with no attention to the transitions. Any such short-run or transitional analysis raises difficult problems of specifying how expectations are formed when the economy is not on a steady-state growth path.

3. Deficits, Inflation, and Capital Intensity

The model developed in Section 2 can now be used to analyze how changes in the government deficit affect the rate of inflation and the capital intensity of the economy. Can the government increase the real steady-state deficit in this fully employed economy without causing either inflation, reduced capital intensity, or both? What policies can be pursued to mitigate the adverse effects of the deficit? What happens when the policy options of the government are restricted?

To answer these questions, it is useful to collect the four equations [(8), (13), (12), and (20), respectively] that describe the steady-state behavior of the economy:

$$\delta = (\pi + n)(m + b), \tag{21}$$

$$m = L(i)f(k), \tag{22}$$

$$b = \beta\left[(1-\tau)f'(k) + (1-\tau\lambda)\pi - i\right]k, \tag{23}$$

$$\sigma\left[(1-\gamma)f(k) + nm + nb\right] = n(k + m + b), \tag{24}$$

where $f(k)$ has been substituted for y in (22) and (24). The policy instruments controlled by the government are the size of the deficit δ, the share of government spending in national income γ, the interest rate on government bonds i,[16] and the tax rates on capital income τ and λ. For given values of these policy instruments and the exogenous growth rate n the four equations determine the values of k, π, m, and b.

It is clear from these four equations that the government can increase its deficit without inducing any changes in inflation or capital intensity if it can vary all of the other policy instruments (γ, i, τ, and λ). In practice, however, the government does not alter the share of government spending in national income γ in order to neutralize the effect of a deficit.[17] It is tempting to conclude that, even if γ is held constant, the government can still increase the deficit without changing π or k because it still has three unconstrained instruments. It is easily shown, however, that this is not true; an increased deficit must then be accompanied by a change in either inflation, capital intensity, or both. To see this, note that with γ constant (24) implies that if $dk = 0$, it is also true that $d(m + b) = 0$. Equation (21) shows that $d(m + b) = 0$ and $d\pi = 0$ together imply $d\delta = 0$. The deficit must be unchanged if both inflation and capital intensity are unchanged.

The government can, however, affect the combination of changes in inflation and capital intensity that occurs by its debt management policy and its tax policy. Because changes in tax policy (in τ and λ) are not a

[16] Recall that this would not in general equal the rate of return on private capital. This interest rate could equivalently be regarded as endogenous if the government is assumed to choose the supply of nominal bonds, or the supply of money, or the ratio of these two.

[17] This would in particular require reducing the share of government spending in national income. To see this, note that (21) implies $d\delta = (\pi + n)\,d(m + b)$ if $d\pi = 0$. Equation (24) implies $-k\sigma f\,d\gamma = (1 - \pi)n\,d(m + b)$ since $dk = 0$. Combining these two shows $d\gamma/d\delta < 0$.

typical government response, most of this section will assume that τ and λ as well as γ are unchanged. My analysis focuses on debt management policy—the way that the government adjusts the relative supply of money and bonds or, equivalently, the rate of interest on government debt.

A. A Deficit Causing Both Increased Inflation and Reduced Capital Intensity

With the type of debt policy that has been pursued in the United States an increase in the steady-state deficit is likely to cause both a higher rate of inflation and a reduced capital intensity of production. More specifically, most empirical research indicates that the government has issued a mix of money and debt in such a way that the *real* interest rate on government debt remains approximately unchanged.[18] Section 3.A analyzes the consequences of this policy; alternative debt policies are examined in the subsequent section. To analyze the effect of an increased deficit with a constant *real* interest rate on government debt, (21)–(24) are totally differentiated subject to the condition $di = d\pi$.

The key to the adverse effect of inflation on capital intensity is seen in the total differential of (23), subject to $di = d\pi$:

$$db = \left[\beta + k\beta'(1-\tau)f'' \right] dk - k\beta'\tau\lambda\, d\pi. \tag{25}$$

The partial effect of an increase in inflation is to increase the demand for bonds rather than capital because the real yield on bonds is maintained while the real yield on capital falls by $\tau\lambda\, d\pi$. If this positive effect of inflation on the demand for bonds is large enough to outweigh the negative effect of inflation on the demand for money that is implied by (22) with $di = d\pi$:

$$dm = Lf'\, dk + fL'\, d\pi, \tag{26}$$

the effect of an increased deficit can be shown unambiguously to reduce k. To see this, note first that (24) implies

$$d(m+b) = \frac{\sigma(1-\gamma)f' - n}{(1-\sigma)n}\, dk. \tag{27}$$

[18] Evidence that the nominal interest rate rises by approximately the rate of inflation was presented by Fisher (1954) and has been verified by Yohe and Karnovsky (1969), Feldstein and Eckstein (1970), Feldstein and Summers (1977), and others. The assumption in Tobin (1965) that $di = 0$ is clearly inconsistent with experience when i is interpreted as the yield on government debt rather than the yield on money.

Adding (25) and (26) and then using (27) to eliminate $d(m+b)$ yields

$$\frac{(1-\gamma)f'-n}{(1-\sigma)n}\,dk = \left[Lf' + \beta + k\beta'(1-\tau)f''\right]dk + (fL' - k\beta'\tau\lambda)\,d\pi. \tag{28}$$

Similarly, differentiating (21) and using (27) yields

$$\lambda\delta = \frac{\sigma(1-\gamma)f'-n}{(1-\sigma)n}\,dk + (m+b)\,d\pi. \tag{29}$$

Using (28) to eliminate $d\pi$ from (29) yields

$$\left.\frac{dk}{d\delta}\right|_{di=d\pi} = \frac{(1-\sigma)n(fL'-k\beta'\tau\lambda)}{(\pi+n)\left[\sigma(1-\gamma)f'-n\right](fL'-k\beta'\tau\lambda) + (m+b) \times \{\sigma(1-\gamma)f'-n-n(1-\sigma)\}\left[Lf'+\beta+k\beta'(1-\tau)f''\right]}. \tag{30}$$

With the increased demand for bonds induced by higher inflation greater than the reduced demand for money $fL' - k\beta'\tau\lambda > 0$, and the numerator is positive. Note that stability of the simpler nonmonetary economy requires $\sigma(1-\gamma)f' - n < 0$; with this assumption the denominator is negative. Under these quite plausible conditions a higher deficit reduces capital formation. Since (28) implies that dk and $d\pi$ are of opposite signs, the higher deficit also increases inflation.

B. A Deficit without Inflation

The bleak outcome of increased inflation and reduced capital intensity is not a necessary implication of a greater deficit. A different debt policy would permit a deficit with no inflation. By totally differentiating (21) through (24) with the constraint that $d\pi = 0$ it is possible to find the change in the interest rate and corresponding debt policy that permits such a noninflationary increase in the deficit:

$$d\delta = (\pi+n)\,d(m+b), \tag{31}$$

$$d(m+b) = (fL' - k\beta')\,di + \left[Lf' + \beta + k\beta'(1-\tau)f''\right]dk, \tag{32}$$

and

$$\left[\sigma(1-\gamma)f' - n\right]dk = (1-\sigma)n\,d(m+b). \tag{33}$$

The separate behavior of m and b is irrelevant for determining the change in i that is required to keep the inflation rate unchanged. Equation (33) can be substituted into (32) to eliminate dk, and (31) can then be used to eliminate $d(m + b)$. The resulting equation shows that

$$\left.\frac{di}{d\delta}\right|_{d\pi=0} = \frac{\sigma(1-\gamma)f' - n - \left[Lf' + \beta + k\beta'(1-\tau)f''\right](1-\sigma)n}{(\pi + n)\left[\sigma(1-\gamma)f' - n\right](fL' - k\beta')}. \quad (34)$$

The numerator is unambiguously negative since

(a) $\sigma(1-\gamma)f' - n < 0$ was assumed from stability considerations and

(b) $f' > 0$, $\beta' < 0$, and $f'' < 0$ make $-[Lf' + \beta + k\beta'(1-\tau)f''](1-\sigma)n < 0$.

The first term of the denominator is positive while, as already noted, the second term is negative. The final term in the denominator is the difference between the effect on the demand for money of an increase in the interest rate on government debt and its effect on the demand for the bonds themselves. Since a higher value of i can be expected to increase the demand for bonds by more than it reduces the demand for money, this term will be taken to be positive. The denominator as a whole is therefore negative. Thus $di/d\delta > 0$.

In short, the interest rate must increase when the deficit increases if the inflation rate is to remain constant. It is easy to understand why this interest rate increase is necessary. Equation (31) indicates that a stable inflation rate requires that $m + b$ must increase with the deficit. This is so because a higher value of $m + b$ permits the larger annual increase in the money supply and/or government borrowing that must accompany an increased deficit to be absorbed without a higher proportional rate of growth of either money or bonds. To state this same point in a slightly different way, the faster growth of government liabilities can be absorbed without increasing the *proportional* growth rate of either money or bonds if the *level* of money and bonds that is demanded (in other words, the denominators of the proportional growth rates) is increased. The higher interest rate makes this possible by increasing the demand for bonds by more than it decreases the demand for money.

Note that in practice the required change would come about by financing the increased deficit with a higher ratio of bonds to money than that which prevailed in the initial equilibrium. Achieving this reduction in liquidity would require paying a higher rate of interest on those bonds.

It is clear that this policy of a higher interest rate and an increased supply of real government debt must reduce the capital intensity of production. This can be seen directly by combining Eqs. (31) and (33):

$$\left.\frac{dk}{d\delta}\right|_{d\pi=0} = \frac{(1-\sigma)n}{(\pi+n)\left[\sigma(1-\gamma)f' - n\right]} < 0. \tag{35}$$

The cost of avoiding the higher inflation rate that would otherwise accompany an increased deficit is a lower level of capital intensity and a smaller real income.

C. A Deficit without Reduced Capital Intensity

The crowding out of real capital accumulation by the government deficit can be avoided by allowing inflation to occur. It is worth examining how much inflation and what change in the interest rate are needed to keep capital intensity unchanged.

Differentiating (24) with $dk = 0$ shows immediately that $m + b$ must also remain unchanged. Equation (21) then implies that $d\delta = (m + b)\,d\pi$; that is, an increase in the deficit must increase inflation. With $d(m + b) = 0$ (22) and (23) together imply

$$0 = (fL' - k\beta')\,di + (1 - \tau\lambda)k\beta'\,d\pi. \tag{36}$$

Substituting $(m + b)^{-1}\,d\delta$ for $d\pi$ yields the change in i required to keep k fixed:

$$\left.\frac{di}{d\delta}\right|_{dk=0} = \frac{-(1-\tau\lambda)k\beta'}{(m+b)(fL' - k\beta)} \tag{37}$$

As explained previously, the denominator is positive in the likely case that a rise in the interest rate increases the demand for bonds by more than it decreases the demand for money. The value of λ would be zero if the tax law did not cause inflation to reduce the real net return on capital. In that case the numerator is positive, and $di/d\delta > 0$. More generally, even when historic cost depreciation rules do raise the effective tax rate on real profits ($\lambda > 0$), the numerator will still be positive as long as inflation raises the *nominal* after-tax return on capital.[19]

The mechanism by which a higher interest rate permits a constant value of k is clear from the derivation. A constant value of k implies a constant value of $m + b$ and therefore an increased value of π. With a constant value of k a higher rate of inflation would actually decrease b (and therefore $m + b$) unless i is raised to prevent this.

Comparing (37) and (34) shows that the increase in i that keeps k

[19] The nominal after-tax return on capital is $(1-\tau)f' + (1-\tau\lambda)\pi$.

unchanged is less than the increase in i that keeps π unchanged:

$$\left.\frac{di}{d\delta}\right|_{d\pi=0} - \left.\frac{di}{d\delta}\right|_{dk=0} = \frac{\begin{array}{r}\sigma(1-\gamma)f' - n - \left[Lf' + \beta + k\beta'(1-\tau)f''\right](1-\sigma)n(m+b) \\ -(\pi+n)\left[\sigma(1-\gamma)f' - n\right](1-\tau\lambda)k\beta'\end{array}}{(m+b)(fL' - k\beta')(\pi+n)\left[\sigma(1-\gamma)f' - n\right]} > 0. \tag{38}$$

The reason for this is clear. Holding k and therefore $m + b$ constant implies $d\pi > 0$. Making $d\pi = 0$ requires an increase in $m + b$ and therefore a higher rate of interest.

D. A Deficit Financed by Interest-Bearing Debt

A particularly interesting debt policy requires that any increase in the deficit be financed only by additional borrowing. The real growth of the money supply remains constant. This section looks briefly at the effect of such a policy. This specification of debt policy implies that the real rate of new money creation remains unchanged: DM/pN is constant. Since $DM/pN = m(DM/M) = m(\pi + n)$, this debt policy implies $m(\pi + n) = c$, a constant. The implication of this for capital intensity and inflation depends on the interest elasticity of the demand for money. On the simplifying assumption that the money demand is completely inelastic ($L' = 0$) it is easily shown that the deficit unambiguously decreases capital intensity and increases inflation.

With $m(\pi + n) = c$

$$d\delta = (\pi + n)\,db + b\,d\pi \tag{39}$$

and

$$dm = \left[-m/(\pi + n)\right]d\pi. \tag{40}$$

Combining $m = Lf$ and $m(\pi + n) = c$ yields

$$(\pi + n)f'\,dk = -f\,d\pi. \tag{41}$$

Thus inflation and capital intensity move in opposite directions. The growth equilibrium condition of (24) implies

$$\frac{\sigma(1-\gamma)f' - n}{(1-\sigma)n}\,dk = db + dm. \tag{42}$$

Using (40) and (41) to eliminate dm yields

$$db = \left[\frac{\sigma(1-\gamma)f' - n}{(1-\sigma)n} - \frac{mf'}{f} \right] dk. \tag{43}$$

Equation (39) can thus be rewritten using (41) and (43) as

$$d\delta = (\pi + n)\left[\frac{(1-\gamma)f' - n}{(1-\sigma)n} - \frac{mf'}{f} - \frac{bf'}{f} \right] dk. \tag{44}$$

This shows that $dk/d\delta < 0$, and (41) then implies that $d\pi/d\delta > 0$. Thus even with a debt policy that keeps the growth of real money balances unchanged, the deficit increases inflation and reduces capital intensity.

4. Fiscal Incentives, Saving, and Aggregate Demand

The three-asset growth model can be used to analyze the effects of an exogenous increase in the saving rate.[20] The most important issue to be examined is the possibility of excess saving. Under quite reasonable conditions an increase in the saving rate will be absorbed into higher capital intensity without any problem for aggregate demand if there is accommodating monetary policy. The possibility of excess saving arises when investors are unwilling to hold real capital in their portfolio at a lower rate of return; we shall refer to this as a "safety trap" by analogy to the traditional Keynesian liquidity trap. The problem is exacerbated if the yield on government bonds also cannot be lowered, that is, if the economy is also in a liquidity trap.

The problem of excess saving can manifest itself in two ways. Under some conditions the extra saving could be absorbed in additional capital if the steady-state rate of inflation is reduced. If there is no inflation in the initial equilibrium, the increased saving rate would involve a continuous price deflation. While there may be no theoretical problem with this, as a practical matter the downward rigidity of money wages could prevent this from occurring. The additional saving would not be absorbed, but would result in unemployment. The problem is even worse when the safety trap and liquidity trap conditions both prevail. Under these conditions the extra savings cannot be absorbed in increased capital even if the inflation rate could be permanently reduced.

The problem of excess saving arises only if the government restricts its accommodating action to monetary policy. This section shows how tax

[20] Such an increase in the saving rate σ may reflect a change in taste or a change in institutions such as social security that are not explicitly included in the model.

incentives, or under some conditions an increased deficit, can be used to assure that an increase in the saving rate results in a greater rate of capital formation.

A. Increased Saving with Accommodating Monetary Policy

Before studying the problem of excess saving, it is useful to examine the nature of the well-behaved equilibrium in which additional saving can be absorbed with the help of only accommodating monetary policy. Let us impose the requirement that the real deficit δ, the share of the government in national income γ, and the tax rates on capital income τ and γ remain constant. The rate of inflation will also be required to remain unchanged, thus precluding the problem of unattainable price deflation.

The key change from the analysis of Section 3 is that the differential of the growth equilibrium condition, (24), now involves a change in the saving rate:

$$\left[(1-\gamma)f + n(m+b)\right]d\sigma + \left[\sigma(1-\gamma)f' - n\right]dk - (1-\sigma)n\,d(m+b) = 0. \tag{45}$$

With a constant deficit $d\delta = 0$ and constant inflation rate $d\pi = 0$ the government budget constraint

$$d\delta = (\pi + n)\,d(m+b) + (m+b)\,d\pi \tag{46}$$

implies $d(m+b) = 0$. Together with (45) this shows immediately that the higher saving rate increases capital intensity:

$$\frac{dk}{d\sigma} = -\frac{(1-\gamma)f + n(m+b)}{\sigma(1-\gamma)f' - n} > 0. \tag{47}$$

The required change in the interest rate can then be derived from the money demand relation (22) and the bond demand relation (23). Together these imply

$$\begin{aligned} d(m+b) = {} & \left[Lf' + \beta + k\beta'(1-\tau)f''\right]dk \\ & + (fL' - k\beta')\,di + k\beta'(1-\tau\lambda)\,d\pi. \end{aligned} \tag{48}$$

With $d(m+b) = d\pi = 0$

$$\frac{di}{dk} = -\frac{Lf' + \beta + k\beta'(1-\tau)f''}{fL' - k\beta'}. \tag{49}$$

If the effect of a change in the interest rate on the demand for bonds exceeds its effect on the demand for money, the denominator is positive and $di/dk < 0$. To achieve this reduction in the equilibrium interest rate on government debt, the money supply must be increased relative to real income, and the supply of bonds must be reduced relative to the capital stock. The precise changes are indicated by (22) and (23) and satisfy $d(m + b) = 0$.

In short, if investors are willing to accept a lower return on capital accompanied by a less than equal reduction in the yield on government debt, an increase in the saving rate can raise capital intensity without any change in inflation or other government policies.[21]

B. Safety Preference and Excess Saving

The basic insight of the Keynesian analysis is that, in a monetary economy, additional saving will not automatically be invested. When the yield on real capital becomes too low, individuals will prefer to hold government bonds rather than to assume the greater risk associated with the ownership of real capital. More precisely, the demand for government bonds becomes infinitely elastic at some low differential between the yield on real capital $[(1-\tau)f' + (1-\tau\lambda)\pi]$ and the yield on government bonds i. In the notation of the bond demand equation

$$b = k\beta\left[(1-\tau)f' + (1-\tau\lambda)\pi - i\right], \tag{50}$$

$\beta' = -\infty$ at some low value of $(1-\tau)f' + (1-\tau\lambda)\pi - i$. We can refer to this situation as being in a "safety trap."

When the economy has reached this condition, a further fall in $(1-\tau)f' + (1-\tau\lambda)\pi - i$ is not possible. This additional constraint on the adjustment of the economy can be the source of an excess saving problem. When certain further conditions exist, the increase in capital intensity could only occur if the rate of inflation could be reduced. If the initial equilibrium had no inflation (or a very low rate), the required reduction in inflation might not be achievable, and the extra saving would result in an unemployment disequilibrium.[22]

To see the conditions under which this problem would arise, note that the safety trap condition implies

$$(1-\tau)f''\,dk + (1-\tau\lambda)\,d\pi - di = 0. \tag{51}$$

[21] If the interest rate on government debt cannot be reduced, an increase in the rate of inflation could achieve the same thing (as long as $1 - \tau\lambda > 0$). This is essentially Tobin's (1965) solution since he assumes $di = 0$. The implication of Section 4.A and the remainder of Section 4 is that Tobin's inflationary policy is unnecessary and may be counterproductive.

[22] The dynamics of such an employment disequilibrium will not be considered. The relative strength of the Pigou effect and Wicksell effect would influence the ultimate path. For the current purpose it is sufficient that price deflation and unemployment would be required for at least some period of time.

This in turn implies that $db = \beta\, dk$ and therefore that

$$d(m + b) = fL'\, di + (Lf' + \beta)\, dk. \tag{52}$$

With no change in the government deficit the government budget constraint entails

$$(\pi + n)d(m + b) + (m + b)\, d\pi = 0 \tag{53}$$

Using this equation to eliminate $d(m + b)$ from (52) and using (51) to rewrite di in terms of $d\pi$ and dk yields

$$\frac{d\pi}{dk} = -\frac{fL'(1 - \tau)f'' + Lf' + \beta}{\left[(m + b)/(\pi + n)\right] + fL'(1 - \tau\lambda)}. \tag{54}$$

The numerator is unambiguously positive. If the denominator is also positive, an increase in capital intensity must be accompanied by a lower rate of inflation. There are two different plausible conditions under which the denominator will be positive. If the demand for money is interest inelastic ($L' = 0$) or, more generally, if the effect of interest on money demand is small [that is, if $(\pi + n)fL'(1 - \tau\lambda) < m + b$], the denominator will be positive. Alternatively, regardless of the size of L', if inflation raises the effective tax rate on capital income by enough to make the nominal after-tax yield on capital vary inversely with inflation ($1 - \tau\lambda < 0$), both terms in the denominator will be positive. In either case increased capital intensity could not accompany a higher saving rate unless the rate of inflation could be reduced.

It is easy to see why the safety trap condition implies that a greater capital intensity entails a lower rate of inflation. Consider the case of inelastic money demand. The safety trap implies that the demand for bonds increases in proportion to the capital stock: $db = \beta\, dk$. With inelastic money demand the money supply also increases with the capital stock: $dM = Lf'\, dk$. But with no change in the government deficit the steady-state value of $m + b$ can increase only if the inflation rate is lower. In the alternate case in which inflation increases the effective tax rate the analysis is only slightly more complex. If there were no change in inflation, the interest rate would have to fall to maintain the minimum yield differential with greater capital intensity. But this would increase the demand for money, raising $m + b$. This is incompatible with a constant inflation rate. If the inflation rate increased, this would further reduce the yield on capital relative to government bonds.

The problem of excess saving under these conditions can be avoided if the government uses fiscal policy as well as monetary policy to accommodate the additional saving. Consider first the possibility of responding to a higher saving rate by reducing the rate of tax on capital income τ. With a lower tax rate, the net of tax yield on the real capital stock can be maintained while the greater capital intensity depresses the pretax yield. To confirm explicitly that this fiscal incentive is sufficient to permit greater capital intensity with no change in the rate of inflation, consider the four equations that describe the "safety trap" equilibrium with $d\tau \neq 0$. The government budget constraint with $d\pi = 0$ and $d\delta = 0$ implies $d(m + b) = 0$. Substituting this into the growth equilibrium (45) shows $dk/d\sigma > 0$ exactly as in (47). The two remaining conditions that must be satisfied are the "safety trap" condition with $d\pi = 0$:

$$(1 - \tau) f'' \, dk - di - (f' + \lambda\pi) \, d\tau = 0 \tag{55}$$

and the condition that the change in the demands for debt and money leave $m + b$ unchanged:

$$0 = fL' \, di + (\beta + Lf') \, dk. \tag{56}$$

Equation (56) shows that the interest rate must rise, reducing the demand for money per unit of capital. With the unique increase in di determined by (56) and the unique increase in k determined by (47) the required decrease in the tax rate τ is shown by (55).

A higher saving rate can be transformed into greater capital intensity with no change in inflation even without changing the tax rate on capital income by an accommodating increase in the government deficit accompanied by a lower rate of interest. The lower rate of interest balances the fall in the return on real capital, permitting the real capital to be absorbed. The greater deficit with the unchanged rate of inflation permits an increase in both money and bonds that is required by the fall in i and increase in k.

To see all of this explicitly, note that with $d\tau = d\pi = 0$, the safety trap condition becomes

$$(1 - \tau) f'' \, dk - di = 0. \tag{57}$$

The increased demand for money and bonds is

$$d(m + b) = fL' \, di + (Lf' + \beta) \, dk, \tag{58}$$

which from (57) is

$$d(m + b) = \left[fL'(1 - \tau) f'' + Lf' + \beta \right] dk. \tag{59}$$

Substituting this value of $d(m + b)$ into the growth equilibrium (45) yields

$$\frac{dk}{d\sigma} = - \frac{(1 - \gamma) f + n(m + b)}{(1 - \gamma) f' - n - \left[fL'(1 - \tau) f'' + Lf' + \beta \right]} \, . \tag{60}$$

This is unambiguously positive. The last term in the denominator, which reflects the increased deficit [that is, $d(m + b)$], reduces the size of $dk/d\sigma$, but does not alter the fact that it is positive. With dk determined by (60)

Eq. (59) implies a unique value of $d(m + b) > 0$. The government budget constraint with $d\pi = 0$ then gives the required change in the deficit, $d\delta = (\pi + n)d(m + b) > 0$.

Although both the reduced tax on capital income and the increased deficit are capable of turning additional saving into greater capital intensity without a change in the price level (and therefore without the possibility of a deflationary unemployment disequilibrium), the reduced tax on capital income has at least three advantages over the increased government deficit. First, and probably most important, the equilibrium capital intensity is greater if the increased saving is accommodated by a lower tax rate. Second, the lower tax rate on capital income reduces the excess burden caused by a distorting tax.[23] Finally, the tax reduction can be effective under special conditions when the increased deficit would fail. More specifically, the lower interest rate that must accompany the increased deficit would not be possible if the economy is also in a liquidity trap, that is, if investors are unwilling to hold any asset other than money at a lower rate of interest.[24] Even in this case, the tax reduction (and increased rate of interest) can be used to accommodate a higher rate of saving.

5. Some Conclusions

This paper has studied the long-run impact of fiscal policies on inflation and capital formation. The analysis uses an expanded monetary growth model in which the government finances its deficit by issuing both money and interest-bearing debt.

One major focus of the paper is the effect of a permanent increase in the government's real deficit in a fully employed economy. An important conclusion is that such an increased deficit must raise the rate of inflation or lower the capital intensity of production or both. The analysis shows that the combination of *both* increased inflation and reduced capital intensity is a likely outcome with current U.S. tax rules and the prevailing monetary

[23]The welfare gain from reducing the tax rate on capital income depends on the way in which the lost tax revenue is recovered. Feldstein (1978b) shows that even when the uncompensated elasticity of saving with respect to its return is zero, the excess burden of the tax system would be reduced by lowering the tax on capital income and raising it on labor income. In the current context there is the further complication that the increased deficit and lower interest rate would permit lower total taxes.

[24]In the notation of the model $L' = -\infty$ at some low level of i. This implies the extra constraint $di \geqslant 0$ which is consistent with (56) in the context of a tax rate reduction but not with (57) when $d\tau = 0$ and $d\delta > 0$. An increased deficit could avoid unemployment by the Keynesian remedy of absorbing all of the additional saving, that is, with $dk = 0$.

policy of allowing the interest rate to rise with inflation in a way that keeps the real interest rate unchanged. Section 3 determines the debt management policy (and the corresponding change in the interest rate) that would be required to maintain either a constant inflation rate or a constant capital–labor ratio.

The second purpose of the paper is to analyze the effect of an exogenous increase in the saving rate and the possibility of "excessive saving." The problem of "excessive saving" arises when the yield on capital becomes so low that individuals prefer to hold government bonds rather than the more risky claims to real capital. Under some conditions an increased rate of saving could only be absorbed in increased capital intensity if the rate of inflation could be permanently reduced. This requirement might entail a negative inflation rate which, as a practical matter, would be precluded by the downward rigidity of money wages. In this case the additional saving would not be absorbed, but would result in unemployment.

Section 4 shows first that there is no problem of excessive saving if

(a) investors are willing to hold real capital even though the differential between its yield and that on government bonds is narrowed and if

(b) the government reduces the interest rate on government bonds by expanding the money supply more rapidly than the stock of bonds. When these conditions are met, an increase in saving can be absorbed in greater capital intensity without any change in either inflation or the government deficit.

A problem can arise if the economy is in a "safety trap," that is, if investors would be unwilling to hold real capital if the difference between its yield and that on government debt were reduced. In that case an increased saving rate can imply price deflation and therefore possible unemployment. This problem can be avoided however by reducing the tax on capital income (or, in some cases, by an increased deficit that absorbs some but not all of the higher savings rate). In short, by using fiscal incentives as well as monetary accommodation an increased saving rate can be converted to greater capital intensity.

The analysis as a whole, although clearly a theoretical study of a simplified economy, suggests some insights that may help in understanding the unsatisfactory macroeconomic experience of the past decade and in designing more appropriate economic policies for the future. The recent years have been characterized by substantial inflation, a low rate of investment, and large government deficits. Section 3 shows how an increased government deficit can give rise to both greater inflation and reduced capital intensity. The combination of inflation and historic cost depreciation raised the effective tax rate on the income from real capital while the monetary and debt management policies have kept the real interest rate on government debt unchanged. The reduced equilibrium capital–labor ratio that this implies manifests itself as a lower rate of investment. The problem is then exacerbated when the government responds to decreased investment by further enlarging its deficit. The analysis suggests that a more appropriate solution would be to reduce the deficit while stimulating investment through a lower tax rate and a depreciation method based on current rather than historic costs.

I have argued in previous papers (Feldstein, 1976, 1977) that the United States should increase its saving rate to take advantage of the high social rate of return on additional investment. Such an increase in the private saving rate could be achieved by reducing the growth of social security benefits or by tax reforms that make the personal income tax more like a consumption tax. These proposals implicitly assumed that such extra saving would result in greater capital intensity rather than in a fall in aggregate demand. Section 4 implies that this assumption is warranted. With appropriate fiscal incentives and accommodating monetary policies an increase in saving can be absorbed in greater capital intensity without any change in the rate of inflation.

REFERENCES

Baumol, W. J. (1952). The Transactions Demand for Cash: An Inventory Theoretic Approach. *Quarterly Journal of Economics* **66**, 545–556.

Eckstein, O., and Brinner, R. (1972). *The Inflation Process in the United States* (A Study for the Joint Economic Committee, U.S. Congress). U.S. Government Printing Office, Washington, D.C.

Feldstein, M. S. (1976). Inflation, Income Taxes and the Rate of Interest: A Theoretical Analysis. *American Economic Review* **66**, 809–820.

Feldstein, M. S. (1977). Does the U.S. Save Too Little? *American Economic Review* **67**, 116–121.

Feldstein, M. S. (1978a). The Effect of Inflation on the Prices of Land and Gold. NBER Working Paper No. 296, November.

Feldstein, M. S. (1978b). The Welfare Cost of Capital Income Taxation. *Journal of Political Economy* **86**, Part 2, S2–S51.

Feldstein, M. S. (1979). National Savings in the United States. In *Productivity and Jobs*, pp. 124–154. American Assembly, New York.

Feldstein, M. S. (1980). Inflation and the Stock Market. *American Economic Review* (to be published).

Feldstein, M. S., and Chamberlain, Gary (1973). Multimarket Expectations and the Rate of Interest. *Journal of Money, Credit and Banking* **5**, 873–902.

Feldstein, M. S., and Eckstein, O. (1970). The Fundamental Determinants of the Interest Rate. *Review of Economics and Statistics* **52**, 363–375.

Feldstein, M. S., and Flemming, J. S. (1964). The Problem of Time-Stream Evaluation. *Bulletin of the Oxford Institute of Statistics* Feb., pp. 79–85.

Feldstein, M. S., and Rothschild, M. (1974). Towards an Economic Theory of Replacement Investment. *Econometrica* **42**, 393–423.

Feldstein, M. S., and Summers, Lawrence (1977). The Rate of Profit: Falling or Cyclical? *Brookings Papers on Economic Activity* **1**, 211–228.

Feldstein, M. S., and Summers, L. (1979). Inflation and the Taxation of Capital Income in the Corporate Sector. *National Tax Journal*, pp. 445–470.

Feldstein, M. S., Green, Jerry, and Sheshinski, Eytan (1978). Inflation and Taxes in a Growing Economy with Debt and Equity Finance. *Journal of Political Economy* **86**, Part 2, S53–S70.

Feldstein, M. S., Green, Jerry, and Sheshinski, Eytan (1979). Corporate Financial Policy and Taxation in a Growing Economy. *Quarterly Journal of Economics* **93**, 411–432.

Fisher, I. (1954). *The Theory of Interest*. Kelly & Millman, New York. (Reprint.)

Friedman, Benjamin J. (1977). Financial Flow Variables and the Short-Run Determination of Long-Term Interest Rates. *Journal of Political Economy* **85**, 661–689.

Friedman, Benjamin J. (1979). Crowding Out or Crowding In? Economic Consequences of Financial Government Deficits. *Brookings Papers on Economic Activity* **3**, 593–654.

Gordon, Robert J. (1967). The Incidence of the Corporation Income Tax in U.S. Manufacturing. *American Economic Review* **57**, 731–758.

Gordon, R. (1971). Inflation in Recession and Recovery. *Brookings Papers on Economic Activity* **1**, 105–166.

Green, Jerry, and Sheshinski, Eytan (1977). Budget Displacement Effects of Inflationary Finance. *American Economic Review* **67**, 671–682.

Harberger, Arnold C. (1962). The Incidence of the Corporate Income Tax. *Journal of Political Economy* **70**, 215–240.

Harris, Seymour (1941). *Economics of Social Security*. McGraw-Hill, New York.

Harrod, R. F. (1948). *Towards a Dynamic Economics*. Macmillan, London.

Keynes, John M. (1936). *The General Theory of Employment, Interest and Money*. Macmillan, London.

Krzyzaniak, M., and Musgrave, R. (1963). *The Shifting of the Corporation Income Tax*. John Hopkins Press, Baltimore, Maryland.

Levhari, David, and Patinkin, Don (1968). The Role of Money in a Simple Growth Model. *American Economic Review* **58**, 713–753.

Oakland, W. (1972). Corporate Earnings and Tax Shifting in U.S. Manufacturing, 1930–1968. *Review of Economics and Statistics* **54**, 235–244.

Sargent, Thomas J. (1973). Rational Expectations, the Real Rate of Interest, and the Natural Rate of Unemployment. *Brookings Papers on Economic Activity* **2**, 429–472.

Sargent, Thomas J. (1976). Interest Rates and Expected Inflation: A Selective Summary of Recent Research. *Explorations in Economic Research, Occasional Papers of the National Bureau of Economic Research*. Summer, pp. 303–325.

Shoven, J. B., and Whalley, J. (1972). A General Equilibrium Calculation of the Effects of Differential Taxation of Income from Capital in the U.S. *Journal of Public Economy* **1**, 281–321.

Stiglitz, Joseph (1973). Taxation, Corporate Financial Policy and the Cost of Capital. *Journal of Public Economy* **2**, 1–34.

Stiglitz, Joseph (1976). The Corporation Income Tax. *Journal of Public Economy* **5**, 303–311.

Tobin, James (1965). Money and Economic Growth. *Econometrica* **33**, 671–684.

Tobin, James, and Buiter, W. (1978). Fiscal and Monetary Policies, Capital Formation and

Economic Activity. In *The Government and Capital Formation* (George von Furstenberg, ed.), pp. 73–151.
Yohe, William, P., and Karnovsky, Denis S. (1969). Interest Rates and Price Level Changes, 1952–69. *Federal Reserve Bank of St. Louis Review*, pp. 18–38.

DEPARTMENT OF ECONOMICS
HARVARD UNIVERSITY
CAMBRIDGE, MASSACHUSETTS

and

NATIONAL BUREAU OF ECONOMIC RESEARCH
CAMBRIDGE, MASSACHUSETTS

On the Almost Neutrality of Inflation

Notes on Taxation and the Welfare Costs of Inflation

*JOSEPH E. STIGLITZ**

Inflation is almost universally considered to be a bad thing, a symptom of mismanagement of the economy on the part of the government. It is now widely thought that, like many diseases, it can appear in a variety of forms. The kind of inflation that seems to be present in most countries is a kind which, evidently, can be kept under control, although the only medicines promising anything near a full cure are so strong that the patient is likely to die in the process. If properly kept under control, it appears that we can learn to live with inflation, even inflation at moderately high rates. Much of the unhappiness over inflation arises from the failure to anticipate it, and much of that unhappiness is not concerned with welfare losses but with unintended transfers of purchasing power (for example, from creditors to debtors).

If inflation were fully anticipated, would there be any welfare loss associated with it? And if there is some uncertainty about the rate of inflation, to what extent can it be alleviated by indexing and other institutional reforms?

In this paper I attempt to clarify the nature of the losses associated with inflation within a conventional model of a competitive economy. I shall argue that were inflation fully anticipated, it would be "almost neutral" provided (a) that the tax system were fully indexed and (b) that interest were paid on bank deposits (as to an increasing extent it is in the United States). However, unanticipated inflation may have significant effects.

*Research support from the National Science Foundation is gratefully acknowledged. The author is indebted to Mark Gersovitz for helpful comments.

ISBN 0-12-259750-8

When there is uncertainty about the rate of inflation, the distinction between anticipated and unanticipated inflation may no longer be meaningful. Nevertheless, it can be shown that, under not implausible assumptions, inflation with proper indexing is neutral or "almost" neutral.

Perhaps the most serious distortions associated with inflation arise from the failure of the tax system to be fully indexed. Part II is therefore devoted to analyzing the distortionary effects of our present (nonindexed) tax system.

The results of this paper may be viewed in two different ways. The first is that if only the government were to index the tax system properly, inflation would be easy to live with; in this view, the policy prescription of this paper is clear.

The second view is somewhat more skeptical. The widespread concern over inflation is real. It existed in earlier economies in which taxation was not of the primary importance that it is in modern capitalist economies. Moreover, it probably should not be attributed to myopia (that is, that individuals perceive the increases in costs more strongly than they perceive the increase in wages). In this view the simple model of inflation presented in this paper is inadequate: inflation arises from and is associated with the presence of conflicting forces, inflexibilities, and so forth not fully reflected in the competitive model underlying this analysis. It is the resolution of these underlying problems—not the resolution of their symptom, inflation—which is of central concern. There are those who would argue that by making the symptom, inflation, easier to live with (for example, by indexing taxation and providing indexed bonds) it becomes easier to avoid dealing with these underlying problems.

I INFLATION IN A FULLY INDEXED ECONOMY

1. Perfectly Anticipated Inflation

Let us imagine an economy in which all contracts and transactions are fully indexed. The government would daily conduct a large sample of prices and use this to form a price index which would be announced each morning over the radio and television. All futures contracts (that is, bonds, promises today to undertake certain services in the future, and so forth) would be indexed, so that neither sellers nor buyers would face any risk in terms of "general purchasing power." There would, of course, still be risks: future short term (real) interest rates are uncertain, and this risk would not be eliminated by indexing, but neither would it be exacerbated. Checking accounts would be interest bearing, so the only "monetary" distortion associated with inflation would be that currency would be less attractive. In more advanced economies, where checking accounts are an almost perfect substitute for cash, the welfare loss associated with this may be viewed as negligible. The tax system is also assumed to be fully indexed, so that taxes are only paid on real returns (not nominal returns) to assets, depreciation allowances are "appropriately adjusted for inflation,"[1] and so forth.

It is apparent that in such an economy the rate of inflation would have no real effects: inflation would be perfectly neutral. To see this most clearly, consider the standard neoclassical growth model with interest-bearing money. (The results would extend to a variety of other models as well.) The aggregative behavior of the economy can be described by the following basic equations[2]:

(a) *The portfolio equilibrium equation.* We postulate a demand for real balances of the form[3]

$$m = m(r, i - \dot{p}/p, y, k), \tag{1}$$

where m is the real supply of money per capita (the nominal supply of money, per capita, divided by the price level p), p the price level, i the rate of interest earned by money, r the return to capital, k the per capita capital, and y the real income per capita. Output is described by a conventional neoclassical production function (constant returns to scale in inputs, quasi-concave)

$$Y = F(K, L),$$

where Y is (net) output, K is capital, and L is the labor supply. Hence per capita income is $y = f(k)$, where $k = K/L$, the capital–labor ratio. The real return to capital is assumed to be equal to its marginal productivity

$$r = f'(k). \tag{2}$$

Equation (1) asserts that the demand for real balances is a function of the opportunity cost (the return on capital), the return to holding the real

[1] What precisely is entailed by perfect indexing of the tax system is a subject we shall deal with at greater length in Part II of this paper.

[2] In the model presented in this section there is no uncertainty; all inflation is perfectly anticipated. As we note below, in this environment there is no need (apart from savings on transaction costs) to index. The more general case with uncertainty is considered in Section 4.

[3] In this equation, as well as in the savings equation to be described below, we can easily introduce tax variables. We assume, however, that all taxes are functions of real magnitudes: real rates of return, real incomes, and so forth.

balances, and the level of real income and wealth (for convenience everything is expressed in per capita terms).[4]

The rate of change of the real money supply per capita is simply the rate of monetary expansion θ minus the rate of growth of population n and minus the rate of increase in prices:

$$\dot{m}/m = \theta - n - \dot{p}/p. \tag{3}$$

(b) *The savings equation.* Real savings per capita s are postulated to be a function of the real rates of return on the various assets $(r, i - \dot{p}/p)$, the level of real income and wealth of individuals, and the rate of real monetary expansion[5]

$$s = s(r, i - \dot{p}/p, y(k), \dot{m}, m + k). \tag{4}$$

Several special cases of this savings functions have been discussed in the literature. For instance, in the earlier monetary growth model of Shell *et al.* (1969) $s = s^*[y(k) + \dot{m}]$. They assumed, in other words, that individuals treated capital gains and losses on their money on par with other forms of income. This formulation follows naturally from the Haig-Simons approach to the definition of income.

On the other hand, it has been widely argued that since the real opportunity set of the economy is unchanged by the change in the real money supply, it ought to have no effect on an individual's behavior.[6]

In that case $s_m = s_{\dot{m}} = 0$. Fortunately, for our purposes any specification of savings behavior which does not show "money illusion" will work as well.

(c) *Real capital accumulation.* Savings are allocated between increases (decreases) in real balances and capital accumulation: $s = (\dot{K}/L) + (\dot{m} + nm)$, or

$$\frac{\dot{k}}{k} = \frac{s}{k} - \left(\theta - \frac{\dot{p}}{p}\right)\frac{m}{k} - n. \tag{5}$$

[4]The simple model presented here assumes that there are only two assets, real balances and capital, but it should be apparent that the model admits of considerable generalization. This formulation incorporates both the transactions demand for real balances and the asset demand.

[5]A still more general specification of the savings function would let the savings rate be a function of the rates of return, incomes, and so forth expected to prevail in the future. Such a generalization would also be consistent with the results reported here. What is critical about the savings function postulated here is that nominal values—nominal price levels, the expansion of the nominal money supply, and so forth—do not enter.

[6]This would be particularly apparent if the economy were to consist of individuals whose lives are infinite, but even in the more realistic models with overlapping generations, changes on the part of the government can be "undone" by changes in bequest behavior of individuals. See, for instance, Barro (1974). For a more extended discussion see Atkinson and Stiglitz (1980).

Equations (1)–(5) provide a completely determined model of the economy. At each date the price level, real money supply, and per capita capital stock (p, m, k) are given. Equation (1) can then be used to solve for the rate of inflation which will equate the demand and supply for money, given a particular level of interest i on monetary deposits. Then (3) can be solved, given the rate of nominal monetary expansion, for the increase in real monetary balances. This allows us, in (4), to determine the level of real per capita savings and hence, through (5), the increment in the capital stock. Thus, given p, m, and k in one period, we can solve for p, m, and k at the next.

2. Changes in the Rate of Inflation

We now need to ask What are the consequences of a change in the rate of inflation? This, in itself, is not quite a meaningful question since the rate of change of prices in the economy is an *endogenous* variable, not an exogenous variable. We therefore need to ask What is the effect of a change in some policy which leads to a higher rate of inflation? But clearly, the answer to that question is likely to depend on the particular policy chosen.

If the government increases the rate of monetary expansion θ *and at the same time increases the interest payment on debt proportionately, then the resulting inflation is perfectly neutral: Nothing real changes.* More formally, there exists a new equilibrium in which $m(t)$, $k(t)$, and $\theta - \dot{p}/p$ are identical at all t to the initial equilibrium.

To see this, observe that if $\theta - \dot{p}/p$ remains unchanged, from (3) $\dot{m}/m$ remains unchanged, from (4) s remains unchanged, and hence from (5) k remains unchanged. Moreover, from (1), on such a path the portfolio balance equation is satisfied at each moment of time.

In the model presented above there are no government expenditures and no taxes. The analysis may, however, easily be extended to include these. If the government's expenditure (in real terms) is fixed and all taxes are perfectly indexed (in the manner to be described in Part II of this paper), then inflation is perfectly neutral. The real value of the government deficit will be independent of the rate of inflation.

3. Limitations on the Basic Theorem

The result of the previous section is very strong. Inflation is not, in general, viewed to be neutral, and we need to ask which of our assumptions accounts for the apparent unrealism of our conclusion.

In this section we shall discuss two limitations which imply that inflation will not be neutral: the fact that money does not bear interest and that it is costly to raise prices. I do not, however, believe that in the present economy either of these are significant enough to explain the widespread concern over inflation.

In Sections 4 and 5 I consider the effects of unanticipated inflation, and more generally, the effects of uncertainty about the rate of inflation. These effects, I argue, are likely to be significant, but could be directly alleviated with appropriately indexed bonds.

Part II of the paper is concerned with what is perhaps the most significant source of distortion arising from inflation in the modern economy: the failure to index taxes.

A. Interest on Money

Rates of expansion of the monetary supply are often not immediately accompanied by corresponding increases in the payments on government debt. This may, as in the usual money and growth models, have a significant effect on the patterns of capital accumulation. These effects, however, ought not really be attributed to inflation; it is to be hoped that they are the result of deliberate decisions on the part of government concerning the intertemporal allocation of resources. To the extent that the resulting path results in a pattern of intertemporal resource allocation considered undesirable, there is an easy remedy: simply change the rate of interest on government debt.

In practice, the rate of interest on government debt is set freely by the market and moves, accordingly, with the (expected) rate of inflation. What has *not* been fixed by the market in the United States and in many other countries is the rate of return on bank deposits: this is set by government regulation at zero. In the last few years, however, this has changed: now demand deposits (or financial holdings essentially equivalent to demand deposits) yield rates of return which are also market determined. Thus the only form of financial asset not effectively indexed is cash and currency. At the rates of inflation currently experienced in the United States and other Western economies it is hard to believe this results in significant distortion in the allocation of resources. (This may not, of course, be the case at much higher rates of inflation, and there may have been significant costs associated with this distortion in the past.)

B. Transaction Costs

The previous analysis also assumed that there were no costs associated with changing the prices marked on various goods. In effect, prices were continuously being revised for all commodities, so that all relative prices remained unchanged as we changed θ and i. (Since we assumed that the inflation was perfectly anticipated, it made no difference whether we assumed that prices were fully indexed or simply changed with time.)

Assume, however, that there are significant fixed costs associated with changing prices. Firms will thus change prices at discrete intervals. If information costs were zero, then there could exist coordinated price changes, such that at each moment of time relative prices among goods still remained unchanged. If, on the other hand, the average rate of change in prices remains what it would have been in the absence of transaction costs, in intervals between the changes in goods prices the real return on holding money would exceed that on capital; while during periods in which price changes occur, the real return on goods (capital) would exceed that on money. Thus, if individuals could costlessly shift their portfolio between financial and nonfinancial assets, there would be significant swings in portfolio composition, and if there were no costs of adjustment associated with the level of investment, there would be great variability in the level of investment.

These assumptions are clearly unrealistic: their purpose is to show that even perfectly anticipated inflation can have real distortionary costs associated with it. How significant these costs are is, however, another matter. Since there are significant costs of adjustments in investment, the variations in demands for real and financial assets are not likely to have a significant effect on the pattern of capital accumulation; the swings in demand will have an effect on the relative price of the two kinds of assets.

More important, however, is the fact that changes in price are never fully coordinated. Each firm must decide when, and by how much, to increase its price. Presumably, this is a result of costly information, which, as I have shown elsewhere (Salop and Stiglitz, 1977; Stiglitz, 1973), gives rise to a dispersion in the prices charged by various stores (the wages received by different workers). Again, we can show that a change in the rate of inflation will not be neutral: the magnitude of dispersion will be altered.

To see this most clearly, assume initially some store increases its prices at dates $t_1, t_2, \ldots$, and some other store increases its prices at dates $t'_1, t'_2, \ldots$. Thus on each of the dates there will be changes in the relative prices, which will induce *some* individuals to shift their patterns of purchase. Now assume that the rate of monetary expansion doubles, and assume that on each of the dates each of the firms increases its prices accordingly. It is immediately obvious that, with fixed intervals of price adjustment, the magnitude of price dispersion at each date is increased. This will induce increased search.

Note that all the firms could increase their prices more frequently and, by doing so, maintain relative prices at each of the dates at which price changes occur (regardless of the rate of inflation). If there were no costs of changing prices, this too would have no effect (but then price adjustments would be instantaneous). But clearly, if price adjustments are costly, this will necessitate a larger expenditure of resources on price adjustments.

However, neither this pattern of price increase nor the earlier pattern constitutes an equilibrium. In both cases search behavior will be altered, and it will not be optimal for firms to adjust their prices in this manner. For certain simple models (such as those with quadratic adjustment costs) the equilibrium frequency of adjustment of prices as a function of the rate of inflation may be easily derived; as expected, the frequency increases with the rate of inflation but less than proportionately. In equilibrium there are thus more resources spent on price adjustments. There is some presumption that more resources are spent on search, and there is some loss in economic efficiency arising out of the increased price dispersion.[7]

Again, we have established the nonneutrality of inflation, but again, I am not persuaded that this is a quantitatively significant effect. When price changes are frequent, routines are developed which significantly reduce the cost of price changes—for instance, printing menus which allow new prices to be inserted, or developing computer routines which allow prices to be adjusted to changed costs. Even if firms went to the (clearly suboptimal) pattern of increasing prices twice as frequently when the rate of inflation doubles, the total present discounted value of the increased cost of pure changes is not likely to be significant.

4. Unanticipated Inflation

The previous discussion established the neutrality (or near neutrality) of fully anticipated inflation. What happens if inflation is not fully anticipated? The question, as posed, is not completely meaningful. We have to describe the unanticipated change in the economy which gives rise to the unanticipated inflation—for prices, in the model that we have developed, are an *endogenous* variable.

The natural "experiment" to consider is the following: assume that the economy is in long-run equilibrium, with a given rate of monetary expansion and a corresponding rate of interest paid on monetary assets. Assume,

[7]Normally, one might expect that increased dispersion would lead to greater search; however, for items which are repeatedly purchased, when the price of one store is changing frequently relative to another, the value of search will be lower than when relative prices are stable.

moreover, that the rate is expected to continue indefinitely into the future. Then assume that in a particular period the government increases the rate of monetary expansion, but then announces that it will return to the old rate of monetary expansion thereafter. (And assume, less plausibly, that everyone believes this.) Then in the discrete time version of the simple model presented in Section 2 the rate of inflation in the given period will be faster than anticipated, but there will be no effects outside the period if the savings function does not exhibit "money illusion" in the particular sense to be described below. Prices rise so that the real money supply is identical, at each date, to what it would have been had the government followed the anticipated rate of increase in the money supply. Clearly, if an individual's investment in capital during the given period is unaffected, then since all the state variables are the same as they would have been had the government not increased its money supply faster than anticipated, the subsequent history of the economy is unaltered.

There are three critical assumptions in this analysis:

1. The savings function does not exhibit "money illusion," in the sense that the level of real capital accumulation is unchanged. If all individuals are identical, this will be the case if savings rates are a function of anticipatory variables (such as expected real rates of return on money and capital), real state variables, capital stock, real money supply, and change in the real money supply. But it cannot be a function of the current-period real return on money—because of the increased rate of inflation, this will be lower than on the original path. Note that in many of the savings functions traditionally analyzed, current real returns on money do affect savings rates.

2. Normally, we postulate that values of variables anticipated to prevail in the future depend on past values. In the particular model examined this link is explicitly denied. When it is present, unanticipated inflation has an effect because of its effects on anticipations of further inflation.

3. Perhaps the most significant effects of unanticipated inflation are distributive: contracts are denominated in monetary terms. Individuals who are net lenders are worse off as a result of inflation; those who are net borrowers are better off. This, in turn, may have a significant effect on the aggregate evolution of the economy if, as one might expect, *lenders and borrowers have different savings functions or hold different portfolios of assets*. For instance, owners of equities are better off, owners of debt worse off. If, on average, those who own equities are less risk averse than those who own debt, this may increase the demand for capital relative to the demand for monetary assets. This, in turn, may imply that the increased supply of money gives rise to a more than proportionate rise in prices. Whether lenders have a higher or lower marginal propensity to save depends, in part,

on whether the primary motive for savings is life cycle or intergenerational transfer. In the former case it is the old who are net lenders, the young who are net borrowers. The old are the ones "robbed" by inflation (these, indeed, are the victims in the popular folklore), and since they have a higher marginal propensity to consume, inflation increases the savings rate. On the other hand, in the model of "capitalists" who lend to the profligate workers who cannot limit their spending to their income, it is the capitalists who are worse off, and in that case savings rates decrease.

Although the exact effect of unanticipated inflation on the evolution of the economy is not clear, what *is* obvious is that unless there is indexing, it is not neutral. There is no once-and-for-all adjustment of the price level to a change in the monetary supply; indeed, the effects may be long lived.

With full indexing the distinction between anticipated and unanticipated inflation disappears. Unanticipated inflation has no effect (or negligible effects) for exactly the same reason as it did before. But for this result to be true, it is necessary that there be no nonindexed monetary assets, as the discussion of the next section hopefully will make clear.

5. Uncertain Rates of Inflation

In general, inflation is neither anticipated nor unanticipated. Individuals have a probability distribution associated with different rates of price increases. So long as there was some positive probability associated with the observed rate of inflation occurring, it was, in a sense, anticipated; so long as that probability was less than unity, it was, in a sense, not fully anticipated. The distinction between anticipated and unanticipated inflation does not seem to be particularly useful.

An increase in uncertainty about the rate of inflation (say, a mean-preserving spread in the probability distribution of the rate of increase in prices) has real effects. Monetary assets become riskier, so presumably the demand for them decreases. (However, anyone familiar with the literature on the effects of uncertainty on portfolio composition will recognize that it is possible that an increase in the riskiness of the return associated with an asset *may* increase its demand. There are, as usual, income and substitution effects.) This leads to increased capital accumulation with easily traced effects on the evolution of the economy.

We are concerned here, however, with the effect of an increased average rate of inflation. Again, as I have emphasized throughout, since we assume prices to be endogenous, we have to ask what generates both the uncertainty about the rate of inflation and the changes in the average level of inflation.

Earlier, we assumed that the government increased the money supply at a deterministic rate θ. Now, let us assume that θ is a random variable with a given mean and coefficient of variation. Now let us increase the mean, keeping the coefficient of variation constant. For simplicity we assume θ_t and θ_{t+j} for all j are identically distributed independent random variables. We assume, moreover, that when the government increases mean θ, the nominal interest rate i is increased correspondingly. Under this assumption, in the case of no uncertainty, monetary policy was completely neutral; now, however, it is not, provided only that individuals are risk averse. To see this, let us consider the special case where $\theta_t^* = \lambda\theta_t$. That is, we shall compare two economies which, at each date, are identical except that in one the rate of monetary expansion is λ times that of the other, with a nominal interest rate correspondingly greater.

Now assume the two economies are identical in all real respects. Let us consider the real return to holding money is any period. It is a random variable

$$i - (\tilde{p}_{t+1}/p_t) + 1$$

in the first economy and

$$i^* - (\tilde{p}_{t+1}^*/p_t) + 1 = i + (\lambda - 1)(Ep_{t+1}/p_t) - \lambda(\tilde{p}_{t+1}/p_t) + 1$$

in the second.

Clearly, the expected rate of return on money is unchanged, but the variance of the rate of return on money is increased by a factor of λ^2. Thus, even though the coefficient of variation in the rate of increase in the money supply is unchanged, the coefficient of variation in the rate of return on money is increased. Money becomes less attractive. But this contradicts our original assumption that the increase in the rate of monetary expansion was neutral.

Thus, unless all individuals are risk neutral, if there is uncertainty in the rate of monetary expansion, a higher average rate of monetary expansion, with a given degree of "risk," will lead to a shift away from monetary assets.

What happens now if we have fully indexed bonds? Then, of course, although there is uncertainty about the rate of inflation, there is no uncertainty about the return to holding monetary assets, and with savings functions which exhibit no "monetary illusion" in the sense defined earlier, there will be no effect on the equilibrium path of the economy. But note that this result depends on all bonds being fully indexed. If there are some unindexed bonds, then inflation will again not be neutral, as we shall see.

There are two questions which naturally arise at this juncture: (1) If the distortions associated with inflation could be alleviated by issuing indexed bonds, why are they not issued, at least by the private sector? (2) If such bonds were issued by the government, would there still be any contractual obligations which were not fully indexed?

There are two possible answers to the first question. The first is that were such securities to be offered, there would be little demand for them. The second is that the "market" simply has not recognized the potential demand for such securities. (There is, in a sense, a market imperfection. The successes of the new futures markets and the greatly expanded options markets suggests that this explanation may be the appropriate one.)

The need for indexed securities is limited under two circumstances. First, there will be no need for indexing if there is no uncertainty about the rate of inflation—all inflation is fully anticipated. Thus in periods in which the rate of inflation is negligible (or varies within small bounds) there would be little need for an indexed bond; there is no distinction between an indexed and an unindexed bond (or other contract); the unindexed bond would in its provisions fully provide for the future inflation.

Second, even if there is uncertainty about the rate of inflation, there will be no need for indexing if all individuals have the same belief about the probability distribution of the rate of inflation and have the same attitudes towards the risks associated with variability in the inflation rate. This might typically be the case in the aggregate models commonly employed in macroeconomic analysis, but in any disaggregate model individuals differ in their expectations [even if they all have "rational" expectations; if they have access to different information, their beliefs will still differ, as in the recent models of Grossman and Stiglitz (1976, 1980)]; and even if they have identical expectations, their attitudes towards the risks associated with price variability will be markedly different since some individuals are net lenders and some are net borrowers.

Thus in periods, such as the present, when there is significant uncertainty about the rate of inflation, there would seem to be a *prima facie* gain from the introduction of an indexed bond.

If *fully* indexed bonds were introduced, then[8] changing the rate of inflation—even though there is uncertainty about the rate of inflation—would have no effect on the economy. The analysis follows precisely along the lines of the argument presented in Section 3.B: since i, the interest paid on a bond, increases to offset exactly changes in the rate of inflation $\dot{p}/p$, there is no uncertainty about the rate of return on money; the differential equations describing the dynamics (which now need to be viewed as stochastic differential equations) are unchanged, provided that there is no money illusion (that is, savings rates do not depend on the rate of nominal increase in the money supply). With fully indexed bonds and contracts even a change in the uncertainty about the rate of inflation has no effect.

[8] Ignoring the two limitations noted in Section 3.

Assume now both fully indexed bonds and nonindexed bonds (and other contracts) are available on the market. For the above result on the neutrality of the rate of inflation to go through, we need there to be no demand for nonindexed bonds (contracts). If all individuals are risk averse, clearly there exists an equilibrium with this characteristic. For assume that no one purchases nonindexed bonds; then, as we argued, the rate of increase in prices would have no real effects on the economy; hence for the individual's savings–consumption–portfolio allocation decision the rate of inflation would be as irrelevant as the number of sunspots, but this means that there would be no market for nonindexed securities, provided individuals were risk averse.

If, however, not all government bonds were fully indexed, the rate of inflation would not be neutral. Provided there were some partially indexed bonds, it might be thought that an individual, by arranging his portfolio appropriately, could effectively obtain 100% hedging; in a partial equilibrium context that is correct. To see this, assume $\gamma\%$ indexing: every time prices rise by 1%, the return on the bond rises by $\gamma\%$. Assume now there is another nonindexed bond, yielding a return of $\hat{i}$. If the individual borrows (sells short) at the nonindexed rate an amount α and buys $1 + \alpha$ of the (partially) indexed bond, his real return per dollar is

$$i(1+\alpha) - \alpha\hat{i} + (\dot{p}/p)\left[(\gamma - 1)(1+\alpha) + \alpha\right],$$

which is perfectly certain, independent of the rate of inflation, if $\alpha/(1+\alpha) = 1 - \gamma$. Thus all that is required for full hedging of the rate of inflation within a partial equilibrium context is that there be a partially indexed bond.

But this argument does not extend to a general equilibrium context. For note, to accomplish the full hedging, someone needed to lend at a nonindexed rate. Thus it is not possible for all individuals simultaneously to hedge completely if there are some government bonds which are nonindexed or only partially indexed. It immediately follows that in this context inflation will not be neutral.

One could, moreover, attempt to ascertain which groups would in such cases be "less covered" than others. Assume, for instance, that there are some individuals who are less risk averse than others. Then they would normally be expected to absorb willingly some of the risk of the more risk averse individuals. Thus, in those particular states of nature where the rate of expansion of the money supply is large, there will be a real transfer from the less risk averse individuals to the more risk averse individuals. This redistribution will, in turn, affect the real evolution of the economy, as described earlier. Thus, if the less risk averse individuals also have higher savings rates and invest in more "risky" capital ventures, the shift in the distribution of wealth may have a significant effect on the aggregate savings rate and on the composition of the demand for new investment.

II TAXATION

In Part I we considered the effect of inflation on an economy without taxation (or in which taxation is fully indexed). It was emphasized that inflation is virtually neutral if there is no uncertainty, or would be neutral, even with uncertainty, if all contracts (bonds) were fully indexed. Although there are certain limitations on this basic result, I consider them minor: they would suggest that inflation is almost neutral.

We now consider the effects of taxation: the present tax system is far from fully indexed, and as a result, inflation is far from neutral. The objectives of Part II are to ascertain what exactly would be entailed by full indexing, to suggest that a nondistortionary tax system is in fact not completely attainable, and to analyze the kinds of distortions which arise in the absence of full indexing.

The focal point of our concern is the taxation of capital with a proportional tax.[9] There are three sets of provisions with which we are concerned: the tax treatment of depreciation, the tax treatment of interest payments, and the tax treatment of capital gains. As we shall see, full indexing requires that

(a) depreciation must be at replacement cost and at the "correct" rate;

(b) only real interest is taxed, and only real interest is tax deductible; the particular manner in which this must be done requires careful attention;

(c) capital gains and losses need to be taxed (at full rates) on an accrual basis rather than on a realization basis. I argue that the latter is not feasible and show that the commonly suggested approaches to dealing with it are, in fact, distortionary.

Although I argue that taxation is not neutral and that there is no way of designing a fully neutral tax policy, appropriate indexing can make the magnitude and direction of the distortions independent of the inflation rate: although taxation is not neutral, inflation, in this sense, is. (There are other important aspects of tax policy which are important in the presence of inflation, such as the treatment of inventories, which we shall not discuss in this paper.)

[9] In such a tax system there is absolutely no need for indexing of wage taxes; indexing of wage taxes is only important within a progressive tax structure. There is thus an important difference between the consequences of the failure to index a wage tax and a capital tax.

6. Depreciation

A. Introduction

There are two sets of conditions under which taxation will not be distortionary on the level or allocation of investment: (a) if interest payments are tax deductible and if depreciation allowances are equal to "true economic depreciation"—the change in the market value of the asset and (b) if interest payments are not tax deductible and if there is instantaneous depreciation (immediate write-off), in which case the tax is equivalent to a pure profits tax.

Current tax codes do not correspond to either of these idealized systems. As a result, they introduce distortions both in the level and direction of investment. One of our objectives here is to clarify the nature of these distortions and the effect of inflation on the magnitude of these distortions. We focus the analysis on tax systems in which interest is fully deductible. There are four important discrepancies between the idealized capital tax described above and current U.S. practices:

1. Physical depreciation rates allowed do not correspond to true physical depreciation.

2. Depreciation is valued at book (historical) cost rather than replacement cost. If the price of machines is rising, this means that the value of the depreciation allowances for the same machine will be higher if the investment is postponed. Thus inflation serves to discourage investment. The relative magnitude of this effect will depend on the lifetime of the machine.

3. Capital gains are taxed at realization rather than accrual, and when taxed, are taxed at much lower rates. This implies that there is a distortion in favor of assets whose relative price is increasing. To the extent that capital gains are taxed, the effective tax rate rises with the rate of inflation, and this reduces the return on capital.[10]

4. Nominal interest payments, rather than real interest payments, are tax deductible. The effect of this depends on the extent to which increases in inflation are reflected in increases in pretax rates of interest. Although there are some grounds for suggesting that the rate of interest may increase more than proportionately to the rate of inflation, because of the taxation of interest income, with full indexing it would increase precisely by the amount of the rate of inflation, and full indexing, both of payments and receipts, would result in inflation neutrality.

In the remainder of this section we develop a simple model which

[10]The implications of the tax treatment of capital gains are analyzed in greater detail in Section 7.

illustrates these distortions and which enables us to make a precise calculation of the magnitude of the biases introduced.

B. The Basic Model

We consider a firm on an equilibrium investment path. We then consider what happens if it perturbs its investment strategy by bringing forward a small investment by one period. If, in fact, the original investment strategy was optimal, this must have a negligible effect on profits.

We first review the standard analysis for the case without taxation. The gain in profits from an increased investment at time $t-1$ is simply the value of the marginal product $p_0^t MPK^t$, where p_0^t is the price of output at date t and MPK^t is the marginal product at date t.

Assume that the machine suffers from exponential depreciation at the rate δ. (More general patterns of depreciation may also be handled easily.) Then next period the firm will reduce its expenditures by $(1-\delta)p_K^t$, where p_K^t is the price of capital at date t.

To finance its original investment, assume that it borrows an amount p_K^{t-1}. (Since, at the margin, the firm should be indifferent between equity and bond finance so long as it can borrow and lend, the assumption that the investment is financed by debt is inconsequential.) This means that to repay the bondholders, it will have to pay $p_K^{t-1}(1+r)$, where r is the rate of interest (for simplicity assumed to be invariant with time). Thus equilibrium requires that the net financial flow from this perturbation be zero, or

$$\begin{aligned} p_0^t MPK^t &= (1+r)p_K^{t-1} - (1-\delta)p_K^t \\ &= p_K^{t-1}\left[r + \delta - (1-\delta)(\Delta p_K^t / p_K^{t-1})\right] \equiv c, \end{aligned} \tag{6}$$

where $\Delta p_K^t = p_K^t - p_K^{t-1}$, the change in price between $t-1$ and t. The right-hand side of (6) is sometimes referred to as the cost of capital. Expression (6) says that the value of the marginal product is, in equilibrium, equal to the cost of capital. The cost of capital is equal to the rate of interest plus the rate of depreciation minus the rate of increase in the price of the capital good. This can be viewed in another way. The net return from holding a capital asset is the rental plus the capital appreciation minus the depreciation, and in equilibrium this must be equal to the rate of interest:

$$\left(p_0^t / p_K^{t-1}\right)MPK^t + (1-\delta)\left(\Delta p_K^t / p_K^{t-1}\right) - \delta = r. \tag{7}$$

We shall say that the tax system is neutral if the tax leaves the equilibrium condition (6) unaltered. In general, with taxation we obtain an expression, say, of the form

$$p_0^t MPK^t = c + D, \tag{8}$$

where D is the distortionary impact of the tax system. We shall be concerned with three critical questions:

1. Under what assumptions concerning the provisions of the tax code is taxation nondistortionary ($D = 0$)?

2. In general, $D \neq 0$; that is, taxation is distortionary. Either the aggregate level of investment may be distorted or the pattern of investment may be distorted. That is, D may vary from one kind of investment project to another. Hence the second question is to ascertain the parameters of the project which determine the "bias" under various provisions of the tax code; for example, are long-lived projects encouraged or discouraged?

3. When taxation is distortionary, how does an increase in the rate of inflation affect the magnitude and directions of the distortions?

We proceed in stages. First, we consider three special cases: no depreciation, instantaneous depreciation, and true physical depreciation. We then consider the general case. We assume throughout a fixed taxed rate and that interest is tax deductible.[11]

C. No Depreciation

The firm receives only $1 - \tau$, where τ is the tax rate, of the value of the marginal product, but because of the interest deductibility, the cost of borrowing is $r(1 - \tau)$ rather than r. Thus the equilibrium condition is

$$p_0^t MPK^t(1-\tau) = \left[1 + r(1-\tau)\right] p_K^{t-1} - (1-\delta) p_K^t$$

or

$$p_0^t MPK^t = p_K^{t-1}\left[\left(r + \delta - \frac{\Delta p_K^t(1-\delta)}{p_K^{t-1}}\right) + \frac{\tau}{1-\tau}\left(\delta - \frac{\Delta p_K^t(1-\delta)}{p_K^{t-1}}\right)\right]. \tag{9}$$

Note that such a tax is clearly distortionary. The magnitude of the distortion depends on the magnitude of

$$\frac{\delta}{1-\delta} - \frac{\Delta p_K^t}{p_K^{t-1}},$$

that is, the difference between the rate of appreciation in the value of the asset from price increases and the rate of depreciation in the value of the asset from physical depreciation. Thus the tax system is biased *against* assets which depreciate rapidly and biased *in favor* of assets whose relative price is increasing more rapidly.

[11] We also ignore the complications introduced by investment tax credits, accelerated depreciation, and so forth, leaving these as exercises for the reader.

D. Instantaneous Depreciation

The value of the tax reduction at time $t-1$ is thus τp_K^{t-1}, so the amount to be borrowed is $(1-\tau)p_K^{t-1}$. Hence the equilibrium condition is now

$$p_0^t MPK^t(1-\tau) = \left[1 + r(1-\tau)\right](1-\tau)p_K^{t-1} - (1-\tau)(1-\delta)p_K^t$$

or

$$p_0^t MPK^t = p_K^{t-1}\left[\left(r + \delta - \frac{\Delta p_K^t(1-\delta)}{p_K^{t-1}}\right) - \tau r\right]. \tag{10}$$

Again, there is a tax distortion, but now the magnitude does not vary with the project. With instantaneous depreciation the cost of capital is reduced, and investment is increased.

Note that if interest is not deductible, the equilibrium condition becomes

$$p_0^t MPK^t = p_K^{t-1}\left(r + \delta - \frac{\Delta p_K^t(1-\delta)}{p_K^{t-1}}\right). \tag{11}$$

Thus with full depreciation and instantaneous write-off the tax system is nondistortionary. In this case the tax is simply a pure profits tax (Stiglitz, 1976).

E. True Depreciation Rates

Now assume that the government allows depreciation at the rate γ.

The changes in depreciation allowances at each date are set forth in the first two columns of Table 1. The net change at date $t+n$ is

$$A_{t+n} \equiv \gamma(1-\gamma)^n p_K^{t-1} - (1-\delta)\gamma(1-\gamma)^{n-1} p_K^t. \tag{12}$$

TABLE 1

Change in Depreciation Allowances

Period	Increase from depreciation allowed on investment at $t-1$	Decrease from reduced investment at time t	Net change with replacement depreciation
	p_K^{t-1} times	p_K^t times	—
t	γ	—	γp_K^t
$t+1$	$\gamma(1-\gamma)$	$(1-\delta)\gamma$	$\gamma(\delta-\gamma)(1+g)p_K^t$
$t+2$	$\gamma(1-\gamma)^2$	$\gamma(1-\delta)(1-\gamma)$	$(\delta-\gamma)\gamma(1-\gamma)(1+g)^2 p_K^t$
$t+n$	$\gamma(1-\gamma)^n$	$(1-\delta)\gamma(1-\gamma)^{n-1}$	$\gamma(1-\gamma)^{n-1}(\delta-\gamma)(1+g)^n p_K^t$

If $p_K^{t-1} = p_K^t$, this equals $p_K^t\, \gamma(1-\gamma)^{n-1}(\delta-\gamma) \gtrless 0$ as $\delta \gtrless \gamma$. Thus with true economic depreciation (depreciation at the true rate) the perturbation in the investment at date $t-1$ has no effect on depreciation allowances at dates $t+1$ and beyond.

Thus, when prices are constant and depreciation is allowed at the rate δ, the equilibrium condition becomes simply

$$\begin{aligned}(1-\tau)p_0 MPK^t &= p_K^{t-1}[1+r(1-\tau)] - (1-\delta)p_K^t - \tau\delta p_K^{t-1}\\ &= p_K[r(1-\tau)+\delta(1-\tau)]\end{aligned}$$

or $p_0 MPK^t = p_K(r+\delta)$. Thus, once again, the tax is nondistortionary. Again, this result is not surprising since, in the absence of changes in prices of capital goods, setting $\delta = \gamma$ is equivalent to true economic depreciation, which, with interest deductibility, is known to be nondistortionary.

However, when prices are changing or $\delta \neq \gamma$, (12) is not identically zero; we cannot simply employ the myopic rules for investment employed so far, which enabled us to concentrate on the effects of a perturbation in the investment pattern at date $t-1$ only at dates $t-1$ and t. In the more general case we need to discount these future cash flows originating from the changed depreciation allowances. Since individuals can borrow and lend at an aftertax rate of interest of $r(1-\tau)$, it seems natural to use this as the discount rate. Then the present discounted value of the depreciation allowances from $t+1$ on is

$$\frac{\gamma[p_K^{t-1}(1-\gamma) - p_K^t(1-\delta)]}{r(1-\tau)+\gamma}, \tag{13}$$

so firms will set

$$\begin{aligned}(1-\tau)p_0^t MPK^t = rp_K^{t-1}(1-\tau) &+ p_K^{t-1}\left[\delta - \tau\frac{\gamma(\delta-\gamma)}{\gamma+r(1-\tau)}\right]\\ &- \tau\gamma p_K^{t-1} - \Delta p_K^t\left[1-\delta-\tau\frac{\gamma(1-\delta)}{\gamma+r(1-\tau)}\right]\end{aligned}$$

or

$$\begin{aligned}p_0^t MPK^t = p_K^{t-1}\Bigg\{r+\delta &- \frac{\Delta p_K^t(1-\delta)}{p_K^{t-1}} + \frac{r\tau}{\gamma+r(1-\tau)}\\ &\times\left[(\delta-\gamma) - \frac{\Delta p_K}{p_K^{t-1}}(1-\delta)\right]\Bigg\}.\end{aligned} \tag{14}$$

Thus, even with true physical depreciation ($\delta = \gamma$), the tax system is distortionary.

The effective cost of capital is decreased if the price of the capital good is rising. This result at first appears a little surprising: since for purposes of depreciation capital is valued at historical costs, with rising prices the depreciation allowances are smaller than they should be; firms postpone investment in order to increase the "value" of the depreciation allowances. But at the same time the firm ought to pay a tax on the (unrealized) value of its capital gain. Equation (14) says that the former effect is dominated by the latter effect (the failure to tax capital gains).

The percentage decreases in the cost of capital are significant. The percentage bias when there is true physical depreciation can be written as

$$|\hat{D}| = gr\tau(1-\delta)/[\delta + r(1-\tau)][r+\delta-g(1-\delta)], \tag{15}$$

where $g = \Delta p_K^t / p_K^{t-1}$, the rate of increase in the price of the capital good. Thus $\hat{D}$, the magnitude of the bias, decreases with δ (that is, long-lived investments are favored more than short-lived investments), but increases with g, the rate of growth of the relative price.

With $r = 0.1$, $\tau = 0.5$, and $g = 0.1$, if $\delta = 0.1$ (a ten-year life), then $\hat{D} = 27\%$ (the tax system lowers the cost of capital by 27%), while if $\delta = 0.02$ (a fifty-year capital good), $\hat{D} = 318\%$. The distortion imposed is, indeed, very significant.

F. The General Case

As has been emphasized elsewhere, to attain neutrality requires the use of true *economic* depreciation: taxing capital gains on an accrual basis and allowing depreciation at replacement costs. The net effect of our tax system in the absence of inflation arises from three distinct errors:

1. The depreciation rate allowed generally does not correspond to the true physical depreciation rate; that is, $\gamma \neq \delta$ (in general, $\gamma > \delta$).
2. Capital gains are not taxed on an accrual basis, but only upon realization.
3. Depreciation is taken at historical costs, rather than at replacement (current value). If the price of machines is falling (in real terms), this implies a bias in favor of investment).

Expression (14) allows us to estimate the *net* effect of all three distortions taken together.

Clearly, if $\gamma > \delta$, the tax system reduces the cost of capital, and the magnitude of the distortion is even greater than in the case where $\delta = \gamma$. To ascertain the pattern of distortions, we need to know the relationship between γ and δ. For instance, if $\delta/\gamma =$ a constant, then if the constant is small enough, the bias may be larger for shorter-lived investments rather than longer-lived investments, so that the direction of the bias may be the opposite of what it was with true economic depreciation.

G. Depreciation at Replacement Cost

It has often been suggested that it would be desirable to switch to replacement cost depreciation rather than historical cost depreciation. In the presence of the other two imperfections in the depreciation allowances such a switch may *increase* the magnitude of the distortion, although it may make it less sensitive to the value of δ.

Let the firm value the depreciation at time $t + n$ at the price prevailing at that date. Then the change in depreciation allowance A at $t + n$ is

$$A_{t+n} = p_K^{t+n}\gamma(1-\gamma)^{n-1}(\delta - \gamma).$$

Thus with depreciation at the true physical rate there is no change in depreciation allowances from date $t + 1$ onwards. More generally, the change in the present discounted value of future depreciation allowances (from $t + 1$ on, valued as t), if prices are rising at the rate g, is approximately

$$\frac{\gamma(\delta-\gamma)p_K^{t-1}(1+g)^2}{r(1-\tau)+\gamma-g+\gamma g},$$

and the equilibrium condition becomes

$$p_0^t MPK^t = p_K^{t-1}\left\{r + \delta - \frac{\Delta p_K^t(1-\delta)}{p_K^{t-1}} + \frac{\tau}{1-\tau}\right.$$
$$\left.\times\left[(\delta-\gamma)\left(1+g-\frac{\gamma(1+g)^2}{r(1-\tau)+\gamma-g+\gamma g}\right)-g\right]\right\}. \qquad (16)$$

It is thus apparent that if $\gamma = \delta$, taxes reduce the cost of capital by an amount proportional to the rate of increase in the price of the capital good. (Capital goods whose prices are falling have their cost of capital raised by taxation.)

Allowing depreciation at replacement costs without correcting the other distortions could exacerbate the distortions in the economy. (This result needs to be modified when we come to inflation.)

H. Inflation

The previous analysis focused on an economy in which there was no inflation but in which there were changes in relative prices. It is easy to show that if there is a general rise in the price level, say at the rate λ, then if all bonds are short term, neutrality of taxation requires allowing the deductibility of only real interest payments, but using replacement cost rather than historical costs to evaluate depreciation. In addition, as before, we require that the physical rates of depreciation allowed must correspond to the true rates of depreciation, and that there must be instantaneous taxation of *real* capital gains. Thus, in addition to the "errors" noted earlier, in inflationary periods the tax system introduces one further error: all interest payments (rather than just "real" interest payments) are deductible. In addition, however, the failure to evaluate depreciation t at replacement costs may become more serious in inflationary periods. We are concerned with the nature of the biases introduced. It is not apparent, however, what the appropriate way to calculate these biases is. Whenever a nonneutral tax is imposed, it will have general equilibrium effects on the economy, just as whenever bonds are not fully indexed and there is uncertainty about the rate of inflation (inflation is not perfectly anticipated), there are general equilibrium effects resulting from inflation. Although the precise nature of these general equilibrium effects may be difficult to estimate, they may be quite significant. If the tax system results in the return to housing and land relative to physical capital goods increasing with the rate of inflation, then an unanticipated increase in the rate of inflation may result in a significant redistribution of wealth. This redistribution of wealth may, in turn, have important effects on savings and demands for assets in subsequent periods. The full ramifications of an unanticipated increase in inflation may extend far beyond the direct effects on debtors and creditors which are the usual focus of concern. In particular, the pretax rate of interest is likely to change as a result of inflation. This change in the pretax rate of interest may partially offset, or may more than offset, the direct effects of the tax, say, on the level of investment.

For analytical purposes in our discussion below we focus on three polar cases.

We first consider what would be the nature of the bias if taxation were not indexed and, as in the traditional Fisherian theory, the nominal rate of interest increases by the rate of inflation. Thus, if r is the nominal rate of interest, r^* the real rate of interest, and λ is the rate of inflation,

$$r = r^* + \lambda.$$

Fisher's argument applied, of course, to an economy in which there were no taxes. It is not immediately apparent that this is the appropriate assumption in an economy in which there is a tax distortion.

We next consider the bias if the pretax interest rate is adjusted to keep the individual's marginal rate of substitution between consumption at different dates unchanged. Again, we assume taxes are not fully indexed. This could, of course, be a full equilibrium only if inflation were fully anticipated (so there were no distributive effects of taxes) and if, with interest rates adjusted in the manner described, there were no distortion in the pattern and level of investment. We show, however, that with present provisions there will be a bias, although the direction depends on the rate of inflation. We conjecture (but have not proved) that under the usual stability conditions full general equilibrium biases will be of the same sign, but will be smaller in magnitude. The precise magnitude will, however, depend on a number of factors: (a) As we have noted several times, with imperfect indexing inflation will have significant redistributive effects which alter the aggregate level of savings and the demand for different kinds of assets; (b) the changes in the rate of return on investment will lead to changes in savings behavior; the magnitude of these changes will depend on the elasticity of savings; (c) since the tax system is not fully indexed, inflation will affect the real value of the government's deficit (surplus), and this, in turn, may have significant effects on the economy; if the government attempts to keep the real value of its deficit constant, it will have to change some tax rates. The incidence of inflation will then depend on the particular way in which taxes or the real deficit will be adjusted to keep the government's budget constraint satisfied. No a priori or general theory predicting the effect of inflation on the general equilibrium in an economy with an incompletely indexed tax system would thus seem possible.

The third case is the only one where a full general equilibrium analysis is possible: if there is full indexing, then the Fisherian result, that the before-tax rate of interest will rise by the ratio of inflation, will be true.

We begin our analysis with the Fisherian case ($r = r^* + \lambda$) with the nonindexed tax system.

Letting g represent, as before, the increase in the relative price of the capital good ($g + \lambda$ therefore being the increase in the "money" price of the capital good), we can rewrite (14) as[12]

$$p_0^{*t} MPK^t \approx p_K^{*t-1} \left\{ r^* + \delta - \lambda - g^* + \frac{\tau(r^* + \lambda)}{\gamma + (r^* + \lambda)(1 - \tau)} (\delta - \gamma - g^* - \lambda) \right\}, \tag{17}$$

where asterisks denote "real" (deflated) values.

What is apparent from (17) is that an increase in the rate of inflation actually may lower the cost of capital. The gain from the tax deductibility of interest more than offsets the loss from the depreciation allowances not corresponding to replacement costs.

Note that the smaller γ the larger is the bias. Thus, if $\gamma = \delta$, inflation has a larger effect on longer-lived investments. Thus, if depreciation is

[12] We assume the time period is sufficiently small that terms of order $g\delta$, $g\lambda$, and so forth can be dropped.

allowed at replacement value *and* the other distortions are not simultaneously corrected, the magnitude of the bias could be increased still further.

I. Explanations for Distortions

The failure to tax capital gains on an accrual basis and the failure to use true depreciation rates should not be viewed as simply a reflection of the incompetency or perversity of politicians and government bureaucrats. Both unrealized capital gains and depreciation are unobservable variables. Not only may it be difficult, if not impossible, for the government accurately to observe these variables, it may not even be possible for the owner of the capital to ascertain them with any degree of precision. Even if it were, he would not have any incentive to reveal these parameters to the government. Indeed, since the design of machines is constantly changing, even the notion of replacement cost may not be well defined.

For the analysis of the behavior of firms what is of relevance, of course, is their perceptions (beliefs) concerning depreciation rates and capital gains. Our problem is that for neutrality we need to know their beliefs—for example, about the relative prices of capital goods at different dates. Even if firms could articulate these beliefs (and they would not, in general, be adequately described by a single number), they would not do so.

J. Indexing as a Remedy

Given the impossibility (or difficulty) of correctly ascertaining capital gains on an accrual basis and depreciation at true rates, what can we say about the other two distortions?

I wish to argue that the distortion arising out of the failure to allow only real interest payments to be deductible is not as serious as the failure to allow depreciation at an indexed value. The reason for this is that although nominal interest payments are deductible to the corporation, they are taxable to the individual. If the individual and the corporation are at similar tax rates, these effects precisely cancel out.

The matter may be looked at another way. We assume that the individual's marginal rate of substitution (MRS) between consumption at date t and $t + 1$ remains unchanged, and ask what this implies for the adjustment in pretax interest rates as a result of inflation. (Recall from our earlier discussion that in the general equilibrium the marginal rate of substitution will in general change; we make this assumption simply to provide ourselves a benchmark.) We require

$$MRS = 1 + r(1-\tau) - \lambda = 1 + r^*(1-\tau)$$

or

$$r = r^* + \frac{\lambda}{1-\tau}.$$

Thus the equilibrium condition is now not (17) but

$$p_0^{*t} MPK^t \approx p_K^{*t-1}\left[r^* + \delta - g^* - \lambda + \frac{\tau[r^* + \lambda/(1-\tau)]}{\gamma + r^*(1-\tau) + \lambda}(\delta - \gamma - g^* - \lambda)\right]. \tag{18}$$

If the individual's marginal rate of substitution remains unchanged, with indexing of the individual income tax we would obtain

$$MRS = 1 + r(1-\tau) - \lambda + \tau\lambda = 1 + r^*(1-\tau)$$

or

$$r = r^* + \lambda.$$

This is precisely the original (Fisherian) model analyzed earlier.

It also follows that full indexing of both corporate and individual taxation results in inflation being nondistortionary. Instead of (18) we obtain

$$p_0^{*t} MPK^t \approx p_K^{*t-1}\left\{ r^* + \delta - g(1-\delta) + \frac{1}{\gamma + r^*(1-\tau)} \times \tau[(\delta - \gamma) - g(1-\delta)r^*]\right\}. \tag{19}$$

It is also apparent that full indexing of taxation—allowing depreciation at replacement costs and allowing the deduction only of real interest payments—would not result in the tax system being neutral. The other two sources of distortion (the failure to tax capital gains on an accrual basis and the failure of allowed depreciation rates to correspond to true depreciation rates) would remain. (Indeed, as we have noted, the total distortion may actually be increased by partial reforms.) On the other hand, full indexing would imply that inflation would, itself, not be distortionary. That is, with full indexation the rate of inflation would have no effect on the cost of capital. It would ensure neutrality of inflation, not of taxation. (Note that full indexation would also mean that government *real* income would be invariant with respect to the rate of inflation.)

The argument that full indexation would result in inflation being neutral needs to be modified in one critical respect. Earlier I argued that if there are costs of adjustment associated with changing prices and if price changes are not coordinated, the dispersion in relative prices would, in general, increase with the rate of inflation. Full indexation would not, as we noted, affect the distortions arising from the failure to tax changes in *relative* prices. If the increased dispersion in prices is significant, then the magnitude of the distortions introduced by the tax system may be increased significantly as a result of inflation.

K. Progressive Taxation and Distributive Effects of Anticipated Inflation

The analysis presented so far assumes that all individuals face the same marginal (equal average) tax rate. This implies that the change in the pretax rate of interest as a result of inflation has exactly the same impact on everyone within the economy. When different individuals face different marginal tax rates, the aftertax rate of interest facing different individuals may change significantly. Thus in the absence of tax indexation even perfectly anticipated inflation may have significant distributive effects. Assume, for instance, that there is no indexation and that *most* individuals in the economy face a tax rate of τ^*. Assume, moreover, that the pretax rate of interest adjusts so that the aftertax rate of return (which equals the individual's marginal rate of substitution) remains unchanged, or as we showed earlier, $r = r^* + \lambda/(1 - \tau^*)$. Then the real rate of interest facing individuals who happen to face a lower tax rate (say, poor individuals who face no taxation) rises by $\lambda(\tau^* - \tau)/(1 - \tau^*)$, while the real rate of interest facing individuals who have a higher marginal tax rate falls. If the former group of individuals are net borrowers, they become worse off, although tax exempt institutions will, by the same token, become better off.

Again, it is easy to show that with full indexing inflation is completely neutral; not only does it have no aggregative effects, it has no distributive effects.

L. Multiperiod Bonds

The analysis so far has implicitly assumed all bonds are one-period bonds; in that case there is little difficulty in indexing. For such bonds payments of interest coincide with the repayment of principal.

To see the problems that arise more generally, consider an individual borrowing \$100 for a project, which at the end of two years is worth \$120 and yields \$10 income at the end of the first year. Assume the interest rate is 10%. The individual borrows \$100. Thus his income in the first period is just enough to pay the interest. At the end of the second period he obtains a net return of \$20. Now assume that the rate of inflation increases to 10%, for the moment ignore taxes, and assume that his nominal interest payments therefore rise correspondingly to 20%. Inflation increases his receipts the first period by 10% to \$11, but he still cannot meet his interest obligations: he needs to borrow an additional \$9. It would appear that inflation has had a real effect on the economy. But this is misleading. The "real" indebtedness of the individual has decreased from \$100 to \$90 as a result of inflation (measured in constant dollars). Thus to maintain indebtedness at the same real level requires that interest payments for multiperiod bonds prior to repayment of principal be indexed, but not be increased by the rate of inflation, although the final payment of principal needs to be indexed. That is, if the real interest rate is r^* and the inflation rate is λ, the interest payment during the first period should not be $r^* + \lambda$, but $r^*(1 + \lambda)$. In our example this would imply again during the first period zero net cash receipts for the borrower and a constant real income for the lender, and that real income at the end of the second period is unaffected by the rate of inflation.

Now let us introduce taxation at a uniform rate t. Suppose the tax were applied only to the amount by which interest exceeded the rate of inflation [a tax equal to $t(r - \lambda)$] and similarly deductions were allowed only on real interest payments. Clearly, such a straightforward extension of the appropriate indexing policy for one-period bonds will be neutral. Neutrality requires that the borrower's real net income in the first period be zero. If π is his first period profit and B is the amount of borrowing, then

$$\frac{(1+\lambda)\pi(1-t) - (r - t(r-\lambda))B}{1+\lambda} = \pi(1-t) - \frac{B(r - t(r-\lambda))}{1+\lambda}$$

must be unchanged, which means that

$$r = r^*(1+\lambda) - \frac{t\lambda}{1-t},$$

where r^* is the interest rate without inflation. But now the net real return to the lender is

$$\begin{aligned}\frac{r - t(r-\lambda)}{1+\lambda} &= r^*(1-t) + \frac{t\lambda}{1+\lambda} - \frac{t\lambda}{1+\lambda}\\ &= r^*(1-t).\end{aligned}$$

Note however that *if the lender and borrower are at different tax brackets, any adjustment in nominal interest rates which leaves the borrower's real income unchanged must affect the real income of the lender*. Letting t_B and t_L be the marginal tax rate of the borrower and lender, the change in real income of the lender per dollar loaned is equal to

$$\frac{t_L - t_B^{\lambda}}{(1+\lambda)(1-t_B)} \, .$$

That is, the change in real income is proportional to the differences in tax rates and the rate of inflation.

In this particular instance a policy which is neutral is simply to index the final repayment of principal, that is, in the first period

$$\frac{r(1-t)}{1+\lambda} = \text{independent of } \lambda,$$

which is to say

$$r_1 = r^*(1+\lambda),$$

and at the end of the second period the real income of the lender is

$$\frac{r_2(1-t)}{(1+\lambda)^2} \, ,$$

which is independent of λ if $r_2 = r^*(1+\lambda)^2$, where r_2 is the nominal interest payable in the second period of the loan.

Finally, we note that with or without inflation, there is an incentive to relabel the first period interest payments as principal when the borrower is in a lower tax bracket than the lender provided $t_L \leqslant 0.5$. The present value of tax savings to the lender is

$$\frac{t_L r^{*2}(1-t_L)}{1+r^*(1-t_L)} \, ,$$

while the cost to the borrower is only

$$\frac{t_B r^{*2}(1-t_B)}{1+r^*(1-t_B)} \, .$$

If the rate of inflation increases, the gain to the lender is increased in money terms but not real terms.

7. Tax Treatment of Capital Gains

There are two aspects of the tax treatment of capital gains that have been extensively discussed in the literature: (a) capital gains are taxed at lower rates than ordinary income, and (b) capital gains are taxed only upon realization rather than upon accrual. Our concern here is primarily with the latter, although in Section 7.G we shall have a few words to say about the former.

In our earlier discussion we noted how the failure to tax *real* capital gains introduced a distortion into the tax system, which favored capital goods whose price was increasing relative to other goods. To the extent that inflation does not affect *relative* prices and to the extent that the real value of the tax liabilities can be reduced by postponing realization, an increase in the actual rate of inflation has no real effect on the cost of capital.

In fact, of course, the capital gains tax is only postponed; when the capital gain is realized, a tax becomes due. In an inflationary period the tax which becomes due is largely on purely nominal capital gains. As a result, inflation increases the cost of capital and, perhaps more importantly, interferes with the allocative efficiency of the economy. The reason that we would argue that this allocative effect is more significant is that while there may be other instruments available to the government for controlling the overall level of investment in the economy (and thus "correcting" any distortion in the overall savings rate), it is likely to be far more difficult to have specific remedies for various categories of capital goods which would correct the allocative inefficiencies with which we are concerned here.

The capital gains tax also introduces significant inequities: even individuals who have a negative real income may have to pay a tax.

A particular allocative effect which has received widespread attention arises from the taxation of capital gains on the basis of realization rather than accrual: the so-called locked-in effect. When individuals sell an asset whose value (in money terms) has increased, a tax is due. The tax can be postponed (and thus its present discounted value reduced) by not realizing the return. Thus individuals are induced to postpone realization beyond the point where the expected return is equal to the rate of interest. Our analysis suggests that under certain circumstances this locked-in effect may not be as serious as is widely believed; we show, moreover, that the kinds of remedies often suggested (some method of "constructive" realization) are distortionary. The magnitude of the locked-in effect is likely, however, to increase with the rate of inflation.

We develop these results within the context of a simple capital-theoretic model.

A. The Model

We assume that there is an investment opportunity, the cost of which is a unit, and the real value of which increases with time according to the function $f(T)$. To finance the investment opportunity, the individual borrows a dollar at an interest rate per unit of time of r. In the absence of

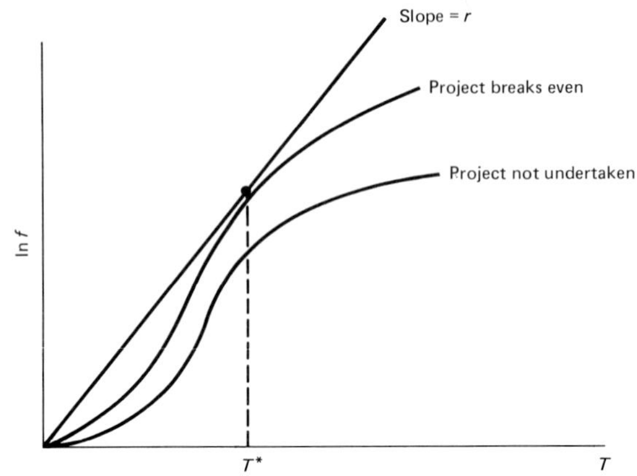

Fig. 1. Rate of interest in alternative investment projects.

inflation and taxation the individual chooses T to maximize

$$e^{-rT}f(T) - 1; \tag{20}$$

that is,

$$f'(T)/f(T) = r. \tag{21}$$

The rate of growth of the asset equals the rate of interest as depicted in Fig. 1. The investment is undertaken if

$$\max_T \left[e^{-rT}f(T) - 1 \right] > 0.$$

Figure 1 depicts two different projects, one of which is undertaken, the other of which is not.

Now let us introduce taxation. Assume that interest payments are tax deductible, so the aftertax rate of interest is $r(1 - \tau)$. Assume too that upon realization of the investment a capital gains tax is paid at the rate τ_c. Then the individual maximizes

$$e^{-r(1-\tau)T}\left[(1 - \tau_c)f + \tau_c \right] - 1. \tag{22}$$

The investment is held until

$$\frac{f'}{f + \tau_c/(1 - \tau_c)} = r(1 - \tau). \tag{23}$$

There is a slight *negative* locked-in effect arising from the capital gains taxation. To obtain an order of magnitude estimate of this effect, assume we are considering a ten-year investment with an average real interest rate of 7%. Then with $\tau_c = 0.2$ the denominator of the left-hand side is 10% greater than it would be in the absence of capital gains taxation. But notice that the right-hand side is also smaller than it would be in the absence of taxation because of interest deductibility. While the first effect results in a smaller T, the second effect results in a larger T: for reasonable values of the parameters the net effect of the tax system is to lead to longer holding periods but *not* because of the taxation of capital gains on an accrual basis.

Now let us assume that there is inflation at the rate λ. The firm maximizes

$$e^{-r^*(1-\tau)T}\left[(1-\tau_c)f+\tau_c e^{-\lambda T}\right]-1, \tag{24}$$

where we have assumed that the real aftertax interest rate remains unchanged. Thus

$$(1-\tau_c)f' = \left[(1-\tau_c)f+\tau_c e^{-\lambda T}\right]r^*(1-\tau)+\lambda e^{-\lambda T}\tau_c. \tag{25}$$

Apparently, the locked-in effect is even more strongly negative than before: if the purchase price of the capital asset were not deductible for purposes of capital gains taxation, and if interest were not tax deductible, the tax system would be neutral with respect to the date of termination of the investment project. The source of nonneutrality is that there is a deduction allowed for the original purchase price. The present discounted *real* value of this declines faster the faster is the rate of inflation. Thus there is an incentive for earlier termination. For reasonable values of the parameters, however, it would not appear that this effect is particularly significant.

It is apparent from (25) that at each value of T an increase in the rate of inflation lowers the value of the project. Thus with fixed tax rates, as inflation increases, some projects which previously were just viable will no longer be undertaken.

B. Multistage Projects

The analysis can be extended to an individual who, over his lifetime, is planning a sequence of investments. The question is Does taxation of capital gains affect the date at which he switches from one project to the next? For simplicity assume there are only two stages and that there are constant returns to scale in the second stage. Let V_2^* be the (optimized) value of the second stage per unit of investment, evaluated as of the date of the beginning of the second stage: $V_2^* = \max_T[f_2(T)e^{-rT}-1]$. Then the value of an investment program which terminates the first stage at time T_1 and invests the proceeds in the second stage is (in the absence of taxation)

$$e^{-rT_1}f_1(T_1)V_2^*.$$

Maximization of this again entails $f_1'/f_1 = r$. Now let us assume there is a sales tax. The firm then maximizes

$$e^{-rT_1} f_1(T_1)(1-\tau)V_2^*.$$

It is immediately apparent that the time of termination of the first project is completely unaffected by such a tax. Again, if we introduce a capital gains tax (with an allowance for the original purchase price), we maximize[13]

$$e^{-rT_1}\left[f_1(T_1)(1-\tau)+\tau\right]V_2^*.$$

As before, the capital gains tax leads to an *earlier* termination of the first project rather than a later termination.

C. The Locked-in Effect and Inflation

The same argument can be used to extend the analysis to any *fixed* number of stages. The locked-in effect only appears when there is a discrete change in the number of investment projects undertaken in the individual's life. Thus Fig. 2 depicts a case where the individual prefers to stick with a single investment project yielding relatively low marginal returns rather than switch to the new investment project. The fixed cost of the switch (the

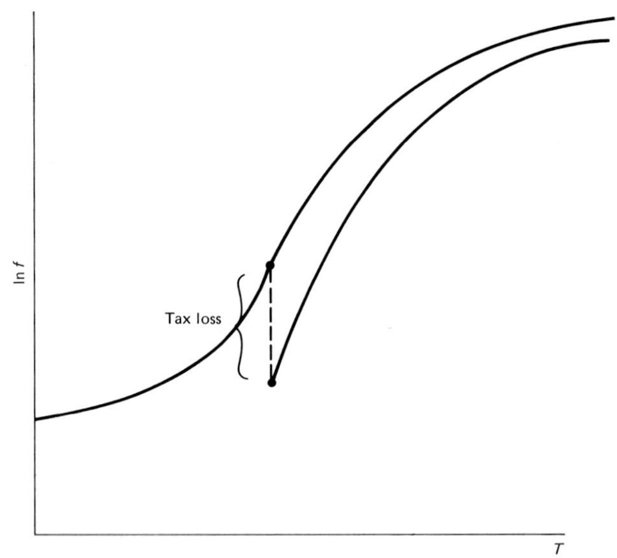

Fig. 2. The locked-in effect.

[13]If there is no interest income tax; with an interest income tax the modification required is straightforward.

capital gains tax) does in fact "lock" the individual into the unproductive investment.

Moreover, one can easily show not only that the monetary value of the tax liability due at a switch increases with inflation, but also the real value. If the value of the asset is $qe^{\lambda t}$, the real value of the tax liability at sale is

$$\tau e^{-r^*(1-\tau)T}(q - e^{-\lambda T}).$$

This also makes clear the inequity arising from the tax: even if there is a real loss on the investment ($q < 1$), there may be a tax due, particularly on long-lived investment. The magnitude of this clearly increases both with the rate of inflation and the length T of the investment project.

D. Roll-Over Provisions: A Simple Remedy

There is a simple remedy for this. If we introduce a "roll-over" provision (as in housing), then the individual simply wishes to maximize the present discounted value of his terminal wealth, and capital gains taxation has no locked-in effect; the entire sequence of projects can be viewed as a single project. As in our earlier analysis of a single project, the individual will terminate the project (begin consuming) earlier than he otherwise would.

E. The Distortionary Impact of Constructive Realization

While the above proposal constitutes a further departure from taxation on the basis of accrual rather than realization, there have been a number of proposals attempting to make the tax more like a tax on accrual. In this section I shall attempt to show why no nondistortionary scheme of this type is possible if market price is not continuously observable.

Assume the tax authority postulates that the asset has grown exponentially at the rate g between purchase p_o and sale (in fact, g is not constant)

$$p(T) = p_o e^{gT}.$$

If we impose a tax *as if* the capital gain were continuously realized, the present discounted value of tax payments would be

$$\tau g \int p_o e^{gt} e^{-rt}\, dt = \frac{\tau g p_o}{g - r}\left[e^{(g-r)T} - 1\right].$$

Firms thus maximize

$$\left[p(T) - \frac{\tau g}{g - r}\, p_o(e^{gT} - e^{rT})\right] e^{-rT};$$

that is,

$$p' - rp = -\frac{\tau g r}{g-r} p_0\left[e^{gT} - e^{rT}\right] + \frac{\tau}{g-r}\left[g(p' - rpe^{(r-g)T}) - \frac{r}{g-r} p_0(e^{gT} - e^{rT})\frac{dg}{dT}\right] > 0$$

since at $p' = rp$, $g > r$ (the average rate of growth exceeds the marginal) and $dg/dT < 0$ (by the second-order condition). Thus this tax results in premature sale of the asset.

This shows that the simplest, and most natural, approach to constructive realization is distortionary. I now show that there exists no nondistortionary system.

The general problem can be formulated as follows: does there exist a tax rule based on observables (say, the length of the holding period and the growth rate over the holding period) which is nondistortionary? I now show that, for a particular example, provided the growth functions of different assets are different, no such nondistortionary rule exists.

Assume the individual has a single investment opportunity, a tree which grows at the rate g_1. At some subsequent (random) date a new investment opportunity becomes available, which grows at the rate g_2, where $g_2 > g_1$. To avail himself of this new opportunity, the individual cannot borrow, but must sell the original tree. Clearly, it is desirable for him to do so, provided only that $g_2 > g_1$. With capital gains taxation he will not do so; g_2 must exceed g_1 by an amount which depends on the rate of taxation. The critical value of τ is given by the solution to

$$e^{g_1 T} - \tau(e^{g_1 T} - 1) = e^{g_2 T + (g_1 - g_2)t}\left[1 - \tau(e^{-g_2(T-t)} + e^{-g_1 t} - 2) + \tau^2(e^{g_2 T + (g_1 - g_2)T} - e^{g_1 t} - e^{g_2(T-t)} + 1)\right].$$

Clearly, at $\tau = 0$, $g_1 = g_2$. To see more clearly what g_2 depends on, let us calculate

$$\frac{dg_2}{d\tau}_{|\tau=0} = \frac{e^{g_2 T}(2 - e^{-g_2(T-t)} - e^{-g_1 t}) - (e^{-g_1 t} - 1)}{(T-t)e^{g_2 T}}$$

$$\approx \left[\frac{g_1}{1 + g_2 T} + g_2 T\right]\frac{1}{T-t}.$$

Clearly, if g_1 were observable, one could make the capital gains tax a function of the holding period to obtain neutrality:

$$e^{gT} - \tau_1(e^{gT} - 1) = e^{gT}\left[1 + \tau_1(e^{-gt} - 1) - \tau_2(e^{-g(T-t)} - 1)\right] + \tau_1\tau_2(e^{gT} - e^{gt} - e^{g(T-t)} + 1).$$

If all assets grew at a constant exponential rate, this "first-best" solution could easily be obtained, for g_1 could be inferred from its past growth rate. But in reality growth rates vary over time (and, indeed, are stochastic). Assume that at the date at which the new investment opportunity becomes available, the past growth rate has been $\bar{g}_1$, but the future growth rate is expected to be $\hat{g}_1$. Neutrality clearly requires that the individual be indifferent to switching if $\hat{g}_1 = g_2$. But with taxation, even depending on holding periods, we require for neutrality

$$
\begin{aligned}
& e^{\bar{g}_1 t+\hat{g}_1(T-t)} - \tau_1(e^{\bar{g}_1 t+\hat{g}_1(T-t)} - 1) \\
& \quad = e^{g_2 T+(\bar{g}_1-g_2)t}\left[1+\tau_1(e^{-g_1 t}-1)+\tau_2(e^{-g_2(T-t)}-1)\right] \\
& \qquad + \tau_1\tau_2(1-e^{g_2(t-T)}).
\end{aligned}
$$

It is immediately apparent that this cannot hold for all values of $\bar{g}_1$, $\hat{g}_1$; thus, unless there is a *unique* relationship between past growth rates and future growth rates for assets, one cannot design a neutral tax structure. (It may, of course, be possible to design second-best tax structures, but to do so requires detailed knowledge of the asset structures, time horizons, and so forth within the population.)[14]

F. Welfare Implications

The discussion so far has focused on a descriptive analysis of the effects of capital gains taxation. We now turn, in a somewhat broader framework, to an analysis of the welfare implications.

The social losses associated with the locked-in effect are of two types:

1. Exchange inefficiency. There are exchanges of assets between two individuals, which in the absence of taxation would increase both individuals' expected utility, but which do not occur as a result of the tax. These trades are motivated by three considerations: (a) differences in attitudes towards risk associated with different stages in the life cycle, (b) other differences in circumstances (changes in sources of wage income) which lead to a change in portfolio composition, and (c) differences in beliefs. It would seem that a considerable proportion of trades which do not occur as a result of the capital gains tax are motivated by differences in beliefs (information). The appropriate criterion for measuring welfare losses associated with inhibiting such trades is a matter of some dispute; under some criteria (involving ex post evaluations) there may even be a welfare gain.

[14] For an extremely insightful and more extensive discussion of the issue of locked-in effects, see Green and Sheshinski (1978).

2. Production efficiency (for example, when a tree should be felled). Our analysis has been primarily directed towards this. It has shown that taxation will interfere with allocative efficiency, but it appears that although fewer projects will be undertaken, some will be sustained longer while others will be terminated earlier.

G. Inflation, Indexation, and Capital Gains

Again, it is important to observe, as we have throughout this paper, that although indexation will not eliminate the distortion arising from these provisions of the tax code, it will result in the neutrality of inflation.

It is sometimes argued that the lower tax rates on capital gains can be justified as compensation for the failure to index for inflation. Although these special provisions do reduce the effective tax rate and, correspondingly, reduce the magnitude of the locked-in effect, they introduce further distortions between those assets which yield their returns in the form of capital gains and those which yield direct returns. These allocative effects may be significant.[15]

8. Concluding Comments

In a world in which there was no uncertainty about the rate of inflation, full indexing could eliminate inflation-induced tax distortions. This would require: (a) allowing deductions for real interest payments only, (b) taxing real capital gains only, and (c) taxing real returns on capital.[16]

The issue of indexing the taxation of capital is completely separate from the issue of indexing the taxation of wages, where the primary issue is simply whether, in the absence of indexing, the change in the progressivity of the tax induced by inflation is desirable. The issue in the case of capital taxation is far more fundamental: the absence of indexing leads to rates of taxation on the *real* return to capital which are extremely high even at moderate rates of inflation. For instance, with a 10% rate of inflation and a 2% real rate of interest, a 50% nominal tax rate is equivalent to a tax of

[15]There is also an increased incentive to convert ordinary income into capital gains. Although such financial effects clearly reduce the effective tax rate, their implications for real resource allocation are more ambiguous.

[16]As we noted above, full indexing would require a "credit" on the value of currency held in one's portfolio. However, to do so might be administratively difficult, while ignoring this is not likely to introduce significant distortions; in any case there is some distortion associated with the fact that the "liquidity" returns to money are not taxed.

300% on the real return; the aftertax real return is -4%. A slight increase in the rate of inflation to 12% increases the tax rate to 350% while a slight decrease to 8% reduces it to 250%. It was probably never the intention of tax authorities to impose taxes at these rates; even if one believes on equity grounds that income from capital ought to be taxed, it is hard to argue that it should be taxed at these rates.

Moreover, the distortionary effects both in the level of savings and the patterns of investment may be significant.

Although the government may have instruments by which it can offset the effects on the overall rate of investment, it may be far more difficult to offset the allocative effects. We have seen in Sections 6 and 7 how nonindexed taxation leads to a distortionary impact on different classes of assets.

It is important to realize, however, that one cannot ascertain the full effect of inflation on any single class of assets in isolation. What is critical is the effect on the relative returns to different assets. Thus, to the extent that inflation increases the effective rate of taxation on capital gains, it reduces the return on assets subject to capital gains taxation relative to those upon which the effective capital gains tax rate is negligible, like housing and durable goods.

Moreover, one cannot necessarily infer the effect of taxation on the marginal cost of capital from observing the effect on the average return to capital. If the inflation was unanticipated, there is a transfer of wealth from bondholders to equity holders: the value of shares should (in real terms) accordingly increase. But the rate of interest charged on new loans is increased to reflect the rate of inflation. We noted that the marginal cost of capital could, accordingly, increase with the rate of inflation, even though the average price of equities on the stock market also increased.

Indexing would eliminate the tax-induced distortions associated with inflation. At the same time it is important to emphasize that indexing itself will not eliminate the distortions arising in the tax system from changes in relative prices, for example, if depreciation rates are not "true real economic depreciation rates" and nominal interest is tax deductible.[17] As I have suggested, these may be significant, but they arise from the fundamental nonobservability of asset values (prices), knowledge of which would be required for the implementation of a system of true economic depreciation.

The other distortion widely associated with the taxation of capital gains —the locked-in effect, which arises from the taxation on realization rather than on accrual—may also be attributed to the nonobservability of asset

[17] The tax would also be nondistortionary if there is an immediate write-off of capital and interest is not tax deductible, but such a tax is a tax on pure profits, not on interest income.

prices. Although the magnitude of the distortion as well as the welfare implications may be in question, the most obvious remedy seems to introduce a possibly significant distortion. In any case indexing would cause these and other distortions to remain just as they would have been in the absence of inflation.

The analysis of indexing in a world in which inflation is perfectly anticipated is, in a sense, embarrassingly simple. The more interesting questions arise when there is uncertainty about the rate of inflation. The distinction between anticipated and unanticipated inflation becomes, at this point, blurred: individuals have a probability distribution of the rate of inflation; they may indeed have "rational expectations." Still there is a sense in which one could say that every outcome is anticipated; and another sense in which one could say that no outcome is fully anticipated.

If the joint probability distribution of all relative (goods) prices remains unchanged, full indexing would again leave the economy unaffected by the rate of inflation. I have argued, however, that the higher rates of inflation may be associated with greater variability in relative (real) prices; moreover, I have identified certain distortions in our present tax system which are associated with changes in relative prices. To the extent that this is the case, indexing will not be sufficient to eliminate the effects of inflation on the economy.

In the absence of full indexing of bonds and taxes, inflation may well have a significant effect on the general equilibrium of the economy. Three important categories of effects have been discussed:

(a) the direct distributive effects, between creditors and lenders, which have been the traditional focus of concern,

(b) the direct allocative effects, arising out of failure of the tax system to be fully indexed, and

(c) the indirect general equilibrium effects, arising out of the first two.

The direct distributive and allocative effects have effects on the price of different assets and on the pretax rate of interest which may give rise in turn to possibly significant and reinforcing redistributive and allocative effects. Without full indexation, when the rate of inflation changes, either government expenditure, the real value of the deficit, or taxation rates will have to adjust. The precise nature of the equilibrium which emerges will depend on the nature of these adjustments.

The problems with which we have been concerned here arise from the difficulties, particularly in the presence of inflation, of defining the return to capital. More fundamentally, we may ask whether a simpler and more direct way of dealing with the problems we have been discussing is to eliminate the taxation of capital. The advantages of such a change in the basis of taxation have been well argued elsewhere.

REFERENCES

Atkinson, A., and Stiglitz, Joseph E. (1980), *Lectures in Public Economics*. McGraw-Hill, New York.

Barro, R. J. (1974). Are Government Bonds Net Wealth? *Journal of Political Economy* **82**, 1095–1117.

Diamond, Peter A. (1975). Inflation and the Comprehensive Tax Base, *Journal of Public Economics* **4** (3), 227–244.

Feldstein, Martin, and Slemrod, Joel (1978). Inflation and the Excess Taxation of Capital Gains on Corporate Stock. *National Tax Journal* **XXXI** (2), 107–118.

Feldstein, Martin, and Summers, Lawrence (1977). Is the Rate of Profit Falling? *Brookings Papers on Economic Activity* **1**, 211–227.

Green, Jerry R., and Sheshinski, Eytan (1978). Optimal Capital-Gains Taxation under Limited Information. *Journal of Political Economy* **86**(6), 1143–1158.

Grossman, S., and Stiglitz, Joseph E. (1976). Information and Competitive Price Systems. *American Economic Review* **66**(2), 246–253.

Grossman, S., and Stiglitz, Joseph E. (1980). On the Impossibility of Informationally Efficient Markets. *American Economic Review* **70**(3), 393–408.

Salop, S., and Stiglitz, Joseph E. (1977). Bargains and Ripoffs. *Review of Economic Studies* **44**, 493–510.

Samuelson, Paul A. (1964). Tax Deductibility of Economic Depreciation to Insure Invariant Valuation. *Journal of Political Economy* **72**, 604–606.

Shell, Karl, Sidrauski, M., and Stiglitz, Joseph E. (1969). Capital Gains, Income and Saving. *Review of Economic Studies* **36**, 15–26.

Stiglitz, Joseph E. (1973). Taxation, Corporate Financial Policy, and the Cost of Capital. *Journal of Public Economics* **2**, 1–34.

Stiglitz, Joseph E. (1976). Corporation Tax. *Journal of Public Economics* **5**, 303–311.

Stiglitz, Joseph E. (1981). Equilibrium Wage Distributions. *Economic Journal*, (to be published).

DEPARTMENT OF ECONOMICS
PRINCETON UNIVERSITY
PRINCETON, NEW JERSEY

PART 7

Review and Critique

Critique I

RUDIGER DORNBUSCH

The conference papers in this volume present a rich menu on macroeconomics and finance in the open economy. They deal with a range of topics from methodology and modeling through economic history to the very hot issue of the costs of economic stabilization. They decidedly do not present themselves as a unified body, but rather as lots and chunks of stimulating variety. In my own remarks I will therefore not even try to pretend at structure and unity, but will simply pick on a few points. I used the occasion of the oral presentation to hand out all possible compliments and shall thus feel free here to remark on shortcomings and possible extensions of the work we have seen.

The first paper I will comment on is that by **Knobel**, which discusses the implications of indexation for open-economy macroeconomic stability. Knobel compares wage indexation that maintains the real wage constant, on one side, with a situation of fixed money wages, (and thus, potentially, flexible real wages) on the other. How do these two regimes compare under various domestic and external shocks?

This is a very important issue, and the open-economy extension of the Fischer–Gray analysis is certainly timely. What are the answers? If we have purely nominal shocks, full indexation is optimal to maintain the initial (full-employment?) real equilibrium. If we have real shocks, on the contrary, then the question is by how much equilibrium real wages will have to change and whether the fixed nominal or the indexed wage achieves the optimal position more nearly. Here the answers are not very satisfying and, indeed, the question may be ill posed.

First, one ought not to compare full indexation with fixed nominal

ISBN 0-12-259750-8

wages. The realistic alternative is a particular indexation or rule versus a wage adjustment process based on expectations and employment. The realistic comparison differs from the Knobel scenario in three respects. The first is that, in my judgment, the main interest here is in the dynamics. We can really not, with any seriousness, consider comparative statics with permanently fixed money wages; rather we want to know whether indexation or the wage process—to use the loose and suggestive term—makes for more stability as the economy is subjected to shocks. The point of comparison is between, say, the United Kingdom with one regime and Italy with another.

A second point, in a realistic setting, is to ask what the indexation rule might look like. Should it include import prices, direct taxes, and the like? That question is of importance because, in the presence of real shocks, flexibility of the real wage is required to accommodate terms of trade changes or changes in fiscal policy.

The last paragraph suggests another basic point that one would hope to find in further work on open economy indexation, that is, a more refined treatment of the disturbances. We should look for a distinction between various real disturbances, but also a distinction between transitory and permanent disturbances. The distinction between various real disturbances is essential because it brings in, for example, the terms of trade as one of the important real variables. (Incidentally, I should think that the terms of trade would be more important in a first modeling effort than the relative price of home goods.) The distinction between transitory and permanent disturbances is important because the former call for accommodation and financing while the latter require adjustment, and the implications for indexation differ quite dramatically.

A last comment on the indexation topic concerns the specification of the stabilization objective. Knobel uses current-account balance as a target. Clearly imposing the constraint of current-account balance is quite suboptimal for transitory disturbances. With the possibility of external borrowing we should look for external accommodation as part of the optimal response. In this context it is interesting to note that Knobel's work should have a natural counterpart in the question of how indexation in financial markets affects economic performance in the open economy. The question is particularly important in those countries where capital markets remain imperfect but where the presence of exchange rate rules and official indexation of debt are prevalent.

The work by **Parkin** and his associates presents an important effort to specify the Lucas tests of rational expectations and money in an open economy. At the conceptual level the authors are to be applauded for the recognition that the open economy imposes structure that should be exploited in the empirical tests. Their modeling presents a useful first step. Much is left to do here, and the first results are not too strong, but this should not detract from an imaginative line of research.

Frenkel presents an integration of his research effort: reevaluating the evidence on flexible rates in the 1920s. The 1920s have long been the main source of anecdote and prejudice about the performance of flexible rate systems. Nurkse's (1944) work drew attention to the experience, and Friedman (1953) implicitly challenged the interpretation. Now what does Frenkel's work offer as insight? His questions center on three issues: first, the monetary approach to the determination of exchange rates; second, purchasing power parity; third, the efficiency of foreign exchange markets.

Frenkel finds that the evidence supports, strongly or weakly, but invariably, his priors. With so thorough a research effort we should take a closer look to see whether or not there are definitive lessons. The reason a close look is warranted is that the evidence for the 1970s—with data that are incommensurably better and with many more countries to consider—offers us rather exactly the opposite conclusions. Some of the issues follow.

The Frenkel view, not surprisingly, is that money demand and supply determine the price level instantaneously, and the instantaneous purchasing power parity links price levels and the exchange rate. What support is there for this view? While Frenkel finds that it holds in the 1920s, the 1970s show no support whatsoever for this specification or for its various nested hypotheses. Of course, a more basic question with respect to the Frenkel tests is: What is the alternative hypothesis? Few would argue that money should not, somehow, appear in an exchange rate equation. But surely an alternative view is that money is endogenous and that accordingly a more structural model is called for to test hypotheses. Another argument is that the alternative hypothesis is a portfolio balance approach where, in addition to money, domestic and foreign debt would appear in the equation. Still another approach would emphasize that the entire equation is misspecified because only unanticipated variables should appear as determinants of (interest-differential adjusted) exchange rate changes. Accordingly, I find that the basic question of the monetary approach is much more wide open than a first reading of Frenkel's evidence might lead us to expect.

I would also argue that the purchasing power parity and efficiency questions remain quite open. For the 1970s, where we do know a bit about the price indices, there is no question that purchasing power parity does *not* hold by the week, month, or year. If it did in the 1920s, where is the difference? On efficiency, Ralph Tryon (1979) has suggested an interesting idea. He argues that conventional tests of efficiency—running the spot rate at $t + 1$ on the forward rate at t—are only weak tests. A stronger test recognizes that the forward rate is the spot rate adjusted for the interest differential. Thus, using separately the lagged spot rate at t and the interest differential, Tryon finds strong evidence against efficiency. The appearance of efficiency only arises from the inclusion of a lagged dependent variable.[1]

I conclude then that the Frenkel work presents an important contribution to our understanding of flexible rates, but perhaps more than that, it opens up the area to many more questions then answers. Among these questions I see as the central issue the serious testing of models that permit real events to affect the exchange rate.

I turn next to a few remarks on the **Blejer–Leiderman** contribution. This paper is central to the topic of the conference and it presents a very serious and noteworthy attempt to analyze the inflation process. The basic hypothesis modeled and econometrically implemented is the following: Inflation is created by excess domestic credit creation; during the adjustment process to a change in credit creation there is a change in relative prices but output, velocity, and real balances are constant throughout. The model is estimated for Brazil, but it is quite apparent that it is a specification that is readily applied to any developing country.

Here are some problems that I see with the model and that perhaps help explain the econometric performance. First, the assumption of constant output during an adjustment process is quite unrealistic. On the contrary, accelerations and decelerations in domestic credit expansion do have systematic effects on real growth. This is surely true for Brazil, as Lemgruber's (1978) work has amply demonstrated, and as a brief look at the 1963–1968 experience will persuade any observer. Second, along the same lines, the omission of financial markets (and in particular, indexed public debt), which we should expect to affect the adjustment process. Capital market considerations are particularly important to the extent that they have a direct, rapid impact on the external balance and therefore on the money supply process.

There are two other important issues in the Blejer–Leiderman paper that need further thought. One is the implicit assumption that only variations in domestic credit are a source of changes in inflation. Neither fiscal policy nor variations in the world price of coffee, for example, are admitted as sources of disturbances. The second point concerns dynamics, and here is certainly one explanation for the implausible empirical results they obtain. In their specification the world rate of inflation spills over into

[1] Let F and S be the logs of forward and spot rates. And let $F_t \equiv S_t + \pi_t$, where π_t is the interest differential. The Tryon equation is $S_{t+1} = a_0 + a_1 S_t + a_2 \pi_t$ and differs from the ordinary specification that amounts to $S_{t+1} = a_0 + a_1(S_t + \pi_t)$. The latter does support efficiency $\{a_0 = 0, a_1 = 1\}$, while the former does not since a_2 shows up with significant negative coefficients.

domestic inflation with a factor of 0.9 within a quarter. Even for a vastly open economy that number is implausibly high. For Brazil, with an import-to-GNP ratio much like that of the United States, it is an entirely implausible restriction, arising entirely from the constraint that money and exchange rates have only contemporaneous effects on prices and demand. Such an assumption, of course, receives very little empirical support in other studies of the transmission process or of inflation. I see no reason why the authors should not allow a more flexible specification that allows for adjustment lags.

The papers by **Razin** and **Helpman**—the Tel Aviv School—are broadly characterized by their challenge to "ad hocery," their insistence on formal maximization considerations, and their emphasis on theoretical propriety. It is hard to disagree with these purposes, although much of the charge is lost once we see that standard gross substitute assumptions, separability, and the like, when everything is said and done, give us the structural equations that bolder or more ignorant practitioners assume off the cuff.

There is, though, a sense in which these papers make an important contribution, and I would single out the Razin paper in particular. We might ask for what questions a more formal maximization approach will give us insights that are not readily available in the fast-and-easy way of open economy macroeconomics? I would point out as an example the Laursen–Metzler (1950) effect—the effect of a change in the terms of trade on saving and spending. The question is clearly important since it is central to balance of trade theory; it is also a question that is traditionally mishandled by a nonchalant application of Keynesian consumption functions that make spending a function of income.

The approach adopted by Razin would treat the problem as one of intertemporal maximization by households that consider their lifetime budget constraint and the path of prices. The spending response to a current terms of trade change will depend, among other things, on whether it is transitory or permanent. The adjustment will show income effects and substitution, possibly current and intertemporal. There is thus scope for a much richer analysis of a key effect in trade balance theory.

Another example where I should think the Razin approach is promising is in the question of fiscal policy. Here the question is to what extent—and in what particular way—individuals may see through the veil of public debt and thus simply offset in the world capital market the financial effects of budget deficits.

I would thus conclude that the formal approach of the Tel Aviv School is well recognized as suitable for particular problems that get mishandled in the unthinking aggregation of Keynesian economics; I should also think, however, that the usefulness is limited to such questions and not to a reworking of all known propositions.

I have reserved **Harberger's** contribution for special discussion. His present paper and accompanying papers already published constitute a major effort to review in a large cross section of countries what we know about inflation—the sources of inflation and the costs of stabilization. I emphatically endorse such an effort, and I fully share Harberger's suggestion that the large LDC inflation experience should not go untapped as a major source of information on the inflation process.

I have serious reservations, however, concerning the evidence that Harberger presents and particularly the two suggestions that (a) the chances that inflation is not due to deficit finance are one in a million and (b) that disinflation is *not* painful. As to the former proposition I would simply note that the evidence is drawn from various time periods for the same group of six countries. With four chronic-inflation countries, how many are in the first quartile of the Harberger distributions?

The more serious question and one that is really not to be handled lightly since it involves too much economic and social dynamite, is the question of disinflation. Harberger shows a group of Latin American countries with their episodes of disinflation. He reports in each case the inflation rates and real growth rates for the year preceding a decline in inflation and likewise for subsequent years where inflation actually falls. Taking these latter years alone, he calculates the frequency distribution of real growth. He comes out with the amazing conclusion that even during disinflation growth performance was laudable, or to put it differently, disinflation is not "so" painful.

For reasons that are altogether baffling Harberger actually excludes from his cost measure the year preceding disinflation. This is, of course, the year where the restrictive aggregate demand policy takes place and where accordingly most of the costs show up. What Harberger records is the "high-growth recovery" from the bottom of the pit, ignoring the downward route completely. Even including the year immediately preceding disinflation would possibly bias the measure of cost; we can well imagine circumstances where a restrictive policy taking hold progressively would result in protracted low growth. A case in point is that of Brazil in the mid-1960s. The data are reported in Table 1.

We note the 1963–1964 wage explosion that leads to sharp inflation increases. Nominal money grows substantially less than inflation and accordingly real balances fall. Thus, as of 1963, real growth tumbles. It is hard, of course, to split up the decline in real balances into the part due to an adjustment in velocity, and the exogenous reduction in real money growth that forces the recession. While we cannot point to an exact

TABLE 1

ANNUAL PERCENTAGE RATES FOR GROWTH IN BRAZIL 1960–1969[a]

	M_1	CPI	Real GDP[b]	Wages	Budget/GDP
1960	37.9	29.6	9.7	n.a.	2.8
1961	45.0	32.4	10.3	n.a.	3.4
1962	53.4	51.1	5.3	n.a.	4.3
1963	57.3	71.0	1.5	95.5	4.2
1964	87.1	91.6	2.9	95.9	3.2
1965	83.6	65.8	2.7	50.7	1.6
1966	38.5	41.3	3.8	48.5	1.1
1967	34.5	30.5	4.8	28.5	1.7
1968	42.0	22.0	11.2	30.5	1.2
1969	32.3	22.7	10.0	25.5	.6
Average 1960–1969	49.2	44.2	6.2	n.a.	2.4

[a]Source: *Conjuntura Economica* and *International Financial Statistics* and Bacha, E., *et al.* (1975, p. 165).

[b]Note: The real GDP series has a break in 1964. Growth rates shown here through 1965 use the old series and from 1966 on the new series. Harberger mistakenly reports for 1965 a growth rate of 23.6%, failing to recognize the break in the series.

measure of monetary tightness, there is little doubt that we should date the start of the disinflation in 1963. The disinflation, reinforced by a fiscal tightening and wage controls, continues until 1967. Low growth—by far lower than that of the early or late 1960s—prevails throughout. Suggesting that the low growth is not painful strikes me as gratuitous, taking real growth as the only criterion as frivolous.

There is a separate question that deserves attention and it relates so the distinction between *inertia inflation* and *bubble inflation*. The former is characteristic of industrialized countries, proceeds typically at rates below 20 or 30%, and is compatible with long-term contracts. Indeed, its existence and the high costs of disinflation may well arise from the overlapping long-term contracts that we observe. Bubble inflation is at the other end of the spectrum. It is highly volatile and typically occurs in a setting where expectations and spot markets, not long-term contracts, set the pattern for inflation. We should expect the latter to be an environment where important inroads on inflation can be made with relatively great ease. An example might be the reduction of inflation in Indonesia from 900 to 170%. The interesting question is to know where the dividing line is and what institutions account for the high costs of disinflation in countries with relatively stable and low inflation.

REFERENCES

Bacha, E., *et al.* (1972). *Encargos Trabalhistas e Absorçao de Mão-de-Obra*. Instituto de Pesquisa e Planejamenta, Rio de Janeiro.

Friedman, M. (1953). The Case for Flexible Exchange Rates. In *Essays in Positive Economics*. Univ. of Chicago Press, Chicago, Illinois.

Laursen, S., and Metzler, L. (1950). Flexible Exchange Rates and the Theory of Employment. *Review of Economics and Statistics* **32** (November), 281–299.

Lemgruber, A. (1978). *Inflação, Moeda & Modelos Macroeconomicos*. Editora da Fundação Getulio Vargas, Rio de Janeiro.

Nurkse, R. (1944). *International Currency Experience*. League of Nations, Geneva.

Tryon, R. (1979). Testing for Rational Expectations in Foreign Exchange Markets. International Finance Discussion Paper, Board of Governors of the Federal Reserve, May.

DEPARTMENT OF ECONOMICS
MASSACHUSETTS INSTITUTE OF TECHNOLOGY
CAMBRIDGE, MASSACHUSETTS

Critique II

*DOUGLAS D. PURVIS**

As Rudiger Dornbusch has noted in his comments, this volume contains a larger number of papers covering a diverse range in terms of issues addressed as well as in terms of method and scope of analysis. My comments are intended to supplement those presented by Dornbusch; his assignment was to comment on the papers dealing with open economies, my assignment was to deal with the "residual" which, in this case, means those papers dealing primarily with closed economy aspects of inflation and development. The comments are intended partly as a "reader's guide" and partly as a reflection of the conference discussion, although no attempt is really made at summarizing the latter. But more importantly, and in the same spirit as Dornbusch, these comments will also try to focus on the shortcomings of the papers and to note the implications for suggestions for future research.

The first part of the volume presents relatively informal papers by Lerner, Tobin, Harberger, and Patinkin, drawn together under the title, "Inflation: Causes, Characteristics, Cure(s)." The unifying theme, to the extent that there is one, is that they in one way or another focus on the important question of the *costs of disinflation*; hence we are to be saved from yet another exchange on "Is the Phillips curve vertical?" Dornbusch discusses the Harberger paper in detail; hence I shall focus on the other three.

*These comments were written while I was visiting the Institute for International Economic Studies, Stockholm. I am grateful to that Institute for its hospitality.

ISBN 0-12-259750-8

Lerner proposes establishing "property rights" in "price increases." These rights must be purchased by firms wishing to raise prices; establishing a "penalty" for raising prices and a corresponding reward (through sales of such property rights) for lowering prices would create private incentives for limiting inflation. A major benefit of this plan, according to Lerner, is that it would eliminate the lag in the response of prices to anti-inflation policy that most economists believe to be a feature of the current economic environment.

Needless to say, Lerner's paper stimulated much discussion and controversy. Several commentators, especially those who hold that "inertial inflation" is a major problem, were sympathetic to the general view that conventional monetary and fiscal policy tools need to be supplemented with an auxiliary policy; Lerner's proposal was compared to various sorts of incomes policies, especially to the tax based incomes policy (TIP), with which he has been associated along with Henry Wallich, Sydney Weintraub, and Arthur Okun. The essential ingredient of Lerner's plan, common to the various TIP plans, is that it taxes those who raise prices. And this in turn is the critical point on which such plans can be criticized. They do not identify any particular market failure or externality to justify the intervention they put forward (although Lerner does refer to a "social" flaw in the private accounting of firms). Instead, they simply identify those who raise prices as the "villains" in the inflationary process. This of course stands in contrast to the usual view that economists attach to price changes as being efficient responses to market forces. The criticism then is that the plan uses market participants as scapegoats rather than attributing responsibility to the true sources of inflationary pressures, much like punishing the bearer of bad news. Of course, one part of the response to this criticism would draw the distinction between comparisons of long-run equilibrium positions and the process of adjustment between such positions, while another would argue that this plan is designed primarily to aid the process of adjustment.

A second criticism that can be made of the Lerner proposal is that no mechanism is suggested by which to control the supply of the "property rights"; governments may well find reasons to increase the supply at an inflationary rate just as they find reasons to print money.

Tobin outlined a taxonomy of alternative theories of inflation, none of which were meant to be exclusive. Tobin's paper is brief and clearly written; hence it needs no extensive summary. He examines the conventional view of government (and, in particular, monetary) authorities as being the "cause" of inflation in terms of providing the initial stimulus, and finds it wanting. The Friedman view that instability is caused by the central banks focusing on interest rates also does not wash here since the increase in inflation of the 1970s coincided with the conversion of central bankers to focusing on monetary aggregates. Tobin also rejects "political business cycle" arguments and the view that governments have deliberately inflated in an attempt to eliminate unemployment. Rather, he considers the government an unwilling accomplice in the inflationary process, being faced with cruel choices and needing to "accommodate" inflationary trends in order to avoid unacceptable levels of unemployment.

Tobin argues that for the United States at least, *inertial inflation* was a major factor, thus taking the view that "disinflation" would be extremely costly. This view of the U.S. experience is supported by the figures presented in Assar Lindbeck's 1979 Gaston Eÿskens Lectures in Leuven, and supporting evidence for a number of other countries is found in the paper in the present volume by Dornbusch and Fischer, which I discuss below. The role of overlapping contracts in explaining this phenomenon is just beginning to be understood [see Taylor (1980)], and much further work needs to be done.

Patinkin takes up a related theme, also found in the Tobin and the Dornbusch–Fischer papers. That theme is Why do governments print money? Or, pushing the question a bit further, How do we explain the cyclical and secular patterns of monetary creation?. Here he gives some historical perspective to popular notions such as accommodation and inflation–taxation; as well, he makes some interesting suggestions on more novel approaches including bureaucratic or "coalition" theories of government behavior. If economists are serious about wanting their advice to be taken seriously, then further work exploring the question of why governments behave the way they do is essential.

The next group of papers that I wish to discuss are the essentially empirical papers.

The **Dornbusch–Fischer** paper outlines an eclectic macroeconomic model in which aggregate supply and demand combine to determine inflation and unemployment. The major novelty in their analysis is the attention they give to explaining monetary growth. The particular question they pose is whether it is the financing requirements caused by large government deficits which lie at the heart of the inflation process. Perhaps surprisingly, their empirical results lend little support to this commonly held view, and they find instead a "stronger link between monetary growth and the rate of increase of wages, indicating typically accommodative monetary policies." A related result is that inflation (what Tobin calls "inertial inflation") is very sluggish and hence the major effect of contractionary policy tends to be an increase in unemployment.

These results, of course, are extremely interesting; if they are "true," they are extremely important. But they must be regarded as very provisional, and there is much further work to be done. The data used cover an extremely short period, and the sample of countries used is neither very broad nor representative. There are econometric difficulties which the authors fully acknowledge but tend to understate. Considerable further work could be done on modeling the behavioral setting of the money supply process, in particular the portfolio balance decision of the central bank, and the need for extensive further work explaining the "autonomy" of wages is apparent if this view is to be made more credible.

Cavallo's econometric analysis of the supply-side effects of contractionary policy in Argentina is closely related. While Cavallo pays very close attention to the "persistence" aspects of expected inflation by detailed modeling of "economically rational" (or, in his terms, "best you can do") expectations, his main focus is on the recurrent question "Is a rise in the interest rate inflationary?". This question is often given a central place in the public debate on policy, but has not been given adequate treatment in either the theoretical or empirical literature on inflation. Cavallo's careful and stimulating paper helps fill that gap, and I hope it will provoke further research on this topic.

His model focuses on the role of working capital due to the lag between labor payments and the sale of output. Essentially, he finds that an increase in the real interest rate raises the effective real wage by an amount dependent on the length of the lag. Unfortunately, he provides us with very little evidence about the magnitude of the lag u, but one would expect that in Argentina's volatile environment it would be rather short and that hence the cost-push effects of an increase in the real interest rate would be rather minor. His results, however, suggest that for Argentina for the period 1963–1973 this was not the case. These results will be very surprising to most economists, as they go beyond the Dornbusch–Fischer argument that disinflation policy will be costly. Cavallo argues that contractionary monetary policy will not only cause an increase in unemployment but also an *increase* in inflation. "Disinflation" is not only costly; in the short run it is counterproductive!

Essentially, restrictive monetary policy in this model has the usual effect of causing a leftward shift in the aggregate demand curve but in addition a *leftward shift of the aggregate supply curve* due to the cost-push effect of higher interest rates discussed above. His empirical results suggest that this additional effect is actually stronger than the former, so that prices rise. This striking result warrants further attention: Is it a peculiar feature of the Argentine economy, or does it have broader applicability? Does it depend upon the particular lag structure, in combination with the specification that aggregate demand depends upon the expected equilibrium interest rate while aggregate supply reacts to the current rate, or will it prove robust in the face of alternative specifications?

The above papers address the issue of the effectiveness of disinflation, but that is really only half the story. To assess the desirability of contractionary policy, one must also have some framework in which to assess the relative social costs of inflation and unemployment; unfortunately little is known about these, especially with regard to the former. The paper by **Sheshinski, Tishler, and Weiss** constitutes an attempt to measure one aspect of the welfare costs of inflation. They draw on earlier theoretical work in which nominal price adjustment is costly, giving rise to a price adjustment policy analogous to (s, S) rules in optimal inventory models. With inflation the relative price thus falls continuously to some critical value and is then raised discretely to S, only to start its decline again. Increased inflation leads to larger price dispersion and hence to larger social costs; the larger $s - S$ gap is not, in their framework, offset by *more frequent* adjustment of prices which could, in principle, reverse the result.

The present paper tests the model in the context of the price of instant coffee produced by an Israeli monopoly. As the authors recognize, the results are suggestive at best, but so little is known about this important problem of price-setting behavior that one welcomes any results at all; still, there is much more theoretical and empirical work to be done before we have even an adequate understanding of this issue. Their measure of expected inflation—a three-month moving average—was extensively criticized during the discussion; a rational expectations framework was proposed in its stead since this might permit time-dependent inflationary expectations rather than a constant level subject to revision. It was also suggested that treating expectations as endogenous would add greatly to the applicability of the model and that more care might be given to modeling the demand side since the pricing policy included in the model might well induce speculative demand behavior. The authors themselves make a number of salient comments about the "negative" results and note the implications for future work. I hope they follow these up.

Zilberfarb takes up the question of the destabilizing effect of tax indexation. He simulates an annual model of the U.S. economy "which is close in nature to the Wharton model." The analysis is relatively straightforward with the only real wrinkle being that one of the experiments deals with a "stagflationary" disturbance, so the presumptions about the destabilizing effects of tax indexation are not unambiguous. While some aspects of the model can be criticized—especially the treatment of expectations and dynamics—the results are also straightforward and not surprising; the usual presumption is supported, and when that presumption is ambiguous, the calculated effects are negligible.

Blinder gives a detailed (Keynesian) analysis of the U.S. experience between 1971 and 1976, presenting a strident defense of the case for the use of accommodating monetary policy. This was one of the most interesting papers of the conference, and it certainly created a lively discussion.

Blinder's review of the "great stagflation" of the 1970s argues that a coherent explanation can be given by introducing supply shocks into an orthodox Keynesian model. Further, in a bit of comparative hypothesis testing that is all too rare in economics, he conducts some simple tests to show that the inflation of the 1970s *cannot* be explained by monetary phenomena alone. As Sachs pointed out in his discussion at the conference, this is not, however, such a telling blow to monetarism, if monetarism is interpreted not as Friedman's aphorism that inflation is a monetary phenomenon but rather as Friedman's (1970) position that nominal income is a monetary phenomenon. Sachs argues that $M2$ does explain nominal income well over the period (though neither prices nor output individually), and hence Blinder's supply-shock analysis is compatible with both monetarist and Keynesian views.

Blinder argues that monetary policy *can* and *should* be used to accommodate such supply shocks. He presents some estimates of the inflationary cost of accommodation in a Keynesian context and then uses some estimates from Barro and Rush to show that a "rational expectations" context would not alter this view very much. (Essentially, the latter suggests that both output and inflation would be a bit more responsive to accommodation than the Keynesian estimates.) Up to this point the case for accommodation is based on nominal wage rigidity, arising either as a "given" in the Keynesian model or from "confusion" in the case of the Barro–Rush model.

Blinder goes on to analyze the case for accommodation in the context of rational expectations models. He considers three such models in which the possibility of incorporating the price of oil and in which the possibility of monetary policy being potent arises from either sticky wages (Fischer-type contracts) or from some nominal ridigity in oil prices. In all three models there is full current information. Unanticpated OPEC price rises generate stagflation in all three models; monetary accommodation is effective but, of course, faces an output–inflation trade-off. *Anticipated* OPEC price rises have rather different effects in the three models. In the wage-contracts model, as long as some contracts have been settled before the shocks occur (and before they are anticipated), there is a role for monetary accommodation. This is also true if OPEC is setting an exogenous *nominal* price, although one might not expect to be able to play this game repeatedly. If OPEC sets an exogenous *real* price, full monetary accommodation would render the nominal price level indeterminate while yielding no positive effects on the output level. In fact, as Blinder concedes, this is the one case where *anti-accommodation* may be optimal, as many monetarists advocated following the 1973 oil crisis. Such a result, of course, hinges crucially on the assumption of completely flexible wages.

There is clearly much food for thought in this analysis. Blinder's arguments for accommodation are persuasive. His facts are clearly presented, as in his framework of analysis. He has laid an excellent groundwork for the debate, and those who wish to reinforce or take issue with his arguments for accommodation of supply shocks have a clearly laid out starting point. I expect that we will hear a good deal more about this issue in the next few years.

Barro, Feldstein, and Stiglitz deal with various aspects of the relationship between inflation, taxation, and capital formation. **Barro**'s paper is essentially a restatement of his earlier work, which takes a "Ricardian" position that there is no first-order difference between tax and debt finance of government expenditure. This so-called neutrality proposition, with its associated implication that government bonds do not constitute net wealth, contradicts the intuitive position taken by most economists on these issues. Accordingly, this view is highly controversial, and Barro's earlier writings have elicited a number of critical responses and generated considerable debate within the profession. The controversy is not lessened by the obvious connection with monetarist–Keynesian divisions about the efficacy of fiscal policy and with the implications for various forms of social security systems.

The thrust of Barro's analysis is that channels for intergenerational transfer in the form of bequests already exist, and hence a debt-issue accompanied by increased future taxes does not represent a really new option for shifting a burden onto future generations.

Much of the response at the conference mimicked that already in the published record and hence can be given rather short shrift here. The possibility of capital market imperfections was raised; individuals currently borrowing privately at high interest rates might well be made "wealthier" by the option to borrow through the government bond market at lower rates. A related point dealt with the conversion of human wealth into marketable wealth and the associated implications for consumption. Barro's rather casual treatment of uncertainty was the subject of extensive criticism as was his treatment of distribution effects as being of "second-order" importance. Stiglitz made a particularly salient comment reinforcing Feldstein's well-known argument that individuals are likely to be at a corner solution in terms of current options for intergenerational transfer, and hence the neutrality position will not be supported. He then argued that there is a theory of inheritance consistent with observed patterns of inheritance, but in which the assumption of identical individuals is dropped. He contended that incorporating features such as correlation of abilities and wages of parents and children (with a process of regression towards the mean), uncertain life times, and imperfect capital markets as a result of adverse selection phenomena would not support the neutrality proposition. While there is much empirical work that can and should be done, Stiglitz's comments reinforce the point that the theoretical work is not yet complete.

Part of the discussion surrounding Barro's paper reflected a broader debate within the profession, and this surfaced elsewhere in the conference. This debate is between those who wish to use the concepts of rationality and equilibrium as the only "inputs" into their analytical framework and to relate conclusions directly to these foundations, and those who believe that macroeconomics is an interesting subject precisely because there are departures from these "ultra neoclassical" situations. The latter group held that models have to be more "descriptive" of the real world, and hence they draw policy conclusions *necessarily* based in part on these ad hoc elements. This issue could profitably be faced more explicitly in future discussions.

Feldstein uses a neoclassical money and growth model to analyze the long-run impact of fiscal policies on inflation and capital formation. As is well known, the standard models emphasize that an increase in the rate of inflation is a tax on money, and asset holders will switch their portfolios in favor of real capital, which is likely to increase long-run capital intensity. Feldstein incorporates government bonds into the model so that the rate of return of the asset alternative to capital does not necessarily fall with inflation. Further he models features of the U.S. tax system which imply that the tax liability per unit of capital increases with the rate of inflation. Hence, in his model, the standard results are reversed and an increase in inflation reduces long-run capital intensity.

As Levhari and Patinkin (1968) have shown, the standard results are not robust in the fall of alternative assumptions about saving. This of course reduces the novelty of Feldstein's result as well as raising doubts about their robustness. Further, the fact that his model ignores the taxation of bond interest seems to be important for the results. Tobin also suggested that it may be unfair to hold that current inflation-related distortions in the tax system will be unchanged in the face of a *permanent* rise in the inflation rate (as Feldstein quipped, "In the long run we are all indexed"), so that the association between inflation and increased taxes on capital is therefore also unfair.

Stiglitz examines the nonneutralities or distortions associated with inflation and finds the major distortions to be associated with the tax system, in particular with the taxation of capital. He proceeds by first reviewing the standard money and growth literature (also discussed in Drazen's paper) under the assumption that the tax system is somehow fully indexed.

In a world of certainty anticipated inflation is "almost neutral" as long as interest is paid on money at a constant real rate ("almost" because interest can only be paid on deposits and not on currency, an effect that is likely to be very minor). Unanticipated inflation arising from a temporary burst in the rate of monetary expansion will also be "almost neutral" as long as expectations and savings behavior are not affected and there are no distributional effects. With uncertainty these results can be essentially replicated as long as there are fully indexed bonds. The problem of uncertainty as to the *source* of changes in the price level, a distinction which is important in establishing the neutrality (and desirability) of most indexing schemes, is not raised here.

While most of this is pretty standard, there are several interesting points raised: the roles of savings behavior and distributional effects are highlighted; the surprising result that an increase in the mean rate of monetary expansion (with a constant covariance) increases the variance of the rate of return on money is developed; and the impossibility of "homemade indexation" in a general equilibrium context is shown.

Stiglitz then turns to the analysis of the taxation of capital. As is well known, the tax system distorts capital accumulation in several ways, including tax deductability of interest payments, differences between actual and allowed depreciation rates, and capital gains taxation. With inflation additional sources of distortion arise due to the distinction between real and nominal interest rates, the distinction between historical and replacement cost and the distinction between changes in the nominal and the relative price of capital goods. These possibilities combine to generate a large taxonomy of results, most of which are discussed in some detail; many of the results illustrate the second-best nature of the problem in that eliminating one distortion in the presence of others may worsen the situation. Stiglitz also argues that while it is nearly impossible to remove all distortions, it is possible to make such distortions as do remain independent of the mean rate of inflation; in this sense inflation is neutral.

Perhaps the most interesting aspect of the paper is when Stiglitz focuses on the fundamental problems associated with the inherent unobservability of the real price of capital goods. This, of course, makes taxation of capital gains potentially distorting since such taxes are usually levied on a realization basis rather than on an accrual basis. This problem has led to "constructive realization" schemes of calculating taxable income addressed to that particular distortion. Stiglitz argues that even with the imposition of such schemes (or because of them) a serious distortion remains. There is a "locked-in effect" which causes individuals to hold on to assets too long, generating a potentially large productive inefficiency. This distortion is not a marginal one, and thus it is extremely difficult to devise schemes to rectify it. Stiglitz concludes on a pessimistic note about the potential for redressing the problem and suggests that perhaps the only way is to not tax capital income at all.

The work of **Karni** is representative of work in the recent tradition of macroeconomic theory, which attempts to analyze and explain phenomena that are simply assumed or asserted in traditional Keynesian theory. Karni extends the incomplete-information-based equilibrium theory of the business cycle to include economy-wide markets. The title of Karni's paper is, in fact, slightly misleading. He is concerned with the possibility that "confusion effects" will lead to monetary disturbances generating real output responses *on impact* à la Lucas (1972) rather than with the potential for such effects to persist over *several* periods so as to generate "business cycle" phenomenon, à la Lucas (1975). In Karni's own terms, he is interested in the "trigger" mechanism rather than the "propagation" mechanism.

He shows first that, in a model wherein the equilibrium price in the economy-wide market is independent of relative or market-specific disturbances, if there is only one aggregate disturbance, its *current* realization will be fully revealed by the (observed) price in the economy-wide market. This, of course, is a very straightforward result; it does, however, tell us that models which tend to limit aggregate disturbances to *only* monetary disturbances are of very limited interest. Karni goes on to show that in a multi-aggregate-disturbance context where information is incomplete, the usual positive association between unobserved monetary disturbances and output can be expected only with particular assumptions about the effect of the (unobserved) nonmonetary aggregate disturbance upon relative prices; otherwise, the association will be negative. Thus, just as the Lucas (1972) model requires certain restrictions on the form of the expected utility function (in particular that leisure be an inferior good) in order to generate a negatively sloped Phillips curve and a "monetary" explanation of business cycles, so do the more ad hoc models of the type employed by Karni require particular restrictions in order to be consistent with the stylized facts outlined in Lucas's 1977 paper.

While these results are of some interest, they seem to hinge on the particular specification, based on the use of the central limit theorem, that relative market shocks do not generate "noise" in aggregate markets. While this model, like its predecessors, persists in not paying enough attention to the distinction between transitory and permanent disturbances, it does show the shortcoming of associating monetary disturbances with aggregate.

Drazen's provocative and challenging paper is one of the most interesting contributions in the present volume. Also, it is perhaps the one paper that deals directly with the conference title, *Inflation and Development*. It is an attempt to explore some very new and unfamiliar ground relating to the potential for "hysteresis" effects arising from technical innovation induced by firms being stuck in a disequilibrium situation. In the first part of the paper he presents a clear and insightful discussion of the sources of the differences between two opposing views of the influence of inflation on capital intensity. One the one hand is the "orthodox-Tobin" view, which emphasizes that money and capital are substitutes; inflation is a tax on money, which leads to an increased demand for capital. The other view is the Shaw–McKinnon model of countries with less-developed capital markets so that commercial bank intermediation is an important mechanism by which household savings get channeled into real investment. Here inflation is a tax on such savings since money is the main asset available to savers, and hence inflation leads to a reduction in *investment*.

Drazen goes on to show that the difference may well be important in a way not recognized elsewhere in the literature. He argues that capital rationing of the McKinnon–Shaw type combined with a particular type of learning by doing may lead to a bias in favor of *labor intensive techniques*. The mechanism is that the *short-run* constraints imposed by capital rationing may lead to induced technical change in the specific labor intensive technique used during that regime. This in turn renders some alternative techniques unprofitable and may well lead to a different *long-run* steady state being attained after the removal of the capital rationing. (Parts of this analysis are similar in spirit to the analysis of hysteresis effects in the presence of adjustment costs by Wan and Kemp in the Metzler *Festschrift*, although they were not interested in capital rationing.) The analysis is rather special and therefore can be only suggestive; as Drazen recognizes, a great deal more theoretical work is needed to see how robust and general the results are. There is also obviously room for careful examination of their empirical relevance. But as he emphasizes, the policy implications are potentially very important.

REFERENCES

Friedman, M. (1970). A Theoretical Framework for Monetary Analysis. *Journal of Political Economy* **78**, 193–238.

Levhari, D., and Patinkin, D. (1968). The Role of Money in a Simple Growth Model. *American Economic Review* **58** (September), 713–753.

Lucas, R. E. (1972). Expectations and the Neutrality of Money. *Journal of Economic Theory* **4**, 103–123.

Lucas, R. E. (1975). An Equilibrium Model of the Business Cycle. *Journal of Political Economy* **83**, 1113–1144.

Lucas, R. E. (1977). Understanding Business Cycles. *Journal of Monetary Economics* (*Supplement on Stabilization of the Domestic and International Economy*) pp. 7–21.

Taylor, J. B. (1980). Aggregate Dynamics with Staggered Contracts. *Journal of Political Economy* **88** (1), 1–23.

DEPARTMENT OF ECONOMICS
QUEEN'S UNIVERSITY
KINGSTON, CANADA

Conference Participants*

Tamir Agmon, Tel Aviv University, Israel
*Chaim Barkai, Hebrew University of Jerusalem, Israel
Robert J. Barro, University of Rochester, U.S.A.
*Simon Beninga, Tel Aviv University, Israel
Haim Ben-Shahar, President, Tel Aviv University, Israel
Uri Ben-Zion, Ben-Gurion University of the Negev, Israel
Eitan Berglas, Tel Aviv University, Israel
*Mario J. Blejer, Hebrew University of Jerusalem, Israel
*Alan S. Blinder, Princeton University, U.S.A.
Michael Bruno, Hebrew University of Jerusalem, Israel
Domingo F. Cavallo, Institute of Economic Studies, Cordoba, Argentina
*Hollis B. Chenery, International Bank for Reconstruction and Development
*Alex Cukierman, Tel Aviv University, Israel
*Leif Danziger, Tel Aviv University, Israel
Rudiger Dornbusch, Massachusetts Institute of Technology, U.S.A.
*Allan Drazen, University of Chicago, U.S.A.
*Benjamin Eden, Hebrew University of Jerusalem, Israel
Martin S. Feldstein, Harvard University; President, National Bureau of Economic Research, U.S.A.
*Stanley Fischer, Massachusetts Institute of Technology, U.S.A.
Gideon Fishelson, Tel Aviv University, Israel
*M June Flanders, Tel Aviv University, Israel
*Jacob Frenkel, University of Chicago, U.S.A.
*Giora Hanoch, Hebrew University of Jerusalem, Israel
*Arnold C. Harberger, University of Chicago, U.S.A.
*Milton Harris, Carnegie-Mellon University, U.S.A.
*Elhanan Helpman, Tel Aviv University, Israel
*Edi Karni, Tel Aviv University, Israel
*Ephraim Kleiman, Hebrew University of Jerusalem, Israel
Abraham Knobel, Tel Aviv University, Israel
Leonardo Leiderman, Tel Aviv University, Israel
Abba P. Lerner, Florida State University, U.S.A.
*Nissan Liviatan, Hebrew University of Jerusalem, Israel
*Yoram Mayshar, Hebrew University of Jerusalem, Israel
Arie Melnik, Haifa University, Israel

*Discussants of papers presented in this volume are starred.

Michael Michaely, Hebrew University of Jerusalem, Israel
Yair Mundlak, Hebrew University of Jerusalem, Israel
Aharon R. Ofer, Tel Aviv University, Israel
Michael Parkin, University of Western Ontario, Canada
Don Patinkin, Hebrew University of Jerusalem, Israel
Yakir Plessner, Hebrew University of Jerusalem, Israel
*Douglas D. Purvis, Queen's University, Kingston, Canada
Assaf Razin, Tel Aviv University, Israel
*Eytan Sheshinski, Hebrew University of Jerusalem, Israel
Zalman Shiffer, Bank of Israel, Israel
Joseph E. Stiglitz, Oxford University, U.K.
*Jeffrey Sachs, Harvard University, U.S.A.
Zvi Sussman, Deputy Governor, Bank of Israel, Israel
Arie Tamir, Tel Aviv University, Israel
Asher Tishler, Tel Aviv University, Israel
James Tobin, Yale University, U.S.A.
Orhan Turkay, Ankara University, Turkey
*Yoram Weiss, Tel Aviv University, Israel
Shlomo Yitzhaky, Hebrew University of Jerusalem, Israel
Ben-Zion Zilberfarb, Bar-Ilan University, Israel

Author Index

Numbers in italics refer to the pages on which the complete references are listed.

Subject Index

Country Index

M

N

P

R

S

T

U

V

ECONOMIC THEORY, ECONOMETRICS, AND MATHEMATICAL ECONOMICS

Consulting Editor: Karl Shell

University of Pennsylvania
Philadelphia, Pennsylvania

Franklin M. Fisher and Karl Shell. **The Economic Theory of Price Indices: *Two Essays on the Effects of Taste, Quality, and Technological Change***

Luis Eugenio Di Marco (Ed.). **International Economics and Development: *Essays in Honor of Raúl Presbisch***

Erwin Klein. **Mathematical Methods in Theoretical Economics: *Topological and Vector Space Foundations of Equilibrium Analysis***

Paul Zarembka (Ed.). **Frontiers in Econometrics**

George Horwich and Paul A. Samuelson (Eds.). **Trade, Stability, and Macroeconomics: *Essays in Honor of Lloyd A. Metzler***

W. T. Ziemba and R. G. Vickson (Eds.). **Stochastic Optimization Models in Finance**

Steven A. Y. Lin (Ed.). **Theory and Measurement of Economic Externalities**

David Cass and Karl Shell (Eds.). **The Hamiltonian Approach to Dynamic Economics**

R. Shone. **Microeconomics: *A Modern Treatment***

C. W. J. Granger and Paul Newbold. **Forecasting Economic Time Series**

Michael Szenberg, John W. Lombardi, and Eric Y. Lee. **Welfare Effects of Trade Restrictions: *A Case Study of the U.S. Footwear Industry***

Haim Levy and Marshall Sarnat (Eds.). **Financial Decision Making under Uncertainty**

Yasuo Murata. **Mathematics for Stability and Optimization of Economic Systems**

Alan S. Blinder and Philip Friedman (Eds.). **Natural Resources, Uncertainty, and General Equilibrium Systems: *Essays in Memory of Rafael Lusky***

Jerry S. Kelly. **Arrow Impossibility Theorems**

Peter Diamond and Michael Rothschild (Eds.). **Uncertainty in Economics: *Readings and Exercises***

Fritz Machlup. **Methodology of Economics and Other Social Sciences**

Robert H. Frank and Richard T. Freeman. **Distributional Consequences of Direct Foreign Investment**

Elhanan Helpman and Assaf Razin. **A Theory of International Trade under Uncertainty**

Edmund S. Phelps. **Studies in Macroeconomic Theory, Volume 1:** ***Employment and Inflation.*** **Volume 2:** ***Redistribution and Growth.***

Marc Nerlove, David M. Grether, and José L. Carvalho. **Analysis of Economic Time Series:** ***A Synthesis***

Thomas J. Sargent. **Macroeconomic Theory**

Jerry Green and José Alexander Scheinkman (Eds.). **General Equilibrium, Growth and Trade:** ***Essays in Honor of Lionel McKenzie***

Michael J. Boskin (Ed.). **Economics and Human Welfare:** ***Essays in Honor of Tibor Scitovsky***

Carlos Daganzo. **Multinomial Probit:** ***The Theory and Its Application to Demand Forecasting***

L. R. Klein, M. Nerlove, and S. C. Tsiang (Eds.). **Quantitative Economics and Development:** ***Essays in Memory of Ta-Chung Liu***

Giorgio P. Szegö. **Portfolio Theory:** ***With Application to Bank Asset Management***

M June Flanders and Assaf Razin. **Development in an Inflationary World**

Thomas G. Cowing and Rodney E. Stevenson (Eds.). **Productivity Measurement in Regulated Industries**

Robert J. Barro (Ed.). **Money, Expectations, and Business Cycles:** ***Essays in Macroeconomics***

In preparation

Giorgio Szegö (Ed.). **New Quantitative Techniques for Economic Analysis**

Advances in Computer Vision and Pattern Recognition

For further volumes:
www.springer.com/series/4205

Giovanni Maria Farinella · Sebastiano Battiato ·
Roberto Cipolla
Editors

Advanced Topics in Computer Vision

Springer

Editors
Dr. Giovanni Maria Farinella
Dipartimento di Matematica e Informatica
Università di Catania
Catania, Italy

Prof. Roberto Cipolla
Department of Engineering
University of Cambridge
Cambridge, UK

Prof. Sebastiano Battiato
Dipartimento di Matematica e Informatica
Università di Catania
Catania, Italy

Series Editors
Prof. Sameer Singh
Research School of Informatics
Loughborough University
Loughborough, UK

Dr. Sing Bing Kang
Interactive Visual Media Group
Microsoft Research
Redmond, WA, USA

ISSN 2191-6586 ISSN 2191-6594 (electronic)
Advances in Computer Vision and Pattern Recognition
ISBN 978-1-4471-5519-5 ISBN 978-1-4471-5520-1 (eBook)
DOI 10.1007/978-1-4471-5520-1
Springer London Heidelberg New York Dordrecht

Library of Congress Control Number: 2013950636

Printed on acid-free paper

Springer is part of Springer Science+Business Media (www.springer.com)

Preface

Computer vision is the science and technology of making machines that see. It is concerned with the theory, design and implementation of algorithms that can automatically process visual data to recognize objects, track and recover their shape and spatial layout.

This edited volume contains a selection of articles covering both theoretical and practical aspects of the three main area in Computer Vision: Reconstruction, Registration, and Recognition. The book provides both, an in-depth overview of challenging areas, as well as novel advanced algorithms which exploit Machine Learning and Pattern Recognition techniques to infer the semantic content of images and videos. The topics covered by the chapters include visual feature extraction, feature matching, image registration, 3D reconstruction, object detection and recognition, human actions recognition, image segmentation, object tracking, metric learning, loopy belief propagation, etc. Each chapter contains key references to the existing literature.

The authors of the chapters have been selected among the best students who attended the International Computer Vision Summer School (ICVSS) in the last years, and are co-authored by world renowned researchers in Computer Vision. ICVSS was established in 2007 to provide both an objective and clear overview and an in-depth analysis of the state-of-the-art research in Computer Vision. The courses are delivered by experts in the field, from both academia and industry, and cover both theoretical and practical aspects of real Computer Vision problems. The school is organized every year by University of Cambridge (Computer Vision and Robotics Group) and University of Catania (Image Processing Lab). Different topics are covered each year. A summary of the past Computer Vision Summer Schools can be found at: http://www.dmi.unict.it/icvss.

It is our hope that graduate students, young and senior researchers, and academic/industrial professionals will find the book useful for understanding and reviewing current approaches in Computer Vision, thereby continuing the mission of the International Computer Vision Summer School.

Sicily, Italy
June 2013

Giovanni Maria Farinella
Sebastiano Battiato
Roberto Cipolla

Acknowledgements

We would like to take this opportunity to thank all contributors of this book, and all people involved in the organization of ICVSS.

Contents

Contributors

Editors' Biographies

Giovanni Maria Farinella

Giovanni Maria Farinella obtained the Master degree in Computer Science (egregia cum laude) from University of Catania in 2004. He was awarded a Ph.D. degree (Computer Vision) in 2008. He became Associate Member of the Computer Vision and Robotics Research Group at University of Cambridge in 2006. He joined the Image Processing Laboratory (IPLAB) at the Department of Mathematics and Computer Science, University of Catania in 2008 as Contract Researcher. He is Contract Professor of Computer Vision at the School of Arts of Catania (since 2004) and Adjunct Professor of Computer Science at the University of Catania (since 2008). His research interests lie in the fields of Computer Vision, Pattern Recognition and Machine Learning. He has edited three volumes and co-authored more than 50 papers in international journals, conference proceedings and book chapters. He is a co-inventor of 3 international patents. Dr. Farinella also serves as a reviewer and on the programme committee for major international journals and international conferences. He has participated to several international and national research projects. Dr. Farinella founded (in 2006) and currently directs the International Computer Vision Summer School (www.dmi.unict.it/icvss).

Sebastiano Battiato

Sebastiano Battiato received his degree in computer science (summa cum laude) in 1995 from University of Catania and his Ph.D. in computer science and applied mathematics from University of Naples in 1999. From 1999 to 2003 he was the leader of the "Imaging" team at STMicroelectronics in Catania. He joined the Department of Mathematics and Computer Science at the University of Catania as assistant professor in 2004 and became associate professor in the same department in 2011. His research interests include image enhancement and processing, image coding, camera imaging technology and multimedia forensics. He has edited 4 books and co-authored more than 150 papers in international journals, conference proceedings and book chapters. He is a co-inventor of about 15 international patents, reviewer for several international journals, and he has been regularly a member of numerous international conference committees. Professor Battiato has participated in many international and national research projects. Chair of several international events (IWCV2012, ECCV2012, VISAPP 2012-2013-2014, ICIAP 2011, ACM MiFor 2010-2011, SPIE EI Digital Photography 2011-2012-2013, etc.). He is an associate editor of the IEEE Transactions on Circuits and System for Video Technology and of the SPIE Journal of Electronic Imaging. Guest editor of the following special issues: "Emerging Methods for Color Image and Video Quality Enhancement" published on EURASIP Journal on Image and Video Processing (2010) and "Multimedia in Forensics, Security and Intelligence" published on IEEE Multimedia Magazine (2012). He is the recipient of the 2011 Best Associate Editor Award of the IEEE Transactions on Circuits and Systems for Video Technology. He is director (and co-founder) of the International Computer Vision Summer School (ICVSS). He is a senior member of the IEEE.

Roberto Cipolla

Roberto Cipolla obtained the B.A. degree (Engineering) from the University of Cambridge in 1984 and an M.S.E. (Electrical Engineering) from the University of Pennsylvania in 1985. From 1985 to 1988 he studied and worked in Japan at the Osaka University of Foreign Studies (Japanese Language) and Electrotechnical Laboratory. In 1991, he was awarded a D.Phil. (Computer Vision) from the University of Oxford and from 1991–1992 was a Toshiba Fellow and engineer at the Toshiba Corporation Research and Development Centre in Kawasaki, Japan. He joined the Department of Engineering, University of Cambridge in 1992 as a Lecturer and a Fellow of Jesus College. He became a Reader in Information Engineering in 1997 and a Professor in 2000. He is a Fellow at the Royal Academy of Engineering (since 2010); also a Professor of Computer Vision at the Royal Academy of Arts, London (since 2004) and Director of Toshiba's Cambridge Research Laboratory (since 2007). His research interests are in computer vision and robotics and include the recovery of motion and 3D shape of visible surfaces from image sequences; object detection and recognition; novel man–machine interfaces using hand, face and body gestures; real-time visual tracking for localization and robot guidance; applications of computer vision in mobile phones, visual inspection and image-retrieval and video search. He has authored 3 books, edited 8 volumes and co-authored more than 300 papers. Professor Cipolla founded (in 2006) and currently directs the International Computer Vision Summer School.

List of Contributors

Lamberto Ballan Media Integration and Communication Center, University of Florence, Florence, Italy

Michel Barlaud I3S Laboratory, University of Nice-Sophia Antipolis, Sophia Antipolis, France

Kobus Barnard University of Arizona, Tucson, USA

Wafa Bel Haj Ali I3S Laboratory, University of Nice-Sophia Antipolis, Sophia Antipolis, France

Marco Bertini Media Integration and Communication Center, University of Florence, Florence, Italy

Horst Bischof Institute for Computer Graphics and Vision, Graz University of Technology, Graz, Austria

Michael Bleyer Vienna University of Technology, Vienna, Austria; Microsoft Redmond, Redmond, USA

Christian Breiteneder Vienna University of Technology, Vienna, Austria

Minsu Cho INRIA/École Normale Supérieure, Paris, France

Aaron Courville Université de Montréal, Montréal, Quebec, Canada

Daniel Cremers Department of Informatics, TU München, Garching, Germany

Gabriela Csurka Xerox Research Centre Europe, Meylan, France

Alberto Del Bimbo Media Integration and Communication Center, University of Florence, Florence, Italy

Luca Del Pero University of Arizona, Tucson, USA

Sandra Ebert Max Planck Institute for Informatics, Saarbrücken, Germany

Maria Klodt Department of Informatics, TU München, Garching, Germany

Kyoung Mu Lee Seoul National University, Seoul, Korea

Thomas Mensink LEAR Team – INRIA Grenoble, Montbonnot, France

Ross Messing University of Rochester, Rochester, NY, USA; Tandent Vision Science, Inc., Pittsburgh, PA, USA

Frank Nielsen Department of Fundamental Research, Sony Computer Science Laboratories, Inc., Tokyo, Japan; LIX Department, Ecole Polytechnique, Palaiseau, France

Richard Nock CEREGMIA, Université Antilles-Guyane, Martinique, France

Takahiro Okabe The University of Tokyo, Tokyo, Japan

Chris Pal École Polytechnique de Montréal, Montréal, Quebec, Canada

Florent Perronnin Xerox Research Centre Europe, Meylan, France

Paolo Piro Istituto Italiano di Tecnologia, Genova, Italy

Peter M. Roth Institute for Computer Graphics and Vision, Graz University of Technology, Graz, Austria

Imari Sato National Institute of Informatics, Tokyo, Japan

Yoichi Sato The University of Tokyo, Tokyo, Japan

Bernt Schiele Max Planck Institute for Informatics, Saarbrücken, Germany

Lorenzo Seidenari Media Integration and Communication Center, University of Florence, Florence, Italy

Giuseppe Serra Media Integration and Communication Center, University of Florence, Florence, Italy

Mihoko Shimano The University of Tokyo, Tokyo, Japan; PRESTO, Japan Science and Technology Agency, Tokyo, Japan

Young Min Shin Seoul National University, Seoul, Korea

Frank Steinbrücker Department of Informatics, TU München, Garching, Germany

Sabine Sternig Institute for Computer Graphics and Vision, Graz University of Technology, Graz, Austria

Radu Timofte VISICS, ESAT-PSI/iMinds, KU Leuven, Leuven, Belgium

Atousa Torabi Université de Montréal, Montréal, Quebec, Canada

Luc Van Gool VISICS, ESAT-PSI/iMinds, KU Leuven, Leuven, Belgium; Computer Vision Lab, D-ITET, ETH Zurich, Zurich, Switzerland

Jakob Verbeek LEAR Team – INRIA Grenoble, Montbonnot, France

Martin Weinmann Institute of Photogrammetry and Remote Sensing, Karlsruhe Institute of Technology (KIT), Karlsruhe, Germany

Andreas Wendel Institute for Computer Graphics and Vision, Graz University of Technology, Graz, Austria

Chapter 1
Visual Features—From Early Concepts to Modern Computer Vision

Martin Weinmann

Abstract Extracting, representing and comparing image content is one of the most important tasks in the fields of computer vision and pattern recognition. Distinctive image characteristics are often described by visual image features which serve as input for applications such as image registration, image retrieval, 3D reconstruction, navigation, object recognition and object tracking. The awareness for the need of adequately describing visual features emerged in the 1920s in the domain of visual perception, and fundamental concepts have been established to which almost every approach for feature extraction can be traced back. After the transfer of the basic ideas to the field of computer vision, much research has been carried out including the development of new concepts and methods for extracting such features, the improvement of existing ideas and numerous comparisons of different methods. In this chapter, a definition of visual features is derived, and different types are presented which address both the spatial and the spatio-temporal domain. This includes local image features, which are used in a variety of computer vision applications, and their evolution from early ideas to powerful feature extraction and matching methods.

1.1 Introduction

"A picture is worth a thousand words." According to this proverb, a single image already contains as much information as a large amount of descriptive text. However, this information has to be extracted and analyzed in an efficient way. Hence, in image processing, it has become popular to transform images or relevant image patches into a compact description using features. The number of different features proposed in literature has increased significantly within the last decades. However, usually features are selected which visually show some special characteristics. These features are now referred to as *visual features*. Such visual features are of great importance in computer vision and pattern recognition as they alleviate crucial tasks such as image registration, image retrieval, object recognition, object tracking, navigation of autonomous vehicles, scene reconstruction or scene interpre-

M. Weinmann (✉)
Institute of Photogrammetry and Remote Sensing, Karlsruhe Institute of Technology (KIT), Englerstr. 7, 76131 Karlsruhe, Germany
e-mail: martin.weinmann@kit.edu

G.M. Farinella et al. (eds.), *Advanced Topics in Computer Vision*,
Advances in Computer Vision and Pattern Recognition,
DOI 10.1007/978-1-4471-5520-1_1, © Springer-Verlag London 2013

tation. Surprisingly, approaches for extracting such features representing important visual details of an image even allow for predicting image memorability [64]. For these reasons, the goal of this chapter is to provide a survey on visual features. In contrast to previous work [85, 103, 136], the contribution of this chapter is to categorize different approaches to different types of visual features, to link all types of visual features to a common source in visual perception as well as to extend the definition from single images to image sequences. Additionally, it is shown for the very popular type of local features arising from image locations with special characteristics within a small spatial neighborhood how these features can be detected, how they can be described and how they can be recognized in a similar image again.

General considerations on visual features are carried out in Sect. 1.2. This includes deriving a definition of the term *visual feature*, checking the traces back to the origin of visual features resulting from investigations on visual perception, considering the suitability of visual features with respect to typical computer vision applications as well as revisiting properties of a *good* visual feature. These general considerations are followed by a brief summary of various existing types of visual features in Sect. 1.3. The intention of this chapter is not to provide a complete and detailed survey over all of the existing approaches for extracting visual features, but rather to revisit the most important ideas. As local features represent a very promising type of visual features suitable for various kinds of applications, they are of great interest in current research. Hence, Sect. 1.4 provides a more detailed analysis by showing how an idea concerning the detection and the description of such features has been transferred to digital image processing and how it evolved over time. Finally, in Sect. 1.5, the chapter is concluded with a summary and an outlook on current research trends related to visual features.

1.2 Visual Features

Throughout the past decades, there has been growing interest in visual features and many investigations have been carried out as such features significantly alleviate common tasks in computer vision. Hence, it seems to be necessary to derive a general definition of the term *visual feature* which is done in Sect. 1.2.1. The idea of using such visual features is then motivated in Sect. 1.2.2, and the necessity of such features for typical computer vision applications is discussed in Sect. 1.2.3. As it is possible to distinguish between different types of visual features, the question about the best feature type might arise which is finally addressed in Sect. 1.2.4.

1.2.1 What Is a Visual Feature?

In order to describe the characteristics of a visual feature, it is worth thinking of the main idea of any feature. In general, a *feature* describes a property by which real or abstract elements or objects can be distinguished. Thus, a feature represents a piece of information which may be relevant for solving a special task. This definition is

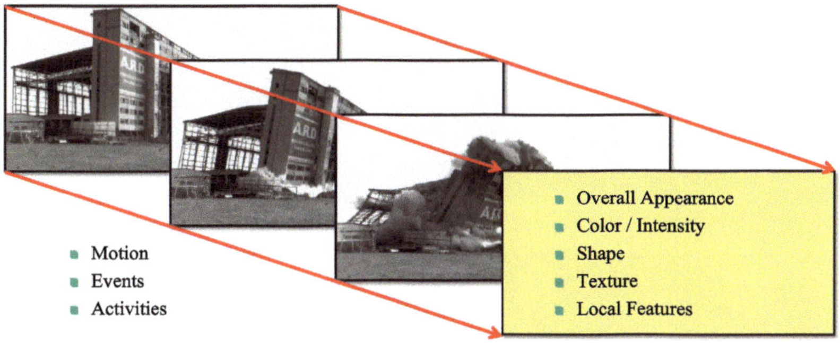

Fig. 1.1 Different types of visual features in images and image sequences

very general and, depending on the respective application, different types of features may differ in their suitability.

The meaning of a visual feature has even been investigated beyond computer vision. According to the *Designs Act 2003* [36], a *visual feature*, in relation to a product, includes the shape, configuration, pattern and ornamentation of the product. Furthermore, a visual feature may serve a functional purpose, but not necessarily, and special attributes like the feel of the product and the materials used in the product are explicitly excluded. Based on this definition, a *design*, in relation to a product, then means the overall appearance of the product resulting from one or more visual features of the product.

In the field of computer vision, a general description of a visual feature can be derived in a very similar way. A visual feature describes a special property of an image as a whole or an object within the image and it can either be a local property or a global characteristic of the image. Thus, for instance, a visual feature might be color in case of color images, intensity in case of grayscale images, shape, size, orientation or texture. Extending this definition to whole image sequences and thus videos, further properties like the motion of objects, the respective velocity, acceleration and direction, single trajectories or the time span within which an object is present may also be considered as visual features. This extension also allows for including more complex features in form of events in an image sequence as well as high-level features like activities describing the behavior of persons or objects within a scene. As a video represents a special image sequence, where the temporal difference between successive images is constant, only the more general term is used in the following. Consequently, a first but very coarse scheme for the classification of different types of visual features can be derived which is illustrated in Fig. 1.1.

1.2.2 What Is the Idea of Using Visual Features?

The derived definition of a visual feature is based on typical characteristics which can be observed in images or image sequences. Early studies on human visual perception can be traced back to ancient Greek theories on how vision is carried out.

Fig. 1.2 Illusion showing that an image might be more than the sum of its parts ("*The Forest Has Eyes*" © Bev Doolittle/The Greenwich Workshop, Inc.)

Since then, many investigations yielded improved insights into human vision. Different psychological theories have been established among which *Structuralism*, *Gestalt Theory* and the *Theory of Ecological Optics* cover important ideas which finally led to cognitive and computational approaches to visual perception. With all these ideas, a growing awareness of the importance of visual features emerged.

Structuralism, where perception is based on a large number of sensory atoms measuring color at specific locations within the field of view, represents a very simple principle of visual perception. However, when considering visual illusions such as the one depicted in Fig. 1.2, it becomes apparent that the whole might be different from the sum of its parts, which has already been that concisely summarized by Aristotle. Hence, visual perception not only involves local image characteristics such as lines, angles, colors or shape, but also grouping processes for what has been detected with the senses and the respective interpretation. In Fig. 1.2, the grouping processes arise from the fact that human vision is biased and trained to see faces. The concept of *Holism* where the whole cannot be represented by utilizing the sum of its parts alone due to relations between the parts has been addressed in Gestalt Theory. The term *gestalt* can be seen as a German synonym for shape, form, figure or configuration. Summarizing the main ideas of Gestalt Theory, it has already been stated in 1924 that "there are entities where the behavior of the whole cannot be derived from its individual elements nor from the way these elements fit together; rather the opposite is true: the properties of any of the parts are determined by the intrinsic structural laws of the whole" [146]. These structural laws of the whole correspond to relations between the parts and, as a consequence, special principles for grouping elements of an image have been proposed. According to [145] and [70], the visual system uses different principles for automatically grouping elements into patterns such as *proximity*, *similarity*, *closure*, *symmetry*, *common fate* (i.e. *common motion*) and *continuity*. In [50], further principles like *homogeneity* and *contour* are proposed.

The homogeneity is introduced as *texture* and the contour represents a physical edge caused by an abrupt change in texture or color. However, describing the whole content of an image might be very complex and therefore, the concept of *Reductionism* according to which an image can be explained by reduction to its fundamental parts became more and more important. In [50] and [51], the Theory of Ecological Optics has been presented which focuses on active and direct perception of visual information. Involving basic principles of Gestalt Theory as well as aspects of information theory, a modified set of 10 principles concerning varieties of continuous regularity, discontinuous regularity or recurrence, proximity and situations involving interaction is presented in [7]. These principles arise from three main observations:

- Information is not uniformly distributed but rather concentrated along contours and especially at points on a contour at which its direction changes, that is, corners.
- Contours are caused by changes of homogeneity with respect to color or texture.
- The degree of homogeneity, that is, texture, can be considered as a characteristic.

Consequently, the perceived information contains a certain degree of redundancy. Visual features should therefore provide a compact representation of the image content. Hence, typical types of visual features in an image might be corners, contours (i.e., shape), color/intensity or homogeneity (i.e., texture). However, exactly these types of visual features have already been addressed in Fig. 1.1.

The cognitive and computational approaches to visual perception are based on combining descriptive principles already proposed in Gestalt Theory and the Theory of Ecological Optics with a model of perceptual processing. According to [87], the early processing of visual information therefore focused on achieving a primitive but rich description of intensity changes present in an image which has been denoted as *primal sketch*. This description is derived from different kinds of intensity changes like edges, lines and blobs as well as additional parameters specifying attributes like position, size, orientation, contrast, termination and fuzziness. As the primal sketch represents a relatively impractical description, further processes for grouping elements are essential which are similar to those of Gestalt Theory. Further involving concepts of Reductionism has proven to be feasible, as an image typically contains very much and redundant information. Exploiting all this information for a special application results in a large amount of input data which leads to problems if tasks cannot be solved fast enough. Hence, only the most significant information of an image can be exploited which typically corresponds to visual features. Thus, feature extraction is commonly introduced for a variety of tasks in computer vision. Suitable features even allow for comparing images or image patches with different size as well as image content in form of objects which vary in scale and orientation.

1.2.3 Are Visual Features Always Necessary?

Although many investigations within the last few decades have clearly demonstrated the high potential of using visual features in a variety of applications, some investigations show that several tasks can also be solved without using such features. The automatic and accurate alignment of captured point clouds, for instance, is an important task for digitization, reconstruction and interpretation of 3D scenes. Active sensors such as terrestrial laser scanners can cope with measuring the 3D distance of scene points and simultaneously capturing image information in form of either co-registered camera images or panoramic reflectance images representing the respective energy of the backscattered laser light. The recorded 3D point clouds typically provide a high point density as well as a high measurement accuracy. Hence, the registration of two partially overlapping scans can be carried out based on the 3D geometry alone and thus without the need of visual features if the 3D structure of the scene is distinctive enough.

Considering the example of point cloud registration, standard approaches such as the *Iterative Closest Point* (*ICP*) *algorithm* [18, 117] or *Least Squares* 3D *Surface Matching* (*LS3D*) [53] only exploit spatial 3D information. Whereas the ICP algorithm iteratively minimizes the difference between two point clouds, the LS3D approach minimizes the distance between matched surfaces. Other approaches focus on the distribution of the points on 2D scan slices [22] or in 3D [86]. For environments with regular surfaces, various types of geometric primitives such as planes [22, 106, 139] or more complex geometric features like spheres, cylinders or tori [109] have been proposed. In scenes without regular surfaces, the registration can rely on descriptors representing local surface patches which may, for instance, be derived from geometric curvature or normal vectors of the local surface [8].

Several investigations, however, have shown that the registration of point clouds can efficiently be supported by involving visual features derived from 2D imagery. As both range and intensity information are typically measured on a regular scan grid resulting from a cylindrical or spherical projection, they can be represented as images. From these images, distinctive feature points can be extracted and reliable feature point correspondences between the images of different scans can be derived. The extraction of such features has been proposed from range images [11, 127], from intensity images [20, 66, 140] and from co-registered camera images [4, 10, 17]. In general, features in the intensity images provide a higher level of distinctiveness than features in the respective range images [122] and, probably, information not yet represented in the range measurements. Projecting the information of distinctive 2D points to 3D space according to the respective range information yields sparse point clouds describing physically almost identical 3D points. The point cloud registration may then exploit the reliable 3D/3D correspondences [122] or 3D/2D correspondences [143, 144] between different scans which typically involves a RANSAC-based scheme [42]. Thus, the reduction to sparse point clouds significantly reduces the time effort and even tends to improve the accuracy of the registration results as the amount and influence of outliers can be reduced [140, 143, 144]. Furthermore, these approaches can directly be transferred to Time-of-Flight cameras or devices based on the use of structured light (e.g., Microsoft Kinect). Consequently, most of the current approaches addressing point cloud registration consider both range and intensity information for reaching an increased performance, although the alignment can also be carried out without using visual features if the scene provides a sufficiently distinctive 3D structure.

1.2.4 What Is the Best Visual Feature?

Considering the very general definition, a large variety of visual feature types can be extracted which indicates that, depending on the respective application and the data available, different types of visual features will surely differ in their suitability. For instance, it might be sufficient to detect people via skin color extraction or to extract bright objects in front of a dark background by simple thresholding techniques. Both tasks can be realized very easily but if additional aspects are essential, for example, when the detected persons or objects should be identified by comparison to elements of a large database, the selected visual features may not provide enough information. For this purpose, other feature types are more appropriate. This example clearly shows that, instead of searching for the *best* feature type, it is more desirable to get characteristics for a *good* feature type.

Based on approaches for extracting adequate features in pattern recognition, it can be noticed that several ideas may obviously be adapted to characterize visual features. Thus, in general, besides being observable, a good visual feature could at least satisfy several of the most commonly desired characteristics:

- The extracted features should be *distinctive* and thus significantly differ from their spatial neighborhood.
- The extracted features should be *invariant* to irrelevant changes of the respective image or image sequence from which they have been extracted, and *robust* against noise effects.
- The feature extraction and the comparison of extracted features should be *efficient* with respect to computational effort.
- A visual feature or a set of visual features should be *comparable* and thus allow for detecting similar content in different images or image sequences.
- The feature type should be highly *relevant* with respect to the application. For different classes with (possibly abstract) objects, the features should provide only small variations when comparing objects within the same class and large variations when comparing objects of different classes.

1.3 The Different Types of Visual Features

Once the awareness for transferring the idea of visual features to computational concepts had emerged, different methods for extracting these features evolved. One of the first surveys on feature extraction has already been carried out in 1969 [76]. Since then, a very large number of approaches for detecting different kinds of features has been presented of which only a relatively small number still has significant impact on current research. Hence, describing all of these methods for feature extraction is beyond the scope of this chapter and, as visual features typically correspond to a certain location or region within an image and its temporal behavior, only the most important ideas concerning the *spatial domain* (Sect. 1.3.1) and the *spatio-temporal domain* (Sect. 1.3.2) are considered. The main focus is on spatial

Fig. 1.3 An image and an image sequence showing different types of visual features

features as image analysis is also required when considering image sequences and many ideas concerning spatial features have therefore been transferred to image sequences. The existence of a preferred feature type with almost general applicability is finally discussed in Sect. 1.3.3. For all of the following considerations, an example is provided in Fig. 1.3 which illustrates a variety of visual features in images and image sequences such as color, shape, texture, local features and features arising from scene dynamics.

1.3.1 Spatial Features

Spatial features only address the image domain and can therefore be directly extracted from an image. The variety of such spatial features covers overall appearance, color or intensity, shape, texture and local features. Whereas those features addressing color/intensity, shape and texture may be rather global or local, the local features only rely on a small spatial image neighborhood. Furthermore, visual features may even be defined depending on the respective application. For recognizing the same or similar information in a different image, the features are often assigned a special description encapsulating the respective image properties.

1.3.1.1 Overall Appearance

Currently, several approaches still address the idea of finding an adequate method for achieving a holistic representation of an image. Early approaches were based on the *Fourier transform*, *generic Fourier descriptors* [150] or *moment invariants* [61] and modified variants such as the *Zernike moment invariants* (*ZMIs*) [132, 133] or the *orthogonal Fourier–Mellin moments* (*OFMMs*) [123]. For the latter two, those moments with a lower order capture the low-frequency information and thus the coarse structure of an image, whereas the moments with a higher order capture the high-frequency information and thus image details. Hence, an image can be represented as a superposition of such moments. A further approach exploiting a coarse-to-fine image representation is based on the *Discrete Cosine Transform* (*DCT*) [3] which has proven to be well-suited for image compression. Some more recent approaches directly address the issue of scene recognition. The *GIST descriptor* [105] focuses on obtaining the *gist*, an abstract representation of the scene which spontaneously activates memory representations of scene categories. This descriptor contains perceptual properties (*naturalness*, *openness*, *roughness*, *ruggedness* and *expansion*) which are meaningful to human observers. A further descriptor denoted as *CENTRIST descriptor* [148] is based on the *CENsus TRansform hISTogram* and has been proposed for recognizing topological places or scene categories.

1.3.1.2 Color/Intensity

Considering Fig. 1.3, it becomes obvious that *color* or *intensity* is an important visual feature. The respective information represents a perceptual attribute of objects and might therefore be important to distinguish between different objects or to classify objects. Color usually is represented in a color space with 3 channels of intensity information such as RGB or HSV. However, it strongly depends on the illumination of the scene and therefore, a normalized RGB representation and other invariant color representations have been presented in literature as well as using color ratios between pixels and their neighbors. Furthermore, *color histograms* representing the global distribution of colors and *color correlograms* capturing the spatial correlation of colors have been introduced in [128] and [62]. Using *color moments*, other image properties such as the mean value, the variance and the skewness of color distributions may be derived [41].

Simple thresholding techniques for detecting image regions with special color seem to be quite obvious, but they are only suitable if the colors to be detected are not likely to change which indicates that the illumination of the scene may not change significantly. More sophisticated approaches have been proposed for tasks like skin color detection [65, 107], but these techniques can also be adapted for detecting image regions representing the sky or the respective skyline within an image. The rough color structure of an image can also be derived by segmenting an image into different homogeneous color regions, where the mean-shift based approach yields promising results [31].

1.3.1.3 Shape

The objects present in a scene can often be identified just by considering their *shape*. Hence, different approaches for adequately describing shape have been proposed in the past. Early investigations on descriptions of shape were based on contours as these represent physical edges caused by abrupt changes in color or texture [7, 50]. Such abrupt changes or discontinuities in image brightness, image color or image texture are likely to correspond to discontinuities with respect to distance or orientation of a surface as well as to different material properties. Furthermore, the region within a closed contour may be considered. Hence, shape description techniques can be categorized into contour-based and region-based approaches. According to [151], contour-based approaches focus on either global properties of a contour such as *perimeter*, *compactness*, *eccentricity*, *shape signature*, *Haussdorff distance*, *Fourier descriptors* or *Wavelet descriptors*, or structural properties such as *chain codes*, *polygonal approximations*, *splines* or *boundary moments*. In contrast to this, region-based approaches take the whole region of a shape into consideration and they may cover global properties such as *area*, *eccentricity*, *geometric moments*, *Zernike moments*, *pseudo-Zernike moments*, *Legendre moments* or *generic Fourier descriptors*, or structural properties such as *convex hull*, *media axis* or *core*. Some of these approaches also address *size* and *orientation* which may be useful for typical applications such as object detection and object recognition.

For obtaining the contours within an image, even local techniques exploiting the convolution with different filter masks have been proposed, for example, the *Roberts operator* [110], the *Prewitt operator* [108], the *Sobel operator* [126], the *Canny operator* [26] or the *Laplacian-of-Gaussian (LoG) filter* [88]. The further importance of angles and sides of a shape has been addressed in [113] and [34]. For detecting special kinds of contours which can be described via mathematical models, the *Hough transform* [60] has been proposed, which originally has been designed for extracting lines. In order to achieve a higher level of generality, the Hough transform has been extended to detect circles and ellipses and, finally, to detect arbitrary shapes [9].

1.3.1.4 Texture

When considering Fig. 1.3, it becomes quite obvious that the homogeneity of certain image regions can also be sufficient to distinguish between different objects or whole image regions with a different semantic content. In [50], this homogeneity has been introduced as *texture*. However, in general, texture is very difficult to define and for this reason, many different definitions of texture can be found in literature [27, 56]. A general but very suitable definition for a variety of applications defines texture as a function of the spatial variation of intensity values within an image [27]. This encapsulates a contextual property involving intensity values within a spatial neighborhood as well as the spatial distribution of these intensity values and different scales or levels of resolution. According to [72], texture can be described with respect to *uniformity*, *density*, *coarseness*, *roughness*, *regularity*, *linearity*, *directionality*, *direction*, *frequency* and *phase*. However, not all of these attributes are independent. In general, the approaches for describing texture can be categorized into three different groups:

- *Statistical approaches* describe texture via the statistical distribution of intensity values. They include *Fourier power spectra*, *Tamura features* [131] including *coarseness*, *contrast*, *directionality*, *linelikeness*, *regularity* and *roughness*, *co-occurrence matrices* or measures derived from the co-occurrence matrix such as *energy*, *entropy*, *contrast*, *homogeneity* and *correlation*.

- *Structural approaches* define texture as composed of *texture primitives* or *textural elements* (*texels*) occurring repeatedly with respect to certain placement rules [138, 152]. The structural properties of these elements are commonly described via *average intensity*, *area*, *perimeter*, *eccentricity*, *orientation*, *compactness*, *moments*, etc. [152].
- *Model-based approaches* focus on modeling an image as a probability model or as a set of basis functions [152]. The coefficients of the utilized models are assumed to adequately characterize the image. Such approaches are often based on *simultaneous autoregressive* (*SAR*) *models*, *Wold-like models* describing properties such as *periodicity*, *directionality* or *randomness*, *Markov models* or multi-resolution filtering techniques such as *Gabor transform* and *wavelet transform* [152].

1.3.1.5 Local Features

Features arising from small parts of an image are referred to as *local features*. Using such local features has been investigated since the 1950s, as highly informative image points are located at corners or blobs in an image [7]. Different methods for detecting *convex blobs* [111], *points of inflection* [49] representing zero-crossings of the curvature which separate convex and concave parts of a curve, *maxima or minima of curvature* [113] and *dominant points* [112] have been proposed. Further local features may be derived from *junctions* or *intersection of edges*. As only a small region is involved and not the whole edge, local *edge elements* (*edgels*) can also be defined as local features. Considering the general structure of an image [69], the approaches can be categorized based on the distribution of intensity values, the image derivatives, the spatial frequency, etc. [136].

An analysis of early approaches to corner detection in intensity images has been presented in [154], where a large number of approaches representing template-based corner detection and geometry-based corner detection with respect to edges, topology and autocorrelation have been analyzed. Then, within a few years, other comparisons including existing methods, improved methods and new methods followed [92–97, 118]. Many of these approaches are based on the *structure tensor* or on the *Hessian matrix*. However, the improvements not only addressed feature extraction, but also feature description in order to achieve an increased robustness when comparing images. A performance evaluation of various local feature descriptors has been carried out in [94] and [96]. A valuable survey over different local feature detectors and feature descriptors is provided in [136].

1.3.1.6 Application-Specific Features

Some visual features strongly depend on the respective application. If, for instance, only human faces are to be found within an image, it might be sufficient to shift a small face patch taken from a database over the image and compare it to the respective image content. Then the face patch itself becomes a visual feature. Furthermore, characteristic parts of a human face such as eyes, eyebrows, nose or mouth can also become visual features. Such features are however only important for face detection, and not for other applications. Different approaches for detecting faces are presented in [149]. A further example is the analysis of building façades, where a symmetric arrangement of simple primitives representing windows and doors can be expected [37].

1.3.2 Spatio-Temporal Features

Whereas spatial features cover many characteristics of an image, there are still some further types of visual features which only appear when analyzing image sequences, that is, these features also address the temporal domain. As a consequence, appropriate spatio-temporal features are required. Hence, different types of such spatio-temporal features are presented in the following sections.

1.3.2.1 Motion

When considering an image sequence, a further feature type might arise from moving objects or persons. Sub-categories describing motion could then be defined, for example, direction, velocity, acceleration, the respective trajectory or the time span within which an object or person is visible in the image sequence.

1.3.2.2 Events

It also becomes apparent that special events themselves represent visual features. For instance, in the image sequence depicted in Fig. 1.3, it becomes visible that an event can be located within an image sequence. Other events which might be of importance are shot-boundaries in videos as these usually separate different scenes.

1.3.2.3 Activities

Depending on the scene, activities of objects or persons may be visually perceptible. However, activities might be difficult to detect as they include interpretation as well as context information and thus, activities represent high-level features.

1.3.3 Is There a Preferred Type of Visual Features?

A key desire for many applications would be a type of visual features with almost general applicability. Considering Fig. 1.3, the global information of the whole image leads to the interpretation that the building is in a very bad condition and a demolition by controlled blasting can be expected to follow within the next time.

This is a high-level feature which cannot properly be captured with other feature types. Color or texture information allow for separating special image regions containing sky, building and ground. The shape information is concentrated in the area of the building as well as most of the local features.

For technical and time-critical applications such as object recognition or navigation, the presence of clutter and occlusions represents a major problem to global features, and methods for extracting and comparing color regions, texture information or shape information still remain computationally challenging. In contrast, local features can be extracted very efficiently, and, due to their accurate localization, their stability over time and the possibility of individual identification, they are suited for a wide range of applications such as object recognition, autonomous navigation and exploration, image and video retrieval, image registration or the reconstruction, interpretation and understanding of 3D scenes. Hence, these features tend to provide a well-suited feature type for typical computer vision applications [136]. For this reason, the following section addresses their evolution from early approaches to modern computer vision.

1.4 The Evolution of Local Features

According to [136], a *local feature* is an image pattern varying from its spatial neighborhood. The variation typically arises from a change of one or more image properties such as color, intensity or texture. In general, local features can be corners, blobs, edgels or small image patches. If only the location of the feature is of interest, the term *interest point* is commonly used. For most applications, however, a description of each feature is derived from local image properties in order to identify and match similar features. When localizing or describing features, a local neighborhood has to be analyzed, and thus not only the location of a feature, but also the size and shape of the neighborhood have to be determined. In this section, the basic ideas with the most significant impact on current research are presented. These ideas address both an adequate extraction of the respective image locations, that is, *feature detection* (Sect. 1.4.1), and an adequate representation of the local image characteristics, that is, *feature description* (Sect. 1.4.2). In general, the impact of an approach depends on its performance with respect to common evaluation criteria in reasonable time. Such criteria are considered in Sect. 1.4.3. Finally, in Sect. 1.4.4, the focus of current and future research trends is described which addresses feature detection and feature description (even beyond images and image sequences) as well as challenges arising from more complex scenarios with respect to reflectance behavior.

1.4.1 Feature Detection

Different strategies for feature extraction have been proposed in literature which aim at finding the respective image locations. In general, the definition of a local feature postulates the following characteristics [57, 136]:

- *Distinctiveness/Informativeness*: Local features should significantly differ from their spatial neighborhood within the image and thus be highly distinctive.
- *Repeatability* (*Invariance/Robustness*): A method for extracting local features should be able to produce similar features for similar images. A high degree of reproducibility often is correlated with invariance and robustness. In general, the extraction of local features should be unaffected by simple mathematical transformations of the image, that is, invariant to image rotation and image scaling, and it should be tolerant to image noise, changes in illumination and small deformations arising from minor changes in viewing direction.
- *Locality*: Local features should only depend on a small spatial neighborhood within the image.
- *Quantity*: The total number of local features being extracted from an image should be sufficiently high.
- *Accuracy*: The detected local features should be localized accurately. This includes the spatial location within the image as well as other aspects such as scale and possibly shape.
- *Efficiency*: The extraction of local features should be relatively easy and thus be suited for time-critical applications such as object recognition or navigation.

1.4.1.1 Moravec Corner Detector

The *Moravec corner detector* presented in [99] is based on considering local image patches and determining the average change of intensity resulting from small shifts of the respective patch into various directions (u, v). This average change is measured via the sum of squared differences (SSD) between the two respective patches. Denoting the image intensities with $I(x, y)$ and introducing a window function $w(x, y)$, the change E_{uv} resulting from a shift (u, v) is defined as

$$E_{uv} = \sum_{(x,y)\in\mathcal{A}} w(x, y)\big[I(x+u, y+v) - I(x, y)\big]^2, \tag{1.1}$$

where $\mathcal{A}$ describes the considered spatial neighborhood. If, for all possible shifts $(u, v) \in \mathcal{B}$, the minimum change and thus the measure

$$c_{\text{Moravec}} = \min\{E_{uv}|_{(u,v)\in\mathcal{B}}\} \tag{1.2}$$

is above a given threshold, a *corner* is detected. In literature, this measure is also referred to as *cornerness* or *corner strength*. For pixels within homogeneous regions, nearby image patches look very similar and thus, the cornerness becomes small. For pixels on edges, nearby image patches in direction parallel to the edge are similar, whereas nearby image patches in direction perpendicular to the edge differ significantly, which together yields a small value for the cornerness. Only for pixels showing varying intensities in all directions, nearby image patches will significantly differ and the cornerness reaches higher values. However, the Moravec corner detector is limited on a small number of possible and discrete shifts in discrete directions which, for instance, leads to problems if edges are not oriented along these shifts.

1.4.1.2 Harris Corner Detector and Modified Variants

Overcoming the limitations of the Moravec corner detector, the *Harris corner detector* has been presented in [58] as an improved corner detector directly considering the derivatives of the image $I(x, y)$ instead of shifted patches. Assuming only small shifts (u, v), the term $I(x+u, y+v)$ can be approximated by a Taylor series which ignores the higher order terms. This finally leads to the expression

$$E_{uv} = [u, v]\mathbf{S}[u, v]^T \tag{1.3}$$

with

$$\mathbf{S} = \sum_{(x,y)\in\mathcal{A}} w(x, y) \begin{bmatrix} I_x^2(x, y) & I_x(x, y)I_y(x, y) \\ I_x(x, y)I_y(x, y) & I_y^2(x, y) \end{bmatrix}, \tag{1.4}$$

where $I_x(x, y)$ and $I_y(x, y)$ denote the partial derivatives of the image $I(x, y)$ in x- and y-direction. The function $w(x, y)$ is a window function, and the second moment matrix $\mathbf{S}$ is also referred to as *autocorrelation matrix* or *structure tensor* as it describes the gradient distribution in the local neighborhood and thus local image structures. The eigenvalues λ_1 and λ_2 of $\mathbf{S}$ are proportional to the principal curvatures of the local autocorrelation function and form a rotationally invariant description of $\mathbf{S}$ [58]:

- If both eigenvalues λ_1 and λ_2 are small, the local autocorrelation function is flat. Thus, shifts (u, v) only cause little change in E_{uv}. This indicates a local neighborhood of approximately constant intensity.
- If one eigenvalue is high and the other one is low, the local autocorrelation function is ridge shaped. Thus, only shifts along the ridge (i.e., along the edge) cause little change in E_{uv}. This indicates an edge.
- If both eigenvalues λ_1 and λ_2 are high, the local autocorrelation function is sharply peaked. Thus, shifts in any direction will increase E_{uv}. This indicates a corner.

The direct use of the eigenvalues has been proposed in [124] with

$$c_{\text{ShiTomasi}} = \min\{\lambda_1, \lambda_2\} \tag{1.5}$$

as definition of the cornerness. This definition tends to be robust, but it only determines whether a pixel corresponds to a corner or not. As using the terms trace($\mathbf{S}$) and det($\mathbf{S}$) is computationally less expensive than explicitly calculating the eigenvalues λ_1 and λ_2 of $\mathbf{S}$, the cornerness has been defined as

$$c_{\text{HarrisStephens}} = \lambda_1\lambda_2 - \kappa(\lambda_1 + \lambda_2)^2 = \det(\mathbf{S}) - \kappa\,\text{trace}^2(\mathbf{S}) \tag{1.6}$$

where κ is a tunable sensitivity parameter typically chosen between 0.04 and 0.06 [58, 68]. As a consequence, it is possible to distinguish between edges and corners:

- If both eigenvalues λ_1 and λ_2 are small, both terms are relatively small. Thus, the cornerness reaches a small absolute value which indicates a local neighborhood of approximately constant intensity.

- If one eigenvalue is high and the other one is low, the second term is higher than the first one. Thus, the cornerness is negative which indicates an edge.
- If both eigenvalues λ_1 and λ_2 are high, the first term is much greater than the second one. Thus, the cornerness is high which indicates a corner.

The use of a constant parameter which has to be set empirically, however, is a drawback. Hence, a further definition of the cornerness has been presented in [104] with

$$c_{\text{Noble}} = \frac{\lambda_1 \lambda_2}{\lambda_1 + \lambda_2 + \varepsilon} = \frac{\det(\mathbf{S})}{\text{trace}(\mathbf{S}) + \varepsilon} \tag{1.7}$$

where ε is a very small, but constant value. This value has to be introduced in order to avoid a singular denominator which might occur in case of a rank zero matrix. The values of the cornerness are non-negative and only high values indicate a corner.

As the Harris corner detector is not invariant to changes in image scale, a multi-scale representation has been introduced in [92] in order to reach a scale-invariant corner detector. Using a scale-space has already been introduced in 1983 as this yields a concise but complete qualitative description of an image over all scales of observation [147]. Investigations presented in [69] and [79] showed that the Gaussian function is the most suitable scale-space kernel. If a Gaussian function is utilized, the scale-space of the image is defined as a function $L(x, y, \sigma)$ with

$$L(x, y, \sigma) = G(x, y, \sigma) * I(x, y) \tag{1.8}$$

which is derived by convolving the original image $I(x, y)$ with Gaussians G of variable scale σ. The resulting *multi-scale Harris detector* can be described via the multi-scale second order matrix which includes a parameter σ_D for the scale of Gaussian kernels (*differentiation scale*) and a parameter σ_I for the scale of a Gaussian window used for averaging the derivatives in the local neighborhood (*integration scale*). Thus, the cornerness can again be determined via the measures described above. However, it might not be optimal to select the scale parameters empirically. Hence, it has been proposed in [92] to combine the multi-scale Harris detector with an automatic scale selection involving the scale-normalized Laplacian operator [80] which finally yields the *Harris–Laplace detector*.

The Harris–Laplace detector can further be modified by introducing an iterative procedure proposed in [79] which modifies the location and the scale as well as the shape of the local neighborhood of each detected corner. This yields the *Harris-Affine detector* [93] which allows for an affine invariant detection of corners. An improved Harris corner selection strategy involving the z-score function has recently been published [16] which increases the repeatability as well as the matching score and avoids the use of an empirically determined parameter.

1.4.1.3 Förstner Detector and SFOP

A further method for extracting local features has been introduced with the *Förstner detector* in [47]. This approach is also based on local statistics of the image function encapsulated in the structure tensor. It uses the trace of this tensor for measuring the energy of the image function at the respective image point, the ratio of the eigenvalues as a degree of orientation or of an isotropy, and the largest eigenvalue as estimate for the local gradient [46]. Initially, the existence and the approximate location of features are analyzed. Subsequently, the detected features are precisely localized. As this involves further statistics, the algorithm shows a higher computational effort when compared to other detectors. The original Förstner detector has been extended in [46] by combining it with a spiral feature model proposed in [19] for detecting junctions and spiral features. A further extension involving a scale-space has been proposed with the *Scale-invariant Feature OPerator* (*SFOP*) [48]. In comparison to other feature detectors, the SFOP can be used to detect features with complementary properties over scale-space, even in poorly textured areas, and the high localization accuracy is very suitable for tasks such as camera calibration.

1.4.1.4 Hessian Detector

Characteristic features can also be extracted by exploiting the second order derivatives. The *Hessian detector* presented in [15] is based on the Hessian matrix

$$\mathbf{H}(x, y) = \begin{bmatrix} I_{xx}(x, y) & I_{xy}(x, y) \\ I_{xy}(x, y) & I_{yy}(x, y) \end{bmatrix} \tag{1.9}$$

where $I_{xx}(x, y)$, $I_{xy}(x, y)$ and $I_{yy}(x, y)$ are the second order image derivatives which locally describe how the normal to an isosurface changes [136]. The determinant of this matrix is also known as *discriminant*, and the trace is also referred to as *Laplacian*. These provide two measures for detecting blob-like structures in an image, as blobs are detected where the respective measure reaches a local maximum above a predefined threshold. The determinant of the Hessian matrix is related to the product of the principal curvatures which represents the Gaussian curvature.

The Hessian detector is only invariant to image rotation and for this reason, a multi-scale representation has been introduced in [35] in order to obtain a scale invariant detector. Using the automatic scale selection based on the Laplacian operator which has been presented in [80] yields the *Hessian–Laplace detector* [92]. Alternatively, a scale could be selected for which both the trace and the determinant of the Hessian matrix assume a local extremum [91]. In the same way the Harris–Laplace detector has been extended to the Harris-Affine detector by including an affine adaptation process to obtain invariance to affine image transformations, the Hessian–Laplace detector can be modified to the *Hessian-Affine detector* [97].

1.4.1.5 DoG Detector/SIFT Detector

The *Scale Invariant Feature Transform* (*SIFT*) introduced in [83] and later improved in [84] can be utilized for detecting distinctive keypoints in an image and extracting appropriate local feature descriptors. The detection of keypoints is based on an efficient approximation of the Laplacian function and carried out in two steps:

- *Scale-space extrema detection*: At first, the image I is convolved with Gaussian kernels of variable scale, reduced in size and again convolved with Gaussian kernels of variable scale in order to build the Gaussian scale-space. The blurred images are grouped according to their size and sorted with respect to their scale. Subtracting neighboring images yields the scale-space of Gaussian differences also known as Difference-of-Gaussian (DoG) pyramid. Stable keypoint locations can then be determined by comparing each sample point to its eight neighbors at the same scale and its nine neighbors at both neighboring scales. Resulting from this, local extrema are selected as keypoint candidates.
- *Keypoint localization*: Once keypoint candidates have been found, the next step is to improve their location to subpixel accuracy by fitting a 3D quadratic function to the local sample points in order to determine the interpolated location of the extremum. Furthermore, keypoint candidates with a low stability are removed, that is, points with low contrast which are sensitive to noise or points located along edges which can hardly be distinguished from each other.

1.4.1.6 SURF Detector

A further approach for detecting distinctive features is directly based on a scale-space representation of the Hessian matrix. It involves an approximation of the Hessian matrix via box filters [13, 14]. These filters introduce an equal weight of $+1$ or -1 for the contribution of each pixel within a rectangular area and allow for using integral images which can be computed efficiently. Once such an integral image is available, only three additions are necessary to obtain the sum of all intensities within any upright rectangular area, independent of its size. Distinctive features in an image can be detected at locations where the determinant of the approximated Hessian matrix reaches a maximum. Subsequently, similar to the extraction of SIFT features, the location of the resulting feature points is improved to subpixel accuracy and a non-maximum suppression is carried out by considering $3 \times 3 \times 3$ neighborhoods. The resulting features are denoted as *Speeded-Up Robust Features* (*SURF*).

1.4.1.7 CenSurE Detector

The Harris–Laplace detector [92] and the Hessian–Laplace detector [92] are based on calculating the respective cornerness measure at all locations and all scales, and, additionally, the Laplacian at all scales where peaks of the cornerness have been detected [2]. As the Laplacian is supposed to be very suitable, the *Center Surround Extremas* (*CenSurE*) *detector* presented in [2] uses efficient bi-level approximations of the Laplacian (LoG filter) and thus reaches real-time potential.

At all locations and all scales, center-surround bi-level filters are calculated which multiply the respective image pixel by either $+1$ or -1. Local extrema then indicate potential interest point candidates. Except for the circular symmetric filter, these filters can efficiently be calculated via box filters and thus integral images.

In order to improve the approximation by using polygonal filters, modified versions of integral images covering trapezoidal areas have been proposed in [2], which are derived by combining different slanted integral images. Finally, a non-maximum suppression is performed over the scale space by considering local $3 \times 3 \times 3$ neighborhoods of potential interest point candidates. As the magnitude of the response indicates the strength of a feature and weak responses are less stable, the performance can further be increased by simple thresholding with respect to the filter response, and applying the scale-adapted Harris measure is proposed in order to suppress responses along edges or lines.

A special filter can be derived by utilizing two of the boxes if one is rotated by an angle of 45°. This yields the star detector which is also known as *Star Keypoint detector*. However, as the CenSurE detector does not exploit the sparseness of the filter responses, significant improvements have been proposed with the *Speeded-Up Surround Extremas (SUSurE) detector* in [38].

1.4.1.8 SUSAN Detector

Instead of considering image gradients being sensitive to noise and computationally more expensive, the *Smallest Univalue Segment Assimilating Nucleus (SUSAN) detector* [125] relies on comparing the intensity of each image pixel to the intensities of all pixels within a small circular neighborhood. This comparison yields two sets of pixels, one consisting of those pixels with intensities similar to the intensity of the center pixel and one consisting of pixels with different intensities. Hence, according to [125], the center pixel is referred to as *nucleus*, and all pixels with similar intensities define a local area denoted as *Univalue Segment Assimilating Nucleus (USAN)*. This USAN contains much information about the local structure of the image. Its size is at maximum for a center pixel within homogeneous regions where the USAN covers almost the entire neighborhood. Near edges, the ratio of similar pixels to all pixels within the circular neighborhood decreases to approximately 50 % and near corners even further to approximately 25 % [136]. Thus, interest points can be detected at locations in the image where the size of the USAN reaches a local minimum. At these locations, potential candidates with Smallest Univalue Segment Assimilating Nucleus (SUSAN) are detected. However, these have to be filtered by applying several constraints in order to achieve an increased robustness. This involves a limitation of the maximum size of the USAN as well as a consideration of the distance between centroid and center pixel. If, for instance, the centroid of the USAN is not located close to the center pixel, and all pixels on the line between the center pixel and the centroid and even further to the end of the circular neighborhood are within the USAN, this indicates the presence of a corner more reliably. An additional non-maximum suppression finally yields interest points with a SUSAN.

1.4.1.9 FAST Detector

Based on only a special part of local image neighborhoods, the *Features from Accelerated Segment Test (FAST) detector* has been introduced in [114] which still nowadays is one of the fastest feature detectors. This feature detector is closely related to the SUSAN detector [125] which, for each pixel (x, y) of the image, considers the fraction of pixels within a local neighborhood being similar to the respective center pixel (x, y). Instead of all pixels within a local neighborhood, the FAST detector only uses the pixels on a Bresenham circle [23] of radius $r = 3$ surrounding the center pixel and thus only 16 pixels. Hence, for each pixel (x, y) of the image, a test is performed by comparing the intensity values corresponding to the pixels on the surrounding Bresenham circle to its intensity value $I(x, y)$. Introducing a threshold t, the investigated pixel is assumed to be a potential candidate interest point if the intensities of at least $n = 12$ contiguous pixels are above $I(x, y) + t$ or below $I(x, y) - t$. This test can be optimized by first comparing the pixels in opposite horizontal and vertical direction to the center pixel and checking whether three of the selected pixels satisfy the constraint. Finally, a non-maximum suppression may be carried out in order to avoid adjacent responses. Additionally, *positive features* where the circular pixels are brighter than the center pixel and *negative features* where the center pixel is brighter than the circular pixels can be distinguished. This allows for a more efficient matching process, as positive features do not necessarily need to be compared to negative ones [114].

A modification with enhanced repeatability (ER) and only little loss of efficiency has been proposed with the *FAST-ER detector* in [115] which represents a generalization of the FAST detector involving concepts of machine learning. As the FAST detector is not invariant to changes in image scale, an extension to a multi-scale detector involving a scale selection based on the Laplacian function has been proposed in [74]. Extensions considering scaling and rotation have been proposed with the detector of the *Oriented FAST and Rotated BRIEF (ORB) operator* [116] and the *Binary Robust Invariant Scalable Keypoint (BRISK) detector* [75].

1.4.1.10 Detection of MSERs

A method for detecting distinctive image regions has been presented with *Maximally Stable Extremal Regions (MSERs)* in [89]. Initially, the image pixels are sorted by intensity and placed in the image either in increasing or in decreasing order. The list of connected components and the respective areas is maintained using the union-find algorithm [121]. The whole process yields a data structure where the area of each connected component is stored as a function of intensity. MSERs then correspond to thresholds for which a function describing the relative area change reaches an extremal value. Hence, an MSER is a connected component of an appropriately thresholded image [136], and it is either darker than its surrounding area (dark extremal regions) or brighter (bright extremal regions). For being able to derive point correspondences, the MSERs are assigned the respective centroid and (maybe) the respective threshold value. A further optimized implementation for extracting MSERs has been introduced in [102] which replaces the union-find algorithm with a more efficient strategy and thus allows for faster calculation with less requirements concerning memory. The extension of MSERs to multi-resolution involving a scale pyramid has been proposed as *Multi-Resolution MSERs* in [45], and an extension of MSERs to color images has been presented in [44].

1.4.2 Feature Description

Once a local feature has been detected, it has proven to be feasible to assign an adequate description in order to allow for reliably finding the feature again in different images of the same scene. Hence, in the following, different techniques are considered with respect to the main ideas.

1.4.2.1 Early Approaches

The early feature detectors had no specific descriptors and only relied on the comparison of intensity values in the local neighborhoods. Hence, an interest point is described via a small image patch covering its local neighborhood. For comparing the small image patches, a *template matching* can be carried out between small image patches around the respective interest points. The template matching is typically based on normalized cross-correlation, that is, when comparing the local neighborhood of a feature in one image to the local neighborhoods of the features of the other image, a resulting extremum indicates the most similar feature point in the other image. Consequently, feature correspondences can be derived, and their quality may be measured with respect to the similarity of the respective neighborhoods. Instead of using the intensity values within the local neighborhoods, it is also possible to use different information for establishing feature correspondences, for example, information derived from the respective first or second order derivatives, or the information derived from the *monogenic signal* [39, 40, 130]. In contrast, more modern descriptors rely on a vectorized representation which, for instance, allows for determining the most similar descriptor via Euclidean distances.

1.4.2.2 SIFT Descriptor

The detection of similar image patches is challenging if these provide the respective information at a different scale and maybe even with a different orientation. Hence, in addition to detecting distinctive keypoints in an image, the SIFT algorithm [83, 84] also extracts local feature descriptors which are invariant to image scaling and image rotation, and robust with respect to image noise, changes in illumination and small changes in viewpoint. With these descriptors, it is possible to locate correspondences between different images and, finally, to derive common image contents. The *SIFT descriptor* is calculated in two steps:

- *Orientation assignment*: Based on the local image gradient directions of the closest Gaussian smoothed image, each keypoint is assigned an orientation histogram. Each sample added to this histogram is weighted by its gradient magnitude and a Gaussian window centered on the keypoint. Dominant directions of the local

gradients lead to peaks in the orientation histogram. The highest peak detected describes the orientation of a keypoint, and for all peaks within 80 % of this maximum value, an additional keypoint with the corresponding orientation is generated. Finally, an interpolation of the dominant peaks in the orientation histogram is carried out in order to reach a more accurate orientation assignment.
- *Generation of keypoint descriptors*: The descriptor of each remaining keypoint is derived from the image gradients of the closest Gaussian smoothed image in the local neighborhood of the keypoint. In order to achieve rotational invariance, this gradient information is rotated and aligned with the assigned keypoint orientation. Then, the local neighborhood of each keypoint is divided into 4×4 subregions and, for each of these subregions, an orientation histogram with eight entries is created. Again, the contribution of each pixel in the neighborhood of a keypoint to the corresponding orientation histogram is weighted by the gradient magnitude and by a Gaussian window centered on the keypoint. This yields a local image descriptor with 128 elements. Finally, the feature descriptors are normalized in order to reduce the effects of changes in illumination [84].

For two images of a scene, corresponding SIFT features can then be detected by comparing the Euclidean distances of a keypoint descriptor in the first image to the nearest neighbor and to the second-nearest neighbor in the second image. The ratio of these distances has to be below a given threshold t. This ratio test significantly reduces ambiguities in the matching process.

The SIFT algorithm is probably one of the most powerful algorithms for feature extraction. However, it shows a relatively high computational effort which is the reason for a large amount of investigations based on the general idea of SIFT. For instance, to further improve SIFT, modified variants like *Fast approximated SIFT* [52], *Rotation-Invariant Feature Transform* (*RIFT*) [73], *Gradient Location-Orientation Histogram* (*GLOH*) [96], *Coloured SIFT* (*CSIFT*) [1], *Affine-SIFT* (*ASIFT*) [100], *PCA-SIFT* [67], *Salient-SIFT* [77] or *Kernel Projection Based SIFT* (*KPB-SIFT*) [153] have been proposed. SIFT also inspired establishing the *Mirror Reflection Invariant Feature* (*MIFT*) *descriptor* preserving robustness to changes in image scale, image rotation, affine transformations and mirror reflections [54].

1.4.2.3 HOG Descriptor

A feature descriptor similar to the SIFT descriptor has been presented in [33]. It is based on the distribution of the gradient orientations within a local neighborhood of an interest point from which the *Histogram of Oriented Gradient* (*HOG*) *descriptors* are derived. In the original implementation, the image has been divided into small spatial regions referred to as *cells*. For all pixels within a cell, the gradient orientations are calculated and quantized into a fixed number of angular bins representing an orientation histogram. Concatenating the histogram entries and normalizing the resulting vector finally yields HOG descriptors.

In [81], the HOG descriptors are extracted along the normal direction and along the tangential direction of edges by using slices of six cells, each consisting of oriented gradients quantized into 12 angular bins. The resulting features are then defined as *edge-slice* and *edge-ribbon*. The HOG descriptor has also been combined with the Bag of Visual Words representation which yields the *Pyramid Histogram of Words (PHOW) descriptor*, and it has been extended to using different resolution levels which yields the *Pyramid Histogram of Oriented Gradients (PHOG) descriptor*, to also involving soft connecting edges which yields the *Histogram of Canny Oriented Gradients (CHOG) descriptor*, or to achieving a more dense HOG-based feature type in form of *PixelHOG (PiHOG)* [30].

1.4.2.4 SURF Descriptor

The *SURF descriptor* [13, 14] is aligned to the dominant orientation of an interest point. This dominant orientation is calculated via Haar wavelet responses in x- and y-direction within a circular neighborhood. The respective wavelet responses are weighted by a Gaussian window centered on the keypoint and represented as points in a 2D space derived from the response strengths in x- and y-direction. All points within a sliding orientation window of 60° are summarized which yields a local orientation vector, and the orientation for which this vector reaches the maximum length is defined as dominant orientation.

In order to achieve rotational invariance, the squared region aligned with the assigned keypoint orientation is considered and divided into 4×4 subregions. For each of these subregions, the Haar wavelet responses at 5×5 regularly spaced sample points are calculated with respect to the local x- and y-direction within the subregion. The contribution of each wavelet response is weighted by a Gaussian window centered at the keypoint. For each subregion, the sums over the weighted wavelet responses in x- and y-direction as well as the sums over the weighted absolute wavelet responses in x- and y-direction are computed. This yields four characteristic values. The concatenation of these values for all of the 4×4 subregions yields a vector with 64 elements. Finally, a normalization is carried out in order to increase the robustness with respect to changes in illumination.

A faster method for calculating a descriptor for images where rotations are not likely to occur has also been proposed with the *Upright-SURF (U-SURF) descriptor* which does not rely on an assigned dominant orientation [12–14].

1.4.2.5 CenSurE Descriptor

A further modification of the U-SURF descriptor has been presented in [2] as *Modified Upright-SURF (MU-SURF) descriptor*. In order to avoid boundary effects in which the descriptor changes abruptly, paddings are introduced to each boundary in the descriptor increasing the whole region size. These paddings lead to smoothing effects in the descriptor as the extended subregions overlap. Similar to the extension of the CenSurE detector yielding the SUSurE detector, the MU-SURF or *CenSurE descriptor* has been extended by exploiting sparse sampling for increased efficiency which leads to the *SUSurE descriptor* [38].

1.4.2.6 DAISY Descriptor

Being inspired from earlier descriptors such as SIFT and GLOH, a local descriptor denoted as *DAISY descriptor* has been presented in [134]. This descriptor provides the same properties as the histogram-based descriptors concerning changes in image scale, image quality, illumination and viewpoint. However, the SIFT and GLOH descriptors have been designed for sparse wide-baseline matching, as they are computationally demanding. Their suitability arises from orientation histograms based on gradient information within the local neighborhood of an interest point. Using integral images, the SURF descriptor is computationally more efficient, but the missing spatial weighting results in equally contributing gradients. This causes artifacts when densely computing the descriptor for all image pixels. In contrast, the DAISY descriptor provides both a robustness comparable to the SIFT descriptor and a fast calculation. For this reason, it has even been proposed for dense depth map estimation from wide-baseline image pairs [134, 135].

For establishing the DAISY descriptor, an orientation map G_o is derived for each quantized direction o. For this, usually eight directions with an equal angular spacing are used. Subsequently, each orientation map is convolved with several Gaussian kernels G_σ with different σ values. This yields convolved orientation maps G_o^σ. For an interest point located at (x, y), the respective DAISY descriptor consists of a vector with entries being derived from these convolved orientation maps located at positions (u, v) on concentric circles around (x, y), which is the reason for the name of the descriptor. A normalization is then carried out for each histogram independently. Finally, the full DAISY descriptor $\mathcal{D}(x, y)$ for an interest point at location (x, y) is defined as a concatenation of the respective normalized vectors.

DAISY descriptors share histograms so that a histogram computed for the descriptor belonging to one image pixel does not need to be computed for the descriptors of the surrounding pixels again. This fact in combination with using separable convolutions is the main reason for the efficiency of DAISY. An efficient memory access and the early separation of the histogram layers further improve efficiency. Thus, the computation of the DAISY descriptor allows for a parallelized implementation. According to [135], the current implementation can even further be optimized, and a real-time or even faster implementation for computing the DAISY descriptors for all pixels of an image might be possible. A fast and dense computation of robust image descriptors, however, may also be very useful for applications beyond stereo reconstruction such as object or material recognition.

1.4.2.7 Descriptors for MSERs

A method for describing MSERs has been introduced in [29] and relies on local affine frames derived from triplets of points affine-invariantly selected with respect to contour and centroid of each MSER. Affine invariant shape descriptors for MSERs have been introduced in [45] and using the SIFT descriptor for MSERs has been proposed in [101].

1.4.2.8 Binary Representations

Binary strings have the advantage that they can be compared using the Hamming distance [55] which is much more efficient than using the Euclidean distance. Hence, binary feature descriptors have also been investigated. Originally proposed for texture description, the idea of using *Local Binary Patterns* (*LBPs*) has been transferred in order to describe local regions [59]. Thus, LBPs are derived by thresholding the neighborhood of a feature and considering the result as a binary pattern. For reducing the number of different binary patterns, comparing center-symmetric pairs of pixels has been proposed as *Center-Symmetric Local Binary Patterns* (*CS-LBPs*) [59]. The extension to multi-resolution levels of local image regions has been addressed with *Multi-Resolution Local Binary Patterns* (*MR-LBPs*) in [78].

Exploiting the fact that the relative order of pixel intensities remains unchanged in case of monotonic intensity changes, the *Local Intensity Order Pattern* (*LIOP*) *descriptor* has been proposed in [142]. After using the overall intensity order to divide the local patch into subregions, a LIOP of each point is derived which represents a binary vector and encodes the relative relationships among the intensities of its neighboring sample points. Accumulating the binary LIOPs in each ordinal bin and the respective concatenation for all subregions finally yields the real-valued LIOP descriptor. This descriptor tends to be highly discriminative as both local and overall intensity order information of the local patch are encoded.

Recently, with *Binary Robust Independent Elementary Features* (*BRIEF*), a further descriptor has been presented in [25] which is reported to be highly discriminative and very efficient to compute. This descriptor relies on a number of difference tests with respect to intensity values. However, it is not invariant to changes in scale or rotation which has to be addressed to compete with other current descriptors such as SIFT, SURF or DAISY. The most recent advancements address this issue while maintaining a fast, compact and robust descriptor. For instance, the descriptor calculated with the *Oriented FAST and Rotated BRIEF* (*ORB*) *operator* [116] uses oriented BRIEF descriptors, and the *Binary Robust Invariant Scalable Keypoint* (*BRISK*) *descriptor* [75] is based on a more qualitative variant of difference tests on a circular sampling pattern similar to the DAISY pattern [134, 135], and it also considers orientation and scale. The *Compact and Real-time Descriptor* (*CARD*) [6] exploits lookup tables to extract histograms of oriented gradients from arbitrary layouts of bins and applies learning-based sparse hashing for converting these histograms into short binary codes. Being inspired by the human visual system, a further descriptor denoted as *Fast Retina Keypoint* (*FREAK*) *descriptor* [5] is based on computing a cascade of binary strings for comparing image intensities over a retinal sampling pattern.

1.4.3 Evaluation of Feature Detectors and Feature Descriptors

Depending on the application or the used datasets, the performance of feature detectors and feature descriptors may vary significantly as well as the requirements

Table 1.1 Qualitative comparison of popular feature detectors

Feature Detector	Type	Invariance	Time Efficiency
Harris	corner	rotation	++
DoG / SIFT	blob (corner)	rotation, scale	++
SURF	blob (corner)	rotation, scale	+++
FAST	corner	rotation	+++
MSER	region	rotation, scale, affine	+++
ORB	corner	rotation, scale	+++
BRISK	corner	rotation, scale	+++

Table 1.2 Qualitative comparison of popular feature descriptors

Feature Descriptor	Size	Descriptor Entries	Time Efficiency
SIFT	128	real-valued	+
DAISY	200	real-valued	++
SURF	64	real-valued	++
LIOP	144	real-valued	+
BRIEF	32	binary	+++
ORB	32	binary	+++
BRISK	64	binary	+++

which have to be satisfied. Hence, a certain trade-off has to be found which may, for instance, consider the persistence of features and feature correspondences across a large variety of image transformations involving image rotation, scale change, viewpoint change, illumination change, noise, blur or compression [118]. Furthermore, the trade-off may address different characteristics with respect to computational effort, data storage, geometric accuracy and applicability to different image contents. State-of-the-art measures for evaluation are the *repeatability* measuring the persistence of features in terms of the overlap of the detected feature regions, and the *matching score* measuring the ability to correctly assign corresponding features which also involves the similarity of the respective feature descriptors [96, 118]. Further commonly used measures are the *number of detected correspondences*, the *number of correct correspondences* or *precision-recall characteristics*. Additionally, for feature detection, the *localization accuracy* describing whether an interest point is accurately located at a specific ground-truth location may be important, and, for feature description, the *information content* describing the distinctiveness of a feature seems to be an appropriate measure as well. Following [136] and [98], a qualitative comparison of feature detectors and feature descriptors is provided in Tables 1.1 and 1.2.

1.4.4 The Future of Local Features

Unfortunately, the question concerning the best feature type still remains open. Hence, some approaches are based on using a *Bag-of-Words*, where different types of features are extracted and an appropriate combination of these features is derived by learning processes, for example, for material recognition [81] or visual concept classification [137]. As the performance of a feature descriptor is relatively independent of the feature detector, different detector-descriptor combinations may also be applied [32, 119]. An evaluation for finding the best combination of several feature detectors and various feature descriptors has been carried out in [32] and concludes that the MSER and Difference-of-Gaussian (DoG) detectors combined with a SIFT or DAISY descriptor provide the best performance. Recent comparisons with respect to computational effort show that FAST, STAR, BRISK and ORB provide a fast detector, whereas SURF, BRISK and ORB provide an efficient descriptor [98].

A research topic closely related to the extraction of local features focuses on extracting and describing features from point cloud data, and several of the proposed methods are directly or indirectly linked to the same ideas. Thus, SIFT has been extended to 2.5D [82], to 3D [120] and even to n-dimensional data [28]. Combining a 3D feature detector based on SURF and a 3D descriptor extending SIFT has been presented with *THRIFT* [43]. A method extending the 2D structure matrix to the 3D structure tensor has been proposed for feature detection in depth images which extracts multi-scale *surface normal interest points* (*SNIPs*) [129]. SIFT has also been extended to multispectral images with *multispectral SIFT* (*MSIFT*) [24] and to fused intensity-range images with *Complex SIFT* (*ℂSIFT*) [21]. Besides, interest points have been transferred to the spatio-temporal domain [71, 141].

The focus of this chapter has been set on image features for passive techniques and thus features which arise from natural circumstances, that is, the scene is not actively manipulated. However, there are situations when passive techniques tend to get unreliable. Features relying on texture will not appear on homogeneous objects and hence, no information can be captured for this part of the scene making tasks such as object recognition, autonomous navigation or scene reconstruction more challenging. In contrast, there are active techniques for establishing robust feature correspondences by actively taking influence on the scene by manipulating the illumination, for example, by projecting illumination patterns. Thus, scene points are assigned with particular labels. These labels can be decoded in the images and hence, they can be interpreted as synthetically generated features allowing for a robust matching.

Furthermore, depending on the material of present object surfaces, the occurrence of features and their localization might be affected by the light transport within a scene. Occurring phenomena such as specular highlights or subsurface scattering heavily depend on light- and view-direction. As texture-based approaches towards feature representation usually are based on assuming that object surfaces exhibit a Lambertian reflectance behavior, they are not suited for objects with complex reflectance behavior, where this assumption fails. Then, effects such as specular highlights, interreflections or sub-surface scattering represent serious problems, and a reliable retrieval of the feature classes is very difficult or even impossible [63]. For overcoming these limitations, multiple-view features which exhibit non-Lambertian reflectance have been proposed in [90]. An overview for techniques addressing the reconstruction of objects with complex reflectance behavior can be found in [63].

1.5 Conclusion

In this chapter, visual features have been investigated. A general definition has been derived and the idea of using such features has been traced back far beyond the early days of computer vision. Different types of visual features have been considered among which local features are of special interest due to their almost general applicability. For these, the concepts with the most significant impact on current research have been analyzed and traced over time. The presented concepts provide fundamental ideas still visible in current research, as these are used in a variety of computer vision applications, for example, image registration, image and video retrieval, object recognition, object tracking, navigation of autonomous vehicles, scene reconstruction or scene interpretation. These ideas may further be extended in 2D, to 3D, to the spatio-temporal domain or to more complex scenes with respect to reflectance behavior. The availability of modern active sensors such as Time-of-Flight cameras or the Microsoft Kinect even motivates the combination of 2D images and spatial 3D measurements. Promising results may be expected.

References

1. Abdel-Hakim AE, Farag AA (2006) CSIFT: a SIFT descriptor with color invariant characteristics. In: Proceedings of the IEEE computer society conference on computer vision and pattern recognition (CVPR), vol 2, pp 1978–1983
2. Agrawal M, Konolige K, Blas MR (2008) CenSurE: center surround extremas for realtime feature detection and matching. In: Forsyth D, Torr P, Zisserman A (eds) ECCV 2008, part IV. LNCS, vol 5305. Springer, Heidelberg, pp 102–115
3. Ahmed N, Natarajan T, Rao KR (1974) Discrete cosine transform. IEEE Trans Comput C-23(1):90–93
4. Al-Manasir K, Fraser CS (2006) Registration of terrestrial laser scanner data using imagery. Photogramm Rec 21(115):255–268
5. Alahi A, Ortiz R, Vandergheynst P (2012) FREA: fast retina keypoint. In: Proceedings of the IEEE computer society conference on computer vision and pattern recognition (CVPR), pp 510–517
6. Ambai M, Yoshida Y (2011) CARD: compact and real-time descriptors. In: Proceedings of the IEEE international conference on computer vision (ICCV), pp 97–104
7. Attneave F (1954) Some informational aspects of visual perception. Psychol Rev 61(3):183–193
8. Bae K-H, Lichti DD (2008) A method for automated registration of unorganised point clouds. ISPRS J Photogramm Remote Sens 63(1):36–54
9. Ballard DH (1981) Generalizing the Hough transform to detect arbitrary shapes. Pattern Recognit 13(2):111–122
10. Barnea S, Filin S (2007) Registration of terrestrial laser scans via image based features. Int Arch Photogramm Remote Sens Spat Inf Sci 36(part 3):32–37
11. Barnea S, Filin S (2008) Keypoint based autonomous registration of terrestrial laser point clouds. ISPRS J Photogramm Remote Sens 63(1):19–35
12. Bay H, Fasel B, Van Gool L (2006) Interactive museum guide: fast and robust recognition of museum objects. In: Proceedings of the international workshop on mobile vision
13. Bay H, Tuytelaars T, Van Gool L (2006) SURF: speeded up robust features. In: Leonardis A, Bischof H, Pinz A (eds) ECCV 2006, part I. LNCS, vol 3951. Springer, Heidelberg, pp 404–417

14. Bay H, Ess A, Tuytelaars T, Van Gool L (2008) Speeded-up robust features (SURF). Comput Vis Image Underst 110(3):346–359
15. Beaudet PR (1978) Rotationally invariant image operators. In: Proceedings of the international joint conference on pattern recognition (ICPR), pp 579–583
16. Bellavia F, Tegolo D, Valenti C (2009) Improving Harris corner selection strategy. IET Comput Vis 5(2):87–96
17. Bendels GH, Degener P, Körtgen M, Klein R (2004) Image-based registration of 3D-range data using feature surface elements. In: Proceedings of the international symposium on virtual reality, archaeology and cultural heritage, pp 115–124
18. Besl PJ, McKay ND (1992) A method for registration of 3-D shapes. IEEE Trans Pattern Anal Mach Intell 14(2):239–256
19. Bigün J (1990) A structure feature for some image processing applications based on spiral functions. Comput Vis Graph Image Process 51(2):166–194
20. Böhm J, Becker S (2007) Automatic marker-free registration of terrestrial laser scans using reflectance features. In: Proceedings of the 8th conference on optical 3D measurement techniques, pp 338–344
21. Bradley PE, Jutzi B (2011) Improved feature detection in fused intensity-range images with complex SIFT (ℂSIFT). Remote Sens 3(9):2076–2088
22. Brenner C, Dold C, Ripperda N (2008) Coarse orientation of terrestrial laser scans in urban environments. ISPRS J Photogramm Remote Sens 63(1):4–18
23. Bresenham JE (1965) Algorithm for computer control of a digital plotter. IBM Syst J 4(1):25–30
24. Brown M, Süsstrunk S (2011) Multi-spectral SIFT for scene category recognition. In: Proceedings of the IEEE computer society conference on computer vision and pattern recognition (CVPR), pp 177–184
25. Calonder M, Lepetit V, Strecha C, Fua P (2010) BRIEF: binary robust independent elementary features. In: Daniilidis K, Maragos P, Paragios N (eds) ECCV 2010, part IV. LNCS, vol 6314. Springer, Heidelberg, pp 778–792
26. Canny J (1986) A computational approach to edge detection. IEEE Trans Pattern Anal Mach Intell 8(6):679–698
27. Chen CH, Pau LF, Wang PSP (1998) Handbook of pattern recognition and computer vision, 2nd edn. World Scientific, Singapore
28. Cheung W, Hamarneh G (2007) n-SIFT: n-dimensional scale invariant feature transform for matching medical images. In: Proceedings of the IEEE international symposium on biomedical imaging: from nano to macro, pp 720–723
29. Chum O, Matas J (2006) Geometric hashing with local affine frames. In: Proceedings of the IEEE computer society conference on computer vision and pattern recognition (CVPR), vol 1, pp 879–884
30. Collins M, Zhang J, Miller P, Wang H (2009) Full body image feature representations for gender profiling. In: Proceedings of the ICCV workshop on visual surveillance, pp 1235–1242
31. Comaniciu D, Meer P (2002) Mean shift: a robust approach toward feature space analysis. IEEE Trans Pattern Anal Mach Intell 24(5):603–619
32. Dahl AL, Aanæs H, Pedersen KS (2011) Finding the best feature detector-descriptor combination. In: Proceedings of the joint conference on 3D imaging, modeling, processing, visualization and transmission (3DIMPVT), pp 318–325
33. Dalal N, Triggs B (2005) Histograms of oriented gradients for human detection. In: Proceedings of the IEEE computer society conference on computer vision and pattern recognition (CVPR), vol 1, pp 886–893
34. Davis LS (1973) Understanding shape: angles and sides. IEEE Trans Comput C-26(3):236–242
35. Deriche R, Giraudon G (1993) A computational approach for corner and vertex detection. Int J Comput Vis 10(2):101–124

36. Designs Act 2003 (2003) Office of Legislative Drafting and Publishing, Attorney-General's Department, Canberra
37. Dick AR, Torr PHS, Cipolla R (2004) Modelling and interpretation of architecture from several images. Int J Comput Vis 60(2):111–134
38. Ebrahimi M, Mayol-Cuevas WW (2009) SUSurE: speeded up surround extrema feature detector and descriptor for realtime applications. In: Proceedings of the CVPR workshop on feature detectors and descriptors: the state of the art and beyond, pp 9–14
39. Felsberg M (2007) Optical flow estimation from monogenic phase. In: Jähne B, Barth E, Mester R, Scharr H (eds) IWCM 2004. LNCS, vol 3417. Springer, Heidelberg, pp 1–13
40. Felsberg M, Sommer G (2001) The monogenic signal. IEEE Trans Signal Process 49(12):3136–3144
41. Feng D, Siu WC, Zhang HJ (2003) Multimedia information retrieval and management: technological fundamentals and applications. Springer, Berlin
42. Fischler MA, Bolles RC (1981) Random sample consensus: a paradigm for model fitting with applications to image analysis and automated cartography. Commun ACM 24(6):381–395
43. Flint A, Dick A, Van Den Hengel A (2007) Thrift: local 3D structure recognition. In: Proceedings of the Biennial conference of the Australian pattern recognition society on digital image computing techniques and applications (DICTA), pp 182–188
44. Forssen P-E (2007) Maximally stable colour regions for recognition and matching. In: Proceedings of the IEEE computer society conference on computer vision and pattern recognition (CVPR), pp 1–8
45. Forssen P-E, Lowe DG (2007) Shape descriptors for maximally stable extremal regions. In: Proceedings of the IEEE international conference on computer vision (ICCV), pp 1–8
46. Förstner W (1994) A framework for low-level feature extraction. In: Eklundh J-O (ed) ECCV 1994, part II. LNCS, vol 801. Springer, Heidelberg, pp 383–394
47. Förstner W, Gülch E (1987) A fast operator for detection and precise location of distinct points, corners and centres of circular features. In: Proceedings of the ISPRS conference on fast processing of photogrammetric data, pp 281–305
48. Förstner W, Dickscheid T, Schindler F (2009) Detecting interpretable and accurate scale-invariant keypoints. In: Proceedings of the IEEE international conference on computer vision (ICCV), pp 2256–2263
49. Freeman H (1969) A review of relevant problems in the processing of line-drawing data. In: Automatic interpretation and classification of images, pp 155–174
50. Gibson JJ (1950) The perception of the visual world. Houghton Mifflin, Boston
51. Gibson JJ (1961) Ecological optics. Vis Res 1(3–4):253–262
52. Grabner M, Grabner H, Bischof H (2006) Fast approximated SIFT. In: Narayanan PJ, Nayar SK, Shum H-Y (eds) ACCV 2006, part I. LNCS, vol 3851. Springer, Heidelberg, pp 918–927
53. Gruen A, Akca D (2005) Least squares 3D surface and curve matching. ISPRS J Photogramm Remote Sens 59(3):151–174
54. Guo X, Cao X, Zhang J, Li X (2010) MIFT: a mirror reflection invariant feature descriptor. In: Zha H, Taniguchi R-I, Maybank S (eds) ACCV 2009, part II. LNCS, vol 5995. Springer, Heidelberg, pp 536–545
55. Hamming RW (1950) Error detecting and error correcting codes. Bell Syst Tech J 29(2):147–160
56. Haralick RM (1979) Statistical and structural approaches to texture. Proc IEEE 67(5):786–804
57. Haralick RM, Shapiro LG (1993) Computer and robot vision. Addison-Wesley, Reading
58. Harris CG, Stephens M (1988) A combined corner and edge detector. In: Proceedings of the Alvey vision conference, pp 147–151
59. Heikkilä M, Pietikäinen M, Schmid C (2009) Description of interest regions with local binary patterns. Pattern Recognit 42(3):425–436
60. Hough PVC (1962) Method and means for recognizing complex patterns. United States Patent 3069654

61. Hu M-K (1962) Visual pattern recognition by moment invariants. IRE Trans Inf Theory 8(2):179–187
62. Huang J, Kumar SR, Mitra M, Zhu W-J, Zabih R (1997) Image indexing using color correlograms. In: Proceedings of the IEEE computer society conference on computer vision and pattern recognition (CVPR), pp 762–768
63. Ihrke I, Kutulakos KN, Lensch HPA, Magnor M, Heidrich W (2008) State of the art in transparent and specular object reconstruction. In: STAR proceedings of Eurographics, pp 87–108
64. Isola P, Xiao J, Torralba A, Oliva A (2011) What makes an image memorable? In: Proceedings of the IEEE computer society conference on computer vision and pattern recognition (CVPR), pp 145–152
65. Kakumanu P, Makrogiannis S, Bourbakis N (2007) A survey of skin-color modeling and detection methods. Pattern Recognit 40(3):1106–1122
66. Kang Z, Li J, Zhang L, Zhao Q, Zlatanova S (2009) Automatic registration of terrestrial laser scanning point clouds using panoramic reflectance images. Sensors 9(4):2621–2646
67. Ke Y, Sukthankar R (2004) PCA-SIFT: a more distinctive representation for local image descriptors. In: Proceedings of the IEEE computer society conference on computer vision and pattern recognition (CVPR), vol 2, pp 506–513
68. Kerr D, Coleman S, Scotney B (2008) Comparing cornerness measures for interest point detection. In: Proceedings of the international machine vision and image processing conference (IMVIP), pp 105–110
69. Koenderink JJ (1984) The structure of images. Biol Cybern 50(5):363–370
70. Koffka K (1935) Principles of gestalt psychology. Harcourt, Brace & World, New York
71. Laptev I (2005) On space-time interest points. Int J Comput Vis 64(2–3):107–123
72. Laws KI (1980) Textured image segmentation. PhD thesis, University of Southern California, United States
73. Lazebnik S, Schmid C, Ponce J (2005) A sparse texture representation using local affine regions. IEEE Trans Pattern Anal Mach Intell 27(8):1265–1278
74. Lepetit V, Fua P (2006) Keypoint recognition using randomized trees. IEEE Trans Pattern Anal Mach Intell 28(9):1465–1479
75. Leutenegger S, Chli M, Siegwart RY (2011) BRISK: binary robust invariant scalable keypoints. In: Proceedings of the IEEE international conference on computer vision (ICCV), pp 2548–2555
76. Levine MD (1969) Feature extraction: a survey. Proc IEEE 57(8):1391–1407
77. Liang Z, Fu H, Chi Z, Feng D (2010) Salient-SIFT for image retrieval. In: Blanc-Talon J, Bone D, Philips W, Popescu D, Scheunders P (eds) ACIVS 2010, part I. LNCS, vol 6474. Springer, Heidelberg, pp 62–71
78. Liang P, Li S-F, Qin J-W (2010) Multi-resolution local binary patterns for image classification. In: Proceedings of the international conference on wavelet analysis and pattern recognition (ICWAPR), pp 164–169
79. Lindeberg T (1994) Scale-space theory: a basic tool for analysing structures at different scales. J Appl Stat 21(2):224–270
80. Lindeberg T (1998) Feature detection with automatic scale selection. Int J Comput Vis 30(2):77–116
81. Liu C, Sharan L, Adelson EH, Rosenholtz R (2010) Exploring features in a Bayesian framework for material recognition. In: Proceedings of the IEEE computer society conference on computer vision and pattern recognition (CVPR), pp 239–246
82. Lo T, Siebert JP (2009) Local feature extraction and matching on range images: 2.5D SIFT. Comput Vis Image Underst 113(12):1235–1250
83. Lowe DG (1999) Object recognition from local scale-invariant features. In: Proceedings of the IEEE international conference on computer vision (ICCV), vol 2, pp 1150–1157
84. Lowe DG (2004) Distinctive image features from scale-invariant keypoints. Int J Comput Vis 60(2):91–110
85. Ma Y, Soatto S, Kosecka J, Sastry SS (2005) An invitation to 3-D vision: from images to geometric models. Springer, New York

86. Magnusson M, Lilienthal A, Duckett T (2007) Scan registration for autonomous mining vehicles using 3D-NDT. J Field Robot 24(10):803–827
87. Marr D (1976) Early processing of visual information. Philos Trans R Soc Lond B, Biol Sci 275(942):483–519
88. Marr D, Hildreth E (1980) Theory of edge detection. Proc R Soc Lond B, Biol Sci 207(1167):187–217
89. Matas J, Chum O, Urban M, Pajdla T (2002) Robust wide baseline stereo from maximally stable extremal regions. In: Proceedings of the British machine vision conference (BMVC), vol 1, pp 384–393
90. Meltzer J, Soatto S (2005) Shiny correspondence: multiple-view features for non-lambertian scenes. Technical report CSD2006-004, University of California
91. Mikolajczyk K (2002) Detection of local features invariant to affine transformations. PhD thesis, Institut National Polytechnique de Grenoble, France
92. Mikolajczyk K, Schmid C (2001) Indexing based on scale invariant interest points. In: Proceedings of the IEEE international conference on computer vision (ICCV), vol 1, pp 525–531
93. Mikolajczyk K, Schmid C (2002) An affine invariant interest point detector. In: Heyden A, Sparr G, Nielsen M, Johansen P (eds) ECCV 2002, part I. LNCS, vol 2350. Springer, Heidelberg, pp 128–142
94. Mikolajczyk K, Schmid C (2003) A performance evaluation of local descriptors. In: Proceedings of the IEEE computer society conference on computer vision and pattern recognition (CVPR), vol 2, pp 257–263
95. Mikolajczyk K, Schmid C (2004) Scale & affine invariant interest point detectors. Int J Comput Vis 60(1):63–86
96. Mikolajczyk K, Schmid C (2005) A performance evaluation of local descriptors. IEEE Trans Pattern Anal Mach Intell 27(10):1615–1630
97. Mikolajczyk K, Tuytelaars T, Schmid C, Zisserman A, Matas J, Schaffalitzky F, Kadir T, Van Gool L (2005) A comparison of affine region detectors. Int J Comput Vis 65(1–2):43–72
98. Miksik O, Mikolajczyk K (2012) Evaluation of local detectors and descriptors for fast feature matching. In: Proceedings of the international conference on pattern recognition (ICPR), pp 2681–2684
99. Moravec HP (1977) Towards automatic visual obstacle avoidance. In: Proceedings of the international joint conference on artificial intelligence (IJCAI), vol 2, p 584
100. Morel JM, Yu G (2009) ASIFT: a new framework for fully affine invariant image comparison. SIAM J Imaging Sci 2(2):438–469
101. Nister D, Stewenius H (2006) Scalable recognition with a vocabulary tree. In: Proceedings of the IEEE computer society conference on computer vision and pattern recognition (CVPR), vol 2, pp 2161–2168
102. Nister D, Stewenius H (2008) Linear time maximally stable extremal regions. In: Forsyth D, Torr P, Zisserman A (eds) ECCV 2008, part II. LNCS, vol 5303. Springer, Heidelberg, pp 183–196
103. Nixon MS, Aguado AS (2008) Feature extraction & image processing, 2nd edn. Academic Press, Oxford
104. Noble JA (1988) Finding corners. Image Vis Comput 6(2):121–128
105. Oliva A, Torralba A (2001) Modeling the shape of the scene: a holistic representation of the spatial envelope. Int J Comput Vis 42(3):145–175
106. Pathak K, Birk A, Vaskevicius N, Poppinga J (2010) Fast registration based on noisy planes with unknown correspondences for 3-D mapping. IEEE Trans Robot 26(3):424–441
107. Phung SL, Bouzerdoum A, Chai D (2005) Skin segmentation using color pixel classification: analysis and comparison. IEEE Trans Pattern Anal Mach Intell 27(1):148–154
108. Prewitt JMS, Mendelsohn ML (1966) The analysis of cell images. Ann NY Acad Sci 128(3):1035–1053

109. Rabbani T, Dijkman S, van den Heuvel F, Vosselman G (2007) An integrated approach for modelling and global registration of point clouds. ISPRS J Photogramm Remote Sens 61(6):355–370
110. Roberts LG (1965) Machine perception of three-dimensional solids. In: Tippett J, Berkowitz D, Clapp L, Koester C, Vanderburgh A (eds) Optical and electro-optical information processing. MIT Press, Cambridge, pp 159–197
111. Rosenberg B (1972) The analysis of convex blobs. Comput Graph Image Process 1(2):183–192
112. Rosenberg B (1974) Computing dominant points on simple shapes. Int J Man-Mach Stud 6(1):1–12
113. Rosenfeld A, Johnston E (1973) Angle detection on digital curves. IEEE Trans Comput 22(9):875–878
114. Rosten E, Drummond T (2005) Fusing points and lines for high performance tracking. In: Proceedings of the IEEE international conference on computer vision (ICCV), vol 2, pp 1508–1515
115. Rosten E, Porter R, Drummond T (2010) Faster and better: a machine learning approach to corner detection. IEEE Trans Pattern Anal Mach Intell 32(1):105–119
116. Rublee E, Rabaud V, Konolige K, Bradski G (2011) ORB: an efficient alternative to SIFT or SURF. In: Proceedings of the IEEE international conference on computer vision (ICCV), pp 2564–2571
117. Rusinkiewicz S, Levoy M (2001) Efficient variants of the ICP algorithm. In: Proceedings of the international conference on 3d digital imaging and modeling (3DIM), pp 145–152
118. Schmid C, Mohr R, Bauckhage C (2000) Evaluation of interest point detectors. Int J Comput Vis 37(2):151–172
119. Schmidt A, Kraft M, Kasinski A (2010) An evaluation of image feature detectors and descriptors for robot navigation. In: Bolc L, Tadeusiewicz R, Chmielewski LJ, Wojciechowski KW (eds) ICCVG 2010, part II. LNCS, vol 6375. Springer, Heidelberg, pp 251–259
120. Scovanner P, Ali S, Shah M (2007) A 3-dimensional SIFT descriptor and its application to action recognition. In: Proceedings of the international conference on multimedia, pp 357–360
121. Sedgewick R (1988) Algorithms, 2nd edn. Addison-Wesley, Boston
122. Seo JK, Sharp GC, Lee SW (2005) Range data registration using photometric features. In: Proceedings of the IEEE computer society conference on computer vision and pattern recognition (CVPR), vol 2, pp 1140–1145
123. Sheng Y, Shen L (1994) Orthogonal Fourier–Mellin moments for invariant pattern recognition. J Opt Soc Am A 11(6):1748–1757
124. Shi J, Tomasi T (1994) Good features to track. In: Proceedings of the IEEE computer society conference on computer vision and pattern recognition (CVPR), pp 593–600
125. Smith SM, Brady JM (1997) SUSAN—a new approach to low level image processing. Int J Comput Vis 23(1):45–78
126. Sobel IE (1970) Camera models and machine perception. PhD thesis, Stanford University, United States
127. Steder B, Grisetti G, Burgard W (2010) Robust place recognition for 3D range data based on point features. In: Proceedings of the IEEE international conference on robotics and automation (ICRA), pp 1400–1405
128. Stricker M, Swain M (1994) The capacity of color histogram indexing. In: Proceedings of the IEEE computer society conference on computer vision and pattern recognition (CVPR), pp 704–708
129. Stückler J, Behnke S (2011) Interest point detection in depth images through scale-space surface analysis. In: Proceedings of the IEEE international conference on robotics and automation (ICRA), pp 3568–3574
130. Takaya K (2007) Feature point correspondence of stereo images by monogenic phase. In: Proceedings of the IEEE Pacific Rim conference on communications, computers and signal processing, pp 272–275

131. Tamura H, Mori S, Yamawaki T (1978) Textural features corresponding to visual perception. IEEE Trans Syst Man Cybern 8(6):460–473
132. Teague MR (1980) Image analysis via the general theory of moments. J Opt Soc Am 70(8):920–930
133. Teh C-H, Chin RT (1988) On image analysis by the methods of moments. IEEE Trans Pattern Anal Mach Intell 10(4):496–513
134. Tola E, Lepetit V, Fua P (2008) A fast local descriptor for dense matching. In: Proceedings of the IEEE computer society conference on computer vision and pattern recognition (CVPR), pp 1–8
135. Tola E, Lepetit V, Fua P (2010) DAISY: an efficient dense descriptor applied to wide-baseline stereo. IEEE Trans Pattern Anal Mach Intell 32(5):815–830
136. Tuytelaars T, Mikolajczyk K (2007) Local invariant feature detectors: a survey. Found Trends Comput Graph Vis 3(3):177–280
137. Uijlings JRR, Smeulders AWM, Scha RJH (2010) Real-time visual concept classification. IEEE Trans Multimed 12(7):665–681
138. Van Gool L, Dewaele P, Oosterlinck A (1985) Texture analysis anno 1983. Comput Vis Graph Image Process 29(3):336–357
139. Von Hansen W (2006) Robust automatic marker-free registration of terrestrial scan data. Int Arch Photogramm Remote Sens Spat Inf Sci 36(part 3):105–110
140. Wang Z, Brenner C (2008) Point based registration of terrestrial laser data using intensity and geometry features. Int Arch Photogramm Remote Sens Spat Inf Sci 37(part B5):583–589
141. Wang H, Ullah MM, Kläser A, Laptev I, Schmid C (2009) Evaluation of local spatio-temporal features for action recognition. In: Proceedings of the British machine vision conference (BMVC), pp 127–138
142. Wang Z, Fan B, Wu F (2011) Local intensity order pattern for feature description. In: Proceedings of the IEEE international conference on computer vision (ICCV), pp 603–610
143. Weinmann M, Jutzi B (2008) Fully automatic image-based registration of unorganized TLS data. Int Arch Photogramm Remote Sens Spat Inf Sci 38(part 5):55–60
144. Weinmann Ma, Weinmann Mi, Hinz S, Jutzi B (2011) Fast and automatic image-based registration of TLS data. ISPRS J Photogramm Remote Sens 66(6):S62–S70
145. Wertheimer M (1923) Laws of organization in perceptual forms. Psycologische Forschung 4:301–350
146. Westheimer G (1999) Gestalt theory reconfigured: Max Wertheimer's anticipation of recent developments in visual neuroscience. Perception 28(1):5–15
147. Witkin AP (1983) Scale-space filtering. In: Proceedings of the international joint conference on artificial intelligence (IJCAI), pp 1019–1022
148. Wu J, Rehg JM (2011) CENTRIST: a visual descriptor for scene categorization. IEEE Trans Pattern Anal Mach Intell 33(8):1489–1501
149. Yang M-H, Kriegman DG, Ahuja N (2002) Detecting faces in images: a survey. IEEE Trans Pattern Anal Mach Intell 24(1):34–58
150. Zhang D, Lu G (2002) Generic Fourier descriptor for shape-based image retrieval. In: Proceedings of the 2002 IEEE international conference on multimedia and expo (ICME), vol 1, pp 425–428
151. Zhang D, Lu G (2004) Review of shape representation and description techniques. Pattern Recognit 37(1):1–19
152. Zhang J, Tan T (2002) Brief review of invariant texture analysis methods. Pattern Recognit 35(3):735–747
153. Zhao G, Chen L, Chen G, Yuan J (2010) KPB-SIFT: a compact local feature descriptor. In: Del Bimbo A, Chang S-F, Smeulders AWM (eds) Multimedia 2010. ACM, New York, pp 1175–1178
154. Zheng Z, Wang H, Teoh EK (1999) Analysis of gray level corner detection. Pattern Recognit Lett 20(2):149–162

Chapter 2
Where Next in Object Recognition and how much Supervision Do We Need?

Sandra Ebert and Bernt Schiele

Abstract Object class recognition is an active topic in computer vision still presenting many challenges. In most approaches, this task is addressed by supervised learning algorithms that need a large quantity of labels to perform well. This leads either to small datasets (<10,000 images) that capture only a subset of the real-world class distribution (but with a controlled and verified labeling procedure), or to large datasets that are more representative but also add more label noise. Therefore, semi-supervised learning has been established as a promising direction to address object recognition. It requires only few labels while simultaneously making use of the vast amount of images available today. In this chapter, we outline the main challenges of semi-supervised object recognition, we review existing approaches, and we emphasize open issues that should be addressed next to advance this research topic.

2.1 Introduction

Object recognition is one of the central topics in computer vision and an integral part of many computer vision tasks. To mention only a few, image classification (Fig. 2.1a) is one of the more basic tasks that includes object recognition to classify an image, for example, *duck*. Content-based image retrieval (CBIR, Fig. 2.1b) contains object recognition to search systematically for images that contain these objects. Object detection (Fig. 2.1c) must in addition specify the actual position of the recognized object in the image (marked as a bounding box), thus a clear separation between foreground and background is essential. Tracking (Fig. 2.1d) is based on object detection and tries to track the localized object across a sequence of frames. Finally, scene understanding (Fig. 2.1e) aims to capture the whole scene including all interactions among objects and the environment, for example, to

S. Ebert (✉) · B. Schiele
Max Planck Institute for Informatics, Saarbrücken, Germany
e-mail: ebert@mpi-inf.mpg.de

B. Schiele
e-mail: schiele@mpi-inf.mpg.de

G.M. Farinella et al. (eds.), *Advanced Topics in Computer Vision*,
Advances in Computer Vision and Pattern Recognition,
DOI 10.1007/978-1-4471-5520-1_2,

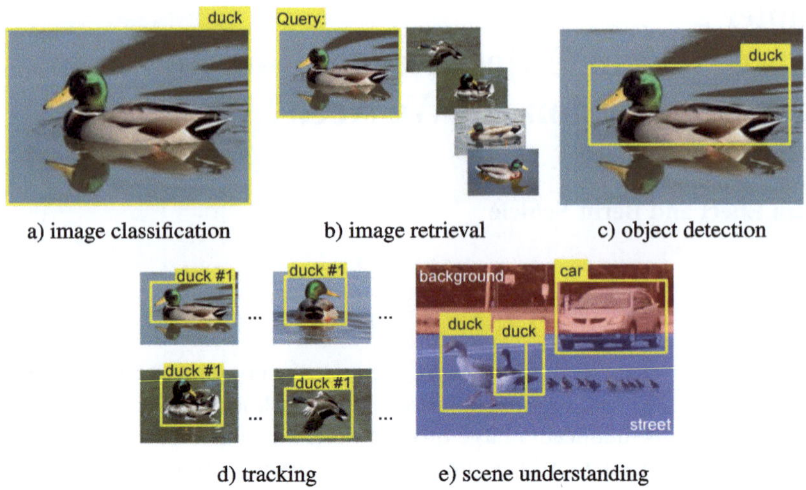

Fig. 2.1 Computer vision applications with object recognition as an integral part

warn the car driver before an accident happens with the ducks. This list of computer vision tasks could be continued arbitrarily. But although object recognition is a crucial part it is surprising that even image classification, which only aims to provide the image label, does not provide satisfactory results on more challenging datasets.

In contrast, humans can quickly and accurately recognize objects in images or video sequences. They can categorize them into thousands of categories [10]. Beyond that they can track objects in videos and they are able to interpret the entire scene and to infer subsequent events. Of course, human perception, recognition, and inference also have their limits but they might serve as a good starting point to improve upon. Therefore it is not surprising that computer vision, in particular the machine learning part of it, is mainly driven by cognitive science—the science of understanding the learning and thinking of humans. But as controversial theories in cognition are, as diverse are the approaches in computer vision and machine learning.

One of these long-lasting debates in cognition focuses on the question whether a human learns exemplar-based or concept-driven. The exemplar-based model [67, 74, 129] assumes that humans store a list of exemplars for each category. A category decision will be made based on a similarity to existing exemplars. One of the most prominent representative in machine learning is the k nearest neighbor classifier visualized in Fig. 2.2a. This classifier looks for the nearest labeled neighbor in the training set marked as red and blue data point and uses the label of this training sample for classification. In contrast, concept-driven learning assumes that people abstract to a model or a prototype that is used for classifying objects [68, 69, 84]. This paradigm can be found in many algorithms that learn a model of a category and do any kind of generalization such as SVM that learns a decision boundary (Fig. 2.2b). More recently, there is a tendency towards the theory that humans use

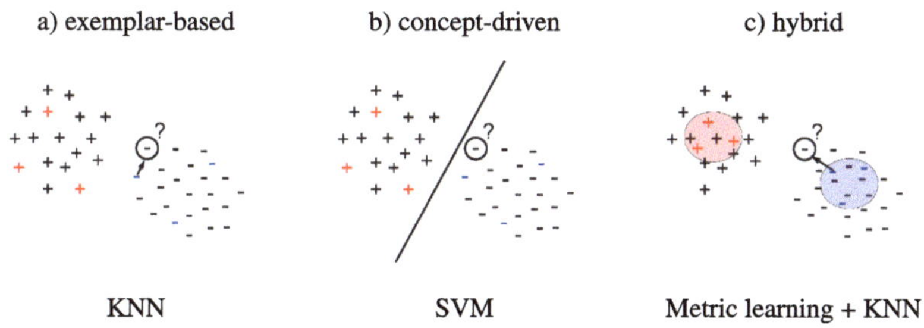

Fig. 2.2 Illustration of several learning principles that are used to classify the marked unlabeled data point: (**a**) exemplar-based learning, e.g., KNN classification, (**b**) concept-driven, e.g., SVM, or (**c**) hybrid approach, e.g., that groups exemplars around a general concept by transformation with metric learning and than applying KNN. *Blue* and *red points* are the labels of two different classes, and *black points* are the unlabeled data

either multiple learning systems in parallel [4, 35] or a hybrid version that groups exemplars around a general concept. This approach can be found for example in a combination of metric learning and KNN that first maps the exemplars to a more discriminative description, that is, examples of the same class are closer together visualized as red and blue area in Fig. 2.2c, and then applies KNN.

Another equally controversial but much older debate revolves around the question how we gain the insight that forms the base of our decisions. This leads to one of the most fundamental questions in machine vision: whether and how much supervision do we need? On one hand, a human learns provable faster with supervised feedback [3]. Therefore, it is not surprising that state-of-the-art performance is achieved by supervised algorithms. However, this success has to be put into perspective as the dataset construction itself contains an enormous amount of supervision. Each method is only as good as the underlying training data. If the learner sees only the side view of a car during training, then the resulting classifier will fail on cars shown in front views or from above. This aspect is often neglected in the subsequent evaluation and leads to datasets that are either small and strongly biased [82, 113] or large and error-prone [124]. On the other hand, it is also clear that many human decisions are driven to some extent by intuition, that is, more or less unsupervised, particularly in unfamiliar or risky situations [51]. But although unsupervised learning is an important research area [103, 123], for example, for object discovery or novelty detection, a minimum level of supervision is required at the end to judge the quality and to gain insight. Therefore, semi-supervised learning (SSL) has to be turn out the paradigm that combines the advantages of supervised learning and unsupervised learning by using both labels as well as the underlying structure or geometry in the data.

In the following, we discuss the large potential of semi-supervised learning in Sect. 2.2. After that, we outline in Sect. 2.3 the main challenges of object recognition with respect to semi-supervised learning and how it is already addressed in previous work. Finally, we point out open issues and we give recommendations how we could tackle those in Sect. 2.4.

2.2 How much Supervision Do We Need?

Mind without structure is empty and
perception without labels is blind.
Translated from [52]

Imitation, intuition, and experience play an important role in human decision making [23] especially under risk [51]. But only a small fraction of this accumulated knowledge is labeled. The discussion around the question on *whether and how much supervision a human need* can be traced back at least to the philosophical theories of the 17th century. [52] was the first who argued that labels (knowledge) and structure (perception or observation) are closely intertwined, summarized in one of his key phrases (see beginning of this section). His theory fundamentally changed and influenced our way of thinking and acting. After 200 years of research, some of his basic assumptions and argumentations might be obsolete. But the underlying theory and the main argumentation itself is still up-to-date. Indeed this theory seems to be obvious because in addition to the things we learn supervised at home or in school, there are many other things that we learn without any teacher. For example, how we move, how we grab a glass, how we use language before we start school, how we make fast decisions and so on. Of course, many of those things are learned feedback-driven in the sense that an action is completed successfully or not. However, there are still many actions or feelings that we cannot explain let alone derive solely based on knowledge. In that sense, semi-supervised learning seems a natural choice to address object recognition as it allows us to improve state-of-the-art supervised learning approaches with more data without the need of correct annotations.

But in defense of the more skeptical people, one has to state that this large unlabeled part of semi-supervised learning is almost impossible to grasp. Actually, it is even not clear whether humans will ever be capable to understand it in their completeness. For the simple reason that in the course of evolution, we only had to understand and infer simple causalities, for example, *I take the glass of water because I am thirsty*. But we were never forced to understand the entire chain of actions and decisions that leads to this final action, for example, *grasping the glass and drinking*. In fact, every physical movement is a highly individual action that is based on imitation and experience. Although this might lead to sub-optimal movements or actions, the acquired knowledge is quite sufficient to survive in everyday life—even if we notice some limitation and ask for more supervision, for example, to get rid of pain induced by suboptimal movements or to run faster in a marathon. Most advices only give a direction and do not describe a muscle-induced action in its full complexity.

One might argue that these examples are indeed more physical. But even if we limit these considerations to our decisions that could be purely driven by our knowledge, we still observe many decision based on the so called *gut feeling* or other feelings that we cannot explain. Why do we know that someone is annoyed or sad or impatient although this person uses exactly the same words as he does every day? Why is it impossible to imagine in advance how we will react or feel after a certain event, for example if we loose a competition. Even more complicated is to infer how other people will react on an event. The reason is simple and devastating at the same

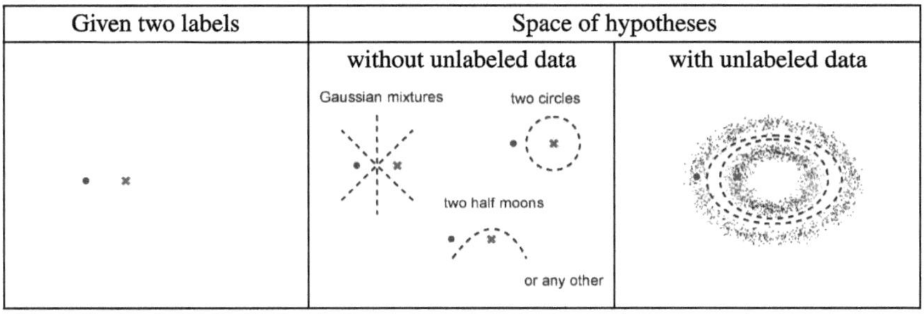

Fig. 2.3 Unlabeled data reduce the space of hypotheses if there are only few labels

time: We are overwhelmed by millions of sensations per minute of which only a small fraction of impressions are processed consciously and the rest subconsciously and this is only a tiny fraction of what the entire world perceives. Thus, to answer at least the questions with respect to our own, we have to assimilate all sensations. With this insight, it becomes clear why research in semi-supervised learning (SSL) is still not where it should be. To bring a machine into the closer range of human thinking, we have to tap into the vast amount of unlabeled data meaning a ratio of 1 labeled to 1 million unlabeled data points and not the common ratio of today's task descriptions of 1 labeled to 100 unlabeled observations.

Besides these more philosophical considerations, there are also many practical reasons for SSL. One obvious argument is the reduction of the hypotheses space [5] in particular if there are only few labels. Figure 2.3 shows one point per class in the leftmost image. Without any additional information, the space of possible hypotheses is less goal-oriented (Fig. 2.3 middle) while unlabeled data reduces this space as shown in the right visualization. This speed up of concept learning through relevant prior knowledge has been also verified in cognition by [70, 78]. A mechanical engineer will be proceed faster and more goal-oriented when assembling a machine in comparison to a layman because he already knows how to use the tools and where the single items should be approximately placed.

Another reason for SSL is the low amount of supervision. In particular for tasks such as semantic image labeling or image understanding, where we need pixel-wise annotations, this advantage becomes increasingly important. But also for tasks such as object detection or recognition, we observe a substantial improvement the more data are used. The most image descriptions are high dimensional resulting in a strong demand for data. But the labeling process is not always reliable—for example, when using Mechanical Turk [124]. Finally, some applications need a continuous update, for example, for separating spam emails from valid emails.

2.3 Challenges of Object Recognition

Semi-supervised learning (SSL) seems a reasonable approach to tackle object recognition as it makes use of both supervision in terms of labels and structure (geom-

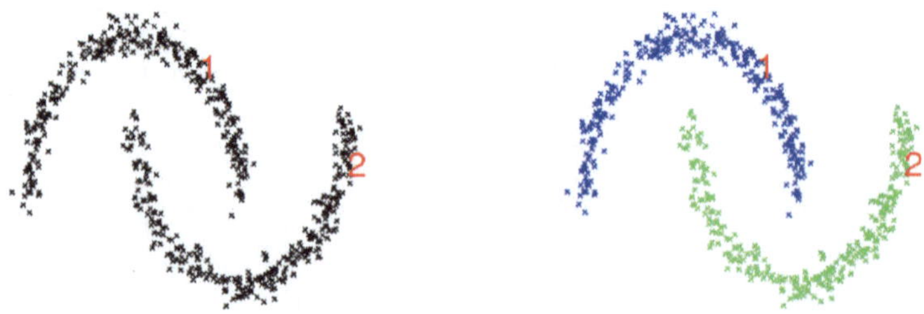

Fig. 2.4 Two half moons dataset with exactly one label per class (marked by a *red number*): before classification (*left*) and after classification (*right*) with 100 % accuracy

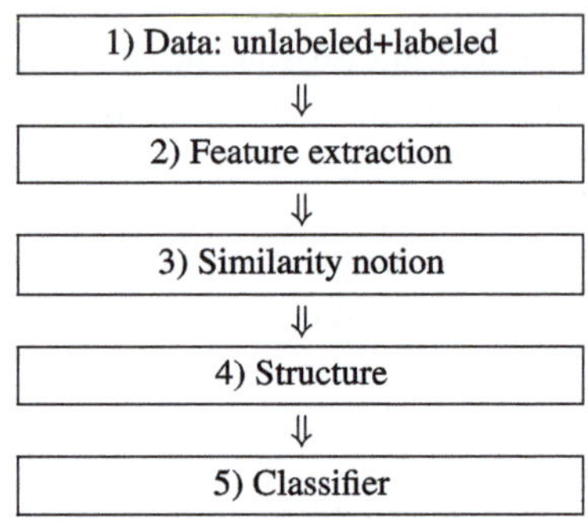

Fig. 2.5 Workflow of semi-supervised learning algorithms in vision

etry) that comes with the unlabeled and labeled data. Therefore, it is obvious that both parts strongly influence the performance of the classifier. In the following, we discuss the challenges of both components separately starting with the structural problems in Sect. 2.3.1 followed by the difficulties in getting representative labels in Sect. 2.3.2.

2.3.1 Structural Problems

The apparently most promising but also much more complicated direction for SSL is the improvement of the structure itself. Imagine a dataset like the *two half moons* shown in Fig. 2.4 with two labels marked with red numbers. It does not matter which label is used for classification. The used SSL algorithm [132] achieves always a classification performance of 100 %. Although this is an artificial example it still reflects our common sense assumption that there is exactly one concept for each class and each instance of this class is organized around this central prototype [19, 75]. But often, there is a large gap between our base assumption and today's computer vision task descriptions and solutions.

Figure 2.5 visualizes the general workflow of object recognition with SSL algorithms: Based on our dataset that consists of labeled and unlabeled data, we compute image descriptors for each image. After that we compute the similarities between each image pair with some measure. The resulting structure is used by SSL algo-

Fig. 2.6 Examples for (**a**) large intra-class variability for the base category *bird* (*top row*) and (**b**) for the subcategory *puffin* of the category *bird*, and (**c**) small inter-class differences (*bottom row*)

rithms, for example, for EM clustering [73], as a regularization term to improve SVM [50, 98], or to build a graph structure and to find a solution with Mincut [12] or by label spreading [132]. However, each of these classifiers can be only as good as the extracted geometry of the data and this strongly depends on three main sources: (1) data, (2) image description, and (3) similarity notion. Furthermore, the quality of each single source is dependent on both the approaches that are used for these steps but also on the quality of the previous steps. This means, information loss for example through an incomplete dataset will be propagated to the classifier and cannot be compensated by one of the intermediate steps. Similar argument holds for image description: if one aspect is neglected, for example, color, the best similarity measure will be not able to properly distinguish between *green apples* and *red tomatoes*. In the following, we discuss each of these three components separately.

2.3.1.1 Data

Most common datasets for image classification like Caltech 101 [38], PASCAL VOC [36], Animals with Attribute [59], LabelMe [114], animals on the web [9], or ImageNet [27], are generated for supervised classification. They provide full label information that might be error-prone in particular when crowd-source services like Mechanical Turk are used [124]. They contain a large intra-class variety within a base category such as *bird* (Fig. 2.6a) but also within one specific subcategory of this class such as *puffin* (Fig. 2.6b). Without a good description and understanding of the concept, it will be difficult to connect those examples and group them together to one class. Small inter-class variation is the other end of the scale (Fig. 2.6c) leading

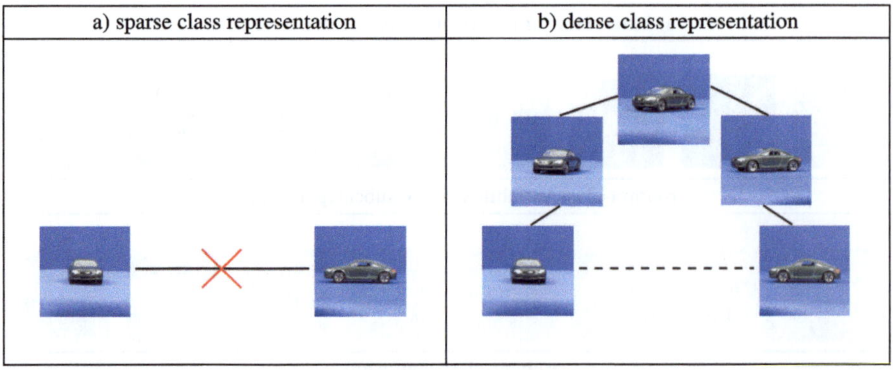

Fig. 2.7 Example of (**a**) a sparse class description that makes it difficult to find a connection between both images and of (**b**) a dense class representation that makes it possible to find a way from the front view to the side view of a car over several viewpoints

to many overlapping and confusing areas that are even for humans difficult to learn. Finally and most unfortunately, they contain usually a limited amount of images because labeling is expensive.

An ideal dataset for SSL should be *dense* enough that means each class should be densely sampled that allows to find compact and well separated clusters. In this dataset, we might be able to connect the front view of a car and a side view of car as in Fig. 2.7. But on the other hand, this dataset should be also *sparse* enough to avoid overheads due to space and time complexity. Usually, SSL approaches such as graph-based algorithms come with a quadratic time complexity in the number of images. Because of this complexity, the *the-more-data-the-better* strategy can usually not be applied.

A second reason why *the-more-data-the-better* strategy does not work well in practice is that only a small fraction of the data, for example, added from the internet, is helpful for our classification task. Furthermore, these data sources often have a certain bias in terms of image type. One example is the data source bias. Flickr, that is the base for PASCAL VOC [36], contains mostly holiday pictures. Therefore *person* is with 31.2 % the most common object in this dataset. The second most frequent object is *chair* with 8.5 %. Another bias can be also seen in Fig. 2.8 (top row) that shows the first results of approx. 5.8 million results for the query *car* in Flickr. In contrast, Google shows more professional images that are often generated for marketing purpose as you can see in Fig. 2.8 (bottom row).

Another problem comes with the capture bias. This is usually a result from human properties such as body height. Most images are taken from an adult person in a standing position thus from an average height of 1.6–1.8 meters (Fig. 2.9a). A simple change to a child position, that is, <1 meter, leads to a different viewpoint and thus perception, for example, some things appear larger (buildings) or more frightening (animals). Furthermore, most people are right handed resulting, for example, in many images of mugs with the handle on the right side. Some objects have a quite different appearance (Fig. 2.9b), e.g., salmon considered as an animal vs. food, and

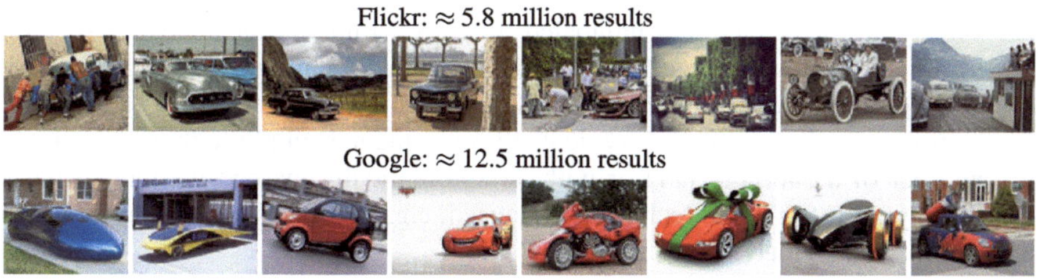

Fig. 2.8 Data source bias: First results for the query *car* with (**a**) Flickr that contains more holiday pictures of cars (*top row*), and (**b**) Google images with focus on racing cars (*bottom row*)

Fig. 2.9 Dataset bias due to (**a**) the sighting angle, (**b**) the semantic of an object, or (**c**) because of historical trends

other categories might change their appearance over time (Fig. 2.9c). Of course, it seems likely that massive amounts of data also contain relevant images but to find these images we have to process over millions of images for this single class.

Related Work Many SSL algorithms in particular graph-based algorithms come at least with a runtime of $O(n^2m)$ with n the number of data and m the number of feature dimensions. This runtime is needed to compute all similarities between image pairs and to construct the graph. Thus, the applied algorithm depends strongly on the number of data and the dimensionality of the features but also on the approach itself. For example, [132] provide both a closed form solution that would need the inversion of a $n \times n$ matrix and an iterative procedure that is faster and often avoids over-fitting. In general, there are two different strategies to reduce the runtime: (i) a reduction of the data space ($\ll n$) to a representative subset of unlabeled data or (ii) an approximation either of the similarity matrix or the eigenvectors.

(i) *Data reduction.* The most common approach to data reduction is clustering to find representative unlabeled data either by hierarchical clustering [64], or by k-means clustering [65, 100]. [26] propose a Greedy approach that starts with the labels only and successively add unlabeled samples farthest away from the current set of labeled and unlabeled data. [37] find similar nodes by spectral decomposition and merge these together. Another technique is to treat this task as an optimization problem that considers each point in a data set as a convex combination of a set of archetypical or prototypical examples either with a fixed number of archetypes [21] or with an automatically learned number of these prototypes [85]. These techniques are used, e.g., to find typical poses [8], or to summarize a video sequence [34].

(ii) *Approximation.* In contrast, Nystroem approximation is employed to approximate the entire kernel matrix. This approximation is estimated also on a subset of data that are retrieved either by random sampling [131] or with k-means clustering [130]. This approximation can then be used to find a segmentation [42], for similarity search [122], or face recognition [109]. To speed up the algorithms, [40] propose an approximation of the eigenvectors of the normalized graph Laplacian. [115] solve the dual optimization problem by introducing a sparsity constraint, and [54] use stochastic gradient descent to solve the TSVM.

In [33], we focus mainly on the question if more unlabeled data have really a positive impact on the classification performance. In particular, we challenge the *the-more-data-the-better* strategy that is common sense in the computer vision community but also comes with an increase in runtime and space. This question is difficult to answer as adding unlabeled data leads to a different field of research due to the dataset bias [82, 113] and the data source bias (Sect. 2.3.1). Therefore, we focus on ILSVRC 2010 with 1 million images and reduce this large amount of data to a representative subset of unlabeled data showing that this representative subset leads to a better graph structure than using all unlabeled data. We compare our approach to [26] and [65] that can be considered state-of-the-art methods to reduce the graph size. But in comparison to previous work, we analyze also the effect of more unlabeled data. Additionally, our work is the first attempt to process more than one million data points that is far more than 30,000 data points used in previous work [26, 65, 130]. But this can be only seen as good starting point to improve on.

2.3.1.2 Image Description

Suppose we have a dataset that captures the broad variety of each class, for example, different viewpoints, several contexts and so on. Thus, there is a chance to build a compact cluster structure similar to Fig. 2.10. Then it does not automatically mean that we are also able to exhaust this potential. Today's image descriptors are far away from capturing all these different aspects that humans can easily recognize. In the following, we list briefly most of the common problems. See also [43] for a short overview of today's problem in computer vision.

Intra-class/Inter-class Variability As it mentioned before, many classes come with a large intra-class variance in their appearance and their surrounding environment. The class *bird* is one of the extreme cases where even the height varies from few centimeters like the hummingbird to almost 2 meters like the flightless ostrich

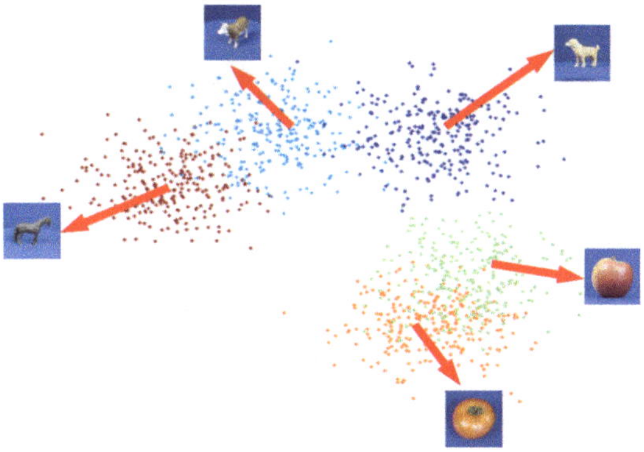

Fig. 2.10 Structure with dense representation but still overlapping regions

(Fig. 2.6a) not to mention the large variation in shape and in color. Of course, a limitation to one species (Fig. 2.6b) might constrain the general appearance of an object but not the number of different poses or the context around this object. On the other side, there are classes that look similar to each other in particular in some poses, for example, a bird and an airplane in the sky (Fig. 2.6c), or when two classes jointly appear in an image, for example, a cat in the arms of a person or a sticker from an animal at a mug.

Background Clutter Some images are dominated by their background as can be seen in Fig. 2.11 where it is almost impossible to see some objects because of the trees. Often, these images are confused because of their similar-looking background. There are images with an overloaded background structure that are similar to many other images in a dataset. Finally, some objects are difficult to distinguish from the background because they are transparent (like glass) [44], or filigree like a bicycle or a chair.

Illumination Changes Another problem is the change in illumination depending on the time of the day and the season (Fig. 2.12). For example, a lake is susceptible to lighting conditions due to its surface and volume properties resulting in a wide color spectrum. But also many other objects look different during the day and at night, for example, trees are green during the day and dark at night.

Truncation and Partial Occlusion Partial occlusions are an omnipresent property. Herd animals like sheep or gazelles occur frequently in groups. As already mentioned before, some objects can be covered to a large extend by a person using that object like a bicycle or chair. And other object classes are very large so that they are only partly captured or truncated like a cathedral (Fig. 2.13).

Shape Variation Some categories have a large variation in shape and appearance, for example, *chair* (Fig. 2.14), *table*, or *lamp*. These categories can be often only described by their function such as *something to sit on*.

Mimesis and Other Another set of problems comes with the evolutionary adaption of some species to their background so that they are difficult to recognize by

Fig. 2.11 Examples with a dominating background that is shared among different classes (*top row*), and examples with overloaded background and object that are transparent or filigree so that background is always a part of the object (*bottom row*)

Fig. 2.12 Examples of a lake with different illuminations depending on the time of day and the season

Fig. 2.13 Examples of truncations and partial occlusions

Fig. 2.14 Examples of the large variety in shape for the class *chair*

other animals, for example, the chameleon or the flounder. Other animals such as zebras are indeed visible but it is difficult to point out an individual animal due to their pattern structure (Fig. 2.15).

Basically, the ideal image descriptor should emerge with some prior knowledge about what and where the object is located in the image, how to separate the background from the main object, which color is trustable or rather how to adjust this color, and what are the possible and feasible poses of an object. Furthermore, this descriptor should have a general idea of the shape and texture of an object to infer which part is occluded or truncated. While a human focuses led on the main object,

Fig. 2.15 Examples of objects that are difficult to distinguish from their background or to identify the object-specific shape

Fig. 2.16 Examples of images that are difficult to understand without color information

many of today's image descriptors such as dense SIFT analyze every single blade of grass or every single leaf from a tree leading to an overcrowded image description that often considers only one aspect in the image like color or gradients. Of course a good similarity metric can handle this high dimensionality. But an information loss in this partial extraction propagates to the classifier. Figure 2.16 shows some examples with and without color information. Even for a human it is hard to follow a soccer game or to distinguish between eatable and poisonous mushrooms by just omitting color, not to mention information such as texture or shape.

Related Work As mentioned before, most image descriptors lack still expressiveness. They consider only one aspect when describing an image, for example, texture, shape or color. This leads inherently to an enormous information loss. Therefore, a combination of several features are essential, for example image-based features with geometry [14, 83, 125], shape with texture [20], several local appearances [94], local and global appearances [61], HOG with texture [121], multiple kernels for global as well as local features learned with an SVM [46, 105, 117], with boosting [28], or with conditional random fields [96].

In SSL, the combination of multiple graphs offers the possibility to capture different aspects in the data. For graph-based methods, there are few works that combine graph structures similar to multiple kernel learning (MKL) [2, 116]. In [55], they learn weights for combining graph Laplacian within an EM framework. [22] propose a method to find one graph from a set of graphs that best fits the data. [112] formulate this combination as a multi-modality learning problem that fuses different modalities either linearly or sequentially. [6] use domain knowledge to extract three different sources, that is, time, color and face features, that are combined with different hyperparameters. Finally, [47] and [110] combine a similarity and a dissimilarity graph and apply label propagation on this mixed graph structure. Most of these previous works are developed for applications in bioinformatics. But more importantly, they combine often only graphs based on different parameters, that is, a different number of neighbors k or different weight functions.

In [30], we show the strong influence on the graph quality when combining different image descriptors leading to a completely different and more powerful graph structure. Additionally, we use the SVM output to construct a new graph. But in comparison to [86] who use the SVM output to delete and insert existing edges, we build a complete new graph based on these decision values and combine this graph with our original graph. This leads to a richer and better connected graph structure than the graph structure in [86].

2.3.1.3 Similarity Notion

The final crucial part of the structure extraction is the similarity measure. Most frequently used is the Euclidean distance with a Gaussian kernel weighting. This is usually a good choice for feature vectors of low dimensionality ($\ll$100) containing only little noise. But as mentioned before, most image descriptors aggregate many not preprocessed information that leads to a high-dimensional vector ($>$10,000) from which only a small fraction of dimensions are relevant for a object class. In particular Euclidean distance is known to be sensitive to noise that becomes more prominent the more dimensions are used. One phenomenon that we observe with Euclidean distance is that some images are similar to almost all other images. The resulting structure (such as shown in Fig. 2.17) harms almost every classification algorithm because there is no clear separation between different classes [119].

Another problem comes with the missing weighting of the single dimensions in the feature space, that is, all dimensions are equally considered. But usually only a small fraction of this high dimensional feature vector is relevant for each class. Finally, we often consider image pairs instead of groups of images. This is easy to implement but seems suboptimal for good generalization. A human who has never seen a zebra before and only gets the first image from Fig. 2.18 will certainly have problems to build a general concept or model of a zebra because there is no information about the shape, the size, or the environment around this animal. Without these higher order relations extracted from a group of images, it might be difficult to distinguish the first image from the sofa shown in the last image.

Related Work Metric learning is a promising direction to tackle this problem. These methods find a better data representation such that examples within a class are close together and examples from different classes are far away, that is, small intra-class distances and large inter-class distances. Metric learning approaches can be split into unsupervised, supervised, and semi-supervised methods that are further divided into global and local learning methods. See also [126] and [29] who provide a more detailed exploration of metric learning methods.

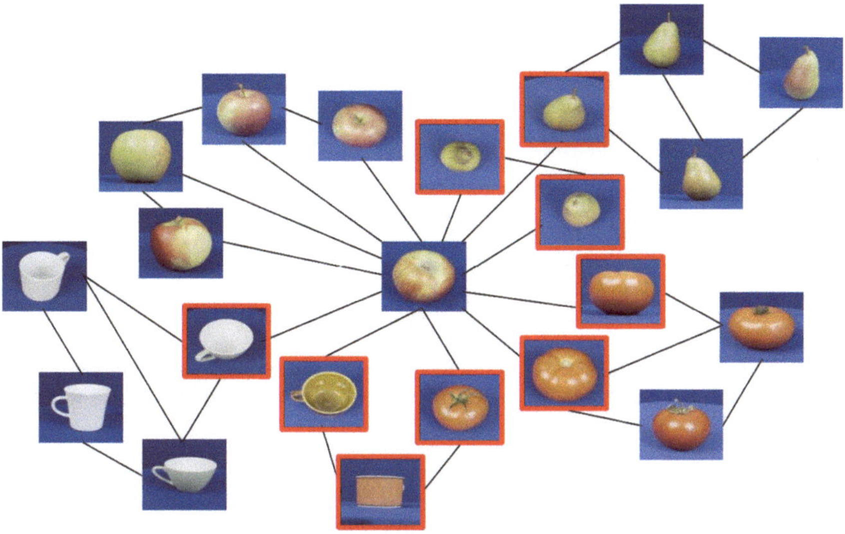

Fig. 2.17 Problem of Euclidean distance in a high dimensional space: The image in the *middle* is similar to many other images. *Red boxes* indicate false neighbors

Fig. 2.18 Pairwise image similarities might be problematic due to the missing generalization. From the *first image* it is not clear how to generalize so that this image do not get confused with the sofa in the *last image*

In [31] and [29], we analyze several supervised and unsupervised metric learning approaches with respect to a better graph construction. Particularly, we apply PCA [79] and LDA [41] to reduce the dimensionality of our feature representation and compare both methods. Furthermore, we also analyze ITML [24]. Instead of reducing the number of dimensions, it learns a weighting of the feature dimensions. The advantage of ITML is that it can be transformed into a kernelized optimization problem. Thus, the runtime depends only on the number of labels that is usually smaller than the number of dimensions ($n \ll d$). Additionally, this approach shows state-of-the-art performance on Caltech 101 [58]. Finally, we integrate ITML in a semi-supervised metric learning scheme that leads to an increased performance.

2.3.2 Labeling Issues

The second import issue besides the structure is the label information. As mentioned before, supervision causes no problems if the structure itself perfectly separates

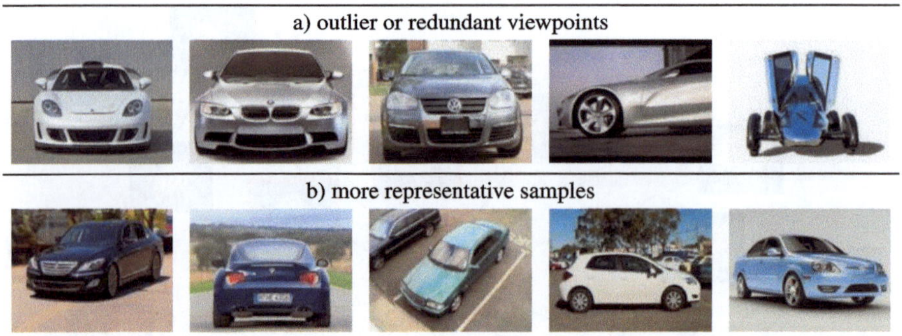

Fig. 2.19 SSL is strongly dependent on the representativeness of the small training set: (**a**) less representative samples for the entire class *car* vs. (**b**) more representative samples in terms of viewpoints

the classes. But usually this is not the case. Therefore, the label information plays an important role in particular for semi-supervised learning where we have only few labels per class. While for supervised learning more data is labeled, in SSL we have to deal with a ratio of 1 %–5 % labeled to 95 %–99 % unlabeled data. Thus, there is a need for high quality labels that are representative for the class and allow a better generalization. Additionally, we have to ensure that there is at least one label for each mixture (e.g., different viewpoints or appearances) of one class otherwise it might be difficult to classify unseen viewpoints. Figure 2.19 shows five less representative samples for the class *car* in the first row, assuming that the test set contains also the back or the side view of a car. In contrast, the second row shows more representative samples of this class so that the main properties of this object will be apparent such as the shape and the surface.

Coming back to Fig. 2.17 if the image in the middle with these many false neighbors is labeled, then most of the neighboring images will be false classified (marked with a red bounding box) because of the strong impact on the direct neighbors. Another problem occurs when a class is split into separate clusters, for example, front view of a car and side view of a car, and there are only labels for one of these sub-clusters. The other sub-clusters cannot be classified correctly anymore. Ideally, we have labels that are representative or prototypical for a class that means they lie in a dense region and consider each aspect or viewpoint of a class.

Related Work Active learning is a well known strategy to reduce the amount of supervision to a small but representative subset and to improve the quality of the learner at the same time. This is also verified by cognitive science as [3] shows that a higher accuracy is achieved with feedback during the learning in comparison to the scenario where supervision is only provided at the beginning. In machine learning, active learning leads in most cases to better performance. [1] show that some NP-complete learning problems become polynomial in computation time. On the other side, active learning in combination with some classification algorithms might lead to poor performance, for example, SVM with few examples at the beginning [120]. Model selection is critical for these algorithms [108].

Most popular is pool-based active learning. These methods consider all unlabeled data as a pool from which samples are drawn to be labeled. In general, pool-based methods can be divided by their sampling strategy into three different types. Exploitation-driven methods [97, 111] focus mainly on uncertain regions during the learning process. In contrast, methods based on exploration sampling [13, 72] estimate the overall distribution of the entire data space and query samples that represent and cover this space. Finally, there are also strategies that combine both exploration and exploitation to get samples that are uncertain but also diverse. We refer also to [99] and [29] who provide a general overview on different active learning strategies.

In [32], we propose a novel sampling criteria for exploration that shows significant better performance in comparison to previous exploration criteria. Furthermore, we address active learning by proposing a reinforced active learning formulation (RALF) that considers the entire active learning sequence as a process. Our approach can deal with multiple criteria, is able to have time-varying trade-offs between exploration and exploitation, and is fast and efficient due to a compact parameterization of the model without dataset-specific tuning. In comparison to [7] who also use a reinforcement procedure, our model comes with fewer parameters, more flexibility in terms of sampling criteria, and provides always a linear combination of exploration and exploitation instead of switching between criteria. For the linear combination, we extend the work proposed by [15] to a time-varying combination that leads to a better adaptivity to dataset requirements. Finally, we show in [33] that a potentially large improvement is possible when applying metric learning with more representative labels. To this end, we combine active learning with metric learning and show improvements of more than 10 % over our previous publication [31] and more than 20 % improvement as compared to our first publication [30].

2.4 Future Perspective

In this last section, we will mention open issues and how we could tackle those in Sect. 2.4.1. These suggestions are closely intertwined to cognitive science for the simple reason that particularly object recognition raises automatically the question how humans form class concepts. Thus, it is not surprising that this close relationship has been studied earlier, for example, in the *Roadmap of Cognitive Vision* [118]. Of course, the human object recognition should be only seen as a good starting point to improve on. Therefore, we finally discuss in Sect. 2.4.2 also the human weaknesses in perception, learning and inference and how we might overcome those with machine learning and computer vision.

2.4.1 What Can We Learn from Human Object Recognition?

Following the general structure of this chapter, we discuss open issues of each of the components of SSL separately, that is, (1) data, (2) image description, (3) sim-

Fig. 2.20 Visualization of an incomplete object class description that makes it difficult to find relation between these images

Fig. 2.21 Visualization of a more complete object class description extracted from a video sequence

ilarity notion and (4) supervision. Additionally, we also challenge the use of label propagation in the last subsection called (5) exemplar-based vs. concept-driven learning.

2.4.1.1 Data

[133] stated in their position paper about graph-based SSL that one of the limitations of these algorithms results from the common sense assumption that each class can be projected to a single manifold. Thus, they suggest to model classes by a mixture of multiple manifolds. This observation is particularly in computer vision not novel. Also [92] distinguish between visual classes and object classes as there are classes such as *chair* that cannot be modeled with one mixture. Even if this is an important aspect, an at least equally important problem is the incompleteness of today's datasets in terms of viewpoints and variations for a class to fully leverage the power of SSL algorithms. In [29], we assume that most classes can be described with one concept and all exemplars of these classes are grouped around this concept [19]. But often we have to deal with class descriptions as shown in Fig. 2.20 for the class *kingfisher*. Even for a human who have never seen this class before might have problems to merge these images in one compact mixture because color, shape, and appearance are quite different. But an image sequence might provide a path among those images as visualized in Fig. 2.21 and helps to extract an object models similar to the work of [90] shown for car tracking.

Fig. 2.22 Visualization of feasible and unfeasible poses and scenes for the class *anteater* that will be more obvious with informations such as 1.5–1.8 m long

In [33], we analyze the problem of incomplete datasets by looking at existing datasets such as ImageNet with more than one million images and their behavior and performance when adding more unlabeled data. But this should be only considered as a first attempt towards a smooth manifold structure. As a next step, we have to get away from this controlled setting because we still depend on the quality of the datasets given by the limited (although larger) amount of images and the quality of labels. Instead, we have to tap into other sources. In general, there are three possibilities: (1) combining several datasets, (2) adding synthetic data or (3) browsing the internet.

Merging different datasets is problematic because most of the available datasets have an inherent bias attached to the dataset [82, 113]. Although there are works that try to undo the damage of dataset by estimating the bias for each dataset [56], combining itself seems an unsatisfactory strategy because each dataset has different classes and the amount of images is also strongly limited. In contrast, adding synthetic data is a more promising direction but is still in a early stage of development. There are only few works that either generate new training images [63, 81], or add synthetic data points (so-called *ghost points*) in the distance space itself [18, 127]. The former approach is currently bound to certain classes such as *people* for where 3D shape models exist that ensure the generation of feasible poses and shape variations. The latter one is hard to control because the semantic meaning of these *ghost points* is not clear and it can lead to a blending of different classes. To expand approaches suggested by [81] to other classes, we have to integrate more physical constraints to guarantee feasible poses and appearances of the object. Figure 2.22 shows some images of the class *anteater*. A human does not necessarily have to know and to observe this animal to decide if a pose is likely or not. Information such as size of 1.5–1.8 m or weight of $\approx$60 kg might be already a good advice.

Another limitation comes with the fixed pool of unlabeled data in particular if we use existing datasets. This is similar to use the knowledge of a child for our entire life without any update. But in fact, our knowledge base will be permanently updated. That is why children regard a lost rabbit in a magic show as the reality while an adult knows that this can be only a trick. However, the internet provides us a large amount of images as well as videos and it is steadily updated with new data. A transformation of current SSL algorithms into on-line learning algorithms might be necessary [48, 89, 107] to benefit from these changes. Nevertheless, tapping into this data source poses many problems and questions: How do we get representative samples for each class out of these large amounts of data? How should we deal with

Fig. 2.23 First examples for the query *fish* in Google images (out of 1.5 billion results) that are not representative for this class

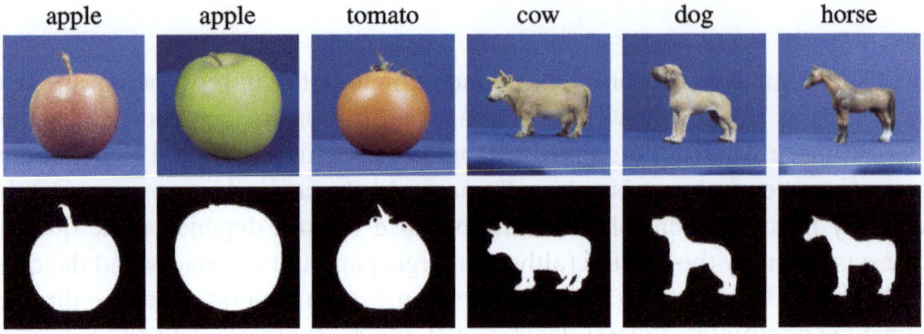

Fig. 2.24 Most confusing classes for ETH-80 although the conditions are optimal for SSL, i.e., smooth manifold structure and no background clutter

incorrect tags? Do we get enough images for each class, for example, endangered animals/plants or deep sea fish? But even the first question is of great importance if we look at the first examples of the query *fish* in Google (Fig. 2.23) that contains drawings, a robot fish (3rd image), body paintings and other atypical examples.

2.4.1.2 Image Description

Missing data is clearly not the only bottleneck that can be seen in [29] for ETH-80. This dataset is well suited for semi-supervised learning because each object is photographed from different viewpoints and there is no background clutter, occlusion, or truncation of the object. But in our experiments, we achieve at most 80 % with 5 randomly drawn labels per class and a combination of three different descriptors. Figure 2.24 shows the most confusing classes for this dataset with the corresponding binary masks, that is, tomatoes are mixed up with apples and the animals (cow, dog, horse) are confused with each other. By using also a color descriptor, we are able to distinguish green apples and red tomatoes but the final improvement is only minor.

This poses many questions. Which information do we miss? Do we need a better texture description to distinguish the different surfaces of tomato and apple? Why can a human easily guess the object class for the animals by only looking at the binary masks in the second row in Fig. 2.24? Do we describe a concept of a class in terms of proportions? It seems obvious that a better shape description is needed. But it is still not clear how to extract, to store and to use this structural description. In [95], they show that only 15 % to 30 % of an object is required to recognize 100 classes correctly independent of the orientation and the view point of the object. But many of today's shape descriptors lack on this generalization. They extract

Fig. 2.25 Representativeness of viewpoints for the class *armadillo*: images on the *left side* show less representative viewpoints as they miss important properties of this species while the viewpoints in the *right images* are most informative for this class

often too detailed and too specific contours of an object and store this description as a template that will be later used for classification by matching. Although this is a good starting point, this approach needs too many templates to perform reasonably well. One promising direction is to use 3D information [80, 106] that allows to extract structural information about the object and to make assumptions about unseen parts in the image. In these mentioned works, they use a CAD model of an object to get this information. In general, this information is difficult to get for the most object classes that we tackle in this work. Furthermore, they consider the detection of the object also as a matching problem. But ideally we would use these rich 3D models to extract structural invariances for a set of viewpoints to get a more general description assuming that we need only a representative set of salient points to maximize the discrimination between objects [91].

Apparently, there is a similar discussion in cognitive science [49]. Supporter of the viewpoint-based model theory believe that we can extract all information from different viewpoints assuming infinite many viewpoints, i.e., templates, that would clearly exceed our brain capacity. In contrast, advocates of the structural description models argue that each object can be explained by viewpoint-independent invariances. For some classes, this assumption might be true such as *bottle* or *orange*. But for many other classes it will be difficult to find such invariances over all viewpoints, for example, the table legs are invisible in the top view. More recently, there is a common agreement that we need both templates for completeness and structural description for generalization. But this trade-off is currently missing in computer vision. Thus, we need a set of representative and most discriminative viewpoints [93] as shown for the class *armadillo* in Fig. 2.25 but we also need a more general description, for example, properties, and proportions that are invariant over a set of different viewpoints.

Another issue in our experimental setting is that we compute the image descriptor on the entire image. In fact, this is a fast and simple way of extraction but it is not clear whether this is an advantage due to the additional context information or a disadvantage because of the background clutter. But this could be analyzed by using for example part-based models [39], or foreground extraction [60].

Finally, we also miss prior knowledge and context to speed up and enhance image description similar to the work of [45] for image segmentation. [70] show that humans learn three times faster and more accurate if the features of an object were related to each other. A human learns even more although this additional knowledge is not strictly necessary for accurate performance [53]. Thus, there is obviously a strong correlation between associations among features and final performance, for example, animals with feathers are more likely to have also wings in comparison to animals with fur. Equally important is the grouping of features or objects otherwise it would be impossible to follow a soccer match if the player do not wear an uniform. But in many applications, the raw image description is fed directly into the classifier without any intermediate steps such as grouping, ranking, or finding associations. This is rather disappointing because we cannot really reconstruct and understand what went wrong during the classification. Apart from that, some categories are almost only defined by their function, for example, *chair*. Thus, to boost the recognition of those classes, we need associations for example with human poses as shown in [25].

2.4.1.3 Similarity Notion

Encouraged from the positive results of previous metric learning literature, we integrate in [29] several of those methods in the graph construction procedure. But the outcome did not meet our expectations. The main reason is that previous work almost exclusively compare their methods to the Euclidean distance (L2). In this work, we also observe a larger improvements for the L2 distance but these final numbers are lower than just applying Manhattan (L1) distance. In fact, it is almost impossible to improve L1 distance with any metric learning procedure. PCA decrease the performance of L1 and also the most supervised metric learning approaches decrease the performance or do not have any effect. Only with ITML [24], we observe a small improvement of approximately 1.5 %. But this benefit seems rather out of proportion if we consider the runtime and the tedious parameter search.

One problem is that the supervised approaches tend to over-fit due to the small amount of labeled data. [66] addresses this problem by including the geometry of the entire dataset as an additional regularization parameter. But this geometry is not updated during the learning that strongly limits the outcome of this algorithm. In principle, any change of the metric space should also cause a change in the geometry of the data. In [31], we tackled this issue by using an interleaved procedure that integrates successively unlabeled data with their highest prediction values. This method works fine for datasets with an already high graph quality. Otherwise the predictions are often incorrect so that the algorithm drifts to a worse solution. Additionally, we cannot control the label distribution leading to an unbalanced metric learning as some classes are more often requested than other classes. To further improve this approach, we have to incorporate a balancing factor and we should find a way to adjust and update the predictions.

In the long term, we require also different models and levels of granularity to express the similarity between objects. The properties and the description is completely different between base categories such as *cat* and *dog* and two species of the base category *dog*. Also [88] argue that basic level categories carry most information of a category and the categorization of objects into sub- or super-categories takes usually longer than the assignment of a base level category because superclasses ask for a generalization and sub-classes need a specification. Therefore, it is not surprising that many learning algorithms do not improve their performance when using also a hierarchy for learning as shown in [87] because they assume always the same level of similarity description. A better approach would be to start with base level categories (mid-level of a hierarchy) and to switch the strategies when learning super- and sub-classes. The general benefit of a hierarchy should be more obvious as it allows to structure our data. Another important issue might be to integrate also relations into the similarity notion such as *larger head*, *more compact body*, *thinner legs* similar to the work of [77] that use relative attributes.

Finally, we also need a better visualization of the resulting graph structure. [11] visualized in their work a neural network to answer the questions what has the network learned and how is the knowledge represented inside this network. For graph structures, similar questions cannot be answered or only insufficiently. In [29], we look usually at the next nearest neighbors. But this is only one aspect of structure. It does not reflect the interactions in the entire graph. The shortest path between two nodes might be an interesting information. But usually this does not offer any valuable clue to the graph structure as the average shortest path length is ≈ 2 due to the previously mentioned *hub* nodes [119]. Also information visualization strategies such as multidimensional scaling do not produce revealing results.

2.4.1.4 Supervision

In [32], we improve the quality of labels with active learning. This is a promising direction and should be always considered within semi-supervised learning due to the small amount of labels and the stronger dependency of the quality of those. However, our model, that automatically estimates the trade-off between exploration and exploitation and combines more than two criteria, has still some open issues. The trade-off is modeled with discrete states and not continuously. The feedback given by the overall entropy might be unreliable. The number of parameters is in comparison to previous work [7, 76] smaller but still to high. Finally, the initialization for this reinforcement learning is difficult and time-consuming as we start with no prior knowledge. Thus, one improvement could be the integration of domain knowledge or by using counterexamples [16].

2.4.1.5 Concept-Driven vs. Exemplar-Based Learning

Graph-based algorithms are a popular choice for SSL. These algorithms reflect more or less the exemplar-based theory in cognition [57, 67, 74] assuming that humans store a list of exemplars and use a nearest neighbor approach to categorize objects. But this theory seems inconsistent as [84] and [128] show that people abstract to prototypes sometimes even without seeing those [68]. Thus, we possess a generalization ability from which the used algorithms are far away. In [31, 33], we approach this problem by combining label propagation with some prototype-based methods. Metric learning transforms the data space such that classes are more compact and in [33] we add prototypical unlabeled examples.

Although these approaches are a step in the right direction, they still miss a notion of the concept that is flexible enough to classify also unseen constellations and appearances of one object. Concepts allows us to go beyond the information given or visible [104], for example, if a human knows that an object is an apple then he also knows that there is most likely a core inside. This leads to one of the fundamental questions: "What makes a category seem coherent?" that is not yet satisfactory answered. [71] argue that similarity alone is not sufficient to describe a concept. We need also feature correlations, a structure of the attributes that are internal to a concept, and background knowledge as already discussed in the previous subsections. Beyond that we also require a relation of the concepts to each other. One possibility to get away from this purely similarity-driven approach of label propagation is to consider groups of images instead of pairwise similarities.

2.4.2 Beyond Human Perception, Learning, and Inference

In the previous subsection, we discussed some future work strongly based on the insight of cognitive science. This focus on human object recognition might serve as a good starting point. But also human perception and inference has their weaknesses that might be tackled by computers. One of these shortcomings is the selective attention also known as *change blindness*. There are several studies showing that a human does not recognize large differences such as a complete different clothing of a person in a video sequence of the same situation when focusing on the conversation [62]. In [102], one person is exchanged by another while the other person explains the direction without noticing the exchange. Most famous is the *invisible gorilla* [17] that runs through a video sequences and most people overlook this disguised person. But 78 % of the people are sure to recognize unexpected objects [101] that is also called *memory illusion* meaning that we have the feeling of continuous attention because we cannot remember the unconscious moments. In this point, computers are trustworthy and this is one reason why most of the assembly line work or other production steps are done by a machine. Also in computer vision we can benefit from this advantage by completely analyzing video sequences (not partially like a human) or by scanning through millions of images to find prototypical examples of one class.

Another problem comes with the limited knowledge base of a human. Even if a person learns day and night, he will never be capable to acquire the entire knowledge and experience existing in our world. Also in the case that we bound this knowledge to a particular area for example a lawyer who read all cases to his topic or a doctor who is specialized to one organ. We cannot be sure that this specialist will remember the appropriate precedent or the disease pattern if it is needed. In contrast, with a computer we are able to get more information at the same time and to remind humans on the existence of some facts, e.g. to assist the diagnosis. This ability is also in computer vision of great importance as we can acquire more and better knowledge from the internet that might be helpful for semi-supervised learning.

Fig. 2.26 Visualization of rare categories and their effect on our inference: (**a**) Wolpertinger a fake object, and (**b**) duckbill platypus a real object that seems like a fake as it mix up properties of different species

Finally, also human inference is highly dependent on the knowledge of a person. Sure we infer quickly the position of a glass and can grasp it within few seconds and we immediately recognize the *Wolpertinger*—a bavarian mythical creature—shown in Fig. 2.26 as a fake because no hare has a dear head and bird wings. But on the other side, rare species such as the duckbill platypus (Fig. 2.26 right) looks also like an elaborate fraud to us as if someone stick the duckbill on this animal. In fact, this species comes with an unusual appearance and atypical properties for a mammal such as laying eggs like a bird or a reptile, having a tail like a beaver, a bill like a duck, and foots like an otter. Assuming that we can collect more knowledge with a computer then this added information should also improve the inference beyond that of a human. In particular in the shown case from Fig. 2.26, a computer should be in a better position to decide which one is a fake. First, each imitation of the *Wolpertinger* looks different in comparison to images of the duckbill platypus. Second, we can also take into account the trustability of the source.

References

1. Angluin D, Laird P (1988) Learning from noisy examples. Mach Learn 2:343–370
2. Argyriou A, Herbster M, Pontil M (2005) Combining graph Laplacians for semi-supervised learning. In: NIPS
3. Ashby FG (1992) Multidimensional models of categorization. In: Multidimensional models of perception and cognition. Erlbaum, Hillsdale, pp 449–483
4. Ashby FG, Todd WT (2011) Human category learning 2.0. Ann NY Acad Sci 1224:147–161
5. Balcan M-F, Blum A (2005) A PAC-style model for learning from labeled and unlabeled data. In: COLT
6. Balcan M-f, Blum A, Pakyan Choi P, Lafferty J, Pantano B, Rwebangira MR, Zhu X (2005) Person identification in webcam images: an application of semi-supervised learning. In: ICML WS
7. Baram Y, El-yaniv R, Luz K (2004) Online choice of active learning algorithms. J Mach Learn Res 5:255–291
8. Bauckhage C, Thurau C (2009) Making archetypal analysis practical. In: DAGM
9. Berg TL, Forsyth DA (2006) Animals on the web. In: CVPR
10. Biederman I (1987) Recognition-by-components: a theory of human image understanding. Psychol Rev 94(2):115–147
11. Bischof H, Pinz A, Kropatsch WG (1992) Visualization methods for neural networks. In: IAPR

12. Blum A, Chawla S (2001) Learning from labeled and unlabeled data using graph mincuts. In: ICML
13. Buhmann JM, Zöller T (2000) Active learning for hierarchical pairwise data clustering. In: ICPR
14. Burl MC, Perona P (1996) Recognition of planar object classes. In: CVPR
15. Cebron N, Berthold MR (2009) Active learning for object classification: from exploration to exploitation. Data Min Knowl Discov 18(2):283–299
16. Cebron N, Richter F, Lienhart R (2012) "I can tell you what it's not": active learning from counterexamples. In: Progress in artificial intelligence
17. Chabris C, Simons D (2010) The invisible gorilla: how our intuitions deceive us. Crown Publishing Group
18. Chawla NV, Bowyer KW, Hall LO, Kegelmeyer WP (2002) SMOTE: synthetic minority over-sampling technique. J Artif Intell Res 16:341–378
19. Cohen B, Murphy GL (1984) Models of concepts. Cogn Sci 8(1):27–58
20. Cootes TF, Edwards GJ, Taylor CJ (1998) Active appearance models. In: ECCV
21. Cutler A, Breiman L (1994) Archetypal analysis. Technometrics 36(4):338–347
22. Daitch SI, Kelner JA, Spielman DA, Haven N (2009) Fitting a graph to vector data. In: ICML
23. Damasio A (1994) Descartes' error: emotion, reason, and the human brain. Penguin Group
24. Davis J, Kulis B, Jain P, Sra S, Dhillon I (2007) Information-theoretic metric learning. In: ICML
25. Delaitre V, Fouhey DF, Laptev I, Sivic J, Gupta A, Efros AA (2012) Scene semantics from long-term observation of people. In: ECCV
26. Delalleau O, Bengio Y, Le Roux N (2005) Efficient non-parametric function induction in semi-supervised learning. In: AISTATS
27. Deng J, Dong W, Socher R, Li L-J, Li K, Fei-Fei L (2009) ImageNet: a large-scale hierarchical image database. In: CVPR, June 2009. IEEE
28. Dubout C, Fleuret F (2011) Tasting families of features for image classification. In: ICCV
29. Ebert S (2012) Semi-supervised learning for image classification. PhD thesis, Saarland University
30. Ebert S, Larlus D, Schiele B (2010) Extracting structures in image collections for object recognition. In: ECCV
31. Ebert S, Fritz M, Schiele B (2011) Pick your neighborhood—improving labels and neighborhood structure for label propagation. In: DAGM
32. Ebert S, Fritz M, Schiele B (2012) Active metric learning for object recognition. In: DAGM
33. Ebert S, Fritz M, Schiele B (2012) Semi-supervised learning on a budget: scaling up to large datasets. In: ACCV
34. Elhamifar E, Sapiro G, Vidal R (2012) See all by looking at a few: sparse modeling for finding representative objects. In: CVPR
35. Erickson MA, Kruschke JK (1998) Rules and exemplars in category learning. J Exp Psychol Gen 127(2):107–140
36. Everingham M, Van Gool L, Williams CK (2008) The PASCAL VOC
37. Farajtabar M, Shaban A, Reza Rabiee H, Rohban MH (2011) Manifold coarse graining for online semi-supervised learning. In: ECML
38. Fei-Fei L, Fergus R, Perona P (2006) One-shot learning of object categories. IEEE Trans Pattern Anal Mach Intell 28(4):594–611
39. Felzenszwalb PF, Girshick RB, McAllester D, Ramanan D (2010) Object detection with discriminatively trained part-based models. IEEE Trans Pattern Anal Mach Intell 32(9):1627–1645
40. Fergus R, Weiss Y, Torralba A (2009) Semi-supervised learning in gigantic image collections. In: NIPS
41. Fisher RA (1936) The use of multiple measurements in taxonomic problems. Ann Eugen 7:179–188
42. Fowlkes C, Belongie S, Chung F, Malik J (2004) Spectral grouping using the Nystrom method. IEEE Trans Pattern Anal Mach Intell 26(2):214–225

43. Freeman WT (2011) Where computer vision needs help from computer science. In: ACM-SIAM symposium on discrete algorithms
44. Fritz M, Black M, Bradski G, Darrell T (2009) An additive latent feature model for transparent object recognition. In: NIPS
45. Fussenegger M, Roth PM, Bischof H, Pinz A (2006) On-line, incremental learning of a robust active shape model. Pattern Recognit 4174:122–131
46. Gehler P, Nowozin S (2009) On feature combination for multiclass object classification. In: ICCV
47. Goldberg AB, Zhu X, Wright S (2007) Dissimilarity in graph-based semi-supervised classification. In: AISTATS
48. Grabner H, Leistner C, Bischof H (2008) Semi-supervised on-line boosting for robust tracking. In: ECCV
49. Hayward WG (2003) After the viewpoint debate: where next in object recognition? Trends Cogn Sci 7(10):425–427
50. Joachims T (1999) Transductive inference for text classification using support vector machines. In: ICML
51. Kahneman D, Tversky A (1979) Prospect theory: an analysis of decision under risk. Econometrica 47(2):263–291
52. Kant I (1781) Kritik der reinen Vernunft. Johann Friedrich Hartknoch Verlag. English edition: Kant I (1838) Critique of pure reason (trans: Haywood F)
53. Kaplan AS, Murphy GL (2000) Category learning with minimal prior knowledge. J Exp Psychol 26(4):829–846
54. Karlen M, Weston J, Erkan A, Collobert R (2008) Large scale manifold transduction. In: ICML. ACM Press, New York
55. Kato T, Kashima H, Sugiyama M (2009) Robust label propagation on multiple networks. IEEE Trans Neural Netw 20(1):35–44
56. Khosla A, Zhou T, Malisiewicz T, Efros AA, Torralba A (2012) Undoing the damage of dataset bias. In: ECCV
57. Kruschke JK (1992) ALCOVE: an exemplar-based connectionist model of category learning. Psychol Rev 99(1):22–44
58. Kulis B, Jain P, Grauman K (2009) Fast similarity search for learned metrics. IEEE Trans Pattern Anal Mach Intell 31(12):2143–2157
59. Lampert CH, Nickisch H, Harmeling S (2009) Learning to detect unseen object classes by between-class attribute transfer. In: CVPR
60. Lee YJ, Grauman K (2009) Foreground focus: unsupervised learning from partially matching images. Int J Comput Vis 85:143–166
61. Leibe B, Seemann E, Schiele B (2005) Pedestrian detection in crowded scenes. In: CVPR. IEEE
62. Levin DT, Simons DJ (1997) Failure to detect changes to attended objects in motion pictures. Psychon Bull Rev 4(4):501–506
63. Li W, Fritz M (2012) Recognizing materials from virtual examples. In: ECCV
64. Li Y-F, Zhou Z-H (2011) Improving semi-supervised support vector machines through unlabeled instances selection. In: AAAI
65. Liu W, He J, Chang SF (2010) Large graph construction for scalable semi-supervised learning. In: ICML, pp 1–8
66. Lu Z, Jain P, Dhillon IS (2009) Geometry-aware metric learning. In: ICML
67. Medin DL, Schaffer MM (1978) Context theory of classification learning. Psychol Rev 85(3):207–238
68. Minda JP, Smith JD (2001) Prototypes in category learning: the effects of category size, category structure, and stimulus complexity. J Exp Psychol Learn Mem Cogn 27(3):775–799
69. Murphy GL (2002) The big book of concepts
70. Murphy GL, Allopenna PD (1994) The locus of knowledge effects in concept learning. J Exp Psychol Learn Mem Cogn 20(4):904–919

71. Murphy GL, Medin DL (1985) The role of theories in conceptual coherence. Psychol Rev 92(3):289–316
72. Nguyen HT, Smeulders A (2004) Active learning using pre-clustering. In: ICML
73. Nigam K, McCallum AK, Thrun S, Mitchell T (2000) Text classification from labeled and unlabeled documents using EM. Mach Learn 39:103–134
74. Nosofsky RM (1984) Choice, similarity, and the context theory of classification. J Exp Psychol 10(1):104–114
75. Osherson DN, Smith EE (1981) On the adequacy of prototype theory as a theory of concepts. Cognition 9(1):35–58
76. Osugi T, Kun D, Scott S (2005) Balancing exploration and exploitation: a new algorithm for active machine learning. In: ICDM
77. Parikh D, Grauman K (2011) Relative attributes. In: ICCV, November 2011. IEEE
78. Pazzani MJ (1991) Influence of prior knowledge on concept acquisition: experimental and computational results. J Exp Psychol 17(3):416–432
79. Pearson K (1901) On lines and planes of closest fit to systems of points in space. Philos Mag 2(6):559–572
80. Pepik B, Stark M, Gehler P, Schiele B (2012) Teaching 3D geometry to deformable part models. In: CVPR
81. Pishchulin L, Jain A, Andriluka M, Thormälen T, Schiele B (2012) Articulated people detection and pose estimation: reshaping the future. In: CVPR
82. Ponce J, Berg TL, Everingham M, Forsyth DA, Hebert M, Lazebnik S, Marszalek M, Schmid C, Russell BC, Torralba A, Williams CKI, Zhang J, Zisserman A (2006) Dataset issues in object recognition. In: Ponce J, Hebert M, Schmid C, Zisserman A (eds) Towards category-level object recognition. LNCS. Springer, Berlin, pp 29–48
83. Pope A, Lowe DG (1996) Learning appearance models for object recognition. In: Object representation in computer vision II
84. Posner MI, Goldsmith R, Welton KE (1967) Perceived distance and the classification of distorted patterns. J Exp Psychol 73(1):28–38
85. Prabhakaran S, Raman S, Vogt JE, Roth V (2012) Automatic model selection in archetype analysis. In: DAGM
86. Rohban MH, Rabiee HR (2012) Supervised neighborhood graph construction for semi-supervised classification. Pattern Recognit 45(4):1363–1372
87. Rohrbach M, Stark M, Schiele B (2011) Evaluating knowledge transfer and zero-shot learning in a large-scale setting. In: CVPR
88. Rosch E, Mervis CB, Gray WD, Johnson DM, Boyes-Braem P (1976) Basic objects in natural categories. Cogn Psychol 8:382–439
89. Saffari A, Godec M, Pock T, Leistner C, Bischof H (2010) Online multi-class LPBoost. In: CVPR, June 2010. IEEE
90. Schiele B (2000) Towards automatic extraction and modeling of objects from image sequences. In: Int sym on intelligent robotic systems
91. Schiele B, Crowley JL (1996) Where to look next and what to look for. In: IROS
92. Schiele B, Crowley JL (1997) The concept of visual classes for object classification. In: Scand conf image analysis
93. Schiele B, Crowley JL (1998) Transinformation for active object recognition. In: ICCV
94. Schiele B, Crowley JL (2000) Recognition without correspondence using multidimensional receptive field histograms. Int J Comput Vis 36(1):31–52
95. Schiele B, Pentland A (1999) Probabilistic object recognition and localization. In: ICCV
96. Schnitzspan P, Fritz M, Roth S, Schiele B, Berkeley Eecs UC (2009) Discriminative structure learning of hierarchical representations for object detection. In: CVPR
97. Schohn G, Cohn D (2000) Less is more: active learning with support vector machines. In: ICML
98. Seeger M (2001) Learning with labeled and unlabeled data. Technical report, University of Edinburgh

99. Settles B (2009) Active Learning Literature Survey. Technical report, University of Wisconsin–Madison
100. Simon I, Snavely N, Seitz SM (2007) Scene summarization for online image collections. In: ICCV. IEEE
101. Simons DJ, Chabris CF (1999) Gorillas in our midst: sustained inattentional blindness for dynamic events. Perception 28(9):1059–1074
102. Simons DJ, Levin DT (1998) Failure to detect changes to people during a real-world interaction. Psychon Bull Rev 5(4):644–649
103. Sivic J, Russell BC, Efros AA, Zisserman A, Freeman WT (2005) Discovering object categories in image collections. In: ICCV
104. Smith E, Medin DL (1981) Categories and concepts. Harvard University Press, Cambridge
105. Sonnenburg S, Rätsch G, Schäfer C, Schölkopf B (2006) Large scale multiple kernel learning. J Mach Learn Res 7:1531–1565
106. Stark M, Goesele M, Schiele B (2010) Back to the future: learning shape models from 3D CAD data. In: BMVC
107. Sternig S, Roth PM, Bischof H (2012) On-line inverse multiple instance boosting for classifier grids. Pattern Recognit Lett, 33(7):890–897
108. Sugiyama M, Rubens N (2008) Active learning with model selection in linear regression. In: DMKD
109. Talwalkar A, Kumar S, Rowley H (2008) Large-scale manifold learning. In: CVPR, June 2008, pp 1–8
110. Tong W, Jin R (2007) Semi-supervised learning by mixed label propagation. In: AAAI, vol 22
111. Tong S, Koller D (2001) Support vector machine active learning with applications to text classification. J Mach Learn Res 2:45–66
112. Tong H, He J, Li M, Zhang C, Ma WY (2005) Graph based multi-modality learning. In: ACM multimedia
113. Torralba A (2011) Unbiased look at dataset bias. In: CVPR
114. Torralba BA, Russell BC, Yuen J (2010) LabelMe: online image annotation and applications. In: Proc IEEE
115. Tsang IW, Kwok JT (2006) Large-scale sparsified manifold regularization. In: NIPS
116. Tsuda K, Shin H, Schoelkopf B (2005) Fast protein classification with multiple networks. Bioinformatics 21:59–65
117. Vedaldi A, Gulshan V, Varma M, Zisserman A (2009) Multiple kernels for object detection. In: ICCV, pp 606–613
118. Vernon D (2005) A research roadmap of cognitive vision. Technical report, ECVision: the European research network for cognitive computer vision systems
119. Von Luxburg U, Radl A, Hein M (2010) Getting lost in space: large sample analysis of the commute distance. In: NIPS
120. Wang L, Chan KL, Zhang Z (2003) Bootstrapping SVM active learning by incorporating unlabelled images for image retrieval. In: CVPR. IEEE Comput. Soc., Los Alamitos
121. Wang X, Han TX, Yan S (2009) An HOG-LBP human detector with partial occlusion handling. In: ICCV, September 2009. IEEE
122. Wang G, Wang B, Yang X, Yu G (2012) Efficiently indexing large sparse graphs for similarity search. IEEE Trans Knowl Data Eng 24(3):440–451
123. Weber M, Welling M, Perona P (2000) Unsupervised learning of models for recognition. In: ECCV
124. Welinder P, Branson S, Belongie S, Perona P (2010) The multidimensional wisdom of crowds. In: NIPS, pp 1–9
125. Wiskott L, von der Malsburg C (1993) A neural system for the recognition of partially occluded objects in cluttered scenes. Int J Pattern Recognit Artif Intell 7(4):935–948
126. Yang L (2006) Distance metric learning: a comprehensive survey. Technical report, Michigan State University

127. Yang X, Bai X, Köknar-Tezel S, Latecki LJ (2013) Densifying distance spaces for shape and image retrieval. J Math Imaging Vis 46:12–28
128. Zaki SR, Nosofsky RM (2007) A high-distortion enhancement effect in the prototype-learning paradigm: dramatic effects of category learning during test. Mem Cogn 35(8):2088–2096
129. Zaki SR, Nosofsky RM, Stanton RD, Cohen AL (2003) Prototype and exemplar accounts of category learning and attentional allocation: a reassessment. J Exp Psychol Learn Mem Cogn 29(6):1160–1173
130. Zhang Z, Zha H, Zhang M (2008) Spectral methods for semi-supervised manifold learning. In: CVPR
131. Zhang K, Kwok JT, Parvin B (2009) Prototype vector machine for large scale semi-supervised learning. In: ICML. ACM Press, New York
132. Zhou D, Bousquet O, Navin Lal T, Weston J, Schölkopf B (2004) Learning with local and global consistency. In: NIPS
133. Zhu X, Goldberg AB, Khot T (2009) Some new directions in graph-based semi-supervised learning. In: ICME

Chapter 3
Recognizing Human Actions by Using Effective Codebooks and Tracking

Lamberto Ballan, Lorenzo Seidenari, Giuseppe Serra, Marco Bertini, and Alberto Del Bimbo

Abstract Recognition and classification of human actions for annotation of unconstrained video sequences has proven to be challenging because of the variations in the environment, appearance of actors, modalities in which the same action is performed by different persons, speed and duration and points of view from which the event is observed. This variability reflects in the difficulty of defining effective descriptors and deriving appropriate and effective codebooks for action categorization. In this chapter, we present a novel and effective solution to classify human actions in unconstrained videos. In the formation of the codebook, we employ radius-based clustering with soft assignment in order to create a rich vocabulary that may account for the high variability of human actions. We show that our solution scores very good performance with no need of parameter tuning. We also show that a strong reduction of computation time can be obtained by applying codebook size reduction with Deep Belief Networks with little loss of accuracy.

3.1 Introduction

With the continuous growth of video production and archiving, the need for automatic annotation tools that enable effective retrieval by content has accordingly gained increasing importance. In particular, action recognition is a very active re-

L. Ballan (✉) · L. Seidenari · G. Serra · M. Bertini · A. Del Bimbo
Media Integration and Communication Center, University of Florence, Viale Morgagni 65, 50134 Florence, Italy
e-mail: lamberto.ballan@unifi.it

L. Seidenari
e-mail: lorenzo.seidenari@unifi.it

G. Serra
e-mail: serra@dsi.unifi.it

M. Bertini
e-mail: marco.bertini@unifi.it

A. Del Bimbo
e-mail: alberto.delbimbo@unifi.it

G.M. Farinella et al. (eds.), *Advanced Topics in Computer Vision*,
Advances in Computer Vision and Pattern Recognition,
DOI 10.1007/978-1-4471-5520-1_3,

search topic with many important applications such as human-computer interaction, video indexing and video-surveillance. Existing approaches for human action recognition can be classified as using holistic or part-based information [3, 45]. Most of the holistic-based methods usually perform better in a controlled environment and are also computationally expensive due to the requirement of pre-processing the input data. Moreover, these representations can be influenced by motions of multiple objects, variations in the background and occlusions. Instead, part-based representations that exploit interest point detectors combined with robust feature descriptors, have been used very successfully for object and scene classification tasks in images [15, 62]. As a result, nowadays most video annotation solutions have exploited the bag-of-features approach to generate textual labels that represent the categories of the main and easiest to detect entities (such as objects and persons) in the video sequence [18, 48].

The definition of effective descriptors that are able to capture both spatial and temporal features has opened the possibility of recognizing dynamic concepts in video sequences. In particular, interesting results have been obtained in the definition of solutions to automatically recognize human body movements, which usually represent a relevant part of video content [38, 40, 41, 50]. However, the recognition and classification of such dynamic concepts for annotation of generic video sequences has proven to be very challenging because of the very many variations in environment, people and occurrences that may be observed. These can be caused by cluttered or moving background, camera motion and illumination changes; people may have different size, shape and posture appearance; semantically equivalent actions can manifest differently or partially, due to speed, duration or self-occlusions; the same action can be performed in different modes by different persons. This great variability on the one hand reflects in the difficulty of defining effective descriptors and on the other makes it hard to obtain a visual representation that may describe such dynamic concepts appropriately and efficiently. Furthermore, these part-based approaches usually do not attempt to localize and track actions that is necessary in video surveillance applications.

3.1.1 Effective Spatio-temporal Descriptors

Holistic descriptors of body movements have been proposed by a few authors. Among the most notable solutions, Bobick et al. [6] proposed motion history images and their low-order moments to encode short spans of motion. For each frame of the input video, the motion history image is a gray scale image that records the location of motion; recent motion results into high intensity values whereas older motion produces lower intensities. Efros et al. [14] created stabilized spatio-temporal volumes for each action video segment and extracted a smoothed dense optic flow field for each volume. They have proved that this representation is particularly suited for distant objects, where the detailed information of the appearance is not available. Yilmaz and Shah [60] used a spatio-temporal volume, built stacking object regions; descriptors encoding direction, speed and local shape of the resulting 3D surface were generated by measuring local differential geometrical properties. Gorelick et al. [17] analyzed three-dimensional shapes induced by the silhouettes and exploited the solution to the Poisson equation to extract features, such as shape structure and orientation. Global descriptors that jointly encode shape and motion were suggested in Lin et al. [29]; Wang et al. [54] exploited global histograms of optic flow together with hidden conditional random fields. Although encoding much of the visual information, these solutions have shown to be highly sensitive to occlusions, noise and change in viewpoint. Most of them have also proven to be computationally expensive due to the fact that some preprocessing of the input data is needed, such as background subtraction, segmentation and object tracking. All these aspects make these solutions only suited for representation of body movements in videos taken in controlled contexts.

Local descriptors have shown better performance and are in principle better suited for videos taken in both constrained and unconstrained contexts. They are less sensitive to partial occlusions and clutter and overcome some of the limitations of the holistic models, such as the need of background subtraction and target tracking. In this approach, local patches at spatio-temporal interest points are used to extract robust descriptors of local moving parts and the bag-of-features approach is employed to have distinctive representations of body movements. Laptev [26] and Dollár [13] approaches have been among the first solutions. Laptev [26, 43] proposed an extension to the Harris–Förstner corner detector for the spatio-temporal case; interesting parts were extracted from voxels surrounding local maxima of spatio-temporal corners, that is, locations of videos that exhibit strong variations of intensity both in spatial and temporal directions. The extension of the scale-space theory to the temporal dimension permitted to define a method for automatic scale-selection. Dollár et al. [13] proposed a different descriptor than Laptev's, by looking for locally periodic motion. While this method produces a denser sampling of the spatio-temporal volume, it does not provide automatic scale-selection. Despite of it, experimental results have shown that it improves with respect to [43].

Following these works, other authors have extended the definition of local interest point detectors and descriptors to incorporate time or combined static local features with other descriptors so to model the temporal evolution of local patches. Sun et al. [49] have fused spatio-temporal SIFT points with holistic features based on Zernike moments. In [56], Willems et al. extended SURF feature to time and defined a new scale-invariant spatio-temporal detector and descriptor that showed high efficiency. Scovanner et al. [44], have proposed to use grouping of 3D SIFT, based on co-occurrence, to represent actions. Kläser et al. [23] have proposed a descriptor based on histograms of oriented 3D gradients, quantized using platonic solids. Gao et al. [16] presented MoSIFT, an approach that extend the SIFT algorithm to find visually distinctive elements in the spatial domain. It detects spatio-temporal points with a high amount of optical flow around the distinctive points motion constraints. More recently, Laptev et al. [27] proposed a structural representation based on dense temporal and spatial scale sampling, inspired by the spatial pyramid approach of [28] with interesting classification results in generic video scenes. Kovashka et al. [25] extended this work by defining a hierarchy of discriminative neighborhoods instead of using spatio-temporal pyramids. Liu et al. [32] combined

MSER and Harris-Affine [37] regions with Dollár's space-time features and used AdaBoost to classify YouTube videos. Shao et al. [46] applied transformation based techniques (i.e., Discrete Fourier Transform, Discrete Cosine Transform and Discrete Wavelet Transform) on the local patches and used the transformed coefficients as descriptors. Yu et al. [61] presented good results using the Dollár's descriptor and random forest-based template matching. Niebles et al. [39] trained an unsupervised probabilistic topic model using the same spatio-temporal features, while Cao et al. [8] suggested to perform model adaptation in order to reduce the amount of labeled data needed to detect actions in videos of uncontrolled scenes. Comparative evaluations of the performance of the most notable approaches were recently reported by Wang et al. [55] and Shao et al. [45].

3.1.2 Suitable Visual Codebooks

According to the bag-of-features model actions are defined as sets of codewords obtained from the clustering of local spatio-temporal descriptors. Most of the methods have used the k-means algorithm for clustering because of its simplicity and speed of convergence [15, 21, 39, 47]. However, both the intrinsic weakness of k-means to outliers and the need of some empirical pre-evaluation of the number of clusters hardly fit with the nature of the problem at hand. Moreover, with k-means the fact that cluster centers are selected almost exclusively around the most dense regions in the descriptor space results into ineffective codewords of action primitives. To overcome the limitations of the basic approach, Liu et al. [30] suggested a method to automatically find the optimal number of visual word clusters through maximization of mutual information (MMI) between words and actions. MMI clustering is used after k-means to discover a compact representation from the initial codebook of words. They showed some performance improvement. Recently Kong et al. [24] have proposed a framework that unifies reduction of descriptor dimensionality and codebook creation, to learn compact codebooks for action recognition optimizing class separability. Differently, Uemura and Mikolajczyk [35] explored the idea of using a large number of features represented in many vocabulary trees instead of a single flat vocabulary. Yao et al. [59] recently proposed a similar framework using a training procedure based on a Hough voting forest. Both these methods require higher efforts in the training phase.

3.1.3 Our Contribution

In this chapter, we propose a novel and effective solution to classify human actions in unconstrained videos. It improves on previous contributions in the literature through the definition of a novel local descriptor and the adoption of a more effective solution for the codebook formation. We use image gradient and optic flow to respectively model the appearance and motion of human actions at regions in the neighborhood of local interest points and consider multiple spatial and temporal scales. These two descriptors are used in combination to model local features of human actions and activities. Unlike similar related works [23, 44], no parameter tuning is required.

In the formation of the codebook, we recognize that the clusters of spatio-temporal descriptors should be both in a sufficiently large number and sufficiently distinguished from each other so to represent the augmented variability of dynamic content with respect to the static case. To this end, radius-based clustering [22] with soft assignment has been used. In fact, with radius-based clustering cluster centers are allocated at the modes corresponding to the maximal density regions, so resulting into a statistics of the codewords that better fits with the variability of human actions with respect to k-means clustering. To obtain a precise spatio-temporal localization of each action, the detected spatio-temporal points are associated to each person, present in the scene, by a particle filter visual tracker. Experiments carried on standard datasets show that the approach followed outperforms the current state of the art methods. To avoid too large codebooks, we performed codebook compression with Deep Belief Networks. The solution proposed shows good accuracy even with very small codebooks. Finally, we provide several experiments on the Hollywood2 dataset [34] and on a new surveillance dataset (MICC-Surveillance), to demonstrate the effectiveness and generality of our method for action recognition in unconstrained video domains.

The rest of the chapter is organized as follows.[1] The full framework of the proposed solution is shown in Sect. 3.2, while the spatio-temporal features are presented in Sect. 3.3. Action representation and categorization is presented in Sect. 3.4. The experimental results, with an extensive comparison with the state-of-the-art approaches, are hence discussed in Sect. 3.5. Here we also included experiments on unconstrained videos to demonstrate the effectiveness of the approach also in this case. Conclusions are drawn in Sect. 3.6.

3.2 Action Classification Architecture

3.2.1 Visual Dictionary Formation

The architectural design of the proposed solution, based on an effective bag-of-features model, is shown in Fig. 3.1. The basic idea of the bag-of-features approach is to represent visual content as an unordered collection of "visual words". To this end, it is necessary to define a visual dictionary from the local features extracted in the video sequences, performing a quantization of the original feature space. The descriptors used to represent the spatio-temporal interest points are presented in the following Sect. 3.3.

The visual dictionary (codebook) is generated by clustering of a set of local descriptors and each cluster is treated as a visual word. Typically it is used the k-means

[1]Please note that an earlier version of this work has recently appeared in *IEEE Transactions on Multimedia* [4].

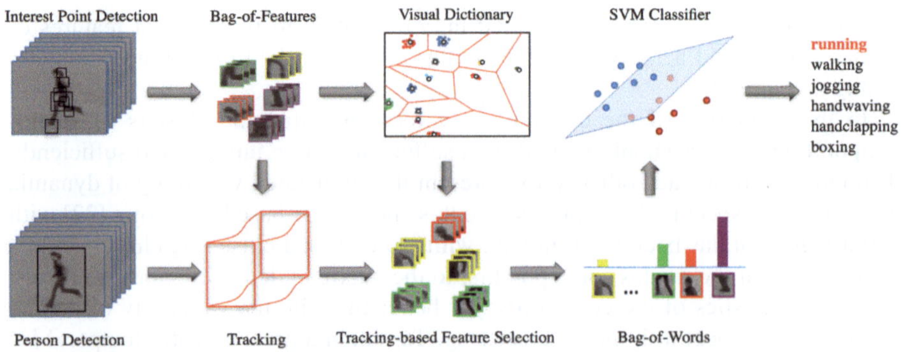

Fig. 3.1 The proposed solution architecture

algorithm because of its simplicity and convergence speed. However, it has been shown that using this algorithm the cluster centers tend to coalesce around the denser regions of the feature space, thus not describing other informative regions. This issue is particularly important in the densely sampled space of the spatio-temporal features used in our approach. In the work of Jurie and Triggs [22] it has been shown that a different approach, namely radius-based clustering, is able to generate better visual dictionaries for the images that arise in natural scenes. We have therefore used a radius-based clustering technique, following a mean-shift approach [11], that improves the performance of the system over k-means. This issue is presented in detail in Sect. 3.4.

3.2.2 Person Tracking and Data Association

Person tracking is used to assign the detected spatio-temporal interest points to each person present in a video, to localize both in space and time each recognized action. The tracker adopted in our system implements a particle filter based tracking algorithm, presented by [2], that tracks position, size and speed of the target, describing the target appearance with its color histogram (using hue and saturation channels). The tracker is initiated using the human detector of [12], implemented in OpenCV. The detector is run frame-wise to obtain both new targets to follow and measures for existing tracks. Measures obtained from the people detector are associated to targets by solving a data association problem, using a fast greedy algorithm that has a much lower complexity than the optimal solution obtainable with the Hungarian algorithm [58]. This greedy algorithm can be executed in real-time, as needed in video-surveillance applications, and works as follows: a matrix M that contains all the matching scores $m_{i,j}$ between the ith target and the jth measure of the person detector is computed. The matching score is computed as:

$$m_{i,j} = e^{-\frac{d_{i,j}^2}{D}} \tag{3.1}$$

where $d_{i,j}$ is the Euclidean distance between the static part of the model (position and size) of the target and the position and size of the detected person (represented using top-left and bottom-right coordinates of the bounding boxes) and D is adaptively chosen based on the target size.

The maximum $m_{i,j}$ are iteratively selected, and the i rows and j columns belonging to target and detector in M are deleted. This is repeated until no further valid $m_{i,j}$ is available. To avoid the erroneous association of a detection to a target two approaches are followed: (i) only the associated detections with a matching score $m_{i,j}$ above a threshold are used, to avoid that a detection that is far from a target is matched; (ii) if a detection overlaps more than one target no association is performed. If a detection is not associated to any target and does not overlap any existing target then it is used to start a new track.

The template of the target appearance is updated every time a new detection is associated to the track. In this way, we prevent template drift and we allow the color histogram to adapt with respect to illumination changes and maneuvers which can change the target appearance. The state update equation, defined over the 8-dimensional state vector x_k (composed by 4 components for position and size and 4 components for their velocities), realizes a 1st-order dynamic model:

$$x_k = Ax_{k-1} + v_{k-1}, \quad A = \begin{bmatrix} I_4 & I_4\Delta t \\ 0 & I_4 \end{bmatrix} \tag{3.2}$$

where I_4 is an 4×4 identity matrix, Δt is the time step and v_{k-1} is an additive, zero mean, isotropic Gaussian uncertainty term that represents the uncertainty in the state update. This uncertainty is parametrized in terms of the standard deviation on each component of the state vector. The measurement model exploits the results of the person detector whenever they are available.

The person detector likelihood is strongly peaked in presence of a target, as shown in the third column of Fig. 3.2. This behavior allows to detect as distinct objects even very close pedestrians, but is not suitable to use it as likelihood of the target [1] since in particle weight computation it could assign very high weights to a few or no particles, and almost uniform low weights to the remaining population, leading thus to a degeneracy problem. To deal with this issue, the target model of the particle filter is based on the color histogram of the tracked object, aiming at robustness against non-rigidity, rotation and partial occlusion; after updating the template histogram with the new measure histogram, weights are computed according to the Batthacharya distance between the particle and the template histograms. On the other hand the color histogram is too weak to be used as an aspect model in a real-world video-surveillance scenario and should not be used as a sole measurement provider, as shown in the second column of Fig. 3.2; this is due to background pixels contaminating the template and the lack of discriminativity of the histogram caused also by its subsampling (we used eight hue bins and eight saturation bins, to reduce sensitivity to light conditions).

To improve the particle filter capability to effectively track the target, even if its appearance is not strongly characterized, the tracking method implements a particular technique, based on the use of the similarity of the current estimate with the orig-

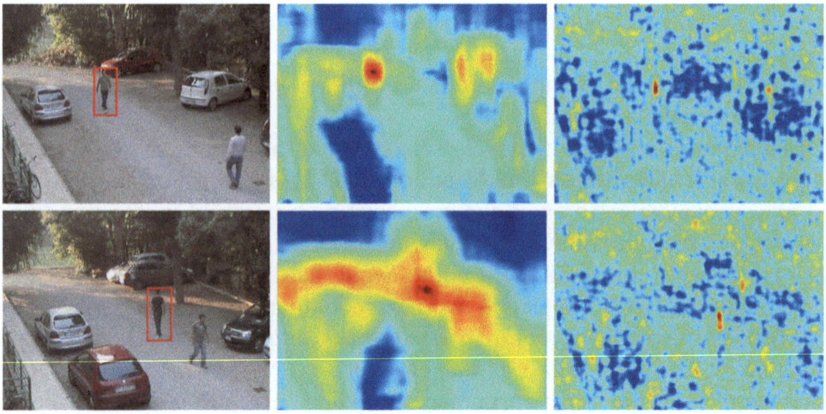

Fig. 3.2 Original frame, hue/saturation histogram and person detector generated likelihood computed for the farthest target (highlighted with *red bounding box*). In this example the pedestrian detector is run at a single scale; histogram likelihood is generated using the values of the Batthacharya distance between the template histogram and a corresponding (same scale and aspect ratio) window. In both cases scale and aspect ratio variations are not considered, for the sake of visualization

inal target histogram as an index of tracking quality, to manage the uncertainty in the state update equation by means of on-line adaptation of the error v_{k-1}. In particular, let us consider the case where the variances of position and size of the target are set to very high values. In this case the filter samples over a wide enough area to maximize the possibility of capturing the target in case of erratic changes in direction or velocity. The pitfall in this strategy, however, is that it also increases the likelihood that the particle filter will become distracted by spurious similar patches in the background. Considering also the variances of the velocities the problem is even worse: from Eq. 3.2, in the update rule for propagating a particle from time $k-1$ to k, the uncertainty in the dynamic component is propagated to the static component. To reduce this effect, a *blindness* value is computed by passing the similarity of estimate and original target histogram through a sigmoid; this *blindness* value is used to adjust the variances in such a way that the noise in the static component of the state observations is never amplified by the noise in the dynamic components. This allows the tracker to switch between two different behaviors: one that relies on the predicted motion of the target and one that behaves like a random-walk model.

3.2.3 Action Classification and Track Annotation

By mapping the features associated to each tracked person in a video to the vocabulary, we can represent it by the frequency histogram of visual words. In order to reduce outliers, histograms of tracks that contain too few interest points, are discarded. Then, the remaining histograms are fed to a classifier to predict the action category. In particular, classification is performed using non-linear SVMs with the χ^2 kernel.

Fig. 3.3 Example of multiple person tracking, spatio-temporal interest point detection and their association to the tracks

To perform multi-class classification we use the *one-vs.-one* approach. To this end we train a binary SVM classifier for each pair of action classes for a total of $\frac{n(n-1)}{2}$ classifiers. Action is predicted considering the output of each SVM as a vote for the correspondent action and using a majority voting procedure. Figure 3.3 shows an example of the tracker results and features association.

3.3 Fusing Spatio-temporal Local Descriptors of Appearance and Motion

Spatio-temporal interest points are detected at video local maxima of the Dollár's detector [13] applied over a set of spatial and temporal scales. Using multiple scales is fundamental to capture the essence of human activity. To this end, linear filters are separately applied to the spatial and temporal dimension: on the one hand, the spatial scale permits to detect visual features of high and low detail; on the other, the temporal scale allows to detect *action primitives* at different temporal resolutions. The filter response function is defined as:

$$R = (I * g_\sigma * h_{ev})^2 + (I * g_\sigma * h_{od})^2 \tag{3.3}$$

where $I(x, y, t)$ is the image sequence, $g_\sigma(x, y)$ is a spatial Gaussian filter with scale σ, h_{ev} and h_{od} are a quadrature pair of 1D Gabor filters that provide a strong response to temporal intensity changes for periodic motion patterns, respectively defined as:

$$h_{ev}(t; \tau, \omega) = -\cos(2\pi t\omega)e^{-t^2/\tau^2} \tag{3.4}$$

$$h_{od}(t; \tau, \omega) = -\sin(2\pi t\omega)e^{-t^2/\tau^2} \tag{3.5}$$

where $\omega = 4/\tau$. In the experiments we used $\sigma = \{2, 4\}$ as spatial scales and $\tau = \{2, 4\}$ as temporal scales. Figure 3.4 shows an example of temporal scaling of human body parts activity during walking: torso has high response at high temporal scale, while limbs respond at the lower scale.

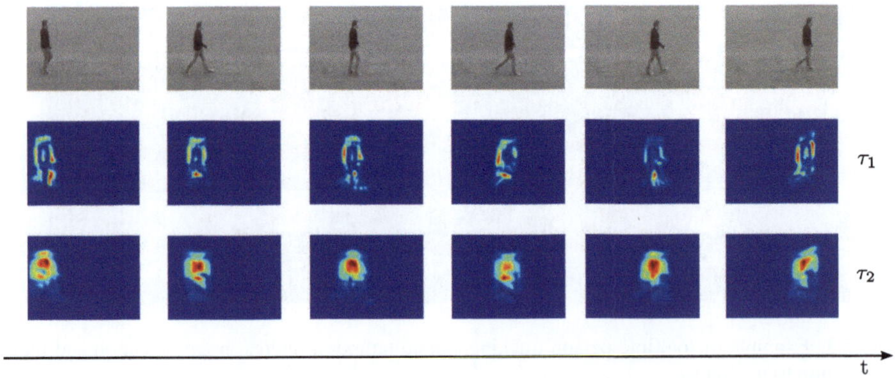

Fig. 3.4 Response of the spatio-temporal interest point detector at two temporal scales $\tau_1 < \tau_2$ (low response in *blue*, high response in *red*); *first row*: original video frames, *second row*: detector response at temporal scale τ_1 (mostly due to motion of human limbs); *third row*: detector response temporal scale τ_2 (mostly due to motion of human torso)

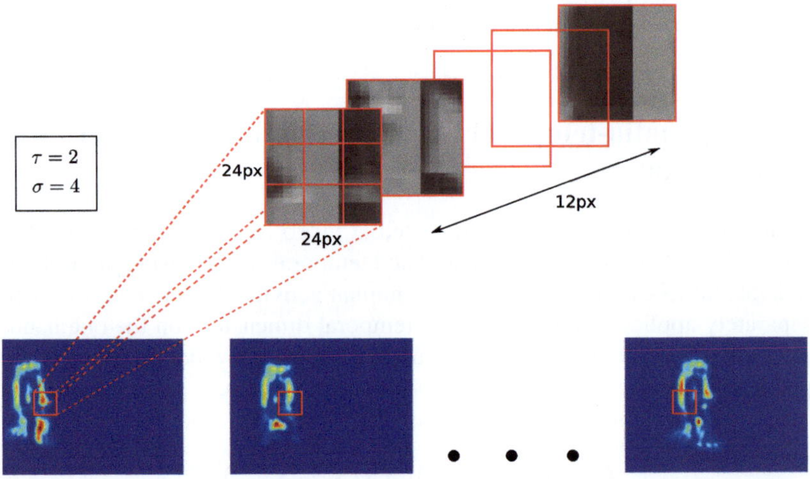

Fig. 3.5 Three-dimensional region at the spatio-temporal interest point corresponding to a swinging arm

Three-dimensional regions of size proportional to the detector scale (6x) are considered at each spatio-temporal interest point, and divided into equally sized sub-regions (three for each spatial dimensions along the x and y, and two for the temporal dimension t), as shown in Fig. 3.5.

For each sub-region, image gradients on x, y and t are computed as:

$$G_x = I(x+1, y, t) - I(x-1, y, t) \tag{3.6}$$

$$G_y = I(x, y+1, t) - I(x, y-1, t) \tag{3.7}$$

$$G_t = I(x, y, t+1) - I(x, y, t-1) \tag{3.8}$$

Table 3.1 Comparison of accuracy and efficiency of our H3DGrad with other gradient based descriptors on KTH and Weizmann datasets. Computation time for a single descriptor measured on a 2.66 GHz Intel Xeon with 12 GB RAM; H3DGrad, [23] and [27] are C++ implementations while [44] is a MATLAB implementation

Descriptor	KTH	Weizmann	Time (ms)
H3DGrad	90.38	92.30	1
Kläser et al. [23]	91.40	84.30	2
Laptev et al. [27]	81.60	–	12
Scovanner et al. [44]	–	82.60	419

and the optic flow with relative apparent velocity V_x, V_y is estimated according to [33].

Orientations of gradients and optical flow are computed for each pixel as:

$$\phi = \tan^{-1}\left(G_t/\sqrt{G_x^2 + G_y^2}\right) \in \left[-\frac{\pi}{2}, \frac{\pi}{2}\right] \tag{3.9}$$

$$\theta = \tan^{-1}(G_y/G_x) \in [-\pi, \pi] \tag{3.10}$$

$$\psi = \tan^{-1}(V_y/V_x) \in [-\pi, \pi] \tag{3.11}$$

where ϕ and the θ are quantized in four and eight bins, respectively.

The local descriptor obtained by concatenating ϕ and θ histograms (H3DGrad) has therefore size $3 \times 3 \times 2 \times (8 + 4) = 216$. There is no need to reorient the 3D neighborhood, since rotational invariance, typically required in object detection and recognition, is not desirable in the action classification context. This approach is much simpler to compute than those proposed in [44] and [23]. In particular, in [44] the histogram is normalized by the solid angle value to avoid distortions due to the polar coordinate representation (instead of quantizing separately the two orientations as in our approach), moreover the size of the descriptor is 2048; in [23] the 3D gradient vector is projected on the faces of a platonic solid. In this latter approach requires additional parameter tuning, to optimize the selection of the solid used for the histogram computation and whether to consider the orientations of its faces or not. Differently from [27] our 12-bin H3DGrad descriptor models the dynamic appearance of the three-dimensional region used for its computation, instead of being a 4-bin 2D histogram cumulated over time. A comparison between our H3DGrad descriptor and the other HOG features (i.e., [23, 27, 44]) is reported in Table 3.1, in terms of both accuracy and feature computation time.

The ψ is quantized in eight bins with an extra "no-motion" bin added to improve performance. The local descriptor of ψ (HOF) has size $3 \times 3 \times 2 \times (8 + 1) = 162$. Histograms of ϕ, θ and ψ are respectively, derived by weighting pixel contributions respectively, with the gradient magnitude $M_G = \sqrt{G_x^2 + G_y^2 + G_t^2}$ (for ϕ and θ), and the optic flow magnitude $M_O = \sqrt{V_x^2 + V_y^2}$ (for ψ).

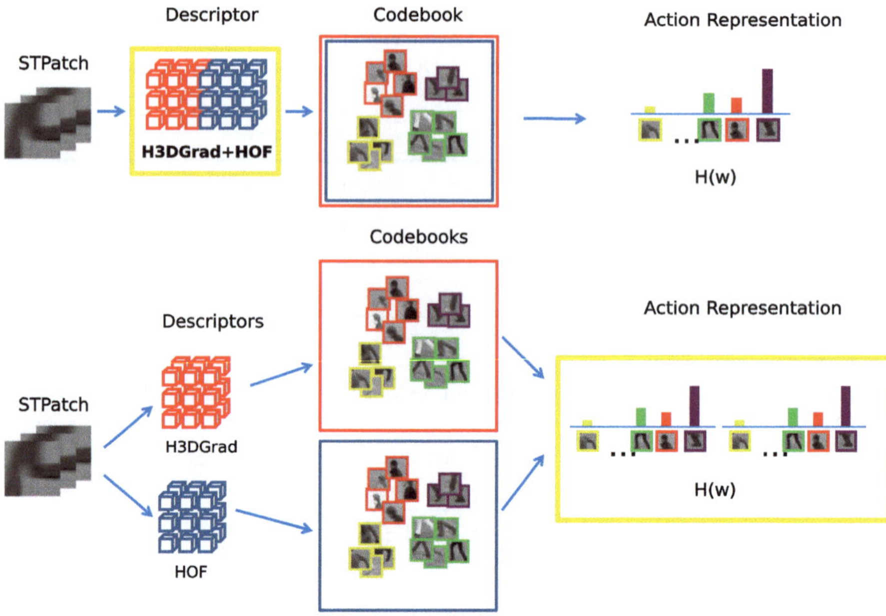

Fig. 3.6 Two fusion strategies: early-fusion (at the descriptor level) and late-fusion (at the codebook level)

In order to obtain an effective codebook for human actions these two descriptors can be combined according to either early or late fusion. In the former case, the two descriptors are first concatenated and the combined descriptor is hence used for the definition of the human action codebook. In the latter, a codebook is obtained from each descriptor separately; then the histograms of codewords are concatenated to form the representation (see Fig. 3.6).

Figure 3.7 shows the classification accuracy measured with the KTH dataset, using codebooks based on the H3DGrad descriptor (a), HOF descriptor (b), and early (c) and late fusion (d), with 4000 codewords. Each action, is represented by an histogram H of codewords w obtained according to k-means clustering with hard assignment:

$$H(w) = \frac{1}{n}\sum_{i=1}^{n}\begin{cases}1 & \text{if } w = \operatorname{argmin}_{v\in V}(D(v, f_i));\\ 0 & \text{otherwise;}\end{cases} \tag{3.12}$$

where n is the number of the spatio-temporal features, f_i is the ith spatio-temporal feature, and $D(v, f_i)$ is the Euclidean distance between the codeword v of the vocabulary V and f_i.

We present in Table 3.2 the average accuracy obtained by H3DGrad and HOF respectively, and by the early and late fusion. From the figures, it appears clearly that late fusion provides the best performance. This can be explained with the fact that H3DGrad and HOF descriptors have quite complementary roles (for example

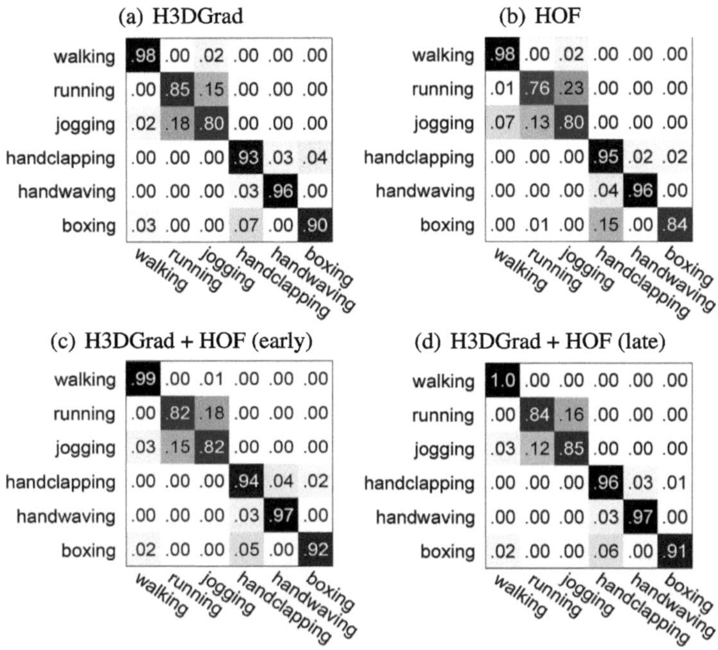

Fig. 3.7 Classification accuracy on the KTH dataset using k-means clustering, hard assignment and different descriptors combination strategies (i.e. early or late fusion)

Table 3.2 Average class accuracy of our descriptors, alone and combined, on the KTH and Weizmann datasets

Descriptor	KTH	Weizmann
H3DGrad	90.38	92.30
HOF	88.04	89.74
H3DGrad + HOF (early fusion)	91.09	92.38
H3DGrad + HOF (late fusion)	*92.10*	*92.41*

the *boxing* action is better recognized when using H3DGrad descriptor while *handclapping* action is better recognized by HOF, as shown in Fig. 3.7(a), (b)). Late fusion improves recognition performance for all the classes except one. A similar behavior was observed with the Weizmann dataset, although in this case the improvement was not so significant mainly due to the limited size and intra-class variability of the dataset (see Table 3.2).

3.4 Action Representation and Classification

In order to improve with respect to k-means and to account for the high variability of human actions in terms of appearance or motion, we used radius-based clustering for codebook formation.

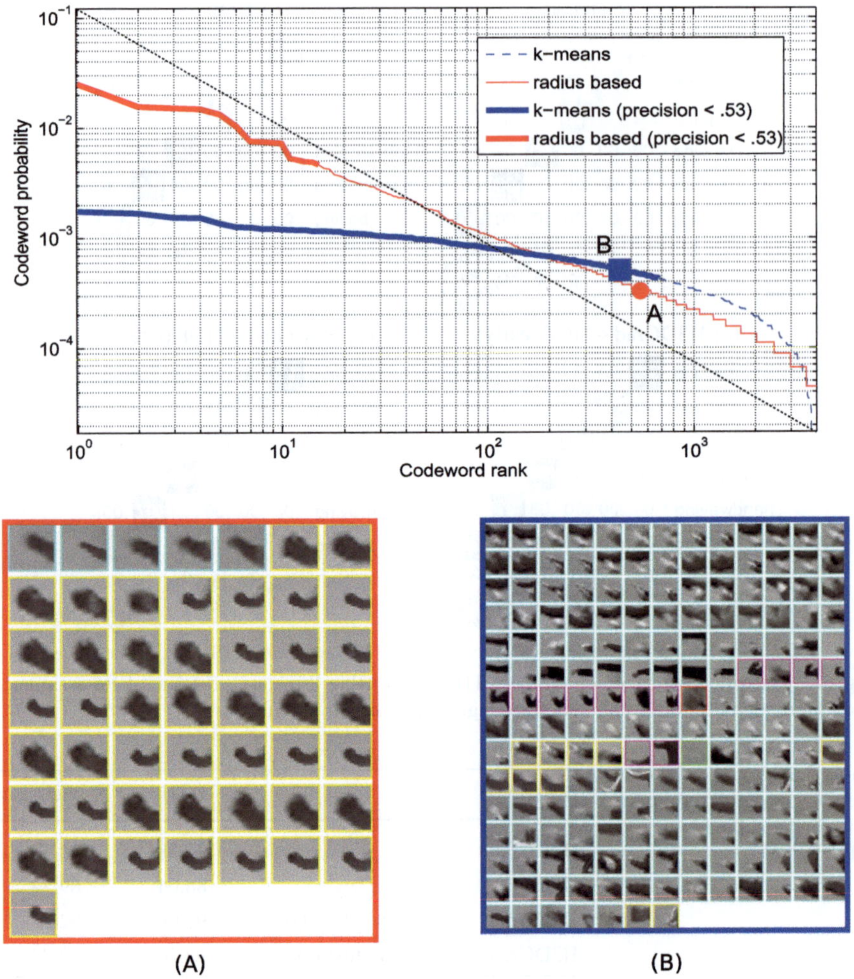

Fig. 3.8 Log–log plots of codeword frequency using k-means and radius-based clustering with hard assignment. *Bold lines* indicate regions where the average cluster precision [36] is below 0.53. The *dotted diagonal line* represents the Zipfian distribution. Two sample clusters are shown at near frequencies, respectively obtained with radius-based clustering (**A**) (most of the features in the cluster represent spatio-temporal patches of the same action) and with k-means (**B**) (features in the cluster represent patches of several actions). Patches of actions have different colors: *boxing (cyan)*, *hand-waving (magenta)*, *hand-clapping (yellow)*, *running (green)*, *walking (red)*, *jogging (blue)*

Figure 3.8 shows the codeword frequency of radius-based clustering and k-means with hard quantization on the KTH dataset. It is interesting to note that with k-means most of the codewords have similar probability of occurrence, so making it difficult to identify a set of words that have at the same time high discrimination capability and good probability of occurrence. In contrast radius-based shows a much less uniform frequency distribution. Interestingly, with radius-based clustering, the codeword distribution of the human action vocabulary is similar to the Zipf's law for textual corpuses. It seems therefore reasonable to assume that codewords at intermediate frequencies are the most informative also for human action classification, and the best candidates for the formation of the codebook.

Due to the high dimensionality of the descriptor, codebooks for human actions usually have cluster centers that are spread in the feature space, so that two or more codewords are equally relevant for a feature point (codeword *uncertainty*); moreover cluster centers are often too far from feature points so that they are not anymore representative (codeword *plausibility*). With radius-based clustering, codeword *uncertainty* is critical because it frequently happens that feature points are close to the codewords boundaries [52]. Instead, codeword *plausibility* is naturally relaxed due to the fact that clusters are more uniformly distributed in the feature space. To reduce the *uncertainty* in codeword assignment, we therefore performed radius-based clustering with soft assignment by Gaussian kernel density estimation smoothing. In this case, the histogram H is computed as:

$$H(w) = \frac{1}{n} \sum_{i=1}^{n} \frac{K_\sigma(w, f_i)}{\sum_{j=1}^{|V|} K_\sigma(v_j, f_i)} \tag{3.13}$$

where K_σ is the Gaussian kernel: $K_\sigma(\cdot,\cdot) = \frac{1}{\sqrt{2\pi}\sigma} e^{(-\frac{d(\cdot,\cdot)^2}{2\sigma^2})}$ being σ the scale parameter tuned on the training set, and $d(\cdot,\cdot)$ is the Euclidean distance.

Figure 3.9 compares the classification accuracy with codebooks obtained with k-means clustering with both hard and soft assignment, and radius-based clustering with soft assignment, respectively, for the KTH and Weizmann dataset. The plots have been obtained by progressively adding less frequent codewords to the codebooks (respectively up to 4000 and 1000 codewords for the two datasets). The performance of k-means is improved by the use of soft assignment. With a small number of words radius-based clustering with soft assignment has lower performance than k-means due to the fact that the codewords used have higher frequency than those used by k-means (see Fig. 3.8). As the number of codewords in the codebook increases, radius-based clustering outperforms k-means, whether with hard or soft assignment. This reflects the fact that in this case radius-based clustering permits to have also sparse regions being represented in the codebook. Besides, soft assignment helps to reduce *uncertainty* in the dense regions. Figure 3.10 shows the confusion matrix for different human actions on KTH and Weizmann datasets with radius-based soft assignment. The average accuracy is respectively, 92.66 % and 95.41 % for the two datasets.

3.5 Experimental Results

We have assessed our approach for categorization of human actions in different conditions. Particularly, it has been tested on the KTH and Weizmann datasets that

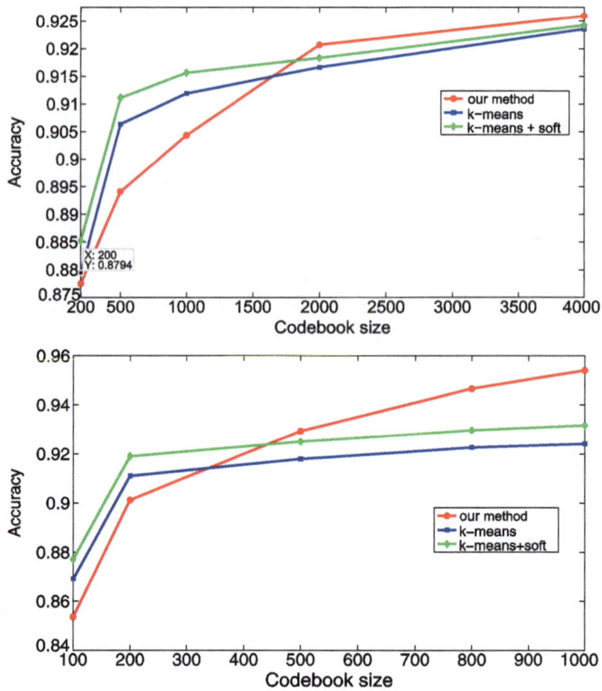

Fig. 3.9 Classification accuracy on KTH (*top*) and Weizmann (*bottom*) datasets with codebooks created with k-means with hard assignment, k-means with soft assignment and radius-based with soft assignment

show staged actions performed by an individual in a constrained non-cluttered environment. Moreover, in order to have a more complete assessment of the performance of the proposed solution even in real world scenes with high variability and unconstrained videos, we also carried out experiments on the Hollywood2 and MICC-UNIFI Surveillance datasets. This latter, made publicly available at www.openvisor.org [53], includes real world video surveillance sequences containing actions performed by individuals with cluttering and varying filming conditions. Experiments were performed using non-linear SVMs with the χ^2 kernel [62].

3.5.1 Experiments on KTH and Weizmann Datasets

The KTH dataset, currently the most common dataset used for the evaluations of action recognition methods [55], contains 2391 short video sequences showing six basic actions: *walking, running, jogging, hand-clapping, hand-waving, boxing*. They are performed by 25 actors under four different scenarios with illumination, appearance and scale changes. They have been filmed with a hand-held camera at 160×120 pixel resolution. The Weizmann dataset contains 93 short video sequences showing nine different persons, each performing ten actions: *run, walk, skip, jumping-jack, jump-forward-on-two-legs, jump-in-place-on-two-legs, gallop-sideways, wave-two-hands, wave-one-hand* and *bend*. They have been filmed with a fixed camera, at 180×144 pixel resolution, under the same lighting condition.

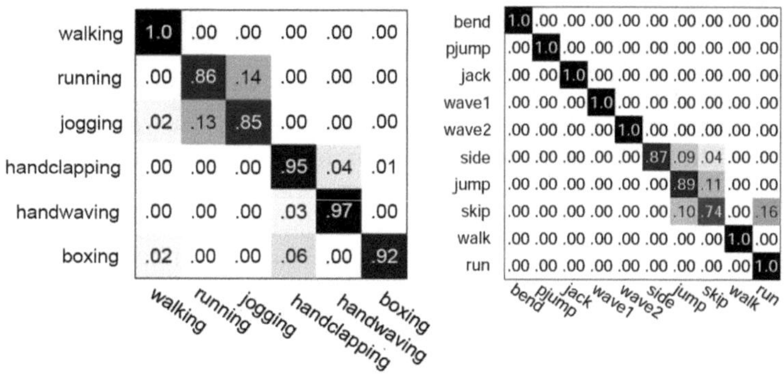

Fig. 3.10 Classification accuracy on KTH (*left*) and Weizmann (*right*) datasets using radius-based clustering with soft assignment

Table 3.3 Comparison of classification accuracy with some state-of-the-art methods on KTH and Weizmann datasets

Method	KTH	Weizmann	Features	Optimizations
Our method	*92.66*	*95.41*	H3DGrad + HOF	–
Yu et al. [61]	91.8	–	HoG + HOF	–
Wang et al. [55]	92.1	–	HOF	–
Gao et al. [16]	91.14	–	MoSIFT	–
Sun et al. [49]	89.8	90.3	2D SIFT + 3D SIFT + Zernike	–
Rapantzikos et al. [42]	88.3	–	PCA-Gradient	–
Laptev et al. [27]	91.8	–	HoG + HOF	codebook, sampling
Dollár et al. [13]	81.2	–	PCA-Gradient	–
Wong and Cipolla [57]	86.62	–	PCA-Gradient	–
Scovanner et al. [44]	–	82.6	3D SIFT	codebook
Niebles et al. [39]	83.33	90	PCA-Gradient	–
Liu et al. [31]	–	90.4	PCA-Gradient + Spin images	codebook
Kläser et al. [23]	91.4	84.3	3D HoG	descriptor
Willems et al. [56]	84.26	–	3D SURF	–
Schüldt et al. [43]	71.7	–	ST-Jets	–

Table 3.3 reports the average accuracy of our method in comparison with the most notable research results published in the literature. The performance figures reported are those published in their respective papers. For a fair comparison, our experiments have been performed with the setup suggested by the creators of the KTH and Weizmann datasets [17, 43], that has been used in [16, 23, 27, 31, 42–44, 49, 55–57, 61]. In particular, with the KTH dataset, SVM classifiers have been trained on sequences of 16 actors and performance was evaluated for the sequences of the remaining 9 actors according to 5-fold cross-validation. With the Weizmann

dataset, SVM classifiers have been trained on the videos of 8 actors and tested on the one remaining, following leave-one-out cross-validation.

While showing the best performance, our solution has also the nice property that it does not require any adaptation to the context under observation. Instead other solutions require some tuning of the descriptor to the specific context. Namely, Laptev et al. [27] perform different spatio-temporal sampling of video frames and define a set of descriptors; hence they represent each action with the best combination of sampling and descriptors; Kläser et al. [23] use a parameterized 3D gradient descriptor; parameter values are optimized for the dataset used; Liu et al. [31] use both local and global descriptors and select the best combination of them according to an optimization procedure; Scovanner et al. [44] optimize the codebook by associating co-occurrent visual words.

Other researchers have claimed higher performance on the KTH dataset: 93.17 % Bregonzio et al. [7]; 94.2 % Liu and Shah [30]; 93.43 % Lin et al. [29]; 95.83 % Chen et al. [10]. However, these results were obtained with a Leave-One-Out Cross-Validation setting that uses more training data and therefore are not directly comparable. For the sake of fairness, they have not been included in Table 3.3. An exhaustive list of the different experimental setups and results has been recently published by Gao et al. [16].

3.5.2 Experiments on MICC-UNIFI Surveillance Dataset

The MICC-UNIFI Surveillance dataset is composed by 175 real world video sequences of human actions with durations ranging from 3 to 20 seconds. The videos have been taken from wall mounted Sony SNC RZ30 cameras at 640 × 480 pixel resolution, in a parking lot. The scenes are captured from different viewpoints, at different degrees of zooming, with different shadowing and unpredictable occlusions, at different duration, speed and illumination conditions. Eight subjects perform seven everyday actions: *walking, running, pickup object, enter car, exit car, handshake* and *give object*. A few examples are shown in Fig. 3.11. We followed a repeated stratified random sub-sampling validation, using 80 % of the videos of each class as training set. Experiments were performed using a 2000 codeword codebook. The confusion matrix of classification accuracy is reported in Fig. 3.12: the average accuracy is 86.28 %. Most of the misclassifications observed with our method occurred with the *give object* and *handshake* actions. They are both characterized by a very fast motion pattern and small motion of the human limbs. Figure 3.13 reports sample sequences of these actions with evidence of details. In Table 3.4, we report a comparison of our method with other codebook creation approaches (k-means with hard and soft assignment) and with other state-of-the-art descriptors that publicly make their implementation available: MoSIFT[2] [16] and Dollár et al.[3] [13]. The results show that the proposed method outperforms the other approaches, and that

[2] http://lastlaugh.inf.cs.cmu.edu/libscom/downloads.htm

[3] http://vision.ucsd.edu/%7epdollar/research.html

(a) Walking

(b) Running

(c) Pickup object

(d) Enter car

(e) Enter car (from a different view point)

(f) Exit car

(g) Handshake

(h) Give object

Fig. 3.11 Sample frames of sequences from the MICC-UNIFI Surveillance dataset

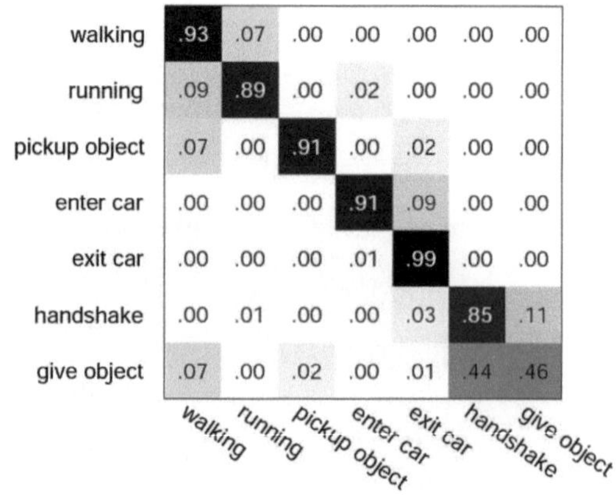

Fig. 3.12 Classification accuracy on the MICC-Surveillance dataset using radius-based clustering with soft assignment

Table 3.4 Comparison of classification accuracy on MICC-Surveillance dataset with our method, k-means with soft assignment, k-means with hard assignment, and with the descriptors proposed in [13] and [16]

Method	MICC-Surveillance
Our method	*86.28*
k-means + soft	83.74
k-means	82.90
Dollár et al. [13]	72.50
MoSIFT [16]	75.88

the proposed codebook creation approach performs better than the typical k-means clustering whether with hard and soft assignment.

3.5.3 Experiments on Hollywood2 Dataset

The Hollywood2 dataset [34] is composed by sequences extracted from DVDs of 69 Hollywood movies, showing 12 different actions in realistic and challenging settings: *answer phone, drive car, eat, fight person, get out of car, handshake, hug person, kiss, run, sit down, sit up, stand up*. We performed our experiments with the same setup of [27, 55] using the "clean" training dataset, containing scenes that have been manually verified. This dataset is composed by 1707 sequences divided in training set (823) and test set (884), with different frame size and frame rate; train and test set videos have been selected from different movies. To be comparable with other experimental results, the performance has been evaluated computing the average precision (AP) for each class and reporting also the mean AP over all classes. Codebooks have been created using 4000 codewords, as in [55]. We have compared our codebook creation approach with k-means clustering using both soft and hard assignments, and with an implementation of the method proposed in [27] using the provided descriptor and detector.[4] Results are reported in Table 3.5, showing that

[4]http://www.irisa.fr/vista/Equipe/People/Laptev/download.html

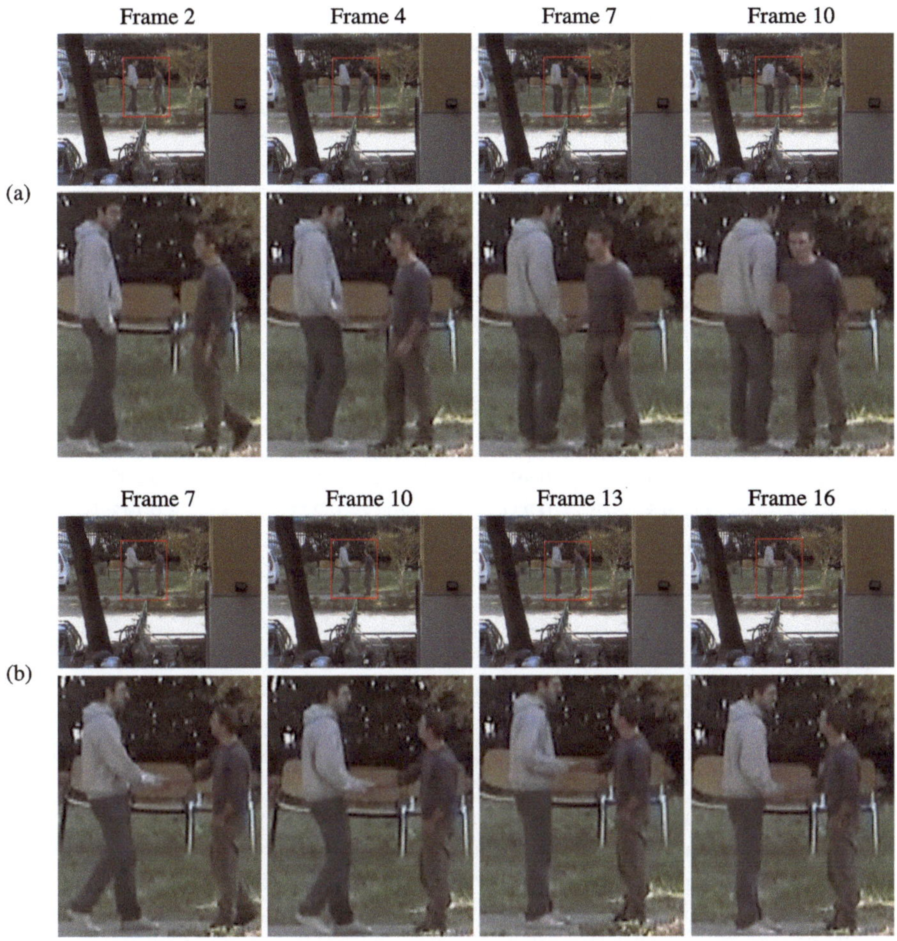

Fig. 3.13 Sample frames of *give object* (**a**) and *handshake* (**b**) action sequences in the MICC–Surveillance dataset. For each sequence, the *second row* shows the detail indicated in *red* in the *first row*

the proposed method outperforms the other approaches in the majority of action classes and in terms of mean AP.

3.5.4 Experiments on Reducing the Codebook Size

Large codebooks, although being able to exploit the most informative codewords as illustrated in Fig. 3.8, imply high time and space complexity. Reduction of codebook size with preservation of descriptive capability is therefore desirable. Linear dimensionality reduction techniques such as Principal Component Analysis or Latent Semantic Analysis, are not suited to this end because they are not able to handle

Table 3.5 Comparison of per-class AP performance on Hollywood2 dataset with codebooks created with our method, k-means with soft assignment, k-means with hard assignment and with the detector+descriptor proposed by Laptev et al. [27]

Action	*k-means*	*k-means + soft*	*Our method*	Laptev et al. [27]
Answer phone	0.178	0.186	*0.195*	0.134
Drive car	0.864	*0.865*	0.863	0.861
Eat	0.552	0.564	0.564	*0.596*
Fight person	0.564	0.557	0.578	*0.643*
Get put of car	0.362	0.364	*0.362*	0.297
Handshake	0.142	0.143	0.167	*0.179*
Hug person	0.251	0.257	0.275	*0.345*
Kiss	0.494	*0.510*	0.503	0.467
Run	0.631	0.636	*0.659*	0.619
Sit down	0.483	0.493	*0.509*	0.505
Sit up	0.215	0.231	*0.227*	0.143
Stand up	0.511	0.513	*0.514*	0.485
Mean AP	0.437	0.443	*0.451*	0.439

high order correlations between codewords that are present in human action representation [51]. We have therefore applied nonlinear dimensionality reduction with Deep Belief Networks (DBNs) [20, 51]. A DBN is composed of several Restricted Boltzmann Machines (RBM) building blocks that encode levels of non-linear relationships of the input vectors. It is pre-trained by learning layers incrementally using contrastive divergence [9]. After pre-training, the auto-encoder is built by reversing the network and connecting the top layer of the network to the bottom layer of its reversed version. The auto-encoder is then used to fine-tune the network using a standard back-propagation algorithm.

Since the action representation $H(w)$ can be considered as a coarse probability density estimation of the features of a human action (see Eq. 3.13), given a set of space-time features $\mathcal{F} = \{f_1, f_2, \dots, f_n\}$, the value of the ith bin of H can be considered as the probability that a space-time descriptor $f \in \mathcal{F}$ is represented by the codeword w_i. This probability can hence be used as an input for an RBM according to [19].

Figure 3.14 reports plots of accuracy measured at different codebook sizes, with PCA, LSA and DBN codebook reduction and radius-based clustering with soft assignment, on the KTH dataset. Codebook reduction was applied to a 4000 codewords codebook. The dimension of the input layer is equal to the size of the uncompressed codebook and the dimension of the output layer is the compressed codebook size. Each hidden layer is one half the dimension of its input layer. The network depth ranges between five and eight depending on the size of the output codebook. The performance of our approach outperforms that of the method recently proposed in [24], especially for the smaller codebook sizes.

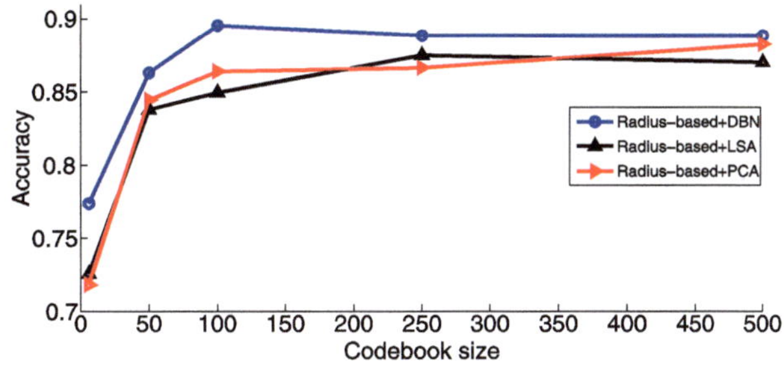

Fig. 3.14 Classification accuracy on KTH dataset at different codebook sizes, with different codebook reduction techniques, for radius-based clustering with soft assignment

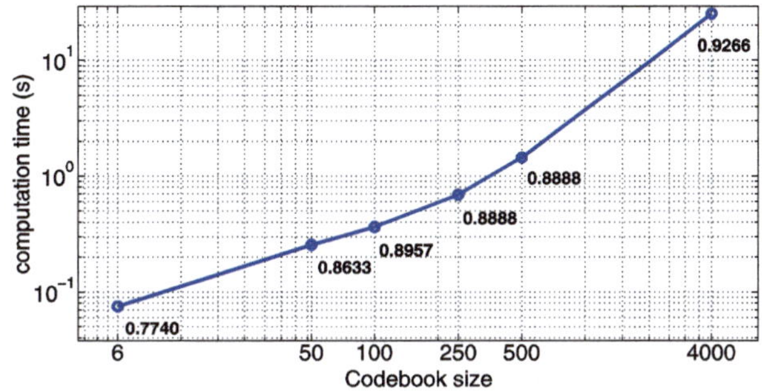

Fig. 3.15 Mean computation times for a KTH video sequence at different codebook sizes with radius-based clustering and DBNs. The numbers associated to the markers indicate the classification accuracy

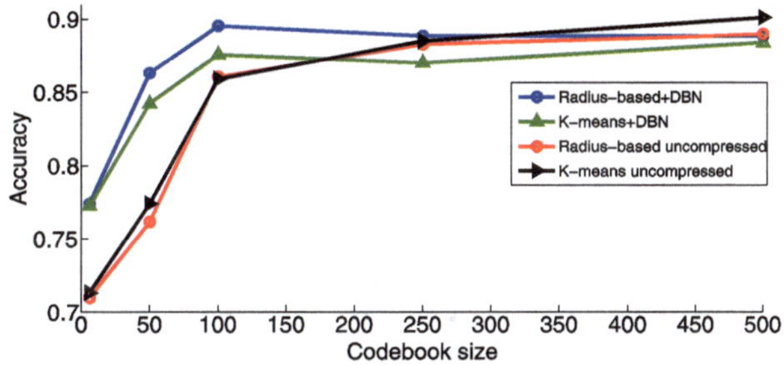

Fig. 3.16 Classification accuracy as a function of codebook size, for DBN-compressed and uncompressed codebooks. Radius-based clustering with soft assignment is compared with k-means clustering with hard assignment

Figure 3.15 reports plots of mean computation times for a KTH video sequence as a function of codebook size for radius-based clustering with soft assignment. The accuracy values of Fig. 3.14 have been reported on the plot for the sake of completeness. It can be noticed that strong codebook size reductions result into time improvements of more than two orders of magnitude. A compressed codebook with 100 codewords scores 89.57 % recognition accuracy with respect to 92.66 % of a 4000 codewords codebook.

Figure 3.16 shows that DBN-compressed codebooks on the one hand provide good accuracy even with very small codebook sizes, and on the other hand make radius-based clustering still competitive with respect to k-means clustering with 100 or less codewords.

Table 3.6 reports a comparison in terms of classification accuracy at different codebook sizes with DBN, PCA and LSA on the MICC-UNIFI surveillance dataset. Codebook reduction was applied to the 2000 codeword codebook obtained with

Table 3.6 Classification accuracy on MICC-UNIFI dataset at different codebook sizes, with different codebook reduction techniques, for radius-based clustering with soft assignment. Using PCA and LSA, it is not possible to create codebooks larger than the number of training videos; using DBNs this issue is not present

Codebook size	6	50	100	250	500
DBN	0.386	0.397	0.412	0.431	0.474
PCA	0.333	0.378	0.405	–	–
LSA	0.330	0.346	0.335	–	–

Table 3.7 Classification of MAP performance on Hollywood2 dataset at different codebook sizes, with different codebook reduction techniques, for radius-based clustering with soft assignment

Codebook size	6	50	100	250	500
DBN	0.281	0.372	0.383	0.375	0.374
PCA	0.191	0.323	0.329	0.337	0.338
LSA	0.204	0.322	0.316	0.311	0.314

radius-based clustering and soft assignment in the previous classification experiment. The smaller number of available training videos, with respect to KTH, is responsible for the reduction in classification accuracy, although the DBNs largely outperform the other methods. This experiment shows another advantage of the use of DBNs over PCA and LSA when the number of sequences available for training is relatively small, that is, the possibility to create larger dictionaries that usually yield higher classification accuracy although maintaining a speed improvement of an order of magnitude. Table 3.7 reports a comparison of MAP performance obtained using compressed codebooks created with DBN, PCA and LSA on the Hollywood2 dataset. Codebook reduction was applied to the 4000 codeword codebook obtained with radius-based clustering and soft assignment used in the classification experiment. Despite the challenging dataset, the performance is still comparable with that obtained with full sized codebooks by several approaches reported in [55].

3.5.5 Tracker Evaluation and Experiments on Recognizing Multiple Actions

These experiments have been performed on a subset of the MICC-UNIFI Surveillance dataset. First of all, we have evaluated our tracking module quality by measuring multiple object tracking accuracy (MOTA) as defined by Bernardin and Stiefelhagen [5]. MOTA is an intuitive performance metric for multiple object trackers and measures a tracker performance at keeping accurate trajectories. For each frame processed a tracker should produce a set of object hypotheses, each of which should ideally correspond to a real visible object. In order to compute MOTA, a consistent

Table 3.8 Multiple object tracking accuracy (MOTA) together with false positive rate (FPR), false negative rate (FPR) and amount of identity switches (SWITCH)

Seq.	FPR	FNR	SWITCH	MOTA
1	27.92	2.92	0	68.35
2	38.56	12.40	2	49.82
3	13.15	32.16	0	54.67
4	23.65	9.18	0	67.20
5	15.02	27.48	0	57.74
6	14.59	3.82	52	79.38

hypothesis-object mapping over time must be produced; the complete procedure to obtain this mapping is specified in detail in [5]. MOTA takes into account all possible errors that a multi-object tracker makes: false positives, missed objects and identity switches. False positives (*fp*) arise when, for example, the tracker is initiated on a false detection or when an object is missed and consequently a wrong pattern replaces the correct object hypothesis. Misses or false negatives (*fn*) arise whenever an object is not mapped to any of the hypotheses proposed by the tracker; finally identity switches (*sw*) happen whenever an object hypothesis is mapped to the wrong object, for example after an occlusion or when an object tracker fails and another tracker is reinitialized. Errors are normalized by the number of objects present (*gt*) with respect to the whole sequence.

MOTA is defined as follows:

$$MOTA = 1 - \frac{\sum_t fp_t + fn_t + sw_t}{\sum_t gt_t} \tag{3.14}$$

We represent persons as bounding boxes and we consider a mapping correct if $\frac{O \cap H}{O \cup H} \geq 0.5$, where O and H are the areas of the object and the hypothesis bounding boxes mapped. We measured MOTA for all five sequences in which our final recognition experiments were performed and another sequence (Table 3.8). The last sequence is recorded with a PTZ camera, panning tilting and zooming on targets and targets are instructed to produce overlapping trajectories in order to create difficult situations for a multiple object tracker. In the first five test sequences, most of the errors are caused by false alarms of the pedestrian detector that cause instantiation of trackers; in the classification stage this empty tracks can be filtered since they usually do not contain enough detected space-time interest points. In the last sequence, most of the errors are due to identity switches since target maneuvers are more complex. MOTA is quite satisfying in all sequences, considering also that, in order to attain real-time performance, our appearance model is weak and no online classifier is used to perform data association or learn the template.

We have further evaluated the performance of our approach on five complex video sequences containing multiple actions performed concurrently (two examples are shown in Fig. 3.17). These sequences have different durations ranging from a minimum of ~120 to a maximum of ~300 frames. Our method has been applied to recognize and localize two basic actions: *walking* and *running*. As training set,

Fig. 3.17 Example of two sequences from our multiple-action surveillance dataset. In the first sequence (*seq.* 3), our actors perform a *pickpocketing* event. In the second sequence (*seq.* 5), a *snatch* is performed

Table 3.9 System performance on complex video sequences: for each sequence the number of tracks, action ground-truth ($\mathbf{W}_{GT}$, $\mathbf{R}_{GT}$, $\mathbf{O}_{GT}$), and classification accuracy are reported

Seq.	Detected	Filtered	$\mathbf{W}_{GT}$	$\mathbf{R}_{GT}$	$\mathbf{O}_{GT}$	Acc
1	8	5	3	2	0	4/5
2	7	6	3	2	1	5/6
3	11	5	2	2	1	4/5
4	8	6	2	3	1	4/6
5	8	5	3	2	0	4/5
						21/27

we used the videos containing a single person performing the same action multiple times.

Table 3.9 shows the performance of our approach on surveillance videos. For each sequence, we report the detected tracks identified from our person detector and tracker. The tracks that contain less than 30 interest points are discarded and the filtered tracks are then used to perform action classification. These tracks are manually annotated in walking, running and other action (reported in Table 3.9 in the columns $\mathbf{W}_{GT}$, $\mathbf{R}_{GT}$, $\mathbf{O}_{GT}$ respectively). Details of classification accuracy are shown. We note that 21/27 tracks are recognized correctly. The performance of action classification is evaluated in terms of two standard metrics that is, precision and recall, defined as:

$$precision = \frac{\text{\# of correctly predicted actions}}{\text{\# of predicted actions}} \tag{3.15}$$

$$recall = \frac{\text{\# of correctly predicted actions}}{\text{\# of ground-truth actions}} \tag{3.16}$$

Precision and recall performance of the action recognition, also shown in Table 3.10, are mostly affected by mistaken classification of the tracks that contain the "other"

Table 3.10 Precision and recall for the *running* and *walking* actions

Action	Precision	Recall
Walking	73 %	85 %
Running	77 %	71 %

action, since only one track that contains a walking action was classified as running action.

3.6 Conclusions

In this chapter, we have presented a novel method for human action categorization that exploits a new descriptor for spatio-temporal interest points that combines appearance (3D gradient descriptor) and motion (optic flow descriptor), and effective codebook creation based on radius-based clustering and a soft assignment of feature descriptors to codewords. The approach was validated on KTH and Weizmann datasets, on the Hollywood2 dataset and on a new surveillance dataset that contain unconstrained video sequences that include more realistic and complex actions. Results outperform the state-of-the-art with no parameter tuning. We have also shown that a strong reduction of computation time can be obtained by applying codebook size reduction with Deep Belief Networks, with small reduction of classification performance.

References

1. Arulampalam M, Maskell S, Gordon N, Clapp T (2002) A tutorial on particle filters for online nonlinear/non-Gaussian Bayesian tracking. IEEE Trans Signal Process 50(2):174–188
2. Bagdanov AD, Dini F, Del Bimbo A, Nunziati W (2007) Improving the robustness of particle filter-based visual trackers using online parameter adaptation. In: Proc of AVSS
3. Ballan L, Bertini M, Del Bimbo A, Seidenari L, Serra G (2011) Event detection and recognition for semantic annotation of video. Multimed Tools Appl 51(1):279–302
4. Ballan L, Bertini M, Del Bimbo A, Seidenari L, Serra G (2012) Effective codebooks for human action representation and classification in unconstrained videos. IEEE Trans Multimed 14(4):1234–1245
5. Bernardin K, Stiefelhagen R (2008) Evaluating multiple object tracking performance: the CLEAR MOT metrics. EURASIP J Image Video Process 2008:246309
6. Bobick AF, Davis JW (2001) The recognition of human movement using temporal templates. IEEE Trans Pattern Anal Mach Intell 23(3):257–267
7. Bregonzio M, Gong S, Xiang T (2009) Recognising action as clouds of space-time interest points. In: Proc of CVPR
8. Cao L, Zicheng L, Huang T (2010) Cross-dataset action detection. In: Proc of CVPR
9. Carreira Perpinan MA, Hinton GE (2005) On contrastive divergence learning. In: Proc of AISTATS
10. Chen MY, Hauptmann AG (2009) MoSIFT: recognizing human actions in surveillance videos. Technical report, CMU

11. Comaniciu D, Meer P (2002) Mean shift: a robust approach toward feature space analysis. IEEE Trans Pattern Anal Mach Intell 24(5):603–619
12. Dalal N, Triggs B (2005) Histograms of oriented gradients for human detection. In: Proc of CVPR
13. Dollár P, Rabaud V, Cottrell G, Belongie S (2005) Behavior recognition via sparse spatio-temporal features. In: Proc of VSPETS
14. Efros AA, Berg AC, Mori G, Malik J (2003) Recognizing action at a distance. In: Proc of ICCV
15. Fergus R, Perona P, Zisserman A (2003) Object class recognition by unsupervised scale-invariant learning. In: Proc of CVPR
16. Gao Z, Chen MY, Hauptmann AG, Cai A (2010) Comparing evaluation protocols on the KTH dataset. In: Proc of HBU workshop
17. Gorelick L, Blank M, Schechtman E, Irani M, Basri R (2007) Actions as space-time shapes. IEEE Trans Pattern Anal Mach Intell 29(12):2247–2253
18. Hauptmann AG, Christel MG, Yan R (2008) Video retrieval based on semantic concepts. Proc IEEE 96(4):602–622
19. Hinton EG, Salakhutdinov R (2006) Reducing the dimensionality of data with neural networks. Science 313(5786):504–507
20. Hinton EG, Osindero S, Teh Y (2006) A fast learning algorithm for deep belief nets. Neural Comput 18(7):1527–1554
21. Jiang YG, Yang J, Ngo CW, Hauptmann AG (2010) Representations of keypoint-based semantic concept detection: a comprehensive study. IEEE Trans Multimed 12(1):42–53
22. Jurie F, Triggs B (2005) Creating efficient codebooks for visual recognition. In: Proc of ICCV
23. Kläser A, Marszałek M, Schmid C (2008) A spatio-temporal descriptor based on 3D-gradients. In: Proc of BMVC
24. Kong Y, Zhang X, Hu W, Jia Y (2011) Adaptive learning codebook for action recognition. Pattern Recognit Lett 32(8):1178–1186
25. Kovashka A, Grauman K (2010) Learning a hierarchy of discriminative space-time neighborhood features for human action recognition. In: Proc of CVPR
26. Laptev I (2005) On space-time interest points. Int J Comput Vis 64(2–3):107–123
27. Laptev I, Marszałek M, Schmid C, Rozenfeld B (2008) Learning realistic human actions from movies. In: Proc of CVPR
28. Lazebnik S, Schmid C, Ponce J (2006) Beyond bags of features: spatial pyramid matching for recognizing natural scene categories. In: Proc of CVPR
29. Lin Z, Jiang Z, Davis LS (2009) Recognizing actions by shape-motion prototype trees. In: Proc of ICCV
30. Liu J, Shah M (2008) Learning human actions via information maximization. In: Proc of CVPR
31. Liu J, Ali S, Shah M (2008) Recognizing human actions using multiple features. In: Proc of CVPR
32. Liu J, Luo J, Shah M (2009) Recognizing realistic actions from videos "in the wild". In: Proc of CVPR
33. Lucas BD, Kanade T (1981) An iterative image registration technique with an application to stereo vision. In: Proc of DARPA IU workshop
34. Marszałek M, Laptev I, Schmid C (2009) Actions in context. In: Proc of CVPR
35. Mikolajczyk K, Uemura H (2008) Action recognition with motion-appearance vocabulary forest. In: Proc of CVPR
36. Mikolajczyk K, Leibe B, Schiele B (2005) Local features for object class recognition. In: Proc of ICCV
37. Mikolajczyk K, Tuytelaars T, Schmid C, Zisserman A, Matas J, Schaffalitzky F, Kadir T, Van Gool L (2005) A comparison of affine region detectors. Int J Comput Vis 65(1/2):43–72
38. Moeslund T, Hilton A, Krüger V (2006) A survey of advances in vision-based human motion capture and analysis. Comput Vis Image Underst 104(2–3):90–126

39. Niebles JC, Wang H, Fei-Fei L (2008) Unsupervised learning of human action categories using spatial-temporal words. Int J Comput Vis 79(3):299–318
40. Poppe R (2007) Vision-based human motion analysis: an overview. Comput Vis Image Underst 108(1–2):4–18
41. Poppe R (2010) A survey on vision-based human action recognition. Image Vis Comput 28(6):976–990
42. Rapantzikos K, Avrithis Y, Kollia S (2009) Dense saliency-based spatiotemporal feature points for action recognition. In: Proc of CVPR
43. Schüldt C, Laptev I, Caputo B (2004) Recognizing human actions: a local SVM approach. In: Proc of ICPR
44. Scovanner P, Ali S, Shah M (2007) A 3-dimensional SIFT descriptor and its application to action recognition. In: Proc of ACM multimedia
45. Shao L, Mattivi R (2010) Feature detector and descriptor evaluation in human action recognition. In: Proc of CIVR
46. Shao L, Gao R, Liu Y, Zhang H (2011) Transform based spatio-temporal descriptors for human action recognition. Neurocomputing 74(6):962–973
47. Sivic J, Zisserman A (2003) Video Google: a text retrieval approach to object matching in videos. In: Proc of ICCV
48. Snoek CGM, Worring M, van Gemert JC, Geusebroek JM, Smeulders AWM (2006) The challenge problem for automated detection of 101 semantic concepts in multimedia. In: Proc of ACM multimedia
49. Sun X, Chen M, Hauptmann AG (2009) Action recognition via local descriptors and holistic features. In: Proc of CVPR4HB workshop
50. Turaga P, Chellappa R, Subrahmanian V, Udrea O (2008) Machine recognition of human activities: a survey. IEEE Trans Circuits Syst Video Technol 18(11):1473–1488
51. van der Maaten L, Postma E, van den Herik H (2009) Dimensionality reduction: a comparative review. Technical report TiCC-TR 2009-005, Tilburg University
52. van Gemert JC, Veenman CJ, Smeulders AWM, Geusebroek JM (2010) Visual word ambiguity. IEEE Trans Pattern Anal Mach Intell 32(7):1271–1283
53. Vezzani R, Cucchiara R (2010) Video surveillance online repository (ViSOR): an integrated framework. Multimed Tools Appl 50(2):359–380
54. Wang Y, Mori G (2009) Max-margin hidden conditional random fields for human action recognition. In: Proc of CVPR
55. Wang H, Ullah MM, Kläser A, Laptev I, Schmid C (2009) Evaluation of local spatio-temporal features for action recognition. In: Proc of BMVC
56. Willems G, Tuytelaars T, Van Gool L (2008) An efficient dense and scale-invariant spatio-temporal interest point detector. In: Proc of ECCV
57. Wong SF, Cipolla R (2007) Extracting spatiotemporal interest points using global information. In: Proc of ICCV
58. Wu B, Nevatia R (2007) Detection and tracking of multiple, partially occluded humans by Bayesian combination of edgelet based part detectors. Int J Comput Vis 75(2):247–266
59. Yao A, Gall J, Van Gool L (2010) A hough transform-based voting framework for action recognition. In: Proc of CVPR
60. Yilmaz A, Shah M (2005) Actions sketch: a novel action representation. In: Proc of CVPR
61. Yu G, Goussies N, Yuan J, Liu Z (2011) Fast action detection via discriminative random forest voting and top-k subvolume search. IEEE Trans Multimed 13(3):507–517
62. Zhang J, Marszałek M, Lazebnik S, Schmid C (2007) Local features and kernels for classification of texture and object categories: a comprehensive study. Int J Comput Vis 73(2):213–238

Chapter 4
Evaluating and Extending Trajectory Features for Activity Recognition

Ross Messing, Atousa Torabi, Aaron Courville, and Chris Pal

Abstract Trajectory features are a powerful new way to describe video data. By leveraging the spatio-temporal range and structure of trajectories, they improve activity recognition performance compared to systems based on fixed local spatio-temporal volumes. This chapter places them in context, compares a sparse, generative model of extended trajectories to a dense, discriminative model of local trajectories, and explores ways to extend the sparse system with new kinds of information.

4.1 Introduction and Background

Activity recognition in video is an increasingly important field of computer vision, with many practical applications in areas like surveillance and smart environments. As activity recognition techniques mature, it is important to take stock of new developments, and evaluate how to integrate them with established techniques.

R. Messing (✉)
University of Rochester, Rochester, NY, USA
e-mail: rmessing@cs.rochester.edu

Present address:
R. Messing
Tandent Vision Science, Inc., Pittsburgh, PA, USA

A. Torabi · A. Courville
Université de Montréal, Montréal, Quebec, Canada

A. Torabi
e-mail: torabi@iro.umontreal.ca

A. Courville
e-mail: courvila@iro.umontreal.ca

C. Pal
École Polytechnique de Montréal, Montréal, Quebec, Canada
e-mail: christopher.pal@polymtl.ca

G.M. Farinella et al. (eds.), *Advanced Topics in Computer Vision*,
Advances in Computer Vision and Pattern Recognition,
DOI 10.1007/978-1-4471-5520-1_4,

4.1.1 Activity Recognition

Early work on activity recognition required very explicit, rigid models of the activities to be recognized, and the people performing those actions [1, 19, 21]. While these systems are not as sophisticated and flexible as modern, state-of-the-art systems, they encoded many important intuitions, like what kinds of information can be usefully combined for activity recognition.

Statistical methods, most notably the bag of words [14] approach to recognition, first became very popular in object recognition in still images [7]. By running an interest point operator to find repeatable interest points in images (usually distinctive corners), extracting a local appearance patch description from the interest point's neighborhood, and codebooking those descriptions, the histogram of local feature codewords becomes a very powerful description of an image, which loses broad spatial structure, but keeps a great deal of local neighborhood structure. This histogram of local patches representation can be treated like a histogram of word counts in a document, and techniques from natural languages processing can be used to classify that histogram.

Statistical approaches inspired by the success of bag-of-words models in still-image object recognition have come to dominate activity recognition in video. A lot of research has gone into the best way to describe small pieces of video, and how to combine those little bits to describe a whole video. The initial work involved straightforward generalization of spatial interest point detectors and descriptors to the temporal dimension [6, 11, 12], recent work has taken a more sophisticated approach to the spatio-temporal structure of video, yielding descriptors that follow trajectories across video [17, 24]. Inspired by psychophysical results showing the power of trajectories in human perception [9], these features seem to outperform local features attached to fixed points.

Trajectory features harness the idea that motion is extremely informative for the perception of human actions. Johansson [9] showed that by attaching point-lights to humans performing actions in the dark, those actions were easily recognizable. Cutting [4] introduced the first computational models of visual trajectories in a psychophysics subfield called "event perception".

4.1.2 Trajectory Features

There are several steps required to use feature trajectories for activity recognition. First, trajectories must be detected in the video. One way to do this is to randomly sample trajectories from uniformly distributed points throughout the video. This is known as dense sampling [23]. Depending on the sampling frequency, it leads to a large number of features, both relevant and irrelevant. The other, more traditional way to detect features is with an interest point detector, just as in still images [20], but with a temporal component as well. By finding reliable corners in space and time, features are more likely to be repeatable, and often result in better tracks.

These interest point detections can be called sparse detection, and leads to fewer features, but often better features, although good features to track that the detector misses may be present with dense features, but absent with sparse features. Recent work by Wang et al. show improved performance with dense local spatio-temporal features [23].

Once features are detected, they must be tracked, generally using optical flow. Optical flow involves finding the velocity transformation between frames, either locally or globally, that minimizes the difference between frames. Sparse trajectory features tend to use local patch-based optical flow, like the KLT tracker [15]. These algorithms tend to be much faster than global optical flow estimates, that compute a full optical flow field across the whole frame. Global optical flow techniques may, on the other hand, offer more robust, non-local motion constraints [3]. Once features are detected, and local or global optical flow is calculated, trajectories are just the concatenation of the optical flow field at the sequence of points indicated by following the optical flow field.

Whole image optical flow techniques consider a broader spatial area than sparse techniques, can incorporate softer constraints, and may be more robust to unusual motion. For example, Brox and Malik integrate rich spatial descriptors into a flow estimator minimizing a variational energy form to produce a more expensive, more robust global optical flow estimate [3]. Depending on how densely dense features are sampled, they can yield a large number of features, some of which are irrelevant, or a small number of features, few of which are irrelevant. When the dense features have some larger fixed distance between them, dense sampling can be much faster than feature detection, as it saves the computational overhead of feature detection. Dense features can still be more expensive than sparse features, however, as computing a dense optical flow field can also be expensive, particularly if it incorporates many global and soft probabilistic constraints.

4.1.3 Recent Developments

Local spatio-temporal features and descriptors in combination with the bag of features models have proven successful for action recognition [12, 16, 18]. In using local descriptors, there is always a trade-off between their discriminative power and their invariance to irrelevant changes in the video, like camera motion and illumination. This limitation causes ambiguities in video representation by local spatio-temporal features, especially when dealing with a large number of actions, resulting in low recognition performance. To cope with this problem, Ullah et al. have proposed an extension of BOF action recognition using non-local cues, including motion-based foreground segmentation, person detection, and object detection [22].

A recent approach to video representation is based on unsupervised feature learning as a way to learn features directly from video rather than applying hand-designed local features described in previous approaches. Le et al. [13] introduce an Independent Subspace Analysis algorithm that learns invariant spatio-temporal features from unlabeled video data. These learned spatio-temporal features achieve state-of-the-art performance on datasets like HoHA2, UCF, and Youtube.

We investigate two state-of-the-art trajectory descriptor systems in Sect. 4.2.

4.2 Trajectory Descriptors for Action Recognition

Activity recognition in video is dominated by approaches based on the bag-of-features models that work so well in still images. As the field matures, descriptors directly extending still-image descriptors into time are being supplanted by descriptors relying more fundamentally on the temporal structure of video. One type of descriptor that has yielded excellent performance is the family of trajectory-based descriptors. These descriptors follow trajectories extracted from the video, and their descriptiveness relies primarily or entirely on their motion, information which is unavailable in still images. We consider two very different kinds of trajectory features. Messing et al. [17] introduced a descriptor based on extended tracking of sparse keypoints, while Wang et al. [24] leverage dense optical flow to track and describe a set of densely-sampled features that span a fixed temporal range, but extend beyond a local spatial window. To our knowledge, these features have never been directly compared. We first review these features, and then compare their performance on a dataset where local spatio-temporal features do not perform well.

4.2.1 Velocity Histories of Sparse Tracked Keypoints

Messing et al. [17] introduce a video descriptor designed to capture the detailed motion of tracked features over long periods of time. By modeling trajectories with a log-polar velocity Markov chain, they naturally deal with variable-length trajectories, something that all other trajectory descriptors have had to deal with by converting them to fixed-length trajectories in one of a variety of ways. Velocity Markov chain parameters are learned via EM as part of a mixture model of velocity Markov chains. Their model can be thought of as extending a kind of supervised topic model, like Latent Dirichlet Allocation [2], to trajectories, where a distribution over discrete words is instead replaced by a Markov chain distribution over sequences of velocity transitions.

These features were explicitly designed to extend beyond local spatio-temporal boundaries of most existing activity recognition features, like Dollar et al.'s cuboids [6], or Laptev et al.'s STIP features [12]. Their performance on small videos with simple motion, where local space-time volumes adequately captured most of the relevant information, was unimpressive. However, on datasets with large videos containing complex, confusable motion, their performance was state-of-the-art. Messing et al. further extended these features by augmenting trajectory features with ancillary position and appearance information. This further improved performance, but at the price of translation-invariance, an important feature for a robust activity recognition system. Examples of Messing et al.'s sparse trajectory features can be seen in Figs. 4.2 and 4.4.

Fig. 4.1 Wang et al.'s dense features found on a sample frame from URADL's Answer Phone activity. *Red dots* denote feature candidates. *Green trails* denote trajectory histories

Fig. 4.2 Messing et al.'s sparse features found on another sample frame from URADL's Answer Phone activity. *Red dots* denote feature candidates. *Green trails* denote trajectory histories

4.2.2 Dense Trajectories

Wang et al. [24] extended existing work on dense local features for activity recognition [23] by linking their dense local features to trajectories. The original dense local feature work showed improved results for activity recognition using densely sampled features, rather than features detected by an interest point detector [23]. Wang et al. describe videos by first extracting a dense optical flow field (which can incorporate non-local constraints, and so may produce higher quality optical flow than the sparse methods used by Messing et al. [17]), densely sampling features across the image frame, and following their trajectories frame-to-frame. As features stop moving, become difficult to track, or reach the fixed trajectory duration of 15 frames, new features are sampled, keeping the total number of features roughly constant. Feature descriptors are applied to each fixed-duration trajectory. Example sparse and dense features extracted with Wang et al.'s detector are shown in Figs. 4.1 and 4.3. The descriptors included histograms of oriented gradients and optical flow (HOG and HOF) descriptors from [12], modified to follow the feature trajectory, but otherwise unchanged. In addition, the velocity history of the trajectory feature was used as a descriptor, differing from Messing et al.'s velocity history descriptor by being fixed-length, and not requiring the discretization required by Messing et al. [17]. Lastly, the motion boundary histogram (MBH), a feature based on motion boundaries detected by the horizontal and vertical gradients of the optical flow field, was introduced to activity recognition.

Fig. 4.3 Wang et al.'s dense features found on a sample frame from URADL's Lookup in Phonebook activity. *Red dots* denote feature candidates. *Green trails* denote trajectory histories

Fig. 4.4 Messing et al.'s sparse features found on another sample frame from URADL's Lookup in Phonebook activity. *Red dots* denote feature candidates. *Green trails* denote trajectory histories

Wang et al. [24] demonstrated impressive performance on established activity recognition datasets, outperforming local spatio-temporal features with their trajectory-linked descriptors.

4.2.3 Comparison

We compare Messing et al.'s [17] sparse, generative trajectory features with Wang et al.'s [24] dense, discriminative trajectory features. We control the high level model, and different kinds of information, to get the closest possible comparison between the two methods. We perform our evaluation on the URADL dataset [17].

Wang et al. [24] efficiently extract the dense trajectories by densely sampling the points in an image grid and tracking them in multiple scales separately using the median filtering in a dense optical flow field. In this way, once the dense optical flow is computed, points can be tracked at no additional cost. Wang et al. impose several heuristic filters to improve the quality of extracted dense trajectories: the length of the trajectories are limited to L frames to avoid drifting problem in tracking, densely sampled points on homogeneous areas are removed using the same criterion as Shi and Tomasi [20], and static trajectories and trajectories with sudden large displacements are pruned since they are most likely to be either erroneous or non-informative. Moreover in their work, dense trajectories are augmented using HOG, HOF, and MBH as trajectory-aligned descriptors in a 3D video volume of size $N \times N$ pixels and L frames around tracked points. The video volume is subdivided into a spatio-temporal grid of size $n_\sigma \times n_\sigma \times n_\tau$ to embed in the feature representation.

Messing et al. [17] use a generative mixture model to describe sparse trajectories found by Laptev et al.'s STIP detector [12] and tracked using the KLT tracker [15] as a mixture of Markov chains. The only limit imposed on trajectories is that they must be at least 10 frames long (Corresponding in this dataset to one third of a second).

4.2.3.1 Method

We implemented Wang et al.'s [24] bag-of-features model. We use the default feature extraction parameters as suggested in this paper. We set, the trajectory length $L = 15$ and video volume sizes $N = 32$, $n_\sigma = 2$, $n_\tau = 3$. In their work, a codebook for each descriptor (dense trajectory, HOG, HOF, MBH) is constructed separately. Since the URADL dataset is smaller than Hollywood2 (i.e., dataset that is used in [24]), we use smaller set of visual words. We construct a set of 100 visual words by clustering 5000 randomly selected training features using k-means.

We implemented Messing et al.'s soft generative bag of features model [17]. We use the same settings as they did for log-polar discretization of trajectories (8 angular bins, 5 magnitude bins), and 100 mixture components.

For classification, we use two approaches: Naive Bayes and the non-linear SVM with chi-squared multi-channel kernel as described by Wang et al. [24], using *SVM-light*'s support vector machine implementation [8].

We extract bags of words from Messing et al.'s generative model by using a video's marginal distribution over mixture component, removing the contribution from the higher level class model's distribution over the mixture component.

We compare bags of Messing et al.'s words against several versions of Wang et al.'s bags of words. First, we compare using just their dense trajectory feature, as it is most similar to Messing et al.'s trajectory features. Messing et al.'s features have longer, variable duration, while Wang et al.'s don't require discretization. We also combine Wang et al.'s dense trajectory features with their histogram of optical flow (HOF) and motion boundary histogram (MBH) features. This could be interpreted as a fairer comparison Messing et al.'s features, as those features only rely on motion, as well, and are cheap to calculate given the dense optical flow required for the dense trajectory features. Lastly, we combine all of Wang et al.'s motion-based features with their histogram of oriented gradients (HOG) appearance descriptor. This uses extra information beyond motion, and so we would expect it to improve performance.

We compare these feature sets using two different high level models. First, we use Naive Bayes, as in Messing et al. [17], a very simple model that applies equal weight to all features, thus penalizing irrelevant features. Naive Bayes is fast and easy to fit, an advantage in datasets like URADL which contain a relatively small number (150 movies) of extremely complex data points. For smoothing, we used a uniform Dirichlet prior, and adjusted it to maximize performance. We also use the multi-channel non-linear SVM described in Wang et al. [24] to illustrate the value of discriminative methods on sparse and dense features.

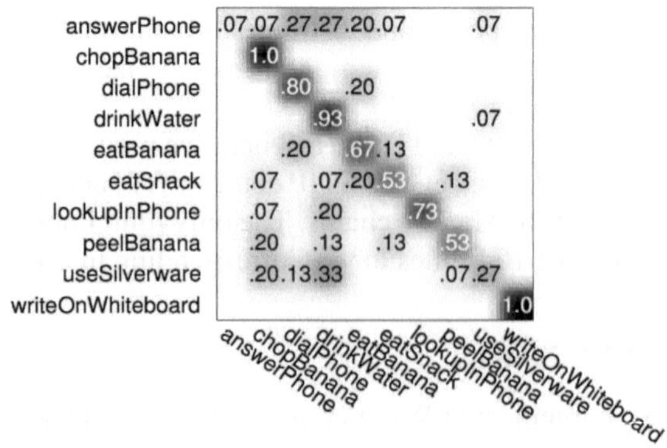

Fig. 4.5 Confusion matrix for Messing et al.'s sparse generative features combined using Naive Bayes. Average accuracy is 65.3 %. Zeros are omitted for clarity

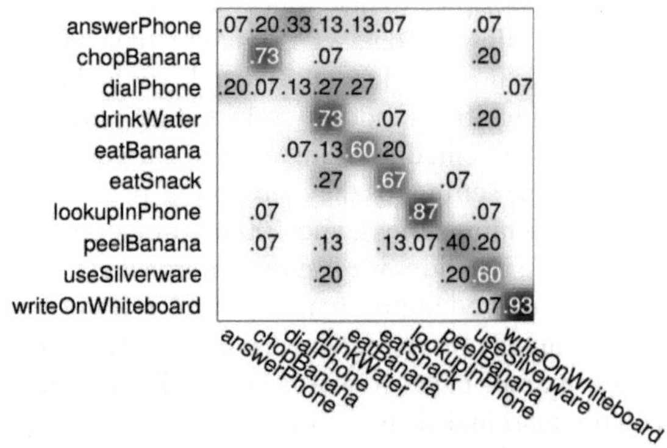

Fig. 4.6 Confusion matrix for Wang et al.'s dense trajectory features combined using Naive Bayes. Average accuracy is 57.3 %. Zeros are omitted for clarity

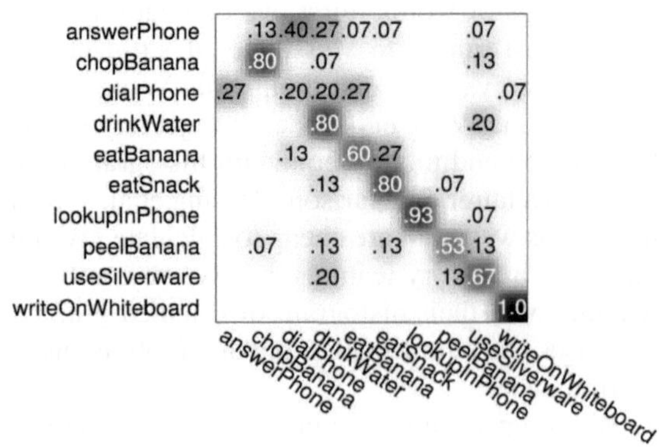

Fig. 4.7 Confusion matrix for Wang et al.'s dense trajectory features, HOF features and MBH features combined using Naive Bayes. Average accuracy is 63.3 %. Zeros are omitted for clarity

4.2.3.2 Results

Figures 4.5–4.12 show confusion matrices for the different experimental conditions. Performance is summarized in Table 4.1.

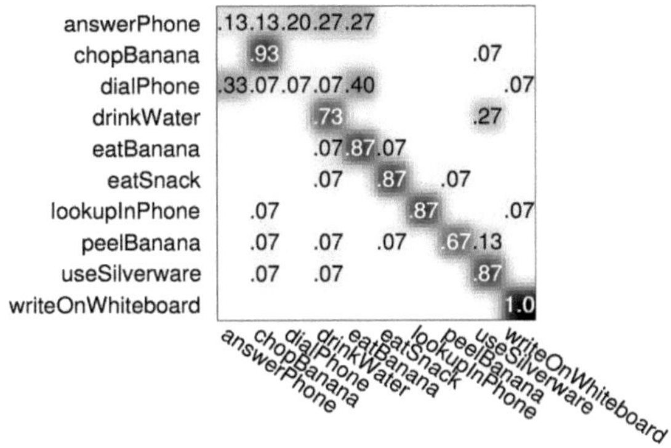

Fig. 4.8 Confusion matrix for Wang et al.'s dense trajectory features, HOF features, MBH features and HOG appearance features combined using Naive Bayes. Average accuracy is 70 %. Zeros are omitted for clarity

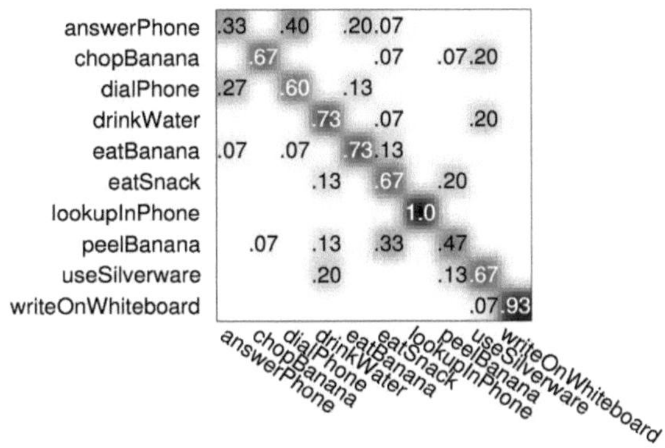

Fig. 4.9 Confusion matrix for Messing et al.'s sparse generative features combined using an SVM. Average accuracy is 68 %. Zeros are omitted for clarity

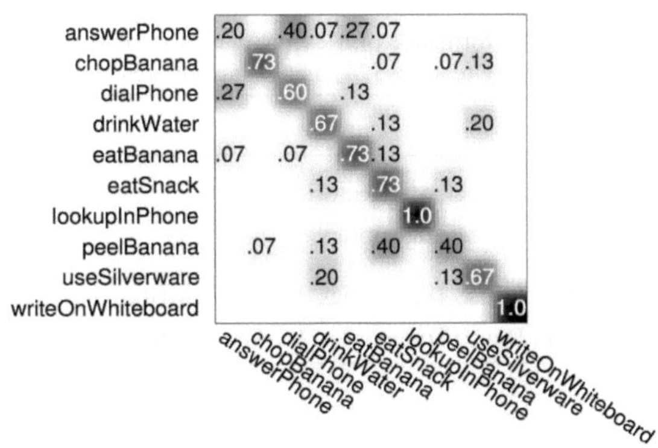

Fig. 4.10 Confusion matrix for Wang et al.'s dense trajectory features combined using an SVM. Average accuracy is 67.3 %. Zeros are omitted for clarity

4.2.4 Discussion

Table 4.1 illustrates the results of our comparison. Unsurprisingly, in the pattern of the dense trajectory results as features are added, we see that adding information improves performance. In comparing the trajectory features themselves, it seems likely that the Messing et al. features, with their extended and variable-length trajectories, are more descriptive than Wang et al.'s fixed-length trajectory features, even though

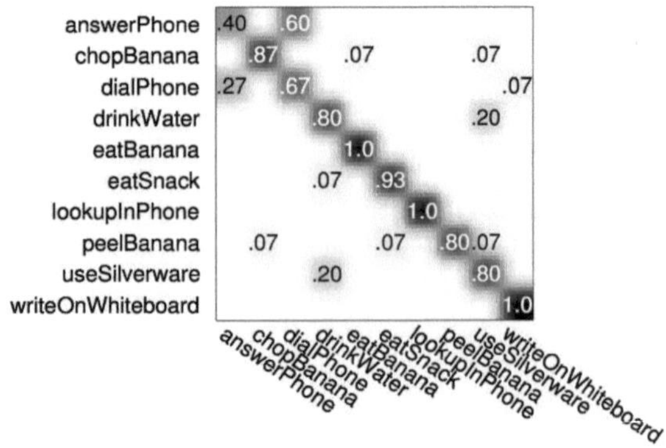

Fig. 4.11 Confusion matrix for Wang et al.'s dense trajectory features, HOF features and MBH features combined using an SVM. Average accuracy is 82.6 %. Zeros are omitted for clarity

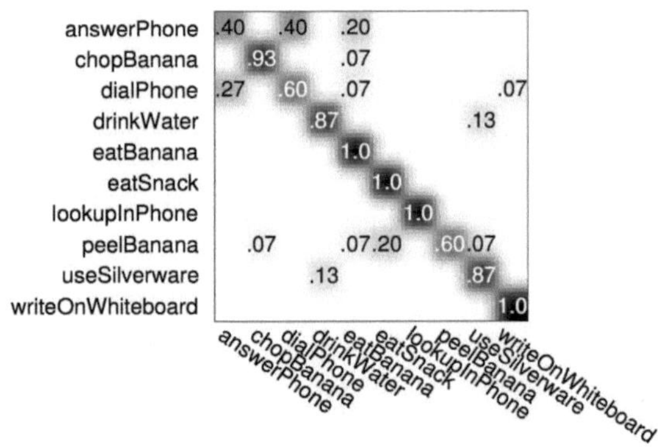

Fig. 4.12 Confusion matrix for Wang et al.'s dense trajectory features, HOF features, MBH features and HOG appearance features combined using an SVM. Average accuracy is 82.6 %. Zeros are omitted for clarity

Table 4.1 Performance of Messing et al.'s velocity history features [17] and sets of Wang et al.'s dense trajectory features [24] using Naive Bayes and SVMs on the URADL dataset

Method	Naive Bayes	SVM
Messing et al. Sparse Trajectories	65.3 %	68.0 %
Wang et al. Dense Trajectories	57.3 %	67.3 %
Wang et al. Dense Trajectories + HOF + MBH	63.3 %	82.6 %
Wang et al. Dense Trajectories + HOF + MBH + HOG	70 %	82.6 %

they are un-discretized. The advantage of Messing et al.'s trajectories goes away once other motion information (HOF and MBH) are added to Wang et al.'s dense trajectories, illustrating the powerful information in an optical flow field. The addition of appearance information substantially improved performance under a generative higher level model, but appears not to have added much to the discriminative model. It is not clear why this is the case, and it may be worth investigating further to maximize performance.

In comparing the performance of the sparse and dense trajectory features using the simple generative and more complex discriminative model, we see that the

Table 4.2 Performance of Messing et al.'s velocity history features [17] using a single augmentation on the URADL dataset

Method	Percent correct
Only Trajectories	69.3 %
Trajectories + Absolute Start and End	78.6 %
Trajectories + Relative Start and End	72.6 %
Trajectories + Appearance	70.6 %

features designed for a generative system receive only a marginal boost from the discriminative model, while the dense features receive a substantial one. Because discriminative models can vary the amount of modeling power applied to a given data point, while generative models spend the same amount of power on each data point, discriminative models are clearly superior for dense features, where many irrelevant features should be ignored. When sparse interest point detectors perform particularly well, and when less data is available, we would suggest sparse features, combined with a simpler, easier-to-fit model like Naive Bayes. The correct choice of a model depends on the problem, but as long as there is sufficient data available, these results argue strongly that discriminative methods should be the default choice.

4.3 Extending Augmentations

Messing et al. [17] used "augmentations" to associate useful information with their velocity history features. In particular, they used absolute position, relative position, and appearance. We extend their initial exploration of augmentations, focusing on the positional augmentations, as position is a very natural kind of information to pair with trajectories.

4.3.1 Messing et al.'s Augmentations

Messing et al. [17] augment their trajectory features with the absolute position of a trajectory's start and end, the position of it's start and end relative to a face, and the PCA-SIFT [10] descriptor appearance of a patch extracted from the feature's initial detection. These augmentations are combined with the trajectories as independent parts of a mixture model. So a mixture component whose parameters include a distribution over discretized velocity sequences also independently included a distribution over feature position, or appearance. In extending this augmentation model, we first examine the augmentations used in the original work [17].

Table 4.2 shows the performance of Messing et al.'s trajectory model with and without each of their augmentations, individually. This table shows two interesting things. First, we see that absolute position is a very powerful source of information. Second, we see that while relative position is more useful than appearance, it doesn't contain as much extra information as absolute position. This is particularly interesting given the powerful boost given by appearance to dense features in Sect. 4.2.3.2, although many other details of the models were different. On close examination, we found that at least part of the performance difference between absolute and relative position is due to unreliable detection of the face, the relative position anchor. Rather than simply relying on absolute position information, we will try to improve relative position information, because position relative to a meaningful landmark can carry a lot of useful information. Additionally, absolute position augmentations yield a model that is not translation-invariant, while relative position augmentations are fully translation invariant, as long as the feature and the positional anchor experience the same translation.

4.3.2 Body Part Anchors

While the face anchor used by Messing et al. [17] proved unreliable, the underlying idea of anchoring features generated by human activities to body parts has obvious merit. To further investigate body-part augmentations, we must first find a set of reliable body part positions to use as anchors. We do this using a combination of hand-annotation and well-established automatic inference methods. The parts we use are the head, hands, and torsos.

4.3.2.1 Acquiring Parts

We use manual annotation to detect hand and head positions in every 50–100 frames of video. We detect bodies on the same frames using Dalal and Triggs' person detector [5]. While there are a number of fully automatic body and pose models, we could have used to find these parts automatically, we are less interested in their reliability than in how a set of good detections could be used. Given these periodic part "detections", we infer the position of parts on every frame in between two detections by using the KLT tracker to track the part forward and backward between those detections, and averaging the position of those forward and backward tracks to find the position at any frame. This technique may seem very simple, but the errors it produces will serve in the place of the noise that would be produced by a fully automatic detection and tracking system.

4.3.3 Feature Selection

Messing et al. [17] used discretized positional information, whether absolute or relative to an anchor, as an augmentation for their trajectory descriptor in their mixture model. We will investigate using the head, hand and body augmentations in this way, but we also consider using this information for feature selection.

Table 4.3 Performance of velocity history features using mean or maximum distance to closest part for feature selection on the URADL dataset. Note that this includes manually detected head and hand parts

Threshold	Percent correct (mean)	Percent correct (max)
All features	69.3 %	69.3 %
50 pixels	65.3 %	44.6 %
100 pixels	70.6 %	66.6 %
200 pixels	70 %	69.3 %

Table 4.4 Performance of velocity history features using mean or maximum distance to either hand for feature selection on the URADL dataset. Note that hand detection was done manually

Threshold	Percent correct (mean)	Percent correct (max)
All features	69.3 %	69.3 %
50 pixels	56 %	36.6 %
100 pixels	68.6 %	61.3 %
200 pixels	72 %	72 %

Feature selection is the practice of selecting a subset of features to consider for a task. It is usually used to speed up a task by limiting the number of features that must be considered, but it can potentially improve performance by throwing out irrelevant features. Most feature-based work practices some form of implicit feature selection, by not considering, for example, feature candidates that are not at the local maximum of interest point detectors, or ignoring trajectories below a duration threshold. Experiments with Messing et al.'s model were slow enough that they explored hardware acceleration, so the primary function of this investigation of feature selection is to accelerate their model without hurting performance.

Feature selection was performed by considering all positions along the course of a trajectory feature. Features were thrown out if either their mean distance to a part, or their maximum distance to a part, exceeded a certain threshold {50, 100, or 200 pixels}. Note that the body parts were used only for feature selection. The velocity history descriptor was the only descriptor used for these experiments.

Tables 4.3 and 4.4 show that using feature selection can maintain and even improve accuracy. In particular, we see that selecting features close to the hands can improve performance while increasing speed, as only a fraction of the trajectory features are near the hands, while most interesting object manipulation involves hand movements.

4.3.4 Feature Augmentation

Messing et al. [17] discretized position, and used that discretized position at the start and end of a trajectory feature as independent parts (called "augmentations") of a mixture component's trajectory model. We consider alternative ways to include the information in position augmentations. One option is to increase the amount of modeling power spent on the position augmentation, by including the position not

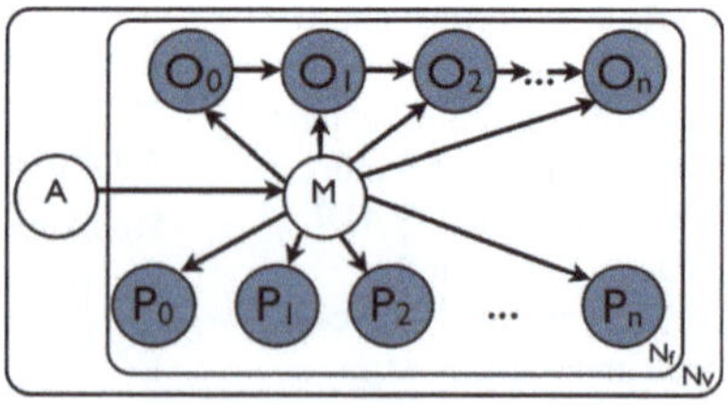

Fig. 4.13 Graphical model for velocity histories with augmentations at each timestep (*dark circles* denote observed variables)

Table 4.5 Performance of velocity history features augmented by their position relative to the body on the URADL dataset. Note that this involved no manual detection of parts

Augmentation	Percent correct
Trajectories Alone	69.3 %
Trajectories + Start and End Relative Position	76.6 %
Trajectories + Relative Position at Each Timestep	47.3 %
Start and End Relative Position	46.6 %
Relative Position at Each Timestep	46 %

only at the start and the end of each trajectory, but every position over the course of the trajectory. We call this a temporal augmentation, and model it similarly to Messing et al.'s model of discrete velocity, but without the dependence on the previous observed position. Using $P_{t,f}$ to denote the position of feature f at time t, the new version of Messing et al.'s PDF becomes

$$\begin{aligned} P(A, P, O) &= \sum_M P(A, M, P, O) \\ &= P(A) \prod_f^{N_f} \sum_i^{N_m} P\big(M_f^i | A\big) P\big(O_{0,f} | M_f^i\big) \\ &\quad \times \prod_{t=1}^{T} P\big(O_{t,f} | O_{t-1,f}, M_f^i\big) P\big(P_{t,f} | M_f^i\big) \end{aligned} \tag{4.1}$$

The graphical model corresponding to (4.1) is shown in Fig. 4.13.

Table 4.5 clearly shows that by themselves the start and end relative position contains about as much information as the relative position at each time step. Despite this, augmenting the trajectory model with the relative position at each time step gives only a marginal performance boost over just using the relative position at each time step. This strongly suggests that the temporal augmentation is dominating the probability model, and swamping the more useful trajectory model. Given that the performance of the temporal augmentation does not exceed that of the start and end position augmentation, it appears that start and end positions convey all or most of the relevant information.

We also consider a reduced-complexity representation of trajectory position relative to body parts. We investigate augmenting the trajectory not with discretized

Table 4.6 Performance of velocity history features augmented in one of several ways by their position relative to one of several parts on the URADL dataset. Parts involving manual detection are marked in *italics*

Augmentation type	Body	*Head*	*Left hand*	*Right hand*
Relative Position	76 %	80.6 %	81.3 %	82 %
Absolute Distance: Mean	75.3 %	75.3 %	75.3 %	73.3 %
Absolute Distance: Max	70.6 %	74.6 %	72.6 %	72 %
Binary: Mean Distance < 200	72 %	72.6 %	73.3 %	71.3 %
Binary: Mean Distance < 100	70 %	70.6 %	72 %	70 %
Binary: Mean Distance < 50	69.3 %	67.3 %	71.3 %	72.6 %
Binary: Max Distance < 200	70.6 %	77.3 %	71.3 %	73.3 %
Binary: Max Distance < 100	70.6 %	68 %	67.3 %	72 %
Binary: Max Distance < 50	68 %	70 %	68.6 %	71.3 %

relative position, but with either mean or maximum absolute distance from the trajectory to the part, and a binary variable indicating whether the part's mean or maximum distance to a feature is within a fixed threshold.

Table 4.6 clearly shows that scalar distance, whether or not it is thresholded, is a less effective representation of position relative to semantic landmarks than is discretized two-dimensional position. This is not very surprising, as distinguishing between "below the hand" and "to the upper right of the hand" are intuitively useful distinction for an activity recognition system to make.

4.3.5 Combining Selection and Augmentation

The relative locations of features to body parts can be used for effective feature selection and augmentation of Messing et al.'s trajectory features. Here, we consider the combination of feature selection and augmentation. For augmentations, we only consider Messing et al.'s original discretized two-dimensional relative position at the start and end of trajectories, as the other representations we have explored are not as effective. For feature selection, we eliminate features that exceed a mean distance of 200 pixels from the parts being considered

Table 4.7 shows that once features are augmented, feature selection reduces performance by a small amount, in exchange for reduced runtime. We also see that of the three relative position augmentations we've added to Messing et al.'s model, the position of trajectories relative to the positions of the hands is the most informative. This is not very surprising, as the dataset is characterized by broad and fine hand motions. If body parts were efficiently and automatically detected, it is likely that good, fast, translation invariant performance could be achieved on tasks like the activities of daily living in Messing et al.'s URADL dataset [17].

Table 4.7 Performance of velocity history features selected for proximity to the part(s) in the first row, and augmented by their start and end position relative to the named semantic parts on the URADL dataset, as measured by percent correct using leave-one-out cross validation. The absolute position augmentation is present for comparison only. Note that the first 3 rows (Trajectories alone, Trajectories and Absolute Position, and Trajectories and Body Position) involve no manual detection of parts, and rows in *italics* involve manual detection

Augmentation	No selection	Hands	All parts
Trajectories Alone	68 %	72 %	71.3 %
Traj. + Abs. Pos	80.6 %	81.3 %	83.3 %
Traj. + Body	76.6 %	82.6 %	77.3 %
Traj. + Head	79.3 %	75.3 %	75.3 %
Traj. + Hands	88.6 %	85.3 %	87.3 %
Traj. + Body + Head	82.6 %	78.6 %	78.6 %
Traj. + Body + Hands	86 %	86.6 %	86.6 %
Traj. + Head + Hands	90.6 %	87.3 %	87.3 %
Traj. + Body + Head + Hands	88 %	84 %	88 %

4.4 Conclusion

Trajectory descriptors are an increasingly important trend as the field of activity recognition in video grows beyond techniques developed for object recognition in still images. As new trajectory-based methods are introduced, it will become increasingly important to carefully consider all parts of the models that use them. Additionally, as trajectory information becomes more standard, it will be more and more important to be able to seamlessly integrate trajectory information with other information, like appearance, or higher level knowledge of scene structure or pose. In comparing Messing et al.'s sparse generative extended trajectory features with Wang et al.'s discriminative dense trajectories, we have provided a template for how to examine new methods, and choose model components. In addition, by illustrating how to add new and more refined augmentations to Messing et al.'s trajectory model, we have illustrated how to explore which new kinds of information are most beneficial to recognition models, and how to add them. It is our hope that these experiments will inform future work developing trajectory-based activity recognition.

Acknowledgements RM thanks the University of Rochester for support and guidance during his graduate education. AT thanks FQRNT for their financial support. CP thanks Ubisoft, NSERC, Google and the University of Rochester for their financial support.

References

1. Black MJ, Yacoob Y (1995) Tracking and recognizing rigid and non-rigid facial motions using local parametric models of image motion. In: ICCV, pp 374–381

2. Blei DM, Ng AY, Jordan MI (2003) Latent Dirichlet allocation. J Mach Learn Res 3:993–1022
3. Brox T, Malik J (2011) Large displacement optical flow: descriptor matching in variational motion estimation. IEEE Trans Pattern Anal Mach Intell 33(3):500–513
4. Cutting JE (1981) Six tenets for event perception. Cognition 10:71–78
5. Dalal N, Triggs B (2005) Histograms of oriented gradients for human detection. In: Proceedings of the 2005 IEEE computer society conference on computer vision and pattern recognition (CVPR'05)—volume 1—volume 01, CVPR'05. IEEE Computer Society, Washington, pp 886–893
6. Dollár P, Rabaud V, Cottrell G, Belongie S (2005) Behavior recognition via sparse spatio-temporal features. In: VS-PETS, October 2005
7. Jebara T (2003) Images as bags of pixels. In: ICCV
8. Joachims T (1999) Making large-scale SVM learning practical. Advances in kernel methods—support vector learning. MIT Press, Cambridge
9. Johansson G (1973) Visual perception of biological motion and a model for its analysis. Percept Psychophys 14:201–211
10. Ke Y, Sukthankar R (2004) Pca-sift: a more distinctive representation for local image descriptors. In: CVPR, pp II-506–II-513
11. Laptev I, Lindeberg T (2004) Local descriptors for spatio-temporal recognition. In: Int workshop on spatial coherence for visual motion analysis
12. Laptev I, Marszalek M, Schmid C, Rozenfeld B (2008) Learning realistic human actions from movies. In: CVPR, Anchorage, Alaska, June 2008, pp 1–8
13. Le QV, Zou WY, Yeung SY, Ng AY (2011) Learning hierarchical invariant spatio-temporal features for action recognition with independent subspace analysis. In: CVPR
14. Lewis D (1998) Naive (Bayes) at forty: the independence assumption in information retrieval. In: ECML
15. Lucas BD, Kanade T (1981) An iterative image registration technique with an application to stereo vision. In: IJCAI, pp 674–679
16. Marszałek M, Laptev I, Schmid C (2009) Actions in context. In: CVPR
17. Messing R, Pal C, Kautz H (2009) Activity recognition using the velocity histories of tracked keypoints. In: ICCV
18. Niebles J-C, Wang H, Fei-fei L (2006) Unsupervised learning of human action categories using spatial-temporal words. In: Proc BMVC
19. Ramanan D, Forsyth DA (2003) Automatic annotation of everyday movements. In: NIPS, December 2003
20. Shi J, Tomasi C (1994) Good features to track. In: CVPR, pp 593–600
21. Sidenbladh H, Black M, Fleet DJ (2000) Stochastic tracking of 3d human figures using 2d image motion. In: ECCV
22. Ullah MM, Parizi SN, Laptev I (2010) Improving bag-of-features action recognition with non-local cues. In: Proc BMVC, pp 95.1–95.11. doi:10.5244/C.24.95
23. Wang H, Ullah MM, Klaser A, Laptev I, Schmid C (2009) Evaluation of local spatio-temporal features for action recognition. In: BMVC
24. Wang H, Klaser A, Schmid C, Liu C-L (2011) Action recognition by dense trajectories. In: CVPR

Chapter 5
Co-recognition of Images and Videos: Unsupervised Matching of Identical Object Patterns and Its Applications

Minsu Cho, Young Min Shin, and Kyoung Mu Lee

Abstract In this chapter, we address the problem of detecting, matching, and segmenting all identical object-level patterns from images or videos in an unsupervised way, called the "co-recognition" problem. In an unsupervised setting without any prior knowledge of specific target objects, it relies entirely on geometric and photometric relations of visual features. To solve this problem, a multi-layer match-growing framework is proposed which explores given visual data by intra-layer expansion and inter-layer merge. We demonstrate the effectiveness of this approach on identical object detection, image retrieval, symmetry detection, and action recognition. These applications will validate the usefulness of co-recognition to several vision problems.

5.1 Introduction

In detection and recognition of visual objects in images or actions in videos, most of computer vision approaches require some level of supervision to specify or learn a model [5, 12, 14, 24, 34, 45, 50, 52]. In such cases, labeled images with bounding boxes or uncluttered video clips are usually adopted for the purpose. Recent categorization methods based on latent topic models have proposed weakly supervised or unsupervised learning approaches using a decent amount of training images [23, 53, 55]. In real-world images or videos, however, multiple objects of similar appearance often show up even in a single view. For example, an image can contain replicas or multiple shots of identical objects, and a video clip often includes the same actions in different spatio-temporal regions. Humans have no difficulty

M. Cho (✉)
INRIA/École Normale Supérieure, Paris, France
e-mail: minsu.cho@ens.fr

Y.M. Shin · K.M. Lee
Seoul National University, Seoul, Korea

Y.M. Shin
e-mail: shinyoungmin@gmail.com

K.M. Lee
e-mail: kyoungmu@snu.ac.kr

G.M. Farinella et al. (eds.), *Advanced Topics in Computer Vision*,
Advances in Computer Vision and Pattern Recognition,
DOI 10.1007/978-1-4471-5520-1_5,

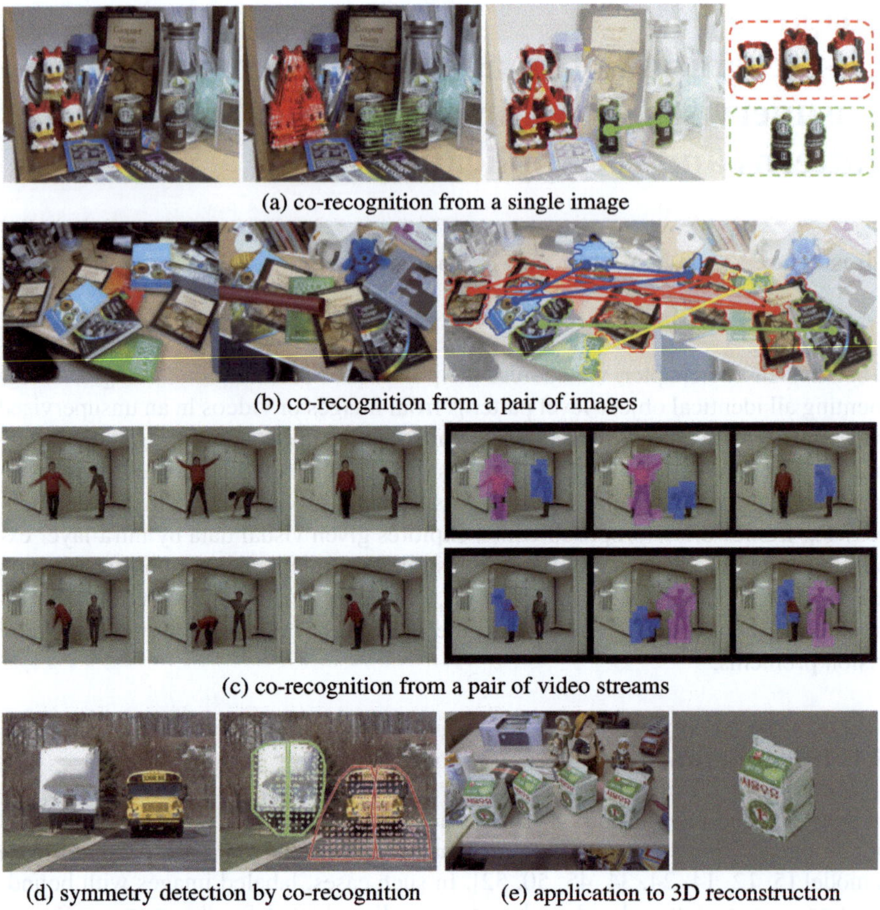

Fig. 5.1 Co-recognition results on images and videos. Our method detects and segments all identical objects in images or actions in video streams without supervision, and can be applied to various applications. (**a**) Two sets of identical objects are detected, matched, and segmented from a single image. (**b**) Many-to-many object matching is obtained across two images. (**c**) Two kinds of actions are matched and segmented from video clips. (**d**) Symmetry detection is done by co-recognition on symmetric feature pairs. (**e**) Matching and segmentation of different views enables object-based 3D reconstruction even from a single image

in finding those visual objects without any prior information, whereas it is still a challenging problem in computer vision.

In this chapter, we pose a problem of detecting, matching, and segmenting all the identical object-level patterns by considering geometric and photometric relations of visual features. It supposes an unsupervised setting without any prior knowledge of specific target objects. According to the naming conventions of related work [49, 56], we term it *co-recognition*, which emphasizes explicit geometric matching unlike other methods. We extend it to video domain and explore further applications. As shown in Fig. 5.1a, our approach can detect, match, and segment identical objects or actions directly from a single image or video clip. Interestingly, this framework generalizes to *many-to-many* object matching across images as in Fig. 5.1b (or action matching across video streams) because two or more images can be treated as a single image by combining all of them; the problem of discovering many-to-many object matches across the original multiple images is addressed by detecting multiple sets of identical objects within the combined single image. We cast it as a maximum a posteriori (MAP) task on a generative model in a Bayesian formulation. Based on it, a multi-layer match-growing algorithm is proposed to detect and segment all the object-level pairwise correspondences in the given images or video streams. The proposed approach goes beyond the conventional assumptions such as one-to-one object matching constraints or model-test settings, and addresses object matching in general. The resultant object correspondence networks can provide useful information for structural pattern analysis and scene understanding in images and videos. As shown in Fig. 5.1, this chapter will present its several applications on unsupervised identical object detection, image retrieval, symmetry detection, action recognition, and object-based reconstruction.

The remainder of this chapter is organized as follows. In Sect. 5.2, we describe our approach and its formulation, and propose the algorithm for co-recognition. In Sects. 5.3, 5.4, and 5.5, the proposed approach is applied to identical object detection, symmetry detection, and action recognition. Experimental evaluations and comparisons are carried out in each section. Finally, in Sect. 5.6, conclusion and future work are stated with some discussions. The research in this chapter has been extended from our previous papers related to this topic [6, 8–10, 51].

5.2 Co-recognition Approach

For the description of our approach, let us take an example of identical object detection problem where two images are given. Relations of matching objects in the images can be represented by networks connecting the object regions as illustrated in Fig. 5.2a. Each isolated network of matching objects means an identical object set detected from the given images. This still holds in general cases where a single or multiple images are given, and the same notion also applies to the spatio-temporal domain of video streams; the more images or videos we consider, the larger networks we obtain. These networks reveal many-to-many object matching relations across images or videos.

Our algorithm is briefly illustrated in Fig. 5.2c. First of all, we separate the whole problem with N images into smaller subproblems. As shown in Fig. 5.2b, since an object correspondence lies either within an image or across two images, object correspondences can be divided into two kinds, intra-matching within an image and inter-matching across two images. Thus, the subproblems are composed of N intra-matching and $\binom{N}{2}$ inter-matching problems. Although they can be considered as one intra-matching problem using a combined image, this decomposition makes the algorithm parallelizable and increases its efficiency by reducing the complexity in

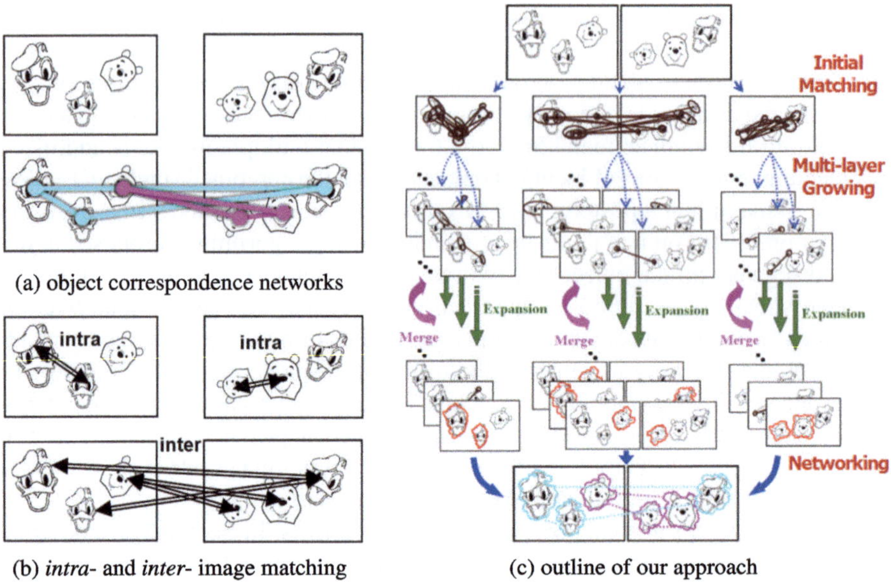

Fig. 5.2 Overview of our approach. (**a**) General object matching relation can be represented by correspondence networks. (**b**) Object correspondences can be divided into two kinds, intra-matching within an image and inter-matching across two images. (**c**) The figure illustrates the outline of our algorithm, where the goal is to detect, match, and segment identical objects from visual data [10]. For more details, see text

the subsequent match-growing process. Second, based on local feature detectors, we obtain a sufficient number of initial matches. In this step, one-to-many feature matching, that allows each feature to match with multiple matching features, is required to deal with the multiple identical patterns in images. Third, the initial matches are progressively updated and expanded by our multi-layer growing algorithm. At the start, singleton match clusters are created from the initial matches, and each of the clusters is endowed with its *expansion layer* that assigns a space for expansion to the match cluster. Then, the match clusters iteratively grow through *intra-layer expansion* and *inter-layer merge* until the posterior probability model of object correspondences is maximized. Finally, reliable object correspondences are selected from the match clusters and are connected into object networks.

In order to model the object correspondences in an unsupervised way, we introduce a perceptually meaningful entity, termed the *Maximal Correspondence* (MC) which is generalized from [8] and is defined as follows:

1. An MC is a semi-global region (or volume) pair, composed of local matches.
2. Matching regions (or volumes) of an MC are mutually consistent in both geometry and photometry.
3. An MC is maximal in its size so that it cannot be further enlarged.

Supposing the appearances of matching objects are not severely deformed in given images (or videos), an MC from given images (or videos) can be detected as an object correspondence under two conditions: (1) Each object correspondence lies on different backgrounds in photometry. (2) Object correspondences appear distinguishable each other in geometry. With the first condition unsatisfied, an MC includes a portion of a common background. With the second unsatisfied, multiple object correspondences can be recognized as one. For example, if two objects always appear aligned next to each other, we cannot discern them as separate objects without additional information. These are common intrinsic ambiguities of unsupervised object discovery. In this work, we explore how we can detect object-level correspondences based on the notion of MC and apply it to vision problems, rather than attempt to eliminate its ambiguities completely.

Here, we formally describe the object correspondences in visual data as a set of MCs Θ consisting of individual MCs Γ_i:

$$\Theta = \{\Gamma_1, \Gamma_2, \dots, \Gamma_K\}, \quad \Gamma_i = \{\mathcal{M}_{m|i} \mid m = 1, \dots, N_i\}, \tag{5.1}$$

where K is the number of MCs in Θ and ith MC Γ_i contains its member matches $\mathcal{M}_{m|i}$. N_i denotes the number of member matches in the match cluster Γ_i. We specifically call an MC in images a Maximal Region Correspondence (MRC) while we term an MC in videos a Maximal Cuboid Correspondence (MCC).

In case of images, each match $\mathcal{M}_{m|i}$ is defined by a local region pair of $(\mathcal{R}_{m|i}, \mathcal{R}'_{m|i})$ and the homography $\mathbf{H}_{m|i}$ between them:

$$\mathcal{M}_{m|i} = \{(\mathcal{R}_{m|i}, \mathcal{R}'_{m|i}), \mathbf{H}_{m|i}\}. \tag{5.2}$$

As shown in Fig. 5.3b–c, each MRC has a pair of corresponding object regions, which in turn consist of local region pairs of matches, $\mathcal{R}_{m|i}$ and $\mathcal{R}'_{m|i}$. Homography $\mathbf{H}_{m|i}$ transforms the points on $\mathcal{R}_{m|i}$ into the points on $\mathcal{R}'_{m|i}$.

On the other hand, Fig. 5.4a illustrates the MCC and its local cuboid matches in video data. In case of videos, due to its spatio-temporal dimension, each match $\mathcal{M}_{m|i}$ is expressed by a local cuboid pair of $(\mathcal{C}_{m|i}, \mathcal{C}'_{m|i})$ and its homography $\mathbf{H}_{m|i}$:

$$\mathcal{M}_{m|i} = \{(\mathcal{C}_{m|i}, \mathcal{C}'_{m|i}), \mathbf{H}_{m|i}\}. \tag{5.3}$$

The detailed description of regions or cuboid matches depends on the type of features in use. In our model of local matches for images, a local region $\mathcal{R}$ is represented by an affine region [41], which has its characteristic orientation estimated by the gradient histogram of the local region [34]. Given two local regions $\mathcal{R}_{m|i}$ and $\mathcal{R}'_{m|i}$, its affine homography $\mathbf{H}_{m|i}$ from $\mathcal{R}_{m|i}$ to $\mathcal{R}'_{m|i}$ is determined by the elliptical parameters and the orientations [10]. Similarly, as for the local matches in videos, we define $\mathcal{C}$ as a local cuboid in 3D coordinates, which occupies σ pixels in width and height, and τ pixels in temporal length. Here, the homography $\mathbf{H}$ transforms a cuboid to another cuboid with translation and scale change. $\mathbf{H}$ becomes a transformation function with 5 degrees of freedom: translation in each coordinates (d_x, d_y, d_t) and spatio-temporal scales (s_σ, s_τ).

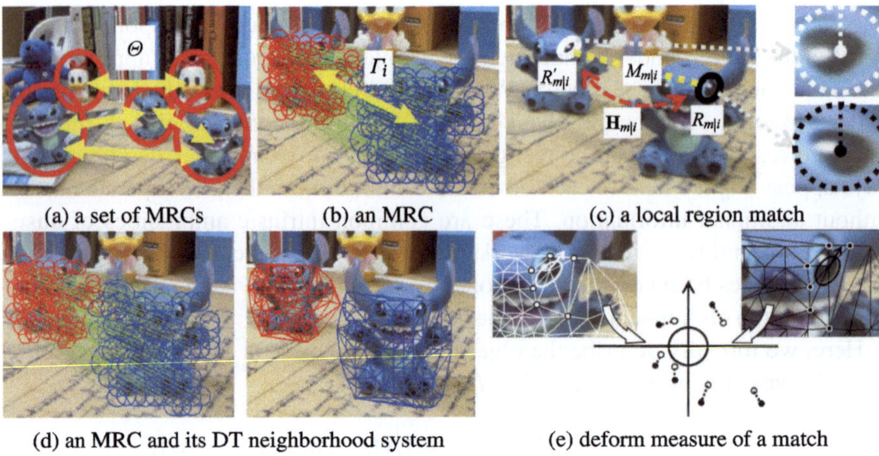

Fig. 5.3 A model of Maximal Region Correspondences (MRC). (**a**) Object correspondences can be represented by a set of MRCs. (**b**) Each MRC consists of local region matches. (**c**) Each local region match is expressed by two affine regions and the homography between them. (**d**) A neighborhood system of the MRC is constructed by Delaunay triangulation. (**e**) Based on this neighborhood system, geometric deformation of a member match is defined as the average transfer error of neighbor points on a normalized domain [10]

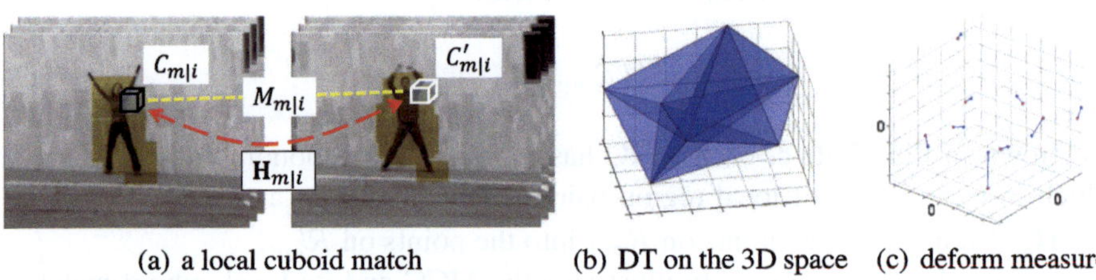

Fig. 5.4 Maximal Cuboid Correspondence (MCC) in video. (**a**) An MCC is composed of local cuboid matches. A local match is defined by two cuboids and the homography between them. (**b**) Three-dimensional Delaunay triangulation on the cuboid centers defines the neighborhood relation. Note that only a part of the DT is displayed here for visibility. (**c**) After normalizing the neighbors to have unit Euclidean distance on average, the geometric deformation is obtained by calculating the average discrepancy between corresponding points

5.2.1 A Bayesian Formulation for Object Correspondence

Based on the concepts described so far, we design a Bayesian model of MCs. The posterior probability $p(\Theta|\mathcal{I})$ is the probability of Θ being a set of MCs given a set of images (or videos) $\mathcal{I}$. In the Bayesian framework, it is decomposed as $p(\Theta|\mathcal{I}) = p(\mathcal{I}|\Theta)p(\Theta)$. In our model, the prior probability $p(\Theta)$ evaluates the geometric coherency and maximality of MCs, and the likelihood probability $p(\Theta|\mathcal{I})$ represents the photometric coherency of MCs. All these terms are defined in the following subsections.

5.2.1.1 Prior

In order to design a robust prior model, we endow each MC Γ_i with a neighborhood system that defines the neighborhood relation of each match $\mathcal{M}_{m|i}$ in Γ_i and adaptively varies with evolution of Γ_i. Suppose an undirected graph $G_i = (\mathcal{V}_i, \mathcal{E}_i)$ where the member matches of Γ_i consist in node set $\mathcal{V}_i = \{\mathcal{M}_{m|i}\}$. Edge set $\mathcal{E}_i$ is constructed by the Delaunay triangulation (DT) [47] on the center points $\mathbf{c}_{m|i}$ of $\mathcal{R}_{m|i}$ as shown in Fig. 5.3d. Then, the neighbor set of $\mathcal{M}_{m|i}$ is defined as $\mathcal{N}_{\mathcal{M}_{m|i}} = \{\mathcal{M}_{n|i} \mid (\mathbf{c}_{m|i}, \mathbf{c}_{n|i}) \in \mathcal{E}_i\}$. Likewise, for video data, 3D neighborhood relations are defined on spatio-temporal (x, y, t) coordinates as shown in Fig. 5.4b. Since DT has low computational complexity of $\mathcal{O}(N_i \log N_i)$ and can be incrementally updated [13], the DT-based neighborhood system is efficiently constructed and evolved along expansion/merge moves.

To evaluate the geometric consistency of an MC Γ_i, we use this neighborhood system. For images, consider a local region match $\mathcal{M}_{m|i}$ in Γ_i, and let $T_{m|i}$ and $T'_{m|i}$ the transformations that map $\mathcal{R}_{m|i}$ and $\mathcal{R}'_{m|i}$ onto a unit circle, respectively. As shown in Figs. 5.3e and 5.4c, the centers of its neighbor nodes $\mathcal{N}_{\mathcal{M}_{m|i}}$ are normalized into the unit domain by $T_{m|i}$ and $T'_{m|i}$, and the distances between the corresponding points in the unit domain are computed as deformation measures [9]. For videos, the normalizing transformations $T_{m|i}$ and $T'_{m|i}$ denotes the transformations that map $\mathcal{C}_{m|i}$ and $\mathcal{C}'_{m|i}$ onto a unit cuboid [51].

The local deformation measure of $\mathcal{M}_{m|i}$ is formulated as

$$d_{\mathrm{G}}(\mathcal{M}_{m|i}) = \frac{1}{|\mathcal{N}_{\mathcal{M}_{m|i}}|} \sum_{\mathcal{M}_{n|i} \in \mathcal{N}_{\mathcal{M}_{m|i}}} \left| T_{m|i}(\mathbf{c}_{n|i}) - T'_{m|i}\left(\mathbf{c}'_{n|i}\right) \right|, \tag{5.4}$$

where $\mathbf{c}_{n|i}$ and $\mathbf{c}'_{n|i}$ denote the center points of $\mathcal{R}_{n|i}$ and $\mathcal{R}'_{n|i}$, or $\mathcal{C}_{n|i}$ and $\mathcal{C}'_{n|i}$. This measure represents the average transfer error of neighbors on the normalized domain. Summing up all the local deformations, the geometric energy of the MC Γ_i is defined as

$$E_{\mathrm{G}}(\Gamma_i) = \sum_{m=1}^{N_i} d_{\mathrm{G}}(\mathcal{M}_{m|i}). \tag{5.5}$$

Due to the DT-based neighborhood system, it effectively adapts to variation of the MC configuration and generates robust deformation measures for smoothly deformed surfaces or volumes.

In addition, to grow MCs to larger ones satisfying the maximality in their sizes, rewards for both expansion and merge are required in the prior model. Thus, we design the maximality energy as

$$E_{\mathrm{M}}(\Theta) = \sum_{i=1}^{K} \left(-N_i - |\Delta_i|\right), \tag{5.6}$$

where N_i and $|\Delta_i|$ denote the number of member matches and the number of Delaunay triangles of Γ_i, respectively. Since expansion of any MC increases the total

(a) flow feature (b) spatial shape feature

Fig. 5.5 Features used in the video data. (**a**) The flow feature in the cuboid is represented as the field of optical flow displacement vectors computed between the consecutive frames. (**b**) The local shape of the edge map is described by the log-polar descriptor. Each pixel within the log-polar bin casts a vote to the corresponding histogram channel. Then, the shape feature of the cuboid is described by the normalized histogram

number of local matches, the first term encourages them to expand. On the other hand, the second term provides a reward for merge of MCs because merge makes additional triangles of DT in a merged MC.

5.2.1.2 Likelihood

The likelihood probability $p(\mathcal{I}|\Theta)$ evaluates the photometric coherency based on local appearance of images or videos $\mathcal{I}$.

For images, we define the dissimilarity [8] of two local image regions in a member match $\mathcal{M}_{m|i}$ by

$$d_{\mathrm{P}}(\mathcal{M}_{m|i}) = 1 - \mathrm{NCC}(\mathcal{R}_{m|i}, \mathcal{R}'_{m|i}) + \frac{\mathrm{dRGB}(\mathcal{R}_{m|i}, \mathcal{R}'_{m|i})}{100}, \tag{5.7}$$

where $\mathrm{NCC}(\cdot,\cdot)$ is the normalized cross-correlation between the gray patterns of two regions, while $\mathrm{dRGB}(\cdot,\cdot)$ is the average pixel-wise Euclidean distance in a normalized RGB color-space [8, 14].

For videos, we use both optical flow and spatial edge shape information in local spatio-temporal cuboids. As shown in Fig. 5.5, the optical flow for a cuboid is computed across adjacent frames by the Lucas–Kanade algorithm [36], and the edge map is obtained by the Berkeley edge detector [38]. The dissimilarity of two local cuboids in a member match $\mathcal{M}_{m|i}$ is described by

$$d_{\mathrm{P}}(\mathcal{M}_{m|i}) = \left(\frac{\sum_{x,y,t} \|F_{x,y,t} - F'_{x,y,t}\|}{\frac{1}{2}\sum_{x,y,t}(\|F_{x,y,t}\| + \|F'_{x,y,t}\|)}\right)^2 + \left(\frac{\|D - D'\|}{\|D\| + \|D'\|}\right)^2, \tag{5.8}$$

where the vector fields $F_{x,y,t}$ and $F'_{x,y,t}$ denote the optical flow vectors at (x, y, t), and D and D' means the edge descriptor extracted from $\mathcal{C}$ and $\mathcal{C}'$, respectively.

$\|\cdot\|$ denotes L2 norm. D is a 40-dimensional log-polar descriptor similar to the *shape context* descriptor [2] with 5 bins of log-polar location grid and 8 orientation bins.

Assuming that local matches in images or videos are mutually independent in photometric coherency, the photometric energy of MC Γ_i is measured by

$$E_P(\Gamma_i) = \sum_{m=1}^{N_i} d_P(\mathcal{M}_{m|i}). \tag{5.9}$$

Finally, using Eqs. (5.5)–(5.7), we formulate the overall prior and the likelihood in the posterior model as follows:

$$p(\Theta) \propto \exp\left(-\sum_{i=1}^{K} E_G(\Gamma_i) - E_M(\Theta)\right), \qquad p(\mathcal{I} \mid \Theta) \propto \exp\left(-\lambda_P \sum_{i=1}^{K} E_P(\Gamma_i)\right), \tag{5.10}$$

where λ_P controls the balance between the likelihood and the prior in the model. Hence, given image or video observation $\mathcal{I}$, an optimal set of MCs Θ^* is obtained by maximizing the posterior probability $p(\Theta|\mathcal{I})$ as

$$\Theta^* = \arg\max_{\Theta} p(\mathcal{I}|\Theta)p(\Theta). \tag{5.11}$$

5.2.2 Algorithm for Co-recognition

In this section, we explain our algorithm for co-recognition. As briefly illustrated in Fig. 5.2, the proposed algorithm consists of three main phases: initial matching, multi-layer growing, and object correspondence networking, which will be described one by one in the following subsections.

5.2.2.1 Initial Matching

To form seeds for MCs, initial matches are established using local feature detectors [27, 29, 42, 57]. Basically, feature pairs having similar descriptors consist in the initial seed matches. For images, we adopted Harris-affine [40] and MSER [39] detectors and the SIFT descriptor [34]. For videos, the spatio-temporal interest point (STIP) detector [27] and the HOG-HOF descriptor [29] are used. In initial matching, the nearest neighbor (NN) matching schemes are widely used in the literature [8, 14, 22, 34, 52]. The NN methods, however, severely degrade inlier detection in the presence of multiple identical objects or similar patterns because in those cases the features have multiple matching features rather than the NN feature. To avoid this problem, we allow each feature to pair with multiple features under a loose threshold; all the matching feature pairs exceeding a loose similarity threshold are simply collected among the possible feature pairs. Matching a feature with itself is avoided in intra-matching within one image.

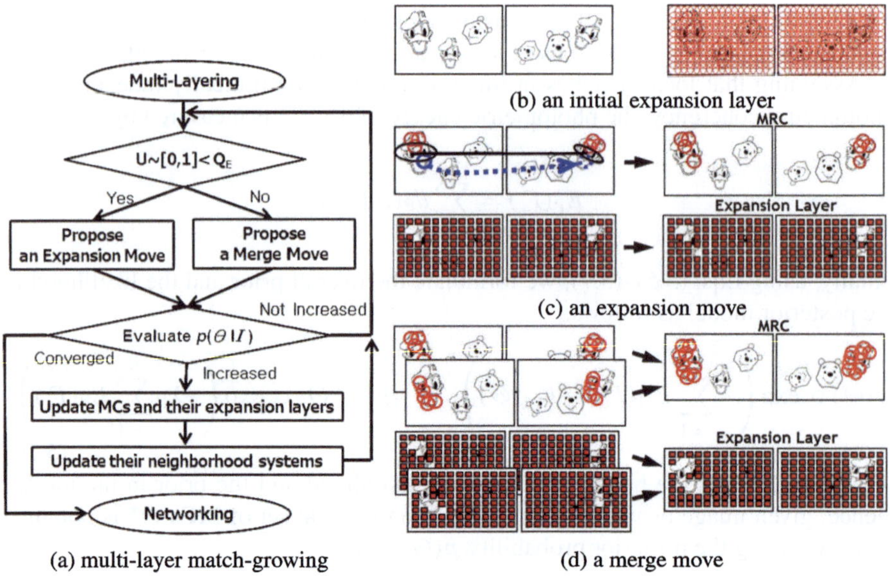

Fig. 5.6 Multi-layer match-growing. (**a**) After multi-layering is performed using the initial seed matches, the iterative growing loop starts. At each iteration, the algorithm grows the matches by intra-layer expansion or inter-layer merge, and increases the posterior probability $p(\Theta|\mathcal{I})$. The growing procedure is iterated until $p(\Theta|\mathcal{I})$ no longer increases. (**b**) Each expansion layer consists of overlapping circular regions covering the image domain. (**c**) In an expansion proposal, a cluster attempts to expand a region (*blue circle in the bottom*) using a support match (*solid black line*). When the proposal is accepted, the MC and its expansion layer is updated. (**d**) In a merge proposal, two clusters attempt to merge into one. When the proposal is accepted, the MC and their expansion layers are combined into one. In (**c**) and (**d**), local regions in expansion layers are represented by *red squares* for better visualization. Expansion and merge in videos works in the similar manner but in spatio-temporal dimensions. For details, refer to [9, 10]

5.2.2.2 Multi-layer Growing

For growing initial seed matches to object-level correspondences, we propose a multi-layer growing algorithm driven by expansion/merge moves. The growing procedure is summarized in Fig. 5.6a. First, multi-layering is performed using the initial seed matches. Each initial seed match forms an initial singleton MC having its own expansion layer that provides space for expansion. As shown in Fig. 5.6c, each expansion layer consists of an overlapping circular grid of regular local regions that covers the entire image [8] or an overlapping spatio-temporal grid that covers the entire video [51]. In the iterative growing loop, expansion is proposed with probability Q_E or merge with probability $1 - Q_E$. In an expansion proposal illustrated in Fig. 5.6c, a match in an MC is selected as a *supporter* match (shown as the black solid line), and a local region around it is chosen as a *target* region (shown as the blue circle) on the expansion layer of the MC. Then, the target region establishes a new match (the blue dotted arrow), which is propagated using the support match and refined by a local search [9]. Likewise, for videos as depicted in Fig. 5.7, an expan-

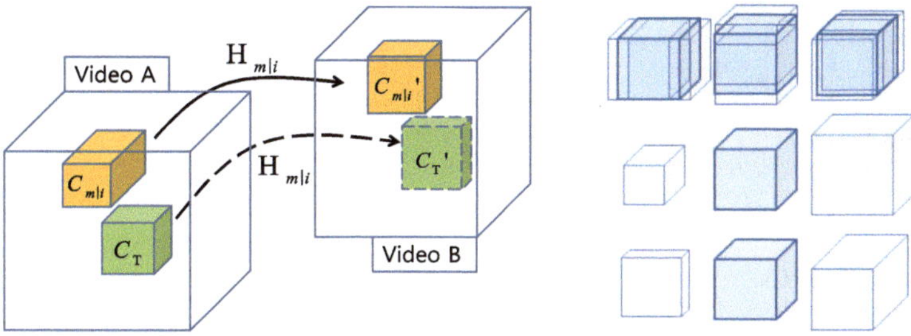

Fig. 5.7 Expansion move in video data. (**a**) The support match $\mathcal{M}_{m|i}$ propagates a target cuboid $\mathcal{C}_\mathrm{T}$ by applying transform $\mathbf{H}_{m|i}$ (**b**) Local search around $\mathbf{H}_{m|i}$ along the coordinate axis (*top row*), spatial scale s_σ (*second row*), and temporal scale s_τ (*third row*) refines the new match to adapt to the deformation

sion proposal propagates a new cuboid match and then refines it by a local search in a 5-dimensional parameter space [51]. If the expansion proposal is accepted, the propagated match is included in the MC and the target region is eliminated from the expansion layer. On the other hand, in a merge move proposal illustrated in Fig. 5.6d, two geometrically similar MCs are selected and proposed to merge. If the merge move proposal is accepted, the expansion layers are also combined into their intersection. The algorithm accepts the expansion/merge proposals when it increases the posterior probability $p(\Theta|\mathcal{I})$. The growing procedure is iterated until $p(\Theta|\mathcal{I})$ no longer increases.

Although the multi-layer approach multiplies expansion layers at the start, merge moves gradually reduce the number of layers and guide expansion moves to concentrate on potentially matching region. Likewise, expansion moves also guide merge moves to find compatible clusters by gradually growing them. Through these cooperative moves, our algorithm efficiently finds object correspondences in spite of significant number of outliers in initial matches. Therefore, while the multi-layer growing algorithm maximizes the posterior probability of MCs in a greedy manner, its expansion/merge proposals efficiently drive the solution to a good local optimum. We refer the reader to [9, 10] for details concerning the expansion/merge proposals.

5.2.2.3 Networking of Maximal Correspondences

To reveal the relations of detected object regions, we establish the object correspondence networks from the set of MCs Θ^*. Since the resultant set of MCs usually includes trivial MCs arising from outliers of initial matches, we first eliminate such unreliable MCs from Θ^*. Typically, object region correspondences are likely to grow larger and have distinctive textures in their regions. Thus, we evaluate the reliability of an MC by its expanded area and its mean variance of the intensity patterns, and discard MCs not satisfying the threshold values. Then, the reliable MCs are considered as object correspondences and connected to construct the networks

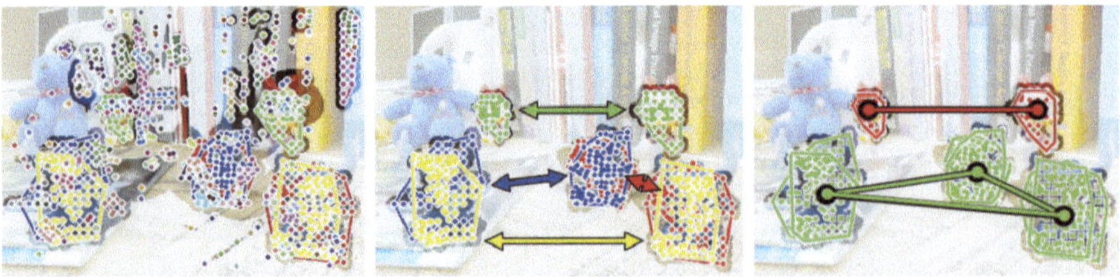

(a) all MRCs (b) reliable MRCs (c) networking

Fig. 5.8 Object correspondence networking. (**a**) Each MRC obtained from the growing step is represented by convex hull region pairs of the same color. Many small and spurious MRCs are observed arising from outliers of initial matches. (**b**) Based on the reliability criteria, MRCs are selected as object correspondences. (**c**) Reliable MRCs are connected by SL-HAC based on region overlaps, and constitutes the object correspondence networks [10]

according to their overlapping regions. In this work, we use a simple and popular algorithm of the Single-Link Hierarchical Agglomerative Clustering (SL-HAC) [20] to group the MCs. Similarity between two MCs is defined as the ratio of overlapping area to the area of the smaller MC region, and SL-HAC sequentially connects the most similar MC pairs until the similarity becomes less than 0.8. As shown in Fig. 5.8, the procedure assembles MRCs of the given image into networks, each representing connected object correspondences, and the detected object regions are all classified into sets of identical objects. The same scheme can be used likewise for networking MCCs in videos. Notably, this networking scheme does not require the pre-determined number of identical object sets, and is robust to missing object correspondences since others can provide indirect pathways. More advanced clustering algorithms could be adopted for this purpose as well. In particular, the partial linkage HAC [7] or the noise-robust spectral clustering [32] could make the networks robust to falsely detected MCs.

5.3 Unsupervised Object Detection, Matching, and Segmentation

In this section, we demonstrate the proposed method on unsupervised object detection and segmentation tasks. Among early works closely related to this topic are co-segmentation [49], co-saliency [56], and common visual pattern discovery [59]. Rother et al. [49] defined co-segmentation as segmenting common regions from two images. They exploited a generative MRF-based graph model and the color histogram similarity measure. Toshev et al. [56] proposed co-saliency matching that searches for region pairs with strong intra-image coherency and high inter-image similarity. Yuan and Wu [59] used spatial random partition to discover common visual patterns from a collection of images. However, none of these methods recognize multiple common objects as distinct entities, and they do not consider sufficient geometrical consistency in the detected region. To handle these limitations, we adopt a match-growing approach that has been developed in several computer vision tasks to boost initial putative matches and eliminate the matching ambiguities [14, 31, 52, 54, 58]. Recently, Cho et al. [8] and Kannala et al. [22] used it to demonstrate unsupervised object matching beyond the limitation of conventional model-test settings in image matching and registration. All these previous methods however, commonly rely on the restrictive assumptions of one-to-one constraints both in feature matching and in object matching to make their problems simpler.

The experimental results in this section suggest that our method can solve general problems of many-to-many object matching, and also outperforms the previous methods [8, 22, 49, 56, 59] even under the one-to-one constraint. The experiments were performed under the following settings. In the initial matching step, affine region detectors of MSER [39] and Harris-affine [40] are used for extracting features, and the SIFT descriptor [34] to measure the similarity between the features. The threshold value for initial matching was set to 0.4 of distance in the SIFT descriptor space. The multi-layer growing was performed with $Q_E = 0.9$, $\lambda_P = 2.0$. In networking step, the thresholds for reliable MRCs as the expanded area over 3 % of the given image and the mean intensity variance over 0.005.

5.3.1 Common Object Detection and Segmentation

In the first experiment, we perform common object detection and segmentation, which is restricted to the case of one-to-one object matching, and compare our results with those of other related methods [22, 49, 56, 59]. All their results are borrowed from the papers.

Fig. 5.9 shows comparative examples with the methods of co-segmentation [49], co-saliency matching [56], common pattern discovery [59]. Co-segmentation, which segments a common part based on a Markov random field model encoding both of spatial coherency and histogram similarity, showed that its result can be used as more robust similarity measure than conventional global histogram comparison [49]. As shown in Fig. 5.9a, our co-recognition provides an even better measure than both co-segmentation and global histogram comparison. Since co-recognition discovers common image regions based on dense correspondences, it does not suffer from accidental similarity of color histogram and gives a more discriminative measure. Figure 5.9b compares ours with co-saliency matching, which jointly segment and match common region based on spectral analysis [56]. While co-saliency matching does not cover all the common regions and gives inaccurate region correspondences, co-recognition generates more dense and accurate region matching. Similarly, it also show better performance than common pattern discovery of [59] in Fig. 5.9c. Unlike all these methods, co-recognition provides object-level correspondence as well as its dense correspondence.

Figure 5.10 shows comparative examples on segmentation of deformed object with the quasi-dense matching method [22] and single-layer match-growing [8]. As can be observed in the detailed segmentation boundaries, other methods fail to segment severely deformed regions, for example, the corner part of the deformed magazine, but our method discovers the deformed common parts with better accu-

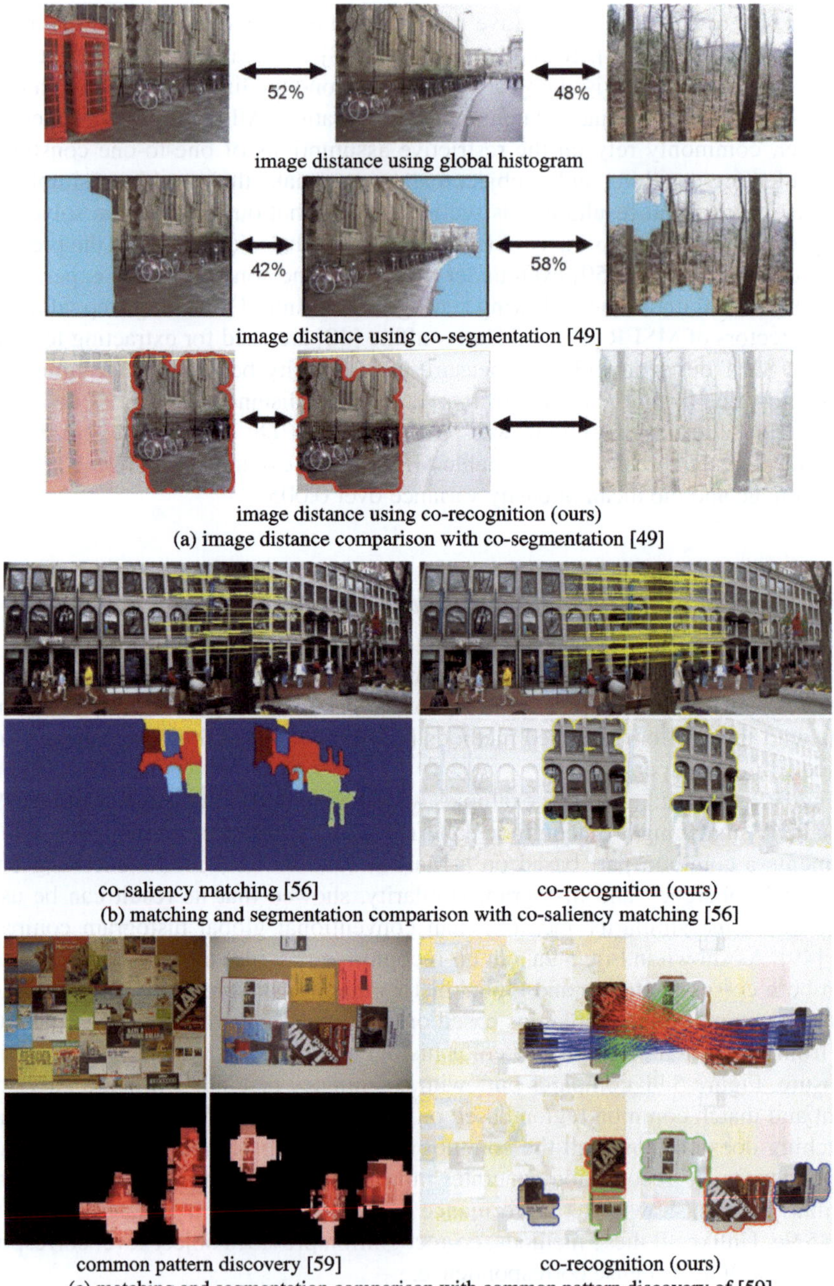

Fig. 5.9 Comparison with other methods. (**a**) Co-recognition gives a more discriminative measure of image distance than co-segmentation of [49] as well as conventional global histogram comparison. (**b**) Co-recognition generates more dense and accurate matching than co-saliency matching [56]. (**c**) Co-recognition achieves better segmentation and matching than common pattern discovery of [59]

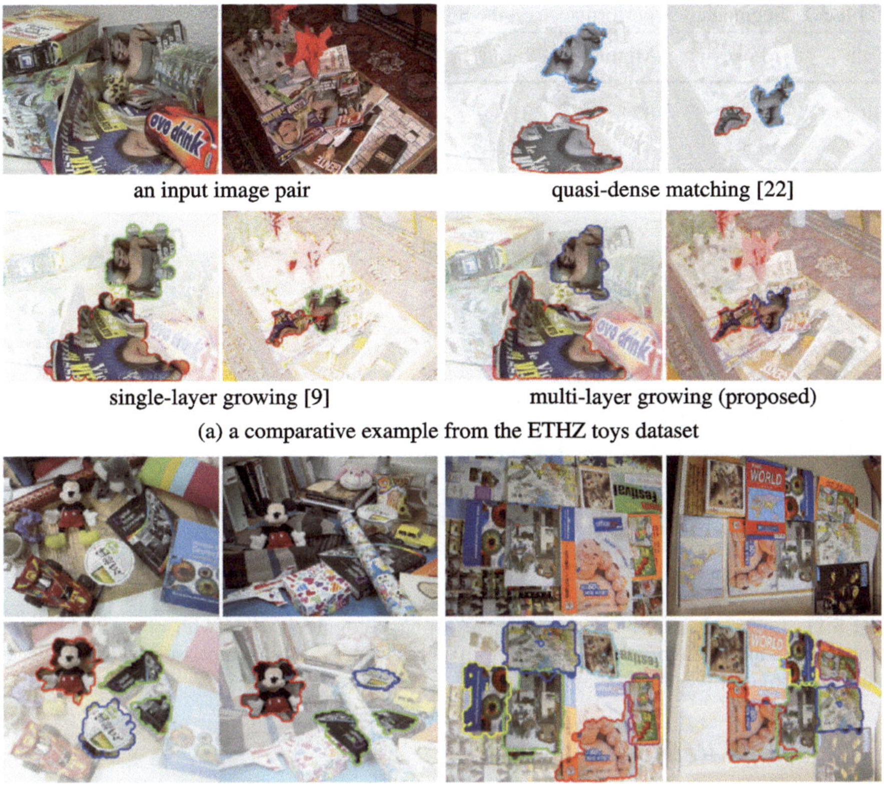

(b) multi-layer growing results on the SNU dataset

Fig. 5.10 Common object detection and segmentation. (**a**) Compared to results of quasi-dense matching [22] and single-layer growing [8], the proposed multi-layer growing shows better robustness to non-rigid deformation so that it covers the whole deformed part more accurately. (**b**) Two example results on the image pairs from the SNU dataset are shown

racy than quasi-dense matching as well as single-layer match-growing. It shows that the proposed multi-layer growing based on the dynamic neighborhood system effectively adapts to deformed surfaces of the objects. We performed quantitative evaluation and comparison on the SNU dataset,[1] that is organized for common object matching and segmentation [8]. The results of segmentation accuracy are reported in Table 5.1, where the higher hit ratios (Hit) and the lower background ratios (Bk) represents the better results. It indicates that the proposed multi-layer growing gives better performance than the previous single-layer growing used in [8]. Figure 5.10b shows two of the results, where detected common objects are delineated by the same color and the background is faded. Object boundaries could be further refined by seeded segmentation algorithms [26, 30, 48] using the current result as seeds.

[1]http://cv.snu.ac.kr/~corecognition

Table 5.1 Segmentation performance on the SNU dataset [8]

Data	Mickey's	Minnie's	Jigsaws	Toys	Books	Bulletins	Avg.	[8]
Hit (%)	84.4	87.8	81.6	85.2	97.2	93.8	*88.3*	85.5
Bk (%)	19.4	31.1	19.4	20.8	11.3	15.2	*19.5*	22.4

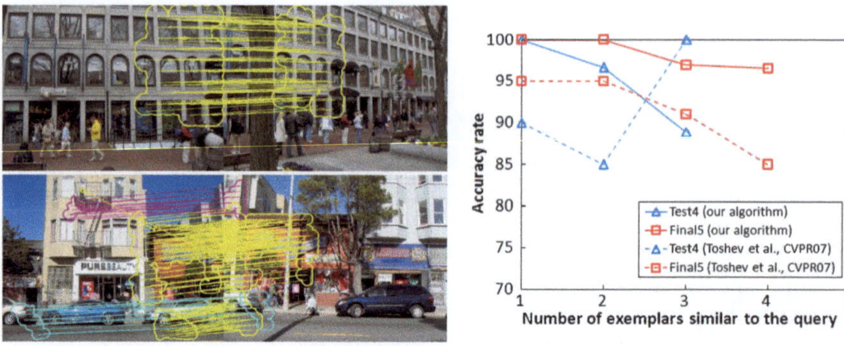

(a) co-recognition on ICCV2005 datasets (b) accuracy rate for Test4 and Final5

Fig. 5.11 Image retrieval by co-recognition. (**a**) Co-recognition deals with object-level correspondence, which is higher than segment-level correspondence. (**b**) Comparison with co-saliency matching [56] on ICCV2005 datasets

5.3.2 Image Retrieval

In the second experiment, we have conducted the image retrieval as in [56] on the ICCV 2005 place recognition contest datasets. Each of two datasets (*Test4* and *Final5*) has been split into exemplar and query set. *Test4* has 19 query images and 9 exemplar images, while *Final5* has 22 query images and 16 exemplar images. Each of query images is compared with all exemplar images, and all the matched image pairs are ranked according to the total area of reliable MRCs. For every query image having at least k similar exemplars, the accuracy rate is evaluated with how many of them are included in top k ranks.

The result in Fig. 5.11 reveals that our co-recognition outperforms co-saliency matching [56] in this experiment. The reason can be explained by comparing our result of the top in Fig. 5.11a with the result of the same pair in [56]. Co-recognition deals with object-level correspondences, which are higher than segment-level correspondences as [56], our method generates larger, denser, and more accurate correspondences.

5.3.3 Identical Object Matching and Segmentation

In the third experiment, we tested the proposed method on a more general problem beyond the one-to-one matching assumptions, which the previous methods

Fig. 5.12 Unsupervised object matching and segmentation on single images. For each result, the input images, segmentation with object correspondence networks, and their classified regions are shown. *Each color* illustrates the identity of an object. In the *last row*, additional results are shown on images with repetitive patterns. For details, see text

[8, 22, 49, 56, 59] cannot deal with. This experiment aimed at demonstrating unsupervised identical object matching and segmentation on various real-world images. For evaluation, we constructed a dataset of 30 images, each image of which has several identical objects with occlusion and clutter.

Figure 5.12 shows some results from the dataset. The object boundaries are determined based on the local regions of MRCs, and delineated by lines of different colors that indicate which object set they belong to. The object correspondence networks are represented by thick lines connecting detected object regions. In the third

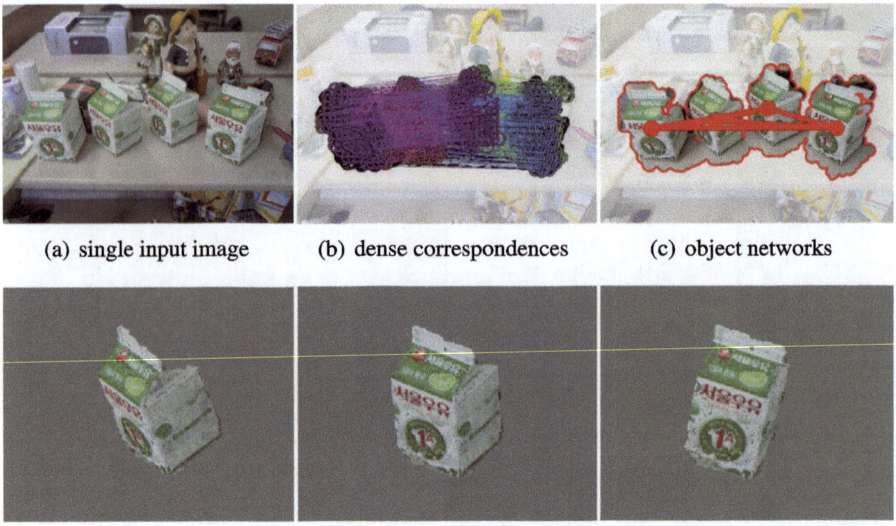

(a) single input image (b) dense correspondences (c) object networks

(d) reconstructed 3D object

Fig. 5.13 3D object reconstruction from a single image. The detected regions of identical objects from a single image provide multiple-views of an object, which are used to reconstruct 3D shape of the object. See text

column of each result, object regions of each identical object are displayed in groups to better understand the object matching results. Our method provides impressive detection and segmentation results in spite of deformation, occlusion, and clutters. Although some false pairwise object correspondences were detected and some were missing, most of the identical objects were correctly localized and classified into identical object groups by the networking step. For evaluating the detection accuracy of the pairwise object correspondences, we computed recall and precision rates for our dataset considering all the possible pairwise correspondences. For the detection criterion, we used the standard detection criterion of 50 % area overlap with the ground truth. The average precision and recall rates are 0.92 and 0.75, respectively. The loss of the recall rate was mainly due to the challenging cases of densely stacked objects as shown in the bottom of Fig. 5.12. In those results, several identical objects often merged into one, thus object correspondences were not distinguishable within the merged MRCs. For more results on the dataset, refer to [10].

5.3.4 Application to 3D Reconstruction

Since co-recognition detects and segments identical objects in an unsupervised way, we can obtain multiple views of an object from the result and use them for the object-based 3D reconstruction. It enables multi-view reconstruction even from a single image. Figure 5.13 shows such a result of unsupervised 3D object reconstruction.

Given a single image containing 4 instances of the same object, the differences in relative camera poses between identical objects offer multi-view observations of the object. Each of the detected object regions is separated and treated as independent images of the same object taken at different viewpoints. The separated segments are camera-calibrated using the conventional structure-from-motion algorithm [17]. Here, we assumed the square pixel aspect ratio, and exploited the prior information that all the separated image segments have same intrinsic camera parameters. The final 3D shape of the object is obtained using the multi-view stereo reconstruction of Furukawa et al.'s [16]. As shown in Fig. 5.13d, the rendered images of the target object in novel views reveal that the 3D model of the object is successfully reconstructed from the single image. This approach enables to reconstruct multiple objects from unsupervised images.

5.4 Symmetry Detection

A variety of symmetries occur in nature, living organisms, and manufactured artifacts, and provide humans with pre-attentive cues that enhance object recognition. Despite the long history of the research, the recent performance evaluation [46] shows that we are still short of a robust and widely applicable symmetry detector. The previous methods for symmetry detection can be broadly classified into global and local feature-based methods. The global methods [25, 37] treat the entire image as a signal from which symmetric patterns are inferred, but are limited to detecting a single incidence of symmetry, and also greatly influenced by background clutters. On the contrary, the local feature-based methods [11, 35] use local features such as edges, contours, boundary points, and regions to detect symmetry by grouping symmetric sets of local features. Their main advantage is to more efficiently detect local symmetries against background clutters in images that are not globally symmetric. However, they are largely influenced by feature detection step, and cannot exploit further information beyond the detected features.

Co-recognition approach can apply to localizing and segmenting symmetric patterns [6]. It overcomes the limitations of the previous local-feature based approaches by efficiently exploring the image space beyond the detected symmetric features. Multiple clusters of consistent symmetric feature pairs are directly detected in our growing process without conventional voting procedure like the Hough transform or RANSAC used in the local feature-based methods [11, 35]. Here, we aim to detect and segment the bilaterally symmetric patterns.

For symmetry detection, the algorithm takes initial matches of symmetric feature pairs and grows them in a symmetric manner. The main difference lies on *symmetric expansion* in multi-layer growing as illustrated in Fig. 5.14. Suppose that a local symmetry match $(\mathcal{R}_a, \mathcal{R}_b)$ and its neighboring region $\mathcal{R}_c$ are given. Then, using the reflective homography T_i from $\mathcal{R}_a$ to $\mathcal{R}_b$, a new symmetric match $(\mathcal{R}_c, \mathcal{R}_d)$ is propagated and refined in expansion.

A brief overview of the approach is illustrated in Fig. 5.15. Using the appearance around the detected features and its mirrored features, we obtain potential symmet-

Fig. 5.14 Symmetric expansion in multi-layer growing. (**a**) A support match $(\mathcal{R}_a, \mathcal{R}_b)$ and its neighboring region $\mathcal{R}_c$. (**b**) Propagation of the region $\mathcal{R}_c$ by symmetric homography of the supporter match. (**c**) Refinement by locally fitting the ellipse parameters

Fig. 5.15 Overview of our symmetry-growing approach. (**a**) Input image. (**b**) Local feature extraction. (**c**) Initial matches of symmetric feature pairs. (**d**) Expansion layers. (**e**)–(**g**) Multi-layer symmetry-growing. (**h**) Segmented symmetric object. For details, see text

ric matching pairs of features [35] as depicted in Fig. 5.15c. Then, starting from singleton symmetry clusters each containing a single symmetry match, we simultaneously expand and merge the symmetry clusters by exploring the image space in our multi-layer growing framework. The algorithm gradually grows reliable symmetry clusters as shown in Fig. 5.15e–f, where the dots with the same color represent features in the same cluster. Finally, the reliable symmetric patterns grown well enough are chosen in Fig. 5.15h, where the detected symmetry is indicated by the convex hull of the features.

We quantitatively evaluated our method on the test dataset of 91 images used in the performance evaluation of symmetry detection [46]. Examples of our results are

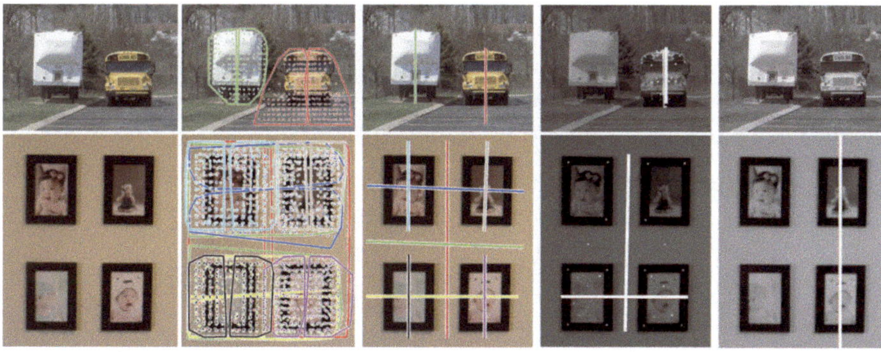

Fig. 5.16 Symmetry detection comparison on the dataset of [46]. LE06 and LHXS05 denote the methods of [35] and [33], respectively

shown in Figs. 5.16–5.17[2] where the convex-hull segmentation and the major axis of each symmetry cluster are visualized. Each color represents the identity of each symmetry cluster. The examples demonstrate that our symmetry-growing method detects the entire region of symmetric pattern with dense correspondences in each symmetry cluster, so that it provides more accurate and robust performance than the previous methods.

Park et al. [46] compared two state-of-the-art bilateral symmetry detection algorithms [33, 35] in their evaluation. We compared our results with them. For comparison, sensitivity and false positive rate are measured. Suppose *TP* is the number of true positives (correctly detected symmetries), and *FP* is the number of false positives (wrongly detected symmetries), and *GT* is the number of ground truth symmetries. Then, the sensitivity is defined as $S_0 = TP/GT$ and the false positive rate as $R_{FP} = FP/GT$. All the results are summarized in Table 5.2. Note that the results of [35] and [33] are obtained by testing the algorithms on four image scales (from 1 to 1/4 of the original size) and choosing the best result [46], whereas our results are obtained by testing only on the original size of the images. Nevertheless, for sensitivity S_0, our algorithm clearly outperforms the methods of [33, 35] in all image types. In the sense of false positive rate R_{FP}, our method appears not clearly better than the two other methods except for the case of real images with multiple symmetry. However, the reason is that our method detects more true symmetric patterns than the ground truth labels of the dataset. That is, a great portion of our false positive detections are not false in fact. For examples, each image at the 3rd and 4th row in Fig. 5.17 has only one symmetric pattern according to the ground truth data, but our method detects even more true bilateral symmetric patterns. It also happens in multiple symmetry dataset as images in the bottom row. These cases were prevalent in our results. These results demonstrate that our method is highly robust to deformation and is effective for real-world complex images.

[2]The dataset, the ground truth, and the result images of [35] and [33] are borrowed from http://vision.cse.psu.edu/evaluation.html.

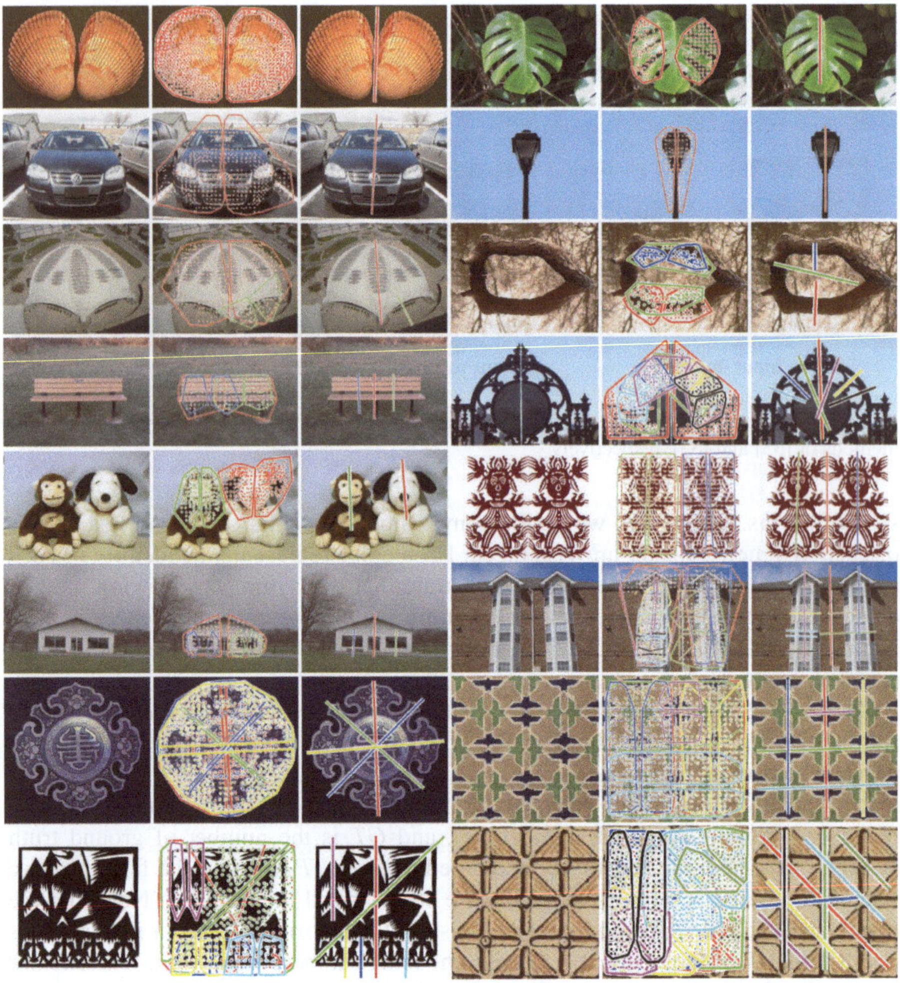

Fig. 5.17 Examples of symmetry detection and segmentation on the dataset of [46]. See text

Table 5.2 Performance comparison on the dataset of 91 images from [46]

Image type	Synthetic single			Synthetic multiple		
Algorithm	LE06	LHS05	*Ours*	LE06	LHS05	*Ours*
S_0	92 %	62 %	*100 %*	35 %	28 %	*77 %*
R_{FP}	15 %	0 %	*15 %*	4 %	8 %	*33 %*

Image type	Real single			Real multiple		
Algorithm	LE06	LHS05	*Ours*	LE06	LHS05	*Ours*
S_0	84 %	29 %	*94 %*	43 %	18 %	*68 %*
R_{FP}	68 %	3 %	*69 %*	44 %	0 %	*17 %*

5.5 Action Recognition

Action recognition is a challenging problem since there are rich intra-class variations and clutter signals. The intra-class variations come from the diversity of actions such as the actor's appearance, performing style, performing speed, and spatial scale. Thus, we are unlikely to obtain identical observations even if the actions are perceived to belong to the same class. The clutter signals are induced by the other motions of the actors or the visual stimuli from the background part of the video, which make unwanted noise and degrade the performance of the system. Thus, for robust action recognition, we need to deal with these ambiguity of action and clutters. Several approaches have been proposed to tackle the challenges [3, 4, 12, 24, 28, 44, 50]. They can be roughly divided into global approaches [3, 12, 24, 50] and local approaches [4, 28, 44] according to the feature types they rely on. The global methods classify human actions based on global descriptors of human centered windows such as optic flow descriptors [12], correlation of 3D gradients [50], space-time shape of silhouettes [3], and the flow features combined with shape [24]. On the contrary, the local methods extract local features from the video sequences, and they represent the action as a set of spatio-temporal interest points(STIP) [28, 44] or composition of local cuboids [4]. The local methods are found to be generally more robust to the recording conditions, action variance, and occlusion. Although they have achieved significant progress in action recognition, most of them required manually supervised input data or a number of category-specific training data to overcome the aforementioned challenges.

The co-recognition approach naturally extends to the action recognition in the video domain based on the spatio-temporal features [51]. Our intuition is that similar human actions occupy similar spatio-temporal regions with consistent local correspondence topology, and they share similar visual features. The match-growing technique is applied to detect and segment the same actions without manually supervised input videos. In this experiment, there are slight differences in implementation of expansion move. We explicitly designed the *contraction* move to prevent the algorithm from being stuck in bad local optimum. The contraction move selects a target cluster with probability proportional to the cluster size, and a target match in it with probability proportional to the deformation error and photometric error. Half of the expansion move is converted to the reversible contraction move. The overlapping latent cuboids are generated every $7 \times 7 \times 3$ pixels. The density of the cuboids in the expansion layer determines the localization accuracy. Although the use of denser cuboids will generate smoother result of the detected action, it requires to deal with larger solution space at the cost of more computation time.

To evaluate our algorithm quantitatively, we performed an action classification test on the Weizmann human action dataset [3]. The Weizmann dataset contains 10 categories of actions {*walk, run, jump, gallop sideways, bend, one-hand wave, two-hand wave, jump inplace, jumping jack, skip*}, which are performed by 9 subjects. In our experiment, we used 9 actions excluding two-hand wave, because one-hand wave is a sub-action of two-hand wave. Prior to running the proposed algorithm, some of the video clips are mirror-reflected to make the actors move to the same direction, and some periodic actions are temporally cropped to remove the periodicity.

	bend	jack	jump	pjump	run	side	skip	walk	wave1
bend	100	0	0	0	0	0	0	0	0
jack	0	100	0	0	0	0	0	0	0
jump	0	0	87.5	1.25	0	11.3	0	0	0
pjump	0	0	0	100	0	0	0	0	0
run	0	0	0	0	87.5	0	12.5	0	0
side	0	0	0	0	0	100	0	0	0
skip	0	0	18.8	0	18.8	0	62.5	0	0
walk	0	0	0	0	0	0	6.25	93.8	0
wave1	0	0	0	0	0	0	0	0	100

(a) flow+shape

	bend	jack	jump	pjump	run	side	skip	walk	wave1
bend	87.5	12.5	0	0	0	0	0	0	0
jack	0	68.8	0	31.3	0	0	0	0	0
jump	0	0	62.5	0	12.5	12.5	12.5	0	0
pjump	0	12.5	0	87.5	0	0	0	0	0
run	0	0	12.5	0	50	0	25	12.5	0
side	0	0	31.3	0	0	68.8	0	0	0
skip	0	0	50	0	25	0	25	0	0
walk	0	12.5	0	0	0	0	0	87.5	0
wave1	30.8	7.69	0	11.5	0	0	0	0	50

(b) flow only

	bend	jack	jump	pjump	run	side	skip	walk	wave1
bend	87.5	12.5	0	0	0	0	0	0	0
jack	0	87.5	0	12.5	0	0	0	0	0
jump	0	0	50	0	12.5	37.5	0	0	0
pjump	0	37.5	0	62.5	0	0	0	0	0
run	0	0	12.5	0	62.5	12.5	0	12.5	0
side	0	0	0	12.5	0	87.5	0	0	0
skip	0	0	0	0	25	0	75	0	0
walk	0	12.5	0	0	0	0	12.5	75	0
wave1	0	0	0	0	0	0	0	0	100

(c) shape only

feature	accuracy
flow + shape	92.4%
flow only	65.3%
shape only	76.4%

(d) accuracy

Fig. 5.18 Classification confusion matrices on Weizmann dataset. (**a**)–(**c**) Different types of features are used to measure the likelihood. (**d**) The accuracy is calculated by taking average of the diagonal entries of confusion matrix. See text

We conducted a leave-one-out cross validation to measure the performance. One of the video clips of an action category is removed from the database and serves as a reference video to all of the remaining videos one by one. The similarity score between two video clips is evaluated by the number of expanded cuboids and classified using the nearest neighbor procedure.

To test the effectiveness of the features, we also examined the performance of the proposed algorithm on different feature types. We performed the experiments on the same dataset using the flow and the shape features separately. The classification confusion matrices and accuracy table are shown in Fig. 5.18. The result suggests that the shape feature has more discriminative power than the flow feature and the composition of flow and shape features is superior to using only one type of feature. We interpret this superiority of the shape feature to the flow feature in terms of the ambiguity. The flow feature has the explicit movement information of the cuboid, but the erroneous value at the object boundary is the major drawback of the flow feature. On the other hand, the shape feature effectively captures the local

Table 5.3 Comparison results on Weizmann dataset

	Classification accuracy
Co-recognition	92.4 %
Boiman et al. [4]	97.5 %
Jhuang et al. [21]	93.8 %
Filipovych et al. [15]	88.9 %
Niebles et al. [43]	72.8 %

pose information of the actor. The shape feature is computed from the 2D image at the center of the cuboid, thus it does not contain any explicit movement information. However, since the MCCs are composed of many overlapping cuboids, their configuration indirectly represents the movement of the actor.

The comparison with other methods on Weizmann dataset is given in Table 5.3. Note that it does not provide the best comparison because each of them has its own limitations and constraints. For example, [4, 15, 43] cannot distinguish multiple actions within a video, and [15, 21, 43] require many training data which are separated by each action class. Our co-recognition shows fair performance as compared with other approaches, considering that only ours has the ability to handle multiple actions without manually split training data.

Since the Weizmann dataset contains a single action per each video, we captured the videos that contain multiple different actions in a clip, and tested our algorithm on them.

Figure 5.19a displays co-recognition results between two actions performed in different temporal order. The actor in the first video performs 'kick' and 'punch' actions sequentially, while the actor in the second video performs 'punch' first and 'kick' later. Figure 5.19b shows another scenario. In the videos, the actors perform two actions in different spatial configuration. The video in the top row shows two actors performing 'jumping jack' and 'bend' simultaneously. The bottom row depicts 'bend' and 'jumping jack' actions performed in different spatial positions. We ran the co-recognition on the video pairs containing multiple actions. The qualitative results are overlaid on the video frames shown in Fig. 5.19. We display the detected location of spatio-temporal cuboids in color-shaded region of the scene. Each color means the identity of each action. The results indicate that the proposed algorithm successfully recognized the multiple common actions and their correspondences in the video pairs. Our results on the video clips are encouraging since we can obtain the action-level correspondence information between videos with their spatio-temporal location despite the presence of multiple actions. These results can provide very useful information for further analysis of video data.

5.6 Summary and Future Work

In this chapter, we have presented the co-recognition approach to images and videos that detects, matches, and segments multiple sets of identical objects or actions in

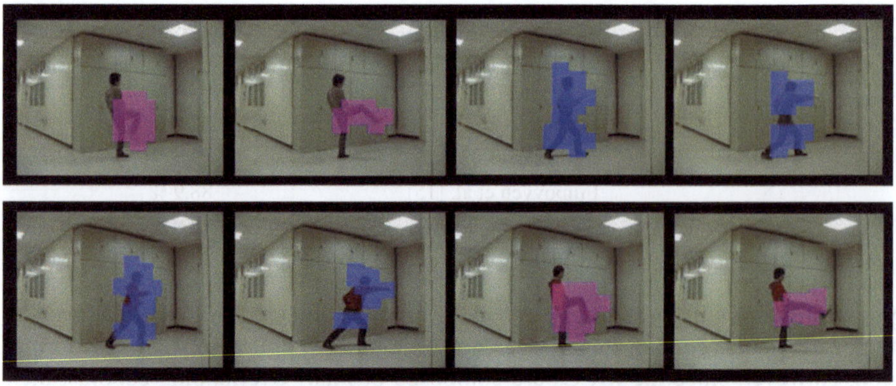

(a) upper:'kick-punch' , lower:'punch-kick'

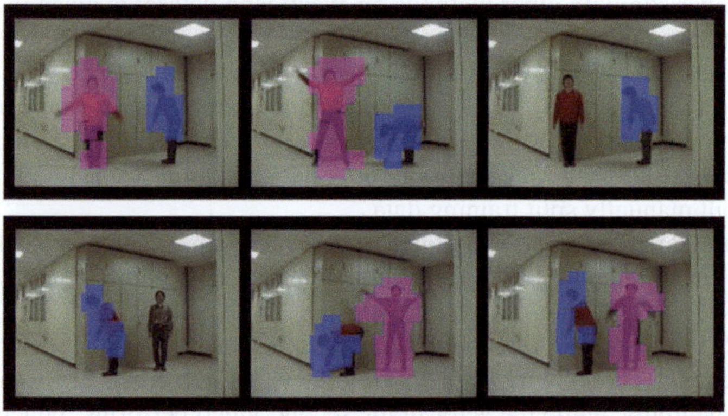

(b) upper:'jack-pick' , lower:'pick-jack'

Fig. 5.19 The qualitative results of the proposed algorithm on our dataset containing multiple actions in a video clip. (**a**) Selected frames from two videos containing temporally distinguished actions. (**b**) Selected frames from two videos containing spatially distinguished actions

an unsupervised way. The basic idea is to grow initial matches into reliable object correspondences in a multi-layer match-growing framework and analyze their relations by their matching regions or volumes. Unlike other unsupervised segmentation or object discovery methods, it effectively considers both geometry and appearance to discover the detailed dense matches and segmentation from complex images or videos. We have shown its robust performance on a variety of unsupervised vision applications, such as unsupervised object detection and segmentation [8, 9], image retrieval, symmetry analysis [6], action detection [51], and 3D reconstruction.

While the proposed approach provides wide applications and impressive results on complex scenes and videos, the current method still has some limitations. As already noted in Sect. 5.2, co-recognition can detect an object correspondence under the geometric and photometric distinctiveness of the objects appeared in given images or videos. The condition, however, is not strictly satisfied in usual data.

As the consequences, in the presence of similar background or clutter, the detected object regions are over-expanded or non-object regions are falsely detected. To deal with these ambiguity of foreground, the foregroundness [18, 19] or objectness [1] could be further incorporated for better results. In the case of geometrically similar arrangements of objects such as stacked objects or cycling actions, the visual data has intrinsic ambiguity between repetitive patterns of one object and dense arrangements of several objects. This problem requires a statistical inference on more observations of various scenes. Thus, to address this, further analysis on larger networks of object correspondences needs to be investigated to infer the objects, their whole-part relations, as well as object interactions. In the future, pursuing the direction, we plan to improve the co-recognition approach for more complex scene understanding based on mutual relations of various objects.

References

1. Alexe B, Deselaers T, Ferrari V (2010) What is an object? In: IEEE conference on computer vision and pattern recognition
2. Belongie S, Malik J, Puzicha J (2002) Shape matching and object recognition using shape contexts. IEEE Trans Pattern Anal Mach Intell 24(4):509–522
3. Blank M, Gorelick L, Shechtman E, Irani M, Basri R (2005) Actions as space-time shapes. In: IEEE international conference on computer vision
4. Boiman O, Irani M (2006) Similarity by composition. In: Neural information processing system
5. Cho M, Lee KM (2007) Partially occluded object-specific segmentation in view-based recognition. In: IEEE conference on computer vision and pattern recognition
6. Cho M, Lee KM (2009) Bilateral symmetry detection and segmentation via symmetry-growing. In: British machine vision conference
7. Cho M, Lee KM (2009) Feature correspondence and deformable object matching via agglomerative correspondence clustering. In: IEEE international conference on computer vision
8. Cho M, Shin YM, Lee KM (2008) Co-recognition of image pairs by data-driven Monte Carlo image exploration. In: European conference on computer vision
9. Cho M, Shin YM, Lee KM (2010) Unsupervised detection and segmentation of identical objects. In: IEEE conference on computer vision and pattern recognition
10. Cho M, Shin YM, Lee KM (2011) Object correspondence networks for unsupervised recognition of identical objects. In: Emerging topics in computer vision and its applications, vol 1, p 313
11. Cornelius H, Perd'och M, Matas J, Loy G (2007) Efficient symmetry detection using local affine frames. In: SCIA, pp 152–161
12. Efros AA, Berg AC, Mori G, Malik J (2003) Recognizing action at a distance. In: IEEE international conference on computer vision
13. Faugeras O (1993) Three-dimensional computer vision: a geometric viewpoint. MIT Press, Cambridge
14. Ferrari V, Tuytelaars T, Gool L (2006) Simultaneous object recognition and segmentation from single or multiple model views. Int J Comput Vis 67(2):159–188
15. Filipovych R, Ribeiro E (2008) Learning human motion models from unsegmented videos. In: IEEE conference on computer vision and pattern recognition
16. Furukawa Y, Ponce J (2007) Accurate, dense, and robust multi-view stereopsis. In: IEEE conference on computer vision and pattern recognition
17. Hartley R, Zisserman A (2004) Multiple view geometry in computer vision. Cambridge University Press, Cambridge

18. Hou X, Zhang L (2007) Saliency detection: a spectral residual approach. In: IEEE conference on computer vision and pattern recognition
19. Itti L, Koch C, Niebur E (1998) A model of saliency-based visual attention for rapid scene analysis. IEEE Trans Pattern Anal Mach Intell 20:1254–1259
20. Jain AK, Dubes RC (1998) Algorithms for clustering data. Prentice Hall, New York
21. Jhuang H, Serre T, Wolf L, Poggio T (2007) A biologically inspired system for action recognition. In: IEEE international conference on computer vision
22. Kannala J, Rahtu E, Brandt S, Heikkila J (2008) Object recognition and segmentation by non-rigid quasi-dense matching. In: IEEE conference on computer vision and pattern recognition
23. Karlinsky L, Dinerstein M, Levi D, Ullman S (2008) Unsupervised classification and part localization by consistency amplification. In: European conference on computer vision
24. Ke Y, Sukthankar R, Hebert M (2007) Event detection in crowded videos. In: IEEE international conference on computer vision
25. Keller Y, Shkolnisky Y (2004) An algebraic approach to symmetry detection. In: IEEE international conference on pattern recognition
26. Kim TH, Lee KM, Lee SU (2010) Nonparametric higher-order learning for interactive segmentation. In: IEEE conference on computer vision and pattern recognition
27. Laptev I (2005) On space-time interest points. Int J Comput Vis 64(2/3):107–123
28. Laptev I, Lindeberg T (2003) Space-time interest points. In: IEEE international conference on computer vision
29. Laptev I, Marszałek M, Schmid C, Rozenfeld B (2008) Learning realistic human actions from movies. In: IEEE conference on computer vision and pattern recognition
30. Lempitsky V, Kohli P, Rother C, Sharp T (2009) Image segmentation with a bounding box prior. In: IEEE international conference on computer vision
31. Lhuillier M, Quan L (2002) Match propagation for image-based modeling and rendering. IEEE Trans Pattern Anal Mach Intell 24(8):1140–1146
32. Li Z, Liu J, Chen S, Tang X (2007) Noise robust spectral clustering. In: IEEE international conference on computer vision
33. Liu Y, Hays JH, Xu YQ, Shum HY (2005) Digital papercutting. Technical sketch, SIGGRAPH
34. Lowe DG (1999) Object recognition from local scale-invariant features. In: IEEE international conference on computer vision
35. Loy G, Eklundh JO (2006) Detecting symmetry and symmetric constellations of features. In: European conference on computer vision, pp II-508–II-521
36. Lucas BD, Kanade T (1981) An iterative image registration technique with an application to stereo vision. In: DARPA image understanding workshop
37. Marola G (1989) On the detection of the axes of symmetry of symmetric and almost symmetric planar images. IEEE Trans Pattern Anal Mach Intell 11:104–108
38. Martin D, Fowlkes C, Malik J (2004) Learning to detect natural image boundaries using local brightness, color, and texture cues. IEEE Trans Pattern Anal Mach Intell 26(5):530–549
39. Matas J, Chum O, Urban M, Pajdla T (2002) Robust wide baseline stereo from maximally stable extremal regions. In: British machine vision conference
40. Mikolajczyk K, Schmid C (2002) An affine invariant interest point detector. In: European conference on computer vision
41. Mikolajczyk K, Schmid C (2004) Scale and affine invariant interest point detectors. Int J Comput Vis 60(1):63–86
42. Mikolajczyk K, Schmid C (2005) A performance evaluation of local descriptors. IEEE Trans Pattern Anal Mach Intell 27(10):1615–1630
43. Niebles JC, Fei-Fei L (2007) A hierarchical model of shape and appearance for human action classifination. In: IEEE conference on computer vision and pattern recognition
44. Niebles JC, Wang H, Fei-Fei L (2006) Unsupervised learning of human action categories using spatial-temporal words. In: British machine vision conference
45. Obdržálek S, Matas J (2002) Object recognition using local affine frames on distinguished regions. In: British machine vision conference

46. Park M, Lee S, Chen PC, Kashyap S, Butt AA, Liu Y (2008) Performance evaluation of state-of-the-art discrete symmetry detection algorithms. In: IEEE conference on computer vision and pattern recognition
47. Preparata F, Shamos M (1985) Computational geometry. Springer, Berlin
48. Rother C, Kolmogorov V, Blake A (2004) Grabcut—interactive foreground extraction using iterated graph cuts. In: ACM SIGGRAPH
49. Rother C, Minka TP, Blake A, Kolmogorov V (2006) Cosegmentation of image pairs by histogram matching—incorporating a global constraint into MRFs. In: IEEE conference on computer vision and pattern recognition, pp 993–1000
50. Shechtman E, Irani M (2005) Space-time behavior based correlation. In: IEEE conference on computer vision and pattern recognition
51. Shin YM, Cho M, Lee KM (2010) Co-recognition of actions in video pairs. In: International conference on pattern recognition
52. Simon I, Seitz SM (2007) A probabilistic model for object recognition, segmentation, and non-rigid correspondence. In: IEEE conference on computer vision and pattern recognition
53. Sivic J, Russell BC, Efros AA, Zisserman A, Freeman WT (2005) Discovering object categories in image collections. In: IEEE international conference on computer vision
54. Steele KL, Egbert PK (2005) Correspondence expansion for wide baseline stereo. In: IEEE conference on computer vision and pattern recognition
55. Todorovic S, Ahuja N (2007) Unsupervised category modeling, recognition, and segmentation in images. IEEE Trans Pattern Anal Mach Intell 30(12):2158–2174
56. Toshev A, Shi J, Daniilidis K (2007) Image matching via saliency region correspondences. In: IEEE conference on computer vision and pattern recognition
57. Tuytelaars T, Mikolajczyk K (2008) Local invariant feature detectors: a survey. Found Trends Comput Graph Vis 3(3):177–280
58. Vedaldi A, Soatto S (2006) Local features, all grown up. In: IEEE conference on computer vision and pattern recognition
59. Yuan J, Wu Y (2007) Spatial random partition for common visual pattern discovery. In: IEEE international conference on computer vision, pp 1–8

Chapter 6
Stereo Matching—State-of-the-Art and Research Challenges

Michael Bleyer and Christian Breiteneder

Abstract Stereo matching denotes the problem of finding dense correspondences in pairs of images in order to perform 3D reconstruction. In this chapter, we provide a review of stereo methods with a focus on recent developments and our own work. We start with a discussion of local methods and introduce our algorithms: geodesic stereo, cost filtering and PatchMatch stereo. Although local algorithms have recently become very popular, they are not capable of handling large untextured regions where a global smoothness prior is required. In the discussion of such global methods, we briefly describe standard optimization techniques. However, the real problem is not in the optimization, but in finding an energy function that represents a good model of the stéreo problem. In this context, we investigate data and smoothness terms of standard energies to find the best-suited implementations of which. We then describe our own work on finding a good model. This includes our combined stereo and matting approach, Surface Stereo, Object Stereo as well as a new method that incorporates physics-based reasoning in stereo matching.

6.1 The Stereo Matching Problem

This chapter concentrates on the stereo matching problem, which is one of the oldest, but still yet unsolved problems in computer vision. Solving this matching problem is the central step in a shape from stereo method. Figure 6.1 outlines the pipeline of this approach. In analogy to human depth perception that uses two eyes, there are two cameras. These cameras are slightly displaced such that they see the same scene

M. Bleyer (✉) · C. Breiteneder
Vienna University of Technology, Vienna, Austria
e-mail: bleyer@ims.tuwien.ac.at

C. Breiteneder
e-mail: breiteneder@ims.tuwien.ac.at

M. Bleyer
Microsoft Redmond, Redmond, USA

G.M. Farinella et al. (eds.), *Advanced Topics in Computer Vision*,
Advances in Computer Vision and Pattern Recognition,
DOI 10.1007/978-1-4471-5520-1_6,

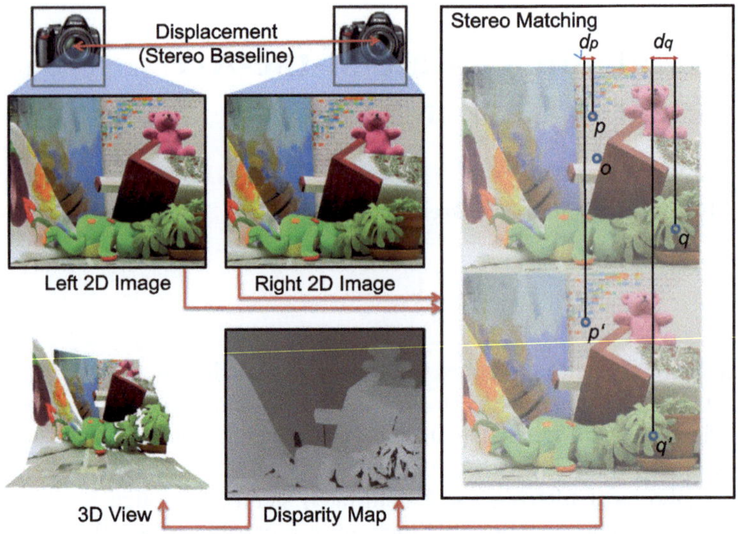

Fig. 6.1 Depth reconstruction via stereo. Two slightly displaced cameras record the scene. The stereo matching module finds dense correspondences between left and right images and encodes them in a disparity map. This disparity map is sufficient to reconstruct the 3D coordinates of each pixel

from different viewpoints.[1] Note that throughout this chapter we will assume that the stereo pair has been rectified such that corresponding points lie on the same horizontal scanlines in left and right views.[2]

Left and right images then form the input for the stereo matching module. In stereo matching, the task is to find a corresponding pixel in the right image for each pixel of the left image. Let us look at Fig. 6.1 where we have placed the left image on top of the right one to understand why this allows depth reasoning. We have marked the background pixel p of the left image as well as its corresponding pixel p' in the right view. Note that p and p' are displaced in horizontal direction due to the different perspectives under which left and right images have been recorded. The amount of this displacement (in pixels) is called disparity (d_p in the figure). We have also marked a pixel q and its correspondence q' of a foreground object. The important observation is that the disparity of the foreground pixel is larger than that of the background pixel (compare d_p and d_q in Fig. 6.1) and it is easy to show (e.g., in [29]) that disparity is inversely proportional to the distance of a pixel to the camera. Note that also the human brain perceives depth using disparity information.

In computational stereo, disparity information is typically stored in an intensity image (a so-called disparity map) where dark pixels encode low disparity val-

[1]The distance between the cameras is thereby referred to as the stereo baseline.

[2]Rectification can be accomplished using standard methods (e.g., [29]), once the stereo camera system has been calibrated.

ues (high distances from the camera) and bright intensities encode large disparities (close distances to the camera). See Fig. 6.1 for an example. In a calibrated stereo system, the disparity map is sufficient to reconstruct a metric 3D model of the recorded scene, which is the final goal in a shape from stereo approach.

The challenge in shape from stereo is to solve the stereo correspondence problem. This problem is permanently and unconsciously solved in the human brain, but turns out to be very challenging for a computer. This is for various reasons. First, as common in computer vision, images are usually contaminated by sensor noise. Second, in the absence of texture, stereo matching becomes highly ambiguous. Note that also a human is not able to perceive the correct depth if, for example, standing in front of a completely white wall without any texture. Third, not every pixel of one image has a correspondence in the other image, because due to the different image perspectives, a pixel can be occluded. To illustrate this, we have also marked a pixel o in Fig. 6.1. Note that this pixel cannot be found in the right view, that is, it is occluded.

Being able to solve the stereo matching problem is important in two respects. First, it may help to get a better understanding of how human depth perception works. Second, there are various applications in computer vision. For example, 3D reconstruction of cities from internet photography has recently gained popularity [1, 70]. Depth maps can also be fused to automatically generate high-quality 3D models of persons or even whole rooms as demonstrated by KinectFusion [56]. Stereo reconstructions can be applied for robot navigation (e.g., autonomously driving car), but also in human motion capture where Microsoft Kinect has recently demonstrated that depth information is vital [68]. There is also potential in next generation television where depth maps enable novel view synthesis, which allows the user to interactively control its viewing perspective [90]. Other applications include 3D tracking (surveillance, pose estimation, augmented reality, human-computer interaction), depth segmentation (z-keying) and industrial applications (quality assurance), to name just a few of them. Basically, whenever one needs to infer geometric information from the surrounding world, stereo vision represents a low-cost and non-intrusive alternative to active devices such as range finders.

In the following, we give a review of stereo methods with a focus on recent developments. This review provides the context for our own algorithms. We follow Scharstein and Szeliski [67] by dividing stereo algorithms in local and global ones.

6.2 Local Methods

A Naive Approach Let us start by describing the simplest possible stereo algorithm. It is reasonable to assume that corresponding pixels in left and right images have similar colors, which is known as the photo consistency assumption. Furthermore, we know that corresponding pixels lie on the same horizontal scanline as we assume that our images have been rectified. Hence a simple algorithm works as follows. For each pixel p of the left image, we search along the corresponding scanline

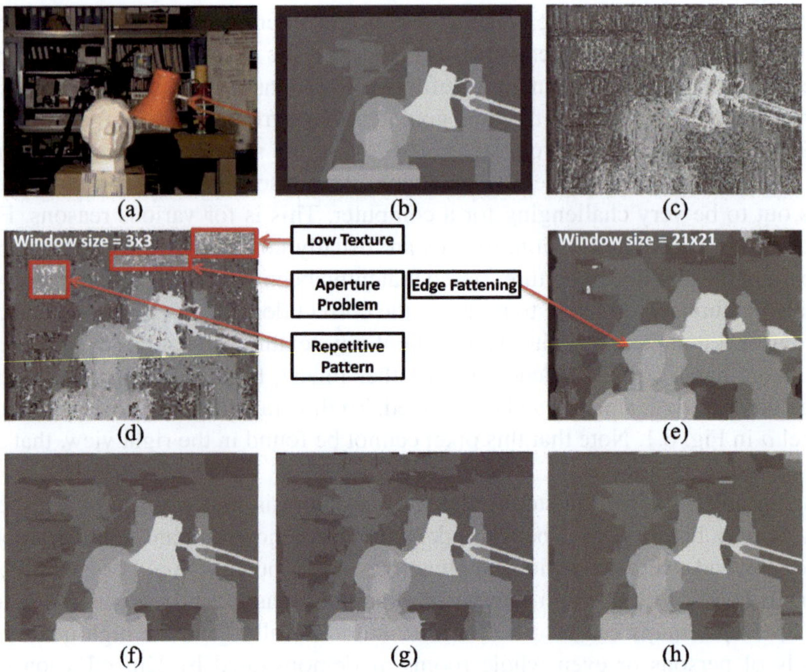

Fig. 6.2 Local methods. (**a**) Left image of the Middlebury Tsukuba image. (**b**) Ground truth disparity map. (**c**) Result of a naive algorithm. (**d**) Window-based aggregation with a 3 × 3 window. (**e**) Aggregation with a 21 × 21 window. (**f**) Result of the adaptive support weight approach [86]. (**g**) Our geodesic approach [36]. (**h**) Our cost filter method [61]

in the right image. We then select the pixel p' whose color is most similar to that of p as a matching point.

Figure 6.2c shows the disparity map of this naive approach which is very noisy. The problem is the high ambiguity of the data, i.e., if we want to find the correspondence of a red pixel of the left image (e.g., on the Tsukuba lamp of Fig. 6.2a) there is usually a relatively large candidate set of red pixels in the right image. The common approach taken in computer vision (and in all stereo algorithms) is to regularize the problem by imposing a smoothness assumption in order to cope with this ambiguity. This smoothness assumption means that spatial neighboring pixels are likely to have similar disparities. Stereo algorithms differ in the way how this assumption is implemented, which defines the difference between local and global methods [67].

The Principle of Local Algorithms Let us now come back to the naive approach above. Instead of matching single pixels, we can match small image areas.[3] It is important to note that by using areas we have made use of the smoothness assumption

[3]This is the reason why local algorithms are also sometimes referred to as area-based methods in literature.

in an implicit way, that is, we assume that all pixels of the area have exactly the same disparity. Let us now formulate the corresponding algorithm. For each pixel p of the left image, we compute its disparity d_p as

$$d_p = \operatorname*{argmin}_{0 \le d \le d_{\max}} \sum_{q \in W_p} c(q, q - d). \tag{6.1}$$

Here, $d_{\max}$ is a parameter defining the maximum allowed disparity. W_p denotes a square window centered on p. The function $c(p, q)$ computes the color dissimilarities between a pixel p of the left and a pixel q of the right image (e.g., summed-up absolute differences in RGB values). We write $q - d$ to denote the pixel coordinate that is derived by subtracting d from q's x-coordinate.

Selecting an Appropriate Window Size The local algorithm above has one important parameter, i.e., the size of the window W. From a computational point of view, the algorithm's runtime complexity is $\mathcal{O}(N \cdot d_{\max} \cdot |W|)$ where N is the number of pixels in the image and $|W|$ denotes the number of pixels in the window. Hence, larger windows would lead to higher run times if the algorithm was implemented in a naive way. However, in an efficient implementation, one can take advantage of high redundancy in the computation to reduce runtime complexity to $\mathcal{O}(N \cdot d_{\max})$ so that run time no longer depends on the size of the support window. The trick is to use a so-called sliding window technique [21, 55]. However, the size of the support window has a large effect on the quality of the disparity map as discussed next.

The problem of small support windows is that they may not capture enough texture variation to resolve matching ambiguities. In particular, the algorithm fails in untextured regions, areas with only horizontal texture (aperture problem) and repetitive image regions. This is illustrated in Fig. 6.2d where we have used a 3×3 window to compute the disparity map. However, note that disparity discontinuities are well preserved as a consequence of the small window size.

A remedy to overcome the ambiguity problem is the use of large support windows. A matching result using a large 21×21 window is shown in Fig. 6.2e. While this disparity map is considerably smoother than that of Fig. 6.2d, it is evident that object borders are badly preserved. The problem is our implicit smoothness assumption, that is, pixels within the window are supposed to have constant disparity. In the proximity of depth discontinuities, this assumption is broken as the window captures a mixture of foreground and background disparities. Whether the foreground or the background disparity leads to lower color dissimilarity depends on the texturedness of objects. In many cases the foreground's texture is dominant, which leads to the well-known foreground fattening problem (see Fig. 6.2e).

The traditional problem of local algorithms is that there is no ideal setting for the parameter defining the window size such that the algorithm gives correct results in low textured areas and regions close to object borders at the same time. Almost all work on local stereo matching focuses on the use of adaptive windows.

Adaptive Windows The idea of adaptive window algorithms is to select an individual window at each pixel such that the support region of a pixel remains large (in order to capture enough intensity variation), but does not overlap a disparity discontinuity (in order to avoid the edge fattening problem). For example, Fusiello et al. [24] test nine different square windows of constant size per pixel. These windows differ from each other in that they are centered at different positions, and the hope is that at least on one of these positions the window does not overlap a depth discontinuity. Hirschmüller et al. [34] divide the search window into a set of nine sub-windows. Only five of these sub-windows are used to compute the aggregated matching costs, that is, if the other four subwindows capture a different disparity than the center pixel they do not have any influence. As a final example, Veksler [78] estimates an arbitrarily sized and shaped window per pixel by optimizing over a large class of compact windows. In practice, none of the above methods has been able to compete with the quality of global methods (described in Sect. 6.3). Hence, the local stereo approach has been believed to be obsolete for some time.

Adaptive Support Weights In recent years, local stereo has experienced a renaissance due to the introduction of adaptive support weights [86].[4] The key idea is to assign an individual weight to each pixel that determines the pixel's influence in the matching process. Let us reformulate (6.1) accordingly as

$$d_p = \operatorname*{argmin}_{0 \le d \le d_{\max}} \sum_{q \in W_p} w(p,q) \cdot c(q, q-d). \tag{6.2}$$

We have now introduced a weight function $w(p,q)$ which should ideally return a value of 1 if pixel q lies on the same disparity as the center pixel p and 0 otherwise. Since disparities are not known in advance, defining $w(p,q)$ is challenging, that is, leads to a chicken-and-egg problem. Adaptive support weight algorithms differ in the way how they define $w(p,q)$ and we discuss this below. To our knowledge, all of them use the color cue for computing this function.

The Weight Function The original adaptive support weight paper [86] makes the assumption that spatially close pixels that are similar in color are likely to originate from the same scene object. Hence, they are also likely to share the same disparity. We define the corresponding function $w_{BL}(p,q)$ as

$$w_{BL}(p,q) = \exp\left(-\left(\frac{color(p,q)}{\gamma_c} + \frac{spatial(p,q)}{\gamma_s}\right)\right). \tag{6.3}$$

Here, $color(p,q)$ computes the color dissimilarity of p and q as the Euclidean distance between p's and q's color values in RGB space. The function $spatial(p,q)$ computes the Euclidean distance between p's and q's image coordinates. γ_c and γ_s are user-defined parameters. Note that a pixel q obtains high weight only if it is similar to the center pixel p in terms of color and spatial position (see assumption

[4]It is interesting to note that the majority of recent submissions to the Middlebury benchmark [67] are adaptive support weight techniques.

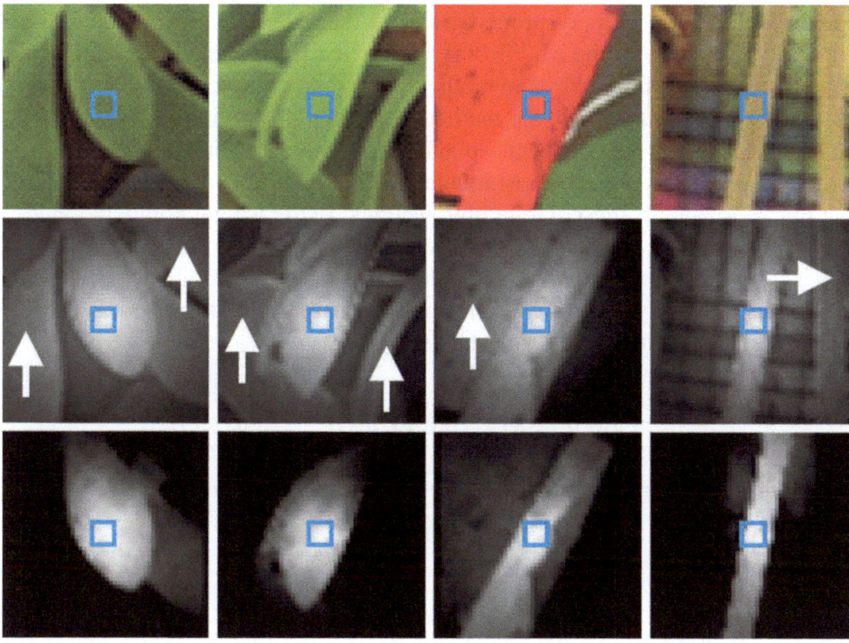

Fig. 6.3 Our geodesic approach [36]. We show adaptive support windows for the Middlebury Teddy and Cones images. (**a**) Color patch. The window's center pixel is marked by a *blue rectangle*. (**b**) Support weights computed by [86]. *Bright values* mean high weight. As marked by the *white arrows*, high weights are assigned to pixels that lie on a different disparity than the center pixel (e.g., the background leaves in the two left-most images). (**c**) Our geodesic support weights [36]. We avoid these wrong high weights by enforcing connectivity

above). Also note that the function above is equivalent to the weighting function of the bilateral filter.

Yoon and Kweon's work [86] has been a breakthrough in local stereo matching as (at least in the Middlebury benchmark) results on-par with global methods could be achieved for the first time. To illustrate the good quality of disparity maps, we plot the Tsukuba result of [86] in Fig. 6.2f. The downside of this approach is that these good-quality results come at the price of considerably increased run times. Due to the weighting function the sliding window technique (mentioned above) can no longer work and the algorithm's run time depends on the size of the support window. This is particularly bad as adaptive support weight techniques typically operate on large windows (e.g., 33×33 pixels in [86]). We will discuss later on one of our techniques [61] that has a considerably better runtime property, i.e., runs in real time, and even outperforms [86] in terms of quality of results.

Our Contribution—Geodesic Stereo [36] Our paper [36] proposes a new weight function. The idea is to introduce a connectivity property, i.e., two pixels are likely to lie on the same object (and disparity, respectively) if they are connected by a path of approximately the same color. Let us look at Fig. 6.3 to explain the advantage of this connectivity property. Figure 6.3a shows four image crops taken from the left images of the Middlebury Teddy and Cones pairs. Figure 6.3b shows that the weights computed by the method of [86] are not ideal. By only looking at color and spatial differences, the method assigns high weights to pixels that lie on a different disparity than the center pixel, which happens, for example, at the background leaves in the two left-most images of Fig. 6.3b. In contrast, our method [36] (see Fig. 6.3c) avoids these wrong high weights. In the weight computation at each pixel q, we check if q is connected to the center pixel p by a path of constant color. This is not the case in the leaves example as the foreground and background leaves are separated by a color edge. More formally, our weighting function $w_{\mathrm{GEO}}(p,q)$ is inversely proportional to the geodesic distance:

$$w_{\mathrm{GEO}}(p,q) = \exp\left(-\frac{geo(p,q)}{\gamma}\right) \tag{6.4}$$

where the parameter γ controls the strength of the segmentation. $geo(p,q)$ is defined as

$$geo(p,q) = \min_{P \in \mathcal{P}_{p,q}} d(P). \tag{6.5}$$

Here $\mathcal{P}_{p,q}$ denotes all possible paths $\langle p_1, p_2, \ldots, p_n \rangle$ that connect p and q within the support window, that is, $p_1 = p$ and $p_n = q$. The costs of a path $d(P)$ are computed as

$$d(P) = \sum_{i=2}^{i=n} color(p_i, p_{i-1}). \tag{6.6}$$

In our experiments on the Middlebury data, we demonstrate that our geodesic approach outperforms the original adaptive support weight method [86]. At the time of publication (2009), our method has been the top-performer among all local methods in the Middlebury benchmark. The disparity map generated for the Tsukuba images is shown in Fig. 6.2g. In a follow-up work [37], we have shown how to speed up our geodesic approach such that near real time frame rates can be achieved without considerable loss of quality.

Adaptive Support Weight Stereo via Image Filtering As stated above, the weight function of the original adaptive support weight function [86] corresponds to the filter weights of a bilateral filter. It is known that the aggregation step of Yoon and Kweon's method [86] can be understood as filtering the cost volume with a joint bilateral filter (see our cost filter paper [61] and [62]). This insight forms the basis for speeding up the adaptive support weight approach. To be more precise, the cost volume is a three-dimensional array that is derived by computing the costs for matching each pixel (x, y) at each allowed disparity d. The joint bilateral filter is then applied on each individual xy-slice of this volume where filter weights are computed from the left color image. Finally, a disparity map is obtained by selecting the disparity of minimum costs in the filtered volume at each pixel.

Fig. 6.4 Our cost filter approach [61] applied on problems outside of stereo. (**a**) Optical flow. We use the *color coding* of [3] for visualization of the flow field. Our approach accurately reconstructs flow borders and thin structures. (**b**) Large displacement optical flow. In contrast to many competing algorithms, our method handles large motions. (**c**) Interactive segmentation. User input is given by drawing the *yellow rectangle* (see *left image*). Our method then computes a binary segmentation using cost filtering (see *right image*)

Being able to implement the original adaptive support weight approach with runtime independent of the window size boils down to the question whether it is possible to implement joint bilateral filtering with runtime complexity independent of the filter kernel size. According to the current state of research, a so-called O(1) implementation only works for approximations of the joint bilateral filter. Several authors [42, 62, 89] have used such approximations to derive fast implementations of Yoon and Kweon's algorithm [86]. In [42] and [89], the joint bilateral filter is approximated by using integral histograms as described in [60], while [62] uses an approximation based on the bilateral grid of [59]. The problem of these approximative approaches is that they sacrifice quality of disparity maps for speed.

A different strategy to derive an O(1) implementation of adaptive support weight matching is to replace the joint bilateral filter with a different filter that shares the joint bilateral filter's edge-preserving property, but can innately be implemented with runtime independent of the filter kernel size. In this line of research, [53, 88] use a cross-shaped filter. Due to using a cross-shaped support region, the algorithm fails at fine structures that are neither horizontal nor vertical. A better alternative is discussed next.

Our Contribution—Cost Filter [61] In [61], we propose to use the very recent guided filter [31] for cost filtering. This filter is similar to the bilateral one in that it shares its edge-preserving property. However, the advantage is that an exact (non-approximative) implementation can be accomplished by running a series of box filters so that the filter's runtime does not depend on the filter kernel size. We show in [39] that a GPU-based implementation runs at 33.3 frames per second for 640×480 pixel images and 40 allowed disparity levels. This makes it the fastest available adaptive support weight algorithm. Apart from that, our method has also been the best-performing method among all local algorithms in the Middlebury table [67] at the time of publication in 2011. In particular, this also means that it outperforms Yoon and Kweon's algorithm [86]. An example result is shown in Fig. 6.2h. In [38], we show how to extend the cost filter approach in order to compute temporally consistent disparity maps given a stereo video as an input.

An important contribution of our paper [61] is to show that the concept of cost filtering is not restricted to stereo, but can be applied to other computer vision tasks

Fig. 6.5 Our PatchMatch Stereo algorithm [14]. (**a**) Left image and ground truth disparities of the Corridor pair that contains highly slanted surfaces. (**b**) The disparity map computed with fronto–parallel windows approximates the slanted surfaces via many fronto-parallel ones. (**c**) PatchMatch Stereo correctly reconstructs the scene as a collection of slanted planar surfaces via using slanted support windows and continuous sub-pixel disparities

that can be formulated as labeling problems. We first instantiate our framework for optical flow computation and show that our algorithm can reach a top position in the Middlebury optical flow benchmark [3] using almost identical parameter settings as for the stereo problem. Figure 6.4a shows a flow map for the Middlebury Schefflera test set. As seen from Fig. 6.4b, an advantage of our optical flow method is that it can handle large displacements, which is challenging for most competing methods.

We then instantiate our framework for interactive image segmentation, which is a very different problem from stereo or optical flow computation. Note that in this case, the cost volume does not store color dissimilarities, but the likelihood to which a pixel belongs to a foreground and a background color model, respectively. The other steps, that is, filtering of the cost volume and minimum selection, remain the same. We show that our segmentation method can compete with a state-of-the-art method, that is, GrabCut [63], but runs considerably faster. It takes 5 milliseconds to segment a 1000×1000 pixel image. An example result is shown in Fig. 6.4c.

Slanted Surfaces and Sub-pixel Precision Let us now come back to the implicit smoothness assumption of local algorithms, that is, all pixels within the support window have the same disparity. We have already discussed that this assumption is broken at disparity borders and that adaptive support weight algorithms represent a good remedy to this problem. However, there are two additional problems. (1) Disparity values of pixels within the support window will be different if the window captures a slanted (non-fronto-parallel) surface. (2) So far we have only spoken about integer-valued disparities and ignored that we should ideally match at continuous sub-pixel disparity values.

Figure 6.5b shows the effect of these two problems on the Corridor test set that contains highly slanted surfaces. To derive the disparity map, we have used fronto-parallel windows that are matched at integer-valued disparities. Note that this is exactly what all algorithms described above do. As can be seen from Fig. 6.5b, the 3D model derived from the computed disparity map is relatively poor, as the slanted planes are reconstructed via many fronto-parallel surfaces. It is known that this problem can be overcome by using slanted planar support windows matched at continuous sub-pixel disparities. However, this model leads to a difficult optimization problem as it is not known in advance which slanted windows occur in the scene and the number of candidate planes is infinite. After discussing previous methods, we will present our algorithm [14] that can effectively handle this complex optimization problem. The result of our algorithm on the Corridor scene is shown in Fig. 6.5c.

Previous Sub-pixel/Slanted Window Algorithms Some local methods (e.g., [84]) obtain sub-pixel precision in a post-processing step by fitting a parabola in the cost volume. From our experience, this method leads to relatively noisy sub-pixel information. A better option is to account for sub-pixel displacements directly in the matching process. This can be accomplished by extending the label space, that is, some fractional disparity values (half- or quarter-pixel) are considered in addition to the integer-valued ones (e.g., in [26]). Note that this is still a discrete approach and that run time doubles (quadruples) if half-pixel (quarter-pixel) precision is used. The same principle works for slanted windows, that is, in addition to fronto-parallel windows a set of slanted windows can be included in the label space (e.g., in [25]). This is known as plane sweeping in the literature. As before, this is a discrete approach, that is, the chances for not having the correct plane in the label space are high, and this strategy leads to considerably longer run times.

Finally, we also want to mention the approach of [87]. The authors first compute an initial disparity map and then apply plane fitting at each pixel. The extracted slanted planes are then used in a second matching round. The problem is that this method fails for highly slanted surfaces as the disparity results of the first round are too poor to extract the correct planes.

Our Contribution—PatchMatch Stereo [14] Let us reformulate (6.2) such that optimization is now performed over the set of all possible 3D planes, that is,

$$d_p = \operatorname*{argmin}_{f \in \mathcal{F}} \sum_{q \in W_p} w(p,q) \cdot c\big(q, q - (a_f q_x + b_f q_y + c_f)\big). \tag{6.7}$$

Here $\mathcal{F}$ is the set of all disparity planes and a_f, b_f and c_f are the three parameters of a plane f. We write q_x and q_y to denote pixel q's x- and y-coordinates. Note that we also use an adaptive weight function $w(p,q)$ to handle the edge fattening problem. For simplicity, we use the one of [86] (see (6.3)). As stated above, minimizing (6.7) is difficult as the set $\mathcal{F}$ has infinite cardinality. Hence, the approach of checking all possible labels (implemented by all algorithms above) can no longer work. We propose an algorithm based on PatchMatch [4] to approximate the minimum of (6.7) at each pixel.

The basic observation is that relatively large regions of an image can be modeled by approximately the same plane. In the initialization step of the algorithm, each pixel is assigned to a plane with random parameters. It is relatively obvious that most of these random planes will be wrong, but the hope is that at least one pixel of a region carries a plane that is close to the optimal one. Note that this is very likely, since we have many guesses. For example, in the Corridor scene of Fig. 6.5a the ground plane consists of approximately 25000 pixels, that is, we have 25000

(a) (b) (c) (d)

Fig. 6.6 3D reconstructions of our algorithm [14] and its competitors. (**a**) Crop of the Middlebury Cones image. (**b**) Matching using fronto-parallel windows and integer disparities. (**c**) Matching using fronto-parallel windows and continuous disparities. (**d**) Our PatchMatch stereo algorithm that uses slanted windows and continuous disparities. Note that the *rounded shape* of the cup's handle is well reconstructed

guesses to find the correct plane for this object. If there is at least a single correct guess, then this is already sufficient, since our algorithm propagates this plane to neighboring pixels. We implement three different forms of propagation, that is, spatial propagation, view propagation and temporal propagation (see our paper [14] for details).

Our PatchMatch stereo algorithm is currently the top performer among all local algorithms when sub-pixel precision is considered (Middlebury error threshold 0.5). It is even the top performer among all algorithms for the challenging Teddy set (Middlebury default error threshold 1.0) that has a highly slanted ground plane where competing methods run into problems. Figure 6.6 demonstrates the high amount of disparity detail that our method achieves. In contrast to competing methods (Figs. 6.6b and 6.6c), our method successfully reconstructs the handle of the cup in Fig. 6.6d.

Limitations of Local Methods Despite of the high research attention that local methods have gained over the last couple of years, they do not render global approaches useless. The problem is that even large support windows are not sufficient for handling highly ambiguous data, that is, very untextured image regions. To illustrate this, we have used our PatchMatch stereo algorithm [14] that is considered to represent the state-of-the-art in local matching to compute the disparity map for the Middlebury Plastic image. As can be seen from Fig. 6.7c, the algorithm fails to handle the completely untextured yellow surface, as this high ambiguity cannot be resolved completely locally. In such cases, a global smoothness prior is essential. To demonstrate this, we have embedded PatchMatch stereo as a data term in a variant of the second order stereo algorithm of [81] (see our paper [14] for details on how this is accomplished). As can be seen from Fig. 6.7d, the yellow plastic surface can now be handled successfully. Note that while local stereo approaches have started to take over the top positions in the Middlebury benchmark [67] from global methods, this is not the case on more realistic imaginary such as that of the very recent KITTI street scene benchmark [27] that is dominated by global methods.

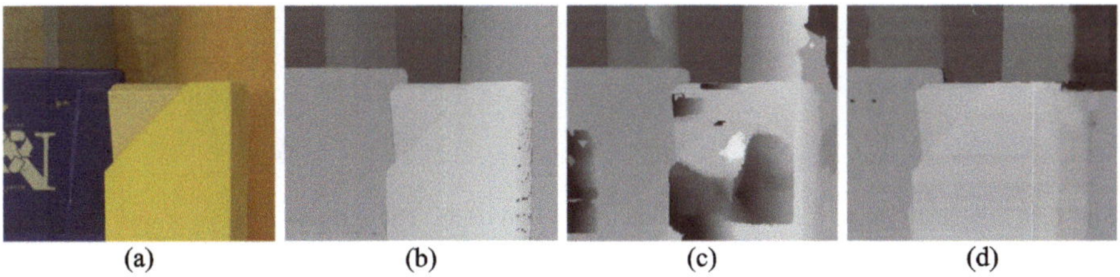

Fig. 6.7 Limitations of local methods. (a) Left image of the Middlebury Plastic pair. (b) Ground truth disparity map. (c) Results of our local algorithm PatchMatch stereo [14]. The *yellow plastic surface* is poorly reconstructed due to the lack of texture. (d) Result of a global method. The global smoothness prior is essential to correctly reconstruct the *yellow surface*

The important point is that the aggregation schemes of local methods can supplement global methods in the form of a stronger (less ambiguous) data term. Due to the use of adaptive support weights, aggregation also improves the performance of global methods near depth discontinuities. Slanted support windows may also improve the results of global algorithms at highly slanted surfaces. Finally it is important to note that many robust match measures require a window to be computed (e.g., Census or Normalized Cross Correlation). As described later, such window-based measures are specifically important on realistic images with illumination differences, for example, the left image is darker than the right one.

Finally, we would also like to mention another limitation of local algorithms, that is, it is difficult to incorporate occlusion handling directly in the matching process. Typically occlusions are treated in a post-processing step by left-right consistency checking [23]. This means that the disparity map for the right image is computed in addition to that of the left view. The check then invalidates pixels of the left view whose disparity value is different in the right image. In the final step, these invalidated pixels are filled by replicating disparities of spatially close valid pixels (e.g., see our filling procedure in [61]). As we will see in the next section, global methods allow for occlusion handling directly in the matching process by modeling the occlusion problem in their energy functions.

6.3 Global Methods

The Principle of Global Algorithms Global methods differ from local ones in that they express the smoothness assumption in an explicit form via a so-called smoothness term. Global algorithms define an energy function $E(D)$ that measures the quality of a disparity map D. In the subsequent optimization step, the goal is to find the disparity map of lowest energy, that is, of highest quality according to our energy function. The typical form of a stereo energy function is:

$$E(D) = E_{\text{data}}(D) + \lambda \cdot E_{\text{smooth}}(D). \tag{6.8}$$

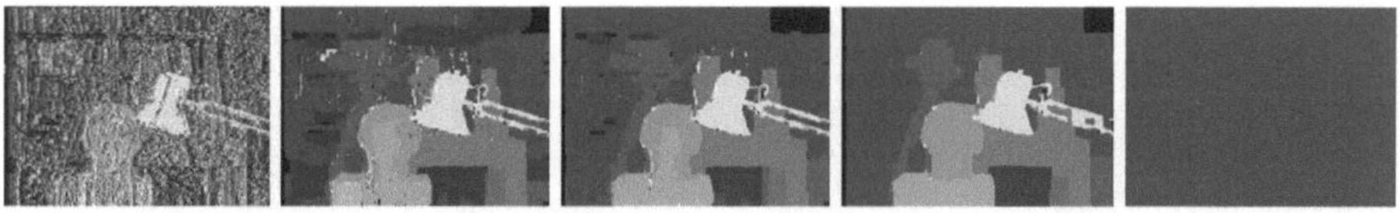

Fig. 6.8 Disparity maps for increasing values of λ in (6.8). The *left-most image* shows the result that is optimal according to the data term ($\lambda := 0$), while the *right-most image* shows the disparity map optimal according to the smoothness term ($\lambda := \infty$)

Here, λ is a user-defined parameter that balances the influence of E_{data} and E_{smooth}. The data term E_{data} measures photo consistency and is defined as

$$E_{\text{data}}(D) = \sum_{p \in I_l} c(p, p - d_p) \tag{6.9}$$

where I_l denotes all pixels of the left image and $c(p, p')$ computes the pixel dissimilarity between pixel p of the left view and pixel p' of the right image (e.g., absolute difference of intensity values). d_p represents the disparity value of pixel p in disparity map D. Let us now focus on the smoothness term E_{smooth}. It is responsible for preferring disparity maps that are spatially smooth over such that are not by assigning lower energy. E_{smooth} is defined as

$$E_{\text{smooth}}(D) = \sum_{\langle p,q \rangle \in \mathcal{N}} s(d_p, d_q) \tag{6.10}$$

where $\mathcal{N}$ denotes all pairs of spatially neighboring pixels in the left image. Note that since the term is defined on pairs of pixels, it is often referred to as pairwise term, whereas the data term is referred to as unary term. The function $s(d_p, d_q)$ assigns a penalty if p's disparity is different from that of q. As discussed below, there are different options for implementing the smoothness function $s()$, which also defines the complexity of the optimization problem. To show the influence of E_{data} and E_{smooth}, we plot disparity maps for the Tsukuba images using different settings of λ in (6.8) in Fig. 6.8. Note that if we set $\lambda := 0$, that is, switch off the smoothness term, then our method "degenerates" to a purely local one.

Optimization Let us now focus on the problem of finding a disparity map that minimizes (6.8). This problem is difficult as the disparity assignment of each pixel influences the disparity assignment of every other pixel of the image via the smoothness term. This is known as the "Knock-on" effect in literature. It is known that even for the simplest discontinuity-preserving smoothness function, that is, the Potts model where $s(d_p, d_q) = 0$ if $d_p = d_q$ and $s(d_p, d_q) = 1$ otherwise, finding the global minimum of (6.8) is an np-complete problem (see [18] for a formal proof). However, there exist powerful optimization strategies that approximate the energy minimum. In the following, we will discuss three of them, that is, (1) dynamic programming, (2) graph-cuts and (3) message passing. Note that there is also

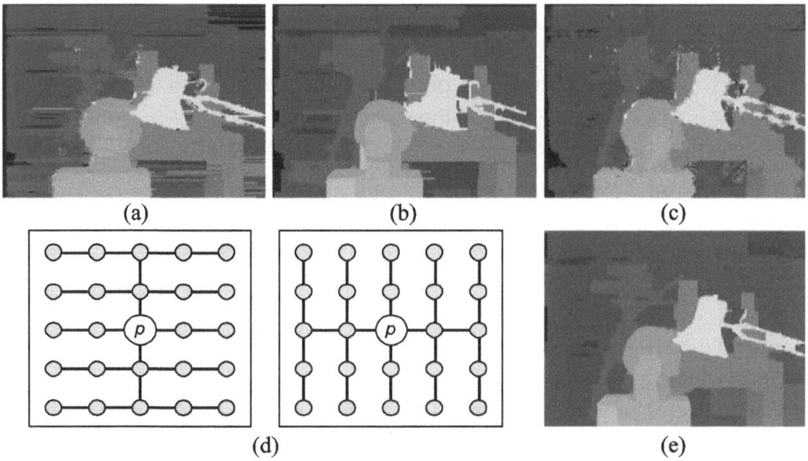

Fig. 6.9 Dynamic programming-based methods. (**a**) The scanline optimization method of [67]. The disparity map suffers from horizontal streaks. (**b**) The tree-based method of [79]. The streaking problem is reduced, but in addition to horizontal streaks, vertical streaks are introduced. (**c**) Our reimplementation of [32]. The streaking problem is eliminated, but the algorithm produces isolated pixels. (**d**) The tree structures used in our work [10]. (**e**) Corresponding disparity map. Our disparity result does not suffer from streaks or isolated pixels

an online competition [74] that compares the effectiveness of optimization strategies.

Dynamic Programming As stated above, exact minimization of (6.8) is an np-complete problem in general. However, there exists a special case. If the smoothness interactions ($\mathcal{N}$ in (6.10)) form a tree in the image grid, the global optimal solution can efficiently be computed via dynamic programming (DP). The simplest method to modify $\mathcal{N}$ such that this set does not contain cycles is to remove all vertical smoothness interactions and this is exactly what most DP-based algorithms do (e.g., [6, 17, 58] or the scanline optimization method of [67]). In this case, each horizontal scanline is optimized independently from the others and this leads to the well-known scanline streaking problem (see Fig. 6.9a). This streaking problem is the reason why such methods clearly fall behind the state-of-the-art in stereo matching [67].

Veksler [79] proposes a smarter way to transform $\mathcal{N}$ into a tree that contains horizontal as well as vertical smoothness edges. The idea is that some smoothness edges are more important than others. In particular, if two neighboring pixels are similar in color, they are likely to lie on the same disparity. Hence, the corresponding smoothness edge is more important than one connecting two pixels of different color. This prioritization is then transformed into weights and the tree is built using a minimum spanning tree algorithm. While this approach reduces horizontal streaks, it, however, introduces vertical streaks (see Fig. 6.9b).

One of the most popular stereo algorithms (e.g., implemented in the Open Computer Vision library) is the semi-global matching approach [32]. Note that we will describe it from the viewpoint of tree DP, which is very different from the description given in [32].[5] Each pixel p represents the root of a tree. This tree has a star-shaped form, i.e., captures all pixels that lie on p's horizontal, vertical and diagonal scanlines. The root p is then assigned to the disparity of optimal costs on this tree structure. As can be seen from Fig. 6.9c, the approach effectively overcomes the scanline streaking problem, but produces isolated pixels. The problem is that the star-shaped tree is composed only of a subset of all image pixels. This subset may not capture enough texture to derive the correct disparity at the tree's root.

Our Contribution—Simple Trees [10] Our Simple Tree approach [10] also constructs individual trees per pixel. However, in contrast to [32], our trees contain all pixels of the reference view and hence the problem of missing texture (see above) is avoided. As shown in Fig. 6.9d, we use two different trees at each pixel p. The horizontal tree (Fig. 6.9d (left)) captures all horizontal smoothness edges as well as the vertical smoothness links of p's scanline. The vertical tree (Fig. 6.9d (right)) represents the complementary tree, i.e., captures all vertical smoothness links and the horizontal edges of p's scanline. Note that there is high redundancy in computation of all tree's optima. This can be accomplished with a few DP scanline passes, which takes less than a second on standard images and in a CPU-based implementation.[6] Hence, the algorithm shows an excellent speed versus quality trade-off. We show our Tsukuba result in Fig. 6.9e. As can be seen, this result is free of scanline streaks and isolated pixels.

Graph-Cuts Graph-cuts have been used in stereo vision for some years (e.g., [66]). In the following, we will speak about "modern" graph-cut based algorithms, so-called move making algorithms. These algorithms are capable of effectively minimizing (6.8) and have been the winner in the optimization benchmark of [74] on some problem instances. The idea is to start with an arbitrary disparity map[7] and then to iteratively apply moves. Here, a move leads to a new disparity map of lower (or at least the same) energy. There are two well-known moves, that is, $\alpha\beta$-swaps and α-expansions [18]. We will focus on α-expansions, because they are known to outperform $\alpha\beta$-swaps. To apply an α-expansion, a discrete disparity label d_α is selected. The α-expansion move changes the disparity map such that each pixel either keeps its current disparity or changes it to d_α. The challenge is to compute the α-expansion that leads to the largest decrease of energy (6.8) among all possible α-expansions. This problem can be solved exactly by computing the minimum cut

[5] Hirschmüller stresses a relationship to local methods. He calls the method semi-global matching, as he uses the aggregation step of local methods, but aggregates (global) DP path costs instead of pixel dissimilarities of spatially close pixels.

[6] It is likely that the approach would run in real time if implemented on a modern GPU.

[7] Note that although we speak about disparity, these move making algorithms can be applied to arbitrary computer vision labeling problems outside stereo vision.

/ maximum flow in a special purpose graph.[8] Note that this is only true if the energy is sub-modular [18], which is for example, the case for the Potts model. There are many stereo algorithms that apply α-expansions as their optimization engine (e.g., [35, 46, 47, 52] or our algorithm [9]). Note that graph-cuts can optimize more complex energies than that of (6.8) such as that discussed below.

Lempitsky et al. [50] have recently proposed a new move, that is, the fusion move that is interesting because it enables graph-cut-based optimization over continuous disparity values. The idea is to have two proposal disparity maps. In a fusion move, each pixel either takes the disparity of proposal 1 or that of proposal 2. Note that if proposal 2 only has a single disparity for all pixels, then this fusion move is identical to an α-expansion. Hence, fusion moves are a generalization of α-expansions. The problem is that in the general case the optimization graph contains non-submodular edges, and hence computing the optimal fusion move becomes an np-complete problem. However, there are graph-cut based algorithms, i.e., quadratic pseudo-boolean optimization (QPBO) [45] that can handle non-sub-modular energies.[9] The fusion move framework has been used in the second order stereo algorithm [81] and our algorithms [13, 15].

Message Passing The most prominent algorithm based on message passing is Belief Propagation (BP) [22]. BP is an iterative procedure where each pixel communicates with its four spatial neighbors via sending messages. A message is thereby a vector that has an entry for each allowed disparity. A message $m^t_{pq}(d_q)$ sent from pixel p to pixel q at iteration t encodes p's belief that q should be assigned to a particular disparity d_q and is computed as

$$m^t_{pq}(d_q) = \min_{0\leq d_p \leq d_{\max}} \left(s(d_p, d_q) + c(p, p - d_p) + \sum_{r \in \mathcal{N}(p) \setminus \{q\}} m^{t-1}_{rp}(d_p) \right) \quad (6.11)$$

where $d_{\max}$ is the maximum allowed disparity and $\mathcal{N}(p)\setminus\{q\}$ denotes p's spatial neighbors excluding q. After T iterations the final disparity d^*_q at pixel q is computed as

$$d^*_q = \operatorname*{argmin}_{0\leq d_q \leq d_{\max}} \left(c(q, q - d_q) + \sum_{p \in \mathcal{N}(q)} m^T_{pq}(d_q) \right). \quad (6.12)$$

Note that by using the strategy of [22] the computational complexity of calculating the messages (6.11) for all image pixels can be reduced to $\mathcal{O}(N \cdot d_{\max})$ where N is the number of pixels. This makes BP fast and GPU-based real time implementations

[8] This is why these algorithms are referred to as graph-cuts.

[9] Due to the np-hardness of the problem, QPBO can only guarantee to find a part of the global optimal solution and will, in general, leave a subset of pixels unlabeled. The autarky property of QPBO guarantees that by assigning unlabeled pixels to the disparities of proposal 1 the energy of the fusion result will be lower or the same as that of proposal 1. Alternative ways for handling these unlabeled pixels are QPBO-I and QPBO-P [64].

for stereo are available [83]. BP forms the optimization engine for many stereo algorithms (e.g., [43, 71, 72, 75]).

Finally, we also mention tree-reweighted message passing (TRW) [80], which is similar to BP, but uses a different message update rule. TRW allows to compute a lower bound on the energy. Comparison of the current energy against this lower bound gives an estimate of how close the current solution is to a global optimal one [54, 74], that is, if the energy is equal to the lower bound, a global energy optimum has been found.

The Problem Is the Model In general, when an energy minimization approach delivers suboptimal results, there are two reasons: (1) The energy function does not represent a good model of the stereo problem or (2) the optimization technique fails to effectively minimize the energy. The problem is that one often does not know whether bad performance is for the first or the second reason (or a combination thereof), since the global energy optimum is usually unknown.

Recent studies give indication that with the use of modern optimization schemes (graph-cuts or TRW) the formulation of the energy function has become the limiting factor. For example, in the above mentioned optimization algorithm comparison [74], the authors have shown that the best-performing optimization algorithms applied on the energy of (6.8) are capable of computing local energy minima extremely close to the exact solution. However, it has been pointed out that, due to flaws in the energy formulation, this does not necessarily translate into improved reconstruction performance (with respect to ground truth data). A specifically interesting result of this study (also noted in [77]) is that the energy of the ground truth image is considerably higher than that produced by modern optimization algorithms. This clearly shows that the energy function represents an unsatisfactory model for the stereo problem.

This is also consistent with the findings of Meltzer et al. [54], who have shown that, despite the np-hardness of the optimization problem, an exact optimum can be obtained for some standard benchmark stereo pairs (the old Middlebury set [67]) using tree-reweighted message passing. The corresponding results are shown in Fig. 6.10. Even the global optimal solution has not led to a better disparity reconstruction in comparison to standard energy minimization approaches. Consequently, the authors have concluded that "*the problem is not in the optimization algorithm, but rather in the energy function*". In other words, progress in stereo can only be achieved by improving the energy function. In the remainder of this chapter, we will discuss options to improve the stereo model.

Data Term Let us start by investigating the data term ((6.9) of our energy (6.8)). Note that from our experience, the match measure has a very large influence on the quality of disparity maps (also see our papers [7, 11]), which is oftentimes larger than the influences of smoothness terms and optimization algorithms.

There are various options to implement the pixel dissimilarity function $c()$. The simplest strategy is to compute the absolute difference (AD) of intensity values, that is, $c(p,q) = |I_p - I_q|$ where I_p denotes the intensity at pixel p. An alternative

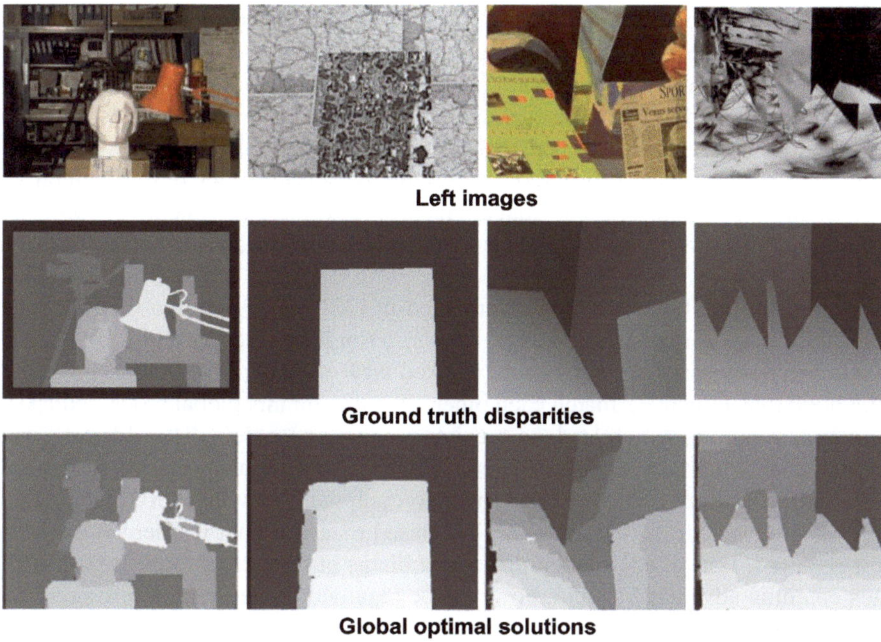

Fig. 6.10 Global optimal solutions for energy (6.8) on the old Middlebury set. (The Potts model is used to implement the smoothness function.) Images are taken from [54]. Note that even the global energy minimum leads to disparity maps that are relatively far off from the ground truth solution (e.g., see handle of the lamp or the camera in the Tsukuba image). This suggests that the energy formulation does not represent an ideal model for the stereo problem

approach is to calculate the squared difference (SD), that is, $c(p,q) = (I_p - I_q)^2$. According to the experiments of [67], there is relatively little performance difference between AD and SD, although SD is potentially more sensitive to outliers. It makes sense to truncate AD and SD values to reduce the influence of outlier pixels. While this improves matching performance [67], the selection of the threshold value that should be chosen according to the images' noise level represents a problem. Birchfield and Tomasi [5] present a match measure that reduces the influence of image sampling. The idea is to perform linear interpolation to derive the intensity at sub-pixel locations and to check whether these sub-pixel intensities lead to lower matching costs. From our experience, this match measure does not necessarily improve quality.

An important weakness of all above dissimilarity functions is that they cannot handle radiometric distortions (e.g., the left image is darker than the right one). Note that in practical stereo such radiometric distortions are almost always present and the treatment of this problem is vital. There are various competing radiometric insensitive measures and an evaluation of which has been conducted in [33].

The first option is to transform left and right images via a filter in a pre-processing step. Matching is then performed on the filtered images using a standard measure such as AD or SD. An edge filter (e.g., Sobel) is an obvious choice. Note that the gradient is not affected if radiometric differences are due to a constant intensity offset, e.g., the intensity of corresponding points is always 10 levels higher in the right image.[10] An alternative filter to handle intensity offsets is to subtract the mean computed in a window from the original intensity images. Note that since the mean is computed within a window, this leads to edge fattening. Hence, a better option is to subtract the image processed by an edge-preserving filter (e.g., bilateral or guided filter) from the original image. According to the experiments of [33], the filter-based methods fall behind the match measures discussed next in terms of quality.

Mutual Information (MI) as implemented in [32] builds a single model of the intensity change for the whole image, that is, given intensities I_p and $I_{p'}$ of pixels in left and right images, the MI score (looked up from the global model) gives the likelihood that I_p and $I_{p'}$ match each other. To compute this global model a disparity map is required, which leads to a chicken-and-egg problem. This dilemma can be solved in an iterative fashion. Given an initial disparity map, the MI scores are computed. These MI scores are then used to compute a new disparity map and so on.[11] The advantage is that MI is a pixel-based measure, that is, there is no window required. Hence, edge fattening and problems at slanted surfaces are avoided. This potential advantage should, however, be regarded in the light of new aggregation schemes that use adaptive support weights and slanted windows as discussed in Sect. 6.2. The main disadvantage is that radiometric distortions are usually not the same all over the image (e.g., only the left bottom image part is darker in the left view). Such local changes cannot be handled by the global distortion model, which may represent the reason why MI has been outperformed by the window-based measures described next in the study of [33].

Zero mean Normalized Cross-Correlation (ZNCC) is a window-based measure than can handle intensity offsets and gains. It is defined as

$$c(p, p-d) = \frac{\sum_{q \in W_p} (I_q - \overline{I_p})(I_{q-d} - \overline{I_{p-d}})}{\sum_{q \in W_p} (I_q - \overline{I_p})^2 \sum_{q \in W_p} (I_{q-d} - \overline{I_{p-d}})^2} \tag{6.13}$$

where W_p represents a squared window centered at p and $\overline{I_p}$ denotes the mean intensity computed over all pixels inside W_p. A second popular window-based measure is Census. Instead of directly matching intensities (that may be affected by radiometric distortion), Census generates a bit string representation that describes the texture within the window. Each pixel q of the window is thereby compared against the center pixel p. If $I_q < I_p$ then 0 is concatenated to the bit string and 1 otherwise. The Census costs between the reference window and the window in the match frame are then computed as the Hamming distance between the corresponding two bit strings.

[10] In practice, it is sufficient to compute the gradient in x-direction, as vertical edges contain more disparity information than horizontal ones.

[11] Hirschmüller [32] uses a hierarchical approach to speed up this iterative procedure.

Our Contribution—The Role of Color [7] So far we have only spoken about matching intensities and ignored the fact that color information is typically available. Note that although color obviously represents additional information, many researcher still convert the input images to grey-scale when computing the match measure. We have published two evaluation papers [7, 11] that investigate the usefulness of color.

In the first paper [11], we have concentrated on the standard match measures AD and SD (see above) that we compute in eight different color spaces[12] as well as on the intensity images. We apply the Simple Tree method [14] (see above) to optimize energy (6.8) using the resulting match measures as data terms. We evaluate on a relatively large test set of 30 Middlebury ground truth pairs. We report a considerable quality improvement when using color. The best-performing color space gives 25 % less disparity errors in comparison to only using intensity.

In our follow-up paper [7], we take a closer look at the image regions where color improves matching performance over intensity-based matching when using AD or SD. The key insight is that these regions correspond to image areas that are affected by radiometric distortions. The paper shows that the benefit of color is small, given that considerably better performance at radiometric distorted regions is achieved by directly using a radiometric insensitive measure such as ZNCC and Census instead of color-based AD. An interesting observation is that in comparison to the intensity-based versions of ZNCC and Census, performance even decreases if these measures are "enriched" with color information. Therefore, we suggest not to use color at all, but radiometric insensitive measures computed on intensity images.

Occlusion-Aware Data Term The data term defined in (6.9) has a systematical problem in that it does not consider the occlusion problem. It does not make sense to compute a match measure for occluded pixels, as the matching point in the other image does not exist. Note that ignoring the occlusion problem leads to wrong disparity results near disparity discontinuities, that is, in occluded regions and their proximity. For example, in the second column of Fig. 6.10, the disparity to the left side of the foreground object is completely wrong due to this problem.

Let us now redefine (6.9) such that it accounts for occlusions:

$$E_{\text{data}}(D) = \sum_{p \in I_l} c(p, p - d_p)\big(1 - O(p)\big) + \lambda_{\text{occ}} O(p). \tag{6.14}$$

Here $O(p)$ is a function that returns 1 if pixel p is occluded and 0 otherwise. λ_{occ} is a user-defined penalty for occlusion. This parameter is required to prevent the algorithm from maximizing the number of occluded pixels. Note that according to (6.14) the match measure is only evaluated for visible pixels, while we impose the occlusion penalty for occluded ones. The challenge is to implement the occlusion

[12] In our study, the extension of AD and SD to color works by computing AD and SD for each color channel separately. We then sum up the differences over the 3 color channels.

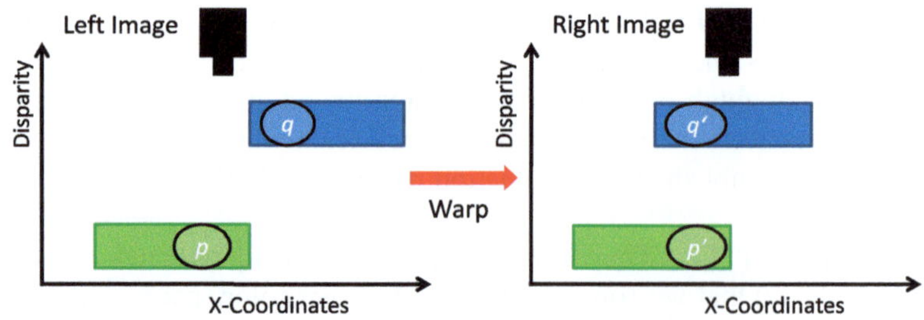

Fig. 6.11 Occlusion Reasoning. The pixel p is occluded by pixel q, because both of them project to the same pixel in the *right image* and q has higher disparity than p

function $O(p)$ and we follow the definition of [81]:

$$O(p) = \begin{cases} 1 & \text{if } \exists q \in I_l : p - d_p = q - d_q \text{ and } d_p < d_q \\ 0 & \text{otherwise.} \end{cases} \tag{6.15}$$

Let us use Fig. 6.11 to explain this equation. We have two pixels p and q. We can use their disparity values d_p and d_q to warp them into the geometry of the right view, that is, we compute $p' = p - d_p$ and $q' = q - d_q$. In our example, p' and q' both lie on the same x-coordinate in the right view and given that the pixels lie on opaque (non-transparent) objects, only one of them can be seen by the right camera. From Fig. 6.11 it is clear that the visible pixel is q' as it has higher disparity, that is, lies closer to the camera. This is exactly what is written in (6.15), that is, a pixel p is occluded if there exists a pixel q such that both pixels project to the same pixel in the right image and p's disparity is smaller than that of q. Note that this data term can be optimized via graph-cuts, which has been done in [81].

Other approaches that handle occlusions in their energy functions are based on a symmetrical formulation, that is, disparity maps are computed for both images and not just for the left one as we have done above. This makes sense as there is no plausible reason for treating the left image different from the right one.[13] Most authors (e.g., [46, 47, 52] and our paper [9]) implement the uniqueness assumption. This assumption enforces that each pixel has at most one matching point. Note that this assumption is broken for highly slanted surfaces where due to surface slant one pixel may have multiple (visible) correspondences in the other view [57]. Sun et al. [72] proposes a so-called visibility constraint to handle this problem and we show that the problem can be overcome using a surface-based representation in [13].

Smoothness Term Let us now concentrate on the smoothness term. As stated above, there are several possibilities to implement the smoothness function $s()$ of (6.10). We will first focus on first order functions that penalize the gradient of the disparity map. Let us start with the linear smoothness function, i.e.,

[13]The stereo problem is symmetrical.

$s(d_p, d_q) = |d_p - d_q|$. Note that from the viewpoint of optimization this linear function represents an interesting special case as exact optimization of (6.8) does no longer represent an np-complete problem, but can be accomplished by computing a single cut in a graph [66].[14] The problem of a linear function is that it is not ideal for the stereo problem. Let us assume that we want to reconstruct a disparity border where disparity abruptly changes from 5 to 15. The problem of the linear term is that reconstructing this disparity discontinuity via several small jumps (e.g., from disparity 5 to 10 and then a few pixels later from 10 to 15) is as expensive as the large jump (from 5 to 15) that we prefer. Hence, disparity borders are blurred.

As stated above, the simplest discontinuity preserving function is the Potts model, that is, $s(d_p, d_q) = 0$ if $d_p = d_q$ and $s(d_p, d_q) = 1$ otherwise. While this term works well for reconstructing depth discontinuities, it is suboptimal for reconstructing slanted surfaces where there is a gradual change of disparity. Note that each of these small disparity transitions receives a large penalty, that is, the same penalty that we assign to depth discontinuities. The consequence is that slanted surfaces are reconstructed via various fronto-parallel ones.

A compromise between accuracy at disparity borders and accuracy at slanted surfaces is the truncated linear function, that is, $s(d_p, d_q) = \min(|d_p - d_q|, k)$ where k is a user-defined truncation value. Let us assume that we set $k := 3$ and again consider the example of reconstructing a depth discontinuity where disparity changes from 5 to 15. The costs of using two jumps (from disparity 5 to 10 and from 10 to 15) is 6, while that of the single large jump (from 5 to 15) is 3, that is, the single large jump is cheaper. This means that the model is discontinuity preserving. Let us now consider a small disparity transition (e.g., from 5 to 6) that occurs at a slanted surface. This transition only obtains a small penalty (1 in our example). The truncated linear term works well in practice and is implemented in many global stereo approaches (e.g., [32, 72, 85] to cite a few).

Note that none of the above first order smoothness functions is ideal for handling slanted surfaces. All of them assign higher energy to slanted surfaces than to fronto-parallel ones. This fronto-parallel bias cannot be justified as slanted surfaces are as likely to occur in natural images as fronto-parallel ones. The solution is to put a penalty on the curvature of the disparity map [51, 81], which is a so-called second order smoothness prior. This term is defined as $s(d_o, d_p, d_q) = |d_o - 2d_p + d_q|$ and penalizes the deviation of the three disparity values from a line (regardless of the line's slant). Note that minimization of energy (6.8) under second order smoothness becomes complex as the smoothness function has three arguments, that is, leads to higher-order cliques in the optimization graph. However, for the triple cliques of the second order term, a scheme for transformation into pairwise cliques is known [48] and has provided the basis for the graph-cut-based optimization algorithm used in the second order stereo method of [81].[15]

[14] In general, such a construction works if the smoothness term is convex [40].

[15] Note that in [81], the smoothness term is also truncated to make it discontinuity preserving.

Edge-Sensitive and Highly-Connected Smoothness Terms In Sect. 6.2 on local stereo, we have stressed that the color image provides valuable information about the location of depth discontinuities. In particular, in most natural images, a disparity discontinuity is more likely to occur between neighboring pixels of different color than between homogeneously colored neighbors. Let us reformulate the smoothness term of (6.10) such that it incorporates this observation:

$$E_{\text{smooth}}(D) = \sum_{\langle p,q\rangle \in \mathcal{N}} w(p,q) \cdot s(d_p, d_q). \tag{6.16}$$

This is known as an edge-sensitive smoothness term. The difference to the standard term is the weighting function $w()$. This function can, for example, be implemented using the color term of the bilateral weight function in (6.3), that is, $w(p,q) = \exp(-color(p,q)/\gamma_c)$. Note that a high weight is assigned if p and q are similar in color and a low weight otherwise. Hence, the energy for aligning depth discontinuities with color edges is lower than for placing depth discontinuities inside a homogeneously colored region.

The standard smoothness term has a bias towards reconstructing compact objects, because it assigns low energy if the length of a disparity border is small. Hence, it is not well-suited for reconstructing complex outlines and thin structures. This is known as the edge shrinking bias in literature. The edge-sensitive smoothness term attenuates this shrinking bias to some extent, but does not work sufficiently well in practice.

A promising approach to overcome the shrinking bias[16] is to increase the neighborhood, which leads to a so-called highly-connected smoothness term defined as

$$E_{\text{smooth}}(D) = \sum_{p \in I_l} \sum_{q \in W_p} w(p,q) \cdot s(d_p, d_q) \tag{6.17}$$

where I_l denotes all pixel coordinates of the left image. Note that the smoothness function $s()$ is no longer only evaluated between a pixel p's four spatial neighbors, but within a window W_p centered on p. An obvious choice for $w()$ is the bilateral function of (6.3), that is, the strength of the smoothness connection decreases proportional to the distance and color dissimilarity of connected pixels. Note that this approach can be regarded as the "global version" of the (local) adaptive weight approach [86] and Smith et al. [69] have shown that it achieves impressive results on the stereo problem. However, due to the large number of smoothness edges, optimization (e.g., via graph-cuts) is computationally very expensive. To reduce the number of edges, Smith et al. [69] eliminate "less important" smoothness connections using a strategy similar to Veksler's tree DP [79] (see paragraph on DP above), but their approach is still slow.

Ideally, the window W_p in (6.17) should capture all pixels of the whole image. This leads to a so-called fully-connected smoothness term where each pixel is directly connected to every other pixel via a smoothness link. Optimization of the

[16]There are also alternative methods (e.g., cooperative cuts [41]).

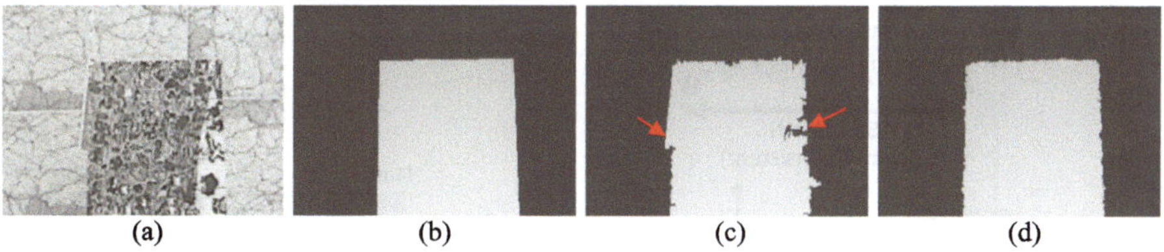

Fig. 6.12 Limitations of segmentation-based methods. (**a**) The intensity image of the Middlebury Map pair. (**b**) Ground truth disparity map. (**c**) Due to segments that overlap disparity discontinuities, our segmentation-based method [8] produces inaccurate results at depth discontinuities (see *red arrows*). (**d**) Our method [13] that uses segmentation only as a soft constraint can successfully handle this image pair

resulting energy is intractable using standard methods (e.g., graph-cuts or standard BP) even on small images. Krähenbühl and Koltun [49] have recently presented an efficient optimization algorithm for this problem based on message passing. The "trick" is to compute message updates via a fast edge-preserving filter operation.[17]

Segmentation-Based Methods Segmentation-based algorithms (e.g., [20, 35, 76, 90] and our papers [8, 9]) also use the color cue. They apply a color segmentation of the left input image. The assumption of segmentation-based algorithms is that disparity varies smoothly within a region of homogeneous color (i.e., within a segment), while depth discontinuities coincide with segment borders. Hence, instead of matching individual pixels, these methods match whole segments at once. Disparity within a segment is thereby assumed to be constant [90] or (in a more sophisticated approach) to lie on a slanted 3D plane [8, 9, 76].

Segmentation-based methods have been very popular for some time, most likely due to their excellent performance on the (new) Middlebury benchmark [67]. However, generalization to other images represents an issue. To illustrate this, we plot results on the Map test set in Fig. 6.12 that has traditionally represented a pitfall for segmentation-based methods in the old Middlebury benchmark. When segmenting the image of Fig. 6.12a there occur segments that overlap a depth discontinuity. Segmentation-based methods cannot recover from such situations, because they model whole segments via a single plane (see errors of our method [8] along the depth discontinuity in Fig. 6.12c). The second problem is the planar model that oversimplifies the 3D shape in the presence of rounded objects. To alleviate both issues, segmentation-based methods apply a strong oversegmentation, but as seen from Fig. 6.12c, this cannot completely overcome these problems. At a later point, we will discuss our Surface Stereo method [13] that can effectively handle both problems. We show the result of this method in Fig. 6.12d.

Stereo and the Matting Problem Before presenting our first algorithm that aims at providing a better model for the stereo problem, let us discuss the following problem. Natural images usually contain pixels that receive contributions from more

[17] It is interesting to note some similarity to cost filter approaches discussed in Sect. 6.2.

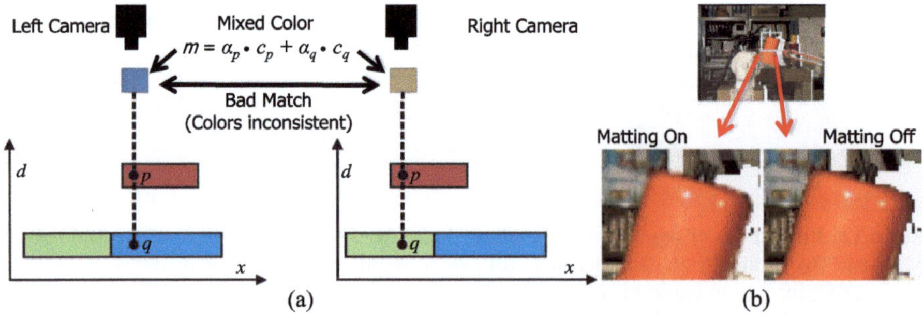

Fig. 6.13 The matting problem in stereo matching and results of our approach [12]. (**a**) Due to lense blur, the *color* of pixels at object borders is a mixture between the *colors* of foreground and background objects. The problem is that this mixture is different in left and right images, which leads to color inconsistencies. (**b**) We use our stereo and matting results for novel view synthesis. Due to using our matting information, the lamp naturally melts with its new background in the *left image*. The *right image* is generated without matting information. Notice disturbing artifacts at the lamp's border

than one real-world object as a consequence of lense blur. Such mixed pixels occur along depth boundaries where a point's color is the composite of colors reflected by background and foreground objects. This so-called matting problem is well-known in photo-montaging. When cutting out an object and pasting it against a new background without considering mixed pixels, the results at the object's border look unnatural as colors are "contaminated" by the color of the old background.

Let us look at Fig. 6.13a to understand the relevance of the matting problem in stereo matching. In this example, the goal is to reconstruct the depth of point p. Due to lense blur, the left camera sees a pixel color that is a mixture between the red foreground and the blue background, whereas in the right camera the red color of p is mixed with the green background. Hence p has different colors in left and right images, i.e., the photo consistency assumption is broken. This makes stereo matching difficult.

Although early work [2, 73] on stereo matching in combination with matting dates back 15 years, there has been relative little progress since then. Some authors [30, 90] compute alpha matting information in a postprocessing step, that is, after computing a disparity map. Xiong and Jia [82] propose a method that can handle the color inconsistency problem of Fig. 6.13a using a joint stereo and matting formulation. However, their approach only works for images that consist of exactly two layers (i.e., foreground and background layers) and generalization to other images is an issue. Taguchi et al. [75] propose a method that can handle an arbitrary number of layers. However, they do not use matting information to overcome the color inconsistency problem.

Our Contribution—Combined Stereo and Matting [12] We present an algorithm for solving the stereo matching and alpha matting problems simultaneously. In contrast to the papers above, our method operates on an arbitrary number of layers and still handles the color inconsistency problem. Our algorithm is based on image segmentation (see discussion of such methods above). Hence, we first apply color segmentation to the left image. Each segment is then enlarged using morphological dilation. The idea is that since mixed pixels typically occur at disparity (segment) borders (see discussion above), we only allow transparencies in a small band around segment borders. In accordance to alpha matting literature, we call this band a segment's unknown region. Note that due to this enlargement, we have many overlapping segments.

We now estimate a disparity plane for each overlapping segment and an alpha value as well as the true color for each pixel via energy minimization. Given alpha values and colors, our energy function computes the mixed colors for the left view. If alpha values and colors were correct, the resulting artificial image should be very similar to the real left view. Our energy function also computes an artificial right view via warping the pixels into the geometry of the right image according to our current disparity solution. This artificial right view is then compared against the real right image to measure the quality of alpha values, colors and disparity planes. The crucial question in generating the artificial right view is how alpha-values are affected by image warping. To correctly perform the warping operation, we introduce the concept of solidity (see our paper).

In the experimental results, we show that our method can compete with the state-of-the-art on the Middlebury benchmark [67]. More importantly, in contrast to all methods listed on Middlebury, our method also provides matting information. This makes it an ideal algorithm for performing depth segmentation and novel view generation. Figure 6.13 shows a novel view example, that is, an image that shows the scene from a virtual viewpoint not recorded by the stereo cameras. As can be seen, our matting information leads to realistic results at object borders when a foreground object is pasted against a new background.

Let us recall a limitation of segmentation-based methods, that is, they fail if a segment overlaps a depth discontinuity. This is only partially true for our method, as it can change the shape of segments by adjusting the alpha values within a segment's unknown region. However, the algorithm fails in the presence of large segmentation errors. A more sophisticated solution is discussed next.

Our Contribution—Surface Stereo [13] In our paper [13], we stress the importance of a surface-based representation. Instead of directly assigning pixels to disparity values, we assign them to 3D surfaces. In our implementation, surfaces thereby correspond to planes and B-Splines (to model rounded surfaces). We claim that this surface-based representation is superior in comparison to the commonly-used disparity-based one as it allows incorporating energy terms that are very challenging or even impossible in the disparity-based representation.

Our approach simultaneously infers (1) which surfaces are present in the scene and (2) which pixels belong to which surface. We search an assignment of pixels to surfaces that minimizes an energy. Apart from data and smoothness terms (as in the standard energy of (6.8)), our energy function includes three new terms, that is, (1) a soft segmentation term, (2) a minimum description length (MDL) term and (3) a curvature term. We will discuss these terms in the following.

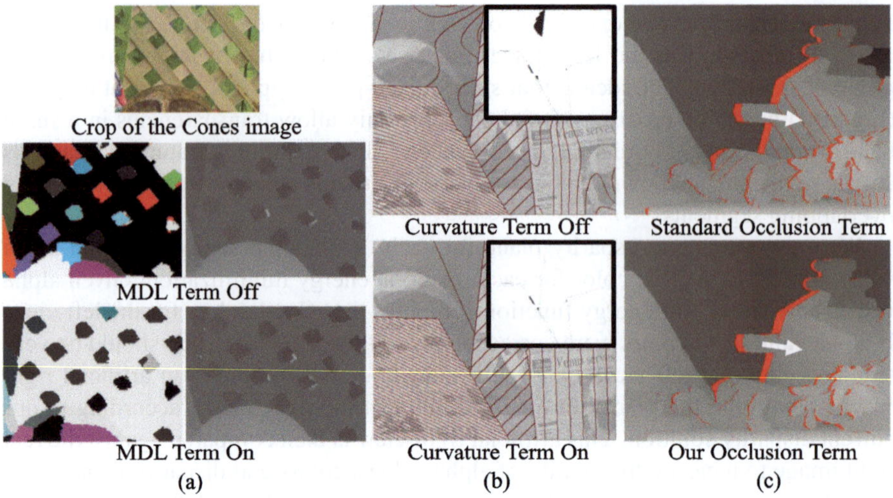

Fig. 6.14 Effect of different terms in the energy of Surface Stereo [13]. (**a**) MDL term. (**b**) Curvature term. *Contour lines* of the disparity maps are superimposed on the left intensity image. (**c**) Our improved occlusion handling strategy. See text for explanation

As stated above, segmentation-based methods fail if (1) segments overlap disparity discontinuities (see Fig. 6.12c) or (2) if the planar model oversimplifies the real 3D shape (e.g., rounded objects). Note that we handle problem (2) by using a more general surface model, that is, a B-spline model. Problem (1) is handled by our soft segmentation term. This term prefers disparity maps that are consistent with a precomputed color segmentation over such that are not by assigning lower energy. Note that in contrast to most segmentation-based methods, inconsistent disparity maps are allowed (at the price of higher energy) and hence segmentation is only used as a soft constraint. For each pixel p, the soft segmentation term builds the intersection of p's segment with a squared window centered at p, which gives us p's subsegment. The soft segmentation term imposes 0 costs if all pixels within p's subsegment are assigned to the same surface and a constant penalty, otherwise.[18] Fig. 6.12d demonstrates that our soft segmentation term can handle the Map test set where color segmentation is misleading. The reason is that the data term of our energy overrules the segmentation term and supports the correct disparity solution.

The MDL term implements the assumption that a simple scene explanation is better than an unnecessarily complex one. We therefore impose a penalty on the number of surfaces, that is, a solution containing five surfaces is cheaper than one

[18]This term forms a higher-order clique in the optimization step. In general, optimization of such higher-order cliques is intractable. We take advantage of the fact that these cliques are sparse, i.e., only one state generates 0 costs and all other states generate constant costs. There exist graph-cut based algorithms that can "efficiently" optimize such sparse higher-order cliques [44, 65] and we make use of them.

with 100 surfaces. Figure 6.14a shows the effect of the MDL term on a crop of the Middlebury Cones images. The interesting part is the background surface behind the fence. If the MDL term is switched off, the green squared background regions are all modeled by different surfaces. (We use a color coding in Fig. 6.14a where all pixels assigned to the same surface carry the same color.) In contrast, a large portion of the isolated background regions are correctly modeled by a single surface if our MDL term is switched on.

Our curvature term puts a penalty on the second order derivative of surfaces. Note that this term is very similar to the second order smoothness term of [81] (see paragraph about smoothness terms), but has two advantages. First, we can analytically and exactly compute the second order derivative, because we have a surface-based representation. This is in contrast to [81] where curvature is only approximated from the disparity values of three neighboring pixels. Second, our curvature term represents a unary potential in optimization and we can therefore avoid the complex and time-consuming triple clique construction of [81]. Figure 6.14b shows the effect of the curvature term. We switch off the curvature term in the top figure. Due to low texture and no penalization of curvature, the spline in the background (top left part of the image) erroneously adapts to the data. This leads to a large disparity error (see black pixels in the error image). When using the curvature term (see bottom figure) representation of the background via a plane leads to lower energy than modeling it as a spline and hence the correct disparity solution is obtained.

Finally, we also make a contribution in the context of occlusion treatment. As stated in the paragraph on occlusion handling, the uniqueness assumption is broken for slanted surfaces where a pixel of one view may have multiple correspondences in the other view. This leads to wrongly detected occlusions. For example, in the top image of Fig. 6.14c, occlusions are erroneously detected on the roof of the toy house. (We use red color to mark occlusions.) We overcome this problem by stating that two pixels must not occlude each other if they originate from the same surface. As seen from the bottom image of Fig. 6.14c, this avoids wrongly detected occlusions on the roof.

Let us now focus on optimization of the resulting energy, which is accomplished using fusion moves [50] (see paragraph on graph-cuts). We start with an initial solution. We have a proposal generator that produces six different types of proposal solutions (see paper for details). We now compute the "optimal" fusion move of our current solution and a proposal obtained from our generator.[19] The fusion result is then fused with the next proposal of our generator and so on.

In the experiments, we show that our method achieves an excellent Middlebury ranking, that is, rank six out of 74 methods at the time of publication. On the complex Teddy test set, our method even takes the first rank on all error measures. Moreover, we demonstrate that each term of our energy contributes to the quality of results (see paper for more information).

[19]By optimal we mean the solution that leads to the largest energy decrease according to our energy function among all possible fusion moves.

(a) (b) (c)

Fig. 6.15 Object Stereo [15]. (**a**) Left image of a stereo pair that forms the input of the algorithm. (**b**) Computed object labeling. (Pixels of the *same color* lie on the same object.) (**c**) Computed disparity map

Our Contribution—Object Stereo [15] In [15], we combine stereo matching with the object segmentation problem where the task is to label pixels that belong to the same object. Figure 6.15 gives an example. The method's input is formed by left and right views of a stereo pair. Our algorithm then jointly computes a segmentation of the image into objects (Fig. 6.15b) and a disparity map (Fig. 6.15c). The idea is that there exist synergies between the stereo and object segmentation problems. We describe our model that is encoded in an energy function in the following.

Our model considers the scene as a collection of a small number of objects.[20] An object is characterized by two aspects. First, an object contains a color model. We use this color model to implement the assumption that pixels of the same object are similar in appearance, that is, in color. The distribution of colors is thereby modeled using a Gaussian mixture model. Second, an object is characterized by a surface model, which implements the assumption that pixels of the same object lie approximately on the same 3D plane. We use a plane-plus-parallax model to allow deviations from this plane. An obvious aspect of our model is that disparities of pixels shall be estimated such that photo consistency is maximized (which represents a standard stereo data term). Finally, we introduce a constraint stating that an object shall be connected in 3D and describe this in more detail below.

Our model allows depth reasoning based on the appearance cue. This is because pixels of similar appearance (color) are grouped in the same object and the disparities for these pixels are biased to lie on the object's plane. Advantages of our color-based depth reasoning are twofold. First, similar to Surface Stereo, this allows implementing color segmentation as a soft constraint. Second and more importantly, this allows to recover disparity for regions where stereo information is poor (low texture) or not present at all (occlusions).

For example, consider the image of Fig. 6.16a1 that has a challenging background of very low texture. Especially, the background region marked by the arrow poses a problem as the data costs for this region are highly ambiguous (no texture) and the pairwise smoothness term motives to assign this isolated region to the foreground disparity. Our algorithm looks at the color of this small region. It finds that

[20] Small number means that we apply the MDL term above to penalize the number of objects.

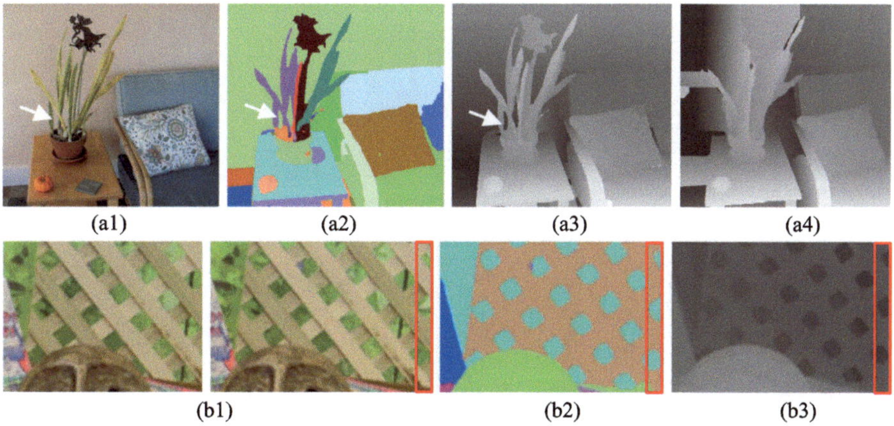

Fig. 6.16 Results of Object Stereo [15]. We can handle regions of very low texture (**a**) and regions that are completely occluded (**b**). (**a1**) Left image of our Fairy test set. The region marked by the *white arrow* is difficult to match. (**a2**) Computed object labeling. (**a3**) Computed disparity map. Note that the disparity of the background is correctly recovered, whereas the competitor Surface Stereo [13] fails badly in these areas as shown in (**a4**). (**b1**) Left and right images of a crop of the Cones images. Note that the *red rectangle* marks pixels that are completely occluded in the left view. Our method combines all *green* pixels in a single background object as shown in (**b2**). This helps to find the correct depth even for the completely occluded image regions (**b3**)

the color matches that of the background object "Wall" and biases the disparity towards the plane of the object "Wall" (Fig. 6.16a3). Note that our Surface Stereo method described above fails on this challenging pair (Fig. 6.16a4), because it does not apply color-based depth reasoning.

Figure 6.16b shows a challenging occlusion case. We show crops of left and right views of the Middlebury Cones images in Fig. 6.16b1. Note that the isolated green background regions inside the red rectangle are only visible in the right image, that is, they are completely occluded in the left image. This makes correct computation of depth impossible for standard algorithms. Note that standard methods would extrapolate disparity via the smoothness term, that is, they would assign the occluded background regions to the disparity of the (foreground) fence. In contrast, our method combines all isolated squares into a single background object based on their green color (Fig. 6.16b2). Disparities inside the isolated regions are then biased towards the disparity of the background plane, which gives the correct disparity despite of some green regions being completely occluded (Fig. 6.16b3).

Let us now focus on our 3D connectivity constraint mentioned above. This constraint states that disconnected 2D regions in an image may belong to the same object only if they are separated by an occluding object with smaller depth (that is, closer to the camera). According to this constraint, the green squared background regions of Fig. 6.16b1 may all belong to the same object, because they are separated by an occluder of smaller depth, that is, the fence. In contrast to this, the two green cones of Fig. 6.15a must not lie in the same object. Although both cones are similar in color and depth, there is no occluder that separates them. Note that our 3D con-

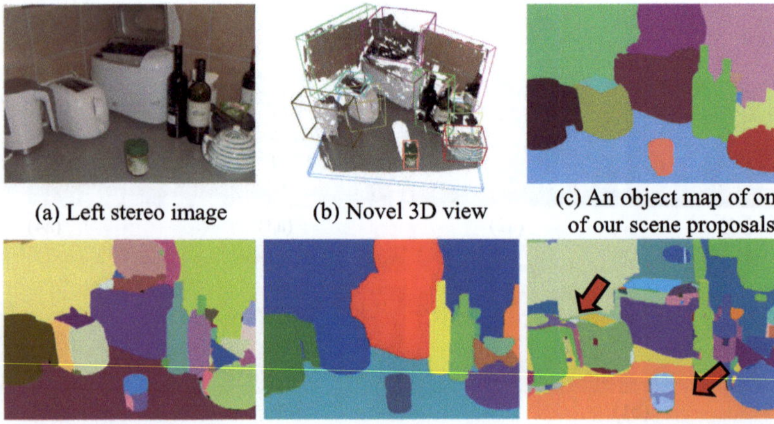

(a) Left stereo image (b) Novel 3D view (c) An object map of one of our scene proposals

(d) An object map of one of our scene proposals (e) Ground truth object labelling (f) Result of object stereo

Fig. 6.17 Our approach [16]. Given a stereo pair (**a**), our algorithm jointly estimates a 3D reconstruction (**b**) and object maps (**c**), (**d**) using physics-based reasoning. The result is considerably closer to ground truth (**e**) than the one of Object Stereo [15] (**f**)

nectivity constraint demonstrates the usefulness of depth information for the object segmentation task, that is, this constraint can only work, because we have depth. In practice, it helps to improve object segmentation results.

At the time of publication of the corresponding paper [15], Object Stereo has taken rank 10 on Middlebury and the first rank on the challenging Cones images. Note that the major advantage over other stereo algorithms is that Object Stereo also provides a segmentation of the input images into objects.

Our Contribution—Physics-Based Segmentation and Stereo [16] As in Object Stereo, our paper [16] concentrates on jointly computing a disparity map as well as a segmentation of the input images into objects. One main difference to Object Stereo is that we give objects a third dimension. In contrast to stating that an object is approximately planar (as in Object Stereo), we compute an enclosing 3D bounding box per object where the bounding box represents a proxy for the real 3D extent of the object. One of our 3D reconstructions and bounding boxes of extracted objects are shown in Fig. 6.17b. Note that this bounding box representation is more general than the "billboard" world of Object Stereo. For example, in Fig. 6.17f, the water kettle is not flat and hence Object Stereo oversegments the kettle using multiple flat objects (see left arrow in Fig. 6.17f). In contrast, our bounding box representation allows modeling the water kettle as a single object (see Figs. 6.17c and 6.17d). However, the main argument for using objects with 3D extents is that it enables modeling physical constraints [28], which is discussed in the following.

In particular, we model intersection and gravity constraints. The intersection constraint thereby reasons about occupancy in 3D space, that is, the spatial extents of 3D objects should not intersect each other. For example, in Fig. 6.17f (right arrow),

Object Stereo assigns the top and the bottom part of the can to the same object, while the middle part is assigned to a different object. This volume intersection is physically very unlikely, whereas our results in Figs. 6.17c and 6.17d are physically plausible. Our second physics-based constraint, that is, the gravity constraint, encodes the observation that objects usually do not float in the air, but stand on top of each other due to gravity. Analogously to the intersection constraint, this could not be realized using Object Stereo's surface-based representation.

In the experimental results, we demonstrate that our approach is on par with the state-of-the-art in stereo matching. We also demonstrate that matching accuracy is improved if our physics-based constraints are enabled. A major focus lies on the object segmentation results. We show that our method can be applied to generate a large set of object proposals. This large set of object proposals has been the key to success in [19], which is the recent winner of the PASCAL object recognition challenge. After automatically ranking the proposals we show experimentally that our results are considerably closer to ground truth than state-of-the-art techniques which either use stereo or monocular images.

6.4 Summary

In this chapter, we have reviewed the state-of-the-art in stereo matching and highlighted our contributions in this field. We have followed the standard categorization of stereo methods and divided them between local and global algorithms.

Local algorithms operate on windows that are displaced in the right image to find the matching point of lowest color dissimilarity. The implicit assumption that all pixels within the support window have constant disparity is broken at disparity borders, which leads to edge fattening. We have discussed that adaptive weights [86] represent a remedy to the edge fattening problem and have presented our contributions in this domain. We have first presented our geodesic support weight algorithm [36]. A limitation of [36] and [86] is the relatively slow runtime. In this context, we have presented our cost filter approach [61] that allows high-quality adaptive support weight matching in real-time. We have then focused on the problem of reconstructing slanted surfaces where standard local methods show poor performance due to using fronto-parallel windows. We have presented our PatchMatch Stereo work [14] that overcomes this problem by using slanted support windows.

In the discussion of global methods, we have started by describing a standard stereo energy function and then briefly focused on the problem of optimizing this energy. We have discussed the following optimization techniques: dynamic programming (including our Simple Tree method [10]), graph-cuts and message passing. However, the real problem is not in the optimization, but in finding an energy function that represents a good model of the stereo problem. Hence, we have concentrated on improving the model in the remainder of this chapter.

We have discussed the data term of our energy and presented different match measures. In the context of data terms, we have presented our work [7], which investigates the usefulness of color information in stereo matching. We have then explained how to incorporate occlusion treatment into the data terms of global methods. In the discussion of smoothness terms, we have presented first and second order terms and stressed the importance of edge-sensitive and highly-connected smoothness terms. After a brief overview of segmentation-based methods, we have explained our combined stereo and matting method [12]. Finally, we have presented our other papers on improving the stereo model. This has included Surface Stereo [13], Object Stereo [15] and our physics-based approach [16].

Acknowledgements This work was supported in part by the Vienna Science and Technology Fund (WWTF) under project ICT08-019.

References

1. Agarwal S, Snavely N, Simon I, Seitz S, Szeliski R (2009) Building Rome in a day. In: ICCV
2. Baker S, Szeliski R, Anandan P (1998) A layered approach to stereo reconstruction. In: CVPR, pp 434–441
3. Baker S, Scharstein D, Lewis J, Roth S, Black M, Szeliski R (2011) A database and evaluation methodology for optical flow. Int J Comput Vis 92(1):1–31
4. Barnes C, Shechtman E, Finkelstein A, Goldman D (2009) PatchMatch: a randomized correspondence algorithm for structural image editing. ACM Trans Graph 28(3):24 (SIGGRAPH Proc)
5. Birchfield S, Tomasi C (1998) A pixel dissimilarity measure that is insensitive to image sampling. IEEE Trans Pattern Anal Mach Intell 20(4):401–406
6. Birchfield S, Tomasi C (1999) Depth discontinuities by pixel-to-pixel stereo. Int J Comput Vis 35(3):269–293
7. Bleyer M, Chambon S (2010) Does color really help in dense stereo matching? In: International symposium on 3D data processing, visualization and transmission (3DPVT)
8. Bleyer M, Gelautz M (2005) A layered stereo matching algorithm using image segmentation and global visibility constraints. ISPRS J Photogramm Remote Sens 59(3):128–150
9. Bleyer M, Gelautz M (2007) Graph-cut-based stereo matching using image segmentation with symmetrical treatment of occlusions. Signal Process Image Commun 22(2):127–143
10. Bleyer M, Gelautz M (2008) Simple but effective tree structures for dynamic programming-based stereo matching. In: VISAPP, vol 2, pp 415–422
11. Bleyer M, Chambon S, Poppe U, Gelautz M (2008) Evaluation of different methods for using colour information in global stereo matching. In: International archives of the photogrammetry, remote sensing and spatial information sciences, vol XXXVII, pp 415–422
12. Bleyer M, Gelautz M, Rother C, Rhemann C (2009) A stereo approach that handles the matting problem via image warping. In: CVPR, pp 501–508
13. Bleyer M, Rother C, Kohli P (2010) Surface stereo with soft segmentation. In: CVPR
14. Bleyer M, Rhemann C, Rother C (2011) PatchMatch stereo—stereo matching with slanted support windows. In: BMVC
15. Bleyer M, Rother C, Kohli P, Scharstein D, Sinha S (2011) Object stereo—joint stereo matching and object segmentation. In: CVPR
16. Bleyer M, Rhemann C, Rother C (2012) Extracting 3D scene-consistent object proposals and depth from stereo images. In: ECCV
17. Bobick A, Intille S (1999) Large occlusion stereo. Int J Comput Vis 33(3):181–200
18. Boykov Y, Veksler O, Zabih R (2001) Fast approximate energy minimization via graph cuts. IEEE Trans Pattern Anal Mach Intell 23(11):1222–1239

19. Carreira J, Li F, Sminchisescu C (2012) Object recognition by sequential figure-ground ranking. Int J Comput Vis 98(3):243–262
20. Deng Y, Yang Q, Lin X, Tang X (2005) A symmetric patch-based correspondence model for occlusion handling. In: ICCV, pp 542–567
21. Faugeras O, Hotz B, Mathieu H, Viéville T, Zhang Z, Fua P, Théron E, Moll L, Berry G, Vuillemin J, Bertin P, Proy C (1996) Real time correlation based stereo: algorithm implementations and applications. Technical report, RR-2013, INRIA
22. Felzenszwalb P, Huttenlocher D (2006) Efficient belief propagation for early vision. Int J Comput Vis 70(1):41–54
23. Fua PV (1991) Combining stereo and monocular information to compute dense depth maps that preserve depth discontinuities. In: International joint conference on artificial intelligence, pp 1292–1298
24. Fusiello A, Roberto V, Trucco E (1997) Efficient stereo with multiple windowing. In: CVPR, pp 858–863
25. Gallup D, Frahm J, Mordohai P, Yang Q, Pollefeys M (2007) Real-time plane-sweeping stereo with multiple sweeping directions. In: CVPR
26. Gehrig S, Franke U (2007) Improving sub-pixel accuracy for long range stereo. In: ICCV VRML workshop
27. Geiger A, Lenz P, Urtasun R (2012) Are we ready for autonomous driving? The KITTI vision benchmark suite. In: CVPR
28. Gupta A, Efros A, Hebert M (2010) Blocks world revisited: image understanding using qualitative geometry and mechanics. In: ECCV
29. Hartley R, Zisserman A (2003) Multiple view geometry in computer vision
30. Hasinoff S, Kang SB, Szeliski R (2006) Boundary matting for view synthesis. Comput Vis Image Underst 103(1):22–32
31. He K, Sun J, Tang X (2010) Guided image filtering. In: ECCV
32. Hirschmüller H (2005) Accurate and efficient stereo processing by semi-global matching and mutual information. In: CVPR, vol 2, pp 807–814
33. Hirschmüller H, Scharstein D (2009) Evaluation of stereo matching costs on images with radiometric differences. IEEE Trans Pattern Anal Mach Intell 31:1582–1599
34. Hirschmüller H, Innocent P, Garibaldi J (2002) Real-time correlation-based stereo vision with reduced border errors. Int J Comput Vis 47:229–246
35. Hong L, Chen G (2004) Segment-based stereo matching using graph cuts. In: CVPR, vol 1, pp 74–81
36. Hosni A, Bleyer M, Gelautz M, Rhemann C (2009) Local stereo matching using geodesic support weights. In: ICIP
37. Hosni A, Bleyer M, Gelautz M (2010) Near real-time stereo with adaptive support weight approaches. In: 3DPVT
38. Hosni A, Rhemann C, Bleyer M, Gelautz M (2011) Temporally consistent disparity and optical flow via efficient spatio-temporal filtering. In: PSIVT
39. Hosni A, Rhemann C, Bleyer M, Rother C, Gelautz M (2013) Fast cost-volume filtering for visual correspondence and beyond. IEEE Trans Pattern Anal Mach Intell 35(2):504–511
40. Ishikawa H (2000) Global optimization using embedded graphs. PhD thesis, New York University
41. Jegelka S, Bilmes J (2011) Submodularity beyond submodular energies: coupling edges in graph cuts. In: CVPR
42. Ju M, Kang H (2009) Constant time stereo matching. In: MVIP, pp 13–17
43. Klaus A, Sormann M, Karner K (2006) Segment-based stereo matching using belief propagation and a self-adapting dissimilarity measure. In: ICPR, pp 15–18
44. Kohli P, Kumar M, Torr P (2007) P3 & beyond: solving energies with higher order cliques. In: CVPR
45. Kolmogorov V, Rother C (2007) Minimizing non-submodular functions with graph cuts—a review. IEEE Trans Pattern Anal Mach Intell 29(7):1274–1279

46. Kolmogorov V, Zabih R (2002) Computing visual correspondence with occlusions using graph cuts. In: ICCV, vol 2, pp 508–515
47. Kolmogorov V, Zabih R (2002) Multi-camera scene reconstruction via graph cuts. In: ECCV
48. Kolmogorov V, Zabih R (2004) What energy functions can be minimized via graph cuts? IEEE Trans Pattern Anal Mach Intell 26(2):147–159
49. Krähenbühl P, Koltun V (2011) Efficient inference in fully connected CRFs with gaussian edge potentials. In: Advances in neural information processing systems
50. Lempitsky V, Rother C, Blake A (2007) Logcut—efficient graph cut optimization for Markov random fields. In: ICCV
51. Li G, Zucker SW (2006) Surface geometric constraints for stereo in belief propagation. In: CVPR, pp 2355–2362
52. Lin M, Tomasi C (2003) Surfaces with occlusions from layered stereo. In: CVPR, pp 710–717
53. Mei X, Sun X, Zhou M, Jiao S, Wang H, Zhang X (2011) On building an accurate stereo matching system on graphics hardware. In: GPUCV, pp 467–474
54. Meltzer T, Yanover TC, Weiss Y (2005) Globally optimal solutions for energy minimization in stereo vision using reweighted belief propagation. In: ICCV, pp 428–435
55. Mühlmann K, Maier D, Hesser J, Männer R (2002) Calculating dense disparity maps from color stereo images, an efficient implementation. Int J Comput Vis 47(1):79–88
56. Newcombe R, Izadi S, Hilliges O, Molyneaux D, Kim D, Davison A, Kohli P, Shotton J, Hodges S, Fitzgibbon A (2011) KinectFusion: real-time dense surface mapping and tracking. In: ISMAR
57. Ogale AS, Aloimonos Y (2004) Stereo correspondence with slanted surfaces: critical implications of horizontal slant. In: CVPR, pp 568–573
58. Ohta Y, Kanade T (1985) Stereo by intra- and inter-scanline search. IEEE Trans Pattern Anal Mach Intell 7(2):139–154
59. Paris S, Durandi F (2009) A fast approximation of the bilateral filter using a signal processing approach. Int J Comput Vis 81:24–52
60. Porikli F (2005) Integral histogram: a fast way to extract histograms in cartesian spaces. In: CVPR, vol 1, pp 829–836
61. Rhemann C, Hosni A, Bleyer M, Rother C, Gelautz M (2011) Fast cost-volume filtering for visual correspondence and beyond. In: CVPR
62. Richardt C, Orr D, Davies I, Criminisi A, Dodgson NA (2010) Real-time spatiotemporal stereo matching using the dual-cross-bilateral grid. In: ECCV, vol 6313, pp 510–523
63. Rother C, Kolmogorov V, Blake A (2004) GrabCut: interactive foreground extraction using iterated graph cuts. ACM Trans Graph 23:309–314
64. Rother C, Kolmogorov V, Lempitsky V, Szummer M (2007) Optimizing binary MRFs via extended roof duality. In: CVPR
65. Rother C, Kohli P, Feng W, Jia J (2009) Minimizing sparse higher order energy functions of discrete variables. In: CVPR, pp 1382–1389
66. Roy S, Cox I (1998) A maximum-flow formulation of the n-camera stereo correspondence problem. In: ICCV, pp 492–499
67. Scharstein D, Szeliski R (2002) A taxonomy and evaluation of dense two-frame stereo correspondence algorithms. Int J Comput Vis 47(1/2/3):7–42. http://vision.middlebury.edu/stereo/
68. Shotton J, Fitzgibbon A, Cook M, Sharp T, Finocchio M, Moore R, Kipman A, Blake A (2011) Real-time human pose recognition in parts from a single depth image. In: CVPR
69. Smith B, Zhang L, Jin H (2009) Stereo matching with nonparametric smoothness priors in feature space. In: CVPR, pp 485–492
70. Snavely N, Seitz S, Szeliski R (2006) Photo tourism: exploring photo collections in 3D. ACM Trans Graph 25:835–846 (SIGGRAPH Proc)
71. Sun J, Zheng NN, Shum HY (2003) Stereo matching using belief propagation. IEEE Trans Pattern Anal Mach Intell 25(7):787–800
72. Sun J, Li Y, Kang SB, Shum HY (2005) Symmetric stereo matching for occlusion handling. In: CVPR, vol 25, pp 399–406

73. Szeliski R, Golland P (1998) Stereo matching with transparency and matting. In: ICCV, pp 517–525
74. Szeliski R, Zabih R, Scharstein D, Veksler O, Kolmogorov V, Agarwala A, Tappen M, Rother C (2006) A comparative study of energy minimization methods for Markov random fields. In: ECCV, vol 2, pp 19–26
75. Taguchi Y, Wilburn B, Zitnick L (2008) Stereo reconstruction with mixed pixels using adaptive over-segmentation. In: CVPR, pp 1–8
76. Tao H, Sawhney H, Kumar R (2001) A global matching framework for stereo computation. In: ICCV, pp 532–539
77. Tappen MF, Freeman WT (2003) Comparison of graph cuts with belief propagation for stereo, using identical MRF parameters. In: ICCV, vol 2, pp 900–906
78. Veksler O (2002) Stereo correspondence with compact windows via minimum ratio cycle. IEEE Trans Pattern Anal Mach Intell 24(12):1654–1660
79. Veksler O (2005) Stereo correspondence by dynamic programming on a tree. In: CVPR, pp 384–390
80. Wainwright M, Jaakkola T, Willsky A (2003) Tree reweighted belief propagation algorithms and approximate ML estimation by pseudo-moment matching. In: AISTATS
81. Woodford O, Torr P, Reid I, Fitzgibbon A (2008) Global stereo reconstruction under second order smoothness priors. In: CVPR
82. Xiong W, Jia J (2007) Stereo matching on objects with fractional boundary. In: CVPR, pp 1–8
83. Yang Q, Wang L, Yang R, Wang S, Liao M, Nister D (2006) Real-time global stereo matching using hierarchical belief propagation. In: BMVC
84. Yang Q, Yang R, Davis J, Nister D (2007) Spatial-depth super resolution for range images. In: CVPR
85. Yang Q, Wang L, Yang R, Stewenius H, Nister D (2009) Stereo matching with color-weighted correlation, hierarchical belief propagation and occlusion handling. IEEE Trans Pattern Anal Mach Intell 31(3):492–504
86. Yoon KJ, Kweon IS (2005) Locally adaptive support-weight approach for visual correspondence search. In: CVPR
87. Zhang Y, Gong M, Yang Y (2008) Local stereo matching with 3D adaptive cost aggregation for slanted surface modeling and sub-pixel accuracy. In: ICPR
88. Zhang K, Lu J, Lafruit G (2009) Cross-based local stereo matching using orthogonal integral images. IEEE Trans Circuits Syst Video Technol 19:1073–1079
89. Zhang K, Lafruit G, Lauwereins R, Gool L (2010) Joint integral histograms and its application in stereo matching. In: ICIP, pp 817–820
90. Zitnick L, Kang S, Uyttendaele M, Winder S, Szeliski R (2004) High-quality video view interpolation using a layered representation. ACM Trans Graph 23(3):600–608

Chapter 7
Visual Localization for Micro Aerial Vehicles in Urban Outdoor Environments

Andreas Wendel and Horst Bischof

Abstract Accurate localization of a micro aerial vehicle (MAV) with respect to a scene is important for a wide range of applications, in particular autonomous navigation, surveillance, and inspection. In this context, visual localization in urban outdoor environments is gaining importance as common methods such as GPS positioning are often not accurate enough or even fail. We present recent approaches and results for robust 3D reconstruction of suitable visual landmarks, for the alignment in a world coordinate system, and for fast, high-accuracy monocular localization. We introduce a scalable representation of the prior knowledge about the scene and demonstrate how in-flight information can be integrated to facilitate long-term operation. Our method outperforms a state-of-the-art visual SLAM approach and achieves localization accuracies comparable to differential GPS.

7.1 Introduction

Micro aerial vehicles (MAVs) are gaining importance as image acquisition tools in photogrammetry, but also for industrial applications such as power-line inspection or building reconstruction [16, 31]. Areas of interest for close-up aerial images are often in urban environments, close to the ground, close to buildings, and possibly close to human beings. Therefore, we see the need for intelligent autonomy in terms of systems which can navigate accurately and safely in an urban outdoor environment.

The usage of unmanned aerial vehicles with an integrated global positioning system (GPS) for photogrammetric applications started as early as 1995 [8]. These systems had the dimensions of a small aircraft to be able to carry the camera systems of the time, which allowed them to fly only above an altitude of about 300 meters. With the advent of MAVs in form of very small and light aircraft or quad-rotor helicopters it became possible to fly much closer to buildings. While this permits to

A. Wendel (✉) · H. Bischof
Institute for Computer Graphics and Vision, Graz University of Technology, Graz, Austria
e-mail: wendel@icg.tugraz.at

H. Bischof
e-mail: bischof@icg.tugraz.at

G.M. Farinella et al. (eds.), *Advanced Topics in Computer Vision*,
Advances in Computer Vision and Pattern Recognition,
DOI 10.1007/978-1-4471-5520-1_7,

obtain high-quality, close-up images of scenes, it also poses a problem to localization. GPS can be replaced by much more accurate differential GPS, if high costs are acceptable; still, both technologies are not able to detect obstacles and are prone to shadowing effects caused by neighboring buildings.

While GPS is still the most widely used sensor for outdoor localization, the trend goes towards visual localization. Zufferey et al. [77] combined GPS-based path following with vision-based collision avoidance. Their bio-inspired approach allowed them to fly close to the ground, approx. 9 m above the terrain, while effectively detecting and avoiding trees during flight. Hrabar and Sukhatme [22] used a similar approach based on optical flow and differential GPS to navigate an autonomous helicopter safely through a simulated urban canyon. Both approaches focus on responding to obstacles using vision, but not on accurate localization of the vehicle. Other approaches focus on marker-based visual localization [51] or visual outside-in tracking [40] which is not suitable for outdoor usage.

Visual SLAM (simultaneous localization and mapping) dominates the field of visual localization in aerial robotics. Bloesch et al. [4] first used Parallel Tracking and Mapping (PTAM) [28] for monocular MAV navigation in unstructured indoor environments. Recent work of Achtelik et al. [1] showed how the same approach can be used outdoors by fusing it with additional sensors available to an MAV. They demonstrate that visual input can be successfully used for the control of an MAV despite the insufficient pose update rates on constrained hardware. However, their localization framework requires a nadir view of the camera and a textured ground plane. This significantly limits the possible applications, as for instance paved roads or grass cause problems.

In contrast, we rely on a prior reconstruction in form of a visual landmark which allows us to localize the MAV with respect to this map. Such a method has several key advantages over a traditional SLAM approach that solves the mapping and localization problem simultaneously. First, given a geo-registered visual 3D model of the environment, localization can be done in a metric scale. This would not be possible for a monocular SLAM approach without considering additional input modalities. Moreover, once a detailed visual model of an environment is available, the localization approach is fully scalable and allows direct data fusion with other sensors such as GPS or inertial measurement units (IMU). Obstacles or points of interest defined in world coordinates can be easily integrated in the map. Finally, once a good localization is available, it is much easier to fill the gaps of the rough model with dynamic visual data.

In this work, we present a framework (Fig. 7.1, Fig. 7.2) which aims for long-term visual localization. We create metric, geo-referenced 3D models [66, 68] by reconstructing and aligning an unordered set of images. Monocular localization in such a landmark can then be achieved based on the concept of virtual views and incremental feature updates [67, 69], with an accuracy comparable to differential GPS in a global coordinate system, and at a speed of 4 frames per second.

We first give an overview of image-based techniques to model an urban outdoor environment in Sect. 7.2. The resulting 3D reconstructions are then aligned to a geo-referenced digital surface model as presented in Sect. 7.3. In Sect. 7.4, we introduce

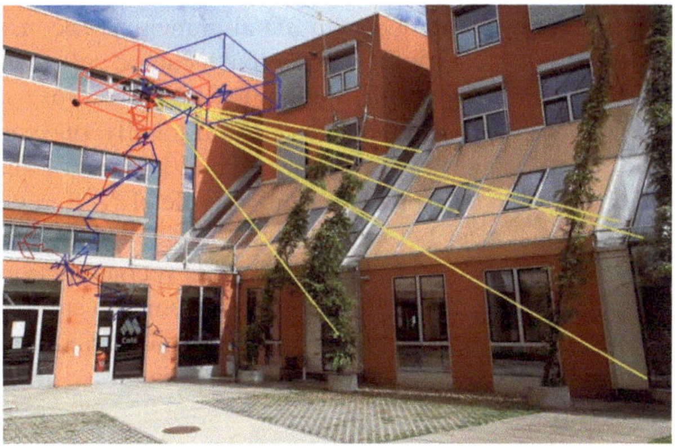

Fig. 7.1 We present an approach to visual localization which exploits prior knowledge in form of pictures taken at ground-level to enhance the accuracy and reliability of position and attitude estimation. Our algorithm (*red trajectory*) is neither prone to drift nor bias and therefore outperforms pure SLAM approaches (*blue trajectory*). ©2011 IEEE. Reprinted, with permission, from [67]

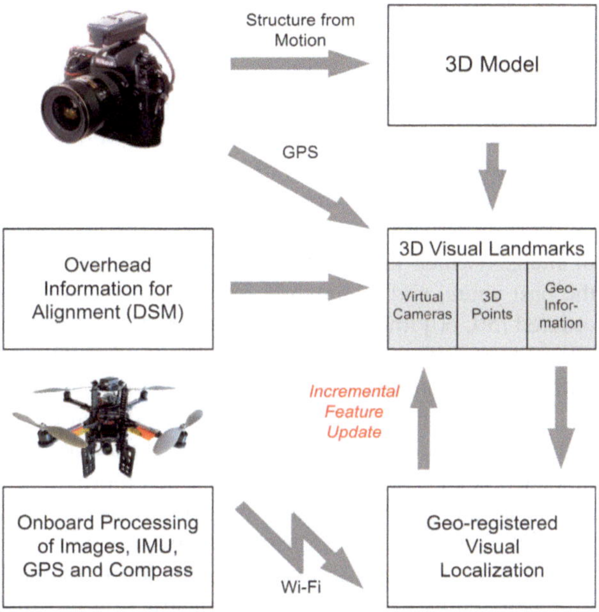

Fig. 7.2 Our framework for visual localization is based on *Visual Landmarks*. 3D models of the environment are geo-referenced and a set of virtual views is generated for the area. The proposed system is able to provide geo-localizations to an MAV with about 4 frames per second in an outdoor environment. This is not fast enough to navigate the vehicle based on vision only, but a bias-free pose estimate is crucial to correct the drift of other sensors. ©2012 IEEE. Reprinted, with permission, from [69]

our method for fast and drift-free localization. Our framework is finally evaluated in Sect. 7.5, and Sect. 7.6 concludes the chapter.

7.2 Scene Reconstruction

Visual landmarks are the fundamental concept of our work. We assume that significant parts of the scene such as buildings or trees do not alter their geometry for days, probably even years, and can therefore serve as natural landmarks. To cope with appearance changes we rely on imagery taken at different times of the day and in different seasons, which should be directly integrated in the 3D reconstruction if possible, or combined by a 3D alignment of reconstructions as discussed in the next section. Imagery for our approach can be collected from many sources such as Microsoft Bing Streetside or Google Street View, or by manually taking pictures of the area with a consumer camera. Additionally, one can exploit novel image acquisition tools such as micro aerial vehicles in form of quad- or octo-rotor helicopters which allow to take pictures from completely different points of view with ground sampling distances below 1 cm.

In the following, we present our 3D reconstruction pipeline and highlight important algorithmic details. We also present two approaches to densify the resulting sparse point cloud, which is an important contribution to subsequent proper alignment and occlusion handling during localization.

7.2.1 Related Work

Structure from Motion (SfM) deals with the problem of estimating the 3D structure of a scene while simultaneously solving for camera orientations using only 2D image measurements. It is a fundamental and well studied problem in both computer vision and photogrammetry [19]. In contrast to approaches which directly estimate a dense depth map for every acquired frame, for instance, by using stereo imaging [42] or active sensing [45], SfM systems extract depth information from a set of images which are acquired one after another. SfM has reached maturity over the past years, and meanwhile fully automatic pipelines for ordered [49] and unordered [59, 60] image collections exist. Processing is typically done offline, which allows to quickly capture images in the field and then do the processing in the lab with powerful hardware.

The recent success of Structure from Motion techniques can be traced back to significant advances in wide-baseline feature matching [39] and multiple-view geometry [46, 64]. Also, the advent of much more powerful computational hardware, and especially general-purpose graphic processing units (GPGPU) [12], supported the applicability of 3D reconstruction from image sequences. Still, exhaustive pairwise feature matching to find correspondences in the individual views is the most time demanding task in today's reconstruction pipelines. To circumvent this issue, Agarwal et al. [2] introduced a two-stage matching approach which is now considered best practice. First, every image is described by a single feature vector and coarse matches between images are detected. This process is based on image retrieval and bag-of-words concepts [58]. Then, only those image pairs which achieve a high similarity score are used for detailed feature matching. Our pipeline incorporates all of these ideas to create robust and accurate 3D models.

7.2.2 Sparse Structure-from-Motion Modeling

For sparse 3D model reconstruction, we rely on a Structure from Motion (SfM) approach that is able to reconstruct a scene from unorganized image sets. Our solution to the 3D reconstruction problem is based on the work of [25] and [67]. It is widely applicable since no prior knowledge about the scene is necessary (i.e., no sequential ordering of the input images has to be provided) and can therefore be used to create 3D models from terrestrial as well as aerial imagery. To accelerate the computations, we take advantage of graphic processing units (GPUs) for efficient parallelized computing. A typical SfM framework consists of three processing steps, namely feature extraction, matching, and geometry estimation. These steps are summarized in the following paragraphs.

7.2.2.1 Establishing the Epipolar Graph

First, salient features are extracted from each frame. Our method utilizes the very effective combination of DoG keypoint detector and SIFT descriptor [39] which achieves excellent repeatability performance for wide baseline image matching [43]. In particular we rely on the publicly available SiftGPU [72] software.

We then match keypoint descriptors between each pair of images. A variety of approaches has been proposed to speedup nearest neighbor matching in high-dimensional spaces (like the 128-dimensional SIFT descriptor space). Among the most promising methods are randomized kd-trees [57] with priority search and hierarchical k-means trees [14]. These algorithms are in general designed to run on a single CPU and are known to provide speedups of about one or two orders of magnitude over linear search, but the speedup comes with the cost of a potential loss in accuracy [44]. On the other hand, given that the number of features is limited to some thousands, nearest neighbor search, implemented as a dense matrix multiplication on recent graphics hardware, can achieve an equivalent speedup but delivers the exact solution. Hence, we employ a GPU-accelerated feature matching approach based on the CUBLAS library with subsequent instructions to apply the distance ratio test and to report the established correspondences.

After matching relevant images to each query view, geometric verification based on the Five-Point algorithm [47] is performed. Since matches that arise from descriptor comparisons are often highly contaminated by outliers, we employ the random sample consensus (RANSAC) [11] algorithm for robust estimation. In its basic implementation, RANSAC acts as a hypothesize-and-verify approach. From a minimal set of samples, several hypotheses are generated and the consensus of the model is evaluated on the full set of observations. The RANSAC termination confidence,

$$p = 1 - \exp\bigl(N \log\bigl(1 - (1 - \varepsilon)^s\bigr)\bigr) \tag{7.1}$$

is used to decide whether two images satisfy the epipolar geometry. Here, N is the total number of evaluated models, $w = 1 - \varepsilon$ the probability that any selected data point is an inlier, and $s = 5$ is the cardinality of the sample point set used to compute a minimal model. We require $p > 0.999$ in order to accept an epipolar geometric relation. In our experiments, we use up to $N = 2000$ models which corresponds to a maximal outlier fraction of $\varepsilon = 0.67$.

The matching output is a graph structure denoted as epipolar graph, that consists of the set of vertices $\mathcal{V} = \{I_1 \dots I_N\}$ corresponding to the images and a set of edges $\mathcal{E} = \{e_{ij} | i, j \in \mathcal{V}\}$ that are pairwise reconstructions, that is, relative orientations between view i and j, $e_{ij} = \langle P_i, P_j \rangle$,

$$P_0 = K_0[I, 0] \quad \text{and} \quad P_1 = K_1[R, t] \tag{7.2}$$

and a set of triangulated points with respective image measurements. Since the cameras are calibrated, a linear triangulation method [18] is sufficient to accurately estimate the 3D point location. This procedure is followed by a pruning step that discards ill-conditioned 3D points (points that do not satisfy the cheirality criterion) and points that have a high depth uncertainty (points where the roundness of the confidence ellipsoid [3] is larger than a given threshold).

7.2.2.2 Structure Initialization

Our SfM method follows an incremental approach [59] based on the epipolar graph. In order to reconstruct a consistent 3D model, a robust and reliable start configuration is required. When the initial structure is prone to errors, a subsequent iterative optimization procedure will eventually end up in a wrong local minimum, hence good initialization is critical. As proposed in [30], we initialize the geometry in the most connected parts of the graph, therefore the vertex I^* with highest degree, that is the node having the largest number of edges, is determined. We start from the vertex I^* and determine all connected neighbors. Next, all pair-wise measurements are linked into point tracks and the global scale factor of the initial structure is estimated. Then, bundle adjustment [64] is used to optimize camera orientations P_i and 3D points $\mathbf{X}_j$ by minimizing the reprojection error,

$$\mathcal{C}(P, \mathbf{X}) = \sum_i \sum_j v_{ij} d(P_i \mathbf{X}_j, \mathbf{x}_{ij})^2 \tag{7.3}$$

where $\mathbf{x}_{ij}$ are 2D point measurements of observed 3D points and v_{ij} is an indicator variable that is 1 if the point $\mathbf{X}_j$ is visible in camera P_i and 0 otherwise. To limit the impact of outliers, we use a robust Huber M-Estimator [23] to compute the costs d.

Given the initial optimized structure, each 3D point is back-projected and searched for in every image. We utilize a 2D kd-tree for efficient search and restrict the search radius to a constant factor r_t. Again, given the new measurements, bundle adjustment is used to optimize 3D points and camera parameters. This method ensures strong connections within the current reconstruction.

7.2.2.3 Incremental Reconstruction

Next, for every image I that is not reconstructed and has a potential overlap to the current 3D scene (estimated from the epipolar graph), 2D-to-3D correspondences are established. A three-point pose estimation algorithm [17, 32] inside a RANSAC loop is used to insert the position of a new image. When a pose can be determined

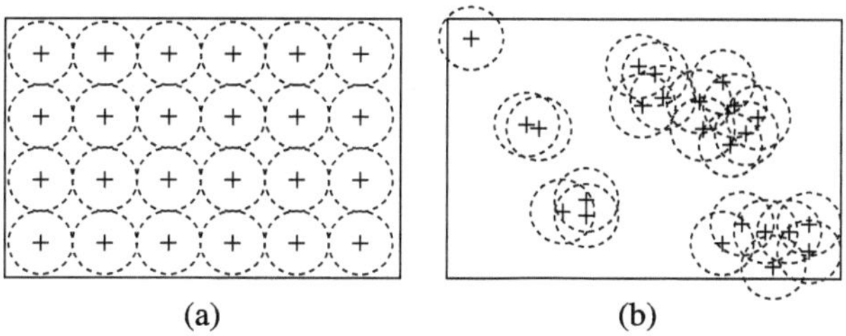

Fig. 7.3 Effective inlier measure. Coverage of (**a**) uniformly and (**b**) non-uniformly distributed image measurements. ©2011 IEEE. Reprinted, with permission, from [67]

(i.e., a sufficient inlier confidence is achieved), the structure is updated with the new camera and all measurements visible therein. A subsequent procedure expands the current 3D structure by triangulation of new correspondences. We follow the approach of Snavely et al. [59] and use a priority queue to guide the insertion order. Our insertion order is based on a saliency measure that favors early insertion of images that have a strong overlap with the given 3D structure. Rather than using the raw number of potential 2D-to-3D matches, we compute an effective matching score that further takes the spatial match distribution into account. This idea is depicted in Fig. 7.3. While the number of features is equal in (a) and (b), the uniform spatial distribution of point features in (a) can be regarded as more reliable than the one shown in (b). Hence, we weight the raw number of features by an estimate for the covered image fraction yielding the effective inlier count.

Whenever a number of N images is added (we use $N = 10$), bundle adjustment is used to simultaneously optimize the structure and all camera poses. The iterative view insertion procedure is repeated until the priority queue is empty. The sparse reconstruction result can be seen in Fig. 7.4(b).

7.2.3 Structure Refinement

Structure from Motion yields camera orientations and a sparse set of triangulated points. These entities are sufficient for a localization task, however for geo-referencing and occlusion handling a denser model is required. We thus apply two stages of refinement to our models: First, we densify the point cloud using a patch-based multiview stereo approach, and then we generate a surface mesh using Delaunay triangulation and free space carving.

The publicly available patch-based multiview stereo (PMVS) software of Furukawa and Ponce [15] is one of the most popular approaches to automatically reconstruct a scene when the camera positions are known. One of the main benefits is that this approach densifies a point cloud directly in 3D space rather than estimating the depth of every pixel which would introduce noise in untextured regions. PMVS initially estimates the position and orientation of small rectangular patches on the surface of the object based on sparse feature matching. Then, an expansion procedure iteratively adds patches in the neighborhood of already known regions. The approach successfully copes with outliers and thus is very robust, but the computational effort is also considerable. Since our structure from motion pipeline de-

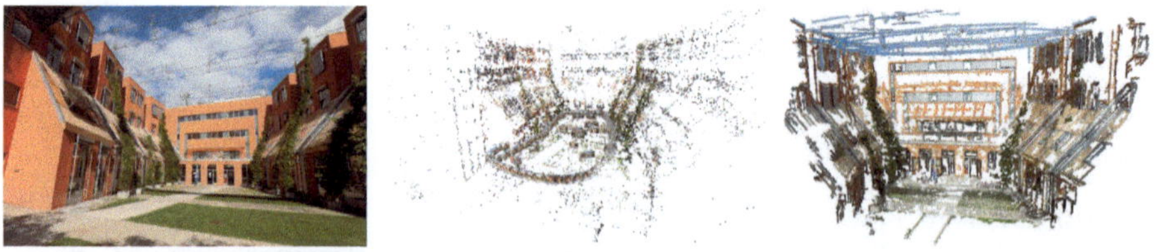

(a) (b) (c)

Fig. 7.4 Atrium scene reconstruction from 157 views. (**a**) Original view of the scene. (**b**) Sparse model and source cameras obtained by structure from motion reconstruction. (**c**) Semi-dense point model obtained by refining the sparse model with PMVS [15]. ©2011 IEEE. Reprinted, with permission, from [67]

livers sub-pixel accurate 3D camera orientations, PMVS can be run at full image resolution. However, even PMVS requires at least weakly textured surfaces for densification, thus a constant ground sampling distance cannot be guaranteed. The PMVS dense reconstruction result of the captured atrium scene is depicted in Fig. 7.4(c).

An alternative to point cloud densification, or as in our case a further refinement step, is to create watertight 3D models by performing a 3D Delaunay triangulation [5] followed by probabilistic space carving based on visibility information. Specifically, we employ the approach of Labatut et al. [34] who minimize an energy consisting of two terms to model the surface of objects: First, the visibility-based energy term votes for tetrahedra as being part of the object or part of free space, and it penalizes the number of conflicts of the line of sight with triangles crossing the surface. The second term takes care of the smoothness of the surface. It geometrically constrains the shape of a tetrahedra by penalizing the surface area, and by constraining the size of the circumsphere of the two adjacent tetrahedra of a triangle. This removes for example tiny elongated facets which are not desired in the resulting mesh. Finally, this energy functional is optimized via graph cuts [6]. The approach is very robust against outliers, and it preserves edges and fine structures while the result is at the same time free of self-intersections. However, the accuracy of the surface estimation depends on the number of 3D points in the mesh, as triangles between points can only linearly interpolate the surface. Therefore, the densification using PMVS as mentioned above is very beneficial to increase the level of detail in the model. The meshing results given a sparse point cloud versus a densified point cloud are compared in Fig. 7.5.

7.2.4 Discussion

We have described a state-of-the-art Structure from Motion pipeline and two additional steps for densification and meshing of the resulting point cloud. This process delivers the required input for subsequent geo-referencing and localization tasks.

While we carefully extract as much information of the input data as possible, the reconstruction quality and completeness heavily depends on the acquisition strategy

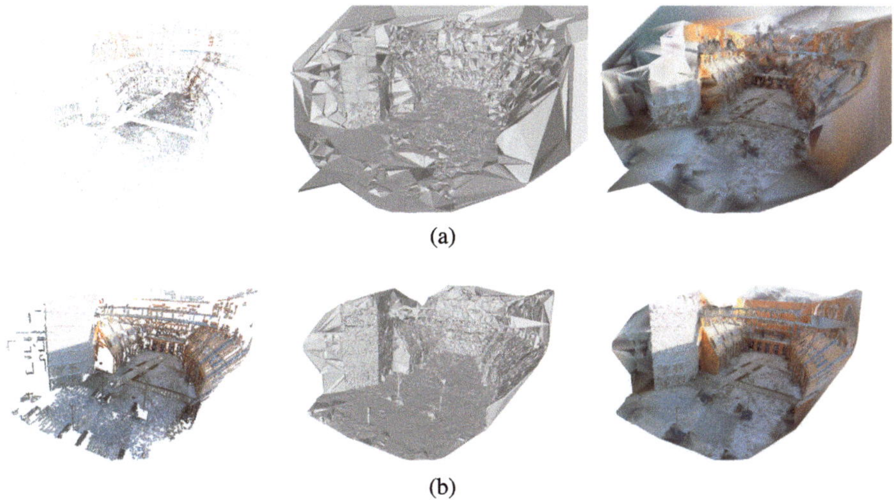

Fig. 7.5 Meshing results based on the approach of [34]. From left to right, the point cloud, the surface mesh, and a textured mesh are visualized, based on (**a**) the SfM point cloud (36,948 points), and (**b**) the densified point cloud (318,540 points). The densification procedure clearly supports the extraction of the true surface and leads to visually appealing results

and can typically only be assessed after the offline processing step has finished; this is the major drawback of current systems. Therefore, we have recently worked on assessing and refining the acquisition strategies for Structure from Motion [20, 21]. We have come up with several requirements which have to be fulfilled: First, the viewing angle between two images must not be too large to allow feature matching, and the viewing cones need to overlap. Second, the images have to be textured, but the texture should not be too repetitive and the illumination must not change too much between images. Finally, the entire scene needs to be covered with sufficient overlap. For a typical user it is impossible to estimate if the acquired images fulfill all demands, so Hoppe et al. [20] have come up with an SfM system which meshes and visualizes the overlap and resolution of the model in real-time (Fig. 7.6(a)). When a prior model of the same scene is available, for instance for an evolving construction site or when the geometry can be estimated using geographic information systems (GIS), a sophisticated approach for automated view planning [21] has been proposed (Fig. 7.6(b)). Finally, our recent system for dense reconstruction on-the-fly [70] can also provide a live preview of the scene geometry and thus facilitates user interaction. We expect that future research in SfM techniques will increasingly incorporate the important aspect of acquisition strategies.

7.3 Alignment in a Global Coordinate System

Alignment of visual maps in a global coordinate system is important for several reasons: First, it facilitates the incorporation of additional sensors at flight time and for

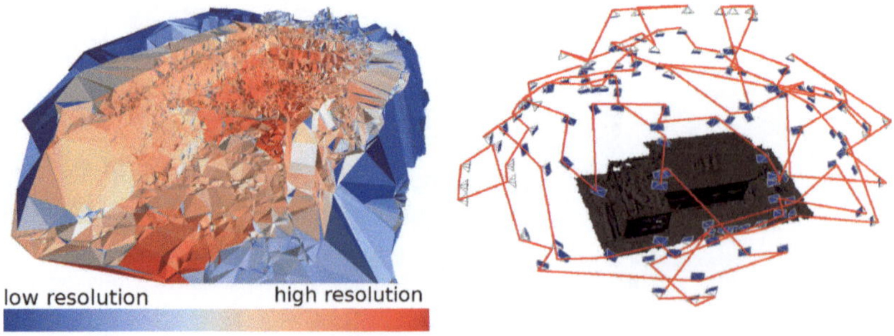

(a) (b)

Fig. 7.6 Optimization of the acquisition strategy. (**a**) The user can get live feedback during the acquisition process by visualizing pose estimation failures as well as overlap and resolution per triangle [20]. (**b**) Alternatively, automatic view planning algorithms [21] can be employed. Blue acquisition positions and orientations are connected by the optimal flight path for an MAV

evaluation, as coordinates obtained by visual localization are directly comparable to IMU and GPS readings. This also allows an MAV to switch seamlessly between GPS waypoint mode and visual localization, which is very important when connecting different visual landmarks, and it allows to represent point clouds with metric scaling. Second, proper alignment is beneficial to applications where the model should be set into context, for instance in industrial applications such as construction site monitoring [31], or whenever further algorithmic steps depend on it as in automatic view planning [21, 56].

However, two major challenges have to be tackled. On the one hand, georeferencing of 3D reconstructions is often difficult because of shadowed GPS signals in urban areas, so accurate alignment purely based on GPS information is not possible. On the other hand, flight space might be restricted in urban areas, which leads to missing views for accurate 3D reconstruction and causes fracturing of large models. This could also happen due to vegetation or simply a change of illumination during image acquisition. For the resulting fractured models, no visual feature correspondences—or at least not enough for fusing the models—can be established.

In this section, we therefore address the automatic alignment of such partial Structure from Motion (SfM) reconstructions to an overhead digital surface model (DSM) [66, 68] as depicted in Fig. 7.7. Our approach is to get an initial rough estimate of the model's pose using noisy GPS locations delivered by the consumer camera, and subsequently refine the pose based on a 2D correlation of the DSM height map with a projected model height map.

7.3.1 Related Work

The problem of aligning 2D images or 3D models to a 3D structure is well studied, especially in the context of large-scale city modeling. Frueh and Zakhor [13] present

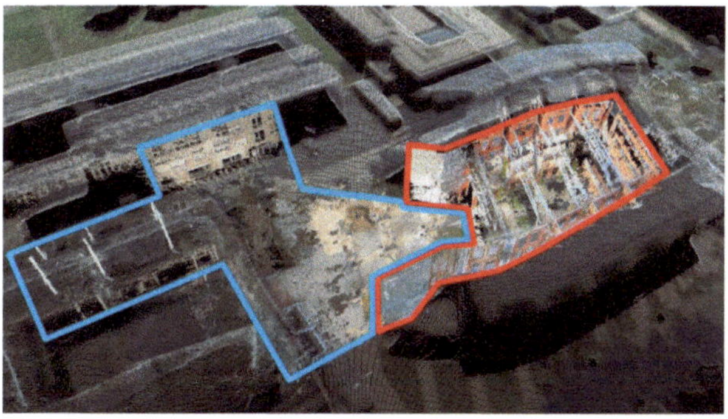

Fig. 7.7 Automatic fusion of two semi-dense 3D point clouds with an overhead, textured Digital Surface Model (DSM). The atrium model (*red*) has been reconstructed from ground-level, whereas the images for the campus model (*blue*) originate from a micro aerial vehicle. ©2011 IEEE. Reprinted, with permission, from [66]

an algorithm to fuse close-range facade models acquired at ground level with a far-range DSM recorded by a plane. The models are created using both ground-based and airborne laser scanners, as well as digital cameras for texturing. Their approach is based on registering the edges of the DSM image to the horizontal scans of a ground model using Monte-Carlo-Localization. Similarly, Strecha et al. [62] register facades segmented from a 3D point cloud to building footprints. Their approach combines various visual and geographical cues in a generative model, which allows robust treatment of outliers. However, both approaches are focused on large-scale city models with flat facades to both sides, resulting in fairly clean edges. In contrast, our approach takes the height over ground into account and therefore even benefits from complex structures.

A popular approach to aligning and fusing SfM point clouds is to use random sample consensus (RANSAC)-based geometric verification [11]. A typical issue is the estimation of a reasonable inlier threshold, however this has been resolved in recent work [50]. Still, such an approach is not feasible for our purpose as on the one hand feature correspondences cannot be established and the algorithm would have to solve a huge combinatoric problem. On the other hand, we want to align data with significant variations of the ground sampling distance which would not be possible either.

Another well-known method of aligning two point clouds is the Iterative Closest Points (ICP) algorithm [74]. ICP estimates a transformation to minimize the overall distance between points by iteratively assigning closest points as correspondences and solving for the best rigid transform. While ICP is mainly used for registering 3D laser scans, Zhao et al. [75] use it to align dense motion stereo from videos to laser scan data. However, 3D ICP can take very long and suffers from getting stuck in local minima due to its typically small convergence radius. In other words, a very good initialization is necessary for ICP to converge. However, using a point-to-plane variant [38] the ICP method can still be exploited on top of our method to improve the results.

Kaminsky et al. [27] use 2D ICP to compute the optimal alignment of a sparse SfM point cloud to an overhead image using an objective function that matches 3D points to image edges. Additionally, the objective function contains free space constraints which avoid an alignment to extraneous edges in the overhead image.

While their approach is suitable to align many 3D models obtained from ground level, it has problems with points on the ground and would therefore fail to align the models acquired using our micro aerial vehicle. Typical models presented in their paper show vertical walls which can be easily projected to the ground and fitted to respective edges. However, when many extraneous edges are visible in the overhead image their method fails. In contrast, given a sufficient point density in the reconstruction, our approach is less prone to errors caused by objects on the ground, it implicitly follows a free-space constraint and it works with models covering a small area.

7.3.2 Surface Model Reconstruction

A digital surface model (DSM) is a 2.5D height representation of the Earth's surface and all objects on it as seen from an orthogonal aerial viewpoint. In contrast to a full 3D model, just the maximum height over ground is considered, rather than looking at all structures that might be below. In other words, for instance the space underneath a bridge is filled instead of empty. The DSM can thus be stored in form of a 2D grayscale image with bright values reflecting a large height over ground.

The creation of a DSM typically requires a set of aerial images acquired by a plane or a micro aerial vehicle. After recovering the sparse geometry and camera orientations using Structure from Motion techniques, a dense 3D reconstruction is generated. Our method of choice is the multi-view plane sweep algorithm [7]. In short, the scene is traversed by planes parallel to the key view as shown in Fig. 7.8(a). For each discrete depth d, the sensor images are projected onto the plane and the similarity $C_i(x, y, d)$ between pixels of the key view and the sensor view i are calculated as the zero-mean normalized cross correlation (ZNCC). Once the cost volume C_{total} is filled with the accumulated matching scores, a variational optimization problem in 3D voxel space as proposed by Irschara et al. [26] is solved to recover the final depth value for every pixel. The resulting depth maps are smoothed but edges are preserved, as can be seen in Fig. 7.8(b). In contrast to close-up scenes as discussed in the previous section, this approach works very well here because the distance between individual cameras is small compared to the distance between the cameras and the surface.

High-quality aerial photographs or digital surface models may not be accessible for everyone, and they may not be available for some locations on earth. However, web-based map providers such as OpenStreetMap provide fairly accurate information not only regarding roads and directions, but also concerning buildings and vegetation. We have shown in [52, 66] that it is straight-forward to estimate a rough DSM by assigning a single, estimated height to all buildings. While the resulting building heights are obviously not correct and thus cause errors, the estimate is in our experience good enough to align a 3D model using the proposed approach, with a better accuracy than the raw GPS alignment.

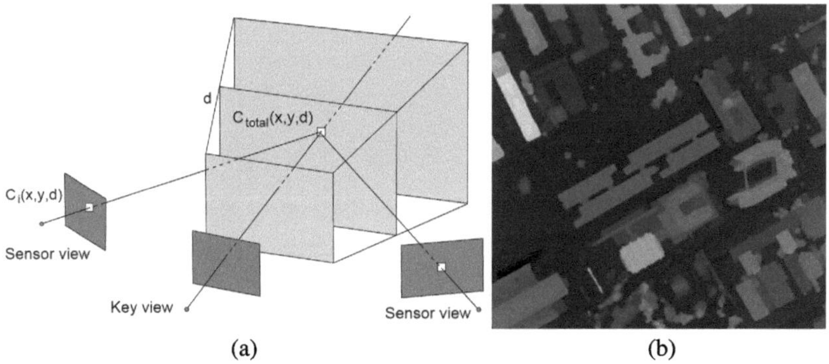

Fig. 7.8 Surface Model Reconstruction. (**a**) Given the camera orientations as a result of the SfM reconstruction, the multi-view plane sweep approach [7] is used to generate dense 3D reconstructions. (**b**) Combined with a variational refinement [26] accurate digital surface models are created

7.3.3 Alignment to an Overhead Surface Model

Our alignment pipeline is based on the registration of 2D depth maps showing the scene in a nadir view, rather than 3D point clouds. We can thus handle geometric configurations where ICP fails due to unknown correspondences or local minima, as well as significant differences in appearance because there is no need to establish sparse feature correspondences. We follow a three step approach: First, we convert all GPS and pixel coordinates into a local, metric coordinate system. Second, we roughly align the acquired 3D point cloud to the DSM by exploiting the available GPS information. Finally, we search for the best height map alignment between the DSM and the semi-dense model point cloud using normalized cross-correlation.

7.3.3.1 Conversion to Local ECEF Coordinates

Geo-referenced model coordinates are represented in a local Earth-centered, Earth-fixed (local ECEF) coordinate system. While the global ECEF coordinate system has its origin at the center of the Earth, with the x axis passing through the equator at the prime meridian and the z axis passing through the north pole, local ECEF employs a tangent plane to the Earth's surface at a reference point (Fig. 7.9). By definition, the x axis heads East, the y axis North, and the z axis up into the sky, thus it is also called *ENU* coordinate system. While the individual reference point needs to be known using this representation, the benefits include a more intuitive Cartesian system which allows to obtain metric measurements in the transformed point cloud, and a better numerical stability of the transformations. We choose the reference point to be the arithmetic center of the DSM's known corner points.

7.3.3.2 Rough Alignment Using GPS Information

We exploit the GPS information available for every camera in our 3D models for rough alignment to the DSM. If the coordinates measured by the GPS system were

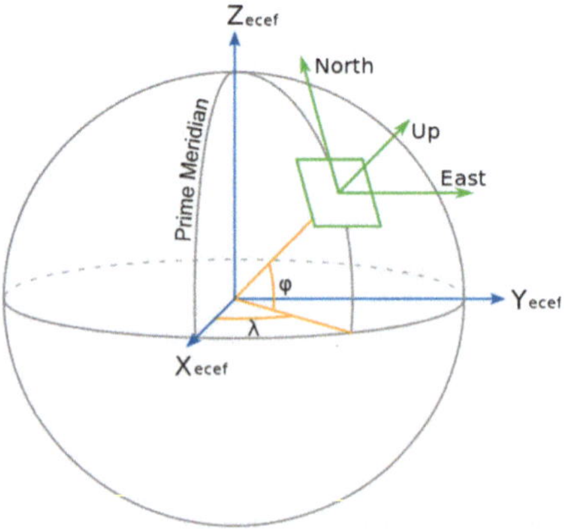

Fig. 7.9 Relationship between GPS coordinates (λ, ϕ) and the Cartesian local ECEF coordinate system (east, north, up). A tangent plane to the Earth's surface at a reference point is established for a more intuitive and numerically stable representation

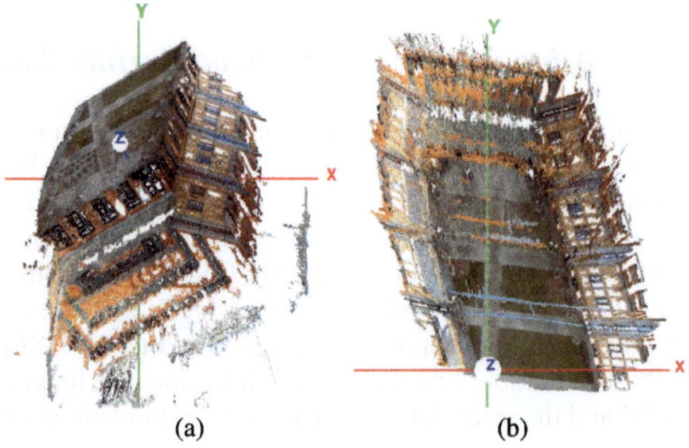

Fig. 7.10 Rotation for ground plane alignment based on the method of [63]. (**a**) SfM model in the coordinate system of the first model camera. (**b**) SfM model after performing the estimated rotation. ©2011 IEEE. Reprinted, with permission, from [66]

correct, it would be straightforward to estimate a 3D similarity transform. However, longitude and latitude are noisy, and especially the altitude estimate can be very inaccurate.

Therefore, our approach is to solve for a 2D similarity transform between the camera positions $(x_{\mathrm{sfm},i}, y_{\mathrm{sfm},i})$ in the SfM model and the GPS coordinates $(x_{\mathrm{gps},i}, y_{\mathrm{gps},i})$, both in local ECEF coordinates. Neglecting the altitude is just possible when the ground planes are aligned. However, SfM pipelines typically store resulting models in the coordinate system of the first camera. As a result, the axes of partial reconstructions do not align and have to be rotated to a common ground plane. We employ a reasonable assumption to approximate this plane, namely that the horizontal axis in every image coordinate system is approximately parallel to the ground plane, which is the case when taking upright photographs from the ground but also when taking nadir and oblique pictures on a micro aerial vehicle. The approach of Szeliski [63] can then be used to compute the ground plane normal and the corresponding rotation, as visualized in Fig. 7.10. Finally, a robust 2D similarity transformation can be found using RANSAC [11].

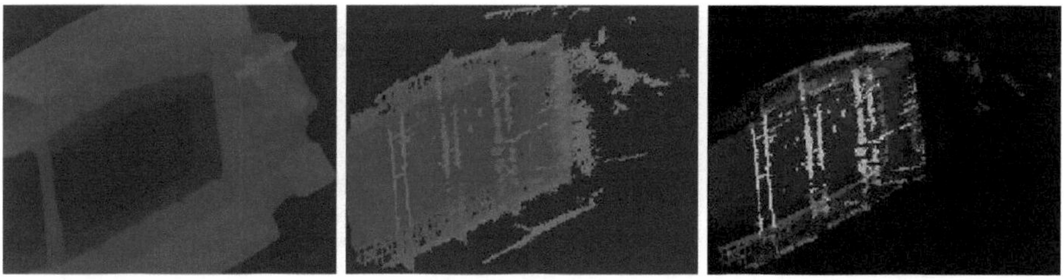

(a) Ground Height (b) Model Height (c) Difference

Fig. 7.11 Precise Alignment using Correlation. The normalized height values G of the ground (**a**) are compared to those of the projected SfM model M_t (**b**), with undefined points marked in *black*. (**c**) Differences occur not only when a building height does not fit, but also when the ground height does not fit. ©2011 IEEE. Reprinted, with permission, from [66]

7.3.3.3 Precise Alignment Using Correlation

Given the rough alignment, we use correlation for precise alignment. We project the semi-dense 3D point cloud into the pixel grid of the DSM image, storing only the maximum height value per pixel. Pixel clusters with a radius $r \leq 2px$ are removed using morphological operations to get rid of reconstruction outliers. The model template M_0 is finally created by cropping an axis-aligned box containing the defined values. The template is visualized in Fig. 7.11(b), with undefined values in black color.

As the uncertainty of the rough alignment can introduce rotation and scale errors next to the translational uncertainty ΔT, we rotate the model by the angles $\Delta\phi$, $\Delta\theta$, and $\Delta\psi$ (roll, pitch, yaw) and scale it with a factor $s = 1.0 \pm \Delta s$ to generate the model templates M_t. We cover the search space using the coarse-to-fine approach by [27] to speed up computation, and crop the ground template G_{gsd} from the DSM image according to the pyramid level gsd (Fig. 7.11(a)).

The score of template t is finally computed by normalized cross-correlation of ground and model templates,

$$d(t) = \frac{1}{n_t - 1} \sum_{x,y} \frac{(G_{\text{gsd}}(x, y) - \overline{G_{\text{gsd}}})(M_t(x, y) - \overline{M_t})}{\sigma_{G_{\text{gsd}}} \sigma_{M_t}}, \tag{7.4}$$

where n_t is the number of *defined* pixels for every template t, and $\overline{G_{\text{gsd}}}$, $\sigma_{G_{\text{gsd}}}$, $\overline{M_t}$ as well as σ_{M_t} are computed only for *defined* pixels. Additionally, we introduce a term for penalizing alignments which contain a large amount of *undefined* pixels,

$$r(t) = \frac{n_t}{N_t}, \tag{7.5}$$

where N_t is the number of all pixels in template t. The best height map alignment is then associated with the best model template

$$t_{\text{best}} = \arg\max_t d(t) + \lambda r(t). \tag{7.6}$$

(a) (b)

Fig. 7.12 Season-Invariant Matching. (**a**) Accurate alignment allows to collect local features in different seasons (*blue*, *red*) and fuse the overlapping point clouds. (**b**) The aligned models have been acquired in different seasons (summer and winter), as can be seen when looking at the vegetation. ©2011 IEEE. Reprinted, with permission, from [66]

The mode of the difference between the ground template and the best model template, and the ratio of the respective variances, can finally be used to estimate the translation and scaling on the vertical axis.

Using height maps for alignment can be seen as an implicit free space constraint, if compared to the work of Kaminsky et al. [27]. Differences between ground and model templates as in Fig. 7.11(c) occur not only when a building height does not fit, but also when the ground height does not fit.

7.3.4 Discussion

In this section, we have presented an algorithm for the automatic alignment of partial 3D reconstructions based on [66]. Given an overhead Digital Surface Model (DSM) and approximate GPS tags for the individual camera positions, we refine the alignment based on the correlation of orthographic depth maps. We can handle complex cases where previous methods had problems, including models which do not share any appearance features and models with considerably different ground sampling distances. This allows not only to fuse data acquired by an MAV, but also combining aerial and terrestrial data sources. The accuracy of our approach mainly depends on the ground sampling distance of the overhead digital surface model, which is in the range of 5–30 cm per pixel for modern cameras.

Our alignment approach has several applications: Accurate alignment helps to fuse partial SfM models which could not be connected in the original reconstruction process, and detailed SfM model information can be fused into the original DSM. The alignment of models also helps to achieve season-invariant matching, as models with different appearance and therefore different feature descriptors can be placed in the same coordinate system. The concept of virtual cameras, as presented in the next section, fully integrates this increased amount of descriptors during a localization task. A visualization of two overlapping and two adjacent models, taken in different seasons, can be found in Fig. 7.12.

Fig. 7.13 Localization in a geo-referenced, metric visual landmark allows to convert the resulting local ECEF coordinates back to a GPS position. It is therefore possible to seamlessly switch between GPS and visual navigation, as well as to exploit onboard GPS and IMU data in the localization process. ©2012 IEEE. Reprinted, with permission, from [69]

7.4 Image-Based Localization

A large number of interesting applications for micro aerial vehicles such as surveillance, agriculture, inspection, or simply 3D reconstruction for visualization share one common feature: The need for highly accurate localization of the vehicle with respect to the scene. According to the work of Konolige and Bowman [33] on life-long maps, long-term visual localization requires an accurate map with good features, but should also allow incremental mapping and recovery from localization failures. An additional requirement for MAVs is the possibility to switch between GPS and visual localization, as visual maps are unnecessary when flying high above buildings or in wide open spaces.

In the previous sections, we have shown how to create metric, geo-referenced 3D models by taking pictures with a consumer camera from eye-level above ground or by using micro aerial vehicles as acquisition tools. Now we demonstrate how the concept of virtual views helps to incorporate prior knowledge and fulfills the requirements listed above. We present a method for monocular localization with an accuracy comparable to differential GPS in a global coordinate system (Fig. 7.13). Further, we introduce an incremental feature update step which allows to fuse in-flight information back into the original scene model, and we exploit additional sensor information to ensure localization robustness.

7.4.1 Related Work

The problem of vision-based MAV navigation in unstructured environments has been addressed only recently. To retrieve position estimates for visual control, most systems [1, 4, 65] employ simultaneous localization and mapping (SLAM) techniques in indoor and outdoor settings.

SLAM addresses the problem of exploring a previously unknown environment. This requires to determine the sensor pose given an estimated map, and to optimize the map given the sensor information at the estimated pose; two tasks which highly depend on each other and thus have to be solved simultaneously. Early SLAM systems using a single camera as the main perceptual sensor were based on filtering approaches. Davison [9] fused measurements from a sequence of images by updating probability distributions over features and extrinsic camera parameters using an Extended Kalman Filter (EKF). This requires tracking and mapping to be closely linked, as the camera pose and feature locations are updated together at every single frame. In contrast, Klein and Murray [28, 29] presented a real-time visual SLAM system based on keyframes named Parallel Tracking and Mapping. PTAM employs two separate threads, one for tracking the camera pose through every single frame, and another for mapping the environment by applying bundle adjustment to a set of spatially distributed keyframes. The major drawback of filtering approaches, namely the limited number of features that can be updated in between two frames, is circumvented in PTAM by leaving more time to the parallel mapping process. Strasdat et al. [61] experimentally showed that localization using a large amount of features measured at low temporal frequency is in general superior to a small amount of features measured at every frame, thus keyframe-based methods typically outperform filtering approaches. Still, as the reconstruction is created online, the mapping process is affected by drift and does not scale well to outdoor environments.

We thus want to emphasize the importance of prior knowledge for vision-based navigation tasks. Model-based localization approaches have been extensively investigated over the past decade [37, 55, 73, 76]. Most closely related to our approach is the urban localization approach of Irschara et al. [24] which uses image retrieval-based methods for location recognition. Compared to this class of methods, considerable improvements have recently been achieved [36, 53] using prioritized, direct matching of 3D points to 2D features. However, Sattler et al. [54] have investigated this performance gap. It turns out that it is caused by a large number of incorrect votes cast by standard re-ranking schemes, and can be fixed using their proposed method. Instead, in this work we employ a motion prior to select a small, feasible set of virtual views which is then ranked. The search space is thus much smaller and we are hardly affected by the issue. Apart from that, our approach using virtual views has many benefits over direct matching as described in the next section.

7.4.2 Scalable Localization Using Virtual Cameras

Our framework provides a visual landmark in terms of a large geo-registered 3D point cloud with associated visual features. However, the information in the landmark is based on a low number of fixed viewpoints and thus does not provide views which are sufficiently close to the images taken by an MAV. Additionally, matching descriptors of a query image against thousands of descriptors in the model is infeasible as it would result in a high number of non-unique matches, and would not scale in terms of computational effort. In contrast, the partitioning of the search space using virtual cameras [24, 67] enables efficient visual localization in outdoor environments. Combined with an incremental feature update step [69] to cope with missing viewing angles in the original model, a robust and scalable localization system is proposed.

7.4.2.1 Placement of Virtual Cameras

Virtual cameras hold the correspondences of only those 3D points and features which are visible given the respective camera center, camera orientation, and occlusion surfaces. Motivated by [24], who use synthetic views for fast location recognition in a flat environment, we have extended the concept to 3D space in [67]. We sample camera centers on a regular grid G, and camera vectors in uniform angular steps of γ on a unit sphere. Additionally, we use the intrinsics of the camera mounted on the MAV to retrieve the correct scale of the features.

After setting up the necessary views, we project all 3D points into the respective cameras. A projected feature has to be in front of the camera and within the extent of the image, and it needs to have a scale larger than one pixel after projection. Additionally, if a surface mesh is available for the model, we restrict the maximum distance of projected points to the distance of the closest surface in viewing direction; this approach avoids adding occluded features. For every 3D point X, we use the SIFT descriptor [39] with the smallest extraction angle

$$\delta_{\min}(X, i) = \min_{j} \arccos\left(\frac{\mathbf{XV_i}}{\|XV_i\|} \cdot \frac{\mathbf{XE_j}}{\|XE_j\|}\right) \tag{7.7}$$

between the virtual camera V_i and the model camera E_j. Consequently, $\delta_{\min}(X, i)$ increases with any deviation from the camera positions used for acquisition, but especially in higher altitudes when using images taken at ground level to create the model. This increase in extraction angle is visualized in Fig. 7.16(a). However, according to Mikolajczyk et al. [43] SIFT is only robust to off-image-plane rotations up to $\delta_{\min} < 30°$. Given, for instance, a distance between camera and point of 10 m, this would mean that the localization only works up to a height of 5 m above the acquisition height, because for higher altitudes matching fails and the pose cannot be estimated robustly. This problem can be circumvented by adding in-flight information to the model; our approach called *incremental feature updates* is described in detail in Sect. 7.4.2.3.

We determine the number of necessary virtual cameras based upon the 3D reconstruction of the scene. The extent and the alignment of the grid G are defined by the 3D point cloud. To ensure overlapping coverage of the entire model, we increase the number of grid points along each axis until the number of feature points which are visible in less than N_{coverage} cameras converges. During this process, all views with less than $|F|_{\min}$ features are removed. The placement of virtual cameras is visualized in Fig. 7.14.

7.4.2.2 Localization Using Virtual Cameras

The resulting virtual cameras V provide a highly redundant representation of the scene. At first sight, the usage of synthetic views seems to cause an enormous need for feature matching. However, the approach scales very well for image sequences,

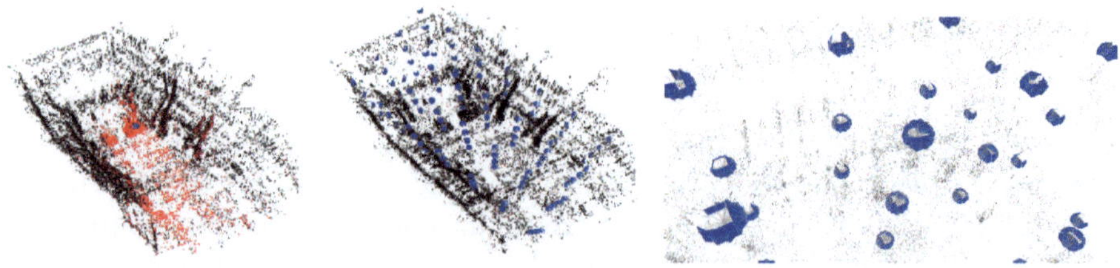

(a) (b) (c)

Fig. 7.14 Placement of virtual cameras. (**a**) A placement with $G = \{1, 1, 1\}$ and $\gamma = 30°$ does not satisfy the required coverage of $N_{\text{coverage}} = 3$. Uncovered points are marked in *red*, virtual cameras in *blue*. (**b**) The coverage converges for $G = \{7, 4, 4\}$ and $\gamma = 30°$. (**c**) A detailed view of the same grid highlights the removal of cameras with less than $|F|_{\min} = 200$ projected features. ©2011 IEEE. Reprinted, with permission, from [67]

as MAVs do not exceed a predetermined translational and rotational speed in normal operation. The feasible set of virtual cameras V_t at a certain time t is defined by the spatial distance to the previously estimated position and orientation of the camera. We define the translational and rotational search radii $t_{\max}$ and $R_{\max}$ around that position, which are enlarged in case the MAV cannot localize its position for a number of frames, for instance due to close-up views of an obstacle or unusual movements.

Virtual cameras within that search area are ranked based on appearance using a vocabulary tree [48] and corresponding inverted files. Restricting the search space by cascading prior knowledge and appearance features to the feasible set V_t allows our approach to handle scenes with unlimited size, and successfully copes with repetitive structures. We sort V_t according to the scores obtained by the vocabulary tree query, and subsequently use the top-scoring k views $V_t^{1:k}$ to geometrically verify the pose of the MAV.

For geometric verification, SIFT features extracted in the query view are matched to those in the virtual view using the GPU and the distance ratio test (see Sect. 7.2.2). We then exploit the knowledge about the 2D to 3D correspondences of points in the virtual view, and estimate a robust absolute pose from three point correspondences (P3P) [32] using fast RANSAC methods [11]. Finally, only poses with a minimal number of effective inliers, $I_{\text{eff}} \geq th_{\text{eff}}$, are accepted. The measure of effective inliers [24] reports the spatial distribution of inliers within the image (Fig. 7.3); a high value indicates that the inliers are well distributed and therefore more reliable. Figure 7.15 visualizes the top three virtual cameras $V_t^{1:3}$ and the corresponding estimated absolute poses P_t for selected query images.

In summary, the main idea is to fill a scene with a large number of virtual cameras which each hold N_{V_i} correspondences between visible 3D points and features, given the respective camera center and orientation. This overcomes the problem of matching all N_{query} features from a query image to all features in the model. Instead, we match only $N_{\text{query}} \times N_{V_i} \times k$ features for a small, feasible subset of k virtual cameras. As a result, the approach scales very well and it can cope with ambiguous environments.

(a) (b)

Fig. 7.15 Localization initiated by virtual cameras. (**a**) In most cases, pose estimation based on the virtual cameras $V_t^{1:3}$ (visualized without texture) results in the same final absolute pose P_t (textured with the query image). (**b**) If the results do not coincide, the pose P_t with most effective inliers I_{eff} (*red matches*) is preferred to other poses (*blue matches*). ©2011 IEEE. Reprinted, with permission, from [67]

Due to the previously discussed process of creating and aligning visual landmarks, the result of the localization process is a metrically correct position which can be converted back to GPS coordinates. The concept of virtual cameras supports the storage of feature descriptors from different acquisition days, thus it is possible to localize the camera in different seasons if the necessary data is available. It is also possible to update virtual cameras, as discussed in the next section.

7.4.2.3 Incremental Feature Update

The previously presented approach has a major drawback, which is the lack of good features whenever the angle to the closest view used for modeling the scene is large. As images are typically taken at ground level, this especially applies when the MAV flies in altitudes higher than 5 m, but may also occur in many other scenarios.

In [69], we have proposed to tackle this issue by adding in-flight information to the model, which we call incremental feature update. The visual localization of every single frame results in a set of inlier features which each correspond to a 3D point X. We evaluate the new extraction angle

$$\delta_{\text{update}}(X, i) = \delta_{\min}(X, i) - \arccos\left(\frac{\mathbf{XL}}{\|XL\|} \cdot \frac{\mathbf{XV_i}}{\|XV_i\|}\right) \tag{7.8}$$

between the localized camera L and the virtual camera V_i. Respective inlier features in virtual camera i are updated, if $\delta_{\text{update}}(X, i) > th_{\text{update}}$, that is, if the new extraction angle is at least th_{update} smaller than the previous one. Note that just the descriptor has to be exchanged; 3D points and 2D feature positions in the virtual camera remain constant. This update step is very fast and does not reduce the localization rate of 4 fps, as we exploit a precomputed list of relevant virtual cameras for every 3D point. By computing the extraction angle for every virtual view individually, we ensure that the average extraction angle is optimized. Figure 7.16(b) visualizes

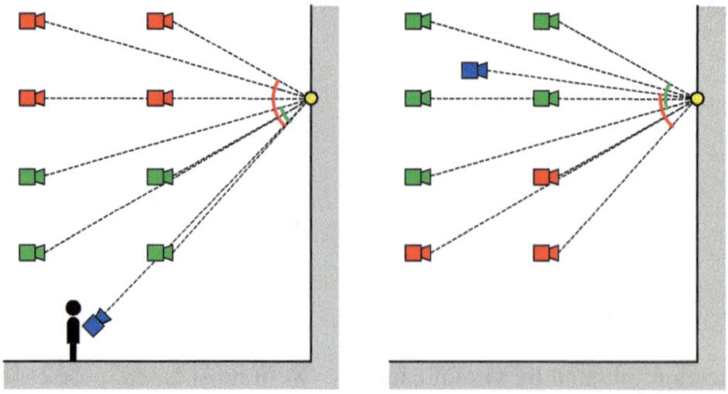

Fig. 7.16 Incremental feature update. (**a**) Depending on the acquisition strategy, some virtual views (*red cameras*) might have an extraction angle larger than 30° compared to the model view (*blue camera*) which contains the real visual information. (**b**) The problem can be circumvented by incrementally updating virtual cameras with in-flight information (*blue camera*). The extraction angle for *green cameras* is reduced and features are updated; the extraction angle for *red cameras* would be increased so the features stay the same. ©2012 IEEE. Reprinted, with permission, from [69]

the update of cameras which initially had a high extraction angle $\delta_{\min}(X, i)$. Virtual cameras in high altitudes are updated, while the features for lower altitudes remain the same.

Incremental feature updates are generally applied in an *online* fashion during the flight of the MAV. This allows a large boost in performance, but early frames do not profit from new information in later stages of the flight. Therefore, we run an additional *batch* update with several iterations (until convergence) after the flight. Even a single additionally registered camera can provide the necessary descriptors for later iterations. During the batch update process, we also update the inverted file tables which are used in vocabulary tree ranking.

7.4.2.4 Validation Using Additional Sensors

A well-known problem in online learning and tracking is drift due to wrong feature updates, called the *template update problem* [41]. If wrong localizations are taken to be correct, the model is disturbed and the localization drifts towards the erroneous features. Incremental feature updates as presented in the previous section can also be affected by these issues, even though robust methods are applied already. To overcome this limitation, we propose to validate visual localization by using the additional global sensors available to an MAV.

We employ the magnetic field sensors and compass of the IMU to validate the estimated attitude, and the GPS readings and pressure sensor to evaluate the estimated position. Thanks to the alignment of our visual landmark introduced in Sect. 7.3, the comparison in a global coordinate system is straight-forward.

For representing the attitudinal error, we choose a measure based on a quaternion representation. A quaternion is defined as $Q = [\boldsymbol{\rho}^T \; q_w]^T$, with $\boldsymbol{\rho} = \boldsymbol{a}\sin(\frac{\theta}{2})$ and $q_w = \cos(\frac{\theta}{2})$, where $\boldsymbol{a}$ corresponds to the axis and θ to the angle of rotation. Thus, the attitude error between the camera attitude quaternion Q_{cam} and the IMU attitude quaternion Q_{magnetic} is calculated as

$$e_{\text{attitude}} = 2\arccos\left(\left\| Q_{\text{cam}}^{-1} Q_{\text{magnetic}} \right\|_w\right), \tag{7.9}$$

where $\| \cdot \|_w$ is an operation that first normalizes the quaternion resulting from the quaternion multiplication and then extracts q_w. The position error is given as

$$e_{\text{position}} = \left\| \begin{pmatrix} x_{\text{cam}} \\ y_{\text{cam}} \\ z_{\text{cam}} \end{pmatrix} - \begin{pmatrix} x_{\text{latitude}} \\ y_{\text{longitude}} \\ z_{\text{pressure}} \end{pmatrix} \right\|, \tag{7.10}$$

with x_{latitude} and $y_{\text{longitude}}$ as GPS position converted to a local ECEF coordinate system, and z_{pressure} as pressure height over ground. These error measures are required to be smaller than a threshold th_{attitude} and th_{position}, respectively. Shadowing effects, weather changes, and magnetic fields may disturb these sensors as well, so the validation should serve as a sanity check rather than a narrow rejection criterion.

The combination of information about the rough orientation and position of the MAV in a world coordinate system also allows us to switch seamlessly between GPS and visual localization, for instance when navigating between several visual landmarks. Moreover, it enhances scalability to a world environment as the feasible set of virtual cameras discussed before is further restricted.

7.4.3 Discussion

We have presented an algorithm for monocular visual localization of MAVs using prior knowledge about the scene. Our work is based on the concept of virtual views in 3D space, which allows to partition the search space for speeding up localization in large environments, but also supports the integration of in-flight information to improve the initial scene representation. Localization results generated by our algorithm are in a world coordinate system, which allows the MAV to switch seamlessly between GPS and visual localization.

In contrast to visual SLAM, our localization method directly allows global registration and is neither prone to drift nor bias. However, with 4 fps it is also much slower than typical feature tracking approaches, and a speed of at least 25 fps is required for effective visual serving [1, 71]. Using our distributed visual SLAM approach [70] which tracks features onboard the MAV but sources the mapping task out, it is straight-forward to achieve short-term localization on the vehicle and correct its map with geo-registered, drift- and bias-free information delivered by our approach. This would push our framework even more in the direction of long-term operation.

7.5 Experiments and Results

In the following paragraphs, we evaluate our localization approach, and accordingly the visual landmark creation and alignment compared to visual and GPS-based groundtruth. The evaluation site, the atrium of a modern building, has already been used to visualize the individual steps of our approach. This environment is very challenging, as there is little texture on the facades and repetitive structures such as windows and vegetation prevail.

7.5.1 Evaluation Dataset and Hardware

For the creation of the initial visual landmark we captured 157 images from eye-level above ground using a Canon EOS 5D. This SLR camera has a resolution of 5616×3744 pixels with a fixed 20 mm lens.

Aerial imagery is obtained using a Pelican quad-rotor MAV by Ascending Technologies and a single industrial camera (IDS UI-1240SE) with a resolution of 1280×1024 pixels, global shutter, and a 12 mm lens. Thanks to the on-board computer running the Robot Operating System (ROS) and a wireless 802.11n link, we are able to stream high-quality images to the ground at 4 fps. Our ground station is equipped with a powerful graphics card running NVIDIA CUDA, which allows highly parallel data processing for feature extraction and matching.

Additional sensor data from the inertial measurement unit (IMU), compass, and global positioning system (GPS) are automatically preprocessed and fused by the MAV. While hardware synchronization with the camera trigger would be desirable, we currently exploit the high update rates of the sensors and collect IMU and GPS messages between triggering and receiving an image. Attitude and position are then estimated using robust statistics.

For the iterative update of the model, we acquired two image sequences (1280×1024 px at 4 fps) of 260 (*flight1*) and 230 images (*flight2*) by exploring the atrium in manual flight mode. Each flight started at the ground and covered a volume of about $10 \times 10 \times 15\ m^3$. Additionally, we have acquired a video stream showing the flight from an observer's point of view. This stream has been recorded with a resolution of 1920×1028 pixels at 25 fps, and is used as groundtruth for evaluating our localization performance qualitatively. Finally, for a quantitative validation of the position accuracy we captured images at fixed points which were globally localized using differential GPS (D-GPS).

The localization process including the online update runs at 4 fps. The runtime of a batch update depends on the length of the flight and the number of modified virtual cameras, and results to approx. 5 min per iteration on our datasets. For the following experiments, a minimal virtual camera coverage $N_{\text{coverage}} = 3$ is achieved by setting the grid to $G = \{7, 4, 4\}$ and the angular step to $\gamma = 30°$. This results in $112 \times 62 = 6944$ virtual cameras, which are reduced to a set of 1903 virtual views

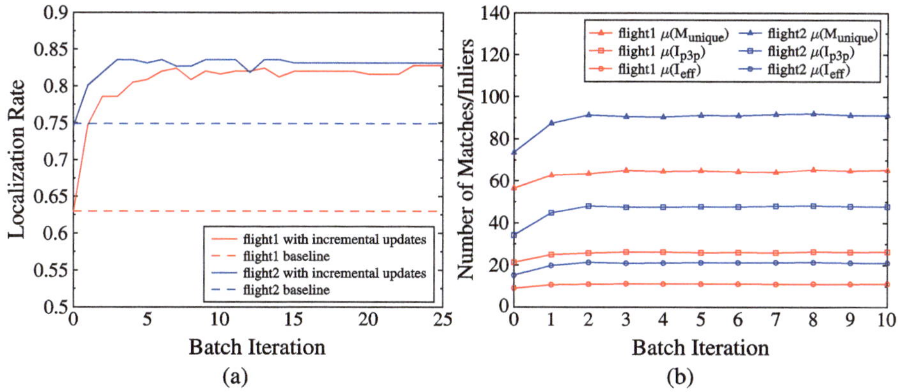

Fig. 7.17 Localization improvement for two test sets. (**a**) *Dashed lines* show the baseline using the non-adaptive algorithm [67] whereas *solid lines* depict correctly localized frames (R_{valid}) based on IMU validation. Our adaptive method improves the localization performance R_{valid} from 62.8 % to 83.1 % for *flight1*, and 74.5 % to 83.5 % for *flight2*. (**b**) For both testsets, all quality measures improve as well when applying incremental feature updates. ©2012 IEEE. Reprinted, with permission, from [69]

by thresholding the minimal number of features to $|F|_{\min} = 200$. For localization, we estimate the pose of at most $k = 3$ top-scoring views in a neighborhood of $t_{\max} = 1.0$ m and $R_{\max} = 45°$ with respect to the previously established pose, and accept the pose if it contains at least $th_{\text{eff}} = 3$ effective inliers. Incremental updates are evaluated with $th_{\text{attitude}} = 10°$, $th_{\text{position}} = 20$ m, and $th_{\text{update}} = 1°$.

7.5.2 Comparison of Adaptive and Non-adaptive Localization

Our first experiment evaluates the localization performance as the ratio of correctly localized frames based on additional sensor data, as previously described in Sect. 7.4.2.4. The ratio of frames which are localized correctly is named R_{valid}. R_{invalid} describes the ratio of frames which exceed th_{attitude} or th_{position} and therefore fail validation.

We achieve a baseline of 63 % for *flight1* and 75 % for *flight2* using the non-adaptive approach [67]. Our evaluation shows that issues with high-altitude views occur starting at a height of about 6 m, which corresponds to the theoretical result shown in the previous section. In contrast, Fig. 7.17(a) shows that adaptive localization can considerably improve these results. After applying 25 incremental updates, meaning that the inliers of all frames were taken into account at every iteration except for the first, we achieve a localization rate of 83 % for both *flight1* and *flight2*. This corresponds to an improvement of up to 30 % in comparison to non-adaptive localization. Even using just the online update during the flight, and neglecting the batch updates afterwards, localization rates of 71 % and 80 % are reached. The on-

Table 7.1 Localization Results for Different Attitude Errors after 25 Incremental Update Iterations. ©2012 IEEE. Reprinted, with permission, from [69]

Flight	th_{attitude}	R_{valid}	R_{invalid}	$\mu(e_{\text{attitude}})$
1	5°	43.7 %	41.4 %	$3.61° \pm 1.03°$
1	10°	82.8 %	2.3 %	$5.04° \pm 1.85°$
1	15°	84.3 %	0.8 %	$5.05° \pm 1.90°$
2	5°	53.2 %	42.0 %	$3.52° \pm 0.96°$
2	10°	83.1 %	12.1 %	$4.77° \pm 2.00°$
2	15°	86.5 %	8.7 %	$5.12° \pm 2.55°$

line update heavily depends on the flight trajectory, as early frames do not benefit from later frames and thus many camera poses might be initially unknown.

Not only the localization rate but also the localization quality in terms of matches and pose estimation inliers is improved by using the adaptive localization. Figure 7.17(b) thus compares the mean values of unique matches (M_{unique}), inliers (I_{p3p}) and effective inliers (I_{eff}). These values considerably increase during the first update and then converge to a maximum, for both test datasets. Especially, I_{eff} is important to reliably estimate the MAVs pose, as it additionally incorporates the distribution of RANSAC inliers in an image. $\mu(I_{\text{eff}})$ increases from 9 to 12 points for *flight1*, and from 15 to 21 points for *flight2*.

The update of the model is a critical point because miss-aligned frames degrade the model quality. We expect that all localizations passing the additional validation step are correct. However, this heavily depends on the parameters th_{attitude} and th_{position}, so the residual errors have to be checked. The selection of the attitude threshold th_{attitude} was done by evaluating the valid localizations, the according drop rates by validation, and the resulting mean attitude errors $\mu(e_{\text{attitude}})$. Table 7.1 shows that for increasing th_{attitude} the ratio R_{valid} and $\mu(e_{\text{attitude}})$ increase, whereas R_{invalid} decreases. The selection of the threshold, in our case $th_{\text{attitude}} = 10°$, is a trade-off between detection rates, outlier removal, and expected IMU accuracy, and it corresponds to earlier work on comparing visual and inertial data [35]. In contrast, GPS is in our experience very noisy. We use the real-time accuracy delivered by the GPS receiver, which results in an average position threshold of $\mu(th_{\text{position}}) = 16.2$ m. It thus only acts as a sanity check for localization in models with repetitive structures.

Figure 7.18 shows the resulting camera positions after applying our approach. Initially localized cameras are depicted in gray, positions found after several batch updates are marked in red. A common source of error are frames distorted by motion blur and joggle, because only little features can be detected. Nevertheless, our proposed approach is able to handle such local failures since it automatically recovers with the next successful pose estimate. Qualitative examples for localization can be found online[1] in form of a video.

[1]http://aerial.icg.tugraz.at

Fig. 7.18 Visual localization result for an entire MAV flight. In a non-adaptive setting, we can localize 62.8 % of all frames of this dataset (*gray camera positions*). By using our technique of incremental feature updates, we are able to boost the localization performance to 83.1 %, especially for high-altitude views (*red camera positions*). ©2012 IEEE. Reprinted, with permission, from [69]

7.5.3 Comparison to Visual SLAM

We compare our approach to localization using PTAM [28], which has recently been proposed for MAV navigation [1, 4, 65, 71]. While this is an unfair comparison as PTAM has to create the map on-the-fly while we use prior knowledge, our intention is to demonstrate the significance of using prior information. Our experiments showed that the camera positions obtained by running the original PTAM code vary considerably according to the stereo initialization. Therefore, we used the recorded stream of images (with radial distortion corrected) and selected the initialization which showed best results for comparison. As the global coordinate system and the scale are not defined and differ in every execution, we aligned the camera centers of PTAM to those retrieved by our proposed algorithm in a least-squares sense.

Figure 7.19 depicts the reconstructed flight path from take-off to landing. While PTAM can compete with our approach locally, that is, in the environment it was initialized, it only returns a valid pose for 36 % of all frames. In a direct comparison to our approach, it is clearly visible that PTAM misses large parts of the flight. As soon as the track is lost, the relative pose cannot be established anymore and the localization fails. Another problem is the repetitiveness of the scene, which causes misleading model updates and inhibits successful re-localization within a larger space.

7.5.4 Comparison to Visual Groundtruth

We use the video stream showing the quad-rotor's flight from a ground observer's viewpoint as a visual groundtruth. It shares the set of virtual cameras, so we can localize the video within our scene using the same localization method as above.

(a) (b)

Fig. 7.19 Visual localization results. (**a**) *Top*: Flight path of our visual landmark-based approach with 83 % of all frames correctly localized. *Bottom*: In comparison, a state-of-the-art visual SLAM approach (PTAM [28]) is not suitable for such a large-scale outdoor environment, and achieves a localization rate of only 36 %. (**b**) The overlay of both paths shows that PTAM has lost track of its initial map at some point during the flight and is not able to recover. ©2011 IEEE. Reprinted, with permission, from [67]

(a) (b)

Fig. 7.20 Visual comparison of the localization results via registered groundtruth video stream. (**a**) Oblique view of registered groundtruth showing the current camera frame and MAV positions (*path and bounding box*) estimated by our localization approach (*red*) and the aligned PTAM result (*blue*). (**b**) Back-projected bounding box from the observer's point of view. ©2011 IEEE. Reprinted, with permission, from [67]

Under the premise of synchronized video streams and a correct current pose estimate from the quad-rotor's flight and ground observing video, the backprojection of the MAV camera center must coincide with the quad-rotor position in the observer's view.

Figure 7.20(a) shows the 3D box of the tracked quad-rotor and the respective ground video frame. We use the widespread PASCAL criterion [10] and consider

(a) (b)

Fig. 7.21 Evaluation of visual and GPS accuracies. Camera poses based on GPS, vision, and differential GPS as reference point are visualized in (**a**) a nadir view and (**b**) an oblique view. Visual localization has been performed on a visual landmark trained by *flight2* to overcome the height limitation, and performs considerably better than GPS. ©2012 IEEE. Reprinted, with permission, from [69]

the back-projected quad-rotor bounding box $\mathcal{B}_Q$ as successfully registered if the criterion,

$$\frac{\mathcal{B}_Q \bigcap \mathcal{B}_G}{\mathcal{B}_Q \bigcup \mathcal{B}_G} > 0.5 \tag{7.11}$$

is satisfied. $\mathcal{B}_G$ denotes the bounding box of the quad-rotor in the groundtruth view. By visual inspection, we conclude that the localization approach as presented in this paper satisfies the overlap criterion in all frames. This is not very surprising, as the automatic validation process using the IMU removes erroneous localizations. In contrast, visual SLAM without validation (PTAM) is only correct in 22 % of all frames. Figure 7.20(b) gives an example of the typical offset. As such an image can just give an impression, the annotated groundtruth video is again available online.

7.5.4.1 Comparison to Differential GPS

For the evaluation of the on-board sensors, we acquired images as well as GPS and IMU data at a fixed reference point. Further, at the same point we recorded groundtruth position data using a Novatel OEMV-2 L1/L2 Real-Time Kinematic (RTK) receiver with an estimated precision of 0.02 m at the time of image acquisition. Figure 7.21 depicts the results in a nadir and oblique view. The reference point has been chosen on the bridge of the atrium scene because even D-GPS was not able to measure accurate positions on the ground. The mean offset in the xy-plane for 10 measured GPS points is 9.76 ± 1.31 m, whereas the mean offset of the 10 localized cameras is 0.31 ± 0.04 m. In comparison to our previous work [69], we were able to

Table 7.2 Long-Term Localization Results: Localization based on the initial visual landmark (flight 1@0, flight 2@0) is compared to localization based on adapted visual landmarks. No further incremental updates were performed on the result.

Flight	R_{valid}	$R_{invalid}$	$\mu(M_u)$	$\mu(I_{p3p})$	$\mu(I_{eff})$
1@0	62.8 %	3.1 %	56.6	21.4	9.1
1@2	73.6 %	2.7 %	60.4	23.7	10.2
2@0	74.5 %	11.3 %	73.5	34.1	15.2
2@1	79.7 %	11.3 %	80.4	38.9	17.4

further reduce the constant offset from 0.52 m to 0.31 m by refining the calibration of the camera. The residual error depends on accurate alignment in a global coordinate system, which in turn depends on the ground sampling distance of the given digital surface model. However, we want to highlight the very good standard deviation of 4 cm in a global coordinate system given the distance to the scene of approx. 20 m; this clearly shows that visual localization is capable of outperforming GPS in urban environments.

We made another interesting observation in the course of producing these ground-truth results: Visual localization did not work for any acquired image on the atrium's bridge in a height of approx. 13 m over ground when using the initial visual landmark. Only after updating the landmark using our adaptive localization algorithm were we able to localize the MAV, which again shows that our proposed incremental update approach is beneficial.

7.5.5 Visual Landmarks for Long-Term Localization

Long-term localization represents the localization of a flight using a model that has been updated by previous flights. In this experiment, we evaluate the improvements in localization rate and quality from the initial model to an automatically adapted model. Table 7.2 shows that using a model updated by previous flights improves the detection rate by up to 17 %, and the measurements for the localization quality $\mu(M_{unique})$, $\mu(I_{p3p})$, and $\mu(I_{eff})$ are also improved.

In other words, flying several times in the same area and using the updated model of previous flights improves the localizations of the current flight and allows incremental improvement of the visual landmark. In contrast to visual SLAM, where the environment is expected to be unknown and the map is recreated for every flight, our approach is able to incorporate and propagate prior knowledge in a certain area to improve localization results. We expect that many other localization algorithms which rely on prior knowledge, such as [37], will also benefit from our findings.

7.6 Conclusion

We have presented a framework for visual localization of micro aerial vehicles in outdoor environments. Our approach makes use of metric, geo-referenced 3D models. Visual landmarks serve as prior knowledge to the MAV and allow robust, high-accuracy localization in urban environments at 4 frames per second. We have demonstrated an incremental feature update algorithm which fuses in-flight information back into the original scene model and improves localization results by up to 30 %, reaching a total localization rate of 83 % in two experiments. Convergence is ensured by comparing the visual localization to attitude and position information obtained from magnetic sensors and GPS. The ground-truth evaluation using an observer's view and a differential GPS receiver shows an excellent localization accuracy comparable to differential GPS. Our framework is applicable to long-term localization tasks in urban environments and facilitates the combination with short-term, dynamic visual SLAM in future work.

Acknowledgements This work has been supported by the Austrian Research Promotion Agency (FFG) projects FIT-IT Pegasus (825841), Construct (830035), and Holistic (830044). The authors would like to thank Arnold Irschara, Christof Hoppe, Michael Maurer, Markus Rumpler, and Christian Mostegel for contributions to earlier work on this topic.

References

1. Achtelik M, Achtelik M, Weiss S, Siegwart R (2011) Onboard IMU and monocular vision based control for MAVs in unknown in- and outdoor environments. In: IEEE international conference on robotics and vision (ICRA)
2. Agarwal S, Snavely N, Simon I, Seitz SM, Szeliski R (2009) Building Rome in a day. In: IEEE international conference on computer vision (ICCV)
3. Beder C, Steffen R (2006) Determining an initial image pair for fixing the scale of a 3d reconstruction from an image sequence. In: Proc DAGM, pp 657–666
4. Bloesch M, Weiss S, Scaramuzza D, Siegwart R (2010) Vision based MAV navigation in unknown and unstructured environments. In: IEEE international conference on robotics and vision (ICRA)
5. Boissonnat J-D, Yvinec M (1998) Algorithmic geometry. Cambridge University Press, Cambridge
6. Boykov Y, Veksler O, Zabih R (2001) Fast approximate energy minimization via graph cuts. IEEE Trans Pattern Anal Mach Intell 23(11):1222–1239
7. Collins RT (1996) A space-sweep approach to true multi-image matching. In: IEEE conference on computer vision and pattern recognition (CVPR)
8. Conway AR (1995) Autonomous control of an unstable model helicopter using carrier phase GPS only. PhD thesis, Stanford University, USA
9. Davison AJ (2003) Real-time simultaneous localisation and mapping with a single camera. In: IEEE international conference on computer vision (ICCV)
10. Everingham M, Van Gool L, Williams CKI, Winn J, Zisserman A (2007) The PASCAL visual object classes challenge 2007 results. http://www.pascal-network.org/challenges/VOC/voc2007/workshop/index.html
11. Fischler MA, Bolles RC (1981) Random sample consensus: a paradigm for model fitting with application to image analysis and automated cartography. Commun ACM 24(6):381–395

12. Frahm J-M, Georgel P, Gallup D, Johnson T, Raguram R, Wu C, Jen Y-H, Dunn E, Clipp B, Lazebnik S, Pollefeys M (2010) Building Rome on a cloudless day. In: European conference on computer vision (ECCV)
13. Frueh C, Zakhor A (2003) Constructing 3D city models by merging ground-based and airborne views. In: IEEE conference on computer vision and pattern recognition (CVPR)
14. Fukunaga K, Narendra PM (1975) A branch and bound algorithm for computing k-nearest neighbors. IEEE Trans Comput C-24(7):750–753
15. Furukawa Y, Ponce J (2009) Accurate, dense, and robust multi-view stereopsis. In: IEEE transactions on pattern analysis and machine intelligence (PAMI)
16. Golparvar Fard M, Peña-Mora F, Savarese S (2011) Monitoring changes of 3D building elements from unordered photo collections. In: IEEE international conference on computer vision (ICCV) workshops
17. Haralick RM, Lee C, Ottenberg K, Nölle M (1991) Analysis and solutions of the three point perspective pose estimation problem. In: IEEE conference on computer vision and pattern recognition (CVPR), pp 592–598
18. Hartley RI, Sturm PF (1997) Triangulation. Comput Vis Image Underst 68(2):146–157
19. Hartley RI, Zisserman A (2004) Multiple view geometry in computer vision, 2nd edn. Cambridge University Press, Cambridge
20. Hoppe C, Klopschitz M, Rumpler M, Wendel A, Kluckner S, Bischof H, Reitmayr G (2012) Online feedback for structure-from-motion image acquisition. In: British machine vision conference (BMVC)
21. Hoppe C, Wendel A, Zollmann S, Pirker K, Irschara A, Bischof H, Kluckner S (2012) Photogrammetric camera network design for micro aerial vehicles. In: Computer vision winter workshop (CVWW)
22. Hrabar S, Sukhatme G (2009) Vision-based navigation through urban canyons. J Field Robot 26:431–452
23. Huber PJ (1981) Robust statistics. Wiley, New York
24. Irschara A, Zach C, Frahm JM, Bischof H (2009) From structure-from-motion point clouds to fast location recognition. In: IEEE conference on computer vision and pattern recognition (CVPR)
25. Irschara A, Kaufmann V, Klopschitz M, Bischof H, Leberl F (2010) Towards fully automatic photogrammetric reconstruction using digital images taken from UAVs. In: Proceedings of the ISPRS symposium, 100 years ISPRS—advancing remote sensing science
26. Irschara A, Rumpler M, Meixner P, Pock T, Bischof H (2012) Efficient and globally optimal multi view dense matching for aerial images. In: ISPRS annals of photogrammetry, remote sensing and spatial information sciences
27. Kaminsky RS, Snavely N, Seitz SM, Szeliski R (2009) Alignment of 3D point clouds to overhead images. In: IEEE conference on computer vision and pattern recognition (CVPR) workshops. IEEE, pp 63–70
28. Klein G, Murray DW (2007) Parallel tracking and mapping for small AR workspaces. In: International symposium on mixed and augmented reality (ISMAR)
29. Klein G, Murray D (2008) Improving the agility of keyframe-based SLAM. In: European conference on computer vision (ECCV)
30. Klopschitz M, Irschara A, Reitmayr G, Schmalstieg D (2010) Robust incremental structure from motion. In: International symposium on 3D data processing, visualization and transmission (3DPVT)
31. Kluckner S, Birchbauer JA, Windisch C, Hoppe C, Irschara A, Wendel A, Zollmann S, Reitmayr G, Bischof H (2011) Construction site monitoring from highly-overlapping MAV images. In: IEEE international conference on advanced video- and signal-based surveillance (AVSS)
32. Kneip L, Scaramuzza D, Siegwart R (2011) A novel parametrization of the perspective-three-point problem for a direct computation of absolute camera position and orientation. In: IEEE conference on computer vision and pattern recognition (CVPR)

33. Konolige K, Bowman J (2009) Towards lifelong visual maps. In: International conference on intelligent robots and systems (IROS)
34. Labatut P, Pons JP, Keriven R (2007) Efficient multi-view reconstruction of large-scale scenes using interest points, delaunay triangulation and graph cuts. In: IEEE international conference on computer vision (ICCV)
35. Labrosse F (2006) The visual compass: performance and limitations of an appearance-based method. J Field Robot 23(10):913–941
36. Li Y, Snavely N, Huttenlocher DP (2010) Location recognition using prioritized feature matching. In: European conference on computer vision (ECCV)
37. Lim H, Sinha SN, Cohen MF, Uyttendaele M (2012) Real-time image-based 6-dof localization in large-scale environments. In: IEEE conference on computer vision and pattern recognition (CVPR)
38. Low K (2004) Linear least-squares optimization for point-to-plane ICP surface registration. Technical report, TR04-004, University of North Carolina
39. Lowe D (2004) Distinctive image features from scale-invariant keypoints. Int J Comput Vis 60(2):91–110
40. Lupashin S, Schoellig A, Sherback M, D'Andrea R (2010) A simple learning strategy for high-speed quadrocopter multi-flips. In: IEEE international conference on robotics and vision (ICRA)
41. Matthews L, Ishikawa T, Baker S (2004) The template update problem. In: IEEE transactions on pattern analysis and machine intelligence (PAMI)
42. Mei C, Sibley G, Cummins M, Newman P, Reid I (2009) A constant-time efficient stereo SLAM system. In: British machine vision conference (BMVC)
43. Mikolajczyk K, Tuytelaars T, Schmid C, Zisserman A, Matas J, Schaffalitzky F, Kadir T, Van Gool L (2005) A comparison of affine region detectors. Int J Comput Vis 65:43–72
44. Muja M, Lowe DG (2009) Fast approximate nearest neighbors with automatic algorithm configuration. In: International conference on computer vision theory and applications (VISAPP), pp 331–340
45. Newcombe RA, Davison AJ, Izadi S, Kohli P, Hilliges O, Shotton J, Molyneaux D, Hodges S, Kim D, Fitzgibbon A (2011) KinectFusion: real-time dense surface mapping and tracking. In: International symposium on mixed and augmented reality (ISMAR)
46. Nistér D (2003) An efficient solution to the five-point relative pose problem. In: IEEE conference on computer vision and pattern recognition (CVPR), pp 195–202
47. Nistér D (2004) An efficient solution to the five-point relative pose problem. IEEE Trans Pattern Anal Mach Intell 26(6):756–770
48. Nistér D, Stewenius H (2006) Scalable recognition with a vocabulary tree. In: IEEE conference on computer vision and pattern recognition (CVPR)
49. Pollefeys M, Van Gool L, Vergauwen M, Verbiest F, Cornelis K, Tops J, Koch R (2004) Visual modeling with a hand-held camera. Int J Comput Vis 59(3):207–232
50. Raguram R, Frahm J-M (2011) RECON: scale-adaptive robust estimation via residual consensus. In: IEEE international conference on computer vision (ICCV)
51. Rudol P, Wzorek M, Doherty P (2010) Vision-based pose estimation for autonomous indoor navigation of micro-scale unmanned aircraft systems. In: IEEE international conference on robotics and vision (ICRA)
52. Rumpler M, Irschara A, Wendel A, Bischof H (2012) Rapid 3d city model approximation from publicly available geographic data sources and georeferenced aerial images. In: Computer vision winter workshop (CVWW)
53. Sattler T, Leibe B, Kobbelt L (2011) Fast image-based localization using direct 2d-to-3d matching. In: IEEE international conference on computer vision (ICCV)
54. Sattler T, Weyand T, Leibe B, Kobbelt L (2012) Image retrieval for image-based localization revisited. In: British machine vision conference (BMVC)
55. Schindler G, Brown M, Szeliski R (2007) City-scale location recognition. In: IEEE conference on computer vision and pattern recognition (CVPR)

56. Schmid K, Hirschmueller H, Doemel A, Grixa I, Suppa M, Hirzinger G (2012) View planning for multi-view stereo 3d reconstruction using an autonomous multicopter. J Intell Robot Syst 65:309–323
57. Silpa Anan C, Hartley RI (2008) Optimised KD-trees for fast image descriptor matching. In: IEEE conference on computer vision and pattern recognition (CVPR)
58. Sivic J, Zisserman A (2003) Video google: a text retrieval approach to object matching in videos. In: IEEE international conference on computer vision (ICCV), pp 1470–1477
59. Snavely N, Seitz S, Szeliski R (2006) Photo tourism: exploring photo collections in 3D. In: ACM SIGGRAPH
60. Snavely N, Seitz SM, Szeliski RS (2008) Modeling the world from internet photo collections. Int J Comput Vis 80(2):189–210
61. Strasdat H, Montiel JMM, Davison AJ (2010) Real-time monocular SLAM: why filter? In: IEEE international conference on robotics and vision (ICRA)
62. Strecha C, Pylvaenaeinen T, Fua P (2010) Dynamic and scalable large scale image reconstruction. In: IEEE conference on computer vision and pattern recognition (CVPR)
63. Szeliski R (2006) Image alignment and stitching: a tutorial. Found Trends Comput Graph Vis 2(1):1–104
64. Triggs B, McLauchlan P, Hartley R, Fitzgibbon A (2000) Bundle adjustment—a modern synthesis. In: Vision algorithms: theory and practice, pp 298–375
65. Weiss S, Achtelik M, Kneip L, Scaramuzza D, Siegwart R (2011) Intuitive 3D maps for MAV terrain exploration and obstacle avoidance. J Intell Robot Syst 61:473–493
66. Wendel A, Irschara A, Bischof H (2011) Automatic alignment of 3D reconstructions using a digital surface model. In: IEEE international conference on computer vision and pattern recognition (CVPR), workshop on aerial video processing
67. Wendel A, Irschara A, Bischof H (2011) Natural landmark-based monocular localization for MAVs. In: IEEE international conference on robotics and vision (ICRA)
68. Wendel A, Hoppe C, Bischof H, Leberl F (2012) Automatic fusion of partial reconstructions. In: ISPRS annals of photogrammetry, remote sensing and spatial information sciences
69. Wendel A, Maurer M, Bischof H (2012) Visual landmark-based localization for MAVs using incremental feature updates. In: Joint 3DIM/3DPVT conference: 3D imaging, modeling, processing, visualization & transmission (3DIMPVT)
70. Wendel A, Maurer M, Graber G, Pock T, Bischof H (2012) Dense reconstruction on-the-fly. In: IEEE conference on computer vision and pattern recognition (CVPR)
71. Wendel A, Maurer M, Katusic M, Bischof H (2012) Fuzzy visual servoing for micro aerial vehicles. In: Austrian robotics workshop (ARW)
72. Wu C (2007) SiftGPU: a GPU implementation of scale invariant feature transform (SIFT). http://cs.unc.edu/~ccwu/siftgpu
73. Zamir AR, Shah M (2010) Accurate image localization based on google maps street view. In: European conference on computer vision (ECCV)
74. Zhang Z (1994) Iterative point matching for registration of free-form curves and surfaces. Int J Comput Vis 13(2):119–152
75. Zhao W, Nister D, Hsu S (2005) Alignment of continuous video onto 3D point clouds. In: IEEE transactions on pattern analysis and machine intelligence (PAMI), pp 1305–1318
76. Zhu ZW, Oskiper T, Samarasekera S, Kumar R, Sawhney HS (2008) Real-time global localization with a pre-built visual landmark database. In: IEEE conference on computer vision and pattern recognition (CVPR)
77. Zufferey J-C, Beyeler A, Floreano D (2010) Autonomous flight at low altitude with vision-based collision avoidance and GPS-based path following. In: IEEE International conference on robotics and vision (ICRA)

Chapter 8
Moment Constraints in Convex Optimization for Segmentation and Tracking

Maria Klodt, Frank Steinbrücker, and Daniel Cremers

Abstract Convex relaxation techniques have become a popular approach to shape optimization as they allow to compute solutions independent of initialization to a variety of problems. In this chapter, we will show that shape priors in terms of moment constraints can be imposed within the convex optimization framework, since they give rise to convex constraints. In particular, the lower-order moments correspond to the overall area, the centroid, and the variance or covariance of the shape and can be easily imposed in interactive segmentation methods. Respective constraints can be imposed as hard constraints or soft constraints. Quantitative segmentation studies on a variety of images demonstrate that the user can impose such constraints with a few mouse clicks, leading to substantial improvements of the resulting segmentation, and reducing the average segmentation error from 12 % to 0.35 %. GPU-based computation times of around 1 second allow for interactive segmentation.

8.1 Introduction

Shape optimization is at the heart of several classical computer vision problems such as image segmentation and multi view reconstruction. Following a series of seminal papers [1, 12, 19], functional minimization has become the established paradigm to solve shape optimization problems such as image segmentation or 3D reconstruction. In the spatially discrete setting the study of the corresponding binary labeling problems goes back to the spin-glas models introduced in the 1920s [11]. Popular algorithms to solve the arising shape optimization problems include level set methods [20], graph cuts [9] or convex relaxation [4].

M. Klodt (✉) · F. Steinbrücker · D. Cremers
Department of Informatics, TU München, Garching, Germany
e-mail: klodt@tum.de

F. Steinbrücker
e-mail: steinbrf@tum.de

D. Cremers
e-mail: cremers@tum.de

G.M. Farinella et al. (eds.), *Advanced Topics in Computer Vision*,
Advances in Computer Vision and Pattern Recognition,
DOI 10.1007/978-1-4471-5520-1_8,

In this chapter, we focus on a class of functionals of the form:

$$E(S) = \int_{\text{int}(S)} f(x)\,\mathrm{d}x + \int_S g(x)\,\mathrm{d}A, \tag{8.1}$$

where S denotes a hyper surface in $\mathbb{R}^d$, that is, a set of closed boundaries in the case of 2D image segmentation or a set of closed surfaces in the case of 3D segmentation and multi view reconstruction. The functions $f:\mathbb{R}^d \to \mathbb{R}$ and $g:\mathbb{R}^d \to \mathbb{R}^+$ are application dependent. In a statistical framework for image segmentation, for example,

$$f(x) = \log p_{\text{bg}}\big(I(x)\big) - \log p_{\text{ob}}\big(I(x)\big), \tag{8.2}$$

may denote the log likelihood ratio for observing the color $I(x)$ at a point x given that x is part of the background or the object, respectively. A common choice for g is the function

$$g(x) = \frac{1}{1+\beta|\nabla I_\sigma(x)|^2} \tag{8.3}$$

with suitable choices for the parameters β and σ. Here, I_σ is a Gaussian smoothed version of the input image.

The second term in (8.1) corresponds to the area (for $d = 3$) or the boundary length (for $d = 2$), measured in a metric given by the function g. In the context of image segmentation, g may be a measure of the local edge strength—as in the geodesic active contours [3, 13]—which energetically favors segmentation boundaries along strong intensity gradients. In the context of multi view reconstruction, $g(x)$ typically measures the photo-consistency among different views of the voxel x, where low values of g indicate a strong agreement from different cameras on the observed patch intensity (Fig. 8.1).

8.1.1 Shape Priors for Image Segmentation

There has been much research on imposing prior shape knowledge into image segmentation. While it was shown that segmentation results can be substantially improved by imposing shape priors [5, 8, 10], existing approaches typically suffer from the following problems:

- Apart from a few exceptions such as [23]—computable solutions are only *locally* optimal. As a consequence, one typically needs appropriate initializations and solutions may be arbitrarily far from the globally optimal ones. Other notable exceptions were designed by Veksler and coworkers for specific scenarios such as "compact objects" [6] or "star-shaped objects" [25].
- Many shape priors have a rather fine granularity in the sense that they impose the object silhouette to be consistent with those silhouettes observed in a training set [5, 7]. The degree of abstraction is typically rather small. In particular, deviations of the observed shape from the training shapes are (elastically) suppressed by the

Fig. 8.1 We propose a convex formulation for interactive image segmentation which allows to impose constraints on moments of arbitrary order. In particular, constraints on the lower order moments (area, centroid, covariance) are easily transmitted through mouse interaction (*left*). They allow to stabilize the segmentation process while preserving fine-scale details of the shape (*right*)

shape prior. This is particularly undesirable in medical image segmentation where malformations of organs (that make it deviate from the training shapes of healthy organs) should be detected rather than ignored. It may therefore be of interest to merely impose some coarse-level shape information rather that imposing the exact form of the object.

An alternative approach that may provide a remedy for both of the above problems is to impose moment constraints. In particular, the lower-order moments allow to constrain the area/volume, the centroid and the size or covariance of objects without imposing any constraints on their local shape. A related idea of using *Legendre moments* (albeit in a local optimization scheme) was developed in [8].

In a convex formulation of multiple view 3D reconstruction, it was recently shown [15] that one can impose additional convex constraints which assure that the computed minimal surfaces are silhouette-consistent. Essentially this constraint can be seen as a *volume constraint*: The volume along any ray from the camera center must be at least 1 if that ray passes through the silhouette and zero otherwise. In the two-dimensional case, a related constraint was recently proposed as a bounding box prior for image segmentation [17].

8.1.2 Contribution

We show that one can impose an entire family of moment constraints in the framework of convex shape optimization, thereby generalizing from the zeroth order moment (volume) to higher order moments (centroid, scale, covariance, etc). In particular, all moment constraints—both soft or hard—correspond to convex constraints.

As a consequence we can compute moment-constrained shapes which are independent of initialization and lie within a bound of the optimum.

The outline of the paper is as follows. In Sect. 8.2, we will briefly review a framework for convex relaxation and thresholding which allows to efficiently compute global minima of the above energies in a spatially continuous setting. In Sect. 8.3, we will then show that moment constraints can be imposed as convex constraints within the optimization framework. In Sect. 8.4, we show how the arising optimization problem can be minimized using efficient GPU-accelerated PDE solving. We will furthermore show that computing projections onto the moment constraint sets reduces to solving systems of linear equations. Section 8.5 shows how the presented method for image segmentation with moment constraints can be extended to a method for object tracking in videos. In Sect. 8.6, we present experimental results and a quantitative evaluation showing that interactive segmentation results can be drastically improved using moment constraints.

8.2 Shape Optimization via Convex Relaxation

Functionals of the form (8.1) can be globally optimized in a spatially continuous setting by means of convex relaxation and thresholding [4]. To this end, one reverts to an implicit representation of the hyper surface S using an indicator function $u \in BV(\mathbb{R}^d; \{0, 1\})$ on the space of binary functions of bounded variation, where $u = 1$ and $u = 0$ denote the interior and exterior of S. The functional (8.1) defined on the space of surfaces S is therefore equivalent to the functional

$$E(u) = \int_{\Omega} f(x)u(x)\,\mathrm{d}x + \int_{\Omega} g(x)\big|Du(x)\big|, \tag{8.4}$$

where the second term in (8.4) is the weighted total variation. Here Du denotes the distributional derivative which for differentiable functions u boils down to $Du(x) = \nabla u(x)\,\mathrm{d}x$. By relaxing the binary constraint and allowing the function u to take on values in the interval between 0 and 1, the optimization problem becomes that of minimizing the convex functional (8.4) over the convex set $BV(\mathbb{R}^d; [0, 1])$. Global minimizers u^* of this relaxed problem can therefore efficiently be computed, for example by a simple gradient descent procedure.

The thresholding theorem [4] assures that thresholding the solution u^* of the relaxed problem preserves global optimality for the original binary labeling problem. We can therefore compute global minimizers for functional (8.4) in a spatially continuous setting as follows: Compute a global minimizer u^* of (8.4) on the convex set $BV(\mathbb{R}^d; [0, 1])$ and threshold the minimizer u^* at any value $\mu \in (0, 1)$.

The following theorem [4] assures that thresholding the solution u^* of the relaxed problem provides a minimizer of the original binary labeling problem (8.4), in other words the convex relaxation preserves global optimality for the original binary labeling problem.

Theorem 8.1 *Let $u^* \in BV(\mathbb{R}^d; [0, 1])$ be a global minimizer of the functional* (8.4). *Then all upper level sets* (*i.e. thresholded versions*)

$$\Sigma_{\mu,u^*} = \{x \in \mathbb{R}^d \mid u^*(x) > \mu\}, \quad \mu \in (0, 1), \tag{8.5}$$

of u^* are minimizers of the original binary labeling problem (8.1).

Proof Using the layer cake representation of the function $u^* \in BV(\mathbb{R}^d; [0, 1])$:

$$u^*(x) = \int_0^1 1_{\Sigma_{\mu,u*}} \, \mathrm{d}\mu \tag{8.6}$$

we can rewrite the first term in the functional (8.4) as

$$\int_{\mathbb{R}}^d f u^* \, \mathrm{d}x = \int_{\mathbb{R}}^d f \left(\int_0^1 1_{\Sigma_{\mu,x}} \, \mathrm{d}\mu \right) \mathrm{d}x = \int_0^1 \int_{\Sigma_{\mu,u^*}} f(x) \, \mathrm{d}x. \tag{8.7}$$

As a consequence, the functional (8.4) takes on the form:

$$E(u^*) = \int_0^1 \left\{ \int_{\Sigma_{\mu,u^*}} f \, \mathrm{d}x + |\partial \Sigma_{\mu,u^*}|_g \right\} \mathrm{d}\mu \equiv \int_0^1 \widehat{E}(\Sigma_{\mu,u^*}) \, \mathrm{d}\mu, \tag{8.8}$$

where we have used the coarea formula to express the weighted total variation norm in (8.4) as the integral over the length of all level lines of u measured in the norm induced by g. Clearly the functional (8.8) is now merely an integral of the original binary labeling problem $\widehat{E}$ applied to the upper level sets of u^*.

Assume that for some threshold value $\tilde{\mu} \in (0, 1)$ Theorem 8.1 was not true, that is, there exists a minimizer Σ^* of the binary labeling problem with smaller energy:

$$\widehat{E}(\Sigma^*) < \widehat{E}(\Sigma_{\tilde{\mu},u^*}). \tag{8.9}$$

Then—using continuity arguments—we have for the indicator function $1_{\Sigma*}$ of the set Σ^*:

$$E(1_{\Sigma*}) = \int_0^1 \widehat{E}(\Sigma^*) \, \mathrm{d}\mu < \int_0^1 \widehat{E}(\Sigma_{\mu,u^*}) \, \mathrm{d}\mu = E(u^*), \tag{8.10}$$

which contradicts the assumption that u^* was a global minimizer of (8.4). □

The above theorem allows to compute global minimizers of the functional (8.4) in a spatially continuous setting as follows:

1. Compute a global minimizer u^* of (8.4) on the convex set $BV(\mathbb{R}^d; [0, 1])$.
2. Threshold the minimizer u^* at any value $\mu \in (0, 1)$ to obtain a binary solution of the original shape optimization problem.

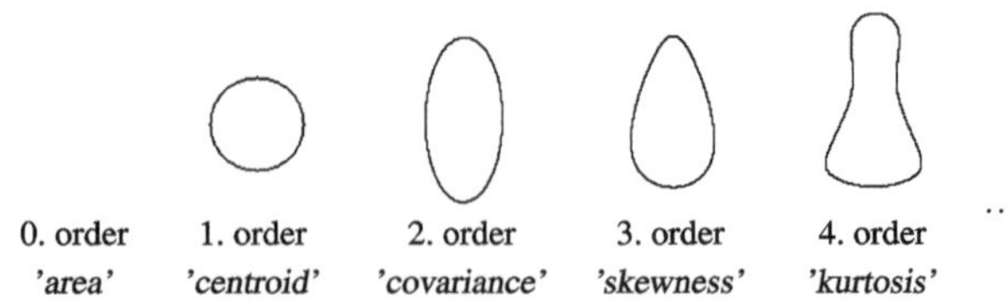

Fig. 8.2 2D central moments of a shape. With increasing order of the moment more details of the shape can be described

8.3 Moment Constraints for Segmentation

In the following, we will describe the moment constraints presented in [14]. We will successively constrain the moments of the segmentation and show how all of these constraints give rise to nested convex sets. To this end, we will represent shapes in d dimensions as binary indicator functions $u \in BV(\Omega; \{0,1\})$ of bounded variation on the domain $\Omega \subset \mathbb{R}^d$. We will denote the convex hull of this set by $\mathcal{B} = BV(\Omega; [0,1])$.

Figure 8.2 shows examples for the first five 2D central moments of a shape. The first order moment describes the centroid of a shape, the second describes the covariance, that is, the relation between width and height of an object. While with the third order moment egg-shapes of shapes can be described, for the fourth order moments the effect on the shape already becomes less intuitive. The figure shows how the higher the order of a moment, the more sophisticated properties can be imposed on the corresponding shape. In the following, we will show how these moments can be used to constrain properties of shapes for segmentation in a convex framework, and how especially the lower order moments can constrain shape optimization in a very intuitive way.

8.3.1 Area Constraint

We can impose that the area of the shape u to be bounded by a constant $c \in \mathbb{R}^+$ by constraining u to lie in the set:

$$\mathcal{C}_0 = \left\{ u \in \mathcal{B} \;\Big|\; \int_\Omega u \,\mathrm{d}x = c \right\}. \tag{8.11}$$

In the case of a 3 dimensional domain Ω, the constant c constrains the volume of a shape.

Proposition 8.1 *For any constant $c \geq 0$, the set $\mathcal{C}_0$ is convex.*

Proof Let $u_1, u_2 \in \mathcal{C}_0$ be two elements from this set. Then for any convex combination $u_\alpha = \alpha u_1 + (1-\alpha)u_2$, $\alpha \in [0,1]$ of these elements we have:

$$\int_\Omega u_\alpha \,\mathrm{d}x = \alpha \int_\Omega u_1 \,\mathrm{d}x + (1-\alpha) \int_\Omega u_2 \,\mathrm{d}x. \tag{8.12}$$

As a consequence, we have $\int_\Omega u_\alpha \,\mathrm{d}x = c$ such that $u_\alpha \in \mathcal{C}_0$. □

In practice, we can either impose an exact area or we can impose upper and lower bounds on the area with two constants $c_1 \leq c_2$ and constrain the area to lie in the range $[c_1, c_2]$

Alternatively, we can impose a soft area constraint by enhancing the functional (8.4) as follows:

$$E_0(u, \lambda_0) = E(u) + \lambda_0 \left(\int u \, \mathrm{d}x - c \right)^2, \tag{8.13}$$

which imposes a soft constraint with a weight $\lambda_0 > 0$ favoring the area of the estimated shape to be near $c \geq 0$. Clearly, the functional (8.13) is also convex.

8.3.2 Centroid Constraint

Assume that someone gave us some bounds about the centroid (center of gravity) for the object we want to reconstruct. We can impose the centroid of the shape by constraining the solution u to the set $\mathcal{C}_1$:

$$\mathcal{C}_1 = \left\{ u \in \mathcal{B} \,\middle|\, \frac{\int_\Omega x u \, \mathrm{d}x}{\int_\Omega u \, \mathrm{d}x} = \mu \right\}, \tag{8.14}$$

where equality is to be taken point wise and $\mu \in \mathbb{R}^d$. Alternatively, we can impose the centroid to lie between two constants $\mu_1, \mu_2 \in \mathbb{R}^d$. For $\mu_1 = \mu_2$, the centroid is fixed. $\mathcal{C}_1$ contains all shapes whose first order moment is μ. In probability theory, the first order moment is also called the expected value.

Proposition 8.2 *For any constant $\mu \geq 0$, the set $\mathcal{C}_1$ is convex.*

Proof The equality constraint in (8.14) is equivalent to

$$\int_\Omega x u \, \mathrm{d}x = \mu \int_\Omega u \, \mathrm{d}x, \tag{8.15}$$

which is clearly a linear constraint. □

Reformulating the constraint equation in (8.14) leads to

$$\int_\Omega (\mu - x) u \, \mathrm{d}x = 0, \tag{8.16}$$

allowing us to impose the centroid as a soft constraint by minimizing the energy:

$$E_1(u, \lambda_1) = E(u) + \lambda_1 \left(\int_\Omega (\mu - x) u \, \mathrm{d}x \right)^2. \tag{8.17}$$

Energy (8.17) is also convex in u. Interestingly this soft constraint does not minimize the quadratic difference to the specified center μ; the latter would not be convex. In contrast to the hard constraint, this soft constraint unfortunately exhibits a preference toward smaller shapes as it vanishes with decreasing object size:

$$\left(\int_\Omega (\mu - x)u\,\mathrm{d}x\right)^2 = \left(\mu - \frac{\int_\Omega xu\,\mathrm{d}x}{\int_\Omega u\,\mathrm{d}x}\right)^2 b^2, \tag{8.18}$$

where $b = \int u\,\mathrm{d}x$ denotes the size of the object.

8.3.3 Covariance Constraint

The proposed concept can be generalized to moments of successively higher order, where we shall focus on so-called central moments (i.e., moments with respect to a specified centroid). In particular, the respective structures will generally be tensors of higher dimension. One can impose the covariance structure by considering the following convex set:

$$\mathcal{C}_2 = \left\{u \in \mathcal{B} \mid \frac{\int_\Omega (x-\mu)(x-\mu)^\top u\,\mathrm{d}x}{\int_\Omega u\,\mathrm{d}x} = A\right\}, \tag{8.19}$$

where the equality constraint should be taken element wise. Here $\mu \in \mathbb{R}^d$ denotes the center and $A \in \mathbb{R}^{d\times d}$ denotes a symmetric matrix. Alternatively, we can impose the covariance to lie in a range between two symmetric matrices $A_1, A_2 \in \mathbb{R}^{d\times d}$ such that $A_1 \leq A_2$ element-wise. Constraining the covariance, that is, the second order moment, we are able to constrain the relation between width and height of an object. This constraint is particularly meaningful if one additionally constrains the centroid to be μ, that is, considers the intersection of the set (8.19) with a set of the form (8.14).

Proposition 8.3 *For any constant $A \geq 0$, the set $\mathcal{C}_2$ is convex.*

Proof The proof is analogous to that of Proposition 8.2. □

We can derive the corresponding soft constraint on the covariance matrix by adding a respective term to the original energy:

$$E_2(u, \lambda_2) = E(u) + \lambda_2\left(\int_\Omega \left(A - (x-\mu)(x-\mu)^\top\right)u\,\mathrm{d}x\right)^2. \tag{8.20}$$

Note that this allows, in particular, to constrain the scale σ of the object, because:

$$\sigma^2 = \frac{\int_\Omega (x-\mu)^2 u\,\mathrm{d}x}{\int_\Omega u\,\mathrm{d}x} = \operatorname{tr}\frac{\int_\Omega (x-\mu)(x-\mu)^\top u\,\mathrm{d}x}{\int_\Omega u\,\mathrm{d}x}. \tag{8.21}$$

(a)	(b)	(c)	(d)	(e)	(f)	(g)	(h)
Input	no constr.	0th order	up to 1st	up to 2nd	up to 3rd	up to 6th	up to 12th

Fig. 8.3 Segmentation results with higher order moment constraints: By imposing constraints of increasing order (up to 12th order), more and more fine scale details of the shape are restored

From the constraint in (8.19), it follows that:

$$\mathrm{tr}(A_1) \leq \sigma^2 \leq \mathrm{tr}(A_2). \tag{8.22}$$

Here, tr denotes the trace of a matrix.

8.3.4 Higher Order Moment Constraints

In general, we can impose constraints on moments of any order $k \in \mathbb{N}$:

$$\mathcal{C}_k = \left\{ u \in \mathcal{B} \;\Big|\; \frac{\int_\Omega (x_1 - \mu_1)^{i_1} \dots (x_d - \mu_d)^{i_d} u \,\mathrm{d}x}{\int_\Omega u \,\mathrm{d}x} = a_{i_1 \dots i_d} \right\}, \tag{8.23}$$

where $i_1 + \dots + i_d = k$ and $a_{i_1 \dots i_d}$ can be chosen arbitrarily to constrain the moment tensor of order k. Here x_i and μ_i denotes the ith component of x and μ, respectively.

Proposition 8.4 *For all* $i_1, \dots, i_d \in \mathbb{N}$ *and for any constants* $a_{i_1 \dots i_d} \leq b_{i_1 \dots i_d}$, *the set* $\mathcal{C}_{i_1 \dots i_d}$ *is convex.*

Proof The proof is analogous to that of Proposition 8.2. □

The above properties allow to impose various constraints on the shape associated with the indicator function u. Imposing more and more constraints of increasingly higher order leads to a smaller and smaller intersection of the associated convex sets as a feasible domain of the shape and a corresponding hierarchy of shape details being imposed in the segmentation. How much shape detail can one impose in this manner?

Proposition 8.5 *Similarity to any given shape can be imposed at arbitrary detail by imposing convex moment constraints of increasingly higher order.*

Proof According to the uniqueness theorem of moments [21], the function u is uniquely defined by its moment sequence. □

Figure 8.3 shows an example of segmentations with high order moment constraints: While the higher-order moments allow to recover fine-scale shape details, the shape improvements due to higher order constraints are fairly small. Furthermore imposing moments of higher order is not very practical: First, the user cannot estimate these moments visually. Second, the user cannot transmit respective higher-order tensors through a simple mouse interaction. Instead, having the image data determine the shape's fine scale structure turns out to be far more useful.

Figure 8.3(a) shows the manually segmented input shape which is used to compute color histograms for foreground and background, as well as the moments that constrain the subsequent image segmentation. Figure 8.3(b) shows that color-only segmentation based on color histograms for foreground and background is not sufficient in this example image to correctly segment one red pepper from the others. Figure 8.3(c)–(e) show that the first three moment constraints—area, centroid and covariance—are able to substantially improve segmentations, however are in this hard case, not enough for an exact segmentation. In Fig. 8.3(f)–(h), we can see how with increasing order of moment constraints more and more fine scale details of the shape can be reconstructed. Even the 12th order moment constraint still results in an improvement of segmentation.

In the example of Fig. 8.3, the respective higher order moment constraints have been learned from a training shape. For interactive applications however, the higher order moments are too less intuitive to be applicable. Therefore, for the application we consider—namely interactive image segmentation—we shall in the following limit ourselves to imposing moments up to 2nd order (area/volume, center of mass, scale and covariance).

8.4 Shape Optimization with Moment Constraints

Shape optimization and image segmentation with respective moment constraints can now be done by minimizing convex energies under respective convex constraints.

Let $\mathcal{C}$ be a specific convex set containing knowledge about respective moments of the desired shape—given by an intersection of the above convex sets. Then we can compute segmentations by solving the convex optimization problem

$$\min_{u \in \mathcal{C}} E(u), \tag{8.24}$$

with $E(u)$ given in (8.4). In this work, we solve the Euler–Lagrange equation:

$$0 = \operatorname{div}\left(g \frac{\nabla u}{|\nabla u|} \right) - f. \tag{8.25}$$

The equation system can be solved using gradient descent, or the lagged diffusivity approach that was presented in [16]. We use the latter because in our experiments it achieves a speed up of computation times of a factor of $\sim$5. An update step for u at pixel i and time step k yields

$$\begin{aligned} u_i^{l,k+1} &= (1-\omega) u_i^{l,k} \\ &\quad + \omega \frac{\nu \sum_{j \in \mathcal{N}(i), j<i} g \cdot g_{i\sim j}^l u_j^{l,k+1} + \nu \sum_{j \in \mathcal{N}(i), j>i} g \cdot g_{i\sim j}^l u_j^{l,k} - f_i}{\nu \sum_{j \in \mathcal{N}(i)} g \cdot g_{i\sim j}^l}, \end{aligned} \tag{8.26}$$

where $g^l_{i\sim j}$ is the diffusivity between pixel i and j, and $\mathcal{N}(i)$ is the 4-connected neighborhood around i. The method converges for overrelaxation parameters $\omega \in (0, 2)$. We obtained the fastest convergence rate for $\omega = 1.85$.

In the case of segmentation without moment constraints, there is only the constraint that $u \in \mathcal{B}$, where we project u such that $u \in [0, 1]$. This constraint can be enforced by clipping the values of u at every point x after each iteration:

$$u(x) = \begin{cases} 0 & \text{if } u(x) < 0, \\ u(x) & \text{if } 0 \leq u(x) \leq 1, \\ 1 & \text{if } 1 < u(x). \end{cases} \tag{8.27}$$

8.4.1 Minimization with Soft Constraints

Soft constraints are implemented by adding additional terms to the cost function, as has been done in (8.13), (8.17) and (8.20). Minimization is then performed by computing the corresponding Euler–Lagrange equations with the additional terms. This leads to solutions that prefer shapes that fulfill the constraints, but do not necessarily exactly fulfill them.

For the area constraint, the corresponding Euler–Lagrange equation is computed by derivation of (8.13). We obtain the equation system:

$$0 = \operatorname{div}\left(g \frac{\nabla u}{|\nabla u|}\right) - f - 2\lambda_0 \left(\int_\Omega u - \frac{c}{|\Omega|} \, \mathrm{d}x\right). \tag{8.28}$$

Note that the area update term for u is equal for all points in Ω since the last term is completely independent of x. A positive value is added in the case that the area of the current segmentation is smaller than the desired area constraint, and a negative value in the case that it is greater. The term is zero in the case that the constraint is exactly fulfilled. The constraint parameter c is divided by the size of the image domain $\int_\Omega \mathrm{d}x = |\Omega|$ in order to equally distribute the update value over all points.

The centroid soft constraint (8.17) yields an Euler–Lagrange equation where the update term for the centroid constraint is dependent on the location of x:

$$0 = \operatorname{div}\left(g \frac{\nabla u}{|\nabla u|}\right) - f - 2\sum_{i=1}^{d} \lambda_{1i} \left(\int_\Omega (\mu_i - x_i) u \, \mathrm{d}x \, (\mu_i - x_i)\right), \tag{8.29}$$

where μ_i and x_i denote the ith elements of vectors μ and x. Note that it yields d additional terms to the equation system, as well as d additional optimization parameters $\lambda_{11}, \dots, \lambda_{1d}$.

Similar functions can be derived for the soft covariance and higher order moment constraints. The corresponding Euler–Lagrange term for an arbitrary moment of order k gives the following more general formulation:

$$0=-2\sum_{i_1=1}^{d}\cdots\sum_{i_k=1}^{d}\lambda_{ki_1i_k}\left[\int_{\Omega}\left(a_{i_1\dots i_k}-\prod_{l=1}^{k}(\mu_{i_l}-x_{i_l})\right)u\,\mathrm{d}x\left(a_{i_1\dots i_k}-\prod_{l=1}^{k}(\mu_{i_l}-x_{i_l})\right)\right].$$

In this formulation, some terms appear multiple times. This is due to the fact that for all permutations σ of $i_1 \dots i_k$ we have $a_{i_1\dots i_k} = a_{\sigma(i_1)\dots\sigma(i_k)}$, because of the symmetry of the constraint tensors.

For all soft constraints, the additional parameters $\lambda_{k1}, \dots, \lambda_{kd}$ have to be optimized, with k being the order of the respective moment.

8.4.2 Computing Projections to Moment Constraint Sets

The moment hard constraints can be implemented by projecting onto the constraint sets during optimization. In our implementation we prefer the projection method over soft constraints, because firstly the constraints can be fulfilled exactly, and secondly there are no additional parameters that need to be optimized.

In the case of moment hard constraints, we enforce all constraints during the optimization by back-projecting the current segmentation onto the constraint set after every iteration. Segmentations u are projected onto the intersection of two convex sets:

1. the convex set [0, 1] and
2. the intersection of the respective moment constraints.

Since all moment constraints presented in this chapter are linear in u an orthogonal projection can be directly computed for all combinations of moment constraints. Hence, iterative projections are needed between two sets only—independent of the order or the number of moment constraints. In the following, we will show how these projections can be easily computed and implemented. A special case arises in the case of the area constraint, because the projection can be computed in a single step. In all other cases, we use the algorithm of [2] to iteratively project onto the intersection of the convex sets.

8.4.2.1 Projection to Area Constraint

The projection onto the range [0, 1] and onto the area constraint in (8.11) can be combined in one step.

For any $u_0 \in \mathcal{B}$, the projection u onto those constraints has to solve the convex program

$$\begin{aligned} u = \arg\min_{v\in\mathcal{B}} &\frac{1}{2}\|v-u_0\|_2^2 \\ \text{s.t.}\quad v(x)-1 &\le 0 \quad \forall x \\ -v(x) &\le 0 \quad \forall x \\ \|v\|_1 - c &= 0 \end{aligned}$$

By means of the Karush–Kuhn–Tucker conditions for convex problems, if we can find the functions u, ξ_1, and ξ_0 and a scalar ν that fulfil the following conditions

$$u(x) - u_0(x) + \xi_1(x) - \xi_0(x) + \nu = 0 \quad \forall x \tag{8.30}$$

$$u(x) \leq 1 \wedge \xi_1(x) \geq 0 \quad \forall x \tag{8.31}$$

$$u(x) \geq 0 \wedge \xi_0(x) \geq 0 \quad \forall x \tag{8.32}$$

$$\xi_1(x) = 0 \vee u(x) = 1 \quad \forall x \tag{8.33}$$

$$\xi_0(x) = 0 \vee u(x) = 0 \quad \forall x \tag{8.34}$$

$$\|u\|_1 = c, \tag{8.35}$$

then u is the correct projection.

With the following method we can find a solution for the conditions above:

1. Set $u := u_0$, $\xi_1 := 0$, $\xi_0 := 0$, $\nu := 0$
2. On all positions where $u(x) > 1$, set $u(x) := 1$, $\xi_1(x) := u_0(x) - 1$
3. On all positions where $u(x) < 0$, set $u(x) := 0$, $\xi_0(x) := -u_0(x)$

All constraints but the area constraint are now fulfilled.

Without loss of generality, let the projection of u_0 to $[0, 1]$ have a smaller norm than c. If not, set $u_2(x) := 1 - u(x)$ and $c_2 := \|\Omega\| - c$, switch ξ_0 and ξ_1, perform the projection onto the volume c_2 as described in the following, and afterwards again reflect u_2 at 1 and switch ξ_0 and ξ_1.

To fulfill the area constraint (8.35), we can now raise the sum $u(x) + \xi_1(x) - \xi_0(x)$ by the same amount in all pixels, and adjust ν such that (8.30) is fulfilled. If $0 < u(x) < 1$, raise $u(x)$, if $u(x) = 1$, raise $\xi_1(x)$, if $\xi_0(x) > 0$, lower $\xi_0(x)$.

Unfortunately, the difference ν is nontrivial, because the area constraint (8.35) depends on u, not on $u + \xi_1 - \xi_0$. Therefore, we have to employ Algorithm 1: Afterwards, we have to adjust the last iteration, if $\Delta_c < 0$. This algorithm computes the desired projection and it does not require to explicitly store ξ_0 and ξ_1, as the sum in (8.30) can be stored in one field u and the checks in the algorithm above can be performed on u as well. Unfortunately though, the algorithm requires several $O(n)$ computations in the regression to find the minima and in the update steps.

However, if we sort the discrete pixel positions by their value u_0, and remap them after the projection, the projection can be performed very easily with Algorithm 2. Let us assume now, that u_0 is stacked to a vector and monotonically decreasing in x from pixel $x = 1$ to pixel $x = |\Omega|$.

Figure 8.4 demonstrates the input and output of Algorithm 2, assuming that u_0 and u are sorted in decreasing order. The optimal value ν that needs to be added to u_0 in order to fulfill both the area constraint $\int u \, dx = c$ and the constraint $u \in [0, 1]$, is computed in one step of Algorithm 2.

After Algorithm 2 terminates, we simply subtract ν from $u_0(x)$ in every pixel to get u, x, clamp u to $[0, 1]$ and put the difference into the (virtual) ξ_0 and ξ_1.

Algorithm 1 Simple projection algorithm

$\nu \leftarrow 0$
$\Delta_c \leftarrow c - \|u\|$
while $\Delta_c > 0$ **do**
  $\Delta_u \leftarrow \min\{\min_{\{x\in\Omega|\xi_0(x)>0\}}\{\xi_0(x)\}, \min_{\{x\in\Omega|u(x)<1\}}\{1-u(x)\}\}$
  $\Delta_k \leftarrow 0$
  for all $x \in \Omega$ **do**
    if $\xi_0(x) > 0$ **then**
      $\xi_0(x) \leftarrow \xi_0(x) - \Delta_u$
    else if $u(x) < 1$ **then**
      $u(x) \leftarrow u(x) + \Delta_u$
      $\Delta_k \leftarrow \Delta_k + \Delta_u$
    else
      $\xi_1(x) \leftarrow \xi_1(x) + \Delta_u$
    end if
    $\nu \leftarrow \nu + \Delta_u$
  end for
  $\Delta_c \leftarrow \Delta_c - \Delta_k$
end while

Algorithm 2 Projection algorithm with sorting

$\nu \leftarrow 0$
$\Delta_c \leftarrow c - \|u_0\|$
$x_1 \leftarrow \min\{x|u_0(x) < 1\}$
$x_2 \leftarrow \min\{x|u_0(x) < 0\}$
while $\Delta_c > 0$ **do**
  $\Delta_1 \leftarrow 1 - u_0(x_1) + \nu$
  $\Delta_2 \leftarrow -u_0(x_2) + \nu$
  if $\Delta_1 > \Delta_2$ **then**
    $\nu \leftarrow \nu - \min\{\Delta_2, \frac{\Delta_c}{x_2-x_1}\}$
    $\Delta_c \leftarrow \Delta_c - \min\{(x_2-x_1)\Delta_2, \Delta_c\}$
    $x_2 \leftarrow \min\{x|u_0(x) - \nu < 0\}$
  else
    $\nu \leftarrow \nu - \min\{\Delta_1, \frac{\Delta_c}{x_2-x_1}\}$
    $\Delta_c \leftarrow \Delta_c - \min\{(x_2-x_1)\Delta_1, \Delta_c\}$
    $x_1 \leftarrow \min\{x|u_0(x) - \nu < 1\}$
  end if
end while

Now all KKT conditions are fulfilled and u is the desired projection. Note that every assignment in the algorithm is performed at most $2n$ times and the algorithm only requires constant memory. Therefore, its complexity is dominated by the sorting algorithm.

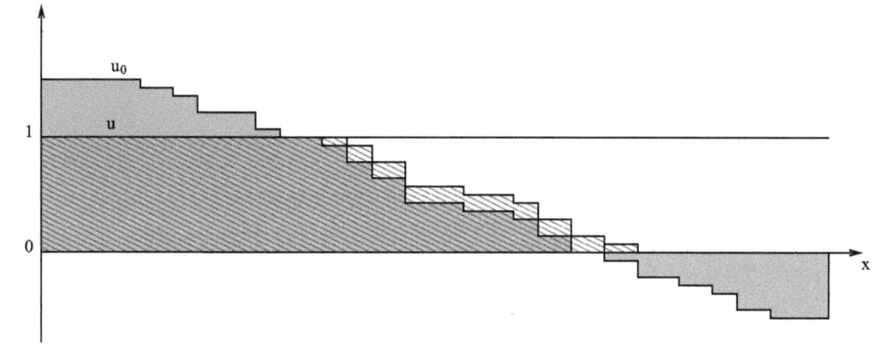

Fig. 8.4 Area of u before and after applying Algorithm 2. The *gray area* denotes the area before the projection: neither the area constraint $\int u\,\mathrm{d}x = c$ nor the constraint $u \in [0, 1]$ is fulfilled. The *shaded area* shows the area of u after projection: both constraints are fulfilled after two steps of the algorithm

8.4.2.2 Projection to Higher Order Moment Constraints

For moments of an order higher than 0, we use the method of [2] to iteratively compute projections of u onto the intersection of the convex set $[0, 1]$ and the linear moment constraints. The algorithm of [2] projects to the intersection of convex sets by alternatingly projecting to the respective sets. The correct solution is found by remembering the previous projection for each step. This leads to an algorithm that converges to the solution, although slow.

We can summarize all projections to an arbitrary number of moment constraints in one projection step because all moment constraints are linear sets. Hence, we project between the two sets $[0, 1]$ and the intersection of the moment constraints.

Centroid Constraint We will in the following show the projection formula for the centroid constraint.

An equivalent formulation of (8.14) is the constraint set

$$\mathcal{C}_1 = \left\{ u \in \mathcal{B} \;\middle|\; \int_\Omega (\mu_i - x_i)\, u\,\mathrm{d}x = 0, \forall 1 \le i \le d \right\}. \tag{8.36}$$

We are looking for the orthogonal projection $\hat{m}$ that projects u to the nearest $\hat{u}$ in $\mathcal{C}_1$ s.t. $\hat{u} = u + \hat{m}$. Since $\mathcal{C}_1$ is linear in u this projection is unique. We have

$$\hat{m} = \arg\min_{m \in \mathcal{M}} \|m\| \tag{8.37}$$

with

$$\mathcal{M} = \left\{ m \in \mathcal{B} \;\middle|\; \int_\Omega (\mu_i - x_i)\, m\,\mathrm{d}x = -\int_\Omega (\mu_i - x_i)\, u\,\mathrm{d}x, \forall 1 \le i \le d \right\}. \tag{8.38}$$

The left-hand sides of the constraint equations in $\mathcal{M}$ are linear in m, and the right-hand sides are constants (independent of m).

Then the following projection theorem [18] holds.

Theorem 8.2 *The orthogonal projection* $\hat{m}$ *(projection of minimum norm) to a set of constraints* $(m, y_i) = c_i, \forall 1 \leq i \leq d$ *is given by*

$$\hat{m} = \sum_{i=1}^{d} \beta_i y_i \tag{8.39}$$

where the coefficients $\beta_i \in \mathbb{R}$ *are the solution to the linear equation system*

$$(y_1, y_i)\beta_1 + \cdots + (y_d, y_i)\beta_d = c_i. \tag{8.40}$$

Proof A proof can be found in [18]. □

In our case, the y_i and c_i are given by

$$y_i = \mu_i - x_i, \quad c_i = -\int_{\Omega} (\mu_i - x_i)\, u \,\mathrm{d}x, \quad \forall 1 \leq i \leq d, \tag{8.41}$$

reducing the problem to solving a linear system of equations of the size $d \times d$ to obtain the coefficients $\beta_1, \ldots, \beta_d$ and the resulting projection is

$$\hat{m} = \sum_{i=1}^{d} \beta_i (\mu_i - x_i). \tag{8.42}$$

This means in particular, that points that have a high distance to the constraint centroid μ, get assigned a higher value to change. The reason is the orthogonal projection that finds a projection where the smallest change in u is achieved that fulfills the constraint. Points with a high distance to μ contribute higher values to the sum (8.42).

Covariance Constraint Similarly, we can compute the projection to the covariance constraint which yields

$$\hat{m} = \sum_{i=1}^{d} \sum_{j=1}^{d} \beta_{ij} \big(a_{ij} - (\mu_i - x_i)(\mu_j - x_j)\big), \tag{8.43}$$

where a_{ij} are the entries of constraint matrix A. Here we solve a $d^2 \times d^2$ system of linear equations to obtain the coefficients β_{ij}. If we exploit the symmetry of A and merge terms that appear duplicate times in the sum, the number of coefficients reduces to

$$d' = \sum_{i=1}^{d} \sum_{j=i}^{d} 1 = \frac{1}{2} d(d+1), \tag{8.44}$$

which is still in the same complexity class $O(d^2)$, however reduces the number of coefficients that need to be computed by a factor of almost 2.

Moment Constraints of Arbitrary Order Higher order moment constraints and combinations of different order moment constraints can be computed in an analogous way.

The general projection for a moment of order k can be computed by

$$\hat{m} = \sum_{i_1=1}^{d} \cdots \sum_{i_k=1}^{d} \beta_{i_1 \ldots i_k} \left(a_{i_1 \ldots i_k} - \prod_{l=1}^{k} (\mu_{il} - x_{il}) \right). \tag{8.45}$$

The corresponding linear equation system has d^k unknowns $\beta_{i_1 \ldots i_k}$.

8.4.3 *Optimality Bound*

Unfortunately, the threshold theorem [4] guaranteeing optimality for the unconstrained binary labeling problem does not generalize to the constrained optimization problems considered here. Nevertheless, we can prove the following optimality bound:

Proposition 8.6 *Let $u^* = \arg\min_{u \in \mathcal{C}} E(u)$ be a minimizer of the relaxed problem and E_{opt} the (unknown) minimum of the corresponding binary problem. Then any thresholded version $\hat{u}$ of the relaxed solution u^* is within a computable bound of the optimum E_{opt}.*

Proof Since E_{opt} lies energetically in between the minimum of the relaxed problem and the energy of the thresholded version, we have:

$$E(\hat{u}) - E_{\text{opt}} \le E(\hat{u}) - E(u^*). \tag{8.46}$$

□

For all experiments in this paper, this bound is on average around 5 %. How to assure that the binarized version still exactly fulfills the moment constraints remains an open challenge.

8.5 Moment Constraints for Object Tracking

Object tracking over a sequence of images is the problem of finding the shape of an object that was given in the first frame in the subsequent frames of the sequence. This section shows how segmentation with moment constraints can be generalized with a few modifications to a method for object tracking.

Constraining the moments of a shape during a sequence of images leads—in combination with the presented method for image segmentation—to a method for object tracking. Given the moments of the shape in the first frame, we can constrain these moments for all subsequent frames as well. u is now a function defined on the image plane Ω evolving over time $T \subseteq \mathbb{R}^+$, that is, $u : \Omega \times T \to [0, 1]$.

First, we will show how the area constraint can be used to track an object over time: We assume that the area of the shape should not change over time, and therefore constrain the area of a shape at time t to be equal to the area of the shape in the previous frame $t-1$:

$$\min_{u\in\mathcal{B}} E(u) \quad \text{s.t.} \quad \left|\int_{\Omega} u(x,t)\,\mathrm{d}x - c_{t-1}\right| = 0, \quad \forall t \in T, \tag{8.47}$$

where c_{t-1} is the area of the shape in time frame $t-1$ and we define c_{-1} as the area of the ellipse drawn by the user in the first frame.

Alternatively, we can allow for a small change of area and thereby model motion of the object towards or away from the camera (or the camera towards/away from the object) by replacing the $=0$ in (8.47) by $\leq v$ with a constant value $v \in \mathbb{R}$. Here, v corresponds to the amount that the area of the shape is allowed to change from one frame to the next, that is, depends on the velocity of the motion.

Equally, we can impose a constraint that the object should not move too far from one frame to the other: The centroid of the shape should not change more than a given value v which corresponds to the velocity of the object:

$$\min_{u\in\mathcal{B}} E(u) \quad \text{s.t.} \quad \left|\frac{\int_{\Omega} x u(x,t)\,\mathrm{d}x}{\int_{\Omega} u(x,t)\,\mathrm{d}x} - \mu_{t-1}\right| \leq v, \quad \forall t \in T, \tag{8.48}$$

where v corresponds to the maximum length of the vector between the centroid in one frame and the centroid in the next frame, and μ_{t-1} is the centroid of u in the previous frame. Again, we define μ_{-1} as the centroid of the ellipse drawn by the user in the first frame in order to obtain an initialization for $t=0$.

Similar constraints can be imposed on the covariance and higher order moment constraints. For the covariance constraint, for example, rotation of the object can be constrained by assuming that the covariance matrix should not change more than a given value.

Optimization can be performed with the same method as explained in Sect. 8.4 while the respective moment constraints are updated in each frame.

8.6 Experimental Results

In this section, we present a qualitative and quantitative evaluation of the proposed method on medical imagery and other real-world images and videos. For all experiments, we use $g(x)=1$ and $f(x)=\log(p_{\mathrm{bg}}(I(x))/p_{\mathrm{obj}}(I(x)))$ with input image $I:\Omega\to\mathbb{R}$. We compute the likelihoods p_{obj} and p_{bg} using color or gray-scale histograms from inside and outside regions defined by the user input. Respective moment constraints on centroid, area or covariance structure are easily imposed by simple mouse interactions. Solutions to the constrained convex optimization problems are computed on the fly. In all experiments shown, moment constraints are enforced by iteratively projecting solutions to the respective constraint sets after each iteration of optimization. Typical run-times on the GPU are around 1 second for an image of the size 300×400.

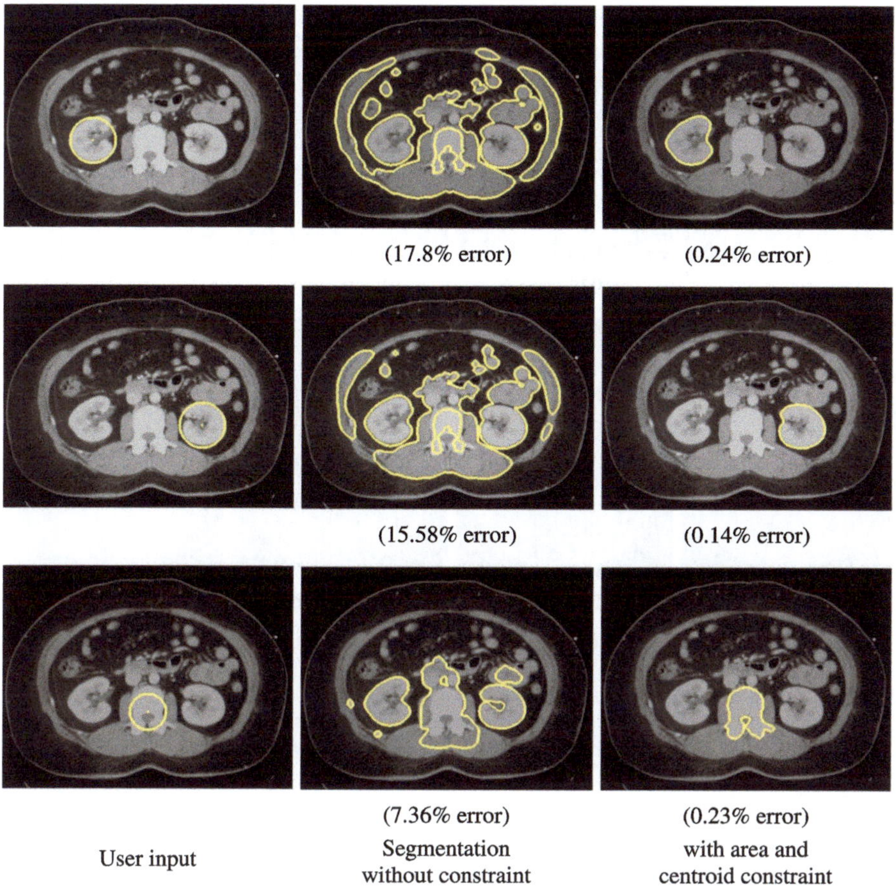

Fig. 8.5 Segmentation of a CT image with kidneys and spine. The centroid and area constraints enable the user to specify the approximate location and size of the desired object that should be segmented. Imposing these moment constraints during optimization leads to drastic improvements in the segmentation

8.6.1 Quantitative Evaluation on Medical Images

We evaluate segmentations with and without moment constraints on a set of medical images and quantitatively compare the results to a manually labelled ground truth.

8.6.1.1 Area and Centroid Constraints

Figure 8.5 shows a comparison of segmentation with and without a constraint on the area and centroid for a CT image of kidneys and spine: without constraints no shape information is taken into account for the segmentation, resulting in a segmentation that includes many different regions. Enabling the area and centroid con-

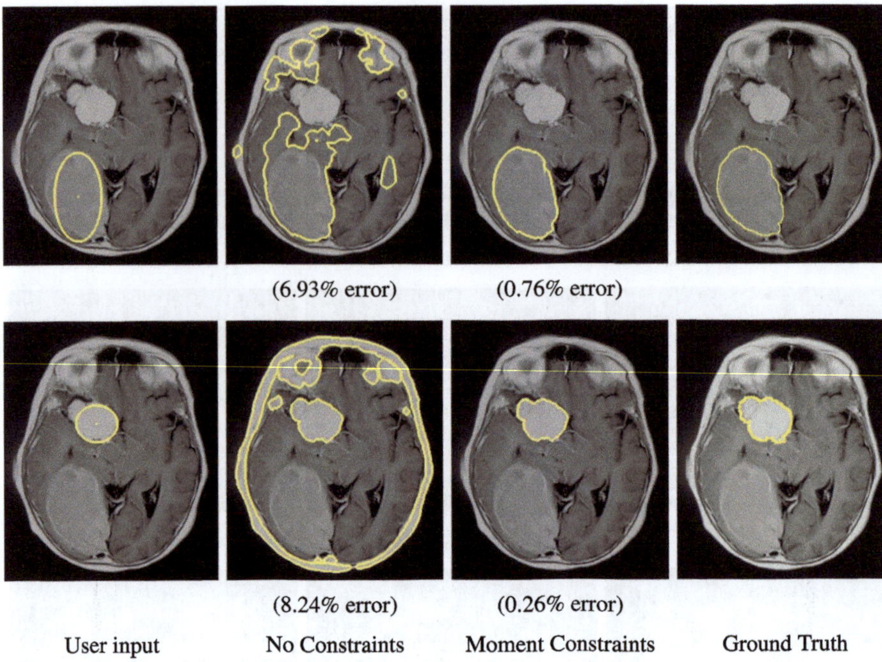

Fig. 8.6 Tumor extraction in brain MR images using segmentation with and without constraints on covariance and area. While the algorithm does not require any local boundary information, constraining its second order moments by a simple user interaction suffices to generate the desired segmentation

straints leads to segmentations that prefer the center and the size of the circle that was clicked by the user. This leads to substantial improvements of the segmentations without affecting the fine-scale boundary estimation.

8.6.1.2 Higher Order Constraints

More sophisticated structures can be specified with higher order moments. Since covariance matrices can be represented by ellipsoids, an intuitive user input is achieved by clicking an ellipse with the mouse. The axes of the ellipse define the entries of the corresponding covariance matrix, while the center and area of the ellipse define the centroid and area constraints. Figures 8.6 and 8.7 show segmentations with and without constraints resulting from user defined ellipses describing the approximated size, location and shape of the desired object.

8.6.1.3 Quantitative Performance Evaluation

Clearly, the user-specified moment constraints allow to visibly improve the segmentation. To quantify this improvement, Table 8.1 shows average relative errors (i.e.

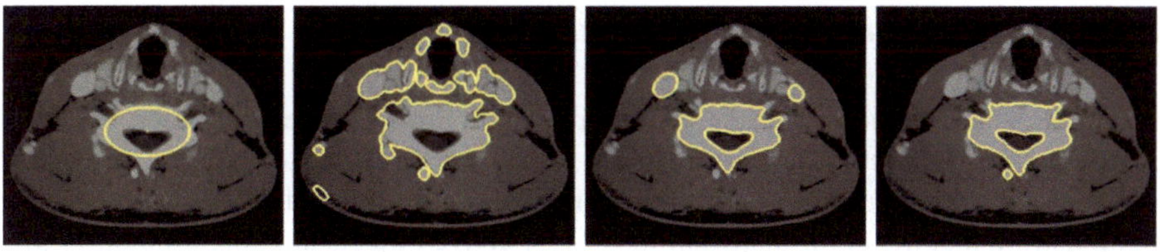

User input	(6.14% error) Segmentation without constraints	(1.41% error) Segmentation with area constraint	(1.04% error) with covariance and area constraint

Fig. 8.7 Segmentation without and with constraints for a CT image of the neck. Constraining the area yields a segmentation which prefers the size of the ellipse that was clicked by the user, resulting in less incorrectly labeled pixels, compared to the segmentation without constraints. The covariance constraint additionally considers the dimensions of the ellipse yielding an even more accurate segmentation. Again, the convex constraints merely constrain respective moments of the solution leading to drastic improvements of the segmentation results

Table 8.1 Average relative errors with standard deviations for segmentation without and with moment constraints

	Average relative error
segmentation without constraint	12.02 % ± 0.89 %
with area constraint	2.36 % ± 0.11 %
with area and centroid constraint	0.41 % ± 0.05 %
with area, centroid and covariance	0.35 % ± 0.09 %

the percentage of incorrectly labeled pixels per image) with standard deviations for an evaluation of the segmentation without constraint, with area constraint only, and with area and centroid and covariance constraint, respectively. Some of the images that were used for the tests and their segmentations are shown in Figs. 8.5, 8.6 and 8.7. The table shows that the use of these rather simple and easy to transmit constraints yield a reduction of incorrectly classified pixels by a factor of about 10.

8.6.2 Computation Times for Moment Constraint Projections

Figure 8.9 shows run times in seconds for projections onto the presented moment hard constraints. We computed the number of seconds that were needed on a 3.4 GHz Intel Core i7-2600 CPU to compute one projection onto all moment constraints of order 0 to k for $k \in \{0, \dots, 30\}$ using the projection formula (8.45). The respective constraints were obtained by computing the moments of the manually segmented reference shape shown in Fig. 8.3(a). While projections onto the lower order moment constraints are computed in just a few milliseconds, the figure implies exponentially growing run time for an increasing number of constraints.

We conclude that segmentation with moment constraints is applicable to real-time tasks for the lower order moments, whereas higher order moments that can theoretically constrain arbitrary shapes, are applicable only to off-line tasks.

8.6.3 Segmentation of Real-World Images

Figure 8.8 shows how moment constraints can improve segmentation of non-medical images. Here the data term is based on RGB histograms. The purely color-based segmentations without moment constraints shown in the second column demonstrate that the color distributions of respective objects are not sufficiently different to discriminate the objects of interest. The third column of Fig. 8.8 shows the segmentation results with constraints on area, centroid and covariance. All moment constraints are extracted from the user-specified ellipse, allowing a deviation of 10 % for each constraint to handle imprecise user input. The moment constraints allow to quickly disambiguate the color information leading to substantial improvements of the segmentation.

8.6.4 Optimality Bounds

The threshold theorem [4] states that in the unconstrained case the thresholded version is a globally optimal solution of the binary energy (8.4). Since this is not the case when we impose additional moment constraints on the segmentation, we analyzed the distance of the continuous result to the thresholded version. To this end, we compute the relative energy bound

$$\frac{E(\hat{u}) - E(u^*)}{E(u^*)}, \tag{8.49}$$

where u^* is the continuous solution before thresholding and $\hat{u}$ is the solution after thresholding. Figure 8.10 shows segmentation results for u before thresholding. The percent values below the images refers to the energy bound (8.49). In all four experiments that are shown in the figure, the distance to the thresholded version is below 1 %. In our experiments, we further observed that the more constraints are imposed on a segmentation, the larger the distance to the thresholded version increases.

8.6.5 Comparison to Segmentation with User Scribbles

Many interactive segmentation methods that utilize manual input from the user implement scribbles to obtain initial values for the histograms that generate the data term f. Scribbles in this context are arbitrary pixels marked by the user with the mouse while different labels are used for foreground and background pixels. The methods are implemented in discrete, for example [22], or continuous, for example [24], settings.

Figure 8.11 shows a comparison of two segmentation methods with priors on color and location from user input: first the presented method with moment constraints and second a segmentation method based on user scribbles. The purpose of

(a) User Input (b) No Constraints (c) Moment Constraints

Fig. 8.8 Segmentation of real world images without and with moment constraints. (**a**) The user marks an ellipse at the approximate size and location of the object with two mouse clicks. Color histograms for foreground and background are determined from the inside and outside of the ellipse, respectively. (**b**) Segmentation results without constraints using only the histograms. (**c**) Segmentation results with constraints on area, centroid and covariance. Parameters of the constraints are derived from the ellipse marked by the user

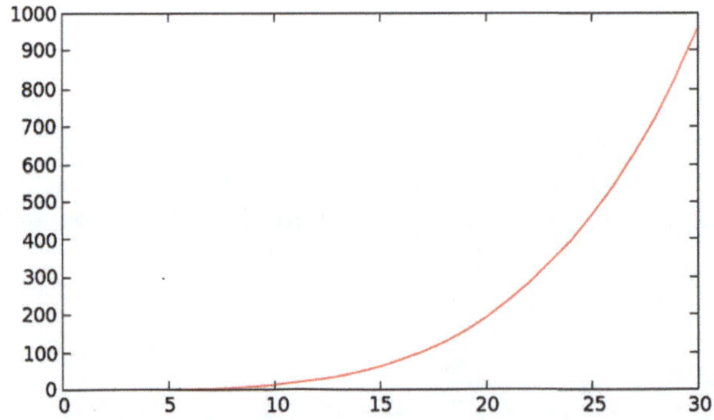

Fig. 8.9 Run time (in seconds) vs. number of moment constraints k in projection. The *plot* shows the number of seconds needed to compute a projection onto the moments of order 0 to k. While lower order moment constraints are computed in a few milliseconds, computation times appear to grow exponentially for increasing numbers of constraints. Fortunately, for interactive segmentation applications one is mostly interested in constraining the low-order moments only, leaving the fine-scale details to be determined by the image data

this experiment was to compare the effort that needs to be brought in by the user in order to sufficiently segment the respective object of interest from the background. For the scribble segmentation the user draws mouse strokes in two different colors: blue for foreground and green for background. Histograms for the data term f are computed from these marked pixels. Segmentation results with user scribbles were computed by minimizing functional (8.4), using the same method and same parameters as in the case of the moment constraints, except that the moment constraints were replaced by a constraint that all pixels that were marked as foreground by the user belong to the segmented region, and that the background pixels are not contained by the segmented region.

The figure shows that segmentations with user scribbles need much more mouse interaction compared to segmentation with moment constraints and therefore are able to substantially simplify the task of image segmentation for the user.

8.6.6 Tracking with Moment Constraints

Figures 8.12 and 8.13 show how the proposed method can be applied to tracking objects in videos. As can be seen in Fig. 8.13, the purely color-based segmentation does not suffice to correctly segment object from background in the case of non-unique color distributions.

We impose shape information by constraining the low order moments (area, centroid and covariance) throughout the entire image sequence. As can be seen in the first image of each sequence, the user initializes the method with two mouse clicks: an ellipse of the approximate size and location of the object is drawn on the first frame of the sequence. This is sufficient user input, since histograms and moment

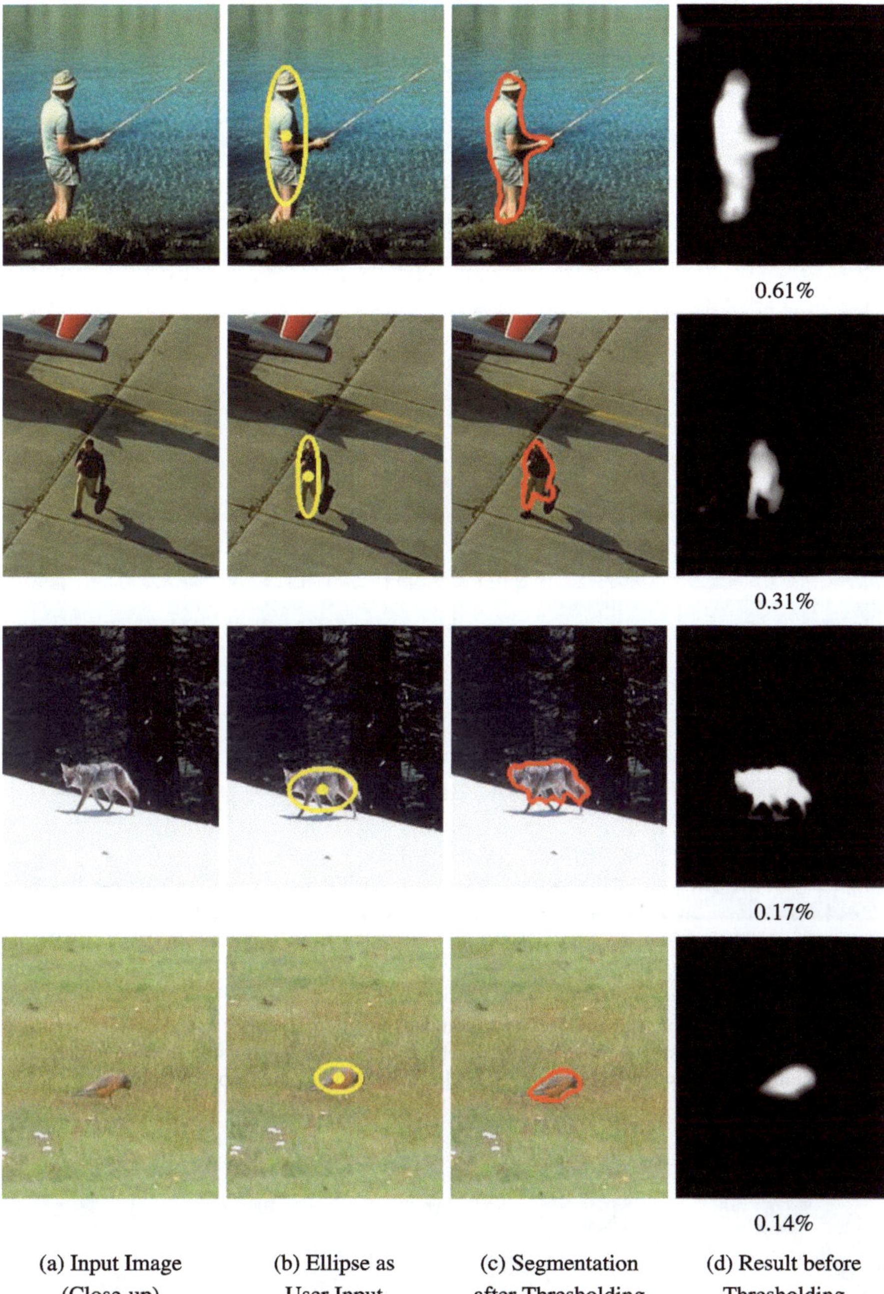

Fig. 8.10 Segmentation with the convex moment constraints converges to nearly binary solutions, making the method robust to the chosen threshold. The percentage below the images in (**d**) refers to the distance between the continuous result and its corresponding thresholded version

(a) Input Ellipse for Moment Constraints (b) Segmentation with Moment Constraints (c) User Scribbles (d) Segmentation with Scribbles

Fig. 8.11 Comparison of segmentation with moment constraints and user scribbles: Segmentation with user scribbles needs more mouse interaction to obtain similar results, since the implementation with moment constraints needs just two mouse clicks for drawing the respective ellipse

Fig. 8.12 Moment constraints for object tracking. The user initializes the tracking by clicking an ellipse in the *first frame*, the moments of which constrain the segmentation in subsequent images. A small deviation of the centroid is allowed to track the moving object. Note that this approach is generic, as no shapes have to be previously learned

Fig. 8.13 Moment constraints for object tracking. The user initializes the tracking in form of an ellipse in the *first frame* (*left*), from which histograms and constraint parameters are derived. The *first row* shows results with moment constraints, where a deviation of the centroid is allowed from each frame to the next one to account for the object's motion. The *second row* shows results of histogram based tracking without constraints. This comparison shows that moment constraints can realize acceptable real-world object tracking with no previous learning of shapes

constraint parameters are derived from the ellipse: again, histograms for foreground and background are computed from the inside and outside of the ellipse, respectively, and the constraint parameters for area, centroid and covariance are derived from the ellipse's area, center point and principal axes. The subsequent frames of the video use the histograms and moment constraints from the first frame, allowing a small deviation of the centroid from each frame to the next, which corresponds to a constraint on the maximum velocity. Since no previous learning of shapes is necessary, the approach naturally applies to arbitrary object shapes.

8.7 Conclusion

In this chapter, we proposed the use of moment constraints in a convex shape optimization framework. In particular, we showed that for an entire family of constraints on the area, the centroid, the covariance structure of the shape and respective higher-order moments, the feasible constraint sets are all convex. While we cannot guarantee global optimality of the arising segmentations, all computed solutions are independent of initialization and within a known bound of the optimum. In both qualitative and quantitative experiments on interactive image segmentation, we demonstrated that respective moment constraints are easily imposed by the user and lead to drastic improvements of the segmentation results, reducing the average segmentation error from 12 % to 0.35 %. In contrast to existing works on shape priors in segmentation, the use of low-order moment constraints does not require shape learning and is easily applied to arbitrary shapes since the recovery of fine scale shape details is not affected through the moment constraints. Efficient GPU-accelerated PDE solvers allow for computation times of about one second for images of size 300×400, making this a practical tool for interactive image segmentation.

References

1. Blake A, Zisserman A (1987) Visual reconstruction. MIT Press, Cambridge
2. Boyle JP, Dykstra RL (1986) An method for finding projections onto the intersection of convex sets in Hilbert spaces. In: Lecture Notes in Statistics, vol 37, pp 28–47
3. Caselles V, Kimmel R, Sapiro G (1995) Geodesic active contours. In: Proc IEEE int conf on computer vision, Boston, USA, pp 694–699
4. Chan T, Esedoḡlu S, Nikolova M (2006) Algorithms for finding global minimizers of image segmentation and denoising models. SIAM J Appl Math 66(5):1632–1648
5. Cremers D, Osher SJ, Soatto S (2006) Kernel density estimation and intrinsic alignment for shape priors in level set segmentation. Int J Comput Vis 69(3):335–351
6. Das P, Veksler O, Zavadsky V, Boykov Y (2008) Semiautomatic segmentation with compact shape prior. Image Vis Comput 27(1–2):206–219
7. Etyngier P, Segonne F, Keriven R (2007) Shape priors using manifold learning techniques. In: IEEE int conf on computer vision, Rio de Janeiro, October 2007
8. Foulonneau A, Charbonnier P, Heitz F (2006) Affine-invariant geometric shape priors for region-based active contours. IEEE Trans Pattern Anal Mach Intell 28(8):1352–1357
9. Greig DM, Porteous BT, Seheult AH (1989) Exact maximum a posteriori estimation for binary images. J R Stat Soc B 51(2):271–279
10. Grenander U, Chow Y, Keenan DM (1991) Hands: a pattern theoretic study of biological shapes. Springer, New York
11. Ising E (1925) Beitrag zur theorie des ferromagnetismus. Z Phys 23:253–258
12. Kass M, Witkin A, Terzopoulos D (1988) Snakes: active contour models. Int J Comput Vis 1(4):321–331
13. Kichenassamy S, Kumar A, Olver PJ, Tannenbaum A, Yezzi AJ (1995) Gradient flows and geometric active contour models. In: IEEE int conf on computer vision, pp 810–815
14. Klodt M, Cremers D (2011) A convex framework for image segmentation with moment constraints. In: IEEE int conf on computer vision, Barcelona, Spain
15. Kolev K, Cremers D (2008) Integration of multiview stereo and silhouettes via convex functionals on convex domains. In: European conference on computer vision (ECCV), Marseille, France, October 2008
16. Kolev K, Klodt M, Brox T, Cremers D (2009) Continuous global optimization in multiview 3d reconstruction. Int J Comput Vis 84(1):80–96
17. Lempitsky V, Kohli P, Rother C, Sharp T (2009) Image segmentation with a bounding box prior. In: IEEE int conf on computer vision, Kyoto, Japan
18. Luenberger DG (1997) Optimization by vector space methods, 1st edn. Wiley, New York
19. Mumford D, Shah J (1989) Optimal approximations by piecewise smooth functions and associated variational problems. Commun Pure Appl Math 42:577–685
20. Osher SJ, Sethian JA (1988) Fronts propagation with curvature dependent speed: algorithms based on Hamilton–Jacobi formulations. J Comp Physiol 79:12–49
21. Papoulis A, Pillai SU (2002) Probability, random variables, and stochastic processes, 4th edn. McGraw-Hill, New York
22. Rother C, Kolmogorov V, Blake A (2004) GrabCut: interactive foreground extraction using iterated graph cuts. ACM Trans Graph 23(3):309–314
23. Schoenemann T, Cremers D (2009) A combinatorial solution for model-based image segmentation and real-time tracking. IEEE Trans Pattern Anal Mach Intell 32(7):1153–1164
24. Unger M, Pock T, Cremers D, Bischof H (2008) Tvseg—interactive total variation based image segmentation. In: British machine vision conference (BMVC), Leeds, UK, September 2008
25. Veksler O (2008) Star shape prior for graph-cut image segmentation. In: Europ conf on computer vision, pp 454–467

Chapter 9
Large Scale Metric Learning for Distance-Based Image Classification on Open Ended Data Sets

Thomas Mensink, Jakob Verbeek, Florent Perronnin, and Gabriela Csurka

Abstract Many real-life large-scale datasets are open-ended and dynamic: new images are continuously added to existing classes, new classes appear over time, and the semantics of existing classes might evolve too. Therefore, we study large-scale image classification methods that can incorporate new classes and training images continuously over time at negligible cost. To this end, we consider two distance-based classifiers, the k-nearest neighbor (k-NN) and nearest class mean (NCM) classifiers. Since the performance of distance-based classifiers heavily depends on the used distance function, we cast the problem into one of learning a low-rank metric, which is shared across all classes. For the NCM classifier, we introduce a new metric learning approach, and we also introduce an extension to allow for richer class representations.

Experiments on the ImageNet 2010 challenge dataset, which contains over one million training images of thousand classes, show that, surprisingly, the NCM classifier compares favorably to the more flexible k-NN classifier. Moreover, the NCM performance is comparable to that of linear SVMs which obtain current state-of-the-art performance. Experimentally we study the generalization performance to classes that were not used to learn the metrics. Using a metric learned on 1,000 classes, we show results for the ImageNet-10K dataset which contains 10,000 classes, and ob-

This chapter is largely based on previously published work [30, 31].

T. Mensink (✉) · J. Verbeek
LEAR Team – INRIA Grenoble, 655 Avenue de l'Europe, 38330 Montbonnot, France
e-mail: thomas.mensink@inria.fr

J. Verbeek
e-mail: jakob.verbeek@inria.fr

F. Perronnin · G. Csurka
Xerox Research Centre Europe, 6 chemin de Maupertuis, 38240 Meylan, France

F. Perronnin
e-mail: florent.perronnin@xrce.xerox.com

G. Csurka
e-mail: gabriela.csurka@xrce.xerox.com

G.M. Farinella et al. (eds.), *Advanced Topics in Computer Vision*,
Advances in Computer Vision and Pattern Recognition,
DOI 10.1007/978-1-4471-5520-1_9,

tain performance that is competitive with the current state-of-the-art, while being orders of magnitude faster.

9.1 Introduction

In the last decade, we have witnessed an explosion in the amount of images and videos that are digitally available, for example, in broadcasting archives or social media sharing websites. Scalable automated methods are needed to handle this huge volume of data, for retrieval, annotation and visualization purposes. This need has been recognized in the computer vision research community and large-scale methods have become an active topic of research in recent years. The introduction of the ImageNet dataset [9], which contains more than 14M manually labeled images of 22K classes, has provided an important benchmark for large-scale image classification and annotation algorithms.

In this chapter, we focus on the problem of large-scale, multi-class image classification, where the goal is to assign automatically an image to one class out of a finite set of alternatives, for example, the name of main object appearing in the image, or a general label like the scene type of the image. The predominant approach to this problem is to treat it as a classification problem. To ensure scalability, often linear classifiers such as linear SVMs are used [27, 39]. Additionally, to speed-up classification, dimension reduction techniques could be used [46], or a hierarchy of classifiers could be learned [2, 12]. Recently, impressive results have been reported on 10,000 or more classes [10, 39, 46]. For all these methods hold that they are trained by using stochastic gradient descend (SGD) algorithms, which access only a small fraction of the training data at each iteration [3].

Many real-life large-scale datasets are open-ended and dynamic: new images are continuously added to existing classes, new classes appear over time, and the semantics of existing classes might evolve too. At first glance, one-vs.-rest classifiers (such as SVMs) trained with SGD algorithms appear to be the perfect solution. Indeed, classes can be trained independently, thus enabling to easily add new classes. Also since SGD algorithms are online algorithms they can accommodate for new samples easily. However, in order to apply these algorithms successfully we need to address several challenging problems. First, it is unclear to which classifier a new training sample should be fed; surely the sample should be used for the corresponding class, however feeding it as a negative sample to all other classes is not only costly but also suboptimal [36]. Second, for state-of-the-art performance the parameters of the SVM (such as the regularizer and the balance between positive and negative samples) are set by cross validation. The optimal value of these parameters depend, among others, on the number of training samples and classes, and it is unclear how these should be adapted when applied on open ended datasets to allow for an increasing number of samples and classes over time. Therefore, we believe that standard one-vs.-rest SVM classifiers are unsuitable for this task.

In this work, as an alternative, we explore distance-based classifiers which enable the addition of new classes and new images to existing classes at (near) zero cost. These methods can be used continuously as new data becomes available, and

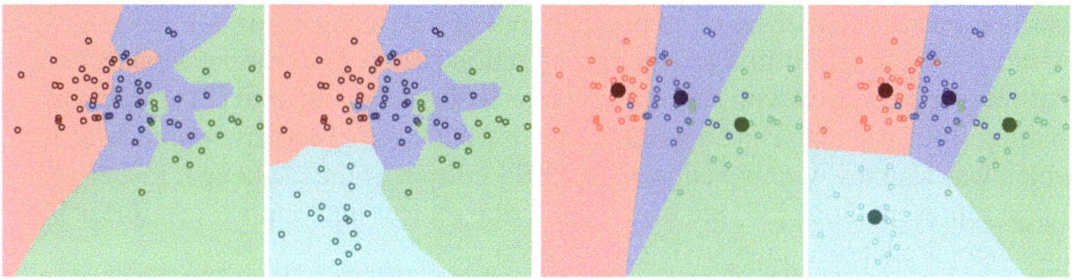

(a) K-NN Classification (b) NCM Classification

Fig. 9.1 Illustration of the classification rules of k-NN (**a**) and NCM (**b**). We also illustrate the effect of adding data from a new class to the data set

additionally alternated from time to time with a computationally heavier method to learn a good metric using all available training data. In particular, we consider two distance-based classifiers.

The first is the k-nearest neighbor (k-NN) classifier, which uses all examples to represent a class, and is a highly nonlinear classifier that has shown competitive performance for image classification [10, 18, 46]. New images (of new classes) are simply added to the database, and can be used for classification without further processing, see Fig. 9.1(a) for an illustration.

The second is the nearest class mean classifier (NCM), which represents classes by their mean feature vector of its elements, see, for example, [42]. Contrary to the k-NN classifier, this is an efficient linear classifier. To incorporate new images (of new classes), the relevant class means have to be adjusted or added to the set of class means, see Fig. 9.1(b) for an illustration. In Sect. 9.3, we introduce an extension which uses several prototypes per class, allowing a trade-off between the model complexity and the computational cost of classification.

The success of these methods critically depends on the used distance functions. Therefore, we cast our classifier learning problem as one of learning a low-rank Mahalanobis distance which is shared across all classes. The dimensionality of the low-rank matrix is used as regularizer, and to improve computational and storage efficiency. In this chapter, we explore several strategies for learning such a metric. For the NCM classifier, we propose a novel metric learning algorithm based on multi-class logistic discrimination (NCMML), where a sample from a class is enforced to be closer to its class mean than to any other class mean in the projected space. We show qualitatively and quantitatively the advantages of our NCMML approach over the classical Fisher Discriminant Analysis [42]. For k-NN classification, we rely on the Large Margin Nearest Neighbor (LMNN) framework [44] and investigate two variations similar to the ideas presented in [6, 44] that significantly improve classification performance.

Most of our experiments are conducted on the ImageNet Large Scale Visual Recognition Challenge 2010 (ILSVRC'10) dataset, which consists of 1.2M training images of 1,000 classes. To apply the proposed metric learning techniques on such a large-scale dataset, we employ stochastic gradient descend (SGD) algorithms, which access only a small fraction of the training data at each iteration [3]. To allow metric learning on high-dimensional image features of datasets that are too large to fit in memory, we use in addition product quantization [17], a data compression technique that was recently used with success for large-scale image retrieval [21] and classifier training [39]. As a baseline approach, we use the state-of-the-art approach of [39], which was also the winning entry in the 2011 edition of the challenge: Fisher vector image representations [35] are used to describe images and one-vs.-rest linear SVM classifiers are learned independently for each class.

Surprisingly, we find that the NCM classifier outperforms the more flexible k-NN classifier, after learning a low-rank metric on the Fisher vector image representations. Moreover, the NCM classifier performs on par with the SVM baseline, and results are improved when we use the extension to allow for multiple centroids per class. Further we consider, among others, the generalization performance to new classes on the ImageNet-10K dataset (which consist of 4.5M training images of 10K classes) [10], a zero-shot setting where we estimate the mean of novel classes based on related classes in the ImageNet hierarchy, and image retrieval where we use a metric learned with our NCM classifier on the ILSVRC'10 dataset, to retrieve the most similar images for a given query on the INRIA Holidays [20] or the University of Kentucky Benchmark dataset (UKB) [32].

The rest of the chapter is organized as follows. In Sect. 9.2, we discuss a selection of related work which is most relevant to this chapter. In Sect. 9.3, we introduce the NCM classifier and the NCMML metric learning approach, together with an extension to use multiple centroids (NCMC). In Sect. 9.4, we review LMNN metric learning for k-NN classifiers, and present two variants. We present extensive experimental results in Sect. 9.5, analyzing different aspects of the proposed methods and comparing them to the current state-of-the-art in different application settings such as large scale image annotation, transfer learning and image retrieval. Finally, we present our conclusions in Sect. 9.6.

9.2 Related Work

In this section, we review related work on large-scale image classification, metric learning, and transfer learning.

9.2.1 Large-Scale Image Classification

The ImageNet dataset [9] has been a catalyst for research on large-scale image annotation. The current state-of-the-art [27, 39] uses efficient linear SVM classifiers trained in a one-vs.-rest manner in combination with high-dimensional bag-of-words [8, 47] or Fisher vector representations [35]. Besides one-vs.-rest training, large-scale ranking-based formulations have also been explored in [46]. Interestingly, their WSABIE approach performs joint classifier learning and dimensionality reduction of the image features. Operating in a lower-dimensional space acts as a regularization during learning, and also reduces the cost of classifier evaluation at test time. Our proposed NCM approach also learns low-dimensional projection matrices but the weight vectors are constrained to be the projected class means. This allows for efficient addition of novel classes.

In [10, 46] k-NN classifiers were found to be competitive with linear SVM classifiers in a very large-scale setting involving 10,000 or more classes. The drawback of k-NN classifiers, however, is that they are expensive in storage and computation, since in principle all training data needs to be kept in memory and accessed to classify new images. The storage issue is also encountered when SVM classifiers are trained since all training data needs to be processed in multiple passes. Product quantization (PQ) was introduced in [21] as a lossy compression mechanism for local SIFT descriptors in a bag-of-features image retrieval system. It has been subsequently used to compress bag-of-words and Fisher vector image representations in the context of image retrieval [22] and classifier training [39]. We also exploit PQ encoding in our work to compress high-dimensional image signatures when learning our metrics.

9.2.2 Metric Learning

There is a large body of literature on metric learning, but in this section we limit ourselves to highlight just several methods that learn metrics for (image) classification problems. Other methods aim at learning metrics for verification problems and essentially learn binary classifiers that threshold the learned distance to decide whether two images belong to the same class or not, see, for example, [19, 23, 33]. Yet another line of work concerns metric learning for ranking problems, that is, to learn a metric between a query and the documents in the database, for example to address text retrieval tasks as in [1].

Among those methods that learn metrics for classification, the Large Margin Nearest Neighbor (LMNN) approach of [44, 45] is specifically designed to support k-NN classification. It tries to ensure that for each image a predefined set of target neighbors from the same class are closer than samples from other classes. Since the cost function is defined over triplets of points—that can be sampled in an SGD training procedure—this method can scale to large datasets. The set of target neighbors is chosen and fixed using the ℓ_2 metric in the original space; this can be problematic as the ℓ_2 distance might be quite different from the optimal metric for image classification. Therefore, we explore two variants of LMNN that avoid using such a pre-defined set of target neighbors, similar to the ideas presented in [6, 44], both variants leading to significant improvements.

The large margin nearest local mean classifier [5] assigns a test image to a class based on the distance to the mean of its nearest neighbors in each class. This method was reported to outperform LMNN but requires computing all pairwise distances between training instances and therefore does not scale well to large datasets.

The TagProp method of [18] is a probabilistic nearest neighbor classifier; it consists in assigning weights to training samples based on their distance to the test instance and in computing the class prediction by the total weight of samples of each class in a neighborhood. However, similar as [5], for training also TagProp requires pairwise distances between all training examples. Other closely related methods are metric learning by collapsing classes [14] and neighborhood component analysis [15]. As TagProp, for each data point these define weights to other data points proportional to the exponent of negative distance. In [14], the target is to learn a distance that makes the weights uniform for samples of the same class and close to zero for other samples. While in [15], the target is only to ensure that zero weight is assigned to samples from other classes. These methods also require computing distances between all pairs of data points, and therefore we do not consider any of these methods in our experiments.

Closely related to our NCMML metric learning approach for the NCM classifier is the LESS model of [41]. They learn a diagonal scaling matrix to modify the ℓ_2 distance by rescaling the data dimensions, and include an ℓ_1 penalty on the weights to perform feature selection. However, in their case, NCM is used to address small sample size problems in binary classification, that is, cases where there are fewer training points (tens to hundreds) than features (thousands). Our approach differs significantly in that (i) we work in a multi-class setting and (ii) we learn a low-dimensional projection which allows efficiency in large-scale.

Another closely related method is the Taxonomy-embedding method of [43], where a nearest prototype classifier is used in combination with a hierarchical cost function. Documents are embedded in a lower dimensional space in which each class is represented by a single prototype. In contrast to our approach, they use a predefined embedding of the images and learn low-dimensional classifies, and therefore their method resembles more to the WSABIE method of [46].

The centroid-based classification method explored in [48] is also related to our method. It uses a NCM classifier and an ℓ_2 distance in a subspace that is orthogonal to the subspace with maximum within-class variance. To obtain the optimal subspace, it computes the first eigenvectors of the within-class covariance matrix, which has a computational cost between $O(D^2)$ and $O(D^3)$, this is undesirable for high-dimensional feature vectors. Moreover, this metric is heuristically obtained, rather than directly optimized for maximum classification performance.

9.2.3 Transfer Learning

The term transfer learning is used to refer to methods that share information across classes during learning. Examples of transfer learning in computer vision include the use of part-based or attribute class representations. Part-based object recognition models [11] define an object as a spatial constellation of parts, and share the part detectors across different classes. Attribute-based models [24] characterize a category (e.g., a certain animal) by a combination of attributes (e.g., is yellow, has stripes, is carnivore), and share the attribute classifiers across classes. Other approaches include biasing the weight vector learned for a new class towards the weight vectors of classes that have already been trained [40]. Zero-shot learning [25] is an extreme case of transfer learning where for a new class no training instances are available but a description is provided in terms of parts, attributes, or other relations to already learned classes. Transfer learning is related to multi-task learning, where the goal is to leverage the commonalities between several distinct but related classification problems, or classifiers learned for one type of images (e.g., ImageNet) are adapted to a new domain (e.g., imagery obtained from a robot camera), see for example, [34, 38].

In [37], various transfer learning methods were evaluated in a large-scale setting using the ILSVRC'10 dataset. They found transfer learning methods to have little added value when training images are available for all classes. In contrast, transfer learning was found to be effective in a zero-shot learning setting, where classifiers were trained for 800 classes, and performance was tested in a 200-way classification across the held-out classes.

In this chapter, we also aim at transfer learning, in the sense that we allow only a trivial amount of processing on the data of new classes (storing in a database, or averaging), and rely on a metric that was trained on other classes to recognize the new ones. In contrast to most works on transfer learning, we do not use any intermediate representation in terms of parts or attributes, nor do we train classifiers for the new classes. While also considering zero-shot learning, we further evaluate performance when combining a zero-shot model inspired by [37] with progressively more training images per class, from one up to thousands. We find that the zero-shot model provides an effective prior when a small amount of training data is available.

9.3 The Nearest Class Mean Classifier

The nearest class mean (NCM) classifier assigns an image to the class $c^* \in \{1, \dots, C\}$ with the closest mean:

$$c^* = \underset{c \in \{1,\dots,C\}}{\operatorname{argmin}}\ d(\boldsymbol{x}, \boldsymbol{\mu}_c), \tag{9.1}$$

$$\boldsymbol{\mu}_c = \frac{1}{N_c} \sum_{i:y_i=c} \boldsymbol{x}_i, \tag{9.2}$$

where $d(\boldsymbol{x}, \boldsymbol{\mu}_c)$ is the Euclidean distance between an image $\boldsymbol{x}$ and the class mean $\boldsymbol{\mu}_c$, and y_i is the ground-truth label of image i, and N_c is the number of training images for class c. The NCM classifier is a linear classifier, which allows for efficient evaluation at test time, see Fig. 9.1(b) for an illustration.

Next, we introduce our NCM metric learning approach, and its relations to existing models. Then, we present an extension to use multiple centroids per class, which transforms the NCM into a non-linear classifier. Finally, we explore some variants of the objective which allow for smaller SGD batch sizes, and we give some insights in the critical points of the objective function.

9.3.1 Metric Learning for the NCM Classifier

In this section, we introduce our metric learning approach, which learns a metric by maximizing the log-likelihood of correct classification. We will refer to our method as "nearest class mean metric learning" (NCMML). In our method, we replace the Euclidean distance in NCM, Eq. (9.1), by a learned (squared) Mahalanobis distance:

$$d_M(\boldsymbol{x}, \boldsymbol{x}') = (\boldsymbol{x} - \boldsymbol{x}')^\top M(\boldsymbol{x} - \boldsymbol{x}'), \tag{9.3}$$

where $\boldsymbol{x}$ and $\boldsymbol{x}'$ are D dimensional vectors, and M is a positive definite matrix. We focus on low-rank metrics with $M = W^\top W$ and $W \in \mathbb{R}^{d\times D}$, where $d \leq D$ acts as regularizer and improves efficiency for computation and storage. The Mahalanobis distance induced by W is equivalent to the squared ℓ_2 distance after linear projection of the feature vectors on the rows of W:

$$\begin{aligned} d_W(\boldsymbol{x}, \boldsymbol{x}') &= (\boldsymbol{x} - \boldsymbol{x}')^\top W^\top W(\boldsymbol{x} - \boldsymbol{x}') \\ &= \|W\boldsymbol{x} - W\boldsymbol{x}'\|_2^2. \end{aligned} \tag{9.4}$$

In this chapter, we do not consider using the more general formulation of $M = W^\top W + S$, where S is a diagonal matrix, as in [1]. While this formulation requires only D additional parameters to estimate, it still requires computing distances in the original high-dimensional space. This is costly for the dense and high-dimensional (4K–64K) Fisher vectors representations we use, as detailed in Sect. 9.5.

We formulate the NCM classifier using a probabilistic model based on multi-class logistic regression and define the probability for a class c given a feature vector $\boldsymbol{x}$ as:

$$p(c|\boldsymbol{x}) = \frac{\exp(-\frac{1}{2} d_W(\boldsymbol{x}, \boldsymbol{\mu}_c))}{\sum_{c'=1}^{C} \exp(-\frac{1}{2} d_W(\boldsymbol{x}, \boldsymbol{\mu}_{c'}))}. \tag{9.5}$$

This definition may also be interpreted as giving the posterior probabilities of a generative model, where $p(\boldsymbol{x}|c) = \mathcal{N}(\boldsymbol{x}; \boldsymbol{\mu}_c, \Sigma)$, is a Gaussian with mean $\boldsymbol{\mu}_c$, and a covariance matrix $\Sigma = (W^\top W)^{-1}$, which is shared across all classes.[1] Using Bayes rule, we obtain:

$$p(c|\boldsymbol{x}) = \frac{p(\boldsymbol{x}|c)p(c)}{p(\boldsymbol{x})} = \frac{\mathcal{N}(\boldsymbol{x}_i; \boldsymbol{\mu}_c, \Sigma)p(c)}{\sum_{c'} \mathcal{N}(\boldsymbol{x}_i; \boldsymbol{\mu}_{c'}, \Sigma)p(c')} \tag{9.6}$$

$$= \frac{Z(\Sigma)\exp(-\frac{1}{2}(\boldsymbol{x} - \boldsymbol{\mu}_c)^\top \Sigma^{-1}(\boldsymbol{x} - \boldsymbol{\mu}_c))p(c)}{\sum_{c'} Z(\Sigma)\exp(-\frac{1}{2}(\boldsymbol{x} - \boldsymbol{\mu}_{c'})^\top \Sigma^{-1}(\boldsymbol{x} - \boldsymbol{\mu}_{c'}))p(c')} \tag{9.7}$$

[1] Strictly speaking the covariance matrix is not properly defined as the low-rank matrix $W^\top W$ is non-invertible.

$$= \frac{\exp(-\frac{1}{2}d_W(\boldsymbol{x}, \boldsymbol{\mu}_c))}{\sum_{c'=1}^{C} \exp(-\frac{1}{2}d_W(\boldsymbol{x}, \boldsymbol{\mu}_{c'}))}, \tag{9.8}$$

where the class probabilities $p(c)$ are set to be uniform over all classes. Later, in Eq. (9.27), we formulate an NCM classifier with non-uniform class probabilities.

We learn the projection matrix W in a discriminative manner, by maximizing the log-likelihood of the correct predictions of the training images:

$$\mathcal{L} = \frac{1}{N} \sum_{i=1}^{N} \ln p(y_i | \boldsymbol{x}_i). \tag{9.9}$$

The gradient of the NCMML objective Eq. (9.9) is:

$$\nabla_W \mathcal{L} = \frac{1}{N} \sum_{i=1}^{N} \sum_{c=1}^{C} \alpha_{ic} W \boldsymbol{z}_{ic} \boldsymbol{z}_{ic}^{\top}, \tag{9.10}$$

where $\alpha_{ic} = p(c|\boldsymbol{x}_i) - [\![y_i = c]\!]$, $\boldsymbol{z}_{ic} = \boldsymbol{\mu}_c - \boldsymbol{x}_i$, and we use the Iverson brackets $[\![\cdot]\!]$ that equals one if its argument is true and zero otherwise.

Although not included above for clarity, the terms in the log-likelihood in Eq. (9.9) could be weighted in cases where the class distributions in the training data are not representative for those when the learned model is applied.

9.3.2 Relation to Existing Linear Classifiers

In this section, we related the NCM classifier and the proposed NCMML approach to other linear models.

First, we compare the NCMML objective with the classical Fisher Discriminant Analysis (FDA). The objective of FDA is to find a projection matrix W that maximizes the ratio of between-class variance to within-class variance:

$$L_{\text{FDA}} = \operatorname{tr}\left(\frac{W S_{\text{B}} W^{\top}}{W S_{\text{W}} W^{\top}}\right), \tag{9.11}$$

where $S_{\text{B}} = \sum_{c=1}^{C} \frac{N_c}{N} (\boldsymbol{\mu} - \boldsymbol{\mu}_c)(\boldsymbol{\mu} - \boldsymbol{\mu}_c)^{\top}$ is the weighted covariance matrix of the class centers (and $\boldsymbol{\mu}$ is the data center), and $S_{\text{W}} = \sum_{c=1}^{C} \frac{N_c}{N} \Sigma_c$ is the weighted sum of within class covariance matrices Σ_c. Also to obtain a well-defined problem, W has a constraint on the norms of its columns. See, for exmaple, [42] for more details on the FDA.

In the case where the within class covariance for each class equals the identity matrix, the FDA objective seeks the direction of maximum variance in S_{B}. This equals to a PCA projection on the class means, which has the objective to maximize $\operatorname{tr}(W^{\top} S_{\text{B}} W)$, also with a constraint on the norms of W. The result of using the unsupervised PCA technique, is that it ignores the class information in the projected space, it just maximizes the variance between all class means. To illustrate this,

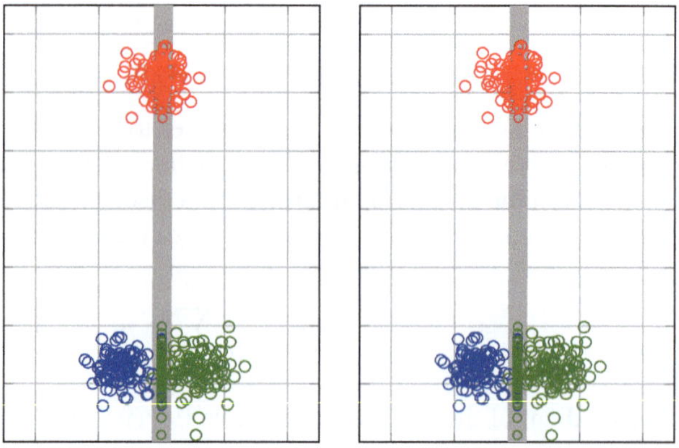

Fig. 9.2 Illustration to compare FDA (*left*) and NCMML(*right*), the obtained projection direction is indicated by the *gray line* on which also the projected samples are plotted. For FDA, the result is clearly suboptimal since the *blue* and *green* classes are collapsed in the projected space. While the proposed NCMML method finds a projection which separates the classes reasonably well

we show an example of a two-dimensional problem with three classes in Fig. 9.2. In contrast to FDA, our NCMML method only aims at separating class means which are nearby in the projected space, so as to ensure correct predictions. The resulting projection direction separates the three classes reasonably well.

To relate the NCM classifier to other linear classifiers, we represent them with the class specific score function:

$$f(c, \boldsymbol{x}) = \boldsymbol{w}_c^\top \boldsymbol{x} + b_c, \tag{9.12}$$

that assigns a sample $\boldsymbol{x}$ to the class with maximum score. NCM can be seen as a linear classifier by defining f_{NCM} with bias and weight vectors given by:

$$b_c = -\frac{1}{2}\|W\boldsymbol{\mu}_c\|_2^2, \tag{9.13}$$

$$\boldsymbol{w}_c = W^\top W\boldsymbol{\mu}_c. \tag{9.14}$$

This is proportional to the Mahalanobis distance up to an additive constant that is constant with respect to the class c, and therefore irrelevant for classification.

These definitions allows us relating the NCM classifier to other linear methods. For example, we obtain standard multi-class logistic regression, if the restrictions on b_c and $\boldsymbol{w}_c$ are removed. Note that these are precisely the restrictions that allows us adding new classes at near-zero cost, since the class specific parameters b_c and $\boldsymbol{w}_c$ are defined by just the class means $\boldsymbol{\mu}_c$ and the class-independent projection W.

In the WSABIE method [46], the classifier f_{WSABIE}, is defined using $b_c = 0$ and,

$$\boldsymbol{w}_c = W^\top \boldsymbol{v}_c \tag{9.15}$$

where $W \in \mathbb{R}^{d\times D}$ is also a low-rank projection matrix shared between all classes, and $\boldsymbol{v}_c$ is a class specific weight vector of dimensionality d, both learned from data. This is similar to NCM if we set $\boldsymbol{v}_c = W\boldsymbol{\mu}_c$. As in multiclass logistic regression, however, for WSABIE the $\boldsymbol{v}_c$ need to be learned from scratch for new classes.

The NCM classifier can also be related to the solution of ridge-regression (RR, or regularized linear least-squares regression), which also uses a linear score function. The parameters b_c and $\boldsymbol{w}_c$ are learned by optimizing the squared loss:

$$L_{RR} = \frac{1}{N} \sum_i \bigl(f_{RR}(c, \boldsymbol{x}_i) - y_{ic} \bigr)^2 + \lambda \|\boldsymbol{w}_c\|_2^2, \tag{9.16}$$

where λ acts as regularizer, and where $y_{ic} = 1$, if image i belongs to class c, and $y_{ic} = 0$ otherwise. The loss L_{RR} can be minimized in closed form and leads to:

$$b_c = \frac{N_c}{N}, \tag{9.17}$$

$$\boldsymbol{w}_c = \frac{N_c}{N} \boldsymbol{\mu}_c^\top (\Sigma + \lambda I)^{-1}, \tag{9.18}$$

where Σ is the (class-independent) data covariance matrix, see, for example, [42]. Just like the NCM classifier, the RR classifier also allows to add new classes at low cost, since the class specific parameters can be found from the class means and counts once the data covariance matrix Σ has been estimated. Moreover, if N_c is equal for all classes, RR is similar to NCM with W set such that $W^\top W = (\Sigma + \lambda I)^{-1}$.

Finally, the Taxonomy-embedding method of [43], can be rewritten such that it equals the linear classifier f_{TAX} using:

$$b_c = -\frac{1}{2} \|\boldsymbol{v}_c\|_2^2, \tag{9.19}$$

$$\boldsymbol{w}_c = W^\top W \boldsymbol{v}_c, \tag{9.20}$$

where the class-specific weight vectors $\boldsymbol{v}_c$ are learned from the data and $W \in \mathbb{R}^{C \times D}$ projects the data to a C dimensional space. The projection matrix W is set using a closed-form solution based on ridge-regression. This method relates to the WSABIE method since it also learns the classifier in low-dimensional space (if $C < D$), however in this case the projection matrix W is given in closed-form. It also shares the disadvantage of the WSABIE method: it cannot generalize to novel classes without retraining the low-dimensional class-specific vectors $\boldsymbol{v}_c$.

9.3.3 Nonlinear NCM with Multiple Class Centroids

In this section, we extend the NCM classifier to allow for more flexible class representations, which result in non-linear classification, see Fig. 9.3 for an illustration. The idea is to represent each class by a set of centroids, instead of only the class mean. Assume that we have obtained a set of k centroids $\{\boldsymbol{m}_{cj}\}_{j=1}^k$ for each class c. We define the posterior probability for a centroid $\boldsymbol{m}_{cj}$ as:

$$p(\boldsymbol{m}_{cj}|\boldsymbol{x}) = \frac{1}{Z} \exp\left(-\frac{1}{2} d_W(\boldsymbol{x}, \boldsymbol{m}_{cj}) \right), \tag{9.21}$$

where $Z = \sum_c \sum_j \exp(-\frac{1}{2} d_W(\boldsymbol{x}, \boldsymbol{m}_{cj}))$ is the normalizer. The posterior probability for class c is then given by:

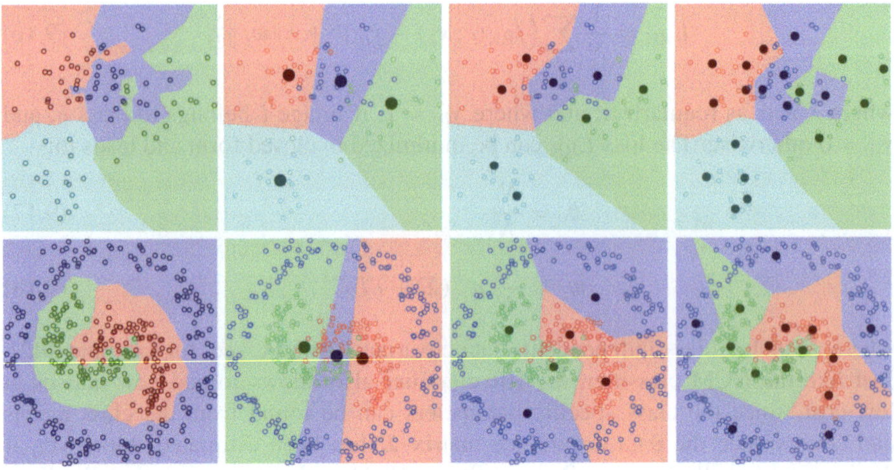

Fig. 9.3 Illustration of nonlinear classification using multiple centroids on not linearly separable data. From left to right we show, k-NN classification ($k = 1$), NCM classification, and NCMC classification with 2 and 5 centroids, respectively

$$p(c|\boldsymbol{x}) = \sum_{j=1}^{k} p(\boldsymbol{m}_{cj}|\boldsymbol{x}). \tag{9.22}$$

This model also corresponds to a generative model, where the probability for a feature vector $\boldsymbol{x}$, to be generated by class c, is given by a Gaussian mixture distribution:

$$p(\boldsymbol{x}|c) = \sum_{j=1}^{k} \pi_{cj} \mathcal{N}(\boldsymbol{x}_i; \boldsymbol{m}_{cj}, \Sigma), \tag{9.23}$$

with equal mixing weights $\pi_{cj} = 1/k$, and the covariance matrix Σ shared among all classes. We refer to this method as the nearest class multiple centroids (NCMC) classifier. A similar model was independently developed recently for image retrieval in [29]. Their objective, however, is to discriminate between different senses of a textual query, and they use a latent model to select the sense of a query.

To learn the projection matrix W, we again maximize the log-likelihood of correct classification, for which the gradient w.r.t. W in this case is given by:

$$\nabla_W \mathcal{L} = \frac{1}{N} \sum_{i,c,j} \alpha_{icj} W \boldsymbol{z}_{icj} \boldsymbol{z}_{icj}^{\top}, \tag{9.24}$$

where $\boldsymbol{z}_{icj} = \boldsymbol{m}_{cj} - \boldsymbol{x}_i$, and

$$\alpha_{icj} = p(\boldsymbol{m}_{cj}|\boldsymbol{x}_i) - [\![c = y_i]\!] \frac{p(\boldsymbol{m}_{cj}|\boldsymbol{x}_i)}{\sum_{j'} p(\boldsymbol{m}_{cj'}|\boldsymbol{x}_i)}. \tag{9.25}$$

To obtain the centroids of each class, we apply k-means clustering on the features $\boldsymbol{x}$ belonging to that class, using the ℓ_2 distance. The value k offers a transition between NCM ($k = 1$), and a weighted k-NN (k equals all images per class), where the weight of each neighbor is defined by the soft-min of its distance, c.f. Eq. (9.21). This is similar to TagProp [18], used for multi-label image annotation, which assigns a probability to a class c based on the class labels and distances of the images in the training set:

$$p(c|\boldsymbol{x}_i) = \sum_j \pi_{ij} [\![y_j = c]\!], \qquad \pi_{ij} = \frac{\exp(-\frac{1}{2} d_W(\boldsymbol{x}_i, \boldsymbol{x}_j))}{\sum_{j'} \exp(-\frac{1}{2} d_W(\boldsymbol{x}_i, \boldsymbol{x}_{j'}))}. \tag{9.26}$$

In Fig. 9.3, we illustrate the influence of increasing k on the obtained classification boundaries, and made the comparison with the k-NN ($k = 1$) classifier.

Instead of using a fixed set of class means, it could be advantageous to iterate the k-means clustering and the learning of the projection matrix W. Such a strategy allows the set of class centroids to represent more precisely the distribution of the images in the projected space, and might further improve the classification performance. However, the experimental validation of such a strategy falls beyond the scope of this paper.

9.3.4 Alternative Objective for Small SGD Batches

Computing the gradients for NCMML in Eq. (9.10) and NCMC in Eq. (9.24) is relatively expensive, regardless of the number of m samples used per SGD iteration. The cost of this computation is dominated by the computation of the squared distances $d_W(\boldsymbol{x}, \boldsymbol{\mu}_c)$, required to compute the $m \times C$ probabilities $p(c|\boldsymbol{x})$ for C classes in the SGD update. To compute these distances we have two options. First, we can compute the $m \times C$ difference vectors $(\boldsymbol{x} - \boldsymbol{\mu}_c)$, project these on the $d \times D$ matrix W, and compute the norms of the projected difference vectors, at a total cost of $O(dD(mC) + mC(d + D))$. Second, we can first project both the m data vectors and C class centers, and then compute distances in the low dimensional space, at a total cost of $O(dD(m + C) + mC(d))$. Note that the latter option has a lower complexity, but still requires projecting all class centers at a cost $O(dDC)$, which will be the dominating cost when using small SGD batches with $m \ll C$. Therefore, in practice we are limited to using SGD batch sizes with $m \approx C = 1{,}000$ samples.

In order to accommodate for fast SGD updates based on smaller batch sizes, we replace the Euclidean distance in Eq. (9.5) by the dot-product plus a class specific bias s_c. The probability for class c is now given by:

$$p(c|\boldsymbol{x}_i) = \frac{1}{Z} \exp\big(\boldsymbol{x}_i^\top W^\top W \boldsymbol{\mu}_c + s_c\big), \tag{9.27}$$

where Z denotes the normalizer. The objective is still to maximize the log-likelihood of Eq. (9.9). The efficiency gain stems from the fact that we can avoid projecting the class centers on W, by twice projecting the data vectors: $\hat{\boldsymbol{x}}_i = \boldsymbol{x}_i^\top W^\top W$, and then

Table 9.1 Comparison of complexity of the considered alternatives to compute the class probabilities $p(c|\boldsymbol{x})$

Distances in D dimensions	$O(dD(mC) + mC(d + D))$
Distances in d dimensions	$O(dD(m + C) + mC(d))$
Dot product formulation	$O(dD(m) + mC(D))$

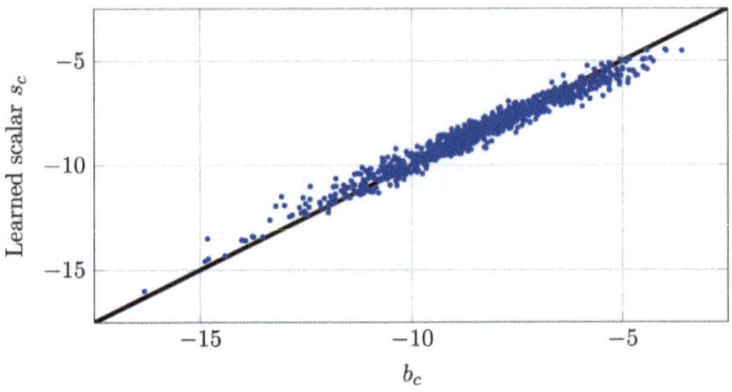

Fig. 9.4 The learned class-specific biases s_c and the norm of the projected means b_c are strongly correlated

computing dot-products in high dimensional space $\langle \hat{\boldsymbol{x}}_i, \boldsymbol{\mu}_c \rangle$. For a batch of m images, the first step costs $O(mDd)$, and the latter $O(mCD)$, resulting in a complexity of $O(dD(m) + mC(D))$. This complexity scales linearly with m, and is lower for small batches with $m \leq d$, since in that case it is more costly to project the class vectors on W than on the double-projected data vectors $\hat{\boldsymbol{x}}_i$. For clarity, we summarize the complexity of the different alternatives we considered in Table 9.1.

A potential disadvantage of this approach is that we need to determine the class-specific bias s_c when data of a new class becomes available, which would require more training than just computing the data mean for the new class. However, we expect a strong correlation between the learned bias s_c and the biased based on the norm of the projected mean b_c. Similar as used for Eq. (9.5), we could interpret the class probabilities in Eq. (9.27) as those being generated by a generative model where the class-conditional models $p(\boldsymbol{x}|c)$ are Gaussian with a shared covariance matrix. We continue from Eq. (9.7) and obtain:

$$p(c|\boldsymbol{x}) = \frac{Z(\Sigma)\exp(-\frac{1}{2}(\boldsymbol{x} - \boldsymbol{\mu}_c)^\top \Sigma^{-1}(\boldsymbol{x} - \boldsymbol{\mu}_c))p(c)}{\sum_{c'} Z(\Sigma)\exp(-\frac{1}{2}(\boldsymbol{x} - \boldsymbol{\mu}_{c'})^\top \Sigma^{-1}(\boldsymbol{x} - \boldsymbol{\mu}_{c'}))p(c')} \tag{9.28}$$

$$= \frac{\exp(\boldsymbol{x}_i^\top W^\top W \boldsymbol{\mu}_c - \frac{1}{2}\|W\boldsymbol{\mu}_c\|_2^2)p(c)}{\sum_{c'} \exp(\boldsymbol{x}_i^\top W^\top W \boldsymbol{\mu}_{c'} - \frac{1}{2}\|W\boldsymbol{\mu}_{c'}\|_2^2)p(c')}. \tag{9.29}$$

In this interpretation, the class specific biases s_c define class prior probabilities given by $p(c) \propto \exp(\frac{1}{2}\|W\boldsymbol{\mu}_c\|_2^2 + s_c)$. Therefore, a uniform prior is obtained by setting $s_c = -\frac{1}{2}\|W\boldsymbol{\mu}_c\|_2^2 = b_c$. A uniform prior is reasonable for the ILSVRC'10 data, since the classes are near uniform in the training and test data.

Experimentally, we find that using this formulation yields comparable results as using the Euclidean distance. As expected, we find a strong correlation between the learned bias s_c and the norm of the projected mean b_c, shown in Fig. 9.4. Indeed, the classification performance differs insignificantly if at evaluation time we set $s_c = b_c$ instead of the value that was found during training.

Thus, even if we train the metric by using class-specific biases, we can use the learned metric in the NCM classifier with the bias based on the norm of the projected mean, which is easily computed for data of new classes.

9.3.5 Critical Points of Low Rank Metric Learning

We use a low-rank Mahalanobis distance where $M = W^\top W$, as a way to reduce the number of parameters and to gain in computational efficiency. Learning a full Mahalanobis distance matrix M, however, has the advantage that the distance is linear in M and that the multi-class logistic regression objective of Eq. (9.9) is therefore concave in M [4, p. 74]. Using a low-rank formulation, on the other hand, yields a distance which is quadratic in the parameters W, therefore the objective function is no longer concave. In this section, we investigate the critical-points of the low-rank formulation by analyzing W when the optimization reaches a (local) minimum, and considering the gradient for the corresponding full matrix $M = W^\top W$.

The gradient of the objective of Eq. (9.9) w.r.t. to M is:

$$\nabla_M \mathcal{L} = \frac{1}{N} \sum_{i,c} \alpha_{ic} z_{ic} z_{ic}^\top \equiv H, \tag{9.30}$$

where $\alpha_{ic} = p(c|\boldsymbol{x}_i) - [\![y_i = c]\!]$, and $z_{ic} = \boldsymbol{\mu}_c - \boldsymbol{x}_i$. Then Eq. (9.10) follows from the matrix chain rule, and we redefine $\nabla_W \mathcal{L} \equiv 2WH$. From the gradient w.r.t. W, we immediately observe that $W = 0$ leads to a degenerate case to obtain a zero gradient, and similarly for each row of W. Below, we concentrate on the non-degenerate case.

We observe that H is a symmetric matrix, containing the difference of two positive definite matrices. Further, we observe that when $H = 0$, that is, when we reach the minimum of the full Mahalanobis distance, we obtain zero gradient for W. Here we analyze H when the gradient w.r.t. W reaches a zero point. In the analysis below, we use the eigenvalue decomposition of $H = V \Lambda V^\top$, with the columns of V being the eigenvectors, and the eigenvalues are on the diagonal of Λ.

We can now express the gradient for W as

$$\nabla_W \mathcal{L} = 2WV\Lambda V^\top \equiv G. \tag{9.31}$$

Thus the gradient of the ith row of W, which we denote by $\boldsymbol{g}_i$, is a linear combination of the eigenvectors of H:

$$\boldsymbol{g}_i \equiv \sum_j \lambda_j \langle \boldsymbol{w}_i, \boldsymbol{v}_j \rangle \boldsymbol{v}_j, \tag{9.32}$$

where $\boldsymbol{w}_i$ and $\boldsymbol{v}_j$ denote the ith row of W and the jth column of V, respectively. Thus, an SGD gradient update will drive a row of W towards the eigenvectors of H that (i) have a large positive eigenvalue, and (ii) are most aligned with that row

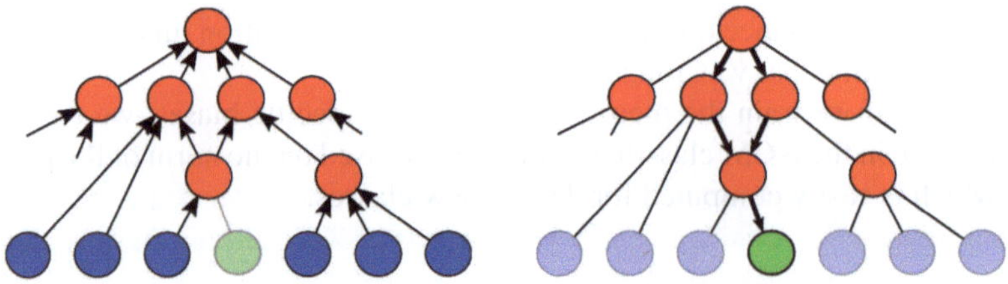

Fig. 9.5 Illustration of the estimation of the zero-shot prior on a mean. In the first step (*left*), the means of train classes (*blue*) are propagated upwards in the ImageNet hierarchy to the internal nodes (*red*). In the second step (*right*), the prior is estimated as the average of all the ancestor nodes of the new class (*green*)

of W. This is intuitive, since we would expect the low-rank formulation to focus on the most significant directions of the full-rank metric.

Moreover, the expression for the gradient in Eq. (9.32) shows that at a critical point W^* of the objective function, all linear combination coefficients are zero: $\forall_{i,j}$: $\lambda_j \langle \boldsymbol{w}_i^*, \boldsymbol{v}_j \rangle = 0$. This indicates that at the critical point, for each row $\boldsymbol{w}_i^*$ and each eigenvector $\boldsymbol{v}_j$ it holds that either $\boldsymbol{w}_i^*$ is orthogonal to $\boldsymbol{v}_j$, or that $\boldsymbol{v}_j$ has a zero associated eigenvalue, that is, $\lambda_j = 0$. Thus, at a critical point W^*, the corresponding gradient for the full rank formulation at that point, with $M^* = W^{*\top} W^*$, is zero in the subspace spanned by W^*.

Given this analysis, we believe it is unlikely to attain poor local minima using the low rank formulation. Indeed, the gradient updates for W are aligned with the most important directions of the corresponding full-rank gradient, and at convergence the full-rank gradient is zero in the subspace spanned by W. To confirm this, we have also experimentally investigated this by training several times with different random initializations of W. We observe that the classification performance differs at most ± 0.1 % on any of the error measures used in Sect. 9.5, and that the number of SGD iterations selected by the early stopping procedure are of the same order.

9.3.6 Transfer Learning with the Nearest Class Mean Classifier

In this section, we describe how we can use the NCM classifier in a zero-shot setting. Inspired by [37], we propose to use the ImageNet hierarchy to estimate the mean of novel classes from the means of related training classes, see Fig. 9.5 for an illustration. We follow ideas of [37] and estimate the mean of a novel class $\boldsymbol{\mu}_z$ using the means of its ancestor nodes in the ImageNet class hierarchy:

$$\boldsymbol{\mu}_z = \frac{1}{|\mathcal{A}_z|} \sum_{a \in \mathcal{A}_z} \boldsymbol{\mu}_a, \tag{9.33}$$

where $\mathcal{A}_z$ denotes the set of ancestors of node z, and $\boldsymbol{\mu}_a$ is the mean of ancestor a. The mean of an internal node, $\boldsymbol{\mu}_a$, is computed as the average of the means of all its descendant training classes. In our experiments, the classes of interest are always leaf-nodes of the hierarchy.

In the setting where we also have a few images of the new class, we can combine the zero-shot prior with the mean of the sample images. If we view the estimation of each class mean as the estimation of the mean of a Gaussian distribution, then the mean of a sample of images $\boldsymbol{\mu}_s$ corresponds to the Maximum Likelihood (ML) estimate, while the zero-shot estimate $\boldsymbol{\mu}_z$ can be thought of as a prior. We can combine the prior with the ML estimate to obtain a maximum a-posteriori (MAP) estimate $\boldsymbol{\mu}_p$ on the class mean. The MAP estimate of the mean of a Gaussian is obtained by:

$$\boldsymbol{\mu}_p = \frac{n\boldsymbol{\mu}_s + m\boldsymbol{\mu}_z}{n+m}, \qquad (9.34)$$

where n is the number of images used to compute the ML estimate of the sample mean $\boldsymbol{\mu}_s$, and the prior obtains a weight m determined on the validation set [13].

9.4 k-NN Metric Learning

We compare the NCM classifier to the k-NN classifier, a frequently used distance based classifier. The k-NN classifier is attractive since it is very intuitive, just assigning the class of the nearest neighbors to a test image, see Fig. 9.1(a) for an illustration. Just as for the NCM classifier, the k-NN classifier relies on distances, and thus it is essential to use a metric in which nearby images are also semantically related. In this section we discuss metric learning for k-NN classifiers, used to learn a low-rank Mahalanobis distance $M = W^\top W$, where $W \in \mathbb{R}^{d\times D}$.

For successful k-NN classification, the majority of the nearest neighbors should be of the same class. This is reflected in the Large Margin Nearest Neighbors (LMNN) metric learning objective of [44, 45]. LMNN is defined over triplets consisting of a query image q, a positive image p from the same class, and a negative image n from another class. The objective is to get the distance between q and p smaller than the distance between q and n, using the hinge-loss to upper bound the zero/one loss:

$$L_{qpn} = \big[1 + d_W(\boldsymbol{x}_q, \boldsymbol{x}_p) - d_W(\boldsymbol{x}_q, \boldsymbol{x}_n)\big]_+, \qquad (9.35)$$

where $[z]_+ = \max(0, z)$ is the positive part of z. The hinge-loss for a triplet is zero if the negative image n is at least one distance unit farther from the query q than the positive image p, and the loss is positive otherwise. The final learning objective sums the losses over all triplets:

$$L_{\mathrm{LMNN}} = \sum_{q=1}^{N} \sum_{p\in P_q} \sum_{n\in N_q} L_{qpn}, \qquad (9.36)$$

where P_q and N_q denote a predefined set of positive and negative images for each query image q. An important design choice is how to set P_q and N_q for each query.

For the set of negative images N_q, we follow [44] and use all images not belonging to the class of the query image. Below, we describe several variants for the set of positive images P_q.

Also in this case we can weight the terms in the loss function to account for non-representative class proportions in the training data.

9.4.1 Choice of Target Neighbors

For LMNN a set of target P_q for a query q is set to some images from the same class. The rationale is that if we ensure that these targets are closer than the instances of the other classes, then the k-NN classification will succeed. To select the set of targets, we consider three alternatives:

1. In the basic version of LMNN the set of targets P_q is set to the query's k nearest neighbors from the same class, using the ℓ_2 distance. Since this selection method tries to ensure that the ℓ_2-targets will also be the closest points using the learned metric, it implicitly assumes that the ℓ_2 distance in the original space is a good similarity measure. In practice, however, this might not be the case.
2. The set of targets P_q is defined to contain all images of the same class as q, hence the selection is independent on the metric. This is similar to [6] where the same type of loss was used to learn image similarity defined as the scalar product between feature vectors after a learned linear projection.
3. The set of targets P_q is dynamically updated to contain the k images of the same class that are closest to q using the current metric W. Hence, different target neighbors can be selected depending on the current metric. This method corresponds to minimizing the loss function also with respect to the choice of P_q. A similar approach has been proposed in [44], where every T iterations P_q is redefined using target neighbors according to the current metric.

A potential disadvantage of the last method is that it requires frequent recomputation of the target neighbors. However, below we describe an efficient gradient evaluation method, which allows to approximate the dynamic set of P_q at each iteration at a negligible additional cost compared to using a fixed set of target neighbors or using all images of the same class as targets.

Next, we will discuss an efficient triplet sampling and gradient evaluation algorithms to increase the efficiency of the SGD training.

9.4.2 Triplet Sampling Strategy

Here, we describe a sampling strategy which obtains the maximal number of triplets from m images selected per SGD iteration. Using a small m is advantageous since the cost of the gradient evaluation is in large part determined by computing the projections Wx of the images, and the cost of decompressing the PQ encoded signatures, if these are used.

To generate triplets, we first select uniformly at random a class c, that will provide the query and positive images. When P_q is set to contain all images of the same class, we sample ρm images from class c, with $0 < \rho < 1$, and the remaining $(m - \rho m)$ images are uniformly sampled from the other classes. We can consider the number of triplets t we can generate as a function of ρ for a given 'budget' of m images to be accessed. In the case where P_q is set to contain all images from the same class, the number of triplets t we can generate for a specific ρ is given by:

$$t(\rho) = (\rho m)(\rho m - 1)(m - \rho m), \tag{9.37}$$

since we can pair the ρm images with the $\rho m - 1$ other images from the same class, and each pair forms a triplet with any of the $m - \rho m$ negative sampled images. The number of triplets t can be approximated by:

$$t(\rho) \approx m^3 \rho^2 (1 - \rho), \tag{9.38}$$

and hence, the number of triplets is maximized when we choose $\rho \approx \frac{2}{3}$, in which case we can construct about $\frac{4}{27}m^3$ triplets. In our experiments, we use $\rho = \frac{2}{3}$ and $m = 300$ images per iteration, leading to about 4 million triplets per iteration.

For other choices of P_q, we do the following:

- For a fixed set of target neighbors, we still sample $\frac{1}{3}m$ negative images, and take as many query images together with their target neighbors until we obtain $\frac{2}{3}m$ images allocated for the positive class.
- For a dynamic set of target neighbors, we simply select the closest neighbors among the $\frac{2}{3}m$ sampled positive images using the current metric W. Although approximate, this avoids computing the dynamic target neighbors among all the images in the positive class.

An alternative to obtain roughly 4 million triplets is to sample two images from each of the $C = 1{,}000$ classes. In this case, there are two query images per class, each forming a pair with the other positive image, and each pair can form a triplet with the $2(C - 1)$ images of other classes, leading to $4C(C - 1) \approx 4$ million triplets. A potential advantage of this method is that the gradient is computed in each iteration from triplets generated using all possible combinations of classes, and therefore, the gradient might be more informative. However, this sampling strategy does not allow for fast approximation of the dynamic neighbors, and we would need to access $m = 2{,}000$ images, which is about 7 times more costly than using the described approach with $m = 300$.

9.4.3 *Efficient Gradient Evaluation*

For either choice of the target set P_q, the gradient can be computed without explicitly iterating over all triplets. In this section, we introduce an efficient gradient evaluation method, which uses sorting of the distances w.r.t. query images.

Algorithm 1 Compute coefficients A_{qn} and A_{qp}

1. For positive images redefine $d_W(\boldsymbol{x}_q, \boldsymbol{x}_p) \leftarrow d_W(\boldsymbol{x}_q, \boldsymbol{x}_p) + 1$ to account for the margin.
2. Sort distances w.r.t. q in ascending order.
3. $C_n(i) \leftarrow \sum_{j=1}^{i} [\![j \in N_q]\!]$, the number of negative images up to each position.
4. $C_p(i) \leftarrow \sum_{j=i+1}^{m} [\![j \in P_q]\!]$, the number of positive images after each position.
5. Read-off the number of hinge-loss generating triplets of image p or n:

$$A_{qn} = -2C_p\big(\text{rnk}(q, n)\big), \qquad A_{qp} = 2C_n\big(\text{rnk}(q, p)\big),$$

where $\text{rnk}(q, p)$ indicates the rank of document p for the query q, and similar for $\text{rnk}(q, n)$.

The sub-gradient of the loss of a triplet is given by:

$$\nabla_W L_{qpn} = [\![L_{qpn} > 0]\!] 2W\big(\boldsymbol{x}_{qp}\boldsymbol{x}_{qp}^\top - \boldsymbol{x}_{qn}\boldsymbol{x}_{qn}^\top\big), \tag{9.39}$$

where $\boldsymbol{x}_{qp} = \boldsymbol{x}_q - \boldsymbol{x}_p$, and $\boldsymbol{x}_{qn} = \boldsymbol{x}_q - \boldsymbol{x}_n$. By observing that the gradient takes the form of outer products of the feature vectors, we can write the gradient w.r.t. $L_q = \sum_{p,n} L_{qpn}$ in matrix form as:

$$\nabla_W L_q = 2WXAX^\top, \tag{9.40}$$

where X contains the m feature vectors used in an SGD iteration, and A is a coefficient matrix. This shows that once A is available, the gradient can be computed in time $O(m^2)$, even if a much larger number of triplets is used.

When P_q contains all images of the same class, the gradient per query can be rewritten as:

$$\begin{aligned} \nabla_W L_q = {} & +2W \sum_p \Big(\sum_n [\![L_{qpn} > 0]\!] \Big) \big(\boldsymbol{x}_p \boldsymbol{x}_p^\top - \boldsymbol{x}_q \boldsymbol{x}_p^\top - \boldsymbol{x}_p \boldsymbol{x}_q^\top \big) \\ & - 2W \sum_n \Big(\sum_p [\![L_{qpn} > 0]\!] \Big) \big(\boldsymbol{x}_n \boldsymbol{x}_n^\top - \boldsymbol{x}_q \boldsymbol{x}_n^\top - \boldsymbol{x}_n \boldsymbol{x}_q^\top \big). \end{aligned} \tag{9.41}$$

Which shows that the coefficient matrix A can be computed from the number of hinge-loss generating triplets in which each $p \in P_q$ and each $n \in N_q$ for a query q occurs:

$$A_{qn} = 2 \sum_p [\![L_{qpn} > 0]\!], \qquad A_{pq} = -2 \sum_n [\![L_{qpn} > 0]\!], \tag{9.42}$$

$$A_{qq} = \sum_p A_{qp} - \sum_n A_{qn}, \qquad A_{pp} = \sum_q A_{qp}, \qquad A_{nn} = \sum_q A_{qn}. \tag{9.43}$$

In Algorithm 1, we describe how to efficiently compute the coefficients, which sorts the distances w.r.t. the query q and then can read of the number of hinge-loss generating triplets. The same algorithm can be applied when using a small set of fixed, or dynamic target neighbors. In particular, the sorted list allows to dynamically determine the target neighbors at a negligible additional cost. In this case only the selected target neighbors obtain nonzero coefficients, and we only accumulate the number of target neighbors after each position in step 3 of the algorithm.

The cost of this algorithm is $O(m \log m)$ per query, and thus $O(m^2 \log m)$ when using $O(m)$ query images per iteration. This is significantly faster than explicitly looping over all $O(m^3)$ triplets.

Note that while this algorithm enables fast computation of the sub-gradient of the loss, the value of the loss itself cannot be determined using this method. However, this is not a problem when using an SGD approach, as it only requires gradient evaluations, not function evaluations.

9.5 Experimental Evaluation

In this section, we experimentally validate our models described in the previous sections. We first describe the dataset and evaluation measures used in our experiments, followed by the presentation of the experimental results.

9.5.1 Experimental Setup and Baseline Approach

In this section, we describe the experimental setup, our image representations and our baseline methods.

Dataset In most of our experiments, we use the dataset of the ImageNet Large Scale Visual Recognition 2010 challenge (ILSVRC'10),[2] see Fig. 9.6 for a few examples. This dataset contains 1.2M training images of 1,000 object classes (with between 660 to 3047 images per class), a validation set of 50K images (50 per class), and a test set of 150K images (150 per class).

In some of the experiments, we use the ImageNet-10K dataset introduced in [10], which consists of 10,184 classes from the nodes of the ImageNet hierarchy with more than 200 images. We follow [39] and use 4.5M images as training set, 50K as validation set and the rest as test set.

Image Representation We represent each image with a Fisher vector (FV) [35] computed over densely extracted 128 dimensional SIFT descriptors [28] and 96 dimensional local color features [7], both projected with PCA to 64 dimensions. FVs are extracted and normalized separately for both channels and then combined by concatenating the two feature vectors. We do not make use of spatial pyramids. In our experiments, we use FVs extracted using a vocabulary of either 16 or 256 Gaussians. For 16 Gaussians, this leads to a 4K dimensional feature vector, which re-

[2]See http://www.image-net.org/challenges/LSVRC/2010/index.

Park bench — *A bench in a public park*

Mortar — *A bowl-shaped vessel in which substances can be ground and mixed with a pestle*

Carousel — *A large, rotating machine with seats for children to ride or amusement*

Brace — *Elastic straps that hold trousers up (usually used in the plural)*

Crab apple — *Small sour apple; suitable for preserving; "crabapples make a tangy jelly"*

Leaf beetle — *Brightly colored beetle that feeds on plant leaves; larvae infest roots and stems*

Violoncello — *A large stringed instrument; seated player holds it upright while playing*

Tile roof — *A roof made of fired clay tiles*

Fig. 9.6 Example images from the ILSVRC'10 data set, with their class names and descriptions. The data set contains 1.2M training images of 1,000 different classes

quires about 20GB for the 1.2M training set (using 4-byte floating point arithmetic). This fits into the RAM of our 32GB servers.

For 256 Gaussians, the FVs are 16 times larger, that is, 64K dimensional, which would require 320GB of memory. To fit the data in memory, we compress the feature vectors using product quantization [17, 21]. In a nutshell, it consists in splitting the high-dimensional vector into small sub-vectors, and vector quantizing each sub-vector independently. We compress the dataset to approximately 10GB using 8-dimensional sub-vectors and 256 centroids per sub-quantizer, which allows storing each sub-quantizer index in a single byte, combined with a sparse encoding of the zero sub-vectors, c.f. [39]. In each iteration of SGD learning, we decompress the features of a limited number of images, and use these (lossy) reconstructions for the gradient computation.

Evaluation Measures We report the average top-1 and top-5 flat error used in the ILSVRC'10 challenge. The flat error is one if the ground-truth label does not correspond to the top-1 label with highest score (or any of the top-5 labels), and zero otherwise. The motivation for the top-5 error is to allow an algorithm to identify multiple objects in an image and not being penalized if one of the objects identified was in fact present but not included in the ground truth of the image which contains only a single object category per image. Unless specified otherwise, we report the top-5 flat error on the test set using the 4K dimensional features; we use the validation set for parameter tuning only.

Baseline Approach For our baseline, we follow the state-of-the-art approach of [36] and learn weighed one-vs.-rest SVMs with SGD, where the number of negative images in each iteration is sampled proportional to the number of positive images for that class. The proportion parameter is cross validated on the validation set. The results of the baseline can be found in Table 9.3 and Table 9.6. We see that the 64K dimensional features lead to significantly better results than the 4K ones, despite the lossy PQ compression.

In Table 9.3, the performance using the 64K features is slightly better than the ILSVRC'10 challenge winners [27] (28.0 vs. 28.2 flat top-5 error), and very close to the results of [39] (25.7 flat top-5 error), wherein a much higher dimensional image representation of more than 1M dimensions was used. In Table 9.6, our baseline shows state-of-the-art performance on ImageNet-10K when using the 64K features, obtaining 78.1 vs. 81.9 flat top-1 error [36]. We believe this is due to the use of the color features, in addition to the SIFT features used in [36].

SGD Training and Early Stopping To learn the projection matrix W, we use SGD training and sample at each iteration a fixed number of m training images to estimate the gradient. Following [1], we use a fixed learning rate and do not include an explicit regularization term, but rather use the projection dimension d, as well as the number of iterations as an implicit form of regularization. For all experiments, we use the following early stopping strategy:

- we run SGD training for a large number of iterations ($\approx$750K–2M),
- the performance on the validation set is computed every 50k iterations (for the k-NN) or every 10k iterations (for the NCM), and
- the metric which yields the lowest top-5 error on the validation set is selected.

In case of a tie, the metric giving the lowest top-1 error is chosen. Similarly, all hyper-parameters, like the value of k for the k-NN classifiers, are validated in this way. Unless stated otherwise, training is performed using the ILSVRC'10 training set, and validation using the described early stopping strategy on the provided 50K validation set.

It is interesting to notice that while the compared methods (k-NN, NCM, and SVM) have different computational complexities, the number of images seen by each algorithm before convergence is rather similar. For example, training of the SVMs, on the 4K features, converge after $T \approx 100$ iterations, and each iteration takes about 64 negative images per positive image, per class. In the ILSVRC'10 dataset, each class has roughly $p = 1{,}200$ positive images, and consist of $C = 1{,}000$ classes. Therefore, the total number of images seen during training of the SVMs is $TC(65p) = 7.800$M images. The NCM classifier requires much more iterations, $T \approx 500$K, but uses at each iteration only $m = 1{,}000$ images, and trains only a single metric. Therefore, the total number of images seen during training is roughly $Tm = 500$M. Finally, the k-NN classifier, requires even more iterations, $T \approx 2$M, but uses only $m = 300$ images per iteration, the total number of images seen before convergence is therefore about $Tm = 600$M.

Table 9.2 Comparison of flat error for different k-NN classification methods using 4K dimensional features. For all methods, except those indicated by 'Full', the data is projected to a 128 dimensional space

		k-NN classifiers						
	SVM	ℓ_2	ℓ_2	LMNN		All	Dynamic	
	Full	Full	+ PCA	10	20		10	20
Top-5	*38.2*	55.7	57.3	50.6	50.4	44.2	*39.7*	40.7

9.5.2 k-NN Metric Learning Results

We start with an assessment of k-NN classifiers in order to select a baseline for comparison with the NCM classifier. Given the cost of k-NN classifiers, we focus our experiments on the 4K dimensional features, and consider the impact of the different choices for the set of target images P_q (see Sect. 9.4), and the projection dimensionality.

We initialize W as a PCA projection, and determine the number of nearest neighbors to use for classification on the validation set. Typically using 100 to 250 neighbors is optimal, which is rather large for k-NN classification, for example in [44] $k = 3$ is used, and indicates that the classification function is rather smooth.

9.5.2.1 Target Selection for k-NN Metric Learning

In the first experiment, we compare the three different options of Sect. 9.4 to define the set of target images P_q, while learning projections to 128 dimensions. For LMNN and dynamic targets, we experimented with various numbers of targets on the validation set and found that using 10 to 20 targets yields the best results.

The results in Table 9.2 show that all methods lead to metrics that are better than the ℓ_2 metric in the original space, or after a PCA projection to 128 dimensions. Furthermore, we can improve over LMNN by using all within-class images as targets, or even further by using dynamic targets. The success of the dynamic target selection can be explained by the fact that among the three alternatives, the learning objective is the most closely related to the k-NN classification rule. The best performance on the flat top-5 error of 39.7 using 10 dynamic targets is, however, slightly worse than the 38.2 error rate of the SVM baseline.

9.5.2.2 Impact of Projection Dimension on k-NN Classification

Next, we evaluate the influence of the projection dimensionality d on the performance, by varying d between 32 and 1024. We only show results using 10 dynamic targets, since this performed best among the evaluated k-NN methods. From the results in Table 9.3 we see that a projection to 256 dimensions yields the lowest error of 39.0, which still remains somewhat inferior to the SVM baseline.

Table 9.3 Flat top-5 error of k-NN and NCM classifiers, as well as baselines, using the 4K and 64K dimensional features, for various projection dimensions, and comparison to related methods, see text for details

	4K dimensional features							64K dimensional features			
Proj. dim.	32	64	128	256	512	1024	Full	128	256	512	Full
SVM baseline							*38.2*				*28.0*
k-NN, dynamic 10	*47.2*	*42.2*	39.7	39.0	39.4	42.4					
NCM, NCMML	49.1	42.7	*39.0*	*37.4*	*37.0*	*37.0*		*31.7*	31.0	30.7	
NCM, FDA	65.2	59.4	54.6	52.0	50.8	50.5					
NCM, PCA + ℓ_2	78.7	74.6	71.7	69.9	68.8	68.2	68.0				63.2
NCM, PCA + inv. cov.	75.5	67.7	60.6	54.5	49.3	46.1	43.8				
Ridge-regression, PCA	86.3	80.3	73.9	68.1	62.8	58.9	54.6				
WSABIE	51.9	45.1	41.2	39.4	38.7	38.5		32.2	*30.1*	*29.2*	

9.5.3 Nearest Class Mean Classifier Results

We now consider the performance of NCM classifiers and the related methods described in Sect. 9.3. In Table 9.3, we show the results for various projection dimensionalities.

We first consider the results for the 4K dimensional features. As observed for the k-NN classifier, using a learned metric outperforms using the ℓ_2 distance (68.0), which is far worse than using the k-NN classifier (55.7, see Table 9.2). However, unexpectedly, with metric learning we observe that our NCM classifier (37.0) outperforms the more flexible k-NN classifier (39.0), as well as the SVM baseline (38.2) when projecting to 256 dimensions or more. Our implementation of WSABIE [46] scores slightly worse (38.5) than the baseline and our NCM classifier, and does not generalize to new classes without retraining.

We also compare our NCM classifier to several algorithms which do allow generalization to new classes. First, we consider two other supervised metric learning approaches, NCM with FDA (which leads to 50.2) and ridge-regression (which leads to 54.6). We observe that NCMML outperforms both methods significantly. Second, we consider two unsupervised variants of the NCM classifier where we use PCA to reduce the dimensionality. In one case, we use the ℓ_2 metric after PCA. In the other, inspired by ridge-regression, we use NCM with the metric W generated by the inverse of the regularized covariance matrix, such that $W^\top W = (\Sigma + \lambda I)^{-1}$, see Sect. 9.3.2. We tuned the regularization parameter λ on the validation set, as was also done for ridge-regression. From these results, we can conclude that, just like for k-NN, the ℓ_2 metric with or without PCA leads to poor results (68.0) as compared to a learned metric. Also, the feature whitening implemented by the inverse covariance metric leads to results (43.8) that are better than using the ℓ_2 metric, and also substantially better than ridge-regression (54.6). The results are however significantly worse than using our learned metric, in particular when using low-dimensional projections.

Fig. 9.7 The nearest classes for two reference classes using the the ℓ_2 distance and metric learned by NCMML. Class probabilities are given for a simulated image that equals the mean of the reference class, see text for details

When we use the 64K dimensional features, the results of the NCM classifier (30.8) are somewhat worse than the SVM baseline (28.0); again the learned metric is significantly better than using the ℓ_2 distance (63.2). WSABIE obtains an error of 29.2, in between the SVM and NCM.

9.5.3.1 Illustration of Metric Learned by NCMML

In Fig. 9.7, we illustrate the difference between the ℓ_2 and the Mahalanobis metric induced by a learned projection from 64K to 512 dimensions. For three reference classes we show the five nearest classes, based on the distance between class means. We also show the posterior probabilities on the reference class and its five neighbor classes according to Eq. (9.5). The feature vector $\boldsymbol{x}$ is set as the mean of the reference class, that is, a simulated perfectly typical image of this class. For the ℓ_2 metric, we used our metric learning algorithm to learn a scaling of the ℓ_2 metric to minimize Eq. (9.9). This does not change the ordering of classes, but ensures that we can compare probabilities computed using both metrics. We find that, as expected, the learned metric has more visually and semantically related neighbor classes. Moreover, we see that using the learned metric most of the probability mass is assigned to the reference class, whereas the ℓ_2 metric leads to rather uncertain classifications.

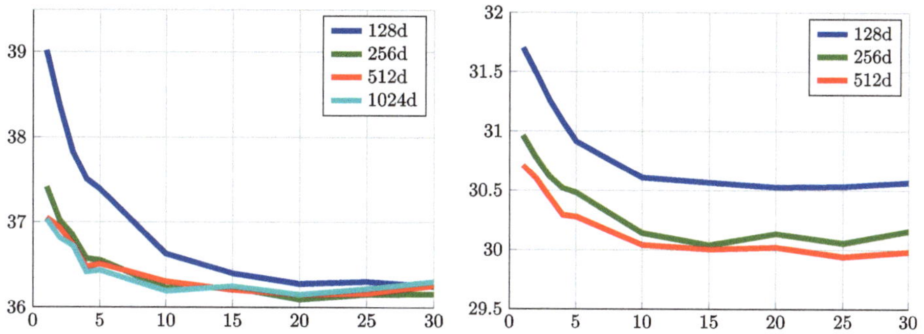

Fig. 9.8 The flat top-5 error of the NCMC-test classifier, which at test time uses $k > 1$ on a metric obtained with $k = 1$, for the 4K features (*left*) and the 64k (*right*) features

Table 9.4 The flat top-5 error of the NCMC classifier using the 4K features, compared to the NCM baseline and the best NCMC-test classifier (with k in brackets)

Method	NCM	NCMC-test		NCMC		
Proj. dim.			(k)	5	10	15
128	39.0	36.3	(*30*)	36.2	*35.8*	36.1
256	37.4	36.1	(*20*)	35.0	*34.8*	35.3
512	37.0	36.2	(*20*)	34.8	*34.6*	35.1

9.5.3.2 Non-linear Classification Using Multiple Class Centroids

In these experiments, we use the non-linear NCMC classifier, introduced in Sect. 9.3.3, where each class is represented by a set of k centroids. We obtain the k centroids per class by using the k-means algorithm in the ℓ_2 space.

Since the cost of training these classifiers is much higher, we run two sets of experiments. In Fig. 9.8, we show the performance of using the NCMC classifier only at test time with $k = [2, \ldots, 30]$, while using a metric obtained by the NCM objective ($k = 1$). This method is denoted as NCMC-test. In Table 9.4, we show the performance of the NCMC classifier, trained with the NCMC objective, using the 4K features. In the same table, we compare the results to the NCM method and the best NCMC-test method.

From the results, we observe that a significant performance improvement can be made by using the non-linear NCMC classifier, especially when using a low number of projection dimensionalities. When learning the NCMC classifier, we can further improve the performance of the nonlinear classification, albeit for a higher training cost. When using as little as 512 projection dimensions, we obtain a performance of 34.6 on the top-5 error, using $k = 10$ centroids. That is an improvement of about 2.4 absolute points over the NCM classifier (37.0), and 3.6 absolute points over SVM classification (38.2), c.f. Table 9.3.

For the 64K features learning for the NCMC objective (with, $k = 10$ and $d = 512$) improves the performance to 29.4, about 1.3 points over the NCM classifier.

Table 9.5 Flat top-5 error for 1,000-way classification among test images of 200 classes not used for metric learning, and control setting with metric learning using all classes

	4K dimensional features									64K dimensional features				
Method	SVM	k-NN			NCM					SVM	NCM			
Proj. dim.	Full	128	256	ℓ_2	128	256	512	1024	ℓ_2	Full	128	256	512	ℓ_2
Trained on all	37.6	39.0	38.4		38.6	36.8	36.4	36.5		27.7	31.7	30.8	30.6	
Trained on 800		42.2	42.4	54.2	42.5	40.4	39.9	39.6	66.6		39.3	37.8	37.8	61.9

9.5.4 Generalizing to New Classes with Few Samples

Given the encouraging classification accuracy of the NCM classifier observed above—and its superior efficiency as compared to the k-NN classifier—we now explore its ability to generalize to novel classes. We also consider its performance as a function of the number of training images available to estimate the mean of novel classes.

Generalization to Classes not Seen During Training In this experiment, we use approximately 1M images corresponding to 800 random classes to learn metrics, and evaluate the generalization performance on 200 held-out classes. The error is evaluated in a 1,000-way classification task, and computed over the 30K images in the test set of the held-out classes. The early stopping strategy uses the validation set of the 200 unseen classes. Performance among test images of the 800 train classes changes only marginally and would obscure the changes among the test images of the 200 held-out classes.

In Table 9.5, we show the performance of NCM and k-NN classifiers, and compare it to the control setting where the metric is trained on all 1,000 classes. The results show that both classifiers generalize remarkably well to new classes. For comparison, we also include the results of the SVM baseline, and the k-NN and NCM classifiers using the ℓ_2 distance, evaluated over the 200 held-out classes. In particular for 1024 dimensional projections of the 4K features, the NCM classifier achieves an error of 39.6 over classes not seen during training, as compared to 36.5 when using all classes for training. For the 64K dimensional features, the drop in performance is larger, but still surprisingly good considering that training for the novel classes consists only in computing their means.

To further demonstrate the generalization ability of the NCM classifier using learned metrics, we also compare it against the SVM baseline on the ImageNet-10K dataset. We use projections learned and validated on the ILSVRC'10 dataset, and only compute the means of the 10K classes. The results in Table 9.6 show that even in this extremely challenging setting the NCM classifier performs remarkably well compared to earlier mentioned SVM-based results of [10, 36, 39] and our baseline, all of which require training 10K classifiers. We note that, to the best of our knowledge, our baseline results exceed the previously known state-of-the-art [26, 36] on this dataset. Training our SVM baseline system took 9 and 280 CPU days respec-

Table 9.6 Flat error rate of the NCM classifier on the ImageNet-10K dataset, using metrics learned on the ILSVRC'10 dataset, with comparison to the baseline SVM, the NCM using ℓ_2 distance (denoted as full), and previously reported SVM results [10, 36, 39] and the Deep Learning framework of [26]

	4K dimensional features						64K dimensional features					Previous Results			
Method	NCM					SVM	NCM				SVM	[10]	[39]	[36]	[26]
Proj. dim.	128	256	512	1024	Full	Full	128	256	512	Full	Full	21K	128K	128K	
Top-1 err.	91.8	90.6	90.5	90.4	95.5	86.0	87.1	86.3	86.1	93.6	78.1	93.6	83.3	80.9	80.8
Top-5 err.	80.7	78.7	78.6	78.6	89.0	72.4	71.7	70.5	70.1	85.4	60.9				

tively for the 4K and 64K features, while the computation of the means for the NCM classifier took approximately 3 and 48 CPU minutes, respectively. This represents roughly a 8,500 fold speed-up as compared to the baseline, without counting the time to learn the projection matrix.

Accuracy as Function of Sample Size of Novel Classes In this experiment, we consider the error as a function of the number of images that are used to compute the means of novel classes. Inspired by [37], we also include results of a zero-shot learning experiment, where we use the ImageNet hierarchy to estimate the mean of novel classes from the means of related training classes, see Sect. 9.3.6 for details.

In Fig. 9.9, we analyze the performance of the NCM classifier trained on the images of the same 800 classes used above, with a learned projection from 4K and 64K to 512 dimensions. The metric and the parameter m are validated using the images of the 200 held-out classes of the validation set. We again report the error on the test images of the held-out classes, both in a 1,000-way classification as above, and in a 200-way classification as in [37]. We repeat the experiment 10 times, and show error-bars at three times standard deviation. For the error to stabilize, we only need approximately 100 images to estimate the class means.

The results also show that the prior leads to zero-shot performance of 66.5 (4K features) and 64.0 (64K features), in the 200-way classification setting. These results are comparable to the result of 65.2 reported in [37], even though a different set of 200 test-classes were used. Note that they also used different features, however their baseline performance of 37.6 top-5 error is comparable to our 4K features (38.2).

More importantly, we show that the zero-shot prior can be effectively combined with the empirical mean to provide a smooth transition from the zero-shot setting to a setting with many training examples. Inclusion of the zero-shot prior leads to a significant error reduction in the regime where ten images or less are available.

9.5.5 Instance Level Image Retrieval

Query-by-example image retrieval can be seen as an image classification problem where only a single positive sample (the query) is given and negative examples

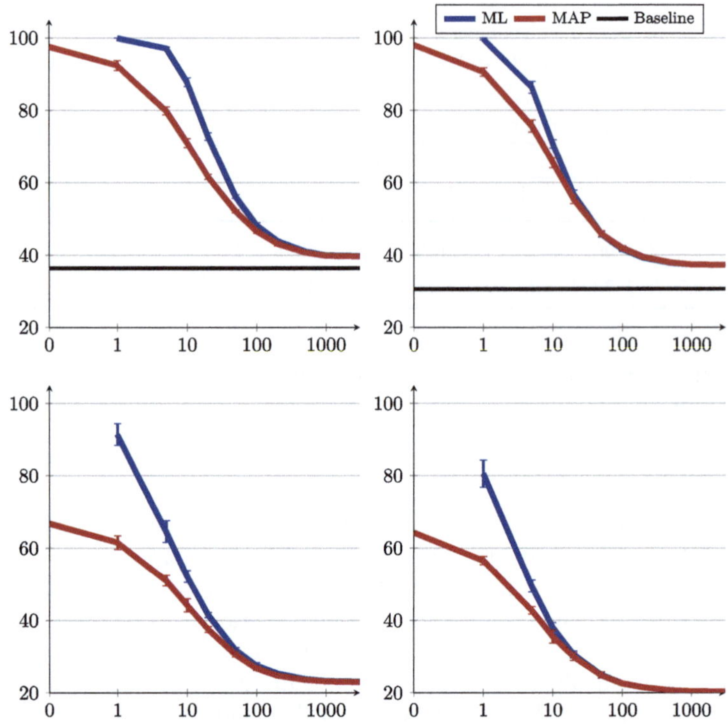

Fig. 9.9 Flat top-5 error of NCM as a function of the number of images used to compute the means for test classes. We compare the ML (*blue*) and MAP (*red*) mean estimates, for the 4K (*left*) and 64K (*right*) features. We show the results for 1,000-way (*top*), including baseline when trained on all classes in *black*, and 200-way classification (*bottom*)

are not explicitly provided. In this case, the class mean simplifies to the query. We propose to use a metric learned for our NCM classifier on an auxiliary supervised dataset to retrieve the most similar images for a given query.

Using classifiers to learn a metric for image retrieval was recently considered also in [16]. They found the Joint Subspace and Classifier Learning (JSCL) method to be most effective. This basically amounts to jointly learning a set of classifiers and a projection matrix W using the WSABIE scoring function, Eq. (9.15), and minimizing the hinge-loss on class labels. After training, the classifiers are discarded and only the learned projection matrix W is used to compute distances between query and database images.

For this experiment, we use the same public benchmarks as in [16]. First, the INRIA Holidays data set introduced by [20] consists of 1,491 images of 500 scenes and objects. In the standard evaluation protocol, one image per scene/object is used as query to search withing the remaining images. The accuracy is measured as the mean average precision over the 500 queries (mAP). Second, the University of Kentucky Benchmark dataset (UKB) introduced by [32], which contains of 4 images for each of the 2,550 objects (10,200 images). We follow the standard evaluation

Table 9.7 Instance level image retrieval accuracy on the Holidays dataset, and the UKB dataset. NCMML is compared to a PCA baseline and the JSCL method [16]

	INRIA Holidays dataset No projection: 77.4 %				UKB dataset No projection: 3.19		
Dim.	PCA	JSCL	NCM	NCM*	PCA	JSCL	NCM
32	61.3	67.7	*69.3*	63.3	2.82	3.04	*3.07*
64	68.0	73.6	*75.4*	68.8	3.01	*3.23*	*3.23*
128	72.3	76.4	*79.6*	73.1	3.08	3.31	*3.33*
256	75.0	78.3	*80.2*	74.0	3.15	*3.36*	3.32
512	76.8	78.9	*80.6*	73.5	3.18	*3.36*	3.31

protocol, where each image is used as query to search in the database. The performance is measured by 4×recall@4 averaged over all queries, hence the maximal score is 4. For both datasets, we extract the 4K image features also used in our earlier experiments, which are the same ones as those used in [16]. To compute the distance between two images, we use the cosine-distance, that is, the dot-product on ℓ_2-normalized vectors.

In analogy to [16], we use NCMML to train a metric from the ILSVRC'10 data set, and do the early stopping based on retrieval performance. To avoid tuning on the test data, the cross-validation is performed on the other dataset, that is, when testing on UKB and we regularize based on Holidays and vice-versa. In Table 9.7, we compare the performance of the NCM based metric with that of JSCL, and also include a baseline PCA method and the performance using the high-dimensional descriptors without any projection. Finally, for the Holidays dataset we included the NCM metric while using early-stopping based on classification performance on the ILSVRC'10 validation data set (NCM-class).

From the results, we observe that the NCM metric yields similar performance gains as the JSCL method on both datasets. In both cases, a projection to only 128 dimensions yields an equal or better retrieval performance as using the original 4K dimensional features. On the Holidays dataset, the NCM metric outperforms the JSCL metric, while on the UKB dataset JSCL slightly outperforms NCM. Both the NCM and JSCL methods are effective to learn a projection metric for instance level retrieval, employing class level labels, and outperform the unsupervised PCA projection.

Note that it is crucial to use retrieval performance for early stopping; without it the results (see NCM*) are in fact worse than the original descriptors, and comparable to using PCA. Thus, the classification objective determines a good "path" through the space of projection matrices, yet it is crucial to regularize for retrieval performance, where the selected number of iterations is typically an order of magnitude smaller than for classification. We explain this discrepancy by the fact that instance level retrieval does not require the suppression of the within class variations needed for good classification. This observation suggests also that even better metrics may be learned by training NCM on a large set of queries with corresponding matches.

9.6 Conclusions

In this chapter, we have considered distance-based classifiers for large-scale image classification. The advantage of distance-based classifiers is that new data (possibly of new classes) can be integrated at a negligible cost. This advantageous property is not shared by the one-vs.-rest SVM approach that is used in most current state-of-the art approaches, but is essential when dealing with real-life open-ended datasets where new images and classes are continuously added over time.

Since the performance of distance-based classifiers is heavily dependent on the used metric, we employ supervised metric learning techniques to improve classification performance. For k-NN classifiers, we rely on the large margin nearest neighbor (LMNN) framework, and consider several variants to select the set of target neighbors. For the NCM classifier, we have introduced a new metric learning technique, which we coined NCMML. It is based on maximizing the log-likelihood of correct prediction using a soft-min over the distances to class centers to define the class probabilities of a sample. Moreover, we introduced the NCMC classifier, a non-linear extension of the NCM classifier, that uses multiple centroids to represent each class. The used number of centroids offers a complexity trade-off from the linear NCM classifier to the non-linear and non-parametric k-NN classifier where all samples are used as a class centroids.

We have experimentally compared the k-NN and NCM classifiers to a strong baseline, the one-vs.-rest SVM approach. Using a high-dimensional Fisher vector image representation, our baseline attains current state-of-the-art results. Surprisingly we found that the NCM classifier outperforms the more flexible k-NN approach. Moreover, the performance of the NCM classifier is comparable to that of SVM baseline (slightly better with 4K dimensional features, but somewhat worse using the 64K dimensional features), while projecting the data to as few as 256 dimensions. Furthermore, we find that using multiple centroids per class improves the performance of the NCM classifier.

Our learned metrics generalize well to unseen classes, as shown by the experiments where the metric is learned on a subset of 800 classes and evaluated on the 200 held out classes. In this case we observe only a modest drop in performance, in spite of the fact that for the held-out classes "training" consists only in computing the mean vector of each class. These results are further corroborated by our experiments on the ImageNet-10K dataset, where we obtain competitive performance at a negligible cost compared to the feature extraction process. We only need to compute the class means, as opposed to training 10,000 binary one-vs.-rest SVM classifiers, which represents roughly a 8,500 fold speedup.

In addition, we have shown that our NCM classifiers can be used in a zero-shot setting where no training images are available for novel classes, and that the zero-shot prior significantly improves performance when combined with a class mean estimated from a limited amount of training images.

Finally, we have shown that NCM provides a unified way to treat classification and retrieval problems, as query-by-example image retrieval can be seen as a classification problem where only a single positive sample per class is provided. We have evaluated the NCM metric for image retrieval and found performance that is comparable to previous published metric learning approaches.

References

1. Bai B, Weston J, Grangier D, Collobert R, Qi Y, Sadamasa K, Chapelle O, Weinberger K (2010) Learning to rank with (a lot of) word features. Inf Retr 13(3):291–314 (special issue on learning to rank)
2. Bengio S, Weston J, Grangier D (2011) Label embedding trees for large multi-class tasks. In: NIPS
3. Bottou L (2010) Large-scale machine learning with stochastic gradient descent. In: COMPSTAT
4. Boyd S, Vandenberghe L (2004) Convex optimization. Cambridge University Press, Cambridge
5. Chai J, Liua H, Chenb B, Baoa Z (2010) Large margin nearest local mean classifier. Signal Process 90(1):236–248
6. Checkik G, Sharma V, Shalit U, Bengio S (2010) Large scale online learning of image similarity through ranking. J Mach Learn Res 11:1109–1135
7. Clinchant S, Csurka G, Perronnin F, Renders J-M (2007) XRCE's participation to ImagEval. In: ImageEval workshop at CVIR
8. Csurka G, Dance C, Fan L, Willamowski J, Bray C (2004) Visual categorization with bags of keypoints. In: ECCV int workshop on stat learning in computer vision
9. Deng J, Dong W, Socher R, Li L-J, Li K, Fei-Fei L (2009) ImageNet: a large-scale hierarchical image database. In: CVPR
10. Deng J, Berg A, Li K, Fei-Fei L (2010) What does classifying more than 10,000 image categories tell us? In: ECCV
11. Fei-Fei L, Fergus R, Perona P (2006) One-shot learning of object categories. IEEE Trans Pattern Anal Mach Intell 28(4):594–611
12. Gao T, Koller D (2011) Discriminative learning of relaxed hierarchy for large-scale visual recognition. In: ICCV
13. Gauvain J-L, Lee C-H (1994) Maximum a posteriori estimation for multivariate Gaussian mixture observations of Markov chains. IEEE Trans Speech Audio Process 2(2):291–298
14. Globerson A, Roweis S (2006) Metric learning by collapsing classes. In: NIPS
15. Goldberger J, Roweis S, Hinton G, Salakhutdinov R (2005) Neighbourhood component analysis. In: NIPS
16. Gordo A, Rodríguez J, Perronnin F, Valveny E (2012) Leveraging category-level labels for instance-level image retrieval. In: CVPR
17. Gray R, Neuhoff D (1998) Quantization. IEEE Trans Inf Theory 44(6):2325–2383
18. Guillaumin M, Mensink T, Verbeek J, Schmid C (2009) TagProp: discriminative metric learning in nearest neighbor models for image auto-annotation. In: ICCV
19. Guillaumin M, Verbeek J, Schmid C (2009) Is that you? Metric learning approaches for face identification. In: ICCV
20. Jégou H, Douze M, Schmid C (2008) Hamming embedding and weak geometric consistency for large scale image search. In: ECCV
21. Jégou H, Douze M, Schmid C (2011) Product quantization for nearest neighbor search. IEEE Trans Pattern Anal Mach Intell 33(1):117–128
22. Jégou H, Perronnin F, Douze M, Sánchez J, Pérez P, Schmid C (2012) Aggregating local image descriptors into compact codes. IEEE Trans Pattern Anal Mach Intell 34(9):1704–1716
23. Köstinger M, Hirzer M, Wohlhart P, Roth P, Bischof H (2012) Large scale metric learning from equivalence constraints. In: CVPR
24. Lampert C, Nickisch H, Harmeling S (2009) Learning to detect unseen object classes by between-class attribute transfer. In: CVPR

25. Larochelle H, Erhan D, Bengio Y (2008) Zero-data learning of new tasks. In: AAAI conference on artificial intelligence
26. Le Q, Ranzato M, Monga R, Devin M, Chen K, Corrado G, Dean J, Ng A (2012) Building high-level features using large scale unsupervised learning. In: ICML
27. Lin Y, Lv F, Zhu S, Yang M, Cour T, Yu K, Cao L, Huang T (2011) Large-scale image classification: fast feature extraction and SVM training. In: CVPR
28. Lowe D (2004) Distinctive image features from scale-invariant keypoints. Int J Comput Vis 60(2):91–110
29. Lucchi A, Weston J (2012) Joint image and word sense discrimination for image retrieval. In: ECCV
30. Mensink T, Verbeek J, Perronnin F, Csurka G (2012) Metric learning for large scale image classification: generalizing to new classes at near-zero cost. In: ECCV
31. Mensink T, Verbeek J, Perronnin F, Csurka G (2013) Distance-based image classification: generalizing to new classes at near-zero cost. IEEE Trans Pattern Anal Mach Intell (to appear)
32. Nistér D, Stewénius H (2006) Scalable recognition with a vocabulary tree. In: CVPR
33. Nowak E, Jurie F (2007) Learning visual similarity measures for comparing never seen objects. In: CVPR
34. Parameswaran S, Weinberger KQ (2010) Large margin multi-task metric learning. In: NIPS
35. Perronnin F, Sánchez J, Mensink T (2010) Improving the Fisher kernel for large-scale image classification. In: ECCV
36. Perronnin F, Akata Z, Harchaoui Z, Schmid C (2012) Towards good practice in large-scale learning for image classification. In: CVPR
37. Rohrbach M, Stark M, Schiele B (2011) Evaluating knowledge transfer and zero-shot learning in a large-scale setting. In: CVPR
38. Saenko K, Kulis B, Fritz M, Darrell T (2010) Adapting visual category models to new domains. In: ECCV
39. Sánchez J, Perronnin F (2011) High-dimensional signature compression for large-scale image classification. In: CVPR
40. Tommasi T, Caputo B (2009) The more you know, the less you learn: from knowledge transfer to one-shot learning of object categories. In: BMVC
41. Veenman C, Tax D (2005) LESS: a model-based classifier for sparse subspaces. IEEE Trans Pattern Anal Mach Intell 27(9):1496–1500
42. Webb AR (2002) Statistical pattern recognition. Wiley, New York
43. Weinberger KQ, Chapelle O (2009) Large margin taxonomy embedding for document categorization. In: NIPS
44. Weinberger K, Saul L (2009) Distance metric learning for large margin nearest neighbor classification. J Mach Learn Res 10:207–244
45. Weinberger K, Blitzer J, Saul L (2006) Distance metric learning for large margin nearest neighbor classification. In: NIPS
46. Weston J, Bengio S, Usunier N (2011) WSABIE: scaling up to large vocabulary image annotation. In: IJCAI
47. Zhang J, Marszałek M, Lazebnik S, Schmid C (2007) Local features and kernels for classification of texture and object categories: a comprehensive study. Int J Comput Vis 73(2):213–238
48. Zhou X, Zhang X, Yan Z, Chang S-F, Hasegawa-Johnson M, Huang T (2008) Sift-bag kernel for video event analysis. In: ACM multimedia

Chapter 10
Top–Down Bayesian Inference of Indoor Scenes

Luca Del Pero and Kobus Barnard

Abstract The task of inferring the 3D layout of indoor scenes from images has seen many recent advancements. Understanding the basic 3D geometry of these environments is important for higher level applications, such as object recognition and robot navigation. In this chapter, we present our Bayesian generative model for understanding indoor environments. We model the 3D geometry of a room and the objects within it with non-overlapping 3D boxes, which provide approximations for both the room boundary and objects like tables and beds. We separately model the imaging process (camera parameters), and an image likelihood, thus providing a complete, generative statistical model for image data. A key feature of this work is using prior information and constraints on the 3D geometry of the scene elements, which addresses ambiguities in the imaging process in a top–down fashion. We also describe and relate this work to other state-of-the-art approaches, and discuss techniques that have become standard in this field, such as estimating the camera pose from a triplet of vanishing points.

10.1 Introduction

There has been much recent interest in estimating the 3D layout of indoor scenes from monocular images [4, 9–11, 15, 16, 20, 24], as this provides crucial geometric context for higher level tasks, such as object recognition and prediction of human activities. Consider for example, Fig. 10.1. From just a single image, human observers can infer the 3D structure of the room, even when many cues are hidden. For example, we can estimate the boundary between the floor and the walls, even if it is mostly occluded by furniture. This kind of geometric understanding informs interaction with the environment. For example, one could infer that the bed provides a surface for sitting, or that a possible path to the couch goes around the bed.

L. Del Pero (✉) · K. Barnard
University of Arizona, Tucson, USA
e-mail: delpero@email.arizona.edu

K. Barnard
e-mail: kobus@sista.arizona.edu

G.M. Farinella et al. (eds.), *Advanced Topics in Computer Vision*,
Advances in Computer Vision and Pattern Recognition,
DOI 10.1007/978-1-4471-5520-1_10,

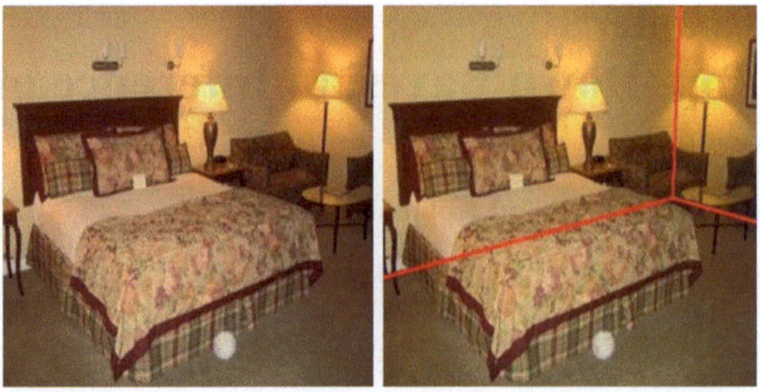

Fig. 10.1 Inferring the 3D layout of a room from an image is challenging due to occlusions and clutter. Here, the boundary between floor and walls is occluded by the furniture. We show on the *right* the correct position of the 3D box approximating the room

A number of computational methods for recovering the 3D scene layout have been recently developed based on modeling rooms with simple geometric primitives, such as sets of orthogonal surfaces [15], or 3D boxes [9, 16]. Despite the coarse geometric approximation, these approaches have enabled several interesting applications. For example, Gupta et al. [7] used extracted 3D information to identify locations where people can sit or lie, while Hedau et al. [10] showed how knowledge of the 3D environment helps detecting pieces of furniture, such as beds. Other notable applications include inserting realistic computer graphics objects into indoor images [14], and robot navigation [22].

This chapter extends our previous work on indoor scene understanding [2, 3]. Specifically, we provide additional details on the model and the inference discussed in these papers. New contributions include making the inference multi-threaded by allowing threads to exchange information (Sect. 10.3.4), a new method to make the inference more robust (Sect. 10.3.1.4), and a comprehensive evaluation of all the techniques proposed (Sect. 10.4).

10.1.1 Background

In the domain of inferring 3D geometry from indoor images, it is common to parametrize the scene layout as a 3D box [9–11, 16, 20, 24]. This is often referred to as *room box*, as it coarsely models the space of a room as if it were empty. An example is shown in Fig. 10.1, where the estimated room box is shown on the right. Inferring the room box from an image entails determining the 3D position and orientation of the floor, ceiling and walls that typically define an indoor environment. This process presents two main challenges. First, recovering the 3D box requires inferring the perspective transformation that generated the image (camera estimation). Second, clutter and occlusions are a major source of confusion, since the room box boundaries are often mostly hidden (Fig. 10.1).

Estimating the camera in indoor scenes has been tackled by using a strong model [9–11, 16, 20, 24], specifically the Manhattan world assumption [1]. This states that most surfaces in the scene are aligned with three principal orthogonal directions, which can be estimated by detecting a triplet of orthogonal vanishing points on the image plane [18]. The parameters of the perspective projection can then be recovered analytically from the position of the vanishing points, and this is a well understood problem [8]. In Manhattan world indoor scenes, the three orthogonal directions are invariably those of the room box.

Addressing occlusions and clutter requires reasoning about the objects in the room. Hedau et al. [9] detect clutter in 2D with an appearance based classifier. More recently, Lee et al. [15] showed the benefits of reasoning about objects in 3D. Specifically, they proposed modeling objects as 3D boxes, which provide reasonable bounding approximations of objects typically found in rooms, such as beds and tables, and further exploit the Manhattan assumption by constraining these boxes to be aligned with the room box. Their results showed that joint inference of the room and the 3D objects, which addresses ambiguities caused by clutter and occlusions in a top–down fashion, improves on estimating the room box. Our approach is related to Lee's work [15], but we advocate an even more top–down approach with a more unified representation.

10.1.2 Overview of Our Approach

Similarly to Lee et al. [15], our goal is to simultaneously estimate the camera, detect and localize in 3D the floor, ceiling, and walls comprising the room "box", and determine the position of the objects in the room. However, instead of using an object box only to explain occlusions, we want to identify it (e.g., a couch or a bed) as well. This simultaneously achieves a fuller understanding of the scene, and allows object knowledge to help fit the overall geometry. For example, knowing that a specific block is approximating a bed rather than, say, a wardrobe, adds constraints on the box's 3D size and position, as a bed is typically much lower. Conversely, the size and position of a 3D block provide strong cues on the identity of the object.

Our goal is to provide a comprehensive parsing of the scene that is globally consistent in 3D, both geometrically and semantically, which is on the lines of the work of Hoiem et al. [13]. This introduces complex constraints, which make the inference process challenging. Examples of constraints include preventing objects from overlapping in 3D, and enforcing that each object is contained in the room box. Previous work [9, 16, 20] relied on the framework of structured prediction for inferring indoor scene models, where inference and modeling are strongly coupled. This makes it harder to adapt the method to handle more complex sources of information, such as conditioning the position and size of objects on their identity.

Bayesian inference is a natural way to handle these complexities, as it allows to separate the modeling and the inference. Specifically, we propose a Bayesian generative model for images of indoor scenes, where we separately model the 3D geometry (room box and objects), the imaging process (camera parameters), and an image likelihood. We assume that the image features are generated statistically from the projected 3D scene under the camera parameters. We impose further structure by introducing the notion of an object type. The Bayesian framework naturally allows using prior information of the world, which in our case are prior distributions on a box's 3D size and position conditioned on its type and on the room box. For example, beds are typically against a wall, while tables are likely found in the center of the room. In this work, we allow four different types of object boxes, approximating beds, cabinets, couches and tables. We also introduce the notion of *frames*, which are thin boxes "anchored" to a wall, to approximate objects such as doors. We use three types of frames: doors, picture frames, and windows.

Bayesian inference allows us to jointly infer all the elements in our model, without having to commit to partial solutions. For example, previous work [9–11, 16, 20, 24] rely on initial estimates of the camera parameters, and they cannot recover from mistakes in this step. Similarly, both Hedau et al. [9] and Gupta et al. [7] use an initial estimate of the room box for identifying beds and predicting human activities in the room, respectively. Again, errors in the estimate of the room box cannot be recovered from. In principle, our approach does not have this problem.

In what follows, we detail with our model for the 3D scene geometry and the camera (Sect. 10.2). We then develop priors that distinguish among object boxes based on their position and size (Sect. 10.2.1), and then detail the imaging model (Sect. 10.2.2), including an analysis of the standard image features used in this field. We then describe the Markov chain Monte Carlo sampling method that we use for inference (Sect. 10.3). Important aspects include how to handle constraints during sampling, how to use data-driven methods for efficient sampling, and how to do inference with multiple threads. Finally, we provide extensive evaluation of our approach on two standard datasets (Sect. 10.4).

10.2 A Bayesian Generative Model for Indoor Scenes

We use a Bayesian generative model, where we assume that images are generated by the projection of the 3D scene. We partition model parameters, θ, into scene parameters, s, encoding the 3D geometry, and camera parameters, c, modeling the perspective transformation

$$\theta = (s, c). \tag{10.1}$$

We define the posterior distribution as

$$p(\theta|D) \propto p(D|\theta)p(\theta), \tag{10.2}$$

where D are features detected on the image plane and $p(\theta)$ is the prior distribution over model parameters.

Scene parameters include the room box and objects in it

$$s = (r, o_1, \ldots, o_n), \tag{10.3}$$

where the number of objects n and their type are not known a priori. We model the room as a right-angled parallelepiped whose floor is parallel to the x–z plane of the world reference frame. It is defined by its 3D center, width, height, length, and rotation angle, γ_r, around an axis parallel to the world y-axis and through the room center (yaw):

$$r = (x_r, y_r, z_r, w_r, h_r, l_r, \gamma_r). \tag{10.4}$$

Objects in the room are similarly modeled by blocks, but include an object category, t_i, (e.g., bed, table, door). A block on the floor could approximate a convex object such as a bed, or provide a bounding box for a more complex object, such as a table. Windows, doors and pictures are approximated with thin blocks (frames) attached to a wall. All objects share the same orientation γ_r of the room block, following the Manhattan world assumption. Objects must be entirely inside the room box, and they can not intersect each other.

Objects coordinates are relative to the coordinate frame defined by the room center, and whose axes are aligned with the room walls, which we call "room coordinates". We define a coordinate transformation function $r_{\text{coord}}(x, y, z) = (x^r, y^r, z^r)$ for later use, to transform a point defined relatively to the world coordinate system (x, y, z) into room coordinates. Since the world x–z plane is parallel to the room floor, r_{coord} simply applies a translation and a rotation around the y-axis defined by the room yaw γ_r. An advantage of storing objects in room coordinates, is that it allows for efficient computation of intersections among objects, and between an object and the room box.

Each object is "anchored" to a room surface, whose index is stored as a discrete variable (s_i). Furniture objects lie on the floor $(s_i = 4)$, implying that, given the object height, the y coordinate of the object center is not a free parameter. Specifically, $y_i = -(y_r/2) + (h_i/2.0)$, where $-(y_r/2)$ is the position of the floor in room coordinates. Similarly, frames are anchored to one of the walls, which analogously constrains their parameters (see Fig. 10.2). To summarize the object parameters,

$$o_i = (t_i, s_i, x_i, y_i, z_i, w_i, h_i, l_i). \tag{10.5}$$

The imaging process is modeled with a standard perspective camera

$$c = (f, \phi, \psi), \tag{10.6}$$

where f, ϕ and ψ are, respectively, the focal length, the pitch, and the roll angle. Since absolute positions cannot be determined when reconstructing from single images, we arbitrarily position the camera at the origin of the world coordinate system, pointing down the z-axis. The extrinsic camera rotations, specified by three degrees of freedom, are fully determined by ϕ, ψ and the yaw γ_r of the room (see Fig. 10.3). Pitch and roll are constrained within ranges of plausible values for indoor scenes ($\phi \in [-60°, 60°]$), $\psi \in [-10°, 10°]$), while the focal length has to be positive. We further assume unary aspect ratio, no skew, and that the principal point coincides with the image center.

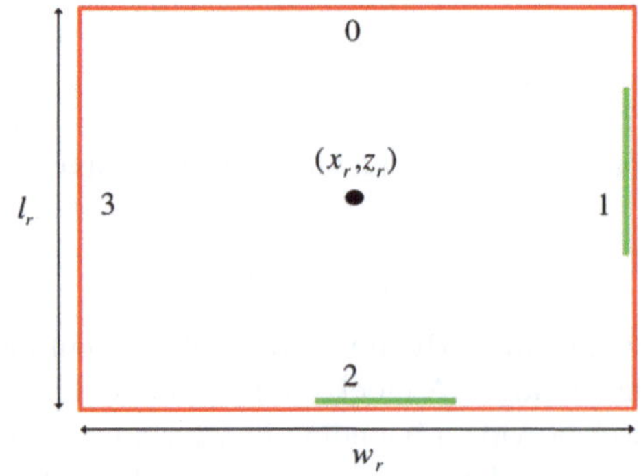

Fig. 10.2 The coordinates of the objects are stored in a coordinate frame relative to the center of the room box, and whose axes are aligned with the room walls. Here, two frames are "anchored" to a wall of the room box, seen from above. Walls are numbered from 0 to 3, and this index is stored in variable s_i, which imposes constraints on the parameters in Eq. 10.5. For example, for the frame on the *right*, we have $s_i = 1$ and $x_i = (w_r/2)$. Further, since frames are approximated with thin blocks, we set $w_i = \varepsilon$, with $\varepsilon = 0.01$ units. For the frame at the *bottom*, $s_i = 2$, $z_i = (l_r/2)$, and $l_i = \varepsilon$

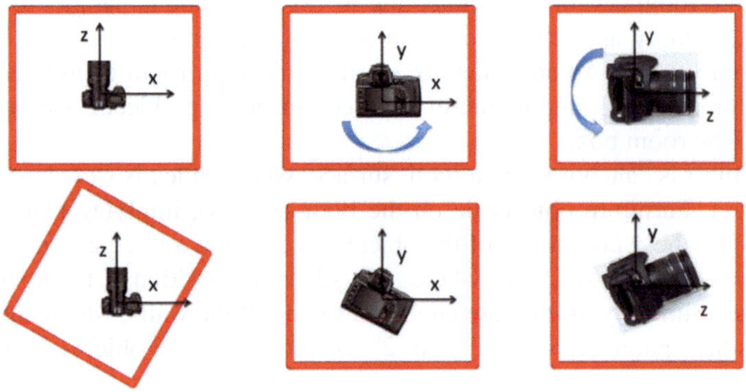

Fig. 10.3 Camera parameters. The extrinsic parameters define the position and orientation of the camera with respect to the world reference frame. Since absolute sizes and position cannot be determined, we arbitrarily position the camera at the origin of the world coordinate system, pointing down the negative z-axis. The room box can rotate around its y-axis, thus determining the yaw of the camera (*left column*). Two more angles, a rotation around the camera z-axis (roll, *mid column*) and a rotation about the x-axis (pitch, *right column*) complete the camera orientation specification

10.2.1 Model Priors

Priors on scene elements improve global scene understanding by helping resolve ambiguity during inference, and also support identifying objects based on geometry cues, such as size and location, alone. Previous work has used blocks in the scene to explain occlusions [16] and to infer what regions of the 3D space are occupied by generic objects [11]. In this work, we assign a semantic label to our blocks (e.g., couch, door, etc.), with each label corresponding to specific prior probabilities on object size and position in 3D. Because we are reconstructing from a single image, we have one overall scale ambiguity, and thus priors on object "size" and position are defined relatively to the room box.

As an example of information captured by the priors, wardrobe cabinets are tall and narrow and typically against a wall, while tables are usually shorter, wider, and in the middle of the room. Similarly, a door is quite tall and touches the floor, while picture frames are much shorter and are typically found in the higher half of a wall.

Assuming independence, the overall prior for the model parameters is given by

$$p(\theta) = \pi(r)\pi(c)\prod_{i=1}^{n}\pi(o_i), \tag{10.7}$$

where $\pi(r)$ is the prior on the room box, $\pi(c)$ is the prior on camera parameters, and $\pi(o_i)$ is the prior for one of n objects in the room. We now describe each of these components and how we set their parameters from training data.

10.2.1.1 Prior on Room Box

The room box is defined in terms of the center position in 3D (x_r, y_r, z_r) and its width, height, and length (w_r, h_r, l_r). First, we define a prior over the ratio between the long dimension to the short dimension, with

$$r_{r1} = \frac{\max(w_r, l_r)}{\min(w_r, l_r)}. \tag{10.8}$$

We use this formulation since we do not know in advance which dimension is the largest. We also put a prior on the ratio of the long dimension to the height

$$r_{r2} = \frac{\max(w_r, l_r)}{h_r}. \tag{10.9}$$

The prior distributions over these two quantities are set to be relatively non-informative, but help reduce the time spent in regions of the sampling space with low probability, especially during the early stages of the inference process. We set both parameters to be normal distributions, independent from each other

$$\pi(r) = \mathcal{N}(r_{r1}, \mu_{r1}, \sigma_{r1})\mathcal{N}(r_{r2}, \mu_{r2}, \sigma_{r2}). \tag{10.10}$$

10.2.1.2 Prior on Camera Parameters

We found that the camera height from the floor c_h is a particularly indicative property in indoor scenes, as small variations in this quantity result in major changes in the image plane. Intuitively, pictures of indoor images are rarely taken by putting

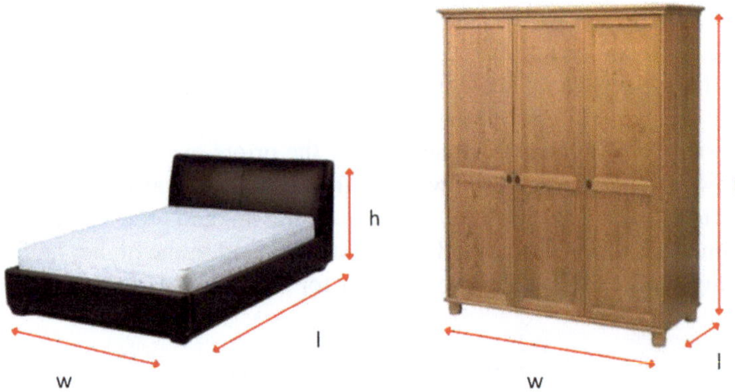

Fig. 10.4 Distinguishing objects using their size. The ratio between the height of an object and the largest between its width and length varies considerably between beds and cabinets. In this example, also the ratio between width and length is quite discriminative

the camera close to the floor or to the ceiling. Since we cannot use absolute sizes, the prior is defined on the ratio r_{ch} between camera height and room height

$$\pi(c) = \mathcal{N}(r_{\text{ch}}, \mu_{\text{ch}}, \sigma_{\text{ch}}). \tag{10.11}$$

10.2.1.3 Prior on Objects

Several categories of furniture and frames have a very distinctive size (Fig. 10.4). Here we introduce a general formulation for a prior for a specific object of category $t_i = \tau$ that exploits this intuition. Given an object o_i defined in terms of its size (w_i, h_i, l_i), and a room with dimensions (w_r, h_r, l_r), we use the following quantities

- Ratio between the object height and its largest other dimension $r_{i1} = h_i / \max(w_i, l_i)$ (Fig. 10.4). This helps distinguish between categories that are taller than they are wide, such as wardrobes, and short and wide objects, such as beds.
- Ratio between the object long and short dimensions, $r_{i2} = \max(w_i, l_i)/\min(w_i, l_i)$ (Fig. 10.4). Again, we use this formulation since we do not know in advance which dimension is the largest. This quantity discriminates between furniture with a roughly square base, and furniture with a rectangular base. This component is not used for frames, since one of their width or length is always negligible.
- Ratio between room height and object height $r_{i3} = h_r / h_i$. Intuitively, the height of a bed is quite small with respect to the room height, whereas the height of a wardrobe or of a door is quite large (Fig. 10.5).
- Whether the object is against a wall or not. This is based on the intuition that some objects tend to be against a wall (e.g., beds) more than others (tables). For frames, we use whether or not the frame touches the floor. For example, doors touch the floor, while windows typically do not.

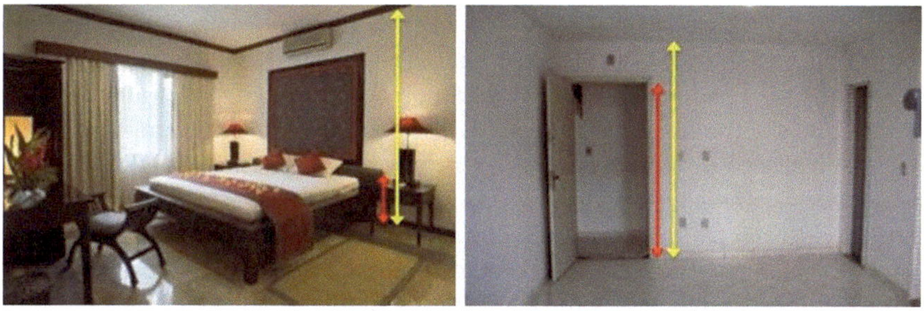

Fig. 10.5 Learning the ratio between room height and object height. This quantity is very informative, and we estimate its statistics from training images. We use the ratio between the two arrows, provided that the object is against or close to a wall. While ratios of lengths of collinear segments are normally not preserved by projective transformations (only affine), in this domain the vanishing point for vertical segments is usually at infinity, and this method provides a reasonable approximation

The first two ratios carry information on the object structure, and do not depend on the scene, while the last two encode information on the size and position of an object relatively to the room box. The first three quantities follow a normal distribution

$$\pi_j(o_i|t_i=\tau)=\mathcal{N}(r_{ij};\mu_{\tau_j},\sigma_{\tau j}), \qquad (10.12)$$

for $j=1,2,3$. Each category τ has different $(\mu_{\tau j},\sigma_{\tau j})$, and for object o_i we use the prior distribution for the category it belongs to, denoted by t_i. Notice that from now on we will use the shorthand $\pi_j(o_i)$ for $\pi_j(o_i|t_i=\tau)$. Last, d_i follows a Bernoulli distribution $\pi(d_i)$. Given an object o_i, we combine the components of its prior probability as follows

$$\pi(o_i)=\pi(d_i)\prod_{j=1}^{3}\pi_j(o_i). \qquad (10.13)$$

10.2.1.4 Setting Prior Probabilities from Data

As mentioned above, the first two components of the object prior do not depend on the scene. For each category τ, we set $(\mu_{\tau 1},\sigma_{\tau 1},\mu_{\tau 2},\sigma_{\tau 2})$ using fifty random examples selected from online furniture and appliances catalogs. We recorded their dimensions, provided in the text description, and the means and variances of the relevant ratios. We used the Ikea catalog[1] for beds, couches, cabinets and tables, and the Home Depot catalog[2] for windows, doors and picture frames.

Setting the parameters for the remaining two priors is more challenging, since they relate the size of an object category to that of the room, and this information is

[1] http://www.ikea.com/us/en/catalog/categories/departments/bedroom/

[2] http://www6.homedepot.com/cyber-monday/index.html

not available in furniture catalogs. In this case, we use image data, and set (μ_{c3}, σ_{c3}) as explained in Fig. 10.5. We also use images to set $\pi(d)$, which we approximate as the frequency at which an instance of an object of category τ is against a wall, or floor if it is a frame. For training, we used the images in the training split of the Hedau dataset [9], omitting images where we could not tell whether a piece of furniture was against the wall or not.

Last, we set the parameters of the priors on camera and room box from training images. We manually fit an empty room box and the camera to images in the Hedau training set, from which we set the parameters [3].

10.2.2 The Image Model

Our image model is similar to the one used by Schlecht and Barnard [19]. Specifically, we assume that image features $D = (f_1, \ldots, f_s)$ are generated by the projection of the 3D scene under the given camera. We use three feature types that proved useful in this domain, specifically edges [2, 3, 15], orientation surfaces [15, 16], and geometric context [9, 16].

10.2.2.1 Image Edges

We assume image edges to be generated by the blocks in the scene. We measure the quality of a fit by comparing the set of edges E_d detected on the image plane to the set of edges E_θ generated by projecting the model. As in Schlecht et al. [19], we define a likelihood function $p(E_d|E_\theta)$, which we specify using the following intuitions:

- An edge point $e_{dj} \in E_d$ detected in the image plane should be matched to an edge point $e_{\theta k} \in E_\theta$ generated by the model. If the match is good the two points should be very close to each other, and the difference in orientation between the two edges should be minimal. We use $p(e_{dj}|e_{\theta k}) = \mathcal{N}(d_{jk}, 0, \sigma_d)\mathcal{N}(\phi_{jk}, 0, \sigma_\phi)$, where d_{jk} is the distance between the points, and ϕ_{jk} the difference in orientation between the edges.
- We penalize a detected edge point that is not matched to any model edge (noise). We define p_n as the probability of such an event occurring.
- We explain points in E_θ not matched to any point in E_d as missing detections, and define probabilities p_{hmiss} and p_{smiss}. The former is used for "hard" edges arising from occlusion boundaries, such as the edges that belong to the silhouette of an object. The latter is used for "soft" edges that are less likely to be found by the edge detector, such as the room edges and non-silhouette edges from objects. It is less likely that a detector will miss a "hard" edge compared with a "soft" edge. Note that one of the advantages of using a full 3D model, is that we can determine whether hypothesized edge points in E_θ are hard or soft.

We then have

$$\tilde{p}(E_d|E_\theta) = p_n^{N_n} p_{\text{smiss}}^{N_{\text{smiss}}} p_{\text{hmiss}}^{N_{\text{hmiss}}} \prod_{(j,k)\in\text{matches}} p(e_{dj}|e_{\theta k}), \tag{10.14}$$

where N_n is the number of edge points labeled as noise, and $N_{\text{smiss}}(N_{\text{hmiss}})$ the number of missed soft (hard) edges. We match points in a greedy fashion by finding the closest point e_θ to a data edge e_d along the edge gradient, provided that this distance is smaller than 40 pixels, and the difference in orientation is less than 0.7 radian. We further adjust this likelihood function to make it less sensitive to the number of edge points, which we found makes it more stable over a larger variety of input data. Specifically, we use

$$p(E_d|E_\theta) \approx \tilde{p}(E_d|E_\theta)^{(N_{\text{hmiss}}+N_{\text{smiss}}+N_n+N_{\text{matches}})^{-1}}. \tag{10.15}$$

10.2.2.2 Orientation Surfaces

Based on the Manhattan world assumption, most pixels in the scene are generated by a plane aligned with one of three orthogonal directions, and we can estimate which one using the approach by Lee et al. [15]. We compare the pixel orientation O_d detected from the image plane with the orientation surfaces O_θ generated by projecting our model. We approximate $p(O_d|O_\theta)$ by the ratio between the number of pixels where the orientation detected on the image plane agrees with the orientation predicted by the model, and the total number of pixels.

10.2.2.3 Geometric Context

Following Hedau et al. [9], we also consider geometric context labels, which estimate the geometric class of each pixel, choosing between object, floor, ceiling, left, middle and right wall. This is done using a probabilistic classifier trained on a mixture of color and oriented gradient features [12]. We use the code and the pre-trained classifier available online [12]. For each pixel p_k, this provides a probability distribution $gc_k = [gc_{k1}, \ldots, gc_{k6}]$ over the six classes. Given the label l predicted by the model for pixel p_k, we define $p(gc_k|p_k) = p(gc_k|p_k = l) = gc_l$, and

$$p(GC|\theta) = \frac{\sum_{p_k \in I} p(gc_k|p_k)}{\text{size}(I)}, \tag{10.16}$$

where we average the contributions of all image pixels. Since the available classifier was trained against data where only furniture was labeled as objects, and not frames, we consider frames as part of the wall they are attached to, and not as objects when we evaluate on geometric context.

10.2.2.4 Combining the Three Features

Assuming independence among the features, we define our likelihood function

$$p(D|\theta) = p(E_d|E_m)p(O_d|O_m)^{\alpha} p(GC|\theta)^{\beta}, \tag{10.17}$$

where α and β weigh the importance of the orientation and geometric context likelihoods, relative to the edge likelihood. We set $\beta = 12$ and $\alpha = 6$ by running our algorithm on the training portion of the Hedau dataset [9]. Here we used a coarse grid search over α and β, with a step of 2, using the room box layout error (defined in Sect. 10.4) as an objective function.

Later, in the results (Fig. 10.18), we illustrate how these three features work together. Errors in the edge detection process can be fixed using orientation surfaces and geometric context, and vice versa. Using edges also helps improving the camera fit when starting from a wrong estimate of the vanishing points, which are detected at the beginning and used to initialize the camera parameters. In fact, since the algorithms for computing orientation maps and geometric context depend on the initial vanishing point estimation, this feature is compromised by this initial error, whereas edges are not.

10.3 Inference

We use Markov chain Monte Carlo (MCMC) sampling to search the parameter space, defined by camera and room box parameters, the unknown number of objects, their type, and the parameters of each object. To change the discrete structure of the model, which includes the unknown number of objects, and the type of each of them, we use reversible jump Metropolis-Hastings (MH) [5, 6]. To change the continuous parameters, which comprise the room box, the camera, and size and position of each object, we use Hamiltonian dynamics sampling [17]. The proposals from these two samplings strategies are often referred to as "jump" and "diffusion" moves [23].

The 3D structure of the model introduces several constraints and dependencies among parameters, which must be carefully taken into account during inference. Specifically, objects cannot overlap in 3D, and they have to be entirely inside the room box. Further, the camera must be inside the room box, and not within the volume occupied by any of the objects. Enforcing these constraints during inference can introduce several ambiguities, as illustrated in Fig. 10.6(g), using a birdview of the room box. Consider sampling over objects A and B simultaneously. This could result in a conflict where object B tries to expand towards the left, and A towards the right, as illustrated by the arrows. A similar situation can happen when the room box is trying to shrink and object B is trying to expand Fig. 10.6(h).

To avoid these ambiguities, we use three different types of continuous moves over subsets of the scene parameters, and define rules for adapting the model so that no constraint is violated. In the first one, we sample over the parameters of a single object, and we enforce constraints by shrinking other objects in case of overlap, and expanding the room box in case it is not big enough to contain the

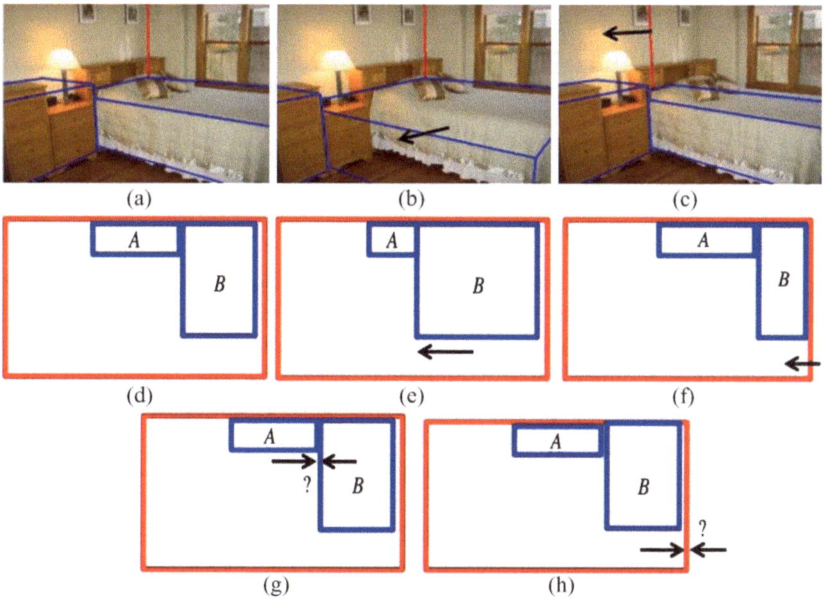

Fig. 10.6 Sampling over subsets of parameters handles containment constraints (*top two rows*) and avoids ambiguities (*bottom row*). Consider sampling over the parameters of a single object at a time. As the object expands, other objects have to shrink to avoid overlap. For example, A has to shrink to allow B to grow (**a**)–(**b**), as shown also in the corresponding birdviews (**d**)–(**e**). Similarly, when sampling over the room box only, objects have to shrink so that they are entirely in the room, like object B in (**c**) and (**f**). Instead, sampling over two objects at the same time could result in conflicts such as in (**g**), where both A and B are contending the same 3D space. Sampling over the room box and an object jointly would create similar conflicts (**h**)

object (Fig. 10.6(a)–(b)). The second move samples over the parameters of the room box only, and adapt the objects to respect the constraints. As the room box becomes smaller, we shrink objects in case they end outside the room (Fig. 10.6(c)). Third, we jointly sample over camera and room box parameters, by enforcing constraints as in the previous move. Further, for all the three moves just discussed, we enforce that the camera is inside the room box, and is not within the volume occupied by an object. These are corner cases that occur less often, and we simply reject samples violating these constraints.

Diffusion moves and Jump moves are alternated throughout inference. We summarize the entire process here, and describe each component in detail in the following sections:

1. Initialize the parameters of the camera and of the room box
2. Repeat K times

    a. Generate a new sample with one of the following moves, chosen randomly

        - Jump 1: add an object to the scene (furniture of frame)
        - Jump 2: remove an object from the scene

- Jump 3: pick a random object, and change its type
- Diffusion 1: pick a random object and sample over its parameters
- Diffusion 2: sample over the room box parameters only
- Diffusion 3: sample over room box and camera parameters

b. Reject samples that violate the constraints on the camera position (camera outside the room or inside an object).

3. Return the sample with the highest posterior

We rely on a multi-threaded strategy to efficiently explore more of the space on modern multi-core workstations. Each thread executes the procedure above, and, at the end, threads are allowed to exchange information, as some of the objects might be found by a thread and missed by the others, and vice versa (Sect. 10.3.4). This exchanging procedure is followed by additional sampling, and we output the best sample found. In our experiments we used 20 threads, and the whole inference process takes on average ten minutes per image.

In what follows, we first detail with the diffusion moves in Sect. 10.3.1, where we develop concepts needed to better discuss the Jump moves Sect. 10.3.2, and how we initialize the room box and the camera Sect. 10.3.3. Last, we explain how to exchange objects among threads Sect. 10.3.4.

10.3.1 Diffusion Moves

As illustrated in Fig. 10.6, we sample over subsets of the scene parameters and specify rules to make the model comply with all constraints. We use Hamiltonian dynamics sampling, which were used by Schlecht et al. [19] for learning the continuous parameters of geometric models for furniture with a similar parametrization.

We use Neal's formulation of Hamiltonian dynamics [17] to sample over phase space, where the energy function is defined in terms of the joint distribution of the parameters and the image data $p(\theta, D)$

$$E(\theta) = -\log\bigl(p(D|\theta)\bigr) - \log\bigl(p(\theta)\bigr). \qquad (10.18)$$

We follow the dynamics using leapfrog discretization [17], and compute the derivative of the potential energy with numerical approximation, which is the current bottleneck for computation.

10.3.1.1 Sampling over the Continuous Parameters of an Object (Diffusion 1)

When sampling the parameters of object o_i, we adapt the room box and the other objects so that no constraints are violated. When we detect an overlap with another object, we shrink the latter, and delete it if it is completely contained in o_i. We also check whether o_i is partly outside the room. If this is the case, we expand the room box so that o_i is entirely inside, and further adjust the position of the other objects (Sect. 10.3.1.2).

To reduce the sampling time, we designed efficient ways for sampling object parameters. For example, consider the window in Fig. 10.7(a). To find the correct fit, the window height must be stretched, and its center must be shifted downwards. To do this efficiently, we vary the height of the window by keeping the upper edge fixed. In this example, we would run Hamiltonian dynamics on the object height h_i. At each leapfrog step t, a proposed change in the height $h_i^t = h_i^{t-1} + \delta$ is followed by changing the y position of the object center as $y_i^t = y_i^{t-1} - \frac{\delta}{2}$, achieving the result in Fig. 10.7(b). This technique is effective in our framework, since typically one edge of the object is correctly "latched" to an image edge, given our proposal mechanism from image corners discussed in Sect. 10.3.2.1, and we thus want to find the correct size of the object without displacing that edge. There are four directions to sample a frame using this strategy, and six for furniture objects, as illustrated in Fig. 10.7(c), (d) and (e). When executing move Diffusion 1 for object o_i, we iterate over all four possible directions if o_i is a frame, six if it is a furniture object. For each direction, we use 20 leapfrog steps, and at each step we enforce the containment constraints.

10.3.1.2 Sampling over the Continuous Parameters of the Room Box (Diffusion 2)

When sampling the parameters of the room box r, we adapt all the objects so that no constraints are violated. When we detect that an object is partly outside the box, we shrink it, and delete it if it is completely outside. As for the object parameters, we sample along one direction of the room by keeping one edge "latched" (Fig. 10.7, third row). Six sampling directions are available (fourth row), and we use 20 leapfrog steps per direction. At each leapfrog step, we enforce the containment constraint, and we further apply a transformation to the objects in the room, to preserve their projection on the image plane. Since room objects parameters are relative to the room box coordinate system, changing the 3D position of the room box would not preserve the projection of the room objects. An example is shown in Fig. 10.7(g)–(h), where a small change in the room center causes the object to move as well.

We address this as follows. We define the room 3D center $(r_x + \delta_{rx}, r_y + \delta_{ry}, r_z + \delta_{rz})$ at leapfrog step t, where all the parameters are relative to the world coordinate system, and (r_x, r_y, r_z) is the room center at leapfrog step $(t-1)$. Let us also define (x_i, y_i, z_i) as the center of object o_i at $(t-1)$, this time in room coordinates. For each object o_i, we compute the position of its center at step t as $(x_i + \delta_{rx}^r, y_i + \delta_{ry}^r, z_i + \delta_{rz}^r)$, where $(\delta_{rx}^r, \delta_{ry}^r, \delta_{rz}^r) = r_{\text{coord}}(\delta_{rx}, \delta_{ry}, \delta_{rz})$. The result of applying this transformation is shown in Fig. 10.7(i), where the room box has changed, but the object block kept its position on the image plane.

10.3.1.3 Sampling over Camera and Room Box Parameters (Diffusion 3)

We sample over camera and room box parameters jointly, for a total of 10 parameters. We found that sampling over the camera parameters independently typically produces samples with a lower posterior, due to correlations with other scene pa-

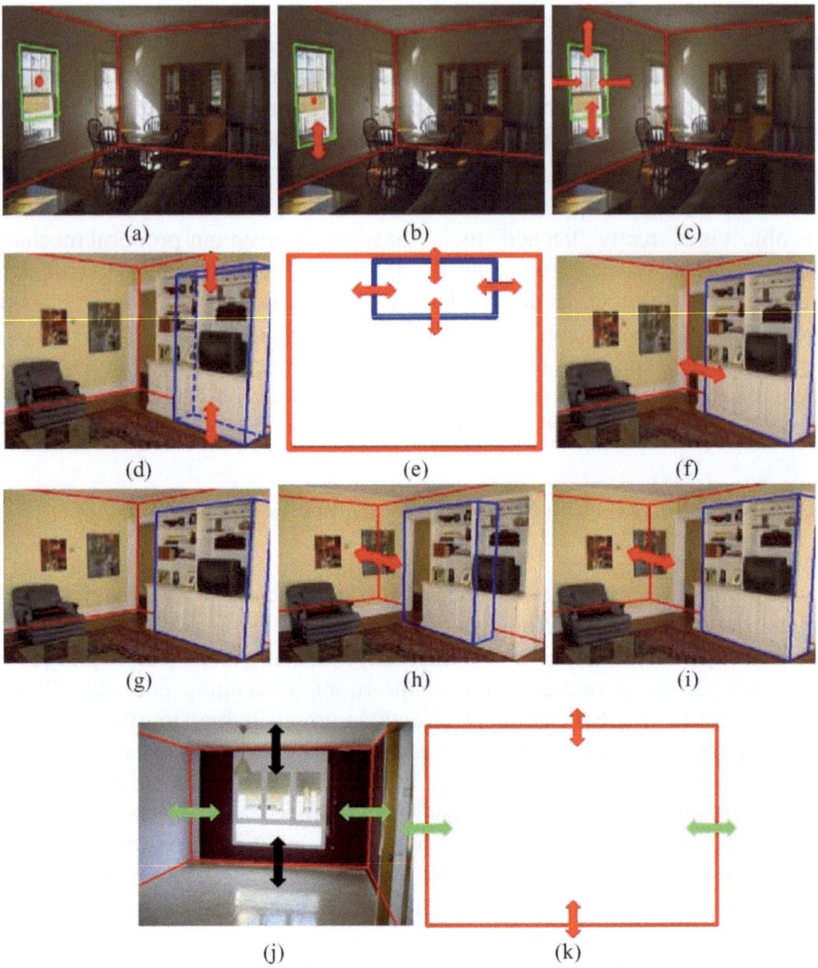

Fig. 10.7 Efficient strategies for sampling over continuous parameters. The upper edge of the window in (**a**) is positioned correctly, and the correct fit for the window can be obtained efficiently by dragging down the lower edge while keeping the upper edge fixed (**b**). We designed moves that achieve this by sampling the continuous parameters of the window in 3D (see text). For a frame, this principle can be applied to any of the edges, and this creates four possible sampling directions, denoted by the *arrows* in (**c**). For furniture we have six alternatives, as illustrated in (**d**) and (**e**), which is a birdview of the model. (**f**) is an example of the effects of this move when sampling over the direction denoted by the *arrow*. The same strategy is also used when sampling over the room box (*third row*), where we have six possible directions, illustrated in (**j**) and (**k**) (two of those are shown in both, denoted by the *green arrows*). Since object coordinates are relative to the room box, changes in the latter have the undesirable effect of changing the projection of objects already in the room. For example, we only changed the 3D center of the room box from (**g**) to (**h**), and this "shifted" the projection of the *blue block* as well. By introducing a transformation that preserves the projection of the objects in the room (see text), we obtain the result in (**i**)

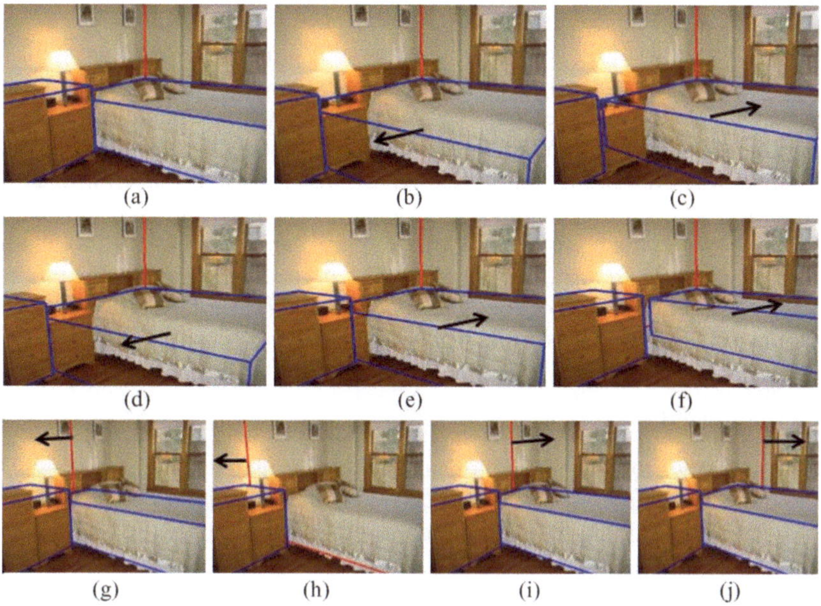

Fig. 10.8 Sensible sampling with interacting boxes. Suppose sampling over the block projected over the bed (**a**), along the direction denoted by the *arrow* (**b**) for N leapfrog steps. For a few steps, the bed tries to expand, and the containment constraints force the block on the left to shrink (**b**). Then, the bed tries to shrink (**c**), but we see that the *left block* does not return to its initial position. The behavior in the *second row* is more desirable, where the *left block* "grows" back to its initial location as the bed shrinks (**e**), but does not grow beyond that point (**f**). In the *third row*, we show the desired behavior of the sampler when the room box is trying to expand along the direction of the *arrow*. As the room shrinks, so does the bed (**g**), which completely disappears when it is fully outside the room (**h**). When the box starts to expand again, the bed grows back to its initial size (**i**), but no further (**j**)

rameters. For example, sampling over the focal length should drive the model to the current perspective distortion, which provides a better alignment of the projected model edges and the image edges. However, changing the focal length also modifies the size of the projection of the 3D scene, and these two forces are conflicting.

Hence, we jointly sample over camera and room box, as this allows to account for some of the correlations between camera and scene parameters. For this move, we use Hamiltonian dynamics for 20 iterations. At each step, we enforce the same constraints as in the case where we sample over the room box only.

10.3.1.4 Sensible Dynamics with Multiple Boxes

The constraints in the model give rise to an additional problem illustrated in Fig. 10.8. Suppose sampling over the block projected over the bed Fig. 10.8(a), along the direction denoted by the arrow Fig. 10.8(b) for N leapfrog steps. For a few steps, the bed tries to expand, and the containment constraints force the block on the left to shrink Fig. 10.8(b). Then, the bed tries to shrink Fig. 10.8(c), but we see that the left block does not return to its initial position. The behavior in the second row is more desirable, where the left block "grows" back to its initial location as the bed shrinks Fig. 10.8(e), but does not grow beyond that point Fig. 10.8(f). In the third row, we show a similar situation, where we show the desired behavior of the sampler when the room box is trying to expand. As the room shrinks, so does the bed Fig. 10.8(g), which completely disappears when it is fully outside the room Fig. 10.8(h). When the box starts to expand again, the bed grows back to its initial size Fig. 10.8(i), but no further Fig. 10.8(j). The procedure implementing this strategy for the sampling of a set of continuous parameters is as follows (θ_{in} is the initial sample, and θ_{out} is the sample after N leapfrog steps).

1. Set $\theta_0 = \theta_{\text{in}}$
2. For every step $i = 1, \ldots, N$
   a. Compute θ_i from θ_{i-1} by following the Hamiltonian dynamics
   b. Whenever the posterior needs to be evaluated, compute it on a copy of θ_{i-1} where we apply the containment constraints. Never apply the constraints on either θ_i or θ_{i-1}
3. Set $\theta_{\text{out}} = \theta_N$
4. Apply the containment constraints on θ_{out}

This procedure implements the desired behavior illustrated in Fig. 10.8, by keeping track of the initial positions and sizes of all objects in the model, and applying the containment constraints only when the posterior needs to be evaluated. Finally, these constraints are applied to the last sample, which will be the starting point for the next sampling move.

10.3.2 Jump Moves

One of the main challenges in the inference process is designing jump moves to efficiently add objects to the scene. Since the sampling space is so large, naive jump proposals, such as samples from a prior distribution, are unlikely to be accepted, and this leads to unacceptably long running times. To face this challenge, we introduced a data-driven strategy [23, 26] to condition the sampling on the data, by proposing samples from image evidence in a bottom–up fashion. Further, we exploit the Manhattan world assumption [1] that most surfaces in the world are aligned with one of three orthogonal directions, as this provides strong constraints on the parameter space.

In Fig. 10.9, we illustrate how our proposal mechanism combines the Manhattan world constraints and the advantages of data-driven inference. Here, we show that intersections of line segments on the image plane, which we call *image corners*, typically correspond to the projection of corners that are orthogonal in the 3D world. Using projective geometry and Manhattan orthogonality constraints, an image cor-

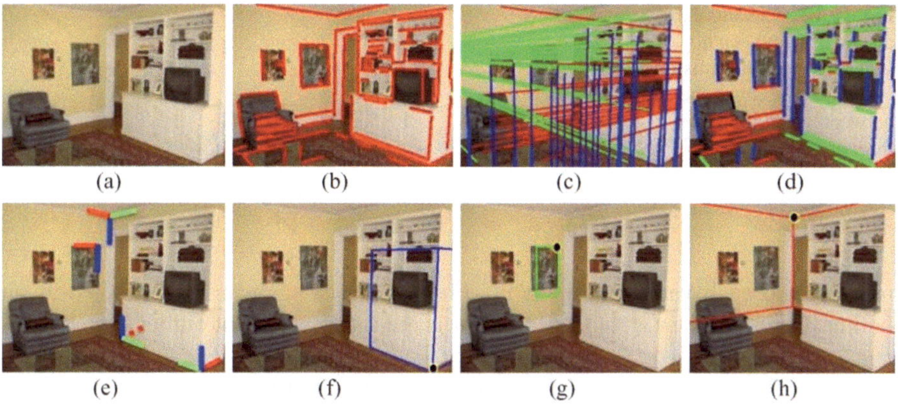

Fig. 10.9 Detecting vanishing points (*top*) to find orthogonal corners (*bottom*). Most surfaces in indoor scenes are aligned with three principal orthogonal directions. This defines a triplet of orthogonal vanishing points in the image plane, which we find in a RANSAC fashion (**c**) from straight detected segments (**b**). Segments are assigned to one of three groups based on the vanishing point they converge to (**d**). Intersections of edges in different groups, which we call image corners, are typically generated by the projection of an orthogonal 3D corner (**e**). Given an estimate of the camera pose computed from the vanishing points, an image corner can be used to propose a furniture object (**f**), a frame (**g**), or the room box (**h**)

ner can be used to propose furniture objects (Fig. 10.9(f)), frames Fig. 10.9(g) and room box candidates Fig. 10.9(h), which are accepted with high probability.

To achieve this goal, we first estimate the triplet of orthogonal vanishing points defining the Manhattan world directions [18]. This provides a good estimate of the camera focal length and pose, which are needed to propose 3D blocks from image corners. In what follows, we describe the procedure for estimating the vanishing points (Sect. 10.3.2.1), how to detect image corners (Sect. 10.3.2.2), and how to use them to propose both objects in the scene (Sect. 10.3.2.3) and room box candidates (Sect. 10.3.3).

10.3.2.1 Vanishing Point Estimation

We first detect straight edges and fit line segments to them using the straight connected edge detector by Hoiem et al. [12]. Then, we detect vanishing points following the RANSAC procedure proposed by Lee et al. [15]. At each step, we randomly select three pairs of line segments and position a vanishing point at the intersection of each pair. We then check the orthogonality of the vanishing points and reject triplets that are not orthogonal. We then estimate the intrinsic camera matrix K from the Choleski decomposition of the absolute conic matrix [8], which is fully determined by the position of the three vanishing points. We reject triplets that provide a non realistic focal length ($f \notin [50, 2000]$, measured in pixel).

For each valid triplet $V_t(v_1, v_2, v_3)$, we compute the objective function $f(V_t)$ as follows. First, we compute the angular distance $\alpha(s_i, v_k)$ between each line seg-

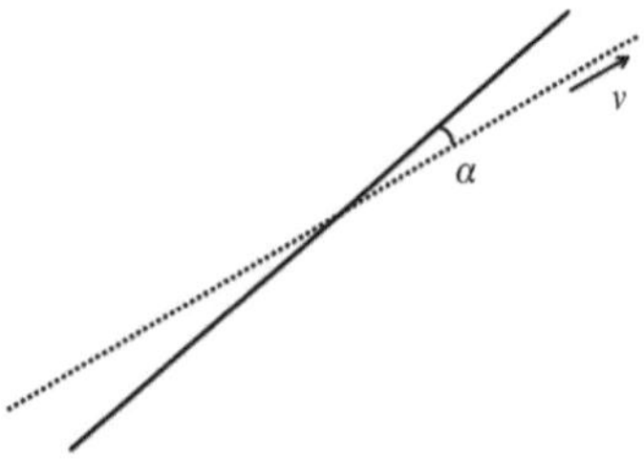

Fig. 10.10 The angular distance α between a segment s and its vanishing point v. α measures the angle between s and the line through the mid point of s and v

ment s_i and each vanishing point v_k (Fig. 10.10). A segment s_i is labeled as an outlier if $\min_{k=1,2,3} \alpha(s_i, v_k) > 0.06$. If n is the total number of outliers, we have

$$f(V_t) = \left(\sum_{i=1}^{n} \frac{\min_{k=1,2,3} \alpha(s_i, v_k)}{l_i} \right) / n \tag{10.19}$$

where n is the number of inlier line segments in the RANSAC procedure. l_i is the length of segment s_i, and is used to assign a larger weight to long segments.

We keep the valid triplet of vanishing points minimizing $f(V_t)$ and such that the ratio r_{out} between the number of outliers and the total number of segments is less than 0.1. If no triplet satisfying these constraints is found, we increase this threshold by 0.1 and repeat until a triplet is found. This allows for considering first only triplets supported by a large number of segments, and, if none is available, we allow a larger number of outliers.

10.3.2.2 Image Corners

Given the estimated triplet of vanishing points, each line segment is assigned to the vanishing point minimizing the angular distance α [9], thus partitioning them in three groups. Segments with $\alpha > 0.12$ are not assigned to any group and considered as outliers. Notice that this threshold is less strict than the one used during RANSAC, as we want to have more candidates at this point. An example is shown in Fig. 10.9(d), where the three different groups are shown, respectively, in green, red and blue, and the outliers in black.

We assume that two image segments in different groups were generated by segments that are orthogonal in 3D. The intersection of two such segments, which we call image corner, is thus likely to be generated by a 3D orthogonal corner, such as the corners of the cabinet or the inner corner of the room shown in Fig. 10.9(e). Given an image corner and an estimate for the camera pose, we can propose 3D objects in likely positions. However, this requires knowing the three segments forming the image corner, but typically only two are visible due to occlusions, like the bottom left corner of the cabinet in Fig. 10.9(e). We address this problem by "hallucinating" the third segment when it is not visible. In the case of the bottom left cabinet corner, we consider the intersection between the two visible segments, which converge to two different vanishing point, and hypothesize that the third segment converges to the remaining vanishing point in the triplet. This is discussed in detail in Fig. 10.11,

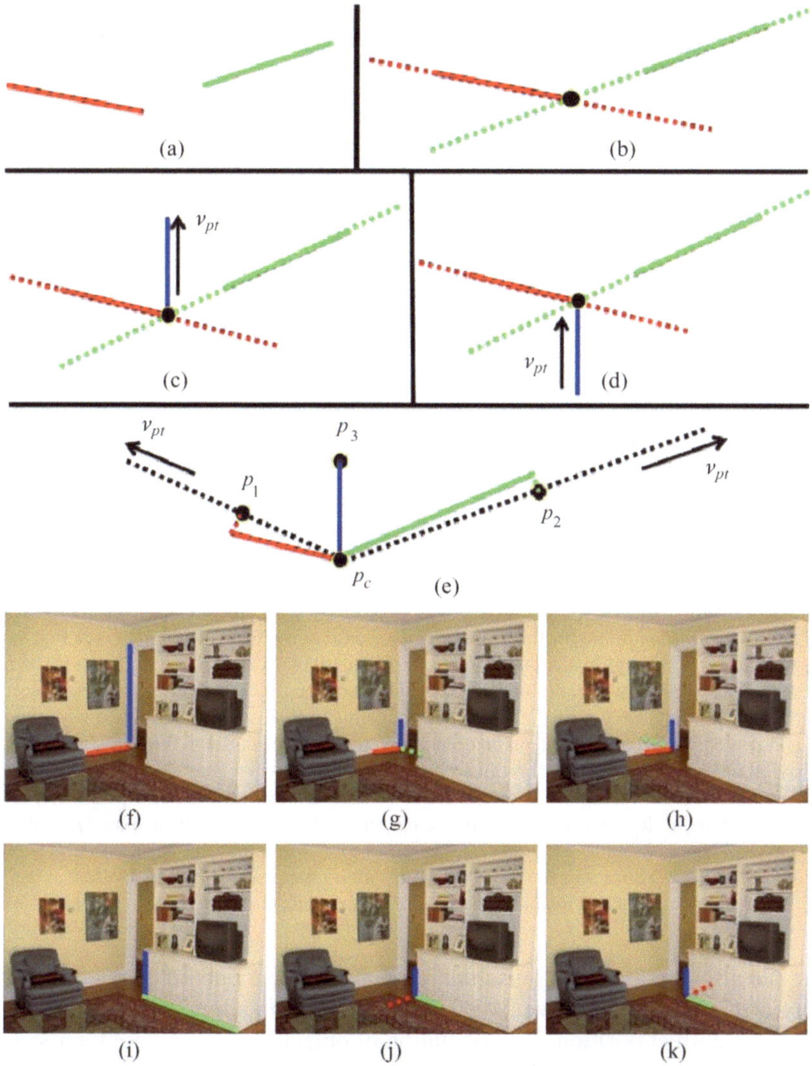

Fig. 10.11 Creating orthogonal corners from line segments. Given a pair of segments converging to different vanishing points (**a**), we first find their intersection (**b**). We do not create corners if the distance between the intersection and each segment is larger than 30 pixels. We position the third segment of the corner on the line through the corner position and the third vanishing point (**c**). Two corner configurations are possible (**c**)–(**d**). Last, we "rectify" the corner (**e**), to make sure it satisfies the orthogonality constraint imposed by the Manhattan world, which is needed to propose 3D objects from a 2D corner. In fact, corners are created from detected image segments, which do not necessarily satisfy these constraints due to errors in the edge detection. Specifically, instead of using the image segments, we consider their projections on the line through the corner center and the vanishing points (**e**), which are guaranteed to be orthogonal. The final corner is centered in p_c, and defined by segments p_1p_c, p_2p_c and p_3p_c. Notice that p_3p_c was hallucinated by using a vanishing point, and does not need to be "rectified". In the *last two rows*, we show examples of corners created from pairs of segments

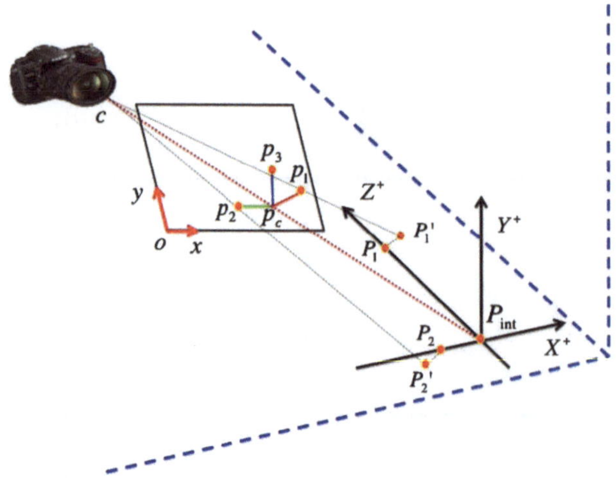

Fig. 10.12 Finding the 3D corner of a furniture object from an image corner, conditioned on the current room box. $p_c = (p_{cx}, p_{cy})$ denotes the position of the corner on the image plane, and $P_c = (p_{cx}, p_{cy}, -f)$ is the corner in the 3D camera reference frame, where f is the focal length. We first consider the segment $p_3 p_c$: if $p_{3y} > p_{cy}$ in the image reference frame, the image corner is pointing upwards, and we assume that it was generated by an object corner on the room floor, delimited by the *dashed lines* (for the complimentary case of a downwards corner, see Fig. 10.13). Then, we cast a ray through the camera center c and the image corner P_c, and find its intersection with the room floor P_{int}, which defines the 3D position of the object corner. Assuming objects are aligned with the walls, we define the coordinate system (X, Y, Z), which is aligned with the room walls and centered in P_{int}, the XZ plane coinciding with the room floor. We know the 3D corner will expand along the positive Y axis, and we use the rays between the camera and p_1 and p_2 to determine the directions along the X and Z axis. We first find the intersection P_1' between ray $p_1 c$ and the floor, which, due to small errors in the camera estimate, does not lie exactly on the Z or the X axis. We then compute P_1 as the closest point to P_1' on either the X or the Z axis, which determines that the 3D corner in the picture expands along the positive Z axis. We repeat the same for P_2 by using p_2, and in this example the 3D corner expands along the negative X axis

where we also explain how to use the Manhattan constraints to ensure the orthogonality of the corner. Last, we stress that, since the main purpose of corners is to propose the correct position and orientation of objects in 3D, and not their size, the length of corner segments in 2D does not provide any valuable information, as long as their direction is correct.

10.3.2.3 Adding Objects in the Scene Using Image Corners

As discussed above, we create image corners by considering the intersection of each pair of segments converging to different vanishing points. A corner is then used to add an object to the scene in a bottom–up data-driven fashion, in order to increase the acceptance probability in the MH acceptance formula [5].

First, the image corner is used to estimate the position of the furniture object in 3D (Figs. 10.12 and 10.13). The proposal is conditioned on the current estimate of both camera pose and room box. Second, we randomly select the type of the object,

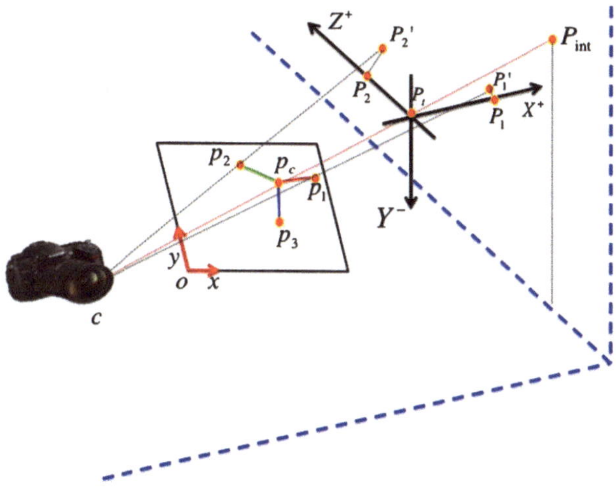

Fig. 10.13 Finding the 3D corner of a furniture object from a downwards image corner. We assume that a downwards image corner is generated by a corner on the *top* of a 3D object (For the complimentary case of an upwards corner, see Fig. 10.12). We cast a ray through the camera center and the corner position in the image P_c, and find the intersection P_{int} between this ray and the closest room wall. The 3D position of the corner can lie anywhere on the line $((1-t)c + tP_{\text{int}})$ between P_{int} and the camera center c. Any $t \in [0, 1]$ defines a valid 3D position P_t for the corner, and we choose t by randomly choosing from the interval [0.4, 1.0]. We set the lower bound to 0.4, since values of t too close to 0 result in positioning the corner too close to the camera, which is a non realistic configuration. We assume that the object is aligned with the room walls and floor, and knowing that the 3D corner is pointing downwards, only the directions along the X and Z axis are left to be determined. Similarly to Fig. 10.12, we find the intersection P_1' between ray p_1c and a plane parallel to the room floor and passing through P_t, and P_1 as the closest point to P_1' on either the X or the Z axis. P_1 and P_2 determine the corner directions in 3D along X and Z, which in this example are the positive X axis and the positive Z axis

such as bed, and use the priors for that category to propose the size of the object. Third, to further increase the acceptance ratio of jump moves, we use a delayed acceptance mechanism. In fact, corners help propose objects at the right position, but the size sampled from the prior is often inaccurate. Hence, we briefly sample over the continuous parameters of the newly added object before consulting the MH acceptance formula to decide whether to accept or reject the sample.

The full proposal procedure to add a furniture object in the scene is as follows.

1. Randomly choose an image corner, and determine whether it is pointing up or down (Fig. 10.12).
2. Determine the object category τ by randomly choosing from the four available classes (bed, cabinet, couch, table), where each class has the same probability.
3. If the corner is pointing up, find the position of the 3D corner on the floor as explained in Fig. 10.12, otherwise find the position of the 3D corner as explained in Fig. 10.13.
4. Sample $\mathcal{N}(r_{i3}; \mu_{\tau_3}, \sigma_{\tau 3})$ to propose the ratio r_{i3} between the room height and that of the proposed object height h_i. Set $h_i = \frac{h_r}{r_{i3}}$, where h_r is the current height of the room box.

5. Sample u from uniform distribution $\mathcal{U}(0, 1)$. If $u > 0.5$, set the width w_i of the object to be larger than its length l_i, if $u \leq 0.5$ set l_i to be larger. The next two steps are defined for the case $u > 0.5$, and can be adapted to the opposite case by swapping w_i with l_i.
6. Sample from $\mathcal{N}(r_{i1}; \mu_{\tau_1}, \sigma_{\tau 1})$ to propose the ratio r_{i1} between h_i and its largest dimension w_i. Set $w_i = \frac{h_i}{r_{i1}}$ using h_i from the previous step.
7. Sample from $\mathcal{N}(r_{i2}; \mu_{\tau_2}, \sigma_{\tau 1})$ to propose the ratio r_{i2} between the object largest and shortest dimensions (w_i and l_i). Set $l_i = \frac{w_i}{r_{i2}}$ using w_i from the previous step.
8. Shrink any furniture object in the scene colliding with the proposed one.
9. In case the object does not fit in the room, expand the room box. This might involve lowering the position of the floor, raising the ceiling, or increasing the room width and/or length.
10. Briefly sample over the object continuous parameters using Diffusion move 3 (delayed acceptance).
11. Accept or reject the proposed object by consulting the MH acceptance formula.

Similarly, the procedure to add a frame in the scene is summarized below. Notice that the move adding an object chooses whether to add a furniture object or a frame with 0.5 probability.

1. Randomly choose an image corner.
2. Determine the object category τ by randomly choosing from the three available classes (door, picture frame, window), where each class has the same probability.
3. Find the position of the 3D corner, and the room wall s_i it is anchored to as explained in Fig. 10.14.
4. Sample $\mathcal{N}(r_{i3}; \mu_{\tau_3}, \sigma_{\tau 3})$ to propose the ratio r_{i3} between the room height and that of the proposed frame height h_i. Set $h_i = \frac{h_r}{r_{i3}}$, where h_r is the current height of the room box.
5. Conditioned on s_i, the frame has either negligible width or negligible length. In the latter case, sample from $\mathcal{N}(r_{i1}; \mu_{\tau_1}, \sigma_{\tau 1})$ to propose the ratio r_{i1} between h_i and width w_i. Set $w_i = \frac{h_i}{r_{i1}}$ using h_i from the previous step. When w_i is negligible, set $l_i = \frac{h_i}{r_{i1}}$.
6. Shrink any frame in the scene colliding with the proposed one.
7. If the frame does not fit on the wall, expand it.
8. Briefly sample over the object continuous parameters using Diffusion move 3 (delayed acceptance).
9. Accept or reject the proposed frame by consulting the MH acceptance formula.

10.3.2.4 Other Jump Moves

The remaining two jump moves respectively remove an object from the room, or change the type of one of the objects. The former simply deletes a randomly selected object, and the proposed change is accepted or rejected using the MH acceptance formula. Instead, changing the type of an object involves only changes in the prior.

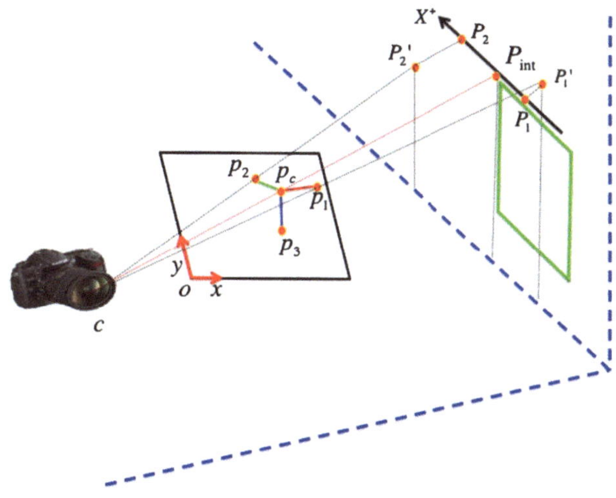

Fig. 10.14 Finding the 3D corner of a frame from an image corner. We cast a ray between the camera center c and P_c, and find the intersection P_{int} with the closest wall, which determines the position of the corner in 3D. We know that the frame will expand downwards on the wall, as the corner on the image plane is pointing down, but we have to determine the 3D corner direction along the X axis. We do so by considering P_1' and P_2', which are obtained by intersecting rays p_1c and p_2c with the wall the frame is anchored to. Due to errors in the camera estimate, we cannot expect P_1' and P_2' to lie exactly on X, and we then consider their projections on X, P_1 and P_2. P_1 defines the direction if the distance between P_1 and P_1' is smaller than the distance between P_2 and P_2', and use P_2 otherwise. This is equivalent to choosing the direction that best satisfies the orthogonality constraints. In this example, we used P_1 to set the direction of the frame drawn on the wall

First, an object is randomly selected, and we propose changing its current type τ to a different category, also randomly selected. For example, changing the label of an object from "bed" to "couch" results in using the distribution on size and position for couches when evaluating the object prior probability, while before the prior for beds was used. Again, the proposed change is evaluated using the MH acceptance formula. Last, we do not propose changing furniture objects into frames or vice versa. This means that, for example, a couch can only be changed into a table, a bed or a cabinet, while a door only into a picture frame or a window.

10.3.3 Initializing the Room Box and the Camera Parameters

We initialize the parameters of the camera and of the room box by proposing candidates from the orthogonal corners detected on the image plane. Each corner is used to generate a candidate, and we use the N room box candidates with the highest posterior to initialize the N threads used for inference. While we do not solely commit to these proposals, since the inference process will modify room box and camera parameters, we found that a good initial estimate of the room box parameters makes

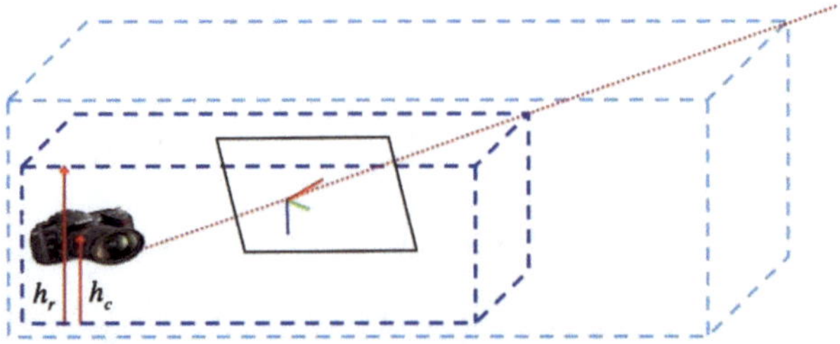

Fig. 10.15 Finding the position of a 3D room corner from an image corner. We first cast a ray between the corner in the image and the camera center. We then position the 3D room corner along this line. Different positions generate different room boxes, as illustrated by the *two dashed examples* above. Once the 3D position is chosen, we set the room height h_r such that the ratio between the height of the camera from the floor h_c and h_r falls in the range of plausible values (see text). Further, we have to enforce that the room box is big enough to contain the camera

the inference more efficient. We now discuss how a corner is used to generate a candidate.

Shi et al. [21] showed how to estimate the camera pose from the projection of an orthogonal corner and the known focal length. We follow their procedure to estimate the pitch ϕ, the roll ψ of the camera and the yaw γ_r of the room, which in our framework define the camera pose. Notice that the focal length is available from the estimated triplet of orthogonal vanishing points.

The method by Shi et al. [21] also recovers the 3D directions of the lines forming the corner. However, we still need to determine the 3D position of the corner, which can lie anywhere on the line defined by the camera center and the corner position on the image plane, as illustrated in Fig. 10.15. Since we cannot determine absolute positions and sizes from a single image, we arbitrarily position the corner on the line such that the distance between the corner and the camera center is 10 units.

This still leaves the room dimensions (h_r, w_r, l_r) as free parameters. Since absolute sizes cannot be used when reconstructing from a single image, we set the room height such that the ratio between the height of the camera from the floor h_c and h_r takes plausible values (Fig. 10.15). Specifically, we sample uniformly from the interval $[\mu_{\text{ch}} - 2\sigma_{\text{ch}}, \mu_{\text{ch}} + 2\sigma_{\text{ch}}]$, with step $\frac{\sigma_{\text{ch}}}{5.0}$. For each different height, we set w_r and l_r such that $\frac{w_r}{h_r} = \mu_{r2}$ and $\frac{l_r}{h_r} = \mu_{r2}$, and if the room box is not big enough to contain the camera, we expand it. We then briefly sample over room box and camera parameters by alternating Diffusion moves 1 and 2, and keep the sample with the highest posterior.

10.3.4 Exchanging Information Among Threads

At the end of the inference process, each thread outputs the sample with the highest posterior. In most cases, we found that some objects are found only by some of the threads, as illustrated in Fig. 10.16. One thread did not find the picture Fig. 10.16(a), while the other did not find the nightstand Fig. 10.16(b). While a longer running

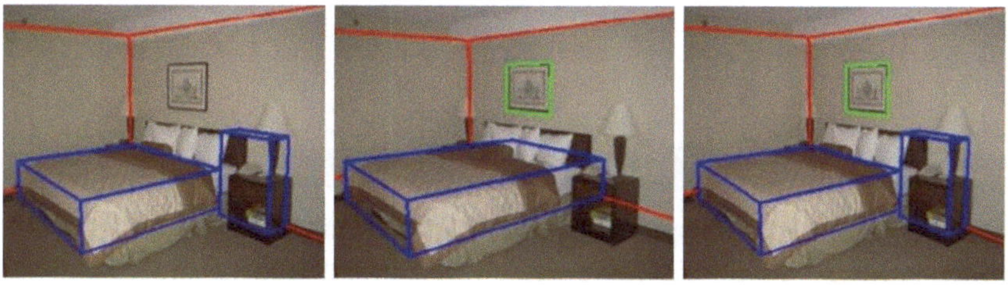

(a) (b) (c)

Fig. 10.16 The result (**c**) of exchanging objects between the samples found by two different threads (**a** and **b**)

time could potentially allow each thread to find all objects, we propose instead to let threads exchange objects at the end of the inference Fig. 10.16(c).

Since object position and size is defined relatively to the room, we need an exchanging mechanism taking into account that different threads have different estimates of the room box. Further, the camera parameters found by each thread are potentially different. Hence, we exchange an object between a source thread and a destination thread by enforcing that the projection of the object in the source matches as closely as possible the projection of the object in the destination (Fig. 10.17).

At the end of inference, we add to the best sample found by a thread all the objects found by the other threads, one at a time, and keep the one that provides the best posterior. We repeat this $K = 10$ times, or until there is no improvement in the posterior. While less greedy methods are possible, this approach works well in practice. The complete procedure for exchanging objects among N threads is as follows:

1. For each thread i, save in θ_i^0 the best sample found by thread i
2. For each θ_i^0, and for $k = 1, \ldots, K$

   a. Set $\theta_i^k = \theta_i^{k-1}$. Compute the posterior p_i^k of θ_i^k. Get all the objects found by other threads $O = \cup_{j=1}^N O_j$ with $j \neq i$, where $O_j = (o_{j1}, \ldots, o_{jn})$ is the list of objects in θ_j^0.
   b. For each object o_w in O, create $\theta_i^{k\_w}$ by adding o_w to θ_i^k, and compute the posterior $p_i^{k\_w}$. Set $\theta_{i\_\max}^k = \theta_i^{k\_w}$ such that $p_i^{k\_w} = \max_{w'} p_i^{k\_w'}$.
   c. If the posterior of $\theta_{i\_\max}^k$ is larger that p_i^k, set $\theta_i^k = \theta_{i\_\max}^k$. Otherwise, stop and return $\theta_i^K = \theta_i^k$.

3. Return θ_i^K with the largest posterior.

10.4 Results

We start by evaluating the performances of the various components of our algorithm in terms of the error on the room layout estimation [9, 16, 24], which is a standard

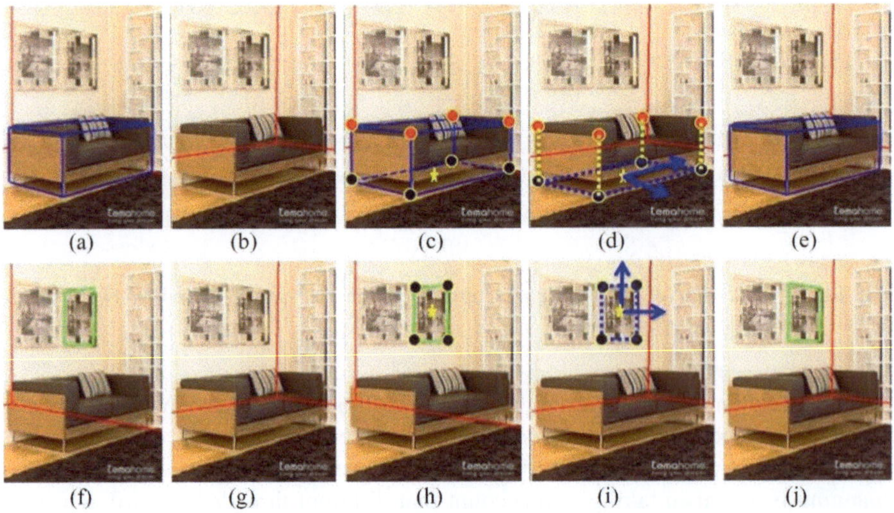

Fig. 10.17 Exchanging furniture objects (*top row*) and frames (*bottom row*) between two samples. Consider adding the object in (**a**) to (**b**): the camera parameters and the room boxes are different, and this is a problem since object coordinates are relative to the room reference frame. We address this by making sure that the projection of the transferred object (**e**) matches that of the original one (**a**). First, we use the original camera to project the object corners that touch the floor, shown in *black* in (**c**). The *star* indicates the projection of the center of the object "floor". We then cast a ray between the destination camera and the *star*, and intersect it with the floor of the destination room. This gives us the object "floor" center in the coordinate system defined by the destination room box. The transferred object will be aligned with the walls of the destination room, denoted by the *arrows* in (**d**). We determine the object width and length by intersecting the *arrows* with the *dashed lines* (**d**), which might not be aligned with the destination walls due to the differing camera parameters. The object height is found by projecting the corners on the top of the object under the original camera (**c**). For each corner c, we consider ray r_1 through its projection and the destination camera, and ray r_2 orthogonal to the room floor and through the corresponding corner of the object on the floor. The 3D position of c in the destination room is given by the point on r_2 closest to r_1. The 3D length of the *vertical dashed lines* determines the height of the transferred object. This length might not be the same for all four lines, and we set the height of the object by averaging them. The final transferred object is shown in (**e**). The *second row* illustrates the equivalent procedure for frames, where we consider the projection of the frame's corners on the closest wall

measure in this field. This error compares the projection of the estimated room box against the ground truth, where each pixel was labeled according to the room face it belongs to (ceiling, floor, left, middle and right wall), by computing the ratio of misclassified pixels.

In Table 10.1, we evaluate the impact of the different components of our approach on the test portion of the Hedau dataset [9], consisting of 104 color images. In the left column we show the contribution of the priors in the scenario where the likelihood function uses edges and orientation maps, as in our 2012 CVPR paper [3]. We see that the room prior reduces the layout error, and so do priors on objects.

Table 10.1 Analysis of the components of our approach based on room layout error, evaluated on the Hedau test set [9]

	Edges + OM
No prior	20.4 %
Room prior	19.7 %
Room + obj prior	*17.8 %*

	Edges	Edges + OM	Edges + OM + GC
No objects	24.1 %	*21.3 %*	21.8 %
Objects	20.7 %	17.8 %	*17.2 %*
Exchange objects	14.2 %	14.6 %	*13.6 %*

This suggests that adding realistic objects in the room drives the inference towards better spatial configurations.

We then evaluate the benefits of the different components of the likelihood, considering three cases: (1) we do not allow any object in the room, (2) we allow objects in the scene, and (3) we allow exchanging information among threads. Interestingly, exchanging objects allows choosing a better room box, since more objects provide more evidence on the correct room layout. There is no improvement when only edges are used, and we believe this happens because the likelihood is not robust enough in this case. Qualitative examples of these improvements are shown in Fig. 10.18.

Table 10.2 shows that our method is comparable to the state-of-the-art on the Hedau dataset, and also report results on the UCB dataset [25], consisting of 340 black and white images. When comparing with state-of-the-art, we consider our full algorithm, including all the likelihood components, and with the object exchange enabled.

Then, we evaluate on object recognition. We ground truthed the UCB [25] and Hedau dataset [9] by manually identifying the seven object classes we experimented with, not considering objects occupying less than 1 % of the image. To evaluate detection, we project the 3D object hypothesized by our model onto the image, and compare this with the ground truth object position. If the intersection of the two areas is more than 50 % of their union, we consider it a correct detection. We first measure how many objects we correctly identified for each of the two main categories (furniture and frames), even if there is confusion within the subcategories (e.g., when we label a table as a couch, or a window as a door). We provide precision and recall scores based on this criterion. Second, we measure the accuracy we achieved within each of the two categories, as the percentage of objects that were assigned to the correct subcategory.

We report in Table 10.3 that using object priors greatly improves precision and recall, for both furniture and frames. When we do not use priors, objects are not labeled (e.g., we do not know whether a furniture object is a couch or a bed), and subcategory accuracy cannot be evaluated. Table 10.4 shows that geometric context improves all recognition scores, except for frame subcategory classification on the

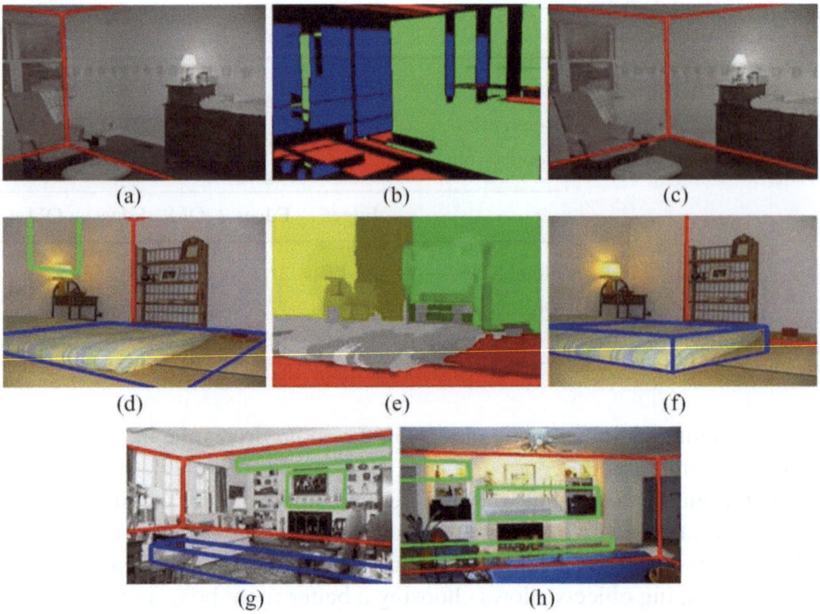

Fig. 10.18 Effects of the individual components of our model. Using only edges we get a poor estimate of the room box, due to the edge detector missing the wall edges (**a**). By adding orientation maps to the likelihood (**b**), where we draw in *green* and *blue* the pixels assigned to the two orthogonal vertical surfaces and in *red* the horizontal pixels, we obtain a better room box (**c**). Also adding geometric context helps. In (**d**), the algorithm is confused by several mistakes made in estimating the orientation maps, but geometric context (**e**) helps the reconstruction process (**f**). In (**e**), we used *red* for pixels labeled as floor, *yellow* for left wall, *green* for middle wall, and *gray* for objects. Last, using priors on object 3D position and size avoids proposing objects with unrealistic size, which would otherwise often "latch" to image features (**g**)–(**h**)

Table 10.2 Comparison with state-of-the-art on room layout error

Dataset	Hedau [9]	Lee [16]	Schwing [20]	Our full approach
Hedau [9]	21.2 %	16.2 %	*12.8 %*	13.6 %
UCB [25]	NA	NA	NA	*14.2 %*

Hedau dataset. In general, performances are more modest on the UCB dataset, and this includes also the room layout error. This black and white dataset is in fact more challenging, as several images are extremely blurry. We also notice that in general geometric context only introduces small improvements in the subcategory classification, if we exclude furniture on the UCB dataset. This is because adding a new feature allows to obtain more accurate object fits, but the "burden" of classification is still entirely on the prior on size and position. We posit that having different geometric models for object classes, such as tables with legs or couches with backrests, as well as class-dependent appearance models, would improve this score.

Table 10.3 Benefits of object priors evaluated on UCB and Hedau datasets. P, R, and S denote Precision, Recall and Subcategory Accuracy

	UCB [25]			Hedau [9]		
	P	R	S P	R	S	
Furn no prior	19.4 %	10.4 %	NA	27.1 %	9.2 %	NA
Furn prior	*31.0 %*	*20.1 %*	*38.0 %*	*32.5 %*	*20.3 %*	*50.0 %*
Frames no prior	21.8 %	14.0 %	NA	23.1 %	19.5 %	61.2 %
Frames prior	*27.2 %*	*19.7 %*	*60.0 %*	*36.1 %*	*27.5 %*	*62.6 %*

Table 10.4 Benefits of geometric context evaluated on UCB and Hedau datasets

	UCB [25]			Hedau [9]		
	P	R	S	P	R	S
Furn no gc	31.0 %	20.1 %	38.0 %	32.5 %	20.3 %	50.0 %
Furn gc	*33.7 %*	*27.7 %*	*50.1 %*	*50.0 %*	*24.2 %*	*51.6 %*
Frames no gc	27.2 %	19.7 %	60.0 %	36.1 %	27.5 %	*62.6 %*
Frames gc	*28.2 %*	*24.3 %*	*60.8 %*	*38.4 %*	*28.3 %*	61.2 %

Table 10.5 Effects of exchanging objects among threads on UCB and Hedau datasets

	UCB [25]			Hedau [9]		
	P	R	S	P	R	S
Furn no swap	*33.7 %*	27.7 %	*50.1 %*	50.0 %	24.2 %	*51.6 %*
Furn swap	33.0 %	*29.7 %*	50.0 %	*53.5 %*	*28.5 %*	51.3 %
Frames no swap	28.2 %	24.3 %	*60.8 %*	*38.4 %*	28.3 %	61.2 %
Frames swap	*28.4 %*	*37.3 %*	59.8 %	37.5 %	*35.5 %*	*66.0 %*

The effects of exchanging objects among threads are available in Table 10.5. There is a trend showing that exchanging objects achieves better recall at similar or slightly lower levels of precision. This is because adding objects from other threads allows to find many more objects, at the cost of a few additional mistakes. Variations in subcategory classification are mostly negligible. Last, we report confusion matrices for both furniture and frames on the Hedau dataset (Table 10.6). We here consider our full approach, including edges, orientation maps, geometric context, priors and object exchanging. We see that we recognize more objects in categories that are better approximated by a single block, such as beds and cabinets. Performances decrease for concave objects like table, that are not well approximated by a convex box. Also, there is more confusion between object categories similar in size, such as couches and tables, or windows and picture frames.

Qualitative results are available in Fig. 10.19, where we show the scene reconstructions provided by the full algorithm. The most typical failures are shown in Fig. 10.20.

Fig. 10.19 Scene reconstructions provided by our full approach. We show the room box in *red*, furniture in *blue* and frames in *green*

Table 10.6 Confusion matrices on Hedau test set [9]

	Bed	Cabinet	Couch	Table
Bed	14	1	7	1
Cabinet	1	12	2	2
Couch	6	1	7	5
Table	4	3	4	6

	Door	Picture	Window
Door	7	0	7
Picture	0	29	13
Window	8	5	28

10.5 Conclusions

Our top–down Bayesian approach for understanding indoor scenes is competitive with state-of-the-art approaches on the task of recovering the room box. Interestingly, priors on 3D geometry both improved object recognition scores, and provided better room box estimates. We believe this is an interesting finding towards providing top–down scene interpretations that are globally consistent in terms of geometry

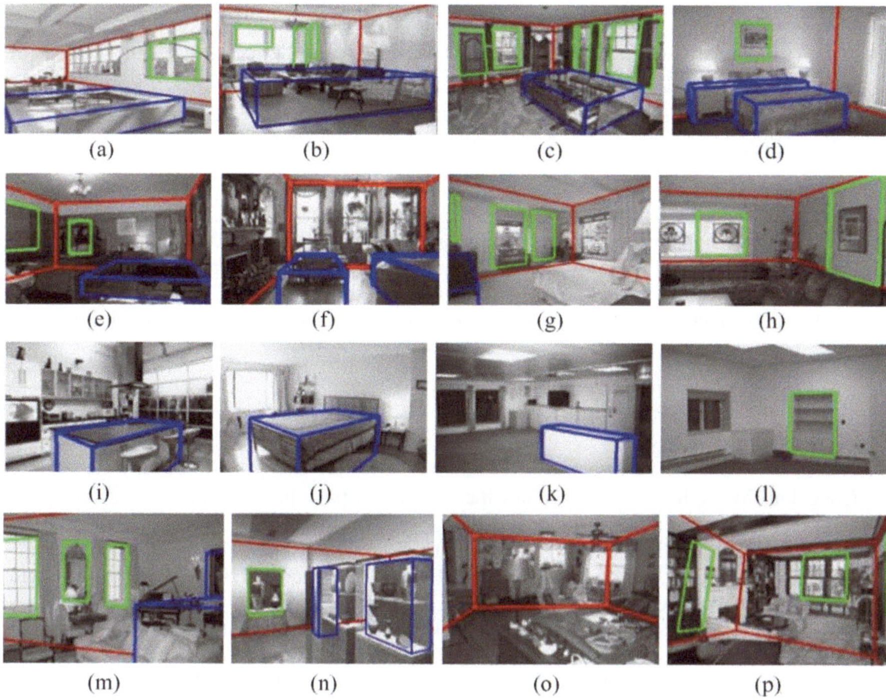

Fig. 10.20 Some typical failures. Due to clutter we often hallucinate objects (**a**)–(**d**). For example, in (**b**) we propose a bed whose edges "latch" to those of the carpet, and to the top of the armchairs. However, in this case our approach still provides a reasonable approximation of the space occupancy of the scene. In other situations (**e**)–(**f**), we hallucinate boxes in the gap among objects, thus providing a wrong estimate of the occupied space, or completely miss objects (**g**)–(**h**). This mostly happens when faint edges are missed by the edge detector, such as those of the bed in (**g**). Further, we often confuse object categories similar in size and position. For example, the table in (**i**) is wrongly labeled as a bed, and the opposite happens in (**j**). The wall in (**k**) is labeled as a cabinet, and we sometimes confuse an object that is directly facing the camera for a frame (**l**). We also show some cases where the algorithm estimated the wrong room box (**m**)–(**n**). In (**m**), this is caused by the edge detector missing the edge between the room walls and the ceiling completely. Other more catastrophic failures are due to bad initial estimates of the camera, from which the algorithm could not recover (**o**)–(**p**)

and semantics. Another strength of this method is that it does not commit to partial configurations, and can recover from initial errors, one example being the improvements on the initial estimate of the room box.

We posit that our method will prove more powerful as it integrates more sophisticated object models, including non convex-approximations such as tables with legs. In fact, more detailed geometry should help distinguish between classes that are similar in position and size. Also, recent work by Hedau et al. [11] showed that scene interpretation is enhanced by more accurate geometric models, such as blocks with backrests. More sophisticated models introduce additional complex constraints on the structure of objects (for example, chairs with four symmetric legs), which our

Bayesian framework could accommodate relatively easily. Further, the Bayesian formulation also allows integrating additional image evidence that would make the model more robust. For example, visual inspection of the results suggested that adding category dependent appearance models is a promising direction of research, as well as enforcing that projections of objects are uniform in terms of color and texture.

Acknowledgements This material is based upon work supported by the National Science Foundation under Grant No. 0747511. We thank Joseph Schlecht for his contributions and suggestions in designing the code base. We also acknowledge the valuable help of Joshua Bowdish, Ernesto Brau, Andrew Emmott, Daniel Fried, Jinyan Guan, Emily Hartley, Bonnie Kermgard, and Philip Lee.

References

1. Coughlan JM, Yuille AL (1999) Manhattan world: compass direction from a single image by Bayesian inference. In: ICCV
2. Del Pero L, Guan J, Brau E, Schlecht J, Barnard K (2011) Sampling bedrooms. In: CVPR
3. Del Pero L, Bowdish J, Fried D, Kermgard B, Hartley E, Barnard K (2012) Bayesian geometric modeling of indoor scenes. In: CVPR
4. Delage E, Lee HL, Ng AY (2005) Automatic single-image 3d reconstructions of indoor Manhattan world scenes. In: ISRR
5. Green PJ (1995) Reversible jump Markov chain Monte Carlo computation and Bayesian model determination. Biometrika 82(4):711–732
6. Green PJ (2003) Trans-dimensional Markov chain Monte Carlo. In: Highly structured stochastic systems
7. Gupta A, Satkin S, Efros AA, Hebert M (2011) From 3D scene geometry to human workspace. In: CVPR
8. Hartley RI, Zisserman A (2004) Multiple view geometry in computer vision. Cambridge University Press, Cambridge
9. Hedau V, Hoiem D, Forsyth D (2009) Recovering the spatial layout of cluttered rooms. In: ICCV
10. Hedau V, Hoiem D, Forsyth D (2010) Thinking inside the box: using appearance models and context based on room geometry. In: ECCV
11. Hedau V, Hoiem D, Forsyth D (2012) Recovering free space of indoor scenes from a single image. In: CVPR
12. Hoiem D, Efros AA, Hebert M (2005) Geometric context from a single image. In: ICCV
13. Hoiem D, Efros AA, Hebert M (2006) Putting objects in perspective. In: CVPR
14. Karsch K, Hedau V, Forsyth D, Hoiem D (2011) Rendering synthetic objects into legacy photographs. In: SIGGRAPH Asia
15. Lee DC, Hebert M, Kanade T (2009) Geometric reasoning for single image structure recovery. In: CVPR
16. Lee DC, Gupta A, Hebert M, Kanade T (2010) Estimating spatial layout of rooms using volumetric reasoning about objects and surfaces. In: NIPS
17. Neal RM (1993) Probabilistic inference using Markov chain Monte Carlo methods. Technical report
18. Rother C (2002) A new approach to vanishing point detection in architectural. Image Vis Comput 20(9–10):647–655
19. Schlecht J, Barnard K (2009) Learning models of object structure. In: NIPS
20. Schwing A, Hazan T, Pollefeys M, Urtasun R (2012) Efficient structure prediction with latent variables for general graphics models. In: CVPR

21. Shi F, Zhang X, Liu Y (2004) A new method of camera pose estimation using 2D-3D corner correspondence. Pattern Recognit Lett 25(10):1155–1163
22. Tsai G, Xu C, Liu J, Kuipers B (2011) Real-time indoor scene understanding using Bayesian filtering with motion cues. In: ICCV
23. Tu Z, Zhu S (2002) Image segmentation by data-driven Markov chain Monte-Carlo. In: PAMI
24. Wang H, Gould S, Koller D (2010) Discriminative learning with latent variables for cluttered indoor scene understanding. In: ECCV
25. Yu SX, Zhang H, Malik J (2008) Inferring spatial layout from a single image via depth-ordered grouping, In: POCV
26. Zhu S-C, Zhang R, Tu Z (2000) Integrating top–down/bottom–up for object recognition by data driven Markov chain Monte Carlo. In: CVPR

Chapter 11
Efficient Loopy Belief Propagation Using the Four Color Theorem

Radu Timofte and Luc Van Gool

Abstract Recent work on early vision such as image segmentation, image denoising, stereo matching, and optical flow uses Markov Random Fields. Although this formulation yields an NP-hard energy minimization problem, good heuristics have been developed based on graph cuts and belief propagation. Nevertheless both approaches still require tens of seconds to solve stereo problems on recent PCs. Such running times are impractical for optical flow and many image segmentation and denoising problems and we review recent techniques for speeding them up. Moreover, we show how to reduce the computational complexity of belief propagation by applying the Four Color Theorem to limit the maximum number of labels in the underlying image segmentation to at most four. We show that this provides substantial speed improvements for large inputs, and this for a variety of vision problems, while maintaining competitive result quality.

11.1 Introduction

Much recent work on early vision algorithms—such as image segmentation, image denoising, stereo matching, and optical flow—models these problems using Markov Random Fields (MRF). Although this formulation yields an NP-hard energy minimization problem, good heuristics have been developed based on graph cuts [3] and belief propagation [21, 29]. A comparison between the two different approaches for the case of stereo matching is described in [23]. Both approaches still require tens of seconds to solve stereo problems on recent PCs. Such running times are impractical for many stereo applications, but also for optical flow and many image segmentation

R. Timofte (✉) · L. Van Gool
VISICS, ESAT-PSI/iMinds, KU Leuven, Leuven, Belgium
e-mail: Radu.Timofte@esat.kuleuven.be

L. Van Gool
e-mail: Luc.VanGool@esat.kuleuven.be

L. Van Gool
Computer Vision Lab, D-ITET, ETH Zurich, Zurich, Switzerland
e-mail: vangool@vision.ee.ethz.ch

G.M. Farinella et al. (eds.), *Advanced Topics in Computer Vision*,
Advances in Computer Vision and Pattern Recognition,
DOI 10.1007/978-1-4471-5520-1_11,

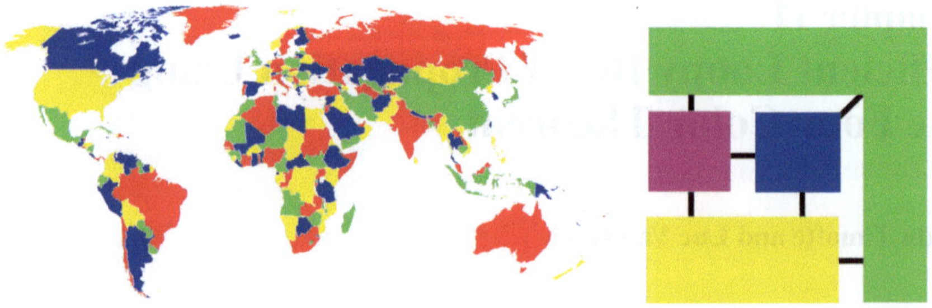

Fig. 11.1 Planar graphs: political world map colored with 4 colors illustrating the FCT (*left*, only the land boundaries are considered) and an example with 4 connected regions showing that less than 4 colors would indeed not suffice (*right*)

and denoising problems. Alternative, faster methods are available but generally give inferior results.

In the case of Belief Propagation (BP), a key reason for its slow performance is that the algorithm complexity is proportional to both the number of pixels in the image, and the number of *labels* in the underlying image segmentation, which is typically high. If we could limit the number of labels, its speed performance should improve greatly. Our key observation is that by modifying the propagation algorithms we can use a low number of placeholder labels, that we can reuse for non-adjacent segments. These placeholder labels can then be replaced by the full set of actual labels. Since image segments form a planar graph, they therefore require at most four placeholder labels by virtue of the Four Color Theorem (FCT) [17] to still have different colors for all adjacent segments. A joint optimization process provides a fast segmentation through the placeholder labels and a fine-grained labeling through the actual labels. The computational time is basically dependent on the number of placeholder rather than actual labels. This chapter is an extended version of our previous published work [24]. For the sake of self-consistency, the FCT is explained next.

The FCT states that for any 2D map there is a four-color covering such that contiguous regions sharing a common boundary (with more than a single point) do not have the same color. F. Guthrie first conjectured the theorem in 1852 (*Guthrie's problem*). The consequence of this theorem is that when an image, seen as a planar graph, is segmented into contiguous regions, there are only four colors to be assigned to each pixel/node for all segments to be surrounded only by segments of different colors (see Fig. 11.1). Once such 4-color scheme is adopted, for each pixel/node there is only one of four decisions that can be taken.

This work exploits the FCT result to substantially improve the running time of BP, thus providing fast alternatives to local methods for early vision problems. Our approach assigns one of 4 colors, that is, one of 4 placeholder labels, to each pixel, in order to arrive at a stable segmentation of the image. At the same time it assigns a more fine-grained label, like the intensities, disparities, or displacements to each of the 4 possible colors. The resulting fine-grained labeling—the actual outcome of the algorithm—changes continuously within the segments and abruptly across their boundaries. In doing so, our approach provides a fast approximation to optimal MRF labeling. Henceforth, we will systematically refer to placeholder labels as *colors*, and to actual, fine-grained labels as *labels*.

In the case of image segmentation, we obtain results that are qualitatively comparable to traditional log-linear Minimum Spanning Tree (MST)-based methods [6], but with computation times only linear in the number of pixels. Also for image denoising, stereo matching, and optical flow, we obtain computation times linear in the number of pixels but independent of the number of labels (resp. intensities, disparities, and displacements). The results are as accurate as for the (slower) multi-scale loopy belief propagation proposed in [7].

The remainder of the chapter is structured as follows. Section 11.2 surveys the (recent) MAP inference literature focusing on Loopy Belief Propagation for MRF labeling and provides the links between the graph coloring theory and our settings. Section 11.3 goes into more details about the implementation of Loopy Belief Propagation (LBP). In Sect. 11.4, the Four Color Theorem-based techniques are incorporated in both the LBP framework and a fast forward BP approximation. Section 11.5 describes the experiments that were conducted, and how the proposed techniques can be used for tasks like image segmentation, image denoising, stereo matching, and optical flow. The conclusions are drawn in Sect. 11.6.

11.2 Related Literature

So far, the FCT has been used only sporadically in computer vision. To the best of our knowledge, Vese and Chan [26] were the first to use the FCT in computer vision for their multiphase level set framework, in the piecewise smooth case. Agarwal and Belongie [1] showed that the two bit upper bound for per-pixel label storage in color-coded image partitions as a result of FCT, still is sub-optimal according to information theory. As said, this work for the first time introduces the use of the FCT in MAP inference for MRF labeling. In what follows, we review the state-of-the-art in MRF labeling and provide further background information on graph coloring.

11.2.1 MAP Inference—Discrete MRF

The general framework for the problems we consider here can be defined as follows (we use the notation and formulation from [7]). Let $\mathcal{P}$ be the set of pixels p in an image and $\mathcal{L}$ be a set of labels. The labels correspond to the quantities that we want to estimate at each pixel, such as disparities, intensities, or classes. A labeling f then assigns a label $f_p \in \mathcal{L}$ to each pixel $p \in \mathcal{P}$. Typically, a labeling varies smoothly except for a limited number of places, where it changes discontinuously, that is, at segment edges. A labeling is evaluated through an energy function,

$$E(f) = \sum_{(p,q)\in\mathcal{N}} V(f_p, f_q) + \sum_{p\in P} D_p(f_p) \tag{11.1}$$

where the (p, q) in $\mathcal{N}$ are the edges in the four-connected image grid. $V(f_p, f_q)$ is the pairwise cost or 'discontinuity cost' of assigning labels f_p and f_q to two neighboring pixels p and q. $D_p(f_p)$ is the unary cost or 'data cost' of assigning label f_p to pixel p. Finding a labeling with minimum energy corresponds to the maximum a posteriori (MAP) estimation problem for an appropriately defined MRF.

The MAP inference for discrete MRFs is NP-hard except for tree-structured MRFs, and pairwise MRFs with submodular energies, where

$$V(a, a) + V(b, b) \leq V(a, b) + V(b, a) \tag{11.2}$$

for two neighboring pixels and the labels $a, b \in \mathcal{L}$. In practice, approximate optimization methods are proposed [22, 28] for minimizing the energy in (11.1). Iterated Conditional Modes (ICM) [2], Simulated Annealing [10] and Highest Confidence First (HCF) [4] are among the oldest such methods. The 1990s turned Loopy Belief Propagation (LBP) [15] and Graph Cuts [11] into mainstream methods. A lot of recent efforts are going into optimization methods such as quadratic pseudo-boolean optimization [18], linear programming primal-dual, or other dual methods [28].

In this work, we focus mainly on LBP methods, and more particular on the max-product approach [29], which we adapt based on the FCT. Other variants include: factor graph BP higher-order factors [13], particles for continuous variables—non-parametric BP [20], top M solutions [33], tree-reweighted message passing BP [27].

When it comes to speeding up LBP, again several approaches can be mentioned: Felzenszwalb and Huttenlocher [7] introduce a distance transform and multiple scale guided LBP, Coughlan and Shen [5] employ a dynamic quantization of the state space, while Potetz and Lee [16] propose higher-order factors with linear interactions. Other solutions are tailored towards specific applications, for example, Yang et al. [32] propose a constant-space BP variant for stereo matching.

11.2.2 Graph Coloring

In graph theory, graph coloring is a subclass of graph labelings [9], which is the assignment of labels to the edges and/or vertices of a graph. We focus on vertex coloring, that is, the assignment of different labels to adjacent vertices. Traditionally, the labels were called "colors", as coloring the countries on a map was the first problem tackled (see Fig. 11.1 (left)). This problem was later generalized to coloring the faces of a graph embedding in the plane. By planar duality, it became a vertex coloring problem.

A (proper) k-coloring is a vertex coloring using at most k different colors, with all neighboring vertices differing in color. Then, the graph is called k-colorable. The chromatic number of a graph is the smallest number of colors needed to color the graph. A k-colorable graph is k-chromatic when k is its chromatic number.

Deciding for an arbitrary graph if it admits a proper vertex k-coloring is NP-complete. Finding the chromatic number is thus an NP-hard problem. While there are greedy algorithms able to achieve $(d + 1)$-coloring solutions, where d is maximum degree (adjacencies) of any node in the graph, these do not allow for the deriva-

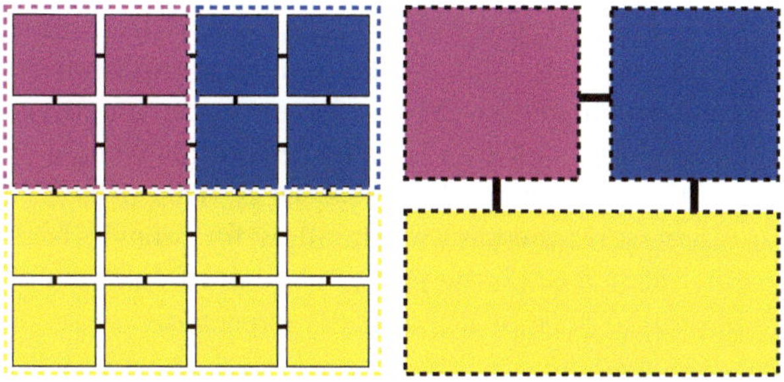

Fig. 11.2 Girth. While the 2D grid connectivity is a girth 4 planar graph (*left*), at a higher level, after merging the grid vertices into regions/segments the new planar graph can have girth 3 (*right*)

tion of the chromatic number, as the actual coloring uses at most $d+1$ colors, not exactly $d+1$ [31]. Providing a proper vertex k-coloring solution or counting the number of k-coloring solutions has been proven to have exponential time complexity.

The MRF labeling problems we work with are defined on grids, which often are combined with a 4-connectivity (see Fig. 11.2). This representation corresponds to a planar graph, that is, a graph that can be drawn in the plane without edge crossings. According to the FCT [17] the chromatic number of the graph is 4—at most 4 different colors are needed such that no adjacent vertices have the same color. For vertex coloring any map on a torus maximum 7 colors are necessary. On a projective plane, Klein bottle, or Moebius strip, one needs 6 colors. For spheres just 4 are necessary, as for planes. For more details, we refer the reader to [30]. Another vertex coloring result is given by Groetzsch's theorem [12]. If the planar graph is triangle-free, that is, the length of the shortest cycle (or girth, see Fig. 11.2) is at least 4, then the chromatic number of the graph is 3 (see Fig. 11.1 (right) for an example with girth 3 and thus requiring at least 4 colors).

The MRF labeling problems working on image grids can be seen as a joint optimization for the optimal image/grid segmentation into regions sharing the same label and the optimal assignment of such labels for each segmented region. The underlying segmentation can be seen as a planar graph, as if the regions are the equivalent of countries on a map and the region adjacencies are inherited from the local adjacencies on the initial grid. Thus, we have a vertex coloring problem for a planar graph. Provided that the regions/countries/segments are fixed, the four-color theorem guarantees that 4 colors are sufficient for a 4-coloring solution of the underlying segmentation. For each 4-colored segment, a final label assignment is to be optimized. Each image pixel is part of one color segment, and the number of color states is bounded by 4 as a result of the FCT. Moreover, the MRF label is carried at color state level as a property of each color segment, that is, for each color a single label is carried. During the MRF optimization process, both label and color state segment are continuously estimated by means of message passing under the Loopy Belief Propagation umbrella. Graph coloring theory thus provides a powerful argument that we can reduce the number of states when segmenting an image using an MRF labeling formulation.

Note that starting from the triangle-free planar graph of pixels does not imply that the planar graph of the underlying segmentation is a triangle-free planar graph as well. These segment adjacencies follow from merging the pixel-wise adjacencies. On the other hand, edge crossings are still impossible as a planar graph is still a planar graph whenever two adjacent nodes are merged. In summary, we still have a planar graph, but it no longer needs to be triangle-free and the girth can thus decrease to 3 (one example in Fig. 11.2). This calls for not using only 3 color states (as Groetzsch's theorem would allow for triangle-free planar graphs). In the experimental Sect. 11.5.5, the proper number of color states is empirically validated and comes out to be 4, as theoretically expected.

11.3 Loopy Belief Propagation

For inference on MRFs, Loopy Belief Propagation can be used [29]. In particular, the max-product approach finds an approximate minimum cost labeling of energy functions in the form of (11.1). Indeed, as an alternative to a formulation in terms of probability distributions, an equivalent formulation uses negative log probabilities, where the max-product becomes a min-sum. Following Felzenszwalb and Huttenlocher [7], we use this formulation as it is numerically more robust and makes more direct use of the energy function.

The max-product BP algorithm passes messages around on a graph defined by the 4-connected image grid. Each message is a vector, with the number of possible labels as dimension (some examples in Fig. 11.3). Let $m^t_{p\rightarrow q}$ be the message that node p passes on to a neighboring node q at time (iteration) t, $0 < t \leq T$, $p, q \in \mathcal{P}$. T is the total number of iterations. Consistent with the negative log formulation, all entries in $m^0_{p\rightarrow q}$ are initialized to zero. At each iteration t, new messages are computed based on the previous ones from iteration $t-1$, as follows:

$$m^t_{p\rightarrow q}(f_q) = \min_{f_p}\left(V(f_p, f_q) + D_p(f_p) + \sum_{g\in\mathcal{N}(p)\setminus q} m^{t-1}_{g\rightarrow p}(f_p)\right) \tag{11.3}$$

where $\mathcal{N}(p)\setminus q$ denotes all of p's neighbors, except q, and $f_q \in \mathcal{L}$ is the label of q. After T iterations, a belief vector $\hat{m}_q$ is computed for each node $q \in \mathcal{P}$. $\hat{m}_q$ is of size equal with the number of labels, $|\mathcal{L}|$, having one entry for each potential label $f_q \in \mathcal{L}$, and $\mathcal{N}(q)$ is the set of neighbors for q:

$$\hat{m}_q(f_q) = D_q(f_q) + \sum_{p\in\mathcal{N}(q)} m^T_{p\rightarrow q}(f_q) \tag{11.4}$$

Finally, for each node q, the best label $\hat{f}_q$ that minimizes $\hat{m}_q(f_q)$ is selected:

$$\hat{f}_q = \arg\min_{f_q} \hat{m}_q(f_q) \tag{11.5}$$

The standard implementation of this message passing algorithm runs in $O(nk^2T)$ time, with n the number of pixels, $n = |\mathcal{P}|$, k the number of possible labels, $k = |\mathcal{L}|$,

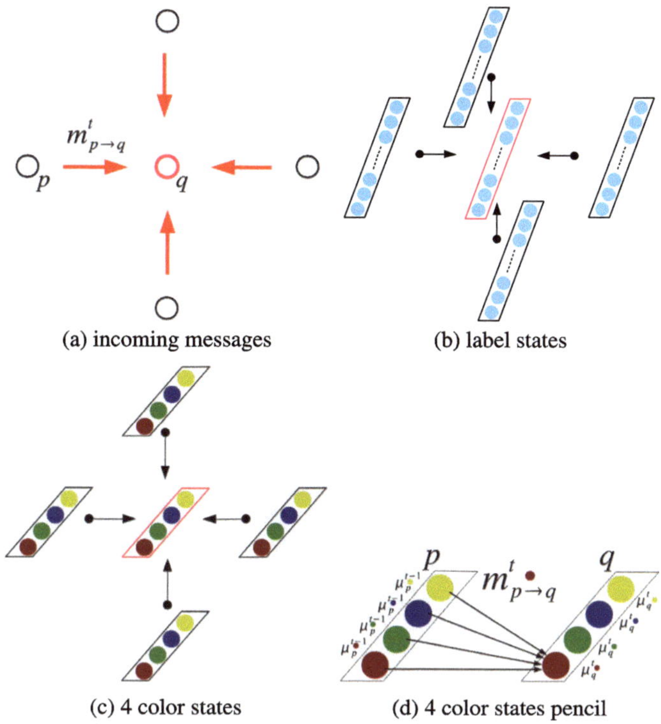

Fig. 11.3 Local neighborhoods in BP with message passing (**a**) and a pencil example (**d**). Note the reduction in working states from the traditional approaches (= number of labels) (**b**) to only 4 color states (**c**)

and T the number of iterations. Essentially it takes $O(k^2)$ time to compute each message vector between neighboring nodes (see (11.3)) and there are $O(n)$ messages per iteration. In [7], the time of computing each message is reduced to $O(k)$. This acceleration is based on the distance transform for particular classes of data cost functions D such as truncated linear and quadratic models combined with a Potts model for the discontinuity cost V. Thus, the algorithm has $O(nkT)$ time complexity.

11.3.1 Multiscale BP on the Grid Graph

As in [7], we can partition the 2D grid in a checkerboard pattern where every edge connects nodes of different partitions, so that the grid graph is bipartite (see Fig. 11.4(c)). We then compute only half of the messages, for example, from the green nodes to the blue nodes in Fig. 11.4(c). Then we swap partitions and do the same. This process of partial message passing in 2 subsequent tacts is repeated until convergence or a maximum number of iterations has been reached. This scheme has

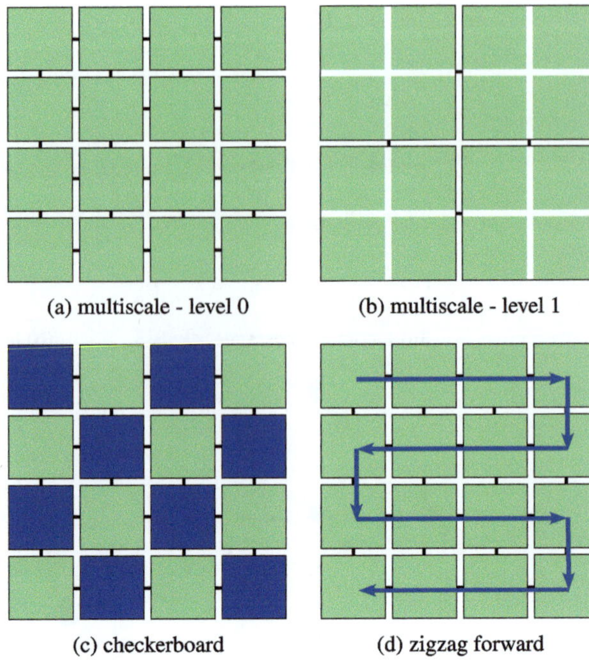

Fig. 11.4 Levels in multiscale (**a**), (**b**), a checkerboard (**c**), and zigzag forward traversal for a 2D grid (**d**)

the advantage of requiring no additional memory space for storing the updated messages. Another technique explained in [7] and also used here addresses the problem of needing many iterations of message passing to cover large distances. One solution is to perform BP in a coarse-to-fine manner, so that the long-range interactions between nodes are captured by shorter ones in coarser graphs. The minimization function does not change. In this hierarchical approach, BP runs at one resolution level in order to get estimates for the next finer level. Better initial estimates from the coarser level help to speed up the convergence at the finer level. The pyramidal structure works as follows. The zero-th level is the original image (see Fig. 11.4(a)). The ith level corresponds to a lower-resolution version with blocks of $2^i \times 2^i$ pixels grouped together. The resulting blocks are still connected in a grid structure (see Fig. 11.4(a), (b), showing the first two levels as an example). For a block $\mathcal{B}$, the adapted data cost of assigning label $f_{\mathcal{B}}$ is

$$D_{\mathcal{B}}(f_{\mathcal{B}}) = \sum_{p \in \mathcal{B}} D_p(f_p) \tag{11.6}$$

where the sum runs over all pixels p in the block $\mathcal{B}$. The multiscale algorithm first solves the problem at the coarsest level, where the messages are initialized to zero. Subsequent, finer levels take the previous, coarser level as initialization. In the 4-connected grid each node p sends messages in all 4 directions, *right*, *left*, *up*, *down*. Let r_p^t be the message sent by node p to the *right* at iteration t, and similarly l_p^t, u_p^t, d_p^t for the other directions. This is just a renaming. If q is the right neighbor of p, then $r^t_p = m^t_{p\to q}$ and $l^t_q = m^t_{q\to p}$. If q is the upper neighbor of p, then $u^t_p = m^t_{p\to q}$ and $d^t_q = m^t_{q\to p}$. For a node p at level $i-1$, the messages $(r^0_{p,i-1}, l^0_{p,i-1}, u^0_{p,i-1}, d^0_{p,i-1})$ will be initialized with the ones obtained by solving the level i for the containing block $\mathcal{B}$, $p \in \mathcal{B}$:

$$\begin{aligned} r^0_{p,i-1} &\leftarrow r^T_{\mathcal{B},i} \\ l^0_{p,i-1} &\leftarrow l^T_{\mathcal{B},i} \\ u^0_{p,i-1} &\leftarrow u^T_{\mathcal{B},i} \\ d^0_{p,i-1} &\leftarrow d^T_{\mathcal{B},i} \end{aligned} \tag{11.7}$$

The total number of nodes in a quad-tree is upper bounded by

$$n\left(1+\frac{1}{4}+\frac{1}{16}+\frac{1}{64}+\cdots\right)=n\sum_{i=0}^{\infty}\frac{1}{4^i}=n\frac{4}{3} \tag{11.8}$$

where n is the number of nodes at the finest level, that is, in our case, the number of pixels in the image, $n = |\mathcal{P}|$. We have $4/3$ the number of nodes at the finest level, n, so the overhead introduced by the multiscale approach amounts to only $1/3$ of the original single scale approach, but it results in a greatly reduced number of iterations (between five and ten iterations per scale instead of hundreds at the finest) for convergence. In general, the number of levels needed is proportional to $\log_2$ of the image diameter. The diameter is defined as the longest shortest path between any two nodes (pixels) in the connected grid (graph) representation (of the image). The traditional LBP scheme using one level requires at least a number of iterations equal with the diameter of the image in order to allow information propagation between any two nodes.

11.3.2 Forward Belief Propagation

While, in theory, the LBP messages are updated simultaneously, we propose a traversing order for the nodes in the 2D grid as another way to speed up the propagation of beliefs. Sequentially applying the message updates in the imposed order allows a belief from one node to influence all the following nodes in the traversing order.

Once the traversal order has been fixed, updating the messages in that order corresponds to a Forward Belief Propagation (FBP), whereas Backward Belief Propagation (BBP) corresponds to going in the reverse order of the traversal. Here we consider the traversing order to be in a zigzag/square wave pattern (see Fig. 11.4(d)). Starting from top-left we first go to the top-right, then we go down one line and take the path back to the left, where we move to the next line and repeat the procedure until no line remains unvisited. This traversing order has some advantages in canceling/reducing the incorrectly propagated beliefs.

The message costs have to be normalized. One way of doing this is to simply divide by the number of messages used for computing them. In our 4-connected grid graph, we divide the costs of the newly updated messages by 4.

Note that our zigzag FBP and BBP can be used in the multiscale framework as described in Sect. 11.3.1. In our implementations, we use the forward traversal order (see Fig. 11.4(d)) in the odd iterations and the backward traversal order in the even iterations. Replacing the checkerboard scheme with FBP traversing in the multiscale BP framework (BP-FH) from [7] provides very similar performance in the stereo and denoising tasks. We refer to this method as Forward Belief Propagation-Multi Scale (FBP-MS). Without multiscale guidance, FBP usually gets stuck in a poor solution.

11.4 Four Color Theorem in BP

The Four Color Theorem guarantees us, that with only four colors, neighboring segments can always be colored differently. This is important for all low-level processes where keeping boundaries intact is crucial. Examples are segmentation, but also stereo, optical flow, and image denoising. Within the resulting segments, more refined labels have to be assigned to the different pixels (e.g., gradually changing disparities, displacements, or intensities). With only 4 colors to be considered, we have—at a single pixel—the limitation that we can associate with each of the 4 colors only 1 label. This may sound like a drastic restriction. Yet, one should consider the different pixels within the segments, that can each bring 4 such labels to the table. The total number of labels that are considered is therefore a lot larger. The hope is that the message passing will distribute the truly relevant labels. Messages actually contain both color and label information. Following our experimental results, the proper label is, at least for sufficiently large segments, seen to prevail. Note that one could add robustness by additionally considering a randomly selected label for each pixel when the message passing updates are computed. Our results did not call for such addition, however.

Importantly, by keeping only *four* labels, one for each possible color state of one pixel/node in the 2D grid graph, we obtain an algorithm that is linear in the number of pixels but not labels, and therefore is very fast. Moreover, our results are comparable to those obtained when using standard max-product BP, efficient multiscale BP [7], or graph cuts algorithms to minimize energy functions in the form of (11.1).

In Fig. 11.3(d), we show two neighboring nodes/pixels with 4 color states and a *pencil*. The pencil shows the possible connections between one state and the states of a neighboring node/pixel. Here, as usual, only the best connection is used, that is, the one that minimizes a certain energy.

The Four Color Theorem says that we can cover an image with disjoint segments, where each segment has one of no more than four colors, and no two segments sharing a border of more than one pixel have the same color. The total number of

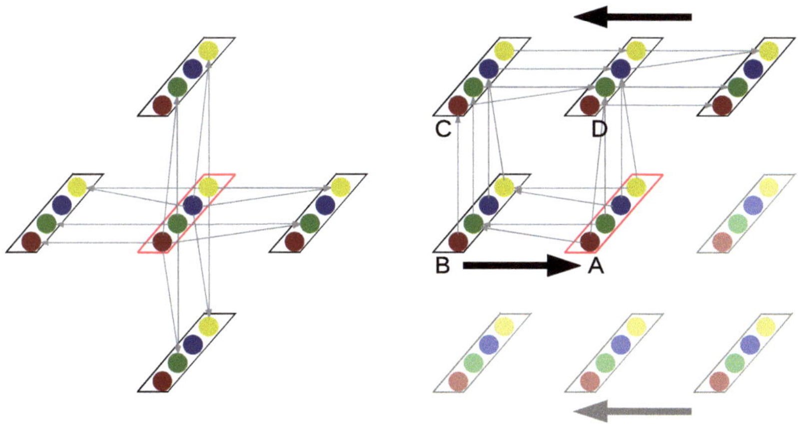

Fig. 11.5 Four color states pixel neighborhood used in computing message updates, the case for BP-FCT (*left*) and FBP-FCT (*right*)

segments for the problems considered here is a priori unknown but upper bounded by the number of image pixels, $n = |\mathcal{P}|$. Let $\mathcal{S}$ be the set of segments. Thus, locally each pixel can belong to one of four color states and the color itself represents the segment of pixels connected through the same color. In (11.1), the labeling f should assign each pixel p from $\mathcal{P}$ to a segment from $\mathcal{S}$.

In the next sections, *color state* is the term used to refer to the construct where for each of the 4 colors used for the underlying segmentation we keep energies, estimated labels, and possibly other parameters, locally assigned to each underlying color segment.

11.4.1 BP with Four Colors

In order to work with four color states, the labeling f, in our new formulation, assigns $f_p \in \mathcal{C}$ to each pixel $p \in \mathcal{P}$, where the cardinality of $\mathcal{C}$ is 4 ($|\mathcal{C}| = 4$). In the left part of Fig. 11.5 a 4-connected grid neighborhood is depicted for the four colors case. The edges/connections to the neighboring nodes are picked to minimize the energies in the BP formulation. For each pixel $p \in \mathcal{P}$, each possible color state of that pixel $c \in \mathcal{C}$, and each of its neighbors $q \in \mathcal{N}(p)$, we have a data parameter that is continuously updated through message passing, $\mu^t_{p\to q}(c)$ at iteration t. Thus, $\mu^t_q(c)$ is updated by using all the incoming messages, including $\mu^t_{p\to q}(c)$. The data parameter μ^t_q (see Fig. 11.3), which represents a quantity to be estimated in each pixel, is the equivalent of the labels in the original BP formulation, where there is a bijection between labels and quantities to be estimated.

The initial values for $\mu^0_p(c)$ and $\mu^0_{p\to q}(c)$ depend on the data; we set them to the best observation we have. For example, in stereo matching, these will be the best scoring disparities in each pixel (in a *winner-take-all* sense) and in image denoising, the pixel values. When we compute the new messages (using (11.3)), we also store the color of the state, $\hat{c}^t_{p\to q}$, for which we have the minimum message energy at iteration t:

$$\hat{c}^t_{p\to q}(f_q) = \arg\min_{f_p\in\mathcal{C}}\left(V(f_p, f_q) + D_p(f_p) + \sum_{g\in N(p)\backslash q} m^{t-1}_{g\to p}(f_p)\right) \tag{11.9}$$

for every color state $f_q \in \mathcal{C}$. Also, at each iteration, part of the message is the data parameter estimation:

$$\mu^t_{p\to q}(f_q) = \mu^{t-1}_p\left(\hat{c}^t_{p\to q}(f_q)\right) \tag{11.10}$$

for every color state $f_q \in \mathcal{C}$. The exact nature of V and D_p depends on the application and will be specified in Sect. 11.5.

We call this formulation BP-FCT, standing for Belief Propagation with Four Color Theorem principle.

11.4.2 FBP with Four Colors

FBP (see Sect. 11.3.2) does not produce good quality results on its own (e.g., in the absence of multiscale guidance). A solution is to consider a different updating scheme at each step, employing local consistency. Standard message updating assumes that the history and neighborhood belief are stored/propagated in all the messages reaching the current node and takes the best updates. Instead, we exploit the ordering introduced in FBP, and keep track of the links/connections/edges which provided the best costs for each node and color state in the grid. Thus the nodes are processed sequentially, following the imposed order (see Fig. 11.5). We compute the current best costs only based on the connections to the previously processed nodes. These are (for an inner node, i.e., A in Fig. 11.5) the previously processed node (in the traversal order, B in Fig. 11.5) and the neighboring node from the previously processed line (D in Fig. 11.5).

For each pixel p from the image, $p \in |\mathcal{P}|$, and each possible color state $c \in \mathcal{C}$, we keep the minimum obtained energy $E(p,c)$, the estimated average image intensity/color coined $\mu_{p,c}$ (the estimated label) of the segment where p belongs to, and the estimated number of pixels in the current segment $N_{p,c}$.

We use the following notations:

- $c_{\leftarrow}(p,c)$ the color state from the preceding pixel in the FBP traversing order for p that contributed to the energy $E(p,c)$, $\forall c \in \mathcal{C}$ (e.g., $c_{\leftarrow}(A, \mathit{blue}) = \mathit{yellow}$ in Fig. 11.5).
- $l_{\leftarrow}(p)$ the link to the preceding pixel according to the FBP traversing order for p (e.g., $l_{\leftarrow}(A) = B$ in Fig. 11.5).
- $c_{\uparrow}(p,c)$ the color state from the neighboring pixel in the previous computed raw of pixels in the FBP traversing order for p that contributed to the energy $E(p,c)$, $\forall c \in \mathcal{C}$ (e.g., $c_{\uparrow}(A, \mathit{red}) = \mathit{green}$ in Fig. 11.5).

$l_{\uparrow}(p)$ the link to the neighboring pixel in the previous raw of pixels according to the FBP traversing order for p (e.g., $l_{\uparrow}(A) = D$ in Fig. 11.5).

The right part of Fig. 11.5 shows the general case where for the current node A we only use what we know from the already traversed nodes (B, C, D). To enforce local consistency, we calculate the energy of each possible color state of a pixel A not only from the previous pixel B, but also from the color state of the pixel D that, through C influenced that particular color state in B. For example, in Fig. 11.5, to compute the energy to go from the *green* state in B to the *red* state in A we observe that if B is green, then D is also green (via the C node). Therefore, the possible energy in A's red state, if B's green state is considered as connection, is the sum of the transition energy from B's green state and D's green state. Computing the best energy for each of A's 4 color states requires to first consider all of B's states leading there, each time paired with the corresponding state in D, and to then take the minimum energy among these alternatives.

Thus, the energy $E(p, c)$ is computed consistently if the links point correctly on the grid:

$$l_{\uparrow}(p) = l_{\leftarrow}\big(l_{\uparrow}\big(l_{\leftarrow}(p)\big)\big) \tag{11.11}$$

and

$$c_{\uparrow}(p, c) = c_{\leftarrow}\big(l_{\uparrow}\big(l_{\leftarrow}(p)\big), c_{\uparrow}\big(l_{\leftarrow}(p), c_{\leftarrow}(p, c)\big)\big) \tag{11.12}$$

which enforces that the connecting color state $c_{\leftarrow}(p, c)$ of the previously processed pixel results from the connecting color state $c_{\uparrow}(p, c)$ of the neighboring pixel from the previously processed line.

In order to compute $E(p, c)$, we first compute for each possible color state $i \in \mathcal{C}$ of the previously processed pixel the energy

$$\begin{aligned} E_{\leftarrow}(p, c, i) = {} & E\big(l_{\leftarrow}(p), i\big) + h\big((p, c), \big(l_{\leftarrow}(p), i\big)\big) \\ & + h\big((p, c), \big(l_{\uparrow}(p), c_{\leftarrow}\big(l_{\uparrow}\big(l_{\leftarrow}(p)\big), c_{\uparrow}\big(l_{\leftarrow}(p), i\big)\big)\big)\big) \end{aligned} \tag{11.13}$$

cumulating the energy $E(l_{\leftarrow}(p), i)$ of the previously processed pixel, the energy for color states of the previous and current pixels, as well as the energy for corresponding color states of the current pixel and the connected one on the previous line. Now we can take the lowest energy over all possible color states i as

$$E(p, c) = \min_{i \in \mathcal{C}} E\big(l_{\leftarrow}(p), c, i\big) \tag{11.14}$$

and store the color state from the previously processed pixel which provides the best energy:

$$c_{\leftarrow}(p, c) = \arg\min_{i \in \mathcal{C}} E\big(l_{\leftarrow}(p), c, i\big) \tag{11.15}$$

The energy $h((p,c_p),(q,c_q))$ between two pixels $p,q \in \mathcal{P}$, given their corresponding color states $c_p, c_q \in \mathcal{C}$, is:

$$h\big((p,c_p),(q,c_q)\big) = \begin{cases} D(I(p),I(q),\sigma_c) + D(\mu_{p,c_p},\mu_{q,c_q},\sigma_m) & \text{if } c_p = c_q \\ 2 - [D(I(p),I(q),\sigma_c) + D(\mu_{p,c_p},\mu_{q,c_q},\sigma_m)] & \text{if } c_p \neq c_q \end{cases} \tag{11.16}$$

where $I(p)$ is the color value of the pixel p, σ_x indicates a noise level for x used in some of our applications, $D(I(p),I(q),\sigma_c)$ is the smoothness cost between two pixels p and q with color values $I(p)$ and $I(q)$, and $D(\mu_{p,c_p},\mu_{q,c_q},\sigma_m)$ is the data cost agreeing between the estimated working labels/quantities at color segment level μ_{p,c_p} and μ_{q,c_q}.

The distance/penalty $D(u,v,\sigma)$ between pixel values penalizes for segment discontinuities between similar values ($\|u-v\|_1 < 2\sigma^2$), whereas if the pixels are very different, the penalty is reasonably small.

$$D(u,v,\sigma) = 1 - \exp\left(-\frac{\|u-v\|_1}{2\sigma^2}\right) \tag{11.17}$$

The function models the distribution of the label noise among neighboring pixels, with σ its variance. For the smoothness cost, we can take a different σ than for the data cost. Here we use σ_c for agreement between pixel color values and σ_m for the agreement between the average labels of segments.

The link to the corresponding pixel state at the previous line is stored in

$$c_\uparrow(p,c) = c_\leftarrow\big(l_\uparrow(l_\leftarrow(p)), c_\uparrow(l_\leftarrow(p), c_\leftarrow(p,c))\big) \tag{11.18}$$

Given the previous notations, the estimated label $\mu_{p,c}$ for a pixel p and color state c in a segment and the approximated number of pixels belonging to the segment, $N_{p,c}$, are obtained as follows:

$$N_{p,c} = \begin{cases} N_{l_\leftarrow(p),c_\leftarrow(p,c)} + 1 & \text{if } c = c_\leftarrow(p,c) \\ N_{l_\uparrow(p),c_\uparrow(p,c)} + 1 & \text{if } c = c_\uparrow(p,c) \wedge c \neq c_\leftarrow(p,c) \\ 1 & \text{otherwise} \end{cases} \tag{11.19}$$

and

$$\mu_{p,c} = \begin{cases} (\mu_{l_\leftarrow(p),c_\leftarrow(p,c)} N_{l_\leftarrow(p),c_\leftarrow(p,c)} + I(p))/N_{p,c} & \text{if } c = c_\leftarrow(p,c) \\ (\mu_{l_\uparrow(p),c_\uparrow(p,c)} N_{l_\uparrow(p),c_\uparrow(p,c)} + I(p))/N_{p,c} & \text{if } c = c_\uparrow(p,c) \wedge c \\ & \quad \neq c_\leftarrow(p,c) \\ I(p) & \text{otherwise} \end{cases} \tag{11.20}$$

For $N_{p,c}$, we either increment the estimated number of pixels of the color segment to which the current pixel is assigned, or we put it to 1 if a new color segment is formed. Following the same logic, the estimated label in the current pixel changes by taking a weighted average over that pixel's label ($I(p)$) and the label of at most one of its neighbors: the previously updated neighbor if it lies in the same 4-color segment; if not, the neighbor on the previous line if that falls within the same segment; and none if both neighbors fall outside.

11.5 Experiments

We now demonstrate how the proposed methods can be used in different early vision applications that can be formulated as energy minimization problems through an MRF model.

For all those applications, we provide details about discontinuity/pairwise costs ($V(f_p, f_q)$), data/unary costs ($D_p(f_p)$), and message updates/computations ($\mu^t_p(f_p)$, $m^t_{p\to q}(f_q)$). Also, we provide a comparison with well-known standard methods. The images used are from the Berkeley Segmentation Dataset [14], the Middlebury Stereo Datasets [19], and enhancement images from [7].

All the provided running times were obtained on an Intel Core 2 Duo T7250 (2.0 GHz/800 Mhz FSB, 2 MB Cache) notebook with 2 GB RAM. More results are available at: http://homes.esat.kuleuven.be/~rtimofte/.

11.5.1 Image Segmentation

For comparison, we use our proposed method based on the Four Color Theorem—FBP-FCT (see Sect. 11.4.2) versus a standard Minimum Spanning Tree based method—MST-FH from [6].

The oversegmentation in our FBP-FCT is addressed in a similar fashion to MST-FH in [6]. The smaller (than an imposed minimum size) segments are merged with other segments until no segment with a size less than the imposed minimum remains. We use the original MST-FH implementation with the original parameters ($\sigma = 0.8$, $k = 300$). Our FBP-FCT method uses an initial smoothing of the image with $\sigma = 0.7$, $\sigma_c = 3.2$, and $\sigma_m = 4.2$ (see (11.17)). We set $k = 300$ and the minimum segment size for both methods is 50 pixels. Figure 11.6 depicts the image segmentation results for several cases.

MST-FH is an $O(n \log n)$ algorithm, while FBP-FCT is $O(n|\mathcal{C}|^2)$, where n is the number of pixels in the image, i.e. $n = |\mathcal{P}|$. This means (and our tests show) that FBP-FCT and MST-FH have comparable running times on low resolution images while for high resolution images ($\log n > |\mathcal{C}|^2$), the FBP-FCT is faster. For example, the *Venus* RGB image with 434 × 383 pixels (top-left in Fig. 11.6) is processed by MST-FH in about 250 milliseconds, while our approach takes 320 milliseconds. For the upscaled image with 3472 × 3064 pixels our FBP-FCT runs in 16 seconds, half a second less than the MST-FH method. Using fewer than 4 color states largely improves the running time of our method, as we show in Sect. 11.5.5.

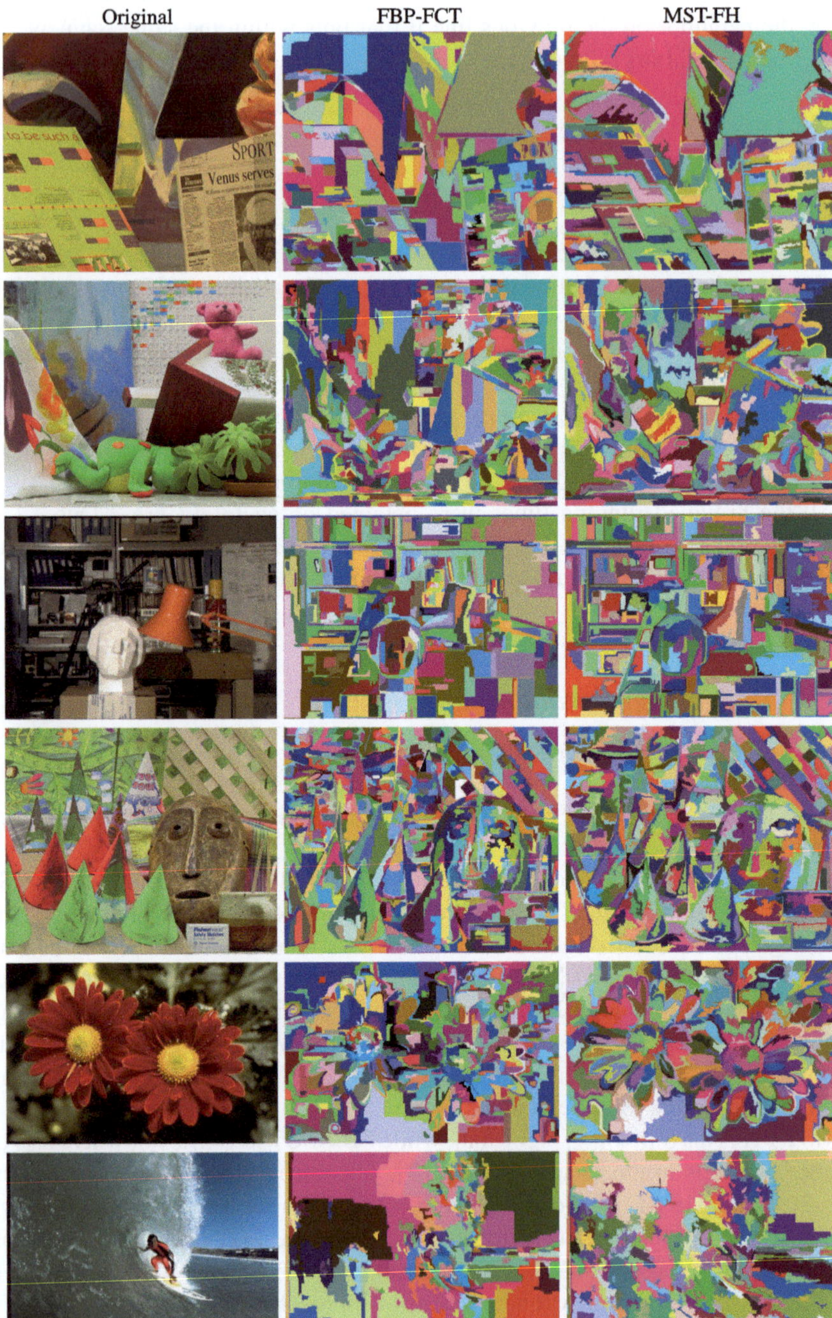

Fig. 11.6 Segmentation results. Minimum segment size set to 50 pixels

11.5.2 Image Denoising

The image denoising problem is a case where usually the number of labels (in an MRF/BP formulation) is very large since it is equal to the number of intensity levels/colors used. We argue that this way of seeing the problem, besides being computationally demanding, does not take advantage of the relation that exists between labels as intensities. The intensity values are obtained through uniform sampling of a continuous signal, therefore carry direct information on their relative closeness. Instead of updating labels through selection from neighboring labels, as with standard BP, our scheme—which maintains the discrete nature of the 4 colors—can submit the actual, neighboring labels to mathematical operations such as averaging.

In the BP-FCT formulation (see Sect. 11.4.1) we take the following updating function for the intensity data at each message:

$$\mu_q^t(f_q) = \frac{\alpha I(q) + \sum_{p\in\mathcal{N}(q)\backslash q}(\mu_{p\to q}^t(f_q)[\hat{c}_{p\to q}^t(f_q) = f_q])}{\alpha + \sum_{p\in\mathcal{N}(q)\backslash q}[\hat{c}_{p\to q}^t(f_q) = f_q]} \tag{11.21}$$

where $[\cdot = \cdot]$ is the Iverson bracket for Kronecker's delta, that is, it returns 1 for equality, 0 otherwise, and α is the weight/contribution of the observed value $I(q)$ in the updated data term. Here we use $\alpha = 0.25$. $\hat{c}_{p\to q}^t(f_q)$ is defined by (11.9) and represents the best color state for which we achieved the minimum message energy at iteration t.

The data cost for a pixel p, at iteration t is taken as

$$D_p(f_p) = \min\left(\left\|I(p) - \mu_p^{t-1}(f_p)\right\|_2, \tau_1\right) \tag{11.22}$$

where τ_1 acts as a truncation value, that is empirically set. D_p depends on the difference between the estimated intensity value $\mu_p^t(f_p)$ at iteration t and the observed one $I(p)$ for the pixel p under the labeling (color state assignment) f_p.

The discontinuity cost is given by:

$$V(f_p, f_q) = \beta \min\left(\left\|\mu_p^{t-1}(f_p) - \mu_q^{t-1}(f_q)\right\|_2, \tau_2\right) \tag{11.23}$$

where β is a scaling factor and τ_2 acts as a truncation value.

We compare BP-FCT (Sect. 11.4.1) and FBP-FCT (Sect. 11.4.2) with BP-FH [7]. For this purpose the gray-scale images are corrupted by adding independent and identically-distributed Gaussian noise with zero-mean and variance 30. We use the original available implementation for multiscale BP-FH. We apply for FBP-FCT a Gaussian smoothing with standard deviation 1.5 before processing the corrupted images, while BP-FH was demonstrated using a Gaussian filtering with a standard deviation of 1.5. We set $\sigma_c = \sigma_m = 3.2$ for FBP-FCT, while BP-FCT uses for discontinuity truncation $\tau_2 = 200$, for data truncation $\tau_1 = 10000$ and for the rate of increase the cost $\beta = 1$. While BP-FH uses 5 iterations, BP-FCT uses 20.

Reducing the number of labels when $|\mathcal{L}| \gg |\mathcal{C}|^2$ assures a considerable speed-up of our proposed methods (BP-FCT—$O(n|\mathcal{C}|^2T)$, FBP-FCT—$O(n|\mathcal{C}|^2)$), over

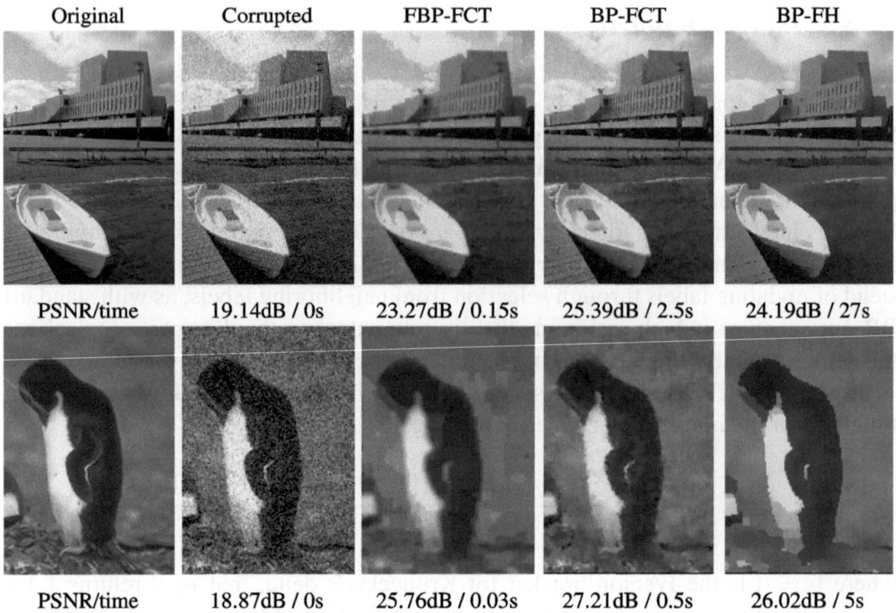

Fig. 11.7 Denoising results. BP-FCT and FBP-FCT perform better or similar when compared with BP-FH (in terms of PSNR) while being 1 up to 2 orders of magnitude faster

the standard multi-scale BP-FH which has a time complexity of $O(n|\mathcal{L}|T)$ (with n the number of pixels and T the number of iterations). Image denoising results are shown in Fig. 11.7. For all the test images BP-FCT and FBP-FCT had a better or similar denoising performance (in terms of PSNR) than the BP-FH method, while being up to 100 times faster. For example, the *Boat* gray-scale corrupted image with 321×481 pixels (top row in Fig. 11.7) is processed by FBP-FCT in about 150 milliseconds, by BP-FCT in 2.5 seconds, while BP-FH takes more than 27 seconds. The computed PSNR (in decibels) for the *Penguin* images are: $PSNR_{\text{Corrupted}} = 18.87$, $PSNR_{\text{FBP-FCT}} = 25.76$, $PSNR_{\text{BP-FCT}} = 27.21$, $PSNR_{\text{BP-FH}} = 26.02$. We refer the reader to the figure for the complete set of numbers for all images. Having a denoising method that works for a single channel image (gray levels), usually the multi-channel images (e.g., RGB) are processed for each channel individually and the denoised image is the union of the denoised channels.

11.5.3 Stereo Matching

For stereo matching, in the BP-FCT (see Sect. 11.4.1) framework we define the following cost and update functions. We employ the standard settings using a Disparity Space Image (DSI) computed as follows using the left and right intensity images, I_l and I_r.

For a pixel $p=(i,j)$ whose intensity is $I_l(i,j)$ in the left camera image, the cost for a disparity of d is:

$$DSI(p,d)=\beta\min\big(\big\|I_l(i,j)-I_r(i-d,j)\big\|^2,\tau_s\big) \tag{11.24}$$

where $\beta=0.1$ and $\tau_s=10000$.

The data cost at iteration t is defined for each point p in the left image and color state $f_p\in\mathcal{C}$ as:

$$D_p(f_p)=DSI\big(p,\mu_p^{t-1}(f_p)\big) \tag{11.25}$$

where $\mu_p^{t-1}(f_p)$ is the previous disparity estimate for the pixel p and the same color state $f_p\in\mathcal{C}$.

The data update at iteration t is:

$$\mu_q^t(f_q)=\begin{cases}\arg\min_d DSI(p,d) & \text{if } \mathcal{W}(q)=\emptyset\\ \arg\min_{\mu_{p\to q}^t(f_q),p\in\mathcal{W}(q)}(DSI(p,\mu_{p\to q}^t(f_q))) & \text{otherwise}\end{cases} \tag{11.26}$$

where $\mathcal{W}(q)$ is

$$\mathcal{W}(q)=\big\{p\in\mathcal{N}(q)|\hat{c}_{p\to q}^t(f_q)=f_q\big\} \tag{11.27}$$

and represents the set of neighbors from the 4-neighborhood $\mathcal{N}(q)$, as picked in the best energy computation that share the same color state f_q (thus underlying color segment) with q. $\hat{c}_{p\to q}^t(f_q)$ is computed using (11.9).

The discontinuity cost is given by:

$$V(f_p,f_q)=\begin{cases}0 & \text{if } f_p=f_q\\ \tau_v & \text{otherwise}\end{cases} \tag{11.28}$$

where $\tau_v=40$ in our experiments.

Figure 11.8 depicts results of the BP-FCT method in comparison with BP-FH. Here we see a case where our approach does not improve upon the full BP-FH [7] formulation. The main reason for the poorer performance is the discrete nature of the cost function. There is no smooth transition in costs from one disparity to a neighboring one with respect to difference in absolute values. This makes it difficult to define an updating function for the data estimation when we work with four colors. Our intuition is to pick the best disparity from the same color segment and in the absence of connections to neighbors with the same color, to return to the best observed disparity (see (11.26)). The drawback is that our proposed method needs more iterations per level to achieve a performance similar to BP-FH. In our experiments, it takes between five and ten times more iterations than BP-FH to achieve similar performance, however this is not directly seen in the running time for large inputs, since our method has $O(n|\mathcal{C}|^2T)$ complexity and BP-FH $O(n|\mathcal{L}|T)$. Starting from the case where $|\mathcal{L}|>4|\mathcal{C}|^2$ our proposed method (BP-FCT) is similar or considerably faster ($|\mathcal{L}|\gg 4|\mathcal{C}|^2$).

For stereo matching based on image segmentation, our proposed segmentation method (FBP-FCT) can be integrated as a fast oversegmentation step. Figure 11.8

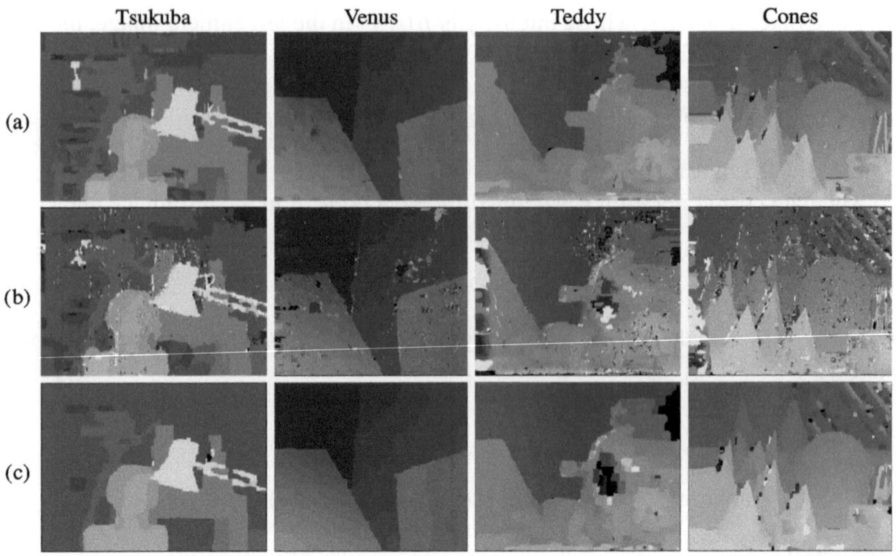

Fig. 11.8 Stereo matching results. (**a**) Our implementation of [25] where for image segmentation we use our FBP-FCT, (**b**) BP-FCT, (**c**) BP-FH from [7]

depicts results where we used our segmentation and our implementation of the pipeline from [25]. This is a *winner-take-all* method that combines fast aggregation of costs in a window around each pixel with costs from the segment support to which the pixel belongs. According to the Middlebury benchmark [19], this implementation ranks 76th out of 88 current methods.

11.5.4 Optical Flow

In motion flow estimation, the labels correspond to different displacement vectors. While in stereo matching the disparities were evaluated along the scanline, here the displaced/corresponding pixels are to be found in a surrounding two-dimensional window in the paired images. Thus, the set of labels goes quadratic when compared with stereo. We are using the cost functions as defined for stereo matching in the BP-FCT framework (see Sect. 11.5.3), where d is a mapping for displacements. For a pixel $p = (i, j)$ whose intensity is $I_l(i, j)$ in the first (left) image, the cost for a displacement of $d(i, j) = (d_i, d_j)$ is:

$$DSI(p, d) = \beta \min\left(\left\| I_l(i, j) - I_r(i - d_i, j - d_j)\right\|^2, \tau_s\right) \tag{11.29}$$

where $\beta = 0.1$ and $\tau_s = 10000$. The other cost functions are given by the (11.25), (11.26), and (11.28). We keep the same parameter values as in the stereo case, Sect. 11.5.3.

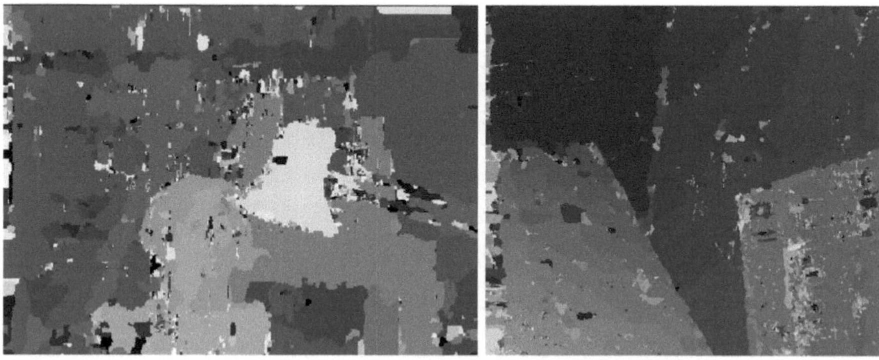

Fig. 11.9 Optical flow results for the *Tsukuba* and *Venus* image pairs

Note that increasing the set/space of displacement values will not increase the computational time of our Four-Color Theorem based BP approach, since the size of the actual label set is decoupled from that of the placeholder labels, that is, the four colors. However, the *DSI* still needs to be computed for having good initial estimates. In our case, the optical flow case takes as much running time as the stereo case (see Sect. 11.5.3) for the same image size, apart from differences in initialization and the selection of the best energy displacement per pixel which is slower for optical flow, given its higher number of actual labels. Figure 11.9 shows the results for the optical flow computation on the same standard stereo image pairs. For this, we are considering as disparity the distance from the left pixel to the corresponding pixel in the right image. We see that the results are worse but very close to the ones obtained in the stereo-specific formulation (from Fig. 11.8). Increasing the number of displacements from 16(20) in the *Tsukuba* (*Venus*) pair in the stereo case to as much as 1024(1600) (about two orders magnitude bigger) causes a drop of only 4 % in the quality of the results, but does not increase the computational time of the BP-FCT algorithm. However, the *DSI* computation time (and the winner-take-all initialization) taken individually increases linearly with the number of possible displacements.

11.5.5 Theory and Parameters in Practice

In Sect. 11.2.2, we reviewed the graph theoretical foundations supporting our choice of 4 color states, which was based on the four-color theorem. Here we empirically verify that indeed 4 color states is the right number in our conditions. We want to prove that using more than 4 color states is: (i) suboptimal, slowing down the BP inference, and (ii) the solution does not improve. Also, if we reduce the number of color states below 4 then we have: (i) insufficient color states, but faster BP inference, and (ii) the obtained solution worsens.

We use the previous settings for image segmentation (Sect. 11.5.1) and image denoising (Sect. 11.5.2). For image segmentation with FBP-FCT, we first apply a

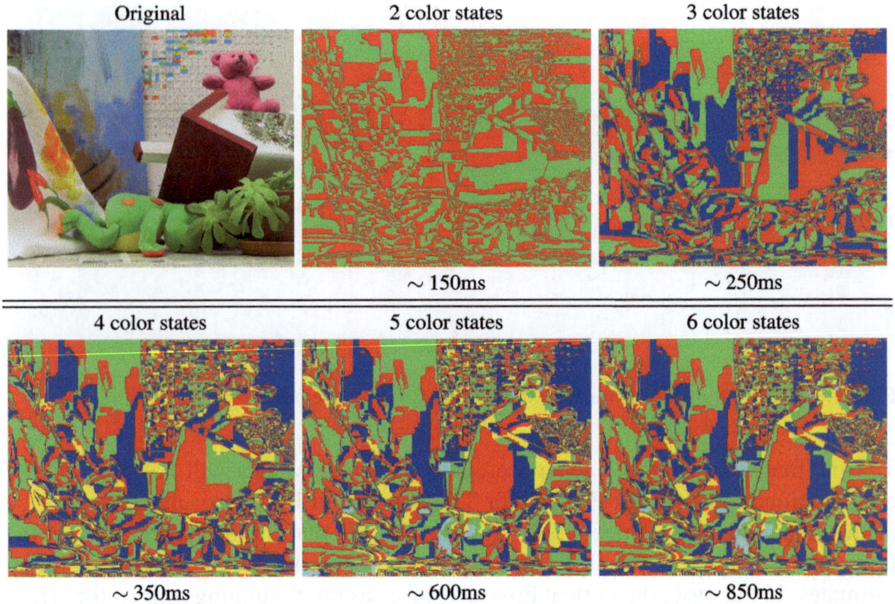

Fig. 11.10 Number of color states versus FBP-FCT segmentation results on *Teddy* image. Using more than 6 color states usually does not change the segmentation. Already from 5 to 6 color states the changes in segmentation are minor

Gaussian smoothing with standard deviation 0.7, followed by our method with $\sigma_c = 4.2$ for pairwise costs (at pixel level) and $\sigma_m = 3.2$ for data costs (at color segment level).

For image denoising results with FBP-FCT, we apply a Gaussian smoothing of the image with standard deviation 0.8, followed by our method with $\sigma_c = 3.2$ for pairwise costs (at pixel level) and $\sigma_m = 3.2$ for data costs (at color segment level). For image denoising with BP-FCT, no prior smoothing is employed and the number of iterations of message passing updates per each scale is fixed to 20.

In Figs. 11.10, 11.11, and 11.12, we depict the impact of the number of color states, as used in the Forward BP algorithm, on the segmentation results. Figure 11.10 shows the underlying segmentation as obtained for different numbers of color states used for FBP-FCT, as well as the running times. Figures 11.11 and 11.12 illustrate the segmentation by filling in the segments with the color of the first pixel of the segment in forward traversal order (Fig. 11.11) or an average of such pixel colors whenever the segments were merged to meet the minimum 50 pixels size (Fig. 11.12). We qualitatively see that the best image segmentation results are achieved for 4 color states, and quantitatively, as expected, the running time increases quadratically with the number of color states. Also, the changes from 4 color states to 5 are small, while between 5 color states and 6 color states the differences are hardly noticeable. Using more than 6 color states does not change the segmentation when compared with the 6 color states result.

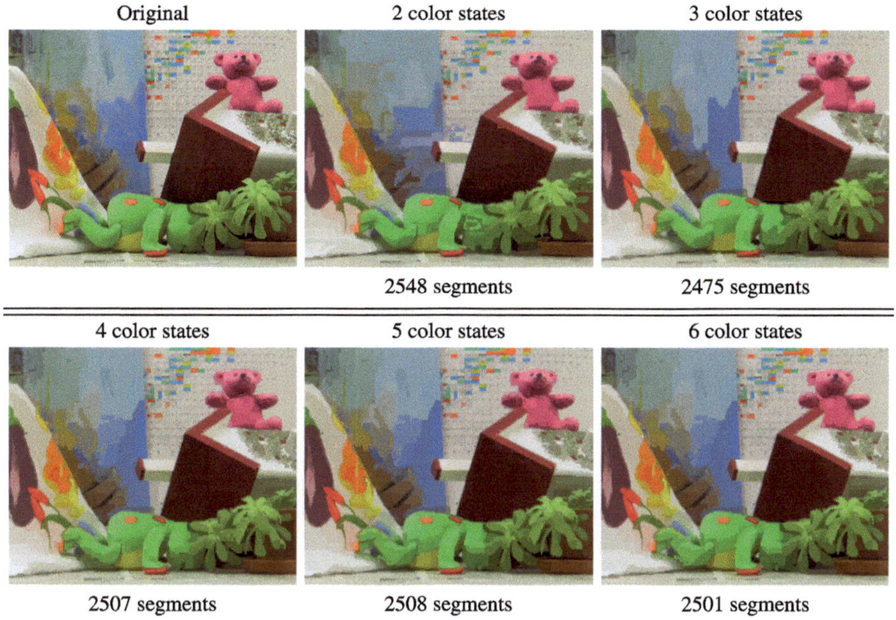

Fig. 11.11 Number of color states versus FBP-FCT segmentation results on *Teddy* image. The minimum segment size is 1. Each segment is colored using the color of the first pixel in the segment in the forward traversal order

For the denoising experiment, we report the running time (in seconds, s) and the PSNR (in decibels, dB) for each FBP-FCT and BP-FCT setting with 2 up to 6 color states. As seen in Fig. 11.13, the best PSNR is reached for 4 color states. Using more color states does not necessarily help the denoising results but slows down the process. Note that the underlying segmentation of FBP-FCT does not necessarily imply pixelwise equal denoised labels/intensities within each color state segment. This is because FBP-FCT actually is a single, consistent FBP iteration and the assigned denoised intensities are the best as computed locally in the forward traversal order. Thus, locally within each color state segment the labels can evolve smoothly. The larger the segments are, the bigger the label differences within them can get.

In the underlying segmentations for both the segmentation and denoising experiments, the segments only change visibly up to the use of 6 colors. Within that initial range, the changes get smaller as the number of colors increases. We did not even try and match colors between corresponding segments. Anyway, these experimental results are in agreement with graph coloring theory. As a matter of fact, that theory also states that at most 6 colors are required to color any map on the plane or the sphere [8]. Of course, and as repeatedly mentioned in the paper, the Four Color Theorem [17] demonstrates that the necessary number of colors is 4. Yet, such coloring is NP-complete and using more colors relaxes the situation, allowing for polynomial time complexity colorings. Increasing the number of colors further eases the task.

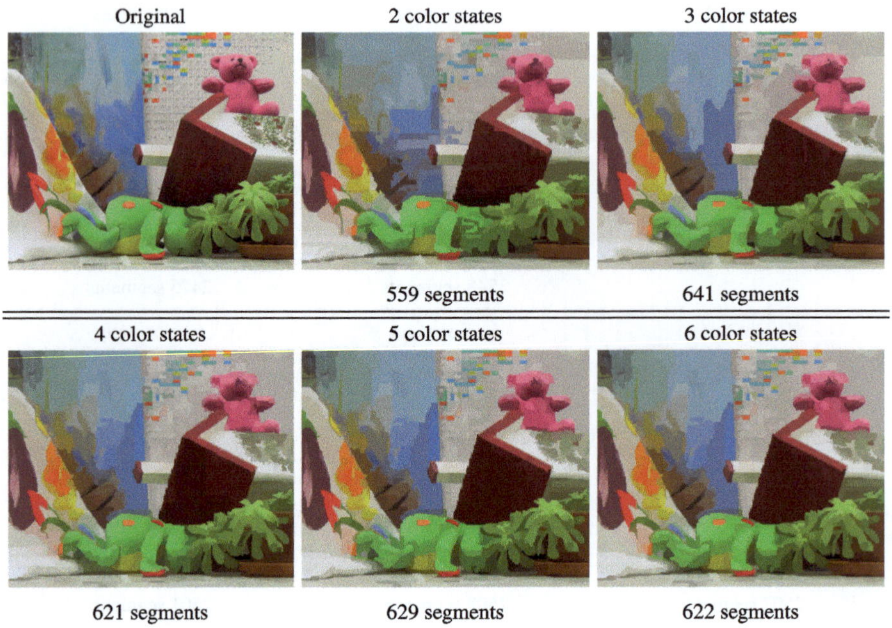

Fig. 11.12 Number of color states versus FBP-FCT segmentation results on *Teddy* image. The minimum segment size is 50. Each segment is colored using the color of the first pixel in the segment in the forward traversal order or the average of such colors when where merged to form segments with ≥50 pixels

Our task is even harder, as we not only optimize the colors but also the number of segments, their labels, and their boundaries.

From these experiments we can empirically conclude that, under our settings, the four color theorem holds in practice. Four color states suffice for the best trade-off between performance and running time of our BP variants.

11.6 Conclusions

We have presented how the Four-Color Theorem based on the max-product belief propagation technique can be used in early computer vision for solving MRF problems where an energy is to be minimized. Our proposed methods yield results that are comparable with other methods, but improve either the speed for large images and/or large label sets (the case of image segmentation, stereo matching and optical flow), or both the performance and speed (the case of image denoising).

The Four Color Theorem principle is difficult to apply in cases where the label set is discrete and no natural order/relation between them can be inferred. This is the case for stereo matching and optical flow, where the disparity cost function takes discrete, unrelated values. This causes slower convergence, but is compensated by the low time complexity of the methods, independent of the number of labels. Thus,

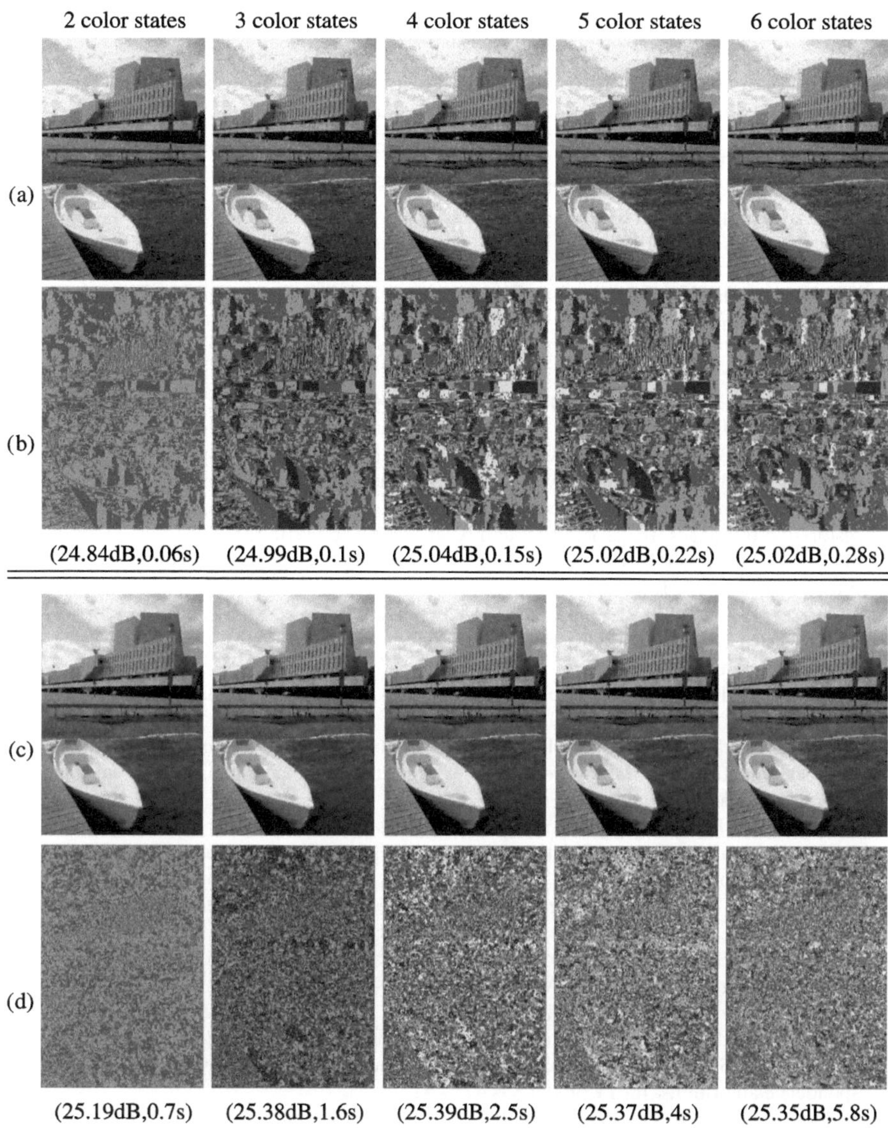

Fig. 11.13 Number of color states versus denoising results for the *Boat* image with FBP-FCT (**a**), (**b**) and BP-FCT (**c**), (**d**). We report (PSNR, running time) and show the final denoised images together with the underlying segmentations and corresponding color states. The PSNR peaks at 4 color states. Adding more color states does not improve on it

the proposed methods perform faster than the standard methods considered here, at least for large inputs.

Acknowledgements This work was supported by the Flemish Hercules Foundation project RICH and the Flemish iMinds project on Future Health.

References

1. Agarwal S, Belongie S (2002) On the non-optimality of four color coding of image partitions. In: IEEE international conference on image processing
2. Besag J (1986) On the statistical analysis of dirty pictures Julian Besag (with discussion). J R Stat Soc B 48(3):259–302
3. Boykov Y, Veksler O, Zabih R (2001) Fast approximate energy minimization via graph cuts. IEEE Trans Pattern Anal Mach Intell 23:1222–1239
4. Chou PB, Brown CM (1990) The theory and practice of Bayesian image labeling. Int J Comput Vis 4(3):185–210
5. Coughlan J, Shen H (2007) Dynamic quantization for belief propagation in sparse spaces. Comput Vis Image Underst 106(1):47–58
6. Felzenszwalb PF, Huttenlocher DP (2004) Efficient graph-based image segmentation. Int J Comput Vis 59:167–181
7. Felzenszwalb PF, Huttenlocher DP (2006) Efficient belief propagation for early vision. Int J Comput Vis 70:261–268
8. Franklin P (1934) A six colour problem. J Math Phys 13:363–369
9. Gallian JA (2011) A dynamic survey of graph labeling. Electron J Comb 18:1–256
10. Geman S, Geman D (1984) Stochastic relaxation, Gibbs distributions, and the Bayesian restoration of images. IEEE Trans Pattern Anal Mach Intell 6(6):721–741
11. Greig DM, Porteous BT, Seheult AH (1989) Exact maximum a posteriori estimation for binary images. J R Stat Soc B 51:271–279
12. Groetzsch H (1958/1959) Zur Theorie der diskreten Gebilde. VII. Ein Dreifarbensatz für dreikreisfreie Netze auf der Kugel. (German) Wiss Z, Martin-Luther-Univ Halle-Wittenb, Math-Natwiss Reihe 8:109–120
13. Kschischang FR, Frey BJ, Loeliger H-A (2001) Factor graphs and the sum-product algorithm. IEEE Trans Inf Theory 47:498–519
14. Martin D, Fowlkes C, Tal D, Malik J (2001) A database of human segmented natural images and its application to evaluating segmentation algorithms and measuring ecological statistics. In: International conference on computer vision
15. Pearl J (1982) Reverend Bayes on inference engines: a distributed hierarchical approach. In: Second national conference on artificial intelligence, AAAI-82, Pittsburgh, PA. AAAI Press, Menlo Park, pp 133–136
16. Potetz B, Lee TS (2008) Efficient belief propagation for higher-order cliques using linear constraint nodes. Comput Vis Image Underst 112(1):39–54
17. Robertson N, Sanders DP, Seymour PD, Thomas R (1996) A new proof of the four colour theorem. Electron Res Announc Am Math Soc 2:17–25
18. Rother C, Kolmogorov V, Lempitsky V, Szummer M (2007) Optimizing binary MRFs via extended roof duality. In: IEEE conference on computer vision and pattern recognition
19. Scharstein D, Szeliski R (2002) A taxonomy and evaluation of dense two-frame stereo correspondence algorithms. Int J Comput Vis 47:7–42
20. Sudderth E, Ihler A, Freeman W, Willsky A (2003) Nonparametric belief propagation. In: Conference on computer vision and pattern recognition
21. Sun J, Zheng NN, Shum HY (2003) Stereo matching using belief propagation. IEEE Trans Pattern Anal Mach Intell 25:787–800
22. Szeliski R, Zabih R, Scharstein D, Veksler O, Kolmogorov V, Agarwala A, Tappen M, Rother C (2008) A comparative study of energy minimization methods for Markov random fields with smoothness-based priors. IEEE Trans Pattern Anal Mach Intell 30(6):1068–1080
23. Tappen MF, Freeman WT (2003) Comparison of graph cuts with belief propagation for stereo, using identical MRF parameters. In: International conference on computer vision
24. Timofte R, Van Gool L (2010) Four color theorem for fast early vision. In: Asian conference on computer vision
25. Tombari F, Mattoccia S, Di Stefano L, Addimanda E (2008) Near real-time stereo based on effective cost aggregation. In: International conference on pattern recognition

26. Vese LA, Chan TF (2002) A multiphase level set framework for image segmentation using the Mumford and Shah model. Int J Comput Vis 50:271–293
27. Wainwright M, Jaakkola T, Willsky A (2005) Map estimation via agreement on trees: message-passing and linear programming. IEEE Trans Inf Theory 51:3697–3717
28. Wang C, Paragios N (2012) Markov random fields in vision perception: a survey. INRIA research report, 25 September (2012), pp 1–42
29. Weiss Y, Freeman WT (2001) On the optimality of solutions of the max-product belief propagation algorithm in arbitrary graphs. IEEE Trans Inf Theory 47:723–735
30. Weisstein EW (2012). Map coloring. From MathWorld—a Wolfram web resource. http://mathworld.wolfram.com/MapColoring.html
31. Welsh DJA, Powell MB (1967) An upper bound for the chromatic number of a graph and its application to timetabling problems. Comput J 10(1):85–86
32. Yang Q, Wang L, Ahuja N (2010) A constant-space belief propagation algorithm for stereo matching. In: IEEE conference on computer vision and pattern recognition, pp 1458–1465
33. Yanover C, Weiss Y (2003) Finding the M most probable configurations using loopy belief propagation. In: NIPS

Chapter 12
Boosting k-Nearest Neighbors Classification

Paolo Piro, Richard Nock, Wafa Bel Haj Ali, Frank Nielsen, and Michel Barlaud

Abstract A major drawback of the k-nearest neighbors (k-NN) rule is the high variance when dealing with sparse prototype datasets in high dimensions. Most techniques proposed for improving k-NN classification rely either on deforming the k-NN relationship by learning a distance function or modifying the input space by means of subspace selection. Here we propose a novel boosting approach for generalizing the k-NN rule. Namely, we redefine the voting rule as a strong classifier that linearly combines predictions from the k closest prototypes. Our algorithm, called UNN (Universal Nearest Neighbors), rely on the k-nearest neighbors examples as weak classifiers and learn their weights so as to minimize a *surrogate risk*. These weights, called *leveraging coefficients*, allow us to distinguish the most relevant prototypes for a given class. Results obtained on several scene categorization datasets display the ability of UNN to compete with or beat state-of-the-art methods, while achieving comparatively small training and testing times.

P. Piro (✉)
Istituto Italiano di Tecnologia, Via Morego 30, 16163 Genova, Italy
e-mail: paolo.piro@iit.it

R. Nock
CEREGMIA, Universitè Antilles-Guyane, Campus de Schoelcher, Martinique, France
e-mail: rnock@martinique.univ-ag.fr

W. Bel Haj Ali · M. Barlaud
I3S Laboratory, University of Nice-Sophia Antipolis, 06903 Sophia Antipolis, France

W. Bel Haj Ali
e-mail: belhajal@i3s.unice.fr

M. Barlaud
e-mail: barlaud@i3s.unice.fr

F. Nielsen
Department of Fundamental Research, Sony Computer Science Laboratories, Inc., Tokyo, Japan

F. Nielsen
LIX Department, Ecole Polytechnique, Palaiseau, France
e-mail: nielsen@lix.polytechnique.fr

G.M. Farinella et al. (eds.), *Advanced Topics in Computer Vision*,
Advances in Computer Vision and Pattern Recognition,
DOI 10.1007/978-1-4471-5520-1_12,

12.1 Introduction

In this chapter, we describe the proposed approach to k-NN boosting. First, we introduce the scope of our work, which aims at automatic visual categorization of scenes (Sect. 12.1.1) and relies on prototype-based classification (Sect. 12.1.2). Then, in Sects. 12.2.1–12.2.3 we present the key definitions for surrogate risk minimization. Our UNN algorithm is detailed in Sect. 12.2.4 for the case of the exponential risk. Section 12.2.5 presents the generic convergence theorem of UNN and the upper bound performance for the exponential risk minimization. Then, in Sect. 12.3, we report our experiments on simulated and real data, comparing UNN with k-NN, support vector machines (SVM) and AdaBoost, using Gist and/or Bag-of-Feature descriptors. Real datasets include those proposed in [10, 30, 43], with a number of categories ranging from 8 to 60. Then, in Sects. 12.4 and 12.5 we discuss results, mention future works, and conclude. Finally, we postpone the general form and analysis of UNN to other surrogate risks to the Appendix.

12.1.1 Visual Categorization

In this work, we address the problem of generic visual categorization. This is a relevant task in computer vision, which aims at automatically classifying images into a discrete set of categories, such as *indoor* vs *outdoor* [15, 32], *beaches* vs *mountains*, *churches* vs *towers*. Generic categorization is distinct from object and scene recognition, which are classification tasks concerning particular instances of objects or scenes (e.g., *Notre Dame Cathedral* vs *St. Peter's Basilic*). It is also distinct from other related computer vision tasks, such as content-based image retrieval (that aims at finding images from a database, which are semantically related or visually similar to a given query image) and object detection (which requires to find both the presence and the position of a target object in an image, e.g., person detection).

Automatic categorization of generic scenes is still a challenging task, due to the huge number of natural categories that should be considered in general. In addition, natural image categories may exhibit high inter-class variability (i.e., visually different images may belong to the same category) and low inter-class variability (i.e., distinct categories may contain visually similar images). Classifying images requires an effective and reliable description of the image content, for example, location and shape of specific objects or overall scene appearance. Although several approaches have been proposed in the recent literature to extract semantic information from images [36, 42], most of the state-of-the-art techniques for image categorization still rely on low-level visual information extracted by means of image analysis operators and coded into vector descriptors.

Examples of suitable low-level image descriptors for categorization purposes are Gist, that is, global image features representing the overall scene [30], and SIFT descriptors, that is, descriptors of local features extracted either at salient patches [24] or at dense grid points [23]. A Gist descriptor is based on the so-called "spatial envelope" [30], which is a very effective low dimensional representation of the overall scene based on spectral information. Such a representation bypasses segmentation, extraction of key-points and processing of individual objects and regions, thus enabling a compact global description of images. Gist descriptors have been successfully used for categorizing locations and environments, showing their ability to provide relevant priors for more specific tasks, like object recognition and detection [40]. Another successful tool for describing the global content of a scene is the Bag-of-Features scheme [38], which represents an image by the histogram of occurrences of vector quantized local descriptors like SIFT.

12.1.2 k-NN Classification

Apart from the descriptors used to compactly represent images, most image categorization methods rely on supervised learning techniques for exploiting information about known samples when classifying an unlabeled sample. Among these techniques, k-NN classification has proven successful, thanks to its easy implementation and its good generalization properties [37]. A generalization of the k-NN rule to the multi-label classification framework has been also proposed recently by [46], whose technique is based on the maximum-a-posteriori principle applied to multi-labeled k-NN. A major advantage of the k-NN rule is not to require explicit construction of the feature space and be naturally adapted to multi-class problems. Moreover, from the theoretical point of view, straightforward bounds are known for the true risk (i.e., error) of k-NN classification with respect to the Bayes optimum, even for finite samples [29].

Although such advantages make k-NN classification very attractive to practitioners, it is an algorithmic challenge to speed-up k-NN queries. It is also a statistical challenge to further improve the risk bounds of k-NN. In part due to the simplicity of the classification rule, many methods have been proposed to address either of these challenges. For example, many methods have been proposed for speeding up nearest neighbor retrieval, including locality sensitive hashing (LSH, [13]), product quantization for nearest neighbor search [21], and vector space embedding with boosting algorithms [2, 25].

It is yet another challenge to reduce the true risk of the k-NN rule, usually tackled by data reduction techniques [17]. In prior work, the classification problem has been reduced to tracking ill-defined categories of neighbors, interpreted as "noisy" [6]. Most of these recent techniques are in fact partial solutions to a larger problem related to the nearest neighbors' true risk, which does not have to be the discrete prediction of labels, but rather a continuous estimation of class membership probabilities [19]. This problem has been reformulated by [7] as a strong advocacy for the formal transposition of *boosting* to nearest neighbors classification. Such a formalization is challenging as nearest neighbors rules are indeed not *induced*, whereas all formal boosting algorithms induce so-called *strong* classifiers by combining *weak* classifiers—also induced, such as decision trees—[35].

A survey of the literature shows that at least four different categories of approaches have been proposed in order to improve k-NN classification:

- learning local or global adaptive distance metric;
- embedding data in the feature space (kernel nearest neighbors);
- distance-weighted and difference-weighted nearest neighbors;
- boosting nearest neighbors.

The earliest approaches to generalizing the k-NN classification rule relied on learning an adaptive distance metric from training data (see the seminal works of [11]). An analogous approach was later adopted by [18], who carried out linear discriminant analysis to adaptively deform the distance metric. Recently, [31] has proposed a method for learning a weighted distance, where weights can be either global (i.e., only depending on classes and features) or local (i.e., depending on each individual prototype as well).

Other more recent techniques apply the k-NN rule to data embedded in a high-dimensional feature space, following the kernel trick approach of support vector machines. For example, [44] have proposed a straightforward adaptation of the kernel mapping to the nearest neighbors rule, which yields significant improvement in terms of classification accuracy. In the context of vision, a successful technique has been proposed by [47], which involves a "refinement" step at classification time, without relying on explicitly learning the distance metric. This method trains a local support vector machine on nearest neighbors of a given query, thus limiting the most expensive computations to a reduced subset of prototypes.

Another class of k-NN methods relies on weighting nearest neighbors votes based on their distances to the query sample [8]. Recently, [49] have proposed a similar weighting approach, where the nearest neighbors are weighted based on their vector difference to the query. Such a difference-weight assignment is defined as a constrained optimization problem of sample reconstruction from its neighborhood. The same authors have proposed a kernel-based non-linear version of this algorithm as well.

Finally, comparatively few work have proposed the use of boosting techniques for k-NN classification [1, 2, 12, 25, 33]. [1] use AdaBoost for learning a distance function to be used for k-NN search. [12] adopt the boosting approach in a non-conventional way. At each iteration a different k-NN classifier is trained over a modified input space. Namely, the authors propose two variants of the method, depending on the way the input space is modified. Their first algorithm is based on optimal subspace selection, that is, at each boosting iteration the most relevant subset of input data is computed. The second algorithm relies on modifying the input space by means of non-linear projections. But neither method is strictly an algorithm for inducing weak classifiers from the k-NN rule, thus not directly addressing the problem of boosting k-NN classifiers. Moreover, such approaches are computationally expensive, as they rely on a genetic algorithm and a neural network, respectively. [2, 25] map examples in a vector space by using the outputs of (Ada)boosted weak classifiers. It is not known whether these algorithms formally keep (or improve) the boosting properties known for AdaBoost [35]. More recently, [33] have built upon the works of [27, 28] (see also the survey of the approach in [9]) to provide a provable boosting algorithm for k-NN classifiers. Guaranteed convergence speed is obtained for AdaBoost's famed exponential loss, under a weak index assumption which parallels the weak learning assumption of boosting algorithms, making the approach of [33] among the first to provide a provable boosting algorithm for k-NN [7].

We propose in this work a full-fledged solution to the problem of boosting k-NN classifiers in the general multi-class setting and for general classes of losses. Namely, we propose the first provable boosting algorithm, called UNN, which *induces* a *leveraged* nearest neighbor rule that generalizes the uniform k-NN rule, and whose convergence rate is guaranteed for a wide (i.e., infinite) set of losses, encompassing popular choices such as the logistic loss or the squared loss. The voting rule is redefined as a strong classifier that linearly combines weak classifiers of the k-NN rule (i.e., the examples). Therefore, our approach does not need to learn a distance function, as it directly operates on the top of k-NN search. At the same time, it does not require an explicit computation of the feature space, thus preserving one of the main advantages of prototype-based methods. Our boosting algorithm is an iterative procedure which learns the weights for examples called *leveraging coefficients*. Then, our class encoding allows to generalize the guarantees on convergence *rates* for an *infinite* number of *surrogate risks.*[1] The generalization is highly desirable, not only for experimental purposes related *for example,* to no-free-lunch Theorems [28]: our generalization encompasses many *classification calibrated* surrogates, functions exhibiting particularly convenient guarantees in the context of classification [4]. Finally, an important characteristic of UNN is that it is naturally able, through the leveraging mechanism, to discriminate the most relevant prototypes for a given class.

12.2 Method

12.2.1 Preliminary Definitions

In this work, we address the task of *multi-class, single-label* image categorization. Although the multi-label framework is quite well established in literature [5], we only consider the case where each image is constrained to belong to one single category among a set of predefined categories. The number of categories (or classes) may range from a few to hundreds, depending on applications. For example, categorization with 67 indoor categories has been recently studied by [34]. We treat the multi-class problem as multiple binary classification problems as it is customary in machine learning. Hence, for each class c, a query image is classified either

[1] A *surrogate* is a function which is a suitable upperbound for another function (here, the non-convex non-differentiable empirical risk).

to c or to $\bar{c}$ (the complement class of c, which contains all classes but c) with a certain confidence (*classification score*). Then the label with the maximum score is assigned to the query. Images are represented by descriptors related to given local or global features. We refer to an image descriptor as an *observation* $\boldsymbol{x} \in \mathcal{X}$, which is a vector of n features and belongs to a *domain* $\mathcal{X}$ (e.g., $\mathbb{R}^n$ or $[0, 1]^n$). A label is associated to each image descriptor according to a predefined set of C classes. Hence, an observation with the corresponding label leads to an *example*, which is the ordered pair $(\boldsymbol{x}, \boldsymbol{y}) \in \mathcal{X} \times \mathbb{R}^C$, where $\boldsymbol{y}$ is termed the *class vector* that specifies the class memberships of $\boldsymbol{x}$. In particular, the sign of y_c gives the membership of example $(\boldsymbol{x}, \boldsymbol{y})$ to class c, such that y_c is negative iff the observation does not belong to class c, positive otherwise. At the same time, the absolute value of y_c may be interpreted as a relative confidence in the membership. Inspired by the multi-class boosting analysis of [48], we constrain class vectors to be *symmetric*, that is:

$$\sum_{c=1}^{C} y_c = 0. \tag{12.1}$$

Hence, in the single-label framework, the class vector of an observation $\boldsymbol{x}$ belonging to class $\tilde{c}$ is defined as:

$$y_{\tilde{c}} = 1, \qquad y_{c \neq \tilde{c}} = -\frac{1}{C-1}. \tag{12.2}$$

This setting turns out to be necessary when treating multi-class classification as multiple binary classifications, as it balances negative and positive labels of a given example over all classes. In the following, we deal with an input set of m examples (or prototypes) $\mathcal{S} = \{(\boldsymbol{x}_i, \boldsymbol{y}_i), i = 1, 2, \ldots, m\}$, arising from annotated images, which form the *training set*.

12.2.2 Surrogate Risks Minimization

We aim at defining a one-versus-all classifier for each category, which is to be trained over the set of examples. This classifier is expected to correctly classify as many new observations as possible, that is, to predict their true labels. Therefore, we aim at determining a classification rule $\boldsymbol{h}$ from the training set, which is able to minimize the classification error over all possible new observations. Since the underlying class probability densities are generally unknown and difficult to estimate, defining a classifier in the framework of supervised learning can be viewed as fitting a classification rule onto a training set $\mathcal{S}$, with the hope to minimize overfitting as well. In the most basic framework of supervised classification, one wishes to train a *classifier* on $\mathcal{S}$, that is, build a function $\boldsymbol{h} : \mathcal{X} \to \mathbb{R}^C$ with the objective to minimize its *empirical risk* on $\mathcal{S}$, defined as:

$$\varepsilon^{0/1}(\boldsymbol{h}, \mathcal{S}) \doteq \frac{1}{mC} \sum_{c=1}^{C} \sum_{i=1}^{m} \left[\varrho(\boldsymbol{h}, i, c) < 0\right], \tag{12.3}$$

with [.] the indicator function (1 iff true, 0 otherwise), called here the 0/1 *loss*, and:

$$\varrho(\boldsymbol{h}, i, c) \doteq y_{ic} h_c(\boldsymbol{x}_i) \tag{12.4}$$

the *edge* of classifier $\boldsymbol{h}$ on example $(\boldsymbol{x}_i, \boldsymbol{y}_i)$ for class c. Taking the sign of h_c in $\{-1, +1\}$ as its membership prediction for class c, one sees that when the edge is positive (resp. negative), the membership predicted by the classifier and the actual example's membership agree (resp. disagree). Therefore, (12.3) averages over all classes the number of mismatches for the membership predictions, thus measuring the goodness-of-fit of the classification rule on the training dataset. Provided the example dataset has good generalization properties with respect to the unknown distribution of possible observations, minimizing this empirical risk is expected to yield good accuracy when classifying unlabeled observations.

However, minimizing the empirical risk is computationally not tractable as it deals with non-convex optimization. In order to bypass this cumbersome optimization challenge, the current trend of supervised learning (including boosting and support vector machines) has replaced the minimization of the empirical risk (12.3) by that of a so-called *surrogate risk* [4], to make the optimization problem amenable. In boosting, it amounts to sum (or average) over classes and examples a real-valued function called the *surrogate loss*, thus ending up with the following rewriting of (12.3):

$$\varepsilon^{\psi}(\boldsymbol{h}, \mathcal{S}) \doteq \frac{1}{mC} \sum_{c=1}^{C} \sum_{i=1}^{m} \psi\big(\varrho(\boldsymbol{h}, i, c)\big). \tag{12.5}$$

Relevant choices available for ψ include:

$$\psi^{\mathrm{sqr}} \doteq (1 - x)^2, \tag{12.6}$$

$$\psi^{\exp} \doteq \exp(-x), \tag{12.7}$$

$$\psi^{\log} \doteq \log\big(1 + \exp(-x)\big); \tag{12.8}$$

(12.6) is the squared loss [4], (12.7) is the exponential loss [35], and (12.8) is the logistic loss [4]. Such surrogates play a fundamental role in supervised learning. They are upper bounds of the empirical risk with desirable convexity properties. Their minimization remarkably impacts on that of the empirical risk, thus enabling to provide minimization algorithms with good generalization properties [28].

In the following, we move from recent advances in boosting with surrogate risks to redefine the k-NN classification rule. Our algorithm, UNN (Universal Nearest Neighbors), is first proposed for the exponential surrogate. We describe in the appendix the general formulation of the algorithm, not restricted to this surrogate. We show that UNN converges to the optimum of many surrogates with guaranteed convergence rates under mild assumptions, and more generally converges to the global optimum of the surrogate risk for an even wider set of surrogates.

12.2.3 Leveraging the k-NN Rule

We denote by $\mathrm{NN}_k(\boldsymbol{x})$ the set of the k-nearest neighbors (with integer constant $k > 0$) of an example $(\boldsymbol{x}, \boldsymbol{y})$ in set $\mathcal{S}$ with respect to a non-negative real-valued "distance" function. This function is defined on domain $\mathcal{X}$ and measures how much two observations differ from each other. This dissimilarity function thus may not necessarily satisfy the triangle inequality of metrics. For sake of readability, we let $i \sim_k \boldsymbol{x}$ denote an example $(\boldsymbol{x}_i, \boldsymbol{y}_i)$ that belongs to $\mathrm{NN}_k(\boldsymbol{x})$. This neighborhood relationship is intrinsically asymmetric, that is, $\boldsymbol{x}_i \in \mathrm{NN}_k(\boldsymbol{x})$ does not necessarily imply that $\boldsymbol{x} \in \mathrm{NN}_k(\boldsymbol{x}_i)$. Indeed, a nearest neighbor of $\boldsymbol{x}$ does not necessarily contain $\boldsymbol{x}$ among its own nearest neighbors.

The k-nearest neighbors rule (k-NN) is the following multi-class classifier $\boldsymbol{h} = \{h_c : c = 1, 2, \ldots, C\}$ (k appears in the summation indices):

$$h_c(\boldsymbol{x}) = \sum_{j \sim_k \boldsymbol{x}} [y_{jc} > 0], \tag{12.9}$$

where h_c is the one-versus-all classifier for class c and square brackets denote the indicator function. Hence, the classic nearest neighbors classification is based on majority vote among the k closest prototypes.

We propose to weight the votes of nearest neighbors by means of real coefficients, thus generalizing (12.9) to the following *leveraged* k-NN rule $\boldsymbol{h}^\ell = \{h_c^\ell : c = 1, 2, \ldots, C\}$:

$$h_c^\ell(\boldsymbol{x}) = \sum_{j \sim_k \boldsymbol{x}} \alpha_{jc} y_{jc}, \tag{12.10}$$

where $\alpha_{jc} \in \mathbb{R}$ is the leveraging coefficient for example j in class c, with $j = 1, 2, \ldots, m$ and $c = 1, 2, \ldots, C$. Hence, (12.10) linearly combines class labels of the k nearest neighbors (defined in Sect. 12.2.1) with their leveraging coefficients.

Our work is focused on formal boosting algorithms working on top of the k-NN methods. These algorithms do not affect the nearest neighbor search when inducing weak classifiers of (12.10). They are thus independent on the way nearest neighbors are computed, unlike most of the approaches mentioned in Sect. 12.1.2, which rely on modifying the neighborhood relationship via metric distance deformations or kernel transformations. This makes our approach fully compatible with any underlying (metric) distance and data structure for k-NN search, as well as possible kernel transformations of the input space.

For a given training set $\mathcal{S}$ of m labeled examples, we define the k-NN *edge matrix* $\mathrm{R}^{(c)} \in \mathbb{R}^{m \times m}$ for each class $c = 1, 2, \ldots, C$:

$$\mathrm{r}_{ij}^{(c)} \doteq \begin{cases} y_{ic} y_{jc} & \text{if } j \sim_k i \\ 0 & \text{otherwise.} \end{cases} \tag{12.11}$$

The name of $\mathrm{R}^{(c)}$ is justified by an immediate parallel with (12.4). Indeed, each example j serves as a classifier for each example i, predicting 0 if $j \notin \mathrm{NN}_k(\boldsymbol{x}_i)$,

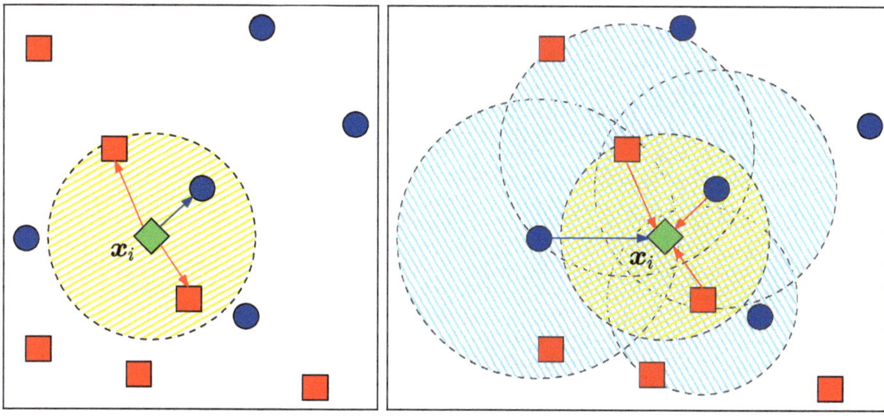

Fig. 12.1 Schematic illustration of the *direct* (*left*) and *reciprocal* (*right*) k-nearest neighbors ($k = 1$) of an example $\boldsymbol{x}_i$ (*green diamond*). *Red squares* and *blue circles* represent examples of positive and negative classes. Each *arrow* connects an example to its k-nearest neighbors

y_{jc} otherwise, for the membership to class c. Hence, the jth column of matrix $\mathrm{R}^{(c)}$, $\boldsymbol{r}_j^{(c)}$, which is different from $\boldsymbol{x}$ when choosing $k > 0$, collects all edges of "classifier" j for class c. Note that nonzero entries of this column correspond to the so-called *reciprocal nearest neighbors* of j, that is, those examples for which j is a neighbor (Fig. 12.1). Eventually, the edge of the leveraged k-NN rule on example i for class c reads:

$$\varrho\big(\boldsymbol{h}^\ell, i, c\big) = \big(\mathrm{R}^{(c)}\boldsymbol{\alpha}^{(c)}\big)_i, \quad c = 1, 2, \ldots, C, \tag{12.12}$$

where $\boldsymbol{\alpha}^{(c)}$ collects all leveraging coefficients in a vector form for class c: $\alpha_i^{(c)} \doteq \alpha_{ic}$, $i = 1, 2, \ldots, m$. Thus, the induction of the leveraged k-NN classifier $\boldsymbol{h}^\ell$ amounts to fitting all $\boldsymbol{\alpha}^{(c)}$'s so as to minimize (12.5), after replacing the argument of $\psi(\cdot)$ in (12.5) by (12.12).

12.2.4 UNN Boosting Algorithm

We explain our classification algorithm specialized for the exponential loss minimization in the multi-class one-versus-all framework, with pseudo-code shown in Algorithm 1. Like common boosting algorithms, UNN operates on a set of weights w_i ($i = 1, 2, \ldots, m$) defined over training data. Such weights are repeatedly updated to fit all leveraging coefficients $\boldsymbol{\alpha}^{(c)}$ for class c ($c = 1, 2, \ldots, C$). At each iteration, the index to leverage, $j \in \{1, 2, \ldots, m\}$, is obtained by a call to a *weak index chooser* oracle WIC(., ., .), whose implementation is detailed later in this section.

Figure 12.2 presents a block diagram of UNN algorithm. In particular, notice how the initialization step, relying on k-NN and edge matrix computation, is clearly

Algorithm 1 Universal Nearest Neighbors UNN($\mathcal{S}$) for $\psi = \psi^{\exp}$

Input: $\mathcal{S} = \{(\boldsymbol{x}_i, \boldsymbol{y}_i), i = 1, 2, \dots, m, \ \boldsymbol{x}_i \in \mathcal{X}, \ \boldsymbol{y}_i \in \{-\frac{1}{C-1}, 1\}^C\}$

$\mathrm{r}_{ij}^{(c)} \doteq \begin{cases} y_{ic} y_{jc} & \text{if } j \sim_k \boldsymbol{x}_i \\ 0 & \text{otherwise} \end{cases} \quad \forall i, j = 1, 2, \dots, m, \ c = 1, 2, \dots, C$ ▷ k-NN edge matrix

for $c = 1, 2, \dots, C$ **do**

  $\alpha_{jc} \leftarrow 0, \quad \forall j = 1, 2, \dots, m$ ▷ Leveraging coefficients

  $w_i \leftarrow 1, \quad \forall i = 1, 2, \dots, m$ ▷ Example weights

  for $t = 1, 2, \dots, T$ **do**

    [I.1] $j \leftarrow \textsc{Wic}(\{1, 2, \dots, m\}, t)$ ▷ Weak index chooser oracle

    [I.2]

$$w_j^+ = \sum_{i:\mathrm{r}_{ij}^{(c)}>0} w_i, \qquad w_j^- = \sum_{i:\mathrm{r}_{ij}^{(c)}<0} w_i \tag{12.13}$$

$$\delta_j \leftarrow \frac{1}{2} \log\left(\frac{w_j^+}{w_j^-}\right) \tag{12.14}$$

    [I.3]

$$w_i \leftarrow w_i \exp\left(-\delta_j \mathrm{r}_{ij}^{(c)}\right), \quad \forall i : j \sim_k \boldsymbol{x}_i \tag{12.15}$$

    [I.4] $\alpha_{jc} \leftarrow \alpha_{jc} + \delta_j$

  end for

end for

Output: $h_c(\boldsymbol{x}) = \sum_{i \sim_k \boldsymbol{x}} \alpha_{ic} y_{ic}, \quad \forall c = 1, 2, \dots, C$

distinguished from the iterative procedure, where a new prototype is added at each iteration t, thus updating both the strong classifier $\boldsymbol{h}(\boldsymbol{x})$ and the weights w_i.

The training phase is implemented in a one-versus-all fashion, that is, C learning problems are solved independently, and for each class c the training examples are considered as belonging to either class c or the complement class $\bar{c}$, that is, *any other class*. Eventually, one leveraging coefficient (α_{jc}) per class is learned for each weak classifier (indexed by j).

The key observation when training weak classifiers with UNN is that, at each iteration, one single example (indexed by j) is considered as a prototype to be leveraged. Indeed, all the other training data are to be viewed as observations for which j may possibly vote. In particular, due to k-NN voting, j can be a classifier only for its reciprocal nearest neighbors (i.e., those data for which j itself is a neighbor, corresponding to nonzero entries in matrix (12.11) on column j). This brings to a remarkable simplification when computing δ_j in step [I.2] and updating weights w_i in step [I.3] (Eqs. (12.14), (12.15)). Indeed, only weights of reciprocal nearest neighbors of j are involved in these computations, thus allowing us not to store the entire matrix $\mathrm{R}^{(c)}$, $c = 1, 2, \dots, C$. Note that the set of reciprocal neighbors is split in two subsets, each containing examples that agree (disagree) with the class membership of j, thus yielding the partial sums w_j^+ and w_j^- of (12.13).

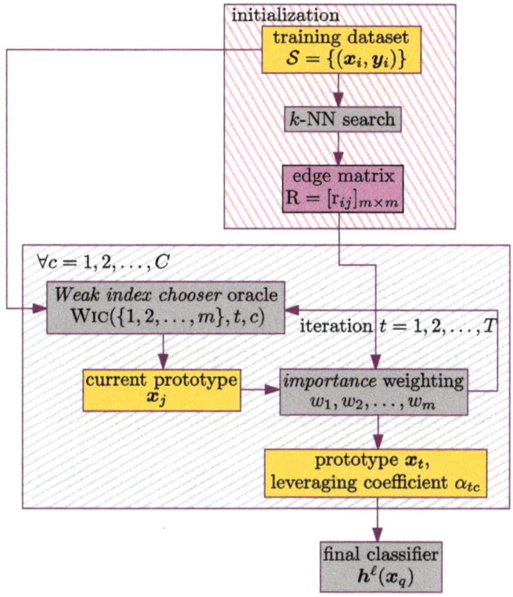

Fig. 12.2 Block diagram of the UNN learning scheme

Note that when whichever w_j^+ or w_j^- is zero, δ_j in (12.14) is not finite. There is however a simple alternative, inspired by [35], which consists in smoothing out δ_j when necessary, thus guaranteeing its finiteness without impairing convergence. More precisely, we suggest to replace:

$$w_j^+ \leftarrow w_j^+ + \frac{1}{m}, \tag{12.16}$$

$$w_j^- \leftarrow w_j^- + \frac{1}{m}. \tag{12.17}$$

Also note that step [I.1] relies on oracle $\mathrm{WIC}(., ., .)$ for selecting index j of the next weak classifier. We propose two alternative implementations of this oracle, as follows:

(a) a *lazy* approach: $T = m$, $\mathrm{WIC}(\{1, 2, \ldots, m\}, t, c) \doteq t$;
(b) the *boosting* approach: we pick $T \geq m$, and let j be chosen by $\mathrm{WIC}(\{1, 2, \ldots, m\}, t, c)$ such that δ_j is large enough. Each j can be chosen more than once.

There are also schemes *mixing* (a) and (b): for example, we may pick $T = m$, choose j as in (b), but exactly once as in (a).

12.2.5 UNN Convergence

The main properties of UNN are summarized by the following three fundamental theorems. The first theorem ensures general *monotonic convergence* to the optimal surrogate loss, for *any* given surrogate function. The second theorem further refines this general convergence theorem by providing an effective convergence bound for the exponential loss.

Suppose that ψ meets the following conditions:

(i) $\mathrm{im}(\psi) = \mathbb{R}_+$;
(ii) $\nabla_\psi(0) < 0$ (∇_ψ is the conventional derivative);
(iii) ψ is strictly convex and differentiable.

Theorem 12.1 *As the number of iteration steps T increases, UNN converges to $\boldsymbol{h}^\ell$ realizing the* global *minimum of the surrogate risk at hand* (12.5), *for any ψ meeting conditions* (i), (ii) *and* (iii) *above.*

Proof A proofsketch is given in Appendix. □

Then, in order to obtain the specific convergence rate for $\psi^{\exp}$, suppose the following *weak index assumption* (WIA) holds. (See Eq. (12.13) in Algorithm 1 for the definition of $w_j^{(c)+}$ and $w_j^{(c)-}$.)

(WIA) There exist some $\gamma > 0$ and $\eta > 0$ such that the following two inequalities hold for index j returned by WIC(., ., .):

$$\left| \frac{w_j^{(c)+}}{w_j^{(c)+} + w_j^{(c)-}} - \frac{1}{2} \right| \geq \gamma, \tag{12.18}$$

$$\frac{w_j^{(c)+} + w_j^{(c)-}}{\|\boldsymbol{w}\|_1} \geq \eta. \tag{12.19}$$

Theorem 12.2 *If the* (WIA) *holds for $\nu \leq T$ steps in UNN (for each c), then* $\varepsilon^{0/1}(\boldsymbol{h}^\ell, \mathcal{S}) \leq \exp(-\Omega(\eta\gamma^2\nu))$.

Proof A proofsketch is given in Appendix. □

Theorems 12.1 and 12.2 show that UNN converges (exponentially fast) to the global optimum of the surrogate risk on the training set. Most of the recent works that can be associated to boosting algorithms, or more generally to the minimization of some surrogate risk using whichever kind of procedure, have explored the universal consistency of the surrogate minimization problems (see [4, 26, 45], and references therein). The problem can be roughly stated as whether the minimization of the surrogate risk guarantees in probability for the classifier built to converge to the Bayes rule as $m \to \infty$. This question obviously becomes relevant to UNN given our results. Among the results contained in this rich literature, the one whose consequences directly impact on the universal consistency of UNN is Theorem 3 of [4]. We can indeed easily show that all our choices of surrogate loss are classification calibrated, so that minimizing the surrogate risk in the limit ($m \to \infty$) implies minimizing the true risk, and implies uniform consistency as well. Moreover, this result, proven for $C = 2$, holds as well for arbitrary $C \geq 2$ in the single-label prediction problem. [3] proved an additional result for AdaBoost [35]: if the algorithm is run for a number $T \geq m^{\eta}$ boosting rounds, for $\eta \in (0, 1)$, then there is indeed minimization in the limit of the exponential risk, and so AdaBoost is universally consistent. From our theorems above, this implies the consistency of UNN, and this even has the consequence to prove that the filtering procedure described in the experiments is also consistent, since indeed [3]'s bound implies that we leverage a proportion of $1/m^{1-\eta}$ examples, "filtering out" the remaining ones.

Moreover, the results of [26] are also interesting in our setting, even when they are typically aimed at boosting algorithms with weak learners like decision-tree learning algorithms, that define *quantizations* of the observations (each decision tree defines a new description variable for the examples). They show that there exists conditions on the quantizers that yield conditions on the surrogate loss function for universal consistency. It is interesting to notice that the universal consistency of UNN does not need such assumptions, as weak learners are examples that do not make quantizations of the observation's domain. Finally, the work of [45] explores the consistency of surrogate risk minimization in the case where rejects are allowed by classifiers, somehow refusing to classify an observation at a cost smaller than misclassifying. While this setting is not relevant to UNN in the general case, it becomes relevant as we filter out examples (see the experiments), which boils down to stating that they systematically reject on observations.

On the one hand, [45] show that filtering out examples does not impair UNN universal consistency, as long as filter thresholds are locally based. On the other hand, they also provide a way to quantify the actual loss $\ell_{r,j}$ caused by filtering out example j, which we recall is in between 0 (the loss of good classification) and 1 (the loss of bad classification). For example, choosing the exponential loss and using Theorem 1 in [45] reveals that the reject loss is:

$$\ell_{r,j} = \frac{\min\{w_j^+, w_j^-\}}{w_j^+ + w_j^-}.$$

Let us now complete further the picture of boosting algorithms for k-NN, by showing that, under a mild additional assumption on ψ, we obtain a guaranteed convergence rate for UNN. Of particular interest is the assumption under which we are able to prove this result. Following [27, 28], we make a "Weak Edge Assumption":

(WEA) There exists some $\vartheta > 0$ such that the following inequality holds for index j returned by WIC(., ., .):

$$\left| \sum_{i:j \sim_k i} \mathrm{r}_{ij}^{(c)} w_i \right| \geq \vartheta. \tag{12.20}$$

This assumption states that the average value (in absolute value) of $y_{ic} y_{jc}$ over the reciprocal neighborhood of example j cannot be smaller than some constant ϑ. It is *weak* for the following reason. If the classes in the reciprocal neighborhood were picked at random, the quantity inside the absolute value in (12.20) would be zero in average because of the way we model classes in (12.1). So, we are assuming that, regardless of weights, we can always pick an example $(\boldsymbol{x}_j, \boldsymbol{y}_j)$ "beating" random by a potentially small advantage ϑ. Note that (WEA) is weaker than (WIA) in the sense that we do not make any coverage assumption like (12.19).

Let us now turn to the assumption on ψ:

(iv) ψ is locally ω strongly smooth, for some $\omega > 0$:

$$D_\psi(x' \| x) \leq \frac{\omega}{2}(x' - x)^2, \tag{12.21}$$

where x, x' range through the values $\varrho(\boldsymbol{h}, i, c)$ over which UNN is run, and

$$D_\psi(x' \| x) \doteq \psi(x') - \psi(x) - (x' - x)\nabla_\psi(x) \tag{12.22}$$

is the Bregman divergence with generator ψ. There is an important duality between strong smoothness and strong convexity, with applications in machine learning and optimization [22]. The proof of the following theorem, in the Appendix, is another example of its applicability in these fields.

Theorem 12.3 *If the* (WEA) *holds and ψ meets assumptions* (i)–(iv), *then for any user-fixed $\tau \in [0, 1]$, UNN has fit a leveraged k-NN classifier with empirical risk no greater than τ provided the number of boosting iterations T satisfies*:

$$T \geq \frac{2(1-\tau)\psi(0)\omega k m}{\vartheta^2 (C-1)} = \Omega\left(\frac{\omega k m}{\vartheta^2}\right). \tag{12.23}$$

Theorem 12.3 does not obliterate the (better) convergence results for the exponential loss of Theorem 12.2, yet it opens the guarantees of convergence under weak assumptions to some of the most interesting surrogates in classification. These include *permissible convex surrogates* (PCS, [27]), a set containing as special cases the squared and logistic surrogates in (12.6), (12.8). Informally, any loss which meets regularity conditions and common requirements about losses, such as lower-boundedness, symmetry and the proper scoring property, can be represented by a PCS [27]. The exponential surrogate in (12.7) is not a PCS, yet it is a first-order approximation to the logistic surrogate. Up to translating and scaling by constants, any PCS meets $\operatorname{im}(\nabla_\psi) \subseteq [-1, 0]$ [27]. Reasoning on the second derivative of ψ, we see that there is not much room to violate (12.21), thus making many PCS ω strongly smooth for small values of ω. Simple calculations yield that we can take for example $\omega = 1/4$ for the logistic loss (12.8), and $\omega = 2$ for the squared loss (12.6), making the bound in (12.23) more favorable to the former. As a last example, consider the following parameterized choice for ψ, with $\mu \in (0, 1)$:

$$\psi_\mu^{\mathrm{mat}} \doteq \frac{1}{1-\mu}\left(-x + \sqrt{(1-\mu)^2 + x^2}\right);$$

this choice, which gives rise to Matsushita's loss for $\mu = 0$, has important convexity properties [27]. In this case, we easily obtain that we can pick $\omega = 1/(1-\mu)$.

12.3 Experiments

In this section, we present experimental results of UNN for image categorization. In order to reduce numerical problems on the large databases on which we test UNN, we normalize weights to unity after the update in (12.15). Our experiments aim at carefully quantifying and explaining the gains brought by boosting on k-NN voting on real image databases. In particular, we propose in Sects. 12.3.1 and 12.3.2 an analysis and comparison of UNN vs k-NN for Gist and Bag-of-Features descriptors on two broadly used datasets of natural images. In Sect. 12.3.3, we drill down into precision and execution times comparisons between UNN vs k-NN, SVM and AdaBoost. We also introduce in this section a soft version of UNN which, to classify new observations, convolutes weighting with a simple density estimation suggested by boosting.

12.3.1 Image Categorization Using Global Gist Descriptors

We tested UNN on global descriptors for the categorization of natural images. In particular, we used the database of natural scenes collected by [30], which has been successfully used to validate several classification techniques relying on Gist image descriptors. A Gist descriptor provides a global representation of a scene directly, without requiring neither an explicit segmentation of image regions and objects nor an intermediate representation by means of local features. In the standard setting, an image is first resized to square, then represented by a single vector of d components (typically $d = 512$ or $d = 320$), which collects features related to the spatial organization of dominant scales and orientations in the image. The one-to-one mapping between images and Gist descriptors is one of the main advantages of using such a global representation instead of local descriptors. In particular, the ability to map any instance to a single point in the feature space is crucial for the effectiveness of k-NN methods, where computing the one-to-one similarity between testing and training instances is explicitly required at classification time. Conversely, representing an image with a set of multiple local descriptors is not directly adapted to such discriminative classification techniques, thus generally requiring an intermediate (usually unsupervised) learning step in order to extract a compact single-vector descriptor from the set of local descriptors [14]. For example, this is the case for Bag-of-Features methods, that we discuss in Sect. 12.3.2 along with an experimental comparison to our method. Finally, although Gist is not an alternative image representation method with respect to local descriptors, it has proven very successful in representing relevant contextual information of natural scenes, thus allowing, for instance, to compute meaningful priors for exploration tasks, like object detection and localization [40].

In the following, we denote as 8-*cat* the database of [30], which contains 2,688 color images of outdoor scenes of size 256 × 256 pixels, divided in 8 categories: *coast*, *mountain*, *forest*, *open country*, *street*, *inside city*, *tall buildings* and *highways*. One example image of each category is shown in Fig. 12.3. In addition, we

Fig. 12.3 Examples of annotated images from the 8 categories database of [30]

Fig. 12.4 Examples of the five additional categories included in the 13 categories database of [10]

Fig. 12.5 Gist image classification performances of UNN compared to k-NN on the 8-cat database (see text for details)

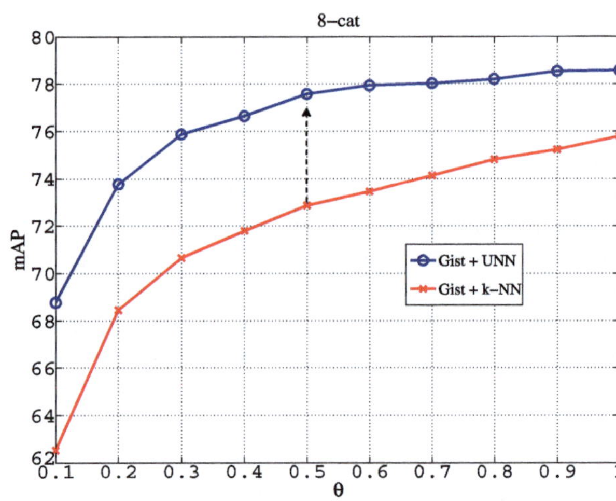

carried out categorization experiments on a larger database of 13 categories as well, denoted as 13-*cat*. This dataset was firstly proposed by [10] and contains five more categories, as shown in Fig. 12.4. We extracted Gist descriptors from these images with the most common settings: 4 resolution levels of the Gabor pyramid, 8 orientations per scale and 4×4 blocks.[2]

We evaluated classification performances when filtering the prototype dataset, that is, retaining a proportion θ of the most relevant examples as prototypes for classification.

[2]The implementation by the authors is available at: http://people.csail.mit.edu/torralba/code/spatialenvelope/sceneRecognition.m.

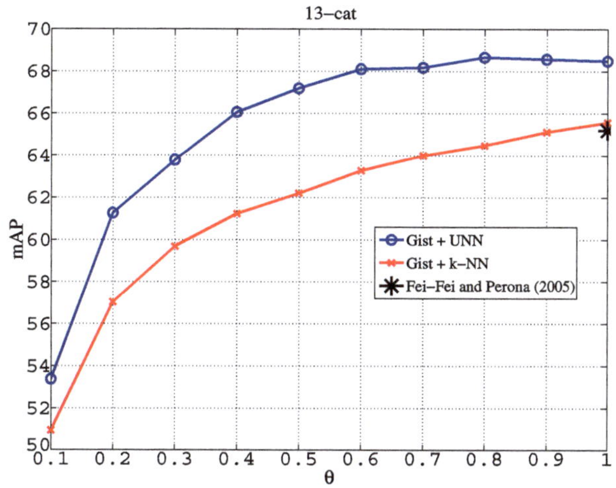

Fig. 12.6 Gist image classification performances of UNN compared to k-NN on the 13-cat database (see text for details)

In Figs. 12.5 and 12.6, we show classification performances in terms of the mean Average Precision (MAP)[3] as a function of θ. We randomly chose half images to form a training set, while testing on the remaining ones. In each UNN experiment, we fixed the value of $\theta = T/m$, thus constraining the number of training iterations T such that at most T examples could be retained as prototypes.

We compared UNN with the classic k-NN classification. Namely, in order for the classification cost of k-NN be roughly the same as UNN, we carried out random sampling of the prototype dataset for selecting proportion θ (between 10 % and the whole set of examples). UNN significantly outperforms classic k-NN. Take for example $\theta = 0.5$ in Fig. 12.5: UNN not only outperforms k-NN with $\theta = 0.5$, its MAP also exceeds that of k-NN with all data ($\theta = 1$) by almost 2 %. Moreover, on the 13-cat database, UNN outperforms the technique proposed by [10] by 3 % (the asterisk in Fig. 12.6, which corresponds to the best result reported in their paper).

12.3.2 Image Categorization Using Bags-of-Features

We now describe experiments with UNN on the Bag-of-Features (BoF) image classification approach. This technique is based on extracting a "bag" of local descriptors (e.g., SIFT descriptors) from an image and vector quantizing them on a precomputed vocabulary of so-called "visual words" [38]. An image is then represented by the histogram of visual word frequencies. This approach provides an effective tool

[3]The MAP was computed by averaging classification rates over categories (diagonal of the confusion matrix) and then averaging those values after repeating each experiment 10 times on different folds.

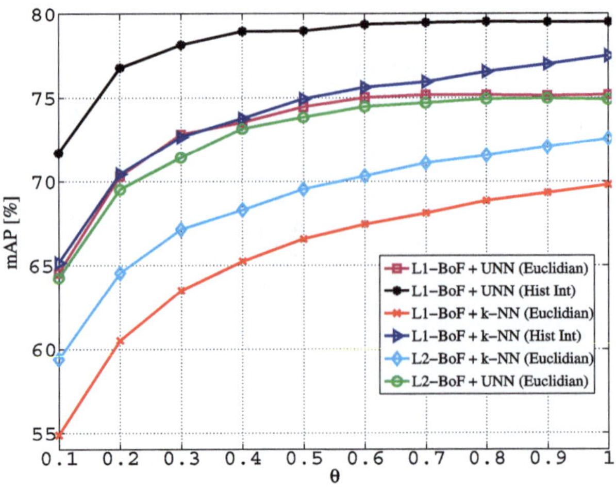

Fig. 12.7 Overall results of BoF classification with UNN compared to k-NN for different settings of histogram normalization (either L1- or L2-norm) and nearest neighbor matching (either Euclidean distance or Histogram Intersection)

for image categorization, as it relies on one single compact descriptor per image, while keeping the informative power of local features. We compare UNN and k-NN on the 8-cat database (see Sect. 12.3.1).

We used the VLFeat toolbox [41][4] for extracting gray-scale dense SIFT descriptors at four resolution levels. In particular, a regular grid with spacing 10 pixels was defined over the image and at each grid point SIFT descriptors were computed over circular support patches with radii 4, 8, 12 and 16 pixels. As a result, each point was represented by four different SIFT descriptors. Therefore, given the image size 256×256, we obtained about 2,500 SIFT descriptors per image. Then we split the database in two distinct subsets of images, half for training and half for testing (i.e., 1,344 images in each dataset). In order to build the dictionary of visual words, we applied k-means clustering on 600,000 SIFT descriptors extracted from training images. For this purpose, we first selected a random subset of training images (about 30 images per class), then we collected all SIFT descriptors of these images and run k-means. In all the experiments, we computed dictionaries of 500 visual words.

The results obtained with the three different settings are depicted in Fig. 12.7. Notice that UNN using the Histogram Intersection matching outperforms all the compared curves. We also note an improvement (up to 5 % gap for k-NN and 7 % for UNN) when using L1-normalized Bag-of-Features descriptors compared to Euclidean distance. This similarity measure was firstly proposed by [39] for image indexing based on color histograms, and, more recently, it has been successfully used by [23] in the context of Bag-of-Features image categorization.

[4]Code available at http://www.vlfeat.org/.

12.3.3 Comparison with SVM and AdaBoost on Image Categorization

Two major issues arise when implementing our UNN algorithm in practice. The first one concerns the distance (or, more generally, the *dissimilarity*) measure used for the k-NN search. The second one consists in setting the value of k for both training and testing our prototype-based classifiers.

On the one hand, defining the most appropriate dissimilarity measure for k-NN search is particularly challenging when dealing with very high-dimensional feature vectors like image descriptors commonly used for categorization. Indeed, the classic metric distances may be inadequate when such vectors are generated by sophisticated pre-processing stages (e.g., vector quantization or unsupervised dictionary learning), thus lying on complex high-dimensional manifolds. In general, this should require an additional distance learning stage in order to define the optimal dissimilarity measure for the particular type of data at hand. In this respect, our UNN method has the advantage of being fully complementary with any metric learning algorithm, acting on the top of the k-NN search. In Sect. 12.3.2, we have described some examples of using different distances for k-NN search, particularly focusing on the most suitable dissimilarity measure for histogram-based descriptors.

On the other hand, selecting a good value for k amounts to learning parameter-dependent weak classifiers, where the parameter k specifies the size of the voting neighborhood in classification rule (12.10). From the theoretical standpoint, a brute-force approach is possible with boosting: one can define multiple candidate weak classifiers per example, one for each value of k, that is, for each neighborhood size, and then learn prototypes by optimizing the surrogate risk function over k as well. This strategy has the advantage of enabling direct learning of k at training time. However, training several weak classifiers per example without computation tricks would potentially severely impair the applicability of the algorithm on huge datasets. The solution we propose is subtler, as it relies on weighting the neighbors, exploiting the trick that boosting locally fits particular maximum likelihood estimators of class memberships [27]. Using (12.14), we can indeed rewrite (12.10) as:

$$h_c^\ell(\boldsymbol{x}) \approx \log \prod_{j \sim_k \boldsymbol{x}, y_{jc}>0} \frac{\hat{p}(c|j)}{\hat{p}(\bar{c}|j)} - \log \prod_{j \sim_k \boldsymbol{x}, y_{jc}<0} \frac{\hat{p}(c|j)}{\hat{p}(\bar{c}|j)}, \tag{12.24}$$

where $\hat{p}(c|j)$ (resp. $\hat{p}(\bar{c}|j)$) models a conditional probability (resp. not) to belong to class c. To make the right-hand side of (12.24) closer to a full-fledged maximum likelihood, we have to integrate the density estimators for nearest neighbors, $\hat{p}(j)$. We can obviously make the assumption that they are all equal: this would multiply the right-hand side of (12.24) by a positive constant factor, and would not change the outcome of (12.10). Instead, we have modified the classification phase of UNN, and tried a *soft* solution which considers a logistic estimator for a Bernoulli prior which vanishes with the rank of the example in the neighbors, thus decreasing the importance of the farthest neighbors:

$$\hat{p}(j) = \beta_j = \frac{1}{1 + \exp(\lambda(j-1))}, \qquad (12.25)$$

with $\lambda > 0$. The shape prior is chosen this way because it was shown that boosting, as carried out in a number of algorithms—not restricted to the induction of linear separators [27]—locally fits logistic estimators for Bernoulli priors. The soft version of UNN we obtain, called UNN$_s$ (for "Soft UNN"), replaces (12.10) by:

$$h_c^{\ell}(\boldsymbol{x}) = \sum_{j \sim_k \boldsymbol{x}} \beta_j \alpha_{jc} y_{jc}. \qquad (12.26)$$

Notice that it is useless to enforce the normalization of coefficients β_j in (12.25), because it would not change the classification of UNN$_s$. Notice also that the β_js in (12.26) are used only to classify new observations: the training steps of UNN$_s$ are the same as UNN, and so UNN$_s$ meets the same theoretical properties as UNN described in Theorems 12.1, 12.2 and 12.3.

We selected 100 categories from the SUN database [43]. We kept all the images of each category and the inherent unbalancing of the original database. We randomly chose half images to form a training set, while testing on the remaining ones. The MAP was computed by averaging classification rates over categories (diagonal of the confusion matrix) and then averaging those values after repeating each experiment 10 times on different folds. To speed-up processing time, we used the fast implementation of k-NN proposed by [21].[5] Furthermore, we also developed an optimized version of our program, which exploits *multi-thread* functionalities. We denote this version as UNN$_s$(MT). All the experiments were run on an Intel Xeon X5690 12-cores processor at 3.46 GHz.

We compared UNN$_s$, SVM with Gaussian RBF Kernel, and AdaBoost with decision stumps[6] (i.e., decision trees with a single internal node), using BoF descriptors. In particular, we followed the guidelines of [20] for carrying out the SVM experiments, thus carrying out cross-validation for selecting the best parameters values for SVM. For the sake of completeness, we also provide results for Gist descriptors with UNN$_s$ and k-NN.

In Table 12.1, we report the MAP for each classification method. Results in these tables are provided as a function of the number of image categories. The most relevant results obtained are also displayed in Fig. 12.8 (mAP as a function of the number of categories) and Figs. 12.9 and 12.10, for the training and classification times, respectively.

[5]Code available at http://www.irisa.fr/texmex/people/jegou/src.php.

[6]For AdaBoost, we used the code available at http://www.mathworks.com/matlabcentral/fileexchange/22997-multiclass-gentleadaboosting.

Table 12.1 Classification performances of the different methods we tested in terms of the Mean Average Precision (MAP) as a function of the number of categories

# categories	10	20	30	40	50	60	100
k-NN BoF	76.38	57.28	45.00	40.27	36.09	32.30	24.67
SVM BoF	83.85	67.65	58.21	*53.45*	*47.81*	*44.09*	*35.31*
AdaBoost BoF	75.37	58.21	45.57	37.75	32.41	29.01	26.72
UNN$_s$ BoF	*84.28*	*70.44*	*58.49*	51.07	46.34	41.80	31.61
k-NN Gist	64.22	51.48	43.65	39.04	35.65	32.27	25.50
UNN$_s$ Gist	77.84	66.80	56.37	50.45	46.48	42.75	32.71

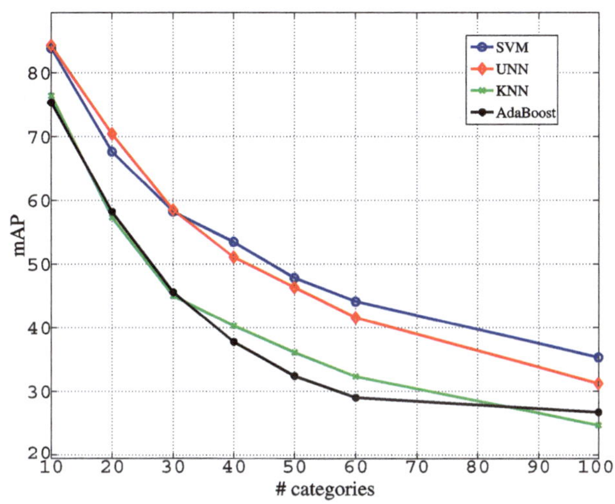

Fig. 12.8 Classification performances of the tested methods as a function of the number of image categories

We can first notice that BoF descriptors generally outperform Gist, even when this phenomenon is dampened as the number of categories increases (above 30). This, overall, follows the trend generally reported in the literature.

MAP results display that UNN$_s$ dramatically outperforms AdaBoost (and k-NN as well); this result, which somehow experimentally confirms that UNN successfully exploits the boosting theory, was quite predictable, as UNN builds a piecewise linear decision function in the initial domain $\mathcal{O}$, while AdaBoost builds a linear separator in this domain. SVM, on the other hand, have access to non-linear fitting of data, by lifting the data to a domain whose dimension far exceeds that of $\mathcal{O}$. Yet, SVM's testing results are somehow not as good as one might expect from this clearcut theoretical advantage over UNN, and also from the fact that we carried out SVMs with significant parameters optimization [20]. Indeed, UNN$_s$ even beats SVMs over 10 to 30 categories, being slightly outperformed by them on more categories.

In Tables 12.2 and 12.3, we report the corresponding computation time (in seconds) for the training and classification phase, respectively. Obviously, the computation times over training and testing are also a key for exploiting the experimental re-

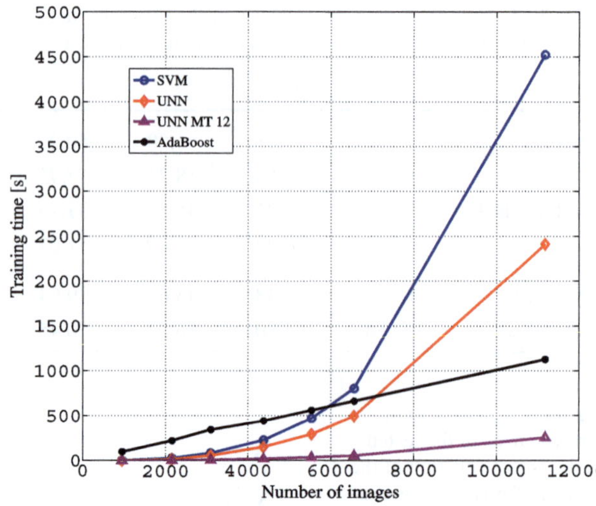

Fig. 12.9 Training time as a function of the number of image categories

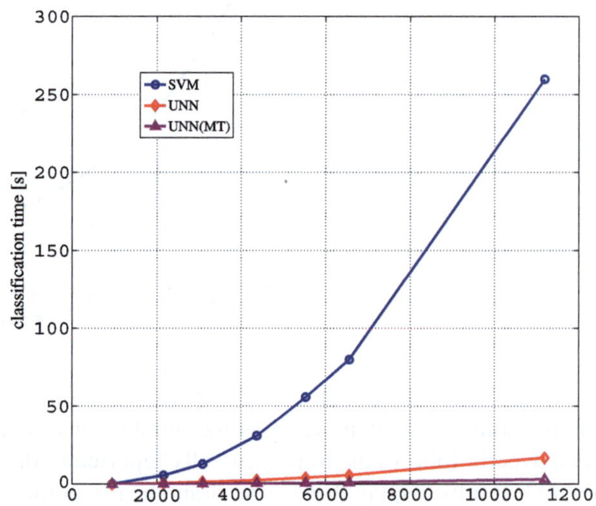

Fig. 12.10 Classification time for UNN_s vs SVM as a function of the number of image categories with BoF

sults. Table 12.2 displays that, while the training time of AdaBoost is linear, UNN_s is a logical clearcut winner over SVM for training: it achieves speedups ranging in between two and more than seventeen over SVM. To assess the validity of these comparisons, we have computed least-square fittings of the training and testing times of UNN_s vs AdaBoost vs SVM (all with BoF), with both linear ($s = aC + b$, s being the time in *s*econds, and C the number of categories) and polynomial ($s = bC^a$) fittings, with the objective to foresee on the best models what might happen on domains with classes ranging from hundreds to (tens of) thousands. The best models are displayed in Table 12.4. The coefficients of determination show that only a slim portion of the data is not explained by the models shown.

Table 12.2 Computation time [s] for the training phase

# categories	10	20	30	40	50	60	100
# training images	951	2,162	3,099	4,381	5,540	6,568	11,186
k-NN BoF				0			
SVM BoF	2.4	27	83	226	472	806	4526
AdaBoost BoF	96	218	341	442	559	662	1128
UNN$_s$ BoF	1.7	16	58	150	295	498	2146
UNN$_s$(MT) BoF	0.3	2.5	7.8	19	36	53	257

Table 12.3 Computation time [s] for the testing phase

# categories	10	20	30	40	50	60	100
# test images	951	2,162	3,099	4,381	5,540	6,568	11,186
k-NN BoF	0.20	1.0	2.0	4.0	6.0	9.0	22.0
SVM BoF	0.25	5.7	13	31	56	80	260
AdaBoost BoF	0.02	0.1	0.25	0.43	0.67	0.95	2.74
UNN$_s$ BoF	0.21	0.72	1.6	2.7	4.2	5.9	17
UNN$_s$(MT) BoF	0.08	0.2	0.37	0.58	0.84	1.11	3.25

Models confirm that the training time of AdaBoost is linear. This is not a surprise, as it is ran with stumps as weak classifiers. Allowing decision trees with more than one internal node would have certainly blown the linear time barrier. While they are roughly equivalent for UNN$_s$ and AdaBoost (Table 12.3), testing times reveal a much bigger gap between UNN$_s$ and SVM, as displayed in Fig. 12.10. Exploiting the models of Table 12.4, we obtain the ratio:

$$s_{\mathrm{SVM}}/s_{\mathrm{UNN}} \approx \Omega(m), \tag{12.27}$$

while, for the multi-thread implementation, we obtain:

$$s_{\mathrm{SVM}}/s_{\mathrm{UNN}_s\mathrm{MT}} \approx \Omega\left(m^{1.3}\right). \tag{12.28}$$

The ratio is always in favor of UNN, and of order the number of examples. Hence, the execution time for UNN$_s$ should allow to classify many images in reduced time compared to SVM: from Table 12.4, UNN should already classify almost twenty times as many images as SVM in a single minute. In such a case, UNN$_s$ should also classify almost twice as many images as AdaBoost. Thus, UNN provides the best MAP/time trade-off among the tested methods, which suggests that UNN might well be more than a legal contender to classification methods dealing with huge domains, or domains where the testing set is huge compared to the training set, which is the case, for instance, for cell classification in biological images [16]. Finally, we have only scratched experimental optimizations for UNN, and have not optimized

Table 12.4 Best fits for training/testing times [s] as a function of the number of classes C, or the number of images m in the training sample/to be tested. The model indicated is the best fit among models of the type $y = ax + b$ and $y = bx^a$, according to the coefficient of determination r^2. For all but two models, $r^2 > 0.999 \approx 1.0$ (the exceptions are (*), for which $r^2 \approx 0.97$, and (**), for which $r^2 \approx 0.99$). $m_{1\text{m}}$ is the number, estimated by the model, of images that can be processed in 1 minute (see text for details)

	Training		Testing		
	$s = f(C)$	$s = f(m)$	$s = f(C)$	$s = f(m)$	$m_{1\text{m}}$
SVM BoF	$s = (1.42 \times 10^{-3}) \times C^{3.25}$	$s = (1.9 \times 10^{-9}) \times m^{3.05}$	$s = (4.94 \times 10^{-4}) \times C^{2.94}$ (*)	$s = (2.11 \times 10^{-9}) \times m^{2.77}$	5 942
AdaBoost BoF	$s = -11.40 + 11.37 \times C$	$s = 7.63 + 0.10 \times m$	$s = (2.16 \times 10^{-4}) \times C^{2.05}$	$s = (4.19 \times 10^{-8}) \times m^{1.93}$	55 643
UNN$_s$ BoF	$s = (1.24 \times 10^{-3}) \times C^{3.16}$	$s = (2.43 \times 10^{-9}) \times m^{2.96}$	$s = (2.49 \times 10^{-3}) \times C^{1.90}$	$s = (9.19 \times 10^{-7}) \times m^{1.78}$	24 567
UNN$_s$ MT BoF	$s = (3.85 \times 10^{-4}) \times C^{2.91}$	$s = (2.07 \times 10^{-9}) \times m^{2.74}$	$s = (1.82 \times 10^{-3}) \times C^{1.58}$	$s = (2.57 \times 10^{-6}) \times m^{1.48}$ (**)	95 175

UNN from the complexity-theoretic standpoint, so we expect room space for further significant improvement of its training/testing times.

12.4 Discussion and Perspectives

UNN provides us with a sound blend of two powerful yet simple classification algorithms: nearest neighbors and boosting. While the analysis of the mixing is not straightforward—such as for the convergence and boosting properties in Theorems 12.1–12.3—UNN remains simple to state and implement, even in the multiclass case. It also appears to be a interesting contender to SVM: without using the kernel trick mapping examples to high dimensional feature spaces, UNN manages to fit nonlinear classifiers in the initial feature space whose accuracy clearly compete with SVM's.

We think that this simplicity opens avenues for future research on the way separate extensions and improvements of nearest neighbors and boosting might be transferred to UNN. One example is the inclusion of powerful density estimation techniques that would fit better than our simple logistic convolution of priors in (12.25).

Another example involves improved sophistication from the classifier's standpoint, in particular with metric distance learning and the kernelization of the input space [47]. This, we expect, would enable significant improvements of categorization performances.

A third example involves improvements from the nearest neighbor search standpoint. Novel techniques exist that make embeddings in a real-valued vector space of nearest neighbors queries, thus transforming the data space with the hope to achieve good compromises between reducing the processing complexity of nearest neighbor queries while not reducing the accuracy of (vanilla) nearest neighbors in the space learnt [2, 25]. Clearly, such approaches do not tackle the same problem as us, as UNN directly processes nearest neighbors on the data's ambient space. Nevertheless, they are very interesting from the perspective standpoint because this new data space is learnt with (Ada)boosting. A neat combination with UNN might thus offer the possibility to kill two birds in one boosting shot for nearest neighbors: learn an improved data space, *and* learn in this data space an improved nearest neighbor classifier with UNN. The questions raised by such perspective are not only experimental, as basically only the contractiveness of the approach of [2] is formally known to date. Transferring, or even improving, the boosting properties of UNN in such sophisticated blends would thus be more than interesting.

12.5 Conclusion

In this work, we contribute to fill an important void of NN methods, showing how boosting can be transferred to k-NN classification, with convergence rates guarantees for a *large* number of surrogates. Our UNN algorithm generalizes classic k-NN to weighted voting where weights, the so-called leveraging coefficients, are iteratively learned by UNN. We prove that this algorithm converges to the global optimum of many surrogate risks in competitive times under very mild assumptions.

Our work is also the first extensive assessment of UNN to computer vision related tasks. Comparisons with k-NN, support vector machines and AdaBoost, using Gist or Bag-of-Feature descriptors, on simulated and real domains, display the ability of UNN to be competitive with its contenders, achieving high mAP in comparatively reduced training and testing times.

Avenues for future research include blending UNN with other approaches that bias the domain towards the improvement of nearest neighbors rules, or that learn more sophisticated metrics over data.

Appendix

Generic UNN Algorithm The general version of UNN is shown in Algorithm 2. This algorithm induces the leveraged k-NN rule (12.10) for the broad class of surrogate losses meeting conditions of [4], thus generalizing Algorithm 1. Namely, we constrain ψ to meet the following conditions: (i) $\mathrm{im}(\psi) = \mathbb{R}_+$, (ii) $\nabla_\psi(0) < 0$ (∇_ψ is the conventional derivative of ψ loss function), and (iii) ψ is strictly convex and differentiable. (i) and (ii) imply that ψ is *classification-calibrated*: its local minimization is roughly tied up to that of the empirical risk [4]. (iii) implies convenient algorithmic properties for the minimization of the surrogate risk [28]. Three common examples have been shown in Eqs. (12.7)–(12.6).

The main bottleneck of UNN is step [I.1], as Eq. (12.30) is non-linear, *but* it always has a solution, finite under mild assumptions [28]: in our case, δ_j is guaranteed to be finite when there is no total matching or mismatching of example j's memberships with its reciprocal neighbors', for the class at hand. The second column of Table 12.5 contains the solutions to (12.30) for surrogate losses mentioned in Sect. 12.2.2. Those solutions are always exact for the exponential loss (ψ^{exp}) and squared loss (ψ^{squ}); for the logistic loss (ψ^{log}) it is exact when the weights in the reciprocal neighborhood of j are the same, otherwise it is approximated. Since starting weights are all the same, exactness can be guaranteed during a large number of inner rounds depending on which order is used to choice the examples. Table 12.5 helps to formalize the finiteness condition on δ_j mentioned above: when either sum of weights in (12.29) is zero, the solutions in the first and third line of Table 12.5 are not finite. A simple strategy to cope with numerical problems arising from such situations is that proposed by [35]. (See Sect. 12.2.4.) Table 12.5 also shows how the weight update rule (12.31) specializes for the mentioned losses.

Proofsketch of Theorem 12.1 We show that UNN converges to the global optimum of any surrogate risk (Sect. 12.2.5). For this purpose, let us consider the

Algorithm 2 Universal Nearest Neighbors UNN($\mathcal{S}$, ψ)

Input: $\mathcal{S} = \{(\boldsymbol{x}_i, \boldsymbol{y}_i), \quad i = 1, 2, \ldots, m, \quad \boldsymbol{x}_i \in \mathcal{X}, \quad \boldsymbol{y}_i \in \{-\frac{1}{C-1}, 1\}^C\}$, ψ meeting (i), (ii), (iii) (Appendix);

$\mathrm{r}_{ij}^{(c)} \doteq \begin{cases} y_{ic} y_{jc} & \text{if } j \sim_k i \\ 0 & \text{otherwise} \end{cases} \quad \forall i, j = 1, 2, \ldots, m, \; c = 1, 2, \ldots, C$ ▷ k-NN edge matrix

for $c = 1, 2, \ldots, C$ **do**

$\alpha_{jc} \leftarrow 0, \quad \forall j = 1, 2, \ldots, m$ ▷ Leveraging coefficients

$w_i \leftarrow -\nabla_\psi(0) \in \mathrm{R}_{+*}^m, \quad \forall i = 1, 2, \ldots, m$ ▷ Example weights

for $t = 1, 2, \ldots, T$ **do**

[I.0] $j \leftarrow \text{WIC}(\{1, 2, \ldots, m\}, t)$ ▷ Weak index chooser oracle

[I.1]

$$w_j^+ = \sum_{i:\mathrm{r}_{ij}^{(c)} > 0} w_i, \qquad w_j^- = \sum_{i:\mathrm{r}_{ij}^{(c)} < 0} w_i, \tag{12.29}$$

Let $\delta_j \in \mathbb{R}$ solution of:

$$\sum_{i=1}^m \mathrm{r}_{ij}^{(c)} \nabla_\psi\big(\delta_j \mathrm{r}_{ij}^{(c)} + \nabla_\psi^{-1}(-w_i)\big) = 0; \tag{12.30}$$

[I.2] $\forall i : j \sim_k i$, let

$$w_i \leftarrow -\nabla_\psi\big(\delta_j \mathrm{r}_{ij}^{(c)} + \nabla_\psi^{-1}(-w_i)\big). \tag{12.31}$$

[I.3] $\alpha_{jc} \leftarrow \alpha_{jc} + \delta_j$

end for

end for

Output: $h_c(\boldsymbol{x}_{i'}) = \sum_{i \sim_k i'} \alpha_{ic} y_{ic}, \quad \forall c = 1, 2, \ldots, C$

Table 12.5 Three common loss functions and the corresponding solutions δ_j of (12.30) and w_i of (12.31). (Vector $\boldsymbol{r}_j^{(c)}$ designates column j of $\mathrm{R}^{(c)}$ and $\|.\|_1$ is the L_1 norm.) The rightmost column says whether it is (A)lways the solution, or whether it is when the weights of reciprocal neighbors of j are the (S)ame

Loss function	δ_j in (12.30)	w_i in (12.31)	Opt
$\psi^{\exp} \doteq \exp(-x)$	$\frac{1}{2}\log(\frac{w_j^{(c)+}}{w_j^{(c)-}})$	$w_i \exp(-\delta_j \mathrm{r}_{ij}^{(c)})$	A
$\psi^{\mathrm{squ}} \doteq (1-x)^2$	$\frac{w_j^{(c)+} - w_j^{(c)-}}{2\|\boldsymbol{r}_j^{(c)}\|_1}$	$w_i - 2\delta_j \mathrm{r}_{ij}^{(c)}$	A
$\psi^{\log} \doteq \log(1+\exp(-x))$	$\log(\frac{w_j^{(c)+}}{w_j^{(c)-}})$	$\frac{w_i \exp(-\delta_j \mathrm{r}_{ij}^{(c)})}{1 - w_i(1+\exp(-\delta_j \mathrm{r}_{ij}^{(c)}))}$	S

surrogate risk (12.5) for a given class $c = 1, 2, \ldots, C$:

$$\varepsilon_c^\psi(\boldsymbol{h}, \mathcal{S}) \doteq \frac{1}{m} \sum_{i=1}^m \psi\big(\varrho(\boldsymbol{h}, i, c)\big). \tag{12.32}$$

In this section, we use the following notations:

- $\tilde{\psi}(x) \doteq \psi^\star(-x)$, where $\psi^\star(x) \doteq x\nabla_{\psi}^{-1}(x) - \psi(\nabla_{\psi}^{-1}(x))$ is the Legendre conjugate of ψ, which is strictly convex and differentiable as well. ($\tilde{\psi}$ is related to ψ in such a way that: $\nabla_{\tilde{\psi}}(x) = -\nabla_{\psi}^{-1}(-x)$.)
- $D_{\tilde{\psi}}(w_i \| w_i') \doteq \tilde{\psi}(w_i) - \tilde{\psi}(w_i') - (w_i - w_i')\nabla_{\tilde{\psi}}(w_i')$ is the Bregman divergence with generator $\tilde{\psi}$ [28].

Let $\boldsymbol{w}_t$ denote the tth weight vector inside the "**for** c" loop of Algorithm 2 (assuming $\boldsymbol{w}_0$ is the initialization of $\boldsymbol{w}$); similarly, $\boldsymbol{h}_t^\ell$ denotes the tth leveraged k-NN rule obtained after the update in [I.3]. The following fundamental identity holds, whose proof follows from [28]:

$$\psi\left(\varrho\left(\boldsymbol{h}_t^\ell, i, c\right)\right) = g + D_{\tilde{\psi}}(0 \| w_{ti}), \tag{12.33}$$

where $g(m) \doteq -\tilde{\psi}(0)$ does not depend on the k-NN rule. In particular, Eq. (12.33) makes the connection between the real-valued classification problem and a geometric problem in the non-metric space of weights. Moreover, Eq. (12.33) proves in handy as one computes the *difference* between two successive surrogates: $\varepsilon_c^\psi(\boldsymbol{h}_{t+1}^\ell, \mathcal{S}) - \varepsilon_c^\psi(\boldsymbol{h}_t^\ell, \mathcal{S})$. Indeed, plugging Eq. (12.33) in Eq. (12.32), and computing δ_j in Eq. (12.30) so as to bring $\boldsymbol{h}_{t+1}^\ell$ from $\boldsymbol{h}_t^\ell$, we obtain the following identity:

$$\varepsilon_c^\psi\left(\boldsymbol{h}_{t+1}^\ell, \mathcal{S}\right) - \varepsilon_c^\psi\left(\boldsymbol{h}_t^\ell, \mathcal{S}\right) = -\frac{1}{m}\sum_{i=1}^{m} D_{\tilde{\psi}}(w_{(t+1)i} \| w_{ti}). \tag{12.34}$$

Since Bregman divergences are non negative and meet the identity of the indiscernibles, (12.34) implies that steps [I.1]–[I.3] *guarantee* the decrease of (12.32) as long as $\delta_j \neq 0$. But (12.32) is lowerbounded, hence UNN must converge.

In addition, it converges to the global optimum of the risk (12.5). Since predictions for each class are independent, the proof consists in showing that (12.32) converges to its global minimum for each c. Let us assume this convergence for the current class c. Then, following the reasoning of Nock and Nielsen [28], (12.30) and (12.31) imply that, when any possible $\delta_j = 0$, the weight vector, say $\boldsymbol{w}_\infty$, satisfies $\mathrm{R}^{(c)\top}\boldsymbol{w}^\top = \boldsymbol{0}$, *that is*, $\boldsymbol{w}_\infty \in \ker \mathrm{R}^{(c)\top}$, and $\boldsymbol{w}_\infty$ is unique. But the kernel of $\mathrm{R}^{(c)\top}$ and $\overline{\mathbb{W}}$, the closure of $\mathbb{W}$ (i.e., the manifold where $\boldsymbol{w}$'s live), are provably Bregman orthogonal [28], thus yielding:

$$\underbrace{\sum_{i=1}^{m} D_{\tilde{\psi}}(0 \| w_i)}_{m\varepsilon_c^\psi(\boldsymbol{h}^\ell, \mathcal{S}) - mg} = \underbrace{\sum_{i=1}^{m} D_{\tilde{\psi}}(0 \| w_{\infty i})}_{m\varepsilon_c^\psi(\boldsymbol{h}_\infty^\ell, \mathcal{S}) - mg} + \underbrace{\sum_{i=1}^{m} D_{\tilde{\psi}}(w_{\infty i} \| w_i)}_{\geq 0}, \quad \forall \boldsymbol{w} \in \overline{\mathbb{W}}. \tag{12.35}$$

Underbraces use (12.33) in (12.32), and $\boldsymbol{h}^\ell$ is a leveraged k-NN rule corresponding to $\boldsymbol{w}$. One obtains that $\boldsymbol{h}_\infty^\ell$ achieves the global minimum of (12.32), as claimed.

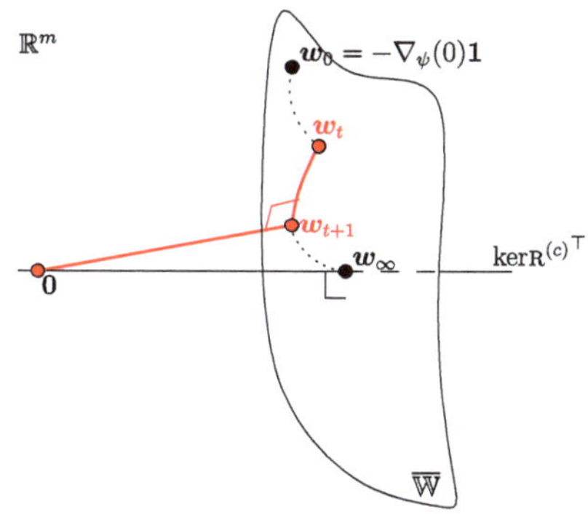

Fig. 12.11 A geometric view of how UNN converges to the global optimum of (12.5). (See Appendix for details and notations.)

The proofsketch is graphically summarized in Fig. 12.11. In particular, two crucial *Bregman orthogonalities* are mentioned [28]. The red one symbolizes:

$$\sum_{i=1}^{m} D_{\tilde{\psi}}(0\|w_{ti}) = \sum_{i=1}^{m} D_{\tilde{\psi}}(0\|w_{(t+1)i}) + \sum_{i=1}^{m} D_{\tilde{\psi}}(w_{(t+1)i}\|w_{ti}), \tag{12.36}$$

which is equivalent to (12.34). The black one on $\boldsymbol{w}_\infty$ is (12.35).

Proofsketch of Theorem 12.2 Using developments analogous to those of [28], UNN can be shown to be equivalent to AdaBoost in which m weak classifiers are available, each one being an example. Each weak classifier returns a value in $\{-1, 0, 1\}$, where 0 is reserved for examples outside the reciprocal neighborhood. Theorem 3 of [35] brings in our case:

$$\varepsilon^{0/1}(\boldsymbol{h}^\ell, \mathcal{S}) \leq \frac{1}{C}\sum_{c=1}^{C}\prod_{t=1}^{T} Z_t^{(c)}, \tag{12.37}$$

where $Z_t^{(c)} \doteq \sum_{i=1}^{m} \tilde{w}_{it}^{(c)}$ is the normalizing coefficient for each weight vector in UNN. ($\tilde{w}_{it}^{(c)}$ denotes the weight of example i at iteration (t, c) of UNN, and the Tilda notation refers to weights normalized to unity at each step.) It follows that:

$$\begin{aligned}
Z_t^{(c)} &= 1 - \tilde{w}_{jt}^{(c)+-}\left(1 - 2\sqrt{p_{jt}^{(c)}(1 - p_{jt}^{(c)})}\right) \\
&\leq \exp\left(-\tilde{w}_{jt}^{(c)+-}\left(1 - 2\sqrt{p_{jt}^{(c)}(1 - p_{jt}^{(c)})}\right)\right) \\
&\leq \exp(-\eta(1 - \sqrt{1 - 4\gamma^2})) \leq \exp(-2\eta\gamma^2),
\end{aligned}$$

where $\tilde{w}_{jt}^{(c)+-} \doteq \tilde{w}_{jt}^{(c)+} + \tilde{w}_{jt}^{(c)-}$, $p_{jt}^{(c)} \doteq \tilde{w}_{jt}^{(c)+}/\tilde{w}_{jt}^{(c)+-} = w_{jt}^{(c)+}/w_{jt}^{(c)+-}$. The first inequality uses $1 - x \leq \exp(-x)$, and the second the (WIA). Since even when the (WIA) does not hold, we still observe $Z_t^{(c)} \leq 1$, plugging the last inequality in (12.37) yields the statement of the theorem.

Proofsketch of Theorem 12.3 We plug in the weight notation the iteration t and class c, so that $w_{ti}^{(c)}$ denotes the weight of example $\boldsymbol{x}_i$ prior to iteration t for class c in UNN (inside the "**for** c" loop of Algorithm 2, letting $\boldsymbol{w}_0$ denote the initial value of $\boldsymbol{w}$). To save space in some computations below, we also denote for short:

$$\bar{\varepsilon}^{\psi}\left(\boldsymbol{h}_T^{\ell}, \mathcal{S}\right) \doteq \frac{1}{C}\sum_{c=1}^{C}\varepsilon_c^{\psi}\left(\boldsymbol{h}_T^{\ell}, \mathcal{S}\right). \tag{12.38}$$

ψ is ω strongly smooth is equivalent to $\tilde{\psi}$ being strongly convex with parameter ω^{-1} [22], that is,

$$\tilde{\psi}(w) - \frac{1}{2\omega}w^2 \tag{12.39}$$

is convex. Here, we have made use of the following notations: $\tilde{\psi}(x) \doteq \psi^{\star}(-x)$, where $\psi^{\star}(x) \doteq x\nabla_{\psi}^{-1}(x) - \psi(\nabla_{\psi}^{-1}(x))$ is the Legendre conjugate of ψ. Since a convex function h satisfies $h(w') \geq h(w) + \nabla_h(w)(w' - w)$, applying inequality (12.39) taking as h the function in (12.39) yields, $\forall t = 1, 2, \ldots, T, \forall i = 1, 2, \ldots, m$, $\forall c = 1, 2, \ldots, C$:

$$\begin{aligned} D_{\tilde{\psi}}\left(w_{(t+1)i}^{(c)} \| w_{ti}^{(c)}\right) &= D_{\tilde{\psi}}\left(w_{ti}^{(c)} + \left(w_{(t+1)i}^{(c)} - w_{ti}^{(c)}\right) \| w_{ti}^{(c)}\right) \\ &\geq \frac{1}{2\omega}\left(w_{(t+1)i}^{(c)} - w_{ti}^{(c)}\right)^2, \end{aligned} \tag{12.40}$$

where we recall that D_{ψ} denotes the Bregman divergence with generator ψ (12.22). On the other hand, Cauchy–Schwarz inequality yields:

$$\begin{aligned} \forall j \in \mathcal{S}, \quad \sum_{i:j\sim_k i}\left(\mathrm{r}_{ij}^{(c)}\right)^2 \sum_{i:j\sim_k i}\left(w_{(t+1)i}^{(c)} - w_{ti}^{(c)}\right)^2 &\geq \left(\sum_{i:j\sim_k i}\mathrm{r}_{ij}^{(c)}\left(w_{(t+1)i}^{(c)} - w_{ti}^{(c)}\right)\right)^2 \\ &= \left(\sum_{i:j\sim_k i}\mathrm{r}_{ij}^{(c)} w_{ti}^{(c)}\right)^2. \end{aligned} \tag{12.41}$$

The equality in (12.41) holds because $\sum_{i:j\sim_k i}\mathrm{r}_{ij}^{(c)} w_{(t+1)i}^{(c)} = 0$, which is exactly (12.30). We obtain:

$$\begin{aligned} \frac{1}{m}\sum_{i=1}^{m} D_{\tilde{\psi}}\left(w_{(t+1)i}^{(c)} \| w_{ti}^{(c)}\right) &= \frac{1}{m}\sum_{i:t\sim_k i} D_{\tilde{\psi}}\left(w_{(t+1)i}^{(c)} \| w_{ti}^{(c)}\right) \\ &\geq \frac{1}{2\omega m}\sum_{i:t\sim_k i}\left(w_{(t+1)i}^{(c)} - w_{ti}^{(c)}\right)^2 \end{aligned} \tag{12.42}$$

$$\geq \frac{1}{2\omega m} \frac{(\sum_{i:t\sim_k i} \mathrm{r}_{it}^{(c)} w_{ti}^{(c)})^2}{\sum_{i:t\sim_k i} (\mathrm{r}_{it}^{(c)})^2} \tag{12.43}$$

$$\geq \frac{\vartheta^2}{2\omega m} \times \frac{1}{\sum_{i:t\sim_k i} (\mathrm{r}_{it}^{(c)})^2} \tag{12.44}$$

Here, (12.42) follows from (12.40), (12.43) follows from (12.41), and (12.44) follows from (12.20). Adding (12.44) for $c = 1, 2, \ldots, C$ and $t = 1, 2, \ldots, T$, and then dividing by C, we obtain:

$$\frac{1}{C}\sum_{c=1}^{C}\sum_{t=1}^{T}\frac{1}{m}\sum_{i=1}^{m} D_{\tilde{\psi}}\left(w_{(t+1)i}^{(c)} \| w_{ti}^{(c)}\right)$$

$$\geq \frac{T\vartheta^2}{2\omega m} \times \left(\frac{1}{TC} \times \sum_{c=1}^{C}\sum_{t=1}^{T} \frac{1}{\sum_{i:t\sim_k i} (\mathrm{r}_{it}^{(c)})^2}\right). \tag{12.45}$$

We now work on the big parenthesis which depends solely upon the examples. We have:

$$\left(\frac{1}{TC} \times \sum_{c=1}^{C}\sum_{t=1}^{T} \frac{1}{\sum_{i:t\sim_k i} (\mathrm{r}_{it}^{(c)})^2}\right)^{-1}$$

$$\leq \frac{1}{TC}\sum_{c=1}^{C}\sum_{t=1}^{T}\sum_{i:t\sim_k i} \left(\mathrm{r}_{it}^{(c)}\right)^2 \tag{12.46}$$

$$= \frac{1}{TC}\sum_{c=1}^{C}\sum_{t=1}^{T}\sum_{i\in \mathrm{NN}_k(\boldsymbol{x}_t)} y_{tc}^2 y_{ic}^2$$

$$\leq \frac{1}{TC}\sum_{c=1}^{C}\sum_{t=1}^{T}\sum_{i\in \mathrm{NN}_k(\boldsymbol{x}_t)} \left(\frac{|y_{tc}|}{2} + \frac{|y_{ic}|}{2}\right) \tag{12.47}$$

$$= \frac{k}{TC}\sum_{t=1}^{T}\sum_{c=1}^{C}\frac{|y_{tc}|}{2} + \frac{1}{TC}\sum_{t=1}^{T}\sum_{i\in \mathrm{NN}_k(\boldsymbol{x}_t)}\sum_{c=1}^{C}\frac{|y_{ic}|}{2}$$

$$= \frac{k}{(C-1)}. \tag{12.48}$$

Here, (12.46) holds because of the Arithmetic-Geometric-Harmonic inequality, and (12.47) is Young's inequality[7] with $p = q = 2$. Plugging (12.48) into (12.45), we obtain:

[7] We recall young inequality: for any p, q Hölder conjugates ($p > 1$, $(1/p) + (1/q) = 1$), we have $yy' \leq y^p/p + y'^q/q$, assuming $y, y' \geq 0$.

$$\frac{1}{C}\sum_{c=1}^{C}\sum_{t=1}^{T}\frac{1}{m}\sum_{i=1}^{m}D_{\tilde{\psi}}\left(w_{(t+1)i}^{(c)}\|w_{ti}^{(c)}\right)\geq\frac{T(C-1)\vartheta^2}{2\omega mk}. \tag{12.49}$$

Now, UNN meets the following property, which can easily be shown to hold with our class encoding as well:

$$\varepsilon_c^{\psi}\left(\boldsymbol{h}_{t+1}^{\ell},\mathcal{S}\right)-\varepsilon_c^{\psi}\left(\boldsymbol{h}_{t}^{\ell},\mathcal{S}\right)=-\frac{1}{m}\sum_{i=1}^{m}D_{\tilde{\psi}}\left(w_{(t+1)i}^{(c)}\|w_{ti}^{(c)}\right). \tag{12.50}$$

Adding (12.50) for $t=0,2,\ldots,T-1$ and $c=1,2,\ldots,C$, we obtain:

$$\frac{1}{C}\sum_{c=1}^{C}\varepsilon_c^{\psi}\left(\boldsymbol{h}_{T}^{\ell},\mathcal{S}\right)-\psi(0)=-\frac{1}{C}\sum_{c=1}^{C}\sum_{t=1}^{T}\frac{1}{m}\sum_{i=1}^{m}D_{\tilde{\psi}}\left(w_{(t+1)i}^{(c)}\|w_{ti}^{(c)}\right). \tag{12.51}$$

Plugging (12.49) into (12.51), we obtain:

$$\bar{\varepsilon}^{\psi}\left(\boldsymbol{h}_{T}^{\ell},\mathcal{S}\right)\leq\psi(0)-\frac{T(C-1)\vartheta^2}{2\omega mk}. \tag{12.52}$$

But the following inequality holds between the average surrogate risk and the empirical risk of the leveraged k-NN rule $\boldsymbol{h}_{T}^{\ell}$, because of (i):

$$\begin{aligned}\bar{\varepsilon}^{\psi}\left(\boldsymbol{h}_{T}^{\ell},\mathcal{S}\right)&=\frac{1}{C}\sum_{c=1}^{C}\varepsilon_c^{\psi}\left(\boldsymbol{h}_{T}^{\ell},\mathcal{S}\right)\\&=\frac{1}{mC}\sum_{c=1}^{C}\sum_{i=1}^{m}\psi\left(y_{ic}\sum_{j:j\sim_k i}\alpha_{jc}y_{jc}\right)\\&\geq\frac{\psi(0)}{mC}\sum_{c=1}^{C}\sum_{i=1}^{m}\left[y_{ic}\sum_{j:j\sim_k i}\alpha_{jc}y_{jc}<0\right]\\&=\psi(0)\varepsilon^{0/1}\left(\boldsymbol{h}_{T}^{\ell},\mathcal{S}\right),\end{aligned} \tag{12.53}$$

so that, putting altogether (12.52) and (12.53) and using the fact that $\psi(0)>0$ because of (i)–(ii), we have after T rounds of boosting for each class: *that is*,

$$\varepsilon^{0/1}\left(\boldsymbol{h}_{T}^{\ell},\mathcal{S}\right)\leq 1-\frac{T(C-1)\vartheta^2}{2\psi(0)\omega mk}. \tag{12.54}$$

There remains to compute the minimal value of T for which the right-hand side of (12.54) becomes no greater than some user-fixed $\tau\in[0,1]$ to obtain the bound in (12.23).

References

1. Amores J, Sebe N, Radeva P (2006) Boosting the distance estimation: application to the k-nearest neighbor classifier. Pattern Recognit Lett 27(3):201–209
2. Athitsos V, Alon J, Sclaroff S, Kollios G (2008) BoostMap: an embedding method for efficient nearest neighbor retrieval. IEEE Trans Pattern Anal Mach Intell 30(1):89–104
3. Bartlett P, Traskin M (2007) Adaboost is consistent. J Mach Learn Res 8:2347–2368
4. Bartlett P, Jordan M, McAuliffe JD (2006) Convexity, classification, and risk bounds. J Am Stat Assoc 101:138–156
5. Boutell MR, Luo J, Shen X, Brown CM (2004) Learning multi-label scene classification. Pattern Recognit 37(9):1757–1771
6. Brighton H, Mellish C (2002) Advances in instance selection for instance-based learning algorithms. Data Min Knowl Discov 6:153–172
7. Cucala L, Marin JM, Robert CP, Titterington DM (2009) A bayesian reassessment of nearest-neighbor classification. J Am Stat Assoc 104(485):263–273
8. Dudani S (1976) The distance-weighted k-nearest-neighbor rule. IEEE Trans Syst Man Cybern 6(4):325–327
9. Escolano Ruiz F, Suau Pérez P, Bonev BI (2009) Information theory in computer vision and pattern recognition. Springer, London
10. Fei-Fei L, Perona P (2005) A bayesian hierarchical model for learning natural scene categories. In: IEEE computer society conference on computer vision and pattern recognition (CVPR), pp 524–531
11. Fukunaga K, Flick T (1984) An optimal global nearest neighbor metric. IEEE Trans Pattern Anal Mach Intell 6(3):314–318
12. García-Pedrajas N, Ortiz-Boyer D (2009) Boosting k-nearest neighbor classifier by means of input space projection. Expert Syst Appl 36(7):10,570–10,582
13. Gionis A, Indyk P, Motwani R (1999) Similarity search in high dimensions via hashing. In: Proc international conference on very large databases, pp 518–529
14. Grauman K, Darrell T (2005) The pyramid match kernel: discriminative classification with sets of image features. In: IEEE international conference on computer vision (ICCV), pp 1458–1465
15. Gupta L, Pathangay V, Patra A, Dyana A, Das S (2007) Indoor versus outdoor scene classification using probabilistic neural network. EURASIP J Appl Signal Process 2007(1): 123
16. Bel Haj Ali W, Piro P, Crescence L, Giampaglia D, Ferhat O, Darcourt J, Pourcher T, Barlaud M (2012) Changes in the subcellular localization of a plasma membrane protein studied by bioinspired UNN learning classification of biologic cell images. In: International conference on computer vision theory and applications (VISAPP)
17. Hart PE (1968) The condensed nearest neighbor rule. IEEE Trans Inf Theory 14:515–516
18. Hastie T, Tibshirani R (1996) Discriminant adaptive nearest neighbor classification. IEEE Trans Pattern Anal Mach Intell 18(6):607–616
19. Holmes CC, Adams NM (2003) Likelihood inference in nearest-neighbour classification models. Biometrika 90:99–112
20. Hsu CW, Chang CC, Lin CJ (2003) A practical guide to support vector classification. Technical report
21. Jégou H, Douze M, Schmid C (2011) Product quantization for nearest neighbor search. IEEE Trans Pattern Anal Mach Intell 33(1):117–128
22. Kakade S, Shalev-Shwartz S, Tewari A (2009) Applications of strong convexity–strong smoothness duality to learning with matrices. Technical report
23. Lazebnik S, Schmid C, Ponce J (2006) Beyond bags of features: spatial pyramid matching for recognizing natural scene categories. In: IEEE computer society conference on computer vision and pattern recognition (CVPR), pp 2169–2178
24. Lowe DG (2004) Distinctive image features from scale-invariant keypoints. Int J Comput Vis 60(2):91–110

25. Masip D, Vitrià J (2006) Boosted discriminant projections for nearest neighbor classification. Pattern Recognit 39(2):164–170
26. Nguyen X, Wainwright MJ, Jordan MI (2009) On surrogate loss functions and f-divergences. Ann Stat 37:876–904
27. Nock R, Nielsen F (2009) Bregman divergences and surrogates for learning. IEEE Trans Pattern Anal Mach Intell 31(11):2048–2059
28. Nock R, Nielsen F (2009) On the efficient minimization of classification calibrated surrogates. In: Advances in neural information processing systems (NIPS), vol 21, pp 1201–1208
29. Nock R, Sebban M (2001) An improved bound on the finite-sample risk of the nearest neighbor rule. Pattern Recognit Lett 22(3/4):407–412
30. Oliva A, Torralba A (2001) Modeling the shape of the scene: a holistic representation of the spatial envelope. Int J Comput Vis 42(3):145–175
31. Paredes R (2006) Learning weighted metrics to minimize nearest-neighbor classification error. IEEE Trans Pattern Anal Mach Intell 28(7):1100–1110
32. Payne A, Singh S (2005) Indoor vs. outdoor scene classification in digital photographs. Pattern Recognit 38(10):1533–1545
33. Piro P, Nock R, Nielsen F, Barlaud M (2012) Leveraging k-NN for generic classification boosting. Neurocomputing 80:3–9
34. Quattoni A, Torralba A (2009) Recognizing indoor scenes. In: IEEE computer society conference on computer vision and pattern recognition (CVPR)
35. Schapire RE, Singer Y (1999) Improved boosting algorithms using confidence-rated predictions. Mach Learn J 37:297–336
36. Serrano N, Savakis AE, Luo JB (2004) Improved scene classification using efficient low-level features and semantic cues. Pattern Recognit 37:1773–1784
37. Shakhnarovich G, Darell T, Indyk P (2006) Nearest-neighbors methods in learning and vision. MIT Press, Cambridge
38. Sivic J, Zisserman A (2003) Video google: a text retrieval approach to object matching in videos. In: IEEE international conference on computer vision (ICCV), vol 2, pp 1470–1477
39. Swain MJ, Ballard DH (1991) Color indexing. Int J Comput Vis 7:11–32
40. Torralba A, Murphy K, Freeman W, Rubin M (2003) Context-based vision system for place and object recognition. In: IEEE international conference on computer vision (ICCV), pp 273–280
41. Vedaldi A, Fulkerson B (2008) VLFeat: an open and portable library of computer vision algorithms. http://www.vlfeat.org
42. Vogel J, Schiele B (2007) Semantic modeling of natural scenes for content-based image retrieval. Int J Comput Vis 72(2):133–157
43. Xiao J, Hays J, Ehinger KA, Oliva A, Torralba A (2010) SUN database: large-scale scene recognition from abbey to zoo. In: IEEE conference on computer vision and pattern recognition (CVPR), pp 3485–3492
44. Yu K, Ji L, Zhang X (2002) Kernel nearest-neighbor algorithm. Neural Process Lett 15(2):147–156
45. Yuan M, Wegkamp M (2010) Classification methods with reject option based on convex risk minimization. J Mach Learn Res 11:111–130
46. Zhang ML, Zhou ZH (2007) ML-kNN: a lazy learning approach to multi-label learning. Pattern Recognit 40(7):2038–2048
47. Zhang H, Berg AC, Maire M, Malik J (2006) SVM-kNN: discriminative nearest neighbor classification for visual category recognition. In: IEEE computer society conference on computer vision and pattern recognition (CVPR), pp 2126–2136

48. Zhu J, Rosset S, Zou H, Hastie T (2009) Multi-class adaboost. Stat Interface 2:349–360
49. Zuo W, Zhang D, Wang K (2008) On kernel difference-weighted k-nearest neighbor classification. Pattern Anal Appl 11(3–4):247–257

Chapter 13
Learning Object Detectors in Stationary Environments

Peter M. Roth, Sabine Sternig, and Horst Bischof

Abstract The most successful approach for object detection is still applying a sliding window technique, where a pre-trained classifier is evaluated on different locations and scales. In this chapter, we interrogate this strategy in the context of stationary environments. In particular, having a fixed camera position observing the same scene a lot of prior (spatio-temporal) information is available. Exploiting this specific scene information allows for (a) improving the detection performance and (b) for reducing the model complexity; both on reduced computational costs! These benefits are demonstrated for two different real-world tasks (i.e., person and car detection). In particular, we apply two different evaluation/update strategies (holistic, grid-based), where any suited online learner can be applied. In our case we demonstrate the proposed approaches for different applications and scenarios, clearly showing their benefits compared to generic methods.

13.1 Introduction

A very prominent approach for object detection is to use a sliding window technique (e.g., [7, 28, 31, 42]). Each patch of an image is tested if it is consistent with a previously estimated model or not. Finally, all consistent patches are reported. The model may either represent a specific object (e.g., a specific cup, that is represented by different views) or a class of objects (e.g., faces, pedestrians, cars, or bikes), where specific instances are not distinguished. These models are mostly based on local features described by a classifier, (e.g., AdaBoost [12] or support vector machine [40]), which is typically obtained by learning. Hence, when discussing the problem of object detection, implicitly, the problem of visual learning is addressed.

The goal of all of such approaches is to build a generic object model that is applicable for all possible scenarios and tasks (e.g., [7, 10, 20]). The drawback of these methods, however, is that the detectors are usually not very specific (i.e., they return false alarms). As can be seen from Fig. 13.1 even if general classifiers ("broad application") are trained from a very large number of training samples, they often fail for

P.M. Roth (✉) · S. Sternig · H. Bischof
Institute for Computer Graphics and Vision, Graz University of Technology, Graz, Austria
e-mail: pmroth@icg.tugraz.at

G.M. Farinella et al. (eds.), *Advanced Topics in Computer Vision*,
Advances in Computer Vision and Pattern Recognition,
DOI 10.1007/978-1-4471-5520-1_13,

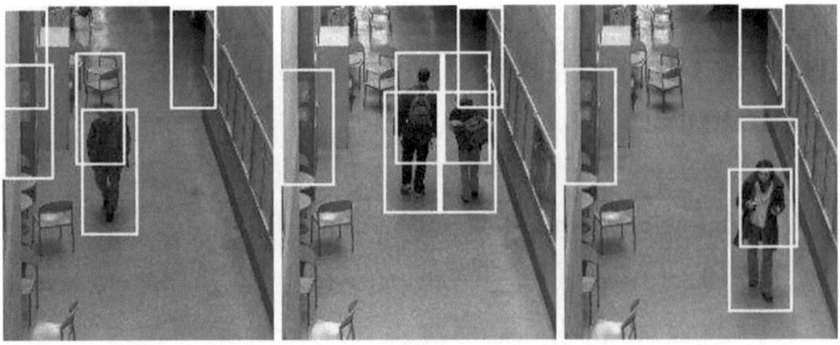

(a) (b) (c)

Fig. 13.1 Typical false positives obtained from generic object detectors: background patches that are similar to persons and partially detected persons

specific situations. This is caused by the main limitation of such approaches—a representative dataset is needed, which is not available for many applications. Since not all variability, especially for the negative class (i.e., all possible backgrounds), can be captured this results in a low recall and an insufficient precision.

One way to overcome this problem is to additionally use scene specific information to reduce the number of false alarms [18]. To further improve the classification results specific classifiers ("narrow applications") can be applied, which are designed to solve a specific task. In fact, for most object detection problems (e.g., visual surveillance) we can assume a stationary camera, allowing us also to include scene specific information also during training. Even though this aspect is often ignored, it was shown that in this way not only less training data is required but that such classifiers are usually also better in terms of accuracy and efficiency [22, 28, 31, 46]. Moreover, an online learning algorithm can be applied [19, 28, 46]. Thus, the system can adapt to changing environments (e.g., changing illumination conditions) and these variations need not to be handled by the model. In fact, in this way the complexity of the problem is reduced and a more efficient classifier can be trained.

Adaptive systems, however, suffer from one main problem: new unlabeled data has to be robustly included into an already built model. Typical approaches are self-training (e.g., [24, 30]), co-training (e.g., [6, 22]), semi-supervised learning (e.g, [15]), or the application of oracles[1] (e.g., [28, 45]. Semi-supervised methods, however, are often biased by the prior and thus only a "limited" information gain can be achieved whereas oracles often provide too less new information. Self- or co-training suffer from the problem that the theoretical constraints can not be assured in practice or that they rely on a direct feedback of the current classifier—both resulting in unreliable classifiers.

In this chapter, we address the problem of making the learning of adaptive scene-specific detectors more stable. Therefore, we discuss two different approaches to

[1]We refer a classifier to as an oracle, if it has a high precision, even at a low recall, and can thus be used to generate new training samples.

cope with this problem: *Conservative Learning* and *Classifier Grids*. The main idea of Conservative Learning is to use a small number of labeled samples to train a discriminative classifier and then to online adapt it to a specific scene. For that purpose, additionally a generative model, that can even be estimated from a smaller number of samples, is used to verify the discriminative model. In this way, using an active learning strategy the most valuable samples can be recognized, ensuring both, a fast adaption to the scene and a very powerful detector. Classifier Grids further simplify the task's complexity by reducing the problem from the static scene to just a small spatio-temporal region. The main idea is to apply a separate classifier on each image location (grid element) to learn an adaptive but still robust scene specific object representation.

The proposed learning strategies are quite general, and any suitable online learner can be applied. For our specific tasks, however, we found that online Boosting (see Sect. 13.2) is a valid choice. In the experiments, we demonstrate the benefits of both approaches for the task of object detection from stationary cameras and give a detailed comparison to state-of-the-art methods. Even just demonstrated for person and car detection, the approach is quite general and not limited to these specific applications.

The chapter is structured as follows. First, in Sect. 13.2 we review online GradientBoost and its variants, where our online learned detectors build on. Next, in Sects. 13.3 and 13.4 we discuss the ideas of Conservative Learning and Classifier Grids. Experimental results for both approaches compared to existing generic approaches are given in Sect. 13.5. Finally, we summarize and conclude our findings in Sect. 13.6.

13.2 Online Learning for Object Detection

The scene-specific object detection approaches presented in Sects. 13.3 and 13.4 are quite general and any suitable learning method could be applied. However, having real-world scenarios we would require classifiers which are efficient during training and evaluation, online capable, and easy to adapt to different applications. Therefore, we propose to use *Online GradientBoost* [21], which is not only very efficient but can also easily be adapted for the different requirements given by our specific tasks. In the following, we first summarize the main concept of online GradientBoost in Sect. 13.2.1 and then introduce two extensions coping better with unreliable data, that is, TransientBoost [36] and inverse MILBoost [37], in Sects. 13.2.2 and 13.2.3.

13.2.1 Online GradientBoost

Given a labeled dataset, $\mathcal{X} = \{(x_1, y_1), \ldots, (x_N, y_N)\}$, $x_n \in \mathbb{R}^D$, $y_n \in \{-1, +1\}$, the goal of Boosting [33] is to estimate a strong classifier

$$H(x) = \sum_{j=1}^{M} \alpha_j h_j(x) \tag{13.1}$$

via a linear combination of M weak classifiers $h_j(x)$, which have only to perform better than random guessing. During evaluation then for a sample x the label $\hat{y} = \text{sign}(H(x))$ should be predicted. Due to its effectivity various different variants such as [11, 14, 26, 34] have been proposed. In particular, in computer vision Boosting for Feature Selection [38, 41] has gained a lot of interest. The main idea is that each feature f_j within a feature pool $\mathcal{F}$ corresponds to a single weak classifier h_j and to use AdaBoost [12] to select an informative subset of M features.

In particular, we adopt these ideas for use with GradientBoost [13]. Let $\ell(\cdot)$ be a loss function and

$$\mathcal{L}\big(H(x)\big) = \sum_{n=1}^{N} \ell\big(y_n H(x_n)\big) \tag{13.2}$$

be the empirical loss, the goal of GradientBoost is to estimate the strong classifier $H(x)$ such that this loss is minimized. Hence, at stage t, we are searching a base function h_t which maximizes the correlation with negative direction of the loss function:

$$h_t(x) = \arg\max_{h(x)} -\nabla\mathcal{L}^T h(x), \tag{13.3}$$

where $\nabla\mathcal{L}$ is the gradient vector of the loss at $H_{t-1}(x) = \sum_{m=1}^{t-1} h_m(x)$. This can be simplified to

$$h_t(x) = \arg\max_{h(x)} -\sum_{n=1}^{N} y_n \underbrace{\ell'\big(y_n H_{t-1}(x_n)\big)}_{-w_n} h(x_n), \tag{13.4}$$

where $\ell'(\cdot)$ are the derivatives of the loss with respect to H_{t-1} and w_n are the sample's weights. Thus, the optimization is equivalent to maximizing the weighted classification accuracy

$$h_t(x) = \arg\max_{h(x)} \sum_{n=1}^{N} w_n y_n h(x_n). \tag{13.5}$$

This formulation can simply be adopted for online learning by using selectors as introduced in [16]. Each selector $s_m(x)$ holds a set of K weak classifiers $\{h_{m,1}(x), \ldots, h_{m,K}(x)\}$ and is represented by its best weak classifier $h_{m,k}(x)$, that is, the weak classifier with the lowest estimated error $\varepsilon_{m,k}$, which is estimated via

$$\varepsilon_{m,k} \leftarrow \varepsilon_{m,k} + w_n \mathbb{I}\big(\text{sign}\big(h_m^k(x_n)\big) \neq y_n\big), \tag{13.6}$$

where $\mathbb{I}(\cdot)$ is the indicator function. The optimization step in Eq. (13.4) is then performed iteratively by propagating the samples through the selectors and updating

Algorithm 1 On-line GradientBoost

Input: Training sample (x_n, y_n)
Output: Strong classifier $H(x)$

Set $H_0(x_n) = 0$
Set the initial weight $w_n = -\ell'(0)$
for $m = 1$ to M **do**
  for $k = 1$ to K **do**
    Train weak learner $h_{m,k}(x)$ with sample (x_n, y_n) and weight w_n
    Compute the error: $\varepsilon_{m,k} \leftarrow \varepsilon_{m,k} + w_n \mathbb{I}(\text{sign}(h_m^k(x_n)) \neq y_n)$
  end for
  Find the best weak learner: $j = \arg\min_k \varepsilon_{m,k}$
  Set $h_m(x_n) = h_m^j(x_n)$
  Set $H_m(x_n) = H_{m-1}(x_n) + h_m(x_n)$
  Set the weight $w_n = -\ell'(y_n H_m(x_n))$
end for
Output the final classifier $H(x)$

the weight estimate w_n according to the negative derivative of the loss function. Thus, optimizing Eq. (13.4) is independent of the applied loss function. The overall approach is summarized in Algorithm 1.

13.2.2 TransientBoost

On-line GradientBoost was designed for a binary classification problem. However, by introducing weak learners that are able to handle more than two classes, we can extend it to the multi-class domain. For that purpose, any weak learner providing confidence-rated responses can be applied. In particular, following Friedman et al. [14], to define a J-class problem, we use symmetric multiple logistic transformation as weak learners:

$$h_j(x) = \log p_j(x) - \frac{1}{J}\sum_{l=1}^{J} \log p_l(x), \tag{13.7}$$

where $p_j(x) = P(y_j = 1|x)$. In particular, they showed that if the sum over the weak classifier responses over all classes is normalized to zero, that is, $\sum_{j=1}^{J} h_j(x) = 0$, the probability $p_j(x)$ can be estimated by using histograms. Moreover, histograms are highly appropriate for online learning since they can easily be updated.

Now having a multi-class formulation we can model reliable and unreliable data using different classes, that is, $y = [+1, -1]$ for the reliable data and $y = [+2, -2]$ for the unreliable data. Thus, during an update the classifier is provided a sample

x_t and a label $y_t \in \{-2, -1, +1, +2\}$ and depending on the label the corresponding histograms are updated. Moreover, for the reliable samples the histogram updates are performed incrementally whereas for the unreliable transient samples an iir-like filtering of the histogram bins is applied (i.e., the knowledge is scaled down according to its age). In this way the reliable information is accumulated whereas the unreliable information allows higher adaptivity, but is fading out quickly (depending on the forgetting rate), thus, avoiding drifting.

The next, crucial step is to include the uncertainty of the sample $\langle x_t, y_t \rangle$ into the feature selection procedure. In each update step, similar to the binary case, the best weak classifier $h_{m,k}$ within a selector s_m is estimated according to its error. The error is updated depending on the weight of the correct classified samples $\lambda^c_{m,n}$ and the misclassified samples $\lambda^w_{m,n}$ within each weak classifier. However, the error updates must be adapted according to the multi-class formulation. If the prediction was correct, that is, the signum of the classifier response $h_{m,n}$ equals the signum of class label used to update the classifier y_t ($\text{sign}(h_{m,n}(x)) = \text{sign}(y_t)$), the weight $\lambda^c_{m,n}$ is updated:

$$\lambda^c_{m,n} = \lambda^c_{m,n} + w_n; \tag{13.8}$$

otherwise the weight $\lambda^w_{m,n}$ is updated:

$$\lambda^w_{m,n} = \lambda^w_{m,n} + w_n, \tag{13.9}$$

where w_n is the current estimated weight of the current sample. In the original GradientBoost formulation any differentiable loss function ℓ can be used to update the weight by $w_n = -\ell'(y_t H_m(x_t))$, where $H_m(x)$ is the combination of the first m weak classifiers and y_t is the label of the current sample. In our case, however, we have to re-formulate the weight update according to our multi-class model. Otherwise the classifier would try to distinguish between the reliable and the unreliable classes and would penalize samples that are already classified correctly. Hence, since we are interested in discrimination of positive and negative classes, we have to change the weight update to

$$w_n = -\ell'\big(\text{sign}(y_t) H_m(x)\big). \tag{13.10}$$

13.2.3 Inverse MILBoost

A different way to cope with unreliable, ambiguously labeled data is Multiple Instance Learning (MIL), which was first introduced by Dietterich et al. [8]. Since this is a widespread problem, there has been a considerable interest and many popular supervised learning algorithms such as SVM [3] or Boosting [4, 43] have been adapted in order to incorporate the MIL constraints.

In contrast to supervised learning algorithms, where each sample (instance) is provided a label, in multiple-instance learning the training samples are grouped into bags $B_i \subset \mathbb{R}^d$, $i = 1, \ldots, N$. Each bag consists of an arbitrary number of instances:

$B_i = \{x_{1i}, x_{2i}, \ldots, x_{m_i i}\}$. Negative bags B_i^- are required to consist only of negative instances, whereas for positive bags B_i^+ it has only to be guaranteed that they contain at least one positive instance. There are no further restrictions to the non-positive instances within the positive bag B_i^+, they might not even belong to the negative class. The task now is to learn either a bag classifier $f : B \to \{-1, 1\}$ or an instance classifier $f : \mathbb{R}^d \to \{-1, 1\}$. However, a bag classifier can follow automatically from instance prediction, e.g., by using the *max* operator over posterior probabilities over the instances p_{ij} within the ith bag: $p_i = \max_j \{p_{ij}\}$.

In context of GradientBoost this can easily be realized by defining a new loss function, which optimizes the binary log likelihood over bags:

$$\log \mathcal{L} = \sum_i \big(y_i \log p(y_i) + (1 - y_i) \log\big(1 - p(y_i)\big)\big), \tag{13.11}$$

where the instance probability can be estimated using a sigmoid function

$$p(y|x) = \sigma\big(H(x)\big) = \frac{1}{1 + e^{-H(x)}}, \tag{13.12}$$

which requires a gradient descent in function space. The bag probability $p(y|B)$ is modeled by the Noisy-OR (NOR) operator:

$$p(y_i|B_i) = 1 - \prod_{j=1} \big(1 - p(y_i|x_{ij})\big). \tag{13.13}$$

This formulation assumes the ambiguity in the positive data. However, for many tasks the uncertain labeled data mainly concerns the negative samples, requiring to adapt the original MIL idea. In fact, we require that the negative bags B_i^- contain only one negative example whereas the positive bag B_i^+ consists only of positive examples:

$$\forall x_{ij}^+ \in B_i^+ : \quad y\big(x_{ij}^+\big) = 1, \tag{13.14}$$

$$\exists x_{ij}^- \in B_i^- : \quad y\big(x_{ij}^-\big) = -1. \tag{13.15}$$

Thus, in order to correctly calculate the loss $\mathcal{L}$ by inverting the problem, we have to switch the labels between the positive and the negative class (*inverse MIL*). This causes to focus on examples that are more likely to be correct negative examples, which directly fits to our problem.

13.3 Scene-Specific Detectors

The main motivation for training scene-specific detectors is twofold. First, as illustrated for instance, in Fig. 13.1 generic classifiers cannot cope with all variabilities in the data. Second, often only small amount of labeled training data is available, thus, it might be useful also to exploit the information naturally given by unlabeled

Algorithm 2 Active learning

Input: unlabeled samples **U**, classifier C_{t-1}
Output: classifier C_t
1: **while** teacher can label samples u_j **do**
2: Apply C_{t-1} to all samples u_j
3: Let Q find the m most informative samples u_q
4: Let teacher S assign labels y_q to samples u_q
5: Re-train classifier: C_t
6: **end while**

data. Both issues can be addressed by online learning. Thus, a classifier can adapt to environmental conditions, which have not to be modeled in beforehand. Surprisingly a lot of research was focused on developing new (online) learning methods, however, only little work was done on sampling meaningful training data. Hence, typically a *passive learning* strategy [23] is applied, where a huge number of samples are randomly drawn from the training set. In the following, we introduce an approach which samples training data in a more sophisticated way exploiting information given by a fixed camera setup.

13.3.1 Active Learning

To overcome these problems an adaptive learning algorithm taking advantage of the ideas if *active learning* (e.g., [23, 39, 47]) can be applied. In general, an active learner can be considered a quintuple $(C, Q, S, \mathbf{L}, \mathbf{U})$ [23], where C is a classifier, Q is a query function, S is a supervisor (teacher), and $\mathbf{L}$ and $\mathbf{U}$ are a set of labeled and unlabeled data, respectively. First, an initial classifier C_0 is trained from the labeled set $\mathbf{L}$. Given a classifier C_{t-1}, then the query function Q selects the most informative unlabeled samples from $\mathbf{U}$ and the supervisor S is requested to label them. Using the thus labeled samples the current classifier is re-trained obtaining a new classifier C_t. This procedure is summarized in Algorithm 2.

When considering an adaptive system we can start from a small set of labeled data $\mathbf{L}$. But usually the unlabeled data $\mathbf{U}$ is not available in advance. Assuming we have already trained a classifier C_{t-1} the first crucial point at time t is to define a set of unlabeled data $\mathbf{U}_t$ and a suitable query function Q, raising two questions. First, we have to discover the most valuable samples. It has been shown by [29] that it is more effective to sample at the current estimated decision boundary than the unknown true boundary. In context of online learning, the most valuable samples are exactly those that have been misclassified by the current classifier. This is illustrated in Fig. 13.2.

The red and green points indicate the samples that were wrongly classified by the current classifier. Obviously, these points are much better samples than randomly selected points from the class! Hence, the algorithm is focused on the hard samples and the current decision boundary (dashed gray line) can be moved such that those

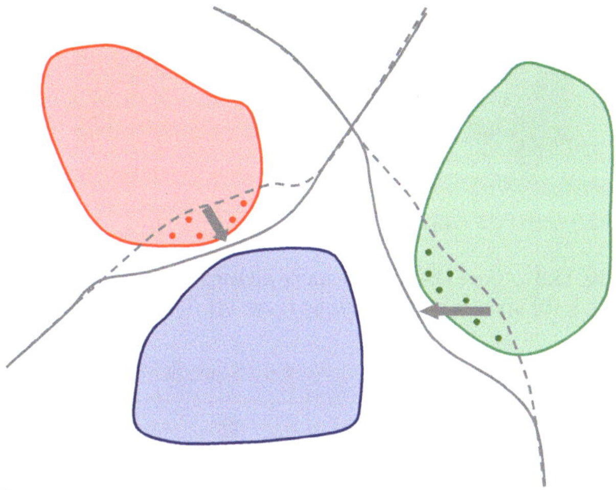

Fig. 13.2 Sampling at the current decision boundary is more efficient than random sampling: updating using only a small number of wrongly classified samples (*red* and *green points*) allows to move the current decision boundary (*dashed gray line*) in the right direction (*solid gray line*)

samples are correctly classified (solid gray line). For a detailed theoretical discussion, see [29].

The second crucial point is the definition of the supervisor S. In fact, new unlabeled data has to be robustly included into the already built model. More formally, at time t given a classifier C_{t-1} and an unlabeled example $x_t \in \mathbb{R}^m$. Then, a reliable supervisor is needed, that robustly estimates a label $y_t \in \{+1, -1\}$ for x_t.

13.3.2 Conservative Learning

The goal now is to identify meaningful choices for the query function Q as well as for the supervisor S for the given task. In fact, considering object detection the misclassified samples are the detected false positives. Thus, it would be desirable to identify those false positives and use them to update the classifier. This is illustrated in Fig. 13.3, where it can be seen that using especially those samples an initially insufficient classifier can be significantly be improved.

The remaining problem is how to conveniently decide if a selected detection is a true or a false positive! In fact, we additionally apply a generative model for this purpose, that is trained from the same (positive) samples. This is motivated by two properties of generative models: first, a sufficient generative model can be trained from a smaller number of samples and, second, generative models are robust against wrongly labeled data (up to some extent). Thus, we use two models in parallel, a discriminative one, which actually performs the detection, and a generative one, which assures robustness and serves for verification.

In this way the output of the discriminative classifier is verified by the generative model. The detected false positives are fed back into the discriminative classifier as negative examples and true positives as positive examples. Since we have a huge amount of unlabeled data, that is readily available (i.e., we have video stream),

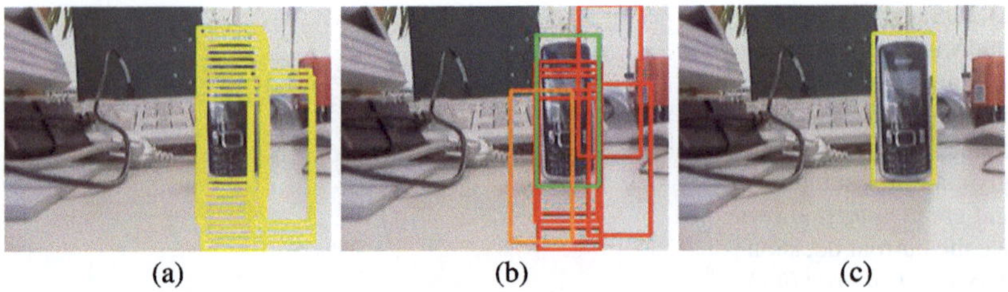

Fig. 13.3 Active learning—suitable updates for learning a detector: (**a**) classifier evaluated at time $t-1$, (**b**) updates selected at time t, and (**c**) classifier evaluated at time $t+1$.

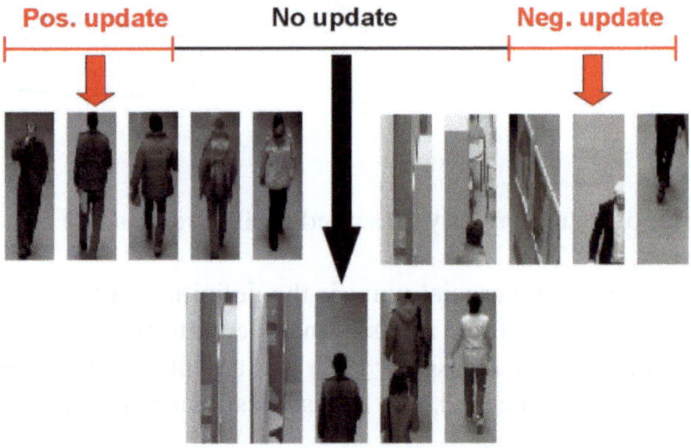

Fig. 13.4 Conservative updating the discriminant classifier using the of the generative model

we can use very *conservative* decision criteria. In fact, the generative model returns a similarity measure and we use two conservative thresholds θ_{pos} and θ_{neg} for this decision. Hence, we refer to this approach as *Conservative Learning*. This update rule is illustrated in Fig. 13.4.

Thus, only a very small number of samples, that were selected by the query function, are labeled by the supervisor and are finally used for updating. In this way we guarantee that the discriminative classifier is only learned from clean correctly labeled samples. In addition, the thus labeled samples can be used to update the generative model. Exploiting the huge amount of video data this process can be iterated to produce a stable and robust classifier. This update learning strategy is summarized more formally in Algorithm 3.

The update rules described here are very general and can be applied to any pair of discriminative/generative online learners. However, in our particular case we apply online boosting (see Sect. 13.2.1) as discriminative model and incremental PCA [35] as generative model.

To illustrate incremental learning process, we visualize the update over time in Fig. 13.5. Therefore, the first, the third, the 34th and the 64th frame of a sequence of total 300 frames are shown. A red bounding box indicates a negative update, a green bounding box a positive update and a white bounding box indicates a detection that is not used for updating the existing classifier. It can be seen that there is a great number of negative updates within the very first frames (see Figs. 13.5(a), (b)). If the

Algorithm 3 Conservative Learning update strategy

Input: discriminative classifier D_{t-1}, generative classifier G_{t-1}, unknown image **I**
Output: classifier D_t, classifier G_t
1: Evaluate D_{t-1} on **I** obtaining J detections x_j
2: **for** $j = 1, \dots, J$ **do**
  if $G_{t-1}(x_j) < \theta_{\text{pos}}$ **then**
    $update(D_{t-1}, x_j, +)$, $update(G_{t-1}, x_j)$
  else if $G_{t-1}(x_j) > \theta_{\text{neg}}$ **then**
    $update(D_{t-1}, x_j, -)$
  end if
3: **end for**

incremental learning process is running for a longer time, we finally get a stable classifier and only a small number of updates are necessary (see Figs. 13.5(c), (d)).

The learning framework discussed so far has two main disadvantages. First, still a small amount of labeled data is required. Second, new positives examples are only obtained from the detection results, that are already described well by the model. Thus, completely different appearances are not captured and the classifier is biased by the very first positive examples. To overcome these problems, we need a robust method to automatically label additionally positives samples. In fact, we can apply low level cues such as motion detection or tracking for this purpose. The whole learning approach is thus summarized in Algorithm 4.

13.4 Classifier Grids

The idea of Classifier Grids is to sample an input image by using a fixed highly overlapping grid (both in location and scale), where each grid element $i = 1, \dots, N$ corresponds to one classifier C_i. This is illustrated in Fig. 13.6. Thus, the classification task that has to be handled by one classifier C_i is reduced to discriminate the background of the specific grid element from the object-of-interest. Due to this simplification, less complex classifiers can be applied.

In particular, the grid-based representation is well suited for compact smart online classifier, which can be evaluated and updated very efficiently. However, as online systems suffer from the problem to robustly include new data they tend to drift, that is, the classifier starts to learn something completely wrong and would yield arbitrarily wrong results. Therefore, we introduce three different update strategies for Classifier Grids that cope with different aspects of online learning.

13.4.1 Fixed Update Rules

The first problem we address is to ensure stability over time. Therefore, we build on two observations. First, for many task labeled positive data, that is, describing the

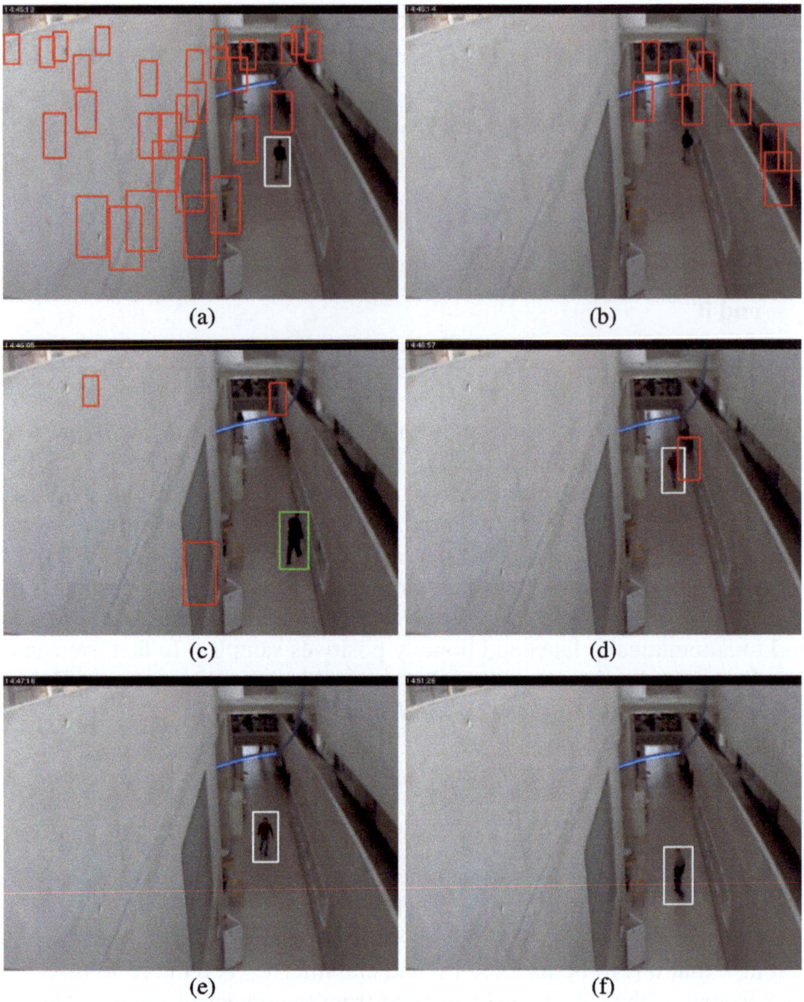

Fig. 13.5 On-line Conservative Learning—learning progress: (**a**) updates for 1st frame, (**b**) updates for 3rd frame, (**c**) updates for 34th frame, and (**d**) update for 64th frame, (**e**) detection but no update for 75th frame, (**f**) detection but no update for 172th frame

object of interest, is available. Second, in a typical fixed camera scenario a specific image position is occupied by an object very rarely. Thus, we can define fixed update rules for online learning that exploit previously given labeled positive data but also sample unlabeled negative information from the scene [17].

More formally, let $\mathcal{X}^+$ be a set of representative positive (hand) labeled examples. Then, using

$$\langle \mathbf{x}, +1 \rangle, \quad \mathbf{x} \in \mathcal{X}^+ \tag{13.16}$$

Algorithm 4 Conservative Learning

```
Automatically collect pos./neg. training samples
Train initial classifier D_0
Train initial classifier G_0
while t do
    update D_t (Algorithm 3)
    update G_t (Algorithm 3)
    Acquire new pos. samples x
    update(D_t, x, +)
    update(G_t, x)
end while
```

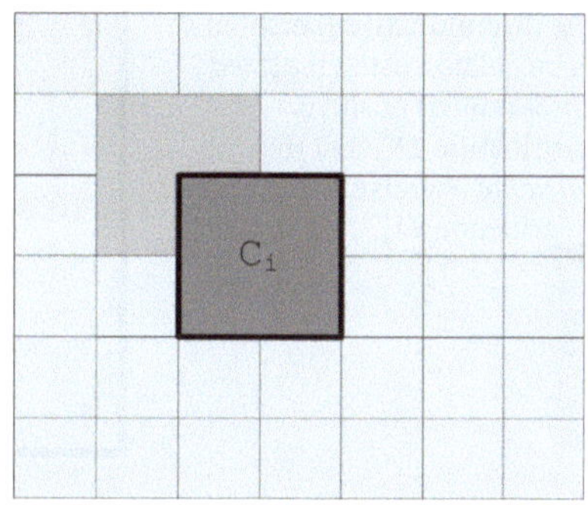

Fig. 13.6 Concept of grid-based classification: a highly overlapping grid is placed over the image, where each grid element corresponds to a single classifier

to update the classifier is a correct positive update by definition. Moreover, the probability that an object is present at patch $\mathbf{x}_i$ is given by

$$P(\mathbf{x}_i = \text{object}) = \frac{\#p_i}{\Delta t}, \tag{13.17}$$

where $\#p_i$ is the number of objects entirely present in a particular patch within the time interval Δt. Thus, the negative update with the current patch

$$\langle \mathbf{x}_{i,t}, -1 \rangle \tag{13.18}$$

is correct most of the time (wrong with probability $P(\mathbf{x}_i = \text{object})$). The probability of a wrong update for this particular image patch is indeed very low. To further decrease this probability instead of sampling from the original images a background model can be applied instead. Even though this strategy is quite general, in our case we apply the online Boosting approach presented in Sect. 13.2.1 within each grid element. The overall approach is illustrated in Fig. 13.7.

To further reduce the computational effort and to increase the stability, more sophisticated weak classifiers can be applied within the online Boosting framework [32]. Since the object-of-interest is known before, its appearance can be described in advance by a finite set $\mathcal{X}^+$ of positive samples. Thus, for each feature

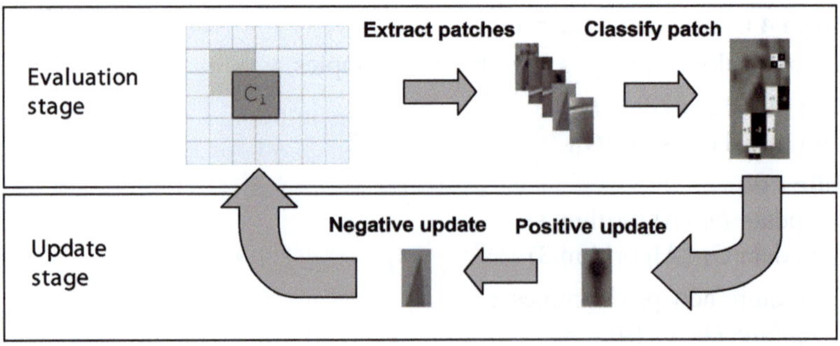

Fig. 13.7 Online updating the classifier grid approach using fixed update rules

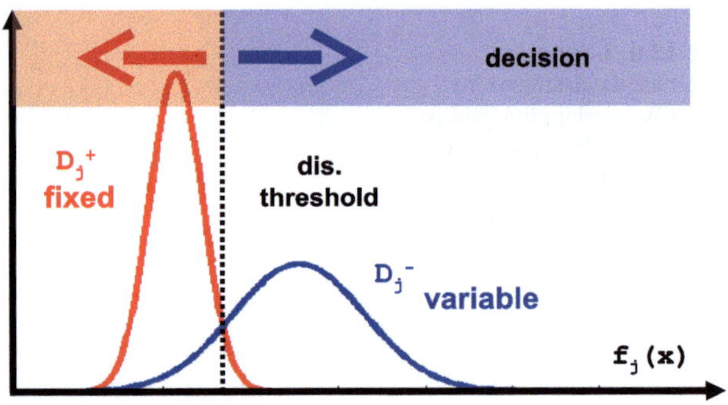

Fig. 13.8 For each feature f_j the discriminative threshold θ is calculated using the *fixed* (pre-trained) positive distribution D_j^+ and the *variable* negative distribution D_j^-

$f_j \in \mathcal{F}$ a generative model can be estimated via the distributions D_j^+. Since $\mathcal{X}^+$ is fixed, the distributions D_j^+ can also be kept fixed and can be calculated in an offline pre-training stage. In contrast, the negative class is changing over time and can therefore not be described by a finite set of samples. However, this information can be extracted online from the scene, that is, from the patch corresponding to the grid-element, as described before. Thus, for each feature f_j we can estimate a distributions D_j^- online over time. Using these distributions, we can define a weak classifier as illustrated in Fig. 13.8.

For the feature selection process, the errors of the features (weak classifiers) have to be calculated to select the best weak classifier within a selector. Since only negative updates are performed during online learning, only the error for negative samples $\varepsilon_-^{\text{online}}$ can be estimated. However, since the distributions D_j^+ were pre-estimated, we can also provide an error for the positive samples: $\varepsilon_+^{\text{offline}}$. Thus, instead of Eq. (13.6) we can use the combined error

$$\varepsilon = \frac{1}{2}\left(\varepsilon_+^{\text{offline}} + \varepsilon_-^{\text{online}}\right) \tag{13.19}$$

to select the best weak classifier within the selector.

Overall, this formulation has two main benefits. On the one hand, we can combine offline and online learning very easily by analyzing distribution on the feature level. On the other hand, compared to typical update schemes such as self-training (e.g., [24, 30]) and co-training (e.g., [6, 22]), we do not rely on a direct feedback of the current classifier. Taking into account both, errors are not accumulated but are fading out, ensuring a stable system, even over a long period of time, which is demonstrated in Sect. 13.5.2.2.

13.4.2 Inverse MIL Updates

Even though the updates generated by the rules discussed before are correct most of the time, they might be wrong if an object is not moving over a long period of time. Hence, foreground information is used to perform negative updates, which causes the positive information to be temporally unlearned. This can be seen in the context of ambiguously labeled samples, which can be resolved with ideas from Multiple Instance Learning.

In particular, we apply the Inverse MILBoost described in Sect. 13.2.3. Since in the classifier grid scenario, the positive samples are well defined (positive samples are hand labeled) and the ambiguity concerns only the negative samples (coming directly from the scene without labeling), the original MIL idea makes only little sense. Therefore, as already defined in Eqs. (13.14) and (13.15), we modify the definition of bags such that the negative bags B_i^- need only to contain one negative example whereas the positive bag B_i^+ consists only of positive examples. To generate the required negative bags, we collect a stack of input images from the image sequence over time, which we refer to as "temporal bag". Having a large stack assures that the assumption for the negative bag containing at least one negative sample is mostly valid, since the probability that an object stays at one specific location over a longer period of time is very low.

Collecting a large stack of input images is adversarial for the runtime behavior. In order to avoid a large stack of input images within the temporal bag, we propose to use a small set of background images which operate on different time scales, which means that they are updated in different time intervals. Any kind of background model can be used. However, in our case we apply the approximated median background model [27]. Since these background models are updated in different time intervals, even a small number ensures that the temporal bags fulfill the MIL constraints. To give enough adaptivity to changing illumination conditions, we have background models which are updated in small time intervals, while to avoid objects staying at the same position for a while to become part of the background we have background models updated in long time intervals. Hence, the multiple instance learning property of inherently dealing with ambiguity in data can be exploited for improving the classifier grid approach and avoiding short-term drifting.

13.4.3 Robust Positive Updates by Co-training

The main focus of the approaches presented in Sects. 13.4.1 and 13.4.1 was to ensure stability over time. In this way, the system is able to adapt to changing environmental

Fig. 13.9 Different illumination conditions with the corresponding background subtracted images. Even in case of totally different illumination conditions and differently appearing objects the background subtracted image gives a similar representation of the object

conditions, however, no new positive, object-specific information is gained. In the following, we introduce an update scheme based on co-training, which allows for adding new information in a robust way.

Co-training [6], in general, exploits the redundancy of unlabeled input data. The main idea is to train two conditionally independent classifiers h_1 and h_2 on some labeled data $\mathcal{D}^L$ and then let these classifiers update each other using unlabeled data $\mathcal{D}^U$. An update is performed if one classifier is confident on a sample whereas the other one is not. Since Abney [1] showed that co-training classifiers aims at minimizing the error on the labeled samples while increasing the agreement on the unlabeled data, it is clear that the unlabeled data can help to improve the margin of the classifiers and to decrease the generalization error. The strong condition of conditionally independent classifiers was later relaxed by several authors (e.g., [1, 5]). Wang and Zhou [44] provided a PAC-style proof that co-training can converge to good accuracy if the classifiers are strong and highly uncorrelated. Thus, co-training can typically also be applied if the learners are strong and low-correlated. Thus, co-training has recently become popular in the field of computer vision and was applied for a variety of applications including background modeling [48], learning an object detector [22], or tracking [25].

For our purpose, we adopt the ideas of Levin et al. [22], who ran co-training on two boosted offline classifiers. Similarly, we train one classifier from gray-value images whereas the other is trained from background subtracted images (i.e., approximated median background model [27]). However, in contrast, we run co-training only in an initial phase to adapt the main classifier to the scene and apply a more sophisticated online learner. In fact, after a settling phase we keep the classifier fixed and use it only as an oracle for two reasons. First, not all situations can be handled by co-training in a robust manner. Hence, if too many wrong updates are performed the co-trained classifier would start to drift and finally fails totally. Second, as illustrated in Fig. 13.9, most environmental changes are eliminated by the background subtraction and the variability in the positive class vanishes. Thus, no further information can be gained.

Algorithm 5 Co-grid initialization

Input: grid-classifier G_j^{t-1}, classifier C^{t-1}
Input: grid-element $\mathbf{X}_j$, BGS patch $\mathbf{B}_j$

```
if C^{t-1}(B_j) > θ then
    update(G_j^{t-1}, X_j, +)
else if C^{t-1}(B_j) < −θ then
    update(G_j^{t-1}, X_j, −)
end if
if G_j^{t-1}(X_j) > θ then
    update(C^{t-1}, B_j, +)
else if G_j^{t-1}(X_j) < −θ then
    update(C_{t-1}, B_j, −)
end if
```

Output: grid-classifier G_j^t, classifier C^t

In general, any online learner can be applied within the co-grid approach. However, to increase the robustness (the co-trained oracle may still suffer from a small amount of label noise), we apply online TransientBoost as introduced in Sect. 13.3.2, which allows to combine reliable (labeled) data with unreliable data (unlabeled from the scene). Thus, robustly new positive information can be gained, especially increasing the recall but preserving the accuracy. In our case, we apply three classes: one for the reliable positive data (+1), one for the possibly unreliable positive data (+2), and one for the classifier-specific background (−1). The class +1 is trained offline and is kept fix whereas the others are updated online over time. In the following, the two main steps are summarized more detailed.

Co-training Stage During the initial stage our system is trained in a co-training manner. Given n grid classifiers G_j operating on gray level image patches $\mathbf{X}_j$ and one compact classifier C operating in a sliding window manner on background subtracted images $\mathbf{B}$. To start co-training, the classifiers G_j as well as the classifier C are initialized with the same offline pre-trained classifier, then the classifiers co-train each other. A confident classification (positive and negative) of a classifier G_j is used to update the classifier C with the background subtracted representation at position j. Vice versa, a confident classification of classifier C at position j generates an update for classifier G_j. Due to the offline pre-trained prior, already capturing the generic information, only a small number of updates is sufficient to adapt the classifiers to a new scene or changing environmental conditions. The update procedure during the initialization for a specific grid element j is summarized in Algorithm 5.

Detection Stage After the initial stage, as described above, the classifier C is not longer updated and is applied as an oracle to generate new positive and negative

Algorithm 6 Co-grid update

Input: grid-classifier G_j^{t-1}, classifier C
Input: grid-element $\mathbf{X}_j$, BGS patch $\mathbf{B}_j$

```
1: if C(B_j) > θ then
2:     ∀i : update(G_i^{t-1}, X_j, +)
3: end if
4: if C(B_j) < −θ then
5:     update(C_j^{t-1}, X_j, −)
6: end if
```

Output: grid-classifier G_j^t

samples. Hence, we can abstain from fixed update rules, which are broadly used for Classifier Grids. Moreover, we perform negative updates for the classifiers G_j only if they are necessary, that is, if the scene is changing. Even if the oracle classifier C has a low recall, the precision is very high. Thus, only very valuable updates are generated, increasing the performance of the classifiers G_j. In particular, a confident classification result of classifier C at position j generates an update for all classifiers G_i, $i = 1, \ldots, n$. In this way, new scene specific positive samples are disseminated over the whole classifier grid. Negative updates are performed for classifiers G_j if there is no corresponding detection reported at this position for classifier C. The update procedure during the detection phase for a specific grid element j is summarized in Algorithm 6.

13.5 Experimental Results

The experimental results are spit into three parts. First, we give an evaluation on scene specific detectors trained using Conservative Learning in Sect. 13.5.1. Then, in Sect. 13.5.2, we give a detailed evaluation on grid-based detectors. Finally, in Sect. 13.5.3 we compare both approaches to state-of-the-art methods for person detection. Even not limited to this specific setups, for all experiments we build on the online learning methods presented in Sect. 13.2 and use Haar-like features as underlying representation. Moreover, as we are dealing with stationary cameras we take into account a simple scene calibration, which allows for reducing the computational effort and also suppressing a number of false positives.

To allow for a fair quantitative evaluation, we build our results on precision $Pr = TP/(TP + FP)$ and recall $R = TP/P$, where TP is the number of true positives, FP is the number of false positives, and P is the number of positives in the test data represented by the given ground-truth. The positives are estimated according to the overlap criterion [2], requiring a minimal overlap of 50 %. Once these parameters are estimated, we can plot recall-precision curves (RPC) [2]. Additionally, we estimate the F-measure $FM = (2 \cdot R \cdot Pr)/(R + Pr)$ [2], which is the harmonic mean between *recall* and *precision*. In particular, the characteristics given in this section are estimated such that the F-measure is maximized.

13.5.1 Scene Specific Classifiers

In the following, we analyze different aspects of Conservative Learning, where the experimental setup is as follows. We use a boosted classifier consisting of 50 selectors each holding 100 weak classifiers. If not stated otherwise, the initial classifier used for all setups is the same and is trained using 50 positive and negative samples, respectively. This classifier is then online trained and the finally obtained classifier is evaluated on an independent test sequence, which was not seen before during training but steaming from the same camera setup. To monitor the progress during online training, a classifier is saved after a pre-defined number of training samples. Thus, the obtained classifiers are evaluated on an independent test sequence and the precision, the recall, and the F-measure are estimated. Hence, we can plot learning curves that show the performance of an online learned classifier over time.

For these experiments, we generated the *CoffeeCam* dataset showing a corridor in a public building near to a coffee dispenser. Hence, we capture various representative real-world scenarios: walking people, people standing around while waiting for their coffee, or people building small crowds while drinking coffee. To create this dataset, we have recorded images over several days. In total, we have recorded over 35000 (gray-value) images, which have a resolution of 192×238. For evaluation purposes, we generated a training sequence containing 1200 frames and a challenging independent test set (containing groups of persons, persons partially occluding each other, and persons walking in different directions) and a corresponding ground-truth. In total, the test sequence consists of 300 frames and contains 224 person. The resulting precision-recall curves for the initial and the final classifier as well as for time steps 50 and 100 are shown in Fig. 13.10.

It can be seen that the performance of the initial classifier can be improved and gets saturated already after a small number (i.e., 50–100) of updates. The same behavior can also be recognized from Fig. 13.11, where precision, recall and F-measure are plotted individually over time. In contrast to Fig. 13.10, this clearly reveals that the main benefits arise from improving the precision. In fact, the recall is already on a satisfying level from the very beginning. Moreover, we also show the effect of using initial classifiers trained using a different number of labeled samples. Figure 13.11(a) depicts the performance curves if 50 labeled samples were used to train the initial classifier. One can see a clear improvement (especially in the first 100 steps), where most of the false positives can be eliminated. Later, if all scene-specific information is acquired the performance gets saturated (around step 500). The same behavior can be recognized from Fig. 13.11(b), which depicts the performance curves if only 10 labeled samples were used to train the initial classifier. Hence, there is a greater number of false positives in the beginning, but finally we get the same performance as for the first test case!

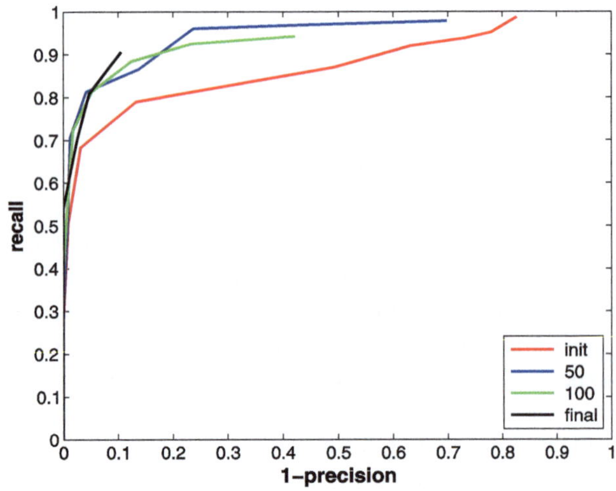

Fig. 13.10 Precision-recall curves for Conservative Learning for different time steps: initial classifier, after 50 frames, after 100 frames, and final classifier

The same performance increase over time can also be seen from the illustrative detection results in Fig. 13.12 for three different online classifiers (initial, after 300, and after 1200 training frames). There are many false positives in the beginning, which are reduced via the online updates and are completely vanishing in the end.

To get a benchmark, we compared this final classifier to two commonly used person detection methods, that is, Dalal and Triggs [7] and Viola and Jones [41]. In particular, we show the detection characteristics that is, recall, precision, and F-measure, which are summarized in Table 13.1. It can be seen, even seeming to be a simple scenario, that the generic detectors yield an insufficient detection performance. In fact, these results show that on the same accuracy level the recall is much lover. Further illustrative detection results for the Conservative Learning are shown in Fig. 13.13.

Next, after we have shown that using the proposed update strategy the detection performance can be improved, we would like to demonstrate that in particular the active sampling strategy is beneficial. For that purpose, we train two detectors in parallel and run the same experiment as before. The first detector was trained using Conservative Learning described in Sect. 13.3. The second detector was trained in the same way, however, the negative samples were randomly selected from the background. Hence, we will further refer to this method as "Random Sampling". To avoid a bias of the positive samples due to differently online trained detectors, the positive updates are generated via tracking. Hence, to avoid tracking confusion due to overlapping instances, for this experiments we created a single face detection setup, once again consisting of independent training and test sequences each consisting of 250 frames. The corresponding results are shown in Fig. 13.14.

From Fig. 13.14(a), it can be seen that for Conservative Learning less than 100 updates are sufficient to derive precision, recall, and hence F-measure of more than 0.90. In contrast, Fig. 13.14(b) shows that Random Sampling requires a longer settling phase. Even though a trend of increasing accuracy can be observed after approximate 150 updates the precision is still insufficient and the precision curve

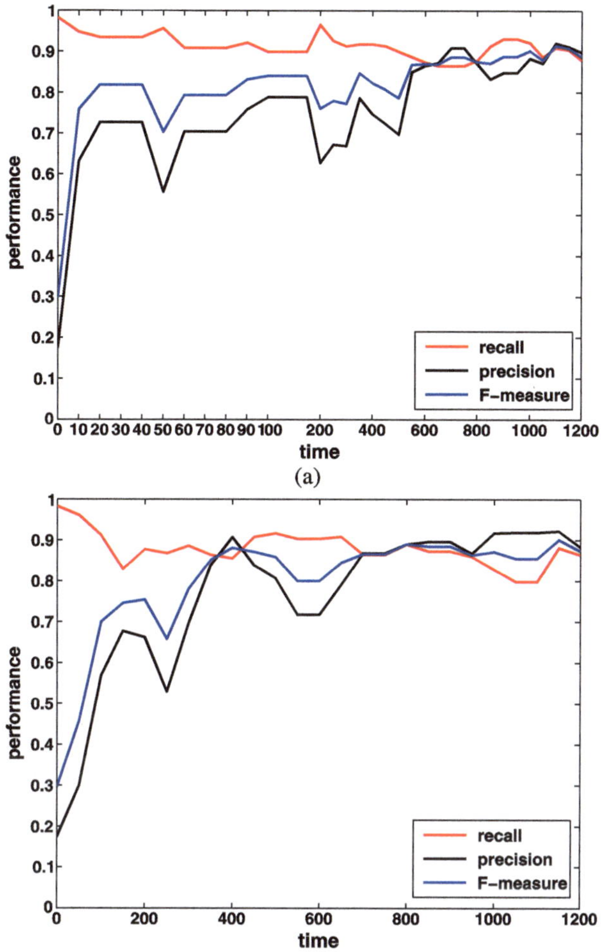

(a)

(b)

Fig. 13.11 Improvement of online classifier: (**a**) started from 50 labeled samples and (**b**) started from 10 labeled samples

shows a stochastic trend. But, in fact, compared to Conservative Learning we have a higher recall. However, both experiments clearly indicate the benefits of the proposed approach: (a) a small number of labeled samples is sufficient to finally obtain a performative classifier, (b) the active learning strategy allows for sampling "better" samples, and thus (c) only a small number of updates is necessary to adapt to the scene.

13.5.2 Classifier Grids

The experiments on Classifier Grids tackle four different aspects. First, in Sect. 13.5.2.1 we give a proof-of-concept study. Next, in Sect. 13.5.2.2 we demon-

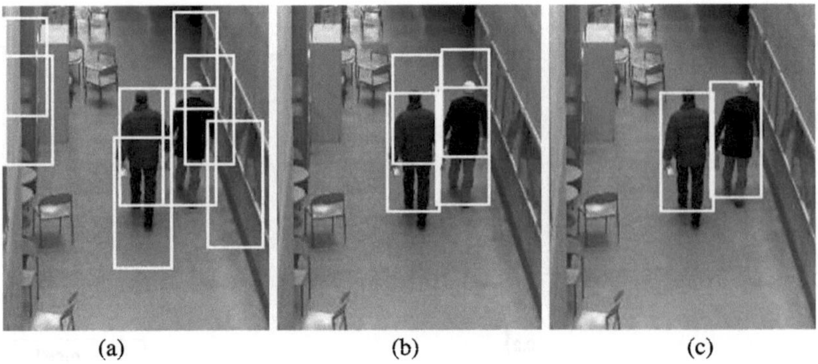

Fig. 13.12 Improvement of online classifier: (**a**) initial classifier, (**b**) after 300 frames and (**c**) after 1200 frames

Table 13.1 Final classifier obtained via Conservative Learning benchmarked against state-of-the-art person detection on the *CoffeeCam* dataset

	Recall	Precision	F-measure
Cons. Learning	0.87	0.96	0.91
Dalal & Triggs	0.37	1.00	0.54
Viola & Jones	0.36	0.95	0.52

strate the key aspects of this approach, i.e., the long-term stability. Finally, in Sects. 13.5.2.4 and 13.5.2.3 we show the benefits of two extensions in sense of increasing the recall and avoiding short term drifting.

13.5.2.1 Not yet Another Background Model

When reviewing Classifier Grids it might seem that they are just "some kind of background model" or a "little bit more sophisticated template matching". Thus, the following experiment faces two goals. First, to alleviate these arguments and, second, to illustrate that even using this quite simple strategy competitive results can be obtained. For that purpose, we generated a challenging pedestrian detection benchmark showing a corridor of a public building (*Corridor sequence*). The main difficulties arise from various moving objects (e.g., a ball, chairs, and an umbrella) and partly overlapping persons, situations that can neither be captured by a simple background model nor by a template matcher. The sequence consisting of 300 frames was taken at a resolution of 320×240 and contains 296 persons in total.

Hence, we compared the Classifier Grid approach to low level methods (i.e., a simple background model (BGM) [27], template matching (TM), and a combination of both (TM+BGM), which might be considered a simple pendent to our method). Additionally, to get a benchmark, we compare these results to two generic state-of-the-art person detectors (i.e., Dalal and Triggs (D&T) [7] and deformable

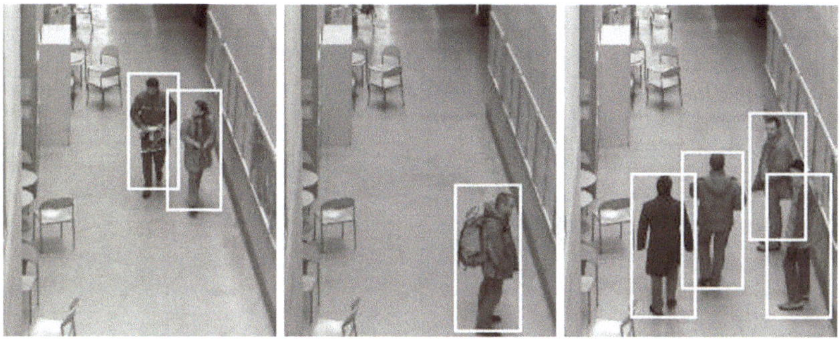

(a) (b) (c)

Fig. 13.13 Illustrative detection results from Conservative Learning on the *CoffeeCam* dataset

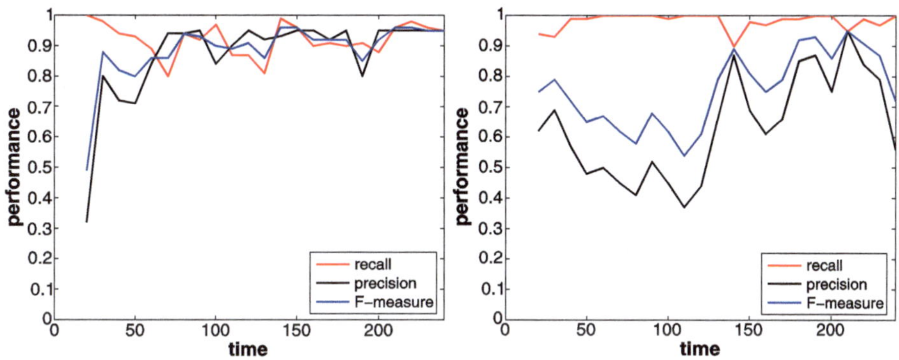

(a) (b)

Fig. 13.14 Importance of negative sampling: (**a**) Active Sampling ensures a faster adaption to the problem and finally yields robust results compared to (**b**) Random Sampling

part model of Felzenszwalb et al. (FS) [10]). The thus obtained results are summarized in Fig. 13.15.

From these results, it can be seen that the generic detectors show an excellent precision, but the recall very low. Moreover, the low level cues totally fail, that is, for BM and TM either the recall or the precision is very poor such that even a combination of both (TM+BGM) yields insufficient results. Hence, we can conclude that these approaches are too weak to provide sufficient detection results. In contrast, the proposed approach yields competitive detection results, even using only very simple update rules and compact classifiers. Finally, typical results of the Classifier Grid approach are depicted in Fig. 13.16.

13.5.2.2 Long-Term Behavior

As illustrated in Fig. 13.18, within realistic setups we have to cope with heavily changing environmental conditions, which have to be handled by the system. Thus,

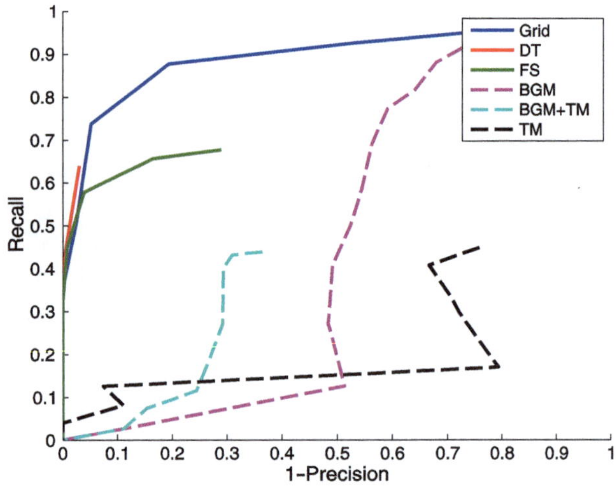

Fig. 13.15 Precision-recall curves for Classifier Grids, simple baselines, and state-of-the-art methods for the *Corridor Sequence*

a main challenge of an online system that is learning 24 hours a day and 7 days a week is to guarantee the stability over time. Therefore, we demonstrate the long-term behavior of the Classifier Grid method by running it for a whole week. In fact, during a period of 7 days we updated our system 580,000 times (i.e., 1 fps). To show that the systems' performance is unchanged over time we provide the evaluations results on four different points in time. Each of these sequences consists of 2,500 frames, corresponding to approx. 40 minutes of video data. The details of the experimental setup are summarized in Table 13.2.

From the results shown in Fig. 13.17, it can be seen that the method is stable over time. The slightly variations in the curves can be explained by the different levels of complexity for the four sequences (i.e., number of persons, density of persons, etc.). These results are in particular of interest considering the significantly changing conditions we had to deal with during these 7 days (i.e., natural light, artificial lighting, inadequate lighting, etc.), as also illustrated in Fig. 13.18. Hence, these drastically changing conditions, which can be handled by our system considerable better than by other methods, clearly show the requirement of an adaptive system.

13.5.2.3 IMIL Grids

After we demonstrated the long-term stability of Classifier Grids, we address short-time drifting if an object might not move for a longer period of time. This problem is illustrated in Fig. 13.19(a).

Thus, in the following we demonstrate that this problem can be alleviated by using the extension introduced in Sect. 13.4.2. For that purpose, we generated two test sequences containing also non-moving objects, *Corridor-Standing* and *Vehicle-Standing*, and compared the IMIL to the standard Classifier Grid approach. The first sequence showing a corridor in a public building consists of 900 frames (640×480)

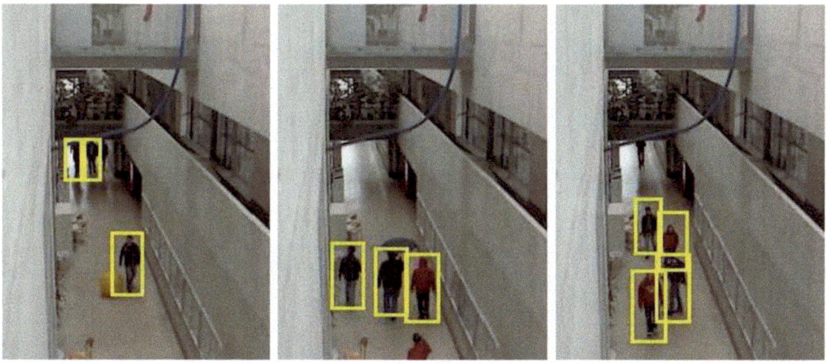

Fig. 13.16 Illustrative detection results of the grid-based person detector for the *Corridor Sequence*

Table 13.2 Description of the selected sequences of the long-term experiment

	# updates yet performed	# persons
1st day	3,390	201
3rd day	179,412	222
6th day	484,891	454
7th day	577,500	316

Fig. 13.17 Recall-precision curves for the *long-term experiment* at different points in time

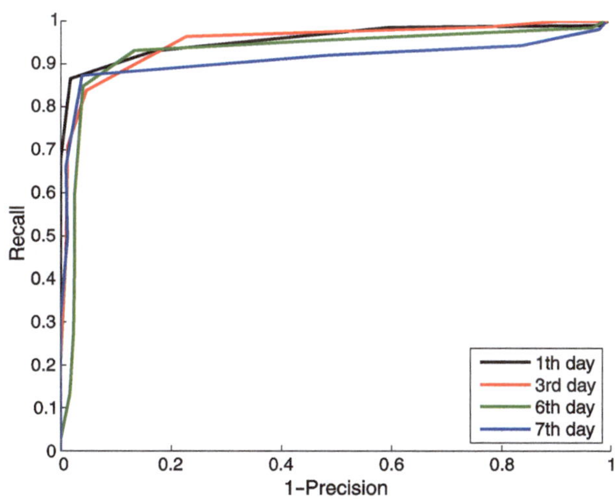

containing 2491 persons, which are staying at the same position over a long period of time. The second one consists of 500 frames (720 × 576), containing 2375 cars. One car broke down within this sequence and is standing at the same position for 400 frames. The obtained recall-precision curves, again for the proposed and the original CG approach, are shown in Fig. 13.20.

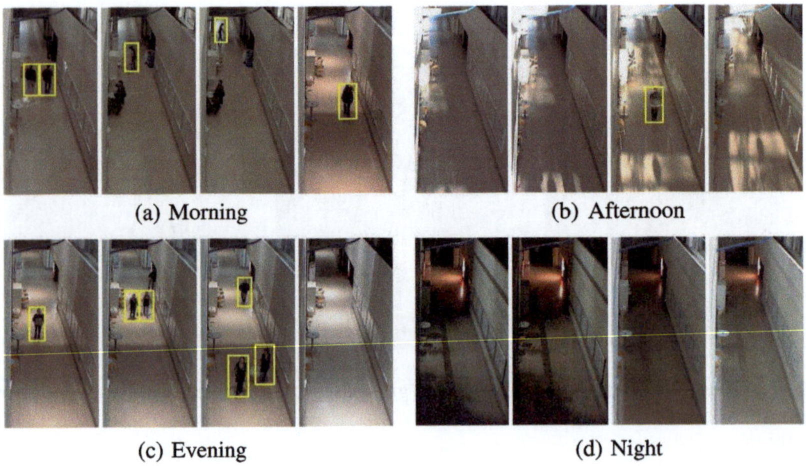

Fig. 13.18 Illustrative detection results of the grid-based person detector obtained during to long-term experiment showing the difficulties over time

Since due to the IMIL formulation we get rid of short-term-drifting for both scenarios, the recall (at a reasonable precision level) can be significantly improved. This is also illustrated in Fig. 13.19, where the first row shows detection results of the original Classifier Grid approach, whereas the second row shows detection results using the proposed inverse multiple-instance learning. It can clearly be seen that the person on the right side, standing at the same position over 175 frames, is detected by the proposed approach whereas it is not in the other case.

13.5.2.4 Classifier Co-grids

Up to now the goal was to establish an efficient, robust object detector, ensuring both, short- and long-time stability. However, in this way we can only guarantee that the accuracy is preserved, but no new (positive) information can be gained. Thus, in the following we show that using the update scheme introduced in Sect. 13.4.3 also the recall can be increased at the same accuracy level.

We evaluated our approach on two publicly available standard benchmark datasets for pedestrian detection, i.e., *PETS 2006*,[2] and for car detection, that is, *AVSS 2007*.[3] The PETS 2006 dataset shows the concourse of a train station from four different views, having a resolution of 720×576. For our experiments we adapted a sequence from Camera view 4 consisting of 308 frames, which contains 1714 persons. The AVSS 2007 dataset is adopted from the i-LIDS Bag and Vehicle Detection Challenge (AVSS 2007). In particular, we run our approach

[2]http://www.cvg.rdg.ac.uk/PETS2006/ (November 30, 2012).

[3]http://www.eecs.qmul.ac.uk/~andrea/avss2007_d.html (November 30, 2012).

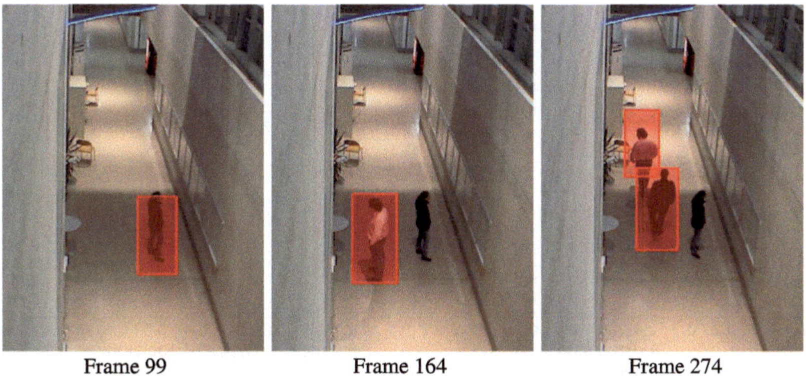

(a) Classifier Grid.

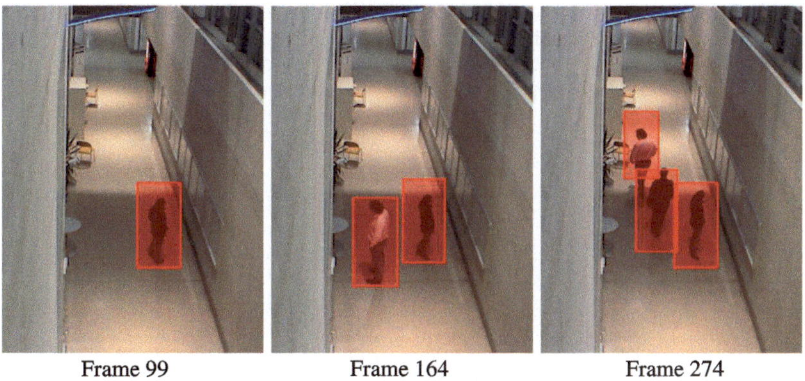

(b) IMIL Grid.

Fig. 13.19 Temporal information incorporation by MIL avoids short-term drifting. The original Classifier Grid approach (*first row*) temporary drifts after about 60 frames whereas the proposed approach (*second row*) avoids temporal drifting even after more than 170 frames

on the first 500 frames (720 × 576 pixels) from the sequence AVSS_PV_Hard, which contains 673 cars. For both approaches, we also generated a corresponding groundtruth.

The estimated recall-precision curves are shown in Fig. 13.21. For the PETS scenario, it can be seen that additionally using object-specific information significantly increases (by 0.3), whereas there is only a little gain for the AVSS 2007 sequence (by 0.1). However, for both scenarios, as indented, the precision is preserved. The different amount of performance gain can be simple described by the nature of the tasks, showing significantly different variability within the positive class. Whereas persons can have a different appearance (frontal, back, or side views), having a stationary camera the cars are mainly shown from frontal and back views. Thus, also the baseline for the car detector is much better. Nevertheless, these experiments show that including scene-specific data is highly beneficial for the given tasks.

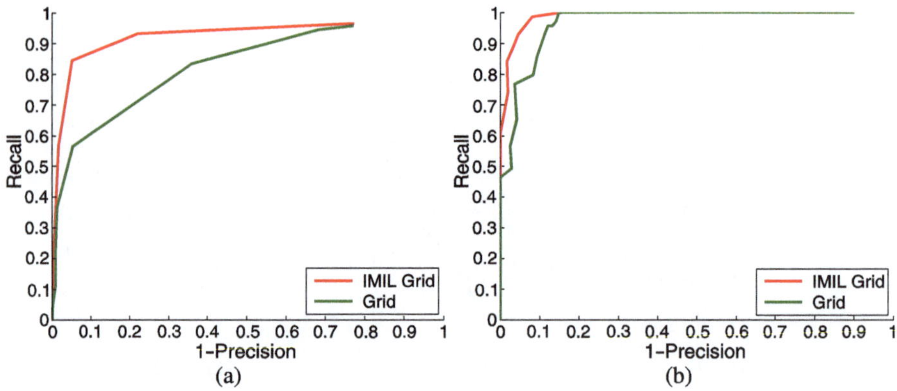

Fig. 13.20 Recall-precision Curves for (**a**) *Corridor-Standing* and (**b**) *Vehicle-Standing* sequences for the original Classifier Grid and the IMIL Grid approach

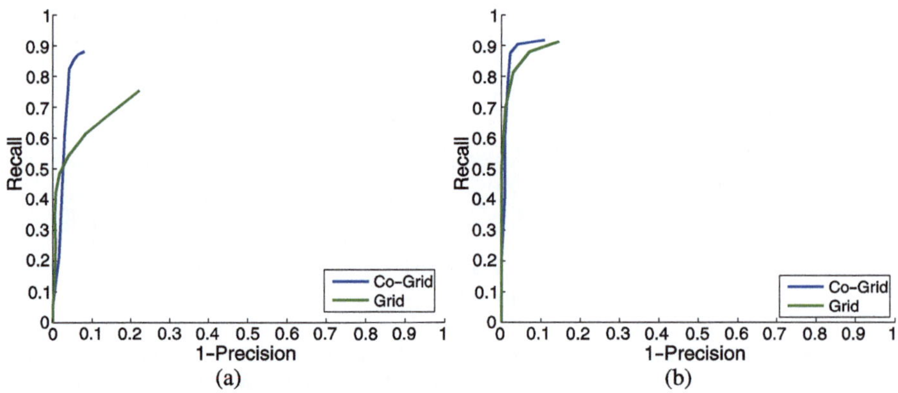

Fig. 13.21 Increasing recall by using classifier co-grids: (**a**) *PETS 2006* and (**b**) *AVSS 2007*

13.5.3 Person Detection

Finally, after analyzing both, the scene specific and the grid approach, in detail, we would like to give a more general evaluation for the task of person detection.[4] Please note, the main emphasis of this experiment is to illustrate that using the proposed online learning strategies competitive detectors can be trained even if only a very limited amount of training data is available and not to learn a perfect person detector. In fact, the approaches are more general and can be also applied for different objects. For a more detailed study on person detection, we would refer to [9].

[4]This particular task was chosen as implementations of existing approaches as well as a number of benchmark datasets are publicly available.

Table 13.3 Person detection results for the *Corridor Sequence*

	Recall	Precision	F-measure
Cons. Learning	0.84	0.94	0.89
Class. Grids	0.88	0.83	0.85
Dalal and Triggs	0.63	0.97	0.76
Viola & Jones	0.00	0.00	0.00
Felzenszwalb et al.	0.61	0.83	0.70

In particular, we give a comparison to the approaches of Dalal and Triggs [7], Viola and Jones [41], and the deformable parts model of Felzenszwalb et al. [10]. All three detectors are general person detectors, which, in contrast to Conservative Learning and the Grid Classifiers, do not use any previous knowledge about the scene. To enable a fair comparison in a post-processing step all detections were removed, that do not fit to the estimated ground-plane. In fact, a detection was removed if the scale was smaller than 50 % or greater than 150 % of the expected patch-size. This post-processing does not reduce the recall since the removed detections would have been counted as false positives otherwise. Considering the evaluation setup, the grid classifiers (standard version as introduced in Sect. 13.4.1) are updated online whereas for Conservative Learning an independent test sequence was used to train a classifier, which is kept fixed later on.

Corridor Sequence Before showing results on publicly available datasets, we first show results for the Corridor Sequence introduced in Sect. 13.5.2.1. This sequence is in particular of interest since a lot of other objects are moving within the scene and there are severe occlusions due to the limited space. Both are typical problems making online learning much more difficult. The corresponding results are given in Table 13.3, which reveal that under the given difficulties the approaches additionally exploiting scene information yield a significantly better recall, that is, plus 0.25 (!), at a comparable or even better precision level.

Caviar Next, we run experiments on the *Caviar* dataset[5] showing a corridor in a shopping mall, taken at a resolution of 384 × 288. For our experiments, we have selected one typical (more complex) sequence for evaluation (*ShopAssistant2cor*). The frame-rate of the original sequence was reduced and the images were converted to gray-scale. In total, the test sequence consists of 144 frames and contains 364 person. The provided ground-truth, which also contains partial persons (hands, head, etc.), was adapted such that only persons are included, that are detectable. For training, the Conservative Learning classifier additionally a training sequence of 1200 frames was used, that was compiled from different sequences.

The estimated characteristics are summarized in Table 13.4. Again we can recognize the same trend that Conservative Learning and Classifier Grids yield a sig-

[5]http://homepages.inf.ed.ac.uk/rbf/CAVIARDATA1 (November 30, 2012).

Table 13.4 Person detection results for the *Caviar* dataset

	Recall	Precision	F-measure
Cons. Learning	0.81	0.92	0.86
Class. Grids	0.76	0.88	0.82
Dalal & Triggs	0.42	0.98	0.59
Viola & Jones	0.32	0.85	0.46
Felzenszwalb et al.	0.55	0.93	0.69

Table 13.5 Person detection results—*PETS 2006* dataset, Camera 4

	Recall	Precision	F-measure
Cons. Learning	0.79	0.94	0.86
Class. Grids	0.78	0.78	0.78
Dalal & Triggs	0.43	0.95	0.60
Viola & Jones	0.16	0.91	0.28
Felzenszwalb et al.	0.73	0.86	0.79

nificantly higher recall (plus 0.20–0.50) compared to the generic classifiers. Representative detection results of our approaches are shown in Fig. 13.22.

PETS 2006 Finally, the last experiment was run on the PETS 2006 dataset, already introduced in detail in Sect. 13.5.2.4. Again, for Conservative Learning additionally a training sequence consisting of 650 frames was generated. From Table 13.5, we can recognize the same trend as for the previous two experiments, however, in this case the approach of Felzenszwalb et al. also yields results comparable to the approaches exploiting scene-specific information. Nevertheless, from these different setups we can clearly conclude that additionally exploiting scene information can help to (significantly) improve the detection performance. Again, illustrative detection results for our approaches are shown in Fig. 13.23.

13.6 Conclusion

In this chapter, we addressed the problem of scene-specific object detection. In particular, by exploiting the fact that many object detection scenarios build on stationary cameras we can drastically ease the task for two main reasons: (a) the complexity of the task is reduced (b) an online classifier can be used and not all variability over time has to be captured. Both allow for using less complex and thus more efficient classifiers. Moreover, also the detection performance can be improved. In particular, we introduced two approaches working on a different scale: Conservative Learning—working on frame level and Classifier Grids—working only at one specific image position.

(a) (b)

Fig. 13.22 Person detection results—*Caviar* dataset

(a) (b)

Fig. 13.23 Person detection results—*PETS 2006* dataset, Camera 4

The main idea of Conservative Learning is to adopt active learning for the task of scene specific object detection. In this way, the most valuable samples are robustly identified, which allow for adapting an offline pre-trained classifier to a new scene as well as to changing environmental condition. To go one step further, Classifier Grids even further decrease the problem's complexity by reducing the problem to discriminate an object from the background on one particular position. Moreover, due to the used update strategy long-term stability can be assured, which is highly beneficial for real-world applications. Additionally, two extensions were discussed that allow fir including further positive information and for further increasing the robustness.

The experimental results show both, a proof-of-concept and competitive results compared to state-of-the-art methods in the field of person and car detection. However, the approaches are quite general and can also be applied for different tasks. Even though not limited to this specific learner, both approaches build on online GradientBoost. In fact, the approach is very efficient and can easily be adapted for different task as the actually used loss function can be defined according to the problems requirements. Future work would include the usage of more efficient and more sophisticated features and to adopt successful developments in the context of Classifier Grids also for Conservative Learning.

Acknowledgements The work was supported by the Austrian Science Foundation (FWF) project Advanced Learning for Tracking and Detection in Medical Workflow Analysis (I535-N23) and by the Austrian Research Promotion Agency (FFG) projects SHARE (831717) in the IV2Splus program and MobiTrick (8258408) in the FIT-IT program.

References

1. Abney S (2002) Bootstrapping. In: Proc annual meeting of the association for computational linguistics, pp 360–367
2. Agarwal S, Awan A, Roth D (2004) Learning to detect objects in images via a sparse, part-based representation. IEEE Trans Pattern Anal Mach Intell 26(11):1475–1490
3. Andrews S, Tsochantaridis I, Hofmann T (2003) Support vector machines for multiple-instance learning. In: Advances in neural information processing systems, pp 561–568
4. Babenko B, Yang M-H, Belongie S (2009) Visual tracking with online mulitple instance learning. In: Proc IEEE conf on computer vision and pattern recognition
5. Balcan M-F, Blum A, Yang K (2004) Co-training and expansion: towards bridging theory and practice. In: Advances in neural information processing systems, pp 89–96
6. Blum A, Mitchell T (1998) Combining labeled and unlabeled data with co-training
7. Dalal N, Triggs B (2005) Histograms of oriented gradients for human detection. In: Proc IEEE conf on computer vision and pattern recognition
8. Dietterich TG, Lathrop RH, Lozano-Pérez T (1997) Solving the multiple instance problem with axis-parallel rectangles. Artif Intell 89(1–2):31–71
9. Dollár P, Wojek C, Schiele B, Perona P (2011) Pedestrian detection: an evaluation of the state of the art. IEEE Trans Pattern Anal Mach Intell 34(4):743–761
10. Felzenszwalb P, McAllester D, Ramanan D (2008) A discriminatively trained, multiscale, deformable part model. In: Proc IEEE conf on computer vision and pattern recognition
11. Freund Y, Schapire RE (1995) A decision-theoretic generalization of on-line learning and an application to boosting. In: Proc European conf on computational learning theory, pp 23–37
12. Freund Y, Schapire RE (1997) A decision-theoretic generalization of on-line learning and an application to boosting. J Comput Syst Sci 55:119–139
13. Friedman J (2001) Greedy function approximation: a gradient boosting machine. Ann Stat 29(5):1189–1232
14. Friedman J, Hastie T, Tibshirani R (2000) Additive logistic regression: a statistical view of boosting. Ann Stat 28(2):337–374
15. Goldberg AB, Li M, Zhu X (2008) Online manifold regularization: a new learning setting and empirical study. In: Proc European conf on machine learning and knowledge discovery in databases, vol I, pp 393–407
16. Grabner H, Bischof H (2006) On-line boosting and vision. In: Proc IEEE conf on computer vision and pattern recognition
17. Grabner H, Roth PM, Bischof H (2007) Is pedestrian detection really a hard task? In: Proc IEEE workshop on performance evaluation of tracking and surveillance
18. Hoiem D, Efros AA, Hebert M (2006) Putting objects in perspective. In: Proc IEEE conf on computer vision and pattern recognition
19. Javed O, Ali S, Shah M (2005) Online detection and classification of moving objects using progressively improving detectors. In: Proc IEEE conf on computer vision and pattern recognition
20. Leibe B, Leonardis A, Schiele B (2008) Robust object detection with interleaved categorization and segmentation. Int J Comput Vis 77(1–3):259–289

21. Leistner C, Amir R, Saffari AA, Roth PM, Bischof H (2009) On robustness of on-line boosting—a competitive study. In: Proc IEEE on-line learning for computer vision workshop
22. Levin A, Viola P, Freund Y (2003) Unsupervised improvement of visual detectors using co-training. In: Proc IEEE int'l conf on computer vision
23. Li M, Sethi IK (2006) Confidence-based active learning. IEEE Trans Pattern Anal Mach Intell 28(8):1251–1261
24. Li L-J, Wang G, Fei-Fei L (2007) Optimol: automatic online picture collection via incremental model learning. In: Proc IEEE conf on computer vision and pattern recognition
25. Liu R, Cheng J, Lu H (2009) A robust boosting tracker with minimum error bound in a co-training framework. In: Proc IEEE int'l conf on computer vision
26. Mason L, Baxter J, Bartlett P, Frean M (1999) Functional gradient techniques for combining hypotheses. In: Advances in large margin classifiers. MIT Press, Cambridge, pp 221–247
27. McFarlane NJB, Schofield CP (1995) Segmentation and tracking of piglets. Mach Vis Appl 8(3):187–193
28. Nair V, Clark JJ (2004) An unsupervised, online learning framework for moving object detection. In: Proc IEEE conf on computer vision and pattern recognition
29. Park J-H, Choi Y-K (1996) On-line learning for active pattern recognition. IEEE Signal Process Lett 3(11):301–303
30. Rosenberg C, Hebert M, Schneiderman H (2005) Semi-supervised self-training of object detection models. In: IEEE workshop on applications of computer vision
31. Roth PM, Bischof H (2008) Conservative learning for object detectors. Machine learning techniques for multimedia. Springer, Berlin
32. Roth PM, Sternig S, Grabner H, Bischof H (2009) Classifier grids for robust adaptive object detection. In: Proc IEEE conf on computer vision and pattern recognition
33. Schapire RE (1990) The strength of weak learnability. Mach Learn 5(2):197–227
34. Schapire RE, Singer Y (2000) Boostexter: a boosting-based system for text categorization. Mach Learn 39(2/3):135–168
35. Skočaj D, Leonardis A (2008) Incremental and robust learning of subspace representations. Image Vis Comput 26(1):27–38
36. Sternig S, Godec M, Roth PM, Bischof H (2010) TransientBoost: on-line boosting with transient data. In: Proc IEEE online learning for computer vision workshop (in conj CVPR)
37. Sternig S, Roth PM, Bischof H (2012) On-line inverse multiple instance boosting for classifier grids. Pattern Recognit Lett 33(1):890–897
38. Tieu K, Viola P (2000) Boosting image retrieval. In: Proc IEEE conf on computer vision and pattern recognition, vol I, pp 228–235
39. Turtinen M, Pietikänien M (2005) Labeling of textured data with co-training and active learning. In: Proc workshop on texture analysis and synthesis, pp 137–142
40. Vapnik VN (1995) The nature of statistical learning theory. Springer, New York
41. Viola P, Jones MJ (2001) Rapid object detection using a boosted cascade of simple features. In: Proc IEEE conf on computer vision and pattern recognition
42. Viola P, Jones MJ, Snow D (2003) Detecting pedestrians using patterns of motion and appearance. In: Proc IEEE int'l conf on computer vision
43. Viola P, Platt JC, Zhang C (2005) Multiple instance boosting for object detection. In: Advances in neural information processing systems
44. Wei W, Zhou Z-H (2007) Analyzing co-training style algorithms. In: Proc European conf on machine learning, pp 454–465
45. Wu B, Nevatia R (2005) Detection of multiple, partially occluded humans in a single image by Bayesian combination of edgelet part detectors. In: Proc IEEE int'l conf on computer vision
46. Wu B, Nevatia R (2007) Improving part based object detection by unsupervised, online boosting. In: Proc IEEE conf on computer vision and pattern recognition
47. Yan R, Yang J, Hauptmann A (2003) Automatically labeling video data using multi-class active learning. In: Proc IEEE int'l conf on computer vision, vol I, pp 516–523
48. Zhu Q, Avidan S, Cheng K-T (2005) Learning a sparse, corner-based representation for background modelling. In: Proc IEEE int'l conf on computer vision, vol I, pp 678–685

Chapter 14
Video Temporal Super-resolution Based on Self-similarity

Mihoko Shimano, Takahiro Okabe, Imari Sato, and Yoichi Sato

Abstract We introduce a method for making temporal super-resolution video from a single video by exploiting the self-similarity that exists in the spatio-temporal domain of videos. Temporal super-resolution is an inherently ill-posed problem because there are an infinite number of high temporal resolution frames that can produce the same low temporal resolution frame. The key idea in this work is exploiting self-similarity for solving this ambiguity. Self-similarity means self-similar motion blur appearances that often reappear at different temporal resolutions. Several existing methods generate plausible intermediate frames by interpolating input frames of a captured video, which has frame exposure time shorter than inter-frame period. In contrast with them, our method can increase the temporal resolution of a given video in which frame exposure time equals to inter-frame period, for instance, by resolving one frame to two frames.

14.1 Introduction

There is a great demand for video enhancement to increase temporal resolution by generating a high-frame rate video from a given video captured at low frame rate. Several methods [3, 6, 9, 10] based on temporal interpolation have been proposed

M. Shimano (✉) · T. Okabe · Y. Sato
The University of Tokyo, 4-6-1 Komaba, Meguro-ku, Tokyo 153-8505, Japan
e-mail: miho@iis.u-tokyo.ac.jp

T. Okabe
e-mail: takahiro@iis.u-tokyo.ac.jp

Y. Sato
e-mail: ysato@iis.u-tokyo.ac.jp

M. Shimano
PRESTO, Japan Science and Technology Agency, Tokyo, Japan

I. Sato
National Institute of Informatics, Tokyo, Japan
e-mail: imarik@nii.ac.jp

G.M. Farinella et al. (eds.), *Advanced Topics in Computer Vision*,
Advances in Computer Vision and Pattern Recognition,
DOI 10.1007/978-1-4471-5520-1_14,

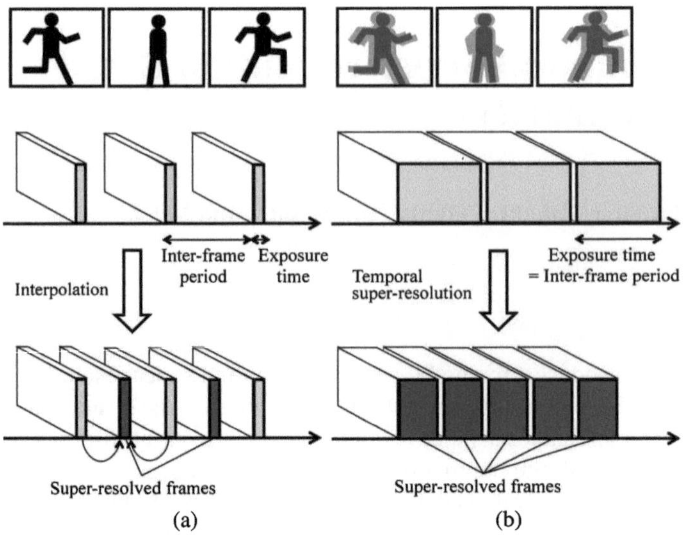

Fig. 14.1 Videos with different exposure times. (**a**) LTR video with sub-exposure time (*upper*), HTR video produced by interpolation (*lower*), (**b**) LTR video with full-exposure time (*upper*), and HTR video produced by temporal super-resolution (*lower*)

for increasing the frame rate of a given video. These techniques produce a high-frame rate video with intermediate frames generated by interpolating input frames with pixel-wise correspondences (Fig. 14.1(a)).

The quality of video largely depends on how much detailed events at different time can be resolved in relation to both the exposure time and frame rate. In a low-frame rate video recorded with *sub-exposure time*, that is, exposure time shorter than inter-frame period (Fig. 14.1(a)) discontinuous motion, called jerkiness, is often observed. On the other hand, motion blur may occur in a low-frame rate video recorded with *full-exposure time*, that is, exposure time equals to inter-frame period (Fig. 14.1(b)), due to camera shake or moving objects in a scene.

Videos often become underexposed if they are taken in sub-exposure time in those scenes like dark cloudy scenes, night scenes, and indoor scenes. To avoid images getting too dark in such cases, full-exposure time (Fig. 14.1(b)) should be selected automatically[1] or manually to capture the enough amount of light for suppressing noise. For such videos recorded with full-exposure time, the above temporal interpolation methods assuming sub-exposure time are not applicable because they cannot resolve one frame into two frames.

In this chapter, we propose a temporal super-resolution method for increasing the temporal resolution of a given video recorded with full-exposure time by resolving one frame to two frames as illustrated in Fig. 14.1(b) [15]. Temporal super-

[1]We confirmed that several consumer cameras automatically selected full-exposure mode for underexposed outdoor and indoor scenes.

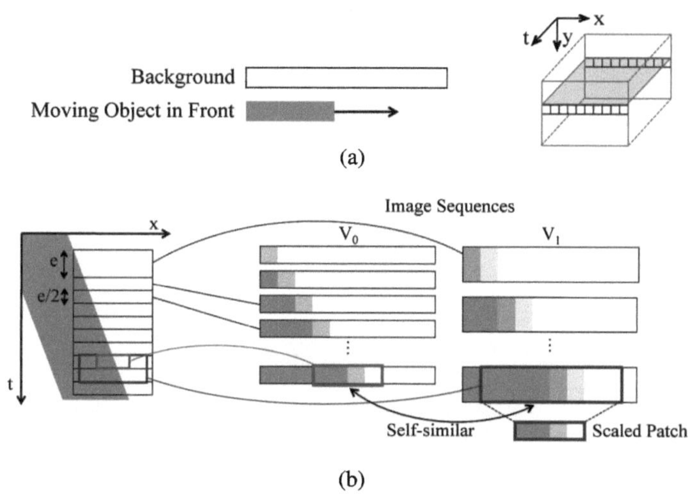

Fig. 14.2 Self-similarity. (**a**) Dynamic scene (*left*) and its continuous spatio-temporal volume of video (*right*), (**b**) x–t plane for single scan line, and 1D image sequences with different temporal resolutions

resolution is inherently ill-posed problem because there are an infinite number of high temporal resolution (HTR) frames that can produce the same low temporal resolution (LTR) frame. The key idea of this work is to exploit *self-similarity* in videos to resolve this ambiguity in creating HTR frames from LTR frames of the original video. Here, self-similarity means self-similar motion blur appearances in the spatio-temporal volume of videos with different temporal resolutions. This self-similar appearance in videos occurs because the appearance represents integrated motion of objects during each exposure time of videos with different temporal resolutions. Such self-similarity is often observed in various types of videos.

For simplicity, let us consider self-similarity in the case of 1D image sequences of a uniformly moving object (Fig. 14.2). Figure 14.2(a) shows a spatio-temporal slice of video (right) representing the dynamic scene (left). Figure 14.2(b) illustrates two image sequences, V_0 and V_1, with exposure time (= inter-frame period) $e/2$ and e. Consider, for example, a small bordered 1D image patch of V_0 with exposure time $e/2$. In a bordered 1D image patch captured with exposure time e at the same position in x–t plane, the same object moves twice the distance. If the spatial size of the bordered patch of V_1 is twice as that of the bordered patch of V_0, the bordered patch becomes similar to the corresponding bordered patch because the object moves twice the distance in the image of V_1. This self-similar relationship can be extended to a 2D-image patch (Fig. 14.3).

We exploit not only the self-similar relationship at the same position but also the relationship between different spatio-temporal positions in a video. A moving object in the scene can be recursively seen at many positions along its moving path in a spatio-temporal volume of video. It is also reported that patches in a natural still image tend to recur inside the image with different scales [8]. Due to these recurrences

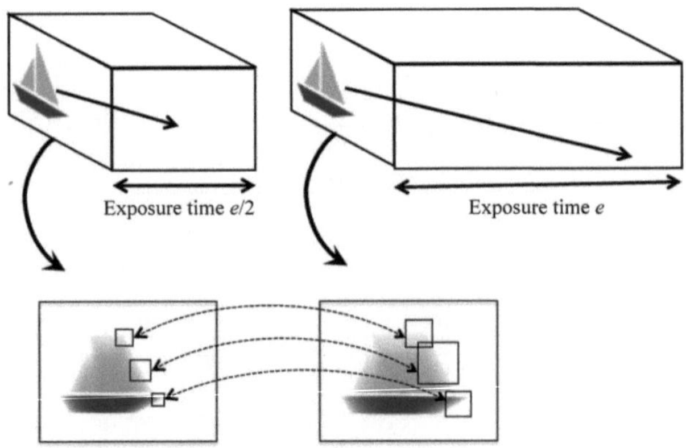

Fig. 14.3 Self-similarity in 2D image sequences. Two image sequences of a uniformly moving sailboat with exposure time (= inter-frame period) $e/2$ and e (*upper*) and their captured frames (*lower*). In the *right frame* captured with exposure time e, the same sailboat moves twice the distance. The *blurred* appearance of a small patch in the *left frame* is similar to that in the *right frame*, due to moving twice the distance in the *right frame*. Such self-similar appearance is observed in videos with different temporal resolutions

of the same and different objects, a lot of self-similar appearances between different positions can be found through a video. More thorough discussion on self-similarity will be given in Sect. 14.3.

On the basis of the self-similar appearances, we formulate the problem of temporal super-resolution as a Maximum a Posteri (MAP) estimate. Here, we use reconstruction constraints: a single frame of LTR video is equal to the average of the two corresponding frames of HTR video. Also, the following self-similar exemplar is utilized for computing a prior probability. We consider similarity at the different temporal resolutions. As shown in Fig. 14.4, consider patches in three videos of different temporal resolutions: HTR video V_0 which we try to create, the original LTR video V_1, and another video V_2 with even lower temporal resolution created by taking the average of two successive frames of V_1. If an image patch of V_2 is similar to a patch in V_1, a patch of V_0 is expected to be similar to the patch of V_1. In this way, we can create the prior probability of an HTR video V_0 from scaled self-similar exemplars of LTR video V_1.

The contribution of this work is that we propose a video temporal super-resolution method from a single image sequence by exploiting the self-similarity in the spatio-temporal domain. Such self-similarity helps us to make the unconstrained problem of temporal super-resolution tractable, while avoiding the explicit motion estimations required for the previous methods. The probabilistic model that reflects both reconstruction constraints and a self-similar prior can yield an HTR sequence, which is consistent with the input LTR sequence.

The rest of this chapter is organized as follows. We briefly summarize related work in Sect. 14.2. We analyze self-similarity in videos with different temporal resolutions in Sect. 14.3. Our temporal super-resolution algorithm is introduced in

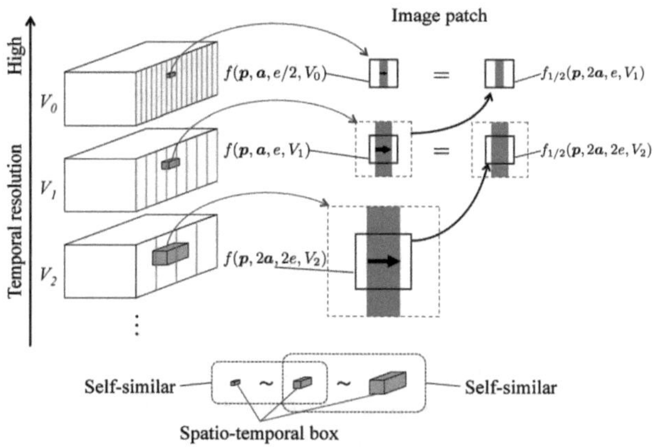

Fig. 14.4 Self-similar exemplars. Videos capture a scene where an edge is in uniform linear motion. Since the exposure time of V_2 is twice as long as that of V_1, the edge moves twice the distance in a frame of V_2. Therefore, the image patch $f(\boldsymbol{p}, \boldsymbol{a}, e, V_1)$ and the image patch $f(\boldsymbol{p}, 2\boldsymbol{a}, 2e, V_2)$ are similar. In other words, $f(\boldsymbol{p}, \boldsymbol{a}, e, V_1)$ is equal to $f_{1/2}(\boldsymbol{p}, 2\boldsymbol{a}, 2e, V_2)$ which can be synthesized from $f(\boldsymbol{p}, 2\boldsymbol{a}, 2e, V_2)$ by scaling the spatial size by $1/2$

Sect. 14.4. This method is validated in our experiments in comparison to the related work in Sect. 14.5. Some applications of our temporal super-resolution techniques are introduced in Sect. 14.6, and concluding remarks are given in Sect. 14.7.

14.2 Related Work

One approach to increasing temporal resolution is frame rate conversion based on temporal interpolation from a single video. It is known that several existing methods have serious limitations, frame repetition suffers from jerky object motion as well as linear interpolation of successive frames enlarges blurred areas because of improperly mixed pixels of different objects. To cope with those problems, a number of methods based on motion compensation have been proposed [3, 6, 9, 10]. For these methods based on motion compensation, motion vectors such as optical flows are commonly used to blend corresponding blocks or pixels. Recently, Mahajan et al. [11] proposed an interpolation method in a gradient domain to get rid of annoying effects such as ghost, blur, and block artifacts caused by errors in motion vectors. These methods achieve good results for videos with sub-exposure times as shown in Fig. 14.1(a), but are not suitable for videos with full-exposure time as shown in Fig. 14.1(b) because establishing dense correspondence is not always possible due to motion blur. Our method has a distinct advantage over those interpolation-based approaches because dense motion estimation is not required.

Another approach to increasing the temporal resolution or deblurring is to use multiple image sequences. Ben-Ezra and Nayar [4] and Tai et al. [18] proposed the use of a hybrid camera system to capture a sequence of low spatial resolution images at high frame rate and a sequence of high spatial resolution images at low frame rate. They estimate motion blur kernels from the former sequence and deblur the latter one. Watanabe et al. [19] proposed a method for combining two captured image sequences in the wavelet domain. Some methods used multiple image sequences that were simultaneously captured by co-located cameras with overlapping exposure times for both spatial and temporal super-resolution [1, 14]. The use of multiple sequences can significantly enhance the resolution of a video. In contrast to methods that use multiple input image sequences captured simultaneously or by using special hardware, our method uses only a single input image sequence for temporal super-resolution by exploiting a self-similar appearance in video. In the context of spatial super-resolution, Glasner et al. [8] reported that natural images have self-similar textures, that is, patches in a natural image tend to redundantly recur many times inside the image, both within the same scale as well as across different scales. On the basis of this observation, they propose a method for spatial super-resolution from a single image. Unlike this spatial super-resolution method using self-similarity in a still image, we focus on self-similarity in video for the first time to increase temporal resolution and can handle the dynamics of the scene. A recent work for a spatial and temporal super-resolution has been proposed [13] that combines the spatial super-resolution method [8] and the temporal super-resolution method [15]. In their method, the motion aliasing has been also resolved by accounting for sub-frame alignments.

In summary, we propose a method for temporal super-resolution from a single input image sequence with full-exposure time by introducing the self-similarity observed in the spatio-temporal domain. Unlike the frame rate conversion approach based on temporal interpolation, our method does not need dense motion estimation. Furthermore, unlike the approach using multiple image sequences, our method does not require multiple image sequences captured simultaneously or the use of special hardware.

14.3 Self-similarity

Here, we explain self-similarity in video in more detail, including the necessary conditions under which self-similarity is observed.

14.3.1 Definition

Let us consider an input video V_1 captured with an exposure time e and construct a video V_2 with an exposure time $2e$ by averaging two adjacent image frames of V_1.[2] In the same manner, we recursively construct a video V_k with an exposure time

[2]We assume that the gain of V_2 is half the gain of V_1. Therefore, an image frame of V_2 is equal to the average of the two corresponding image frames of V_1 rather than their sum.

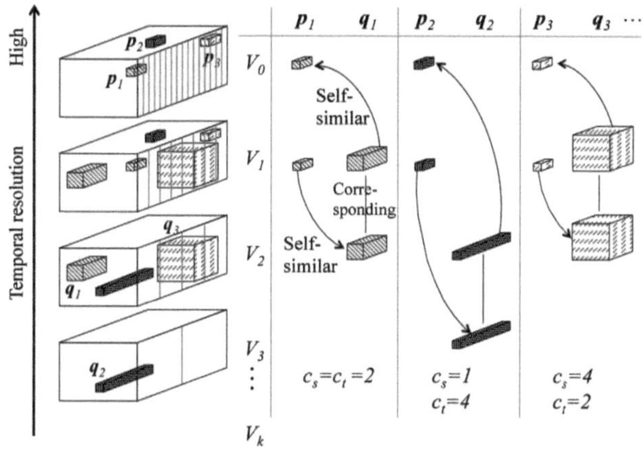

Fig. 14.5 Examples of self-similarity. The self-similar relationship can be observed in the videos with different temporal resolutions. If a spatio-temporal box in V_1 at $\boldsymbol{p_i}$ is similar to a spatio-temporal box in V_2 at $\boldsymbol{q_j}$, a spatio-temporal box in V_0 at $\boldsymbol{p_i}$ is expected to be similar to the corresponding spatio-temporal box in V_1 at $\boldsymbol{q_j}$. Namely, if spatio-temporal boxes with low temporal resolutions are similar, the corresponding spatio-temporal boxes with high temporal resolutions are similar

$2^{k-1}e$ from a video V_{k-1}. Self-similarity is a similarity structure observed among videos with different exposure times constructed from a single input video V_1.

For the sake of simplicity, let us begin with a video V_1 capturing a scene where an edge with an infinite length is in uniform linear motion as shown in Fig. 14.4. We denote a small image patch in V_1 as $f(\boldsymbol{p}, \boldsymbol{a}, e, V_1)$, where $\boldsymbol{p} = (x, y, t)^T$ is the space-time coordinates of the center, $\boldsymbol{a} = (a_x, a_y)$ is the spatial size, and e is the exposure time. Similarly, we denote a small image patch in V_2 as $f(\boldsymbol{p}, \boldsymbol{a}, 2e, V_2)$, and so on. Since the exposure time of V_2 is twice as long as that of V_1, the edge moves twice the distance in a single image frame of V_2. Therefore, the image patch $f(\boldsymbol{p}, \boldsymbol{a}, e, V_1)$ and the image patch $f(\boldsymbol{p}, 2\boldsymbol{a}, 2e, V_2)$ are similar. In other words, $f(\boldsymbol{p}, \boldsymbol{a}, e, V_1)$ is equal to $f_{1/2}(\boldsymbol{p}, 2\boldsymbol{a}, 2e, V_2)$ which can be synthesized from $f(\boldsymbol{p}, 2\boldsymbol{a}, 2e, V_2)$ by scaling the spatial size by 1/2. In the same manner, $f(\boldsymbol{p}, \boldsymbol{a}, e, V_1)$ is equal to $f_{1/4}(\boldsymbol{p}, 4\boldsymbol{a}, 4e, V_3)$, and so on.

Generally, image patches $f(\boldsymbol{p}, \boldsymbol{a}, e, V_1)$ and $f(\boldsymbol{q}, c_s\boldsymbol{a}, c_t e, V_k)$ where $c_t = 2^{k-1}$ are self-similar, if there is a pair of scalars c_s and c_t such that $f(\boldsymbol{p}, \boldsymbol{a}, e, V_1) = f_{1/c_s}(\boldsymbol{q}, c_s\boldsymbol{a}, c_t e, V_k)$. Note that the self-similarity could be observed between image patches at different space-time coordinates as illustrated in Fig. 14.5.

14.3.2 Necessary Conditions

As defined in the previous section, self-similarity among videos with different exposure times requires similarities in both the spatial and temporal domains. For the spatial domain, self-similarity requires that small image patches appear similar when one changes the spatial scale according to the given temporal scale. For some families of images, as Glasner et al. [8] reported, patches in a natural image tend to redundantly recur many times inside the image, both within the same scale as well as across different scales. In addition, since we deal with small patches instead of the entire image, a small patch containing an edge longer than the spatial size of the patch, for example, is considered to be primitives and be invariant to the scale change.

For the temporal domain, self-similarity requires that the motions observed in small patches are similar when one changes the temporal scale in accordance with the given spatial scale. This is exactly true for objects in uniform linear motion (e.g., $c_s = 2$ and $c_t = 2$) and in uniformly-accelerated motion (e.g., $c_s = 4$ and $c_t = 2$) (Fig. 14.5). In addition, since we deal with images captured during the exposure time, that is, a short period of time, the velocity of an object of interest is often considered to be constant. As a result, the behavior of the object such as a complex non-linear motion can often be approximated by uniform linear motion, and then various motions in small patches are similar each other.

Since multiple consecutive patches in a spatio-temporal box are self-similar to those in the corresponding spatio-temporal box, the self-similar relationship can be extended to the self-similar relationship between the spatio-temporal boxes including multiple consecutive patches. Therefore, whereas the spatio-temporal box in Fig. 14.4 or Fig. 14.5 represents an image patch for a simplified notion in the above examples, it can also represent consecutive small image patches. Note that we can use not only the image patches but the difference between image patches for considering self-similar relationship. In fact, multiple patches included in a spatio-temporal box and the difference between them are used in the experiment of Sect. 14.5. Furthermore, the number of the patches in the spatio-temporal box may change at each temporal-scale level. It should be noted here that whereas only two temporal-scale levels are shown in Fig. 14.5, multiple number of temporal-scale levels may be used in the consideration of self-similarity.

14.4 Temporal Super-resolution Algorithm

14.4.1 Overview

We propose an algorithm for increasing the temporal resolution of an input video twice.[3] That is, we reconstruct a video V_0 with an exposure time $e/2$ from a single input video V_1 with an exposure time e and a set of videos V_k $(k = 2, 3, 4, \ldots)$ with an exposure time $2^{k-1}e$ constructed from V_1 by averaging adjacent image frames recursively.

Since we assume that the exposure time of the input video is almost equal to the inter-frame period, a single image frame of V_1 is equal to the average of the

---

[3]The algorithm for increasing the temporal resolution more than twice can be formulated straightforwardly.

two corresponding image frames of V_0. We impose this constraint termed a *reconstruction constraint*[4] in order to decompose a single image frame of V_1 into two image frames of V_0, as described in Sect. 14.4.2. However, this decomposition is an ill-posed problem because an infinite number of combinations of image frames can satisfy the constraint.

To cope with this ill-posedness, we incorporate another constraint based on self-similarity. We take advantage of self-similar exemplars to make the ill-posed problem tractable (Sect. 14.4.3).

To this end, we formulate temporal super-resolution as a MAP estimation. Let us denote the image frame of V_k at time t as $F_k(t)$, or F_k for short. According to Bayes' law, the posterior probability $P(F_0|F_1)$ of the random variable F_0 given an observation F_1 is

$$P(F_0|F_1) = \frac{P(F_1|F_0)P(F_0)}{P(F_1)}. \tag{14.1}$$

Here, $P(F_1|F_0)$ and $P(F_0)$ are the likelihood of F_1 given F_0 and the prior probability of F_0 respectively. Since the probability $P(F_1)$ is constant, the MAP estimation of F_0 results in minimization of the negative logarithm of $P(F_1|F_0)P(F_0)$:

$$F_0^{\mathrm{MAP}} = \arg\min_{F_0}\big[-\ln P(F_1|F_0) - \ln P(F_0)\big]. \tag{14.2}$$

In the next two sections, we describe how the likelihood and the prior probability are computed from the reconstruction constraint and self-similar exemplars.

14.4.2 Likelihood Model

We compute the likelihood from the reconstruction constraint. Assuming that the pixel values of image frame $F_1(t)$ are contaminated by additive noise, the constraint is described as

$$F_1(x, y, t) = \frac{F_0(x, y, t) + F_0(x, y, t + e/2)}{2} + \eta(x, y, t). \tag{14.3}$$

Here, $F_k(x, y, t)$ is a pixel value of the image frame $F_k(t)$ at the image coordinates (x, y), and $\eta(x, y, t)$ stands for additive noise.

We assume that the additive noise obeys an i.i.d. Gaussian distribution with standard deviation σ_{like}. Accordingly, the first term of Eq. (14.2) becomes

[4]Strictly speaking, this constraint assumes a linear camera response function (CRF). However, because adjacent image frames usually have similar pixel values, it is approximately satisfied when the CRF is approximated by a piecewise-linear function. In addition, one could calibrate the CRF and convert the pixel values in advance.

$$-\ln P(F_1|F_0) = \frac{1}{2\sigma_{\text{like}}^2} \sum_{\Omega} \left[F_1(x, y, t) - \frac{F_0(x, y, t) + F_0(x, y, t + e/2)}{2} \right]^2, \tag{14.4}$$

where Ω is the image plane over which the summation is taken, and we have omitted constant terms with respect to F_0.

14.4.3 Prior Model

We compute the prior probability from self-similar exemplars in a similar manner to image hallucination [2, 7]. The self-similar exemplars are exploited on the following assumption: if an image patch $f(\boldsymbol{p}, \boldsymbol{a}, e, V_1)$ and a scaled patch $f_{1/2}(\boldsymbol{q}, 2\boldsymbol{a}, 2e, V_2)$ are similar, the corresponding patch $f(\boldsymbol{p}, \boldsymbol{a}, e/2, V_0)$ and the corresponding scaled patch $f_{1/2}(\boldsymbol{q}, 2\boldsymbol{a}, e, V_1)$ are also similar as shown in Fig. 14.4 and Fig. 14.5.

Specifically, we find an image patch $f_{1/2}(\boldsymbol{q}, 2\boldsymbol{a}, 2e, V_2)$ similar to $f(\boldsymbol{p}, \boldsymbol{a}, e, V_1)$ by approximate Nearest Neighbors [12], and consider $f_{1/2}(\boldsymbol{q}, 2\boldsymbol{a}, e, V_1)$ as a candidate for $f(\boldsymbol{p}, \boldsymbol{a}, e/2, V_0)$. The candidate image patch $\tilde{f}(\boldsymbol{p}, \boldsymbol{a}, e/2, V_0)$ is given by

$$\begin{aligned} &\tilde{f}(\boldsymbol{p}, \boldsymbol{a}, e/2, V_0) = f_{1/2}(\boldsymbol{q}, 2\boldsymbol{a}, e, V_1), \\ &\qquad \text{where } \boldsymbol{q} = \arg\min_{\boldsymbol{p}'} \left| f(\boldsymbol{p}, \boldsymbol{a}, e, V_1) - f_{1/2}(\boldsymbol{p}', 2\boldsymbol{a}, 2e, V_2) \right|. \end{aligned} \tag{14.5}$$

The difference between image patches is defined as the sum of the squared differences (SSD) of the pixel values.

Next, the candidate image patches $\tilde{f}(\boldsymbol{p}, \boldsymbol{a}, e/2, V_0)$ are concatenated into the candidate image frame $\widetilde{F}_0(t)$. Here, we assume that the deviation of F_0 from the candidate $\widetilde{F}_0$ obeys an i.i.d. Gaussian distribution with standard deviation σ_{pri}. In addition, we do not use the image frames but the difference between image frames for modeling the prior probability because it performs better experimentally. Hence, the second term of Eq. (14.2) is given by

$$-\ln P(F_0) = \frac{1}{2\sigma_{\text{pri}}^2} \sum_{\Omega, t'} \left[\Delta F_0(x, y, t') - \Delta \widetilde{F}_0(x, y, t') \right]^2, \tag{14.6}$$

where $t' = t, t + e/2$, and constant terms have been omitted.

Note that we can use more temporal-scale levels for determining a candidate image patch in Eq. (14.6).The current implementation computes the SSD between $f(\boldsymbol{p}, \boldsymbol{a}, 2e, V_2)$ and $f_{1/2}(\boldsymbol{p}', 2\boldsymbol{a}, 4e, V_3)$ in addition to the SSD between $f(\boldsymbol{p}, \boldsymbol{a}, e, V_1)$ and $f_{1/2}(\boldsymbol{p}', 2\boldsymbol{a}, 2e, V_2)$. That is, we use the videos V_k constructed from the input video V_1 up to $k = 3$.

14.4.4 Optimization

To reduce spatial noise and temporal flicker, we add a smoothness term S to Eq. (14.2). Substituting Eq. (14.4) and Eq. (14.6) into Eq. (14.2), the MAP estimation of F_0 results in

$$\begin{aligned} F_0^{\mathrm{MAP}} &= \arg\min_{F_0}\left[-\ln P(F_1|F_0) - \ln P(F_0) + S\right] \\ &= \arg\min_{F_0}\left\{\frac{1}{2\sigma_{\mathrm{like}}^2}\sum_{\Omega}\left[F_1(x,y,t) - \frac{F_0(x,y,t)+F_0(x,y,t+e/2)}{2}\right]^2\right. \\ &\quad + \frac{1}{2\sigma_{\mathrm{pri}}^2}\sum_{\Omega,t'}\left[\Delta F_0(x,y,t') - \Delta\widetilde{F}_0(x,y,t')\right]^2 \\ &\quad \left. + \lambda\sum_{\Omega,t'}\left[\sum_{\Lambda} w(x,y,t',m,n,q)L(m,n,q)F_0(x+m,y+n,t'+q)\right]^2\right\}, \end{aligned} \tag{14.7}$$

where $\Delta F_0(x,y,t') = F_0(x,y,t'+e/2) - F_0(x,y,t')$.

Our smoothness term is based on the discrete Laplacian filter $L(m,n,q)$. To preserve spatiotemporal edges, we incorporate a pixel-wise weight $w(x,y,t',m,n,q)$. It is defined as $w(x,y,t',m,n,q) = w_d(x,y,t',m,n,q)/\sum_{m',n',q'} w_d(x,y,t',m',n',q')$, where $w_d(x,y,t',m,n,q) = \exp[-(F(x,y,t) - F(x+m,y+n,t'+q))^2/2\sigma_s^2]$.

The optimization problem of Eq. (14.7) is iteratively solved according to the following steps.

1. Ignore the smoothness term in Eq. (14.7), and compute the initial estimation $F_0^{r=0}$ by using the least-squares method.
2. Compute the weight $w(x,y,t',m,n,q)$ from F_0^r, and update the estimation as F_0^{r+1} by minimizing Eq. (14.2) via least squares.
3. Repeat step 2 until the difference $|F^{r+1} - F^r|$ converges.

Usually, only a few iterations are needed for convergence.

14.5 Experimental Results

We evaluated various aspects of our approach in experiments using real videos. In Sect. 14.5.1, we compare the performance of our method with that of previously proposed temporal interpolation methods. We then clarified the importance of each component of our algorithm in Sect. 14.5.2.

We used CANON HF-20 and CASIO EX-F1 video cameras. The exposure time of the camera was set almost equal to inter-frame period. Eight kinds of videos were collected as V_0, by capturing dynamic scenes for about a few hundred frames: three videos capturing indoor scenes and five videos captured outside. The video of textured papers 1 and 2 were captured as scenes of uniform circular motion. The video of a small merry-go-round was captured as scenes with uniform linear motion as well as various other motions. Textured paper 1 included repetitions of the same texture, and textured paper 2 included several textures. The videos captured outside included various scenes such as walking people, cars, and trees. The frame images of the captured videos were converted to grayscale in all experiments. The captured videos were considered to be the ground truth high-temporal-resolution video V_0. We reconstructed V_0 from its low-temporal-resolution videos V_1, V_2, and V_3 that were provided from V_0, as mentioned in Sect. 14.3. Our algorithm used 5×5 pixel patches. We empirically set $\sigma_{\text{like}} = 1$, $\sigma_{\text{pri}} = 1.25$, $\lambda = 1.6$, and σ_s was set from 10 to 100 to adjust to the brightness of the frames. The produced grayscale videos were converted to a YUV color space as follows. We obtained the Y channel as the produced grayscale video. For the U and V channels, we used those channels of the original low temporal resolution frame of V_1 for two successive high temporal-resolution frames.

14.5.1 Comparison with Other Methods

We compared the results of our technique with those of three methods: simple frame repetition, linear interpolation, and interpolation based on optical flows [3, 5]. Linear interpolation and optical flow based interpolation generate same number of intermediate frames from input frames. The eight videos were used to examine the performance of each method on various motions.

We made a qualitative comparison of our method and the other interpolation methods. In Fig. 14.6 and Fig. 14.7, (a) shows the ground truth and (f)–(i) show the differences between the ground truth and the reconstructed frame (b)–(e) respectively by various methods ((b) frame repetition, (c) linear interpolation, (d) optical flow based interpolation, and (e) our method). As we see in Fig. 14.6(e) and Fig. 14.7(e), the visual quality of the frames recovered using our method is much better than those of the other interpolation methods. In the results obtained by optical flow based interpolation (d), the motion blur region remained or was enlarged in the interpolated frame. Motion blur likewise remained in the videos produced by frame repetition and was enlarged in the videos produced by linear interpolation. In Fig. 14.8, we show our results, zoom-ups in interesting areas, to compare to those of the input and the results obtained by optical flow based interpolation and the ground truth. In the scene of a crowded intersection with diagonal crosswalks, the moving leg (Fig. 14.8(b)) and coming and going people (Fig. 14.8(c)) in the frames produced by our method matched very closely with the ground truth. On the other hand, the optical flow based interpolation have sometimes failed (compare, e.g., the left leg in frame 3, frame 5 and frame 6 of Fig. 14.8(b) and the lower part of frame 1, frame 3 and frame 5 in Fig. 14.8(c)). Our method could also be used to generate frames to

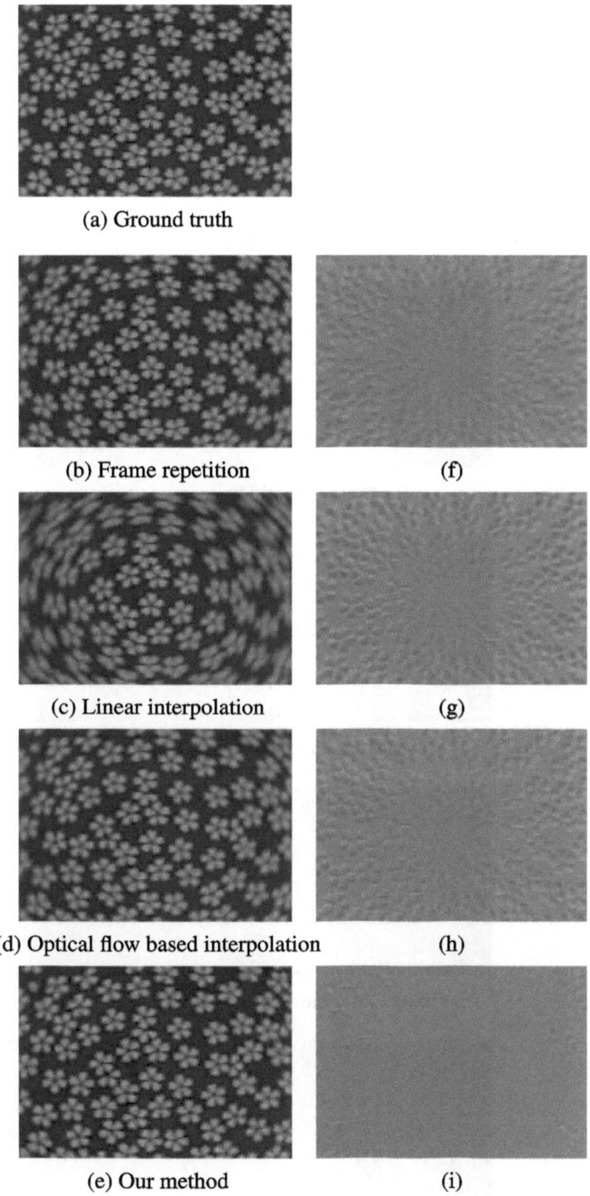

Fig. 14.6 Comparison of our method with other interpolation methods applied video in which textured paper1 rotates uniformly: (**a**) ground truth frame, frames with increased temporal resolution (**b**) frame repetition, (**c**) linear interpolation, (**d**) optical flow based interpolation, and (**e**) our method. (**f**), (**g**), (**h**), (**i**) The difference (image values are added offset 128 to the difference) between each produced frame ((**b**), (**c**), (**d**), or (**e**)) and the ground truth (**a**)

represent correctly two heads moving apart (Fig. 14.9(a)), the changing movie displayed on the big TV screen (Fig. 14.9(b)) and the shadow hovering beyond the vein of the leaf (Fig. 14.9(c)). Note that the information of the input frame was properly resolved to two frames with high temporal resolution produced by our method.

To make a quantitative comparison, we also evaluated the peak signal to noise ratio (PSNR) between the frames produced by all four temporal super-resolution

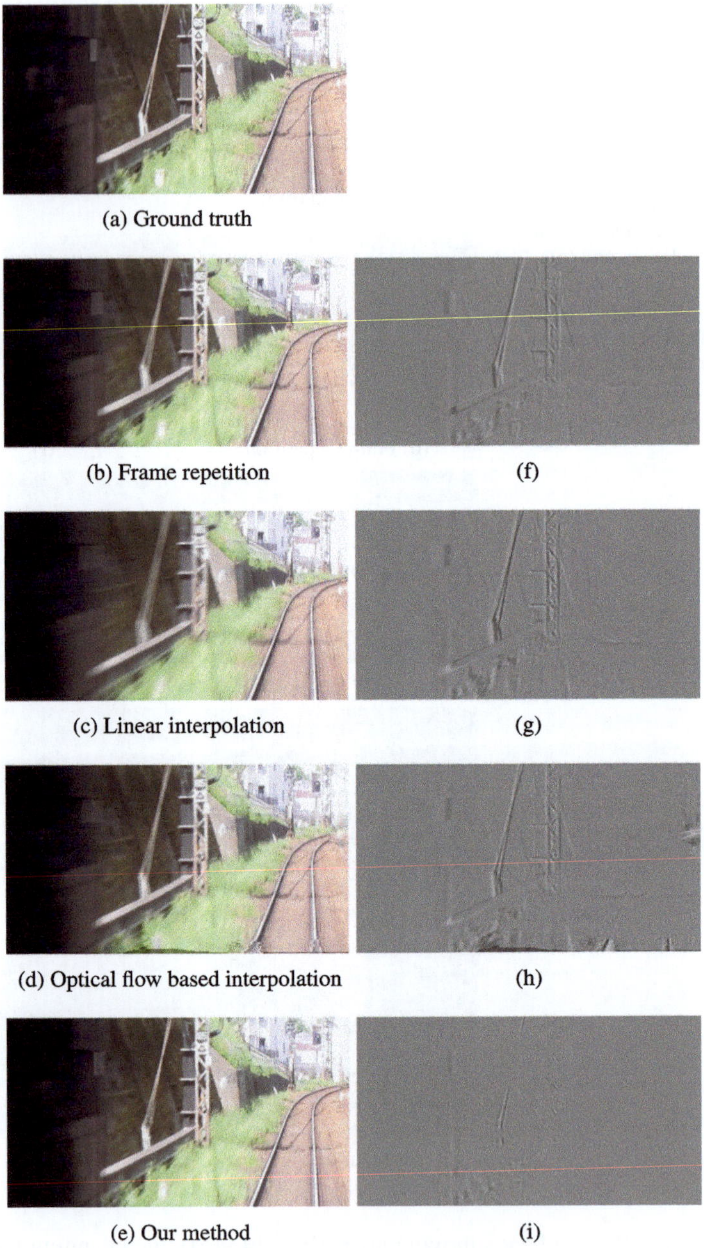

Fig. 14.7 Comparison of our method with other interpolation methods applied to video of outside1. (**a**) Ground truth frame, frames with increased temporal resolution (**b**) frame repetition, (**c**) linear interpolation, (**d**) optical flow based interpolation, and (**e**) our method. (**f**), (**g**), (**h**), (**i**) Difference (image values are added offset 128 to the difference) between each produced frame ((**b**), (**c**), (**d**), or (**e**)) and the ground truth (**a**)

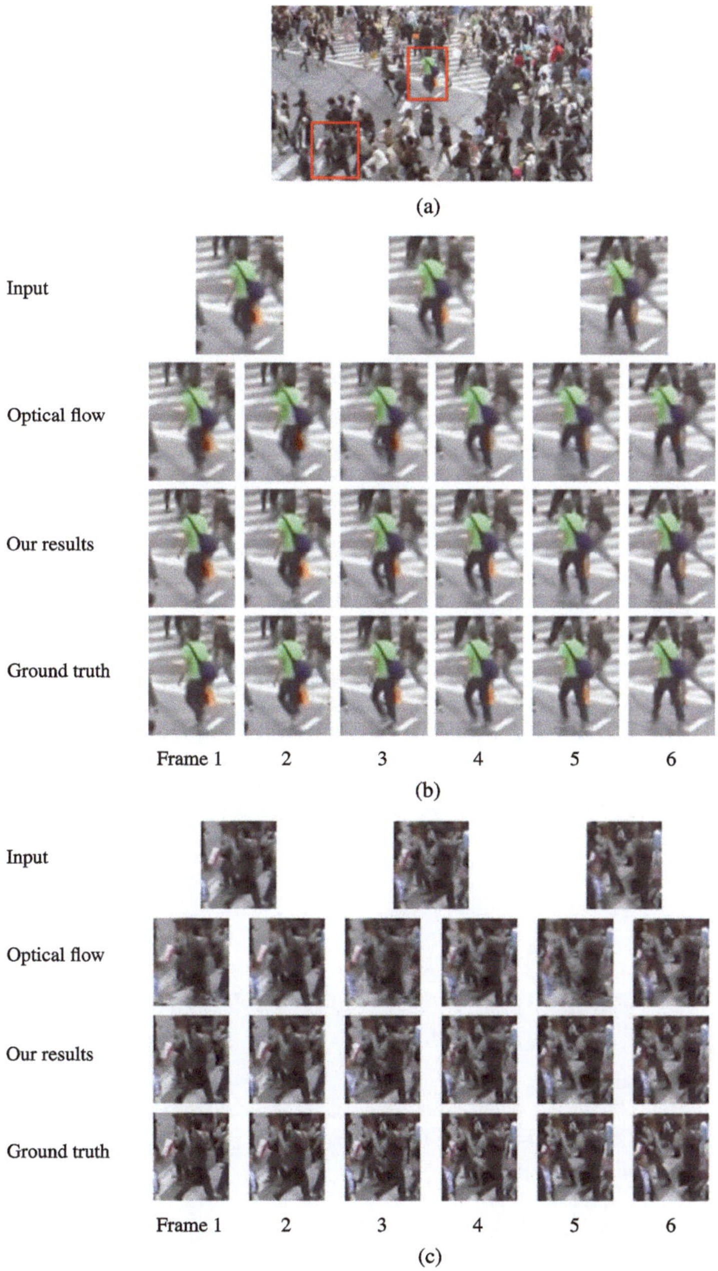

Fig. 14.8 Zoom-ups of high temporal resolution frames produced by our method applied to video of outside2. (**a**) The example input frames, (**b**), (**c**) Zoom-ups of the marked region in the input frames (*first row*), zoom-ups of the marked region in the frames produced by optical flow based interpolation method (*second row*), zoom-ups of the marked region in the frames with increased temporal resolution produced by our method (*third row*), and zoom-ups of the marked region in the ground truth frames (*fourth row*)

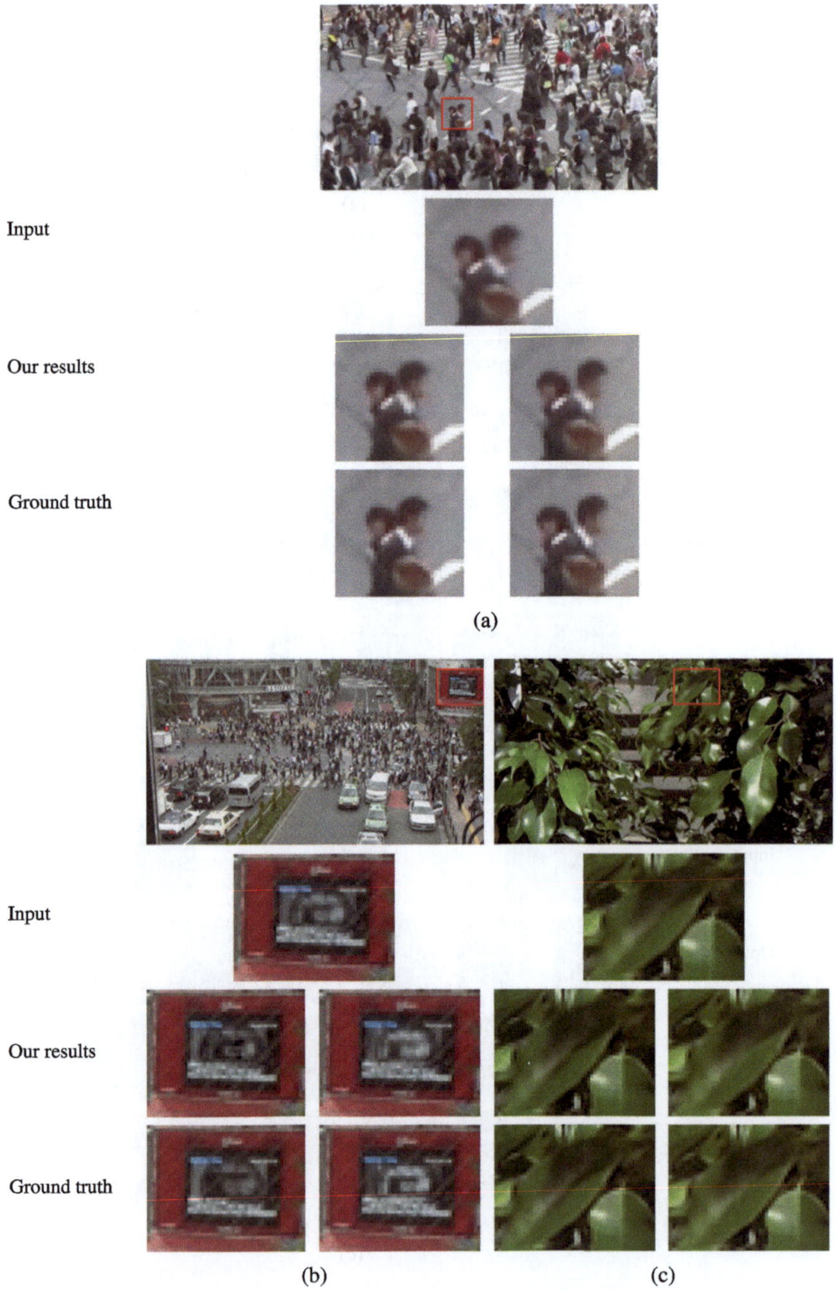

Fig. 14.9 Zoom-ups of high temporal resolution frames produced by our method applied to video of (**a**) outside2, (**b**) outside3, and (**c**) outside4. The example input frames (*first row*), zoom-ups of the marked region in the input frames (*second row*), zoom-ups of the marked region in the two frames with increased temporal resolution produced by our method (*third row*), and zoom-ups of the marked region in the two ground truth frames (*fourth row*)

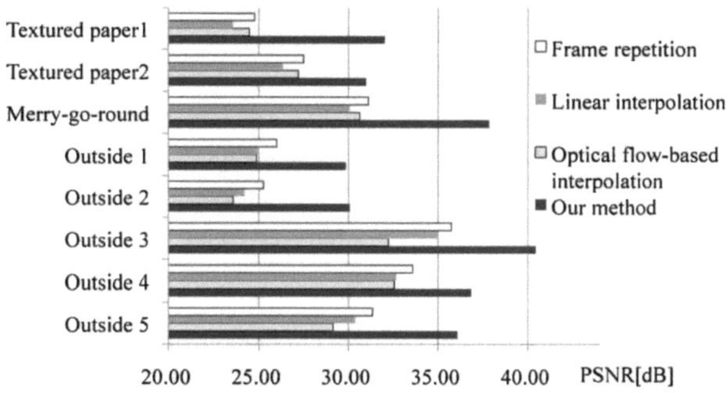

Fig. 14.10 Comparison of our method with other interpolation methods

methods and the ground truth frames. The average PSNRs of all four methods are shown in Fig. 14.10. We clearly see that our method is superior to the other methods for all videos. The optical flow based interpolation have sometimes failed to estimate the optical flows because of the input blurred frames, and these errors may have led to more ghosting and blurring artifacts than in the frame repetition or the linear interpolation video. The qualitative and quantitative comparisons indicated that our method can be effectively used for compensating circular, linear, and various other motions.

14.5.2 Evaluation of Components

We conducted experiments to evaluate the contribution of each component in our method such as reconstruction constraints, the smoothness term, the use of temporal-scale levels up to V_k, and features describing self-similar structures (images or their differences) by using 30 frames each of three captured videos, as follows.

First, we examined the effectiveness of considering multiple temporal-scale levels k of the videos. As shown in Table 14.1, cases using temporal-scale levels up to $k = 3, 4$ superior to the case using temporal-scale levels up to $k = 2$ and achieved a better PSNR. This shows that examining motion at different exposure times (V_1, V_2, and so on) is effective for revealing motion at higher frame rate.

To examine the contribution of each component, we conducted experiments by adding components incrementally. The PSNR of each case is shown in Table 14.2. Here, the quality of the produced videos is improved, as components are added. In other words, all the components play essential roles for improving the resulting image quality.

14.6 Application

The temporal super resolution techniques described in this chapter can be applied to video compression in addition to video enhancement. Some recent work has

Table 14.1 Comparison of different temporal-scale levels. Our algorithm fs results using videos V_k constructed from the input video V_1 up to $k = 4$ are compared

PSNR [dB]			
Sequence	$k=2$	$k=3$	$k=4$
Textured paper1	15.68	24.06	24.01
Textured paper2	18.60	27.45	27.40
Merry-go-round	21.77	34.34	33.19

Table 14.2 Evaluation of a variety of components. Note that use of several temporal-scale levels, image differences, reconstruction constraints, and the smoothness term are all important in our method

Case	$k=3$	Image differences	Reconstruction constraints	Smoothness term	PSNR [dB]		
					Textured paper1	Textured paper2	Merry-go-round
1	–	–	–	–	15.55	19.06	17.96
2	√	–	–	–	22.90	26.26	32.78
3	√	√	–	–	24.06	27.45	34.34
4	√	√	√	–	25.99	28.82	35.49
5	√	√	√	√	26.19	28.72	35.58

started investigating what is the most suitable representation of the video at encoder, since a temporal super resolution video has to be constructed at decoder with low complexity [16, 17]. In order to optimize the rate-distortion performance for video compression, an adaptive encoding strategy to select frames at different temporal resolutions [17] and quantization parameters (QPs) [16] has been proposed as schematically shown in Fig. 14.11. The key idea is to encode at low temporal resolution (and possibly at coarse QP) frames that can be easily synthesized via temporal super-resolution at decoder to save bits, and to encode at high temporal resolution (and possibly at fine QP) frames that are difficult to synthesize after compression to preserve quality. The selection of frames at different temporal resolutions and QPs is formulated as a shortest path problem in a directed acyclic graph (DAG) as illustrated in Fig. 14.11.

14.7 Conclusions

We introduced an approach for making temporal super resolution video from a single input image sequence. To make this ill-posed problem tractable, we focused on *self-similarity* in video which is a self-similar appearances with different temporal resolutions. Our method increases the temporal resolution by using a MAP estimation that incorporates both a prior probability computed from self-similar appearances and reconstruction constraints that is, a single frame of LTR video should

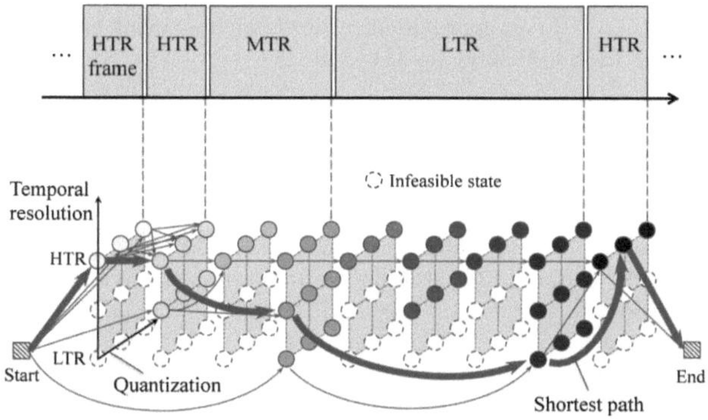

Fig. 14.11 Example of frame selection (*upper*) and a three-dimensional directed acyclic graph (DAG) representing selections of temporal resolutions and corresponding quantization parameters (QPs) for encoding of the sequence (*lower*). The video frames at appropriate temporal resolutions, i.e., HTR, middle temporal resolution (MTR) or LTR, and quantization parameters are selected for encoding by finding a shortest cost path

be equal to the average of the two corresponding frames of HTR video. The experimental results showed that our method could recover a high-quality video with increased temporal resolution, which keeps consistent with the input LTR video. We demonstrated that our approach produce results that are sharper and clearer than those of other techniques based on temporal interpolation.

References

1. Agrawal A, Gupta M, Veeraraghavan A, Narasimhan S (2010) Optimal coded sampling for temporal super-resolution. In: Proc CVPR 2010, pp 599–606
2. Baker S, Kanade T (2002) Limits on super-resolution and how to break them. IEEE Trans Pattern Anal Mach Intell 24(9):1167–1183
3. Baker S, Scharstein D, Lewis J, Roth S, Black M, Szeliski R (2007) A database and evaluation methodology for optical flow. In: Proc ICCV 2007, pp 1–8
4. Ben-Ezra M, Nayar SK (2003) Motion deblurring using hybrid imaging. In: Proc CVPR 2003, pp I-657–I-664
5. Brox T, Bruhn A, Papenberg N, Weickert J (2004) High accuracy optical flow estimation based on a theory for warping. In: Proc ECCV 2004. LNCS, vol 3024, pp 25–36
6. Choi BT, Lee SH, Ko SJ (2000) New frame rate up-conversion using bi-directional motion estimation. IEEE Trans Consum Electron 46(3):603–609
7. Freeman W, Jones T, Pasztor E (2002) Example-based super-resolution. IEEE Comput Graph Appl 22(2):56–65
8. Glasner D, Bagon S, Irani M (2009) Super-resolution from a single image. In: Pro ICCV 2009, pp 349–356
9. Ha T, Lee S, Kim J (2004) Motion compensated frame interpolation by new block-based motion estimation algorithm. IEEE Trans Consum Electron 50(2):752–759
10. Kuo T-Y, Kim J, Kuo C-CJ (1999) Motion-compensated frame interpolation scheme for H.263 codec. In: Proc ISCAS '99, pp 491–494
11. Mahajan D, Huang FC, Matusik W, Ramamoorthi R, Belhumeur P (2009) Moving gradients: a path-based method for plausible image interpolation. In: Proc SIGGRAPH'99, pp 1–11

12. Muja M, Lowe DG (2009) Fast approximate nearest neighbors with automatic algorithm configuration. In: Proc VISSAPP 2009, pp 331–340
13. Shahar O, Faktor A, Irani M (2011) Space-time super-resolution from a single video. In: Proc CVPR 2011, pp 3353–3360
14. Shechtman E, Caspi Y, Irani M (2005) Space-time super-resolution. IEEE Trans Pattern Anal Mach Intell 27(4):531–545
15. Shimano M, Okabe T, Sato I, Sato Y (2010) Video temporal super-resolution based on self-similarity. In: Proc ACCV 2010. LNCS, vol 6492, pp 93–106
16. Shimano M, Cheung G, Sato I (2011) Adaptive frame and qp selection for temporally super-resolved full-exposure-time video. In: Proc ICIP 2011, pp 2253–2256
17. Shimano M, Cheung G, Sato I (2011) Compression using self-similarity-based temporal super-resolution for full-exposure-time video. In: Proc ICASSP 2011, pp 1053–1056
18. Tai YW, Du H, Brown MS, Lin S (2008) Image/video deblurring using a hybrid camera. In: Proc CVPR 2008, pp 1–8
19. Watanabe K, Iwai Y, Nagahara H, Yachida M, Suzuki T (2006) Video synthesis with high spatio-temporal resolution using motion compensation and image fusion in wavelet domain. In: Proc ACCV 2006. LNCS, vol 3851, pp I-480–I-489

Index

G.M. Farinella et al. (eds.), *Advanced Topics in Computer Vision*,
Advances in Computer Vision and Pattern Recognition,
DOI 10.1007/978-1-4471-5520-1, © Springer-Verlag London 2013

MIX
Papier aus verantwortungsvollen Quellen
Paper from responsible sources
FSC® C105338

If you have any concerns about our products,
you can contact us on
ProductSafety@springernature.com

In case Publisher is established outside the EU,
the EU authorized representative is:
Springer Nature Customer Service Center GmbH
Europaplatz 3, 69115 Heidelberg, Germany

Printed by Libri Plureos GmbH
in Hamburg, Germany